The Cambridge Handbook of Psycholinguistics

Our ability to speak, write, understand speech, and read is critical to our ability to function in today's society. As such, *psycholinguistics*, or the study of how humans learn and use language, is a central topic in cognitive science. This comprehensive handbook is a collection of chapters written not by practitioners in the field, who can summarize the work going on around them, but by trailblazers from a wide array of subfields, who have been shaping the field of psycholinguistics over the last decade. Some topics discussed include how children learn language, how average adults understand and produce language, how language is represented in the brain, how brain-damaged individuals perform in terms of their language abilities, and computer-based models of language and meaning. This is required reading for advanced researchers, graduate students, and upper-level undergraduates interested in the recent developments and the future of psycholinguistics.

Michael J. Spivey was on the faculty of Cornell University for twelve years before moving to the cognitive and information sciences unit at the University of California, Merced, in 2008. His research uses dense-sampling methods (such as eyetracking and reach tracking) to explore the real-time interaction between language and vision. He has published in a variety of top-tier journals, including *Science, Cognitive Science, Trends in Cognitive Sciences, Psychological Science*, and *Proceedings of the National Academy of Sciences*. Spivey is the recipient of Sigma Xi's William Procter Prize for Scientific Achievement and multiple teaching awards from Cornell University. The dynamical cognition framework that guides his research is described in his book *The Continuity of Mind* (2007).

Ken McRae has been at the University of Western Ontario since 1993, where he has been studying language and concepts. He has published articles regarding sentence processing and semantic memory from numerous perspectives, including modality-specific representations, the roles of statistical correlations and causal relations in object concepts, category-specific semantic deficits, and the integration of meaning and structure in sentence comprehension. He has also published a number of computational models of these important human abilities. McRae has published in journals such as *Cognition, Journal of Memory and Language, Journal of Experimental Psychology, Cognitive Science*, and *Neuropsychologia*.

Marc F. Joanisse has been at the University of Western Ontario since 2000, studying the cognitive and brain bases of spoken and written language. Work in his laboratory emphasizes the importance of studying multiple aspects of language ability, in a variety of populations, using a range of techniques. His research spans a range of topics encompassing speech perception, spoken word recognition, and reading and grammar abilities in adults and children, using everything from traditional behavioral techniques to eyetracking, event-related potentials, and fMRI. In addition, he has published articles in the field of connectionist modeling of language processing, aphasia following brain injury, and language disorders in children. He has published in a wide range of journals, including the *Proceedings of the National Academy of Sciences, Journal of Cognitive Neuroscience, Cerebral Cortex, NeuroImage, Journal of Memory and Language*, and *Journal of Experimental Psychology: Learning Memory and Cognition*.

The Cambridge Handbook
of Psycholinguistics

Edited by

MICHAEL J. SPIVEY

University of California, Merced

KEN MCRAE

University of Western Ontario

MARC F. JOANISSE

University of Western Ontario

CAMBRIDGE UNIVERSITY PRESS
Cambridge, New York, Melbourne, Madrid, Cape Town,
Singapore, São Paulo, Delhi, Mexico City

Cambridge University Press
32 Avenue of the Americas, New York, NY 10013-2473, USA

www.cambridge.org
Information on this title: www.cambridge.org/9780521677929

First published 2012

Printed in the United States of America

A catalog record for this publication is available from the British Library.

Library of Congress Cataloging in Publication data
The Cambridge handbook of psycholinguistics / [edited by] Michael Spivey, Marc Joanisse, Ken McRae.
    p. cm.
  Includes bibliographical references and index.
  ISBN 978-0-521-86064-2 – ISBN 978-0-521-67792-9 (pbk.)
  1. Psycholinguistics. 2. Cognitive science.   I. Spivey, Michael (Michael James)   II. Joanisse, Marc,
  1972–   III. McRae, Ken, 1962–
  BF455.C36 2012
  401′.9–dc23   2011049753

ISBN 978-0-521-86064-2 Hardback
ISBN 978-0-521-67792-9 Paperback

Shortly after completing her chapter, Rebecca Sandak passed away in an auto accident that also took the life of her husband, Sam. As is evident in her chapter, Rebecca was a promising young scholar who made a number of important contributions to our understanding of the neural bases of skilled reading and dyslexia. We are sad to have lost her, but are proud to include her contribution in this handbook. The Cambridge Handbook of Psycholinguistics *is dedicated to her.*

Contents

Contributors

BLAIR C. ARMSTRONG
Department of Psychology
Carnegie Mellon University

DAVID A. BALOTA
Department of Psychology
Washington University
    in St. Louis

LAWRENCE W. BARSALOU
Department of Psychology
Emory University

JOS J. A. VAN BERKUM
Neurobiology of Language Department
Max Planck Institute for
    Psycholinguistics

LERA BORODITSKY
Department of Psychology
Stanford University

GREGORY A. BRYANT
Department of Communication Studies
Center for Behavior, Evolution, and
    Culture
University of California, Los Angeles

CRISTINA CACCIARI
Dipartimento di Scienze Biomediche
University of Modena and Reggio Emilia

JOANA CHOLIN
Basque Center on Cognition, Brain and
    Language

MORTEN H. CHRISTIANSEN
Psychology Department
Cornell University

STELLA CHRISTIE
Department of Psychology
University of British Columbia

EVE V. CLARK
Department of Linguistics
Stanford University

HERBERT H. CLARK
Department of Psychology
Stanford University

ELIANA COLUNGA
Department of Psychology
University of Colorado, Boulder

JOHN F. CONNOLLY
Department of Linguistics and Languages
McMaster University

MICHAEL J. CORTESE
Department of Psychology
University of Nebraska at Omaha

SEANA COULSON
Department of Cognitive Science
University of California, San Diego

GEORGE S. CREE
Department of Psychology
University of Toronto, Scarborough

CHRISTOPHER M. CREW
Department of Psychology
Columbia University

GARY S. DELL
Department of Psychology
University of Illinois

KEVIN DIEPENDAELE
Department of Experimental Psychology
University of Gent

JUDIT DRUKS
Department of Human Communication
University College London

THOMAS A. FARMER
Department of Psychology
The University of Iowa

ANNE FERNALD
Center for Infant Studies
Stanford University

KELLY FORBES
CAE Professional Services Canada

CAROL A. FOWLER
Haskins Laboratories

MICHAEL FRANK
Department of Psychology
Stanford University

STEPHEN J. FROST
Haskins Laboratories

DEDRE GENTNER
Department of Psychology
Northwestern University

RAYMOND W. GIBBS, JR.
Psychology Department
University of California, Santa Cruz

MONICA GONZALEZ-MARQUEZ
Department of Psychology
Cornell University

ARTHUR C. GRAESSER
The Institute for Intelligent Systems
FedEx Institute of Technology

JONATHAN GRAINGER
National Center for Scientific Research
Université d'Aix-Marseille

ZENZI M. GRIFFIN
Department of Psychology
University of Texas at Austin

MARY HARE
Department of Psychology
Bowling Green State University

HARLAN D. HARRIS
Department of Psychology
New York University

MARC F. JOANISSE
Department of Psychology
Social Science Centre
University of Western Ontario

LEONARD KATZ
Department of Psychology
University of Connecticut

ALBERT KIM
Department of Psychology
   and Neuroscience
University of Colorado at Boulder

GINA R. KUPERBERG
Department of Psychology
Tufts University

NICOLE LANDI
Haskins Laboratories

BIRTE LOENNEKER-RODMAN
International Computer Science Institute

DANIELLE S. MACNAMARA
Department of Psychology
Arizona State University

JAMES S. MAGNUSON
Department of Psychology
University of Connecticut

KEN MCRAE
Department of Psychology
Social Science Centre
University of Western Ontario

W. EINAR MENCL
Haskins Laboratories

DANIEL MIRMAN
Moss Rehabilitation Research Institute

JENNIFER B. MISYAK
Psychology Department
Cornell University

SRINI NARAYANAN
International Computer Science Institute

KATE NATION
Language and Cognitive Development
   Group
Department of Experimental Psychology
St John's College, Oxford

RANDY L. NEWMAN
Department of Psychology
Acadia University

LEE OSTERHOUT
Department of Psychology
University of Washington

ROBERTO PADOVANI
Azienda USL di Modena

KARALYN PATTERSON
MRC Cognition and Brain Sciences Unit

KENNETH R. PUGH
Haskins Laboratories

TERRY REGIER
Department of Linguistics
University of California,
   Berkeley

DOUGLAS ROLAND
Department of Linguistics
University at Buffalo, The State University
   of New York

JAY G. RUECKL
Department of Psychology
University of Connecticut

VASILE RUS
Department of Computer Science
Memphis University

JENNY R. SAFFRAN
Psychology Department
University of Wisconsin-Madison

SARAH D. SAHNI
Psychology Department
University of Wisconsin-Madison

ARTHUR G. SAMUEL
Department of Psychology
Stony Brook University and
   Basque Center on Cognition
   Brain and Language

REBECCA SANDAK
formerly of Haskins Laboratories

DOMINIEK SANDRA
Center for Psycholinguistics
University of Antwerp

SOPHIE SCOTT
Institute of Cognitive Neuroscience
University College London

MARK S. SEIDENBERG
Department of Psychology
University of Wisconsin-Madison

LINDA B. SMITH
Department of Psychological and Brain
   Sciences
Indiana University

MICHAEL J. SPIVEY
Cognitive and Information
    Sciences
University of California, Merced

MEGHAN SUMNER
Department of Linguistics
Stanford University

DANIEL TRANEL
Department of Neurology
University of Iowa Hospitals
    and Clinics

GABRIELLA VIGLIOCCO
Centre for Deafness, Cognition and
    Language
University College London

NICOLE L. WILSON
Pearson Knowledge Technologies

ANNA WOOLLAMS
Neuroscience and Aphasia Research Unit
    (NARU)
School of Psychological Sciences
University of Manchester

Preface

Michael J. Spivey, Ken McRae, and Marc F. Joanisse

In previous years, there have been other handbooks of psycholinguistics, however none of them has been as expansive and comprehensive as this one. With the unusually large number of highly influential authors in this volume, it took a fair bit of time to herd all of these chapters together. But it was definitely worth the wait. We are extremely grateful to Janet Aucoin for assistance in compiling this volume.

The Cambridge Handbook of Psycholinguistics is written not by practitioners in the field who can summarize the work going on around them. It is written by the trailblazers themselves, from a wide array of subfields, who have been forming the field of psycholinguistics and are responsible for its current shape. In addition to its emphasis on comprehensiveness, this handbook displays a commitment to identifying the important changes taking place in various areas of psycholinguistics. In some areas of the cognitive and neural sciences, it could perhaps be argued that the past dozen years have not quite seen enough change in theory and methods to genuinely warrant a new handbook. However, it is abundantly

clear that psycholinguistics has seen more than its usual share of large and small paradigm shifts in just these past dozen years or so – both in the form of transitions of dominance between competing theories and in the form of methodological developments that have changed the way these theories are tested. Thus the field of psycholinguistics unmistakably needs a comprehensive handbook that updates the scientific community (researchers, instructors, and graduate students) on the radically altered empirical and theoretical landscape that has developed.

Several subfields have watched exciting new conceptual developments and previously subordinate theories come to the forefront. For example, the area of language development, from speech perception to sentence comprehension, has experienced a renewed emphasis on the role of the statistical structure in a language learner's input (e.g., Gerken, 2004; Gomez, 2002; Saffran, 2003; Saffran, Aslin, and Newport, 1996). The subfield of sentence processing has been undergoing a shift – already detectable in the textbooks – from a preponderance of stage-based processing accounts to a largely dynamic and interactive (neural net-work–inspired) theoretical framework (e.g., MacDonald, Pearlmutter, and Seidenberg, 1994; Spivey et al., 2002; Tabor and Hutchins, 2004). Furthermore, developmental, adult, modeling, patient, and neurological research is considerably more integrated than was the case ten years ago. The debate over how to represent the morphology of regular and irregular past tenses in English returned with a new vigor (e.g., Joanisse, 2004; Marchman, Plunkett, and Goodman, 1997; Ramscar, 2003; Ullman, 2001). The embodied mean-ings of words, as opposed to amodal sym-bolic representations, is becoming a staple of contemporary literature reviews of semantic memory (e.g., Barsalou, 1999; Glenberg, 1997; Richardson et al., 2003). The field of seman-tic memory has undergone huge changes: the shift from amodal to perceptually based and event-based representations (Barsalou, 1999; Glenberg, 1997), the vastly increased role of patient and neuroimaging research (Martin and Caramazza, 2003), the centrality of con-nectionist modeling (Plaut and Shallice, 1993), and the advent of corpus-based approaches to word meaning (Landauer and Dumais, 1997). The list could go on and on – and in this handbook, it does.

Many of the recent sways in these the-oretical battles have been made possi-ble by major advances in the methods being used by the field in just the past several years. For example, continued development of connectionist modeling techniques has allowed more explicit spec-ification of theories and accommodated new data in the areas of sentence process-ing (e.g., MacDonald and Christiansen, 2002; McRae, Spivey-Knowlton, and Tanenhaus, 1998) word meaning (McRae, de Sa, and Seidenberg, 1997), language acquisition (e.g., Rohde and Plaut, 1999), and language disorders (e.g., Joanisse and Seidenberg, 2003), to name just a few. Moreover, func-tional magnetic resonance imaging has, along with magnetoencephalography and electroencephalography, produced reams of important new neuroimaging results in many areas of language research (e.g., Connolly and D'Arcy, 2000; Martin and

Caramazza, 2003; Osterhout and Nicol, 1999; Pulvermüller, Assadollahi, and Elbert, 2001; Scott and Wise, 2004) that alone could justify a new handbook. And head-mounted eye-tracking – providing the first noninterrup-tive, real-time measure of spoken language comprehension and production in rich situ-ational contexts (e.g., Griffin and Bock, 2000; Tanenhaus et al., 1995) – has been revealing new discoveries in speech perception, spo-ken word recognition, sentence processing, language production, figurative language, and even naturalistic conversation.

Handbook Structure

The Cambridge Handbook of Psycholinguistics provides relatively short reports on the psycholinguistic literature in a wide vari-ety of subfields, written by the experts who made those subfields what they are, with discussions of these many recent theoretical and methodological develop-ments. The *Handbook* is divided into ten sections: Speech Perception, Spoken Word Recognition, Written Word Recognition, Semantic Memory, Morphological Process-ing, Sentence Comprehension, Sentence Production, Figurative Language, Discourse and Conversation, and Language and Thought, in that order. To ensure a wide rep-resentation of empirical methodologies and conceptual issues, and equally important, to highlight the theoretical and methodo-logical advances of the past dozen years or so, each section has chapters that together cover adult behavioral measures, develop-mental research, computational modeling, and patient and neuroimaging research. By having these four perspectives emphasized in each of the ten sections, not only will cur-rent areas of research that strongly integrate those four perspectives receive proper treat-ment (e.g., spoken and written word recogni-tion, semantic memory, sentence processing), but younger areas of experimental psycho-linguistic study (e.g., figurative language, language and thought, discourse and con-versation) will be encouraged to strengthen all four of those perspectives in their future research. Thus, in addition to summarizing the *state of the art* of psycholinguistics, it is our hope that this handbook can bolster the metatheoretical richness and methodological diversity of the *future* of psycholinguistics.

The justification for the ten sections we have chosen is twofold. First, we wish this handbook to be representative of the entire field, so it includes chapters on all active areas of contemporary psycholinguistic research. Second, for those portions of certain fields that have become sufficiently active to warrant being identified as their own subfield, we have given them their own section. Nonetheless, it is neither possible nor desirable to have in-depth chapters on every subfield. Therefore, the reader may indeed find sections that could have been subdivided into two sections, and future editions of this handbook could perhaps purse that finer-grain specification. Later in this preface we provide brief summaries of these sections to help guide the reader.

Speech perception

With chapters from major contributors to this field such as Carol A. Fowler, Sophie Scott, Jenny R. Saffran, and their colleagues, this section focuses on how individuals perceive units of speech such as phonemes. The hot topic of speech perception very much remains what it has been for decades – the question of whether "speech is special." That is, does speech represent a unique mode of perception distinct from other types of auditory perception? This is a contentious issue, and we have selected authors who bring forward a range of perspectives on the topic, including exemplar- and prototype-based models of speech and the revised motor theory of speech perception. This section also addresses the role of statistical learning in speech perception, especially as it relates to suprasegmental phenomena such as word segmentation.

Spoken word recognition

With noticeably less emphasis on the level of acoustic properties and phonological features, and significantly more emphasis on interactions between words, the literature on spoken word recognition is sufficiently distinct from the literature on speech perception – and certainly large enough on its own – to warrant its own section in this handbook. Arthur G. Samuel, James S. Magnuson, Anne Fernald, John F. Connolly, and their colleagues contribute four chapters discussing recent theoretical shifts in the area of spoken word recognition that have been instigated by recent research, including novel eyetracking methods and numerous improvements and comparisons of computational models.

Written word recognition

In many ways this area of research captures what we see as a major trend in psycholinguistics: the move toward using behavioral data to test the quantitative predictions of implemented models. In the past decade we have seen the Seidenberg and McClelland model emerge as a key theory of visual word recognition, though the classical dual-route theory also remains popular. We have selected authors who are conversant in this important theoretical debate (e.g., David A. Balota, Mark S. Seidenberg, Kate Nation, and Rebecca Sandak) in order to best represent the state of the art. A second theme in this section concerns the role of phonology in reading acquisition and disorders (including dyslexia). This is a hot topic addressed not only in the developmental chapter, but also in the neuroimaging and computational modeling chapters.

Semantic memory

The area of semantic memory has changed drastically over the past ten years and become significantly coextensive with psycholinguistics. These three chapters by Lawrence W. Barsalou, George S. Cree, Linda B. Smith, and their colleagues highlight those changes, such as the advances toward perceptually based rather than amodal representations; the (competing) theory of corpus-based representations; the central roles that connectionist modeling, neuroimaging, and patient research play; and the always present and increasing role of the study of the development of concepts and word meaning. This section makes apparent the fact that these four approaches are better integrated than ever, which is, in itself, a very exciting development.

Morphological processing

The debate between single- and dual-mechanism models of past tense processing has reemerged as a major theme in psycholinguistics. In addition to new approaches to modeling morphology, evidence has come from the neuropsychology literature, including work with aphasic patients and neuroimaging studies. That said, these chapters by Jonathan Grainger, Karalyn Patterson, and their colleagues go well beyond past tense, focusing on issues related to how morphology interacts with visual word recognition, how children use different types of evidence to learn morphological patterns, and differences between inflectional and derivational morphology.

Sentence comprehension

Sentence comprehension is a key area where psycholinguists and theoretical linguists have shared structural formalisms and experimental methods to study language processing. The field of sentence comprehension has undergone substantial methodological and theoretical changes over the past dozen years, as documented in these chapters by Lee Osterhout and colleagues, Morten H. Christiansen and colleagues, and Douglas Roland and Mary Hare. These include the introduction of implemented computational models and a plethora of evidence supporting constraint-based models. These advances (as well as the *visual world paradigm* in which auditory instructions are interpreted in the context of a visual display) have played powerful roles in changing both theoretical and empirical work. Analyses of large-scale electronic corpora are now a central part of sentence comprehension research. Finally, neuroimaging research has grown rapidly in this area, as it seems to have across many areas of psycholinguistics.

Sentence production

The raw amount of research on language production, both at the lexical level and at the sentential level, has grown substantially over the past dozen years. Invigorated by new methods such as eyetracking, neuroimaging, and improved computational models, this subfield is approaching the size and visibility of the sentence comprehension subfield. In addition to describing the state of the art of this area of research, these chapters by Zenzi M. Griffin, Gary S. Dell, Gabriella Vigliocco, and their colleagues together provide a vision for the future directions in this subfield, encouraging simultaneous attention to multiple sources of evidence.

Figurative language

Figurative language is where psycholinguists and cognitive linguists share theories and methods to understand the wide array of natural everyday language use patterns (within which nonliteral meanings are actually the norm rather than the exception). In the past dozen years, theoretical cognitive linguists (along with cognitive linguistically minded psycholinguists) have begun to integrate findings from real-time laboratory experiments (even conducting experiments themselves at times), as well as extend their theoretical treatments to explicit computational implementations, formal treatments, and neurophysiological constraints. This growing area of research, well-documented here in chapters by Raymond W. Gibbs, Jr., Srini Narayanan, Cristina Cacciari, Seana Coulson, and their colleagues, holds considerable promise for offering a framework of linguistic representation and processing that treats language as an integral component of cognition in general.

Discourse and conversation

With much of its tradition in the philosophy of language (and also somewhat in artificial intelligence), psycholinguistic research on discourse and conversation has seen a resurgence of interest lately by researchers using real-time measures such as EEG and eyetracking. Computational models have also begun to figure prominently again in the description of specific conversational situations such as question answering. These four chapters, by Herbert H. Clark, Arthur C. Graesser, Danielle S. MacNamara, Eve V. Clark, and Jos J. A. Van Berkum, sample this subfield in a manner that sets the stage for the future of this area of research.

Language and thought

This area of inquiry was once all but discarded in the field of theoretical linguistics on the grounds of specific criticisms of a specific handful of linguistic analyses. However, due significantly to the recent high-profile psycholinguistic research (documented here in chapters by Lera Boroditsky, Terry Regier, Dedre Gentner, and Monica Gonzalez-Marquez), the Whorfian hypothesis – that one's language influences how one thinks – has come again to the table of debate. Psycholinguistic methods and computational models, rather than linguistic analyses, have been producing results that strongly suggest this hypothesis still has some genuine (though perhaps limited) merit. As this field is clearly on the rise once again in psycholinguistics, this collection of chapters will help to frame the contemporary research in, as well as distinguish it from, its historical context.

Acknowledgments

Thanks to David Plaut and Jo Ziegler for helpful discussions.

References

Barsalou, L. (1999). Perceptual symbol systems. *Behavioral and Brain Sciences*, 22, 577–660.

Connolly, J. F. & D'Arcy, R. C. N. (2000). Innovations in neuropsychological assessment using event-related brain potentials. *International Journal of Psychophysiology*, 37, 31–47.

Gerken, L. A. (2004). Nine-month-olds extract structural principles required for natural language. *Cognition*, 93, B89–B96.

Glenberg, A. M. (1997). What memory is for. *Behavioral and Brain Sciences*, 20, 1–55.

Gómez, R. L. (2002). Variability and detection of invariant structure. *Psychological Science*, 13, 431–36.

Griffin, Z. M. & Bock, K. (2000). What the eyes say about speaking. *Psychological Science*, 11, 274–79.

Joanisse, M. F. (2004). Specific language impairments in children: Phonology, semantics, and the English past tense. *Current Directions in Psychological Science*, 13, 156–60.

 & Seidenberg M. S. (2003). Phonology and syntax in specific language impairment: Evidence from a connectionist model. *Brain and Language*, 86, 40–56.

Landauer, T. K. & Dumais, S. T. (1997). A solution to Plato's problem: The latent semantic analysis theory of acquisition, induction, and representation of knowledge. *Psychological Review*, 104, 211–40.

MacDonald, M. C. & Christiansen, M. H. (2002). Reassessing working memory: Comment on Just and Carpenter (1992) and Waters and Caplan (1996). *Psychological Review*, 109, 35–54.

MacDonald, M., Pearlmutter, N., & Seidenberg, M. (1994). The lexical nature of syntactic ambiguity resolution. *Psychological Review*, 101, 676–703.

Marchman, V., Plunkett, K., & Goodman, J. (1997). Over-regularization in English plural and past tense inflectional morphology. *Journal of Child Language*, 24, 767–79.

Martin, A. & Caramazza, A. (2003). Neuropsychological and neuroimaging perspectives on conceptual knowledge: An introduction. *Cognitive Neuropsychology*, 20, 195–212.

McRae, K., de Sa, V., & Seidenberg, M. (1997). On the nature and scope of featural representations of word meaning. *Journal of Experimental Psychology: General*, 126, 99–130.

McRae, K., Spivey-Knowlton, M., & Tanenhaus, M. (1998). Modeling the effects of thematic fit (and other constraints) in on-line sentence comprehension. *Journal of Memory and Language*, 37, 283–312.

Osterhout, L. & Nicol, J. (1999). On the distinctiveness, independence, and time course of the brain responses to syntactic and semantic anomalies. *Language and Cognitive Processes*, 14, 283–317.

Plaut, D. C. & Shallice, T. (1993). Deep dyslexia: A case study of connectionist neuropsychology. *Cognitive Neuropsychology*, 10, 377–500.

Pulvermüller, F., Assadollahi, R., & Elbert, T. (2001). Neuromagnetic evidence for early semantic access in word recognition. *European Journal of Neuroscience*, 13, 201–5.

Ramscar, M. (2003). The past-tense debate: Exocentric form versus the evidence. *Trends in Cognitive Science*, 7, 107–8.

Richardson, D., Spivey, M., Barsalou, L., & McRae, K. (2003). Spatial representations activated during real-time comprehension of verbs. *Cognitive Science*, 27, 767–80.

Rohde, D. L. T. & Plaut, D. C. (1999). Language acquisition in the absence of explicit negative evidence: How important is starting small? *Cognition*, 72, 67–109.

Saffran, J. R. (2003). Statistical language learning: Mechanisms and constraints. *Current Directions in Psychological Science*, 12, 110–14.

Saffran, J., Newport, E., & Aslin, R. (1996). Word segmentation: The role of distributed cues. *Journal of Memory and Language*, 35, 606–21.

Scott, S. K. & Wise, R. J. (2004). The functional neuroanatomy of prelexical processing in speech perception. *Cognition*, 92, 13–45.

Spivey, M., Tanenhaus, M., Eberhard, K., & Sedivy, J. (2002). Eye movements and spoken language comprehension: Effects of visual context on syntactic ambiguity resolution. *Cognitive Psychology*, 45, 447–81.

Tabor, W., & Hutchins, S. (2004). Evidence for self-organized sentence processing: digging-in effects. *Journal of Experimental Psychology: Learning, Memory, and Cognition*, 30, 431–50.

Tanenhaus, M., Spivey-Knowlton, M., Eberhard, K., & Sedivy, J. (1995). Integration of visual and linguistic information during spoken language comprehension. *Science*, 268, 1632–4.

Ullman, M. T. (2001). A neurocognitive perspective on language: The declarative/procedural model. *Nature Reviews Neuroscience*, 2, 717–26.

Section 1

SPEECH PERCEPTION

CHAPTER 1

Speech Perception

Carol A. Fowler and James S. Magnuson

Speech perception refers to the means by which acoustic and sometimes visual or even haptic speech signals are mapped onto the language forms (words and their component consonants and vowels) that language users know. For the purposes of this review, we will address three aspects of the language user's perceptual task. We identify as *phonetic perception* the task of extracting information from stimulation about language forms. Next we address how perceivers cope with or even exploit the enormous variability in the language forms that talkers produce. Finally, we address issues associated with lexical access.

1 Phonetic perception

For spoken messages to have their intended effect, minimally listeners/observers have to recognize the language forms, especially the words, that talkers produce. Having accomplished that, they can go on to determine what speakers mean or intend by what they say. The requirement that listeners characteristically successfully identify speakers'

language forms has been called the *parity requirement* (Liberman and Whalen, 2000), and a benchmark by which a theory of phonetic perception may be evaluated is its ability to explain parity achievement. In this section, we focus specifically on how listeners extract information from acoustic or other-modal stimulation to identify language forms. In later sections, we address other sources of information that listeners may use.

Listeners encounter acoustic speech signals and often the facial speech gestures of the speaker. A task for speech perception researchers is to determine what is immediately perceived that allows perceptual recovery of language forms. One idea is that, because the main source of information that listeners receive is acoustic, they perceive some auditory transformation of an acoustically represented word. For example, Klatt (1979) suggested that words in the lexicon were, among other representations, represented as sequences of spectra that might be matched to spectra of input words.

This view may be short-sighted, however. Language is a generative system, and its generativity depends on its compositionality. At the level of relevance here, consonants and vowels combine systematically into words, enabling language users to know, coin, produce, and perceive many tens of thousands of words. Accordingly, words, consonants, and vowels, among other linguistic units, are components of their language competence. Spontaneous errors of speech production occur in which individual consonants and vowels move or are substituted one for the other (e.g., Shattuck-Hufnagel, 1979; but see later in this chapter for a qualification), so we know that, as speakers, language users compose words of consonants and vowels. The need for parity in spoken communications suggests that listeners typically recover the language forms that talkers produce. Here, we will assume that listeners to speech perceive, among other linguistic units, words, consonants, and vowels.

What are consonants and vowels? In one point of view, they are cognitive categories that reside in the minds of speakers/hearers (e.g., Pierrehumbert, 1990). In another, they are actions of the vocal tracts of speakers (e.g., Goldstein and Fowler, 2003). This theoretical disagreement is important.

From the former perspective, speakers do not literally produce language forms. Among other reasons, they do not because they coarticulate when they speak. That is, they temporally overlap actions to implement one consonant or vowel with actions to implement others. The overlap distorts or destroys the transparency of the relation between acoustic signal and phonological segment. Accordingly, the acoustic signal at best can provide cues to the consonants and vowels of the speaker's message. Listeners perceive the cues and use them as pointers to mental phonological categories. Coarticulation creates the (lack of) invariance problem – that the same segment in different contexts can be signaled by different acoustic structures. It also creates the segmentation problem, that is, the problem of recovering discrete phonetic segments from a signal that lacks discrete acoustic segments.

The second point of view reflects an opinion that, in the course of the evolution of language, the parity requirement shaped the nature of language, and, in particular, of language forms. In consequence, language forms, being the means that languages provide to make linguistic messages public, optimally should be things that can be made public without being distorted or destroyed. In short, language forms should be vocal tract actions (phonetic gestures; e.g., Goldstein and Fowler, 2003). Coarticulation and, in particular, resistance to it when its effects would distort or destroy defining properties of language forms, does not distort or destroy achievement of gestures (e.g., Fowler and Saltzman 1993).

In the remainder of this chapter, we discuss current knowledge about the information that supports phonetic perception by way of a brief historical review of the key acoustic and perceptual discoveries in speech research, and we consider how these discoveries motivated past and current theories of speech perception. Next, we address how variability contributes to the lack of invariance problem – the apparent lack of an invariant mapping from the speech signal to phonetic percepts – and discuss challenges to current theories. Then, we discuss the interface of speech perception with higher levels of linguistic processing. We will close the chapter with a discussion of what we view to be the most pressing questions for theories of speech perception.

1.1 *What information supports phonetic perception?*

In the early years of research on phonetic perception at Haskins Laboratories (for a historical overview see Liberman, 1996), researchers used the sound spectrograph to represent acoustic speech signals in a way that made some of its informative structure visible. In addition, they used a Pattern Playback, designed and built at Haskins, to transform schematic spectrographic displays into sound. With these tools, they could guess from spectrographic displays what acoustic structure might be important to the identification of a syllable or consonant or vowel, preserve just that structure by

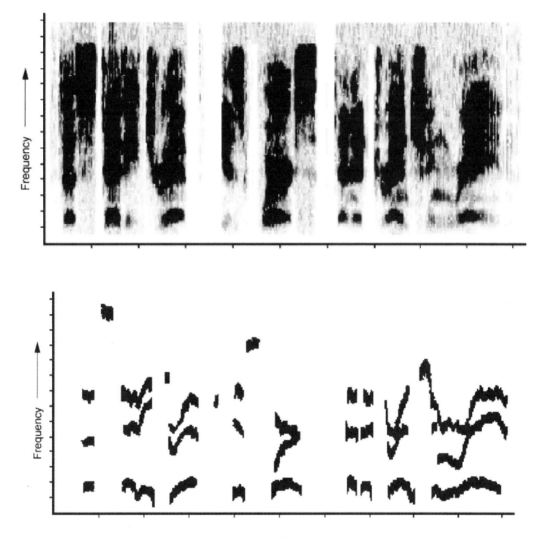

Figure 1.1. A comparison of spectrographic displays of normal (top) and sinewave speech. The sentence depicted in both instances is: "The steady drip is worse than a drenching rain." For more examples, including audio, see http://www.haskins.yale.edu/research/sws.html. Used with the permission of Philip Rubin, Robert Remez, and Haskins Laboratories.

producing a schematic representation of it, and ask whether, converted to sound by the Playback, the schematic representation preserved the phonetic properties of the speech. This research showed them the extent of the acoustic consequences of coarticulation. Acoustic speech signals do not consist of sequences of discrete phone-sized segments, and the acoustic structure that provides information about consonants and vowels is everywhere highly context sensitive. Haskins researchers made an effort to catalogue the variety of acoustic cues that could be used to identify consonants and vowels in their various coarticulatory contexts.

In recent years, researchers have found that the cues uncovered in that early research, acoustic reflections of *formants* – resonant frequencies of the vocal tract that show up as dark horizontal bands in spectrographic displays such as in Figure 1.1 – formant transitions, noise bursts for stops, intervals of noise for fricatives, and so forth, do not exhaust what serves as information for listeners. For example, in sinewave speech, center frequencies of formants are replaced by single sinewaves and even frication noise is represented by a sinewave (see Figure 1.1). These signals are caricatures of speech signals, and they lack most traditional speech cues (e.g., Remez et al., 1981). That is, they lack a fundamental frequency and harmonics: The sinewaves lack the bandwidth of formants; they lack frication noise, stop bursts, and virtually all distinctive cues proposed to support phonetic perception. They leave more or less intact information signaling dynamic change. They sound bizarre, but they can be highly intelligible, permitting phonetic transcription and even identification of familiar speakers (Remez, Fellowes, and Rubin, 1997).

Other radical transformations of the acoustic signal quite different from the sinewave transformation also permit phonetic perception. For example, in noise-vocoded speech, the fine structure of an acoustic speech signal (effectively, the source) can be replaced with noise while the speech envelope (the filter) is retained. If this transformation is accomplished with as few as four frequency bands, speech is highly intelligible (Smith, Delgutte, and Oxenham, 2002). Smith et al. also obtained intelligible speech with chimaeric speech made in the complementary way, with fine structure preserved and envelope replaced by that of another sound.

A conclusion from the findings that these radical transformations of the acoustic signal, so unlike speech and so unlike each other, yield intelligible signals must be that there is massive redundancy in natural speech signals. Signals are informationally rich, not impoverished as implied by early research on speech.

We also know that phonetic information is conveyed by the face. Speech is better identified in noise if perceivers can see the face of the speaker (Sumby and Pollack, 1954). And it can be tracked more successfully in the context of competing speech emanating from the same location in space

if the speaker's face, spatially displaced from the sound source, is visible to the perceiver (Driver, 1996). The much-studied McGurk effect (e.g., McGurk and MacDonald, 1976) also shows that perceivers extract phonetic information from the face. In that phenomenon, a face mouthing one word or syllable, say /da/, is dubbed with a different word or syllable, say /ma/. With appropriate selection of stimuli, perceivers often report hearing a word or syllable that integrates information from the two modalities. A typical percept given the example of visible /da/ and acoustic /ma/ is /na/, which has the place of articulation of the visible syllable, but the voicing and nasality of the acoustic syllable.

Cross-modal integration of phonetic as well, indeed, as indexical information occurs even when the information is highly impoverished. Even when facial gestures are provided by point lights[1] and speech by sinewaves, listeners show McGurk effects (Rosenblum and Saldana, 1998), can identify speakers (Rosenblum et al., 2002) and can determine which visible speaker of two produced a given acoustically presented word (Lachs, 2002; Kamachi et al., 2003).

In summary then, although early findings suggested that the acoustic signal is impoverished in the sense that context sensitivity precludes invariance and transparency, more recent findings suggest that the information available to the perceiver is very rich.

1.2 *Theories of phonetic perception*

Theories of phonetic perception partition into two broad categories. One class of theories (e.g., Diehl and Kluender, 1989; Sawusch and Gagnon, 1995) holds that auditory systems pick out cues in the acoustic speech signal and use the cues to identify mental phonological categories. Another class of theories (e.g., Fowler, 1986; Liberman and Mattingly, 1985) holds that listeners to speech use acoustic structure as information about its causal source, the linguistically

---

1   In this procedure, light reflecting patches are placed on the face and speakers are filmed in the dark so that only the patches can be seen.

significant vocal tract actions of the speaker. Those vocal tract actions are phonological categories (e.g., Goldstein and Fowler, 2003) or else point to them (Liberman and Mattingly, 1985). Gesture theories differ with respect to whether they do (the motor theory of Liberman and colleagues) or do not (the direct realist theory of Fowler and colleagues) invoke a specialization of the brain for speech perception.

An example of an auditory theory is the auditory enhancement theory proposed by Diehl and Kluender (1989). In that theory, as in all theories in this class, identification of consonants and vowels is guided by acoustic cues as processed by the auditory system. The auditory cues are used to identify the consonant or vowel conveyed by the speaker. According to Diehl and Kluender, we can see evidence of the salience of acoustic cues and of auditory processing in phonetic perception in the nature of the sound inventories that language communities develop. Sound inventories in languages of the world tend to maximize auditory distinctiveness in one way or another. For example, approximately ninety-four percent of front vowels are unrounded in Maddieson's (1984) survey of 317 languages; a similar percentage of back vowels are rounded. The reason for that pairing of frontness/backness and unrounding/rounding, according to Diehl and Kluender, is that both the backing gesture and the rounding gesture serve to lengthen the front cavity of the vocal tract; fronting without rounding keeps it short. Therefore, the two gestures conspire, as it were, either to lower (backing and rounding) or to raise the second formant, making front and back vowels acoustically more distinct than if the rounding gesture were absent or, especially, if the pairing were of rounding and fronting rather than backing.

Evidence seen as particularly compatible with auditory theories are findings in some studies that nonhuman animals appear to perceive speech as humans do (see the next section for a more detailed discussion). For most auditory theorists, it is patent that animals are incapable of perceiving human speech gestures. Therefore their perceptions must be guided by acoustic cues mapped neither to gestures nor to phonological categories. Moreover, nonhuman animals do not have a specialization of the brain for human speech perception; therefore, their perception of human speech must be an achievement of their auditory system. Parallel findings between human and nonhuman animals imply that humans do not perceive gestures either and do not require a specialization for speech. Compatibly, findings suggesting that nonspeech signals and speech signals are perceived in parallel ways are seen to contradict the ideas that gestures are perceived and that a specialization of the brain for speech achieves speech perception.

The first impetus for development of gesture theories was a pair of complementary findings. One finding (Liberman, Delattre, and Cooper, 1952) was that, in synthetic syllables, the same stop burst, centered at 1440 Hz placed before steady state formants for /i/ or /u/, led perceivers to hear /p/. Placed before /a/, they heard /k/. The second finding (Liberman et al., 1954), was that two-formant synthetic /di/ and /du/ had remarkably different second formant transitions. That for /di/ was high and rising; that for /du/ was low and falling. Yet the second formant transition was the information that identified the consonants in those synthetic syllables as /d/.

Together these two findings appear to tell a clear story. In the first, to produce a burst at 1440 Hz requires that a labial constriction gesture coarticulate with /i/ or /u/; to produce the same burst before /a/ requires coarticulation of a velar constriction gesture with a gesture or gestures for the vowel. Coarticulation also underlies the second finding. The same alveolar constriction released into a vocal tract configuration for the vowel /i/ will produce a high rising second formant; released into the configuration for /u/, it will produce a low falling second formant. As Liberman put it in 1957, "when articulation and sound wave go their separate ways, which way does perception go? The answer so far is clear. The perception always goes with articulation" (p. 121).

These findings led to the development of the motor theory of speech perception (e.g., Liberman 1957; Liberman et al., 1967; Liberman and Mattingly 1985; Liberman and Whalen, 2000; for a recent evaluation of the motor theory, see Galantucci, Fowler, and Turvey, 2006). In the 1967 version of that theory, coarticulation is proposed to be essential for the efficient transmission of speech. However, it creates difficulties for the perceiver that a specialization of the brain, unique to humans, evolved to handle. The specialization, later identified as a *phonetic module* (Liberman and Mattingly, 1985), was for both production of coarticulated speech and its perception. The evidence that, in the view of Liberman and his colleagues, revealed that listeners perceive speech gestures, suggested to them that the phonetic module involved the speech motor system in the act of perception, using a process of analysis by synthesis.

In a different theory of gesture perception inspired by Gibson's (e.g., 1966; 1979) more general perceptual theory, Fowler (1986; 1994) proposed that listeners perceive linguistically significant actions of the vocal tract (phonetic gestures) because acoustic signals, caused by the gestures, provide information about them. In this direct realist account, speech perception was proposed to be like perception of every other sort (contra occasional claims that direct realism requires special-purpose mechanisms for gesture perception). Perceivers' sense organs are stimulated by proximal stimuli that provide information for their causal source in the environment. Just as perceivers see objects and events rather than reflected light, and just as they feel object properties rather than the skin deformations that inform about them, they hear sounding events, not the acoustic signals that they cause.

The motor theory and direct realism are equally supported or challenged by most relevant evidence. For example, they are equally supported by the findings of Liberman, et al. (1952; 1954) described earlier. They are equally challenged, for example, by certain comparisons of speech

and nonspeech perception. They can be differentiated, however, by research, some of which is described later in this chapter, that addresses the existence of a specialization for speech perception.

Following are some of the research findings that all theories of phonetic perception are required to explain.

1.2.1 CATEGORICAL PERCEPTION
Categorical perception was an early finding in the history of the study of speech perception by experimental psychologists (Liberman et al., 1957). When listeners were asked to identify members of an acoustic continuum of syllables varying in the F_2 transition that ranged from /be/ to /de/ to /ge/, instead of showing a gradual shift in responses, they showed abrupt shifts, shown schematically in Figure 1.2. This occurred despite the fact that there was an equivalent acoustic change at every step along the continuum. A second hallmark of categorical perception, also shown in Figure 1.2, is that discrimination was considerably worse for pairs of syllables labeled as the same syllable than for syllables labeled differently. An early interpretation of this pair of findings was that it indexed a special way of perceiving speech. According to the motor theory of speech perception, listeners do not perceive the acoustic signal, but rather the articulatory gestures that produced the signal. Categorically distinct vocal tract gestures produce /b/, /d/, and /g/. Accordingly, they are perceived categorically as well. Identification functions are sharp, by this early account, because continuum members with the lowest frequency second formant onsets are perceived as bilabial (on the left side of Figure 1.2). Eventually, a syllable is encountered that cannot have been produced by lip closure, and it and the next few syllables are perceived as alveolar; final syllables all must have been produced by the tongue body, and are perceived as velar. Discrimination is near chance within these categories, according to the account, because all category members are perceived as equally bilabial (or alveolar or velar). It is only when one stimulus, say, is perceived as bilabial and one as alveolar that

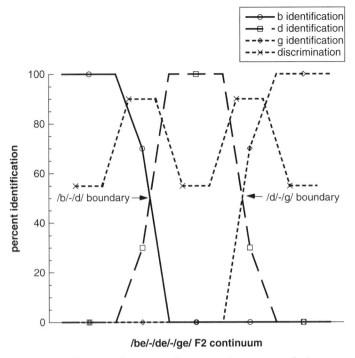

Figure 1.2. Schematic depiction of categorical perception findings. Identification functions are sharp, rather than gradual, and discrimination is poor within as compared to between consonant categories.

discrimination is possible. The categorical nature of speech perception has also been challenged by the findings considered next.

1.2.2 INTERNAL CATEGORY STRUCTURE

The claim (Studdert-Kennedy et al., 1970) that listeners to speech only discriminate syllables that they categorize differently was challenged early. Pisoni and Tash (1974) asked listeners to make same–different judgments of syllables along a /ba/ to /pa/ continuum. "Same" responses to acoustically different syllables were made with longer latencies than "same" responses to identical syllables. McMurray and colleagues have extended this finding by presenting subjects with word–word VOT continua (e.g., bear–pear) and a display of four pictures and asking subjects to click on the picture corresponding to the word they hear. The time course of lexical activation is estimated from eye movements subjects make as they hear the continuum items. Adults show gradient

sensitivity within categories (that is, the farther the stimulus is from the category boundary, the faster they fixate the target picture; McMurray, Tanenhaus, and Aslin, 2002). Infants show similar gradient sensitivity in a head turn preference procedure (McMurray and Aslin, 2005). Accordingly, at least briefly, differences are perceived among syllables ultimately identified as the same syllable.

In fact, they are not perceived only briefly. Miller and colleagues (e.g., Miller and Volaitis, 1989; Allen and Miller, 2001) have shown that listeners give differential goodness ratings to syllables along, for example, a /b/ to /p/ continuum in an unspeeded task.

Kuhl has shown more about internal category structure. Listeners discriminate differentially within a category (Kuhl, 1991; Kuhl and Iverson 1995; but see Lively and Pisoni, 1997). They discriminate stimuli from the best category exemplar more poorly than from a poor category exemplar. Because categories are language-specific, this suggests that a kind of warping of perceptual space occurs in the course of language learning.

1.2.3 DUPLEX PERCEPTION

When all of a syllable that is ambiguous between /da/ and /ga/ is presented to the left ear, and the disambiguating third formant transition is presented to the right ear, listeners hear two things at once (e.g., Mann and Liberman, 1983). They hear /da/ or /ga/ depending on which third formant transition has been presented, and they hear the transition as such, as a chirp that either rises or falls in pitch and that is distinct from the phonetic percept. Mann and Liberman interpreted this as showing that there are two auditory perceptual systems. Otherwise how could the same third formant transition be heard in two ways at the same time? One perceptual system renders a phonetic percept of /d/ or /g/. The other hears the transition literally as a fall or rise in pitch. This interpretation has been challenged, but not entirely successfully, by showing that perception of slamming doors can meet most, but not all, criteria for duplexity (Fowler and Rosenblum, 1990). If slamming door parts can be perceived in two ways at the same time, it cannot be because two perceptual systems, a door-perceiving system and the auditory system, underlie the percepts.

1.2.4 PARSING

Listeners behave as if they are sensitive to coarticulatory information in a speech signal. For example, in a classic finding by Mann (1980), listeners identified more syllables along a /da/ to /ga/ continuum as /da/ in the context of a precursor /ar/ than /al/ syllable. The pharyngeal tongue gesture of /r/ should pull the alveolar gesture of /d/ back, and listeners behave as if they recognize that. For intermediate syllables along the continuum, they behave as if they understand why the syllables are acoustically too far back for /d/ – coarticulation with the /r/ pulled the place of articulation of /d/ back. These findings show that listeners parse the coarticulatory effects of /r/ from acoustic information for /d/, and recent evidence shows that the

parsed information is used as information for the coarticulating segment (e.g., Fowler, 2006). This pair of findings suggests close tracking by listeners of what talkers do.

There are many compatible findings. Listeners compensate for carryover (that is, left-to-right) coarticulation, for example, in the research by Mann (1980). They also compensate for anticipatory coarticulation (e.g., Mann and Repp, 1980). And they compensate for coarticulation that is not directional. For example, different speech gestures have converging effects on fundamental frequency (F0). Other things equal, high vowels, such as /i/, have higher F0 than low vowels such as /a/, a phenomenon known as *intrinsic F0*. Another use of F0 is to realize intonational accents. In research by Silverman (1987), two intonational accents, one on a high vowel and one on a low vowel, sounded equal in pitch when the accent on /i/ was higher in F0 than that on /a/. Listeners parse F0 that they ascribe to intrinsic F0 from F0 that they ascribe to an intonational accent. They do not ignore intrinsic F0 that they parse from an intonational accent. They use it as information for vowel height (Reinholt Peterson, 1986).

One interpretation of these findings is that listeners behave as if they are extracting information about speech gestures and are sensitive to acoustic effects of gestural overlap (Mann, 1980). In an /al/ context, listeners parse the /l/ coloring (fronting) that /l/ should cause from continuum members and hear more /ga/s. Parsing /r/ coloring (backing) leads them to hear more /da/s. However, another interpretation invokes a very general auditory process of spectral contrast (e.g., Lotto and Kluender, 1998). Again with respect to the Mann (1980) example, /al/ has a high ending F_3 that is higher in frequency than the onset F_3 of all members of the /da/ to /ga/ continuum. An /ar/ has a very low F_3 that is lower in frequency than the onset of F_3 of all continuum members. If a high-frequency sound exerts a contrastive effect, it makes following lower frequencies sound even lower than they are. This makes continuum members sound more /ga/-like. A low frequency ending F_3 should have the opposite effect, making continuum members sound more /da/-like.

1.2.5 MULTIMODAL SPEECH

As noted previously, perceivers of speech use more than acoustic information if they encounter it. They perceive speech in noise better if they can see the face of a speaker than if they cannot (Sumby and Pollack, 1954). Moreover, they integrate acoustic and optical speech information in the McGurk effect (McGurk and MacDonald, 1976). If haptic information replaces optical information, a McGurk effect also occurs (Fowler and Dekle, 1991). These effects may occur because listeners hear and see speech gestures. They integrate across the modalities, because the gestures specified by the two modalities of information should be from the same speech event. Alternatively (excepting perhaps the findings of Fowler and Dekle, 1991), the effects may occur because listeners/observers have a lifetime of experience both seeing and hearing speech, so they know what it looks like when various acoustic speech signals are produced. Seeing the speaking face, then, helps them to identify what was said.

Remarkably, Munhall and colleagues (Munhall et al., 2004) have shown that perceivers can extract phonetic information from the visible head movements of a speaker, such that speech is more intelligible in noise when natural head movements as well as facial phonetic gestures are visible to a speaker. Perceivers of speech are information omnivores. This finding awaits interpretation from either a gestural or an auditory theoretical perspective.

1.2.6 PERCEPTION OF SPEECH BY ANIMALS; PERCEPTION OF NONSPEECH BY HUMANS

Two lines of research, often conducted with the intention of challenging either or both of two theoretical claims about speech perception, are to test perception of speech by nonhuman animals (including monkeys, chinchillas, and birds), and to test perception of nonspeech by humans. The challenges are to the motor theory of speech perception, which claims that speech perception is accomplished by a specialization of the brain for phonetic perception, and both the motor theory and direct realism, which claim that listeners perceive vocal tract gestures. The logic of both lines of research is the same. It is that, if response patterns to speech by nonhuman animals or to nonspeech by humans are qualitatively like those to speech by humans, then most likely, perceptual processes applied to the signals are the same. If response patterns are the same, then, both a specialization for phonetic perception by humans and perception of gestures can be ruled out.

There are striking findings in both domains. For example, chinchillas have been found to have boundaries along a voice-onset time continuum similar to those of English listeners, including a shift in the boundary to longer values for farther back places of articulation (Kuhl and Miller, 1978). Japanese quail show compensation for coarticulation like that shown for Mann's (1980) human listeners described earlier (Kluender, Lotto, and Holt, 1997).

As for nonspeech, Lotto and Kluender (1998) showed an effect qualitatively like that of Mann (1980) when precursor syllables /ar/ and /al/ were replaced by tones at the ending F_3s of those syllables. They interpreted their finding as evidence of a contrast effect. The high tones caused the onset F_3s of members of the /da/–/ga/ continuum to sound effectively lower and so more /ga/-like; the low tones caused onset F_3s to sound higher and more /da/-like. There are many like findings (Holt, Lotto, and Kluender, 2000; Holt et al., 2001; Holt and Lotto, 2002). More recently Stephens and Holt (2003) showed a complementary effect. In their research, /al/ and /ar/ syllables were followed by tones tracking F_2 and F_3 transitions of a /da/ to /ga/ continuum. Listeners performed an AX discrimination task on syllable-transition pairs designed either to enhance or diminish discrimination if precursor syllables affected perception of the transitions. On enhanced trials, /al/ syllables, with a high ending F_3, preceded low frequency F_3 transitions, whereas /ar/ syllables, with a low ending F_3, preceded high frequency F3 transitions. On diminished trials the pairing was opposite. As predicted, discrimination performance on enhanced trials exceeded that on diminished trials, demonstrating a contrastive influence of the speech syllables on the nonspeech transitions.

How is this collection of findings to be interpreted? One way is that offered earlier. The findings disconfirm either or both of the claims of the motor theory and the central claim of the direct realist theory. No specialization for speech is required to explain basic speech perception findings. Moreover, animals are not supposed to perceive phonetic gestures; accordingly, when, for example, they show compensation for coarticulation qualitatively like humans do, these findings imply that humans do not perceive gestures. Further, in this view, when nonspeech signals exert context effects qualitatively like context effects exerted by speech signals, one can rule out gesture perception from nonspeech signals, and by implication, from speech signals.

These interpretations can be challenged and have been (e.g., Fowler, 1990). First, they are based on the weak logic that qualitative similarity in behavior implies identity of underlying perceptual processing. Fowler (1990) showed that behavioral responses to the sounds of ball bearings traversing two different kinds of ramps were qualitatively like, in the case of one ramp type, and qualitatively opposite, in the case of the other, to speech-rate normalization responses found by Miller and Liberman (1970) to syllables identified as /ba/ or /wa/. It is unlikely that processing of either sound type was like that for perception of /ba/ and /wa/.

As for the findings with nonhuman listeners, Best (1995) remarks that they do not disconfirm direct realism. Nonhuman animals also perceive sounding events directly, in terms of the forces structuring the acoustics. Nothing in the theory requires perfect perception, or that an organism have a particularly deep understanding of the specific physical objects and forces structuring the environment (consider, for example, our ability to identify general characteristics that cause the acoustic patterns that accompany

bursting bubbles of various sorts of liquids). Therefore, when the speech categories tested involve rather large changes in causes (e.g., in place of articulation, or voicing) it is not surprising that nonhuman animals can perceive (or learn to perceive) the distinction. More crucial cases would involve categories that involve more subtle distinctions, and especially those that require substantial experience to acquire even by humans.

As for findings comparing perception of speech to nonspeech, a recent finding (Holt, 2005) suggests another perspective on the large majority of findings that are contrastive in direction. In Holt's experiments, she preceded members of a /da/ to /ga/ continuum with "acoustic histories." The histories in her first experiment consisted of twenty-one tones. The final tone in each history had a frequency of 2300 Hz. That tone and its twenty predecessors had an average frequency of 1800 Hz, 2300 Hz, or 2800 Hz. Holt found that the acoustic histories had a contrastive impact on /da/–/ga/ identifications even when as much as 1,300 ms or thirteen repetitions of the 2300 Hz tones intervened between the histories and the syllables. Histories with a higher average frequency were associated with more /ga/ responses than those with a lower average.

Holt's results support an interpretation that Warren (1985) offered for the ubiquity of contrast effects. Warren proposed that perceivers continuously update perceptual criteria to calibrate them to recently encountered stimuli. For example, perceivers who find themselves in a setting in which they encounter many high-pitched sounds effectively recalibrate what counts as high-pitched, judging as lower in pitch sounds that in other contexts they would judge high. This account invokes higher-level, cognitive sources of influence on speech processing than either auditory or gestural accounts of speech perception have anticipated.

1.3 *Variability, normalization, and phonetic constancy*

Speech is characterized by variability. The production and acoustic realization of speech sounds depend on context – segmental (Liberman et al., 1952), prosodic (Fougeron and Keating, 1997), discourse (old/new: Fowler and Housum, 1987; Fowler, Levy, and Brown, 1997; Nooteboom and Kruyt, 1987), the physical characteristics of talkers (Dorman, Studdert-Kennedy, and Raphael, 1977; Peterson and Barney, 1952), speaking rate (Miller, 1981), and acoustic environment. Phonetic perception is resilient to all of these, and to many other perturbations of speech including novel accents and wide ranges of acoustic environments and conditions (parking garages, anechoic chambers, listening to a child speak with her mouth full).

This *phonetic constancy* despite a *lack of invariance* (the many-to-many mapping between acoustics and phonetic categories) defies easy explanation and poses significant challenges to all theories of speech perception. The flip side to variability, though, is that speech is rich with information beyond phonetic cues.

For example, the listener can glean a tremendous amount of *indexical* information from the speech signal (Ladefoged and Broadbent, 1957), including talker identity (Van Lancker, Kreiman, and Emmorey, 1985), physical characteristics (e.g., sex, age, height, and weight; Krauss, Freyberg, and Morsella, 2002), socioeconomic status (Ellis, 1967), and emotional state (e.g., Murray and Arnott, 1993; Streeter et al., 1983). Some of these qualities obviously co-vary with the elements of the speech signal assumed to carry phonetic information (e.g., differences in dialect specifying the realization of *pen* as /pEn/ or /pIn/; see Niedzielski, 1999 for evidence that *expectations* about dialect influence vowel perception), while others may have greater or lesser effect on phonetic information. An increase in Fo or amplitude in an arousal state has less impact on the realization of phonetic categories than do changes in speaking rate that may accompany an arousal state (e.g., Streeter et al., 1983). Similarly, changes in voice quality associated with aging within adulthood (e.g., Caruso, Mueller, and Shadden, 1995) may have little impact on the realization of speech sounds.

So variability is a double-edged sword: It creates a complex mapping between acoustics and percepts, but carries a tremendous amount of important information, and indexical information in particular. For several decades, there were two strands of talker variability research. Research focused on phonetic information largely took a negative view of variability, and sought to avoid or eliminate it by finding invariant cues or finding a way to transform speech signals to make the acoustic-phonetic mapping invariant. Research focused on indexical variability viewed variability as a rich source of useful information, and largely ignored phonetic perception.

Recently, this separation has been reconsidered in light of evidence that phonetic and indexical variability is preserved in memory and influences perception as well as memory of words. Exemplar and nonanalytic theories motivated by these findings present the possibility that subcategorical phonetic information and even nonlinguistic variability in the speech signal may help solve the lack of invariance problem in understanding phonetic constancy. We will briefly review the two major conventional approaches to phonetic constancy (the search for invariant cues and normalization theories) and then discuss the potential of exemplar theories.

1.4 *Finding invariants*

One possibility is that a larger window of analysis would provide a less variable mapping from acoustics to phonetic categories. Candidates have included syllables (Massaro, 1972), overlapping context-sensitive units (Wickelgren, 1969), or whole phrases (Miller, 1962), but none of these result in an invariant mapping.

Another possibility is that the speech signal contains invariant cues to phonetic categories, but we have not discovered them yet. For example, some evidence suggested context-invariant cues might be found by integrating across time scales not captured in typical acoustical analyses (Kewley-Port, 1983; Stevens and Blumstein, 1978). However, candidate cues have thus far turned out not to provide an invariant mapping. Furthermore, when both candidate invariant and variable cues are present, listeners focus attention on the variable cues (Blumstein, Isaacs, and Mertus, 1982; Walley and Carrell, 1983).

A third possibility is that articulatory actions provide the basis for phonetic categorization. Although the mapping from articulators to vocal tract shapes is indeterminate (e.g., Gopinath and Sondhi, 1970), it does not follow that phonetic gestures cannot be recovered from acoustic signals by listeners. Motor theorists invoke innate mechanisms, special to speech, that provide knowledge (about coarticulation's acoustic effects) that may permit selection among the possible vocal tract configurations consistent with an acoustic signal. However, there is a more fundamental reason why gestures may be recovered from indeterminate acoustic signals: Proofs of indeterminacy are only proofs that not *every* detail of vocal tract configurations is recoverable. However, phonetic gestures are proposed to be coarse-grained vocal tract actions that create and release constrictions in equifinal ways. For example, lip closures for /b/, /p/, and /m/ are achieved by a variety of patterns of jaw and lip movement and, because tongue configuration is irrelevant to that gesture, with a variety of tongue configurations. To detect the lip gesture, listeners only have to detect that the lips have closed. The precise lip, jaw, and tongue configurations need not be recovered.

In the case of variability, then, direct realism presents a promissory note along the following lines. The acoustics researchers extract from speech (spectra, formants, etc.) do not capture the underlying causal structure listeners perceive. The similarity of different tokens of the same gesture is greater than that of the acoustics as we currently analyze them, such that the same lawful relations hold between two speakers' gestures (distal stimuli) and the resulting acoustic structure (proximal stimuli). The heavy lifting of identifying the precise structure remains, but making a distinction between perfect recovery versus good-enough,

coarse-grained recovery of articulation may lead to progress.

It may not be obvious how this approach can handle the sensitivity of listeners to far more in the signal than constriction locations and degrees (such as indexical information and speaking rate). Some indexical information (e.g., differences in vocal tract morphology) may be specified by the acoustic information for vocal tract shape just considered. However, much indexical information as well as information about rate is expected to be specified by acoustic information for vocal tract dynamics.[2]

1.5 *Normalization*

A more common approach for addressing the variability in speech signals is to suppose that phonetic categorization depends on auditory, perceptual, and/or cognitive transformations of speech signals that map them onto speaker- and rate-independent categories. This sort of approach dates at least to Joos (1948), who proposed that either the incoming speech or internal phonetic categories must be warped to bring the two into registration when a talker change is detected. In addition to the descriptive problem that normalization addresses – the apparent lack of invariance – there is behavioral evidence suggesting a perceptual cost to a change in talker. Mullennix, Pisoni, and Martin (1989) found that identification of words presented in noise was less accurate and slower when words in a series of trials were produced by multiple talkers compared to when blocks of trials were produced by a single talker. Nusbaum and Morin (1992) compared phoneme, syllable, and word monitoring in blocked and mixed talker conditions, and found a constant talker variability cost of about thirty ms. The descriptive lack of acoustic–phonetic invariance and perceptual costs motivate *talker normalization theories*.

Normalization theories typically focus on vowels (although similar problems

---

2 We thank Gordon Ramsay for a tutorial on acoustic–articulation indeterminacy.

apply to consonants; Dorman et al., 1977), and hold either that the basis for phonetic constancy comes from *stimulus intrinsic* or *stimulus extrinsic* information (Ainsworth, 1975; Nearey, 1989). Stimulus intrinsic theories hold that each sample of speech (e.g., any vowel) contains sufficient information for accurate classification. For example, Syrdal and Gopal (1986) proposed a normalization algorithm in which F_0 and F_3 are used to rescale F_1 and F_2. This works fairly well but does not result in an invariant mapping (see J. D. Miller, 1989 for a review of formant ratio approaches). Shankweiler, Strange, and Verbrugge (1977) hypothesized that dynamic information from consonant–vowel transitions provide talker-independent phonetic cues; even when vowel nuclei were excised and syllabic onsets and offsets from talkers of different genders were paired, subjects were able to identify vowels with high accuracy (but not perfectly).

However, listeners do not rely solely on information in individual samples. Instead, vowel perception depends on recent context. In the classic experiment by Ladefoged and Broadbent (1957), identical /b/-vowel-/t/ words were identified by listeners following context sentences produced by synthetic speech representing distinct vowel spaces. Perception of a target word depended on the vowel space specified in the context phrase (e.g., with an identical utterance identified as *bit* following one talker and as *bet* following another).[3] Such findings motivate *stimulus extrinsic* theories, in which the listener builds up a talker-specific mapping over multiple samples of speech (possibly initially with mechanisms like those proposed under stimulus intrinsic accounts). Joos (1948) speculated that listeners build up a map of a talker's vowel space from the first few words they hear, gradually improving the mapping as lexical cues (e.g., in conventional greetings) disambiguate acoustic patterns. Algorithmic

approaches in this vein (e.g., classification relative to point vowel measures; Gerstman, 1968) proved quite accurate for isolated samples of speech.

But passive mechanisms such as Gerstman's fail to account for details of behavioral and neural evidence. For example, Nusbaum and Morin (1992) found that the effect of talker variability (blocked versus mixed) in their monitoring tasks interacted with that of cognitive load, a hallmark of active processing (Schneider and Shiffrin, 1977). Wong, Nusbaum, and Small (2004) examined neural activity using fMRI with the blocked/mixed monitoring paradigm. In the mixed talker condition, they found increases in activity in areas associated with speech (posterior superior temporal gyrus) and areas associated with shifts of attentional processing (superior parietal cortex). Magnuson and Nusbaum (2007; see also Nusbaum and Magnuson, 1997) used the monitoring paradigm with two sets of synthetic speech that differed slightly in average F_0 (with some small collateral changes in vowel space). They told one group of subjects they were hearing two talkers and another group that they were hearing one talker; a third group received no special instructions. The latter two groups showed no difference between blocked and mixed conditions, while the group expecting two talkers showed the effect typical of mixing two genuinely different talkers – they were significantly slower in the mixed talker condition. Similarly, Johnson, Strand, and D'Imperio (1999) used instructions to manipulate expectations about talker sex, which caused a shift in vowel category boundaries like those caused by manipulations of F_0 or visual cues to sex. These results suggest that adapting to changes in talker characteristics is an active, resource demanding process subject to cognitive penetration. Nusbaum and Morin (1992) proposed a variant of stimulus extrinsic normalization, *contextual tuning*, which assumes there are active control structures that retune phonetic mappings when talker changes are detected (or even just expected, under certain conditions).

3   For a demonstration, see https://engineering.purdue.edu/~malcolm/interval/1997-056/VowelQuality.html.

1.6 *Exemplar theories*

A radically different proposal is that talker differences do not require normalization – but not because there is invariant information for phonetic categories. Rather, *exemplar theories* (Goldinger, 1998; Johnson, 1997) propose that holistic exemplar traces of speech are stored in memory and form the basis for linguistic perception.[4] As in exemplar models of categorization more generally, the theory is that the exemplars statistically sample the space of talker characteristics (including putatively linguistic and nonlinguistic dimensions). The argument is that phonetic constancy has been misconstrued. The acoustic correlates of talker variability are not random, and this lawful variability (cf. Elman and McClelland, 1986) may constrain rather than complicate the problem of phonetic constancy (and vice versa; cf. Remez et al., 1997). Evidence for this view includes findings that recognition memory improves when talker characteristics are preserved across new and old items[5]

---

[4] Goldinger (1998) claimed his simulations with an exemplar model proved that an exemplar mechanism could solve the lack of invariance problem without normalization. However, the input to his model consisted of presegmented word-length samples of separate units representing phonetic and indexical characteristics; it was prenormalized. In real speech, phonetic information is conditioned by talker characteristics. The episodic model may provide phonetic constancy without normalization, but tests with closer analogs to real speech (or real speech) are needed to evaluate the claim.

[5] One argument proponents of exemplar models sometimes make is that the preservation of surface detail falsifies normalization theories, which they claim require that all information aside from abstract phonetic categories be discarded. There are two problems with this claim. First, normalization does not require that subcategorical detail be discarded, and few accounts of normalization explicitly or implicitly discard it. All it entails is bringing the signal and phonetic categories into registration. Second, preservation of surface detail would not falsify an abstractionist account of normalization, as it would be consistent with multiple parallel representations of different aspects of the signal at varying levels of abstraction, as is found in the visual and auditory systems more generally (Bushara et al., 1999; Mishkin, Ungerleider, and Macko, 1983). Indeed, Belin, Zatorre, Lafaille, Ahad, and Pike (2000) present evidence supporting their model on which a dorsal pathway is specialized for extracting linguistic content, while a ventral pathway is specialized for talker identification.

(e.g., Goldinger, 1996) as does performance in processing tasks like shadowing (Goldinger, 1998).

Goldinger (1998) presented promising simulations with a computational implementation of an exemplar model in which phonetic categorization was accomplished without explicit normalization. However, the inputs to the model were presegmented (exemplars were words) and prenormalized – separate units represented talker and phonetic information. Further tests of the model with more realistic input (in which phonetic information is conditioned by talker characteristics, as in real speech) are needed to evaluate the claim that exemplar models do not require normalization. As Goldinger and Azuma (2003) discuss, *adaptive resonance theory* (e.g., Grossberg, 2003) may provide a framework capable of handling more realistic inputs while incorporating the key principles of Goldinger's *episodic lexicon theory* (see Samuel and Sumner, this volume, for more discussion of the theory).

There is also evidence for *contingency* of linguistic and indexical variability. Task-irrelevant variability in either dimension slows processing (Mullennix and Pisoni, 1990), and training on talker identification facilitates phonetic perception of speech produced by trained-on talkers (Nygaard and Pisoni, 1998; Nygaard, Sommers, and Pisoni, 1994), suggesting that perceptual learning occurs for both types of information no matter which is attended, or, more strongly, that the two dimensions are perceived integrally and nonanalytically – that is, as holistic exemplar traces (Nygaard and Pisoni, 1998).

However, contingency is not always found. Luce and Lyons (1998) found specificity effects in explicit recognition, but not in an implicit priming task. McLennan and Luce (2005) found that specificity effects depend on processing time. When listeners are forced to respond quickly, the advantage for preserving nonlinguistic characteristics of a spoken word disappear. These results challenge strong integrality, but are consistent with the parallel-contingent explanation of Mullennix and Pisoni (1990), who argued that phonetic identification is hierarchically dependent on analyses of talker characteristics.

1.7 *Summary*

Auditory/cognitive accounts assume that phonetic constancy depends on finding one of the following: invariant acoustic cues to phonetic categories; transformations of the speech signal that render talker- (or other context-) specific mappings; or active control structures that, for example, hypothesize mappings and refine them based on success in mapping to phonetic, lexical, or even more complex categories. The motor theory and direct realist theory assume gestures as fundamental units (inferred in the former, directly perceived in the latter based on coarse-grained acoustic information for constriction locations and degrees). *Episodic/exemplar/nonanalytic* theories predict that holistic memory traces of speech will provide a good enough basis for classification to approximate an invariant mapping, and are the only theories to account for specificity effects (e.g., benefits to preserving nonphonetic details of utterances). Each of these approaches continues to hold promise for explaining phonetic constancy. However, none of them can yet specify how information in the speech signal is mapped to phonetic categories in order to achieve phonetic constancy despite variation in talkers, rate, acoustic environment, and other contextual dimensions.

2 Speech perception and lexical access

Psycholinguists tend to classify speech perception and spoken word recognition (and other levels of description) as distinct aspects of spoken language understanding, with most theories postulating distinct levels of representation for each division. Even in theories that posit distinct phonetic-perceptual and lexical levels, the interface between these levels is of great importance. We will focus on three key issues: the lexical segmentation problem, interface representations, and the modularity/interaction debate.

2.1 *Segmentation and interface representations*

The *lexical segmentation problem* (in contrast to the phonemic segmentation problem mentioned earlier) is that fluent speech provides few acoustic cues to word boundaries, and none of those are very reliable (Cole and Jakimik, 1980; Saffran and Sahni, this volume). This fact has helped justify the simplifying assumption that a speech perception mechanism provides a phoneme readout of the speech signal. Thus, phonemes form the interface between perception and a presumably more cognitive word recognition system. This interface assumption simplifies in two directions: Speech perception is given a concrete goal, and word recognition is freed from, for example, the lack of invariance problem. However, it is also a potentially complicating assumption.

Consider the *embedding problem* in spoken word recognition. Assuming that the bottom-up input is a string of phonemes with no cues to word boundaries poses a tremendous parsing challenge. McQueen et al. (1995) estimated that eighty-four percent of polysyllabic words have at least one shorter word embedded within them, and many have more than one (*catalog* has *cat*, *cattle*, *at*, *a*, and *log*) and most short words are embedded within longer words. The problem is compounded by embeddings that straddle word boundaries and phonological processes that create additional ambiguities (e.g., in fluent speech, phonological assimilation can make the realization of *right berry* nearly identical to that of *ripe berry*; Gaskell and Marslen-Wilson, 1996; Gow, 2001). Theories have typically relied on lexical competition to solve the segmentation and embedding problems (e.g., McClelland and Elman, 1986; Norris, 1994).

However, the embedding problem is significantly reduced (but does not go away completely) if we assume that prosodic and subphonemic information is available for word recognition. For example, employing the *metrical segmentation strategy* (Cutler and Norris, 1988) – positing word boundaries before all strong syllables – would correctly segment about ninety percent of (frequency-weighted) words (Cutler and Carter, 1987), but would not completely resolve the segmentation and embedding problems. However, other cues are available. Building on evidence that subcategorical mismatches (misleading coarticulatory cues introduced by splicing parts of two words together, for example, splicing the stop burst of /b/ in *job* onto the *jo* of *jog* so that formant transitions at the end of the vowel signal a forthcoming velar, rather than bilabial stop) influence lexical access (Dahan et al., 2001; Marslen-Wilson and Warren, 1994), Salverda, Dahan, and McQueen (2003) used eyetracking to measure the time course of lexical activation when the first syllable of a word like *hamster* was replaced by a production of an embedded word like *ham* (which was about fifteen ms longer in duration than the *ham* of *hamster*). Not only were listeners sensitive to the manipulation (as revealed by initial biases to look to *ham* rather than *hamster*), they showed differential sensitivity depending on the prosodic context in which the short word was recorded (see Davis, Marslen-Wilson, and Gaskell, 2002 for converging offline evidence from priming). Thus, there is growing evidence that much more detail is available at lexical access than categorical phonemic abstractions (though whether such detail makes direct contact with the lexicon [Gaskell and Marslen-Wilson, 1997] or is mediated by a phonemic or gestural level of representation capable of delivering continuous levels of activation, as in TRACE [McClelland and Elman, 1986; Dahan et al., 2001] or direct realism [Fowler, 1986] remains an open question).

2.2 *Interaction or autonomy?*

A central debate in speech perception and spoken word recognition is whether the influence is bi-directional – whether there is *feedback interaction* between higher and lower levels of representation, or whether

representational organization is strictly *modular* (or *autonomous*).

It is clear that sublexical decisions can be influenced by lexical knowledge. For example, Ganong (1980) spliced identical /t/ to /d/ continua onto following contexts "-ash" and "-ask," creating nonword–word and word–nonword continua, respectively. Lexical status shifted the identification function, such that more steps on each continuum were identified as the stop consistent with a word. Another well-known example is *phoneme restoration*, in which listeners report that they hear a segment that has been completely replaced by noise (e.g., Warren, 1970).

The interpretation of these effects is controversial. They are easily explained by lexical-to-phoneme feedback in an interactive model like TRACE (McCelland and Elman, 1986). But others argue that all effects consistent with feedback could occur prelexically (based on, e.g., transitional probability information stored at a phonemic level) or at a postlexical decision stage in a feedforward, autonomous system (Norris, McQueen, and Cutler, 2000). What is needed to distinguish between the two accounts is evidence for a lexical influence on perception that cannot be attributed to postlexical decisions about phonemes. An ideal task would demonstrate sublexical, perceptual *consequences* of lexical information, ideally after the lexical context has been heard (as in lexically mediated compensation for coarticulation; Elman and McClelland, 1988; Magnuson et al., 2003; Pitt and McQueen, 1998; Samuel and Pitt, 2003), or would not require an explicit phonemic decision (e.g., selective adaptation based on restored phonemes; Samuel, 2001). However, repeated demonstrations of lexical influence on phonemes in these paradigms have not convinced everyone concerned (see Norris, McQueen, and Cutler, 2003, for thoughtful arguments and discussion, and Magnuson, Mirman, and Harris, this volume, for further theoretical and computational details). Thus, there are strong arguments on both sides, but the jury is still out on the empirical evidence.

3 Avenues to progress

We have selectively reviewed the key phenomena and theoretical issues in speech perception. We will close with a discussion of two questions for future research we see as vital for advancing our understanding of speech perception. The issues we have chosen reflect the two main sections of our chapter.

3.1 *What is the basis for phonetic perception?*

The key debate here is between general auditory and gesture theories. Can evidence distinguish the theories in convincing ways? There are some barriers to this. First, neither account is sufficiently developed in critical domains for evidence to make a clear distinction. Theorists in both domains have considerable wiggle room that they will use at least until the accounts are further sharpened or until a superior alternative to both appears. The following, then, is a guess about the kinds of evidence that theorists will seek to confirm or disconfirm either account.

For gesture accounts to be viable, it will be necessary for researchers to address convincingly the proofs of indeterminacy in the mapping from acoustics to articulation. A promising avenue may be the one outlined earlier. The proofs are that not every aspect of vocal tract configuration can be recovered from its acoustic correlates. However, gesture theories do not claim that listeners recover that level of detail. Rather, listeners recover information about gestures, coarse-grained actions that create and release constrictions. Needed now is evidence whether, for the gestures that theorists identify as linguistically relevant across languages of the world, acoustic information can specify them. Proofs that even that level of detail cannot be recovered would disconfirm the direct realist theory, but not necessarily the motor theory, which invokes innate knowledge of coarticulation and its acoustic consequences to assist in gesture recovery.

Neuropsychological evidence that would disconfirm auditory accounts and correspondingly confirm the motor theory would be convincing evidence for a specialization of the brain for speech perception. Such a specialized system should not activate when acoustic signals similar to speech, but not perceived to have phonetic properties, are presented to listeners. The specialized system should also activate when speech is produced or silently mouthed. It might be expected to activate when speech gestures are seen as well as heard. Neuropsychological evidence that would confirm auditory accounts would be evidence that brain areas active for speech signals are also active for acoustically similar nonspeech signals.

As for behavioral evidence, unfortunately it is not obvious what strategies not already adopted would be informative. Strategies already adopted have so far led to inconclusive outcomes.

Direct realists, but not motor theorists or auditory theorists, predict that when nonspeech signals have been caused by real-sounding events (as opposed to being, for example, tones) behavioral response patterns to them should resemble those to speech when distal properties of the speech and nonspeech events are similar in relevant ways. When they are different in relevant ways, response patterns should differ. These predictions hold, in principle, regardless of similarity in acoustic structure. For auditory theorists, the predictions are opposite. Response patterns should be similar when acoustic patterns are similar in relevant ways regardless of the similarity of distal event properties. This distinction in predictions is sharp, but likely difficult to cash out experimentally. Similar event properties are likely most of the time (but not always) to generate similar acoustic patterns.

3.2 *What is the basis for phonetic constancy?*

We described three major approaches to phonetic constancy: auditory/cognitive, gestural invariance, and episodic/exemplar/ nonanalytic. None of the approaches provides a satisfactory answer. Truly invariant acoustic cues to phonetic categories have yet to be identified. Passive normalization algorithms proposed in auditory/cognitive approaches are not capable of human levels of accuracy, nor can they account for evidence for active control in talker adaptation (and note that while talker characteristics have been our focus, rate variability poses similar challenges). Contextual tuning explains evidence for active control (Nusbaum and Magnuson, 1997) and may provide a unitary account of talker and rate adaptation, but as yet, concrete proposals for mechanisms are lacking.

A full account of gestural invariance (the basis for phonetic constancy in motor and direct realist theories) will require identifying the characteristics of the proximal stimulus (acoustics) that map lawfully onto the underlying distal causes (gestures). The possibility that coarse-grained gestural information good enough for phonetic categorization is carried in the acoustics of speech acoustic is promising, but this approach is in very early stages and is thus untested.

Episodic/exemplar/nonanalytic models (Goldinger, 1998) parsimoniously account for effects of linguistic and nonlinguistic variability, and hold promise for the phonetic constancy problem, but a truly convincing theory would require strong support for the claim that exemplar models do not require normalization, including tests with (more) realistic inputs than Goldinger used in his 1998 simulations, and an account of why the impact of linguistic and nonlinguistic information can be dissociated (McLennan and Luce, 2005). As Goldinger and Azuma (2003) discuss, adaptive resonance theory (Grossberg, 2003) may provide a unifying framework that incorporates the key theoretical principles of the exemplar approach as well as mechanisms suited to addressing the challenges of real speech. We are eager to see whether the promise of this approach can be realized.

The truth likely lies somewhere between the theories we have discussed. As Remez (2005) puts it, after reviewing evidence that phonetic perception is resilient against the removal or perturbation of virtually any hypothetical cue to phonetic perception, "perceptual organization [is] attuned to a complex form of regular if unpredictable spectrotemporal variation within which the specific acoustic and auditory elements matter far less than the overall configuration they compose" (2005, pp. 42–3).

References

Ainsworth, W. (1975). Intrinsic and extrinsic factors in vowel judgments. In Fant, G. & Tatham M. (Eds.) *Auditory analysis and perception of speech* (pp. 103–13). London: Academic Press.

Allen, J. S. & Miller, J. L. (2001). Contextual influences on the internal structure of phonetic categories: A distinction between lexical status and speaking rate. *Perception & Psychophysics*, 63, 798–810.

Belin, P., Zatorre, R. J., Lafaille, P., Ahad, P., & Pike, B. (2000). Voice-selective areas in human auditory cortex. *Nature*, 403, 309–12.

Best, C. T. (1995). A direct realist perspective on cross-language speech perception. In Strange, W. (Ed.) *Speech perception and linguistic experience: Theoretical and methodological issues in cross-language speech research* (pp. 167–200). Timonium MD: York Press.

Blumstein, S. E., Isaacs, E., & Mertus, J. (1982). The role of gross spectral shape as a perceptual cue to place of articulation in initial stop consonants. *Journal of the Acoustical Society of America*, 72, 43–50.

Bushara, K. O., Weeks, R. A., Ishii, K., Catalan, M., Tian, B., & Hallett, M. (1999). Modality-specific frontal and parietal areas for auditory and visual spatial localization in humans. *Nature Neuroscience*, 2, 759–66.

Caruso, A., Mueller, P., & Shadden, B. B. (1995). Effects of aging on speech and voice. *Physical and Occupational Therapy in Geriatrics*, 13, 63–80.

Cole, R. & Jakimik, J. (1980). A model of speech perception. In Cole, R. (Ed.) *Perception and Production of Fluent Speech* (pp. 133–63). Hillsdale NJ: Erlbaum.

Cutler, A. & Carter, D. M. (1987). The predominance of strong initial syllables in the English vocabulary. *Computer Speech and Language*, 2, 133–42.

Cutler, A. & Norris, D. G. (1988). The role of strong syllables in segmentation for lexical access. *Journal of Experimental Psychology: Human Perception and Performance*, 14, 113–21.

Dahan, D., Magnuson, J. S., Tanenhaus, M. K., & Hogan, E. M. (2001). Subcategorical mismatches and the time course of lexical access: Evidence for lexical competition. *Language and Cognitive Processes*, 16, 507–34.

Davis, M. H., Marslen-Wilson, W. D., & Gaskell, M. G. (2002). Leading up the lexical garden path: Segmentation and ambiguity in spoken word recognition. *Journal of Experimental Psychology: Human Perception and Performance*, 28, 218–44.

Diehl, R. & Kluender, K. (1989). On the objects of speech perception. *Ecological Psychology*, 1, 121–44.

Dorman, M. F., Studdert-Kennedy, M., & Raphael, L. J. (1977). Stop consonant recognition: Release bursts and formant transitions as functionally equivalent, context-dependent cues. *Perception & Psychophysics*, 22, 109–22.

Driver, J. (1996). Enhancement of selective listening of illusory mislocation of speech sounds due to lip-reading. *Nature*, 381, 66–8.

Ellis, D. S. (1967). Speech and social status in America. *Social Forces*, 45, 431–7.

Elman, J. & McClelland, J. (1988). Exploiting lawful variability in the speech wave. In Perkell, J. S. & Klatt, D. H. (Eds.) *Invariance and variability in speech processes* (pp. 360–80). Hillsdale, NJ: Erlbaum.

Fougeron, C. A. & Keating, P. (1997). Articulatory strengthening at edges of prosodic domains. *Journal of the Acoustical Society of America*, 101, 3728–40.

Fowler, C. A. (1986). An event approach to the study of speech perception from a direct-realist perspective. *Journal of Phonetics*, 14, 3–28.

(1990). Sound-producing sources as objects of speech perception: Rate normalization and nonspeech perception. *Journal of the Acoustical Society of America*, 88, 1236–49.

(1994). The direct-realist theory of speech perception. *The Encyclopedia of Language and Linguistics* 8 (pp. 4199–203). Oxford: Pergamon Press.

(2006). Compensation for coarticulation reflects gesture perception, not spectral contrast. *Perception & Psychophysics*, 68, 161–77.

Fowler, C. A. & Dekle, D. J. (1991). Listening with eye and hand: Crossmodal contributions to speech perception. *Journal of Experimental Psychology: Human Perception and Performance*, 17, 816–28.

Fowler, C. A. & Housum, J. (1987). Talkers' signaling of "new" and "old" words in speech and listeners' perception and use of the distinction. *Journal of Memory and Language*, 26, 489–50.

Fowler, C. A., Levy, E. T., & Brown, J. M. (1997). Reductions of spoken words in certain discourse contexts. *Journal of Memory and Language*, 37, 24–40.

Fowler, C. A. & Rosenblum, L. D. (1990). Duplex perception: A comparison of monosyllables and slamming doors. *Journal of Experimental Psychology: Human Perception and Performance*, 16, 742–54.

Fowler, C. A. & Saltzman, E. (1993). Coordination and coarticulation in speech production. *Language and Speech*, 36, 171–95.

Galantucci, B., Fowler, C. A., & Turvey, M. T. (2006). The motor theory of speech perception reviewed. *Psychonomic Bulletin and Review*, 13, 361–77.

Ganong, W. F. (1980). Phonetic categorization in auditory word perception. *Journal of Experimental Psychology: Human Perception & Performance*, 6, 110–25.

Gaskell, M. G. & Marslen-Wilson, W. D. (1996). Phonological variation and inference in lexical access. *Journal of Experimental Psychology: Human Perception & Performance*, 22, 144–58.

Gaskell, M. G. (1997). Integrating form and meaning: A distributed model of speech perception. *Language & Cognitive Processes*, 12, 613–56.

Gerstman, L. J. (1968). Classification of self-normalized vowels. *IEEE Transactions on Audio Electroacoustics*, AU-16, 78–80.

Gibson, J. (1966). *The senses considered as perceptual systems*. Boston: Houghton-Mifflin.

Gibson, J. (1979). *The ecological approach to visual perception*. Hillsdale, NJ: Lawrence Erlbaum Associates.

Goldinger, S. D. (1996). Words and voices: Episodic traces in spoken word identification and recognition memory. *Journal of Experimental Psychology: Learning, Memory and Cognition*, 22, 1166–83.

Goldinger, S. D. (1998). Echoes of echoes? An episodic theory of lexical access. *Psychological Review*, 105, 251–79.

Goldinger, S. D. & Azuma, T. (2003). Puzzle-solving science: The quixotic quest for units in speech perception. *Journal of Phonetics*, 31, 305–20.

Goldstein, L. & Fowler, C. A. (2003). Articulatory phonology: A phonology for public language use. In Schiller, N. & Meyer, A. (Eds.) *Phonetics and phonology in language comprehension and production: Differences and similarities.* (pp. 159–207) Berlin: Mouton de Gruyter.

Gopinath, B. & Sondhi, M. M. (1970). Determination of the shape of the human vocal tract from acoustical measurements. *Bell Systems Technical Journal*, 49, 1195–214.

Grossberg, S. (2003). Resonant neural dynamics of speech perception. *Journal of Phonetics*, 31, 423–45.

Holt, L. (2005). Temporally nonadjacent nonlinguistic sounds affect speech categorization. *Psychological Science*, 16, 305–12.

Holt, L. & Lotto, A. (2002). Behavioral examinations of the level of auditory processing of speech context effects. *Hearing Research*, 167, 156–69.

Holt, L., Lotto, A., & Kluender, K. (2000). Neighboring spectral content influences vowel identification. *Journal of the Acoustical Society of America*, 108, 710–22.

(2001). Influence of fundamental frequency on stop-consonant voicing perception: A case of learned covariation or auditory enhancement? *Journal of the Acoustical Society of America*, 109, 764–74.

Johnson, K. (1997). Speech perception without speaker normalization: An exemplar model. In Johnson, K. & Mullennix, J. W. (Eds.) *Talker Variability in Speech Processing* (pp. 145–66). San Diego: Academic Press.

Johnson, K., Strand, E. A., & D'imperio, M. (1999). Auditory-visual integration of talker gender in vowel perception. *Journal of Phonetics*, 24, 359–84.

Jones, S. (1996). Imitation or exploration: Young infants' matching of adults' oral gestures. *Child Development*, 67, 1952–69.

Joos, M. (1948). *Acoustic phonetics.* Baltimore, MD: Linguistic Society of America.

Kamachi, M., Hill, H., Lander, K., & Vatikiotis-Bateson, E. (2003). Putting the face to the voice: Matching identity across modality. *Current Biology*, 13, 1709–14.

Kewley-Port, D. (1983). Time-varying features as correlates of place of articulation in stop consonants. *Journal of the Acoustical Society of America*, 73, 322–35.

Klatt, D. H. (1979). Speech perception: A model of acoustic phonetic analysis and lexical access. *Journal of Phonetics*, 7, 279–312.

Kluender, K., Lotto, A., & Holt, L. (1997). Perceptual compensation for coarticulation by Japanese quail (coturnix coturnix japonica).

Journal of the Acoustical Society of America, 102, 1134–40.

Krauss, R. M., Freyberg, R., & Morsella, E. (2002). Inferring speakers' physical attributes from their voices. *Journal of Experimental Social Psychology*, 38, 618–25.

Kuhl, P. (1991). Human adults and human infants show a perceptual magnet effect for the prototypes of speech categories, monkeys do not. *Perception & Psychophysics*, 50, 93–107.

Kuhl, P. & Iverson, P. (1995). Linguistic experience and the perceptual magnet effect. In Strange, W. (Ed.) *Speech perception and linguistic experience, Issues in cross-language research.* (pp. 121–54) Baltimore, MD: York Press.

Kuhl, P. & Miller, J. D. (1978). Speech perception by the chinchilla: Identification functions for synthetic VOT stimuli. *Journal of the Acoustical Society of America*, 63, 905–17.

Lachs, L. (2002). *Vocal tract kinematics and cross modal speech information.* Ph.D Dissertation, Indiana University.

Ladefoged, P. & Broadbent, D. E. (1957). Information conveyed by vowels. *Journal of the Acoustical Society of America*, 29, 98–104.

Liberman, A. M. (1957). Some results of research on speech perception. *Journal of the Acoustical Society of America*, 29, 117–23.

(1996). *Speech, A special code.* Cambridge, MA: Bradford Books.

Liberman, A., Cooper, F. S., Shankweiler, D. P., & Studdert-Kennedy, M. G. (1967). Perception of the speech code. *Psychological Review*, 74, 431–61.

Liberman, A., Delattre, P., & Cooper, F. S. (1952). The role of selected stimulus variables in the perception of the unvoiced-stop consonants. *American Journal of Psychology*, 65, 497–516.

Liberman, A. M., Delattre, P., Cooper, F. S., & Gerstman, L. (1954). The role of consonant-vowel transitions in the perception of the stop and nasal consonants. *Psychological Monographs, General and Applied*, 68, 1–13.

Liberman, A. M., Harris, K. S., Hoffman, H. S., & Griffith, B. C. (1957). The discrimination of speech sounds within and across phoneme boundaries. *Journal of Experimental Psychology*, 54, 358–68.

Liberman, A. M. & Mattingly, I. G. (1985). The motor theory revised. *Cognition*, 21, 1–36.

Liberman, A. M. & Whalen, D. H. (2000). On the relation of speech to language. *Trends in Cognitive Sciences*, 4, 187–96.

Lively, S. & Pisoni, D. B. (1997). On prototypes and phonetic categories: A critical assessment of the perceptual magnet effect in speech perception. *Journal of Experimental Psychology: Human Perception and Performance*, 23, 1665–79.

Lotto, A. & Kluender, K. (1998). General contrast effects in speech perception: Effect of preceding liquid on stop consonant identification. *Perception & Psychophysics*, 60, 602–19.

Luce, P. A., & Lyons, E. A. (1998). Specificity of memory representations for spoken words. *Memory & Cognition*, 26, 708–15.

Maddieson, I. (1984). *Patterns of sounds*. Cambridge: Cambridge University Press.

Magnuson, J. S., Mirman, D., & Harris, H. D. (this volume). Computational models of spoken word recognition.

Magnuson, J. S., & Nusbaum, H. C. (2007). Acoustic differences, listener expectations, and the perceptual accommodation of talker variability. *Journal of Experimental Psychology: Human Perception and Performance*, 33, 391–409.

Magnuson, J., McMurray, B., Tanenhaus, M., & Aslin, R. (2003). Lexical effects on compensation for coarticulation: The ghost of Christmas past. *Cognitive Science*, 27, 285–98.

Mann, V. (1980). Influence of preceding liquid on stop-consonant perception. *Perception & Psychophysics*, 28, 407–12.

Mann, V. & Liberman, A. M. (1983). Some differences between phonetic and auditory modes of perception. *Cognition*, 14, 211–35.

Mann, V. & Repp, B. (1980). Influence of vocalic context on perception of the [s]-[ʃ] distinction. *Perception & Psychophysics*, 28, 213–28.

Marslen-Wilson, W. & Warren, P. (1994). Levels of perceptual representations and process in lexical access: Words, phonemes, features. *Psychological Review*, 101, 653–75.

Massaro, D. W. (1972). Preperceptual images, processing time, and perceptual units in auditory perception. *Psychological Review*, 79, 124–45.

McClelland, J. L., & Elman, J. L. (1986). The TRACE model of speech perception. *Cognitive Psychology*, 18, 1–86.

McGurk, H. & MacDonald, J. (1976). Hearing lips and seeing voices. *Nature*, 264, 746–48.

McMurray, B. & Aslin, R. N. (2005). Infants are sensitive to within-category variation in speech perception. *Cognition*, 95, B15-B26.

McMurray, B., Tanenhaus, M. K., & Aslin, R. N. (2002). Gradient effects of within-category phonetic variation on lexical access. *Cognition*, 86, B33-B42.

McQueen, J. M., Cutler, A., Briscoe, T., & Norris, D. (1995). Models of continuous speech recognition and the contents of the vocabulary. *Language and Cognitive Processes*, 10, 309–31.

Miller, G. A. (1962). Decision units in the perception of speech. *IRE Transactions on Information Theory*, IT-8, 81–3.

Miller, J. L. (1981). Phonetic perception: Evidence for context-dependent and context-independent processing. *Journal of the Acoustical Society of America*, 69, 822–31.

Miller, J. L. & Volaitis, L. (1989). Effect of speaking rate on the perceptual structure of a phonetic category. *Perception & Psychophysics*, 46, 505–12.

Mishkin, M., Ungerleider, L., & Macko, K. (1983). Object vision and spatial vision: Two central pathways. *Trends in Neuroscience*, 6, 414–17.

Mullennix, J. W., & Pisoni, D. B. (1990). Stimulus variability and processing dependencies in speech perception. *Perception & Psychophysics*, 47, 379–90.

Mullennix, J. W., Pisoni, D. B., & Martin, C. S. (1989). Some effects of talker variability on spoken word recognition. *Journal of the Acoustical Society of America*, 85, 365–78.

Munhall, K. G., Jones, J. A., Callan, D. E., Kuratate, T., & Vatikiotis-Bateson, E. (2004). Visual prosody and speech intelligibility: Head movement improves auditory speech perception. *Psychological Science*, 15, 133–6.

Murray, I. R. & Arnott, J. L. (1993). Toward the simulation of emotion in synthetic speech: a review of the literature on human vocal emotion, *Journal of the Acoustical Society of America*, 93, 1097–108.

Nearey, T. M. (1989). Static, dynamic, and relational properties in vowel perception. *Journal of the Acoustical Society of America*, 85, 2088–113.

Niedzielski, N. (1999). The effect of social information on the perception of sociolinguistic variables. *Journal of Language & Social Psychology*, 18, 62–85.

Nooteboom, S. G. & Kruyt, J. G. (1987). Accent, focus distribution, and the perceived distribution of given and new information: An experiment. *Journal of the Acoustical Society of America*, 82, 1512–24.

Norris, D. (1994). Shortlist: A connectionist model of continuous speech recognition. *Cognition*, 52, 189–234.

Norris, D., McQueen, J. M, & Cutler, A. (2003). Perceptual learning in speech. *Cognitive Psychology*, 47, 204–38.

Nusbaum, H. C. & Magnuson, J. S. (1997). Talker normalization: Phonetic constancy as a cognitive process. In Johnson, K. & Mullennix, J. W. (Eds.) *Talker Variability in Speech Processing* (pp. 109–32). San Diego: Academic Press.

Nusbaum, H. C., & Morin, T. M. (1992). Paying attention to differences among talkers. In Tohkura, Y., Sagisaka, Y., & Vatikiotis-Bateson, E. (Eds.) *Speech Perception, Speech Production, and Linguistic Structure.* (pp. 113–34). Tokyo: OHM.

Nygaard, L. C., Sommers, M. S., & Pisoni, D. B. (1994). Speech perception as a talker-contingent process. *Psychological Science*, 5, 42–6.

Nygaard, L. C., & Pisoni, D. B. (1998). Talker-specific learning in speech perception. *Perception & Psychophysics*, 60, 355–76.

Peterson, G. E. & Barney, H. L. (1952). Control methods used in a study of vowels. *Journal of the Acoustical Society of America*, 24, 175–84.

Pierrehumbert, J. (1990). Phonological and phonetic representations. *Journal of Phonetics*, 18, 375–94.

Pisoni, D. B. & Tash, J. (1974). Reaction times to comparisons within and across phonetic boundaries. *Perception & Psychophysics*, 15, 285–90.

Pitt, M. A. & McQueen, J. M. (1998). Is compensation for coarticulation mediated by the lexicon? *Journal of Memory & Language*, 39, 347–70.

Reinholt Peterson, N. (1986). Perceptual compensation for segmentally-conditioned fundamental-frequency perturbations. *Phonetica*, 43, 31–42.

Remez, R. E. (2005). The perceptual organization of speech. In Pisoni, D. B. & Remez, R. E. (Eds.) *The Handbook of Speech Perception*, (pp. 28–50). Oxford: Blackwell.

Remez, R., Fellowes, J., & Rubin. P. (1997). Talker identification based on phonetic information. *Journal of Experimental Psychology: Human Perception and Performance*, 23, 651–66.

Remez, R., Rubin, P., Pisoni, D., & Carrell, T. (1981). Speech perception without traditional speech cues. *Science*, 212, 947–50.

Rosenblum, L. & Saldana, H. (1998). Time-varying information for speech perception. In Campbell, R., Dodd, B., & Burnham, D. (Eds.). *Hearing by eye II, Advances in the Psychology of speechreading and auditory-visual speech.* (pp.61–81) East Sussex, UK: Psychology Press.

Rosenblum, L. D., Yakel, D., Baseer, N., Panchal, A., Nodarse, B., & Niehus, R. (2002). Visual speech information for face recognition. *Perception & Psychophysics*, 64, 220–9.

Saffran, J. R. & Sahni, S. D. (this volume). Learning the sounds of language.

Samuel, A. G. (2001). Knowing a word affects the fundamental perception of the sounds within it. *Psychological Science*, 12, 348–51.

Samuel, A. G. & Pitt, M. A. (2003). Lexical activation (and other factors) can mediate compensation for coarticulation. *Journal of Memory and Language*, 48, 416–34.

Samuel, A. G. & Sumner, M. (this volume). Current directions in research on spoken word recognition.

Sawusch, J. & Gagnon, D. (1995). Auditory coding, cues and coherence in phonetic perception. *Journal of Experimental Psychology: Human Perception and Performance*, 21, 635–52.

Schneider, W. & Shiffrin, R. (1977). Controlled and automatic human information processing: 1. Detection, search and attention. *Psychological Review*, 84, 1–66.

Shankweiler, D., Strange, W., & Verbrugge, R. (1977). Speech and the problem of perceptual constancy. In Shaw, R. & Bransford, J. (Eds.) *Perceiving, acting, and knowing* (pp. 315–45). Hillsdale, NJ: Erlbaum.

Shattuck-Hufnagel, S. (1979). Speech errors as evidence for a serial-ordering mechanism in sentence production. In Cooper, W. & Walker, E. (Eds.) *Sentence processing: Psycholinguistic studies presented to Merrill Garrett.* (pp. 295–342) Hillsdale, NJ: Lawrence Erlbaum.

Silverman, K. (1987). *The structure and processing of fundamental frequency contours*, Ph.D. Dissertation, Cambridge University.

Smith, Z., Delgutte, B., & Oxenham, A. (2002). Chimeric sounds reveal dichotomies in auditory perception. *Nature*, 416, 87–90.

Stephens, J. & Holt, L. (2003). Preceding phonetic context affects perception of non-speech sounds. *Journal of the Acoustical Society of America*, 114, 3036–9.

Stevens, K. N. & Blumstein, S. E. (1978). Invariant cues for place of articulation in stop consonants. *Journal of the Acoustical Society of America*, 64, 1358–68.

Streeter, L. A., Macdonald, N. H., Apple, W., Krauss, R. M., & Galotti, K. M. (1983). Acoustic and perceptual indicators of emotional stress. *Journal of the Acoustical Society of America*, 73, 1354–60.

Studdert-Kennedy, M. & Goldstein, L. (2003). Launching language: The gestural origins of discrete infinity. In Christiansen, M. & Kirby, S. (Eds.) *Language evolution.* (pp. 235–54). Oxford: Oxford University Press.

Studdert-Kennedy, M. G., Liberman, A. M., Harris, K. S., & Cooper, F. S. (1970). The motor theory of speech perception: A reply to Lane's critical review. *Psychological Review*, 77, 234–49.

Sumby, W. H. & Pollack, I. (1954). Visual contributions to speech intelligibility in noise. *Journal of the Acoustical Society of America*, 26, 212–15.

Syrdal, A. K. & Gopal, H. S. (1986). A perceptual model of vowel recognition based on the auditory representation of American English vowels. *Journal of the Acoustical Society of America*, 79, 1086–100.

Van Lancker, D., Kreiman, J., & Emmorey, K. (1985). Familiar voice recognition: Patterns and parameters, part I: Recognition of backward voices. *Journal of Phonetics*, 13, 19–38.

Walley A. D. & Carrell T. D. (1983). Onset spectra and formant transition in the adult's and child's perception of place of articulation in stop consonants. *Journal of the Acoustical Society of America*, 73, 1011–22.

Warren, R. M. (1970). Restoration of missing speech sounds. *Science*, 167, 392–3.

Wickelgren, W. (1969). Context-sensitive coding, associative memory, and serial order in (speech) behavior. *Psychological Review*, 76, 1–15.

(1985). Criterion shift rule and perceptual homeostasis. *Psychological Review*, 92, 574–84.

Wong, PCM, Nusbaum, H. C., & Small, S. L. (2004). Neural bases of talker normalization. *Journal of Cognitive Neuroscience*, 16, 1173–84.

Author Note

Preparation of this manuscript was supported by NICHD grant HD-01994 to Haskins Laboratories. We thank Philip Rubin, Robert Remez, and Yvonne Manning-Jones for making Figure 1 available to us from Haskins Laboratories' Website.

CHAPTER 2

Neural Bases of Speech Perception – Phonology, Streams, and Auditory Word Forms

Sophie Scott

Human speech perception is a very striking skill. We can understand the speech signal, one of the most complex sounds we routinely hear, with rapidity and ease, in a variety of different listening situations, and when confronted with talkers who all speak in their own individual voice. In terms of the neural basis for these perceptual skills, early developments in neuropsychology made important advances in linking structure to function in the human brain. Indeed, the auditory processing of speech was one of the earliest cognitive functions to be localized in the human brain (Wernicke, 1874). This work outlined a role for posterior temporal lobe regions in early mapping from sound to meaning (Bogen and Bogen, 1976), although it has been noted that Wernicke's original description encompassed the entire superior temporal gyrus, not only its posterior extent (Rauschecker and Scott, 2009). Furthermore, as with the delineation of regions of cortex associated with speech production in Broca's area (Broca, 1861), there is a discrepancy between the area and the associated aphasia. True Broca's aphasia occurs after large cortical and white matter

lesions: An infarct of Broca's area results in transient mutism (Mohr, 1976). Likewise, a clear Wernicke's, or receptive, aphasia results from a large lesion of the posterior temporal and inferior parietal lobes: A small lesion of Wernicke's area (when considered to consist of the left posterior superior temporal gyrus) results in conduction aphasia – a patient can understand speech but cannot repeat it (Anderson et al., 1999; Quigg et al., 1999). These discrepancies highlight the problems in using simplistic labels as anatomical constructs, and the problems of mapping between "nature's experiments" and the underlying functional anatomy. In this chapter I will use the patient and functional imaging literature to try and outline an alternative approach to the blanket terminology of Wernicke's area, an approach which my colleagues and I have been developing for the past few years. While other researchers might disagree with the details (Hickok and Poeppel, 2004), all agree that we can start to fractionate Wernicke's area into different functional streams of processing, and that this may be a useful framework in which to think about speech perception.

I will start by outlining the different sources of evidence of the streams of processing. I will then determine the neural basis of different kinds of speech information, including phonological, phonotactic, and cognitive models, within the context of the anatomical framework I have set out.

1 Subsystems within Wernicke's area – evidence from patients

Until recently, the only detailed information about the anatomical damage consequent to brain damage was available at postmortem. The advent of CT scans and more recently MRI scans has dramatically changed this and now it is possible to get detailed anatomical profiles of individual patients' lesions. This has enabled the use of grouped patient data in the analysis of behaviour–brain relationships by using an overlapping lesion approach (e.g. Bates et al., 2003). This identifies the lesions which a group of patients with a particular deficit have in common. Recently, for example, Saygin et al. (2003) demonstrated a role for posterior temporal lobe regions in the processing of both speech and environmental noises. This study revealed that there was a greater association of posterior temporal areas (the core of Wernicke's area) with environmental noises than language, posing some questions for the literal interpretation of Wernicke's area as an exclusively speech related area. Detailed anatomy can also be used in conjunction with functional imaging methods when scanning patients: We recently demonstrated (Sharp, Scott, and Wise, 2004) that patients with left anterior superior temporal lobe lesions show a significantly reduced response to speech in the left basal language area (left anterior fusiform gyrus) (Nobre, Allison, and McCarthy, 1994), a reduced response that can be mimicked in normal listeners by using noise-vocoded speech. Our findings suggest that the aphasic stroke is disconnecting the basal language area, although the basal language area has not itself been directly damaged.

More precise details of functional anatomy can also be seen with patient groups. For example, the role of posterior temporal areas in speech perception has been well-established from the aphasic stroke literature (e.g., Saygin et al., 2003). The core of Wernicke's area is located in the posterior superior temporal sulcus (STS) (Bogen and Bogen, 1976), which fits well with this finding. However, as mentioned in the introduction, a small lesion of the posterior STS does not result in a sensory or receptive aphasia; instead a problem with repetition, with preserved comprehension, is seen – subjects can understand speech but not repeat it (Anderson et al., 1999). Additionally, large lesions centered on the posterior STS seem necessary to develop a true Wernicke's aphasia, with fluent (if unintelligible) output and poor comprehension. This suggests that the posterior STS may not be the only region involved in speech perception. Indeed, work with another group of patients, those with semantic dementia (Snowden, Goulding, and Neary, 1989), suggests that more anterior temporal lobe regions also play a part in the comprehension of speech. In semantic dementia, patients present with word finding difficulties and this tends to develop into problems understanding the meanings of spoken words. As the disease progresses, the patients start to have problems with perceiving speech sounds and with repetition. Semantic dementia (SD) is a variant of frontotemporal dementia, and the initial damage seen on scans is in the left anterior temporal lobe. With time, the atrophy spreads to more posterior and ventral temporal regions and starts to include the right temporal lobe (Lambon Ralph et al., 2001).

The pattern of problems seen in semantic dementia is consistent with a role in left anterior temporal lobe regions for aspects of speech perception – potentially for mapping from sound to meaning, since this is one of the key aspects of early SD. Controversy remains, however, concerning which model – Wernicke's aphasia (posterior STS) or SD (anterior temporal lobes) – is the best for understanding the anatomy of speech perception. Further sections of this chapter will come back to this anterior-posterior superior temporal lobe distinction. However it is also relevant to consider here ways in which stroke and SD differ, since this goes some way to explain some of the differences seen. First, a stroke is often caused by an ischemic event, which starves local areas of blood flow and thus oxygen, damaging both grey and white matter. This damage can be extensive and can disconnect white matter tracts. In contrast, SD involves the selective loss of cortical grey matter, without white matter involvement. Second, strokes typically follow the vasculature of the brain, and the branch of the middle cerebral territory which runs along the superior temporal lobes runs in a posterior-anterior direction. This tends to mean that ischemic damage starts at the posterior aspect of the vasculature and runs forward (Wise, 2003). The corollary of this is that strokes selectively damaging the anterior temporal lobes are rare. Thus a stroke which produces damage homologous to that seen in SD is uncommon.

Some resolution can be seen between the two perspectives: In a recent study by Crinion and colleagues (2006), detailed anatomical scans were used to characterize how much damage had occurred to primary auditory cortical fields following a posterior temporal lobe stroke. This assessment was used to classify those patients in which connections from PAC and anterior temporal lobe regions had been damaged, and it was found that this correlated with the amount of activation in anterior temporal lobe regions. In other words, a posterior stroke can still lead to anterior changes depending on the involvement of primary auditory cortex and the disconnection of anterior fields.

2 Subsystems within Wernicke's area – evidence from nonhuman primates

Detailed anatomical work in the organization of the primate visual system has indicated that there is considerable parallel and hierarchical organization of visual processing. This organization has been associated with distinct streams of processing, with general functional differences. There is a ventral stream, running along the bottom of the temporal lobes, which processes visual objects and identities. A dorsal stream projects towards the parietal cortex, via MT, in the posterior temporal lobe and seems to integrate spatial and sensorimotor organization.

For practical reasons, work dissociating similar streams of processing in the primate auditory system has lagged somewhat; primate primary auditory cortex (PAC) is located on the supratemporal plane, literally tucked into the Sylvian fissure, making it difficult to access. In addition, when recordings were made from PAC, it was hard to demonstrate responses to pure tones, which were used as analogues of the simple visual stimuli used in visual studies. However, technical developments have permitted these problems to be overcome, along with the crucial realization that pure sine tones were not the optimal stimulus for driving auditory cortical responses (Rauschecker, 1998). Most sounds encountered in the environment – especially communicative sounds – are highly complex. Furthermore, unlike the visual system, the auditory system carries out considerable processing of sounds in the ascending auditory pathway, such that the representation at the cortical level is typically of a more complex auditory object (Nelken, 2004; Scott, 2005) – this has implications for the optimal stimuli to drive neurons in PAC.

Since these developments, it has become clear that there are some general parallels between the cortical organization of sound and vision, in the sense that both hierarchical and parallel processing can be seen in auditory processing, and this has some degree of functional specialization (Rauschecker and Scott, 2009). The core of auditory cortex receives all its input from the auditory thalamus, and is organized as three distinct fields in an anterior–posterior orientation (Kaas and Hackett, 1999) (see Figure 2.1). These three fields have different tonotopic organizations, meaning that they represent the pitch height of sounds in different directions. These core areas are connected to surrounding belt and parabelt regions: The anterior–posterior organization

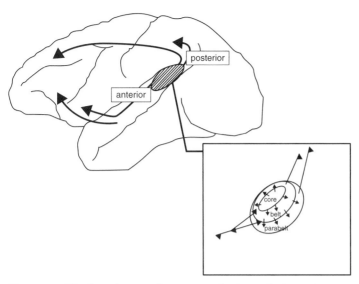

Figure 2.1. The lateral view of a macaque brain, with the major pathways from auditory fields to frontal cortex indicated: The box shows a magnified and schematized image of the core, belt, and parabelt auditory regions and their connectivity. Both belt and parabelt regions project to adjacent regions in frontal cortex.

is maintained within these connections, such that the most anterior core field projects to the anterior and anterior-lateral belt, but not to the posterior belt, and vice versa. The same is true for the projections from the belt and core to parabelt regions. In the medial–lateral direction, further degrees of functional specialization can also be seen. Going from medial to lateral auditory fields, responses are driven by progressively wider bandwidth sounds, with some maintenance of the anterior–posterior tonotopic organization (Rauschecker, 1998). Thus we can see, both in terms of connectivity and function, some evidence for both hierarchical and parallel processing in primate auditory cortex. In terms of streams of processing, the anterior–posterior organization of primate auditory cortex is also maintained in the projections to frontal cortex: There are projections from anterior belt and parabelt to ventral prefrontal regions, and adjacent but none overlapping projections to dorsal prefrontal and premotor cortex from posterior belt and parabelt (Romanski et al., 1999). These two broad streams of processing are associated with different functions:

It has been demonstrated that antero-lateral parabelt cells respond to conspecific vocalizations, while a greater number of more posterior lateral parabelt cells respond preferentially to the localization of calls (Tian et al., 2001). This is strong evidence for functional streams, perhaps similar to those in the visual system, with the anterior "what" stream being functionally and anatomically distinct from a posterior "where" stream. In addition to these, there is also a suggestion of further types of auditory processing: In the medial posterior belt regions, auditory neurons have been identified that respond to touch (Fu et al., 2003). This may form a route for sensorimotor integration.

With respect to speech processing, this review of primate auditory neuroanatomy may not seem directly relevant – nonhuman primates don't speak, and there are no animal models of human language (Wise, 2003). However I would argue that this work is important to the speech scientist in several ways (Rauschecker and Scott, 2009; Scott and Johnsrude, 2003). First, although humans and macaques are very different, we are still primates, and the basic organization of our neural wiring is unlikely to be dramatically different. This in turn means that we can move away from highly simplistic anatomical terms like *Wernicke's area* when considering patient or functional imaging data, and instead use this anatomical information as a framework for our data. Indeed, I would argue that an anatomical framework is essential when interpreting functional imaging data, since methods like fMRI and PET are anatomical tools, and the locations of activations are of critical importance. Second, the work from primates indicates that the primate brain processes sounds in (at least two) different ways – for identity and for location. This is useful for us, as it means that in the human brain one might well not expect speech – which is first and foremost a sound – to be processed along one single dedicated route. Third, although language has no animal model (Wise, 2003), the finding that the "what" pathway in primates is sensitive to conspecific vocalizations suggests that the early acoustic processing of speech, distinct from language abilities, might have developed in a neural system already important in auditory communication. Indeed, there is even evidence that as speech and language are left lateralised in humans, so the processing of conspecific vocalizations is left lateralised in macaques (Poremba et al., 2004). This suggests that understanding the processing of vocalizations by nonhuman primates may well tell us something important about human speech.

In the next sections I am going to describe work on functional imaging of speech, from different perspectives, and try to derive a model of the functional anatomy of human speech processing. I will use the nonhuman primate auditory cortical organization as a general framework to constrain such interpretations.

3 Subsystems within Wernicke's area – evidence from functional imaging studies

One of the more surprising findings of early functional imaging studies of speech

was that considerable bilateral activation was seen when speech was contrasted with silence (Wise et al., 1991), instead of the left lateralised system which was expected, given that left, not right hemisphere lesions result in aphasia. Of course, this was because the results of functional imaging studies are highly dependent on the baselines used, and comparing speech to silence fails to control for acoustic stimulation. Studies from our group, which utilized more sophisticated baselines, have been able to delineate left lateralised systems which seem to be important in early perceptual processing of speech (Narain et al., 2003; Scott et al., 2000). Our initial aim was to identify the neural systems activated by intelligible speech, over and above the neural systems activated by the acoustic structure of speech. To do this, we controlled for early acoustic processing by using a form of transformed speech in which all the acoustic properties are preserved. This transformation, called *spectral rotation*, was developed by Barry Blesser in the 1960s as a way of coding speech so as to evade espionage (Blesser, 1972). It involves taking a low-pass filtered speech signal (e.g., filtered at 4000 Hz) and literally flipping the spectrum around the midpoint of the frequency range – here, the midpoint will be 2000 Hz. This gives a signal in which all the amplitude and spectral structure is maintained, but the information is all now in the "wrong" spectral location. This destroys all the intelligibility, though the pitch and pitch variation of the original signal is roughly maintained and the transformed signal sounds like some*thing* speaking (Blesser, 1972). People can eventually learn to understand spectrally rotated speech, probably since the acoustic-phonetic information has been altered, not destroyed: however this learning takes place on the order of weeks and months. Rotated speech thus overcomes many of the problems of a suitable baseline for speech in functional imaging studies (Scott and Wise, 2004) by maintaining most of the original acoustic structure in the absence of intelligibility.

This study shows a left lateralised response to intelligible speech in the anterior superior

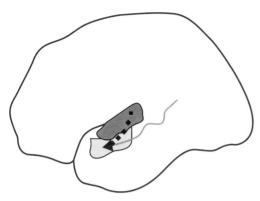

Figure 2.2. The lateral view of a human brain, showing the activations lateral and anterior to primary auditory cortex in Scott et al., 2000. The regions in red respond to speech, noise vocoded speech, and rotated speech; the regions in yellow respond only to speech and vocoded speech.

temporal sulcus (Figure 2.2). Lying lateral and anterior to primary auditory cortex, this looked very much like an early perceptual response to intelligible speech lying within the auditory "what" pathway. Consistent with this, there was extensive activation in the lateral STG to the rotated speech, a response that dropped away in more anterior STS regions. This anterior STS intelligibility response was equivalent to both normal speech and noise-vocoded speech (Shannon et al., 1995), which simulates the percept of a cochlear implant (for further information, see the chapter by Samuel and Sumner, this volume). Thus this anterior STS response did not differentiate between intelligible speech from a human voice and from a robotic sounding harsh whisper.

This study was able to demonstrate a left lateralised response to intelligible speech, which could not be due to simple acoustic differences between the speech and the rotated baseline. Furthermore, this response lay lateral and anterior to PAC, within the territory of the anterior auditory "what" pathway, in a striking parallel to the primate literature. As mentioned earlier, recent work has indicated that the "what" pathway for conspecific vocalizations in primates may also be left lateralised. Poremba and colleagues (2004), using PET activation with macaques, have shown a lateralisation to conspecific vocalizations in the left anterior temporal lobe. Finally, our study suggests that the left anterior STS may process an important initial representation of the speech signal, potentially a well-specified acoustic form, which can be used to access lexical or semantic representations in prefrontal and basal temporal areas (Scott and Johnsrude, 2003). Indeed, some other groups have specifically suggested that the left anterior STS is the auditory word form area, which is a more linguistic formulation of this suggestion (Cohen et al., 2004). However, since our studies used intelligible *sentences*, we cannot dissociate the precise representational characteristics of this response, which could include lexical, semantic, and syntactic factors, although we have also seen similar activation using unconnected single words (Mummery et al., 1999; Scott and Wise, 2004). Following along this reasoning, Angela Friederici and colleagues (Friederici et al., 2003) have demonstrated responses to both semantic and syntactic violations along the left anterior dorsolateral temporal lobe, which might suggest that more linguistic elements are being processed in addition to purely phonological and acoustic processing. However, direct contrasts of these two types of violations did not reveal significant differences in the temporal lobes (though greater responses were seen in the basal ganglia to syntactic violations), suggesting that semantic and syntactic processes may be difficult to precisely distinguish in the temporal lobes (at least with the resolution of current fMRI techniques and subtraction methodologies).

We will return to some of these issues of interpretation later in the chapter, but now I wish to turn to more low-level properties of the speech signal. In Scott et al. (2000), we found extensive activation in the left STG and posterior STS to spectrally rotated speech – a signal matched in acoustic structure to the speech signal, but which is unintelligible. At an acoustic level, spectrally rotated speech preserves the overall temporal sequence of amplitude and spectral variation, as well as the voiced/unvoiced distinction and indeed, some phonetic information (e.g., wide band noise in some fricatives) is little changed. The extensive activation seen to these rotated signals suggests that the lateral STG and posterior STS is sensitive to this acoustic-phonetic detail. In the next sections I will try and unpack these properties further.

4 Phonological information: Phonotactics and features

From a phonetic perspective, the information in speech can be categorized in different ways. One extremely important way attempts to describe characteristics of phonemes in terms of how those phonemes are produced. This can characterize the manner of articulation (e.g., if the outflow of air is completely obstructed then released) or the place of articulation (e.g., the back of the tongue). Such an approach is useful as it suggests a way of identifying ways in which phonemes might be similar, even if they sound perceptually very different. This in turn might be a cue to which the underlying neural system is sensitive. There is some evidence to support this as an aspect of the perceptual processing of speech. For example, Obleser and colleagues, using MEG with source analysis, have indicated that vowels and consonants are apparently processed perceptually using these abstract representations of the place of articulations, despite considerable surface variation (Obleser et al., 2004; 2006). In these studies, multiple exemplars of consonants and vowels were used from different speakers, so the consistency in results was not due to basic acoustic properties of individual tokens. Thus, although different speakers produce speech sounds quite differently with respect to the acoustic pattern, there are responses in the lateral STG which are selective to the place of articulation, across different vowels and consonants. This approach is attractive as it suggests we can successfully use theories of phonetics to drive investigations of the neural basis of speech perception. It also suggests that responses in the lateral STG,

which is auditory association cortex and contains the homologue of primate auditory parabelt regions, may well be tuned to the specific properties of speech sounds.

A second theoretical issue in the speech sciences is the combinatorial structure of speech sounds – phonotactics. This describes how, in different languages, different sequences of speech sounds are possible. One way that this can be described is the legal sequencing of specific phonemes: In British English, the sequence /dl/ is illegal in a syllable initial position, whereas the sequence /dw/ is legal. These rules also govern overall syllable structure. For example, in British English, a syllable can be formed of up to three consonants before a vowel, and up to four afterwards (e.g., *strengths*). Such a structure would be impossible in Japanese, in which syllables have no more than one initial consonant before the vowel, and only a single consonant, either *n* or *ng*, is possible after the vowel. This means that consonant clusters such as *str* are impossible in Japanese, and indeed, there are accounts that Japanese listeners hear a vowel inserted into each appropriate slot to correct for this perceptually. Thus, Japanese listeners report hearing the nonword *ebzu* as *ebuzu* since the sequence *bz* is illegal between two vowels in Japanese. These illusory vowels are termed *epenthetic*. Phonotactics thus captures properties of the syllable structure at both local and global levels.

An fMRI study used phonotactics and featural perception as a way of looking at the early perceptual processing of speech (Jacquemot et al., 2003), and was neatly able to distinguish perceptual from linguistic changes by using two language groups, French and Japanese. French is a language that (like English) does not distinguish vowels as linguistically different based on their length: thus the nonwords *ebuzu* and *ebuuzu* sound like the same nonword to French listeners. In Japanese, however, vowel length is linguistically contrastive: *Ebuzu* and *ebuuzu* sound like two different words. The authors presented the French and Japanese listeners with pairs of nonwords in fMRI that had to be classified as the same or different.

Elegantly, the nonwords which could be distinguished linguistically for one group was an acoustic difference for the other group and vice versa: The French can distinguish between *ebzu* and *ebuzu*, while the Japanese hear them as being the same, and the Japanese can distinguish between *ebuzu* and *ebuuzu*, which the French hear as being the same. Using this design, the researchers were able to identify neural responses in left STG, immediately lateral to primary auditory cortex, which were sensitive to the linguistically relevant stimuli comparisons, but not for the acoustically different but perceptually identical comparisons in both language groups.

What this study is thus able to show is a sensitivity to syllable-level structure that is from one's native language. This activation is early in the perceptual processing of speech, in brain regions that overlap with those that show sensitivity to nonspeech modulations such as amplitude and frequency modulations, and which would correspond to parabelt in the primate brain. It has been claimed speech-specific activations – that is, those not driven by acoustic factors – can only be identified much later in the perceptual system (Davis and Johnsrude, 2003). The Jacquemot et al. (2003) study instead suggests that the influences of language-specific linguistic processing can be seen in early perceptual processing, suggesting that the system has been tuned to these acoustic-phonetic properties of our native language. Consistent with this argument, this same left lateral STG area has been shown to be sensitive to both acoustic and linguistic complexity in degraded speech, in contrast to more anterior left temporal lobe regions that respond solely to more abstract linguistic structure (Scott et al., 2006).

It is also intriguing that these sensitivities to language-specific syllable structure are in broadly similar dorsolateral temporal lobe regions to those involved in featural representations of vowels and consonants (Obleser et al., 2004; 2006). This finding is promising for further elucidation of the perceptual processing of phonetic information: The swathes of STG we saw activated by

rotated speech (Scott et al., 2000) will hopefully be unpacked to reveal the processes and representations important in the fast, plastic, and massively parallel processing of the speech signal which must occur prior to comprehension (Kluender, 2002; Obleser and Eisner, 2009).

5 Cognitive speech constructs: Categorical perception and auditory word forms

More psychological approaches to speech perception have also been attempted in cognitive neuroscientific investigations. Liebenthal and colleagues (Liebenthal et al., 2005) used a categorical perception approach to identify neural responses to CV stimuli. *Categorical perception* describes the twin phenomena of perceptual discrimination being best at the boundary between two classes of sounds, and that a dimension spanning both categories is not classified linearly. This is considered by psychologists to be an important property of speech perception, and potentially explains how listeners cope with the variable speech output produced by speakers. Liebenthal and colleagues generated stimuli along a ba–da continuum, which is perceived categorically by English speakers (see also Fowler and Magnuson, this volume). A form of spectral rotation was used to give an acoustically similar but nonintelligible continuum, which they established was not perceived categorically. The results showed left lateralised response to the ba–da stimuli in the mid STS when contrasted with the rotated stimuli. This was replicated in a recent study (Desai et al., 2008) from the same group, showing that contrasting sinewave analogues of ba–da stimuli before and after training resulted in an increase in activity in the mid STS following training relative to the activity prior to training.

These are important studies and further elegant demonstrations that the left lateralisation of speech is not based on simple acoustic properties of the stimuli (Scott and Wise, 2004); further demonstration is needed before we can conclude that this is the neural basis of *categorical* perception, especially given the controversies over the exact status of categorical perception per se (some have argued that it is an experimental artifact; Schouten and Gerrits, 2004) and its precise utility in speech perception (since several animals, including chinchillas and quail, can perceive speech sounds categorically, can this be considered a mechanism directly linked to speech comprehension?). What needs to be established is whether the neural regions identified demonstrate categorical *responses* to the speech continua. This would be powerful evidence for the categorization of speech sounds in auditory cortex. It would also allow a comparison with the data on featural/phonotactic structure, which tend to give activations somewhat earlier in auditory cortex (Obleser et al., 2004; 2006; Jacquemot et al., 2003).

More recent research has demonstrated a sensitivity to properties of speech sounds which follows the profile expected by categorical perception: Joanisse and colleagues (2007) used a synthesized continuum of speech sounds, manipulating the perceived place of articulation of voiced plosive from *ga* to *da* in eight steps. They used a repetition paradigm with four items rapidly presented. Across the three experimental conditions, these four items were either all the same (*ga*), with the final item crossing a phonetic boundary (between category condition), or with the final item being a different examplar from the same phonetic category (within category condition). Crucially, the authors were careful to ensure that the acoustic differences in the between- and within- category change condition were equivalent. The comparison of the neural activity greater for the between- versus within- category conditions revealed left lateralised activity within the mid STS. This is good evidence that the sensitivity to syllables in the STS (Desai et al., 2008; Liebenthal et al., 2005) can be unpacked to reveal a specific sensitivity to acoustic change which crosses a phonetic boundary – that is, that the STS represents abstract properties of speech sounds.

Another approach to the neural basis of speech perception is that of identifying candidate "auditory word form" areas. This approach is motivated by cognitive neuroscience investigations and cognitive models, and has gained support from PET and fMRI studies of reading, which have consistently identified a response in left extrastriate cortex to written words and orthographically legal nonwords (e.g., McCandliss, Cohen, and Dehaene, 2003). There is much less work on auditory word form areas (a Google search in June 2009 revealed 7,360 hits on the phrase "visual word form area" and 651 hits for "auditory word form area"). A study by Cohen and colleagues (2004) explicitly attempted to address this. As in the study of Joanisse et al. (2007), they used the phenomenon of repetition suppression, whereby the neural response is reduced to the second presentation of a stimulus relative to the first presentation of the same stimulus. This revealed a selective response in the left anterior STS, in a region very similar to our previous demonstration of a neural response to intelligible speech signals, and it seems plausible to consider that the two results are essentially addressing different aspects of the same perceptual phenomenon: not lexical identity per se, but a point along the anterior "what" pathway in the auditory system, consequent upon acoustic, sequential, and featural processing, which is sufficiently well-specified that it can form the basis for access to the lexical and semantic system. From here, one might propose, there is access to and feedback from the lexical and semantic system, in ventral temporal areas, and links with attentional and executive systems in prefrontal cortex.

6 Speech perception–production links

One of the most striking effects in speech perception is the link between speech perception and production. For example, if our language does not discriminate two speech sounds as linguistically distinct, we can have problems hearing or producing the sounds accurately. For example, the /l/ sound in *leaf* and *bell* is very different in standard British English, but we consider it to be linguistically the same phoneme (i.e., the two /l/ sounds are allophones); if British English speakers learnt a language in which these were separate phonemes (e.g., Russian) then we would encounter problems. This is the basis for Japanese mispronouncements of r/l distinctions: These two sounds are two different phonemes in English and two allophones of the same phoneme in Japanese, which leads to problems in accurate articulation. Other, more psychological perspectives have also suggested a role for perception–production links in human language organization. It has been demonstrated that silently mouthing a written word primes a later auditory lexical decision task (Monsell, 1987), suggesting that articulation itself is sufficient to activate the representation of word forms. Indeed, one entire approach to modeling speech perception, the motor theory of speech perception, is focused on the primacy of motor representations in the perception of speech, such that a speaker's articulatory gestures are perceived directly (e.g., Lieberman and Whalen, 2000).

A candidate route for such phenomena is that at some point in the brain, there are some shared resources for the perception and production of speech, be those representational, process-based, or both. Some evidence from patient studies has supported aspects of this suggestion: thus patients with Broca's aphasia (a speech production problem) have been demonstrated to show abnormalities in their ability to categorize phonemes, as do patients with receptive aphasia (Basso, Casati, and Vignolo, 1977). However this deficit did not correlate with the patients' speech comprehension skills for either patient group (Basso et al.), suggesting that this deficit may not reflect perceptual processes which contribute to comprehension (e.g., Hickok and Poeppel, 2004; Scott, McGettigan, and Eisner, 2009). The previous sections of this chapter have suggested that functional imaging studies have been successful at delineating the structures important in the neural basis of speech perception; this next section is targeted at the possibilities for the neural basis of speech perception and production links.

There are several ways in which speech perception–production links can be identified. I am going to take an unashamedly anatomical approach to this topic and split it into two broad themes. The first theme is speech perception regions which are activated in speech production tasks and the second theme is speech production areas which are activated in speech perception tasks.

7 Perception fields important in production

As outlined in the previous sections, speech perception involves regions in the left and right dorsolateral temporal lobes. We have seen that a specific route for speech comprehension runs lateral and anterior to primary auditory cortex. In stark contrast to this, many previous studies have ascribed an important role for the planum temporale in speech perception. Lying lateral and posterior to PAC, this region has been pretty decisively shown to not be important in speech-specific perceptual processing (Binder et al., 1996), and indeed much of the interest in this region has derived from anatomical studies which have indicated that it is larger on the left than on the right (an approach which has come in for criticism [Marshall, 2000]). However, more recent work has suggested that there may well be some more speech-specific functions of the medial planum and that this may form an important sensorimotor integration area.

In 2001 we reanalyzed a PET study which had been originally run to investigate the neural basis of breath control in speech production (Murphy et al., 1997). This study had four conditions: repeating a phrase, mouthing it silently, grunting it (just voicing the rhythm), and rehearsing it silently without articulation. The original analysis identified the neural systems recruited when breathing for speaking (speaking, grunting) and breathing metabolically (mouthing, rehearsing). We reanalyzed the data since it gave us the opportunity to identify neural responses during articulation (speaking, mouthing, grunting, rehearsal), even when that articulation was silent (mouthing) (Wise et al., 2001). This analysis gave us extensive activation in sensorimotor cortex, since all three conditions involved complex motor acts: In addition to this, however, we identified regions of auditory cortex, posterior and medial to primary auditory cortex, which were active in all three articulation conditions. This is a striking activation of auditory cortex in a motor output task, and is all the more impressive for it being seen when the output is mouthed – that is, the response is not solely to the subjects hearing their own voices. One interpretation of this activation, which has also been reported by other labs (Hickok et al., 2000), is that this indicates a guidance of articulation by speech perception mechanisms – that the motor act of speech is guided by representations of the target sound of the utterance. The medial planum temporale is in an optimal place to act as a sensorimotor interface in speech perception and production, being part of the posterior stream of auditory processing, linking into parietal and motor cortex; it also lies just ventral to the secondary face area in sensory cortex. Finally, in nonhuman primates, these medial and posterior auditory areas are activated by sensory stimulation (Fu et al., 2003), again consistent with a role for sensorimotor integration.

Intriguingly, there is some evidence that the more anterior auditory cortical fields implicated in speech comprehension are actually suppressed during overt articulation. This has been demonstrated using PET and a repetition task (Wise et al., 1999): We required subjects to either listen to single words or to repeat them, and we varied the rate of listening or repetition. We were able to identify brain regions which increased with listening or with repetition; we also identified that there was active suppression of activity in the left anterior STG during repetition, since there was significantly less activation in this region during repetition than during listening. Since we controlled the number of lexical items heard

(in the listening task, subjects heard *apple, apple, pencil, pencil* to control for the fact that in the repetition task subjects heard their own voices when they repeated), this result seemed to indicate that anterior auditory fields were suppressed in activity when speaking. Since this study, this reduced response to one's own voice has also been demonstrated using MEG (Numminen et al., 1999), and it has even been demonstrated in single cell recordings from macaques that auditory cortical fields truly are suppressed during vocalization, and that this suppression occurs prior to the onset of vocalization (Eliades and Wang, 2003). The function of this suppression needs to be established: It may be that, since "own voice" appears suppressed in the anterior "what" stream, it reflects own voice not being processed for meaning. In contrast, it may reflect an allocation of auditory processing resources to the more posterior fields which are more active during articulation. What it does mean, however, is that the posterior and anterior streams of processing are responding very differently during perception and production of speech, and that the posterior fields seem to be more likely contenders for production–perception links.

The findings of posterior-medial planum activation in articulation has been extended by some groups to be part of a speech working memory system (Hickok et al., 2003). Indeed, some have claimed that Wernicke's area, the core of which lies in posterior STS, may form an important part of the verbal working memory system. Wise et al. (2001) demonstrated that posterior STS (Wernicke's area) is activated in speech perception (Mummery et al., 1999; Narain et al., 2003; Scott et al., 2000), though its profile of response suggests that it may not be driven solely by intelligibility in speech. Wise et al. (2001) also pointed out that Wernicke's area is differentially activated in verbal fluency tasks, consistent with a role in verbal working memory. This link to controlled speech production may also relate to the known importance of Wernicke's area in conduction aphasia, where it is linked to a deficit in repetition, not comprehension.

8 Production fields activated in speech perception

The cortical systems important in speech production include the left anterior insula, the left dorsolateral frontal cortex (including prefrontal and premotor cortex), supplementary speech area, and bilateral motor cortex, in addition to cerebellar regions and subcortical structures such as the pallidum. The anterior insula has been implicated in speech perception: In our listening and repetition study, it was activated in repetition and also showed some sensitivity to the rate at which words were passively heard (Wise et al., 1999). The anterior insula has also been shown to be activated when subjects listen to perceptually transformed speech (Giraud et al., 2004). In speech production, the anterior insula has been suggested as the location of articulation planning (Dronkers, 1996), and it seems to have a more basic role in speech production than Broca's area (Wise et al., 1999). Its activation in speech perception tasks may thus reflect the activation of complex articulation plans. Another speech production area, the supplementary motor area (SMA), was reported in a study of the neural correlates of masking the speech signal (Scott et al., 2004). When subjects listened to speech embedded in noise, activity in SMA was sensitive to the signal to noise ratio – the higher the masking noise, the greater the SMA activity. This finding was interpreted as indicating that in this difficult speech perception task – noise masking makes the signal hard to hear as it competes with the speech at the level of the auditory periphery – regions associated with explicit articulation are recruited. Of course we cannot tell from this study whether the SMA activation reflects an automatic recruitment of these areas or is a result of explicit strategies (e.g., the subjects trying to sound out what they hear). Even more low levels of speech motor recruitment have suggested in another recent study: Wilson and colleagues (Wilson et al., 2004) used fMRI to scan people listening to syllables and producing syllables aloud. They performed a region of interest analysis on the brain regions activated during speech production, and identified peaks in the left motor and premotor cortex which were also activated during speech perception. This indicated that speech perception recruits motor cortex in a very direct fashion, perhaps along the lines of the classic motor theory of speech. Further work will determine the extent to which this is specific to speech or any vocalizations, and to identify the role of this activation – for example, is it dependent on phonological or semantic processing, and to what extent is it driving the perceptual processes in the temporal lobes? Notably, no functional imaging studies of speech perception have reported motor activity relative to a nonspeech baseline, leading to the suggestion that the motor responses to sound do not underlie phonetic aspects of speech perception (Scott, McGettigan, and Eisner, 2009).

The activation of Broca's area, in left dorsolateral frontal cortex, is also somewhat contentious in speech perception: While commonly seen during active tasks on heard speech input, this has often been ascribed to nonlinguistic aspects of the task (Muller et al., 2003; Thompson-Schill et al., 1997). In contrast, some authors have suggested that its activation by speech is dependent on the task, but in a linguistic fashion, such that more posterior Broca's activation is associated with phonological processing and more anterior regions with more semantic processing (Poldrack et al., 1999). In stark contrast, other papers have firmly identified Broca's area as the centre for grammatical processing (Musso et al., 2003), and it has recently been also construed as the U-space into which phonological, semantic, and syntactic information is integrated in language comprehension (Hagoort, 2005). In functional imaging studies of passive speech perception, Broca's area is rarely activated. Of course, the lack of activation may simply be an issue of power, however this has not prevented other speech production areas being seen in speech perception paradigms.

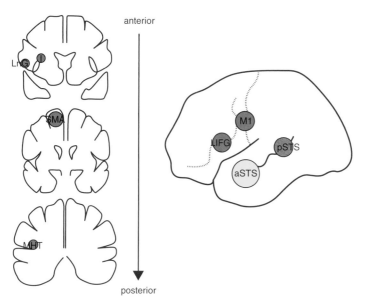

Figure 2.3. The lateral view of a human brain, and three coronal cross-sections, showing rough locations of brain regions activated in perception and in speech production. The regions in green respond during both speech production and speech perception paradigms: SMA – supplementary motor area, I – anterior insula, M1 – primary motor cortex, MPT – medial planum temporale. The region in yellow responds to intelligible speech and also appears to be suppressed during speech production: ASTS – anterior superior temporal sulcus. The region in red is the core of Wernicke's area and is implicated in speech perception and in repetition: PSTS – posterior superior temporal sulcus. The region in dark blue is the core of Broca's area and is potentially more involved in executive control processes, although some have argued for it to have a more purely linguistic function: LIFG – left inferior frontal gyrus.

9 Summary and conclusions

This brief review has thus outlined several candidate anatomical structures important in speech perception: We can identify a sensitivity to the acoustic structure of one's native language early in cortical auditory system, and as we run lateral and anterior to this, we see neural responses becoming progressively more selective for intelligible speech in the left anterior STS. We can see responses in posterior auditory fields that are activated during articulation, even silent articulation. Following on from the work in primate auditory anatomy, we can consider these anterior and posterior streams to have different functional roles in speech perception – an auditory "what" pathway and a posterior "how" pathway. We can see that activity in the "what" pathway appears to be suppressed during speech output. We can also see several different potential loci for speech production and perception links – both in the posterior auditory fields, and also in the anterior insula, SMA, and more controversially in Broca's area. I hope that this has demonstrated some of the utility of primate anatomical models for interpreting functional imaging data, and it helps us to unpack some of the theoretical constructs of Wernicke's and Broca's areas in a meaningful way. This should also help us to start to integrate the neural systems for speech perception into their closely allied processes of verbal working memory (Hickok et al., 2003; Jacquemot and Scott, 2006), as well as provide a framework for considering learning and plasticity in speech perception.

References

Anderson, J. M., Gilmore, R., Roper, S., Crosson, B., Bauer, R. M., Nadeau, S., Beversdorf, D. Q., Cibula, J., Rogish, M., III, Kortencamp, S., Hughes, J. D., Gonzalez Rothi, L. J., & Heilman, K. M. (1999). Conduction aphasia and the arcuate fasciculus: a reexamination of the Wernicke-Geschwind model. *Brain and Language*, 70, 1–12.

Basso, A., Casati, G., & Vignolo, L. A. (1977). Phonemic identification defect in aphasia. *Cortex*, 13, 85–95.

Bates, E., Wilson, S. M., Saygin, A. P., Dick, F., Sereno, M. I., Knight, R. T., & Dronkers, N. F. (2003). Voxel-based lesion-symptom mapping. *Nature Neuroscience*, 6, 448–50.

Binder, J. R., Frost, J. A., Hammeke, T. A., Rao, S. M., & Cox, R. W. (1996). Function of the left planum temporale in auditory and linguistic processing. *Brain*, 119, 1239–47.

Blesser, B. (1972). Speech perception under conditions of spectral transformation. I. Phonetic characteristics. *Journal of Speech and Hearing Research*, 15, 5–41.

Blumstein, S. E., Tartter, V. C., Nigro, G., & Statlender, S. (1984). Acoustic cues for the perception of place of articulation in aphasia. *Brain and Language*, 22, 128–49.

Bogen, J. E. & Bogen, G. M. (1976). "Wernicke's region – where is it?" *Annals (N.Y.) Academic Sciences*, 280, 834–43.

Broca, P. (1861b). Remarques sur le siége de la faculté du langage articulé, suivies d'une observation d'aphémie (perte de la parole) *Bulletin de la Société Anatomique*, 6, 330–57.

Cohen, L., Jobert, A., Le Bihan, D., & Dehaene, S. (2004). Distinct unimodal and multimodal regions for word processing in the left temporal cortex. *Neuroimage*, 23, 1256–70.

Crinion, J. T., Warburton, E. A., Lambon-Ralph, M. A., Howard, D., & Wise, R. J. (2006). Listening to narrative speech after aphasic stroke: the role of the left anterior temporal lobe. *Cerebral Cortex*, 16, 1116–25.

Davis, M. H. & Johnsrude, I. S. (2003). Hierarchical processing in spoken language comprehension. *Journal of Neuroscience*, 23, 3423–31.

Desai, R., Liebenthal, E., Waldron, E., & Binder, J. R. (2008). Left posterior temporal regions are sensitive to auditory categorization. *Journal of Cognitive Neuroscience*, 20, 1174–88.

Dronkers, N. F. (1996). A new brain region for coordinating speech articulation. *Nature*, 384, 159–61.

Dupoux, E., Kakehi, K., Hirose, Y., Pallier, C., & Mehler, J. (1999). Epenthetic vowels in Japanese: A perceptual illusion? *Journal of Experimental Psychology-Human Perception and Performance*, 25, 1568–78.

Eliades, S. J. & Wang, X. (2003). Sensory-motor interaction in the primate auditory cortex during self-initiated vocalizations. *Journal of Neurophysiology*, 89, 2194–207.

Fowler, C. & Magnuson, J. S. (this volume). Speech perception. Friederici, A. D., Ruschemeyer, S. A., Hahne, A., & Fiebach, C. J. (2003). The role of left inferior frontal and superior temporal cortex in sentence comprehension: localizing syntactic and semantic processes. *Cerebral Cortex*, 13, 170–7.

Fu, K. M., Johnston, T. A., Shah, A. S., Arnold, L., Smiley, J., Hackett, T. A., Garraghty, P. E., & Schroeder, C. E. (2003). Auditory cortical neurons respond to somatosensory stimulation. *Journal of Neuroscience*, 23, 7510–515.

Giraud, A. L., Kell, C., Thierfelder, C., Sterzer, P., Russ, M. O., Preibisch, C., & Kleinschmidt, A. (2004). Contributions of sensory input, auditory search and verbal comprehension to cortical activity during speech processing. *Cerebral Cortex*, 14, 247–55.

Hagoort, P. (2005). On Broca, brain, and binding: a new framework. *Trends in Cognitive Science*, 9, 416–23.

Hickok, G., Buchsbaum, B., Humphries, C., Muftuler, T. (2003). Auditory-motor interaction revealed by fMRI: speech, music, and working memory in area Spt. *Journal of Cognitive Neuroscience*, 15, 673–82.

Hickok, G. & Poeppel, D. (2004). Dorsal and ventral streams: a framework for understanding aspects of the functional anatomy of language. *Cognition*, 92, 67–99.

Hickok, G., Erhard, P., Kassubek, J., Helms-Tillery, A. K., Naeve-Velguth, S., Strupp, J. P., Strick, P. L., & Ugurbil, K. (2000). A functional magnetic resonance imaging study of the role of left posterior superior temporal gyrus in speech production: implications for the explanation of conduction aphasia. *Neuroscience Letters*, 287, 156–60.

Jacquemot, C., Pallier, C., LeBihan, D., Dehaene, S., & Dupoux, E. (2003). Phonological grammar shapes the auditory cortex: a functional magnetic resonance imaging study. *Journal of Neuroscience*, 23, 9541–6.

Jacquemot, C. & Scott, S. K. (2006). What is the relationship between phonological short-term memory and speech processing? *Trends in Cognitive Science*, 10, 480–6.

Joanisse, M. F., Zevin, J. D., & McCandliss, B. D. (2007). Brain mechanisms implicated in the preattentive categorization of speech sounds revealed using FMRI and a short-interval habituation trial paradigm. *Cerebral Cortex*, 17, 2084–93.

Kaas, J. H. & Hackett, T. A. (1999). 'What' and 'where' processing in auditory cortex. *Nature Neuroscience*, 2, 1045–7.

Kluender, K. R. (2002). "Speech." In Ramachandran, V. S. (Ed.) *Encyclopedia of the Human Brain*, 4, 433–48. San Diego: Academic Press.

Lambon Ralph, M. A., McClelland, J. L., Patterson, K., Galton, C. J., & Hodges, J. R. (2001). No right to speak? The relationship between object naming and semantic impairment: neuropsychological evidence and a computational model. *Journal of Cognitive Neuroscience*, 13, 341–56.

Liberman, A. M. & Whalen, D. H. (2000). On the relation of speech to language. *Trends in Cognitive Sciences*, 4, 187–96.

Liebenthal, E., Binder, J. R., Spitzer, S. M., Possing, E. T., & Medler, D. A. (2005). Neural substrates of phonemic perception. *Cerebral Cortex*, 15, 1621–31.

Marshall, J. C. (2000). Planum of the apes: a case study. *Brain and Language*, 71, 145–8.

McCandliss, B. D., Cohen, L., & Dehaene, S. (2003). The visual word form area: expertise for reading in the fusiform gyrus. *Trends in Cognitive Sciences*, 7, 293–9.

Mohr, J. P. (1976). Broca's area and Broca's aphasia. In Whitaker, H. & Whitaker, H. A. (Eds.) (1). *Studies in neurolinguistics*. New York: Academic Press.

Monsell, S. (1987). On the relation between lexical input and output pathways for speech. In Allport, A., Mackay, D. G., Prinz, W., & E. Scheerer (Eds.) *Language perception and production: relationships between listening, speaking, reading, and writing* (pp. 273–311). London: Academic Press.

Muller, R. A., Kleinhans, N., & Courchesne, E. (2003). Linguistic theory and neuroimaging evidence: an fMRI study of Broca's area in lexical semantics. *Neuropsychologia*, 41, 1199–207.

Mummery, C. J., Ashburner, J., Scott, S. K., & Wise, RJS (1999). Functional neuroimaging of speech perception in six normal and two aphasic patients. *Journal of the Acoustical Society of America*, 106, 449–57.

Murphy, K., Corfield, D. R., Guz, A., Fink, G. R., Wise, R. J., Harrison, J., & Adams, L. (1997). Cerebral areas associated with motor control of speech in humans. *Journal of Applied Physiology*, 83, 1438–47.

Musso, M., Moro, A., Glauche, V., Rijntjes, M., Reichenbach, J., Buchel, C., & Weiller, C. (2003). Broca's area and the language instinct. *Nature Neuroscience*, 6, 774–81.

Narain, C., Scott, S. K., Wise, RJS, Rosen, S., Leff, A. P., Iversen, S. D., & Matthews, P. M. (2003). Defining a left-lateralised response specific to intelligible speech using fMRI. *Cerebral Cortex*, 13, 1362–8.

Nelken, I. (2004). Processing of complex stimuli and natural scenes in the auditory cortex. *Current Opinions in Neurobiology*, 14, 474–80.

Nobre, A. C., Allison, T., McCarthy, G. (1994). Word recognition in the human inferior temporal lobe. *Nature*, 372, 260–3.

Numminen, J., Salmelin, R., & Hari, R. (1999). Subject's own speech reduces reactivity of the human auditory cortex. *Neuroscience Letters*, 265, 119–22.

Obleser, J., & Eisner, F. (2009). Pre-lexical abstraction of speech in the auditory cortex. *Trends in Cognitive Sciences*, 13, 14–19.

Obleser, J., Lahiri, A., & Eulitz, C. (2004). Magnetic brain response mirrors extraction of phonological features from spoken vowels. *Journal of Cognitive Neuroscience*, 16, 31–9.

Obleser, J., Scott, S. K., & Eulitz, C. (2006). Now You Hear It, Now You Don't: Transient Traces of Consonants and their Nonspeech Analogues in the Human Brain. *Cerebral Cortex*, 16, 1069–76.

Poldrack, R. A., Wagner, A. D., Prull, M. W., Desmond, J. E., Glover, G. H., & Gabrieli, J. D. (1999). Functional specialization for semantic and phonological processing in the left inferior prefrontal cortex. *Neuroimage*, 10, 15–35.

Poremba, A., Malloy, M., Saunders, R. C., Carson, R. E., Herscovitch, P., & Mishkin, M. (2004). Species-specific calls evoke asymmetric activity in the monkey's temporal poles. *Nature*, 427, 448–51.

Quigg, M. & Fountain, N. B. (1999). Conduction aphasia elicited by stimulation of the left posterior superior temporal gyrus. *Journal of Neurology, Neurosurgery and Psychiatry*, 66, 393–6.

Rauschecker, J. P. (1998). Cortical processing of complex sounds. *Current Opinions in Neurobiology*, 8, 516–21.

Rauschecker, J. P., & Scott, S. K. (2009). Maps and streams in the auditory cortex: nonhuman primates illuminate human speech processing. *Nature Neuroscience*, 12, 718–24.

Romanski, L. M., Tian, B., Fritz, J., Mishkin, M., Goldman-Rakic, P. S., & Rauschecker, J. P. (1999). Dual streams of auditory afferents target multiple domains in the primate prefrontal cortex. *Nature Neuroscience, 2*, 1131–6.

Samuel, A. G. & Sumner, M. (this volume). Current directions in research on spoken word recognition.

Saygin, A. P., Dick, F., Wilson, S. M., Dronkers, N. F., & Bates, E. (2003). Neural resources for processing language and environmental sounds: evidence from aphasia. *Brain, 126*, 928–45.

Schouten, M. E. H. & Gerrits, E. (2004). Categorical perception depends on the discrimination task. *Perception and Psychophysics, 66*, 363–76.

Scott, S. K., McGettigan, C., & Eisner, F. (2009). A little more conversation, a little less action: candidate roles for motor cortex in speech perception. *Nature Reviews Neuroscience, 10*, 295–302.

Scott, S. K., Rosen S., Lang, H., & Wise, R. J. S. (2006). Neural correlates of intelligibility in speech investigated with noise vocoded speech – a Positron Emission Tomography study. *Journal of the Acoustical Society of America, 120*, 1075–83.

Scott, S. K., Blank, S. C., Rosen, S., & Wise, R. J. S. (2000). Identification of a pathway for intelligible speech in the left temporal lobe. *Brain, 123*, 2400–06.

Scott, S. K. & Johnsrude, I. S. (2003). The neuroanatomical and functional organization of speech perception. *Trends in Neurosciences, 26*, 100–7.

Scott, S. K., & Wise, R. J. S. (2004). The functional neuroanatomy of prelexical processing of speech. *Cognition, 92*, 13–45.

Scott, S. K. (2005). Auditory processing – speech, space and auditory objects. *Current Opinions in Neurobiology, 15*, 1–5.

Scott, S. K., Rosen, S., Wickham, L., & Wise, R. J. S. (2004). A positron emission tomography study of the neural basis of informational and energetic masking effects in speech perception. *Journal of the Acoustical Society of America, 115*, 813–21.

Shannon, R. V., Zeng, F. G., Kamath, V., Wygonski, J., & Ekelid, M. (1995). Speech recognition with primarily temporal cues. *Science, 270*, 303–4.

Sharp, D. J., Scott, S. K., & Wise, R. J. S. (2004). Retrieving meaning after temporal lobe infarction: the role of the basal language area. *Annals of Neurology, 56*, 836–46.

Snowden, J. S., Goulding, P. J., & Neary, D. (1989) Semantic dementia: a form of circumscribed cerebral atrophy. *Behavioural Neurolology, 2*, 167–82.

Thompson-Schill, S. L., D'Esposito, M., Aguirre, G. K., & Farah, M. J. (1997) Role of left inferior prefrontal cortex in retrieval of semantic knowledge: a reevaluation. *Proceedings of the National Academy of Sciences U S A., 94*, 14792–7.

Tian, B., Reser, D., Durham, A., Kustov, A., & Rauschecker, J. P. (2001) Functional specialization in rhesus monkey auditory cortex. *Science, 292*, 290–293.

Wernicke, C. (1874). Der aphasiche Symptomenkomplex. Breslau: Cohn and Weigert. Republished as: The aphasia symptom complex: A psychological study on an anatomical basis. *Wernicke's Works on Aphasia.* The Hague: Mouton.

Wilson, S. M., Saygin, A. P., Sereno, M. I., & Iacoboni, M. (2004) Listening to speech activates motor areas involved in speech production. *Nature Neuroscience, 7*, 701–702.

Wise, R. J. (2003) Language systems in normal and aphasic human subjects: functional imaging studies and inferences from animal studies. *British Medical Bulletin, 65*, 95–119.

Wise, R. J. S., Greene, J., Buchel, C., & Scott, S. K. (1999). Brain regions involved in articulation. *The Lancet, 353*, 1057–1061.

Wise, R. J. S., Scott, S. K., Blank, S. C., Mummery, C. J., & Warburton, E. (2001). Identifying separate neural sub-systems within Wernicke's area. *Brain, 124*, 83–95.

Wise, R., Chollet, F., Hadar, U., Friston, K., Hoffner, E., & Frackowiak, R. (1991). Distribution of cortical neural networks involved in word comprehension and word retrieval. *Brain, 114*, 1803–17.

CHAPTER 3

Learning the Sounds of Language

Jenny R. Saffran and Sarah D. Sahni

1 Introduction

The infant's world is filled with sound. How do infants begin to make sense of their auditory environment? To do so, infants must discern what is most important in the rich and complex acoustic signal that they receive as input. Infants, however, seem to master this task with remarkable ease. By the end of the first year of postnatal life, infants are sophisticated native language listeners, with knowledge about how individual sounds work in their language and how those sounds combine to make words. Moreover, this ability to process complex linguistic input is not limited to the auditory modality; infants exposed to signed languages exhibit a similar trajectory of language discovery. Even infants exposed to multiple languages somehow appear to discover the structures that are most relevant in each language. How do infants converge on their native language system(s) so rapidly?

Historically, the answer to this question was that infants, like adults, treat speech as "special" – that is, as a privileged auditory input distinct from all other perceptual input distinct from all other perceptual stimuli (e.g., Eimas, et al., 1971). In this view, our brains use specialized processes designed to operate over speech stimuli. This account has spurred decades of research focused on the degree to which the processes subserving speech perception and language acquisition are specific to speech per se, or available more generally for perceptual processing across multiple domains and species (for a current incarnation of this debate, see the exchange between Fitch, Hauser, and Chomsky, 2005 and Pinker and Jackendoff, 2005).

What *is* clear is that the spoken environment (and the signed environment, for infants exposed to signed languages) presents a serious challenge for infant learners. The linguistic structures to be acquired are massively complex, containing multi-tiered layers of information and numerous probabilistic cues. To figure out what matters in the input, infants presumably rely on some set of innate structures (a.k.a. "nature"), which may include learning mechanisms (complete with input representations and computational algorithms) and perceptual biases (inherent preferences for some stimuli over others). This preexisting machinery is then coupled with a rich environment (a.k.a. "nurture"), which includes linguistic, referential, social, and affective information. In this view, learning is an essential bridge between nature and nurture: The learning process makes use of structures internal to the infant to organize incoming information, thereby shaping how new input is processed and represented.

In this chapter, we will briefly review recent developments in the study of how infants learn to perceive the sounds of their native language, focusing on how infants learn about individual native language sounds, how those sounds are combined, and the beginnings of word-level knowledge. We will emphasize what is currently known not just about what babies know and when they know it, but *how* that knowledge is acquired.

2 Background issues: Early research in infant speech perception

The field of *infant speech perception* took off in 1971 with the publication of a seminal paper by Peter Eimas and his colleagues (Eimas et al., 1971). Prior to this study, little research had applied the constructs of adult speech perception to investigate the development of speech perception – no methods were available to study the internal perceptual representations of prelinguistic infants. In the first major study of its kind, Eimas and his colleagues were able to demonstrate a remarkable ability on the part of very young infants (one- and four-month-olds). The syllables /pa/ and /ba/ vary along a dimension known as voice onset time (VOT): the time between the release of the consonant and the opening and closing of the vocal folds. This timing varies reliably across consonants; the VOT for /p/ is longer than the VOT for /b/. Earlier studies with adult participants had demonstrated a phenomenon known as *categorical perception*, which appeared to be specific to speech (e.g., Liberman et al., 1967). Adults reliably discriminated differences in VOT only

when the sounds in question spanned two categories (such as /b/ versus /p/). Using a nonnutritive sucking methodology, in which the rate at which infants sucked on a pacifier determined the presentation of auditory stimuli, Eimas et al. (1971) demonstrated that infants showed equivalent discrimination abilities: good discrimination of token pairs that spanned a category boundary, but poor discrimination of token pairs within a category. These results suggested that, like adults, infants perceived phonemes categorically. The fact that even such young infants demonstrated this hallmark of speech perception is consistent with the hypothesis that the "specialness of speech" previously observed in studies with adult participants might be present from birth.

The second major development in the study of infant speech perception arose from the comparison of younger and older infants. Younger infants, like those studied by Eimas et al. (1971), appeared able to apply their special speech perception abilities, including categorical discriminations, to sound contrasts from many languages of the world, including sound contrasts that did not occur in their native language (e.g., Lasky, Syrdal-Lasky, and Klein, 1975; Trehub, 1976). By contrast, groundbreaking research by Werker and Tees (1984) demonstrated that older infants (ten to twelve months of age) were far less open-minded in the application of their speech perception abilities. By the end of their first year, infants were able to discriminate only those consonant contrasts present in their native language, with a few notable exceptions, such as Zulu clicks (e.g., Best, McRoberts, and Sithole, 1988). The same pattern of initial perception of nonnative contrasts, followed by a tuning of the speech perception system, was observed at a somewhat earlier age for vowel contrasts, by six months of age (Kuhl et al., 1992). This developmental difference between vowels and consonants presumably reflects the fact that vowels are particularly clear and emphasized in infant directed speech (Kuhl et al., 1997).

These results suggest the presence of a powerful mechanism underlying reorganization of perceptual systems as a function of linguistic experience (for recent reviews, see Kuhl, 2004; Werker and Curtin, 2005). Importantly, this tuning of the perceptual system to fit the native language occurs before infants produce their first words – around twelve months of age on average, with great variability (e.g., Fenson et al., 1994). Recent evidence suggests that similar reorganization as a function of perceptual learning occurs during infancy in another domain of auditory experience: musical rhythm (Hannon and Trehub, 2005). As in the linguistic domain, this musical "tuning" occurs well before the onset of infants' productive use of the system, suggesting a process of perceptual learning that is at least somewhat independent of production.[1]

Further evidence to suggest that infants are extremely skilled at extracting structure from speech comes from the domain of *word segmentation*. Speech is typically fluent, and does not contain reliable breaks between words analogous to the white spaces in text; even speech to infants does not contain pauses or other acoustic markers of word boundaries. This raises a potential problem for infants, who must somehow break into the speech in their linguistic environments to find word boundaries. In a seminal paper, Jusczyk and Aslin (1995) demonstrated that after hearing target words in passages (e.g., "The *cup* is filled with milk. Mommy's *cup* is on the table."), seven-month-old infants subsequently listened longer to the familiar target words (e.g., *cup*) than to words that were not contained in the familiarization passages (e.g., *bike*). These findings provided the initial experimental evidence demonstrating that infants can segment word-like sound sequences from fluent speech. Notably, this task is sufficiently difficult that computer speech recognition systems can only segment words from fluent speech following explicit training and instruction. Nevertheless, infants appear to perform this task with ease, and certainly do not require explicit training or feedback. As with the development of phonemic perception, this process clearly occurs independent of word production, and also largely independent of knowledge of the meanings of the newly segmented words – though it is certainly the case that segmentation feeds upon itself; familiar words provide powerful word boundary cues for adjacent novel words (e.g., Bortfeld et al., 2005).

Thus, by the mid-1990s, it was clear that infants can perform complex operations over the speech they hear in the environment. Learning, coupled with potential innate predispositions, was evidently a powerful driving force at the outset of language acquisition. In the remainder of this chapter, we will consider some of the important developments in this area, focusing particularly on the mechanisms that subserve infants' early attainments in becoming native language listeners.

3 Development of speech perception

From the earliest moments of postnatal life, speech – and the human faces that produce it – is a central feature of infants' environments. Indeed, infants begin to discover regularities in speech prior to birth, via sound transmission through the uterine wall. Prenatal exposure provides sufficient information to permit newborn infants to distinguish the prosody (pitch and rhythmic structure) of their mother's language from other languages (Mehler et al., 1988). These musical properties of language appear to be particularly interesting and useful to very young infant perceivers. For example, newborn infants can distinguish between languages that have different characteristic rhythmic patterns (e.g., English versus French), but not those that share rhythmic patterns, such

---

1　*Babbling* – repetitive vocal activity that is not referential – is certainly widespread during the first year. There is some debate as to whether or not babbling is shaped by native language sound structure during the first year (e.g., de Boysson-Bardies et al., 1989; de Boysson-Bardies and Vihman, 1991; Engstrand, Williams, and Lacerda, 2003), at least for spoken languages; signed language exposure does elicit manual babbling that is different from the hand movements of infants not exposed to full signed languages like American Sign Language (e.g., Petitto et al., 2004).

as English versus Dutch (Nazzi, Bertoncini, and Mehler, 1998). Interestingly, both infants and nonhuman primates show evidence of this focus on rhythm in their pattern of discriminating between rhythmically dissimilar languages in forward speech, but not backward speech, which disrupts rhythmic cues (Ramus et al., 2000; Tincoff et al., 2005). Only by five months of age does experience with their native language allow infants to discriminate it from other rhythmically similar languages (e.g., Nazzi, Jusczyk, and Johnson, 2000). This developmental trajectory suggests that we begin postnatal life attending to rhythm in quite a general way, akin to other primates, and that with experience, we learn to attend to rhythm as it functions in our native language.

Speech clearly has great perceptual significance to infants, and is certainly special in that sense. For example, newborns, two-month-olds, and four-month-olds prefer to listen to speech as compared to nonspeech analogues that share many critical acoustic features with speech (Vouloumanos and Werker, 2002; 2004). The brains of young infants also treat speech and nonspeech differently, with greater left hemisphere activation for speech (Dehaene-Lambertz, Dehaene, and Hertz-Pannier, 2002; Peña et al., 2003). Moreover, infants are particularly interested in the kind of speech that adults typically direct to them (e.g., Cooper and Aslin, 1990). Infant-directed speech (IDS) has characteristic features that emphasize its musical components: IDS is higher pitched, slower, and contains larger pitch excursions than adult-directed speech, as measured across a number of different language communities (e.g., Fernald, 1992; Gleitman, Newport, and Gleitman, 1984; Liu, Kuhl, and Tsao, 2003). In addition, the individual sounds in IDS are exaggerated relative to adult-directed speech (Kuhl et al., 1997), and the clarity of maternal speech is correlated with infant speech perception abilities (Liu et al., 2003). Infants' auditory environments and infants' perceptual systems appear to be well-suited to one another, facilitating the learning process.

While speech itself may be a privileged stimulus for infants, the operations performed over speech during language acquisition do not appear to be specialized for speech. For example, consider categorical perception. Once considered a hallmark example of the specialness of speech, categorical perception has since been demonstrated for other stimuli that share the temporal dynamics of speech but that are not perceived as speech, including tone pairs that varied in their relative onset, mimicking the acoustic timing characteristics of VOT (for infant data, see Jusczyk et al., 1980; for adult data, see Pisoni, 1977). In addition, categorical perception has now been demonstrated across many other domains, from musical intervals (e.g., Smith et al., 1994) to facial emotion displays (e.g., Pollak and Kistler, 2002; for review, see Harnad, 1987). As in these nonlinguistic domains, listeners are also sensitive to some within-category differences in speech sounds both during adulthood (e.g., McMurray, Tanenhaus, and Aslin, 2002) and infancy (McMurray and Aslin, 2005).

Additional evidence that many of the operations performed over speech are not specialized for speech processing comes from studies using nonhuman participants, including primates, small mammals, and birds. While the auditory systems of nonhuman animals share many features with our own, these other species presumably did not evolve perceptual systems adapted to process human language. Despite this fact, nonhuman mammals (Kuhl and Miller, 1975, 1978; Kuhl and Padden, 1983) show categorical perception for both voicing (e.g., /pa/–/ba/) and place (e.g., /ba/–/da/) continua, and birds show a warping of their perceptual space to reveal a prototype organization following exposures to vowel categories (e.g., Kluender et al., 1998) as previously seen in human infants (e.g., Kuhl et al., 1992). The body of data from nonhuman animals supports the hypothesis that many aspects of speech perception may have developed to take advantage of existing perceptual discontinuities and learning mechanisms not unique to humans (e.g., Kluender et al., 2006).

Regardless of one's theory of the origins of speech processing in infancy, probably the most remarkable thing about infant speech perception is the pace of the learning that occurs: By six months of age for vowels, and ten months of age for consonants, infants have learned to categorize speech sounds as demanded by the categories present in their native language. How does this learning process unfold? Given the precocity of the nonnative to native language shift in speech processing, it cannot be due to factors like the acquisition of minimal pair vocabulary items (e.g., using the fact that /pat/ and /bat/ have different meanings as evidence that /p/ and /b/ are different phonemes). For this to be the case, we would expect to see extensive vocabulary learning *preceding* the loss of native language speech sounds. Infants do comprehend some words during the first year (e.g., Tincoff and Jusczyk, 1999). However, it is highly unlikely that infants learn enough words, and, critically, the right *kinds* of words (such as minimal pairs), to drive their early achievements in speech perception.

One potentially informative source of information pointing to speech categories lies in the distributions of individual sound tokens. Recent analyses and modeling support the intuition that infant-directed speech contains clumps of exemplars corresponding to native language categories (Vallabha et al., 2007; Werker et al., 2007). Moreover, infants can capitalize on these regularities in lab learning tasks employing an artificial language learning methodology. Maye, Werker, and Gerken (2002) demonstrated that infants' speech categories can be modified by the distribution of speech sound exemplars. When infants heard a *bimodal* distribution (two peaks) of speech sounds on a continuum, they interpreted this distribution to imply the existence of two speech categories. Infants exposed to a *unimodal* distribution (one peak), on the other hand, interpreted the distribution as representing only a single category. These results are remarkable both because they show that young infants possess sophisticated statistical learning abilities – namely, the ability to track and interpret frequency histograms as unimodal or bimodal – and because they suggest that infants are able to represent detailed differences between tokens of the same phoneme in order to generate these histograms. This learning is predicated upon the ability to detect extremely small differences between sounds, a point often overlooked given the characterization of speech perception as categorical (for related evidence, see McMurray and Aslin, 2005). To the extent that infants rely on a statistical learning mechanism of this kind, we have an explanation for how infants adjust their phonemic categories well prior to word learning; according to Maye et al.'s (2002) account, top-down knowledge about words is not needed to drive the reorganization of speech perception in infancy. Recent research suggests that basic Hebbian learning mechanisms could be responsible for maintenance of these established perceptual categories, and for shifting from single-category representations to multiple-category representations (McCandliss et al., 2002).

Infants' early speech perception skills are linked in important ways to later language learning. For example, measures of speech perception in infancy predict later native language outcomes, such as vocabulary size, when infants are assessed months or years later (Kuhl et al., 2005; Tsao, Liu, and Kuhl, 2004). These fine-grained perceptual abilities also appear to be maintained when infants are processing familiar words, allowing infants to distinguish correct pronunciations of known words, such as *baby*, from mispronunciations like *vaby* (e.g., Swingley and Aslin, 2000; 2002). However, the process of learning new words may obscure infants' access to phonetic detail, at least under some circumstances (e.g., Stager and Werker, 1997; Werker et al., 2002). When infants' new lexical representations include phonetic detail, when they do not, and the factors that influence this process are a matter of current active research, with important implications for how speech perception relates to subsequent language acquisition (for recent reviews, see Saffran and Graf Estes, 2006; Werker and Curtin, 2005).

Interestingly, there are features of the interpersonal situation in which infants learn language – which are typically over-looked in experimental studies of infant speech perception – that also appear to matter with respect to the development of speech perception. In a recent study, Kuhl, Tsao, and Liu (2003) demonstrated that social interaction facilitates learning. To do so, they exposed English-speaking infants to speakers of Mandarin, and then tested them on Mandarin consonant contrasts not present in English. Critically, these infants were of an age (nine months) at which perception of nonnative speech contrasts has typically declined. As seen in some nonhuman species (such as zebra finches), only those infants exposed to the speech stimuli in the context of dynamic social interactions learned the contrast; infants who heard the same speech presented via high-quality DVD recordings failed to learn the contrast, despite being able to see and hear the same input as the infants in the face-to-face interactive context. These findings suggest that the presence of an interacting human may facilitate learning, potentially via attentional modulation, affective engagement, or some other feature of the social environment. Goldstein, King, and West (2003) suggest that at least for the development of infant babbling, interaction with adults may provide an important source of reinforcement in shaping infants' subsequent productions. Future research will need to address how social cues are integrated with the kinds of statistical information shown to be relevant in learning, since infants are able to profit from the structure of the input in some noninteractive contexts (see Kuhl, 2004 for discussion).

4 Beginnings of language: Perception of sound combinations

During the first year of life, as infants are busy figuring out which sounds are meaningful in their language, they are also engaged in discovering the patterns that occur over multiple sound units. These patterns occur at many levels (i.e., patterns of syllables cohere into words, patterns of words cohere into grammatical units, etc.). Many of the patterns that are the initial focus of infants' attention are patterns of sounds that are visible to the naked ear – that is, patterns that have salient acoustic structure. From this starting point, infants can continue on to discover more abstract patterns.

One pattern found in many languages that is accessible to infant listeners is an alternation between stressed (strong) and unstressed (weak) syllables, which creates an audible rhythm in many languages, including English. These stress differences are carried by the pitch, amplitude (loudness), duration, and vowel quality (in some languages) of the syllables. Bisyllabic words in English are predominantly trochaic – that is, they consist of strong syllables followed by weak syllables, as in the words *doggie*, *baby*, and *mommy* (e.g., Cutler and Carter, 1987). If one is familiar with this pattern of correlations between a syllable's position within a word and the likelihood that a syllable will receive stress, these lexical stress cues can be used to segment words from fluent speech. By nine months of age, infants have already learned something about the predominant stress pattern of their native language (Jusczyk, Cutler, and Redanz, 1993; Polka, Sundara, and Blue, 2002). Moreover, infants can use this information: When given a stream of fluent speech made up of nonsense words, nine-month-old infants can use stress patterns alone to segment words (Curtin, Mintz, and Christiansen, 2005; Johnson and Jusczyk, 2001; Thiessen and Saffran, 2003), and can integrate stress patterns with other distributional information (e.g., Morgan and Saffran, 1995). Further, infants are able to learn new stress patterns quickly. After just a few minutes of exposure to a novel stress pattern, such as iambic (weak–strong) stress, six-and-a-half- and nine-month-old infants generate iambic word boundary expectations when segmenting words from fluent speech (Thiessen and Saffran, 2007).

Infants are also sensitive to regularities that occur in specific sound combinations. *Phonotactic patterns* define which sound sequences are legal or likely in a given language. For example, English words can end with /fs/, but cannot begin with /fs/. These patterns vary cross-linguistically, and are thus not solely determined by such factors as articulatory constraints and pronounceability. By nine months of age, infants have learned enough about the phonotactic regularities of their native language to discriminate legal from illegal sequences (Jusczyk et al., 1993). This knowledge is sufficiently specific to allow infants to discriminate legal sequences that are frequent from those that are infrequent (Jusczyk, Luce, and Charles-Luce, 1994). Knowledge about the likelihood of phonotactic sequences that occur at word boundaries versus word-medially also plays a role in helping infants to discover word boundaries in fluent speech (Mattys and Jusczyk, 2001; Mattys et al., 1999).

Phonotactic patterns characterize *possible* words in a language – sequences with good English phonotactics are possible words, whether or not they have been "chosen" as actual, meaningful words by a language community. Other types of patterns, which are a subset of phonotactic patterns, characterize the *actual* words that exist in a language. For example, while the sequence *pibay* is a possible English word, it is currently not attested, and reflects a gap in the English lexicon. Infants are able to exploit the differences between particular patterns of phonemes that are likely to occur in a language and patterns that are not when attempting to segment words from fluent speech. To do so, infants make use of sequential statistics in the speech stream. Saffran, Aslin, and Newport (1996) asked whether eight-month-old infants could take advantage of these regularities in a word segmentation task. In this study, syllable pairs contained either high or low transitional probabilities. A high transitional probability indicates that one syllable is highly predictive of the next (e.g., the probability that *pi* will follow *ha*, as in the word *happy*). A low transitional probability indicates that a number of different syllables can follow the given syllable (as in *pibay*, which does occasionally occur in fluent speech, such as when the word

happy is followed by the word *baby*, but which is unlikely in English). These probability differences were the only cue to word boundaries in the nonsense language used by Saffran et al. (1996). Despite the paucity of input and the difficulty of this task, infants were able to use these sequential statistics to discover word-like units in fluent speech (see also Aslin, Saffran, and Newport, 1998).

Similarly, training studies have shown that infants can acquire other types of regularities from brief exposures. Along with novel stress patterns (Thiessen and Saffran, 2007), infants are able to rapidly learn new phonotactic regularities in lab learning tasks (Chambers, Onishi, and Fisher, 2003). They can then use these newly learned phonotactic regularities as cues to word boundaries in fluent speech (Saffran and Thiessen, 2003). Training studies like these demonstrate that infants' strategies based on native language regularities are flexible, allowing learners to take advantage of new patterns in the speech stream following very brief exposures. These findings, along with many others, suggest that language learning is a highly dynamic process, with subsequent learning shaped by prior learning (for a recent review, see Gómez, 2006).

The dynamic processes children use to learn language are not limited to discovering patterns. For example, infants take advantage of previous knowledge when trying to learn language. Once six-month-old infants have segmented a word (such as their own name), that word itself becomes a segmentation cue; infants can now segment words that are presented adjacent to their names in fluent speech (Bortfeld et al., 2005). Similarly, attention-getting features of language assist learners. For example, infants in segmentation tasks are able to take advantage of the infant-directed speech that adults use when speaking to them. In a recent study, Thiessen, Hill, and Saffran (2005) showed that seven-month-old infants found it easier to segment words from infant-directed nonsense speech than adult-directed nonsense speech. Infants heard sentences of nonsense speech that contained pitch contours characteristic of either infant-directed or adult-directed speech. In both conditions, the only cue to word boundaries was the transitional probabilities between syllables, which were uncorrelated with the pitch contours. Participants in the infant-directed condition showed evidence of word segmentation while those in the adult-directed condition did not. Infants were able to capitalize on the added dynamic qualities of IDS to pay more attention, facilitating learning. These results illustrate how infants will readily use a wide array of information at their disposal in order to discover the structure inherent in the language in their environment.

5 Using multiple cues in speech

As researchers, we often investigate infants' abilities to perceive or use specific cues, such as phonotactics, lexical stress, sequential statistics, or pitch contour. However, infants "in the wild" are confronted with rich linguistic input that contains multiple cues to structure. Sometimes these cues are consistent with one another, which can be highly informative, while other times they may conflict, vary in their consistency, or simply provide no useful information at all. How do infants handle the complexity of natural language input, which invariably contains multiple levels of informative (and not so informative) patterns (e.g., Seidenberg, MacDonald, and Saffran, 2002)?

One profitable way to study this problem is to create situations in which cues conflict. In studies of word segmentation that have used this technique, the input intentionally contains two conflicting sources of information, allowing researchers to investigate which of the two cues infants preferentially rely upon (e.g., Johnson and Jusczyk, 2001; Mattys et al., 1999; Thiessen and Saffran, 2003). These studies suggest a developmental trajectory in word segmentation: English-learning infants rely on different word boundary cues at different ages (whether or not this same trajectory emerges in infants learning other native languages has yet to be explored). While six-and-a-half- to seven-month-old infants appear to weight transitional probability cues over lexical stress cues (Thiessen and Saffran, 2003), eight-month-old infants weight coarticulation and stress cues over transitional probability cues (Johnson and Jusczyk, 2001), and nine-month-old infants weight stress cues over phonotactic cues (Mattys et al., 1999).

This trajectory is likely a function of infants' different knowledge states at different ages. Younger infants know less than their older counterparts about how patterns like lexical stress and phonotactics work; these patterns vary from one language to the next, and require infants to know something about the structure of words in their native language. With experience, however, older infants acquire rudimentary lexical items (via sequential statistical learning, hearing words in isolation, and via segmentation of neighbors of known words such as their names). Learning new words provides infants with information about relevant patterns in their native language that may serve as cues for subsequent word segmentation (e.g., Saffran and Thiessen, 2003; Thiessen and Saffran, 2007). This emerging lexicon provides a database for the derivation of new generalizations, allowing infants to discover previously opaque regularities and patterns.

In addition to presenting conflicting information, regularities in natural languages may overlap and agree much of the time. For example, the perception of lexical stress is carried by a combination of multiple dynamic properties in the acoustic signal, including increased duration, fundamental frequency (perceived as pitch), and amplitude (loudness). While nine-month-old infants are willing to rely on any one of these properties of stress as a marker of word boundaries, older infants and adults will not (Thiessen and Saffran, 2004), suggesting that infants eventually learn how these various cues covary. The discovery of this rich correlation of acoustic information likely enhances the status of lexical stress as a word boundary cue in languages such as English.

More generally, the presence and use of multiple converging cues may enhance infants' success in language learning. Computational simulations suggest that attending to multiple cues can lead to better outcomes as compared to learning via single cues (in word segmentation: Christiansen, Allen, and Seidenberg, 1998; in classification of lexical items: Reali, Christiansen, and Monaghan, 2003). Studies with infants also support the hypothesis that multiple cues can affect infants' preferences for nonsense words. In one set of studies, Saffran and Thiessen (2003) taught infants new phonotactic regularities and evaluated their ability to segment novel words that adhere to these regularities. During the first phase of the experiment, infants listened to a list of nonsense words, which all conformed to the new phonotactic regularity. In the second phase of the experiment, infants heard a continuous stream of synthesized speech with no acoustic cues to word boundaries. Two of the words presented in the stream adhered to the phonotactic regularity, while two did not. Given this design, the words that adhered to the regularity were marked by *two* cues to word boundaries, transitional probabilities and the newly learned phonotactic regularities, while the boundaries of the other two words were only marked by the probability cue. In the test phase of the experiment, which used an infant-controlled preferential listening design, infants heard repetitions of all four words from the nonsense language. Infants listened significantly longer to the words that adhered to the phonotactic regularity than the words that did not. This indicates that the pattern induction phase, and possibly the presence of multiple word boundary cues, affected infants' preferences for these words. While the presence of multiple cues increased the complexity of the input, this complexity, paradoxically, likely facilitated learning. The rich structure of infant-directed speech is another example of a place where complexity may enhance learnability (e.g., Thiessen et al., 2005).

6 How does all of this happen? Learning mechanisms

Based on our brief review, which is just a sample of the burgeoning literature on infant speech and language learning (for an extensive review, see Saffran, Werker, and Werner, 2006), it is evident that discovering patterns and extracting regularities are central processes in the earliest stages of speech and language learning. As researchers, we are able to identify regularities in speech that are hypothetically useful for learning language. We then create artificial situations to allow infants to demonstrate that they can take advantage of these abilities when no other information is available. However, infants learning their native language(s) are acquiring a vastly more complex linguistic system. How do they actually go about finding the regularities that matter?

These questions have led researchers to investigate the mechanisms that underlie infants' abilities to find and use regularities in linguistic input. The evidence suggests that mechanisms that support the discovery of patterns in structured input are available early in postnatal life. Kirkham, Slemmer, and Johnson (2002) demonstrated that infants as young as two months of age are sensitive to statistical patterns that occur in sequences of visual shapes, which were created to be analogous to syllable sequences. This predisposition to attend to statistical cues – a capacity that appears to be domain-general rather than specific to the domain of language (for a recent review of the issue of domain-specificity/generality in language acquisition, see Saffran and Thiessen, 2007) – may form a base from which infants can learn other cues, potentially by providing infants with a nascent corpus of words across which to discover new regularities. A recent corpus analysis by Swingley (2005) suggests that the majority of words a child would likely discover by attending to syllable co-occurrence would also reveal the predominant rhythmic pattern of the language. In this way, infants may use the statistics of syllable sequences to begin segmenting words – a cue available across languages – and then discover the language-specific and computationally less intensive strategy of using prosodic patterns to segment words. Lending support to this hypothesis, Sahni, Saffran, and

Seidenberg (2010) have shown that infants can use syllable statistics to extract an over-lapping novel segmentation cue and use it to differentiate items that adhere to and violate the novel cue. They exposed nine-month-old infants to a stream of fluent speech generated by a nonsense language containing two redundant cues to word boundaries: Words always began with /t/ (a novel cue not present in English) and contained high internal transitional prob-abilities (which infants of this age are able to use for word segmentation). Notably, the /t/ cue was not informative to infants prior to learning about it during the exper-iment. Infants next heard bisyllabic test items that either began with a /t/ or had a medial /t/ (*timay vs. fotah*). Infants lis-tened significantly longer to the /t/-initial test items that adhered to the novel cue. Crucially, these items were nonwords from the nonsense language, and therefore had a transitional probability of zero. A con-trol condition with no exposure confirmed that infants did not have a preexisting bias toward the /t/-initial items. Therefore, in order for infants to differentiate these items, they must have extracted the /t/-onset cue.

Work on cue competition (e.g., Johnson and Jusczyk, 2001; Thiessen and Saffran, 2003) and cue bootstrapping (Sahni et al., 2010; Swingley, 2005; Thiessen and Saffran, 2007) implies that infants attend to and use a single reliable source of information at a time. When one cue has proven reli-able, infants examine output learned via that source of information, and can then look for newly discoverable cues. However, computational models have illustrated that sequential bootstrapping of this type may be unnecessary in some cases. When sim-ple learning mechanisms are given noisy systems containing multiple regularities at different levels of input, the system is able to capitalize on the regularities across dif-ferent input units and at multiple levels. A model by Christiansen et al. (1998) shows that the presence of more regularities and patterns available in the input facilitates the model's segmentation of words from fluent speech, even if no single piece of information alone reliably points to a clear answer. Christiansen et al. (1998) trained a simple recurrent network on input from a corpus of child-directed speech. The net-work was presented with words as a series of phonemes. Networks were trained on five different combinations of cues: 1) Phonological information, 2) Phonological and utterance boundary information, 3) Phonological and stress information, 4) Stress and utterance boundary informa-tion, and 5) Phonological, stress, and utter-ance boundary information. None of these cues independently indicated word bound-aries with high reliability. The best perfor-mance was attained when the network was trained with all three cues, illustrating its ability to extract nonexplicit information from the system. It may seem obvious that the more information the network has access to, the better its performance. However, the model's performance illustrates that it is possible to extract nonexplicit informa-tion from inputs that are noisy and look confusing from the outside (like the input to child language learners). Although the model may not accurately capture how an infant receives linguistic input, it illustrates the ability to extract information using multiple probabilistic cues simultaneously. Corpus analyses support the idea that it may be beneficial for infants to use multi-ple segmentation cues in tandem. Curtin et al. (2005) calculated the within-word and between-word transitional probabilities in a child-directed corpus. When syllables with different stress were considered unique (i.e., an unstressed *tar* syllable was treated as a different syllable from a stressed *tar*), within-word transitional probabilities were higher than when a syllable's stress was not considered (unstressed *tar* and stressed *tar* were treated as the same syllable). This indicates that if infants include information about stress levels in their distributional analyses, they may be more successful than when using syllable statistics alone.

When focusing on learning mechanisms, it is important to be clear that invok-ing learning does not imply the presence of a blank slate: all environment, with no internal structure. Indeed, the evidence strongly suggests that constraints on learning play a central role in language acquisition; all patterns are not equally learnable (e.g., Saffran, 2003). For example, Newport and Aslin (2004) demonstrated that when adult learners are exposed to sound sequences containing nonadjacent regularities (e.g., AXB, where X varies such that the relevant dependency is between A and B), some such sequences are more learnable than others. When A, X, and B are individual segments, and A and B are similar in kind (A and B are consonants and X is a vowel, or vice versa), adults succeed at discovering the relevant dependencies. However, when A, X, and B are all syllables, adults fail to find the relevant dependency. These results extend to domains beyond language (Creel, Newport, and Aslin, 2004), and suggest that perceptual constraints on grouping, as suggested long ago by Gestalt psychologists, affect sequence learning. Notably, the same constraints on learning were not observed in nonhuman primates learning the same sequences (Newport et al., 2004). The kinds of patterns most readily learned by humans are those that also are most likely to occur in human languages: for example, phonological systems that include dependencies between consonants that span vowels or vice versa (as in languages that make use of consonant or vowel harmony), but not dependencies between syllables that span syllables. This relationship between learnability and presence in human languages may be nonaccidental; the ease with which humans can learn a particular structure may influence the likelihood that that structure occurs cross-linguistically.

7 Extracting regularities: The gateway to language

The ability to extract regularities over multiple units of sound is extremely helpful when finding and recognizing words. However, there is much more to knowing language than just being able to recognize words. Abilities to recognize and use patterns, in the form of learning mechanisms that extract structure via regularity detection, may be the gateway to language. For example, infants can track patterns of words to find grammar-like sequences, and recognize those same sequences when they are exemplified with novel words (e.g., Gómez and Gerken, 1999; Marcus et al., 1999). Under some circumstances, infants can discover nonadjacent dependencies between elements in sequence, suggesting the availability of learning mechanisms not tightly tied to sequential order (e.g., Gómez, 2002). Infants can even perform word-sequence learning tasks given unsegmented fluent speech: When twelve-month-old infants are exposed to a sequence of syllables organized into words, and words organized into sentences, they can discover and learn both of these layers of patterns superimposed in the same set of stimuli, as in natural languages (Saffran and Wilson, 2003).

It is also clear that early learning about the sound patterns of language influences later language learning. Infants' skill at word segmentation is a predictor of later success at word learning in the native language (Newman et al., 2006). When engaged in word segmentation, even in a novel non-sense language (with English phonology), infants appear to treat the output of the segmentation process as candidate novel words in English (Curtin et al., 2005; Saffran, 2001). Many other features of the sounds of novel words influence the ease with which infants can map them to meanings (for a recent review, see Saffran and Graf Estes, 2006). Learning structures at one level of language – even the lowest levels of sound – has implications for many other language learning problems, including grammatical categories and aspects of syntax (e.g., Kelly and Martin, 1994). Moreover, to the extent that learning is linked to language processing (Seidenberg and MacDonald, 1999), we would expect to see that the factors influencing learning also influence later language processing.

8 What does the future hold?

Modern developmental scientists are focused on investigating questions of how and why, rather than what or when. In order to pursue these deeper questions of mechanism, researchers have begun to harness the power of applying multiple methodologies to individual problems in the development of speech and early language (e.g., Hollich, 2006; Kuhl, 2004). Along with more sophisticated scientific questions, the field requires more sophisticated testing methods. One technological advance has been the use of eyetracking methods in infant speech and language studies (e.g., Aslin and McMurray, 2004; Fernald, Swingley, and Pinto, 2001). Traditionally, researchers have used infants' head movements to assess whether infants are attending to one stimulus over another. However, by using eyetracking methods, we can more accurately assess which stimulus the infant is attending to, as well as the details of infants' phonological and lexical representations. McMurray and Aslin (2004) developed a forced choice paradigm that capitalizes on this technology. In this task, infants concurrently saw a looming circle on a video monitor and heard one of two words, for example, *lamb* or *teak*. Next, the circle moved behind a T-shaped occluder and emerged either on the top right or top left of the T. If the circle was paired with *lamb* it emerged on the top left. If it was paired with *teak* it emerged on the top right. After training, infants were tested to see if they could generalize to other exemplars of *lamb* and *teak* in which duration and pitch were varied. While infants could generalize over different pitch ranges, they had difficulty generalizing over longer durations. By using this forced choice eyetracking method, McMurray and Aslin were able to tap a response that is behaviorally less taxing and capitalizes on infants' tendency to track moving objects. The reduction of task demands is well-known to radically alter the kinds of knowledge that infants can demonstrate in an experiment (for demonstrations elsewhere in infant cognition, see Keen,

2003; Munakata, et al., 1997). It is likely that continued advances in behavioral techniques will permit ever more detailed understanding of infants' internal representations and learning processes.

Noninvasive neuroimaging methods, including fMRI, MEG, and optical imaging, along with the more traditionally used EEG and ERP, are also likely to help us to uncover the underpinnings of language acquisition (e.g., Dehaene-Lambertz et al., 2002; Peña et al., 2003). While these methods, to date, have largely been used to ask "where" and "what" questions, they may be profitably applied to the study of "how" by investigating the circuitry and domain-specificity/generality of the mechanisms that subserve language learning. These methods have been effectively employed in studies of adults that have moved the field beyond old-fashioned general statements concerning hemispheric asymmetries (e.g., "language is localized in the left hemisphere, with music on the right") to more nuanced theoretical constructs (e.g., Scott, this volume; Zatorre and Belin, 2001).

Another innovation that allows researchers to ask deeper questions is the use of cross-species comparisons (Hauser, Chomsky, and Fitch, 2002). Humans are the only species that possesses a full linguistic system. What mechanisms or abilities do humans possess that allow them to have this unique skill? By performing cross-species comparisons we may move closer to answering these questions. For example, the ability of infants to use probability and frequency information to segment words from fluent speech seems to be a powerful mechanism (e.g., Saffran et al., 1996). This may be a crucial early step in the acquisition of language. However, Hauser, Newport, and Aslin (2001) found that adult cotton top tamarins are also able to capitalize on the same frequency and probability information. The fact that both tamarins and human infants are able to use this type of regularity suggests that there must be a more sophisticated skill that is a point of divergence between the two species. By comparing what humans and nonhuman primates can do, we can understand more about the evolution of language. Further work on more sophisticated skills, such as learning nonadjacent dependencies between speech sounds (e.g., Newport et al., 2004) and learning complex grammars (e.g., Saffran et al., 2008) have illuminated points of divergence between the species. By examining the difference in skills between nonhuman primates and humans we can better understand the "how" and "why" questions of language acquisition.

In conclusion, we have seen a great upsurge in research focused on the ontogenesis of speech and language in infancy. It is now evident that however much the infant brings to this task in terms of factory-installed predispositions and perceptual systems, it is our learning mechanisms, operating under the constraints placed by our perceptual and cognitive systems, which become critically important early in postnatal life. There is still much about this process that we do not understand; most notably, the stimuli used in these experiments vastly underestimate the complexity of the problems facing the language learning child. However, increasingly sophisticated methodology in tandem with increasingly rich theorizing are continuously moving researchers closer to understanding the unfolding of infant speech perception and its relationship to the beginnings of language learning.

Acknowledgments

Preparation of this manuscript was supported by grants to JRS from NICHD (R01HD37466) and NSF (BCS-9983630). We thank Jan Edwards, Katie Graf Estes, Jessica Hay, and Erik Thiessen for helpful comments on a previous draft.

References

Aslin, R. N. & McMurray, B. (2004). Automated corneal-reflection eye tracking in infancy: Methodological developments and applications to cognition. *Infancy*, 6(2), 155–63.

Aslin, R. N., Saffran, J. R., & Newport, E. L. (1998). Computation of conditional probability statistics by 8-month-old infants. *Psychological Science*, 9(4), 321–4.

Best, C. T., McRoberts, G. W., & Sithole, N. M. (1988). Examination of perceptual reorganization for nonnative speech contrasts: Zulu click discrimination by English-speaking adults and infants. *Journal of Experimental Psychology: Human Perception and Performance, 14(3)*, 345–60.

Bortfeld, H., Morgan, J. L., Golinkoff, R. M., & Rathbun, K. (2005). Mommy and Me: Familiar Names Help Launch Babies Into Speech-Stream Segmentation. *Psychological Science, 16(4)*, 298–304.

Chambers, K. E., Onishi, K. H., & Fisher, C. (2003). Infants learn phonotactic regularities from brief auditory experiences. *Cognition, 87(2)*, B69-B77.

Christiansen, M. H., Allen, J., & Seidenberg, M. S. (1998). Learning to segment speech using multiple cues: A connectionist model. *Language and Cognitive Processes, 13*, 221–68.

Cooper, R. P. & Aslin, R. N. (1990). Preference for infant-directed speech in the first month after birth. *Child Development, 61(5)*, 1584–95.

Creel, S. C., Newport, E. L., & Aslin, R. N. (2004). Distant Melodies: Statistical Learning of Nonadjacent Dependencies in Tone Sequences. *Journal of Experimental Psychology: Learning, Memory, and Cognition, 30(5)*, 1119–30.

Curtin, S., Mintz, T. H., & Christiansen, M. H. (2005). Stress changes the representational landscape: Evidence from word segmentation. *Cognition, 96(3)*, 233–62.

Cutler, A., & Carter, D. M. (1987). The predominance of strong initial syllables in the English vocabulary. *Computer Speech and Language, 2*, 133–42.

de Boysson-Bardies, B., Hallé, P., Sagart, L., & Durand, C. (1989). A cross-linguistic investigation of vowel formants in babbling. *Journal of Child Language, 16*, 1–17.

de Boysson-Bardies, B., & Vihman, M. M. (1991). Adaptation to language: Evidence from babbling and first words in four language. *Language, 67*, 297–319.

Dehaene-Lambertz, G., Dehaene, S., & Hertz-Pannier, L. (2002). Functional neuroimaging of speech perception in infants. *Science, 298(5600)*, 2013–15.

Eimas, P. D., Siqueland, E. R., Jusczyk, P., & Vigorito, J. (1971). Speech perception in infants. *Science, 171(3968)*, 303–6.

Engstrand, O., Williams, K. A., & Lacerda, F. (2003). Does babbling sound native? Listener responses to vocalizations produced by Swedish and American 12- and 18-month-olds. *Phonetica*, 60, 17–44.

Fenson, L., Dale, P. S., Reznick, J. S., Bates, E., Thal, D. J., & Pethick, S. J. (1994). Variability in early communicative development. *Monographs of the Society for Research in Child Development*, 59(5), v-173.

Fernald, A. (1992). Meaningful melodies in mothers' speech to infants. In Papousek, H. & Jürgens, U. (Eds.) *Nonverbal vocal communication: Comparative and developmental approaches* (pp. xvi, 303). New York, NY; US: Cambridge University Press.

Fernald, A., Swingley, D., & Pinto, J. P. (2001). When half a word is enough: Infants can recognize spoken words using partial phonetic information. *Child Development*, 72(4), 1003–15.

Fitch, W. T., Hauser, M. D., & Chomsky, N. (2005). The evolution of the language faculty: Clarifications and implications. *Cognition*, 97(2), 179–210.

Gleitman, L. R., Newport, E. L., & Gleitman, H. (1984). The current status of the motherese hypothesis. *Journal of Child Language*, 11(1), 43–79.

Goldstein, M. H., King, A. P., & West, M. J. (2003). Social interaction shapes babbling: Testing parallels between birdsong and speech. *Proceedings of the National Academy of Sciences*, 100(13), 8030–8035.

Gómez, R. L. (2002). Variability and detection of invariant structure. *Psychological Science*, 13(5), 431–6.

(2006). Dynamically guided learning. In Munakata, Y. & Johnson, M. H. (Eds.) *Processes of change in brain and cognitive development: Attention and performance*. XXI. Oxford: University Press.

Gómez, R. L. & Gerken, L. (1999). Artificial grammar learning by 1-year-olds leads to specific and abstract knowledge. *Cognition*, 70(2), 109–35.

Hannon, E. E., & Trehub, S. E. (2005). Metrical Categories in Infancy and Adulthood. *Psychological Science*, 16(1), 48–55.

Harnad, S. (1987). Category induction and representation. In Harnad, S. (Ed.) *Categorical perception: The groundwork of cognition*. New York, NY, US: Cambridge University Press.

Hauser, M. D., Chomsky, N., & Fitch, W. T. (2002). The faculty of language: What is it, who has it, and how did it evolve? *Science*, 298(5598), 1569–79.

Hauser, M. D., Newport, E. L., & Aslin, R. N. (2001). Segmentation of the speech stream in a non-human primate: Statistical learning in cotton-top tamarins. *Cognition*, 78(3), B53-B64.

Hollich, G. (2006). Combining Techniques to Reveal Emergent Effects in Infants' Segmentation, Word Learning, and Grammar. *Language and Speech*, 49(1), 3–19.

Johnson, E. K. & Jusczyk, P. W. (2001). Word segmentation by 8-month-olds: When speech cues count more than statistics. *Journal of Memory and Language*, 44(4), 548–67.

Jusczyk, P. W., & Aslin, R. N. (1995). Infants' detection of the sound patterns of words in fluent speech. *Cognitive Psychology*, 29(1), 1–23.

Jusczyk, P. W., Cutler, A., & Redanz, N. J. (1993). Infants' preference for the predominant stress patterns of English words. *Child Development*, 64(3), 675–87.

Jusczyk, P. W., Friederici, A. D., Wessels, J. M., & Svenkerud, V. Y. (1993). Infants' sensitivity to the sound patterns of native language words. *Journal of Memory and Language*, 32(3), 402–20.

Jusczyk, P. W., Luce, P. A., & Charles-Luce, J. (1994). Infants' sensitivity to phonotactic patterns in the native language. *Journal of Memory and Language*, 33(5), 630–45.

Jusczyk, P. W., Pisoni, D. B., Walley, A., & Murray, J. (1980). Discrimination of relative onset time of two-component tones by infants. *The Journal Of The Acoustical Society Of America*, January 1980, Vol. 67 (1), 262–70.

Keen, R. (2003). Representation of objects and events: Why do infants look so smart and toddlers look so dumb? *Current Directions in Psychological Science*, 12(3), 79–83.

Kelly, M. H., & Martin, S. (1994). Domain-general abilities applied to domain-specific tasks: Sensitivity to probabilities in perception, cognition, and language. *Lingua*, 92, 105–40.

Kirkham, N. Z., Slemmer, J. A., & Johnson, S. P. (2002). Visual statistical learning in infancy: Evidence for a domain general learning mechanism. *Cognition*, 83(2), B35-B42.

Kluender, K. R., Lotto, A. J., Holt, L. L., & Bloedel, S. L. (1998). Role of experience for language-specific functional mappings of vowel sounds. *Journal of the Acoustical Society of America*, 104(6), 3568–82.

Kluender, K. R., Lotto, A. J., Holt, L. L., Greenberg, S., & Ainsworth, W. A. (2006). *Contributions of Nonhuman Animal Models to Understanding*

Human Speech Perception. Mahwah, NJ, US: Lawrence Erlbaum Associates Publishers.

Kuhl, P. K. (2004). Early language acquisition: Cracking the speech code. *Nature Reviews Neuroscience, 5(11)*, 831–41.

Kuhl, P. K., Andruski, J. E., Chistovich, I. A., Chistovich, L. A., Kozhevnikova, E. V., Ryskina, V. L., et al. (1997). Cross-language analysis of phonetic units in language addressed to infants. *Science, 277(5326)*, 684–6.

Kuhl, P. K., Conboy, B. T., Padden, D., Nelson, T., & Pruitt, J. (2005). Early speech perception and later language development: Implications for the "critical period." *Language Learning and Development, 1(3)*, 237–64.

Kuhl, P. K., & Miller, J. D. (1975). Speech perception by the chinchilla: Voiced–voiceless distinction in alveolar plosive consonants. *Science, 190(4209)*, 69–72.

(1978). Speech perception by the chinchilla: identification function for synthetic VOT stimuli. *The Journal Of The Acoustical Society Of America*, March 1978, Vol. 63 (3), 905–17.

Kuhl, P. K., & Padden, D. M. (1983). Enhanced discriminability at the phonetic boundaries for the place feature in macaques. *The Journal Of The Acoustical Society Of America*, March 1983, Vol. 73 (3), 1003–10.

Kuhl, P. K., Tsao, F. M., & Liu, H. M. (2003). Foreign-language experience in infancy: Effects of short-term exposure and social interaction on phonetic learning. *Proceedings of the National Academy of Sciences of the United States of America, 100(15)*, 9096.

Kuhl, P. K., Williams, K. A., Lacerda, F., Stevens, K. N., & Lindblom, B. (1992). Linguistic experience alters phonetic perception in infants by 6 months of age. *Science, 255(5044)*, 606–8.

Lasky, R. E., Syrdal-Lasky, A., & Klein, R. E. (1975). VOT discrimination by four to six and a half month old infants from Spanish environments. *Journal of Experimental Child Psychology, 20(2)*, 215–25.

Liberman, A. M., Cooper, F. S., Shankweiler, D. P., & Studdert-Kennedy, M. (1967). Perception of the speech code. *Psychological Review, 74(6)*, 431–61.

Liu, H. M., Kuhl, P. K., & Tsao, F. M. (2003). An association between mothers' speech clarity and infants' speech discrimination skills. *Developmental Science, 6(3)*, F1-F10.

Marcus, G. F., Vijayan, S., Bandi Rao, S., & Vishton, P. M. (1999). Rule learning by seven-month-old infants. *Science* (New York, N.Y.), *283*(5398), 77–80.

Mattys, S. L. & Jusczyk, P. W. (2001). Phonotactic cues for segmentation of fluent speech by infants. *Cognition, 78(2)*, 91–121.

Mattys, S. L., Jusczyk, P. W., Luce, P. A., & Morgan, J. L. (1999). Phonotactic and prosodic effects on word segmentation in infants. *Cognitive Psychology, 38(4)*, 465–94.

Maye, J., Werker, J. F., & Gerken, L. (2002). Infant sensitivity to distributional information can affect phonetic discrimination. *Cognition, 82(3)*, B101-B111.

McCandliss, B. D., Fiez, J. A., Protopapas, A., Conway, M., & McClelland, J. L. (2002). Success and failure in teaching the [r]–[l] contrast to Japanese adults: Tests of a Hebbian model of plasticity and stabilization in spoken language perception. *Cognitive, Affective & Behavioral Neuroscience, 2(2)*, 89–108.

McMurray, B. & Aslin, R. N. (2004). Anticipatory eye movements reveal infants' auditory and visual categories. *Infancy, 6(2)*, 203–29.

(2005). Infants are sensitive to within-category variation in speech perception. *Cognition, 95(2)*, B15-B26.

McMurray, B., Tanenhaus, M. K., & Aslin, R. N. (2002). Gradient effects of within-category phonetic variation on lexical access. *Cognition, 86(2)*, B33-B42.

Mehler, J., Jusczyk, P., Lambertz, G., Halsted, N., Bertoncini, J., & Amiel-Tison, C. (1988). A precursor of language acquisition in young infants. *Cognition, 29(2)*, 143–78.

Morgan, J. L. & Saffran, J. R. (1995). Emerging integration of sequential and suprasegmental information in preverbal speech segmentation. *Child Development, 66(4)*, 911–36.

Munakata, Y., McClelland, J. L., Johnson, M. H., & Siegler, R. S. (1997). Rethinking infant knowledge: Toward an adaptive process account of successes and failures in object permanence tasks. *Psychological Review, 104(4)*, 686–713.

Nazzi, T., Bertoncini, J., & Mehler, J. (1998). Language discrimination by newborns: Toward an understanding of the role of rhythm. *Journal of Experimental Psychology: Human Perception and Performance, 24(3)*, 756–66.

Nazzi, T., Jusczyk, P. W., & Johnson, E. K. (2000). Language discrimination by English-learning 5-month-olds: Effects of rhythm and familiarity. *Journal of Memory and Language, 43(1)*, 1–19.

Newman, R., Bernstein Ratner, N., Jusczyk, A. M., Jusczyk, P. W., & Dow, K. A. (2006). Infants' Early Ability to Segment the Conversational

Speech Signal Predicts Later Language Development: A Retrospective Analysis. *Developmental Psychology, 42(4),* 643–55.

Newport, E. L., & Aslin, R. N. (2004). Learning at a distance I Statistical learning of non-adjacent dependencies. *Cognitive Psychology, 48(2),* 127–62.

Newport, E. L., Hauser, M. D., Spaepen, G., & Aslin, R. N. (2004). Learning at a distance II Statistical learning of non-adjacent dependencies in a non-human primate. *Cognitive Psychology, 49(2),* 85–117.

Peña, M., Maki, A., Kovačić, D., Dehaene-Lambertz, G., Koizumi, H., Bouquet, F., et al. (2003). Sounds and silence: An optical topography study of language recognition at birth. *Proceedings of the National Academy of Sciences, 100(20),* 11702–5.

Petitto, L. A., Holowka, S., Sergio, L. E., Levy, B., & Ostry, D. J. (2004). Baby hands that move to the rhythm of language: Hearing babies acquiring sign languages babble silently on the hands. *Cognition, 93(1),* 43–73.

Pinker, S. & Jackendoff, R. (2005). The faculty of language: What's special about it? *Cognition, 95(2),* 201–36.

Pisoni, D. B. (1977). Identification and discrimination of the relative onset time of two component tones: implications for voicing perception in stops. *The Journal Of The Acoustical Society Of America, 61(5),* 1352–61.

Polka, L., Sundara, M., & Blue, M. (2002). The role of language experience in word segmentation: A comparison of English French and bilingual infants. Paper presented at the 143 Meeting of the Acoustical Society of America: Special Session in Memory of Peter Juszyk, Pittsburgh, PA.

Pollak, S. D. & Kistler, D. J. (2002). Early experience is associated with the development of categorical representations for facial expressions of emotion. *Proceedings of the National Academy of Sciences, 99(13),* 9072–6.

Ramus, F., Hauser, M. D., Miller, C., Morris, D., & Mehler, J. (2000). Language discrimination by human newborns and by cotton-top tamarin monkeys. *Science, 288(5464),* 349–51.

Reali, F., Christiansen, M. H., & Monaghan, P. (2003). Phonological and distributional cues in syntax acquisition: Scaling up the connectionist approach to multiple-cue integration. Paper presented at the 25th Annual Conference of the Cognitive Science Society.

Saffran, J. R. (2001). Words in a sea of sounds: The output of infant statistical learning. *Cognition, 81(2),* 149–69.

(2003). Statistical language learning: Mechanisms and constraints. *Current Directions in Psychological Science, 12(4),* 110–14.

Saffran, J. R., Aslin, R. N., & Newport, E. L. (1996). Statistical learning by 8-month-old infants. *Science, 274(5294),* 1926–8.

Saffran, J. R. & Graf Estes, K. M. (2006). Mapping sound to meaning: Connections between learning about sounds and learning about words. In Kail, R. (Ed.) *Advances in Child Development and Behavior* (pp. 1–38.). New York: Elsevier.

Saffran, J. R., Hauser, M., Seibel, R., Kapfhamer, J., Tsao, F., & Cushman, F. (2008). Grammatical pattern learning by human infants and cotton-top tamarin monkeys. *Cognition,* 107, 479–500.

Saffran, J. R., & Thiessen, E. D. (2003). Pattern induction by infant language learners. *Developmental Psychology, 39(3),* 484–94.

(2007). Domain-general learning capacities. In Hoff, E. & Shatz, M. (Eds.) *Blackwell handbook of language development.* (pp. 68–86). Malden, MA, US: Blackwell Publishing.

Saffran, J. R., Werker, J. F., & Werner, L. A. (2006). The Infant's Auditory World: Hearing, Speech, and the Beginnings of Language. In Kuhn, D. & Siegler R. S. (Eds.) *Handbook of child psychology: Vol 2, Cognition, perception, and language* (6th ed.). (pp. 58–108). Hoboken, NJ, US: John Wiley & Sons Inc.

Saffran, J. R. & Wilson, D. P. (2003). From syllables to syntax: Multilevel statistical learning by 12-month-old infants. *Infancy, 4(2),* 273–84.

Sahni, S. D., Saffran, J. R., & Seidenberg, M. S. (2010). Connecting Cues: Overlapping regularities support cue discovery in infancy. in Word Segmentation. *Child Development,* 81, 727–736

Scott, S. (this volume). Neural bases of speech perception – phonology, streams, and auditory word forms

Seidenberg, M. S. & MacDonald, M. C. (1999). A probabilistic constraints approach to language acquisition and processing. *Cognitive Science, 23(4),* 569–88.

Seidenberg, M. S., MacDonald, M. C., & Saffran, J. R. (2002). Does grammar start where statistics stop? *Science,* 298, 553–4.

Smith, J. D., Kemler Nelson, D. G., Grohskopf, L. A., & Appleton, T. (1994). What child is this? What interval was that? Familiar tunes and music perception in novice listeners. *Cognition,* July 1994, Vol. 52 (1), 23–54.

Stager, C. L., & Werker, J. F. (1997). Infants listen for more phonetic detail in speech perception than in word-learning tasks. *Nature*, 388(6640), 381–2.

Swingley, D. (2005). Statistical clustering and the contents of the infant vocabulary. *Cognitive Psychology*, 50(1), 86–132.

Swingley, D. & Aslin, R. N. (2000). Spoken word recognition and lexical representation in very young children. *Cognition*, 76(2), 147–66.

(2002). Lexical neighborhoods and the word-form representations of 14-month-olds. *Psychological Science*, 13(5), 480–4.

Thiessen, E. D., Hill, E. A., & Saffran, J. R. (2005). Infant-Directed Speech Facilitates Word Segmentation. *Infancy*, 7(1), 53–71.

Thiessen, E. D. & Saffran, J. R. (2003). When cues collide: Use of stress and statistical cues to word boundaries by 7- to 9-month-old infants. *Developmental Psychology*, 39(4), 706–16.

(2004). Spectral tilt as a cue to word segmentation in infancy and adulthood. *Perception & Psychophysics*, 66(5), 779–91.

(2007). Learning to Learn: Infants' Acquisition of Stress-Based Strategies for Word Segmentation. *Language Learning and Development*, 3(1), 73–100.

Tincoff, R., Hauser, M., Tsao, F., Spaepen, G., Ramus, F., & Mehler, J. (2005). The role of speech rhythm in language discrimination: Further tests with a non-human primate. *Developmental Science*, 8(1), 26–35.

Tincoff, R., & Jusczyk, P. W. (1999). Some beginnings of word comprehension in 6-month-olds. *Psychological Science*, 10(2), 172–5.

Trehub, S. E. (1976). The discrimination of foreign speech contrasts by infants and adults. *Child Development*, 47(2), 466–72.

Tsao, F. M., Liu, H. M., & Kuhl, P. K. (2004). Speech Perception in Infancy Predicts Language Development in the Second Year of Life: A Longitudinal Study. *Child Development*, 75(4), 1067–84.

Vallabha, G. K., McClelland, J. L., Pons, F., Werker, J. F., & Amano, S. (2007). Unsupervised learning of vowel categories from infant-directed speech. *Proceedings of the National Academy of Sciences Early Addition*, 1–6.

Vouloumanos, A. & Werker, J. F. (2002, April 18–21). Infants preference for speech: When does it emerge? Poster presented at the 13th biennial International Conference of Infant Studies, Toronto, Ontario.

Vouloumanos, A. & Werker, J. F. (2004). Tuned to the signal: The privileged status of speech for young infants. *Developmental Science*, 7(3), 270–6.

Werker, J. F. & Curtin, S. (2005). PRIMIR: A developmental framework of infant speech processing. *Language Learning and Development*, 1(2), 197–234.

Werker, J. F., Fennell, C. T., Corcoran, K. M., & Stager, C. L. (2002). Infants' ability to learn phonetically similar words: Effects of age and vocabulary size. *Infancy*, 3(1), 1–30.

Werker, J. F., Pons, F., Dietrich, C., Kajikawa, S., Fais, L., & Amano, S. (2007). Infant-directed speech supports phonetic category learning in English and Japanese. *Cognition*, 103, 147–62.

Werker, J. F., & Tees, R. C. (1984). Cross-language speech perception: Evidence for perceptual reorganization during the first year of life. *Infant Behavior & Development*, 7(1), 49–63.

Zatorre, R. J., & Belin, P. (2001). Spectral and temporal processing in human auditory cortex. *Cerebral Cortex*, 11(10), 946–53.

Section 2

SPOKEN WORD RECOGNITION

CHAPTER 4

Current Directions in Research in Spoken Word Recognition

Arthur G. Samuel and Meghan Sumner

Normal adults are quite proficient at understanding utterances in their native language. In this chapter, we will review some of the reasons that make such proficiency a surprising achievement, and some of the experimental findings that help to explain how this proficiency is achieved. To appreciate some of the issues that arise in recognizing what a speaker has said, consider a situation in which a speaker tells a listener, "Chris took the Stucky file to his supervisor."

We will not concern ourselves here with parsing problems, or with matters such as who the referent of *his* is. Rather, our focus is on how listeners map the complex sound stream onto the correct sequence of lexical representations: How do people recognize the words that have been said? Our example poses a number of problems for the listener. For example, in the sound stream there are generally no breaks between the words, so at the point when the vowel in *took* begins, how does the listener know that *Chris* is the first word rather than *Christa*?

The presence of the name *Stucky* potentially creates additional problems. An unfamiliar name is essentially a nonword sitting in the word stream, and the system must be able to reach that conclusion. In this case, the problem is compounded by the fact that the word *stuck* is embedded in the nonword. As we shall see, such embedding is rampant in spoken language, and it potentially creates enormous problems for recognition. Embedding aside, if the system is designed to yield the closest match to a word that can be made with the available input, it might settle on *sticky* in this case, which could potentially be reinforced by misperceiving the following word (*file*) as the very similar, and semantically consistent, word *vile* (i.e., "Chris took the sticky, vile...").

The final two words (*his supervisor*) present additional potential problems. The final sound in *his* is the voiced fricative /z/. However, in this context, the /z/ is likely to be produced more like an /s/, as it assimilates to better match the following /s/ in *supervisor*. This creates two potential problems: How can the listener correctly recognize *his* if the sounds are actually more like the sounds in *hiss*? And, once the assimilation has occurred, one long /s/ now straddles *his* and *supervisor*, yet the listener has to separate them to recognize both. For *supervisor*, the embedding problem is again present, in both the initial form (*sue, soup, super*) we saw for *Stucky*, as well as in additional non-initial positions (e.g., *vie, eyes, visor*).

As we noted, despite all of these potentially severe problems, adults normally are remarkably adept at recognizing spoken words. Researchers have explored the processes that allow this achievement, and have developed models of the representations that are involved. In most current models, the auditory consequences of spoken words are first mapped onto some kind of phonetic features, which in turn comprise some kind of sublexical units, such as phonemes or syllables. These units then map onto lexical representations, yielding word recognition. The dominant metaphor in these models is the notion of "activation" of units: Greater evidence for a unit's presence produces stronger activation of that representation. Recognition of the unit occurs when its activation exceeds either a threshold or some activation state relative to all other units at its level.

Many studies demonstrate the simultaneous activation of multiple lexical candidates, when the information in the speech stream is consistent with more than one word. Some of the best evidence in this literature comes from cross-modal priming experiments. A classic study of this type was conducted by Zwitserlood (1989). She played sentences to Dutch listeners and had them make lexical decisions to printed words that appeared at certain critical points in the speech stream. For example, a listener who heard *cap* (as the first syllable of *capitan* [Dutch for *captain*], or *capital* [capital]) would see the Dutch word for *ship* or for *town*, and would make lexical decisions about the printed probes. Responses were facilitated (relative to an unrelated control word), showing that both *capitan* and *capital* were activated by *cap*. Many studies have shown that word recognition takes place sooner for words that allow this type of ambiguity to be resolved sooner (i.e., words with an early lexical uniqueness point), versus words with longer lasting lexical ambiguity (those with late uniqueness points). For example, Gaskell and Marslen-Wilson (2002) found significantly stronger repetition priming and semantic priming for "early unique" words compared to "late unique" words, suggesting that the former produce faster and stronger lexical activation, yielding the stronger priming effects.

Many other demonstrations of the simultaneous activation of multiple lexical representations have been reported. Allopenna, Magnuson, and Tanenhaus (1998) developed an eyetracking methodology that provides converging evidence. In these experiments, participants see displays of four pictured objects and hear instructions that concern one of them (e.g., "move the beaker"). The participants wear a head-mounted eyetracker, and on critical trials the display includes both the target picture and an item with the same speech onset (e.g., a beetle). The eye movement patterns show that as listeners hear the unfolding speech, they are likely to examine both pictures that are consistent with the input ("bee..."), and then to focus on the one that matches the full word. Thus, just as in the cross-modal priming experiments, it appears that the ongoing speech input activates multiple consistent lexical candidates.

As noted above, the existence of competing lexical possibilities seems to pose a major challenge to a word recognition system. In fact, the *captain–capital* or *beaker–beetle* class of lexical ambiguity represents only one of several such problems. The embedded word situation illustrated in the *stuck–Stucky* and *soup–supervisor* example is potentially even more problematic, because in these cases there really isn't any subsequent information in the signal that makes the shorter word inconsistent with the input (whereas hearing *ker* after *bea* does conflict with a *beetle* representation). There are also cases of potential lexical ambiguity created when adjacent words produce a signal that could match another word (e.g., *two lips → tulips*). Gow and Gordon (1995) demonstrated cross-modal priming of *flowers* when *two lips* had been produced in a neutral sentence context, confirming that such emergent lexical items do indeed generate lexical activation.

At this point, one might be tempted to conclude that spoken word recognition really can't be done – there are simply too many potential complications. However, this is obviously not the case (people actually do successfully talk to each other). The key to overcoming these complications seems to be that there are situations in which the potential problems turn out not to be actual problems. There are many cases in which we might expect to see activation of competing lexical candidates, but no such competition actually exists. For example, although Gow and Gordon (1995) found evidence that *two lips* does engage the *tulips* representation, the reverse was not observed – hearing *tulips* did not produce priming of *kiss*, as might be expected if *lips* were activated by *tulips*.

This limitation on multiple lexical activation was also found in a comprehensive study reported by Vroomen and de Gelder (1997). Using cross-modal priming with Dutch stimuli, Vroomen and de Gelder explored the conditions under which embedded monosyllables get activated within both other monosyllables and in two-syllable utterances. They found that in two-syllable words (e.g., *framboos* [strawberry]), there was significant priming for a word related to the embedded second syllable word *boos* [angry]; this replicates a comparable finding in English by Shillcock (1990), who found that *trombone* produced priming of *rib* (related to *bone*). However, there was very limited multiple lexical activation with monosyllabic carriers. For a word embedded at the end of a monosyllable (e.g., *wijn* [wine] in *zwijn* [swine], or in the nonword *twijn*), no evidence was found for activation of the embedded word. For words embedded in the initial position (e.g., *vel* [skin]), priming was found when the carrier was a nonword (e.g., *velk*), but not when it was a word (e.g., *velg* [rim]), suggesting that longer words have an advantage in the lexical competition. Vroomen and de Gelder concluded that lexical activation depends in part on the presence of a syllable onset that matches the lexical representation.

There appear to be additional ways to mitigate the potential problem of embedded words. Davis, Marslen-Wilson, and Gaskell (2002) used cross-modal repetition priming to investigate whether the acoustic realization of an embedded word is actually different than its realization when it is produced as a full word, and if so, whether listeners can take advantage of the difference. For example, one pair of stimuli was based on the word *cap*, which could be presented either as a full word followed by another word (*cap tucked*), or embedded as the first syllable of a longer word (*captain*). In both cases, the critical information occurred in a plausible but neutral sentence context ("The soldier saluted the flag with his [cap tucked]/[captain]…"). The repetition priming test involved the visual presentation of either *cap* or *captain*, in this example, for a lexical decision. Davis et al. found significant priming effects, and critically, the priming was stronger for trials in which the visual target matched the speech, even when the probe occurred before the end of *cap*. The series of experiments clearly demonstrated that there are acoustic differences between a short word when it stands alone versus when it is embedded in a longer word, and that listeners can use those differences to focus their lexical search.

Salverda, Dahan, and McQueen (2003) replicated and refined this result, using Dutch subjects and stimuli. In an eyetracking paradigm, the authors presented four pictures per trial, with critical stimuli such as *ham* and *hamster*. Sentences involving each of the critical words were recorded, and subjects were told to use a computer mouse to click on and move any pictured object mentioned in a sentence. Two versions of each longer word (e.g., *hamster*) were presented. In one, the first syllable (*ham*) was spliced in from the monosyllable (*ham*); in the other, the first syllable was spliced in from another token of the longer word (*ham*, taken from *hamster*). The central result was that eye movements to the long word occurred later when the first syllable came from a monosyllable, indicating that there were acoustic cues that differed.

Salverda et al. noted that syllables tend to be shorter when they are embedded than when they are not. They therefore manipulated the duration of the spliced first syllables (by selecting tokens that were naturally long or short), and clearly showed that listeners were taking the length of the syllable as a cue to whether it was *ham* or part of *hamster*. Together with the results of Davis et al. (2002), these data show that listeners can use quite subtle acoustic cues to reduce the lexical search space.

There are other ways that one could imagine that the lexical search could be limited. For example, we have known for decades that listeners are better at reporting words heard in noise when the words are predictable from their sentential context (e.g., Miller and Isard, 1963). It would therefore seem plausible that such context could be used to prevent any competition from lexical candidates that are semantically inconsistent. However, as Zwitserlood (1999) argues in a very thorough examination of the literature, the evidence suggests that lexical activation is not affected by semantic plausibility. One of the best illustrations of this is the Zwitserlood (1989) study mentioned earlier (the *capitan–capital* cross-modal priming experiment). Zwitserlood found that providing a sentence context that clearly favored one word over the other did not prevent the activation of both words that were consistent with the initial syllable (e.g., *cap*).

Samuel (1981) also found no evidence that lexical activation is affected by sentential predictability. In that study, listeners heard words in which a phoneme had either been replaced by white noise, or had merely had noise added to it. They were supposed to judge whether any phoneme had been replaced by noise. In a series of experiments, Samuel found that listeners were quite poor at this judgment, because they were perceptually restoring the missing speech (Warren, 1970). When the words were placed in predictive sentence contexts, there was no change in the ability of the listeners to make the discrimination judgment. Recently, Van Berkum et al. (2005) have used an evoked

potentials methodology to reexamine whether predictive sentence context might affect lexical access (see Van Berkum, this volume, for further discussion). They suggest that it can. However, the relevant test involved contexts with exceptionally high predictability (cloze predictability rates averaging almost ninety percent), and there was no direct test of whether the context actually affected decoding of the speech signal. Thus, although their results are interesting, it would be premature to add semantic predictability to the set of cues that listeners use to simplify the lexical competition problem.

Listeners seem to be more successful in using probabilistic cues to aid their word recognition. A widely studied such cue is *metrical stress*. In languages such as English and Dutch, utterances typically consist of a series of metrical feet, with each foot including a relatively strong syllable and a small number of weaker ones. In these languages, most content words begin with a strong syllable, which means that the word recognition system could in principle associate the presence of a strong syllable with the onset of a new word. Cutler and Norris (1988) suggested that listeners do in fact use such a "Metrical Segmentation Strategy" (MSS); see Vroomen, Tuomainen, and de Gelder (1998) for a discussion of whether the relevant property is metrical stress or is instead *lexical stress* (the stress pattern of a word, independent of its role in a metrical foot). Evidence for a stress-based role in word recognition comes from a number of studies (see Cutler, Dahan, and van Donselaar, 1997, for a review). For example, in the Cutler and Norris study that introduced the MSS hypothesis, subjects did a word spotting task in which they listened for monosyllabic targets (e.g., *mint*) embedded in longer nonwords (e.g., *mintesh* or *mintayve*). Detection was slower in carriers like *mintayve*, consistent with the view that the strong final syllable (*tayve*) was treated as a word onset, leaving a remainder (*min*) that did not fully match the target.

Vroomen et al. (1998) have shown that the use of such probabilistic cues is language dependent. For example, in Finnish there are at least two such cues: lexical stress (Finnish words, like Dutch and English ones, strongly favor initial-syllable stress), and vowel harmony. Finnish vowels can be divided into three classes – back, front, and neutral – and within uncompounded words, front and back vowels should not co-occur. Thus, if syllables from these two classes follow one another, this is a strong cue that they are parts of different words. Vroomen et al. showed that word spotting in Finnish was sensitive to both lexical stress and vowel harmony. In contrast, Dutch listeners only showed sensitivity to stress, and French listeners were not affected by either cue. In all cases, the results reflect the probabilistic cues of each language.

A critical role for probability matching in word recognition is also seen in the substantial literature showing that phonotactic properties strongly influence word recognition. The phonotactics of a language can be thought of as the ways in which sounds may occur in a particular language. For example, an English word may begin with the consonant cluster /tr/ as in the word *train*, but it may not begin with the consonant cluster /rt/. This does not mean that this consonant cluster is not possible in the language (cf. *cart*), only that it cannot occur initially. Recent research in spoken word recognition has focused on phonotactic probabilities, or the frequency of a sound or combination of sounds in syllables and words. For example, in English, words may begin with the consonant clusters /tw/ and /tr/ (e.g., *tweet, treat*). The cluster /tr/, however, occurs in the onset two to three times more often than the cluster /tw/. Consequently, in the initial position of a word, or the *onset*, it is more likely that /tr/ occurs than /tw/.

Listeners appear to be sensitive to these probabilistic differences and to use them to facilitate processing. In word spotting experiments, detection performance is enhanced when phonotactic probabilities can be used to predict the segmentation of the embedded word. For example, when phonotactic rules force a syllabic break before the target (e.g., the target *lip* in *venlip*), its detection is better than when such rules do not (e.g., *lip* in *veglip*) (Dumay, Frauenfelder, and Content, 2002; McQueen, 1998).

Recall that most current models of word recognition posit an initial encoding of the signal into sets of phonetic features, followed by some kind of phoneme- or syllable-based code that is mapped onto lexical representations. The phonotactic effects reviewed here would naturally be associated with the intermediate-level codes. There is a corresponding concept at the lexical level – the similarity neighborhood. A *similarity neighborhood* is a group of words that differ from each other in one sound. For example, the words *treat, tweed, twit,* and *sweet* are all neighbors of the word *tweet*. Luce and Pisoni (1998) found that spoken words that are in dense neighborhoods (words that sound like many other words, e.g., *cat*) are recognized more slowly and with less accuracy than words in sparse neighborhoods (words that have fewer neighbors, e.g., *judge*). This finding is akin to the effects of early versus late uniqueness points discussed previously – words that diverge from all others early on are recognized more quickly than words that do not become lexically unique until later in the word.

If we consider these lexical results together with the phonotactic data, a potentially problematic picture emerges. In one case, common sounds lead to better performance (e.g., faster repetition of nonwords), but in the other case, words in dense neighborhoods (which generally have highly probable sounds) have a processing cost. Vitevitch and Luce (1998; 1999; 2005) examined this apparent contradiction by manipulating both phonotactic probabilities and neighborhood density. In a speeded auditory shadowing task, Vitevitch and Luce (1998) found that nonwords with high phonotactic probabilities and dense neighborhoods were repeated more quickly than those with low phonotactic probabilities and sparse neighborhoods, whereas the reverse was found for words: As the Neighborhood Activation Model predicts, words with high phonotactic probabilities and dense neighborhoods were repeated more slowly than words with low phonotactic probabilities and sparse neighborhoods. The relative dominance of phonotactics and neighborhoods can be shifted as a function of task requirements. For example, when a lexical decision task was used (and thus when activation of the lexicon is required to perform the task), neighborhood effects appeared with non-words as well. These results suggest that there are (at least) two distinct levels of representation in recognizing spoken words: a lexical level and a sublexical level. The influence of phonotactic information occurs at the sublexical level, whereas neighborhood effects surface at the lexical level. Lipinski and Gupta (2005) have recently shown that the differences in shadowing times reported by Vitevitch and Luce were in fact confounded with stimulus duration. Although this muddies the water somewhat, Vitevitch and Luce (2005) addressed this concern with a duration-controlled replication of the effect.

Even in tests that use only real words, it is possible to see effects at the sublexical level influencing the processing of real words. For example, Pitt and Samuel (1995) had subjects do a phoneme monitoring task in words like *moccasin* (early uniqueness point) and *discipline* (late uniqueness point), probing at various positions within the words. As expected, probes near the middle of early unique words showed lexical facilitation, compared to such probes in the late unique words. A result that had not been anticipated was better detection of targets at the end of the first syllable in the late unique words, compared to similar targets in early unique words. The authors suggested that this difference reflected a sublexical effect: The early/late uniqueness manipulation was implemented by using words with very common first syllables (like the *dis* in *discipline*), versus those with uncommon ones (e.g., *moc*). This manipulation also corresponds to a manipulation of phonotactics, and it produced a result consistent with the later findings of Vitevitch and Luce.

When we first discussed the large set of potential problems facing a listener when a speaker said, "Chris took the Stucky file

to his supervisor," we noted that this set was extensive enough to make one wonder how word recognition might be possible at all. After our discussion of all of the ways that listeners can use available cues, it might seem that the problem now is to sort out what cues really matter – researchers clearly differ in how they think listeners solve the potential problems. In a very recent and elegant set of experiments, Mattys, White, and Melhorn (2005) have tried to impose some order on the way that all of the available information might be used. In each experiment, their approach was to pit two possible cues against each other and to see which was more important. For example, they constructed stimuli in which lexical stress cues would favor one interpretation of a stimulus, whereas phonotactic cues would favor an alternative. Using word spotting and priming paradigms, they looked at many of the cues we have discussed here, and some additional cues. In addition, they ran each experiment under both clear listening conditions and noisy ones. Their results suggest that when listening conditions are good, sentential and lexical cues dominate word recognition; phonotactics are of moderate value, and stress is least useful. However, when listening conditions are poor, the relative value of the different types of cues reverses. This hierarchy of cue use is generally consistent with the results in the literature and reflects the cleverness of the word recognition process, as it takes advantage of the most useful cues in a given listening situation.

This optimization is necessitated by the considerable amount of variation in the speech signal. Variation in speech can be attributed to speaker characteristics (e.g., gender, age, etc.), phonology (e.g., different pronunciations of /t/ in the words *atom* and *atomic*), and acoustic–phonetic differences (e.g., released versus unreleased stops). Research in variation has grown over the past few years, providing insight into the ability of listeners to cope with variable acoustic information and map it onto particular phonemes and lexical representations.

Much of the variation in a particular sound is subphonetic. For example, voiced and voiceless stops are distinct because of voice onset time (VOT). VOT is the time from the release of an articulator when producing a sound to the onset of voicing of the following sound. In English, voiced stops (b, d, g) have a short lag in VOT, while voiceless stops (p, t, k) have a longer lag in VOT. This gross categorization is ideal for exemplar sounds of each category, and VOT has been shown to affect lexical activation. Andruski, Blumstein, and Burton (1994) showed that a word with a prototypical VOT activates its lexical representation better than a word with a less prototypical VOT. However, in language, the two prototypical categories are not always produced as such; sounds within a category can vary as well. And, in reality, the actual VOTs of voiced and voiceless stops may at times be very close. While Andruski et al. showed that listeners are sensitive to fine-grained acoustic detail when the information is typical of a particular category, McMurray, Tanenhaus, and Aslin (2002) examined whether listeners are sensitive to within-category differences that are more gradient. By monitoring eye movements to pictures that were potential lexical competitors (e.g., bear, pear) and by varying VOT along a zero ms–forty ms continuum, they found that as VOT approaches a boundary, the activation of lexical competitors increases. Therefore, fine-grained acoustic variability is used by listeners, even within a category, in lexical activation.

Additional research in variation has focused on subcategorical mismatches. Both Marslen-Wilson and Warren (1994) and McQueen, Norris, and Cutler (1999) have used cross-spliced words and nonwords to examine the conditions under which acoustic information is mapped onto lexical representations. Subcategorical mismatches occur when information carried by one sound is different from information carried by another sound. For example, vowel formant transitions contain information about the place of articulation of the following sound. So the formants of the vowel in the word *job* are consistent with the place of articulation of the following labial

consonant. To create mismatching stimuli, and to see the effect of subcategorical mismatches on the processing of spoken words, Marslen-Wilson and Warren cross-spliced the onset and vowels of a real word (e.g., *job*) with the coda of the identical word, a different word (e.g., *jog*), or a nonword (e.g., *jod*). Nonwords were also created and cross-spliced in the same manner (e.g., *smob* with *smob*, *smog*, or *smod*). In a series of tasks (lexical decision, gating, and phonetic decision), Marslen-Wilson and Warren found that subcategorical information has immediate consequences for word recognition, as it is more difficult to recognize subcategorical mismatch items than items with no mismatch. By examining both cross-spliced words and nonwords, they also found that perceptual decisions were influenced by the lexical status of the carrier utterance. McQueen et al. (1999) specifically investigated the influence of lexical representations in perceptual decisions. While they, too, found that decisions to items with mismatching vowel formant and consonant release burst information were harder than for those without mismatching information, they suggested that the influence of the lexicon is present only in certain tasks, and is not a general phenomenon.

A number of recent studies have focused on phonological variation and the ways in which it is accommodated by the spoken word recognition system. One example that has received a fair amount of attention in the literature is assimilation. *Assimilation* is the process by which a segment becomes more like a neighboring segment in one or more features. For example, in the phrase *green beans* the /n/ in the word *green* assimilates its place of articulation to match that of the following consonant, making the final consonant more similar to the initial consonant of the following word, yielding *greem beans*. There is a large body of evidence suggesting that assimilation does not disrupt word recognition (Gaskell and Marslen-Wilson, 1996; Gow, 2001; Marslen-Wilson et al., 1995).

Gow (2002) has shown that assimilation does not result in a complete feature change; natural assimilation consists of coarticulated segments that form an intermediate alteration somewhere between the initial segment (e.g., /n/ *bean*) and the theoretically assimilated segment (e.g., /m/ *bean*). He argues that in assimilation, a segment does not change to a completely new segment, and listeners are able to use these acoustic cues in word recognition. These cues are sufficient to eliminate possible ambiguity between assimilated phrases like *right berries* (pronounced as *ripe berries*) and phrases that do not undergo assimilation like *ripe berries* (with *ripe* as the intended word). Gaskell (2003), however, argued that experience with natural variation (rather than residual coarticulated information) enables listeners to compensate for the assimilated sounds.

In addition to assimilation, other areas of variation have been examined as well. LoCasto and Connine (2002) examined schwa deletion and reduction in two- and three-syllable words (e.g., *police, aspirin*) in a form priming paradigm. They argue that knowledge of phonological variation (e.g., systematic deletion of a sound in this case) can be used by listeners when spoken word recognition alone might fail. McLennan, Luce, and Charles-Luce (2003) examined representational issues surrounding intervocalic tapping in American English (e.g., *latter, ladder*) and found support for both abstract and specific representations in a series of long-term priming tasks with varying levels of processing. In addition, Sumner and Samuel (2005) examined three regular variants of the final /t/ in American English using both short-term and long-term priming tests, and found that in the short term, all variants are equal, but in activating a lexical representation over time, the basic or canonical sound is beneficial.

As the preceding discussion shows, listeners are able to accurately perceive the speech signal despite many types of phonetic variation. These studies indicate that listeners essentially normalize the signal, in order to map it onto the appropriate phonemic category. There is also a complementary way that variation from an existing canonical representation could be dealt with – the existing representation could be modified to make it a better match to the input signal. A rapidly growing body of research demonstrates that such modifications do in fact occur. Norris, McQueen, and Cutler (2003) have termed such effects *perceptual learning*; Vroomen and colleagues (Bertelson, Vroomen, and de Gelder, 2003; Vroomen et al., 2004) have called similar cases *perceptual recalibration*. In both cases, stimuli that were designed to be phonetically ambiguous were presented to listeners, and an additional information source was provided that could disambiguate the signal. In the study by Norris et al., the disambiguation was provided by lexical context: The ambiguous sound was a mixture that was midway between /f/ and /s/, and this ambiguous sound was presented at the end of words that normally end in /f/, at the end of words that normally end in /s/, or at the end of nonwords. In the Bertelson et al. study, the ambiguous sound was synthesized to be midway between /b/ and /d/, and the disambiguation was provided by visual information: A video clip either showed the speaker saying a /b/ or a /d/. In both studies, the disambiguation was successful in producing the appropriate percept.

The more interesting results come from identification tests run *after* the portions of these experiments just described. Norris et al. found that listeners who heard the ambiguous sound in the context of /f/-final words later categorized more items on an /f/–/s/ continuum as /f/, whereas listeners who heard this sound in /s/-final words categorized more items on the same /f/–/s/ continuum as /s/. Hearing the ambiguous sound in nonwords produced no such shift. Thus, listeners use lexical knowledge to dynamically "tune" their phonemic representations to reflect the incoming speech signal. Bertelson et al. reported a comparable effect: Subjects who had heard the ambiguous sound as /d/ (due to the video input) later identified more items as /d/ on a /b/–/d/ test series than subjects who had received the /b/ video. In both of these studies, in addition to the immediate perceptual effect provided by the disambiguating information, there was a long-lasting change in the perceptual definition of the speech sounds.

Subsequent studies have started to clarify the nature of the perceptual recalibration. Kraljic and Samuel (2005) focused on how the system can return to its "normal" state. For example, do these context-induced changes only last for a short period of time, as would be expected if they are essentially a kind of priming effect? Or can additional speech input, in which the acoustics of a sound are more typical (rather than an ambiguous, boundary kind of stimulus) reset the phoneme boundaries? Kraljic and Samuel first induced substantial perceptual learning effects, using the Norris et al. (2003) technique. They then measured any identification shifts approximately twenty-five minutes after the perceptual learning phase. These shifts were at least as large after this delay as they had been in an immediate test, contrary to what a simple priming account would predict. Moreover, even if the listener heard dozens of good exemplars of the affected speech sound during the twenty-five minute interval, the perceptual shift remained significant.

There was some reduction in the shift if the good exemplars were presented in the same speaker's voice as the original training stimuli, but none if the voices were different. In fact, Norris et al. (2003) had suggested that the function of perceptual learning was to adapt to a particular speaker's accent, consistent with the somewhat more effective relearning induced by same-voice experience. However, the developing literature in this area indicates that there are both speaker-specific and speaker-general aspects to perceptual learning.

Eisner and McQueen (2005) directly examined the specificity of perceptual learning. Perceptual learning of the /f/–/s/ contrast (as in Norris et al., 2003) was first induced, with stimuli in a female voice. Participants then identified items from /Ef/–/Es/ continua. For some subjects, the continuum was presented in the same female voice that they had heard during the exposure phase. For others, the vowel portion (/E/) of each item was produced in a different, but

similar, female voice; the fricative portion was produced by the same speaker as in the exposure phase. In a third condition, the test items had the original female speaker's fricatives, but the vowel was produced by a male speaker (as a result, these stimuli sounded male); in the final condition, the test series was created entirely from the male speaker's voice. Listeners showed significant perceptual learning in all of the conditions except when both the vowel and fricative were produced by the male speaker. Eisner and McQueen concluded that perceptual learning is speaker-specific, with the learning occurring at a phonemic level.

The situation, however, is more complex, as shown by the conflicting results reported by Kraljic and Samuel (2005; 2006). With fricatives as the critical stimuli (as in Eisner and McQueen's study), Kraljic and Samuel (2005) found results that were generally similar to those of Eisner and McQueen: For the most part, perceptual learning was speaker-specific. However, under certain conditions the recalibration did transfer to a quite different voice. This generality of perceptual learning was much more striking in Kraljic and Samuel's (2006) study that used the stop consonants /d/ and /t/ as the critical stimuli. In this case, the perceptual learning transferred completely across very different voices. Moreover, the perceptual shifts induced for /d/ and /t/ also generalized to a contrast between /b/ and /p/, which like /d/ and /t/, differ in voicing. The results in this literature therefore suggest that the kinds of adjustments that are made will depend on the acoustic details of the speech sounds themselves. As we noted earlier, this area of research is currently expanding rapidly, which should help to resolve some of the outstanding issues. This literature also now includes investigations of perceptual learning for speech in sentences (Davis et al., 2005) and longer passages (Maye, Aslin, and Tanenhaus, 2008).

There is a rather different kind of learning that involves the lexicon – the learning of new words, expanding the lexicon. Although it may seem natural to associate this type of learning primarily with the developmental literature, in fact there is substantial growth of the lexicon in adults. There have been a number of studies of the vocabulary growth over the lifespan, and they consistently show that adults add new words to their lexicons at a surprisingly high rate. Nation and Waring (1997) conclude that a conservative estimate is that people typically add about a thousand new word families (a word and its close morphological relatives) per year, up to a vocabulary size of approximately twenty thousand word families. This means that a typical young adult (and, to a lesser extent, even older adults) learns about three new words a day, every day.

Given such substantial growth, models of spoken word recognition must be able to account for this change in the lexicon over time. At a minimum, we would want to know what mechanisms are involved in adding new lexical entries, and what the consequences of such additions are for the existing lexical representations. At the simplest level, we can think of learning new words as just one example of learning in general: Just as we can learn the name of a new acquaintance, or how to drive from one place to another, we can add information to our memory (in this case, to an organized memory structure that holds the words that we know). From this perspective, learning new words can be studied just like any other learning. A study by Salasoo, Shiffrin, and Feustal (1985) is a good example of this approach. The authors visually presented known words and new "words" (pseudowords) thirty times, with a following mask each time. Subjects were asked to report each item as it was presented. Initially, the known words were recognized better than the new ones were under these challenging perceptual conditions. However, within about six presentations, the difference was eliminated as the new words were learned. Thus, simple repetition of words may be sufficient to establish representations that can aid perception. Moreover, when Salasoo et al. brought these subjects back to the lab a year later, there were still reliable effects of the learning.

Recent work by Gupta and his colleagues (2003; Gupta et al., 2005) has directly tied new word learning into basic memory processes. Gupta (2003) had subjects participate in a small battery of tasks. A digit span task provided an estimate of each person's memory performance, with the goal being to relate this ability to the person's ability to deal with new words (pseudowords). The new words were used in two tasks: immediate nonword repetition and a pseudoword learning task. Gupta argued that if learning new words is essentially a memory process, then there should be correlations among these tasks. In particular, in order to repeat a nonword, the listener must have available the order of the sounds that made it up, just as one must maintain the order of a string of digits in a digit span task. Taking this a step further, in order to learn a new word, one must be able to associate a particular sequence of sounds with the word's referent. Thus, in the pseudoword learning task, subjects had to learn to associate pseudowords with line drawings of either novel animals (Experiment 1) or with various types of "aliens." Gupta found that performance was significantly correlated across the three tasks, as predicted by the view that learning new words is indeed a type of memory process. The correlations were preserved even when a measure of nonverbal ability was factored out. Gupta et al. (2005) extended this perspective by showing that in learning polysyllabic pseudowords, the serial position curve for the syllables comprising a new word was similar to the classic serial position curve for learning lists of words.

A number of other studies in the literature focus on how new lexical entries are created and how such new entries function. Magnuson et al. (2003) developed a procedure for teaching people a set of pseudowords that formed a new, artificial lexicon. The goal was to see whether such a newly acquired lexicon would show some of the classic properties associated with the normal lexicon. For example, as we have discussed, spoken word recognition is affected by the density of a word's lexical neighborhood. Because the structure of an artificial lexicon can be completely determined by the experimenter, neighborhood densities and other such properties can be controlled much more cleanly than is possible with the naturally available lexicon of a given individual. Magnuson et al. therefore taught their subjects the "names" of various visual patterns generated by filling a subset of cells within a four-by-four grid. For example, one such pattern could be a *pibu*, and another might be a *dibu*, or perhaps a *pibo*. After these names were learned, subjects saw arrays of four of these objects, and had to select a specified object as part of the eyetracking paradigm described earlier. Magnuson et al. confirmed that properties such as neighborhood density and word frequency (in both cases, defined within the artificial lexicon itself) affected the eye movement patterns in a manner consistent with the existing word recognition literature (e.g., having a *pibu* in a display when looking for a *pibo* delays recognition). The artificial language learning paradigm thus provides a method that can be used to investigate the acquisition of new words, under very controlled conditions.

Another very interesting recent study of new word acquisition was reported by Gaskell and Dumay (2003). These authors presented listeners with new words that were created by modifying existing words. For example, *cathedruke* and *yathedral* were two of the new words; one of these was derived from *cathedral* by modifying its last syllable, and the other involved a change in the onset. Gaskell and Dumay used these stimulus types because they provide a natural test of lexical competition. Recall that a major problem for the word recognition system is such competition – the system must be able to correctly choose between similar alternatives, such as *sticky* versus *Stucky*. Participants learned a dozen new words in an incidental learning paradigm (they did a phoneme monitoring task with a large set of items, including the critical ones), hearing each critical word a dozen times per day over the course of five days. To test for lexical competition, each day included a lexical decision task that included the real

word items that had been used to generate the new words (e.g., *cathedral*). Gaskell and Dumay reasoned that if a new word establishes a lexical representation, then that new representation could potentially compete with the existing word for recognition. They found that after three days of learning (thirty-six exposures), there was significant competition generated by items like *cathedruke*, but not by items like *yathedral*. This result is consistent with the view that new representations eventually get established, and that two lexical representations with overlapping onsets compete with each other (as shown, for example, by the Zwitserlood [1989] paper discussed previously).

It is worth noting that it took many more presentations for lexical representations to develop in this experiment than in the Salasoo et al. (1985) study (thirty-six versus six). A critical difference is that in the Salasoo et al. study, the measure of lexicality was the ability of the representation to support perception under masked presentation, whereas in Gaskell and Dumay's study the effects depended on lexical competition. One gloss of this difference is that the faster learning in the Salasoo et al. study may reflect its use of a relatively shallow form-based process, whereas the longer developing learning in the Gaskell and Dumay experiment may be a consequence of lexical competition depending on more functional properties of the representations. Work by Leach and Samuel (2007) supports this interpretation. Leach and Samuel found a strong interaction between the conditions under which new words are learned and the measures of their representation. Several different learning situations (e.g., hearing the new words in the context of phoneme monitoring; hearing the words as part of a story; hearing each one with a picture of an unusual object, etc.) all lead to large improvements in the ability to hear the words under masked conditions. However, the training regimes greatly differ in their ability to produce representations with the functionality needed to support perceptual learning. These results converge with those of Gupta and his colleagues in suggesting that classic memory processes play a central role in the expansion of the mental lexicon.

In our discussion of normal adult spoken word recognition, we have noted that the modal model of this system posits some kind of phonetic features used to construct some kind of sublexical units (e.g., phonemes or syllables) that in turn map onto lexical representations. Despite this model's generally wide acceptance, there are many points of considerable disagreement in the field. To provide a more complete sense of the literature, we will briefly mention some current issues impinging on the modal model.

One such issue concerns the nature of the lexical representations themselves. Most theorists have assumed that there is some kind of canonical representation of each word, presumably derived from having heard the word many times; each word has some abstract, prototypical expected pronunciation. It is precisely this assumption that underlies the potential problems posed by the many kinds of variation in the speech input, as each such variation is, by definition, some deviation from a canonical form. Goldinger (1998) has advanced an alternative view of lexical representation that could potentially alleviate many of these problems. He has suggested that for each word in the lexicon there are many "episodic" representations – each time that the person hears the word, such an episodic trace is laid down. From this perspective, when a spoken word is presented it activates all of the existing traces in proportion to their match to the input. The system produces an "echo," which reflects both the intensity of the response (based on the number of matches and their fit to the input), and its content (which can include information from the existing traces, even if that information was not in the input). In a series of shadowing experiments, Goldinger showed that this type of model can accurately predict both the response times and the tendency for subjects to produce an output that matches the acoustic properties of the input.

In recent papers, Goldinger (e.g., Goldinger and Azuma, 2003) has suggested that his episodic representations could

fit within the more general theoretical framework of adaptive resonance theory (ART), a perspective that Grossberg (e.g., 1980; Grossberg and Myers, 2000) has been developing for many years. In fact, the adaptive resonance approach has been gradually gaining adherents, in part because it offers a broadly applicable theoretical perspective. One of the very attractive features of the ART approach is that it naturally avoids a very thorny issue: Exactly what are the intermediate-level units that the modal model posits? In this chapter, we have been intentionally noncommittal about this, largely because the literature does not provide a clear favorite among choices such as phonemes, syllables, or demisyllables (see Goldinger and Azuma's paper for a nice discussion of this problem). In ART, there are such intermediate units, but they are entirely based on the listener's experience rather than being of a particular size a priori. Features are initially bound together into clusters called "items," and items in turn can resonate with larger units ("list chunks"). As noted, these chunks can be of various grain sizes, such as phonemes, syllables, or words, depending on the person's history with similar inputs. Note that the ART approach has much in common with the more standard model that we have described, but its reliance on more opportunistically defined units makes it more flexible, and therefore more able to match the disparate results in the literature. Grossberg and his colleagues have used this model to account for a vast array of findings in perception and cognition.

There is at least one other nonstandard model that has shown notable promise. Gaskell and Marslen-Wilson (e.g., 1997; 2002) have developed their Distributed Cohort Model (DCM), which differs from the typical model in two ways. In the standard model, each lexical representation can be thought of as a localized set of information that is relevant to a particular word. In contrast, in the DCM, all lexical items are represented as vectors in a high-dimensional distributed network; important dimensions can be based on semantic features and on phonetic ones. This lexical representation format naturally leads to another contrast with the standard view: Because features specify the lexical vectors, there is no natural place in the model for the intermediate-level representations. Such intermediate units can be thought of as epiphenomenal, merely reflecting particular regions in this space. Gaskell and Marslen-Wilson have shown that many priming effects fall out naturally from the kinds of "blend states" that this type of model generates, when two words overlap in semantic and/or phonetic features (see also Elman, 2004).

Ongoing studies will ultimately determine the extent to which the standard model will need to develop toward one of these nonstandard forms, or perhaps, toward an as yet unknown form. As we have tried to illustrate, the fundamental problem that faces the listener is one of variation: Selecting the word that the speaker intended is potentially difficult because the instantiation of the word can change due to many influences. The apparent ease with which this task is accomplished by a normal adult belies the complexity of the underlying processes.

References

Allopenna, P. D., Magnuson, J. S., & Tanenhaus, M. K. (1998). Tracking the time course of spoken word recognition using eye movements: Evidence for continuous mapping models. *Journal of Memory and Language*, 38, 419–39.

Andruski, J. E., Blumstein, S. E., & Burton, M. (1994). The effect of subphonetic differences on lexical access. *Cognition*, 52, 163–87.

Bertelson, P., Vroomen, J., & de Gelder, B. (2003). Visual recalibration of auditory speech identification: A McGurk aftereffect. *Psychological Science*, 14, 592–7.

Cutler, A., Dahan, D., & Van Donselaar, W. A. (1997). Prosody in the comprehension of spoken language: A literature review. *Language and Speech*, 40, 141–202.

Cutler, A. & Norris, D. (1988). The role of strong syllables in segmentation for lexical access. *Journal of Experimental Psychology: Human Perception and Performance*, 14, 113–21.

Davis, M. H., Johnsrude, I. S., Hervais-Adelman, A., Taylor, K., & McGettigan, C. (2005) Lexical information drives perceptual learning of distorted speech: evidence from the comprehension of noise-vocoded sentences. *Journal of Experimental Psychology: General*, 134, 222–41.

Davis, M. H., Marslen-Wilson, W. D., & Gaskell, M. G. (2002). Leading up the lexical garden-path: segmentation and ambiguity in spoken word recognition. *Journal of Experimental Psychology: Human Perception and Performance*, 28, 218–44.

Dumay, N., Frauenfelder, U.H., & Content, A. (2002). The role of the syllable in lexical segmentation in french: word-spotting data. *Brain and Language*, 81, 144–61.

Eisner, F. & McQueen, J. M. (2005). The specificity of perceptual learning in speech processing. *Perception and Psychophysics*, 67, 224–38.

Elman, J. L. (2004). An alternative view of the mental lexicon. *Trends in Cognitive Sciences*, 8, 301–6.

Gaskell, M. G. (2003). Modelling regressive and progressive effects of assimilation in speech perception. *Journal of Phonetics*, 31, 447–63.

Gaskell, M. G. & Dumay, N. (2003). Lexical competition and the acquisition of novel words. *Cognition*, 89, 105–32.

Gaskell, M. G. & Marslen-Wilson, W. D. (1996). Phonological variation and inference in lexical access. *Journal of Experimental Psychology: Human Perception and Performance*, 22, 144–58.

(1998). Mechanisms of phonological inference in speech perception. *Journal of Experimental Psychology: Human Perception and Performance*, 24, 380–96.

(1997). Integrating form and meaning: a distributed model of speech perception. *Language and Cognitive Processes*, 12, 613–56.

(1998). Mechanisms of phonological inference in speech perception. *Journal of Experimental Psychology: Human Perception and Performance*, 24, 380–96.

(2002). Representation and competition in the perception of spoken words. *Cognitive Psychology*, 45, 220–66.

Goldinger, S. D. (1998). Echoes of echoes? An episodic theory of lexical access. *Psychological Review*, 105, 251–79.

Goldinger, S. D. & Azuma, T. (2003). Puzzle-solving science: the quixotic quest for units in speech perception. *Journal of Phonetics*, 31, 305–20.

Gow, D. W. (2001). Assimilation and anticipation in continuous spoken word recognition. *Journal of Memory and Language*, 45, 133–59.

Gow, D. W. (2002). Does English coronal place assimilation create lexical ambiguity? *Journal of Experimental Psychology: Human Perception and Performance, 28,* 163–79.

Gow, D. W. & Gordon, P. C. (1995). Lexical and prelexical influences on word segmentation. *Journal of Experimental Psychology: Human Perception and Performance, 21,* 344–59.

Grossberg, S. (1980). How does a brain build a cognitive code? *Psychological Review, 87,* 1–51.

Grossberg, S. & Myers, C. W. (2000). The resonant dynamics of speech perception: Interword integration and duration-dependent backward effects. *Psychological Review, 107,* 735–67.

Gupta, P. (2003). Examining the relationship between word learning, nonword repetition, and immediate serial recall in adults. *Quarterly Journal of Experimental Psychology, 56,* 1213–36.

Gupta, P., Lipinski, J., Abbs, B., & Lin, P. H. (2005). Serial position effects in nonword repetition. *Journal of Memory and Language, 53,* 141–62.

Kraljic, T. & Samuel, A. G. (2006). Generalization in perceptual learning for speech. *Psychonomic Bulletin and Review, 13,* 262–8.

(2005). Perceptual learning for speech: Is there a return to normal? *Cognitive Psychology, 51,* 141–78.

Leach, L. & Samuel, A. G. (2007). Lexical configuration and lexical engagement: When adults learn new words. *Cognitive Psychology, 55,* 306–53.

Lipinski, J., & Gupta, P. (2005). Does neighborhood density influence repetition latency for nonwords? Separating the effects of density and duration. *Journal of Memory and Language, 52,* 171–92.

LoCasto, P. C. & Connine, C. M. (2002). Rule-governed missing information in spoken word recognition: Schwa vowel deletion. *Perception & Psychophysics, 64,* 208–19.

Luce, P. A. & Pisoni, D. B. (1998). Recognizing spoken words: The neighborhood activation model. *Ear & Hearing, 19,* 1–36.

Magnuson, J. S., Tanenhaus, M. K., Aslin, R. N., & Dahan, D. (2003). The time course of spoken word learning and recognition: Studies with artificial lexicons. *Journal of Experimental Psychology: General, 132,* 202–27.

Marslen-Wilson, W. D., Nix, A., & Gaskell, G. (1995) Phonological variation in lexical access: abstractness, inference and English place assimilation. *Language and Cognitive Processes, 10,* 285–308.

Marslen-Wilson, W. D. & Paul Warren. (1994). Levels of perceptual representation and process in lexical access: words, phonemes, and features. *Psychological Review, 101,* 653–75.

Mattys, S. L., White, L., & Melhorn, J. F. (2005). Integration of multiple speech segmentation cues: A hierarchical framework. *Journal of Experimental Psychology: General, 134,* 477–500.

Maye, J., Aslin, R., & Tanenhaus, M. (2008). The weckud wetch of the wast: Lexical adaptation to a novel accent. *Cognitive Science, 32,* 543–62.

McLennan, C. T., Luce, P. A., & Charles-Luce, J. (2003). Representation of lexical form. *Journal of Experimental Psychology: Learning, Memory, & Cognition, 29,* 539–53.

McMurray, B., Tanenhaus, M. K., & Aslin, R. N. (2002). Gradient effects of within-category phonetic variation on lexical access. *Cognition, 86,* B33-B42.

McQueen, J. M. (1998). Segmentation of continuous speech using phonotactics. *Journal of Memory and Language, 39,* 21–46.

McQueen, J. M., Norris, D. G., & Cutler, A. (1999). Lexical influence in phonetic decision making: Evidence from subcategorical mismatches. *Journal of Experimental Psychology: Human Perception and Performance, 25,* 1363–89.

Miller, G. A. & Isard, S. (1963). Some perceptual consequences of linguistic rules. *Journal of Verbal Learning and Verbal Behavior, 2,* 217–28.

Norris, D., McQueen, J. M., & Cutler, A. (2003). Perceptual learning in speech. *Cognitive Psychology, 47,* 204–38.

Nation, P. & Waring, R. (1997). Vocabulary size, text coverage, and word lists. In Schmitt, N., & McCarthy, M. (Eds.) *Vocabulary: Description, acquisition, pedagogy* (pp. 6–19). New York: Cambridge University Press.

Pitt, M. A., & Samuel, A. G. (1995). Lexical and sublexical feedback in auditory word recognition. *Cognitive Psychology, 29,* 149–88.

Salasoo, A., Shiffrin, R. M., & Feustel, T. C. (1985). Building permanent memory codes: Codification and repetition effects in word identification. *Journal of Experimental Psychology: General, 114,* 50–77.

Salverda, A. P., Dahan, D., & McQueen, J. M. (2003). The role of prosodic boundaries in the resolution of lexical embedding in speech comprehension. *Cognition, 90,* 51–89.

Samuel, A. G. (1981). Phonemic restoration: Insights from a new methodology. *Journal of Experimental Psychology: General, 110,* 474–94.

Shillcock (1990). Lexical hypotheses in continuous speech. In Altmann, GTM (Ed.) *Cognitive Models of Speech Processing: Psycholinguistic and Computational Perspectives,* (pp. 24–49). Cambridge: MIT Press.

Sumner, M. & Samuel, A. G. (2005). Perception and representation of regular variation: The case of final /t/. *Journal of Memory and Language, 52,* 322–38.

Van Berkum, JJA (this volume). The electrophysiology of discourse and conversation.

Van Berkum, JJA, Brown, C. M., Zwitserlood, P., Kooijman, V., & Hagoort, P. (2005). Anticipating upcoming words in discourse: Evidence from ERPs and reading times. *Journal of Experimental Psychology: Learning, Memory, and Cognition, 31,* 443–67.

Vitevitch, M. S. & Luce, P. A. (1998). When words compete: Levels of processing in perception of spoken words. *Psychological Science, 9,* 325–29.

—— (1999). Probabilistic phonotactics and neighborhood activation in spoken word recognition. *Journal of Memory and Language, 40,* 374–408.

—— (2005). Increases in Phonotactic Probability. Facilitate Spoken Nonword Repetition. *Journal of Memory & Language, 52,* 193–204.

Vroomen, J. & de Gelder, B. (1997). Activation of embedded words in spoken word recognition. *Journal of Experimental Psychology: Human Perception and Performance, 23,* 710–20.

Vroomen J., Tuomainen J., & de Gelder, B. (1998). The roles of word stress and vowel harmony in speech segmentation. *Journal of Language and Memory, 38,* 133–49.

Vroomen, J., van Linden, S., Keetels, M., de Gelder, B., & Bertelson, P. (2004). Selective adaptation and recalibration of auditory speech by lipread information: Dissipation. *Speech Communication, 44,* 55–61.

Warren, R. M. (1970). Perceptual restoration of missing speech sounds. *Science, 167,* 392–93.

Zwitserlood, P. (1989). The locus of effects of sentential-semantic context in spoken-word processing. *Cognition, 32,* 25–64.

—— (1999). Spoken words in sentence contexts. In Friederici, A. D. (Ed.) *Language comprehension: A biological perspective* (pp. 71–99). Heidelberg/Berlin: Springer.

CHAPTER 5

Computational Models of Spoken Word Recognition

James S. Magnuson, Daniel Mirman, and Harlan D. Harris

1 Preliminaries

A broad distinction can be drawn in psycholinguistics between research focused on how input signals activate representations of linguistic forms, and how linguistic forms are used to access or construct conceptual representations. Words lie at the junction, but do more than simply provide an interface between signals and higher-level structures. Theories in psycholinguistics (e.g., MacDonald, Pearlmutter, and Seidenberg, 1994; Trueswell and Tanenhaus, 1994) and linguistics (e.g., Pustejovsky, 1995) have ascribed increasing syntactic and semantic knowledge and function to the lexical level. This makes theories of spoken word recognition (SWR) key in explaining not just how word forms are recognized, but also in understanding levels upstream (sublexical) and downstream (conceptual, sentential, etc.). While theories of SWR typically take the narrow focus of mapping from phonemes to sound patterns of words, a growing body of empirical results (consistent with the increasing role of the lexicon in linguistic and psycholinguistic theory) suggests that SWR is not so neatly compartmentalized. For example, subphonemic details in the speech signal affect lexical activation (Andruski, Blumstein, and Burton, 1994; Davis, Marslen-Wilson, and Gaskell, 2002; Salverda, Dahan, and McQueen, 2003), revealing that sublexical details are preserved at least to the level of lexical access. Lexical context appears to influence sublexical perception directly (Elman and McClelland, 1988; Samuel, 1981; but see discussion of controversies on this point below), and syntactic context similarly influences lexical activation (Shillcock and Bard, 1993; van Berkum et al., 2005).

Determining what representations are active during any cognitive process is difficult, since many of those representations may no longer be active by the end of the process. The problem is compounded by the nature of the speech signal. The transient acoustic events that make up spoken words must be mapped rapidly onto words in memory, within the limits of echoic and working memory. SWR is further complicated by the many-to-many mapping between acoustics and linguistic categories (Fowler and Magnuson, this volume) and the absence of invariant cues to word boundaries (Samuel and Sumner, this volume), placing speech perception and SWR among the most challenging problems in cognitive science.

In tackling these problems, theories of SWR generally agree on three principles (Dahan and Magnuson, 2006). First, as a word is heard, multiple lexical representations are activated. Second, activation depends on the degree of fit between a lexical item and the incoming speech, and prior probability (frequency of occurrence). Third, recognition is guided by competition among activated representations. Each principle is quite general, and allows for considerable variation in specifics. Theories differ particularly in their similarity metrics and/or bottom-up activation mechanisms (which determine degree of fit), information flow (e.g., only bottom-up or top-down as well), and the nature of the competition mechanisms they assume.

Different assumptions about these principles lead to different predictions about word recognition. Current theories are generally guided by *computational models*, which minimally include *mathematical*, *verbal-algorithmic*, and *simulation* models.[1] In the next section, we will give one example of each of the first two types, and then review several simulation models, introducing additional distinctions among model types as needed. Our review necessarily will be brief and selective, with models chosen to illustrate approaches and principles. For more

comprehensive reviews, see Protopapas (1999) and Ellis and Humphreys (1999). We will then review a recent debate in SWR that hinges on subtle predictions that follow from computational models but have proved elusive in empirical tests. The debate provides useful illustrations of principles of model testing and comparison. We will close the chapter with a discussion of what we see as the most pressing issues for making progress in theories of SWR, and the most promising current modeling approaches.

2 A selective review of SWR models

2.1 *Mathematical models*

The most influential *mathematical* model of SWR is the *Neighborhood Activation Model* (NAM; Luce, 1986; Luce and Pisoni, 1998), which crystallizes the three key SWR principles reviewed above into a simple, but powerful, mathematical form. NAM is also the only SWR model able to generate item-specific and pair-wise competition predictions for thousands of words *easily*. Luce and Pisoni discuss potential connections with simulation models like TRACE (see Section 2.3) and have proposed PARSYN as a simulating instantiation of NAM (Luce et al., 2000), but NAM itself does not specify any algorithms or mechanisms. Rather, it combines general principles and constraints on SWR into a mathematical form that predicts relative ease of lexical access.[2]

This simplicity also places NAM at the fundamentalist end of a *fundamentalist–realist continuum* of models (Kello and Plaut, 2003). Fundamentalist models isolate key theoretical assumptions and implement

---

1   We will stretch *computational model* to mean *formal model*: any formalism that describes a mapping. This definition is broad enough to include nonimplemented descriptions of such a mapping process (verbal-algorithmic), as well as simple mathematical models. Note that there is also unfortunate potential for confusion over the common usage of *computational model* to refer to this range of approaches, and the most abstract of Marr's (1982) levels of information processing theories. A theory at his computational level describes a computed function in terms of input, output, and constraints on the mapping between them, in contrast to theories at the algorithmic and implementational levels (akin roughly to software and hardware, respectively). Mathematical models commonly reside at Marr's computational level, while verbal-algorithmic and simulation models commonly reside at his algorithmic level.

2   While PARSYN is *consistent* with NAM, as we will discuss, NAM's power is in its simplicity and remove from processing details as a choice model. We see PARSYN as complementary to NAM rather than a direct extension. While we are using the label "mathematical" to distinguish NAM from verbal-algorithmic and simulation models, note that this is a weak distinction, as complete mathematical descriptions of processing models may or may not be tractable. The key point here is the simplicity of the model and its relation to Marr's (1982) computational level of information processing theories.

them with as little baggage as possible, with the goal of making transparent tests of the assumptions. Realist models build in as much detail as possible, with the goal of accounting for a broad and deep range of phenomena, often with the goal of seeing whether the complexity of the model engenders emergence of unexpected (positive or negative) behavior.

How does NAM formalize the three core principles of SWR? First, it addresses multiple activation and similarity with a *global similarity metric* that specifies which words will be activated as a word is heard, and how strongly they will be activated. The most familiar NAM metric uses a *one-phoneme DAS (deletion, addition, or substitution) threshold*: Words are neighbors if they differ by no more than one phoneme, whether by deletion (*cat: at*), addition (*cat: scat, cast, cattle*), or substitution (*cat: bat, cot, cab*). More subtle metrics based on empirical measures of sublexical similarity (e.g., perceptual confusion data) can also be used to compute pair-wise positional similarity over all words in the lexicon (where overall similarity of two words is the product of phoneme-by-phoneme similarities). While the more complex metrics do make distinct predictions, such as the priming of *veer* by *bull* (given high similarity at each phoneme; Luce et al., 2000), the two metrics make sufficiently similar predictions that the one-phoneme metric is most frequently used.

Once the neighborhood of a word is defined (or computed, in the case of graded similarity metrics), a word's frequency-weighted neighborhood probability can be computed. We present a slightly modified version of the Luce and Pisoni (1998) form in Equation 1, where $FWNP_t$ is the frequency-weighted neighborhood probability of target word t, f_t is the prior probability (typically, the log frequency of occurrence per million words in a corpus) of a target word t, and s_t is the similarity of the target to itself (1.0). In the denominator, for every word, w, in the lexicon (including the target), f_w is the frequency of word w, and s_{wt} is the similarity of word w with target t. Note that if a threshold rule (like the DAS rule) is not

used to define neighbors, the set of potential neighbors includes every word in the lexicon, though many words will have similarities to t near o. Note also that denominator includes the target, t; even when a threshold is used, t will be a neighbor of itself.

$$FWNP_t = \frac{f_t s_t}{\sum f_w s_{wt}} \qquad (1)$$

This is the most general form of the rule. When the DAS definition of neighbor is used, we can simplify further by dropping the s terms, as items either have similarity of 1.0 (meets DAS definition of neighbor) or 0.0 (not a DAS neighbor).

NAM addresses *prior probability* by weighting each neighbor in the metric by its log frequency. NAM addresses *competition* indirectly, with a choice rule that approximates lexical competition. Ease of recognition of a target word is predicted by the ratio of its log frequency to the sum of all other words' similarities to the target (o or 1 for the DAS rule) weighted by each item's log frequency. Since neighborhood density (summed frequency-weighted neighbor similarities) includes the target (with self-similarity of 1), frequency-weighted neighborhood probability can be stated more simply as *the proportion of the neighborhood frequency contributed by the target word*. NAM predicts that if two words are matched on neighborhood, the one with higher frequency will be recognized more quickly, because it contributes a larger portion of its neighborhood density. If two words are matched on frequency, the one with lower neighborhood density will be recognized more quickly, again because that word's frequency represents a greater proportion of its neighborhood density. Note that the temporal grain size of the model is lexical – it simply predicts the recognition facility of entire words, and does not predict sublexical processing details.

This simple model is surprisingly powerful. NAM accounts for about fifteen percent of the variance (beyond word frequency alone) in tasks like lexical decision and naming (Luce, 1986; Luce and Pisoni,

1998). The next best predictor is frequency alone – which only accounts for about five percent of the variance. Significant effects are commonly found in factorial manipulations of neighborhood density, and again, the complex similarity metric makes surprising pair-wise priming predictions that have been borne out empirically (Luce et al., 2000). NAM has had a large impact on theories and the practice of SWR research (studies of SWR now commonly control neighborhood density).

NAM can be considered a general framework for choice models of SWR, or as a specific, testable model when paired with a particular metric. While the model is strongly associated with the metrics used by Luce and colleagues and the competitor set predictions that follow, using other similarity metrics in the NAM framework would be an excellent strategy for making further progress on identifying general constraints on SWR.

2.2 Verbal-algorithmic models

In *verbal-algorithmic* models, predictions that follow from theoretical assumptions are *described* as an ordered series of processes or computations. The preeminent example in SWR is the *Cohort model* developed by Marslen-Wilson and colleagues (Marslen-Wilson and Tyler, 1980; Marslen-Wilson and Welsh, 1978). The Cohort model illustrates the power of a well-specified verbal-algorithmic model, as it makes many testable predictions and paved the way for the simulation models we describe next. Cohort differs from NAM in three key ways. First, of course, it is a verbal-algorithmic formulation of processing mechanisms that could support SWR rather than a mathematical formulation of general principles. Second, algorithmic choices lead to a similarity metric that differs considerably from NAM's. Third, it grapples explicitly with challenges of processing the speech signal over time, which allows it to generate qualitative time-course predictions and address segmentation of fluent speech.

The original Cohort model was formulated to account for constraints that emerged primarily from experiments that revealed that SWR can occur remarkably early, prior to word offset, depending on possible competitors in the lexicon and higher-level context (Marslen-Wilson and Welsh, 1978). Cohort built on the activation metaphors introduced in Morton's (1969) Logogen theory and broke SWR into three stages: *access* (initial contact of bottom-up perceptual input with lexical representations), *selection* (winnowing the activation *cohort*), and *integration* (retrieving syntactic and semantic properties of a selected word and checking compatibility with higher levels of processing). The key theoretical constraints proposed for models of SWR were multiple access (all lexical items consistent with the input are activated), multiple assessment (the activated items are mapped onto the signal and top-down context in parallel), and real-time efficiency (i.e., a model should make optimal use of available information).

This last constraint is central. Rather than waiting for the best candidate to emerge by simple matching of phonemes to lexical representations, the model posits active removal of words from the recognition cohort (the set of activated candidates). Thus, as a word like *beaker* is heard, initially all words beginning with /b/ would be activated. When /i/ is heard, all items beginning with /bi/ (*beaker*, *beetle*, *bead*, etc.) remain in the cohort, but words that mismatch (*baker*, *batch*, etc.) are removed. In the original model, a top-down mismatch (incompatibilities between the syntactic or semantic properties of the word and sentential context) could also remove an item from the cohort, making "Cohort I" an *interactive* model; although the model assumed bottom-up priority (top-down knowledge did not prevent items from entering the word-initial cohort, it only helped remove them), bottom-up processing was constrained directly by top-down knowledge.

These principles combine to predict that words will often be recognized prior to word offset: Assuming clear speech as input, a word will be recognized prior to its offset if there is a unique completion prior to word offset or if context provides sufficient listener confidence in the as yet incomplete word. A key innovation in the

Cohort model was its implicit segmentation strategy. Utterance onset marks the onset of the first word in a series. As one word is recognized, its offset marks the onset of the next item. The basic principles of the Cohort model, and in particular, the notion that segmentation would emerge from continuous mapping of phonemes to words, have motivated a tremendous amount of research and insight into SWR and paved the way for subsequent models.

The model was revised slightly (Marslen-Wilson, 1987; 1989); "Cohort II" assumes selection must be *autonomous* from integration. This repairs problems with some predictions of Cohort I (e.g., predicting great difficulty recognizing words with low-probability relative to a context, such as *I put on my hiking beetle*). The grain of input was increased from phonemic to featural to allow for a small degree of mismatch tolerance (about one feature), and activation was predicted to be related to goodness of fit weighted by word frequency.

We will turn now to simulation models, which have largely followed from the empirical findings of Marslen-Wilson and colleagues, and the processing principles articulated in the Cohort model.

2.3 *Simulation models*

Mathematical and verbal models can generate specific predictions when their underlying assumptions can be combined in a straightforward way (e.g., when stages of processing are clearly ordered and information only flows forward), especially if they do not address the fine-grained time course of lexical activation. When processing steps cannot be easily ordered or are expected to interact, or fine-grained time course predictions are desired, verbal models become unwieldy, and a mathematical model may be intractable or simply very difficult to derive analytically. In such cases, *simulations* with an implemented processing model (such as a neural network or production system) may be needed.

Simulation presents advantages but also challenges. While all models make simplifying assumptions, implementing a model requires explicit choices about inputs, outputs, and details that may not be part of any underlying theory, but are needed to make a simulating model work. Grappling with such details in order to create a simulation model may identify incorrect or incompatible assumptions that appeared reasonable in a verbal or mathematical model, or may reveal that aspects of human behavior emerge in unanticipated ways from the model. In this section, we review a handful of simulation models chosen to illustrate important developments in SWR modeling. Specifically, we review two hand-wired and four learning models. Parameters in hand-wired models are set by a researcher on the basis of (e.g., phonetic) principle, intuition, trial and error, or algorithmic search. More important than where the parameters come from is the fact that they are fixed by the modeler for a given simulation rather than learned.

2.3.1 HAND-WIRED MODELS

2.3.1.1 *Trace* McClelland and Elman (1986)[3] provided the first major implemented processing model of speech perception and SWR. It remains one of only a few *realist* (Kello and Plaut, 2003) models of SWR (see also Klatt, 1979, and Plaut and Kello, 1999, discussed later in this chapter), and has by far the greatest depth and breadth of empirical coverage. TRACE extended the connectionist interactive activation framework (McClelland and Rumelhart, 1981) from reading to speech and was explicitly motivated by a desire to build and improve upon Cohort (McClelland and Elman, 1986, pp. 52–3). The model has three layers of units: featural, phonemic, and lexical (see schematic in Figure 5.1). Feature nodes are activated by input that roughly represents acoustic-phonetic properties of speech sounds by using nine acoustic-phonetic feature continua, each represented by a bank

---

3   Technically, we are discussing TRACE II; TRACE I (Elman and McClelland, 1986) was focused on the speech-to-phoneme side of the model, but was never linked to TRACE II.

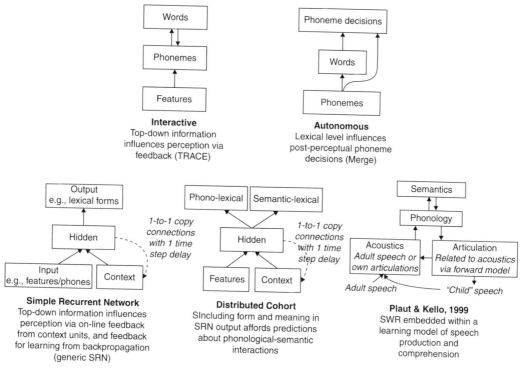

Figure 5.1. Schematics of five of the model types reviewed in this section. TRACE and Merge use localist representations; Distributed Cohort and Plaut & Kello use distributed representations; SRNs can use either.

of seven units. Phoneme patterns are spread out over time, with features ramping on and off over eleven time steps (each corresponding to about ten msecs). Because phonemes spread over many steps, but phoneme centers are only six steps apart, the input includes a coarse analog of coarticulation: On either side of a phoneme center, information about the current phoneme is added to that for the preceding or following segment, making the pattern for each phoneme context-dependent.

Feature nodes send activation forward to the phoneme layer, which consists of banks of phoneme templates aligned at multiple time slices (see more detailed schematic in Figure 5.2). This reduplication of units allows TRACE to handle the temporal extent of speech input by spatializing time. Phoneme templates are maximally activated by a specific feature pattern aligned with them in time. Temporally overlapping phoneme units compete by lateral inhibition, such that ambiguous inputs will

partially activate multiple phoneme units. However, competition will generally lead to a clear "winner" for each phoneme in the input (i.e., a phoneme unit that is substantially more activated than any others for its stretch of time).

The same scheme connects phonemes to words. Lexical templates are duplicated across time and are maximally activated when properly ordered phoneme units aligned with the template are maximally activated. Lexical units also compete with each other through lateral inhibition, with incomplete or ambiguous phoneme sequences partially activating multiple word units, and competition resolving ambiguity. A crucial feature of TRACE's architecture is feedback connections from lexical units to their constituent phoneme units (phoneme-to-feature feedback is typically disabled to speed processing, McClelland and Elman, 1986, p. 23). This feedback makes TRACE interactive (higher levels influence their own sources of input) and is one of the most

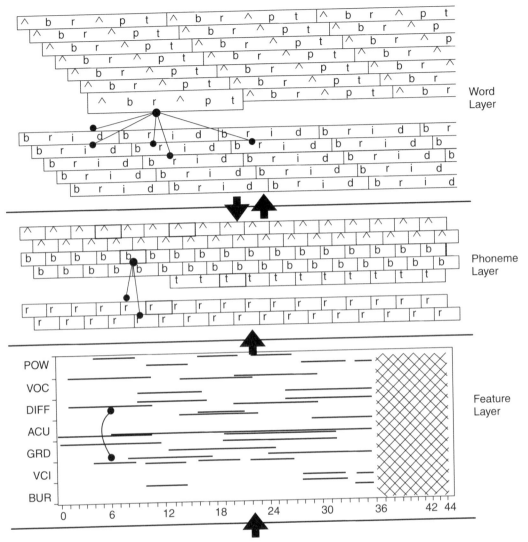

Figure 5.2. More detailed schematic of the TRACE model (adapted from Strauss et al., 2007) only showing four phonemes and two words. TRACE solves alignment and segmentation problems by reduplicating each word and phoneme node at multiple temporal alignments. Arrows stand for forward and backward connectivity (note the absence of phoneme-feature feedback, which is off by default in the model, but can be turned on). Nodes at low levels feedforward to larger units that contain them (e.g., featural patterns corresponding to voicing activate voiced phonemes, such as /b/; /b/ feeds forward to words that contain /b/), and nodes at higher levels feedback to the nodes from which they receive feedforward activation. Connections indicated with filled circles are inhibitory; nodes can inhibit other nodes at their own level ("lateral inhibition") if they overlap with them temporally.

controversial aspects of the TRACE model (discussed later in this chapter; for recent debate see McClelland, Mirman, and Holt, 2006; McQueen, Norris, and Cutler, 2006; Mirman, McClelland, and Holt, 2006a).

TRACE differs from Cohort in that it eschews explicit consideration of mismatch or word boundaries, though it is implicitly sensitive to both. Activation in TRACE is based on *continuous mapping* of bottom-up matches to lexical representations. A bottom-up match to a lexical representation will send activation to that word even if there was an earlier mismatch (Allopenna, Magnuson, and Tanenhaus, 1998, capture this distinction with the terms *alignment* and *continuous mapping* models, where alignment models, such as Cohort, explicitly code mismatches relative to word onset). However, lateral inhibition makes the system sensitive to mismatches and, implicitly, to the position of the mismatch and details of the competition neighborhood. For example, an early mismatch is more penalizing than a late mismatch (given *candle* as input, nodes for *candy* or even *camera* or *cabin* will be activated more strongly than *handle*). This is because by the time the input overlaps with, for example, a rhyme, items overlapping at onset are already activated, and the rhyme must overcome lateral inhibition from the target and its onset cohort. Thus, the competitor set predicted by TRACE is intermediate between Cohort's and NAM's: Onset overlap is an advantage, but items with initial mismatch may still be activated (an effect that is increased if there is uncertainty/noise in the input). Allopenna et al. (1998) found close fits between TRACE's predictions and the time course of phonological competition in human SWR (see Section 3.3).

TRACE depends on a fairly large set of parameters, such as the strength of bottom-up and top-down connections. Unlike most simulation models, in which free parameters are fit to data, the TRACE parameters were fixed by McClelland and Elman, and have been used since then with only small changes. In the original paper, TRACE accounts for more than a dozen aspects of human speech perception and SWR, including categorical perception, segmentation of fluent, multiword utterances, and lexical and phonotactic effects on phoneme recognition. Recent work has shown that TRACE also provides an excellent model of the fine-grained time course details of SWR (Allopenna et al., 1998; Dahan, Magnuson, and Tanenhaus, 2001; Dahan, et al., 2001; Spivey, Grosjean, and Knoblich, 2005).

McClelland (1991) made an important refinement to TRACE – adding intrinsic noise – that allowed it to account properly for joint effects of context and stimulus (see Section 4.2).

Two aspects of TRACE have fueled the development of alternative models. The first is that the strategy of reduplicating phoneme and word templates to solve the temporal extent problem is arguably inelegant and implausible (cf. McClelland and Elman, 1986, p. 77). The second is the theoretical assumption of interaction (lexical-sublexical feedback, which we discuss in detail in Section 4).

2.3.1.2 *Shortlist/Merge* Shortlist (Norris, 1994; Norris, McQueen, and Cutler, 1995) is a fundamentalist simulation model that combines aspects of autonomous, feedforward models like Race (Cutler and Norris, 1979) and Cohort II with the competition dynamics of TRACE. A primary motivation in the development of this model was to keep positive characteristics of TRACE (e.g., competition dynamics) while avoiding weaknesses (e.g., the large number of nodes and connections due to reduplication of nodes over time). In the first stage of processing, bottom-up activation generates word candidates aligned with each phonemic step of input (the bottom-up activation was originally intended to be from a simple recurrent network (SRN); in practice, a dictionary lookup is used). The best candidates (up to thirty) at *each* phonemic input step form the *shortlist* at that position. The items from all shortlists are wired together into an interactive-activation competition network as each new phoneme is heard, and items that overlap in time inhibit one another (see Figure 5.3).[4]

Shortlists are determined by match scores. Words get one point for every phonemic

---

4 Shortlist is often incorrectly described as having a single shortlist, with all items inhibiting each other. Instead, there are shortlists aligned at each input position (making the potential size of the interactive activation network sl: s = maximum size of each shortlist, which is thirty by default; l = phonemic length of the input). Only items that overlap in time inhibit each other. See Figure 5.3.

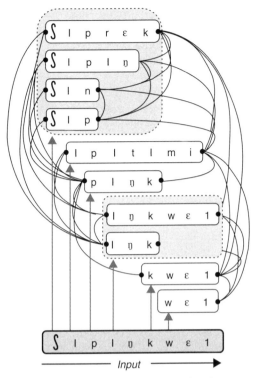

Figure 5.3. Lexical competition in Shortlist. The shaded box at the bottom shows the input ("ship inkwell"). As the input is presented to the model, shortlists of items with positive match scores are constructed for each phoneme position (up to a maximum of thirty items per position). Arrows indicate aligned shortlists. For most positions in this figure, only a single item from the shortlist is shown. Larger subsets of the complete shortlists are shown at positions one and four (shaded groups). Items compete with other items that overlap with them at any position – including items in other shortlists. All inhibitory connections are shown. Only word pairs that do not overlap temporally do not have inhibitory connections. The shortlists shown are an idealization of what might be active at word offset, but are not taken directly from a simulation.

match, and –3 for every mismatch. To enter a shortlist, a word's score must be among the top thirty at a particular position. The mismatch penalty is so strong that the metric functions much like an alignment metric, allowing primarily onset-overlapping words into the shortlists. For example, when the input is *cat*, words beginning with /k/ are

candidates at the first phoneme position when the first phoneme has been presented. When the second phoneme is presented, the shortlist at the first phoneme position is narrowed to words beginning with /kae/, and words beginning with /ae/ are candidates at the second phoneme position. At the third phoneme, words beginning with /kaet/ are candidates for the first phoneme shortlist, words beginning with /aet/ are candidates for the second phoneme shortlist, and words beginning with /t/ are candidates for the third phoneme shortlist. For words that rhyme or otherwise mismatch the input to enter the competitor set, the competition neighborhood must be sparse and the input word must be long. That is, for an initial mismatch to be overcome, a rhyming word would have to match at the next four positions to arrive at a positive score and have some chance of entering the shortlist; for example, given /kaet^lcg/ [*catalog*], /baet^l/ [*battle*] could enter the first phoneme shortlist after /l/ is presented (assuming there were not already thirty words in that shortlist with match scores greater than one). A unique and crucial feature of Shortlist is the use of stress to constrain entry into shortlists (Norris et al., 1995; Norris et al., 1997). This feature could (and should) be added to other models.

This division of labor between lexical search and competition allows Shortlist to use many fewer connections than TRACE. Shortlist is sometimes claimed to require fewer nodes than TRACE as well, but this depends on the nature of the lexical search mechanism. If an SRN were used, the entire lexical search network would have to be replicated at each input step – since a new lexical search is generated for *every* input position as each phoneme is presented. This would result in at least the same number of lexical representations as in TRACE. However, since SRNs also predict a variety of lexical competition effects (Magnuson, Tanenhaus, and Aslin, 2000), there would appear to be no need either for multiple SRNs aligned with each phoneme, or for an interactive activation network – a single

SRN would simultaneously provide lexical search and competition.[5]

Shortlist is a fundamentalist implementation of the theoretical principle that word recognition can be achieved efficiently with a modular division of labor between initial access and selection via competition. It is a fundamentalist model because it incorporates only details necessary for testing those primary assumptions. The *Merge model* (Norris, McQueen, and Cutler, 2000) is a separate but related fundamentalist model that is also purely feedforward. Merge is consistent with the Shortlist framework, but was designed to examine whether lexical effects on phoneme decisions can be predicted without lexical-phonemic feedback by adding postlexical phoneme decision nodes (see Figure 5.1). Merge is meant to be roughly equivalent to the competition network of Shortlist, though it is greatly simplified. Merge has only been demonstrated with a few phonemes and words – up to four words and around six phonemes, depending on the simulation. While the input to the model has a subphonemic grain – phonemes ramp on over three time slices – the architecture does not encode temporal order. Word units have undifferentiated connections from phonemes, such that the inputs *dog, god, odg, ogd, dgo*, and *gdo* would all activate lexical units for *dog* or *god* equally well. All the same, the model qualitatively accounts for several results that previously had been thought to require interaction (see Section 4).

New Bayesian versions of Shortlist and Merge have been proposed (Shortlist B and Merge B; Norris and McQueen, 2008). Shortlist B resides at Marr's (1982) computational level of information processing theories, providing a description of a putatively optimal mapping from speech input to spoken words. It has an unusually fine grain for a computational-level theory: Diphone confusion probabilities from a gating task are used to construct phoneme likelihoods at a subsegmental grain. Those likelihoods are conditioned on lexical knowledge and potentially other context, but with the stipulation that the mechanism for combining these information sources must operate without feedback. This is not a stipulation commonly found in Bayesian approaches to perception; for example, Rao (2004, 2005) demonstrates how Bayesian inference can be implemented in a neural architecture employing feedback, affording optimal combination of top-down and bottom-up information sources, and close fits to behavioral data. Movellan and McClelland (2001) have also proven that the interactive activation framework of a model like TRACE can implement an optimal Bayesian process. Nonetheless, the approach taken with Shortlist B has the potential to generate extremely precise predictions and may lead the way to new approaches. We return to the controversial question of whether feedback occurs in speech perception and SWR in Section 4.

2.3.2 LEARNING MODELS

2.3.2.1 *Simple recurrent networks* SRNs (Elman, 1990) have been applied to SWR with limited coverage. A basic SRN consists of four sets of units: input, hidden, output, and context (see Figure 5.1). There are feedforward connections from input to hidden units and from hidden to output units, as in a standard feedforward network. The context units contain an exact copy of the hidden units at the previous time step and are fully connected to the hidden units (or, equivalently, each hidden unit has a recurrent connection to all other hidden units with a delay of one cycle). This innovation of recurrence, or feedback, provides the network with a limited potential memory for previous time steps. All of the connections (except hidden context, which are one-to-one copy connections) are trained via backpropagation

---

5 Similarly, Scharenborg, Norris, ten Bosch, and McQueen (2005) proposed a Shortlist-inspired model that works on real speech input and replaces Shortlist's modular lexical-lookup and competition components with ASR mechanisms (e.g., rank-ordered hypothesis generation). This "speech-based model" (SpeM) represents a very promising development, though further tests of generalization and psychological tractability will be required.

(where actual input is compared to observed output, and connections receive "blame" for the discrepancy based on how much of the error they contributed, and their weights are changed proportionally; Rumelhart, Hinton, and Williams, 1986). A typical approach is to present a sequence of input vectors corresponding to a sequence of single phonemes and set the desired output to be the next phoneme or the current word. Depending on the nature of the training set and the size of the network, SRNs can develop sensitivity to fairly long stretches of context. While a common approach is to use a series of phonemes as input and localist lexical nodes as output, one can of course use distributed representations, or change the task to predicting the next phoneme, or even the previous, current, and next phonemes. These choices have a significant impact on what the model learns.

Norris (1990) reported SRN simulations in which words in a small lexicon that overlapped at onset activated each other, but words that mismatched at onset and overlapped at offset did not, consistent with predictions of the Cohort model. Although this is a logical result, given the model has explicit access to ordered input, Magnuson et al. (2000) showed that it depends on the training regimen. If the model is given perfectly clear inputs and is trained until error rate asymptotes (the procedure followed by Norris), it will only show onset competition. If instead training continues only until every word in the lexicon is "recognized" correctly using a simple, minimal threshold (only about one-fifth as much training), the network exhibits rhyme effects and will also learn new words more easily and be more tolerant of noisy inputs. Furthermore, early in training, the model shows roughly equivalent rhyme and cohort competition; adults learning novel neighborhoods of words show the same progression (Magnuson, et al., 2003).

There is disagreement about the nature of the architecture of SRNs. Some claim that SRNs are not interactive (Cairns et al., 1995; Norris, 1990), since the input units are not influenced by the output level. Others disagree (e.g., Magnuson, et al., 2003a; McClelland et al., 2006) on the basis that

recurrent connections allow context to have a direct influence on the earliest stage of processing (since feedback from context is mixed with bottom-up input at the hidden unit level), even if the mechanism does not include feedback from explicitly *lexical* nodes. Specifically, the input to the hidden layer at each time step is the current bottom-up input *and* an exact copy of the hidden unit states from the previous time step; the latter are the result of multiplying the previous input and context by the hidden unit weights, so the input includes the output of the first of the two feedforward transformations the model performs.

In summary, SRNs avoid problems of TRACE (reduplicated units, inability to learn), and have the potential to be the basis of a "next generation" of models. Indeed, the next two models are based on this architecture.

2.3.2.2 *Distributed Cohort Model (DCM)* Gaskell and Marslen-Wilson (1997) began pushing beyond the typical focus on sound form recognition by incorporating simultaneous semantic representations in their model. The input (binary phonetic features), hidden, and context layers followed standard SRN design. Their innovation was the use of two output layers: phonology (phonological form) and lexical semantics (an arbitrary, sparse binary vector; see Figure 5.1). Gaskell and Marslen-Wilson (1999) argued that distributed representations and simultaneous activation of phonological and semantic dimensions of words provide fundamentally different ways of thinking about competition. In localist models such as TRACE, when the input supports two lexical items, there is explicit activation of both representations (different nodes at the lexical layer) and explicit competition between them (through mutually inhibitory connections between the lexical units). In a distributed model, all items are represented with the same set of nodes; thus, both activation of and competition between multiple representations is implicit in the *blend* formed by the competing patterns.

Gaskell and Marslen-Wilson (2002) tested a prediction that follows from this conceptualization. Given a word fragment with semantically unrelated phonological completions (e.g., /kaept/ can begin *captive* or *captain*), the system can settle on a *phonological* pattern, but semantic activations will be a blend of the semantics for the phonological competitors. Thus, such a fragment should produce phonological (repetition) priming, but not semantic priming. In contrast, if few completions are possible (e.g., /garm/ can only begin *garment*), the system will settle on single phonological and semantic patterns, and both phonological and semantic priming should be observed. This is precisely what Gaskell and Marslen-Wilson found.

Gaskell and Marslen-Wilson (2002) claimed that only a distributed model could account for such differential activation, though it appears DCM does so by virtue of including both phonological and semantic outputs, not by virtue of using distributed representations. If semantic representations were added to TRACE (e.g., if the phoneme layer simultaneously fed to the current lexical [phonological form] layer, and to a layer of semantic primitives that fed forward to a second lexical [semantic form] layer), it would make similar predictions: /kaept/ would activate mutually reinforcing units (*captain* and *captive*) on the phonological side, predicting strong phonological priming, but /kaept/ would activate disparate semantic representations and predict weak semantic priming. Although localist and distributed models may not make conflicting predictions for currently known empirical results, there are strong arguments for preferring distributed to localist representations (Masson, 1995; Plaut et al., 1996) and the DCM represents a crucial step in that direction among SWR models.

2.3.2.3 *PK99* Plaut and Kello's (1999) model is perhaps the most ambitious model of SWR yet proposed, and it is embedded within a comprehensive model of the development of speech production and speech comprehension (see Figure 5.1). The model learns to control a set of articulatory parameters to generate acoustics based on "adult" input (well-formed acoustics) and self-input

(acoustic results of its own articulations). The acoustics are fairly close analogs of the speech signal (formant frequencies and transitions, frication, plosiveness, loudness, and the visual feature of jaw openness). The model learns a bi-directional mapping between acoustics and articulations and the mapping from both of these phonological representations to an arbitrary set of semantic patterns. The first report was extremely promising; in the domains tested, the model exhibited a range of desirable learning and processing behaviors. We hope development of this model continues, as we find that it provides the most promise for significant progress in modeling the development of speech production and comprehension.

2.3.2.4 *Adaptive Resonance Theory (ART)* ART is a powerful connectionist learning framework. Inputs are initially mapped to early representations in a working memory stage. These then map (through bi-directional links, allowing feedback) to *list chunks* (combinations of lower-level units that have co-occurred over learning). Chunks of equal length inhibit each other and longer chunks mask smaller chunks contained within them. The framework has allowed for an impressive array of fundamentalist models (separate models for processing aspects of real speech [ARTSTREAM; Grossberg et al., 2004], phonological patterns [ARTPHONE, Grossberg, Boardman, and Cohen, 1997], and word segmentation [ARTWORD, Grossberg, and Myers, 2000]), which suggests great promise for a comprehensive, realist model, but such a model has not yet been reported (see also Goldinger and Azuma, 2003, for suggestions of how Goldinger's [1988] episodic lexicon model might be combined with the ART framework).

An intriguing aspect of ART's processing assumptions is that its version of top-down feedback cannot cause hallucinatory representations. A *2/3 rule* means that weak inputs (e.g., phonetic features corrupted by noise) can be strengthened once recognized by higher levels of processing, but completely absent inputs cannot be created from nothing. As we discuss later in this chapter, a common criticism of feedback in TRACE is that it could make the system hallucinate (Norris et al., 2000). Although, in practice, misperception in TRACE seems generally similar to misperception in humans (Mirman et al., 2005) and the default TRACE parameters also give it strong, bottom-up priority, future modeling efforts might benefit from nonsymmetrical feedback rules such as those implemented in ART.

3 Evaluating and comparing models

The recent history of SWR includes disagreements about whether particular models succeed or fail to account for various phenomena. There has been a salient absence of agreed upon principles for gauging model success or failure and for comparing models. We will argue that assessing success requires (1) clear *linking hypotheses* (links between the tasks performed by human subjects and the measurable properties of a model), and (2) attributing a success or failure to one of four levels (in decreasing order of importance): theory, implementation, parameters, and linking hypotheses. After introducing these issues, we will illustrate them with recent examples from the literature and propose a set of candidate principles for assessing success and comparing models. These principles will frame a larger discussion of the feedback debate in Section 4.

3.1 *Linking hypotheses*

The first question for comparing model behavior to human behavior is how to link properties of the model to the task performed by human subjects. The simplest approach is to look for qualitative similarity between a model and human data. For example, if lexical node activations correlate inversely with human response times and error rates in some task, it is reasonable to accept this as a model success, though this is a weak standard. One would do better to ask whether the model also provides good *quantitative* fits, and whether the fits are to condition means or individual items (e.g., does it predict errors on the correct class

of items, or depending on the task, does it predict appropriate errors?). As the quantitative fit and grain of prediction increases, so should the standard for success. The standard can be strengthened further by examining how closely the model's task resembles the human subjects' task by establishing explicit linking hypotheses: concrete operational definitions tying features of model performance to human behaviors and tasks.

Linking hypotheses typically receive little attention. However, one cannot say a *model* has failed unless one has first appropriately linked (a) model performance to human performance, (b) stimulus materials for human subjects to model materials, and (c) task constraints faced by humans to task constraints on models (e.g., through choice models).

3.2 *Model successes and failures: levels of analysis*

A model success or failure can be linked to one of four levels of decreasing importance: theory, implementation, parameters, or linking hypotheses. As we have just discussed, a failure or success due to improper linking hypotheses is not informative in the same way that an experimental failure due to improper operational definitions is not informative. A failure at the level of theoretical assumptions is of greatest interest and holds the greatest possibility for progress (i.e., theory falsification). Before a model failure can be attributed to underlying theoretical assumptions, one must establish that the failure cannot be attributed to implementational details or to parameter settings. Implementational details include factors such as input representation, numbers of units in a neural network model, and details of processing dynamics (e.g., activation functions). Parameter settings play a critical role in simulating models, so, for example, if TRACE model simulations suggest competitors are inhibited too much, one cannot conclude that lateral inhibition is fundamentally flawed without testing different values of lexical inhibition, phoneme inhibition, bottom-up excitation, and so forth. Likewise, in a learning model, performance may change radically as a function of amount of training, as we mentioned earlier in our discussion of SRNs.

Parameters are of particular importance, as there have been suggestions that a model as complex as TRACE should only be tested with minor deviations from the original parameter set. It is true that if different parameter sets are used to model different results, the model loses its generality – the breadth of model successes cannot be attributed to underlying theoretical assumptions if each success requires different parameters. On the other hand, equating a model with a parameter set produces a similar problem: The model loses generality because the constraints of the parameter set are placed on a par with underlying theoretical assumptions. The simple alternative is not to limit model explorations to a "standard" parameter set, but the onus is on the modeler to test whether parameter changes needed for one phenomenon prevent the model from fitting results it was known to fit with the previous settings.[6]

We will now review a case in which proper linking hypotheses provide insight into how task constraints shape behavior, and other cases in which apparent model failures were actually due to improper linking hypotheses. Then we will turn to candidate principles for gauging success and comparing two models.

3.3 *Improving models with linking hypotheses*

An interesting outcome of the use of simulation models is that for more than a decade, models made predictions at a finer grain than could be tested with standard psycholinguistic tasks. Models like TRACE (McClelland and Elman, 1986) make explicit predictions about the parallel activation of similar items and the time course of competition between

them. For example, Panel B of Figure 5.4 shows the complex pattern of activation and competition among TRACE's lexical nodes for items like *beaker, beetle, speaker,* and *carriage* when the input is an item like *beaker.*

Fine-grained lexical activation predictions began to be testable with the advent of the "visual world" eyetracking paradigm (Tanenhaus et al., 1995). In this paradigm, participants see multiple objects and their eye movements are tracked as they follow spoken instructions to perform visually guided movements (e.g., "click on the beaker"). At any instant, participants can fixate only one object, but time course can be estimated from average fixation proportions over time. Panel A of Figure 5.4 shows data from Allopenna et al. (1998), who presented subjects with displays of four items like (on critical trials) *beaker, beetle, speaker,* and *carriage,* and examined fixations as subjects followed an instruction like *click on the beaker.* While there is an obviously strong qualitative fit between the data and the TRACE activations in Panel B, Allopenna et al. established a closer link by linking model time to real time (by relating average phoneme duration in real speech materials to TRACE cycles per phoneme) and, more important, by explicitly considering task constraints on human subjects (Panel C). Subjects had four possible fixation outlets – the pictures on the screen. Allopenna et al. assumed that bottom-up lexical activation was not restricted to the displayed items, and based lexical activation on activation and competition in the entire TRACE lexicon. To incorporate the four-choice task constraint, they computed response probabilities based only on the activations of the four displayed items (using a variant of the Luce [1959] choice rule). With one free parameter (a multiplier used in the choice rule[7]), this

---

6 This is no small burden when a model has been shown to account for a wide range of results. However, tools like jTRACE (Strauss, Harris, and Magnuson, 2007) and others listed in the appendix allow one to automate large numbers of simulations in order to explore the robustness of previous simulations throughout parameter spaces.

7 The best fits used a parameter that changed over time to reflect greater confidence as bottom-up evidence increased. With this parameter (k) set to a constant value of seven, competitor fits were reduced slightly. In later work, a constant value of seven provided excellent fits (Dahan, Magnuson, and Tanenhaus, 2001; Dahan et al., 2001).

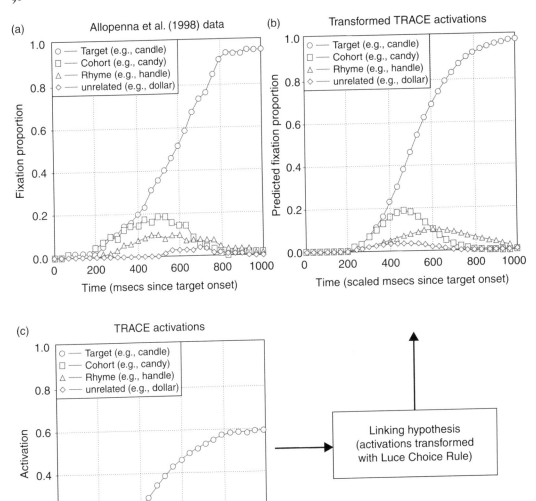

Figure 5.4. Comparison of eyetracking data (A), TRACE activations (B), and TRACE activations transformed into predicted response probabilities via explicit linking hypotheses (C). Adapted from Allopenna et al. (1998).

linking hypothesis greatly improves fit – by taking into account task constraints faced by human subjects and simultaneously providing a "placeholder" model of the decision process (in the sense that it is obviously incomplete). It also suggests the possibility that TRACE activations may surprisingly closely approximate human lexical activations, as a very simple linking hypothesis

taking task constraints into account results in high model-data fits (and this same linking hypothesis allows close fits of changes in looking behavior when cohort competitors are present or absent; Dahan, et al., 2001).

Allopenna et al. calculated fit with $r2$ (do human and model proportions rise and fall together?) and root mean squared (RMS) error (are the actual values close?); $r2$ was

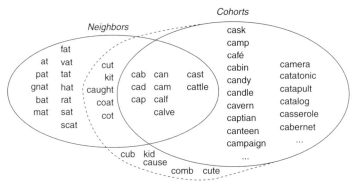

Figure 5.5. The relationships of similarity metrics. Neighbors differ from each other by a single phoneme. Cohorts overlap at onset. Often, the overlap threshold is 200 msecs or approximately the first two phonemes. Less often, overlap in the first phoneme is the threshold (delineated by the dotted curve). The shaded region indicates items that are both neighbors and cohorts. TRACE predicts strongest activation for items that are both (two-phoneme overlap) cohorts and neighbors, then for (two-phoneme overlap) cohorts, then other neighbors, and little activation of items overlapping in a single onset phoneme (though greater activation is predicted for items like *cut* with a single mismatch versus *cub* with two mismatches).

high and RMS was low.[8] The Allopenna et al. (1998) study provided partial resolution to a paradox having to do with similarity metrics (see Figure 5.5). In tasks like cross-modal semantic priming (e.g., Marslen-Wilson, 1990), there is strong evidence for onset (or cohort) competition (e.g., hearing *beaker* primes *insect*, an associate of *beetle*, as *beetle* is strongly activated by phonological similarity to *beaker* and then activates *insect* via spreading semantic activation), but not for rhyme competition (*beaker* would not

detectably prime *stereo*, an associate of *speaker*). In contrast, NAM's similarity metric includes rhymes, and NAM provides the best available predictions for large sets of items (accounting for about fifteen percent of the variance in SWR tasks). TRACE makes an intermediate prediction: Onset competitors have an advantage because they receive substantial bottom-up activation without strong inhibition during the early part of the word. Rhymes are predicted to be activated, but to be at a significant disadvantage: By the time they have bottom-up support, the target and onset competitors are sending strong inhibition. Since the eyetracking data matches TRACE's predictions so closely, this suggests that rhymes are activated, but more weakly than onset competitors. In cross-modal semantic priming, effects depend on phonologically based activation spreading semantic activation. If rhyme activation is weak, it is not surprising that it is difficult to detect it in a mediated task. This case illustrates the symbiotic role of models; this level of resolution of the paradox could only have been attained by use

8 Dahan et al. (2001a; 2001b) extended these linking hypotheses to studies of frequency and subcategorical mismatch. The simple assumptions about the role of the visual display allow accurate predictions of changes in target fixations depending on whether a competitor is present in the display. Norris (2005) suggests that computing response probabilities corresponds to predicting that subjects' eyes instantaneously flit between objects (that is, that each trial must have the same continuous form as the central tendency). However, in choice theory, a response *probability* implies a distribution of responses. Magnuson (2008b) provides simulations demonstrating that a one-parameter stochastic eye movement model quickly recovers the underlying distribution.

of both quantitative empirical methods and an implemented model with an intervening linking hypothesis.

3.4 *Linking to human materials and task constraints*

Marslen-Wilson and Warren (1994) examined the role of lateral inhibition as a competition mechanism in TRACE by creating cross-spliced versions of a word like *net* that combined the initial CV of one word and the final C of another (e.g., the initial CV of *neck* plus the final C of *net*) or the initial CV of a nonword (*nep*) and the final C of the word (*net*). These cross-spliced items included misleading coarticulatory (subcategorical) information about the final C. The baseline item was the initial CV of the target spliced onto the final C of another recording of the same word. The three conditions were labeled W_1W_1 (CV of one recording of *net* spliced onto the final C of another recording of *net*), W_2W_1 (*neck* + *net*), and N_3W_1 (*nep* + *net*). Marslen-Wilson and Warren's simulations indicated that TRACE predicted the following response time pattern: $W_1W_1 < N_3W_1 < W_2W_1$ (with a large increase for W_2W_1), but human lexical decision data showed the pattern $W_1W_1 < N_3W_1 \approx W_2W_1$. Marslen-Wilson and Warren attributed this discrepancy to lateral inhibition in TRACE, which they argued was too strong. Norris et al. (2000) ran simulations with Merge and a radically simplified interactive activation model (the six-phoneme and four-word Merge model with lexical feedback). Merge successfully predicted the response time pattern, as did their interactive analog, but only if it was made to cycle multiple times at each input step, effectively increasing the amount of inhibition that occurred prior to a decision. So Marslen-Wilson and Warren argued TRACE had too much competition, while Norris et al. argued that competition in TRACE was too slow.

Dahan et al., (2001) revisited this paradigm with eyetracking paired with TRACE simulations (see Magnuson, Dahan, and Tanenhaus, 2001 for more simulation

details). Contrary to the lexical decision data, they found that fixation trajectories fit the pattern $W_1W_1 < N_3W_1 < W_2W_1$ (though the pattern was not as extreme as in the Marslen-Wilson and Warren simulations). Magnuson et al. explained the discrepancy between the eye movement and lexical decision data by assuming a "yes" response could be triggered if the activation of *either* W_1 or W_2 reached a threshold. This would decrease average response time for W_2W_1, assuming the activation of W_2 (*neck*) generates infrequent "yes" decisions. In separate lexical decision simulations based on eye movement time course and TRACE activations, there were ranges of parameters where this simple assumption leads to correct RT predictions ($W_1W_1 < N_3W_1 \approx W_2W_1$). Contrary to the Marslen-Wilson and Warren and Norris et al. simulations, new TRACE simulations correctly predicted the data at a very fine grain. Dahan et al. explained the discrepancy between their TRACE simulations and Marslen-Wilson and Warren's by deducing that the latter cross-spliced the TRACE stimuli much too late. Dahan et al. cross-spliced at the latest position possible that still led to the correct recognition of the intended final target. When the splicing is done as late as that reported by Marslen-Wilson and Warren, W_2 is recognized rather than W_1 given W_2W_1, and W_2 is also recognized in a nonword condition (W_2N_1). If this happened with human subjects, the materials would be scrapped and replaced. This illustrates an important principle: The same care that is taken with materials for human subjects must be taken with model testing in order to ensure adequate analogs between human and model conditions. The lexical decision simulations demonstrate that linking hypotheses can radically alter the apparent success or failure of a model.

3.5 *Intuition and logic versus simulation*

Consider the following predictions about TRACE and SWR in general. If word frequency has a prelexical locus, it should have a constant effect, detectable in both fast and slow word recognition responses. If frequency has a postlexical decisional bias, frequency effects might disappear when subjects respond very quickly – before they hit the stage where frequency is integrated with lexical activation. Connine, Titone, and Wang (1993) found that indeed, frequency effects tend not to be detectable in fast responses and concluded that in a model like TRACE, such a result could only occur if frequency were a postlexical bias. Dahan, Magnuson, and Tanenhaus (2001) augmented TRACE with three frequency mechanisms: postlexical (frequency applied in the choice rule rather than activations), resting levels (each word's activation in the absence of input was proportional to frequency), and bottom-up connection strengths (phoneme–word connections were proportional to word frequency). The intuitive expectation was that the latter two would lead to similar predictions and both would differ from the first.

Dahan et al. (2001) compared time course predictions from TRACE to fine-grained time course measurements of frequency effects using eyetracking and the visual world paradigm. Empirically, human listeners showed a continuous influence of frequency that increased as more of a word was heard. Contrary to Connine et al.'s (1993) predictions, all three frequency-augmented versions of TRACE could fit the human fixation proportion data fairly well. Also surprisingly, the resting level and postlexical mechanisms made virtually identical predictions with a constant frequency influence. (To predict a late influence, the postlexical account would require an additional parameter specifying when frequency should be applied.) The bottom-up connection weight mechanism predicted that the effect would be proportional to the amount of evidence, and provided the closest fit to the human data (especially the early time course). This mechanism would account for the Connine et al. results as a matter of task sensitivity: If you sample early in processing (with fast decisions) the magnitude of

the frequency effect would be small. If the sensitivity of the task used were low (as it arguably is in lexical decision), a null result in early responses would not be surprising.

This example demonstrates the value of simulations with complex models over intuition-based expectations. Whenever possible, expectations should be verified with model simulations (see the Appendix for a list of tools that can be used for SWR simulations).

3.6 Comparing models

Assuming two models account for overlapping phenomena, how should we compare them? First, if one appears to fail on some phenomena, the *level* of the failures must be identified, as we have just discussed. If the failures can be argued to be nontrivial, and all else is equal about the models, one has a basis for preferring the one with fewer failures. However, if all else is not equal (e.g., one model uses more realistic input or mechanisms, or one requires different parameter settings for different phenomena), one should prefer the model with greater realism, greater depth and breadth of coverage, or greater parameter stability.

A recent trend in model analysis has been to distinguish between models that fit empirical data because of inherent properties of the model from models that fit only because of specific parameter settings. The standard test of model performance is to compare model and human behavioral data under one specific set of parameter values (or a small range of values). However, a model may be flexible enough to fit any possible data. Ideally, model behavior should be fairly stable over parameter changes and the optimal parameter range should account for a relatively large set of behavioral data (i.e., parameter changes should not be required for each new behavioral data pattern).

Pitt and his colleagues have recently developed a method (called Parameter Space Partitioning, or PSP) for comparing models based on their performance across their parameter space (Pitt et al., 2006).

PSP examines the range of qualitative data patterns (e.g., an ordering of RTs in different conditions) that a model is capable of producing and computes a partitioned map of parameter space in which each partition corresponds to a qualitatively different data pattern generated by the model. This allows one to assess whether a good fit by the model is due to intrinsic properties that follow from the theoretical assumptions of the model, or merely to particular parameter settings. To conclude that a model is reasonably constrained (and cannot predict arbitrary data patterns), the following should hold: (a) the model should produce relatively few data patterns across the parameter space; (b) the empirically observed pattern (human data) should correspond to a relatively large proportion of the parameter space; and (c) most other data patterns the model can produce should be similar to the empirically observed data pattern, with relatively smooth changes in patterns from partition to partition (rather than radically different patterns).

Parameter space partitioning offers a powerful tool for testing and comparing models. However, its results are only as good as the characterizations of models and problems it is given. For example, PSP is extremely computationally intensive, which limits the complexity of models to which it can be applied. When Pitt et al. set out to compare the TRACE and Merge models, they used a "toy" implementation of TRACE like that used by Norris et al. (2000) (with phonemic input and only a subset of TRACE's phonemes, a very small lexicon, and no ability to represent temporal order). This implementation might better be characterized as an extreme fundamentalist version of an interactive model, as it has little in common with TRACE aside from feedback. Similarly, they focused on tests of lexically mediated phoneme inhibition (reviewed in Section 4.2), but based the human behavioral standards on a report by Frauenfelder, Segui, and Dijkstra (1990), which has several problems (Mirman et al., 2005; see Section 4.2), thus undermining their model analysis. Nonetheless, if candidate models are correctly

implemented and human performance is correctly characterized, global qualitative model evaluation approaches such as PSP can offer important new insights into processes underlying SWR.[9]

3.7 *Conclusions*

Currently, there are no generally agreed upon principles for evaluating individual models or comparing two models. Table 5.1 lists a candidate set of heuristics for model evaluation and comparison (Jacobs and Grainger, 1994 provide a more detailed set of principles). However, comparing two models is more difficult than one might expect, especially if they differ in realism and empirical coverage. To illustrate this, we will review a currently central debate in SWR as an example of how model comparison takes place in the literature.

4 The feedback debate

Proponents of interaction in SWR (feedback connections from lexical to sublexical representations) argue that feedback (a) is a logical way to account for the many lexical effects on sublexical tasks that have been reported in SWR (for examples, see McClelland et al., 2006 and Mirman et al., 2006a), (b) makes a model robust to external or internal noise, and (c) provides an implicit representation of sublexical prior probability at multiple scales (e.g., biphone, triphone, ... n-phone). Proponents of autonomous architectures – those with only feedforward connections – argue (a) feedback is unnecessary to account for lexical effects, (b) it cannot improve recognition, and worse, (c) feedback precludes truly veridical perception and predicts perceptual hallucination.

Proponents of the autonomous view have argued against feedback in two ways. First, they argued that all observed lexical effects on sublexical tasks can be explained

9 PSP tools are available from: http://faculty.psy. ohio-state.edu/myung/personal/PSP_PAGE.html.

by postlexical integration of lexical and sublexical information (Norris et al., 2000). More recently, Norris and McQueen (2008) have argued that lexical and other contexts *should* influence word recognition under certain conditions, but only by means of a Bayesian decision process that has pre-perceptual access to context-conditioned probabilities (via an as yet unspecified mechanism). What is required to falsify the autonomous position is empirical data showing lexical influence on predecisional sublexical processing. This has turned out to be a nontrivial enterprise in terms of developing experimental paradigms that proponents of both views would find convincing (for discussion see Dahan and Magnuson, 2006; McClelland et al., 2006; and McQueen et al., 2006). Here, we will focus on model-specific issues that have been important in this debate.

4.1 *What good can feedback do?*

Norris et al. (2000; also Norris and McQueen, 2008) assert that feedback cannot possibly aid recognition. It can neither speed processing nor improve accuracy. Since there is no way to increase the information available in the signal, a system could not do better than simply activating the word with the best bottom-up fit to the signal. One piece of evidence they cite as support comes from TRACE simulations (Frauenfelder and Peeters, 1998; FP98) in which the usefulness of feedback was studied by comparing performance with feedback on and off. For the twenty-one words tested, about half were recognized more quickly with feedback, and about half were recognized more quickly without feedback. Thus, even in TRACE, the flagship interactive model, feedback seemed not to improve recognition.

Magnuson, Strauss, and Harris (2005) revisited this result with three motivations. First, the general argument about the usefulness of feedback can be challenged on logical grounds (since, for example, words provide an implicit coding of prior probability for sublexical phoneme sequences). Second, the FP98 simulations do not address a central motivation for feedback in interactive systems: Feedback makes a system robust against internal or external noise. That is, feedback is useful because it affords context sensitivity by implicitly coding prior probabilities of causes (phonemes, words, etc.), which can be especially useful given uncertain input. Given a sequence of phonemes including noise or ambiguity, the system could perform more quickly and/or accurately if it allowed context (lexical, syntactic, discourse, etc.) to help disambiguate the input as soon as possible. Third, the FP98 simulations only used a small set of words with particular properties (seven phonemes long, with a uniqueness point at the fourth segment). These were chosen for other simulations presented in the same chapter, but are not representative of the lexicon.

Magnuson et al. tested performance with and without feedback on a large (901-word) lexicon with several levels of noise added to the input. At every level of added noise, average accuracy and recognition time were better with feedback on. Without noise, nearly seventy-five percent of the lexical items were recognized more quickly with feedback on. Cases in which words were recognized more quickly *without* feedback resulted from complex neighborhood characteristics; however, when noise was added, feedback preserved accuracy even for these items.

Another benefit of feedback is that it allows top-down knowledge to guide tuning or recalibration of the perceptual system when there are systematic changes in the input; for example, adjusting to a speaker with an unfamiliar accent. There is strong behavioral evidence that listeners use lexical information to tune the mapping from auditory to phonemic representations (Kraljic and Samuel, 2005, 2006; McQueen, Cutler, and Norris, 2006; Norris et al., 2003). However, Norris et al. (2003) describe the possibly game changing insight that one must be careful to distinguish between *online feedback* (as in TRACE) and *feedback for learning* (as in backpropagation). They argue that feedback for learning provides the necessary basis for precompiling context sensitivity into forward connection weights, and suggest that if it turns out that online feedback exists, it may only be an epiphenomenon of the need for feedback for learning. Mirman et al. (2006b) note that both sorts of feedback are a natural consequence of the assumptions of interactive architectures. All the same, this interesting distinction may be the key to resolving the debate (Magnuson, 2008a).

4.2 *Lexically mediated phoneme inhibition*

A recurring theme among criticisms of feedback is that it would cause distorted or inaccurate perception at prelexical levels. Massaro (1989) argued that lexical feedback distorts the representation at the phoneme layer, causing TRACE to fail to fit data from experiments that separately manipulate auditory and lexical support for the identity of a phoneme. However, subsequent work showed that if intrinsic variability is implemented, feedback does not distort prelexical processing (McClelland, 1991), and an extension of this work proved that interactive models can implement optimal Bayesian inference for combining uncertain information from independent sources (Movellan and McClelland, 2001).

A related prediction is that if the acoustic input contains a lexically inconsistent phoneme (for example, if the /k/ in *arsenic* is replaced with /t/ to make *arsenit*), lexical feedback would cause a delay in recognition of the acoustically present phoneme. Two sets of experiments failed to find evidence of lexically induced delays in phoneme recognition (Frauenfelder et al., 1990; Wurm and Samuel, 1997), providing a key motivation for the development of the autonomous Merge model (Norris et al., 2000). Mirman et al. (2005) showed that these experiments had conflated the manipulation designed to show lexical inhibition effects with the lexical status and neighborhood structure of target items at the point of the lexically inconsistent phoneme target. The TRACE model predicted lexical inhibition when these factors were controlled, but not under the previously tested conditions, and

behavioral tests were consistent with these predictions. Thus, lexical feedback can slow phoneme recognition.

Proponents of the autonomous view have argued that models with lexical feedback would "hallucinate" lexically consistent phonemes not present in the input (Norris et al., 2000; Norris and McQueen, 2008). This overstates the potential for hallucination in TRACE (as the "trace" preserves details of malformed input and model behavior differs greatly given well- and malformed input; McClelland and Elman, 1986, e.g., figures 7–11). In addition, the hallucination claim is typically described as a thought experiment that falsifies interactive feedback, but this underestimates actual human misperception: In lexical inhibition tests (Mirman et al., 2005), listeners exhibited a tendency toward lexically induced misperception and this finding is consistent with other contextually appropriate but illusory perceptions of speech such as failures to detect mispronunciations (Cole, 1973; Marslen-Wilson and Welsh, 1978), hearing noise-replaced phonemes ("phoneme restoration;" Samuel, 1981, 1996, 1997; Warren, 1970), and similar findings from other modalities, such as illusory visual contours (Lee and Nguyen, 2001). In sum, the pattern of phoneme identification phenomena in the literature, including lexically induced delays and errors, is consistent with direct feedback from lexical to prelexical processing.

4.3 *Lessons from the feedback debate*

The feedback debate continues with researchers on both sides providing new behavioral and computational arguments supporting their view (McClelland et al., 2006; McQueen et al., 2006; Mirman et al., 2006a). Nonetheless, the debate illustrates the critical two-way connection between model simulations and behavioral data: Simulations need to fit the behavioral data and make predictions for new behavioral experiments. For this connection to work, simulation materials and linking hypotheses need to be matched to behavioral experiment materials and task constraints and intuitive model predictions need to be tested with empirical simulations. In addition, resolving the debate may require integration with other domains of cognitive science (e.g., theoretical neuroscience; Friston, 2003; Magnuson, 2008a) and broader scope analyses (e.g., the importance of interactive feedback for learning).

5 Crucial questions and directions for progress

Current computational models of SWR theories require assumptions about the input and output and implementations of three core principles: multiple activation, similarity and priors, and competition. Progress may require us to reconsider where SWR begins and ends. SWR can be construed narrowly, as mapping strings of phonemes onto sound forms associated with words, or as broadly as mapping from the acoustic signal to a comprehensive set of phonological, grammatical, and semantic characteristics as part of the processes of recognizing larger structures like sentences (cf. Dahan and Magnuson, 2006). Whether you adopt a narrow view, broad view, or something in between has dramatic implications for your processing theory. The conventional view is that adopting the simplifying assumptions of the narrow view allows us to break off a tractable piece of the problem. But seemingly minor simplifying assumptions may actually complicate things, because they remove potentially constraining information.

Consider the *embedded word problem*. Most words are embedded in other words, and/or have words embedded within them (depending on dialect, *cat, at, a, cattle, law,* and *log* are embedded in a phonemic transcription of *catalog*), suggesting that models of SWR must somehow inhibit recognition of embedded words. The problem is much less extreme when one considers potential subphonemic cues such as durational differences between short and long words. For example, the syllable /haem/ is longer in the word *ham* than in *hamster*. Salverda et al.

(2003) used eyetracking to measure lexical activation and competition and found that subjects were exquisitely sensitive to vowel duration differences of only about fifteen msecs (see Davis et al., 2002 for converging results from priming studies), suggesting such subphonemic cues may mitigate (but not obviate) the embedding problem. Thus, while adopting the narrow view of SWR may allow traction on significant parts of the problem, it may simultaneously complicate the problem by ignoring useful information. The same holds in the opposite direction: Limiting the scope of SWR to phonological form recognition ignores syntactic, semantic, and pragmatic knowledge that could potentially constrain word recognition. Similarly, eschewing production constraints, as well as learning and developmental trajectories leaves a more tractable problem, but at the peril of missing, for example, ways in which seeming puzzles of adult processing might emerge in unanticipated fashion from developmental pressures (MacDonald, 1999).

In our view, the greatest potential for progress in modeling SWR is in taking increasingly broader views: upstream (by working toward models that operate on raw speech), downstream (by connecting the output of current SWR models with higher order linguistic and cognitive structures), and developmentally. Current debates, like the feedback debate, have little consequence for broad view models; the differences between models are modest and may disappear (or be amplified) as we grapple with greater realism. The model of Plaut and Kello (1999), with its realistic inputs, perception–production connections, and developmental approach, stands out as a promising example of how the field might proceed toward these goals.

References

Allopenna, P. D., Magnuson, J. S., & Tanenhaus, M. K. (1998). Tracking the time course of spoken word recognition using eye movements: Evidence for continuous mapping models. *Journal of Memory & Language*, 38, 419–39.

Andruski, J. E., Blumstein, S. E., & Burton, M. (1994). The effect of subphonetic differences on lexical access. *Cognition, 52*, 163–87.

Cairns, P., Shillock, R., Chater, N., & Levy, J. (1995). Bottom-up connectionist modeling of speech. In Levy, J. P., Bairaktaris, D., Bullinaria, J. A.., & Cairns, P. (Eds.) *Connectionist models of memory and language.* University College London Press.

Cole, R. A. (1973). Listening for mispronunciations: A measure of what we hear during speech. *Perception & Psychophysics, 1*, 153–6.

Connine, C. M., Titone, D., & Wang, J. (1993). Auditory word recognition: Extrinsic and intrinsic effects of word frequency. *Journal of Experimental Psychology: Learning Memory and Cognition, 19(1)*, 81–94.

Cutler, A. & Norris, D. (1979). Monitoring sentence comprehension. In Cooper, W. E. & Walker, ECT (Eds.) *Sentence processing: Psycholinguistic studies presented to Merrill Garrett.* Hillsdale: Erlbaum.

Dahan, D. & Magnuson, J. S. (2006). Spoken-word recognition. In Gernsbacher, M. A. & Traxler, M. J. (Eds.) *Handbook of Psycholinguistics* (pp. 249–83). Elsevier.

Dahan, D., Magnuson, J. S., & Tanenhaus, M. K. (2001). Time course of frequency effects in spoken-word recognition: Evidence from eye movements. *Cognitive Psychology, 42*, 317–67.

Dahan, D., Magnuson, J. S., Tanenhaus, M. K., and Hogan, E. M. (2001). Tracking the time course of subcategorical mismatches: Evidence for lexical competition. *Language and Cognitive Processes, 16 (5/6)*, 507–34.

Davis, M. H., Marslen-Wilson, W. D., & Gaskell, M. G. (2002). Leading up the lexical garden-path: segmentation and ambiguity in spoken word recognition. *Journal of Experimental Psychology: Human Perception and Performance, 28*, 218–44.

Ellis, R. & Humphreys, G. W. (1999). *Connectionist psychology: A text with readings.* Hove, England: Psychology Press/Taylor & Francis (UK).

Elman, J. L. (1990). Finding structure in time. *Cognitive Science, 14(2)*, 179–211.

Elman, J. L. & McClelland, J. L. (1986). Exploiting lawful variability in the speech wave. In Perkell, J. S. & Klatt, D. H. (Eds.) *Invariance and variability in speech processes.* Hillsdale, NJ: Lawrence Erlbaum Associates.

Elman, J. L. & McClelland, J. L. (1988). Cognitive penetration of the mechanisms of perception: Compensation for coarticulation of lexically restored phonemes. *Journal of Memory & Language, 27*, 143–65.

Fowler, C. & Magnuson, J. S. (this volume). Speech perception. In Spivey, M., McRae, K., & Joanisse, M. (Eds.) *The Cambridge Handbook of Psycholinguistics.* Cambridge University Press.

Frauenfelder, U. H. & Peeters, G. (1998). Simulating the time course of spoken word recognition: An analysis of lexical competition in TRACE. In Grainger, J. & Jacobs, A. M. (Eds.) *Localist Connectionist Approaches to Human Cognition* (pp. 101–46). Mahwah, NJ: Erlbaum.

Frauenfelder, U. H., Segui, J., & Dijkstra, T. (1990). Lexical effects in phonemic processing: Facilitatory or inhibitory? *Journal of Experimental Psychology: Human Perception & Performance, 16(1)*, 77–91.

Friston, K. (2003). Learning and inference in the brain. *Neural Networks, 16*, 1325–52.

Gaskell, M. G. & Marslen-Wilson, W. D. (1997). Integrating form and meaning: A distributed model of speech perception. *Language & Cognitive Processes. Special Cognitive models of speech processing: Psycholinguistic and computational perspectives on the lexicon, 12*, 613–56.

(1999). Ambiguity, competition, and blending in spoken word recognition. *Cognitive Science, 23*, 439–62.

(2002). Representation and competition in the perception of spoken words. *Cognitive Psychology, 45(2)*, 220–66.

Goldinger, S. D. (1998). Echoes of echoes? An episodic theory of lexical access. *Psychological Review, 105*, 251–79.

Goldinger, S. D. & Azuma, T. (2003). Puzzle-solving science: The quixotic quest for units in speech perception. *Journal of Phonetics, 31*, 305–20.

Grossberg, S. & Myers, C. W. (2000). The resonant dynamics of speech perception: Interword integration and duration-dependent backward effects. *Psychological Review, 107(4)*, 735–67.

Grossberg, S., Boardman, I., & Cohen, M. (1997). Neural dynamics of variable-rate speech categorization. *Journal of Experimental Psychology: Human Perception and Performance, 23(2)*, 481–503.

Grossberg, S., Govindarajan, K. K., Wyse, L. L., & Cohen, M. A. (2004). ARTSTREAM: a neural network model of auditory scene analysis and source segregation. *Neural Networks, 17(4)*, 511–36.

Hintzman, D. L. (1986). "schema abstraction" in a multiple-trace memory model. *Psychological Review*, 93, 411–28.

Jacobs, A. M. & Grainger, J. (1994). Models of visual word recognition: Sampling the state of the art. *Journal of Experimental Psychology: Human Perception and Performance*, 20(6), 1311–34.

Kello, C. T. & Plaut, D. C. (2003). Strategic control over rate of processing in word reading: A computational investigation of the tempo-naming task. *Journal of Memory and Language*, 48, 207–32.

Klatt, D. H. (1979). Speech perception: A model of acoustic-phonetic analysis and lexical access. *Journal of Phonetics*, 7(3), 279–312.

Kraljic, T. & Samuel, A. G. (2005). Perceptual learning for speech: Is there a return to normal? *Cognitive Psychology*, 51(2), 141–78.

(2006). Generalization in perceptual learning for speech. *Psychonomic Bulletin & Review*, 13(2), 262–8.

Lee, T. S. & Nguyen, M. (2001). Dynamics of subjective contour formation in early visual cortex. *Proceedings of the National Academy of Sciences*, 98(4), 1907–77.

Luce, P. A. (1986). A computational analysis of uniqueness points in auditory word recognition. *Perception & Psychophysics*, 39, 155–8.

Luce, P. A. & Pisoni, D. B. (1998). Recognizing spoken words: The neighborhood activation model. *Ear and Hearing*, 19, 1–36.

Luce, P. A., Goldinger, S. D., Auer, E. T., Jr., & Vitevitch, M. S. (2000). Phonetic priming, neighborhood activation, and parsyn. *Perception and Psychophysics*, 62, 615–25.

Luce, R. D. (1959). *Individual choice behavior*. Oxford, England: John Wiley.

MacDonald, M. C. (1999). Distributional information in language comprehension, production, and acquisition; Three puzzles and a moral. In MacWhinney, B. (Ed.) *The emergence of language* (pp. 177–96). Mahwah, NJ: Erlbaum.

MacDonald, M. C., Pearlmutter, N.* J., & Seidenberg, M. S. (1994). The lexical nature of syntactic ambiguity resolution. *Psychological Review*, 101, 676–703.

Magnuson, J. S. (2008a). Nondeterminism, pleiotropy, and single word reading: Theoretical and practical concerns. In Grigorenko, E. & Naples, A. (Eds.) *Single Word Reading*. Mahweh, NJ: Erlbaum.

(2008b). Generating individual eye movement behavior from central tendency models of spoken word recognition. Technical Report, University of Connecticut. http://magnuson.psy.uconn.edu/pub.html.

Magnuson, J. S., Dahan, D., & Tanenhaus, M. K. (2001). On the interpretation of computational models: The case of TRACE. In Magnuson, J. S. & Crosswhite, K. M. (Eds.) *University of Rochester Working Papers in the Language Sciences*, 2(1), 71–91.

Magnuson, J. S., McMurray, B., Tanenhaus, M. K., & Aslin, R. N. (2003a). Lexical effects on compensation for coarticulation: The ghost of Christmash past. *Cognitive Science*, 27, 285–98.

(2003b). Lexical effects on compensation for coarticulation: A tale of two systems? *Cognitive Science*, 27, 801–5.

Magnuson, J. S., Strauss, T., & Harris, H. D. (2005). Interaction in spoken word recognition models: Feedback helps. *Proceedings of the Annual Meeting of the Cognitive Science Society*, 1379–84.

Magnuson, J. S., Tanenhaus, M. K., & Aslin, R. N. (2000). Simple recurrent networks and competition effects in spoken word recognition. *University of Rochester Working Papers in the Language Science*, 1, 56–71.

Magnuson, J. S., Tanenhaus, M. K., Aslin, R. N., & Dahan, D. (2003). The microstructure of spoken word recognition: Studies with artificial lexicons. *Journal of Experimental Psychology: General*, 132(2), 202–27.

Marr, D. (1982). *Vision*. San Francisco: W.H. Freeman.

Marslen-Wilson, W. D. (1987). Functional parallelism in spoken word-recognition. *Cognition*, 25, 71–102.

(Ed.) (1989). *Lexical representation and process*. Cambridge, MA: The MIT Press.

(1990). Activation, competition, and frequency in lexical access. In Altmann, GTM (Ed.) *Cognitive Models of Speech Processing: Psycholinguistic and Computational Perspectives* (pp.148–72). Cambridge, MA: MIT Press.

Marslen-Wilson, W. D., & Tyler, L.K. (1980). The temporal structure of spoken language understanding. *Cognition*, 8, 1–71.

Marslen-Wilson, W. D., & Warren, P. (1994). Levels of Perceptual Representation and Process in Lexical Access: Words Phonemes and Features. *Psychological Review*, 101, 653–675.

Marslen-Wilson, W. D. & Welsh, A. (1978). Processing interactions and lexical access during word recognition in continuous speech. *Cognitive Psychology*, 10, 29–63.

Massaro, D. W. (1989). Testing between the TRACE model and the fuzzy logical model of speech perception. *Cognitive Psychology*, 21(3), 398–421.

Masson, M. E. J. (1995). A distributed memory model of semantic priming. *Journal of*

Experimental Psychology: Learning, Memory, and Cognition, 21(1), 3–23.

McClelland, J. L. (1991). Stochastic interactive processes and the effect of context on perception. *Cognitive Psychology, 23*(1), 1–44.

McClelland, J. L. & Elman, J. L. (1986). The TRACE model of speech perception. *Cognitive Psychology, 18*, 1–86.

McClelland, J. L. & Rumelhart, D. E. (1981). An interactive activation model of context effects in letter perception: I An account of basic findings. *Psychological Review, 88*(5), 375–407.

McClelland, J. L., Mirman, D., & Holt, L. L. (2006). Are there interactive processes in speech perception? *Trends In Cognitive Sciences, 10*(8), 363–9.

McLeod, P., Plunkett, K., & Rolls, E. T. (1998). *Introduction to Connectionist Modeling of Cognitive Processes.* Oxford: Oxford University Press.

McQueen, J. M. (2003). The ghost of Christmas future: didn't Scrooge learn to be good? Commentary on Magnuson, McMurray, Tanenhaus, and Aslin (2003). *Cognitive Science, 27*(5), 795–9.

McQueen, J. M., Norris, D., & Cutler, A. (2006). Are there really interactive processes in speech perception? *Trends in Cognitive Sciences, 10*(12), 533.

Mirman, D., McClelland, J. L., & Holt, L. L. (2005). Computational and behavioral investigations of lexically induced delays in phoneme recognition. *Journal of Memory & Language, 52*(3), 424–43.

Mirman, D., McClelland, J. L., & Holt, L. L. (2006a). Reply to McQueen et al.: Theoretical and empirical arguments support interactive processing. *Trends in Cognitive Sciences, 10*(12), 534.

Mirman, D., McClelland, J. L., & Holt, L. L. (2006b). An interactive Hebbian account of lexically guided tuning of speech perception. *Psychonomic Bulletin & Review, 13*(6), 958–65.

Morton, J. (1969) The integration of information in word recognition. *Psychological Review, 76*, 165–78.

Movellan, J. R. & McClelland, J. L. (2001). The Morton-Massaro law of information integration: Implications for models of perception. *Psychological Review, 108*(1), 113–48.

Norris, D. (1990). A dynamic-net model of human speech recognition. In Altmann, GTM (Ed.) *Cognitive Models of Speech Processing: Psycholinguistic and Computational Perspectives*, pp. 87–104. Cambridge: MIT.

(1994). Shortlist: A connectionist model of continuous speech recognition. *Cognition, 52*, 189–234.

(2005) How do computational models help us build better theories? In Cutler, A. (Ed.) *Twenty-First Century Psycholinguistics: Four Cornerstones.* Mahwah, NJ: Lawrence Erlbaum.

Norris, D. & McQueen, J. M. (2008). Shortlist B: A Bayesian model of continuous speech recognition. *Psychological Review, 115*, 357–95.

Norris, D., McQueen, J. M., & Cutler, A. (1995). Competition and segmentation in spoken-word recognition. *Journal of Experimental Psychology: Learning, Memory, and Cognition, 21*(5), 1209–28.

(2000). Merging information in speech recognition: Feedback is never necessary. *Behavioral & Brain Sciences, 23*, 299–370.

(2003). Perceptual learning in speech. *Cognitive Psychology, 47*, 204–38.

Norris, D., McQueen, J. M., Cutler, A., & Butterfield, S. (1997). The possible-word constraint in the segmentation of continuous speech. *Cognitive Psychology, 34*(3), 191–243.

O'Reilly, R. C. & Munakata, Y. (2000). *Computational explorations in cognitive neuroscience: Understanding the mind by simulating the brain.* Cambridge, MA: The MIT Press.

Pitt, M. A., Kim, W., Navarro, D. J., & Myung, J. I. (2006). Global model analysis by parameter space partitioning. *Psychological Review, 113*(1), 57–83.

Pitt, M. A., Myung, J. I., & Altieri, N. (2007). Modeling the word recognition data of Vitevitch and Luce (1998): Is it ARTful? *Psychonomic Bulletin & Review, 14*, 442–8.

Plaut, D. C. & Kello, C. T. (1999). The emergence of phonology from the interplay of speech comprehension and production: A distributed connectionist approach. In MacWhinney, B. (Ed.) *The Emergence of Language* (pp. 381–415). Mahwah, NJ: Erlbaum.

Plaut, D. C., McClelland, J. L., Seidenberg, M. S., & Patterson, K. (1996). Understanding normal and impaired word reading: Computational principles in quasi-regular domains. *Psychological Review, 103*(1), 56–115.

Plunkett, K. & Elman, J. L. (1997) *Exercises in Rethinking Innateness: A Handbook for Connectionist Simulations.* Cambridge, MA: MIT Press.

Protopapas, A. (1999). Connectionist modeling of speech perception. *Psychological Bulletin, 125*(4), 410–36.

Pustejovsky, J. (1995). *The generative lexicon*. Cambridge, MA: The MIT Press.

Rao, R. P. N. (2004). Bayesian computation in recurrent neural circuits. *Neural Computation*, 16, 1–38.

(2005). Bayesian inference and attentional modulation in the visual cortex. *Neuroreport*, 16, 1843–48.

Rumelhart, D. E., Hinton, G. E., & Williams, R. J. (1986). Learning internal representations by error propagation. In Rumelhart, D. E. & McClelland, J. L. (Eds.) *Parallel Distributed Processing: Explorations in the Microstructure of Cognition* (Vol. 1, pp. 318–62). Cambridge, MA: MIT Press.

Salverda, A. P., Dahan, D., & McQueen, J. M. (2003). The role of prosodic boundaries in the resolution of lexical embedding in speech comprehension. *Cognition*, 90, 51–89.

Samuel, A. G. (1981). Phonemic restoration: Insights from a new methodology. *Journal of Experimental Psychology: General*, 110, 474–94.

(1996). Does lexical information influence the perceptual restoration of phonemes? *Journal of Experimental Psychology: General*, 125(1), 28–51.

(1997). Lexical activation produces potent phonemic percepts. *Cognitive Psychology*, 32(2), 97–127.

Samuel, A. G. & Sumner, M. (this volume). Current directions in research in spoken word recognition.

Samuel, A. G. & Pitt, M. A. (2003). Lexical activation (and other factors) can mediate compensation for coarticulation. *Journal of Memory & Language*, 48(2), 416–34.

Scharenborg, O., Norris, D., ten Bosch, L., & McQueen, J. (2005) How should a speech recognizer work? *Cognitive Science*, 29, 867–918.

Shillcock, R. C. & E. G. Bard. (1993). Modularity and the processing of closed class words. In Altmann, GTM & Shillcock, R. C. (Eds.) *Cognitive models of speech processing. The Second Sperlonga Meeting* (pp. 163–85). Erlbaum.

Spivey, M., Grosjean, M., & Knoblich, G. (2005). Continuous attraction toward phonological competitors. *Proceedings of the National Academy of Sciences*, 102(29), 10393–8.

Strauss, T., Harris, H. D., & Magnuson, J. S. (2007). jTRACE: A reimplementation and extension of the TRACE model of speech perception and spoken word recognition. *Behavior Research Methods, Instruments and Computers*, 39, 19–30.

Tanenhaus, M. K., Spivey-Knowlton, M. J., Eberhard, K. M., & Sedivy, J. C. (1995). Integration of visual and linguistic information in spoken language comprehension. *Science*, 268(5217), 632–4.

Trueswell, J. C. & Tanenhaus, M. K. (Eds.). (1994). *Toward a lexicalist framework of constraint-based syntactic ambiguity resolution*. Hillsdale, NJ; England: Lawrence Erlbaum Associates, Inc.

Van Berkum, JJA, Brown, C. M., Zwitserlood, P., Kooijman, V., & Hagoort, P. (2005). Anticipating upcoming words in discourse: Evidence from ERPs and reading times. *Journal of Experimental Psychology: Learning, Memory, & Cognition*, 31(3), 443–67.

Warren, R. M. (1970). Perceptual restoration of missing speech sounds. *Science*, 167, 392–3.

Wurm, L. H., & Samuel, A. G. (1997). Lexical inhibition and attentional allocation during speech perception: Evidence from phoneme monitoring. *Journal of Memory & Language*, 36(2), 165–87.

Author notes

Preparation of this chapter was supported by NIDCD grant DC-005765 and NSF grant 0748684 to JSM, and NICHD grants F32HD052364 to DM and HD-01994 to Haskins Laboratories.

Appendix: Modeling tools

This table lists tools useful for modeling spoken word recognition. The list is ordered by ease of use. Many more tools exist (such as the neural network toolbox for Matlab).

Heuristics for evaluating models

1. Model failures should not be accepted lightly
   a. If there is a qualitative failure, determine level of failure
      i. Theoretical (the underlying assumptions are wrong)
      ii. Implementation (an architectural or representational assumption is wrong)
      iii. Parameters (the model could fit the data with changes in parameters, but then previous model predictions must be verified with the new settings)
      iv. Linking hypotheses (are human and model materials and tasks comparable?)

Table: 5.1. Candidate principles for evaluating and comparing models

Tool	Description and URL
tlearn	Simple yet powerful simulator for feedforward and (simple) recurrent networks. No programming experience required. Batch processing possible with X11 version or scripting tools. Useful in conjunction with Plunkett and Elman (1997) and/or McLeod, Plunkett, and Rolls (1998). http://crl.ucsd.edu/innate
lens	Doug Rohde's "light, efficient neural simulator." Flexible tool for very wide range of neural networks. Graphical user interface. Tcl/tk interface makes basic programming skills useful, but not necessary. http://tedlab.mit.edu/~dr/Lens
Emergent	Very powerful tool for "parallel distributed processing" modeling, ranging from high-level cognitive models to neuronal models. Steep learning curve, but incredibly flexible. See O'Reilly and Munakata (2000). http://grey.colorado.edu/emergent/index.php/Main_Page
TRACE	TRACE: Platform-independent reimplementation of the TRACE model in Java. Includes graphical user interface, analysis, graphing, scripting, and sharing tools. No programming experience required. See Strauss et al. (2007). http://magnuson.psy.uconn.edu/jtrace HebbTRACE: Original TRACE code (written in C), revised and augmented with Hebbian learning (Mirman et al., 2006b). http://magnuson.psy.uconn.edu/mirman/research/HebbTRACE.zip Mark Pitt provides a version of the original code that he has modified slightly and augmented with tools that facilitate simulation and analysis. http://lpl.psy.ohio-state.edu/software.php
ART	Mark Pitt provides Matlab code and descriptions of the version of ARTPHONE used by Pitt, Myung, and Altieri (2007). http://lpl.psy.ohio-state.edu/software.php

b. Failures of theory or implementation are strong evidence against a model
c. Failures of parameters are strong evidence against a model only if new parameters are needed for each new data set
d. Failures due to improper linking hypotheses are not model failures

2. In gauging degree of success, strong standards should be preferred to weak standards

   a. Quantitative fits are stronger than qualitative fits
   b. Item-specific predictions are stronger than condition-specific predictions
   c. Specific error predictions are stronger than error rate predictions

d. Constrained models (based on parameter space partitioning) are stronger than unconstrained models (i.e., models that can fit patterns quite different from human performance)

Heuristics for comparing models

The heuristics cannot be strictly ordered; for example, disparity in heuristic (c) might outweigh heuristics (a) and (b)

In comparing two models

a. Prefer the model with greater breadth (range of phenomena it models)
b. Prefer the model with greater depth (the model that can be held to a stronger standard of success, as in (2)

c. Prefer the model with greater realism (e.g., a model with more realistic inputs or outputs)

d. Prefer the more realistically constrained model (e.g., based on *parameter space partitioning*; see text)

e. When all else is equal, apply Occam's razor: prefer the simpler model

CHAPTER 6

Finding the Words

How Young Children Develop Skill in Interpreting Spoken Language

Anne Fernald and Michael Frank

1 Finding the words: How young children develop skill in interpreting spoken language

Studies of spoken word recognition either by adults or by children all explore how listeners perceive and interpret strings of speech sounds. However, they focus necessarily on very different kinds of questions. One reason for this divide is that studies with mature, fluent language users can take it for granted that subjects know the meanings of the words they hear. Research on adult word recognition (reviewed by Samuel and Sumner, this volume) investigates a wide range of questions about factors influencing lexical access and ambiguity resolution in a system where it can be assumed that lexical representations are phonologically and semantically well-established, that sentence processing is guided by mature syntactic knowledge, and that the cognitive capacities involved in processing are highly practiced and stable. With young language learners, the situation is crucially different. Although the "competent infant" has received a lot of press in recent years,

based on many new findings revealing early skill in processing speech sounds (reviewed by Saffran and Sahni, this volume), learning a first language is a long, slow process that begins with gaining familiarity with initially meaningless sound patterns and only gradually moves toward fluent understanding. The young infant's dawning awareness of language occurs over a period when the central nervous system is changing more rapidly than at any other time in postnatal life, a developmental trajectory profoundly influenced by early linguistic and social experience. Thus the child's emerging linguistic knowledge and skill in interpreting spoken language are moving targets for the developmental researcher, influenced by many different endogenous and experiential factors and undergoing continual change on multiple levels from month to month.

If it is challenging for adults to make sense of potentially ambiguous strings of speech sounds as they fly by, it is even more so for the immature language learner, who must first build up initial representations of word forms from the input and then figure out how these word forms are used to convey meaning. Adults know tens of thousands of words in their dominant language, and all but a few of these are still novel words to the one-year-old hearing that language. If we thought about it at all, we would most likely conclude we had understood every sentence heard in our native language that day, at least those that were clearly spoken and attended to, even if they were not directed to us. In contrast, young infants can understand very little of the speech they hear; thus potential ambiguities in strings of speech sounds pose a more fundamental problem. Even when children in their second year begin to show evidence of understanding more and more words, they have rudimentary semantic knowledge compared to that of an older child or an adult. Thus the young child's task is not only to interpret familiar words correctly based on partial knowledge, but also to *discover* the unknown words in speech, discerning the meanings of these new words while also figuring out the grammatical rules that govern how these words can be combined and interpreted.

Our goal in this chapter is to identify central questions motivating current research on children's spoken word recognition and early understanding, and to describe a few of the many recent contributions to this dynamic area of developmental inquiry. Following a brief historical overview, we review new findings showing how infants in the first year of life find the words in speech and begin to associate word forms with meanings, how children in the second and third year develop skill in recognizing familiar words and interpreting words in combination, and how young language learners across this age range deal with pervasive ambiguity as they continually encounter unfamiliar words in the speech they hear.

2 Early research on early understanding: A historical perspective

How infants begin to make sense of speech is an intriguing question with a long history. Reflecting on his own experience as a young child, St. Augustine concluded that "by constantly hearing words, as they occurred in various sentences" in conjunction with gaze and gestural cues from his elders, he "collected gradually for what [these words] stood" (St. Augustine, 398, translated by E. B. Pusey, 1961, p.11). Some fifteen hundred years later, the German philosopher Tiedemann published the first scholarly observations of early language learning, describing his infant son's gradual progress in understanding speech. At eight months of age, his son appeared to recognize names of a few familiar objects, turning to search when he heard the word, and by fourteen months of age he could articulate a few words but did not yet appear to use them intentionally. Tiedemann concluded that at this age "words awakened in him their proper images and ideas, but not conversely, images of objects and desire of them, any concept of the corresponding word; primarily because children begin by learning words more for the sake of understanding the intention of others than in order to impart their own" (Tiedemann, 1787/1927, p. 221). This early insight anticipates a very modern point of view, reflected in the recent research literature on the role of infant mind reading skills in word learning (Tomasello, 2001). A century later, the diary studies of Hippolyte Taine and Charles Darwin also anticipated questions that have proven to be of enduring scientific interest. Taine (1877) noted that when his eleven-month-old daughter was asked, "Where's Mama?" she always turned toward her mother, an example similar to an earlier observation made by Tiedemann: When asked to "make a bow" or "swat the fly," his eight-month-old son also made appropriate gestures. However, their interpretations differed: While Tiedemann asserted that his son had "learned to comprehend" simple sentences, Taine was more cautious, suggesting that "there is nothing more in this than an association." Taine, however, thought his daughter, by the age of twelve months, did demonstrate true comprehension of the word *bébé*. Although the child's understanding did not coincide with the conventional meaning, Taine claimed that *bébé* had "a general signification" for her beyond a limited association between a sound pattern and a gestural response. Such perceptive parental observations reflected curiosity and wonder about the origins of children's understanding, long before language learning was viewed as a legitimate object of scientific inquiry. It is easy to underestimate the originality of these early diary studies given their lack of methodological rigor, but they were the first to raise challenging questions that continue to motivate research on the development of spoken language understanding: When do infants first begin to respond distinctively to words as familiar sound patterns? And when and how do young children learn to apprehend meaning in these sounds?

When experimental research on spoken word recognition by adults began to emerge in the 1950s, studies addressing similar questions in children soon followed. For example, psychoacoustic research on contextual factors influencing the intelligibility of speech in noise (Miller, Heise, and Lichten, 1951) led to parallel studies with children, often motivated by clinical concerns (see Mills, 1975). Over this same period, young children's responsiveness to spoken language was increasingly of interest to linguists and psychologists working in quite different traditions. In the newly emerging field of language acquisition, Roger Brown (1957; 1973) used informal testing methods and naturalistic observation to explore the early development of comprehension. And psychologists studying perceptual development began to devise ingenious new experimental procedures for assessing discrimination and categorization of visual and auditory stimuli by young children. The introduction of an habituation procedure that could be used to investigate categorical perception of speech sounds by two-month-olds (Eimas et al., 1971) enabled and inspired numerous studies of infants' abilities to discriminate and group vowels and consonants (see Aslin, Pisoni, and Jusczyk, 1983). However, it was not until the 1980s that work in these different traditions began to converge, crossing disciplinary boundaries to explore deeper questions related to language learning. As researchers in the field then known

as "infant speech perception" realized how many interests they had in common with some of their colleagues working in the separate field of "language acquisition," there was a significant shift in emphasis: Studies of early speech processing began to focus on the *discovery procedures* infants use to identify words and higher order elements in spoken language.

3 Finding the words in the first year

Even as newborns, infants are more interested in listening to speech than to other engaging forms of auditory stimulation (Vouloumanos and Werker, 2007). But to begin finding meaning in spoken language, infants must detect patterns and regularities in the sequences of sounds produced by speakers of the language they are hearing. Hundreds of experiments on speech perception in the first year of life have shown that infants become attuned to characteristic sound patterns in the ambient language months before understanding or speaking a single word (see Jusczyk, 1997; Kuhl, 2004; Saffran and Sahni, this volume). Here we describe just a few of many recent studies exploring how infants become acquainted with complex distributional patterns in spoken language and how these implicit learning strategies enable them to identify potential words using multiple sources of information available in the sound patterns of continuous speech.

The majority of experiments on speech processing by infants in the first year have investigated their capacity to recall isolated sound sequences, rather than examining associations formed between words and objects or individuals. Much of this research has focused on the task of word segmentation, exploring how infants identify particular sequences of sound within a larger body of fluent speech. In an influential study of early segmentation abilities, Jusczyk and Aslin (1995) asked when infants first showed evidence of being able to identify repeated word forms embedded in fluent speech. Using a head turn preference procedure, infants were first familiarized with multiple repetitions of a single word such as *cup* or *dog* and then tested in an auditory preference procedure with passages that either did or did not contain the familiarized word. While six-month-old infants showed no preference for the passages containing the words with which they had been familiarized, seven-and-a-half-month-olds did show a significant preference, indicating that they recognized the word forms heard earlier in isolation, even in the context of continuous speech. However, when infants were familiarized with nonwords such as *tup* and *bawg* that differed by only one or two phonetic features from the words that were presented at test, they did not show a preference. This finding suggested that infants at this age did not confuse *tup* with *cup* or *bawg* with *dog*, indicating sensitivity to phonetic details. In a follow-up study, Jusczyk and Hohne (1997) found that eight-month-olds exposed to recordings of stories over a ten-day period showed a preference for lists of words from the stories they had heard, even two weeks after familiarization. These and other studies revealed that by the second half of their first year infants are beginning to segment recurrent acoustic patterns corresponding to words from fluent speech, and that they are capable of long-term storage of these segmented word forms.

During this period, infants also begin to show sensitivity to a variety of speech cues used by adults to recognize words in fluent speech, including distributional cues, lexical stress, phonotactic constraints, and allophonic variation (e.g., Mattys, White, and Melhorn, 2005). Saffran and colleagues made the important discovery that seven-month-olds make use of distributional information to segment highly predictable syllable sequences from fluent speech (Aslin, Saffran, and Newport, 1998; Saffran, Aslin, and Newport, 1996). Other studies have asked when infants become aware of characteristic regularities in the ambient language such as phonotactic patterns (Jusczyk et al., (1993) and lexical stress patterns (Jusczyk, Cutler, and Redanz, 1993), and how they make use of such language-specific cues in identifying potential word boundaries (e.g., Johnson and Jusczyk, 2001). For example, by the age of ten and a half months infants can use their knowledge of the typical trochaic stress pattern of English to segment words with an initial stressed syllable. They can also use subtler cues such as allophonic variations (e.g., the difference in aspiration between the /t/ in *nitrates* and the /t/ in *night rates*) as well as phonotactic probabilities or constraints (e.g., that the sequence /kt/ does not appear word initially in English, though it does in Russian) to identify potential word boundaries (Jusczyk, Hohne, and Bauman, 1999; Jusczyk, Houston, and Newsome, 1999). Moreover, infants can also learn *new* phonotactic patterns after only minimal exposure (Chambers, Onishi, and Fisher, 2003) and then quickly exploit such newly learned regularities as cues to identify the boundaries of novel words (Thiessen and Saffran, 2003). Thus although infants in the second half of the first year already show a strong commitment to the particular sound patterns absorbed from hearing their native language, early speech processing remains a highly dynamic process, and infants remain open to new experience as they build on prior learning. Just as recent research on spoken language processing by adults has focused on how listeners integrate probabilistic information from numerous sources (e.g., Seidenberg, 1997), developmental researchers are also now exploring how infants integrate multiple sources of information to find potential words in strings of speech sounds. (e.g., Curtin, Mintz, and Christiansen, 2005; Mattys et al., 2005; Thiessen and Saffran, 2003, 2004).

In the studies exploring early skill in segmentation described so far, infants were familiarized with the stimulus words through repeated exposure during the experimental procedure. Other studies have asked when infants begin to recognize familiar sound sequences they have encountered frequently outside of the laboratory. The earliest evidence for sensitivity to familiar words comes from Mandel, Jusczyk, and Pisoni (1995), who found that four-month-olds tested in an auditory preference procedure listened longer to their own name than to a distractor name. Toward the end of their first year, infants demonstrate familiarity with the sound patterns of a broader range of frequently heard words. Research with infants learning French (Halle and de Boysson-Bardies, 1994) and Dutch (Swingley, 2005) found that ten- to eleven-month-olds listened longer to words likely to be familiar in the speech they were hearing, as compared to words less common in infants' experience. Parallel studies using electrophysiological measures confirm the findings based on behavioral measures and also provide information about the time course of infants' responses to familiar and unfamiliar words (Koojiman, Hagoort, and Cutler, 2005). For example, Thierry, Vihman, and Roberts (2003) found that familiar words captured the attention of eleven-month-olds in less than 250 ms, a neural response pattern that differed significantly from responses to control words matched for phonotactic structure but unlikely to be familiar to infants at this age.

There is now abundant evidence that infants in their first year attend to the speech they hear around them, making detailed distributional analyses of acoustic-phonetic features of spoken language, and that words experienced frequently in daily interactions begin to emerge as salient acoustic patterns months before these words are perceived as meaningful. Such accomplishments are often cited as evidence of early "word recognition" by infants, and indeed they create a firm foundation for future learning. For example, a study with seventeen-month-olds showed that the word forms found by mechanisms of auditory pattern learning are good targets for future mapping to objects (Graf Estes et al., 2007). This finding, and others reported in the following sections, suggest that exposure to word forms even in the absence of meaningful interpretation can lay the groundwork for future learning of form–meaning correspondences.

Nevertheless, while research on adult word recognition presupposes that familiar words can be meaningfully interpreted as well as recognized, no such assumption

can be made about semantic processing by infants in the first year. Identifying sequences of sounds as coherent acoustic patterns is obviously an essential step in lexical processing, but such form-based recognition can occur without any link between a particular sound pattern and a semantic representation. Thus although it is clear that infants by the age of ten months have some kind of acoustic-phonetic representation for frequently heard sound patterns, this result is best viewed as evidence of pattern detection abilities that are prerequisite for recognizing words in continuous speech, a selective response to familiar words that constitutes word recognition in a somewhat limited sense since it can occur with no evidence of comprehension.

4 Associating word forms with meanings

At what point do infants begin to link familiar word forms consistently with particular meanings? In a large-scale study of early vocabulary growth using the MacArthur Communicative Development Inventory, the median receptive vocabulary for eight-month-olds was around five words, according to parental report (Fenson et al., 1994). But it is hard to know whether this measure accurately reflects infants' appreciation of correct sound–meaning associations or whether it is an overestimate based on conventionalized responses to frequently heard acoustic patterns. As Tiedemann observed, an infant rewarded for making a stereotyped gesture upon hearing "swat the fly" does not necessarily understand any of the words. Although parents typically report that by the end of the first year their infants can speak a few words and appear to understand many more, growth in receptive language competence is much harder to observe than growth in productive abilities, because the processes involved in comprehension are only partially and inconsistently apparent through the child's spontaneous behavior. Thus researchers have relied more on experimental than observational methods to study the earliest stages of sound–meaning mapping. For example, Woodward, Markman, and Fitzsimmons (1994) taught thirteen- and eighteen-month-olds a new object label by naming an object nine times over the course of a short training session. By using an engaging type of test trial in which the infants chose the named object for use in a game, they found some evidence that thirteen-month-olds were able to identify the object that was paired with the novel label even after a twenty-four hour delay.

More recently, studies using procedures that rely on implicit looking time measures have produced convincing evidence that children around their first birthday begin to make form–meaning mappings, even on the basis of a small amount of laboratory experience. For example, in the "switch" procedure, fourteen-month-olds are habituated to two different novel word–object pairs through repeated presentation of each object accompanied by its label (Stager and Werker, 1997). Once a habituation criterion is met, infants are shown a word–object pair that violates the learned associations. The outcome measure is infants' response to this switch in test trials, when one novel object is paired with the label previously presented with another novel object. Successful detection of the switch is measured by greater looking time to the incongruent pairing, compared to baseline looking to the congruent pairings. In an experiment with eight-, twelve-, and fourteen-month-olds, the two younger groups of infants were able to learn a single word–object association, detecting the substitution of a novel word or object at test; however, when asked to learn two novel associations, they failed to detect a switch in one of the two novel pairings (Werker et al., 1998). Werker et al. concluded that initial successes in this paradigm were due to a simple novelty preference: Infants dishabituated to a switch because they noticed that some unitary stimulus element had changed. In the two-referent case, however, they had to notice a violated association between a word and its referent, and only fourteen-month-olds could do this reliably. Thus, although even very young infants may

be able to learn some words with sufficient exposure, mapping forms to meanings within the timeframe of a laboratory experiment requires cognitive resources that may not be available until after the first birthday.

Most experimental studies of early word learning have focused on children's abilities to form links between words and object referents in unambiguous situations. But these constrained laboratory situations – in which a single, salient referent is named repeatedly – differ in important ways from the noisier, real-world situations in which children typically find themselves. In the context of daily interactions, an infant will often hear an unfamiliar word spoken in a sentence frame, rather than in isolation, with several objects present as potential referents in the field of view. In this more complex environment, the learner may not be able to infer which object the unfamiliar word relates to from a single exposure. Instead, it may be necessary to aggregate information over multiple uses of a word. This kind of aggregation has been termed *cross-situational learning*. For example, if the infant hears the unknown words *ball* and *bat* spoken when both a ball and a bat are present, it will not initially be clear which word goes with which object. But if the words *dog* and *ball* are heard soon afterward in the presence of a dog and a ball, it might be possible for the young learner to keep track of statistical evidence across these two situations, noting that the ball was the only object present on both occasions when the word *ball* was heard. If so, this could help the infant to map *ball* to the appropriate object. In a simple artificial language study, Yu and Smith (2007) demonstrated that adult participants were able to associate unfamiliar words with the appropriate referent even when up to four objects and four words were presented simultaneously. A follow-up experiment using a preferential looking procedure suggested that twelve- and fourteen-month-old infants could also learn word–object associations from individually ambiguous presentations (Smith and Yu, 2008). Thus, some kind of cross-situational learning mechanism is available to very young word learners in

(a)
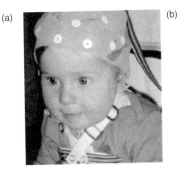

(b)

Known words	Phonetically similar	Phonetically dissimilar
cup	tub	mon
bear	gare	kobe
nose	mose	jud
dog	bog	riss

(c)
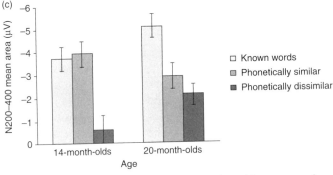

□ Known words
▨ Phonetically similar
▓ Phonetically dissimilar

Figure 6.1. Infants in an ERP paradigm (a) heard known words and nonsense words that were either phonetically similar or dissimilar to those known words, as shown in the abbreviated list of stimulus words (b). The mean amplitude of the N200–400 word recognition component is shown in (c) in response to known words, phonetically dissimilar nonsense words, and phonetically similar nonsense words. At twenty, but not fourteen months, the neural representations accessed for known words are phonetically detailed enough to distinguish similar-sounding foils. Data are from Mills et al. (2004); Figure reprinted from Werker and Yeung (2005), with permission from Elsevier.

attempting to bridge the gap between form and meaning.

What is the nature of this learning mechanism? One of the most exciting features of recent work on cross-situational word learning is the presence of computational proposals that instantiate ideas about mechanisms and make quantitative predictions about human performance. Early work by Siskind (1996) viewed cross-situational learning as involving a deductive inference about which parts of complex, propositional meanings mapped to words in sentences. While this proposal was ambitious and valuable, it also assumed that learners have access to very good guesses about precisely what speakers are talking about, an unrealistic assumption

that limited its applicability to experimental situations. In contrast, more realistic proposals have assumed only that learners have access to their visual environment, but not to the propositional content of the speakers' utterances. For example, both Roy and Pentland (2002) and Yu, Ballard, and Aslin (2005) instantiated models of cross-situational word learning within systems that could parse continuous speech and identify objects via computer vision algorithms. Because they were able to learn word–object pairings using only raw video and audio data as input, these models provided a strong proof of concept that cross-situational mapping can be an effective strategy for acquiring the meanings of object words.

More recent work on this topic has focused primarily on the nature of the mapping mechanisms. Both Yu and Ballard (2007) and Frank, Goodman, and Tenenbaum (2009) have proposed specific mapping mechanisms which could be applied to the schematic output of sensory systems – segmented sets of words and lists of objects. The translation model proposed by Yu and Ballard attempts to estimate direct word–object associations. In contrast, the proposal by Frank et al. posits a specific, though unknown, referential intention – assuming that the speaker most likely intends to talk about only a subset of the objects that are present and uses only a subset of the words she says to refer to them. The idea that speakers' intentions could serve as a mediating variable may prove useful in linking results on early cross-situational word learning to the rich body of research showing that slightly older children soon become expert in using information about speakers' intentions to learn words (e.g., Baldwin, 1993). More broadly, investigations into the learning mechanisms underlying cross-situational learning may provide insights into how to understand the developmental trajectory of early word learning from pure word–form identification through word–object mapping and beyond.

5 Phonological detail in early word representations

Although infants around their first birthday may be able to map words to objects in the lab under the most favorable conditions, more detailed experimental investigations of early word–meaning mapping have produced a striking finding: Early on, infants appear to have difficulty representing the detailed phonetic information in newly learned words. Studies using the switch procedure show that despite being able both to distinguish minimal differences between phonemes and to learn associations between novel words and objects, fourteen-month-olds may not succeed in mapping two new words to two new objects when the labels are a minimal phonetic contrast such as *bih* and *dih* or *bin* and *din* (Pater, Stager, and Werker, 2004; Stager and Werker, 1997). However, infants a few months older are more successful; although fourteen-month-olds fail to dishabituate to violations of the newly learned word–object pairings, seventeen- and twenty-month-olds can correctly recognize this switch (Werker et al., 2002). Convergent evidence for developmental differences in the detail of phonetic representations across the second year comes from research using the electrophysiological method of event-related potentials (ERPs). In a study with fourteen- and twenty-month-olds, Mills and colleagues (2004) compared neural responses to known words (*bear*) with responses to nonwords that were either phonetically similar (*gare*) or dissimilar (*kobe*) to the familiar words. For fourteen-month-olds, ERP responses to known words differed from those to dissimilar nonwords, but did not differ from responses to similar nonwords. In contrast, for the twenty-month-olds, ERP responses to the known words differed from responses to both types of distractor, as shown in Figure 6.2.

The apparent lack of phonetic detail in early word learners' representations is an interesting puzzle in research on early word learning. Given that much younger infants can recognize minimal phonetic differences in the first year of life, why do fourteen-month-olds fail to make use of this ability in the service of word learning? Recall the results by Jusczyk and Aslin (1995) reviewed earlier: Seven-and-a-half-month-old infants can distinguish between *tup* and *cup* or *bawg* and *dog*. Yet when tested in the switch procedure at fourteen months, children cannot learn that a toy labeled *bih* is different from a toy labeled *dih*. This paradox has motivated dozens of experiments, and a variety of possible explanations has been considered, ranging from the proposal that early phonological abilities are discontinuous with later lexical representations, to accounts based on the sparsity of infants' phonological neighborhoods or the limitations of their attentional and information processing abilities.

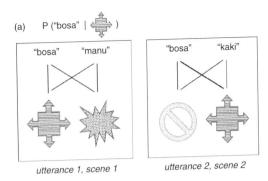

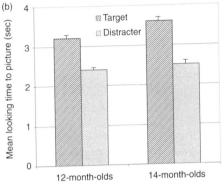

Figure 6.2. A. Schematic of associations among words and referents across two individually ambiguous scenes on sequential trials. If the infant calculates co-occurrence frequencies *across* these two trials, s/he can discover the mapping of the word *bosa* to the appropriate referent. **B.** Mean looking times to target and distracter pictures for younger and older infants. Adapted from Smith and Yu (2008).

One suggestion was that the precise, language-specific, phonetic representations that develop over the first year of life (Jusczyk, 1997; Kuhl et al., 1992; Werker and Tees, 1984) might be unconnected to the level of detail represented in the lexicon. In this account, lexical representations are not continuous with early acoustic-phonetic knowledge but are built as part of a new, holistic representational system which is specific for word forms and contains only the amount of detail that is necessary (Brown and Matthews, 1997; Metsala and Walley, 1998). If young infants initially store words in a vague or underspecified form until word learning begins in the second year, the increasing need to distinguish similar-sounding neighbors might force attention to subtle phonetic detail.

However, this discontinuity view now seems less plausible in light of recent experiments revealing detailed phonological specificity in the representation of highly familiar words by infants early in the second year. Swingley and Aslin (2000; 2002) showed children from fourteen to twenty-three months pairs of pictures of familiar objects and played recorded sentences in which the name of the target object was pronounced either correctly (e.g., *Look at the baby*) or incorrectly (e.g., *Look at the vaby*). If children cannot distinguish *vaby* from *baby*, they should respond identically to both. However, looking to the named picture was significantly above chance across this age range, although it was slower and less reliable in the mispronunciation condition. Based on these findings, Swingley and Aslin concluded that infants as young as fourteen months old have lexical representations that are encoded in fine detail, even when this detail is not yet functionally necessary for distinguishing phonetically similar words in the child's vocabulary. The finding that fourteen-month-olds are sensitive to mispronunciations of highly familiar words in meaningful contexts suggests developmental continuity between the abilities involved in early speech perception and in later lexical learning, consistent with the view that infants beginning to build a vocabulary make full use of the impressive perceptual abilities demonstrated in research with younger infants.

Another possible explanation for the apparent lack of phonetic specificity in newly learned words shown by Stager and Werker (1997) is suggested by the work of Charles-Luce and Luce (1990; 1995), who analyzed the density of adults' and children's lexical neighborhoods (i.e., the number of words differing from a target word by only one phoneme). They found that on average, the lexical neighborhoods of adults' words were denser than those of children, lending support to a view that it may not initially be necessary for children to form highly specific lexical representations, given that fewer competitors to words are present to interfere with recognition (Vitevitch et al., 1999).

However, the work cited above and other recent findings also speak against this view. If fourteen-month-olds are sensitive to mispronunciations within highly familiar words, this accomplishment indicates a level of phonetic detail that should in principle not be necessary if phonetic specificity depends primarily on the size of lexical neighborhoods. Moreover, a series of corpus studies by Coady and Aslin (2003) has reopened the issue of phonological neighborhoods by analyzing transcripts of infants' early speech productions from the CHILDES database. These authors found that when relative vocabulary size is controlled, lexical neighborhoods may actually be *more* rather than less dense earlier in development, presumably because the first words children learn contain highly frequent sound combinations. Thus, the evidence for a large-scale change in the specificity of children's basic lexical representations – whether because of a representational shift or because of sparser phonetic neighborhoods – appears to be limited.

To explain the apparent lack of phonetic specificity in early word learning suggested by the results of Stager and Werker (1997), it may be more productive to focus on other factors that could contribute to children's failure to encode phonetic detail during the period of initial exposure to novel words. One simple explanation for this result is that the novel words taught in brief laboratory experiments differ substantially in frequency of exposure from the familiar words heard over and over during daily life. Recent support for this hypothesis comes from an experiment by Swingley (2007) asking whether previous exposure to a word form influences infants' success in later associating that word form with a meaning. One group of Dutch-learning eighteen-month-olds was familiarized with the acoustic form of a novel word in the context of a storybook, without linking that word to any particular referent; a control group did not receive additional exposure to the novel target word. Infants were then taught to associate the novel target word with an unfamiliar object. While both groups of infants learned to identify the referent of the novel word, only those with additional familiarization showed the mispronunciation effect observed in earlier studies. This result suggests that prior exposure to a particular word form may facilitate early lexical learning by enabling the child to form a phonetic representation that is more detailed and robust when it comes time to associate the word form with a meaning, similar to long-term auditory priming effects observed in adults and older children (Fisher, Church, and Chambers, 2004). However, these results still do not explain the ERP findings of Mills et al. (2004) showing that for fourteen-month-olds, even familiar words like *bear* did not evoke different responses from phonetic neighbors like *gare*. Thus, while a frequency-based explanation is highly parsimonious, there are still other factors that need to be examined.

Werker and colleagues suggest a different kind of explanation for the failures of early word learners to encode phonological details: an attentional resource conflict that impedes access to the full specificity of phonetic representations by infants in difficult word-learning tasks (Werker and Fennell, 2004). When the fourteen-month-old infant has to integrate novel visual and auditory information simultaneously, attempting to categorize an unfamiliar object and at the same time link it to a new word form, the cognitive load interferes with phonological processing. According to the PRIMIR model developed by Werker and Curtin (2005), such attentional demands inherent in the task of word–object mapping account for the failure of infants to detect the switch. However, while this proposal could explain the results of Stager and Werker (1997), it does so in terms of the demands of a particular experimental task. In a novel word learning paradigm that allowed more time for consolidation (e.g., Ballem and Plunkett, 2005), it might still be possible for infants to make use of phonetic detail in learning novel words that are minimal pairs. Support for this view comes from a recent study in which infants tested in a visual preference procedure rather than the switch paradigm were able to identify an object mapped to either *bin* or *din* at greater than chance levels (Yoshida et al., 2009). But although the fourteen-month-old participants' looking to the correct object was significantly greater than chance, their level of preference was very small, suggesting that the difference in results between the visual preference and switch procedures may simply be that one is more cognitively demanding or the other is more precise in its ability to measure fine differences. This result provides further support for the work of Swingley and Aslin (2000; 2002), suggesting that phonetic detail is present even in words learned in the laboratory, however fragile these initial representations may be.

The phonological specificity of the words children learn first has been a source of persistent interest because this question bears directly on the relationship between the sophisticated auditory pattern recognition skills of infants in their first year and their later lexical development. Although the failure in the switch task at fourteen months found by Stager and Werker (1997) remains puzzling, knowledge of the lexical representations of early word learners has increased tremendously. It now appears that young word learners do have access to detailed phonetic information in words, just as they did a few months earlier as infants, contrary to hypotheses positing reorganization or discontinuity. But learning to interpret a new word involves much more than learning to recognize an auditory pattern: Appreciating phonetic and semantic detail in a new word initially requires more attention (Werker and Curtin, 2005) and more exposure (Swingley, 2007) than previously thought. As Naigles (2002) has aptly characterized the situation: "Form is easy, meaning is hard."

6 Developing skill in interpreting familiar words

Over their second year, children typically learn to speak a few hundred words, and beginning around eighteen months, many show evidence of an increase in the rate of lexical learning known as the "vocabulary spurt." Although it is more difficult to track receptive language growth through spontaneous behavior, children reveal progress in understanding through increasingly differentiated verbal and behavioral responses to speech. Until recently, research on early lexical comprehension has focused almost exclusively on questions about what words children "know" and how this knowledge is acquired, that is, the principles that guide their decisions in mapping new words to potential meanings (see Bloom, 2002; Woodward and Markman, 1997). Here we focus on a different aspect of early receptive language competence, reviewing research that explores how children put their lexical knowledge to use. These studies ask how young language learners develop efficiency over the second year in interpreting familiar words in fluent speech.

The majority of research on early comprehension has used methodologies that rely on offline measures (see Bloom, 2002), that is, measures based on children's responses to a spoken word or sentence *after* it is complete rather than as it is heard and processed. For example, with diary observations and parental report checklists of vocabulary, the judgment that a child does or does not "understand" a word such as *cup* or *eat* is made informally by adults interacting with the child in everyday life. In the case of offline experimental measures, judgments are based on the child's behavior in a more controlled situation, with a clearly operationalized response measure such as pointing to an object given two or more alternatives. While offline procedures may enable researchers to assess whether or not a child responds systematically in a way that indicates some understanding, such measures are inherently limited in their potential for illuminating underlying processes in the development of skill in interpreting familiar and novel words. Because offline measures do not tap into the real-time properties of spoken language, they can only capture the endpoint of the process of interpretation. As a consequence, data from offline procedures are often interpreted as all-or-none measures of competence, for example, as evidence that a child either "knows" or "does not know" the word *cup* at fifteen months, revealing little about the child's developing efficiency in identifying and interpreting this and other familiar words in continuous speech.

Of course it is possible that an observable behavior indicating understanding of a particular word at fifteen months reflects a sudden epiphany. However, at this early stage of word learning it is more likely that the child's spontaneous demonstration of knowledge was preceded by a gradual strengthening of the association between this word and the class of objects this word is used to refer to, a process not as easily observed in spontaneous behavior. Haith (1998) has stressed the importance of tracking such incremental progress in cognitive development, urging researchers to think more in terms of graded concepts for the acquisition of "partial knowledge" instead of dichotomous terms that infants at a certain age either have or do not have a mature ability. Maratsos (1998) makes a similar point in discussing methodological difficulties in tracking the acquisition of grammar. Much of language acquisition goes on "underground," he argues, since intermediate stages of developing knowledge systems rarely show up directly in the child's behavior. To understand how the system progresses to mature competence in lexical as well as in grammatical development, it is necessary to gain access to these underground stages of partial knowledge. Researchers using online measures of spoken language processing with infants and young children are now making progress in that direction. Here we review recent findings based on online measures from two different procedures now used to investigate spoken language understanding by very young children: measures of neural responses in an ERP paradigm, and measures of gaze patterns in an eyetracking paradigm. Both procedures yield gradient measures of the young listeners' responses to the speech signal as it unfolds, illuminating different aspects of children's developing skill in making sense of spoken language over the second year.

6.1 *Using ERP measures to investigate early comprehension*

The event-related potential reflects brain activity in response to a specific stimulus event. In studies with adults, particular components of the ERP response to linguistic stimuli have been linked to phonological, semantic, and syntactic processing (Osterhout, McLaughlin, and Bersick, 1997), and recent developmental studies have begun to ask whether and when children show comparable responses in each of these three aspects of language processing (Friederici, 2005). As mentioned earlier, researchers interested in early phonological development have found that infants by the age of ten months show distinctive ERP responses to words presumed to be familiar versus unfamiliar, and that these differential neural responses are evident within 250 ms. of word onset (Kooijman et al., 2005; Thierry et al., 2003). Only a few ERP studies so far have focused on lexical-semantic processing of individual words. Mills, Coffey-Corina, and Neville (1993) compared the responses of thirteen- and twenty-month-olds to words reported by parents to be understood or not understood by the child. They found that patterns of brain activity associated with infants' responses to familiar words became more lateralized over this age range and similar in other ways to those of adults in comprehension tasks. While the younger infants showed bilateral differences in brain activity to known versus unknown words, the older infants showed unilateral differences in activity in the left hemisphere. Moreover, those thirteen-month-olds who were relatively more advanced in lexical development also showed a somewhat more mature ERP response, that is, more similar to that of the twenty-month-olds. However, it was not clear from these results whether it was overall vocabulary size or experience with individual word–object associations that was responsible for the dynamic shifts with age in the pattern of ERP activity. Moreover, because the auditory stimuli in this study were presented with no visual referents, it was also not clear that semantic processing was involved. To address these issues, a follow-up study measured ERPs from twenty-month-old infants with high and low expressive vocabulary scores for novel words they had just learned, either paired with an object or not paired with an object (Mills et al., 2005). The authors concluded that infants' individual experience with words in a meaningful context is a crucial factor in determining the patterns of brain activity that occur during lexical processing. As the child's experience with particular words increases, this leads to increased hemispheric specialization in the brain activity associated with these words.

While the most striking finding in the Mills et al. (1993) study was the extent of change in the *topography* of the ERP response to known and novel words over the second year, other studies have focused on developmental changes in the *time course* of responses to familiar and unfamiliar words. A question of particular interest is when young language learners begin to show neural responses known to be strongly associated with lexical-semantic processing in adults, such as the ERP component known as the N400, a negative waveform peaking at around 400 ms. The N400 effect is manifested in a larger amplitude for a word that is semantically incongruous in a particular context as compared to a word that is expected in that context (e.g., *He wore a hat on his foot/head*). Moreover, the amplitude of the N400, which is thought to indicate semantic integration difficulties, is sensitive to the immediate context of a particular word regardless of whether that context is a single word, a sentence, or a longer discourse (see Kutas and Federmeier, 2000). In a series of studies with German-learning children, Friedrich and Friederici (2005) used an ERP paradigm to investigate the development of semantic knowledge as well as phonological knowledge about possible word forms between the ages of twelve and nineteen months. On each trial they presented a picture of a familiar object accompanied by one of four types of auditory stimulus: a congruent familiar word that matched the name of the object, an incongruent familiar

word that did not match the object, or a "pseudoword" that was either phonotactically legal or illegal in German. Although twelve-month-olds responded differently to congruous and incongruous words paired with familiar pictures, they did not show an N400 effect, which only began to emerge around fourteen months. However, by nineteen months an N400 was more clearly evident in response to both semantically incongruous words and phonotactically legal pseudowords, although not in response to pseudowords that were phonotactically illegal.

The Friedrich and Friederici (2005) findings showed that when infants are tested in a semantic processing task, the ERP response characteristic of adult lexical-semantic processing begins to emerge during the second year. However, when compared to the mature form of the N400 response, the effect observed in fourteen- and nineteen-month-olds began somewhat later and was longer in duration, suggesting that lexical-semantic processing is slower overall in children than in adults. Another important finding was that infants did not respond to psuedowords as adults do. In studies with adults, the N400 amplitude is typically larger for phonotactically legal pseudowords than for real words (e.g., *dottle* versus *bottle*), presumably reflecting the listener's difficulty in accessing a lexical representation for the pseudoword in the mental lexicon. However, infants did not respond differentially to pseudowords and incongruous real words, as long as the nonwords were phonotactically plausible. This result is hardly surprising, given that an infant just beginning to build a vocabulary may be able to distinguish between phonotactically legal and illegal word forms, but cannot possibly know whether a phonotactically legal word form is "pseudo" or not. For a one-year-old who can correctly interpret only 500 words, all but a handful of the tens of thousands of words in the adult vocabulary are not yet represented in the mental lexicon. While an adult native speaker of English can immediately decide that *dottle* is indeed a *possible* word, while rejecting it as an *actual* word in the language, an infant in the second year can only make the first call. An unfamiliar word leads reliably to an N400 response for adult listeners because it is unexpected, although infants encounter unfamiliar words all the time. One interpretation of the finding that nineteen-month-olds responded similarly to known words and pseudowords is that they consider all unfamiliar but phonotactically plausible word forms as potential lexical items for which they will eventually discover meanings, an approach that would seem to be adaptive for the young language learner.

Recent research using measures of neural responses during lexical processing is providing new insights into the development of infants' skill in spoken language understanding, extending previous research based on offline measures in several important ways: ERP studies reveal gradual change over the second year in the brain areas involved in semantic processing, with greater hemispheric lateralization as the child increases in age and experience with language. Moreover, by providing precise measures of the time course of young children's responses to speech, these studies also reveal the gradual emergence of adult-like patterns of response to semantic anomalies in the temporal as well as the spatial domain. These promising recent findings suggest that research using ERP and other more sensitive brain measures will lead to greater understanding of the neural mechanisms that underlie the early development of receptive language skill.

6.2 *Using eyetracking measures to investigate early comprehension*

To understand spoken language, children must learn to make sense of rapidly spoken strings of words, interpreting fluent speech incrementally using different sources of linguistic and nonlinguistic information. Fluent understanding by adults occurs automatically without time for reflection, so it is important to study the listener's online interpretation *during* speech processing using online measures that monitor the time

course of the listener's response in relation to key points in the speech signal. Some of the classic online techniques used in psycholinguistic research with adults (e.g., phoneme monitoring, gating, and cross-modal priming) were adapted for use with school-aged children, but the task demands were problematic for younger children. However, refinements in eyetracking procedures for use with children in recent years have provided a powerful new methodology for exploring the early emergence of skill in language comprehension. Automated eyetracking procedures have been used very productively with adults, (e.g., Tanenhaus et al., 2000) as well as with preschool children (e.g., Snedeker and Trueswell, 2004), although not to the same extent with younger children. In studies with infants, some developmental researchers have used a simpler two-alternative "preferential looking" procedure that relies on summary measures of looking time to a named picture (e.g., Golinkoff et al., 1987; Meints, Plunkett, and Harris, 1999). However, such preferential looking measures do not monitor the time course of the infant's response to the unfolding speech signal. While looking preference can reveal greater attention to one picture over another, it provides no more information than a traditional offline measure of object choice. Another version of the two-alternative procedure is similar in presentation format but differs importantly in measurement techniques and methods of data analysis (e.g., Fernald et al., 1998; Swingley and Aslin, 2002). This "looking-while-listening" procedure incorporates the same online temporal measures of speed and accuracy used in eyetracking studies with adults and older children, enabling more sensitive assessment of children's developing efficiency in interpreting familiar words in different contexts (Fernald et al., 2008).

In a cross-sectional study using the looking-while-listening paradigm, Fernald et al. (1998) found that English-learning infants made dramatic gains in the efficiency of word recognition over the second year. Infants looked at pictures of familiar objects while listening to speech naming

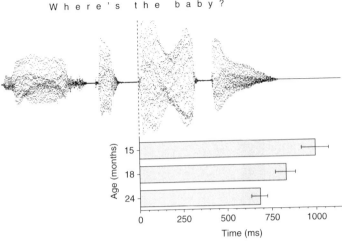

Figure 6.3. Mean latencies to initiate a shift in gaze from the distracter picture to the target picture, measured from the beginning of the spoken target word, for fifteen-, eighteen-, and twenty-four-month-old infants. This analysis included only those trials in which the infant was initially looking at the incorrect picture and then shifted to the correct picture when the target word was spoken. The graph is aligned with an amplitude waveform of one of the stimulus sentences. Figure from Fernald et al. (1998). Reprinted by permission of SAGE Publications.

one of the objects, and their eye movements were coded frame by frame by highly trained coders blind to trial type, yielding a detailed record of gaze patterns time-locked to key points in the auditory stimulus. The developmental changes in the speed and accuracy of understanding were striking: While fifteen-month-olds responded inconsistently and shifted their gaze to the appropriate picture only after the offset of the target word, twenty-four-month-olds were faster and more reliable, initiating a shift in gaze before the target word had been completely spoken (see Figure 6.3). A similar pattern of developmental change in speech processing efficiency across the second year was found in a parallel study with Spanish-learning infants from Latino families living in the United States (Hurtado, Marchman, and Fernald, 2007). Extending these findings in a longitudinal design, Fernald et al. (2006) followed sixty English-learning infants at multiple time points from twelve to twenty-five months, asking whether measures of speed and accuracy in

word recognition were stable over time and to what extent individual differences in processing efficiency were related to traditional offline measures of lexical and grammatical development. Analyses of growth curves showed that those children who were faster and more accurate in online comprehension at twenty-five months were also those who showed faster and more accelerated growth in expressive vocabulary and grammatical complexity across the second year. Infants' success at interpreting familiar words in degraded speech is also correlated with vocabulary size (Zangl et al., 2005), further evidence that early development in speech processing efficiency is related to growth in central domains of language competence.

This impressive increase in speed and accuracy over the second year shows that young children are increasingly able to identify words incrementally, responding based on partial phonetic information rather than waiting to hear the whole word. One consequence of incremental processing is that the young language learner is increasingly confronted with problems of temporary ambiguity. When Allopenna, Magnuson, and Tanenhaus (1998) presented adults with objects that included candy and a candle and asked them to *pick up the can-*, participants waited to hear the next speech sound before orienting to the appropriate object, postponing their response until the final syllable of the target word made it clear which object was the intended referent. The child who hears *Where's the dog?* in the presence of a dog and a doll is also faced with temporary ambiguity, given that *dog* and *doll* overlap phonetically and are thus indistinguishable for the first 300 ms or so. Swingley, Pinto, and Fernald (1999) found that twenty-four-month-olds in this situation also delayed their response by about 300 ms until disambiguating information became available. Even when they heard *only* the initial phonemes in a familiar word (e.g., the isolated first syllable of *baby* or *kitty*), eighteen-month-olds were able to use this limited information to identify the appropriate referent (Fernald, Swingley, and Pinto, 2001). Further evidence that infants interpret phonetic information in a probabilistic fashion during lexical processing comes from the studies by Swingley and Aslin (2000; 2002) mentioned earlier, showing that even younger infants can identify familiar words when they are mispronounced (e.g., *baby* versus *vaby*), although they respond more strongly to the correct than to the incorrect version.

Such results from eyetracking studies that use detailed time course measures show that infants make rapid improvement in both speed and accuracy of spoken word recognition across the second year. Although twenty-four-month-olds are somewhat slower than adults to interpret a familiar object name in a simple sentence frame, consistent with findings of research on ERP responses in lexical processing tasks, two-year-olds can identify the named referent within a fraction of a second of hearing the onset of the noun. Moreover, measures of individual differences in speed of response to familiar words at twenty-five months are related not only to trajectories of vocabulary growth across the second year (Fernald et al.,

2006) but also to traditional offline measures of language and cognitive abilities in middle childhood (Marchman and Fernald, 2008). These findings indicate that developmental gains in the efficiency of online processing in infancy are linked both to concurrent and long-term growth in lexical and grammatical competence.

6.3 *Interpreting words in combination*

Although infants may start making sense of language one word at a time, by their second year they are beginning to combine words in speech production and to understand increasingly complex multiword utterances. The young child learning to interpret fluent speech is confronted constantly with ambiguity on multiple levels, facing the challenges of identifying which unfamiliar sound sequences in the speech stream are possible words, determining what those novel words might refer to, and figuring out how those words can be combined and recombined to convey many different kinds of meaning. As children begin to appreciate regularities at higher levels of linguistic organization in the second and third year, they can increasingly make use of their emerging lexical and morphosyntactic knowledge to identify and interpret new lexical items and find meaning in the strings of words they hear. A review of developmental research on syntactic processing is beyond the scope of a chapter focusing on early word recognition, but we describe here a few recent studies exploring children's early use of morphosyntactic information in the noun phrase, as they attend to (or ignore) determiners in the process of interpreting object names and establishing reference.

Although the article *the* is one of the words English-learning children hear most frequently, it is never among the first words they speak. The observation that children produce dozens of nouns before they begin to use determiners led researchers to wonder whether spontaneous speech really captures what children "know" about language. In an early experimental study, Petretic and Tweney (1977) found that two-year-old children noticed syntactic anomalies in the speech they heard (e.g., *Throw ronta ball* versus *Throw me the ball*), revealing an awareness of linguistic regularities not yet evident in their own productions. Gerken and McIntosh (1993) pursued this question further by more systematically manipulating the functor words preceding familiar object names. In an offline picture book task, children responded more accurately to requests in which the article was grammatical than when the article was replaced by a nonce syllable, confirming that a violation of the determiner–noun pattern could disrupt the process of sentence interpretation. Extending these earlier findings, Zangl and Fernald (2007) used online measures to examine the timing of the disruption in response to an anomalous article before a familiar noun (*Where's po ball?* versus *Where's the ball?)* in children from eighteen to thirty-six months. They found that younger and linguistically less advanced children who did not yet use articles in their own speech were slower and less accurate in recognizing a familiar noun preceded by a nonce syllable than by a grammatical article, with disruption occurring within milliseconds of hearing the target noun. However, older and linguistically more advanced children showed no disruption; they were able to listen through a nonce article preceding a familiar word.

The apparent indifference of linguistically more advanced children to violations of the familiar article–noun sequence in this experiment could at first seem puzzling. One might expect children who produce articles in their own speech to be *more* vulnerable to disruption when encountering an uninterpretable functor-like syllable in the speech stream, as compared to children who have not yet begun to use determiners as grammatical elements in multiword utterances. However, the negative findings with linguistically more advanced children can also be interpreted as a sign of more advanced competence in speech processing, rather than as a paradoxical failure to notice the ungrammatical word. Because the sentences used as stimuli were highly predictable, all

ending in familiar nouns in prosodically similar carrier frames, the words preceding the noun were redundant and uninformative. Efficient processing in this case could take the form of ignoring an ambiguous but irrelevant nonce syllable in the process of rapidly identifying the object name that is the focus of the sentence. The younger children may not have been able to take advantage of this redundancy because the target words were less well known to them, and because they did not yet appreciate articles as grammatical elements separable from the noun that follows.

Zangl and Fernald (2007) explored this possibility in a second experiment using a less predictable processing task, in which thirty-four-month-olds were taught two novel words and then tested on sentences in which the newly learned words were preceded by nonce syllables or grammatical articles. Although more linguistically advanced children at this age could ignore an anomalous article in conjunction with a familiar noun in a highly redundant context, they were significantly slower and less accurate in identifying a newly learned target word when it followed a nonce syllable than a grammatical article. That is, while children could ignore an anomalous functor-like word when interpreting a sentence in a highly redundant context, the same anomalous element was disruptive when they were listening for a less familiar object name and uncertainty was higher, even for linguistically more experienced children. Highly frequent function words are typically much less salient than content words as acoustic elements in the speech stream, and speakers reduce the salience of function words even further when the linguistic context is more predictable (Bell et al., 2003). Skilled listeners can compensate for this reduction in phonological specificity by relying on top-down linguistic knowledge to make sense of the utterance, as long as other features of the sentence context are sufficiently predictable. The Zangl and Fernald findings provide new evidence for the gradual emergence of this kind of flexibility in speech processing over the first three years of life. The young language learner who is just beginning to use words in combination relies on surface regularities and lexical familiarity in the speech input, and so finds it more difficult to interpret a familiar object name when it co-occurs with an unexpected functor-like nonce word. The older and linguistically more advanced child has had more extensive experience with determiners as a class of words that occur in highly constrained contexts with varying pronunciation. Increasingly, acoustic variability within this class of words can be ignored as irrelevant as long as the discourse context is predictable. More advanced language learners are also more efficient in anticipating the focus of the spoken sentence, in this case the upcoming object label, and thus can ignore a "noisy" syllable in place of the article when it is unlikely to modulate the meaning of the focused word.

Although children learning English can afford to ignore a redundant article in some contexts, articles in languages with grammatical gender are potentially more informative. In Spanish, for example, all nouns have grammatical gender, with obligatory gender marking on preceding articles (e.g., $la[_f]$, $el[_m]$, *the*), and adult native speakers of languages with grammatical gender exploit this cue in online sentence interpretation (Dahan, et al., 2000). Although the article *the* reveals little about the English noun that follows, hearing *la* or *el* in Spanish can inform the listener about the gender and number of the upcoming noun and in some contexts can facilitate identification of the referent before the noun is spoken. To investigate the early development of this ability, Lew-Williams and Fernald (2007) tested Spanish-learning children in the looking-while-listening procedure. Children saw pairs of pictures with names of either the same (e.g., *la pelota*, "ball$[_f]$," *la galleta*, "cookie$[_f]$") or different grammatical gender (e.g., *la pelota*, *el zapato*, "shoe$[_m]$"), as they heard sentences referring to one of the pictures (e.g., *Encuentra la pelota*, "Find the ball"). On same-gender trials, the article could not be used to identify the referent before the noun was spoken; on different-

gender trials, the gender-marked article was potentially useful in predicting the referent of the subsequent noun. If young Spanish-learning children are able to take advantage of gender agreement in interpreting speech, they should orient to the correct referent more quickly on different-gender trials than on same-gender trials. Indeed, children were significantly faster to orient to the referent on different-gender trials than on same-gender trials, as were native Spanish-speaking adults tested in the same procedure (see Figure 6.4). Moreover, children's ability to take advantage of grammatical gender cues was correlated with productive measures of lexical and grammatical competence. Although they were slower overall than adults in interpreting spoken language, young Latino children learning Spanish as their first language already demonstrated a significant processing advantage characteristic of adult native speakers but not of second-language learners (Guillelmon and Grosjean, 2001). With only a few hundred words in their productive lexicon, two- to three-year-old Spanish-learning children are able to identify familiar nouns ninety ms faster when a gender-marked article gives them an edge. This ability to exploit morphosyntactic information in the process of establishing reference reveals how the young child learning a richly inflected language makes progress in "becoming a native listener" (Werker, 1989).

7 Conclusions

While early traces of connections among word forms and meanings are evident in the first year of life, learning a word is a gradual process. Much of this learning process occurs underground: Representations of the forms and meanings of words are built up gradually before they begin to surface in children's productive vocabularies. Perhaps the best evidence for this graded, online view of early language understanding comes from measures like eyetracking and event-related potentials. Unlike traditional looking-time or offline measures, these online methods

(a)

¿ Dónde está el pájaro?

SAME
gender

el pájaro   el caballo

DIFFERENT
gender

el pájaro   la vaca

(b)

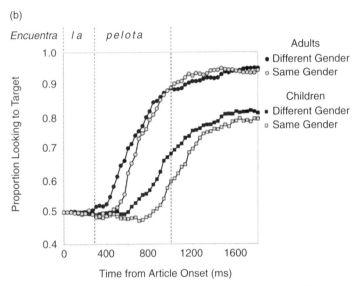

Figure 6.4. A. Examples of stimuli on same-gender and different-gender trials in Spanish. B. Curves depict changes in the proportion shifts from distractor to target picture by three-year-olds and adults as the article and noun unfold, measured from article onset (in ms). Filled squares show responses on different-gender trials, when the article was potentially informative; open squares show responses on same-gender trials when the article was not informative. Vertical dashed lines indicate offsets of article and target word. Adapted from Lew-Williams and Fernald (2007), by permission of SAGE Publications.

allow for the detailed characterization of individual infants, allowing researchers to track the development of "partial knowledge." In addition, going forward, these methods will provide the best chance for researchers to test quantitative as well as qualitative models of development.

This gradualist view contrasts dramatically with the binary construal of word

learning as a process of "fast mapping" between word forms and their meanings, a metaphor that is often used along with statistics about the exponential growth of vocabulary. As demonstrated by the original work on "fast mapping," only a few exposures may be necessary for a veteran word learner to form a partial representation of a word (Carey and Bartlett, 1978). However, much more practice is necessary before the same learner can successfully interpret and produce that word appropriately across a range of contexts. In this review, we have attempted to give an overview both of the developmental progression in skills involved in word recognition by the young language learner, and in the historical progression of research on early spoken word recognition. In many ways, these two trajectories mirror one another, proceeding from the early groundwork laid by studies of auditory language processing and speech perception to a more complete understanding of the complexities involved in learning to communicate using words.

References

Allopenna, P. D., Magnuson, J. S., & Tanenhaus, M. K. (1998). Tracking the time course of spoken word recognition using eye movements: evidence for continuous mapping models. *Journal of Memory and Language*, 38, 419–39.

Aslin, R. N., Pisoni, D. B., & Jusczyk, P. W. (1983). Auditory development and speech perception in infancy. In Haith, M. M. & Campos J. J. (Eds.) *Infancy and the biology of development* (Vol. 2, pp. 573–687). Mussen, P. (Ed.) *Handbook of child psychology* (4th ed.). New York: Wiley.

Aslin, R. N., Saffran J. R., Newport, E. L. (1998). Computation of conditional probability statistics by 8-month-old infants. *Psychological Science*, 9, 321–24.

Ballem, K. D. & Plunkett, KIM (2005). Phonological specificity in children at 1; 2. *Journal of Child Language*, 32(01), 159–73.

Baldwin, D. (1993). Early referential understanding: Infants' ability to recognize acts for what they are. *Developmental Psychology*, 29, 832–43.

Bell, A., Jurafsky D., Fosler-Lussier, E., Girand, C., Gregory, M., & Gildea, D. (2003). Effects of disfluencies, predictability, and utterance position on word form variation in English conversation. *Journal of the Acoustical Society of America*, 113, 1001–24.

Bloom, P. (2002). How children learn the meanings of words: Learning, development, and conceptual change. Cambridge, MA: MIT Press.

Brown, C. & Matthews, J. (1997). The role of feature geometry in the development of phonemic contrasts. In Hannahs, S. J. & Young-Scholten

M. (Eds.) *Focus on Phonological Acquisition* (pp. 67–112). Amsterdam: John Benjamins.

Brown, R. (1957). Linguistic determinism and the part of speech. *Journal of Abnormal and Social Psychology*, 55, 1–5.

(1973). *A first language: The early stages*. Cambridge, MA: Harvard University Press.

Carey, S. & Bartlett, E. (1978). Acquiring a single new word. *Papers and Reports on Child Language Development*, 15, 17–29.

Charles-Luce, J. & Luce, P. A. (1990). Similarity neighbourhoods of words in young children's lexicons. *Journal of Child Language*, 17(1), 205–15.

(1995). An examination of similarity neighbourhoods in young children's receptive vocabularies. *Journal of Child Language*, 22(3), 727–35.

Coady, J. A. & Aslin, R. N. (2003). Phonological neighbourhoods in the developing lexicon. *Journal of Child Language*, 30(02), 441–69.

Curtin, S., Mintz, T. H., & Christiansen, M. H. (2005). Stress Changes the Representational Landscape: Evidence from Word Segmentation. *Cognition*, 96, 233–62.

Dahan, D., Swingley, D., Tanenhaus, M. K., & Magnuson, J. S. (2000). Linguistic gender and spoken-word recognition in French. *Journal of Memory & Language*, 42, 465–80.

Eimas, P., Siqueland, E., Jusczyk, P., & Vigorito, J. (1971). Speech perception in infants. *Science*, 171, 303–06.

Fenson, L., Dale, P. S., Reznick, J. S., Bates, E., Thal, D. J., & Pethick, S. J. et al. (1994). Variability in Early Communicative Development. *Monographs of the Society for Research in Child Development*, 59(5).

Fernald, A. & Hurtado, N. (2006). Names in frames: Infants interpret words in sentence frames faster than words in isolation. *Developmental Science*, 9, F33–F40.

Fernald, A., Pinto, J. P., Swingley, D., Weinberg, A., & McRoberts, G. W. (1998). Rapid gains in speed of verbal processing by infants in the second year. *Psychological Science*, 9, 72–5.

Fernald, A., Perfors, A., & Marchman, V. (2006). Picking up speed in understanding: Speech processing efficiency and vocabulary growth across the second year. *Developmental Psychology*, 42, 98–116.

Fernald, A., Swingley, D., & Pinto, J. P. (2001). When half a word is enough: Infants can recognize spoken words using partial phonetic information. *Child Development*, 72, 1003–15.

Fernald, A., Zangl, R., Portillo, A. L., & Marchman, V. A. (2008). Looking while listening: Using eye movements to monitor spoken language comprehension by infants and young children. In Sekerina I., Fernández E. & Clahsen H., (Eds.), *Language processing in children*. Amsterdam: John Benjamins.

Fisher, C., Church, B. A., & Chambers, K. E. (2004). Learning to identify spoken words. In Hall, D. G. & Waxman, S. R. (Eds.) *Weaving a Lexicon* (pp. 3–40). Cambridge MA: MIT Press.

Frank, M. C., Goodman, N. D., & Tenenbaum, J. B. (2009). Using speakers' referential intentions to model early cross-situational word learning. *Psychological Science, 20*, 578–585.

Friederici, A. D. (2005). Neurophysiological markers of early language acquisition: From syllables to sentences. *Trends in Cognitive Sciences, 9*, 481–8.

Friedrich, M. & Friederici, A. D. (2005). Semantic sentence processing reflected in the event-related potentials of one- and two-year-old children. *Neuroreport, 16*, 1801–4.

Gerken, L., & McIntosh, B. J. (1993). Interplay of function morphemes and prosody in early language. *Developmental Psychology, 29*, 448–57.

Golinkoff, R. M., Hirsh-Pasek, K., Cauley, K. M. & Gordon, L. (1987). The eyes have it: Lexical and syntactic comprehension in a new paradigm. *Journal of Child Language, 14*, 23–45.

Graf Estes, K., Evans, J. L., Alibali, M. W., & Saffran, J. R. (2007). Can infants map meaning to newly segmented words?: Statistical segmentation and word learning. *Psychological Science, 18*, 254–60.

Guillelmon, D. & Grosjean, F. (2001). The gender marking effect in spoken word recognition: The case of bilinguals. *Memory & Cognition, 29*, 503–11.

Haith, M. (1998). Who put the cog in infant cognition? Is rich interpretation too costly? *Infant Behavior and Development, 21*, 167–79.

Hallé, P. & de Boysson-Bardies, B. (1994). Emergence of an early receptive lexicon: Infants' recognition of words. *Infant Behavior and Development, 17*, 119–29.

Hirsh-Pasek, K. & Golinkoff, R. M. (2006). *Action meets word: How children learn verbs*. Oxford UK: Oxford University Press.

Hurtado, N., Marchman, V. A., & Fernald, A. (2007). Spoken word recognition by Latino children learning Spanish as their first language. *Journal of Child Language, 37*, 227–49.

Johnson, E., Jusczyk, P. (2001). Word segmentation by 8-month-olds: When speech cues count more than statistics. *Journal of Memory and Language, 44*, 548–67.

Jusczyk, P. (1997). *The discovery of spoken language*. Cambridge, MA: MIT Press.

Jusczyk, P. & Aslin, R. (1995). Infants' detection of the sound patterns of words in fluent speech. *Cognitive Psychology, 29*, 1–23.

Jusczyk, P., Cutler, A., & Redanz, N. (1993). Infants' preference for the predominant stress patterns of English words. *Child Development, 64*, 675–87.

Jusczyk, P., Friederici, A., Wessels, J., Svenkerud, V., & Jusczyk, A. (1993). Infants' sensitivity to the sound patterns of native language words. *Journal of Memory and Language, 32*, 402–20.

Jusczyk, P. & Hohne, E. (1997). Infants' memory for spoken words. *Science, 277*, 1984–86.

Jusczyk, P., Hohne, E., & Bauman, A. (1999). Infants' sensitivity to allophonic cues for word segmentation. *Perception & Psychophysics, 61*, 1465–76.

Jusczyk, P., Houston, D., & Newsome, M. (1999). The beginnings of word segmentation in English-learning infants. *Cognitive Psychology, 39*, 159–207.

Kooijman, V., Hagoort, P., & Cutler, A. (2005). Electrophysiological evidence for prelinguistic infants' word recognition in continuous speech. *Cognitive Brain Research, 24*, 109–16.

Kuhl, P. K. (2004). Early language acquisition: Cracking the speech code. *Nature Reviews: Neuroscience, 5*, 831–43.

Kuhl, P. K., Williams, K. A., Lacerda, F., Stevens, K. N., & Lindblom, B. (1992). Linguistic experience alters phonetic perception in infants by 6 months of age. *Science, 255(5044)*, 606–8.

Kutas M., Federmeier K. D. (2000). Electrophysiology reveals semantic memory use in language comprehension. *Trends in Cognitive Sciences, 4*, 463–70.

Lew-Williams, C. & Fernald, A. (2007). Young children learning Spanish make rapid use of grammatical gender in spoken word recognition. *Psychological Science, 18*, 193–8.

Mandel, D. Jusczyk, P., & Pisoni, D. (1995). Infants' recognition of the sound patterns of their own names. *Psychological Science, 6*, 314–17.

Maratsos, M. (1998). The acquisition of grammar. In W. Damon (Series Ed.), D. Kuhn, & R. S. Siegler (Vol. Ed.), *Handbook of child psychology. Vol. 2: Cognition, perception and language* (5th ed., pp. 421–66). New York: Wiley.

Marchman, V. A. & Fernald, A. (2008). Speed of word recognition and vocabulary knowledge in infancy predict cognitive and language outcomes in later childhood. *Developmental Science, 11*, F9-F16.

Mattys, S. L., White, L., & Melhorn, J. F. (2005). Integration of multiple speech segmentation cues: A hierarchical framework. *Journal of Experimental Psychology: General, 134,* 477–500.

Meints, K., Plunkett, K., & Harris, P. L. (1999). When does an ostrich become a bird? The role of typicality in early word comprehension. *Developmental Psychology, 35,* 1072 – 78.

Metsala, J. L. & Walley, A. C. (1998). Spoken vocabulary growth and the segmental restructuring of lexical representations: Precursors to phonemic awareness and early reading ability. In Metsala, J. L. & Ehri, L. C. (Eds.) *Word recognition in beginning literacy* (pp. 89–120). New York: Earlbaum.

Miller, G. A., Heise, G. A., & Lichten, W. (1951). The intelligibility of speech as a function of the context of the test materials. *Journal of Experimental Psychology, 41,* 329–35.

Mills, D. L., Prat, C., Zangl, R., Stager, C. L., Neville, H. J., & Werker, J. F. (2004). Language Experience and the Organization of Brain Activity to Phonetically Similar Words: ERP Evidence from 14-and 20-Month-Olds. *Journal of Cognitive Neuroscience, 16,* 1452–64.

Mills, D. L., Coffey-Corina, S. A., & Neville, H. J. (1993). Language acquisition and cerebral specialization in 20-month-old infants. *Journal of Cognitive Neuroscience, 5,* 317–34.

Mills, D. L., Plunkett, K., Prat, C., & Schafer, G. (2005). Watching the infant brain learn words: effects of vocabulary size and experience. *Cognitive Development, 20,* 19–31.

Mills, J. H. (1975). Noise and children: A review of the literature. *Journal of the Acoustical Society of America, 58,* 767–79.

Naigles, L. R. (2002). Form is easy, meaning is hard: Resolving a paradox in early child language. *Cognition, 86,* 157–99.

Naigles, L. R., Bavin, E. L., & Smith, M. A. (2005). Toddlers recognize verbs in novel situations and sentences. *Developmental Science, 8,* 424–31.

Osterhout, L., McLaughlin, J., & Bersick, M. (1997). Event-related potentials and human language. *Trends in Cognitive Science, 1,* 203–9.

Pater, J., Stager, C., & Werker, J. (2004). The perceptual acquisition of phonological contrasts. *Language, 80,* 384–402.

Petretic, P., & Tweney, R. (1976). Does comprehension precede production? The development of children's responses to telegraphic sentences of varying grammatical adequacy. *Journal of Child Language, 4,* 201–9.

Pusey, E. B. (Trans.) (1949). The confessions of Saint Augustine. New York: Random House.

Roy, D. & Pentland, A. (2002). Learning words from sights and sounds: A computational model. *Cognitive Science, 26,* 113–46.

Saffran, J. R. (2003) Statistical language learning: Mechanisms and constraints. *Trends in Cognitive Science, 12,* 110–14.

Saffran, J. R., Aslin, R. N., & Newport, E. L. (1996). Statistical learning by 9-month-old infants. *Science, 274,* 1926–28.

Saffran, J. R. & Sahni, S. D. (this volume). Learning the sounds of language.

Samuel, A. G. & Sumner, M. (this volume). Current directions in research in spoken word recognition.

Seidenberg, M. S. (1997). Language acquisition and use: Learning and applying probabilistic constraints. *Science, 275(5306),* 1599–1603.

Silva-Pereyra, J., Rivera-Gaxiola, M., & Kuhl, P. K. (2005). An event-related brain potential study of sentence comprehension in preschoolers: semantic and morphosyntactic processing. *Cognitive Brain Research, 23,* 247–58.

Siskind, J. M. (1996). A computational study of cross-situational techniques for learning word-to-meaning mappings. *Cognition, 61,* 39–91.

Smith, L. & Yu, C. (2008). Infants rapidly learn word-referent mappings via cross-situational statistics. *Cognition, 106,* 1558–68.

Snedeker, J. & Trueswell, J. C. (2004). The developing constraints on parsing decisions: The role of lexical-biases and referential scenes in child and adult sentence processing. *Cognitive Psychology, 49,* 238–99.

Stager, C. L. & Werker, J. F. (1997). Infants listen for more phonetic detail in speech perception than in word-learning tasks. *Nature, 388(6640),* 381–2.

Swingley, D. (2005). 11-month-olds' knowledge of how familiar words sound. *Developmental Science, 8,* 432–43.

(2007). Lexical exposure and word-form encoding in 1.5-year-olds. *Developmental Psychology, 43(2),* 454–64.

Swingley, D. & Aslin, R. N. (2000). Spoken word recognition and lexical representation in very young children. *Cognition, 76(2),* 147–66.

(2002). Lexical neighborhoods and the word-form representations of 14-month-olds. *Psychological Science, 13,* 480–4.

Swingley, D., Pinto, J. P., & Fernald, A. (1999). Continuous processing in word recognition at 24 months. *Cognition, 71,* 73–108.

Taine, H. (1877). Cerebral vibrations and thought. *British Journal of Psychiatry, 23,* 1–9.

Tanenhaus, M. K., Magnuson, J. S., Dahan, D., & Chambers, C. G. (2000). Eye movements and lexical access in spoken language comprehension: evaluating a linking hypothesis between fixations and linguistic processing. *Journal of Psycholinguistic Research*, 29, 557–80.

Thierry, G., Vihman, M., & Roberts, M. (2003). Familiar words capture the attention of 11-month-olds in less than 250 ms. *Neuroreport*, 14, 2307–10.

Thiessen, E. D. & Saffran, J. R. (2003). When cues collide: Use of stress and statistical cues to word boundaries by 7- to 9-month-old infants. *Developmental Psychology*, 39, 706–16.

(2004). Spectral tilt as a cue to word segmentation in infancy and adulthood. *Perception & Psychophysics*, 66, 779–91.

Thorpe, K. & Fernald, A. (2006). Knowing what a novel word is not: Two-year-olds "listen through" ambiguous adjectives in fluent speech. *Cognition*, 100, 389–433.

Tiedemann, D. (1927). Observations on the development of the mental faculties of children (S. Langer & C. Murchison, Trans.). *Pedagogical Seminary and Journal of Genetic Psychology*, 34, 205–30. (Original work published in 1787)

Tomasello, M. (2001). Perceiving intentions and learning words in the second year of life. In M. Bowerman & S. Levinson (Eds.), *Language Acquisition and Conceptual Development*. Cambridge University Press.

Vitevitch, M. S., Luce, P. A., Pisoni, D. B., & Auer, E. T. (1999). Phonotactics, neighborhood activation, and lexical access for spoken words. *Brain and Language*, 68, 306–11.

Vouloumanos, A. & Werker, J. F. (2007). Listening to language at birth: Evidence for a bias for speech in neonates. *Developmental Science*, 10, 159–64.

Werker, J. F. (1989). Becoming a native listener: A developmental perspective on human speech perception. *American Scientist*, 77, 54–9.

Werker, J. F., Cohen, L. B., Lloyd, V. L., Casasola, M., & Stager, C. L. (1998). Acquisition of word-object associations by 14-month-old infants. *Developmental Psychology*, 34, 1289–1309.

Werker, J. F. & Curtin, S. (2005). PRIMIR: A developmental framework of infant speech processing. *Language Learning and Development*, 1, 197–234.

Werker, J. F. & Fennell, C. T. (2004). Listening to sounds versus listening to words: Early steps in word learning. In D. G. Hall & S. Waxman (Eds.), *Weaving a lexicon* (pp. 79–109). Cambridge, MA: MIT Press.

Werker, J. F., Fennell, C. T., Corcoran, K. M., & Stager, C. L. (2002). Infants' ability to learn phonetically similar words: Effects of age and vocabulary size. *Infancy*, 3, 1–30.

Werker, J. F. & Tees, R. C. (1984). Phonemic and phonetic factors in adult cross-language speech perception. *Journal of the Acoustical Society of America*, 75, 1866–78.

Werker, J. F. & Yeung, H. H. (2005). Infant speech perception bootstraps word learning. *Trends in Cognitive Sciences*, 9, 519–27.

Woodward, A. L. & Markman, E. M. (1997). Early word learning. In Damon, W., Kuhn, D., & Siegler, R. (Eds.) *Handbook of child psychology, (Vol. 2), Cognition, perception, and language*. New York: Wiley.

Woodward, A. L., Markman, E. M., & Fitzsimmons, C. M. (1994). Rapid word learning in 13- and 18-month-olds. *Developmental Psychology*, 30, 553–66.

Yoshida, K. A., Fennell, C. T., Swingley, D., & Werker, J. F. (2009). Fourteen-month-olds learn similar sounding words. *Developmental Science*, 12, 412–418.

Yu, C. & Ballard, D. (2007). A unified model of word learning: Integrating statistical and social cues. *Neurocomputing*, 70, 2149–65.

Yu, C., Ballard, D. H., & Aslin, R. N. (2005). The role of embodied intention in early lexical acquisition. *Cognitive Science*, 29, 961–1005.

Yu, C. & Smith, L. (2007). Rapid Word Learning Under Uncertainty via Cross-Situational Statistics. *Psychological Science*, 18, 414–20.

Zangl, R., Klarman, L., Thal, D. J., Fernald, A., & Bates, E. (2005). Dynamics of word comprehension in infancy: Development in timing, accuracy, and resistance to acoustic degradation. *Journal of Cognition and Development*, 6, 179–208.

Zangl, R. & Fernald, A. (2007). Increasing flexibility of children's online processing of grammatical and nonce determiners in fluent speech. *Language Learning and Development*.

CHAPTER 7

Event-Related Potentials and Magnetic Fields Associated with Spoken Word Recognition

Randy L. Newman, Kelly Forbes, and John F. Connolly

In this chapter we outline aspects of the temporal and spatial features of spoken word recognition (SWR) in the brain as established by event-related potential (ERP) and event-related magnetic field (ERMF) research. We begin with an overview of the ERP component that has had the most significant impact on the field – the N400. It is fair to say that this component's discovery has fuelled and continues to drive much of the ERP and magnetoencephalographic (MEG) research in language, although its functional significance remains controversial. In order to gain a true appreciation for the N400 and what it may tell us about SWR it is essential that we discuss its role in the visual word processing context within which it was discovered. Also, this visual word processing research highlights two of the major themes of this chapter: The N400 is not a unitary phenomenon but rather a response generated by varying collections of neurons that are circumstantially called upon during semantic/conceptual activity; and the N400 is but one of a number of related negativities reflecting stages or subsystems of a semantic/conceptual process.

Also, as will become apparent, both reading and speech perception share certain perceptual mechanisms such as phonological processing as well as neuroanatomical areas of activation. The appreciation of phonological processing in one modality is enhanced by knowledge of its functions in the other just as an understanding of how both reading and spoken word processing activate similar or overlapping brain regions tells us something more about these functions than either does alone.

1 Introduction

Speech comprehension and SWR are processes that seem to proceed with little effort on the part of the listener. It is something we all do automatically even as we do other apparently more complex tasks like driving a car, playing a computer game, or developing our own speech output during a discussion. Yet one need only consider comprehending speech in a nonnative language with which one is only moderately familiar and the complexity of the whole process becomes clear.

In this second language situation, it seems as if word boundary identification and phonemic, syntactic, and semantic processing can be measured not in the milliseconds it takes a native listener but in something approaching geological time! The "automaticity" of speech comprehension in one's native language is a product of repeated practice. Research has shown that this automaticity is based on perceptual learning which can begin at foetal and neonatal developmental stages (see review, Werker and Yeung, 2005). Also, attentional mechanisms linked to the anterior cingulate cortex and the dorsolateral prefrontal cortex are involved in the ability to comprehend language while engaged in other tasks (Botvinick et al., 2004; Roelofs and Hagoort, 2002).

Consider what is accomplished in processing a spoken word. The first element of the process is the disassembling of an acoustic stream into comprehensible linguistic elements. The acoustic and phonetic elements together with the linguistic context establish the bottom-up and top-down features that permit the development of both low-level (e.g., phonological) and high-level (e.g., semantic) expectations that result in the seemingly effortless and automatic processing of speech. Thus, amongst other things, the listener needs to identify word boundaries in order to identify individual word units within a continuous acoustic stream. Again, there is compelling evidence that this capability, which is a primary element of the speech recognition process, develops early in life and is based on phonetic coding (Werker and Yeung, 2005). Having isolated a unit, there follows a series of analyses including phonological, syntactic, and semantic – although such processing need not be as sequential as many accounts suggest (see Jackendoff, 2002). Instead, there is strong evidence from a variety of sources that the processing of the core features of a word proceeds in a cascading fashion from sound through syntax to meaning with one process beginning before the previous process has finished (see Jackendoff, 2002, p. 202).

There are, of course, other sublexical mechanisms such as prosody and tone, the importance of which varies according to the language. These various mechanisms must also be flexible enough to adjust for frequency variations in individual speakers (e.g., between children, men, and women), accent-based variations, and interference caused by environmental noise, be it broadband (e.g., factory) or phonologically based (e.g., a noisy pub) (Davis and Johnsrude, 2003; Scott and Johnsrude, 2003). Speech rate varies from person to person, which has consequences for syllable lengths which, in turn, are influenced by whether they are stressed or unstressed (Crystal and House, 1990). Rates vary even within an individual and potentially from moment to moment, resulting in considerable variability in the mapping of acoustic cues onto phonetic categories (Liberman et al., 1967; see review by Francis and Nusbaum, 1996). The native listener meets all of these challenges, seemingly with little or no effort. However, this apparent automaticity is attributable to the flexibility of the perceptual learning mechanisms which form the foundation of the language processing system(s) leading to findings such as improved perception of distorted speech with more exposure to it.

These issues are critically important for reaching any type of understanding of spoken word processing. In particular, the sublexical elements of speech comprehension will be emphasized in this chapter. These processes are observable in both ERP and ERMF studies and contribute to both the appearance of the N400 and the functions it reflects. As mentioned above, it would be a mistake to discuss the N400 and its appearance during spoken word processing without first discussing its discovery within a reading context.

2 The N400: A brief overview of the principal ERP component associated with language processing

It could be argued that the use of ERP in the study of language blossomed into the active and diverse area it now is with the discovery of the N400 in 1980 (Kutas and Hillyard,

1980). This negative-going waveform that reaches its maximum amplitude at about 400 ms after stimulus onset was seen in response to sequentially presented printed words that were incongruous to the semantic context of the sentences within which they occurred (e.g., "He takes coffee with cream and socks."). The subsequent two and a half decades of research have demonstrated that there is a greater variety of language-related stimulus characteristics that modulate the $N400$ than initially imagined. Thus, within sentence contexts the $N400$ occurs to or is modulated by, for example, congruous words terminating low, contextually constrained sentences (Connolly et al., 1990; 1992). It also occurs to open-class words in a developing sentence context and becomes progressively smaller to such words as the sentence context develops and provides contextual constraints (Van Petten, 1993). The $N400$ is seen in word-pair semantic priming paradigms (e.g., *bread–butter* versus *bread–house*) with the $N400$ amplitude being larger to the second word in a pair when it is *not* primed by the first (e.g., larger $N400$s would be seen to *house* compared to *butter*) (Anderson and Holcomb, 1995; Bentin et al., 1985; Holcomb and Neville, 1990). The $N400$ is also sensitive to a variety of lexical features of words such as being larger to concrete than abstract words (West and Holcomb, 2000), to low than high frequency words (an effect that disappears when the words are placed in a sentence context suggesting the effect is semantically based) (Van Petten, 1993), and to words with higher than lower density orthographic neighbourhoods (Holcomb et al., 2002).

Another feature to which the $N400$ is sensitive is the phonological aspects of written words. For example, there have been demonstrations of larger $N400$-like responses to nonrhyming word pairs during a rhyme judgment task (Rugg, 1984a, b). However, there is controversy as to whether the $N400$-like response observed in these and related studies is, in fact, the classic $N400$ seen to semantically incongruent sentence-ending words or words not primed by a preceding word. This controversy developed for

a variety of reasons, including the atypical scalp distribution of the rhyme generated $N400$ responses. In the intervening years, it has become clear that there are many versions of the $N400$ and more processes with which it is associated than purely semantics. Equally true, however, is that there has been a tendency to ascribe multiple functions to the $N400$ that are more accurately linked to other ERP components. These components are functionally independent of the $N400$ but reflect processes upon which the $N400$-related functions may depend such as form level (orthographic or phonological) analysis within a language context.

Two examples demonstrate $N400$ sensitivity to features of the eliciting stimuli or context and highlight interpretation issues particularly as they relate to other temporally proximal components that may affect $N400$-related processes or alter the $N400$'s appearance. The first example explores $N400$ responses to nonlinguistic stimuli within a priming context and the co-occurring but functionally distinct $N300$. The second example discusses the sensitivity of the $N400$ to phonological features of words during silent reading and the associated but functionally independent $N270$ that maps orthographic form. These two themes provide an essential context in which to discuss the PMN (an auditory modality response related to phonological processing) and $N400$ within SWR.

The $N400$ response was discovered in a linguistic context leading to its strong association with language, but it is *not* a purely linguistic response. For example, a number of studies demonstrate $N400$ modulation to photos and line drawings within priming paradigms. Several studies (Barrett and Rugg, 1989; Barrett et al., 1988) presented photos of faces with subjects being asked to determine whether the second of a pair of sequentially presented photos was the same person (from a different angle) or whether the second face had the same facial expression as the first. In this and other studies, it was reliably found that if the second photo showed either a different person or different facial expression, a negativity peaking at 400 ms was observed. This response was interpreted as being the same component as seen in language studies (i.e., the N400) and that this response could be modulated by both words and nonlinguistic stimuli within an associative priming paradigm. It was also observed that the N400 elicited to faces in the affective judgment study was more evenly distributed along the anterior–posterior axis compared to the language-related N400 that had the typical centro–parietal distribution. A subsequent priming study used line drawings of everyday objects (Barrett and Rugg, 1990). Primes and targets were presented in the usual sequential manner with half of the pairs reflecting matching associative relationships (e.g., *knife–fork*) and the other half characterized by non-matching relationships (e.g., *knife–nut*). Three results came out of these studies: 1. An N400 response was elicited to the second item if it failed to match the first; 2. The N400 occurred ~ 50 ms later than was typically seen in language-related N400 studies; and 3. Another negative component, N300, was found to precede the N400. The authors observed that no language study had found a similar pre-N400 negativity (which, at that time, was correct) and the response was hypothesized to be associated with picture processing in particular.

In a related study, Holcomb and McPherson (1994) used line drawings of objects in an associative priming paradigm in which subjects were not required to make an explicit comparison between the stimuli (as had been done by Barrett and colleagues), but rather simply make a response indicating whether they did or did not recognize the second drawing. This experimental design is procedurally more like language studies using lexical decision tasks. Results replicated the earlier work in finding both an N300 and N400. The atypical scalp distribution of the N400 in comparison to that seen in more traditional lexical decision research was attributed, at least in part, to the frontal distribution of the preceding N300. A subsequent study confirmed and extended these findings by demonstrating dissociation between the N300 and N400 and, on balance,

providing some support for the existence of an amodal semantic system (McPherson and Holcomb, 1999). Briefly, this latter study used photos of familiar and unfamiliar (unidentifiable) objects in an associative priming, object identification task (Experiment 2 in McPherson and Holcomb, 1999) in three conditions that presented: 1. Objects could be identified and also shared a semantic relationship (e.g., a photo of a hamburger followed by a photo of a package of French fries); 2. Objects could be identified but did *not* share a semantic relationship (e.g., a photo of a hamburger followed by a photo of a chair); and 3. Objects could be identified only in the first photo (e.g., a photo of a comb) followed by a second photo of an unidentifiable object. Clear N400 responses to the second member of stimulus pairs in the unrelated and unidentifiable conditions were observed. However, of particular interest was their replication of an earlier result, the dissociation between the N300 and N400, and their repeated assertion that the atypical distribution of the N400 to pictures was attributable to the frontal distribution of the earlier N300. This claim will become relevant when we discuss the PMN (phonological mapping negativity) and N400 responses to spoken word stimuli later.

The second example concerns another factor that can modulate the N400 – phonological compatibility of the target word with the anticipated word (i.e., homophone effects) – and another pre-N400 response, the N270. In a series of studies, we and others have examined the ERP effects associated with the processing of a contextually constrained sentence that ends with a homophone that is semantically inappropriate (e.g., Chocolate tastes very *suite* [sweet].). There is an extensive cognitive linguistics literature spanning more than thirty years that has used a variety of paradigms to examine the roles of orthography and phonology during silent reading (see review, Jared et al., 1999). A seminal model of visual word recognition, the dual-route model (Behrmann and Bub, 1992; Coltheart, 1978, 1985; Coslett, 1991; Funnell, 1983; Herdman and Beckett, 1996) proposed that access to the lexicon is accomplished by a route utilizing orthographic representations that map directly onto lexical items (words) previously encountered (the lexical route) or a route utilizing spelling-to-sound rules to form a phonological code that maps onto the sounds of words in the lexicon (the grapheme-to-phoneme or GPC route, see Venezky, 1970). Both routes acknowledge a phonological code, but while the lexical route represents it as a consequence of lexical access with a secondary integrative role that occurs after word identification (e.g., Daneman and Reingold, 1993), the GPC route envisions the phonological code as the primary method of access to meaning and the lexicon (Ferrand and Grainger, 1994; Lukatela and Turvey, 1994a, b; Van Orden et al., 1990). Recent models offer a more interactive view of how phonology and orthography contribute to visual word recognition. For instance, the most recent version of the dual-route model (Coltheart et al., 2001) allows both routes to be activated in parallel and also incorporates feedback connections between orthographic, phonological, and lexical representations. An alternative to the dual-route model is the connectionist triangle model of reading (Harm and Seidenberg, 2004; Seidenberg and McClelland, 1989). This model proposes a single mechanism for visual word recognition, in which computation of word meaning is achieved via a distributed pattern of activation across orthographic, phonological, and semantic units. The division of labour between these units may be altered, thus permitting phonological or orthographic representations to exert greater influence during the computation of word meaning (Harm and Seidenberg, 2004; Seidenberg and McClelland, 1989). While there are advocates for both dual-route and connectionist models of reading as well as those who support the classic dual-route model with primacy established by a variety of factors such as contextually influenced strategies, it is beyond the scope of this chapter to do any more than provide this sketch of the processes involved in silent reading so that the reader can have some appreciation

of the associated ERP results. As the reader follows the description of ERP work with homophones, he or she should keep the object/face identification and N_{300}/N_{400} research just described in very active working memory. The parallels of N_{400} and related preceding components are striking, and they will recur when we discuss ERP findings for SWR.

Work conducted in our laboratory (Forbes, 1993; 1998) has shown that the N_{400} is modulated by phonology during the silent reading of sentences ending with stimuli that are homophonic to the expected sentence-ending word, and that the N_{400} is preceded by another negative component, the N_{270}, that appears to reflect orthographic form processing and is larger to those stimuli that violate orthographic expectations. The first experiment in the series used homophones to end sentences in one of three ways: 1. congruent to the sentence context (e.g., The knife was made of stainless *steel.*) (congruent homophone); 2. orthographically, phonologically, and semantically incongruent to the sentence context (e.g., The car ran out of *pain/pane* [gas].) (incongruent homophone); and 3. orthographically and semantically incongruent but phonologically identical to its homophonic partner that would have ended the sentence appropriately (e.g., The dove is a sign of *piece* [peace].) (wrong homophonic partner). The congruent homophone condition (e.g., *steel*) resulted in neither a N_{270} nor a N_{400} that was detectable, but instead was characterized by a large P_{300}-like response. The incongruent homophone condition (e.g., *pain*) produced both an N_{270} and N_{400} due to the final word violating orthographic form expectations (the N_{270}) and being phonologically and semantically incongruent to the sentence context (the N_{400}). The question was whether the N_{400} seen in the incongruent homophone condition was attributable to its violation of phonological or semantic expectations, or both. The wrong homophonic partner condition (e.g., *piece*) was particularly interesting inasmuch as it resulted in an N_{270} that was smaller than that seen in the incongruent homophone condition (e.g., *pain*) but larger than that seen in the congruent homophone condition (e.g., *steel*), and a greatly reduced or absent N400. As the study design controlled the level of orthographic similarity, precisely half of the pairs used in the wrong homophonic partner condition (e.g., *piece*) were orthographically different (Olson and Kausler, 1971, criteria) (e.g., *ate–eight*) and half were orthographically similar (e.g., *hear–here*). Separate analysis of these pairs found that the orthographically different pairs produced the large N270 in the wrong homophonic partner condition which was, in fact, as large as the N270 seen in the incongruent homophone condition. There was little N400 activity in either of these two wrong homophonic partner averages – evidence of the importance of phonological recoding during reading.

Two further studies examined the important question of strategy effects in the reading of homophones. In the first study, four sentence types counterbalanced[1] across conditions were used: "Karen went on the Ferris wheel at the county *fair*." (congruent homophone); "Karen went on the Ferris wheel at the county *fare*." (wrong homophone partner); "Karen went on the Ferris wheel at the county *fire*." (orthographically similar); and "Karen went on the Ferris wheel at the county *broom*." (orthographically dissimilar). Three of four conditions involved semantic incongruities and less than twenty percent of the sentences used homophone foils (i.e., *fare* in the wrong homophone partner condition), plus a large number of filler sentences were used in order to prevent participants from adopting a unique processing strategy that favoured the use of phonological codes (e.g., Jared and Seidenberg, 1991). Results replicated earlier work showing reduced N400 responses to the homophone foils used in the wrong homophone partner condition – generally the level of activity in the N400 time window did not differ between the wrong homophone partner and congruent sentences (congruent homophone and fillers) (Figure 7.1.A). N400 amplitudes in the orthographically similar condition in which terminal words were semantically incongruent but orthographically similar to the words primed by the sentence context (e.g., "Karen went on the Ferris wheel at the county *fire*.") and in the orthographically dissimilar condition in which terminal words were both incongruent and orthographically dissimilar (e.g., "Karen went on the Ferris wheel at the county *broom*.") were of similar size. These results indicated that the N400 is *not* sensitive to orthography and by implication not responsive to the orthographic similarity that often exists between homophone pairs. In contrast, the N270 proved to be sensitive to orthographic similarities between anticipated and presented words. The N270 showed reduced amplitude in the congruent homophone, orthographically similar, and wrong homophone partner[2] conditions, demonstrating its sensitivity to orthographic but not semantic violations. Clearly, the reduced N270 in the orthographically similar (and wrong homophone partner) condition together with the large N400 in the orthographically similar condition suggests very different functions underlying the two responses, and also demonstrates that orthographic and phonological codes influence word identification at different processing stages.

The next experiment addressed the finding that inclusion of nonwords diminishes the importance of phonological influences during reading (see Coltheart et al., 1994; Van Orden, 1987). If our interpretation of the earlier studies is correct that modulation

---

1   Sentences in which each ending completed a semantically appropriate sentence were also included: "Karen went on the Ferris wheel at the county *fair*." (congruent homophone, CH); "The driver made change as the passenger did not have the correct *fare*." (incongruent homophone, IH); "The campers cooked on the open *fire*." (orthographically similar, OS); "She swept the porch with a *broom*." (orthographically dissimilar, OD).

2   It should be noted that the N270's sensitivity to orthographically dissimilar homophone partners as seen in the previous study was replicated here in the wrong homophone partner condition when homophone pairs that were orthographically dissimilar were analyzed separately. However, the N270 amplitude for the entire wrong homophone partner condition including similar and dissimilar pairs was reduced in comparison to that seen in the OD condition.

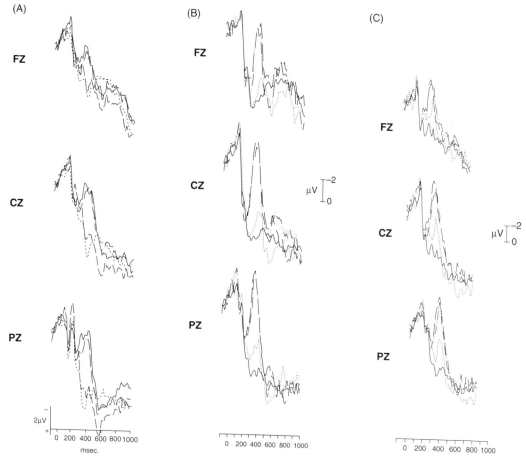

Figure 7.1. A. ERP recordings from three midline sites from experiment manipulating sentence-ending words in one of four ways: with a congruent homophone ["Karen went on the Ferris wheel at the county *fair.*"]; with the wrong (incongruous) homophone partner ["Karen went on the Ferris wheel at the county *fare.*"]; with an orthographically similar word to the congruent ending ["Karen went on the Ferris wheel at the county *fire.*"]; and, with an orthographically dissimilar word to the congruent ending ["Karen went on the Ferris wheel at the county *broom.*"]. **B.** ERP recordings from three midline sites from experiment that used words and nonwords while manipulating orthographic similarity/dissimilarity of sentence-ending words in one of four ways: with a congruent homophone ["The congregation kneeled down to *pray.*"]; with the wrong homophone partner ["The congregation kneeled down to *prey.*"]; with an orthographically similar word/nonword ["The children went outside to *play/prok.*"]; and with an orthographically dissimilar word/nonword ["Pat cut the fabric with a pair of *scissors/corter.*"]. **C.** ERP recordings from three midline sites from experiment that used words and nonwords often homophonic to anticipated sentence-ending words in one of four conditions that ended sentences with: a congruent homophone: "He ordered a T-bone *steak.*"; the wrong homophone partner: "He ordered a T-bone *stake.*"; with a nonword that was a homophone to the congruent ending (a pseudofoil-homophone): "He ordered a T-bone *staik.*"; and with a word that was orthographically similar to its paired homophones/pseudofoils: "He ordered a T-bone *store.*" See text for further details of other conditions.

of the N400 is attributable to a shared phonological code between homophones, then the inclusion of nonwords should reduce this effect – a larger N400 should now be seen to the inappropriately used homophones in sentences such as "The congregation kneeled down to *prey*." This study partnered nonwords with each homophone pair so that, for example, *prok/corter* were partnered with *pray/prey* to complete sentences as orthographically similar/dissimilar nonwords. The conditions and procedures used in this study were similar to those used in the preceding study (except for the inclusion of nonwords) manipulating orthographic similarity/dissimilarity: "The congregation kneeled down to *pray*." (congruent homophone); "The congregation kneeled down to *prey*." (wrong homophone partner); "The children went outside to *play/prok*." (orthographically similar word/nonword); and finally, "Pat cut the fabric with a pair of *scissors/corter*." (orthographically dissimilar word/nonword). The predicted reduction in the phonology effect on the N400 due to the inclusion of nonwords was found – the N400 was larger in the *prey* (wrong homophone partner) than *pray* (congruent) condition. However, a phonology effect was still observable insofar as the N400 in the *prey* condition was smaller than to the incongruent word/nonword sentence endings (Figure 7.1.B).[3]

The final two studies in this series addressed the issue that the presence of pseudohomophones (or pseudohomophonic foils) in the stimulus set can affect the extent to which phonological codes are used for word identification during reading (e.g., Davelaar et al., 1978; Stone and Van Orden, 1993). In this study, the stimulus set consisted

of homophonic stimuli that were words and nonwords: "He ordered a T-bone *steak*." (congruent homophone); "He ordered a T-bone *stake*." (wrong homophone partner); "He ordered a T-bone *staik*." (pseudofoil–homophonic); "He ordered a T-bone *store*." (orthographically similar–homophonic).[4] Aside from filler sentences, control sentences that used nonhomophonic word/nonword stimuli were also included: "The hockey player laced up his *skate*." (congruent–non homophonic); "The hockey player laced up his *skait*." (pseudofoil–non homophonic); "The hockey player laced up his *slime*." (orthographically similar–non homophonic). The results offered strong support for the role of phonology in word identification. N400 amplitudes were similar for nonlexical (the pseudofoil–homophonic and pseudofoil–nonhomophonic conditions) and lexical stimuli (the wrong homophone partner condition) that were phonologically expected, and all were smaller when compared to the two conditions that were not phonologically expected (orthographically similar–homophonic and orthographically similar–nonhomophonic) (Figure 7.1.C). In marked contrast with the findings for the nonlexical stimuli in the preceding experiment, the nonlexical stimuli in this study elicited reduced N400 amplitudes. The difference between the nonlexical items used across the two experiments is that in the current study, they matched phonologically the anticipated endings for the sentences, whereas in the preceding experiment they did not. In support of behavioural research indicating that inclusion of pseudohomophones affects the use of phonological codes, the N400 responses seen in the various homophonic foil conditions (i.e., pseudofoil–homophonic, pseudofoil–nonhomophonic, and wrong homophone partner)

---

3   Unexpectedly, the N270 to orthographically similar and dissimilar words and nonwords that were phonologically unexpected produced similar N270 amplitudes. In fact, when the N270 responses to the orthographically similar words and nonwords were compared with those in wrong homophone partner condition – that is, three conditions in which terminal words were orthographically similar to the congruent homophone ending to the sentence – the N270 to the wrong homophone partner condition proved smaller than to the other two conditions which did not differ.

4   Two conditions that matched the expected terminal word orthographically but not phonologically were used. One condition (orthographically similar–homophonic) was matched orthographically to the homophone pair (in the example used, *steak/stake* and *store*) while the other condition (orthographically similar–non homophonic) was orthographically matched to the nonhomophonic word that ended a sentence congruously (in the example used, *skate/skait* and *slime*).

while smaller than those seen in incongruous conditions, were larger than seen in the congruent condition, a finding that replicates the previous study with its inclusion of nonwords in the stimulus set.

In a follow-up study (Newman and Connolly, 2004), the pseudohomophone work was integrated with a four-condition protocol that manipulated orthographic, phonological, and/or semantic congruency of sentence-terminating words and pseudohomophone foils (nonwords). "Father carved the turkey with a *knife*" is an example of the congruent terminal word condition, while "Joan fed her baby some warm *nose*" [milk] is an example of the incongruent word condition that used sentence-ending words that were orthographically, phonologically, and semantically incongruous to the high cloze ending. "The ship disappeared into the thick *phog*" [fog] represents the congruous nonword pseudohomophone condition that employed nonwords that were orthographically and semantically incongruous but phonologically matched to the high cloze ending. Finally, "The gas station is about two kilometres down the *bole*" [road] is from the incongruous nonword pseudohomophone condition, with sentence-ending nonwords that were homophonic to real words but were orthographically, phonologically, and semantically incongruous to the high cloze ending. Results confirmed earlier work in finding that the introduction of pseudohomophone foils altered strategies so that there remained a discernable $N400$ to items like *phog* although it was significantly smaller than that seen in the *nose* and *bole* conditions. The frontally distributed $N270$ was larger in the *nose*, *bole*, and *phog* compared to the *knife* condition.

The $N270$ described above or a similar pre-$N400$ response has been seen in a number of language studies (e.g., Bentin et al., 1985; Helenius et al., 1999; McPherson et al., 1998). This response appears related to violations of contextually derived orthographic expectancies and may also be related to the $N300$ observed to line drawings and photos. The markedly reduced or virtually absent $N400$ can only be understood within a reading model that places phonological processing of text as an important but strategy dependent route to the lexicon. The reduced $N400$ to phonologically acceptable words/nonwords implies that access to the lexicon is phonologically mediated and that integration of the accessed item into the ongoing context is mediated strongly by the phonological code. What these results tell us about reading and the $N400$ is that: 1. $N400$ amplitude or occurrence is not sensitive to the lexical nature of a sentence-ending item, and 2. phonological processing of text does not occur to homophones only, but to any legal letter string that shares its phonological code with a word, be it a homophone or nonhomophone. The fact that the $N400$ was modulated by manipulations known to affect the use of phonologically based strategies and related task performance suggests these codes *and the $N400$* are activated during the word identification process.

Taken together, these data offer strong support for a parallel processing view of reading given that an orthographic form detector response occurred to some of the stimuli used in these experiments, yet independently, the semantic processor failed to respond – presumably because it is less dependent on orthographic than phonological form. The behavioural response, the last manifestation of this process, would appear to require agreement amongst the orthographic, phonological, and semantic systems because in all of these experiments, behavioural accuracy in deciding which sentences made sense was in the ninetieth percentile.

Finally, it must be noted that others have not found such strong effects of phonology in ostensibly similar tasks. One study used conditions identical to those included earlier: a correct homophone condition in which sentences ended congruously with a homophone, an incorrect homophone condition having sentences that ended with the wrong homophone partner, an orthographic condition having sentences that ended with an orthographically similar but semantically and phonologically incongruous word, and a fourth condition that ended with words that were nonhomophonic and totally incongruous to the sentence context (Niznikiewicz and Squires, 1996). However, this study has serious methodological problems that make interpretation of its results difficult. For example, the peak scored as the N400 had a mean latency of 583 ms, which is far too late for this response (see Kutas and Van Petten, 1994). Also, the response labelled the N400 bore no morphological resemblance to the N400 observed in the literature in any modality.

Another report sought to determine if phonology played a role in accessing word meaning during reading (Ziegler et al., 1999). This study used a semantic categorization task (e.g., participants had to decide if *meat/meet* belonged to the semantic category of food). Behavioural evidence indicated more errors to homophone partners than to orthographic controls (e.g., *melt*). However, the N400 failed to differentiate between homophone partners and orthographic controls, indicating that phonology does not mediate access to meaning and access was achieved by an orthographic not phonological representation of a word. This apparent conflict between Ziegler et al. (1999) and our results is likely due to the different tasks used (sentence reading versus semantic categorization). The categorization task explicitly emphasized orthographic form in mediating meaning and context in contrast to our tasks that used a silent reading environment with strategy manipulated implicitly by fillers, for example. Also, as noted by Ziegler et al. (1999), sentence reading tasks would likely activate phonological working memory which single word reading would not. Taken together, these results emphasize the strategy dependent nature of reading.

This description of reading-related ERP components is related to our primary topic of spoken word-related ERP components because first, it is important to understand the history of the N400 (which is predominantly a visual history); second, it is important to have an appreciation of the fact that there are other, temporally adjacent ERP components that reflect related but quite different functions; and third, and possibly most obviously, there is a clear link between

reading and aural comprehension insofar as, for example, phonological processing features significantly in both. We expand upon this third point in the following section where we discuss the seemingly counterintuitive notion that orthography features just as prominently in SWR and comprehension as phonology does in visual word recognition comprehension.

3 The influence of orthographic knowledge on SWR: Evidence from ERPs

The emergence of written language as a form of communication lags behind SWR both in terms of human evolution and in child development. Despite this primacy of spoken language, however, there is mounting evidence that orthography influences the processing of SWR (Perre and Ziegler, 2008; Taft et al., 2008; Ziegler and Ferrand, 1998; Ziegler et al., 2004). The possibility that orthographic knowledge influences SWR was initially observed in the context of a rhyme judgment task in which adult participants were faster to detect that two words rhymed when they were orthographically similar (e.g., *cot–pot*) than dissimilar (e.g., *yach–pot*; Seidenberg and Tanenhaus, 1979). In addition, several studies have shown that literacy acquisition influences children's performance on phonological awareness tasks (Castles et al., 2003; Ehri and Wilce, 1980; Stuart, 1990). Ehri and Wilce (1980) found that fourth grade children are more apt to say that there are more phonemes in a word like *pitch* than *rich*, presumably because the former has more letters. The influence of reading on a phonological awareness task has also been observed using the phoneme deletion task. For instance, Castles et al. (2003) showed that participants found it easier to perform phoneme deletion when the relationship between the phoneme to be deleted and the letter representing the phoneme was transparent (e.g., /lə/ from slit→/sit/) compared to opaque (e.g., /wə/ from quit→/kit/). These results did not depend on whether items from the two groups (i.e., transparent and opaque) were presented in separate blocks or mixed blocks, suggesting that participants could not inhibit orthographic influences even when it would be advantageous to their task performance. The authors concluded that orthographic representations are automatically activated along with closely linked phonological representations.

Orthographic influences on SWR are not isolated to metaphonological tasks (e.g., rhyming, phoneme deletion), which some suggest encourage the use of an orthographic strategy (i.e., visual imagery) to mediate analysis of phonological information (Taft et al., 2008). Ziegler and Ferrand (1998) manipulated the orthographic consistency of spoken words in a lexical decision task, which is less susceptible to the adoption of orthographic strategies. Words in the consistent condition had rhymes that could only be spelled in one way (e.g., /ʌk/ corresponds only to the orthographic representation /uck/), while words in the inconsistent condition had rhymes that could be spelled in multiple ways (e.g., /-ip/ corresponds to the orthographic representations /eap/ or /eep/). Results showed that inconsistent words were associated with slower and more error prone responses compared to consistent words. This so-called auditory consistency effect has been replicated in several studies (for review, see Ziegler et al., 2008) and has been taken as strong evidence for orthographic influences on auditory processing.

While there is general agreement that orthography does influence SWR, there is debate as to whether such effects occur during or after lexical access (Pattamadilok et al., 2007; Ventura et al., 2004). In an effort to resolve the debate, Ziegler and colleagues have conducted several studies using ERPs in order to track the time course of orthographic influences on SWR. Perre and Ziegler (2008) manipulated the position of orthographic inconsistency in spoken (French) words as participants performed a lexical decision task. In the early inconsistent condition, the initial consonant–vowel segment could be spelled in multiple ways

(e.g., /rym/, in which the phonology /ry/ can be spelled in multiple ways) and in the late inconsistent condition, the final vowel–consonant segment could be spelled in multiple ways (e.g., /nos/, in which the phonology /os/ can be spelled in multiple ways). These two conditions were compared to consistent words (e.g., /lyn/ has only one spelling). ERPs were time-locked to the arrival of orthographic inconsistency. The earliest difference between consistent and inconsistent words was observed at 320 ms in which early inconsistent words exhibited a larger negativity than consistent words. Late inconsistent words did not differ from consistent words in this early time window. A later difference between consistent and inconsistent words was observed at 600 ms for both early and late inconsistent words, but was largest for the former. Evidence that the brain registered the early orthographic inconsistency prior to word offset provides strong support for the early activation of orthography during SWR. These effects were replicated in a recent study that employed a semantic categorization task, which unlike lexical decision and metaphonological tasks, does not draw attention to the orthographic or phonological structure of words (Pattamadilok et al., 2009). Finally, as noted by Perre and Ziegler (2008), the finding that orthographic inconsistency modulated an ERP component, the N320, that has also been observed to mediate spelling-to-sound mapping in the visual modality (Bentin et al., 1999), lends support to bimodal models of word recognition in which the bidirectional coupling between orthography and phonology affects both visual and auditory word recognition (Ferrand and Grainger, 1996; Frost and Ziegler, 2007).

In an effort to identify the cortical generators of orthographic effects on spoken word recognition, Perre et al. (2009b) employed low resolution electromagnetic tomography (LORETA) techniques in a study that replicated the orthographic consistency effect in the context of an auditory lexical decision task (i.e., early inconsistent words differed from consistent words at approximately 330 ms after the onset of the word). The source estimate analysis revealed significant differences between consistent and inconsistent words between 332 ms and 356 ms in the left supramarginal gyrus (SMG) and marginal differences in the same time period in the left superior temporal gyrus (STG) and left inferior parietal lobule (IPL); all regions shown to support aspects of phonological processing (Bitan et al., 2007; Hickok and Poeppel, 2007). There was no evidence of an orthographic consistency effect in the so-called visual word form area, a region in the left occipito-temporal cortex that is proposed to be specialized for processing words' visual form (Cohen et al., 2002). This latter finding cast doubt on the hypothesis that orthographic information is coactivated with phonological information whenever we hear spoken words. Rather, these findings led Perre et al. (2009b) to speculate that reading acquisition changes the very nature of phonological representations. That is, developing orthographic knowledge causes consistent words to develop stronger phonological representations than inconsistent words.

The restructuring of phonological representations by orthographic knowledge was not supported, however, in a recent ERP study by Perre et al. (2009a). Their study employed a priming paradigm in which a target word was preceded by one of three prime types. In the orthographic overlap condition (O+P+), the phonological rhyme of the prime and target was represented by the same letters (e.g., *beef–reef*). In the no-orthographic overlap condition (O-P+), the phonological rhyme of the prime and target was represented by different letters (e.g., *leaf–reef*). Finally, in the unrelated condition (O-P-), primes and targets were phonologically and orthographically unrelated (e.g., *sick–reef*). Results yielded evidence for both phonological and orthographic priming effects. First, targets that rhymed with the prime were associated with a reduced N400 compared to unrelated targets (i.e., a phonological priming effect). Perhaps more interesting was the orthographic priming effect that also modulated the N400 response. Targets that shared both phonological and orthographic overlap with primes elicited

a reduced N400 compared to targets that shared phonological but not orthographic information. The topographical distribution of the orthographic priming effect was distinct from that of the phonological priming effect. Whereas the phonological priming effect displayed a centro-posterior distribution, the orthographic priming effect was more frontally distributed. On the basis of the distinct topographical distributions observed for the phonological and orthographic priming effects, the authors interpreted their results as favouring the "coactivation hypothesis." They suggested that if orthographic knowledge had changed the nature of phonological representations, then phonological and orthographic priming effects would have had more similar distributions.

The results of Perre et al. (2009a) contradict those of Perre et al. (2009b) in terms of which hypothesis best explains the orthographic effects on SWR. There are a number of possible reasons for the discrepant findings, the primary one being the use of different paradigms which in turn elicited different ERP components: the N320 and the N400. The use of source estimate analysis seems a better approach to determining the locus of orthographic effects than reliance on topographical effects, which don't necessarily correspond to the locus of underlying generators. Having said this, it is beyond the scope of this chapter to adjudicate between these two hypotheses. Future studies employing brain imaging techniques will play an important role in determining whether orthographic knowledge is coactivated online or whether it changes the nature of phonological representations. Regardless of whether one hypothesis, or some combination of both, is ultimately seen to provide the best explanation for orthographic effects on SWR, there is little doubt that orthography influences SWR just as phonology influences written language.

The preceding discussion has provided theoretical insights into the effects sublexical processes exert on comprehension within the visual and auditory modality and the neurophysiological manifestations of these effects. These findings demonstrate that although not initially intuitive, phonology and orthography affect the comprehension of both spoken and visual word recognition. The following discussions will now explore factors shown to influence the appearance of ERPs that reliably reflect mechanisms of language processing based upon the modality in which they are elicited and the experimental contexts necessary to elicit them.

4 The N400: A definition, modality differences in its spatial distribution, and its nature as a real-time measure

4.1 A definition

Despite the considerable amount of research conducted with the N400, there is still not a clear consensus on what the N400 reflects functionally. Within the context of the conventional three-stage model of SWR involving lexical selection, lexical access, and lexical integration (see for example, Marslen-Wilson 1987; Zwitserlood, 1989), it can be said that while one view of N400 amplitude modulation sees it as a reflection of a lexical access process, the dominant opinion is that it reflects a lexical integration function. In the former category is the suggestion that the amplitude of the N400 is a marker of the ease of retrieving from memory all of the concepts associated with a word and is dependent on characteristics of that stored representation and the *cues for retrieval* contained in the context in which the word exists (Van Petten and Luka, 2006; see also Kutas and Federmeier, 2000 and Deacon et al., 2000). Others (Brown and Hagoort, 1993, 2000; Connolly and Phillips, 1994; Holcomb, 1993; Rugg, 1990) see the N400 as reflecting a postlexical integration process.

This chapter takes a view of the N400 as a nondiacritic manifestation of a process that uses newly acquired information to construct a working model of a conceptual environment and attempts to integrate it within a developing semantic context. The *onset* of model construction is affected by a variety of domain (e.g., language) specific bottom-up factors such as perceptual quality of the

stimulation (degraded as in Holcomb, 1993; speeded as in Kutas, 1987), or by manipulations that affect bottom-up processing such as "garden pathing" stimulus identification (as in Connolly and Phillips, 1994). The *difficulty* encountered in constructing the model will be dependent upon the degree of contextual guidance (e.g., in the language domain, cloze probability of the critical word), the complexity of the task relevant knowledge base (e.g., vocabulary size), and the extent to which, for instance, memory or attention are required. This multiplicity of factors (bottom-up processing, domain-specific knowledge, recruitment of cognitive processes) together with modality of stimulation will affect appearance (i.e., amplitude, latency, scalp distribution) of the N400.

This view of the N400 as a reflection of a more generalized phenomenon rather than one linked exclusively to language will influence the following discussion only insofar as we will not make reference to N400-like responses, but rather assume that peri-400 ms negativities seen in the cited studies are *the* N400. In a following section (4.0) dealing with speech stimuli, the discussion will follow the theme of the N400 as a nonunitary response that possesses elements sensitive to phonological, orthographic, and semantic features (see Rugg and Barrett, 1987). Furthermore, we will discuss one response known to precede the N400 (e.g., the PMN) with regard to its function(s), its relationship with the N400, and how both components fit into current theories of SWR.

4.2 Spatial distribution

Traditional paradigms that use spoken sentence-ending words that do not integrate easily into the preceding sentence context by virtue of semantic incongruity or low cloze probability often elicit a fronto-central or equally distributed N400 and either a slight left-hemispheric asymmetry or no asymmetry (e.g., Ackerman et al.1994; Bentin et al., 1993; Connolly et al., 1990, 1992; Connolly and Phillips, 1994). However, other studies fail to see such a scalp distribution to speech stimuli (D'Arcy et al., 2004; Holcomb and

Neville, 1990; van den Brink et al., 2001). Nonetheless, for the sake of argument, if we accept the literature trend is for a more fronto-central or equal distribution N400 to spoken words, the question is what causes this different scalp distribution compared to the visually elicited N400 – a different or additional neuronal population or the presence of a preceding negativity? The issue of a different or additional neuronal population can be addressed by equivalent current dipole (ECD) methods while the role of an earlier response is addressed by nothing more than careful observation and additional research.

There is evidence to support both alternatives. A number of studies have shown similar dipole localizations for the N400 in both auditory and visual studies (D'Arcy et al., 2004; Helenius et al., 1998; Helenius et al., 2002) – a result that would, on the face of it, support the distributional differences seen between speech and visual stimuli as being due to a preceding negativity. There are problems with accepting this interpretation unconditionally, however. For one thing, the similarity of visual and auditory N400 dipoles has not been adequately tested. There is, however, one particularly useful study that has examined both visual and auditory word processing in the same participants (Marinkovic et al., 2003). Although the modalities were tested separately on two different occasions (four months apart on average), the participants were young adults and it is not unreasonable to suggest that the sizeable time interval between modality testing was of little consequence. Essentially, they found that early processing followed modality specific ventral routes converging in (predominantly left) anterior temporal and inferior prefrontal areas at around 400 ms post stimulus onset. Subsequent processing (in some cases from about 300 ms onward) appeared to be accomplished in areas including the left temporal region and the left inferior prefrontal cortex and ventromedial prefrontal areas regardless of the modality of stimulation. However, this study does not preclude the possibility of shared neuronal populations or preceding components being the cause of observed scalp distribution differences.

It is equally true that there are shortcomings in any account that attributes the frequently observed visual/auditory N400 distributional differences solely to a preceding negativity. For example, an N270 often precedes the visual N400 during a reading task. If a preceding negativity such as the N300 in the photo/picture priming work described earlier can induce a more frontal distribution to the N400 in the visual modality, then it is unclear why the N270, a similarly preceding and frontally distributed negativity emitted to written words, fails to induce an anterior shift in the subsequent N400. Similarly, any claim that the PMN (Connolly and Phillips, 1994) preceding the N400 during SWR is responsible for the latter's fronto-central scalp distribution would prove difficult to support unequivocally. It seems much more likely that the distributional variations seen within and across modalities for the N400 are due to a number of factors including the strength of preceding components and the effects of subtle variations in task demands on attention and memory functions which, of course, would involve variations in cell populations mediating these functions.

4.3 P300 *in lieu of* N400

A final note for this section provides an example of how the sensitivity and subtlety of task demands can affect the manifestation of the N400. In a study that adapted the Token Test for computer presentation and simultaneous ERP recordings, a procedure was used that was expected to result in N400 elicitation (D'Arcy and Connolly, 1999). Briefly, participants watched tokens (e.g., green squares, red triangles) move about on a computer screen. After a specific movement pattern, participants heard a sentence that described what had just occurred on the screen accurately or inaccurately. Thus, the only demands of this task were that participants attend to the screen, analyze the simple token movements that occurred, retain these movements in working memory, listen to the immediately following descriptive sentence, and press a button to indicate whether the sentence described the movement correctly or incorrectly. Such a design appears unremarkable insofar as it is simply a speech comprehension paradigm containing a word that violates semantic expectations – an N400 paradigm. However, a P300 occurred to the critical word in the incorrect sentences rather than the expected N400. Examination of individual participant waveforms revealed all of them exhibited only P300 responses to the incorrect word. There are several aspects to this study not always seen in typical N400 studies. There is an explicit, if relatively minor, demand on working memory – retaining the memory of token movement for several seconds until a descriptive sentence is presented. However, other studies have manipulated working memory, in some cases substantially, and found reductions in N400 amplitude (e.g., D'Arcy et al., 2005; Fischler et al., 1985), *not* occurrences of P300 responses. This Token study demonstrated the importance of the development of a context within which a subsequent word or sentence must be integrated if one expects to observe an N400. The Token study became more of a matching-to-sample study than a speech comprehension study with participants not having to process much beyond the initial phoneme of the critical word that described the colour or shape of the token to determine if the sentence was accurate or inaccurate. The strict single element that had to be watched for compared to the development of a semantic context (e.g., by sentence or by word or picture priming) resulted in the occurrence of a P300 instead of a N400.

5 The time course of SWR – does one component really fit all?

5.1 *A pre-N400 component during speech comprehension: The role of the PMN in SWR*

Clearly, the process of comprehension, whether reading or speech processing,

unfolds across time in a way that is dependent on the rate of input. This time feature is most apparent and natural during SWR where the auditory signal progresses through a number of stages from the earliest acoustic to the syntactic/semantic. Auditory input reaches the cortex within fifteen ms (Liégeois-Chauvel et al., 1994), while the earliest acoustic-phonetic analyses related to speech processing are typically manifested within fifty to one hundred ms in nonprimary auditory cortex (Eggermont and Ponton, 2002). The first major peak associated with this level of speech processing is the N100m, peaking about 100–150 ms post stimulus onset.

A recent MEG study on the N100m used synthetic vowels (/u/ and /a/) and c-v syllables (/pa/ and /ka/) and acoustically matched complex nonspeech stimuli composed of three sine wave tone components that had the same frequency as each of the formants found in the four speech stimuli (Parviainen et al., 2005). Also, a simple sine wave tone stimulus was composed of the F2 frequency of each speech sound in order to retain the transition difference that existed between the two c-v syllables. The location and orientation of the equivalent current dipoles for the N100m did not significantly vary across stimulus types (including responses to sine wave tones), tending to be in Heschl's sulcus or posterior and lateral to it. However, the strength of the N100m was greater for speech than nonspeech stimuli, but in the left hemisphere only. This greater strength or amplitude was seen for all four speech categories (i.e., vowels and c-v syllables). In contrast, while N100m strength differences were observed between the complex nonspeech and sine wave stimuli, the differences were seen in both hemispheres equally. While onset latency of the N100m did not vary across stimulus type, a steeper slope in the ascending limb of the response (defined as the rate of amplitude increase across time) was observed for speech stimuli in the left compared to the right hemisphere. No hemisphere effect was observed for the nonspeech stimuli. Finally, the N100m reached peak amplitude to speech stimuli later than to complex nonspeech stimuli (two to five ms) and to tones (seven to nine ms) – an effect that was equal for both hemispheres. However, in general N100m peaks occurred on average about twelve ms earlier in the left than right hemisphere.

ERP, MEG, and fMRI studies (Liégeois-Chauvel et al., 1994; Poeppel et al., 1996; Scott and Johnsrude, 2003) have shown the acoustic-phonetic processing associated with this response involves left posterior superior temporal regions and the planum temporale (see also Lütkenhöner and Steinstrater, 1998). While this response (i.e., N100/N100m) is generally viewed as reflecting the acoustic-phonetic processing of an incoming auditory event, an argument has been made that it might also bear some relationship to phonetic-phonological processing. This proposal (Helenius et al., 2002) was based on work suggesting that phonological categories of stimuli have already been accessed when ERP/MEG responses that onset around 150–200 ms post stimulus occur (Phillips et al., 2000; Vihla et al., 2000). In fact, it seems likely that the response involved, the mismatch negativity (MMN), reflects something of a terminal stage of processing for simple stimuli (e.g., c-v syllables) reflecting preattentive, low-level mnemonic functions capable of differentiating, for example, native and nonnative phonetic contrasts at early stages of development (Cheour et al., 1998). What is of particular interest is the large sustained negative potential that onsets at around 200 ms and continues for several hundred milliseconds, often up to 600 ms or later (e.g., Bonte et al., 2006; Helenius et al., 2002; Marinkovic et al., 2003) – the N400.

Over the last few years, increasing attention has been given to the idea that the activity recorded from 200 ms onward in language-related paradigms is not a unitary phenomenon but rather is composed of subcomponents that appear related to mechanisms that are related to and often conceptualized as serving semantic processing and comprehension. We have discussed

TYPICALLY-DEVELOPED READERS

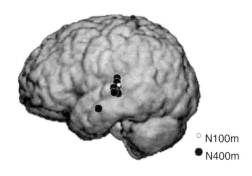

○ N100m
● N400m

SENTENCE-ENDING WORDS

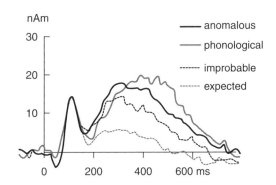

Figure 7.2. The N400m locations in the left hemisphere of typically developed readers with the N100m shown as a white circle. Terminal words of sentences varied semantically, orthographically, and phonologically (see Connolly and Phillips, 1994). The terminal words fell into one of four categories: semantically congruous and phonologically expected (*Father carved the turkey with a knife.*) referred to as "expected;" semantically congruous but phonologically unexpected (*The pigs wallowed in the pen* [mud].) referred to as "improbable;" semantically incongruous but phonologically expected (*The gambler had a streak of bad luggage* [luck].) referred to as "phonological;" and, semantically incongruous and phonologically unexpected (*The winter was harsh this allowance* [year].) referred to as "anomalous." Figure demonstrates the sustained potential characteristic of the N400m (and N400) typically observed in these experiments as well as the localization of the auditory N400m (adapted from Helenius et al., 2002).

this issue to some degree in our earlier evaluation of the visual N400 data. These subcomponents are not always observable in the grand average waveforms because of between-subject variability in these subcomponents so that averaging across participants results in a response that spreads across hundreds of ms, often appears to be "noisy" having one or more bumps across its broad span, and often has an uncharacteristically (compared to other ERP components) slow acceleration to peak. When individual waveforms are examined, the N400 has both a sharper onset slope and a reduced temporal span. The "invisibility" of these components in the grand average appears to be more common in the auditory than visual waveforms and one possible explanation is that it is precisely the combining of a stimulus that unfolds over time and individual differences in processing speeds that sums up to the appearance of a large, undifferentiated, sustained potential (Figure 7.2). So the grand question here is what *are* these other components and what functions do they reflect in SWR?

5.2 *The phonological mapping negativity (PMN)*

Early work on contextually constrained sentence effects on ERP to spoken sentences observed an N400 to semantically congruous words that terminated sentences of low contextual constraint. However, also observed was a negative-going response that occurred between 250–300 ms to all terminal words but was significantly larger to those ending the low contextually constrained sentences that produced N400 responses (Connolly et al., 1990; 1992). Speech comprehension is the classic example of a process that is dependent on a stimulus that unfolds over time. With that in mind, it was proposed that this earlier negativity was a reflection of the ongoing phonological processing that also unfolds over time during SWR (Connolly et al., 1990). Subsequently, a phonological masking stimulus (a "babble" track) was introduced that earlier work had shown interfered with semantic but

not phonological processing of the terminal words of sentences (Kalikow et al., 1977). In support of the proposal that the response preceding the N400 was associated with phonological processing, "babble" interference was observed to reduce the amplitude of the N400 only – not the preceding response (Connolly et al., 1992). This dissociation between the "N200" and the N400 suggested that this peak was of potential functional significance and was not merely an inconsequential morphological perturbation in what was fundamentally a large N400. However, a further attempt at dissociation proved to be decisive in demonstrating the independence of this response (renamed from "N200" to the phonological mismatch negativity, PMN) from the N400 and adding support to its role as a phonologically related response (Connolly and Phillips, 1994) (see Figure 7.3 taken from van den Brink et al., 2001 which included three of the four conditions described later in this chapter). It should be noted that the PMN has since been relabelled as the phonological mapping negativity (still the PMN) to avoid continued confusion with the mismatch negativity or MMN (Steinhauer and Connolly, 2008).

This experiment used sentences with terminal words that varied both in terms of the phonological expectancy of the *initial* phoneme and semantic congruity. The terminal words fell into one of four categories: 1. semantically congruous and phonologically expected (e.g., Father carved the turkey with a *knife*.); 2. semantically congruous but phonologically unexpected (e.g., The pigs wallowed in the *pen* [mud].); 3. semantically incongruous but phonologically expected (e.g., The gambler had a streak of bad *luggage* [luck].); and 4. semantically incongruous and phonologically unexpected (e.g., The winter was harsh this *allowance* [year].). As had been hypothesized, a large PMN/N400 complex was seen to type four (e.g., *allowance*) because the initial phoneme heard was unexpected and the semantics of the word were incongruous to the context. The critical conditions in this study were types two and three where the double dissociation between

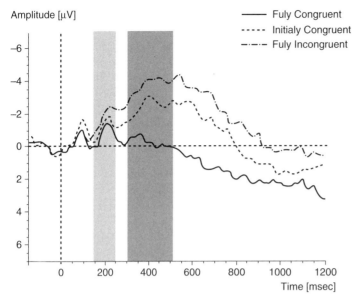

Figure 7.3. Connected speech. Grand average ERPs from the Pz electrode, to sentence-final words that were congruent (solid line), semantically anomalous but shared initial phonemes with semantically congruent completions (dotted line), and semantically anomalous and did not share initial phonemes with congruent completions (alternating dash/dot line), after normalization in the 150-msec prestimulus interval. Time 0 is the onset of the sentence-final words. The time axis is in milliseconds (taken from van den Brink et al., 2001).

the PMN and N400 that had been hypothesized was observed. A prominent PMN to the unexpected initial phoneme of the low cloze probability word (e.g., type two, *pen*) was found coupled with a reduced/virtually absent N400 due to the word's semantic congruity with sentence context; thus, the clear presence of a prominent PMN in the absence of an N400 was demonstrated. The second part of the double dissociation was seen to type three (e.g., *luggage*) where a small PMN to the expected initial phoneme of the word was coupled with a clear N400 due to its semantic incongruity to the context. The reduced or apparently absent PMN to the semantically incongruous words with phonologically expected initial phonemes (e.g., *luggage*) was attributable to the phonemic departure from expectation occurring some point after word onset. Thus, the response would be seemingly lost or reduced in appearance by virtue of the averaging process being time-locked to word

onset while the actual phonemic deviation occurred variably in relation to that onset; a situation analogous to the description given earlier of why some components are lost in grand averaging. Finally, a delayed N400 peak was observed in this condition because the initial phoneme met expectations and thus "garden pathed" the semantic system into an expectancy for the correct word. These findings led us to rename the N200 based on its apparent functional role – the PMN.

Initially, the interpretation of the PMN was that it reflected a point in the auditory word recognition process at the interface of bottom-up sensory information and top-down contextual influences (Connolly and Phillips, 1994). Hagoort and colleagues have proposed that the PMN reflects a lexical selection process occurring at the point where lexical form and contextual influences meet and where the lexical candidates, activated on the basis of lexical form, are evaluated for their semantic appropriateness to the sentence context (Hagoort and Brown, 2000; van den Brink et al., 2001). However, subsequent research has shown that the PMN does not reflect a stage of SWR at which the lexical candidates are established based on lexical form or evaluated semantically. Several studies (e.g., Connolly et al., 2001; Kujala et al., 2004) have demonstrated that the PMN is not dependent on semantic top-down influences because it can be elicited to nonwords. Both words and nonwords were employed in order to test the importance of lexical semantics on the appearance of the PMN. Both studies (Connolly et al., 2001; Kujala et al., 2004) presented three items in sequence: a word/nonword was presented visually followed by a visually presented letter and finally an auditory word/nonword (e.g., *telk/w/welk* or *hat/c/cat*). Prior to the presentation of the auditory word/nonword, participants were asked to replace the "sound" of the first letter in the visually presented word/nonword with the presented letter; thus, instructions emphasized the phonological form of the stimuli. The PMN proved to be independent of lexical semantic top-down influences and showed the largest amplitudes to the mismatching targets (e.g., *telk/w/ket* or *hat/c/bus*) and showed no difference between words and nonwords, suggesting a prelexical stage of processing associated with phonological form processing (Figure 7.4). In fact, Kujala et al. (2004) provided an overview of the progression of speech analysis from about 100 ms describing acoustic-phonetic, sublexical phonological, and whole-word processing stages. Both words and nonwords elicited a bilateral negative response (the N1m) at about 135 ms that was unresponsive to both the lexical and the mismatching features of the stimuli. The next component observed was the PMNm, which peaked at about 280–300 ms and was lateralized to the left anterior temporal cortex (see Price et al., 2005; Scott et al., 2000) (Figure 7.4.A). This response was larger to the phonologically mismatching stimuli but importantly, showed no reliable differences between words and nonwords (Figure 7.4.B). Finally, what was called a "N400-like" response

was also localized to the left hemisphere and appeared sensitive to the phonological form-based nature of the stimuli (Figure 7.4.A). The anatomical relationship amongst these three components indicated that the PMNm was anterior to both the N1m and the "N400m," the latter proving to be posterior to the N1m and having the distribution of the classic N400 in left posterior temporal areas (Halgren et al., 2002; Helenius et al., 1998, 1999; Simos et al., 1997). A final point about the PMN observed in these two studies is that while its appearance was characteristically brief its source (as shown in current source density, CSD, maps) remained active throughout the recording period, leading to the suggestion that it might reflect elements of a phonological working memory process.

Further confirmation that the PMN is not modulated by early lexical and semantic influences has come from studies using a phoneme deletion paradigm (Newman et al., 2003; Newman and Connolly, 2009). In a representative study (Newman et al., 2003), participants performed a metalinguistic analysis of speech stimuli that was independent of lexical/semantic influences. The task was to listen to instructions to omit the initial phoneme of a word (*blink* without the /b/) and to listen to one of a possible four choices of the resulting item: a correct choice (*link*) and three types of incorrect choices involving the deletion of the wrong consonant (*bink*), the consonant cluster, (*ink*), or the introduction of an irrelevant word (*tell*). The PMN (with a latency of around 270 ms) was seen equally to all incorrect choices making no differentiation between word and nonword (*link* and *bink*) or shared rhyme and phonological dissimilarity. Also, in support of earlier work, the presence of a PMN in the correct condition was strongly inferred from distribution maps emphasizing again that the PMN is a response that reflects phonological processing in all relevant circumstances but is larger when the analysis of an incoming acoustic signal mismatches prelexical phonemic expectations.

The work described earlier argues that the PMN reflects bottom-up, as opposed to

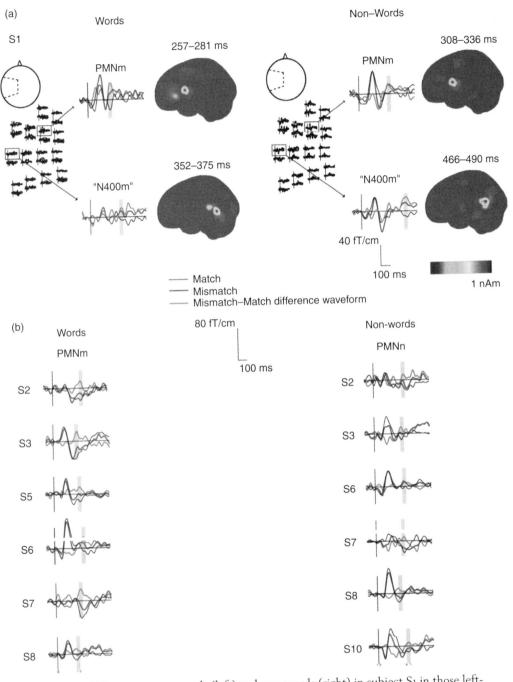

Figure 7.4. A. MEG responses to words (left) and non-words (right) in subject S1 in those left-hemisphere channels with the maximum amplitude for the PMNm and the N400m-like response and the corresponding L1 minimum-norm estimates (MCEs) over a twenty-five ms time window centered at the peak of the response. The gray vertical bars indicate the fifty ms time periods with significant PMNm and N400m-like responses. The MCEs are shown only in the regions of interest (ROIs), with the centers of the ROIs placed at the loci with the strongest current (the radius of the ROIs was always one cm). **B.** MEG responses to words (left) and non-words (right) in all those subjects with PMNm responses at the left-hemisphere channels with maximum response amplitude. Again, the gray vertical bars indicate the fifty ms time periods with significant PMNm responses. Adapted from Kujala et al., (2004), with permission from Elsevier.

top-down, competition effects that occur during SWR. It is tempting to align the PMN with the original cohort model of SWR, which emphasizes the importance of bottom-up competition in the selection of word candidates (Marslen-Wilson and Tyler, 1980). However, a recent study (Desroches et al., 2009) demonstrated how the PMN (and the N400) can fit within the framework of continuous mapping models of speech recognition, and in particular TRACE (McCelland and Elman, 1986). TRACE permits both bottom-up and top-down competition effects such that speech recognition proceeds in a nonlinear fashion. As a result, word candidates that are phonologically similar to the target word are activated, leading to phonological competition at the lexical level. Desroches et al. (2009) used a picture-auditory word matching task in which a visually presented picture either matched a spoken word (e.g., CONE-cone) or mismatched a spoken word in one of three ways: rhyme mismatch (e.g., CONE-bone), cohort mismatch (e.g., CONE-comb), or unrelated mismatch (e.g., CONE-fox). The PMN was largest in the rhyme and unrelated mismatch conditions, a finding consistent with earlier work suggesting the PMN reflects a mismatch between bottom-up input and phoneme expectations derived from the task context (i.e., presentation of the picture in this case).

The PMN was not the only component observed in this study. The N400 was seen in all three mismatching conditions; however, it was largest and more delayed to cohort mismatches and was attenuated to rhyme. The authors attributed the large and delayed N400 seen to cohort mismatches (e.g., comb) as reflecting a miscue in word identification resulting from a combination of misleading bottom-up information and late occurring disambiguating information. The attenuation of the N400 to rhyme mismatches suggested that the rhyme competitor (e.g., bone) had been activated by presentation of the visual image (e.g., cone). Thus, despite the initial phoneme mismatch, which was "registered" by processes mediating the PMN, recognition of the rhyme competitor was facilitated as denoted by reduction of the N400. The fact that both the PMN and the N400 were observed to rhyme mismatches suggests that bottom-up and top-down competition effects operate in parallel, a finding which seems most consistent with models of speech recognition that include both feedforward and feedback connections between phoneme and lexical levels of representation (e.g., TRACE). Finally, this study provided further evidence that the PMN and N400 reflect dissociable aspects of SWR (see Connolly and Phillips, 1994).

Before moving on to other research demonstrating the existence of N400 subcomponents or components preceding/overlapping with the N400, a final issue should be addressed regarding the PMN – its name. Hagoort and colleagues have found it problematic (albeit due to a misunderstanding of some of our findings) and, frankly, so have we. The PMN is a response that is *larger* to stimuli failing to meet phonemic expectations but it always occurs when phonological processing of an acoustic stimulus takes place, a circumstance making the term "mismatch" inappropriate at best and misleading at worst. The PMN has been observed in both metaphonological tasks (e.g., phoneme deletion, phoneme substitution) and tasks that did not require explicit forms of phonological analysis (e.g., sentence processing, picture-auditory matching task). As we have argued previously, the PMN reflects an "automatic" process that unfailingly occurs whenever an acoustic stimulus is phonologically processed. It is, in fact, a response that maps phonological processing in real time, making the decision to rename it the *phonological mapping negativity* an easy one.

5.3 Inferred components and their position in and relevance to the time course of SWR

A number of studies have inferred the existence of subcomponents occurring before the N400 or overlapping with it. Two recent studies can serve as excellent examples demonstrating the presence of other components in the 200–600 ms time interval, their relative invisibility in grand averages, and their relevance to processes that serve auditory processing of spoken words leading ultimately to the activation of a supramodal semantic network.

Marinkovic et al. (2003) used MEG to examine semantic judgments in both the auditory and visual modalities. Their purpose was to investigate the stages of spoken and written word comprehension and track the processing within each modality-specific network to a final common supramodal semantic system. This discussion will only address the auditory element of their study. Participants were asked to make "size" judgments ("larger or smaller than one foot") to words denoting objects, body parts, and animals with a response required to larger items (e.g., *tiger, shirt*) but no response required to items failing to meet the one foot criterion (e.g., *cricket, medal*). During a practice session, ten words were presented repeatedly. These became the "repeated" words that were presented in half (390 trials of a total 780) of the subsequent trials interspersed amongst novel, nonrepeated words heard only once throughout the study. Aside from activating word comprehension functions, the inclusion of repeated stimuli permitted an examination of repetition priming and the brain areas involved in memory-related differential responses to words presented before (i.e., primed) and the time course of this/these processes.

Results for the auditory section of the study showed early activity (fifty-five ms) in the superior temporal area (the P50m), followed at around 100 ms by a negativity (the N100m) located in the perisylvian and superior temporal plane areas. At around 200 ms activity spread from this perisylvian and STP base to include anterior regions and by 250–270 ms there was additional involvement of anterior temporal lobe areas and posterior inferior frontal regions – most of this activity appeared bilaterally. The perisylvian area represented a sustained activation bilaterally, but after about 300 ms anterior temporal lobe and left inferior prefrontal cortex began showing a left-sided bias with bilateral contributions

from ventromedial prefrontal regions. The left-dominant anterior temporal pole activation appeared sustained with waveforms peaking at about 410 ms and other areas such as the anterior left inferior prefrontal cortex peaking slightly later with all activation continuing to about 700 ms. Repetition effects were examined in two latency-based windows, an early window of 250–270 ms and a late window of 300–500 ms. Within the first window of 225–250 ms, novel not repeated stimuli resulted in the stronger responses which centered around anterior temporal (extending to the pole) and the superior temporal plane areas; these areas did not respond to repeated stimuli. In the later window, evidence was found for overlap in activated areas for the auditory and visual stimuli (i.e., an apparent supramodal effect). Novel words produced more activation in left temporal and left prefrontal areas. Specifically, activation was seen at the temporal pole, anterior superior temporal sulcus areas, anterior left inferior prefrontal cortex, and a prefrontal area superior to left inferior prefrontal cortex. Generally speaking, significant activation was observed in many similar areas in the right hemisphere, suggesting a bilateral activation picture for auditory word processing functions – at least in a repetition-novel context. Timings of the activation associated with auditory word processing were sequential with the earliest activation (in this late stage) occurring at about 460 ms in the anterior temporal region followed by two separate activations in anterior left inferior prefrontal cortex (~490 ms and ~600 ms).

These data strongly support the view of a supramodal lexical system accessed by modality-specific lexical elements (e.g., Cabeza and Nyberg, 2000; Geschwind, 1965). However, what is of particular interest in the Marinkovic et al. (2003) study are the modality-specific processes that occur prior to lexical access or integration. These data provide valuable evidence of what appear to be a series of activations spanning as much as 600 ms that are involved in the processing of a spoken word and its novelty or familiarity. Novel words evoked stronger responses in the perisylvian regions in the 225–250 ms period, which the authors attribute to the auditory system's ability to "clearly distinguish the first phoneme of the highly familiar repeated words from the novel words that were presented only once (p. 493)." In other words, the activation was stronger to unfamiliar items and was substantially smaller to those that were familiar. Given the equal probability of occurrence between familiar and novel stimuli and the general context of semantic processing this response seems likely to be a PMN responding to the phonological form of the stimuli rather than, for example, a MMN reflecting some type of very low-level perceptual priming. In fact, the finding resembles a recent finding from our lab (unpublished) that a repeated "wrong choice" in the phoneme deletion task (see Newman as cited earlier in this chapter) produces a PMN that is reduced in size compared to the unique "wrong choices" that occur with equal probability throughout the study. While other "components" were seen in the late window as outlined earlier, what is noteworthy (and relevant to one of the themes of this chapter) is that it is often impossible to observe these components in standard, traditional grand average waveforms (see Marinkovic et al. 2003).

In another recent paper, the time course of bottom-up and top-down processing of syllables was examined and a sustained negativity occurring in the 200–600 ms time frame was found (Bonte et al., 2006). This study examined brain responses to syllable stimuli of two different types: One type was obtained by cutting off the first syllable from the first words of sentences at a point where coarticulatory features were removed (or minimized to the greatest extent possible) and a second type obtained by having someone speak the syllables individually so that there was never a further linguistic context to follow. These two types of stimuli formed the core elements of the study and were presented on their own or mixed together with words and sentences thus forming a linguistic-semantic context within which the syllables were heard.

The field patterns and dipole models obtained in this study found clear dipolar fields in the ~100, ~200, and ~400 ms periods. The N100m was characterized by bilateral dipolar fields with current flow perpendicular to the Sylvian fissure while the ECD analysis indicated the signal was generated just posterior to Heschl's gyrus. In the left hemisphere, the ~200 ms field pattern was due to a strong posterior temporal source that was interspersed with a weaker inferior frontal source. Right hemisphere patterns were more variable but generally showed an anterior temporal source. Although ECDs for this activity could be found in most subjects, they were sufficiently variable to suggest the activation of a network of distributed sources rather than a strong single generating point. This network is reminiscent of the D'Arcy et al. (2004) results showing several sources for PMN, including left-dominant activations in BA44/45 and BA39/40 as well as a dorsolateral prefrontal cortex site. The sustained activity peaking around 400 ms was characterized by bilateral fields perpendicular to the Sylvian fissure with ECDs centering around the posterior region of the superior temporal gyrus with a current flow virtually identical to the N100m.

The data for this study can be categorized with regard to top-down influences and bottom-up effects on syllable processing. Beginning first with the top-down effects, there was a general left hemisphere dominance seen for the syllable stimuli regardless of whether they were syllables cut from words beginning sentences or spoken separately. Also, a main effect for linguistic context was observed reflecting the stronger N400m to both syllable types heard in context rather than in isolation. Finally, a marginal interaction was seen reflecting the fact that the larger N400m responses to syllables heard in context versus syllables heard in isolation was significant in the right hemisphere and marginal in the left. A particularly interesting finding was that when the source waveforms for the isolation condition were subtracted from those for the context condition, a component sensitive to syllable processing within a linguistic context effect was observed. This stronger activation began at about 200 ms and reached a maximum strength around 280 ms with source strength appearing equally large in both hemispheres for syllables cut from sentences and left hemisphere dominant for syllables spoken in isolation: another example of a clear activation level (or component) sensitive to a particular prelexical process involving but possibly not restricted to phonological processing (certainly sharing its timing and field pattern with the PMN) that was not observable in grand average waveforms.

A particular strength of this study is the careful examination of the timing of activations that was undertaken. N400m activations in the left hemisphere began earlier and lasted longer for syllables presented in context compared to in isolation, although context generally had no influence on the timing of N400m peak latency. Also, examination of the ascending and descending limbs of the N400m response found that syllables presented in context produced a more rapid activation (ascending limb) and a more prolonged response (descending limb) than those presented in isolation. An interesting finding was noted when the authors examined the ascending limbs of the N400m to words, syllables in isolation, and syllables in context. They examined the 200–300 ms interval and found that the activation slope of the left hemisphere N400m to words was significantly different from that of the syllables in isolation but not of the syllables in context.

A secondary series of analyses were conducted comparing syllable types – those cut from sentence-initial positions and those spoken separately. Although activity was again observed in the 200–300 ms period to both types of syllables and followed the same hemispheric pattern as seen when the comparison involved context and isolation conditions – the effects were smaller. While the maximum strength of the N400m did not differ between syllable types, the latency of the N400m peak was about twenty-nine ms later to syllables cut from the beginning of sentences compared to those pronounced separately, an effect found regardless of

context (i.e., in word/sentence context or in isolation). This latency effect was found in the left hemisphere only. An examination of the N400m's onset trajectory indicated that it was steeper (as before this is a measure plotting amplitude against time) to the syllables taken from sentence onsets rather than those spoken in isolation and that this effect was found in the left hemisphere only.

The general conclusion drawn from these findings was that when both bottom-up and top-down influences were present, as in the case of syllables taken from sentence onsets and presented amongst words and sentences, responses to these syllables were most word-like. In contrast, when both of these effects were minimized, as seen with syllables spoken in isolation and presented on their own, responses were small and not very word-like. The differences observed between syllables taken from sentences and those created on their own were clearly affected by contextual issues insofar as these differences were seen only when the stimuli were presented in isolation – response to the two syllable types did not differ when they were presented in context. Thus, responses to syllables taken from sentences possessed bottom-up acoustic/phonetic features that evoked larger N400m responses, particularly in the left hemisphere. One of the most fascinating results of this study is that meaningless syllables merely placed in temporal contiguity with linguistic stimuli (words and sentences) resulted in the evocation of processes typically involved in the development of semantic- or meaning-based representations.

What is also important for the theme of this chapter is that an early response beginning at around 200 ms and peaking about eighty ms later, which was hidden by the large N400m seen in the traditional averaged responses, was seen when difference waves were analyzed. The timing of this response and its stronger activation within linguistic contexts (as demonstrated in the comparisons of bottom-up and top-down representations of this response), as well as its apparent network aspect demonstrates again that the N400 is *not* a unitary phenomenon and that subcomponents reflecting significant stages of the construction of meaningful representations of auditory stimulation are present. Also, this response does bear a striking similarity to the PMN.

Hagoort (2005) has suggested that we need to adopt a new framework for modelling or conceptualizing the neural basis of language, one that considers the proliferation of neuroimaging studies of language from a design perspective rather than from an experimental task perspective. While this chapter has studiously avoided such an approach, it is nonetheless a potentially useful one. Hagoort has taken the left inferior frontal gyrus as a point of convergence or unification relevant for phonology, semantics, and syntax. The implication is that these processes, typically conceptualized as discrete entities with their own time-course and localization, occur or co-occur in an overlapping or cascading fashion with one process beginning before another is completed (see also Jackendoff, 2002). Furthermore, it is also likely that a variety of other phenomena (memory and attention to name two) modulate the nature of the overlapping/cascading processes. If nothing else, such an approach could facilitate our appreciation of the morphological, temporal, and spatial variability of ERP/ERMF components associated with language function. Such an approach might also help us appreciate why the best answer to the question "Is the N400 pre or post lexical?" may be "Yes."

References

Ackerman, P. T., Dykman, R. A., & Oglesby, D. M. (1994). Visual event-related potentials of dyslexic children to rhyming and nonrhyming stimuli. *Journal of Clinical & Experimental Neuropsychology*, 16, 138–54.

Anderson, J. E. & Holcomb, P. J. (1995). Auditory and visual semantic priming using different stimulus onset asynchronies: An event-related brain potential study. *Psychophysiology*, 32, 177–90.

Barrett, S. E. & Rugg, M. D. (1989). Event-related potentials and the semantic matching of faces. *Neuropsychologia*, 27, 913–22.

& (1990). Event-related potentials and the semantic matching of pictures. *Brain and Cognition*, 14, 201–12.

Barrett, S. E., Rugg, M. D., & Perrett, D. I. (1988). Event-related potentials and the matching of familiar and unfamiliar faces. *Neuropsychologia*, 26, 105–17.

Behrmann, M. & Bub, D. (1992). Surface dyslexia and dysgraphia: Dual routes, single lexicon. *Cognitive Neuropsychology*, 9, 209–51.

Bentin, S., Kutas, M., & Hillyard, S. A. (1993). Electrophysiological evidence for task effects on semantic priming in auditory word processing. *Psychophysiology*, 30, 161–9.

Bentin, S., McCarthy, G., & Wood, C. C. (1985). Event-related potentials associated with semantic priming. *Electroencephalography and Clinical Neurophysiology*, 60, 343–55.

Bentin, S., Mouchetant-Rostaing, Y., Giard, M. H., Echallier, J. F., & Permier, J. (1999). ERP manifestations of processing printed words at different psycholinguistic levels: time course and scalp distribution. *Journal of Cognitive Neuroscience*, 11, 235–60.

Bitan, T., Burman, D. D., Chou, T. L., Dong, L., Cone, N. E., & Cao, F., et al. (2007). The interaction of orthographic and phonological information in children: An fMRI study. *Human Brain Mapping*, 28, 880–91.

Bloom, P. A. & Fischler, I. (1980). Completion norms for 329 sentence contexts. *Memory & Cognition*, 8, 631–42.

Bonte, M., Parviainen, T., Hytönen, K., & Salmelin, R. (2006). Time course of top-down and bottom-up influences on syllable processing in the auditory cortex. *Cerebral Cortex*, 16, 115–23.

Botvinick, M.. M. M., Cohen, J. D., & Carter, C. S. (2004). Conflict monitoring and anterior cingulate cortex: an update. *Trends in Cognitive Science*, 8, 539–46.

Brown, C., & Hagoort, P. (1993). The processing nature of the N400: Evidence from masked priming. *Journal of Cognitive Neuroscience*, 5, 34–44.

Cabeza, R., & Nyberg, L. (2000). Imaging cognition. II. An empirical review of 275 PET and fMRI studies. *Journal of Cognitive Neuroscience*, 12, 1–47.

Castles, A. C., Holmes, V. M., Neath, J., & Kinoshita, S. (2003). How does orthographic knowledge influence performance on phonological awareness tasks? *The Quarterly Journal of Experimental Psychology*, 56A(3), 445–67.

Cheour, M., Ceponiene, R., Lehtokoski, A., Luuk, A., Allik, J., Alho, K., & Näätänen, R. (1998). Development of language-specific phoneme representations in the infant brain. *Nature Neuroscience*, 1, 351–3.

Cohen, L., Lehéricy, S., Chochon, F., Lemer, C., Rivard, S., & Dehaene, S. (2002). Language-specific tuning of visual cortex? Functional properties of the visual word form area. *Brain*, 125, 1054–69.

Coltheart, M. (1978). Lexical access in a simple reading task. In Underwood, G. (Ed.) *Strategies of information processing* (pp. 151–216). London: Academic Press.

(1985). Cognitive neuropsychology and the study of reading. In Posner, M. I. & Martin, OSM (Eds.) *Attention and performance XI* (pp. 3–37). Hillsdale, NJ: Erlbaum.

Coltheart, M., Davelaar, E., Jonasson, J. T., & Besner, D. (1977). Access to the internal lexicon. In Dornic, S. (Ed.) *Attention and performance VI* (pp.535–55). New York, Academic Press.

Coltheart, M., Patterson, K., & Leahy, J. (1994). When a ROWS is a ROSE: Phonological effects in written word comprehension. *Quarterly Journal of Experimental Psychology*, 47A, 917–55.

Coltheart, M., Rastle, K., Perry, C., Langdon, R., & Ziegler, J. (2001). DRC: A dual route cascaded model of visual word recognition and reading aloud. *Psychological Review*, 108, 204–56.

Connolly, J. F. & Phillips, N. A. (1994). Event-related potential components reflect phonological and semantic processing of the terminal word of spoken sentences. *Journal of Cognitive Neuroscience*, 6, 256–66.

Connolly, J. F., Phillips, N. A., Stewart, S. H., & Brake, W. G. (1992). Event-related potential sensitivity to acoustic and semantic properties of terminal words in sentences. *Brain and Language*, 43, 1–18.

Connolly, J. F., Service, E., D'Arcy, RCN, Kujala, A., & Alho, K. (2001). Phonological aspects of word recognition as revealed by high-resolution spatio-temporal brain mapping. *Neuroreport*, 12, 237–43.

Connolly, J. F., Stewart, S. H., & Phillips, N. A. (1990). The effects of processing requirements on neurophysiological responses to spoken sentences. *Brain and Language*, 39, 302–18.

Coslett, H. B. (1991). Read but not write "idea": Evidence for a third reading mechanism. *Brain & Language*, 40, 425–43.

Crystal, T. H. & House, A. S. (1990). Articulation rate and the duration of syllables and stress groups in connected speech. *Journal of the Acoustical Society of America*, 88, 101–12.

Daneman, M. & Reingold, E. (1993). What eye fixations tell us about phonological recoding during reading. *Canadian Journal of Experimental Psychology*, 47, 153–78.

D'Arcy, R. C. N. & Connolly, J. F. (1999). An event-related brain potential study of receptive speech comprehension using a modified Token Test. *Neuropsychologia*, 37, 1477–89.

D'Arcy, R. C. N, Connolly, J. F., Service, E., Hawco, C. S., & Houlihan, M. E. (2004). Separating phonological and semantic processing in auditory sentence processing: a high-resolution event-related brain potential study. *Human Brain Mapping*, 22, 40–51.

D'Arcy, R. C. N, Service, E., Connolly, J. F., & Hawco, C. S. (2005). The influence of increased working memory load on semantic neural systems: a high-resolution event-related brain potential study. *Cognitive Brain Research*, 22, 177–91.

Davelaar, E., Coltheart, M., Besner, D., & Jonasson, J. T. (1978). Phonological recoding and lexical access. *Memory & Cognition*, 6, 391–402.

Davis, M. H. & Johnsrude, I. S. (2003). Hierarchical processing in spoken language comprehension. *Journal of Neuroscience*, 23, 3423–31.

Deacon, D., Hewitt, S., Yang, C., & Nagata, M. (2000). Event-related potential indices of semantic priming using masked and unmasked words: evidence that the N400 does not reflect a post-lexical process. *Cognitive Brain Research*, 9, 137–46.

Desroches, A. S., Newman, R. L., & Joanisse, M. F. (2009). Investigating the time course of spoken word recognition: Electrophysiological evidence for the influences of phonological similarity. *Journal of Cognitive Neuroscience*, 21, 1893–906.

Eggermont, J. J. & Ponton, C. W. (2002). The neurophysiology of auditory perception: from single units to evoked potentials. *Audiology & neuro-otology*, 7, 71–99.

Ehri, L. C. & Wilce, L. S. (1980). The influence of orthography on readers' conceptualisation of the phonemic structure of words. *Applied Psycholinguistics*, 1, 371–85.

Ferrand, L., & Grainger, J. (1994). Effects of orthography are independent of phonology in masked form priming. *Quarterly Journal of Experimental Psychology*, 47A, 365–82.

(1996). List context effects on masked phonological priming in the lexical decision task. *Psychonomic Bulletin & Review*, 3, 515–19.

Fischler, I., Childers, D. G., Achariyapaopan, T., & Perry, N. W. (1985). Brain potentials during sentence verification: Automatic aspects of comprehension. *Biological Psychology*, 21, 83–105.

Forbes, K. A. K (1993). Memory performance, event-related brain potentials and phonological recoding during silent reading. *Unpublished thesis.*

—— (1998). Event-related brain potentials (ERPs) measure the influences of orthographic, phonological and semantic representations during silent reading. *Unpublished thesis.*

Francis, A. L. & Nusbaum, H. C. (1996). Paying attention to speaking rate. *ICSLP-1996*, 1537–40.

Friederici, A. D., Steinhauer, K., & Frisch, S. (1999). Lexical integration: sequential effects of syntactic and semantic information. *Memory & Cognition*, 27, 438–53.

Frost, R. & Ziegler, J.C. (2007). Speech and spelling interaction: the interdependence of visual and auditory word recognition. In Gaskell, M.G. (Ed.), *The Oxford Handbook of Psycholinguistics.* (pp. 107–18) Oxford University Press: Oxford, UK.

Funnell, E. (1983). Phonological processes in reading: New evidence from acquired dyslexia. *British Journal of Psychology*, 74, 159–80.

Hagoort, P. (2005). On Broca, brain, and binding: A new framework. *Trends in Cognitive Sciences*, 9, 416–23.

Hagoort, P. & Brown, C. M. (2000). ERP effects of listening to speech: semantic ERP effects. *Neuropsychologia*, 38, 1518–30.

Halgren, E., Dhond, R. P., Christensen, N., Van Petten, C., Marinkovic, K., Lewine, J. D., & Dale, A. M. (2002). N400-like magnetoencephalography responses modulated by the semantic context, word frequency, and lexical class in sentences. *NeuroImage*, 17, 1101–16.

Harm, M. & Seidenberg, M. S. (2004). Computing the meanings of words in reading: Cooperative division of labor between visual and phonological processes. *Psychological Review*, 111, 662–720.

Helenius, P., Salmelin, R., Service, E., & Connolly, J. F. (1998). Distinct time courses of word and context comprehension in the left temporal cortex. *Brain*, 121, 1133–42.

—— (1999). Semantic cortical activation in dyslexic readers. *Journal of Cognitive Neuroscience*, 11, 535–50.

Helenius, P., Salmelin, R., Service, E., Connolly, J. F., Leinonen, S., & Lyytinen, H. (2002). Cortical activation during spoken-word segmentation in non reading-impaired and dyslexic adults. *Journal of Neuroscience*, 22, 2936–44.

Herdman, C. M. & Beckett, B. L. (1996). Code-specific processes in word naming: Evidence supporting a dual-route model of word recognition. *Journal of Experimental Psychology: Human Perception and Performance*, 22, 1149–65.

Hickok, G. & Poeppel, D. (2007). The cortical organization of speech processing. *Nature Reviews Neuroscience*, 8, 393–402.

Holcomb, P. J. (1993). Semantic priming and stimulus degradation: implications for the role of the N400 in language processing. *Psychophysiology*, 30, 47–61.

Holcomb, P. J., Grainger, J., & O'Rourke, T. (2002). An electrophysiological study of the effects of orthographic neighborhood size on printed word perception. *Journal of Cognitive Neuroscience*, 14, 938–50.

Holcomb, P. J. & McPherson, W. B. (1994). Event-related brain potentials reflect semantic priming in an object decision task. *Brain & Cognition*, 24, 259–76.

Holcomb, P. J., & Neville, H. J. (1990). Auditory and visual semantic priming in lexical decision: A comparison using evoked potentials. *Language and Cognitive Processes*, 5, 281–312.

Jackendoff, R. (2002). *Foundations of Language: Brain, Meaning, Grammar, Evolution.* Toronto: Oxford University Press.

Jared, D., Levy, B. A., & Rayner, K. (1999). The role of phonology in the activation of word meanings during reading: Evidence from proofreading and eye movements. *Journal of Experimental Psychology: General*, 128, 219–64.

Jared, D. & Seidenberg, M. S. (1991). Does word identification proceed from spelling to sound to meaning? *Journal of Experimental Psychology: General*, 120, 358–94.

Kalikow, D. N., Stevens, K. N., & Elliott, L. L. (1977). Development of a test of speech intelligibility in noise using sentence materials with controlled predictability. *Journal Acoustical Society America*, 61, 1337–51.

Kujala, A., Alho, K., Service, E., Ilmoniemi, R. J., & Connolly, J. F. (2004). Activation in the anterior left auditory cortex associated with phonological analysis of speech input: localization of the phonological mismatch negativity response with MEG. *Cognitive Brain Research*, 21, 106–13.

Kutas, M. (1987). Event-related brain potentials (ERPs) elicited during rapid serial visual presentation of congruous and incongruous sentences: In Johnson Jr., R., Rohrbaugh, J. W., & Parasuraman, R. (Eds.) *Current Trends in Event-Related Potential Research* (EEG Suppl. 40). Elsevier, Amsterdam.

Kutas, M. & Federmeier, K. D. (2000). Electrophysiology reveals semantic memory use in language comprehension. *Trends Cognitive Science*, 2000 *4(12)*, 463–70.

Kutas, M. & Hillyard, S. A (1980). Reading senseless sentences: brain potentials reflect semantic incongruity. *Science*, 207, 203–5.

Kutas, M. & Van Petten, C. K. (1994). Psycholinguistics electrified: event-related brain potential investigations in Gernsbacher, M. A. (Ed.) *Handbook of Psycholinguistics* (pp. 83–143). San Diego, CA: Academic Press.

Liégeois-Chauvel, C., Musolino, A., Badier, J. M., Marquis, P., & Chauvel, P. (1994). Evoked potentials recorded from the auditory cortex in man: evaluation and topography of the middle latency components. *Electroencephalograpy & Clinical Neurophysiology*, 92, 204–14.

Liberman, A. M., Cooper, F. S., Shankweiler, D. P., & Studdert-Kennedy, M. (1967). Perception of the speech code. *Psychological Review*, 74, 431–61.

Lütkenhöner, B. & Steinstrater, O. (1998). High-precision neuromagnetic study of the functional organization of the human auditory cortex. *Audiology & Neuro-otology*, 3, 191–213.

Lukatela, G. & Turvey, M. T. (1994a). Visual lexical access is initially phonological: I. Evidence from associative priming by words, homophones, and pseudohomophones. *Journal of Experimental Psychology: General*, 123, 107–28.

Lukatela, G. & Turvey, M. T. (1994b). Visual lexical access is initially phonological: 2. Evidence from phonological priming by homophones and pseudohomophones. *Journal of Experimental Psychology: General*, 123, 331–53.

Marinkovic, K., Dhond, R. P., Dale, A. M., Glessner, M., Carr, V., & Halgren, E. (2003). Spatiotemporal dynamics of modality-specific and supramodal word processing. *Neuron*, 38, 487–97.

Marslen-Wilson, W. (1987). Functional parallelism in spoken word recognition. *Cognition*, 25, 71–102.

Marslen-Wilson, W. D. & Tyler, L. K. (1980). The temporal structure of spoken language understanding. *Cognition*, 8, 1–71.

McClelland, J. L. & Elman, J. L. (1986). The TRACE model of speech perception. *Cognitive Psychology*, 18, 1–86.

McPherson, W. B., Ackerman, P. T., Holcomb, P. J., & Dykman, R. A. (1998). Event-related brain potentials elicited during phonological processing differentiate subgroups of reading disabled adolescents. *Brain & Language*, 62, 163–85.

McPherson, W. B. & Holcomb, P. J. (1999). An electrophysiological investigation of semantic priming with pictures of real objects. *Psychophysiology*, 36, 53–65.

Newman, R. L. & Connolly, J. F. (2004). Determining the role of phonology in silent reading using event-related brain potentials. *Cognitive Brain Research*, 21, 94–105.

(2009). Electrophysiological markers of pre-lexical speech processing: Evidence for bottom-up and top-down effects on spoken word processing. *Biological Psychology*, 80, 114–21.

Newman, R. L., Connolly, J. F., Service, E., & McIvor, K. (2003). Phonological processing during a phoneme deletion task: Evidence from event-related brain potentials. *Psychophysiology*, 40, 640–7.

Niznikiewicz, M. & Squires, N. K. (1996). Phonological processing and the role of strategy in silent reading: behavioural and electrophysiological evidence. *Brain & Language*, 52, 342–63.

Olson, G. A. & Kausler, D. H. (1971). Orthographic distinctiveness of homonyms. *Behavioural Research Methods and Instruments*, 3, 298–9.

Parviainen, T., Helenius. P., & Salmelin, R. (2005). Cortical differentiation of speech and non-speech sounds at 100 ms: implications for dyslexia. *Cerebral Cortex*, 15, 1054–63.

Pattamadilok, C., Morais, J., Ventura, P., & Kolinsky, R. (2007). The locus of the orthographic consistency effect in auditory word recognition: Further evidence from French. *Language and Cognitive Processes*, 22, 1–27.

Pattamadilok, C., Perre, L., Dufau, S., & Ziegler, J. C. (2009). On-line orthographic influences on spoken language in a semantic task. *Journal of Cognitive Neuroscience*, 21, 169–79.

Perre, L., Midgley, K., & Ziegler, J. C. (2009a). When beef primes reef more than leaf: Orthographic information affects phonological priming in spoken word recognition. *Psychophysiology*, 46, 739–46.

Perre, L., Pattamadilok, C., Montant, M., & Ziegler, J. C. (2009b). Orthographic effects in spoken language: On-line activation or phonological restructuring? *Brain Research*, 1275, 73–80.

Perre, L. & Ziegler, J. C. (2008). On-line activation of orthography in spoken word recognition. *Brain Research*, 1188, 132–8.

Phillips, C., Pellathy, T., Marantz, A., Yellin, E., Wexler, K., Poeppel, D., McGinnis, M., & Roberts, T. (2000). Auditory cortex accesses phonological categories: an MEG mismatch study. *Journal Cognitive Neuroscience*, 12, 1038–55.

Poeppel, D., Yellin, E., Phillips, C. Roberts, T. P., Rowley, H. A., Wexler, K., & Marantz, A. (1996). Task-induced asymmetry of the auditory evoked M100 neuromagnetic field elicited by speech sounds. *Cognitive Brain Research*, 4, 231–42.

Price, C., Thierry, G., & Griffiths, T. (2005). Speech-specific auditory processing: where is it? *Trends in Cognitive Neuroscience*, 9, 271–76.

Roelofs, A. & Hagoort, P. (2002). Control of language use: cognitive modeling the hemodynamics of Stroop task performance. *Brain Research Cognitive Brain Research*, 15, 85–97.

Rugg, M. D. (1984a). Event-related potentials in phonological matching tasks. *Brain & Language*, 23, 225–40.

(1984b). Event-related potentials and the phonological processing of words and nonwords. *Neuropsychologia*, 22, 435–43.

(1990). Event-related brain potentials dissociate repetition effects of high- and low-frequency words. *Memory & Cognition*, 18, 367–79.

Rugg, M. D. & Barrett, S. E. (1987). Event-related potentials and the interaction between orthographic and phonological information in a rhyme judgment task. *Brain & Language*, 32, 336–61.

Scott, S. K., Blank, C. C., Rosen, S., & Wise, R. J. S. (2000). Identification of a pathway for intelligible speech in the left temporal lobe. *Brain*, 123, 2400–6.

Scott, S. K. & Johnsrude, I. S. (2003). The neuroanatomical and functional organization of speech perception. *Trends in Neuroscience*, 26, 100–7.

Seidenberg, M. S. & McClelland, J. L. (1989). A distributed, developmental model of word recognition and naming. *Psychological Review*, 96, 523–68.

Seidenberg, M. S. & Tanenhaus, M. K. (1979). Orthographic effects on rhyme monitoring. *Journal of Experimental Psychology: Human Learning and Memory*, 5, 546–54.

Simos, P. G., Basile, L. F. H., & Papanicolaou, A. C. (1997). Source localization of the N400 response in a sentence-reading paradigm using evoked magnetic fields and magnetic resonance imaging. *Brain Research*, 762, 29–39.

Steinhauer, K. & Connolly, J. F. (2008). Event-related Potentials in the Study of Language. In Stemmer, B. & Whitaker, H. (Eds.) *Handbook of the Neuroscience of Language* (pp. 91–104), Amsterdam: Elsevier.

Stone, G. O. & Van Orden, G. C. (1993). Strategic control of processing in word recognition. *Journal of Experimental Psychology: Human Perception and Performance*, 19, 744–74.

Stuart, M. (1990). Processing strategies in a phoneme deletion task. *Quarterly Journal of Experimental Psychology*, 42A, 305–27.

Taft, M., Castles, A., Davis, C., Lazendic, G., & Nguyen-Hoan, M. (2008). Automatic activation of orthography in spoken word recognition: Pseudohomograph priming. *Journal of Memory and Language*, 58, 366–79.

van den Brink, D., Brown C., & Hagoort, P. (2001). Electrophysiological evidence for early contextual influences during spoken-word recognition: N200 versus N400 effects. *Journal of Cognitive Neuroscience*, 13, 967–85.

Van Orden, G. C. (1987). A ROWS is a ROSE: Spelling, sound, and reading. *Memory & Cognition*, 15, 181–98.

Van Orden, G. C., Pennington, B. F. & Stone, G. O. (1990). Word identification in reading and the promise of subsymbolic psycholinguistics. *Psychological Review*, 97, 488–522.

Van Petten, C. (1993). A comparison of lexical and sentence-level context effects and their temporal parameters. *Language and Cognitive Processes*, 8, 485–532.

Van Petten, C. & Luka, B. J. (2006). Neural localization of semantic context effects in electromagnetic and hemodynamic studies. *Brain & Language*, 97, 279–93.

Venezky, R. (1970). *The structure of English orthography*. The Hague, The Netherlands: Mouton.

Ventura, P., Morais, J., Pattamadilok, C., & Kolinsky, R. (2004). The locus of the orthographic consistency effect in auditory word recognition. *Language and Cognitive Processes*, 19, 57–95.

Vihla, M., Lounasmaa, O.V., & Salmelin, R. (2000). Cortical processing of change detection: dissociation between natural vowels and two frequency complex tones. *Proceedings National Academy Sciences, USA* 97:10590–10594.

Werker, J. & Yeung, H. H. (2005). Infant speech perception bootstraps word learning. *Trends in Cognitive Science*, 9, 519–27.

West, W. C. & Holcomb, P. J. (2000). Imaginal, semantic, and surface-level processing of concrete and abstract words: An electrophysiological investigation. *Journal of Cognitive Neuroscience*, 12, 1024–37.

Ziegler, J. C., Benraiss, A., & Besson, M. (1999). From print to meaning: an electrophysiological investigation of the role of phonology in accessing word meaning. *Psychophysiology, 36*, 775–85.

Ziegler, J. C. & Ferrand, L. (1998). Orthography shapes the perception of speech: The consistency effect in auditory word recognition. *Psychonomic Bulletin & Review, 5*, 683–9.

Ziegler, J. C., Ferrand, L., & Montant, M. (2004). Visual phonology: the effects of orthographic consistency on different auditory word recognition tasks. *Memory and Cognition, 32*, 732–41.

Ziegler, J. C., Petrova, A., & Ferrand, L. (2008). Feedback consistency effects in visual and auditory word recognition: where do we stand after more than a decade? *Journal of Experimental Psychology: Learning, Memory, and Cognition, 34*, 643–61.

Zwitserlood, P. (1989). The locus of the effects of sentential-semantic context in spoken-word processing. *Cognition, 32*, 25–64.

WRITTEN WORD RECOGNITION

CHAPTER 8

Visual Word Recognition in Skilled Adult Readers

Michael J. Cortese and David A. Balota

1 Introduction

Visual word recognition is the foundation of reading. It is the place where form meets meaning and hence is the basis by which higher order semantic and comprehension processes take place. Although evidence suggests that reading is an interactive process, one must be able to recognize a word before one can reliably integrate its meaning into a coherent message. The importance of this process is exemplified by the amount of research that has been conducted on word processing in cognitive psychology and related fields. Word recognition research has been central to developments in cognitive neuroscience (e.g., Frost et al., 2005; Pugh et al., 2005), serial versus parallel processing (e.g., Coltheart and Rastle, 1994; Cortese, 1998; Weekes, 1997), attention (e.g., Neely, 1977; Zevin and Balota, 2000), educational practices (e.g., Harm, McCandliss, and Seidenberg, 2003), connectionism (e.g., Coltheart et al., 2001; Plaut et al., 1996), and much more. In this light, the word can be viewed as important to developments in cognitive psychology as the cell has been to developments in the biological sciences (see Balota, 1994).

In this chapter, we begin by providing an overview of the standard tools employed in visual word recognition research. Next, we discuss some general theoretical issues and controversies, although there are other chapters in this volume dedicated to further specification of these issues. In addition, although we will touch on some evidence from neuroscience and neuropsychology, a more detailed discussion of this topic is covered by Sandak et al. in this volume. The major portion of this chapter will be dedicated toward reviewing the major factors that have been identified in adult word recognition performance, along with some recent methodological developments. Finally, we discuss some continuing controversies covered in the literature and summarize the chapter.

2 Tools of the trade

Although there are many tasks used to measure word recognition, the lexical decision and the naming tasks remain the workhorse tasks in this area (Balota et al., 2004). In the lexical decision task, the subject decides as quickly as possible if a letter string is a word or not and indicates his/her decision by pressing a designated button. In the naming task, the participant simply reads aloud a word as quickly and accurately as possible. In addition, priming paradigms have utilized both naming and lexical decision tasks. In the priming paradigm, two letter strings (i.e., words and/or nonwords) are presented sequentially, and participants either name or make a lexical decision to the second letter string, with the two stimuli varying on some dimension such as relatedness (e.g., *consider dog–cat* versus *pen–cat*).

Although lexical decision and naming are the major tools in this area, there are clearly other important measures. For example, measuring eye movements such as gaze and first fixation durations on a given word has been a very useful tool. These measures may be the best measures of the processes tied to word recognition while reading, and in general converge with the results from naming and/or lexical decision performance (cf. Schilling, Rayner, and Chumbley, 1998). Another useful task involves identifying visually degraded words in which words are briefly presented and often forward and/or backward masked by characters (e.g., Tan and Perfetti, 1999). This task has been viewed as providing an indicant of early visual word processing (but see Broadbent, 1967; Catlin, 1973). Other useful tasks include category verification (i.e., subjects are given a category name followed by a potential exemplar, and they decide if the exemplar is a member of the target category), relatedness judgment (i.e., subjects decide if two words are related or not), and rhyme judgments (i.e., subjects decide if two words rhyme or not). It is important to note that all tasks are likely to engage task-specific processes, and also all have some overlapping processes. Hence, no task is process pure (see Jacoby, 1991). Task differences indicate that one should be cautious in using only one task as a microscope into the processes involved in visual word

recognition (see Grainger and Jacobs, 1996; Jacobs et al., 1998).

3 General theoretical issues

With the previously mentioned tools in hand, it is important to consider some of the important theoretical issues that have shaped this field. The initial attempts to capture word recognition processes involved two distinct classes of models; activation models (Morton, 1969) and search models (e.g., Forster, 1976). In order to glean some understanding of these models, consider the word frequency effect (i.e., the finding that high-frequency words produce faster and more accurate responses than low-frequency words across a wide range of tasks). Because of the robustness of this effect, most researchers consider this as a starting point for any viable modeling endeavor (see Forster, 2004; Murray and Forster, 2004).

In Morton's classic logogen model (1969), frequency is coded in the resting level activations of the logogens (i.e., word recognition devices). Due to the frequency of exposure, high-frequency words have higher resting level activations than low-frequency words. Thus, logogens for high-frequency words need less stimulus driven bottom-up (and contextually driven top-down) activation than low-frequency words in order to reach their threshold for identification. In search models (e.g., Forster, 1976; Forster and Murray, 2004; Rubenstein, Garfield, and Millikan, 1970), the lexicon is ordered by frequency and searched serially. An initial perceptual analysis defines an orthographic bin (i.e., a likely candidate set that could match the stimulus) that is searched in a frequency-ordered manner. Therefore, high-frequency words will be located in the lexicon before low-frequency words (there are also phonological bins for auditory information and syntactic/semantic bins to accommodate context effects). There are also hybrid models (e.g., Becker, 1979; Paap, Newsome, and McDonald, 1982; Taft and Hambly, 1986) that include characteristics of both activation and search models. For example, Becker posits initial activation processes that define both sensory and semantic search sets. The target stimulus is then compared to the search sets via a frequency-ordered search process.

A third class of models involves a connectionist approach. The current interest in connectionist models of word recognition can be traced back to the interactive activation (IA) models proposed by McClelland and Rumelhart. (1981; Rumelhart and McClelland, 1982; also see Paap et al., 1982). These models were a logical extension of Selfridge's (1959; also see Selfridge and Neisser, 1960) pandemonium model of letter recognition and also incorporated aspects of Morton's logogen model. Selfridge hypothesized that letters were initially analyzed in terms of their visual features that communicated with letter-level representations which in turn communicated with a decision component. The pandemonium model was important because it was one of the first computational models of pattern recognition, and it also benefited from the temporal contiguity with evidence that was accumulating from neuroscience. Specifically, there was accumulating evidence that specific neurons appeared to code primitive features (e.g., horizontal lines, vertical lines, intersections) which could then serve as the building blocks for pattern recognition (e.g., Hubel and Weisel, 1962; 1968).

The IA model (see Figure 8.1) consists of feature detectors, letter detectors, and word detectors. Representations at and between these different levels are connected by facilitatory (arrowed lines) and/or inhibitory (knobbed lines) pathways. When processing a letter string, letter-level representations activate word-level representations via facilitatory connections. More interesting, letter-level representations are reinforced via top-down activation from the word level. Also, activated representations inhibit competing representations within and between levels so that, eventually, only the appropriate representation reaches its threshold. For example, when presented with *book*, its word-level representation becomes active

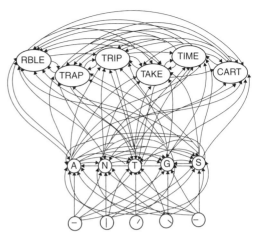

Figure 8.1. The interactive activation (IA) model of McClelland and Rumelhart (1981). Connections marked with arrows denote facilitative connections, and connections marked with circles denote inhibitory connections. This figure was reprinted from McClelland and Rumelhart, "An interactive activation model of context effects in letter perception: Part 1. An account of basic findings." *Psychological Review*, 88, 375–407, 1981, American Psychological Association, reprinted with permission.

across time, and this activation eventually inhibits the word-level representations for *cook*, *boom*, *bock*, etc. Similar inhibitory processing occurs at the feature and letter levels.

Originally, a promising aspect of the IA model was that it could account for the word superiority effect (i.e., the phenomenon that letters are more easily recognized when they occur in words than when they occur in nonwords; cf. Fine, 2001; Reicher, 1969). The explanation is based on the notion of cascadic processing (see Ashby, 1982; McClelland, 1979). Specifically, while information is accumulating in the system, an activated representation does not need to reach its response threshold before it can influence the activation of other representations. Instead, information continuously flows in a bidirectional manner between levels (i.e., among features, letters, and words). Thus, for words, letter-level representations receive bottom-up activation from the feature level and top-down activation from the word level.

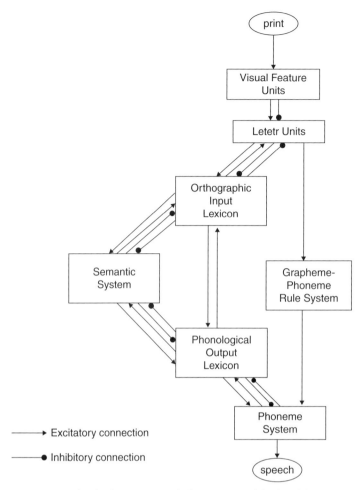

Figure 8.2. The dual-route cascaded (DRC) model of Coltheart et al. (2001). Connections marked with arrows denote facilitative connections, and connections marked with circles denote inhibitory connections. This figure was reprinted from Coltheart et al., "DRC: A dual route cascaded model of visual word recognition and reading aloud. *Psychological Review*, 108, 204–56, 2001; American Psychological Association, reprinted with permission.

Although the original IA model is important, it primarily dealt with letter recognition performance. More recent models have extended this model to capture word recognition performance. For example, an important model that includes an IA component is the dual-route cascaded (DRC) model (e.g., Coltheart et al., 2001). In the DRC model (see Figure 8.2), two routes are used to process words: a lexical route and a sublexical route. The lexical route is a parallel processor that contains an orthographic and phonological representation for each word in the reader's vocabulary, and has some similarity to the IA model. The sublexical route is a serial processor (working from left to right) that employs a set of grapheme-to-phoneme conversion (GPC) rules to convert letter strings into phonological representations. A grapheme consists of one or more letters that symbolizes a single phoneme (e.g., *champ* consists of the graphemes *ch, a, m,* and *p*).

Considerable evidence supports the DRC perspective. For example, consider the performance by skilled readers in naming irregular words and nonwords. An irregular word (e.g., *pint*) has a pronunciation that violates GPC rules. Applying GPC rules to *pint* would yield a pronunciation that rhymes with *mint*. Therefore, a correct reading of *pint* appears to require the lexical route. In contrast, a correct reading of nonwords (e.g., *blask*) requires the sublexical route because nonwords are not represented in the lexicon. In addition, there is evidence from different types of acquired dyslexia. Specifically, individuals with surface dyslexia (e.g., Patterson and Behrmann, 1997) are relatively good at pronouncing nonwords but have difficulty naming low-frequency irregular words, often regularizing these items. These individuals apparently have an intact sublexical route but a disabled lexical route. In contrast, individuals with phonological dyslexia (e.g., Funnell, 1983) have difficulty naming nonwords, but are relatively accurate at naming both irregular and regular words. These individuals apparently have an intact lexical route but a disabled sublexical route. This double dissociation between surface and phonological dyslexics originally was viewed as strong evidence for a dual-route model (but see Patterson et al., 1996; Plaut, 1999 for a more recent discussion of this evidence).

The idea that two routes are necessary to pronounce both irregular words and nonwords was brought into question in 1989, when Seidenberg and McClelland introduced their parallel distributed processing (PDP) model of word recognition. The *parallel* feature of the model means that the processing of different units at a given level occurs simultaneously. The *distributed* feature of the model means that each unique word is associated with a unique pattern of activation across a common set of units that are used to process all words. The Seidenberg and McClelland model consisted of a network of simple processing units, including an orthographic input layer and a phonological output layer. All of these input and output units were connected to all the units of a hidden layer. An important initial advantage of these models is that instead of hard wiring the models to capture

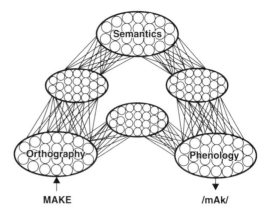

Figure 8.3. The parallel-distributed-processing (PDP) model of Plaut et al. (1996). Reprinted from *Brain and Language*, 52, by Plaut, "Relearning after damage in connectionist networks: Toward a theory of rehabilitation" (1996) with permission from Elsevier.

behavior, the models actually learn via a back propogation algorithm. Specifically, the weights connecting different units are adjusted via exposure to the language in a frequency dependent manner. Weights are adjusted such that the error prone output from the model early during the development is gradually adjusted so that it is more likely to match the desired output in the future. The interesting observation is that the Seidenberg and McClelland model consisted of a single route (from orthography to phonology) that could generate correct pronunciations for both irregular words and nonwords without a lexicon or a set of sublexical rules. However, due to some difficulties with nonword generalization (c.f. Besner et al., 1990) and advances involving recurrent networks (i.e., networks that produce phonological outputs over time), the model was modified by Plaut and colleagues (Plaut et al., 1996) and remains the foremost challenger to the traditional dual-route approach (Figure 8.3).

The Plaut model consists of sets of grapheme units, phoneme units, and semantic units. A layer of hidden units mediates associations between each level of representation, and hence the Plaut model is considerably more complex than the original Seidenberg and McClelland model. As noted, the Plaut model was a recurrent network that eventually settled into a steady state and hence predicted response latencies directly, instead of producing an error measure, which was the output from the original Seidenberg and McClelland model. When recognizing a word, its corresponding grapheme units become activated, and this activation is propagated throughout the network. Knowledge of spelling-to-sound relationships are again contained in the values of weighted connections linking units in the network. The Plaut model demonstrated how to produce codes for regular and irregular words as well as nonwords and eliminated some of the apparent deficiencies with the Seidenberg and McClelland model.

There remains considerable controversy between the connectionist and dual-route models of word recognition (see, for example, Coltheart et al., 2001; Seidenberg, 2005 for recent discussions). In addition, additional models have come online such as the Zorzi, Houghton, and Butterworth (1998) model which combines aspects of the DRC and PDP models. A multiple readout model by Jacobs and colleagues (1998) is also quite important because it emphasizes both task-specific operations and task-general operations in lexical processing. The Ans, Carbonnel, and Valdois (1998) model also has extended this area by providing a computational approach to recognizing multisyllabic words, a deficiency in the previous models dedicated to processing monosyllabic stimuli. Norris (2006) has recently developed a model based on Baysean principles taking into account the probability that a stimulus maps onto a given word given prior probabilities. Also, Perry, Ziegler, and Zorzi (2007) have developed a connectionist model that retains the positive features of earlier models while eliminating many of their weaknesses. As one can see, there is a rich set of theoretical constructs used to capture visual word recognition. Now that we have provided an introduction to the some of the key theoretical issues, we shall turn to the empirical findings that models will need to capture.

4 What variables have been uncovered?

4.1 *The frequency effect*

One of the most robust findings in the literature is that high-frequency words (e.g., *book*) are recognized more quickly and accurately than low-frequency words (e.g., *boom*). In fact, in the large-scale study conducted by Balota and colleagues (2004), word frequency was one of the strongest predictors of performance. In this study, while the word frequency effect was strong for both the naming and lexical decision tasks, the effect was much larger in the lexical decision task.

As noted earlier, although the word frequency effect would appear to be a finding easy to accommodate in models, each model of visual word recognition appears to take a different approach, including thresholds (e.g., Coltheart et al., 2001), weights of connections (e.g., Seidenberg and McClelland, 1989), and locations in frequency-ordered search bins (Murray and Forster, 2004). Others have attempted to argue that task-specific operations contribute to the word frequency effect. For example, consider the lexical decision task. Low-frequency words are more similar to the nonwords than high-frequency words on a familiarity dimension and so are more difficult to accept as a word. Balota and Chumbley (1984) and Balota and Spieler (1999) have argued that this difficulty engages additional analytic processing (also see Besner, 1983), whereas Ratcliff and colleagues (Ratcliff et al., 2004) have recently argued that this will slow the drift rate in a diffusion model. Clearly, the word frequency effect is a classic example of an intuitively simple effect that has been central to theoretical developments in the word recognition literature, and remains a central focus of research.

4.1.1 FAMILIARITY AND SUBJECTIVE FREQUENCY

While objective frequency counts provide good estimates of the frequency of occurrence of words in print, another measure is to have participants rate the subjective familiarity of the stimulus on a numeric scale ranging, for example, from one indicating no familiarity to seven indicating extremely high familiarity. While subjective frequency would be expected to relate to theoretical models in much the same way as objective frequency, this measure may be better because the standard printed frequency counts (e.g., Kučera and Francis, 1967) do not take into consideration spoken word frequency or how often one produces a word through speech or writing. Gernsbacher (1984) argued that objective word frequency estimates are less reliable for low-frequency words than high-frequency words. She noted that *boxer*, *icing*, and *joker* have the same objective frequency value (according to Kučera and Francis, 1967) as *loire*, *gnome*, and *assay*. Fortunately, there are now more extensive word frequency databases than the Kučera and Francis norms (e.g., Baayen, Piepenbrock, and Rijn, 1993; Zeno et al., 1995). However, it is still the case that these researchers typically use the frequency of words in print as their primary measure of frequency. Hence, some researchers still argue that subjective familiarity ratings are a better measure of sheer exposure to a word.

However, familiarity is difficult to define, and familiarity ratings may be influenced by extraneous variables. Standard instructions for familiarity ratings tend to be vague and may encourage the use of other types of information. In fact, Balota, Pilotti, and Cortese (1999) found that the familiarity ratings of Toglia and Battig (1978) were related to meaningfulness, a semantic variable.

As an alternative to standard familiarity ratings, Balota et al.'s (1999) participants rated monosyllabic words in terms of subjective frequency. Participants estimated how often they read, heard, wrote, said, or encountered each word based on the following scale: 1 = never, 2 = once a year, 3 = once a month, 4 = once a week, 5 = every two days, 6 = once a day, 7 = several times a day. They found that these ratings were less influenced by meaningfulness than the Toglia and Battig (1978) familiarity ratings. Therefore subjective frequency ratings may

be more appropriate than traditional familiarity ratings because they are less influenced by semantic factors. In a recent study, Balota et al. (2004) found that the subjective ratings were predictive of lexical and naming performance above and beyond objective word frequency, length, neighborhood size, spelling-to-sound consistency, and so forth.

4.2 Age of acquisition

Recently, researchers have been concerned with the degree to which the age that one acquires a word is related to performance. A number of reports claim that age of acquisition (AoA) influences word recognition performance (e.g., Brown and Watson, 1987; Cortese and Khanna, 2007; Monaghan and Ellis, 2002; Morrison and Ellis, 1995). The intriguing argument here is that early acquired words might provide a special role in laying down the initial representations that the rest of the lexicon is built upon (e.g., Steyvers and Tennenbaum, 2005). Moreover, early acquired words will also have a much larger cumulative frequency of exposure across the lifetime.

There are at least two important methodological issues regarding AoA effects (for a review, see Juhasz, 2005). The first concerns the extent to which AoA affects performance in word recognition tasks like naming and lexical decision. One of the problems with assessing this issue is that AoA is correlated with many other variables including length, frequency, and imageability. Therefore, it may prove difficult to tease apart these correlated factors. The second issue is whether or not AoA should be considered an outcome variable (Zevin and Seidenberg, 2002; 2004) or a standard independent (or predictor) variable. Zevin and Seidenberg have argued that AoA predicts word recognition performance because the age at which a word is learned is affected by many factors. They focus on frequency trajectory. *Frequency trajectory* reflects the distribution of exposures that one has with words over time. Some words such as *potty* occur fairly frequently during early childhood but not adulthood whereas other words such as *fax* occur frequently during adulthood but not childhood. Therefore, frequency trajectory should influence AoA, and indeed the two variables are correlated. In addition, Zevin and Seidenberg (2004) examined the influence of frequency trajectory and cumulative frequency (i.e., the sum of frequency over time) in naming. They found little evidence for frequency trajectory whereas cumulative frequency had a marked effect on performance.

4.3 *Orthographic length*

Effects of orthographic length have proven to be theoretically important (see Coltheart et al., 2001). For example, in naming, Weekes (1997) reported that nonwords produced a large length effect whereas words did not. Balota et al. (2004) found evidence that there was a much larger length effect for low-frequency words than high-frequency words. Note that although Weekes did not find an effect of length for words, the pattern reported by Balota et al. is consistent with the pattern (albeit nonsignificant) found by Weekes. Interestingly, individuals with semantic dementia show exaggerated length effects compared to healthy controls for regular consistent words (Gold et al., 2005).

These findings are important for two reasons. First, the DRC model predicts the length by lexicality interaction reported by Weekes whereas the PDP model has difficulty accounting for this result. The sublexical route that is mainly responsible for nonword pronunciation is a serial processor, and the lexical route that is mainly responsible for word processing is a parallel processor. Hence, length effects should be larger for nonwords that rely on the sublexical route and also for individuals with semantic dementia who rely more on the sublexical route to name words aloud, because their semantic/lexical route is impaired. In contrast, the PDP model processes both words and nonwords via the same parallel architecture. In order to account for greater length effects in nonwords, one must posit that the window available for parallel processing is somehow smaller in nonwords than words

or that each letter in a nonword requires more computational resources than each letter in a word. Interestingly, New et al. (2006) recently reported an analysis on a large data set and found a quadratic relation between length and lexical decision latencies, that is, short words produced a negative correlation between length and lexical decision latencies, whereas long words produced a positive correlation. This pattern may in part be due to a preferred lexical window size based on the most common length of the words readers experience, which are of moderate length.

4.4 *Regularity and consistency*

In many studies, people are slower and less accurate to name irregular words than regular words (e.g., Baron and Strawson, 1976; Gough and Cosky, 1977). As noted, an *irregular word* can be defined as one whose pronunciation violates GPC rules (e.g., *pint*). In the DRC model, when reading an irregular word, the lexical and sublexical routes produce conflicting information to the phonemic output system, that is, the lexical route produces the correct pronunciation for *pint*, and the sublexical route produces the regularized pronunciation (rhymes with *hint*). Hence, there is either a slowdown in response latency or an increase in error rates. In contrast, when processing a regular word (e.g., *punt*), each route produces the same output such that a quick and accurate pronunciation can be made.

In PDP models, regularity effects result from the adjustment of weighted connections during learning. For example, *int* in *mint, tint, hint*, and so forth, is pronounced /Int/. Therefore, in these words, weights are adjusted so that *int* yields /Int/. However, when exposed to *pint*, weight changes occur that lead to the /aint/ pronunciation. Although *pint* will be learned, the connections will be weaker than for a regular word (e.g., *punt*), and these weaker connections produce a slower reaction time.

Note, however, that the word *pint* is irregular at two levels. First, it can be considered irregular because it violates GPC rules (i.e., /I/ is usually pronounced as in *stick*, *lid*, and *dish*). Second, it is irregular (i.e., inconsistent) at the rime level because all other words with the *int* rime, pronounce it as /Int/. Many irregular words are (rime) inconsistent which has led to a confounding of these two variables (i.e., GPC regularity and rime consistency), but they are separable dimensions.

Several studies have demonstrated an effect of rime consistency that is independent of GPC regularity (e.g., Glushko, 1979; Jared, McRae, and Seidenberg, 1990). These studies generally examined regular words (defined by GPC rules) containing consistent (e.g., *spoon*) and inconsistent rimes (e.g., *spook* is inconsistent because of *book*, *took*, etc.). A number of other studies have distinguished regularity from consistency by crossing the two factors factorially (e.g., Andrews, 1982; Cortese and Simpson, 2000; Jared, 1997, 2000). These studies are important because the DRC and the PDP models make contrasting predictions regarding the relative influence of these two factors. The DRC model predicts a large effect of regularity and a small effect of consistency. In contrast, the PDP model predicts a large effect of consistency and a small effect of regularity. The results of these studies have generally found that, in words, rime consistency has a larger influence on latencies and errors than GPC regularity. The PDP model simulates these results well whereas the DRC model does not. Moreover, in studies employing many words, Treiman and colleagues (Kessler, Treiman, and Mullennix, 2002; Treiman et al., 1995) have found that consistency at the rime level is a better predictor of naming performance than consistency at the grapheme-to-phoneme level. Interestingly, Andrews and Scarratt (1998) found that nonword reading is more affected by grapheme-to-phoneme consistency than by rime-level consistency. It is quite possible that subjects may rely on different types of information when pronouncing a set of nonwords. In any case, the procedures used to pronounce nonwords may ultimately be quite useful to the understanding of how subjects bring to bear spelling to sound

correspondences stored in the lexicon to name novel stimuli. However, it should be noted that Zevin and Seidenberg (2005) have recently argued that the consistency effects reported in nonword naming tasks appear to be more consistent with the PDP perspective than the DRC perspective.

4.4.1 POSITION OF IRREGULARITY EFFECT

Notice that an irregular/inconsistent word can be irregular/inconsistent at the first phoneme position (e.g., *chef*), the second phoneme position (e.g., *pint*), the third phoneme position (e.g., *plaid*), or beyond (e.g., *debris*). Interestingly, contemporary models make different predictions about the position of irregularity effect. According to the DRC model, words with early GPC violations are more prone to sublexical interference than words containing later inconsistencies/irregularities because the sublexical route is a serial processor. In contrast, the PDP model processes words in parallel, and so does not predict a position of irregularity effect.

A number of studies have reported a position of irregularity/inconsistency effect (e.g., Coltheart and Rastle, 1994; Cortese, 1998; Rastle and Coltheart, 1999). Although some of these studies have been criticized on methodological grounds (c.f. Cortese, 1998; Zorzi, 2000) the effect appears to be real. That is, latencies are longer for words containing early inconsistencies than words containing later inconsistencies. These results appear to support the DRC model and appear to be more problematic for the PDP model.

4.4.2 FEEDBACK CONSISTENCY EFFECTS

Heretofore, when we have been considering regularity and consistency effects, we have been considering feedforward effects from the orthography of the word to the phonology. For example, *pint* is inconsistent because most words with the *int* orthography produce phonologies that rhyme with *hint*. *Feedback consistency* refers to the likelihood of a given phonological form being spelled in a given manner. For example, the rime in the word *tone* is feedback inconsistent because the /on/ phonological pattern can also be produced via the spelling patterns *own* as in *grown*, and *oan* as in *moan*. As one might guess, many words are both feedforward inconsistent and feedback inconsistent. Stone, Vanhoy, and Van Orden (1997) were the first to decouple feedforward consistency from feedback consistency and observed effects of both variables in lexical decision performance. In addition, Balota et al. (2004) found reliable and equivalent effects of feedback consistency in both lexical decision and naming performance, whereas Ziegler, Montant, and Jacobs (1997) found for French stimuli that the feedback consistency effects were larger in lexical decision than in naming performance. The influence of feedback consistency is quite important theoretically because it suggests a type of resonance in route to the response such that consistent phonological forms provide feedback onto the orthographic patterns (see for example, Pexman, Lupker, and Jared, 2001). However, this area is still controversial, since Peereman, Content, and Bonin (1998) have argued that the feedback consistency effects in French are eliminated when familiarity is controlled (also see Kessler, Treiman, and Mullenix, 2007).

4.5 *Orthographic neighborhood size*

Neighborhood size (i.e., N) refers to the number of words that can be derived from a target word by changing one letter while preserving the other letters and their positions in the word (see Coltheart et al., 1977). For example, *back* has the neighbors *sack*, *buck*, *bask*, and so forth. In the DRC model (Coltheart et al., 2001), inhibitory connections between word-level representations inhibit words with large neighborhoods while facilitatory connections between the lexicon and the phonemic output system and between the lexicon and the letter unit input system facilitate responses to words with large neighborhoods. Therefore, the effect of N will depend on the actual parameter settings in the model (c.f. Coltheart et al., 2001). In PDP models, because the same representations are used to process all words, network connections will be strong

for words sharing similar representations. Therefore, when words are consistent with regard to their spelling-to-sound correspondences, there tends to be less error in orthographic and phonological systems for high-N words than low-N words, and this characteristic facilitates responses (Sears, Hino, and Lupker, 1999).

Coltheart et al. (1977) were the first to examine this factor, and since that seminal study, N has been at the focus of considerable research (for a review see Andrews, 1997). Although the results have been somewhat mixed, a few conclusions can be made. First, there is typically a facilitative effect of N on response latencies that tends to be relatively larger in naming than lexical decision (Balota et al., 2004). Second, increasing N in nonwords increases lexical decision latencies (Coltheart et al., 1977). Third, the list context modulates the effect of N. For example, Johnson and Pugh (1994) found facilitatory effects of N when illegal nonwords served as distracters and inhibitory effects when legal nonwords are used. Therefore, as Andrews notes, it is important to consider task-specific characteristics when interpreting effects of N. Fourth, in naming, N interacts with word frequency such that low-frequency words produce larger effects of N than high-frequency words (Andrews, 1992). Finally, in lexical decision, Balota et al. (2004) found that for younger adults N also interacted with frequency such that having many neighbors facilitated lexical decision latencies for low-frequency words and inhibited decision latencies for high-frequency words. Within a DRC framework, one might argue that high-frequency words are more sensitive to the lexical-level inhibition, whereas low-frequency words are more sensitive to the sublexical facilitation. Clearly further work is needed to understand the complex pattern of N effects across tasks, list contexts, and other variables such as word frequency.

4.6 *Phonological neighborhood size*

Interestingly, recent work by Yates and colleagues (Yates, Locker, and Simpson, 2004) indicates that phonological neighborhood size (i.e., the number of words that can be constructed from a target word by changing one phoneme while preserving the other phonemes and their positions in the word) also facilitates lexical decision performance independently of orthographic neighborhood size. Yates et al. note that in previous work on orthographic neighborhood effects, orthographic neighborhood size is often confounded with phonological neighborhood size. This finding suggests that word recognition models need to accommodate early influences of phonology on recognition (also see Ziegler and Perry, 1998). In addition, these findings along with those reported originally by Abramson and Goldinger (1997) and more recently by Lukatela and colleagues (Lukatela et al., 2004) suggest that visual and auditory word recognition may engage the same phonological processes. Specifically, Lukatela et al. found that lexical decision times were longer for words that, when spoken, produce a long vowel (e.g., *plead*) than those associated with a short vowel length (e.g., *pleat*).

4.7 *Morphological decomposition*

For a more thorough discussion of morphological processing, see chapters in this volume by Diependaele, Grainger and Sandra, and Woolams and Patterson. However, because of the importance this topic has for word recognition, we briefly review some of the literature here as well.

Traditionally, the *morpheme* has referred to the basic unit of meaning in a language (Hockett, 1966). Many words are made up of more than one morpheme. For example, *jumped* consists of the free morpheme *jump* and the bound morpheme *ed*. Taft and Forster (1975; 1976) proposed that readers decompose words into their constituent morphemes when recognizing them. Root morphemes are then used to access their polymorphemic relatives. Evidence for this perspective comes from studies reporting an effect of root frequency when the overall frequency of words has been controlled (e.g., Taft, 1979a; 1979b). In addition,

equivalent long-term priming of roots (e.g., *jump*) from relatives (e.g., *jumped*) and the roots themselves (e.g., *jump*, Stanners et al., 1979) suggests that the root has been accessed during the processing of the more complex relative. It is important to note that these morphemic effects are not due to letter overlap (e.g., Lima, 1987). For example, Lima (1987) reported that while *arson* does not facilitate the recognition of *son*, *dishonest* does facilitate the recognition of *honest*.

In years, research on morphological decomposition has taken on new theoretical significance. This is, in part, due to the fact that the PDP perspective has emerged as a viable general theory of language processing and because PDP models do not possess distinct morphemic representations (e.g., Plaut and Gonnerman, 2000; Rueckl et al., 1997). According to the PDP perspective, morphemic effects emerge from interactions among orthography, phonology, and semantics (Gonnerman, Seidenberg, and Anderson, 2007). Support for this view comes from a recent cross-modal lexical decision study by Gonnerman et al. (2007), who found that the degree of facilitation for visually presented targets was a function of the semantic and phonological overlap found in prime–target pairs regardless of morphemic overlap. For example, *sneer* was just as effective of a prime for *snarl* as *teacher* was for *teach*. In contrast, pairs of items that were more weakly related (e.g., *lately–late*) produced less facilitation.

However, a study by Rastle, Davis, and New (2004) suggests that morphological decomposition does not rely on semantic relationships. In their lexical decision study, target words were preceded by a briefly presented (forty-two ms) masked prime that maintained both a semantic and morphological relationship with the target (e.g., *cleaner–clean*), an apparent morphological relationship only (e.g., *corner–corn*), and a nonmorphological relationship (e.g., *brothel–broth*). Rastle et al. found equivalent priming for targets preceded by primes that appeared to have a morphological relationship with the target regardless of the semantic relationship. Thus, it appears that decomposition is not dependent on semantic information available from the stem. This outcome seems more consistent with localist models (e.g., the DRC model) than distributed models (e.g., PDP models).

4.8 *Pseudohomophone effects*

Pseudohomophones are nonwords that are homophonic with real words (e.g., *brane*). Pseudohomophones are an important stimulus tool because they allow researchers to study the influence of phonology in accessing meaning. With words, meaning can theoretically be accessed via orthography or phonology, but this is probably not the case with pseudohomophones. That is, upon encountering *brane*, there is a high probability that the reader has not seen this letter sequence before. Therefore, if subjects are faster at naming *brane* than *brone* (e.g., McCann and Besner, 1987) or slower at rejecting *brane* than *brone* in lexical decision (e.g., Rubenstein, Lewis, and Rubenstein, 1971), then there is evidence that meaning has been accessed via phonology. Experiments on pseudohomophones have yielded exactly these results, along with a number of additional findings that have important implications for word recognition models (see Reynolds and Besner, 2005 for a review).

In the DRC model, a pseudohomophone will activate a lexical representation due to interactive activation from the phonemic output system via the sublexical route. If the response is naming, the lexical representation reinforces the phonemic output (thus facilitating the response), and if the response is a lexical decision, the latency is increased due to the increased lexical activation. In PDP models (e.g., Harm and Seidenberg, 2004), pseudohomophones activate semantics whereas regular nonwords do not. The activation of semantics will facilitate a naming response by providing additional input into phonology and inhibit a lexical decision because meaning cannot be used to distinguish the pseudohomophone from a word.

4.9 *Semantic characteristics of the word*

For a more thorough discussion of semantic memory, see the chapter by Cree and Armstrong in this volume. At the onset, one should note that semantic effects are larger in lexical decision than naming (Balota et al., 2004). When one considers the nature of the tasks, this finding is not surprising. In lexical decision, because the task is to distinguish between meaningful word stimuli and less meaningful nonword stimuli, participants tend to direct attention to meaning-level information. In contrast, naming only requires one to convert print into phonology, thus meaning is not required to perform the task. Because naming does not require the access of meaning, finding a true semantic effect provides evidence of an interactive word recognition system.

One variable that has sparked interest in the field is *imageability*. Although imageability effects are larger in lexical decision than naming, there are reports of imageability effects in naming. For example, Strain, Patterson, and Seidenberg (1995) crossed imageability and spelling-to-sound consistency in a word naming study for low-frequency words (see Experiment 2). They found that the consistency effect was reduced for words that had highly imageable referents (e.g., *comb* versus *corpse*) compared to words with lowly imageable referents (e.g., *caste* versus *clause*). Recently, however, some researchers have argued that this imageablity effect was confounded with age of acquisition (i.e., AoA or the age at which a person acquires a word, see Monaghan and Ellis, 2002).

In a recent study of lexical decision and naming performance for 2,428 monosyllabic words, Balota and colleagues (2004) found evidence for semantic influences on performance. The basic finding that semantic factors influence lexical decision performance more than naming was clear. However, semantic factors such as imageability and connectivity (i.e., the degree of semantic clustering between a word and other words) were shown to influence naming above and beyond standard lexical and sublexical variables. We note, however, that due to a lack of information regarding AoA for these words, AoA was not included as a predictor variable. Subsequent analyses were performed by Cortese and Khanna (2007) on the same data set. When AoA was included as a predictor variable, imageability no longer accounted for unique variance in naming latencies. Specifically, AoA accounted for unique variance in reaction times for both naming and lexical decision, whereas imageability's influence was limited to lexical decision. It is entirely possible that imageability effects could be due to AoA (or alternatively trajectory frequency, e.g., Zevin and Seidenberg, 2002; 2004).

One intriguing idea about semantic structure that may relate to word recognition performance is the small-world structure described by Steyvers and Tenenbaum (2005; also see Buchanan, Westbury, and Burgess, 2001 for a similar approach). According to Steyvers and Tenenbaum, a relatively small set of concepts serves as a communication hub for the rest of the semantic network. If semantic networks are represented in terms of the structure hypothesized by Steyvers and Tenenbaum, then words characterized by a high degree of connectivity (e.g., Nelson, McEvoy, and Schreiber, 1998) with other words may be processed more quickly than words characterized by sparse connections. In the analyses conducted by Balota et al., connectivity as defined by Nelson et al. was, indeed, related to performance in both naming and lexical decision (albeit more in lexical decision) above and beyond standard sublexical and lexical variables.

5 Priming/context effects

Heretofore, we have focused on isolated word recognition. However, words are most commonly processed in the context of other words. Although there are separate chapters in this book devoted to sentence processing, we will briefly describe the work that has employed the priming paradigm. In this paradigm, a prime word is presented and

followed by a target word that is responded to. Varying the relationship between the prime and target has been instrumental in demonstrating the types of codes activated by the prime used in route to lexical access. For example, the prime and target may be orthographically related (*couch–touch*), phonologically related (*much–touch*), or semantically related (*feel–touch*). Because of space limitations, we only touch upon some of the major themes in this area. For a more detailed discussion of this literature, see Neely (1991), Hutchison (2004), McNamara (2005), and Kinoshita and Lupker (2003).

5.1 *Orthographic priming effects*

One approach to identifying the access code in word recognition is the masked orthographic priming paradigm developed by Evett and Humphreys (1981, also see Forster, Mohan, and Hector, 2003; Humphreys, Besner, and Quinlan, 1998; and Ziegler, Ferrand, and Jacobs, 2000). In this paradigm, subjects are briefly presented two letter strings that are preceded and/or followed by pattern masks. Subjects typically are unable to consciously identify the primes, and hence these effects reflect early access processes. The two letter strings vary in terms of orthographic, phonological, or semantic relatedness. Here, we focus on the orthographic priming conditions. There are a number of interesting findings in the original Evett and Humphreys study: First, subjects were better at identifying the second letter string when it shared letters with the first letter string even though these shared letters appeared in different cases (e.g., *lert–lost*). Second, this effect occurred even when the prime items were nonwords, but only when the naming task is employed (Sereno, 1991); one finds little evidence of masked priming for nonwords in the lexical decision task (Forster, 1987). Furthermore, eyetracking studies by Rayner, McConkie, and Zola (1980) have also provided compelling evidence that case independent orthographic codes can be used to access words in the parafovea while reading (see Balota and Rayner, 1991 for a review).

5.2 *Phonological priming studies*

There has been some debate concerning the mandatory role of phonological codes in word recognition (see Frost, 1998 for an excellent review). In an early study, Evett and Humphreys (1981) used the masked priming paradigm and found priming for pairs that were orthographically and phonologically related (e.g., *bribe–tribe*) compared to pairs that were orthographically related but phonologically unrelated (e.g., *break–freak*). Moreover, the effect occurred across case changes. In addition, in a similar masked priming paradigm, Humphreys, Evett, and Taylor (1982) found that identification accuracy was higher for targets (e.g., *chute*) that followed homophonic primes (e.g., *shoot*) compared to targets that followed graphemically related (e.g., *short*) or unrelated primes (e.g., *trail*). More recently, in a masked priming study conducted in Spanish, Pollatsek, Perea, and Carreiras (2005) found that lexical decisions to targets were facilitated by phonologically consistent primes when as little as sixty-six ms separated the onset of the prime from the onset of the target. Note also that there is evidence of phonological priming in the parafoveal priming paradigm, examining eye movements during the reading of text. Specifically, Pollatsek et al. (1992) found that previews that were homophonic with targets (e.g., *site–cite*) facilitated performance (both in pronunciation latencies and fixation durations) compared to non-homophonic previews controlled for orthographic similarity (e.g., *cake–sake*). Again, this pattern would appear to support a role for phonology as an access code (also see Lee et al., 1999).

5.3 *Semantic priming effects*

The semantic (associative) priming paradigm has been thoroughly investigated, and began with a seminal study by Meyer and Schvaneveldt (1971). They found that subjects were faster to make lexical decisions to pairs of related words (e.g., *cat–dog*) than pairs of unrelated words (e.g., *pen–dog*). This robust effect appeared ideally suited to

map out the architecture of meaning-level representations and the retrieval operations that act upon such representations; both of these issues would appear to be critical to higher level comprehension. We note that semantic/associative priming effects occur not only in standard lexical decision and naming tasks (see Hutchison et al., 2007, for a recent large-scale study), but they also occur cross-modally (i.e., when an auditory prime precedes a visually presented target; cf. Holcomb and Anderson, 1993)

Semantic priming has been a topic of rich empirical and theoretical debate. For example, one might ask if the effect is truly "semantic," that is, reflects similarity in semantic features or category membership, such as *dog* and *cat*, or if it primarily reflects associative relationships among items (e.g., *rat* and *cheese*). Two recent reviews of this topic appear to reach quite different conclusions. Lucas (2000) indicated that there were indeed semantic effects in priming, but Hutchison (2004) concluded that a simple associative account could handle much of this literature. One of the findings that Hutchison focuses on is mediated priming (e.g., Balota and Lorch, 1986; McNamara and Altarriba, 1988). *Mediated priming* refers to priming across intervening nonpresented concepts, that is, from *lion* to *stripes*. Of course, there is very little semantic overlap between *lion* and *stripes*, but there is an associative relationship via *lion* to *tiger* to *stripes*.

A second area where semantic priming has been central concerns *threshold priming*. In threshold priming experiments, the prime item is presented so briefly and patterned masked that subjects are presumably unaware of its presence. Initial experiments reported semantic priming effects under conditions in which subjects apparently can no longer make presence/absence decisions about the prime item (e.g., Balota, 1983; Fowler et al., 1981; Marcel, 1983). This initial work indeed was criticized because of the threshold setting procedures (see Cheesman and Merikle, 1984; Holender, 1986; Merikle, 1982), and the nature of an objective identification threshold still is debated today

(Dosher, 1998; Greenwald and Draine, 1998). The important point here is that one can obtain semantic priming effects under highly degraded situations. This paradigm has been extended to cognitive neuroscience domains (see Dehaene et al. 2005) and social psychology (see Ric, 2004).

A third area of interest regarding priming effects is *backward priming*. There are two types of backward priming effects. First, priming has been reported when the prime is presented after the target (see Balota, Boland, and Shields, 1989; Kiger and Glass, 1983). In this type of experiment, the target that requires a response appears prior to the prime, and then the prime appears afterward, but prior to the response. This finding falls naturally from a cascadic framework in which partial activation is released from representations before such representations have reached threshold (see earlier discussion of the McClelland and Rumelhart model). A second type of backward priming entails direction relations; for example, one finds priming from *boy to bell* in the lexical decision task (c.f. Koriat, 1981; Seidenberg et al., 1984), but not typically in the pronunciation task, at least at long (Stimulus onset synchrony) SOAs. This would appear to support the notion that subjects check back from the target to the prime to bias their lexical decisions. Interestingly, one can find this type of backward priming for non-compounds (e.g., *baby–stork*) at short SOAs (see Kahan, Neely, and Forsythe, 1999) even in naming. This may actually be related to the first type of backward priming, suggesting that when there is close temporal proximity in the presentation of the prime and target, both forward and backward priming effects can be observed, even in a task that does not encourage backward checking such as speeded naming performance (see Hutchison, 2004 for further discussion).

Regarding the theoretical developments, we will only list a few of the mechanisms used to accommodate semantic priming. One of the most popular mechanisms still is some variant of spreading activation theory. The notion that semantic/lexical memory may be represented by nodes that reflect concepts, and that such conceptual nodes are interconnected via associative/semantic pathways has been central to a number of developments in cognitive psychology (e.g., Anderson, 1976; 1983; Collins and Loftus, 1975). When a node in memory becomes activated via stimulus presentation or via internal direction of attention, activation spreads from that node along associative pathways to nearby nodes. Thus, the reason that subjects are faster to recognize *dog* when it follows *cat*, compared to when it follows *pen*, is because the underlying representation for these two words is connected via an associative/semantic pathway and when *cat* is presented activation spreads from its underlying node to the node underlying *dog*. Thus the representation for *dog* has been preactivated and hence needs less stimulus information to surpass threshold.

One of the most compelling studies in support of an automatic spreading activation mechanism comes from Neely's (1977) dissertation. In this study, participants were given category primes and instructions regarding what to expect when a given category was presented. For some categories, subjects were told to expect category exemplars designated by that category (i.e., when you receive the category *bird*, think of *birds*), however, for other categories, subjects received instructions to shift from the designated category to a new category (i.e., when you receive the prime *body*, think of types of building parts). Neely also manipulated the time to process the prime before the target was presented. Amazingly, Neely found full-blown semantic priming at the short prime–target interval that was totally independent of the instructions, that is, there was equal priming from *bird* to *robin* and *body* to *arm* in the previous examples. However, at the long prime–target interval, priming reflected only the subjects' expectancies. For example, Neely found equivalent priming for *bird* to *robin* and *body* to *door*, and the priming observed for *body* to *arm* was equivalent to a totally unrelated condition such as *body* to *maple*. Neely claimed that automatic spreading activation produced priming at the short prime–target interval, and the long prime–target interval reflected a second independent attentional mechanism (also see, Balota, Black, and Cheney, 1992; Favreau and Segalowitz, 1983).

In addition to distinctions between automatic and attentional mechanisms underlying semantic priming effects, there have been many attempts to model such effects (e.g., Becker, 1980; Forster, 1981; Norris, 1986). Most recently, researchers have developed computational models of semantic priming. The problem here is to specify the nature of the underlying semantic/associative representations. One approach has been to model priming in terms of featural overlap between the meanings of the primes and targets (c.f. Cree, McRae, and McNorgan, 1999) or by a temporal contiguity between semantic features of the prime and phonological features of the target (Masson, 1995; Plaut and Booth, 2000). The notion is that when the prime is presented, a set of distributed features is activated, and the extent to which these features overlap with the target modulates the observed priming effects. An alternative approach is Ratcliff and McKoon's (1988) compound cue model. The notion here is that the prime and target serve as a compound cue that is compared to traces already stored in memory, with related cues producing higher familiarity values than unrelated cues. Although each of these models has intriguing components, it is still likely that no single model of priming will be able to handle the rich diversity of this literature, and as Neely (1991) has argued, it is likely that multiple mechanisms will need to be postulated to account for the breadth of priming effects.

6 Recent methodological developments for constraining theories

6.1 *Factorial designs versus large-scale item analyses*

Historically, researchers have employed factorial designs where item variables of interest (e.g., length, frequency, etc.) have been manipulated, and other factors known to affect performance have been controlled. This approach has been useful, but there are potential limitations to this approach (for a discussion of these issues see Balota et al., 2004; Culter, 1981). More recently, researchers have examined word recognition performance for a large set of words (Balota and Spieler, 1998; Besner and Bourassa, 1995; Kessler, Trieman, and Mullennix, 2002; Spieler and Balota, 1997; Trieman et al., 1995). As noted, Balota et al. (2004) examined lexical decision and naming performance in younger and older adults for 2,428 words. Multiple regression techniques were utilized in order to obtain estimates of the unique variance attributable to a set of predictor variables, and these researchers were able to account for .49 of the variance in lexical decision performance and .50 of the variance in naming performance. This is a multifold increase over current computational models (see Balota and Spieler, 1998 and Seidenberg and Plaut, 1998 for a discussion of the pros and cons of this comparison). This outcome was obtained despite the success these computational models have had in accounting for performance at the factor level (but see Perry et al., 2007). The large-scale item level analyses provide another potentially important constraint in the evaluation of theoretical approaches to word processing. More recently, Balota and colleagues have collected naming and lexical decision latencies for over forty thousand words (Balota et al., 2007). The English Lexicon Project website (http://elexicon. wustl.edu) provides a comprehensive data set that researchers can access, via a powerful search engine, performance measures and item characteristics.

In addition to these large-scale behavioral databases, there are also large-scale analyses of the contexts in which words occur in natural language databases. An example of this is the work by Steyvers and Tenenbaum (2005) on the small-scale semantic networks described earlier. This work has been recently reviewed by Cree (2005), and is very exciting because it provides a computational approach of grounding semantics, via the contexts in which words co-occur.

6.2 *Distributional analyses*

Typically, in word recognition experiments, one compares the mean response latency across several conditions to determine if the predictions generated by an experimental hypothesis are correct or not. However, researchers have long noted that means of conditions are only one estimate available from performance. For example, in the Stroop task (i.e., naming the color that a word appears in), Heathcote, Popiel, and Mewhort (1991) provided a useful demonstration of how the shape of a reaction time distribution can provide useful information beyond estimates of central tendency. They found that the incongruent condition (e.g., the word *blue* appearing in the color red) compared to the neutral condition (e.g., the word *block* appearing in the color red) increased both the skewing and the central tendency of the reaction time distribution, but amazingly, the congruent condition (e.g., the word *red* appearing in the color red) increased skewing and decreased the central tendency, which basically masked any effect in means (see Spieler, Balota, and Faust, 1996 for a replication of this pattern). These researchers have fit reaction time distributions to ex-Gaussian functions, but other functions such as the Weibul or ex-Wald could also accomplish the same goals. As theories become more precise regarding the item-level performance, there should be an increased level of sophistication regarding the predictions concerning the underlying reaction time distributions. Balota and Spieler (1999) found that frequency and repetition influenced these parameters differently depending on the task (however, see Andrews and Heathcote, 2001). Ratcliff et al. (2004) have recently used reaction time distributions to more powerfully test a diffusion model of lexical decision performance. We anticipate that the precision of reaction time distribution analyses will be critical in the discrimination of available models (see Balota et al., 2008 for a review).

6.3 *Neuroimaging*

Models of word recognition have been constrained by findings in the neuropsychological literature. For example, early versions of the dual-route model were designed inductively to accommodate certain dyslexia subtypes. More recent findings in the neuroimaging literature have also been important and will continue to influence future theoretical developments (also see Sandak et al., this volume). Some early findings in this literature include those reported by Petersen and colleagues in a positron emission tomography (PET) study (Petersen et al., 1989). For example, Petersen et al. found that passively viewing words was associated with activation of the occipital lobes, reading words aloud was associated with temporal activation, and generating verbs from nouns was associated with frontal lobe activation. Also in a PET study, Fiez and colleagues (Fiez et al., 1999) linked lexicality, frequency, and spelling-to-sound consistency to specific brain regions. Interestingly, spelling-to-sound consistency and lexicality was associated with the activation of an area in the left frontal lobe, suggesting that this region may be involved in orthographic-to-phonological translation. In addition, the primary motor cortex in both hemispheres was associated with greater activation when processing inconsistent words (e.g., *pint*) than consistent words (e.g., *punt*) suggesting that motor production is affected by consistency. Also, processing low-frequency words was associated with activation of a region in the left temporal lobe and supplementary motor area. Finally, more recent studies (as described by Sandak et al., this volume) have attempted to associate these and other regions to dual-route models and parallel distributed processing models. Sandak and colleagues conclude that activation patterns found in the brain are consistent with an interactive PDP framework that divides labor among various codes. Interestingly, the division of labor within this framework depends on the relative acquisition of skill at different levels.

7 Continuing controversies

7.1 *The magic moment*

A reasonable question that one might ask is what does it mean to recognize a word? In other words, is there a "magic moment" (e.g., Balota, 1990) that corresponds to a discrete point in time when a word has been recognized? The answer to this question may depend on the model of word recognition one uses to explain the process. The magic moment for models that contain discrete lexical entries for words (e.g., Coltheart et al., 2001) would occur when a threshold for identification has been reached. In contrast, in models containing distributed representations (e.g., Plaut et al., 1996; Seidenberg and McClelland, 1989), the magic moment is more difficult to discern. In distributed models, there are no separate lexical representations for each individual word and no threshold to be achieved. Therefore, one might posit that the magic moment occurs when the network settles into a stable pattern of activation and that the subject may modulate what "stable" means depending on task, list context, and other variables, that is, there is no single magic moment. In this light, it may be better to consider what the trigger is for a given response in a given task rather than to speculate about a task independent magic moment.

7.2 *Phonological codes in silent reading*

The extent to which readers use phonological codes to access meaning in silent reading has been somewhat controversial (see Frost, 1998 for a review). Representing one side of the issue are those who argue for the mandatory use of phonology in silent reading (e.g., Frost, 1998; Lukatela and Turvey, 1991; Van Orden, 1987). In contrast, some researchers posit that phonological codes play more or less of a role in performance depending upon the nature of the stimulus and/or the ability of the reader. For example, Jared and Seidenberg (1991) and Jared, Levy, and Rayner (1999) argued that phonological codes are used more for infrequent words, and with sufficient exposure, phonology plays a relatively small role. Rather, semantics can be accessed rather directly from orthography. Thus, all reading researchers agree that phonology is used to access meaning at least on a partial basis, and some claim that phonology is mandatory for reading all words.

The role of phonology in reading is quite critical because it influences how educators teach reading in elementary school (also see Nation, this volume). Some advocates of a whole word approach suggest that in learning to read, children can use context to uncover the meaning and most often the phonology of the visual stimulus. The whole word instructional approach exposes children to whole words, their pronunciations, and meanings, both in and out of sentential and discourse context. In contrast, phonics-based approaches emphasize that knowledge of the relationships between graphemes and phonemes is fundamental to skilled reading. The evidence on this issue indicates that phonics-based instruction is a more effective strategy than whole word techniques that do not include phonics (for reviews see Adams, 1990; Rayner et al., 2001; and Snow, Burns, and Griffin, 1998).

7.3 *Attentional control of processing pathways and time criterion*

One question that has received considerable recent interest is the extent to which the lexical processing system adapts to the current processing demands. For example, one might expect different processing of text when proofreading, comprehending, or checking for grammaticality. Indeed, virtually every theory of word recognition posits multiple ways of accessing or computing the phonological code from print. For example, in dual-route models, one can compute a phonological code via the lexical route, which maps the whole word onto a lexical representation to access phonology, or via the sublexical route, which computes the phonology via the spelling-to-sound correspondences in the language. In PDP models, phonology can be computed directly from orthography or indirectly via semantics. The issue addressed here concerns the extent to which attention to a processing pathway can be biased by the experimental operations in a given study. For example, are there procedures that will bias the reader to rely more on the lexical or sublexical pathway within a dual-route framework? This is important because it brings into question the modularity of the lexical processing system (see Fodor, 1983). One way to examine this issue is to present words that place different demands on the lexical and sublexical pathways. For example, nonwords should bias the sublexical pathway and low-frequency exception words should bias the lexical pathway, since the sublexical pathway would lead to regularization errors, that is, pronouncing *pint* such that it rhymes with *hint*. In an early study, Monsell et al. (1992) found that naming latencies to high-frequency irregular words were faster and more accurate when embedded with other irregular words than when mixed with nonwords. This supports the notion that the exception word context directed attention to the lexical pathway, which is more appropriate for naming exception words, than the sublexical pathway. Additional studies have found similar influences of pathway priming (e.g., Rastle and Coltheart, 1999; Reynolds and Besner, 2005; Simpson and Kang, 1994; Zevin and Balota, 2000).

However, the evidence for route priming has been controversial. Specifically, work by Kinoshita and Lupker (2002; 2003) suggests that much of these findings can be accounted for by a time criterion model. Specifically, there is evidence that participants adopt a time criterion whereby they produce a response at a latency biased toward the average of the latencies in a block of trials. Consider the word frequency effect (presumably a reflection of the lexical route). In two pure, independent blocks, assume that a set of low-frequency words produces response latencies on the average of 700 ms and a set of high-frequency words produces response latencies on the average of 600 ms. If one now embeds these same words in the context of nonwords that produce an average response latency of 700 ms, the word frequency effect will likely diminish. Specifically, latencies to the low-frequency words will remain the same (because the latencies are quite similar to the nonwords), whereas latencies to the high-frequency words will increase considerably, that is, migrate toward the time criterion invoked by mean latency of the nonwords. Hence, the word frequency effect will decrease in the context of nonwords not because of a decreased reliance on the lexical pathway, but rather because of a change in the temporal criterion to produce a response.

Although the evidence suggests that participants do adopt a time criterion based on the difficulty of items within a block, we believe that there is also evidence for pathway control. For example, all of the effects reported by Zevin and Balota (2000) hold even after the response latencies to the context items are partialled out via analyses of covariance. Clearly, however, further work is necessary in this area.

8 Summary

In this chapter, we have described the major tasks employed, the different theoretical perspectives, many of the variables that influence word recognition performance, and some of the continuing controversies. Of course, this overview only provides a glimpse of the vast amount of research that has been conducted on visual word recognition. Although much has been accomplished, there is clearly need for continuing work in clarifying the processes engaged in the seductively simple act of visual word recognition.

References

Abramson, M. & Goldinger, S. (1997). What the reader's eye tells the mind's ear: Silent reading activates inner speech. *Perception & Psychophysics*, 59, 1059–68.

Adams, M. (1990). *Beginning to read*. Cambridge, MA: MIT Press.

Anderson, J. R. (1976). *Language, memory, and thought*. Hillsdale, NJ: Erlbaum.

(1983). A spreading activation theory of memory. *Journal of Verbal Learning and Verbal Behavior*, 22, 261–95.

Andrews, S. (1982). Phonological recoding: Is the regularity effect consistent? *Memory & Cognition*, 10, 565–75.

(1992). Frequency and neighborhood effects on lexical access: Lexical similarity or orthographic redundancy? *Journal of Experimental Psychology: Learning, Memory, and Cognition*, 18, 234–54.

(1997). The effect of orthographic similarity on lexical retrieval: Resolving neighborhood conflicts. *Psychonomic Bulletin & Review*, 4, 439–61.

Andrews, S. & Heathcote, A. (2001). Distinguishing common and task-specific processes in word identification: A matter of some moment? *Journal of Experimental Psychology: Learning, Memory & Cognition*, 27, 545–55.

Andrews, S. & Scarratt, D. R. (1998). Rule and analogy mechanisms in reading nonwords: Hough dou peapel rede gnew wirds? *Journal of Experimental Psychology: Human Perception and Performance*, 24, 1052–86.

Ans, B., Carbonnel, S., & Valdois, S. (1998). A connectionst multiple-trace memory model for polysyllabic word reading. *Psychological Review*, 105, 678–723.

Ashby, G. F. (1982). Deriving exact predictions from a cascade model. *Psychological Review*, 89, 599–607.

Baayen, H., Piepenbrock, R., & Van Rijn, H. (1993). *The CELEX lexical database (CD-ROM)*. Linguistic Data Consortium, University of Pennsylvania, Philadelphia, Philadelphia, PA.

Balota, D. A. (1983). Automatic spreading activation and episodic memory encoding. *Journal of Verbal Learning and Verbal Behavior*, 22, 88–104.

(1990). The role of meaning in word recognition. In Balota, D. A., D'Arcais, G. F., & Rayner, K. (Eds.) *Comprehension processes in reading* (pp. 9–32). Hillsdale, NJ: Erlbaum.

(1994). Visual word recognition: The journey from features to meaning. In Gernsbacher, M. A. (Ed.) *Handbook of psycholinguistics* (pp. 303–48). San Diego: Academic Press.

Balota, D. A., Black, S. R., & Cheney, M. (1992). Automatic and attentional priming in young and older adults: Reevaluation of the two-process model. *Journal of Experimental Psychology: Human Perception and Performance*, 18, 485–502.

Balota, D. A., Boland, J. E., & Shields, L. (1989). Priming in pronunciation: Beyond pattern recognition and onset latency. *Journal of Memory and Language*, 28, 14–36.

Balota, D. A. & Chumbley, J. I. (1984). Are lexical decisions a good measure of lexical access? The role of word frequency in the neglected decision stage. *Journal of Experimental Psychology: Human Perception and Performance*, 10, 340–57.

Balota, D. A., Cortese, M. J., Hutchison, K. A., Neely, J. H., Nelson, D., Simpson, G. B., & Treiman, R. (2002). The English Lexicon Project: A web-based repository of descriptive and behavioral measures for 40,481 English words and nonwords. http://elexicon.wustl.edu/. Washington University.

Balota, D. A., Cortese, M. J., Sergent Marshall, S. D., Spieler, D. H., & Yap, M. J. (2004). Visual word recognition for single syllable words. *Journal of Experimental Psychology: General*, 133, 283–316.

Balota, D. A. & Lorch, R. F. (1986). Depth of automatic spreading activation: Mediated priming effects in pronunciation but not in lexical decision. *Journal of Experimental Psychology: Learning, Memory, and Cognition*, 12, 336–45.

Balota, D. A., Pilotti, M., & Cortese, M. J. (2001). Subjective frequency estimates for 2,938 monosyllabic words. *Memory & Cognition (Special Issue)*, 29, 639–47.

Balota, D. A. & Rayner, K. (1991). Word recognition processes in foveal and parafoveal vision: The range of influence of lexical variables. In Besner, D. & Humphreys, G. W. (Eds.) *Basic Processes in Reading* (pp. 198–232). Hillsdale, NJ: Erlbaum.

Balota, D. A. & Spieler, D. H. (1998). The utility of item-level analyses in model evaluation: A reply to Seidenberg and Plaut. *Psychological Science*, 8, 238–40.

(1999). Word frequency, repetition, and lexicality effects in word recognition tasks: Beyond measures of central tendency. *Journal of Experimental Psychology: General*, 128, 32–55.

Balota, D. A., Yap, M. J., Cortese, M. I., & Watson, J. M. (2008). Beyond mean response latency: Response time distributional analyses of semantic priming. *Journal of Memory & Language*, 59, 495–523.

Balota, D. A., Yap, M. J., Cortese, M. J., Hutchison, K. I., Kessler, B., Loftis, B., Neely, J. H., Nelson, D. L., Simpson, G. B., & Treiman, R. (2007). The English Lexicon Project. *Behavior Research Methods*, 39, 445–59.

Baron, J. & Strawson, C. (1976). Use of orthographic and word-specific knowledge in reading words aloud. *Journal of Experimental Psychology: Human Perception and Performance,* 2, 386–93.

Becker, C. (1979). Semantic context and word frequency effects in visual word recognition. *Journal of Experimental Psychology: Human Perception and Performance,* 5, 252–9.

Becker, C. (1980). Semantic context effects in visual word recognition: An analysis of semantic strategies. *Memory & Cognition,* 8, 493–512.

(1983). Basic decoding components in reading: Two dissociable feature extraction processes. *Canadian Journal of Psychology,* 37, 429–38.

Besner, D. & Bourassa, D. C. (June 1995). *Localist and parallel processing models of visual word recognition: A few more words.* Paper presented at the annual meeting of the Canadian Brain, Behavior, and Cognitive Science Society, Halifax, Nova Scotia, Canada.

Besner, D., Twilley, L., McCann, R. S., & Seergobin, K. (1990). On the association between connectionism and data: Are a few words necessary? *Psychological Review,* 97, 432–46.

Broadbent, D. E. (1967). Word-frequency effects and response bias. *Psychological Review,* 74, 1–15.

Brown, GDA & Watson, F. L., (1987). First in, first out: Word learning age and spoken word-frequency as predictors of word familiarity and word naming latency. *Memory & Cognition,* 15, 208–16.

Buchanan, L., Westbury, C., & Burgess, C. (2001). Characterizing semantic space: Neighborhood effects in word recognition. *Psychonomic Bulletin & Review,* 8, 531–44.

Carreiras, M., Perea, M., & Grainger, J. (1997). Effects of the orthographic neighborhood in visual word recognition: Cross-task comparisons. *Journal of Experimental Psychology: Learning, Memory, & Cognition,* 23, 857–71.

Catlin, J. (1973). In defense of sophisticated guessing theory. *Psychological Review,* 80, 412–16.

Cheesmann, J. I. & Merikle, P. M. (1984). Priming with and without awareness. *Perception & Psychophysics,* 36, 387–95.

Collins, A. & Loftus, E. (1975). A spreading activation theory of semantic processing. *Psychological Review,* 82, 407–28.

Coltheart, M., Davelaar, E., Jonasson, J., & Besner, D. (1977). Access to the internal lexicon. In Dornic, S. (Ed.) *Attention and performance VI.* Hillsdale, NJ: Lawrence Erlbaum Associates.

Coltheart, M. & Rastle, K. (1994). Serial processing in reading aloud: Evidence for dual-route models of reading. *Journal of Experimental Psychology: Human Perception and Performance,* 20, 1197–220.

Coltheart, M., Rastle, K., Perry, C., Langdon, R., & Ziegler, J. (2001). DRC: A dual route cascaded model of visual word recognition and reading aloud. *Psychological Review,* 108, 204–56.

Cortese, M. J. (1998). Revisiting serial position effects in reading aloud. *Journal of Memory and Language,* 39, 652–66.

Cortese, M. J. & Khanna, M. M. (2007). Age of acquisition predicts naming and lexical decision performance above and beyond 22 other predictor variables: An analysis of 2340 words. *Quarterly Journal of Experimental Psychology,* 60, 1072–82.

Cortese, M. J. & Simpson, G. B. (2000). Regularity effects in word naming: What are they? *Memory & Cognition,* 28, 1269–76.

Cree, G. S. & Armstrong, B. C. (this volume). Computational models of semantic memory.

Cree, G. S., McRae, K., & McNorgan, C. (1999). An attractor model of lexical conceptual processing: Simulating semantic priming. *Cognitive Science,* 23, 371–414.

Culter, A. (1981). Making up materials is a confounded nuisance: or Will we be able to run any psycholinguistic experiments at all in 1990? *Cognition,* 10, 65–70.

Dehaene, S., Cohen, L., Sigman, M. & Vinckier, F. (2005). The neural code for written words: a proposal. *Trends in Cognitive Sciences,* 9, 335–341.

Dosher, B. A. (1998). The response-window regression method-Some problematic assumptions: Comment on Draine and Greenwald (1998). *Journal of Experimental Psychology: General,* 127, 311–17.

Draine, S.C. & Grrenwald, A.G. (1998). Replicable unconscious semantic priming. *Journal of Experimental Psychology: General,* 127, 286–303.

Ellis, A. W. & Monaghan, J. (2002). Reply to Strain, Patterson, and Seidenberg. *Journal of Experimental Psychology: Learning, Memory, and Cognition,* 28, 215–20.

Evett, L. J. & Humphreys, G. W., (1981). The use of abstract graphemic information in lexical access. *Quarterly Journal of Experimental Psychology,* 33A, 325–50.

Favreau, M. & Segalowitz, N. S. (1983). Automatic and controlled processes in first- and second-language reading of fluent bilinguals. *Memory & Cognition,* 11, 565–74.

Fiez, J. A., Balota, D. A., Raichle, M. E., & Petersen, S. E. (1999). Effects of lexicality, frequency, and spelling-to-sound consistency on the functional anatomy of reading. *Neuron*, 24, 205–18.

Fine, E. M. (2001). The word superiority effect does not depend on one's ability to identify the letter string as a word. *Journal of Vision*, 1, 410.

Fodor, J. (1983). *The modularity of mind: An essay on faculty psychology*. Cambridge, Mass.: MIT Press.

Forster, K. I. (1976). Accessing the mental lexicon. In Wales, R. J. & Walker, E. (Eds.) *New Approaches to Language Mechanisms* (pp. 257–87). Amsterdam: North Holland.

(1979). Levels of processing and the structure of the language processor. In Cooper, W. E. & Walker, E. (Eds.) *Sentence processing: Psycholinguistic essays presented to Merrill Garrett*. Hillsdale, NJ: Lawrence Erlbaum Associates.

(1981). Priming and the effects of sentence and lexical context on naming time: Evidence for autonomous lexical processing. *Quarterly Journal of Experimental Psychology*, 33A, 465–95.

(1987). Form-priming with masked primes: The best match hypothesis. In Coltheart, M. (Ed.), *Attention and Performance 12: The Psychology of Reading* (pp. 127–46). Hillsdale, NJ: Lawrence Erlbaum Associates.

(2004). Category size effects revisited: Frequency and masked priming effects in semantic categorization. *Brain and Language*, 90, 276–86.

Forster, K. I., Mohan, K., & Hector, J. (2003). The mechanics of masked priming. In Kinoshita, S. & Lupker, S. J. (Eds.) *Masked priming: State of the art* (pp. 3–17).

Fowler, C. A., Wolford, G., Slade, R., & Tassinary, L. (1981). Lexical access with and without awareness. *Journal of Experimental Psychology: General*, 110, 341–62.

Frederiksen, J. R. & Kroll, J. F. (1976). Spelling and sound: Approaches to the internal lexicon. *Journal of Experimental Psychology: Human Perception & Performance*, 2, 361–79.

Frost, R. (1998). Toward a strong phonological theory of visual word recognition: True issues and false trails. *Psychological Bulletin*, 123, 71–99.

Frost, S. J., Mencl, W. E., Sandak, R., Moore, D. L., Rueckl, J. G., Katz, L., Fulbright, R. K., & Pugh, K. R. (2005). A functional magnetic resonance imaging study of the tradeoff between semantics and phonology in reading aloud. *Neuroreport: For Rapid Communication of Neuroscience Research*, 16, 621–24.

Funnell, E. (1983). Phonological processes in reading: New evidence from acquired dyslexia. *British Journal of Psychology*, 74, 159–80.

Gernsbacher, M. A. (1984). Resolving 20 years of inconsistent interactions between lexical familiarity and orthography, concreteness, and polysemy. *Journal of Experimental Psychology: General*, 113, 256–81.

Glushko, R. J. (1979). The organization and activation of orthographic knowledge in reading aloud. *Journal of Experimental Psychology: Human Perception and Performance*, 5, 674–91.

Gold, B. T., Balota, D. A., Cortese, M. J., Sergent Marshall, S. D., Snyder, A. Z., Salat, D. H., Fischl, B., Dale, A. M., Morris, J. C., & Buckner, R. L. (2005). Differing neuropsychological and neuroanatomical correlates of abnormal reading in early-stage semantic dementia and dementia of the Alzheimer type. *Neuropsychologia*, 43, 833–46.

Gonnerman, L. M., Seidenberg, M. S., & Andersen, E. S. (2007). Graded semantic and phonological similarity effects in priming: Evidence for a distributed connectionist approach to morphology. *Journal of Experimental Psychology: General*, 136, 323–45.

Gough, P. B. & Cosky, M. L. (1977). One second of reading again. In Castellan, J. N., Pisoni, D. B., & Potts, G. R. (Eds.) *Cognitive Theory (vol. 2)*. Hillsdale, NJ: Lawrence Erlbaum.

Grainger, J. & Jacobs, A. M. (1996). Orthographic processing in visual word recognition: A multiple read-out model. *Psychological Review*, 103, 518–65.

Harm M. W., McCandliss, B. D., & Seidenberg, M. S. (2003). Modeling the successes and failures of interventions for disabled readers. *Scientific Studies of Reading*, 7, 155–82.

Harm, M. W. & Seidenberg, M. S., (2004). Computing the meanings of words in reading: Cooperative division of labor between visual and phonological processes. *Psychological Review*, 111, 662–720.

Heathcote, A., Popiel, S. J., & Mewhort, D. J., (1991). Analysis of response time distributions: An example using the Stroop task. *Psychological Bulletin*, 109, 340–7.

Hino, Y. & Lupker, S. J. (1996). Effects of polysemy in lexical decision and naming: An alternative to lexical access accounts. *Journal of Experimental Psychology: Human Perception and Performance*, 22, 1331–56.

Hockett, C. F. (1966). The problem of universals in language. In Greenberg, J. H. (Ed.) *Universals of Language* (pp. 1–29). Cambridge, MA: MIT Press.

Holcomb, P. J. & Anderson, J. E. (1993). Cross-modal semantic priming: A time-course analysis using event-related brain potentials. *Language and Cognitive Processes*, 8, 379–411.

Holender, D. (1986). Semantic activation without conscious identification in dichotic listening, parafoveal vision, and visual masking: A survey and appraisal. *Behavioral and Brain Sciences*, 9, 1–66.

Hubel, D. H. & Wiesel, T. N. (1962). Receptive fields, binocular interaction and functional architecture in the cat's visual cortex. *Journal of Physiology*, 160, 106–54.

(1968). Receptive fields and functional architecture of monkey striate cortex. *Journal of Physiology*, 195, 215–43.

Humphreys, G. W., Besner, D., & Quinlan, P. T. (1988). Event perception and the word repetition effect. *Journal of Experimental Psychology: General*, 117, 51–67.

Humphreys, G. W., Evett, L. J., & Taylor, D. E. (1982). Automatic phonological priming in visual word recognition. *Memory & Cognition*, 10, 576–90.

Hutchison, K. A. (2004). Is semantic priming due to association strength or feature overlap? A microanalytic review. *Psychonomic Bulletin & Review*, 10, 785–813.

Jacobs, A. M., Rey, A., Ziegler, J. C., & Grainger, J. (1998). MROM-p: An interactive activation, multiple read-out model of orthographic and phonological processes in visual word recognition. In Grainger, J. & Jacobs, A. M. (Eds.) *Localist connectionist approaches to human cognition* (pp. 147–88). Mahwah, NJ, USA: Lawrence Erlbaum Associates.

Jacoby, L. L. (1991). A process dissociation framework: Separating automatic from intentional uses of memory. *Journal of Memory and Language*, 30, 513–41.

Jared, D. (1997). Spelling-sound consistency affects the naming of high-frequency words. *Journal of Memory and Language*, 36, 505–29.

(2000). Spelling-sound consistency and regularity effects in word naming. *Journal of Memory and Language*, 46, 723–50.

Jared, D., Levy, B. A., & Rayner K. (1999). The role of phonology in the activation of word meanings during reading: Evidence from proofreading and eye movements. *Journal*

of Experimental Psychology: General, 128, 219–64.

Jared, D., McRae, K., & Seidenberg, M. S. (1990). The basis of consistency effects in word naming. *Journal of Memory and Language*, 29, 687–715.

Jared, D. & Seidenberg, M. S. (1991). Does word identification proceed from spelling to sound to meaning? *Journal of Experimental Psychology: General*, 120, 358–94.

Johnson, N. F. & Pugh, K. R. (1994). A cohort model of visual word recognition. *Cognitive Psychology*, 26, 240–346.

Juhasz, B. J. (2005). Age-of-acquisition effects in word and picture identification, *Psychological Bulletin*, 131, 684–712.

Kahan, T. A., Neely, J. H., & Forsythe, W. J. (1999). Dissociated backward priming effects in lexical decision and pronunciation tasks. *Psychonomic Bulletin & Review*, 6, 105–10.

Kessler, B., Treiman, R., & Mullennix, J. (2002). Phonetic biases in voice key response time measurements. *Journal of Memory and Language*, 47, 145–71.

(2007). Feedback consistency effects in single-word reading. In Grigorenko, E. J. & Naples, A. J. (Eds.) *Single-word reading: Cognitive, behavioral, and biological perspectives* (pp. 159–74). Mahwah, NJ: Erlbaum.

Kiger, J. L. & Glass, A. (1983). The facilitation of lexical decisions by a prime occurring after the target. *Memory & Cognition*, 11, 356–65.

Kinoshita, S. & Lupker, S. J. (2002). Effects of filler type in naming: Change in time criterion or attentional control of pathways? *Memory & Cognition*, 30, 1277–87.

(2003). Priming and attentional control of lexical and sublexical pathways in naming: A reevaluation. *Journal of Experimental Psychology: Learning, Memory, and Cognition*, 29, 405–15.

Kinoshita, S. & Woollams, A. (2002) The masked onset priming effect in naming: Computation of phonology or speech-planning? *Memory & Cognition*, 30, 237–45.

Koriat, A. (1981). Semantic facilitation in lexical decision as a function of prime-target association. *Memory & Cognition*, 9, 587–98.

Kučera, H. & Francis, W. (1967). *Computational analysis of present-day American English*. Providence, RI: Brown University Press.

Lee, Y., Binder, K. S., Kim, J., Pollatsek, A., & Rayner, K. (1999). Activation of phonological codes during eye fixations in reading. *Journal of Experimental Psychology: Human Perception and Performance*, 25, 948–64.

Lima, S. D. (1987). Morphological analysis in sentence reading. *Journal of Memory and Language*, 26, 84–99.

Lucas, M. (2000). Semantic priming without association: A meta-analytic review. *Psychonomic Bulletin & Review*, 7, 618–630.

Lukatela, G., Eaton, T., Sabadini, L., & Turvey, M. T. (2004). Vowel duration affects visual word identification: Evidence that the mediating phonology is phonetically informed. *Journal of Experimental Psychology: Human Perception and Performance*, 30, 151–62.

Lukatela, G. & Turvey, M. T. (1991). Phonological access of the lexicon: evidence from associative priming with pseudohomophones. *Journal of Experimental Psychology*, 17, 951–66.

Lupker, S. J., Brown, P., & Colombo, L. (1997). Strategic control in a naming task: Changing routes or changing deadlines? *Journal of Experimental Psychology: Learning, Memory, and Cognition*, 23, 570–90.

Masson, M. E. (1995). A distributed memory model of semantic priming. *Journal of Experimental Psychology: Learning, Memory, and Cognition*, 21, 3–23.

Marcel, A. J. (1983). Conscious and unconscious perception: Experiments on visual masking and word recognition. *Cognitive Psychology*, 15, 197–237.

McCann, R. S., & Besner, D. (1987). Reading pseudohomo- phones: Implications for models of pronunciation assembly and the locus of word-frequency effects in naming. *Journal of Experimental Psychology: Human Perception and Performance*, 13, 14–24.

McClelland, J. L. (1979). On the time relations of mental processes: An examination of systems of processes in cascade. *Psychological Review*, 108, 287–330.

McClelland, J. L. & Rumelhart, D. E. (1981). An interactive activation model of context effects in letter perception: Part 1. An account of basic findings. *Psychological Review*, 88, 375–407.

McNamara, T. P. (2005). *Semantic priming: Perspectives from memory and word recognition.* New York: Psychology Press.

McNamara, T. P. & Altarriba, J. (1988). Depth of spreading activation revisited: Semantic mediated priming occurs in lexical decisions. *Journal of Memory and Language*, 27, 545–59.

Merikle, D. (1982). Unconscious perception revisited. *Perception & Psychophysics*, 31, 298–301.

Meyer, D. E. & Schvaneveldt, R. W. (1971). Facilitation in recognizing words: Evidence of a dependence upon retrieval operations. *Journal of Experimental Psychology*, 90, 227–34.

Monaghan, J. & Ellis, A. W. (2002). What exactly interacts with spelling-sound consistency in word naming? *Journal of Experimental Psychology: Learning, Memory, and Cognition*, 21, 116–53.

Monsell, S., Patterson, K., Graham, A., Hughes, C. H., & Milroy, R. (1992). Lexical and sublexical translations of spelling to sound: Strategic anticipation of lexical status. *Journal of Experimental Psychology: Learning, Memory, and Cognition*, 18, 452–67.

Morrison, C. M. & Ellis, E. W. (1995). Roles of word frequency and age of acquisition in word naming and lexical decision. *Journal of Experimental Psychology: Learning, Memory, and Cognition*, 21, 116–53.

Morton, J. (1969). Interaction of information in word recognition. *Psychological Review*, 76, 165–78.

Murray, W. S. & Forster, K.I. (2004). Serial mechanisms in lexical access: The rank hypothesis. *Psychological Review*, 111, 721–56.

Nation, K. (this volume). Decoding, orthographic learning, and the development of visual word recognition.

Neely, J. H. (1977). Semantic priming and retrieval from lexical memory: Roles of inhibitionless spreading activation and limited-capacity attention. *Journal of Experimental Psychology: General*, 106, 226–54.

(1991). Semantic priming effects in visual word recognition: A selective review of current findings and theories. In Besner, D. & Humphreys, G. W. (Eds.) *Basic processes in reading: Visual word recognition* (pp. 236–64), Hillsdale, NJ: Erlbaum..

New, B., Ferrand, L., Pallier, C., & Brysbaert, M. (2006). Re-examining the word length effect in visual word recognition: New evidence from the English Lexicon Project. *Psychonomic Bulletin & Review*, 13, 45–52.

Nelson, D. L., McEvoy, C. L., & Schreiber, T. A. (1998). *The University of South Florida word association, rhyme, and word fragment norms* http://www.usf.edu/FreeAssociation/.

Norris, D. (1986). Word recognition: Context effects without priming. *Cognition*, 22, 93–136.

(2006). The Bayesian reader: Explaining word recognition as an optimal Bayesian decision process. *Psychological Review*, 105, 761–81.

Paap, K. R. & Johansen, L. S. (1994). The case of the vanishing frequency effect: A retest of the verification model. *Journal of Experimental Psychology: Human Perception and Performance*, 20, 1129–57.

Paap, K. R., Newsome, S. L., & McDonald, J. E. (1982). An activation-verification model for letter and word recognition: The word superiority effect. *Psychological Review*, 89, 573–94.

Patterson, K. & Behrmann, M. (1997). Frequency and consistency effects in a pure surface dyslexic patient. *Journal of Experimental Psychology: Human Perception and Performance*, 23, 1217–31.

Patterson, K., Plaut, D. C., McClelland, J. L., Seidenberg, M. S., Behrmann, M., & Hodges, J. R. (1996). Connections and disconnections: A connectionist account of surface dyslexia. In Reggia, J., Berndt, R., & Ruppin, E. (Eds.) *Neural modeling of cognitive and brain disorders* (pp. 177–99). New York: World Scientific.

Peereman, R., Content, A. L., & Bonin, P. (1998). Is perception a two-way street? The case of feedback consistency in visual word recognition. *Journal of Memory & Language*, 39, 151–74.

Perry, C., Ziegler, J. C., & Zorzi, M. (2007). Nested incremental modeling in the development of computational theories: The CDP+ model of reading aloud. *Psychological Review*, 114, 273–315.

Petersen, S. E., Fox, P. T., Posner, M. I., Mintun, M., & Raichle, M. E. (1989). Positron emission tomographic studies of the processing of single words. *Journal of Cognitive Neuroscience*, 1, 153–70.

Pexman, P. M., Lupker, S. J., & Jared, D. (2001). Homophone effects in lexical decision. *Journal of Experimental Psychology: Learning, Memory and Cognition*, 22, 139–56.

Plaut, D. C. (1996). Relearning after damage in connectionist networks: Toward a theory of rehabilitation. *Brain and Language*, 52, 25–82.

(1999). Computational modeling of word reading, acquired dyslexia, and remediation. In Klein, R. M. & McMullen P. A. (Eds.) *Converging methods in reading and dyslexia* (pp. 339–72). Cambridge, MA: MIT Press.

Plaut, D. C. & Booth, J. R. (2000). Individual and developmental differences in semantic priming: Empirical and computational support for a single-mechanism account of lexical processing. *Psychological Review*, 107, 786–823.

Plaut, D. C. & Gonnerman, L. M. (2000) Are nonsemantic morphological effects incompatible with a distributed connectionist approach to lexical processing? *Language and Cognitive Processes*, 15, 445–85.

Plaut, D. C., McClelland, J. L., Seidenberg, M. S., & Patterson, K. E. (1996). Understanding normal and impaired word reading: Computational principles in quasi-regular domains. *Psychological Review*, 103, 56–115.

Pollatsek, A., Lesch, M., Morris, R. K., & Rayner, K. (1992). Phonological codes are used in integrating information across saccades in word identification and reading. *Journal of Experimental Psychology: Human Perception and Performance*, 18, 148–62.

Pollatsek, A., Perea, M., & Carreiras, M. (2005). Does *conal* prime CANAL more than *cinal*? Masked phonological priming effects in Spanish with the lexical decision task. *Memory & Cognition*, 33, 557–65.

Pugh, K. R., Sandak, R., Frost, S. J., Moore, D., & Mencl, W. E. (2005). Examining reading development and reading disabilities in English language learners: Potential contributions from functional neuroimaging. *Learning Disabilities Research & Practice*, 20, 24–30.

Rastle, K., Davis, M., & New B. (2004). The broth in my brother's brothel: Morpho-orthographic segmentation in visual word recognition. *Psychonomic Bulletin & Review*, 11, 1090–8.

Rastle, K. & Coltheart, M. (1999). Serial and strategic effects in reading aloud. *Journal of Experimental Psychology: Human Perception and Performance*, 25, 482–503.

Ratcliff, R., Thapar, A., Gomez, P., & McKoon, G. (2004). A diffusion model analysis of the effects of aging in the lexical-decision task. *Psychology and Aging*, 19, 278–89.

Ratcliff, R. & McKoon, G. (1988). A retrieval theory of priming in memory. *Psychological Review*, 95, 385–408.

Rayner, K. (1998). Eye movements in reading and information processing: Twenty years of research. *Psychological Bulletin*, 124, 372–422.

Rayner, K., Foorman, B. R., Perfetti, C. A., Pesetsky, D., & Seidenberg, M. S. (2001). How psychological science informs the teaching of reading. *Psychological Science in the Public Interest Monograph*, 2, 31–74.

Rayner, K. & Pollatsek, A. (1989). *The psychology of reading*. Englewood Cliffs, NJ: Prentice Hall.

Rayner, K., McConkie, G. W., & Zola, D. (1980). Integrating information across eye movements. *Cognitive Psychology*, 12, 206–26.

Reicher, G. M. (1969). Perceptual recognition as a function of meaningfulness of stimulus material. *Journal of Experimental Psychology*, 81, 275–80.

Reynolds, M. & Besner, D. (2005). Contextual control over lexical and sublexical routines when reading English aloud. *Psychonomic Bulletin & Review*, 12, 113–18.

(2005). Basic processes in reading: A critical review of psuedohomophone effects in naming and a new computational account. *Psychonomic Bulletin & Review*, 12, 622–46.

Ric, F. (2004). Effects of the activation of affective information on stereotyping: When sadness increases stereotype use. *Personality & Social Psychology Bulletin*, 30, 1310–21.

Rubenstein, H., Garfield, L., & Millikan, J. A. (1970). Homographic entries in the internal lexicon. *Journal of Verbal Learning & Verbal Behavior*, 9, 487–94.

Rubenstein, H., Lewis, S. S., & Rubenstein, M. (1971). Homographic entries in the internal lexicon: Effects of systematicity and relative frequency of meanings. *Journal of Verbal Learning and Verbal Behavior*, 10, 57–62.

Rueckl, J. G., Mikolinski, M., Raveh, M., Miner, C. S., & Mars, F. (1997). *Journal of Memory and Language*, 36, 382–405.

Rumelhart, D. E. & McClelland, D. E. (1982). An interactive activation model of context effects in letter perception: II. The contextual enhancement effect and some tests and extensions of the model. *Psychological Review*, 89, 60–94.

Sandak, R. **et al.** (this volume). How does the brain read words?

Schilling, H. E. H., Rayner, K., & Chumbley, J. I. (1998). Comparing naming, lexical decision, and eye fixation times: Word frequency effects and individual differences. *Memory & Cognition*, 26, 1270–81.

Sears, C. R., Hino, Y., & Lupker, S. J. (1995). Neighborhood size and neighborhood frequency effects in word recognition. *Journal of Experimental Psychology: Human Perception and Performance*, 21, 876–900.

(1999). Orthographic neighbourhood effects in parallel distributed processing models. *Canadian Journal of Experimental Psychology*, 53, 220–9.

Seidenberg, M. S. (2005). Connectionist models of word reading. *Current Directions in Psychological Science*, 238–42.

Seidenberg, M. S. & McClelland, J. L. (1989). A distributed developmental model of word recognition and naming. *Psychological Review*, 96, 523–68.

Seidenberg, M. S., Petersen, A., MacDonald, M. C., & Plaut, D. C. (1996). Pseudohomophone effects and models of word recognition. *Journal of Experimental Psychology: Learning, Memory, and Cognition*, 22, 48–62.

Seidenberg, M. S. & Plaut, D. C. (1998). Evaluating word-reading models at the item level: Matching the grain of theory and data. *Psychological Science*, 9, 234–7.

Seidenberg, M. S., Waters, G. S., Barnes, M. A., & Tanenhaus, M. K. (1984). When does irregular spelling or pronunciation influence word recognition? *Journal of Verbal Learning and Verbal Behavior*, 23, 383–404.

Seidenberg, M. S., Waters, G. S., Sanders, M., & Langer, P. (1984). Pre- and post-lexical loci of contextual effects on word recognition. *Memory & Cognition*, 12, 315–28.

Selfridge, O. G. (1959). Pandemonium: A paradigm for learning. In *Symposium of the mechanization of thought processes*. Proceedings of a symposium held at the National Physical Laboratory, U.K. Her Majesty's Stationary Office.

Selfridge, O. G. & Neisser, U. (1960). Pattern recognition by machine. *Scientific American*, 203, 60–8.

Sereno, J. (1991). Graphemic, associative, and syntactic priming effects at a brief stimulus onset asynchrony in lexical decision and naming. *Journal of Experimental Psychology: Learning, Memory, and Cognition*, 17, 459–477.

Simpson, G. B. & Kang, H. (1994). The flexible use of phonological information in word recognition in Korean. *Journal of Memory and Language*, 33, 319–31.

Snow, C. E., Burns, M. S., & Griffin, P. (1998). (Eds.) *Preventing reading difficulties in children*. Washington, DC: National Academy Press.

Spieler, D. H. & Balota, D. A. (1997). Bringing computational models of word naming down to the item level. *Psychological Science*, 8, 411–16.

Spieler, D. H., Balota, D. A., & Faust, M. E. (1996). Levels of selective attention revealed through analyses of response time distributions. *Journal of Experimental Psychology: Human Perception and Performance*, 26, 506–26.

Stanners, R. F., Neiser, J. J., Hernon, W. P., & Hall, R. (1979). Memory representation for morphologically related words. *Journal of Verbal Learning and Verbal Behavior*, 18, 399–412.

Steyvers, M. & Tenenbaum, J. B. (2005). The large-scale structure of semantic networks: Statistical analyses and a model of semantic growth. *Cognitive Science*, 29, 41–78.

Stone, G. O., Vanhoy, M., & Van Orden, G. C. (1997). Perception is a two-way street: Feedforward and feedback phonology in visual word recognition. *Journal of Memory and Language*, 36, 337–59.

Strain, E., Patterson, K., & Seidenberg, M. S. (1995). Semantic effects in single-word naming. *Journal of Experimental Psychology: Learning, Memory, and Cognition, 21,* 1140–54.

(2002). Theories of word naming interact with spelling-sound consistency. *Journal of Experimental Psychology: Learning, Memory, and Cognition, 28,* 207–14.

Taft, M. (1979a). Lexical access via an orthographic code: The basic orthographic syllabic structure (BOSS). *Journal of Verbal Learning and Verbal Behavior, 18,* 21–39.

Taft, M. (1979b). Recognition of affixed words and the word frequency effect. *Memory & Cognition, 7,* 263–72.

Taft, M. & Forster, K. I. (1975). Lexical storage and retrieval of prefixed words. *Journal of Verbal Learning and Verbal Behavior, 14,* 638–47.

(1976). Lexical storage and retrieval of polymorphemic and pollysyllabic words. *Journal of Verbal Learning and Verbal Behavior, 15,* 607–20.

Taft, M. & Hambly, G. (1986). Exploring the Cohort Model of spoken word recognition. *Cognition, 22,* 259–82.

Tan, L. H. & Perfetti, C. A. (1999). Phonological and associative inhibition in the early stages of English word identification: Evidence from backward masking. *Journal of Experiment Psychology: Human Perception and Performance, 25,* 59–69.

Toglia, M. P. & Battig, W. F. (1978). *Handbook of semantic word norms.* Hillsdale, NJ: Erlbaum.

Treiman, R., Mullennix, J., Bijeljac-Babic, R., & Richmond-Welty, E. D. (1995). The special role of rimes in the description, use, and acquisition of English orthography. *Journal of Memory and Language, 124,* 107–36.

Weekes, B. S. (1997). Differential effects of number of letters on word and nonword naming latency. *Quarterly Journal of Experimental Psychology: Human Experimental Psychology, 50A,* 439–56.

Yates, M., Locker, L., & Simpson, G. (2004). The influence of phonological neighborhood on

visual word perception. *Psychonomic Bulletin & Review, 11,* 452–7.

Zeno, S. M., Ivenz, S. H., Millard, R. T., & Duvvuri, R. (1995). *The educator"s word frequency guide.* Brewster, NY: Touchstone Applied Science Associates.

Zevin, J. D. & Balota, D. A. (2000). Priming and attentional control of lexical and sublexical pathways during naming. *Journal of Experimental Psychology: Learning, Memory, and Cognition, 26,* 121–35.

Zevin, J. D. & Seidenberg, M. S. (2002). Age of acquisition effects in word reading and other tasks. *Journal of Memory and Language, 47,* 1–29.

(2004). Age of acquisition effects in reading aloud: Tests of cumulative frequency and frequency trajectory. *Memory & Cognition, 32,* 31–38.

(2006). Simulating consistency effects and individual differences in nonword naming: A comparison of current models. *Journal of Memory & Language, 54,* 145–60.

Ziegler, J. C., Ferrand, L., & Jacobs, A. M. (2000). Visual and phonological codes in letter and word recognition: Evidence from incremental priming. *Quarterly Journal of Experimental Psychology: Human Experimental Psychology, 53A,* 671–92.

(1997). The feedback consistency effect in lexical decision and naming. *Journal of Memory and Language, 37,* 533–54.

Ziegler, J. C. & Perry, C. (1998). No more problems in Coltheart's neighborhood: resolving neighborhood conflicts in the lexical decision task. *Cognition, 68,* 53–62.

Zorzi, M. (2000). Serial processing in reading aloud: No challenge for a parallel model. *Journal of Experimental Psychology: Human Perception and Performance, 26,* 847–56.

Zorzi, M., Houghton, G., & Butterworth, B. (1998). Two routes or one in reading aloud? A connectionist dual-process model. *Journal of Experimental Psychology: Human Perception and Performance, 24,* 1131–61.

CHAPTER 9

Computational Models of Reading

Connectionist and Dual-Route Approaches

Mark S. Seidenberg

Word recognition in reading is one of the most extensively studied topics in cognitive psychology-neuropsychology-neuroscience. Computational models are among the tools available for developing a deeper understanding of cognitive phenomena, and they have played a particularly important role in research on normal and disordered reading. My goal in this chapter is to review some of the historical background for the development of present-day computational models of word reading, and then consider two influential contemporary approaches: the Dual Route Cascade (DRC) approach (Coltheart et al., 1993; 2001) and the triangle connectionist approach (Harm and Seidenberg, 1999, 2004; Plaut et al., 1996; Seidenberg and McClelland, 1989). These are not the only computational models of reading in the marketplace, but I have focused on them for several reasons. One is because it isn't possible to review all the existing models in the available space. Another is because these two frameworks represent very different approaches to computational modeling and so the contrast between them is informative. Finally, these models have engaged

a somewhat broader range of phenomena than other, more specialized models (e.g., ones that focus on a particular task, such as lexical decision (e.g., Wagenmakers et al., 2004).[1]

1 Background

Contemporary computational models of word reading derive from several progenitors that predate the simulation modeling era. The patriarch of the family is perhaps Morton's (1969) logogen model, which was

---

[1] Most people refer to models of word recognition, but I dislike the term because *recognition* seems inconsistent with the kinds of processes that occur in PDP models in which there is no privileged moment of lexical access. It also seems awkward to use this term in reference to tasks as different as determining a word's meaning, reading it aloud, and spelling it. I prefer the term *models of word reading*. This ignores the fact that people also read nonwords, but seems the better alternative, given the artificiality of nonword reading. I am also aware that the term *DRC* was not introduced until Coltheart et al. (2001); however, the model presented in that article was an extension of the 1993 model and so I have used the term to apply to both.

the first, to my knowledge, to utilize the metaphor of a lexicon consisting of entries (logogens, later termed *localist nodes*) corresponding to individual words. The logogen for a word encoded (responded to) information about its visual, semantic, and acoustic codes. These codes were represented by sets of attributes (or "features"). When a word was processed, the numerical value associated with the logogen that encoded any of the word's visual, semantic, or acoustic attributes was incremented. It would be convenient to term this "activating" a logogen, but this term was not introduced until later. Other logogens that encoded these features would also be incremented (e.g., the /b/ in *book* would increment the values for other words containing this phoneme), leading to what would later be called "competition among partially activated alternatives." The "winning" logogen was determined by Luce's choice rule (Luce, 1959). The resemblances to later localist connectionist models (e.g., McClelland and Rumelhart, 1981; the lexical route in Coltheart et al.'s 2001 DRC model, both discussed later in this chapter) are obvious. It is worth pausing for a moment to recognize the sheer number of essential concepts that were introduced in this pioneering work and incorporated in modified or relabeled form in later work.

A second important ancestor was the model developed by Marshall and Newcombe (1973), which introduced the idea of different word processing routines (visual, phonological, semantic). This general framework later became known as the dual-route model (Baron and Strawson, 1976; Coltheart, 1978). Based on a logical analysis of the properties of English spelling, Marshall and Newcombe deduced that people's ability to read aloud irregularly pronounced words (such as *pint* and *give*) as well as unfamiliar, nonce words (such as *nust*) must involve two mechanisms, later termed the *lexical* and *sublexical* routes, respectively. Whereas Morton provided a mathematical characterization of the major tenets of his theory, dual-route models were stated informally in a quasi-computational information processing language. Again it is

worth pausing to acknowledge the extent to which the later computational versions of the dual-route model (i.e., DRC) adhere to these earlier informal proposals.

The dual-route model was the dominant theory of word recognition through the 1980s. As in Marshall and Newcombe's original work, much of the motivation for the model came from studies of patients whose brain injuries impaired their reading in different ways. For example, patients termed "phonological dyslexics" were relatively more impaired at reading nonwords (e.g., *nust, faige*) than "regular" words such as *must* or "exception" words such as *have*. This selective impairment of nonwords was said to imply damage to the nonlexical mechanism responsible for generating the pronunciations of novel letter strings, which Coltheart (1978) construed as "grapheme–phoneme correspondence rules" (GPCs). Conversely, patients termed "surface dyslexics" were relatively more impaired in reading exception words than regular words or nonwords. This implied damage to the lexical naming mechanism responsible for word-specific information. This double dissociation was thought to provide strong evidence for the two independent, isolable naming routines that gave the dual-route model its name. Several variants of the basic dual-route scheme were introduced in attempts to capture other types of impaired reading such as deep dyslexia and letter-by-letter reading (see Coltheart et al., 1980; Patterson et al., 1985). The methodology emphasized the importance of relatively clear cases in which one or another component of the model was impaired while others remained largely intact. Such cases might be highly atypical (insofar as such extreme patterns were rarely observed) but nonetheless highly informative. The co-occurrence of deficits was thought to be less informative than selective impairments; a messy brain lesion might affect several components of the reading system, creating co-occurring but otherwise unrelated deficits.

Such was the state of affairs in the modeling of word recognition circa 1987. Model development was closely tied to the methods, goals, and types of data and theorizing associated with cognitive neuropsychology. Informal "box and arrow" information processing models were proposed as theories of the "functional architecture of the cognitive system;" the pattern of preserved and impaired performance on a set of tasks was used to identify the locus of a brain-injured patient's lesion or lesions within this system. The dual-route model of reading aloud provided the paradigmatic example of the approach. Over time, Marshall and Newcombe's relatively simple and elegant model evolved into more complex systems that dealt with a broader range of behavioral phenomena (e.g., agnosia, dysgraphia). Aside from a brief detour into "analogy" models (Kay and Marcel, 1981), however, the models retained the two naming mechanisms of the dual-route approach at their theoretical core.

1.1 Transitions

In the late 1980s, several developments conspired to disrupt the status quo. One was dissatisfaction in some quarters about the types of theories that resulted from the functional architecture approach. I summarized many of these concerns in Seidenberg (1988). The box and arrow models were static diagrams that left many details about how information was represented and processed unspecified. The diagrams were not well-suited to characterizing the time course of events that occurred in performing a task such as pronouncing a letter string aloud. The absence of these types of information made it difficult to assess the validity of claims pitched at the level of the functional architecture; it was difficult to determine if a proposed mechanism would produce the intended results. The models were unconstrained in the sense that new structures and operations could be added in response to specific phenomena, even the behavior of a single patient. This lent them an ad hoc character. The lack of specificity and the lack of constraints on the formalism created two problems. One is the familiar lack of falsifiability: If it couldn't be determined if proposed

mechanisms would work in intended ways, it couldn't be determined if they would *fail* to work. Moreover, it was too easy to adjust models to fit specific data patterns by adding new modules or processing assumptions. A second, equally important concern is that such models could account for both phenomena that do occur and ones that do not (see Seidenberg, 1993 for discussion). It isn't sufficient that a model account for particular data patterns; given an unconstrained modeling language, and a narrow focus on particular phenomena, any pattern can be mimicked. Considerable explanatory power is gained if a model can simultaneously account for why other outcomes are *not* observed. Whereas falsifiability involves finding data that disconfirm a theory, this second criterion involves showing that a model correctly rules out data that do not occur. The box and arrow models did not meet the latter challenge (Seidenberg, 1988). Rather, they seemed dangerously close to redescriptions of phenomena in a pseudocomputational language.

Other concerns arose about methodology. Numerous battles broke out about best practices. There was an extended debate about the value of single case studies versus analyses of groups of subjects (cf. Caplan, 1988; Caramazza, 1986, and others). Unsurprisingly perhaps, the debate did not yield a consensus, but, utility of group studies aside, one effect was to strengthen arguments in favor of the importance of individual case studies. Eventually, however, additional concerns arose about the interpretation of case studies (Plaut, 1995; Woollams et al., 2006). Another question was whether the methodology was powerful enough to converge on the correct theory of the functional architecture. For example, there was extended debate about whether the functional architecture includes a single semantic system or multiple ones (cf. Caramazza et al., 1990; Shallice, 1993). The conjunction of informal modeling and behavioral data was not sufficient to converge on a clear answer. Concerns were raised about the linkage between data and theory, specifically the kinds of inferences that could be drawn from patient data (Farah, 1994). Many people took issue with the classical interpretation of double dissociations, calling into question whether such dissociations provide airtight evidence for independent components in the functional architecture (cf. Dunn and Kirsner, 2003; Juola and Plunkett, 2000; Plaut, 1995; Van Orden et al., 2001). Such dissociations might arise from other sources: For example, they might represent different points on a distribution of effects created by a combination of factors including different types or degrees of damage to a single system, different degrees of recovery of function or effects of different types of remediation, or different effects of a given type of pathology due to premorbid individual differences. Many of these concerns arose in connection with models of reading, however, they applied more broadly to the functional architecture approach.

1.2 *Enter computational models*

There were several responses to these challenges. Some controversies merely flared and burned out, as researchers lost interest in issues that became bogged down without clear resolution (see, for example, the debate about deficits in access versus representation; Rapp and Caramazza, 1993). Some researchers continued to rely on the traditional approach (see, for example, Miozzo, 2003 and Rapp and Caramazza, 2002, which still use individual case studies and the classical logic governing the identification of components of the functional architecture). However, some researchers took up the challenge of developing models that were more fully specified at the level of how knowledge is represented and processed. The method for achieving this level of mechanistic detail was the implementation of simulation models.

The simulation modeling methodology had been introduced to psychology some years earlier by Newell and Simon (1963). Their models mainly addressed principles of reasoning and problem solving. The pioneering application of this approach to phenomena related to reading was the McClelland

and Rumelhart (1981) model. The main purpose of this model was to examine the role of interactive processing in perception; they happened to use letter and word processing as a domain in which to explore this idea. The model demonstrated how interactivity between levels of information (words, letters, features) allowed the system to converge on the identity of a stimulus. In doing so, the model simulated some counterintuitive behavioral phenomena. Letters are easier to identify in the context of words and pseudowords than in isolation (the word superiority effect; Reicher, 1969). Why would the simpler stimulus (a single letter) be harder to identify than when it occurred as part of a more complicated stimulus (a word or pseudoword)? The interactions between top-down and bottom-up flow of activation in the McClelland and Rumelhart model provided the answer.

McClelland and Rumelhart (1981) did not present a general model of reading. There was no phonology or semantics, even though these codes are crucial to reading. The model was limited in other respects: the levels of representation, the nature of the connections between and within levels, the values of the parameters governing the spread of activation, and other properties of the model were hand-wired. Although sufficient for the purpose of exploring the concept of interactivity, these limitations raised questions that later models of word reading attempted to address.

The McClelland and Rumelhart model provided a vivid demonstration of the value of the simulation modeling framework. The ideas were worked out in sufficient detail to be implemented as a computer program. The program simulated detailed aspects of an empirical literature (on word superiority effects) and generated testable predictions. It instantiated general concepts (e.g., interactive activation) that were relevant to reading but not specifically tailored or limited to the target phenomena. The 1981 article is now among the most highly cited in the history of *Psychological Review*. The presentation of a working model was surely a large part of their appeal; most readers probably have not been that interested in word and letter processing. Moreover, Adams (1979) had also recognized the key idea that the word superiority effect might result from feedback from word to letter levels, and applied this idea to behavioral data, but she lacked a computational model.

Given the availability of simulation modeling techniques, and the apparent limitations of the more informal style of modeling, it was not long before researchers began implementing computational models that addressed the phenomena concerning normal and impaired word and non-word naming that had been the focus of so much research within the functional architecture approach. Research following the McClelland and Rumelhart model branched in three directions. One was the implementation of connectionist models based on the parallel distributed processing approach developed by Rumelhart, Hinton, and McClelland (1986). Another was Coltheart and colleagues' Dual Route Cascade implementation of the dual-route model, which incorporated a McClelland and Rumelhart-style interactive activation model as the lexical route. Finally, some researchers continued to use variants of McClelland and Rumelhart's model to study issues such as the processing of orthographic information and particularly the role of orthographic neighborhoods in performing lexical decisions (e.g., Grainger and Jacobs, 1994). As noted earlier, I will focus on the first two lines of research; for a review of the third, see Grainger and Jacobs (1998).

2 The PDP models

In a 1989 article, McClelland and I outlined the general theoretical framework illustrated in Figure 9.1. The framework assumed that words are represented by patterns of activation over units representing spelling, sound, and meaning. Context units were included in recognition of the fact that words typically occur in contexts that affect their meanings (e.g., *the* rose versus *he* rose). The implemented model computed phonological

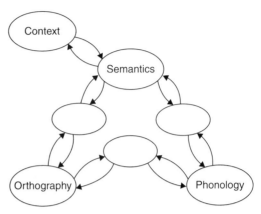

Figure 9.1. General framework for lexical processing introduced by Seidenberg and McClelland (1989). Reprinted with permission.

codes from spellings plus a recreation of the input orthographic pattern. Although the article and implemented model focused on word reading, the framework was intended to represent core processes involved in many uses of words. *Reading* is the process of computing a meaning (or pronunciation) from print. *Spelling* is computing from sound or meaning to print. *Listening*: phonology to meaning. *Production*: meaning to phonology. Seidenberg and McClelland (1989) focused on issues concerning the computation of phonology from print. This seemed like an interesting learning problem insofar as the correspondences between spelling and sound are systematic but include many exceptions, which differ from the central tendencies in differing degrees. I coined the term *quasiregular* to refer to knowledge systems with this character. My interest in the issue arose out of empirical studies of child and adult reading; McClelland's arose out of studies of the past tense in English, which is also quasiregular.

Figure 9.2 illustrates several reading models that have been implemented utilizing principles taken from the PDP framework. The figure brings out the fact that these models bear a family resemblance to each other: They overlap in many respects but no two are identical. What links the models is adherence to PDP principles. None of the models fully incorporate all of the principles, although some principles (e.g.,

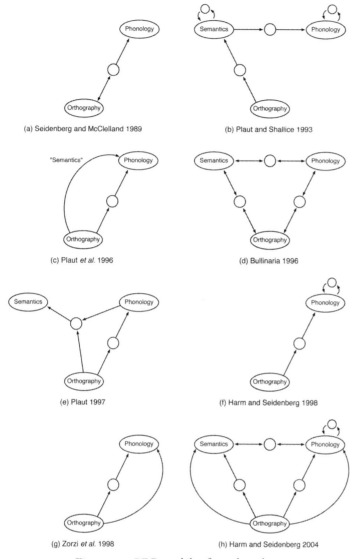

Figure 9.2. PDP models of word reading.

the idea of a multilayer network employing distributed representations with modifiable weights on connections) were employed in all of them. All the models have been concerned with processes involved in reading words, but they have emphasized different aspects of this skill: acquisition; skilled performance; developmental impairments (dyslexia); impairments following brain injury (acquired dyslexia); computation of pronunciations; computation of meanings; naming, lexical decision, and other tasks; bases of individual differences; and others. The models also differ with respect to many properties of the implementations, ranging from network architecture (e.g., number of layers, types of connectivity between layers) to training procedure (e.g., composition of the training corpus) to dependent measures (e.g., summed square error, settling time). Thus there has been a series of models which varied due to differences in focus with respect to behavioral phenomena (e.g., computation of pronunciation versus computation of meaning), and with respect to computational principles (e.g., interactive versus feedforward networks). The models also differ because of advances in understanding both the nature of the phenomena (e.g., the role of the orthography→semantics→phonology component in naming; factors that influence the division of labor between components of a model) and computational issues (e.g., how properties of network representations affect performance).

2.1 *Basic concepts*

The rationale behind this approach to understanding reading and other cognitive phenomena has been discussed extensively elsewhere (e.g., in the 1986 PDP volumes; in sources such as Plaut, 2005; Seidenberg, 1989, 1993; Seidenberg, 2005), and so only an overview is provided here. The goal of our research has been to develop a theoretical understanding of reading and how it is realized in the brain, with computational models providing the interface between the two. The idea is that it is not merely a nice thing to understand the brain bases of reading; rather, characteristics of reading (and other behaviors) arise from the ways in which reading is accomplished by the brain, and thus cannot be fully understood without reference to it.

This view is not universally accepted. The functional architecture style of theorizing assumed that neurobiology contributed very little to understanding the essential nature of the phenomena. The models of that era were not constrained by neurobiological facts (i.e., about how brains acquire, represent, and process information). Even though studies of brain-injured patients played a large role in model development, researchers focused on patterns of behavioral impairment rather than their neurobiological bases. (In fact I have a vivid memory of neurologist Norman Geschwind scolding researchers at an early 1980s conference for failing to report basic information about the nature of patient-subjects' brain injuries.) In part this functional stance was pragmatic, given the amount that was known about the neurobiology of cognition in the 1970s when the dual-route model and other functional style models were developed.

However, this stance did not merely reflect lack of knowledge; in some circles there was also a philosophical commitment to theories of cognitive functions that abstracted away from neurobiology (e.g., Block and Fodor, 1972). Antireductionists such as Fodor (1999) have famously (if recklessly) declared their disinterest in exactly where above the neck cognitive functions are realized. This philosophy is largely retained in the DRC versions of the dual-route model, which are committed to computational explicitness but remain oriented to behavioral generalizations minimally constrained by biology.

In contrast, we assume that cognitive capacities such as reading are shaped by properties of the underlying neural substrate. Thus the methodology employed in our research involves formulating and evaluating computational principles that represent hypotheses about how neural activity gives rise to cognition. The question, then, is not merely what computations are involved or where they are realized in neural circuitry, but rather how the brain enables cognitive functions and why the brain arrived at particular solutions to computational problems. These principles are coupled with domain-specific considerations (e.g., facts and conditions specific to a task such as reading) in developing a theory of the phenomena. Hypotheses are tested by determining whether computational models that embody the proposed principles are, in fact, consistent with relevant behavioral and neurobiological data. Our understanding of these basic principles is partial and thus they are subject to revision as knowledge advances. In fact, there is feedback among all levels of analysis: behavioral, computational, and neurobiological. Discoveries at one level serve to constrain hypotheses at other levels, which in turn feedback on generating and testing hypotheses at other levels. Converging on the correct theory is literally a constraint satisfaction process (Seidenberg and MacDonald, 1999): The correct theory is that which satisfies constraints arising from the biological, computational, and behavioral levels.

The main principles that constitute the PDP framework are well-known: Behavior arises from the cooperative and competitive interactions among large networks of simple, neuron-like processing units; different types of information are represented by distributed patterns of activity over different groups of units, with similarity indexed by pattern overlap; knowledge is encoded as weights on connections between units; learning is the gradual adjustment of these weights based on the statistical structure among inputs and outputs; such networks may include internal, "hidden" representations that allow complex mappings to be learned; processing is constraint satisfaction, that is, the computed output best fits the constraints represented by the weights.

Several other important properties identified in connection with the reading models should also be noted.

1. The PDP principles on which they are based are general rather than domain-specific. Thus the same principles are thought to apply across perceptual, cognitive, and motor domains. That there are such general principles contrasts with the view that the brain has evolved many domain-specific subsystems (Pinker, 1997). One consequence of the domain-general view is that the mechanisms available for modeling are not introduced solely in response to the data from a particular domain, but are constrained to be consistent with applications in other domains. This means that the mechanisms in the reading models have some independent motivation; specifically, they are thought to reflect more general facts about human cognitive functions. This is particularly relevant to reading, a technology invented relatively recently in human history, making use of existing cognitive and perceptual capacities.

2. In the PDP approach, the models are a tool rather than the goal of the enterprise. Modeling is a means of exploring the validity and implications of a set of hypotheses about how cognitive processes are implemented in the brain. The goal is not the development of an individual model that can be taken as the account of some set of phenomena, based on a comfortable degree of fit to empirical data. Rather, the models facilitate converging on the correct set of explanatory principles, which are more general than any individual model, and on theories in particular substantive areas that employ these principles.

This orientation gives rise to two further characteristics of the research. One is that the failures and successes of the models are both sources of insight (McClelland et al., 1995). A classic illustration of this point is the Seidenberg and McClelland model's poor performance on nonwords, which definitely deviated from people's. The nonword generalization problem was soon traced to the imprecise way that phonological information was represented in the model (Plaut et al., 1996). This imprecision had little impact on the pronunciation of words, but affected nonword pronunciation because it is a harder task which requires recombining known elements in novel ways. Models with improved phonological representations yielded much better nonword performance (Harm and Seidenberg, 1999; Plaut et al., 1996). Thus the nonword problem "falsified" our original model, but not the theory it approximated. Moreover, this "failure" led to insights about how representations determine network behavior, to improved models, and to advances in understanding developmental dyslexia, which is associated with phonological impairments (Harm and Seidenberg, 1999). This pattern, in which the limitations of one model lead to deeper insights and improved next-generation models, is a positive aspect of the modeling methodology. However, it complicates the metric by which models are evaluated. A model could be a failure insofar as it did not capture some aspect of human behavior, but a success insofar as this limitation yielded greater insight about it.

A second consequence of the models as tools orientation is that the product of this research is a series of models that address different aspects of reading, which taken together advance the understanding of the phenomena. This approach to modeling is frustrating to some because there is no single simulation that constitutes the model of the domain. The models seem like a moving target: Seidenberg and McClelland's model was interesting but ultimately limited by its phonological representation; Plaut et al. (1996) largely fixed the phonological problem but introduced the idea that the orth→sem→phon pathway also contributes to pronunciation, something Seidenberg and McClelland had not considered. Harm and Seidenberg (1999) used yet another phonological representation and focused on developmental phenomena; Harm and Seidenberg (2004) implemented both orth→sem and orth→phon→sem parts of the triangle but focused on data concerning activation of meaning rather than pronunciation and so forth. Each model shares something with all of the others, namely the computational principles discussed above, but each model differs as well. Where, then, is the integrative model that puts the pieces all together?

The answer, of course, is that there is none. Achieving a complete, integrative model is an ill-conceived goal given the nature of the modeling methodology (particularly the need to limit the scope of a model in order to gain insights from it in finite time) and the goal of the enterprise, which, as in the rest of science, is the development of a general theory that *abstracts away* from details of the phenomena to reveal fundamental principles (Putnam, 1972). The models, as tools for exploring computational and empirical phenomena, change more rapidly than the theory, which is an abstraction away from individual models.

3. The PDP models are intrinsically about learning: They are literally systems that learn. Learning is central to PDP models for many reasons, the least of which is because algorithmic procedures happen to exist for training multilayer networks that employ distributed representations.

(i) The models are intended to address important questions about how people acquire information and represent it in ways that support complex behaviors. In reading (as in other areas such as language acquisition), we want to know how children acquire a skill given the nature of the task, the capacities they bring to the task, and the nature of their experience. Part of the explanation for why the reading system has the character that it does rests with facts about how it is learned.

(ii) Because they are systems that learn, the models provide a unified account of acquisition and skilled performance. The same principles govern both; children and adults represent different points on the developmental continuum represented by states of the model over training time.

(iii) The models address how knowledge representations develop. One consequence is that we avoid having to stipulate in advance how words are represented (e.g., whether there are codes for words, syllables, morphemes, etc.). Whether such representations exist is one of the basic questions and it is not addressed by building them into a model. The representations that the models develop are contingent on the input and output representations and general properties of the architecture such as numbers of units and layers. In fact the input and output representations are themselves learned, something an ideal network would also address. For the moment we can illustrate the general idea as in Figure 9.3. The fact that the models learn also obviates the need to wire a network by hand, as is done in many localist models. The problems associated with hand-wiring are discussed below in connection with DRC. The main problem is that hand-wiring promotes overfitting the results of particular studies. Moreover, the behavior of the models ends up depending on parameter settings that have no independent motivation or theoretical interpretation.

Figure 9.3. The orthographic, phonological, and semantic layers in the Seidenberg and McClelland model can be thought of as interlevel representations that result from sensation, perception, and action, in conjunction with constraints imposed by human biology.

Yet these values are highly important insofar as model performance degrades when other values are used.

The emphasis on learning is one of the main characteristics that distinguishes the PDP and dual-route approaches. Although Coltheart et al. (1993) described an algorithm for deriving grapheme–phoneme correspondence rules, this procedure had little psychological plausibility and the rules that resulted were soon criticized for their oddness (Seidenberg et al., 1994). In later work, this algorithmic approach was abandoned and rules were added to DRC as needed to produce accurate output. The lack of a learning procedure for the lexical and non-lexical procedures in DRC is a serious limitation which extends beyond the need to hand-wire the rules themselves. The DRC models incorporate detailed procedures for applying rules to letter strings, which involve stipulations as to how the database of rules is searched, the order in which rules are applied, the size of the units over which rules apply, and other conditions. How the child would learn such scheduling procedures is also unknown. These gaps raise serious learnability questions: Could a child develop a dual-route system given children's experiences and the capacities and knowledge they bring to the task of learning to read? Coltheart and colleagues' view is apparently that because they model accounts for many aspects of skilled behavior, there must be some way for its components to be acquired. That inference is very weak, however, first because Coltheart et al. overstate the range of phenomena the model actually captures (see later in this chapter), and second because it is just as easy to imagine a model that does about as well as DRC2001 but could not be learned. The same issues do not arise in the PDP approach because learning is intrinsic to the enterprise.

My description of the PDP approach to reading presents an ambitious research agenda; what has actually been accomplished is of course limited in many ways. At this point in the study of reading, I think that having established the utility of the approach is more important than the details of any of the models, which are certain to change. Nonetheless, recognizing the limitations of the models is important and essential to further progress. This chapter is not long enough to tabulate all of these limitations and how they might be addressed in future work. Some examples, however: The goal is to understand reading and its brain bases, but the models have not as yet incorporated constraints arising from discoveries about the brain circuits that support reading. Such information (e.g., about the representation of semantic information in a distributed brain system closely tied to perception, action, and emotion) could be directly incorporated in future models via appropriate changes in the architecture. Many aspects of reading have simply not been addressed; for example, we have not seriously considered the visual front end – the recognition of letters and letter strings – or how context affects processing, particularly the ways in which the meanings of words shift as a function of the contexts in which they occur. The models are simplified at every turn; consider, for example, the differences between how the models learn and how people learn. The problem is not that the brain does not learn according to the backpropagation algorithm; "backpropagation of error" is not one of the foundational principles. More relevant is the fact that the models do not capture the range of experiences that occur in learning. A child is learning to read aloud. Sometimes she receives direct feedback about whether a word has been pronounced correctly or not; sometimes she can determine this herself (e.g., by using her computed pronunciation as the input to the comprehension system); sometimes she receives explicit feedback, other times just a reinforcement signal; sometimes there is no feedback except that provided by the child's own utterance. This variety of learning experiences could of course be incorporated in a model, and my own experience has been that model performance is not hurt by being more faithful to factors that govern human behavior. Whereas the models capture some important aspects of how children learn to read, they clearly do not address many others. The same could be said of almost every aspect of our models. It would be nice to have made further progress by now, but reading is a complex phenomenon involving most of human perception and cognition and most

of the brain, and modeling is hard. Such is life.

3 The DRC models

The Dual-Route Cascade (DRC) model was described in a pair of papers by Coltheart and colleagues (1993; 2001), and its implications concerning reading acquisition, developmental and acquired forms of dyslexia, and other phenomena have been discussed in many additional publications (e.g., Coltheart, 2000; Coltheart, 2006; Jackson and Coltheart, 2001). The DRC framework includes mechanisms for computing both meanings and pronunciations; the implemented models exclusively focus on pronunciation.

Coltheart et al. (2001) offered extensive discussion of the origins of the DRC model and its fundamental assumptions. They linked their models to nineteenth-century diagram makers such as Lichtheim and emphasized continuity between the informal and computational versions of the dual-route model. The approach includes a commitment to a version of the modularity hypothesis (Coltheart, 1999; Fodor, 1983), to theorizing pitched at the level of the functional architecture, and to identifying the modules of the functional architecture primarily through studying brain-injured patients. However, the character of the DRC model is largely a consequence of two types of pretheoretical commitments. One concerns the goals of the modeling enterprise, the other the architecture of the model.

Coltheart et al. (2001) are explicit about their views of modeling. They emphasize the data-driven character of their modeling, endorsing Grainger and Jacobs' (1998, p. 24) view that "in developing algorithmic models of cognitive phenomena, the major source of constraint is currently provided by human behavioral data." They also view models as cumulative: Each model improves upon the previous one by adding to the phenomena covered by a previous version. Thus, the 2001 version of the DRC is said to account for the same facts as the 1999 version but also many others. The models are said to be nested with respect to data coverage. Again they quote Grainger and Jacobs (1998): "[I]n other sciences it is standard practice that a new model accounts for the crucial effects accounted for by the previous generation of the same or competing models."

This gives rise to an approach in which fidelity to behavioral data is the principal criterion for evaluating models. Models are designed to recreate data patterns, and a model is valid unless disconfirmed by making an incorrect prediction. So, for example, in justifying their use of an interactive activation model as a component of DRC, the authors note that the McClelland and Rumelhart IA model had not been refuted by any behavioral data; thus there was no empirical reason to abandon it. The strength of the 2001 version of DRC, then, is the fact that it addresses more than twenty different phenomena. The breadth of the data coverage led Coltheart and colleagues to conclude that "the DRC model is the most successful of the existing computational models of reading" (p. 204).

The second type of commitment is architectural. Coltheart et al. (1993; 2001) retain the central dogma of the dual-route approach, that two mechanisms are required for words and nonwords: a nonlexical route consisting of rules mapping graphemes onto phonemes, and a lexical route involving word-specific knowledge. On the nonlexical side, the implemented models spell out details about what the rules are, expanding the notion of rule to include multiletter graphemes, and adjudicating the order in which rules are applied. They also incorporate assumptions about the timing of rule application, which affects the extent to which output from the lexical and nonlexical routes is combined in generating a pronunciation. On the lexical side, they incorporate a version of the McClelland and Rumelhart (1981) interactive activation model, though with rather different parameter settings than in the original work.

The central dogma reflects a strongly held intuition about the nature of human knowledge and the behaviors it supports, namely that they are rule-governed. Language provides a quintessential example, but the same intuition extends to other areas such as reasoning and social behavior. People being complex organisms, the rules that govern their behavior often have exceptions. Thus the mind/brain has developed other mechanisms for dealing with such deviations (e.g., memorization). Perhaps these intuitions are strong because prior to the development of connectionist models there were few if any alternatives. Perhaps it persists because it meets the requirements of a good folk psychological theory: It is easy to understand and at a very general level seems to be correct. Of course it is trivially true that *any* body of knowledge or behavior can be described as rule-governed if there is a separate mechanism to handle cases that violate the rules. The number of phenomena to be explained (rule-governed cases and exceptions) exactly matches the number of explanatory mechanisms (a rule component, an exception component). Still, the intuition seems to be a strong one, and certainly more accessible than the idea of a multilayer neural network using distributed representations that encode the statistical, probabilistic mappings between spelling and sound. It could also be correct, which of course is the force of Coltheart et al.'s accounting of the many phenomena that DRC simulates.

Given these assumptions, what type of computational model results? Seidenberg and Plaut (2006) discuss this issue. Coltheart et al. (2001) term their approach "Old Cognitivism," identifying it within a longstanding tradition of fitting models to behavioral data. However, they did not discuss longstanding critiques of this approach. The basic problem is that the strategy of accounting for the most data possible is not itself sufficiently powerful to converge on a satisfactory theory. Such models are built out of an ad hoc collection of formalisms such as rules and buffers and decision makers. Elements of the model are configured in response to empirical data; that is the essence of the methodology. This approach does not yield robust theoretical generalizations that explain target phenomena.

As Seidenberg and Plaut argue, the evidence for this conclusion is the fact that the performance of the 2001 version of DRC is closely tied to the specific studies that were simulated. In most cases the authors chose a single study to demonstrate DRC's coverage of a given phenomenon. However, the model fails when tested against other studies of the same type. For example, many studies have reported that frequency and regularity interact in reading aloud (see Seidenberg, 1995 for review). Coltheart et al. simulated the results of one of these studies, Paap and Noel (1989). There are two problems. First, the simulation produces a frequency by regularity interaction, but it is not of the same form as that observed in the behavioral study. Second, the model fails to reproduce the interaction when tested on the stimuli used in other classic studies (e.g., Seidenberg et al., 1984; Taraban and McClelland, 1987). This pattern is repeated for most of the major phenomena that DRC2001 simulates. The best that can be said is that the model's coverage of the data is broad but shallow. The worst is that failures to correctly simulate effects of many studies disconfirm it. Seen in this light, Coltheart et al.'s claim to have tied off a long list of phenomena seems an overstatement of considerable proportion.

Fitting models to a broad range of data is very difficult. DRC does not have a learning procedure and so all of the parameters of the model (Table 1, p. 218, in the 2001 article lists thirty-one, which does not include seven additional parameters for the lexical decision task) must be set by painstakingly searching the parameter space for the values that will best fit the broadest range of studies (i.e., hand-wiring). Coltheart et al. were able to find a set of parameters that correctly simulated individual studies; however these values yield incorrect results when other studies of the same effects are considered. DRC's problem is *overfitting*: The model is too closely tied to the specific studies that were simulated and thus it fails to generalize.

How could this overfitting problem be avoided? One thought is that a model as complex as DRC, with many parameters that can be independently manipulated, should fit any pattern of data. However, that does not turn out to be true. To the contrary, DRC's performance is closely tied to the particular parameter values that were chosen. Changes to the parameters tend to produce worse behavior, not better.[2] Another possibility is that the model fails because it does not operate according to the principles that underlie the corresponding human behavior. This seems likely but ironic given Coltheart et al.'s explicit disavowal of principle-based approaches to modeling.

The validity of these conclusions is also supported by developments since the publication of the 2001 version of DRC. Coltheart and colleagues have presented additional data and arguments favoring the DRC model, primarily focused on atypical cases of developmental or acquired dyslexia with patterns of impaired reading that are said to contradict one or another aspect of the PDP theory (e.g., Blazely, Coltheart, and Casey, 2005; Coltheart, 2006). The interpretation of such "outlier" cases is highly controversial (see Plaut, 1995 and Woollams et al., 2006 for discussion). The more important point is that Coltheart and colleagues' analyses of these cases are not tied to their implemented model. They wish to argue that certain patterns of behavioral impairment are consistent with their model (and not the PDP approach); however, these arguments are not coupled to simulations of the cases in question.

I don't think this is surprising. According to the analysis presented earlier in this chapter, the successes of the 2001 version of DRC are so tightly bound to particular parameter values and other implementation-specific features that it *should* be difficult to extend it to other phenomena, including these case studies. As a result, the most recent arguments on behalf of the dual-route approach

---

2 Exploration of the model suggests that changes to the parameters tend to degrade performance. However, I have no basis for excluding the possibility that slightly better fits might be achieved by searching the parameter space further. Rather, I am suggesting that the problem is deeper than mere parameter search.

have the same form as in the precomputational modeling era discussed in the first section of this chapter. It is almost as though the models (and the insights about the need for such models in order to understand normal and disordered behavior) had never occurred.

4 Hybrid models

Two prominent hybrid models purport to incorporate the best aspects of the dual-route and PDP approaches. The first, by Zorzi, Houghton, and Butterworth (1998), was an SM89-style model of the orthography–phonology mapping that incorporated an additional set of connections between the orthographic and phonological units. Zorzi et al. claimed that the result was a "dual-route connectionist model." The connections between the orthographic and phonological (input and output) units were said to correspond to the sublexical route, whereas the orthography-hidden-phonological pathway corresponded to the lexical route. Thus, the model adhered to the central dogma, but used connectionist machinery. As Harm and Seidenberg (2004) determined, however, the Zorzi et al. model did not create a division of labor such that regulars were handled by one pathway and exceptions by the other. The direct O–P pathway, acting on its own (i.e., with the rest of the model turned off or "lesioned"), read regular words accurately as well as a small percentage of exception words (the latter indicating that it was not strictly nonlexical). With the direct O–P pathway disabled, however, the standard orthography-hidden-phonology pathway – the putative lexical route – read exception words highly inaccurately. In their model, reading exception words requires input from both pathways. This is similar to the account of exception word reading in the triangle framework and quite different from the dual-route approach.

Perry, Ziegler, and Zorzi (2007) created a different type of hybrid. They remain committed to the central dogma that distinct lexical and sublexical procedures are necessary; however they abandoned DRC's commitment to the notion that the sublexical route consists of grapheme-phoneme mapping rules. Instead, they employed a PDP-style model for the nonlexical route. As in DRC, the lexical route is an interactive activation model. This route is thought necessary in order to account for data about lexical decisions.

The CDP+ model has plusses and minuses. On the positive side, Perry et al. incorporated an SM89-style O–P route in recognition of the fact that models like DRC cannot generate consistency effects. They report positive results for a close simulation of a study by Jared (2002). This move further validates the approach we initiated in 1989. But in other ways the Perry et al. model fares less well. The authors emphasize the importance of capturing "benchmark" effects that have the potential to differentiate between alternative theories. Consistency effects are one such benchmark, regularity effects are another, and so on. Targeting theoretically important phenomena is a fine idea and one that the triangle approach instantiated; the question is whether a given model captures them in a principled way or not. Here the Perry et al. model falls into the same trap as DRC2001: It simulates individual studies (such as one experiment out of Jared's 2002 article) but fails when tested on other studies of the same phenomenon. It too overfits the data, but this matters less for CDP+, the authors believe, because they have been selective in choosing which studies to simulate. For example, the Jared experiment is taken as the gold standard for consistency effects and so that is the study they simulate. I share the view that models should aim to account for prominent benchmark phenomena but disagree with their reliance on gold standard experiments. Jared is a fine study, but other experiments that yielded the same effects cannot be dismissed out of hand. The methods in this area of research are weak enough that people have tended to rely on replication with different materials and subjects, across different labs, with the hope of gaining strong converging evidence for a phenomenon. It seems a mistake to use a different method in assessing models of these phenomena. The Perry et al. model also misses many other effects that many people consider benchmarks, including the frequency x regularity interaction in studies by Taraban and McClelland (1987), myself, and others, and the generation of correct pronunciations for complex nonwords.[3]

Perry et al.'s other major theoretical claim is that a localist-style interactive activation model is necessary in order to account for lexical decision phenomena. They therefore incorporated the mechanism from DRC2001 unchanged. This account of lexical decision is highly engineered and performance is brittle, degrading with changes to the seven task-specific parameters. The model captures a narrow range of LD data and again it is easy to find studies on which it fails (e.g., Ziegler and Perry's 1998 study of orthographic versus body neighborhood effects). A flawed account of the lexical decision task does not provide strong motivation for retaining DRC's version of the lexical route. Having incorporated an SM89-style orth–phon system, my suggestion would be to take the next step, which would be to incorporate the orth-sem-phon pathway (as in Harm and Seidenberg, 2004). Lexical decisions might then be based on different patterns of activation produced by words and nonwords over the different types of units, an idea (Seidenberg and McClelland, 1989) that has not been fully explored.

---

3   Perry et al.'s model errs in generating pronunciations for difficult nonwords. They suggest that such data are outside the scope of their model because subjects use metalinguistic problem solving strategies to pronounce them. This is an odd turn of events, since the principal complaint about the SM89 model was its poor performance on such nonwords. By Besner et al.'s (1990) criteria, Perry et al.'s model is in the same boat we were in 1989.
   This was the approach to lexical decision we proposed in SM89. In simulating LD, the model made more errors than people did, but, importantly, it contained no semantics. People do occasionally consult meaning in order to decide if a letter string is a word or not. The idea that lexical decisions are made by comparing the patterns of activation over orthographic, phonological, and semantic representations produced by words versus nonwords remains a viable though underexplored approach to understanding the task.

5 Conclusions

The competition between the dual-route model and the alternative PDP approach has been highly productive in many ways. It stimulated a large amount of excellent empirical research on many aspects of word and nonword reading. It led to more explicit, mechanistic accounts of behavior. The models have grown in sophistication and scope. However, as time has progressed the differences between the approaches have become clearer. The PDP models address a narrower range of phenomena, but aspire to considerable depth insofar as the explanations for the phenomena (e.g., consistency effects, the relationship between frequency and consistency, nonword pronunciation, division of labor between components of a model) are meant to derive from the principles that govern the approach rather than details of how particular models are implemented. In fact the models that we have published could have achieved better fits to particular data sets by manipulating factors such as the composition of the training set or parameters of the learning algorithm. One of the main points of this chapter is that such manipulations are self-defeating unless they are motivated by independently known facts (e.g., about people's experience or how they learn). One can win the best fits battle and lose the correct theory war.

The DRC models' success and failures arise from their creators' data fitting orientation. In advocating this approach, I think that Coltheart and colleagues have misread the history of cognitive science and cognitive modeling. Research has not progressed in the cumulative, nested manner described by Grainger and Jacobs (1998) and endorsed by Coltheart et al. (2001). Researchers who have utilized computational models have tended to develop a series of models that share common principles but differ in detail and address overlapping but nonidentical phenomena (e.g., Roger Ratcliff's diffusion models; John Anderson's ACT models). The same could be said of DRC. The 1993 version of DRC did not start by replicating the results reported by McClelland and

Rumelhart and then extending the model to other phenomena. The two implemented versions of DRC share many properties but also differ in detail; the phenomena they address only partially overlap. In this respect the situation is not very different from the PDP models. I doubt if any science proceeds in a strictly cumulative manner, but that is a matter for philosophers and historians of science to decide.

What about the PDP models? I think we have made considerable progress with respect to those reading phenomena that have been addressed, which include ones that are highly revealing about the basic character of the system (e.g., consistency effects). As noted, however, many aspects of reading remain to be addressed within this framework. The approach has limitations, but of a different character than those of DRC. The main problem seems to be that many researchers think that, despite the talk about principles, the models do little to clarify the bases of complex behavior. These concerns were voiced by McCloskey (1991), who noted that in connectionist models, the explanations for behavior tended to be buried in a mass of units and connections. I think McCloskey was wrong (Seidenberg, 1993), but perhaps this is a minority opinion. Clearly the methodology that underlies DRC can also be applied in developing PDP models, with similar results: creating models to fit the results of particular studies, resulting in brittle models whose performance is highly dependent on unmotivated implementational details. Nor have PDP modelers been exempt from premature declarations of victory. PDP modeling is an approach that can be used in different ways by different people; some applications will be more helpful than others. I think the more important point, however, is that the PDP modelers have apparently not done an adequate job of explaining the philosophy and the approach, the goals of the enterprise, the general principles that underlie the models, and the reasons why models behave the way they do. My own feeling is that these issues have already been addressed in the literature, but perhaps not successfully.

The history of computational models of reading suggest several conclusions that could profitably inform future research: that models are a tool but theories are the goal; that a principled approach is more likely to yield progress than data fitting; that progress has to be assessed in terms of a longer term trajectory toward a goal, rather than comparisons of specific models that only represent points on that trajectory. I hope that researchers continue to recognize the enormous opportunities for making further progress in understanding reading, computation, and the brain.

References

Adams, M. J. (1979). Models of word recognition. *Cognitive Psychology*, 11, 133–76.

Baron, J. & Strawson, C. (1976). Use of orthographic and word-specific knowledge in reading words aloud. *Journal of Experimental Psychology: Human Perception and Performance*, 4, 207–14.

Besner, D., Twilley, L., McCann, R., & Seergobin, K. (1990). On the connection between connectionism and data: Are a few words necessary? *Psychological Review*, 97, 432–46.

Blazely, A. M., Coltheart, M., & Casey, B. J. (2005). Semantic impairment with and without surface dyslexia: Implications for models of reading. *Cognitive Neuropsychology*, 22, 695–717.

Block, N. & Fodor, J. (1972). What psychological states are not. *Philosophical Review*, 81–92.

Caplan, D. (1988). On the role of group studies in neuropsychological and pathopsychological research. *Cognitive Neuropsychology*, 5, 535–47.

Caramazza, A. (1986). On drawing inferences about the structure of normal cognitive systems from the analysis of patterns of impaired performance: The case for single-patient studies. *Brain & Cognition*, 5, 41–66.

Caramazza, A., Hillis, A. E., Rapp, B. C., & Romani, C. (1990). The multiple semantics hypothesis: Multiple confusions? *Cognitive Neuropsychology*, 7, 161–89.

Coltheart, M. (1978). Lexical access in simple reading tasks. In Underwood, G. (Ed.) *Strategies of Information Processing* (pp. 151–216). New York: Academic Press.

(1999). Modularity and cognition. *Trends in Cognitive Sciences*, 3, 115–20.

(2000). Dual routes from print to speech and dual routes from print to meaning: Some theoretical issues. In Kennedy, A., Radach, R., Pynte, J., & Heller, D. (Eds.) *Reading as a Perceptual Process*. Oxford: Elsevier.

(2006). Acquired dyslexias and the computational modeling of reading. *Cognitive Neuropsychology*.

Coltheart, M., Curtis, B., Atkins, P., & Haller, M. (1993). Models of reading aloud: Dual-route and parallel distributed processing approaches. *Psychological Review*, 100, 589–608.

Coltheart, M., Patterson, K. E., & Marshall, J. C. (Eds.) (1980). *Deep dyslexia*. London: Routledge & Kegan Paul.

Coltheart, M., Rastle, K., Perry, C., & Langdon, R. (2001). DRC: A dual route cascaded model of visual word recognition and reading aloud. *Psychological Review*, 108, 204–56.

Dunn, J. C. & Kirsner, K. (Eds.) (2003). Forum on "What Can We Infer From Double Dissociations," *Cortex*, 39, 129–202.

Farah, M. J. (1994). Neuropsychological inference with an interactive brain: A critique of the "locality" assumption. *Behavioral and Brain Sciences*, 17, 43–104.

Fodor, J. A. (1983). *The Modularity of Mind: An Essay on Faculty Psychology*. Cambridge, MA: MIT Press.

(1999). Let your brain alone. *London Review of Books*, September 30.

Glushko, R. J. (1979). The organization and activation of orthographic knowledge in reading aloud. *Journal of Experimental Psychology: Human Perception and Performance*, 5, 674–91.

Grainger, J., & Jacobs, A. M. (1994). Orthographic processing in visual word recognition. *Psychological Review*, 103, 518–65.

(1998). On localist connectionism and psychological science. In Grainger, J. & Jacobs, A. M. (Eds.) *Localist connectionist approaches to human cognition* (pp. 1–38). Mahwah, NJ: Erlbaum.

Harm, M. & Seidenberg, M. S. (1999). Reading acquisition, phonology, and dyslexia: Insights from a connectionist model. *Psychological Review*, 106, 491–528.

(2004). Computing the meanings of words in reading: Division of labor between visual and phonological processes. *Psychological Review*, 111, 662–720.

Jackson, N. E. & Coltheart, M. (2001). *Routes to Reading Success and Failure*. New York: Psychology Press.

Jared, D. (2002). Spelling sound consistency and regularity effects in word naming. *Journal of Memory and Language*, 46, 723–50.

Juola, P. & Plunkett, K. (2000). Why double dissociations don't mean much. In Cohen, G., Johnston, R., & Plunkett, K. (Eds.) *Exploring cognition: Damaged brains and neural networks* (pp. 111–72). New York: Psychology Press.

Kay, J. & Marcel, A. (1981). One process, not two, in reading aloud: Lexical analogies do the work of non-lexical rules. *Quarterly Journal of Experimental Psychology*, 33A, 397–413.

Luce, R. D. (1959). *Individual Choice Behavior*. New York: Wiley.

Marshall, J. C. & Newcombe, F. (1973). Patterns of paralexia: A psycholinguistic approach. *Journal of Psycholinguistic Research*, 2, 175–9.

McClelland, J. L. & Rumelhart, D. E. (1981). An interactive activation model of context effects in letter perception: Part 1. An account of basic findings. *Psychological Review*, 88, 375–407.

McClelland, J. L., McNaughton, B. L., & O'Reilly, R. C. (1995). Why there are complementary learning systems in the hippocampus and neocortex: insights from the successes and failures of connectionist models of learning and memory. *Psychological Review*, 102, 419–57.

McCloskey, M. (1991). Networks and theories: The place of connectionism in cognitive science. *Psychological Science*, 2, 387–95.

Miozzo, M. (2003). On the processing of regular and irregular forms of verbs and nouns: evidence from neuropsychology. *Cognition*, 87, 101–27.

Morton, J. (1969). Interaction of information in word recognition. *Psychological Review*, 76, 165–78.

Newell, A. & Simon, H. (1963). GPS, a program that simulates human thought. In Feigenbaum, E. A. & Feldman, J. (Eds.) *Computers and Thought*. New York: McGraw Hill.

Paap, K. & Noel, R. W. (1989). Dual-route models of print to sound: Still a good horse race. *Psychological Research*, 53, 13–24.

Patterson, K. E., Marshall, J. C., & Coltheart, M. (Eds.) (1985). *Surface dyslexia*. London: Erlbaum.

Perry, C., Ziegler, J. C., & Zorzi, M. (2007). Nested incremental modeling in the development of computational theories: the CDP+ model of reading aloud. *Psychological Review*, 114, 273–315.

Pinker, S. (1997). *How the Mind Works*. New York: Norton.

Plaut, D. C. (1995). Double dissociation without modularity: Evidence from connectionist neuropsychology. *J. Clinical and Exp. Neuropsychology*, 17, 291–321.

(2005). Connectionist approaches to reading. In Snowling, M. J. & Hulme, C. (Eds.) *The Science of Reading: A Handbook* (pp. 24–38). Blackwell: Oxford.

Plaut, D. C., McClelland, J. L., Seidenberg, M. S., & Patterson, K. E. (1996). Understanding normal and impaired word reading: Computational principles in quasiregular domains. *Psychological Review, 103,* 56–115.

Putnam, H. (1972). Psychology and reduction. *Cognition, 2,* 131–46.

Rapp, B. & Caramazza, A. (2002). Selective difficulties with spoken nouns and written verbs: A single case study. *Journal of Neurolinguistics, 15,* 373–402.

(1993). On the distinction between deficits of access and deficits of storage: A question of theory. *Cognitive Neuropsychology, 10,* 113–41.

Reicher, G. M. (1969). Perceptual recognition as a function of meaningfulness of the stimulus material. *Journal of Experimental Psychology, 81,* 274–80.

Riddoch, M. J., Humphreys, G. W., Coltheart, M., & Funnell, E. (1988). Semantic systems or system? Neuropsychological evidence re-examined. *Cognitive Neuropsychology, 5,* 3–25.

Rumelhart, D. E., Hinton, G. E., & McClelland, J. L. (1986). A general framework for parallel distributed processing. In Rumelhart, D. E. & McClelland J. L. (Eds.) *Parallel Distributed Processing: Explorations in the Microstructure of Cognition (vol. 1).* Cambridge, MA: MIT Press.

Seidenberg, M. S. (1989). Word recognition and naming: A computational model and its implications. In Marslen-Wilson, W. D. (Ed.) *Lexical Representation and Process.* MIT Press.

(1988). Cognitive neuropsychology and language: The state of the art. *Cognitive Neuropsychology, 5,* 403–26.

(1993). A connectionist modeling approach to word recognition and dyslexia. *Psychological Science, 4,* 299–304.

(1995). Visual word recognition. In Miller, J. L. & Eimas, P. D. (Eds.) *Handbook of Perception & Cognition, Volume 11, Speech, Language & Communication.* San Diego: Academic Press.

(2005). Connectionist models of reading. *Current Directions in Psychological Science, 14,* 238–42.

Seidenberg, M. S. & MacDonald, M. C. (1999). A probabilistic constraints approach to language acquisition and processing. *Cognitive Science, 23,* 569–88.

Seidenberg, M. S. & McClelland, J. L. (1989). A distributed, developmental model of word recognition and naming. *Psychological Review, 96,* 523–68.

Seidenberg, M. S., & Plaut, D. C. (2006). Progress in understanding word reading: Data fitting vs. theory building. In Andrews, S. (Ed.) *From Ink Marks To Ideas: Current Issues In Lexical Processing.* Hove, UK: Psychology Press.

Seidenberg, M. S., Plaut, D., Petersen, A., McClelland, J. L., & McRae, K. (1994). Nonword naming and models of word recognition. *Journal of Experimental Psychology: Human Perception and Performance, 20,* 1177–96.

Seidenberg, M. S., Waters, G. S., Barnes, M. A., & Tanenhaus, M. K. (1984). When does irregular spelling or pronunciation influence word recognition? *Journal of Verbal Learning and Verbal Behavior, 23,* 383–404.

Shallice, T. (1993). Multiple semantics: Whose confusions? *Cognitive Neuropsychology, 10,* 251–61.

Taraban, R. & McClelland, J. L. (1987). Conspiracy effects in word recognition. *Journal of Memory and Language, 26,* 608–31.

Van Orden, G., Pennington, B. F., & Stone, G. O. (2001). What do double dissociations prove? *Cognitive Science, 25,* 111–72.

Wagenmakers, E. J. M., Steyvers, M., Raaijmakers, J. G. W., Shiffrin, R. M., van Rijn, H., & Zeelenberg, R. (2004). A model for evidence accumulation in the lexical decision task. *Cognitive Psychology, 48,* 332–67.

Woollams, A. M., Lambon Ralph, M. A., Plaut, D. C., & Patterson, K. E. (2006). SD-Squared: On the association between semantic dementia and surface dyslexia. *Psychological Review.*

Ziegler, J. C. & Perry, C. (1998). No more problems in Coltheart's neighborhood: resolving neighborhood conflicts in the lexical decision task. *Cognition, 68(2),* 53–62.

Zorzi, M., Houghton, G., & Butterworth, B. (1998). Two routes or one in reading aloud? A connectionist dual-process model. *Journal of Experimental Psychology: Human Perception & Performance, 24,* 1131–61.

CHAPTER 10

Decoding, Orthographic Learning, and the Development of Visual Word Recognition

Kate Nation

1 Decoding, orthographic learning, and the development of visual word recognition

There's no doubt that learning to read is a complicated business. The first lesson that children must learn is that English is an alphabetic language – that letters and groups of letters map onto pronunciations in a systematic way. This is not easy, particularly in a language such as English where the relationship between orthography and phonology is only quasi-regular. Young children must surely be bemused to learn that the words *beat*, *street*, *ski*, *theme*, and *thief* all contain the same vowel pronunciation; that *steak* and *teak* look very similar yet sound different; and that despite looking different and having distinct meanings, *weak* and *week* have identical pronunciations. Nevertheless, most children crack the code, and reading skills develop rapidly during the elementary school years.

Given the complexities of learning to read, any review chapter can only hope to cover selected aspects of reading development. The aim of this chapter is to review

what we know – and to set out what we don't know – about how children learn to read words. This forms the fundamental basis of reading, as without it there can be no gateway into reading comprehension. Nevertheless, visual word recognition alone is not sufficient to guarantee successful reading comprehension. Nation (2005) and Perfetti, Landi, and Oakhill (2005) provide thorough reviews of other factors that contribute to reading comprehension and its development. In addition, the focus of this chapter is on learning to read English. This is not to deny that cross-linguistic comparisons of children learning to read in different languages provide important insights into the nature of reading development, as evidenced by recent reviews by Ziegler and Goswami (2005), Seymour (2005), and Hanley (2005). Similarly, progress in understanding how reading develops has been fuelled by studies investigating atypical development (Vellutino and Fletcher, 2005), but the focus in this chapter is with typical development. Finally, notwithstanding the fact that reading has its roots in biology (Pennington and Olson, 2005), this chapter presents a perspective from cognitive psychology. The cognitive psychology of reading and reading development has moved apace over recent years and much has been learned. Although there are many questions yet to be answered, the central issue remains simple: How is it that children develop from the effortful decoding attempts that characterise kindergarten children as they painfully decode letter strings to the skilled adult, able to recognise many tens of words per minute?

2 Stage models: Describing reading development

An appropriate starting point for any review of visual word recognition development is stage models. Such models view the process of learning to read as a series of stages through which children need to pass, with each stage qualitatively distinct and characterised by different processing mechanisms and strategies. A number of stage theories have been proposed (e.g., Ehri, 1992; Frith, 1985; Gough and Hillinger, 1980; Marsh et al., 1981). Although these theories differ in detail, broadly speaking, they distinguish three main stages, described here using Frith's (1985) terminology. During the first phase of reading development, children are *logographic* readers. Yet to develop an appreciation of the systematic relationship between letters and sounds, children associate printed words and pronunciations on the basis of idiosyncratic cues, such as the two sticks in the middle of the word *yellow* (Seymour and Elder, 1986). Similarly, children may be adept at reading environmental print (e.g., *McDonalds* or *Pepsi* presented in logo form) but unable to read the words when they are printed out of logo context (Masonheimer, Drum, and Ehri, 1984).

As sight vocabulary expands, children are thought to attend to more detailed orthographic information, as well as to begin to notice the alphabetic relationship between letters and sounds. Once in this *alphabetic* stage, children can apply sequential decoding strategies to sound out words they have never seen before. Consequently, they are prone to over-regularise words, reading *island* as *izland*, for example. Via the opportunities afforded by alphabetic reading, children expand their reading vocabularies enormously and with exposure and experience, they begin to move into the *orthographic* stage of reading development. This is characterised by the presence of word-specific representations that enable fast, efficient, and automatic word recognition.

Stage models have been influential, and they certainly provide a good descriptive account of reading development. However, they are limited in a number of ways. Within each stage, they have little explanatory power in helping us understand underlying processes, and more important, they fail to provide insights into the mechanisms of change that cause children to move from one stage to the next. Over recent years there has been a move away from stage models of reading development, which emphasise qualitative differences between stages, to a view that sees development as more continuous, a trend championed by connectionist frameworks. Before discussing connectionist models of reading development directly, empirical findings are discussed that bring into question the existence of qualitative differences between different stages. These findings serve to highlight the utility of taking a more continuous rather than a stage-like perspective. They also demonstrate what has been at the centre of research into reading development for the past three decades: the fundamental role that phonological sensitivity and phonological awareness play in learning to read (Bowey, 2005; Stanovich and Seigal, 1994).

3 Continuities in reading development

3.1 *Questioning the divide between logographic and alphabetic stages of reading*

The *alphabetic principle* refers to the understanding that letters or letter clusters (graphemes) represent phonemes in spoken words. Results from a number of experiments by

Byrne and colleagues (see Byrne, 1998 for review) make clear that preliterate children do not come to the task of learning to read with a preconceived idea that written language is expressed via an alphabet. However, it is not the case that preliterate children are unable to attend properly to letters. Nor is it the case that they are unable to make mappings between print and oral language. Instead, they lack an appreciation that in an alphabetic language such as English, letters code *phonological* information.

Byrne (1992) taught preliterate children (aged about four years) to read words such as *fat* and *bat*. Once able to read and recognise the two words reliably, they were presented with the printed word *fun* and asked to decide whether it said *fun* or *bun*. Performance was at chance, suggesting that the children had not made connections between the initial letter and sound of *fat* and *bat*, and therefore were not able to transfer this knowledge to other words sharing constituent graphemes and phonemes.

In a follow-up study, Byrne (1996) taught four-year-old preliterate children to recognise and pronounce pairs of words such as *hat–hats* and *small–smaller*. Once learned to criterion (defined as six errorless trials for each pair), Byrne administered two types of transfer test. In one condition, children were presented with pairs of words such as *cup–cups* and *mean–meaner*. For each pair, they were asked to identify which item they thought represented *cup* and *cups* and which represented *mean* and *meaner*. Children found this task relatively straightforward and performance was well above chance, indicating that they were able to generalise knowledge acquired during the learning of *hat–hats* and *small–smaller* to the transfer items. In contrast, however, they performed at chance on transfer items *pur–purs* (pronounced as in *purr* and *purse*) and *corn–corner*, despite the fact that these items shared the same letters and sounds as both the trained words and the first set of transfer items. Why might this be? Byrne argued that the pattern of results across conditions was consistent with children learning mappings between print and *morphemes*, rather than

print and *phonemes*. They failed to notice the phonological role of *s* and *er*, and instead focused on their morphemic function. Put simply, they "seem tuned to detect systematic correspondences between print and meaning" (Byrne, 1998, p. 49) but are blind to the systematic correspondences between print and sound.

It is clear that for most children, this state of alphabetic ignorance does not last very long at all. Rack et al., (1994) provided convincing evidence that young children are sensitive to phonological information in written words from an early age and following minimal instruction. Building on work by Ehri and Wilce (1985), they asked five-year old children to learn to associate printed abbreviations (cues) with phonological forms. For example, children learned to associate the letter cue *dbl* with the word *table*. Rack et al. compared two types of visual cue: phonetic and control. Phonetic cues, like *dbl* for *table*, embodied something of the sound of the base word, but one letter was replaced by a letter representing a sound that differed only in voice, not in place or manner of articulation (in this example, the letter *t* was replaced by the letter *d*). Control cues were identical to phonetic cues except that replaced letters were phonetically more distant (for example, *kbl* for *table*). Children found it easier to learn to associate phonetic cues than control cues. This effect was maintained in children who were completely unable to read a single nonsense word – children traditionally characterised as logographic readers. This shows that beginning readers are sensitive to the relationship between the phonological features of spoken words and letters and that even before sequential decoding skills are in place, learning is facilitated by sensitivity to the phonological content of printed words.

At first sight, these findings seem counter to those reported by Byrne (1992; 1996). If children can readily associate a phonetic cue with a pronunciation, why do they fail to appreciate the role of phonology in Byrne's transfer experiments? One important difference is that in Byrne's studies, children were completely preliterate and were screened to make sure they had no preexisting knowledge of the letters used in the stimuli. Rack et al. did not test letter knowledge, but some children were able to read a small number of words, suggesting that they may have had some insight into the alphabetic principle. This understanding need only be of a very elementary form – recall that the phonetic cue effect was apparent even in children who were completely unable to decode even a very simple nonword.

Given Byrne's observations that young children do not induce the alphabetic principle for themselves, an important question is how children acquire this understanding. A likely answer to this question is that children need for the phonological bases of an alphabet to be made explicit. Byrne and Fielding-Barnsley (1989) showed that even very minimal training in a combination of letter knowledge and phonological awareness allowed children to transfer knowledge between pairs of words in Byrne's paradigm, based on phonological information. This is consistent with a number of more general findings. For example, in longitudinal studies, letter knowledge and phonological awareness measured at school entry predict partially independent variance in later reading skill (e.g., Muter et al., 2004), and intervention programmes for disabled readers are most successful when training combines both letter knowledge and phonological awareness (e.g., Hatcher, Hulme, and Ellis, 1994). Finally, numerous experiments demonstrate the role that letter knowledge plays in making connections between print and speech (e.g., Ross, Treiman, and Bick, 2004; Treiman and Rodriguez, 1999; Treiman, Sotak, and Bowerman, 2001).

Where do these findings leave us with respect to our earlier discussion of stage models? Byrne's experiments suggest that preliterate children are yet to realise that in an alphabetic language, print conveys meaning via sound. Does this correspond to a logographic stage of reading development in which "letter order is largely ignored and phonological factors are entirely secondary" (Frith, 1985, p. 306)? Perhaps, although it is important to point out that the children in

Byrne's experiments were preliterate. Once reading begins, even in an extremely elementary form (as indexed by minimal letter knowledge), children demonstrate sensitivity to the phonological constituents of print and they are able to use this knowledge to bolster learning, as demonstrated by the phonetic cue effect. This casts doubt on the notion of a sharp divide between a logographic stage and an alphabetic stage. Instead, we can think of children becoming increasingly sensitive and refined in their appreciation of spelling–sound mappings over time, rather than switching from one type of processing to another.

3.2 Questioning the divide between alphabetic and orthographic stages of reading

A signature of alphabetic reading is sequential decoding: the application of spelling–sound correspondence rules to decipher words grapheme by grapheme in a context insensitive manner. Clearly however, successful sequential decoding is not enough to guarantee efficient and accurate word recognition in a language such as English where the relationship between letters and sounds is ambiguous and inconsistent. Movement into the orthographic stage of reading development is marked by the availability of word-specific representations, which allow children to perform "instant analysis of words into orthographic units without phonological conversion" (Frith, 1985, p. 306).

Traditionally, orthographic reading is thought to bring with it more flexible reading strategies such as reading by analogy. For example, it is possible to arrive at a number of different pronunciations of a nonsense word such as *juscle*. While alphabetic-stage readers must rely on assembling pronunciations on the basis of applying grapheme–phoneme correspondence rules (*jus-kle*), orthographic-stage readers are also able to read an unfamiliar word by analogy to a known word (for example, *juscle* read to rhyme with *muscle*). As evidence for this developmental progression, Marsh et al. (1981) observed that seven-year-old children produced an analogical response for only fourteen percent of trials, whereas ten-year-olds did so on thirty-four percent of trials. However, these data are difficult to interpret. Analogical responses can only be made if children are familiar with the base word on which an analogy can be made: If a child is not familiar with *muscle*, it is not surprising that they fail to use it as the basis to read *juscle*. This does not mean that children cannot make analogies when reading. A more simple explanation is that they may lack the knowledge on which to base the analogy.

In contrast to the traditional stage view described by Frith (1985) and Marsh et al. (1981), Goswami provided evidence that from the very earliest stages of learning to read, children make orthographic analogies, that is, they pronounce new words by reference to the pronunciation of similarly spelled familiar words. This evidence comes primarily from experiments using the clue word paradigm (e.g., Goswami, 1986; 1993) in which children were shown a clue word (e.g., *beak*), told its pronunciation, and told that the clue word might help them read some other words. They were then shown (one at a time, with the clue word remaining in view) test words, some of which shared orthographic (and phonological) overlap with the clue word (e.g., *bean, peak*). The presence of the clue word was found to enhance children's ability to read similarly spelled test words, but not control words that shared no orthographic or phonological overlap with the clue word. In addition, Goswami found that more analogies were made when clue and test words shared a rime unit (*beak–peak*) than when they shared a beginning (*beak–bean*) and only rime-unit analogies seemed to be available to beginning readers.

These findings led Goswami (1993) to propose an interactive analogy model in which reading development was viewed as a process of increasingly refined use of analogy underpinned by increasingly refined phonological awareness. According to this model, in the earliest stages of reading development, children's phonological awareness is strongest for onset and rime units (e.g., Treiman, 1985)

and therefore, orthographic analogies are made between words that share such units. Increasing awareness of print and reading instruction bolster the development of phonological awareness and as children become sensitive to individual phonemes, they begin to use this knowledge when reading to make more fine-grained analogies between units of spelling–sound correspondence smaller than the rime. This theoretical framework stands in stark contrast to stage models of reading development. Instead of seeing the use of analogy as a late developing strategy the presence of which confirms the transition from an alphabetic stage to an orthographic one, children make analogies from the onset of reading development and they simply get better at doing this over time, as reading develops.

This framework is attractive as it makes explicit a possible link between children's developing phonological awareness and their ability to deploy this knowledge when reading. There are, however, a number of experimental findings that cast doubt on aspects of Goswami's framework. Central to Goswami's theory is the salience and primacy of the rime unit, but some studies have found equivalent transfer to units other than the rime (Bowey, Vaughan, and Hansen, 1998; Bruck and Treiman, 1992; Savage and Stuart, 1998). Concerns have also been raised that the clue word paradigm overestimates the extent to which analogies are used spontaneously by beginning readers (Brown and Deavers, 1999; Muter, Snowling, and Taylor, 1994). Some studies have questioned whether young children make genuine orthographic analogies. For example, Nation, Allen, and Hulme (2001) found that children made analogies to a target such as *peak* even if they had previously only heard (rather than heard and seen) the clue word *beak*; moreover, equivalent transfer was seen between clue–target pairs such as *bone* and *moan* – words that rhyme but do not share orthographic overlap. This suggests that rather than induce orthographic analogies, the clue word in this task serves as a phonological prime that, when combined with children's partial decoding attempts based on limited orthographic knowledge, allows the target word to be read, biased by the sound contained in the clue word.

Taken together, these findings question the importance of orthographic analogy as a primary mechanism driving the development of very early reading skills. Yet it is clear that even beginning readers do not rely solely on simple one-to-one mappings between graphemes and phonemes, although it may be more appropriate to view this as a process of statistical learning (see discussion later in the chapter), rather than orthographic analogy (Nation et al., 2001). What is important for the present purpose is that either characterisation is inconsistent with the view that flexible strategies only become available at a fairly late developing orthographic stage of reading development, once children have fully mastered sequential decoding and alphabetic reading.

4 Mechanisms of orthographic learning

The previously discussed review makes clear that the characterisation of reading development as a series of discrete stages through which children pass is not compatible with experimental evidence pointing to continuities in underlying skills. Yet it is equally clear that developmental change does take place: The five-year-old child who struggles to decipher a word leaves primary school with a reading vocabulary of many thousands of words, and from there, one only needs to fast forward a couple of years to find an adult level of visual word recognition skill. Castles and Nation (2006) reflected on the fact that we understand quite a lot about young children's early reading attempts and the processing skills that underpin them; we also know a huge amount about skilled visual word recognition and the lexical and other variables that influence processing (e.g., Balota et al., 2004). However, we understand relatively little about how children move from novice to expert, a process termed *orthographic learning* by Castles and Nation (2006). The issue is summarised

nicely by Andrews and Scarratt (1996, p. 141): "[T]he existing literature provides little insight into exactly what is required for development of an optimal expert strategy for word identification in reading. The *outcome* of making the transition to this stage of development is assumed to be an 'autonomous lexicon' (Share, 1995) which allows 'automatic word identification' but how does that happen? What changes in the representations or processes underlying reading behaviour to afford these outcomes?" Two strands of research offer some insight on this issue: the self-teaching hypothesis and the notion that children engage in implicit or statistical learning of lexical properties. These accounts are not necessarily mutually exclusive, but as they have evolved from different literatures, they are described separately here.

4.1 *The self-teaching hypothesis*

The self-teaching hypothesis, first described by Share (1995), is an item-based account and as such, it differs radically from traditional stage models that see a child moving from one mode of processing to another. Instead, at any particular point in time, a child may be reading some words slowly and with great effort, while other words are read accurately and fluently. The hypothesis comprises two basic principles. First, letter-sound knowledge and rudimentary decoding skills provide young children with a means of translating a printed word into its spoken form. In turn, this successful (but potentially fairly laborious) decoding experience provides an opportunity to acquire word-specific orthographic information of the nature needed to support fast and efficient word recognition. Central to this hypothesis is the view that phonological decoding provides the essential and fundamental basis for reading development – or as Share describes it, phonological decoding is the *sine qua non* of reading acquisition.

Orthographic learning via self-teaching is tested by asking children to read novel words embedded in stories (e.g., *yait*, introduced in a story context as the name of the coldest city in the world). Following a number of repetitions and decoding attempts, children are asked to choose the name of the coldest city from a number of alternatives, including a homophone foil (e.g., *yate*). If relying on alphabetic decoding skills alone, children should be as likely to choose *yate* as *yait*. However, children as young as second grade show evidence of orthographic learning, both in Hebrew (Share, 1999) and in English (Cunningham et al., 2002). Remarkably, by third grade, a single decoding opportunity following a single exposure to an orthographic form is enough to induce orthographic learning of that item (Nation, Angell, and Castles, 2007; Share, 2004). This observation suggests that orthographic learning may be similar to *fast mapping* – the term used to describe rapid oral vocabulary acquisition following only a few incidental exposures to a new word (e.g., Markson and Bloom, 1997). Although it is clear that by second or third grade, children have amassed a considerable amount of orthographic knowledge, the extent to which self-teaching operates from the beginning of reading remains largely unexplored (Castles and Nation, 2006).

4.2 Statistical learning

It is clear that skilled readers are exquisitely sensitive to consistency – the frequency with which particular letter patterns are associated with particular pronunciations in particular word positions (e.g., Stone, Vanhoy, and Van Orden, 1997; Van Orden and Kloos, 2005; Ziegler, Montant, and Jacobs, 1997). How do children develop this sensitivity? An alternative to the view that children pass through a number of qualitatively distinct stages en route to becoming a skilled reader is the proposal that reading develops gradually with children becoming more skilled at reading over time by virtue of experience and exposure to print. One way to characterise this gradual accumulation of knowledge and experience is as a statistical learning process. Drawing on an example from the language acquisition literature, young infants are sensitive to the

features of spoken language and they use this knowledge to learn about its phonological and phonotactic properties (e.g., Saffran, Aslin, and Newport, 1996). Similarly, children learning to read soon become sensitive to orthographic constraints and regularities, based on the frequency of occurrence of letter combinations in words that they have seen. For example, Cassar and Treiman (1997) reported that by six years of age, children are sensitive to the frequency and legality of different orthographic patterns, and even kindergarten children are able to decide that a written string such as *pess* is more likely to be a word than a string such as *ppes*. Similarly, Pacton et al. (2001) reported a number of experiments demonstrating that following as little as four months of formal education, six-year-old children learning to read French, like the children in Cassar and Treiman's studies of children learning to read English, are sensitive to which consonants can or cannot be doubled in French, and to the fact that consonants are only doubled in medial position, not the initial or final position. Based on these results, Pacton et al. argued that children are very sensitive to distributional information embodied as regularities and patterns in the orthography to which they are exposed. In addition, they speculated that this sensitivity to statistical regularities in the written language domain is subtended by general learning mechanisms akin to those used for other forms of statistical learning (e.g., Bates and Elman, 1996).

These observations demonstrate the utility of the statistical learning approach to understanding young children's sensitivity to orthographic constraints. Is there evidence that statistical learning mechanisms may be at play during reading development itself? Although not directly testing a statistical learning hypothesis, data from a study by Bernstein and Treiman (2004) are relevant to this issue. Bernstein and Treiman (2004) were interested in how children decide to pronounce a vowel grapheme, given that many vowels are ambiguous and can be pronounced in a variety of different ways. If a novel word contained the vowel grapheme *ea*, should it be pronounced as in *meal*, *break*, or *bread*? One factor that influences vowel pronunciation in skilled readers is consonantal context, that is, the letters that precede and follow the vowel (Andrews and Scarratt, 1998). To investigate whether children (aged six to nine years) were sensitive to consonant context, Bernstein and Treiman taught children to pronounce nonwords containing novel vowel grapheme–phoneme correspondences, for example, *zuop* pronounced *zupe*. They then asked children to read other nonwords containing the newly taught vowels. The children were able to learn the pronunciation and showed generalisation. In addition, all age groups showed more generalisation to new words if they shared a consonant as well as a vowel with the trained item. Equivalent transfer was found regardless of whether the shared consonant followed the vowel (e.g., learn *zuop*, test *ruop*) or preceded the vowel (e.g., learn *zuop*, test *tuok*). This suggests that even first grade children are sensitive to co-occurrence between letter combinations and pronunciations and readily generalise this information to new words that share overlapping spelling patterns.

Treiman et al, (2006) provide further evidence to support this view. They examined the spontaneous pronunciations of (real) vowels in novel words and asked whether choice of pronunciation was constrained by the consonant preceding or following the vowel. Once again, even first grade children were influenced by consonantal context such that the particular pronunciation given to a vowel depended on the context in which it occurred. As the vowels were not specifically trained (cf. Bernstein and Treiman, 2004), this knowledge must have been learned implicitly from the children's limited reading experience.

Together with similar findings reported for spelling (Caravolas et al., 2005; Nation and Hulme, 1996; Pacton, et al., 2001), these findings suggest that children become sensitive to statistical properties of orthography, including factors such as sequential constraints and frequency of co-occurrence of letters and their pronunciations. Although sensitivity to these factors increases with age and reading level (Caravolas et al., 2005; Treiman et al., 2006), statistical learning is evident in first grade children, despite their relative inexperience with written language.

5 Computational models and the development of visual word recognition

Both the self-teaching hypothesis and the statistical learning approach point to a gradual accumulation of item-based knowledge over time. This behavioural evidence fits well with attempts to model reading development using connectionist models in which orthographic knowledge emerges gradually from the processing of input, without the specification of inbuilt changes in representational constraint. The triangle framework, first introduced by Seidenberg and McClelland (1989), is an example of a connectionist approach to modelling the reading process and its development. As the triangle model is discussed in detail by Seidenberg (this volume), and reviewed and critiqued at length elsewhere (e.g., Cortese and Balota, this volume; Coltheart, 2005; Lupker, 2005; Plaut, 2005), the focus here is on examining the extent to which it provides a good account of reading development: If the triangle model (or any other computational model) is to have any utility in helping us understand how children learn to read, it is important that it has good psychological validity.

The triangle framework is based on the assumption that word recognition involves three types of mental representation: orthographic, phonological, and semantic. The 1989 simulations focused on the processes of orthography–phonology mapping and reading aloud; the semantic component of the triangle model was not implemented. Building on Seidenberg and McClelland, and on further work by Plaut et al. (1996), Harm and Seidenberg (2004) described a full implementation of a triangle model. At the heart of the triangle approach is the view that information is represented in sets of distributed subsymbolic codes representing the attributes (semantic, phonological, and orthographic) of words that we know. The word recognition process is considered to be the process of activating the appropriate sets of codes from visual input. During development, connections between sets of units need to be learned. The first set of connections learned are those between phonology and semantics. Once the model is able to recognise and produce words, orthography is introduced. This approximates the fact that when children come to the task of learning to read, they have in place well-developed knowledge of the sound and meaning of many words. When presented with a word, units at all levels are activated. The resulting pattern of activation is then compared with the correct pattern of activation. Connection weights between units are then adjusted to reduce error, so that the next time the word is encountered, processing is more accurate. Over time, patterns of activation across one set of units (e.g., phonology) come to produce corresponding patterns of activation across other sets of units in another domain (e.g., orthography). Harm and Seidenberg (2004) describe two pathways to activating meaning from print: a direct pathway from orthography to semantics (O→S) and a phonologically mediated pathway from orthography to phonology to semantics (O→P→S). It is important to note that meanings are not accessed in any sense. Instead, patterns of activation develop over the semantic units continuously, based on input from all sources and from both pathways. Thus, meanings are computed from print by both pathways working simultaneously and in parallel (see Jackson and Colheart, 2001, for a very different characterisation of reading development).

A feature that emerged from Harm and Seidenberg's simulations was that over development, the relative importance of the two pathways to the computation of word meaning changed. Early in development, the network relied heavily on phonological mediation (i.e., the O→P→S pathway). With reading experience, however, the network gradually shifted towards increased reliance on direct mapping (i.e., the O→S pathway), although even at the end of training, both pathways continued to make a contribution to performance. The reason for this developmental change is that O→P connections are easier to form than O→S connections due to the fact that the relationship between O and P (in an alphabetic language) is more systematic than O→S mappings. However, there is pressure for the system to form direct O→S connections as (a) mappings between O→P are inherently ambiguous due to the many homophones in the language and (b) direct mappings are faster as they do not require the intermediate computation from orthography to phonology en route to semantic activation.

This change in the division of labour between the two pathways over training fits well with what we know about children's reading development. Early on, children devote considerable attention to the task of decoding words but with experience, word recognition becomes faster and more automatic. Harm and Seidenberg's simulations suggest that the shift from decoding to automatic word recognition is not a consequence of a qualitative change from one distinct stage to another. Instead, experience with orthography and increased familiarity with the attributes of words leads to more efficient word recognition. While a model with just O→P→S connections can be trained to activate semantics, the additional presence of O→S connections does the job better. This fits with behavioural data showing that while alphabetic decoding accounts for large portions of variance in word recognition, considerable variance is unaccounted for, especially as children get older (Castles and Nation, 2006).

Clearly, Harm and Seidenberg's model learns, and at the end of learning, the model comes to resemble skilled reading well. But, if the model is to inform our understanding of reading development, it is important to reflect on its developmental plausibility. Three issues seem particularly problematic at the present time, although as Harm and Seidenberg point out, these are issues that can be addressed in future modelling attempts. The first issue concerns the nature of orthographic representation employed by Harm and Seidenberg (2004). The model was not pretrained on orthography, unlike semantics and phonology, which were both trained heavily before the onset of reading. Given the importance of letter knowledge during the early stages of word learning (e.g., Byrne and Fielding-Barnsley, 1989; Muter et al., 1998), an elementary introduction to letters early in training is important if psychologically valid orthographic representations are to develop. This point is nicely demonstrated by Powell, Plaut, and Funnell (2006), who made a direct comparison between kindergarten children learning to read and the triangle model (the version reported by Plaut et al., 1996). They noted that early in development, the original model did not generalise its knowledge to novel words very well and levels of non-word reading accuracy were much lower than that which they observed in beginning readers. In a revised model, they mimicked letter-sound knowledge by preexposing the model to grapheme-phoneme correspondences before the introduction of words. This led to faster learning and greater generalisation, bringing the model more in line with data from children.

A second issue concerns the nature of training and the training set of words the network is exposed to. Learning is achieved by a variant of a back-propagation algorithm. This means that learning is *supervised*, in the sense that the output of the network is monitored by an external "teacher," and differences between the actual output and the correct output trigger changes in the network's connections. Although children learn through explicit instruction, they rarely receive feedback on each decoding attempt. Instead, training is much more variable, sometimes comprising direct modelling of an appropriate response, sometimes explicit training in phonological awareness or letter-sound knowledge, and often no feedback at all. Harm and Seidenberg suggest that this rich and varied learning environment may be more advantageous than providing correct

feedback on each trial as it "may discourage the development of overly word-specific representations in favour of representations that capture structure that is shared across words, improving generalisation" (p. 673). This is an interesting issue for future research but at present, it is important to note that the nature of feedback provided to a network differs substantially from the experiences of children learning to read.

A related issue concerning the learning algorithm used by Harm and Seidenberg is that very slow learning rates were employed so as to prevent the network's weights from oscillating wildly. The consequence of this is that many trials were required to learn each word: In Harm and Seidenberg's trial, the very large training set was presented thousands of times. This contrasts sharply with observations from children's learning where initial reading experiences tend to comprise exposure to a small vocabulary of written words that increases in size as proficiency develops (Powell et al., 2006). Despite this incremental and relatively limited training environment, very few exposures may be sufficient for a child to learn a new word (Nation et al., 2007; Share, 2004). Nevertheless, the triangle model demonstrates that progress in learning to read is not necessarily a consequence of qualitative changes in underlying processing mechanisms. Instead, developmental change – and even apparently stage-like changes in surface behaviour – can arise gradually and incrementally as a consequence of the same mechanisms operating across a changing input, as provided by print exposure and experience. This is consistent with experimental work reviewed earlier suggesting that learning may be item-based rather than stage-based, as described by the self-teaching hypothesis or a statistical learning account.

6 From computational models to data

Despite their present limitations, an important feature of computational models is that they are operational and as such, they provide an opportunity to reveal factors that have the power to encourage developmental change. Factors such as the nature of representation, the strength of learning and generalisation, and the lexical characteristics of the reading environment can all be manipulated independently and in interaction, and their effects on word recognition development assessed via simulations. They are also useful in pointing to areas where behavioural data are lacking. This is nicely illustrated by considering the role of semantic knowledge in the development of visual word recognition. Skilled readers demonstrate word recognition skills that are highly sensitive to sources of constraint based on regularities and consistencies that are extracted from reading experience – be they semantic, phonological, or orthographic (Van Orden and Kloos, 2005). This is captured by interactions between semantic, phonological, and orthographic representations in the triangle model. In contrast, experimental studies of learning to read have focused almost exclusively on how children learn to make mappings between orthography and phonology. This is no surprise: Without discovery of this alphabetic principle, reading development will not happen. However, if we are to fully understand how children move from alphabetic decoding to adult levels of visual word recognition, we need to understand more about how sensitivity to lexical properties other than grapheme–phoneme correspondence develops.

A prediction that follows from this is that there ought to be a relationship between factors that underpin the semantic level of representation and word recognition development. Few studies have addressed this issue. Nation and Snowling (2004) reasoned that individual differences in semantic (or nonphonological) aspects of oral language skill may serve to index the proficiency of the semantic pathway. In line with this, they found that nonphonological language skills (e.g., vocabulary knowledge) measured at age eight years predicted individual differences in visual word recognition, even after the powerful effects of decoding (nonword reading) and phonological skills were controlled. In addition, the relationship maintained over time with nonphonological measures taken at eight years predicted unique variance in visual word recognition some four years later when the children were thirteen years old. The basis of this relationship is not clear. As discussed by Nation (2008), it could be an indirect relationship built up over time: Children need to deal with words that are inconsistent and irregular and one way they may do this is to utilise top-down knowledge from oral vocabulary which, in combination with information gleaned from a partial decoding attempt, may help them decipher the appropriate pronunciation of a word (Nation and Snowling, 1998). Over time, this leads to children with good vocabulary knowledge developing a better word recognition system. Alternatively – or additionally – the relationship between semantic factors and word-level reading may be direct in that meaning-based information influences the word recognition process itself, as has been shown to be the case in skilled readers (e.g., Balota et al., 2004). The finding that the rate at which written abbreviations for words could be learned by young children at the earliest stages of reading development depended on the word's imageability is consistent with this view (Laing and Hulme, 1999).

This discussion highlights that there is much to be learned about how factors beyond phonology and orthography contribute to the development of visual word recognition (Nation, 2008). While the triangle model provides a clear prediction that semantic and morphemic resources serve to constrain the development of word recognition, what these constraints are and how they are represented, how they change over time, and how they interact with other lexical properties and reading experience are issues that await thorough testing and specification from behavioural studies.

Acknowledgments

Portions of the text are reprinted from the following article, with kind permission from The Royal Society: Nation, K. (2009).

Form-meaning links in the development of visual word recognition. *Philosophical Transactions of The Royal Society, B, 364, 1536* 3665–367.

References

Andrews, S. & Scarratt, D. R. (1996). What comes after phonological awareness? Using lexical experts to investigate orthographic processes in reading. *Australian Journal of Psychology*, 48(3), 141–8.

(1998). Rule and analogy mechanisms in reading nonwords: Hough Dou Peapel Rede Gnew Wirds? *Journal of Experimental Psychology-Human Perception and Performance*, 24(4), 1052–86.

Balota, D. A., Cortese, M. J., Sergent Marshall, S. D., Spieler, D. H., & Yap, M. J. (2004). Visual word recognition of single-syllable words. *Journal of Experimental Psychology-General*, 133(2), 283–316.

Bates, E. & Elman, J. (1996). Learning rediscovered. *Science, 274(5294)*, 1849–50.

Bernstein, S. E. & Treiman, R. (2004). Pronouncing novel graphemes: The role of consonantal context. *Memory & Cognition, 32(6)*, 905–15.

Bowey, J. A. (2005). Predicting individual differences in learning to read. In Snowling, M. J. & Hulme. C. (Eds.) *The Science of Reading* (pp. 155–72). Oxford: Blackwell Publishing.

Bowey, J. A., Vaughan, L., & Hansen, J. (1998). Beginning readers' use of orthographic analogies in word reading. *Journal of Experimental Child Psychology, 68(2)*, 108–33.

Brown, G. D. A. & Deavers, R. P. (1999). Units of analysis in nonword reading: Evidence from children and adults. *Journal of Experimental Child Psychology, 73(3)*, 208–42.

Bruck, M. & Treiman, R. (1992). Learning to Pronounce Words – the Limitations of Analogies. *Reading Research Quarterly, 27(4)*, 374–89.

Byrne, B. (1992). Studies in the acquisition procedure for reading: Rationale, hypotheses and data. In Gough, P. B., Ehri L. C., & Treiman R. (Eds.) *Reading Acquisition* (pp. 1–34). Hillsdale, NJ: Erlbaum.

(1996). The learnability of the alphabetic principle: Children's initial hypotheses about how print represents spoken language. *Applied Psycholinguistics, 17(4)*, 401–26.

(1998). The foundation of literacy: The child's acquisition of the alphabetic principle. Hove, UK: Psychology Press.

Byrne, B. & Fielding-Barnsley, R. (1989). Phonemic Awareness and Letter Knowledge in the Child's Acquisition of the Alphabetic Principle. *Journal of Educational Psychology, 81(3)*, 313–21.

Caravolas, M., Volin, J., & Hulme, C. (2005). Phoneme awareness is a key component of alphabetic literacy skills in consistent and inconsistent orthographies: Evidence from Czech and English children. *Journal of Experimental Child Psychology*, 92, 107–39.

Cassar, M. & Treiman, R. (1997). The beginnings of orthographic knowledge: Children's knowledge of double letters in words. *Journal of Educational Psychology, 89(4)*, 631–44.

Castles, A. & Nation, K. (2006). How does orthographic learning happen? In Andrews, S. (Ed.) *From inkmarks to ideas: Challenges and controversies about word recognition and reading.* Psychology Press.

Cortese, M. J. & Balota, D. A. (this volume). Visual word recognition in skilled adult readers.

Coltheart, M. (2005). Modeling reading: The dual-route approach. In Snowling, M. J. & Hulme, C. (Eds.) *The Science of Reading* (pp. 6–23). Oxford: Blackwell Publishing.

Cunningham, A. E., Perry, K. E., Stanovich, K. E., & Share, D. L. (2002). Orthographic learning during reading: examining the role of self-teaching. *Journal of Experimental Child Psychology, 82(3)*, 185–99.

Ehri, L. C. (1992). Reconceptulizing the development of sight word reading and its relationship to recoding. In Gough, P. B., Ehri, L. C., & Treiman, R. (Eds.) *Reading Acquisition* (pp. 107–43). Hillsdale, NJ: Erlbaum.

Ehri, L. C. & Wilce, L. S. (1985). Movement into Reading – Is the 1st Stage of Printed Word Learning Visual or Phonetic? *Reading Research Quarterly, 20(2)*, 163–79.

Frith, U. (1985). Beneath the surface of developmental dyslexia. In Patterson, K. E., Marshall, J.C., & Colheart, M. (Ed.) *Surface Dyslexia: Neuropsychological and cognitive studies of phonological recoding* (pp. 301–30). London: Erlbaum.

Goswami, U. (1986). Children's Use of Analogy in Learning to Read – a Developmental Study. *Journal of Experimental Child Psychology, 42(1)*, 73–83.

(1993). Toward an Interactive Analogy Model of Reading Development – Decoding Vowel Graphemes in Beginning Reading. *Journal of Experimental Child Psychology, 56(3)*, 443–75.

Gough, M. & Hillinger, P. (1980). Learning to read: An unnatural act. *Bulletin of the Orton Society*, 30, 1–17.

Hanley, J. R. (2005). Learning to read in Chinese. In Snowling, M. J. & Hulme, C. (Eds.) *The Science of Reading* (pp. 272–95). Oxford: Blackwell Publishing.

Harm, M. W. & Seidenberg, M. S. (2004). Computing the meanings of words in reading: Cooperative division of labor between visual and phonological processes. *Psychological Review*, 111(3), 662–720.

Hatcher, P. J., Hulme, C., & Ellis, A. W. (1994). Ameliorating Early Reading Failure by Integrating the Teaching of Reading and Phonological Skills – the Phonological Linkage Hypothesis. *Child Development*, 65(1), 41–57.

Jackson, N. E. & Coltheart, M. (2001). Routes to reading success and failure. Hove: Psychology Press.

Laing, E. & Hulme, C. (1999). Phonological and semantic processes influence beginning readers' ability to learn to read words. *Journal of Experimental Child Psychology*, 73(3), 183–207.

Lupker, S. J. (2005). Visual word recognition: Theories and findings. In Snowling, M. J. & Hulme, C. (Eds.) *The Science of Reading* (pp. 39–60). Oxford: Blackwell Publishing.

Markson, L. & Bloom, P. (1997). Evidence against a dedicated system for word learning in children. *Nature*, 385(6619), 813–15.

Marsh, G., Friedman, M., Welch, V., & Desberg, P. (1981). A cognitive-developmental theory of reading acquisition. In Mackinnon, G. & Waller, T. (Eds.) *Reading Research: Advances in theory and practice* (pp. 199–221). New York: Academic Press.

Masonheimer, P. E., Drum, P. A., & Ehri, L. C. (1984). Does Environmental Print Identification Lead Children into Word Reading? *Journal of Reading Behavior*, 16(4), 257–71.

Muter, V., Hulme, C., Snowling, M. J., & Stevenson, J. (2004). Phonemes, rimes, vocabulary, and grammatical skills as foundations of early reading development: Evidence from a longitudinal study. *Developmental Psychology*, 40(5), 665–81.

Muter, V., Snowling, M., & Taylor, S. (1994). Orthographic Analogies and Phonological Awareness – Their Role and Significance in Early Reading Development. *Journal of Child Psychology and Psychiatry and Allied Disciplines*, 35(2), 293–310.

Nation, K. (2008). Learning to read words. *Quarterly Journal of Experimental Psychology*, 61, 1121–1133.

(2005). Children's reading comprehension difficulties. In Snowling, M. J. & Hulme, C. (Eds.) *The Science of Reading* (pp. 248–65). Oxford: Blackwell Publishing.

Nation, K., Allen, R., & Hulme, C. (2001). The limitations of orthographic analogy in early reading development: Performance on the clue-word task depends on phonological priming and elementary decoding skill, not the use of orthographic analogy. *Journal of Experimental Child Psychology*, 80(1), 75–94.

Nation, K., Angell, P., & Castles, A. (2007). Orthographic learning via self-teaching in children learning to read English: effects of exposure, durability and context. *Journal of Experimental Child Psychology*, 96, 71–84.

Nation, K. & Hulme, C. (1996). The automatic activation of sound-letter knowledge: An alternative interpretation of analogy and priming effects in early spelling development. *Journal of Experimental Child Psychology*, 63(2), 416–35.

Nation, K. & Snowling, M. J. (1998). Semantic processing and the development of word-recognition skills: Evidence from children with reading comprehension difficulties. *Journal of Memory and Language*, 39(1), 85–101.

(2004). Beyond phonological skills: broader language skills contribute to the development of reading. *Journal of Research in Reading*, 27(4), 342–56.

Pacton, S., Perruchet, P., Fayol, M., & Cleeremans, A. (2001). Implicit learning out of the lab: The case of orthographic regularities. *Journal of Experimental Psychology-General*, 130(3), 401–26.

Pennington, B. F. & Olson, R. K. (2005). Genetics of dyslexia. In Snowling, M. J. & Hulme, C. (Eds.) *The Science of Reading* (pp. 453–72). Oxford: Blackwell Publishing.

Perfetti, C. A., Landi, N., & Oakhill, J. (2005). The acquisition of reading comprehension skill. In Snowling, M. J. & Hulme, C. (Eds.) *The Science of Reading* (pp. 227–47). Oxford: Blackwell Publishing.

Plaut, D. C. (2005). Connectionist approaches to reading. In Snowling, M. J. & Hulme, C. (Eds.) *The Science of Reading* (pp. 24–38). Oxford: Blackwell Publishing.

Plaut, D. C., McClelland, J. L., Seidenberg, M. S., & Patterson, K. (1996). Understanding normal and impaired word reading: Computational principles in quasi-regular domains. *Psychological Review*, 103(1), 56–115.

Powell, D., Plaut, D. C., & Funnell, E. (2006). Does the PMSP connectionist model of single word reading learn to read in the same way as a child? *Journal of Research in Reading*.

Rack, J., Hulme, C., Snowling, M., & Wightman, J. (1994). The Role of Phonology in Young-Children Learning to Read Words – the Direct-Mapping Hypothesis. *Journal of Experimental Child Psychology*, 57(1), 42–71.

Ross, S., Treiman, R., & Bick, S. (2004). Task demands and knowledge influence how children learn to read words. *Cognitive Development*, 19(3), 417–31.

Saffran, J. R., Aslin, R. N., & Newport, E. L. (1996). Statistical learning by 8-month-old infants. *Science*, 274(5294), 1926–8.

Savage, R. & Stuart, M. (1998). Sublexical inferences in beginning reading: Medial vowel digraphs as functional units of transfer. *Journal of Experimental Child Psychology*, 69(2), 85–108.

Seidenberg, M. S. (this volume). Computational models of reading: Connectionist and dual-route approaches.

Seidenberg, M. S. & McClelland, J. L. (1989). A Distributed, Developmental Model of Word Recognition and Naming. *Psychological Review*, 96(4), 523–68.

Seymour, P. H. K. (2005). Early reading development in European orthographies. In Snowling, M. J. & Hulme, C. (Eds.) *The Science of Reading* (pp. 296–315). Oxford: Blackwell Publishing.

Seymour, P. H. K. & Elder, L. (1986). Beginning Reading without Phonology. *Cognitive Neuropsychology*, 3(1), 1–36.

Share, D. L. (1995). Phonological Recoding and Self-Teaching – Sine-Qua-Non of Reading Acquisition. *Cognition*, 55(2), 151–218.

(1999). Phonological recoding and orthographic learning: A direct test of the self-teaching hypothesis. *Journal of Experimental Child Psychology*, 72(2), 95–129.

(2004). Orthographic learning at a glance: On the time course and developmental onset of self-teaching. *Journal of Experimental Child Psychology*, 87(4), 267–98.

Stanovich, K. E. & Siegel, L. S. (1994). Phenotypic Performance Profile of Children with Reading Disabilities – a Regression-Based Test of the Phonological-Core Variable-Difference Model. *Journal of Educational Psychology*, 86(1), 24–53.

Stone, G. O., Vanhoy, M., & Van Orden, G. C. (1997). Perception is a two-way street: Feedforward and feedback phonology in visual word recognition. *Journal of Memory and Language*, 36(3), 337–59.

Treiman, R. (1985). Onsets and Rimes as Units of Spoken Syllables – Evidence from Children. *Journal of Experimental Child Psychology*, 39(1), 161–81.

Treiman, R., Kessler, B., Zevin, J., Bick, S., & Davis, M. (2006). Influence of consonantal context on the reading of vowels: evidence from children. *Journal of Experimental Child Psychology*. 93, 1–24.

Treiman, R. & Rodriguez, K. (1999). Young children use letter names in learning to read words. *Psychological Science*, 10(4), 334–8.

Treiman, R., Sotak, L., & Bowman, M. (2001). The roles of letter names and letter sounds in connecting print and speech. *Memory & Cognition*, 29(6), 860–73.

Van Orden, G. C. & Kloos, H. (2005). The question of phonology and reading. In Snowling, M. J. & Hulme, C. (Eds.) *The Science of Reading* (pp. 61–78). Oxford: Blackwell Publishing.

Vellutino, F. R. & Fletcher, J. M. (2005). Developmental dyslexia. In Snowling, M. J. & Hulme, C. (Eds.) *The Science of Reading* (pp. 362–378). Oxford: Blackwell Publishing.

Ziegler, J. C. & Goswami, U. (2005). Reading acquisition, developmental dyslexia, and skilled reading across languages: A psycholinguistic grain size theory. *Psychological Bulletin*, 131(1), 3–29.

Ziegler, J. C., Stone, G. O., & Jacobs, A. M. (1997). What is the pronunciation for -ough and the spelling for vertical bar u vertical bar? A database for computing feedforward and feedback consistency in English. *Behavior Research Methods Instruments & Computers*, 29(4), 600–18.

CHAPTER 11

How Does the Brain Read Words?

Rebecca Sandak, Stephen J. Frost, Jay G. Rueckl, Nicole Landi, W. Einar Mencl, Leonard Katz and Kenneth R. Pugh

1 Introduction

The investigation of how it is that we are able to read individual words has a long and venerable history in the fields of psychology and neuropsychology, with the earliest findings from patient studies indelibly shaping our theories about the cognitive processes underlying reading. Together with early postmortem patient studies, the selective preservation/impairment of reading skills in the different types of acquired reading disabilities has influenced and constrained the development of models of reading, as well as our understanding of how the brain reads words. With the advent of modern functional neuroimaging techniques it became possible to systematically investigate the cognitive roles played by various parts of the brain during reading. Naturally, the findings from these studies have been interpreted in the context of theoretical and computational models of reading. More recent work has begun to explore the interactions and trade-offs among the cortical regions that have been implicated in reading. Studies that systematically contrast stimulus factors

and learning conditions promise to further constrain neurobiologically based models of reading.

In this chapter, we briefly describe the various types of acquired reading disabilities and their influence on models of reading. We then review findings about the functional neuroanatomy of reading in skilled readers and in readers with developmental reading disabilities (not resulting from brain damage). Finally, we discuss findings from some recent neuroimaging studies and illustrate how they call into question the assumptions made by some models of reading, focusing on general principles of broad classes of models (see Seidenberg, this volume, for a more complete review of models of reading).

2 Patient/lesion studies

Early information about how the brain reads came from patients with brain damage that resulted in acquired reading disabilities. The underlying logic of studying patients with brain lesions is that if damage to a particular region of the brain results in impaired reading, then that region (or part of it) must have been necessary for reading (but see Van Orden and Kloos, 2003 for a critique of this approach). Dejerine (1891; 1892) reported two patients: One had incurred damage to the left angular gyrus and suffered from both reading and writing impairments (dyslexia with dysgraphia), whereas another had incurred damage to the left occipital lobe and had impaired reading but intact writing (dyslexia without dysgraphia, or pure alexia). Through subsequent study of patients with acquired dyslexias, several other left hemisphere brain regions have been identified as involved in reading; these include posterior inferior frontal cortex and posterior and anterior regions of the superior, middle, and inferior temporal lobe. Later in this chapter, we briefly describe the different types of acquired dyslexia and the type of brain damage associated with each, and then consider how patient studies have influenced the development of models of reading.

2.1 *Types of acquired dyslexia*

In addition to identifying candidate brain regions involved in reading, patient studies have uncovered distinct behavioral manifestations of acquired reading impairments. Four types of acquired dyslexias have been observed: pure alexia, surface dyslexia, phonological dyslexia, and deep dyslexia.

In *pure alexia*, patients are impaired in their ability to read all types of words (pseudowords, regular, and irregular) with preserved language and writing abilities; in the other forms of dyslexia, writing, spelling, and language are typically impaired. Pure alexia is also called *letter-by-letter reading* because patients read by first spelling the word or pseudoword aloud (naming each letter in a left-to-right sequence); if all of the letters are named correctly, then the word will usually be read correctly. Reading is very slow for pure alexics, and the time required to read a word is directly related to the number of letters in that word (Montant and Behrmann, 2000). As noted earlier, pure

alexia was first observed by Dejerine (1892) and typically results from damage to the left occipitotemporal region.

Patients with *surface dyslexia* are better at reading novel words (i.e., pseudowords like *fape*) and words with predictable spelling–sound correspondences (regular words; e.g., *mill*), compared to low-frequency words with irregular spelling-to-sound correspondences (e.g., *pint*). Their errors tend to be regularizations of such words, for example, reading *pint* as if it rhymes with *mint* (Marshall and Newcombe, 1973; Patterson et al., 1985; Shallice et al., 1983). Surface dyslexia typically results from antero-lateral temporal lobe damage. Many patients with surface dyslexia also have semantic deficits, including semantic dementia, a neurodegenerative syndrome resulting from focal anterior temporal lobe atrophy, which is characterized by semantic but not phonological deficits (Hodges et al., 1992; Patterson and Hodges, 1992).

Patients with *phonological dyslexia* tend to show the opposite pattern. That is, they are able to read real words, but are relatively impaired in their ability to read pseudowords (Beauvois and Derouesne, 1979; Patterson, 1982; Shallice and Warrington, 1980). Phonological dyslexia typically results from damage to the temporoparietal and frontal cortices (Lambon and Graham, 2000).

Like phonological dyslexia, *deep dyslexia* is also characterized by impaired pseudoword reading. The classic symptom of deep dyslexia is the occurrence of semantic errors while reading (e.g., misreading *dog* for *cat*). These patients also make visual errors (misreading *angle* for *angel*) and morphological errors (misreading *swimmer* for *swimming*), and are more accurate when reading concrete words (*horse* and *boat*) compared to abstract words (*idea* and *life*) and function words (*the* and *or*) (Coltheart, Patterson, and Marshall, 1987; Marshall and Newcombe, 1973). Because both phonological and deep dyslexics show impaired pseudoword reading (with deep dyslexics unable to read pseudowords at all), it has been suggested that phonological dyslexics fall on a continuum of severity of impairment, with deep dyslexia at the most severe end. To this point, it is notable that during recovery from deep dyslexia, semantic errors are the first to disappear, followed by the concreteness effect, then the part of speech effect, then visual and morphological errors, and lastly, nonword reading errors. Deep dyslexia usually occurs following extensive left hemisphere damage, particularly to temporoparietal and parieto-occipital regions; most patients with deep dyslexia are also aphasic (Coltheart et al., 1987).

2.2 Models shaped by patients

The double dissociation observed at the behavioral level in phonological and surface dyslexia has been taken to suggest dissociations at the information processing level and implies that there are at least two ways to identify a written word; indeed virtually all of the current models of reading incorporate at least two strategies for word identification, though the mechanisms underlying these two strategies remains a point of debate (Coltheart et al., 1993; Seidenberg and McClelland, 1989).

In light of the behavioral dissociations seen in neuropsychological case studies, early reading theories proposed that two "routes" were necessary for the reading of pseudowords and words with atypical spelling-to-sound mappings (c.f. Coltheart, 1978; Marshall and Newcombe, 1973). These dual-route theories postulated that pseudowords (and regular words) were assembled via grapheme–phoneme conversion (GPC) rules ("phonologically mediated access" or "sublexical" route), whereas irregular words had to be looked up in a mental dictionary or lexicon (the "direct" or "lexical" route). Besides providing a means to account for stimulus type dissociations seen in patients with acquired dyslexia, these models successfully accounted for many behavioral findings (e.g., word frequency effects and frequency by spelling-to-sound regularity interactions) in nonimpaired readers. In the context of these models, damage to the lexical route will result in surface dyslexia:

Nonwords (and regular words) will still be read correctly, but exception words will often result in regularization errors. In contrast, damage to the sublexical route will result in phonological dyslexia, an inability to read pseudowords. Whereas multiple independent pathway models are usually proposed, it should be noted that connectionist models, which maintain that a single mechanism underlies reading of all words, have also been able to account for the patterns of impairment seen in dyslexic patients (Harm and Seidenberg, 1999; Plaut et al., 1996); this class of model may be more amenable to recent findings from functional neuroimaging studies and will be discussed in more detail later in the chapter.

2.3 Finding the two routes in the brain

Taken together, patient studies and early dual-route cognitive models suggested that discrete types of cognitive processing involved in reading could be localized to discrete regions (or sets of regions) in the brain. For example, because damage to the inferior frontal and temporoparietal regions is associated with phonological and deep dyslexia, it has been suggested that these regions may comprise the sublexical route, whereas the occipito- and antero-temporal regions have been suggested as the primary components of the lexical route due to their association with surface dyslexia and alexia. However, because lesions typically encompass broad cortical regions, the utility of lesion studies is inherently limited: It is not possible to precisely determine which underlying structures (or connections between structures) within those large regions are responsible for particular types of cognitive functioning (but see Cohen et al., 2003 and Price et al., 2003a for methods which may enable patient lesion studies to be more informative in this regard). Moreover, the assumption of selective loss has been questioned (Van Orden and Kloos, 2003). It can be argued that lesion studies are a source of hypotheses regarding functional neuroanatomy, but by themselves are not definitive. Functional neuroimaging techniques allow for new and potentially more ecologically valid investigations into the neurobiological foundations of reading in intact subjects. Initial functional neuroimaging studies of reading focused on localizing the cognitive processes involved in reading to various parts of the brain, with more recent studies investigating the relationships among regions. In the following sections, we review the current literature on the neurobiology of skilled reading, reading development, developmental reading disability, and remediation.

3 Functional neuroanatomy of skilled reading

Evidence from functional imaging studies indicates that skilled word recognition requires the development of a highly organized cortical system that integrates processing of orthographic, phonological, and lexico-semantic features of words (see Pugh et al., 2000a; and Sarkari et al., 2002 for reviews). Illustrated in Figure 11.1, this system broadly includes two posterior subsystems in the left hemisphere (LH): a ventral (occipitotemporal) and a dorsal (temporoparietal) system, and a third area, anterior to the other two, centered in and around the inferior frontal gyrus. All of these regions have been implicated in acquired dyslexia, and extensive neuroimaging research has investigated the degree to which the components of each of these systems are involved in phonological and semantic processing in skilled readers.

The ventral system includes extrastriate areas, a left inferior occipitotemporal/fusiform area, and appears to extend anteriorly into the middle and inferior temporal gyri. It has been suggested that the occipitotemporal (OT) region functions as a presemantic visual word form area (VWFA) by some researchers (c.f. Cohen et al., 2002, but see Price et al., 2003b for an alternative conceptualization). Importantly, the functional specificity of sites along the ventral pathway for reading appears to be late developing and critically related to the acquisition of reading skill (Booth et al., 2001; see Shaywitz

et al., 2002, discussed later in this chapter). More anterior foci within the ventral system extending into the middle to inferior temporal gyri (MTG, ITG) appear to be semantically tuned (Fiebach et al., 2002; Simos et al., 2002; Tagamets et al., 2000). The ventral system, particularly the posterior aspects thought to be prelexical and presemantic, are also fast-acting in response to orthographic stimuli in skilled readers but not in individuals with developmental reading disability (RD; Salmelin et al., 1996). Although there is still disagreement in the literature about the precise taxonomy of critical subregions comprising the ventral system (Cornelissen et al., 2004; Dehaene et al., 2004; Price et al., 2003b), recent studies examining both timing and stimulus-type effects suggest in general terms that subregions respond to word and word-like stimuli in a progressively abstracted and linguistic manner as one moves anteriorly along the ventral pathways (Dehaene et al., 2004; Tagamets et al., 2000; Tarkiainen et al., 2003).

The more dorsal temporoparietal system broadly includes the angular gyrus (AG) and supramarginal gyrus (SMG) in the inferior parietal lobule, and the posterior aspect of the superior temporal gyrus (Wernicke's Area). Among their other functions (e.g., attentionally controlled processing) it has been argued that the areas within this system are involved in mapping visual percepts of print onto the phonological and semantic structures of language (Black and Behrmann, 1994). In skilled readers, certain regions within the LH temporoparietal system (particularly the SMG) respond with greater activity to pseudowords than to familiar words (Price et al., 1996; Simos et al., 2002; Xu et al., 2001). This finding, along with developmental studies (Shaywitz et al., 2002), suggests that the temporoparietal system plays a role in the types of phonological analyses involved in grapheme-phoneme conversion.

The anterior system centered in posterior aspects of the inferior frontal gyrus (IFG) appears to be associated with phonological (possibly articulatory) recoding during reading, among other functions

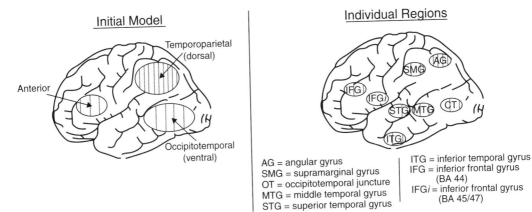

Figure 11.1. Schematics of our initial model and key component regions.

(e.g., phonological memory, syntactic processing); the more anterior aspects of IFG seem to play a role in semantic retrieval (Bookheimer, 2002; Poldrack et al., 1999). The phonologically relevant components of this multifunctional system have been found to function in silent reading and in naming (see Fiez and Petersen, 1998 for review; Pugh et al., 1997) and like the temporoparietal system, is more strongly engaged by low-frequency words (particularly words with irregular/inconsistent spelling-to-sound mappings) and pseudowords than by high-frequency words (Fiebach et al., 2002; Fiez and Peterson, 1998). We have speculated that this anterior system operates in close conjunction with the temporoparietal system to decode new words during normal reading development (Pugh et al., 2000a).

In normally developing beginning readers, the dorsal and anterior systems appear to predominate during initial reading acquisition, given the observation of an increased ventral specialization to print stimuli as proficiency in word recognition increases. Indeed, in our research (Shaywitz et al., 2002) we observed that normally developing children younger than ten and a half years of age showed robust engagement of temporoparietal and anterior systems, but limited engagement of the ventral system during pseudoword and word reading tasks. In contrast, children older than ten and a half years of age tended to show increased engagement of the ventral system, which in

turn was positively correlated with reading skill. Indeed, when multiple regression analyses examined both age and reading skill (measured by performance on standardized reading tests) the critical predictor was reading skill level: the higher the reading skill, the stronger the response in the LH ventral cortex (with several other areas including RH and frontal lobe sites showing age- and skill-related reductions). In contrast, RD readers showed age-related increases in a widely distributed set of regions across both hemispheres. Based on these cross-sectional developmental findings, we have suggested (Pugh et al., 2000a) that a beginning reader on a successful trajectory employs a widely distributed cortical system for print processing including temporoparietal, frontal, and right hemisphere (RH) posterior areas. As reading skill increases, LH ventral sites become more engaged during reading and presumably more central to the rapid recognition of printed (word) stimuli (see Booth et al., 2001; McCandliss et al., 2003; Tarkanien et al. 2003; Turkeltaub et al. 2003 for similar arguments).

More recently, the functional neuroanatomy of visual word recognition in reading has been investigated in mature readers in a variety of languages (which employ both alphabetic and nonalphabetic writing systems) (e.g., Chee et al., 1999; Fiebach et al., 2002; Kuo et al., 2003, 2004; Paulesu et al., 2001; Salmelin et al., 1996). Across languages, neuroimaging studies broadly implicate the same set of LH cortical regions (including occipitotemporal, temporoparietal, and inferior frontal networks) identified in English-language studies. These common networks are almost always engaged by skilled readers irrespective of the specific language and/or writing system under investigation. Language-specific differences usually appear to be a matter of degree, not of kind. That is, in one language, the reading-relevant constituents of a neural network might be more or less activated than in another language, but the general circuitry appears similar in its taxonomic organization (Paulesu et al., 2001). For example, Kuo et al. (2003) examined covert naming of high-frequency and low-frequency Chinese characters and observed greater activation in left premotor/ inferior frontal regions and the left insula for low-frequency characters relative to high-frequency characters. These areas have been implicated in phonological processing in English; in particular, the inferior frontal gyrus is more strongly engaged by low-frequency words and pseudowords than by high-frequency words (Fiebach et al., 2002; Fiez and Peterson, 1998). Moreover, high-frequency characters produced greater activation in the middle temporal/angular gyrus and the precuneus, which have been implicated in lexical-semantic (Fiebach et al., 2002; Price et al., 1997; Simos et al., 2002) and visual imagery (Fletcher et al., 1994) processing, respectively, in neuroimaging studies of English word recognition. In a subsequent study, Kuo and colleagues had participants perform homophone judgments and physical judgments on real characters, pseudo-characters (novel combinations of legal semantic and phonetic radicals that follow the positional architecture of Chinese characters), and nonsense figures modified from Korean characters to be similar to Chinese characters in strokes and use of fixed space (Kuo et al., 2004). A number of regions important for orthographic-to-phonological mapping in English were also more active for the homophone judgment relative to the character judgment in Chinese. These regions included the inferior frontal gyrus, inferior parietal lobule/supramarginal gyrus,

and the fusiform gyrus. Note that some differences have been reported for Mandarin reading with increased reading-related activation at both superior parietal (Kuo et al., 2003), and left middle frontal regions (Tan et al., 2001); however, overall the reading networks appear to be largely similar to those observed for alphabetic writing systems (Kuo et al., 2003; 2004). Examination of both language-specific and language-invariant characteristics of the functional neuroanatomy of reading will be critical for developing proper neurobiologically based models of reading.

4 Functional neuroanatomy of developmental dyslexia

Unlike the acquired dyslexias, developmental dyslexia does not result from known brain damage. However, postmortem observations of subtle cortical anomalies (see Galaburda, 1994 for review) have led some researchers to posit parallels with the lesion literature (Castles and Coltheart, 1993). Nonetheless, no single underlying cause of developmental dyslexia has been identified: It has been argued that the reading difficulties experienced by some children may result from difficulties with processing speed (Wolf and Bowers, 1999), rapid auditory processing (Habib, 2000; Tallal, 1980), general language deficits (Scarborough and Dobrich, 1990), or visual deficits (Cornelissen and Hansen, 1998), and indeed, there may not be a unitary etiology of developmental dyslexia (Grigorenko, 1997). However, there is growing consensus that for the majority of struggling readers with developmental dyslexia, a core difficulty in reading manifests itself as a deficiency within the language system and, in particular, a deficiency at the level of phonological representation and processing (Liberman, 1992; Liberman et al., 1974; Ziegler and Goswami, 2005). Deficits in behavioral performance are most evident at the level of single word and pseudoword reading; reading disabled (RD) individuals are both slow and inaccurate relative to skilled readers.

With regard to functional neuroanatomy, there are clear differences between skilled (or nonimpaired; NI) and RD readers with regard to activation patterns in dorsal, ventral, and anterior sites during reading tasks. In disabled readers, a number of functional imaging studies have observed LH posterior functional disruption at both dorsal and ventral sites during phonological processing tasks (Brunswick et al., 1999; Paulesu et al., 2001; Pugh et al., 2000a; Salmelin et al., 1996; Shaywitz et al., 1998, 2002; Temple et al., 2001). This disruption is instantiated as a relative under-engagement of these regions specifically when processing linguistic stimuli (words and pseudowords) or during tasks that require decoding. This functional anomaly in posterior LH regions has been observed consistently in children (Shaywitz et al., 2002) and adults (Salmelin et al., 1996; Shaywitz et al., 1998). Hypoactivation in three key dorsal and ventral sites, including cortex within the temporoparietal region, the angular gyrus, and the ventral OT skill zone is detectable as early as the end of kindergarten in children who have not reached important milestones in learning to read (Simos et al., 2002).

Most neuroimaging studies have attempted to isolate specific brain regions where activation patterns discriminate RD from NI readers (e.g., Rumsey et al., 1997; Shaywitz et al., 1998; Simos et al., 2002; Temple et al., 2001). However, work in reading disability employing functional connectivity analyses has also provided important insights into functional differences between RD and NI readers in word recognition (Horwitz et al., 1998; Pugh et al., 2000b). In this approach, the primary aim is to consider relations *among* distinct brain regions that function cooperatively as circuits to process information during reading (Friston, 1994). For example, Horwitz, Rumsey, and Donohue (1998) examined correlations (within tasks/across subjects) between activation levels in the LH angular gyrus and other brain sites during two reading aloud tasks (exception word and nonword naming). Correlations between the LH angular gyrus and occipital and temporal lobe sites

were strong and significant in NI readers and weak in RD readers. Such a result suggests a breakdown in functional connectivity across the major components of the LH posterior reading system. A subsequent study by our group (Pugh et al., 2000b) examined functional connectivity between the angular gyrus and occipital and temporal lobe sites on tasks that systematically varied demands made on phonological assembly and showed that for RD readers LH functional connectivity was disrupted on word and pseudoword reading tasks as reported by Horwitz et al. (1998); however, there appeared to be no dysfunction on the tasks which tapped metaphonological judgments only (e.g., a single letter rhyme task), or complex visual-orthographic coding only (e.g., an orthographic case judgment task). The results are most consistent with a specific phonological deficit hypothesis: The data suggest that a breakdown in functional connectivity among components of the LH posterior system manifests only when orthographic-to-phonological assembly is required. The notion of a severe developmental lesion, one that would disrupt functional connectivity in this system across all types of cognitive behaviors, is not supported by this result (or by recent studies of the effects of reading remediation; see later in this chapter). Moreover, Pugh et al. (2000b) found that on word and nonword reading tasks, RH homologues appeared to function in a compensatory manner for RD readers; correlations were strong and stable in this hemisphere for both reading groups with higher values in RD readers.

Because the evidence from neuroimaging studies of skilled reading indicates that different languages and orthographies engage common circuits during reading, we might expect language-invariant neurobiological signatures to be associated with reading disability as well. The evidence to date from alphabetic languages supports this expectation (Paulesu et al., 2001; Salmelin et al., 1996; Shaywitz et al., 2002). Functional disruptions in LH posterior cortex (particularly the occipitotemporal region) in RD individuals performing reading tasks during neuroimaging have been found in several languages that vary in the complexity of mappings between printed and spoken forms (English, Finnish, German, French, and Italian; Paulesu et al., 2001). This common neurobiological signature, within a largely language-invariant circuitry for reading in the LH, reinforces the notion of universality in RD. A recent study of Chinese RD readers (Siok et al. 2004) reported a language-specific difference in the RD signature (specifically diminished activation of middle frontal regions for RD readers relative to controls). This finding has not been reported in alphabetic languages. However, these authors also found diminished activation in RD readers at the same LH ventral regions previously reported by Paulesu and others in RD within alphabetic languages (Brunswick et al., 1999; Paulesu et al., 2001; Salmelin et al., 1996; Shaywitz et al., 2002).

4.1 Potentially compensatory processing in developmental dyslexia

Behaviorally, poor readers compensate for their inadequate phonological awareness and knowledge of letter–sound correspondences by over-relying on contextual cues to read individual words; their word reading errors tend to be visual or semantic rather than phonological (see Perfetti, 1985 for review). These behavioral markers of reading impairment may be instantiated cortically by compensatory activation of frontal and RH regions. For example, Shaywitz et al. (1998; 2002) found that on tasks that made explicit demands on phonological processing (pseudoword and word reading tasks), RD readers showed a disproportionately greater engagement of IFG and prefrontal dorsolateral sites than did NI readers (see also Brunswick et al., 1999; Salmelin et al., 1996 for similar findings). Evidence of a second, potentially compensatory, shift – in this case to posterior RH regions – comes from several findings. Using MEG, Sarkari et al. (2002) found an increase in the apparent engagement of the RH temporoparietal region in RD children. More detailed examination of this trend, using hemodynamic

measures (Shaywitz et al., 1998), indicates that hemispheric asymmetries in activity in posterior temporal and temporoparietal regions (MTG and AG) vary significantly among reading groups: There was greater right than left hemisphere activation in RD readers but greater left than RH activation in NI readers. Rumsey et al. (1999) examined the relationship between RH activation and reading performance in their adult RD and NI participants and found that RH temporoparietal activation was correlated with standard measures of reading performance only for RD readers (see also Shaywitz et al., 2002).

4.2 Neurobiological effects of successful reading remediation

Converging evidence from other studies supports the notion that gains in reading skill resulting from intense reading intervention are associated with a more normalized localization of reading processes in the brain. This rather strongly implies that developmental dyslexia is associated with a poorly trained but not fundamentally lesioned LH system. In a recent MEG study, eight young children with severe reading difficulties underwent a brief but intensive phonics-based remediation program (Simos et al., 2002). After intervention, the most salient change observed on a case-by-case basis was a robust increase in the apparent engagement of the LH temporoparietal region, accompanied by a moderate reduction in the activation of the RH temporoparietal areas. Similarly, Temple et al. (2003) used fMRI to examine the effects of an intervention (FastForword) on the cortical circuitry of a group of eight- to twelve-year-old children with reading difficulties. After intervention, increased LH temporoparietal and inferior frontal increases were observed. Moreover, the LH increases correlated significantly with increased reading scores. Shaywitz et al. (2003) examined three groups of young children (average preintervention age was six and a half years) with fMRI and behavioral indices. A treatment RD group received nine months of an intensive phonologically analytic intervention, and there were two control groups: a typically developing and an untreated RD group. Relative to RD controls, RD treatment participants showed reliable gains on reading measures (particularly on fluency-related measures). When RD groups were compared postintervention, reliably greater activation increases in LH reading related sites were seen in the treatment group. When pre- and postintervention activation profiles were directly contrasted for each group, it was evident that both RD treatment and typically developing, but not RD controls, showed reliable increases in LH reading related sites. Prominent differences were seen in LH IFG, and importantly in LH ventral skill zone. These changes were quite similar to those evidenced by the NI controls as their reading skills also improved over time. Importantly, the treatment group returned one year posttreatment for a follow-up fMRI scan and progressive LH ventral increases along with decreasing RH activation patterns were observed even one year after treatment was concluded (Shaywitz et al., 2003). Taken together, initial neuroimaging treatment studies suggest that a critical neurobiological signature of successful intervention, at least in younger children, appears to be increased engagement of major LH reading related circuits, and reduced compensatory reliance on RH homologues.

5 Toward a neurobiological model of reading

Much of the neuroimaging research on reading has paralleled lesions studies, either explicitly or implicitly interpreting findings in the context of dual-route models and assigning cortical regions to one of the two routes. For example, based on the finding that BA 44 within the inferior frontal gyrus exhibits stronger activation for pseudowords than for words, it has been suggested that this region is part of the sublexical route, responsible for grapheme to phoneme conversion (Fiebach et al., 2002; Fiez et al., 1999; Rumsey et al., 1999). Likewise, some

researchers have associated the direct route with the left inferior temporal cortex based on sensitivity to lexical and semantic manipulations (Price, 2000). Several attempts have been made to assess the degree to which dual-route models can account for neuroimaging findings (Fiebach et al., 2002; Jobard et al., 2003; Price et al., 2000), though few have explicitly contrasted opposing models (but see Binder et al., 2005a).

At this point, we briefly review our early conceptualization of a neurobiological model of reading in which we drew heavily on the dual-route concept in our attempts to integrate evidence concerning the brain systems that support reading with existing models of word reading (Pugh et al., 2000a). We then review some recent experimental findings that have led us to reconsider several of our earlier conclusions and assumptions. We note that this interpretation is but one possible model (cf. Price, 2000) and as will become evident, continues to evolve and be refined as new data are obtained.

5.1 *One initial neurobiological model of reading*

Based on evidence concerning the effects of factors such as lexical status (word–pseudoword), word frequency, and task (e.g., reading aloud, reading for meaning) described earlier, we proposed that the dorsal system uses a relatively slow, algorithmic (rule-based, sublexical) process to recode printed words into phonological representations (a component of phonological mediation); that the ventral system acts as a fast, memory-based word identification system (as in direct, lexical access); and that the anterior system is critical for recoding print into the articulatory code needed for overt naming (Pugh et al., 2000a). According to this view, lexical selection is determined largely by the ventral system when the stimulus is familiar and task demands are appropriate, and largely by the dorsal system, in close conjunction with the inferior frontal gyrus, when the stimulus is novel or low frequency. Thus, in this early conceptualization the two systems were thought to correspond (but only loosely) to the two routes of classical dual-route theory (Coltheart et al., 1993). Like most dual-route models, our initial neurobiological model assumed that the direct and phonologically mediated routes are functionally independent and that their roles change as reading skill develops (Bruck, 1992; see Binder et al., 2005a in which "exclusive" and "parallel" versions of the dual-route model are distinguished and assessed with functional neuroimaging data).

We proposed that the dorsal and anterior routes predominate during initial reading acquisition, and that the ventral system plays the dominant role in skilled reading; thus development of reading skill is characterized by a dorsal-to-ventral shift (Pugh et al., 2000a). In contrast, reading disability was characterized by under-engagement of the ventral system during word reading (Paulesu et al., 2001; Pugh et al., 2000a; Salmelin et al., 1996; Shaywitz et al., 2002). We hypothesized that the reason RD readers tend to strongly engage inferior frontal sites is their increased reliance on covert pronunciation (phonological recoding) in an attempt to cope with their deficient phonological analysis of the printed word. In addition, their heightened activation of the posterior RH regions with reduced LH posterior activation suggests a process of word recognition that relies on letter-by-letter processing in accessing RH localized visuo-semantic representations (or some other compensatory process) rather than relying on phonologically structured word recognition strategies. These differential patterns, especially the increased activation in frontal regions, might also reflect increased effort during reading; under-engagement of LH posterior areas, particularly ventral sites, would not be thought to reflect this increased effort, but rather the failure to engage these areas likely precipitates any change in effort.

Finally, we proposed that the dorsal and anterior circuits play a critical role in the establishment of an effective ventral system, predicting that the ventral circuit would be phonologically sensitive, consistent with evidence that phonology plays an early role in visual word recognition (e.g. Lukatela and Turvey, 1994; Perfetti et al., 1988; Van Orden, 1987).

5.2 Recent findings

Many predictions derived from our initial model have been borne out by research in our labs and others.' Broadly speaking, these results confirm the central importance of the three proposed circuits in skilled reading and support the view that the dorsal and anterior circuits are critical for phonological processing and that the ventral system is a fast, skill-correlated zone (Sandak et al., 2004; Xu et al., 2001), and are consistent with our characterization of normal and impaired reading acquisition (Eden and Moats, 2002; Sandak et al., 2004). At the same time, research conducted during the past few years has led to revisions of the original model. It is now clear that there is greater differentiation within each of the three subsystems than we originally recognized; that these subsystems do not operate independently, but instead engage in cooperative and competitive interactions; and that developmental and learning-related changes in the activation of each subsystem reflect changes in the degree to which each subsystem is engaged and its efficiency rather than a wholesale dorsal to ventral shift. In the following sections, we consider some recent findings that must constrain evolving neurobiological models.

1. *Discovery of differentiation within each of the three subsystems*. Recent evidence about the components of the three subsystems has altered our understanding of their functions and points to important functional distinctions between (a) components of the dorsal (especially SMG) and anterior (IFG) systems (Frost et al., 2005; Katz et al. 2005), and (b) the posterior (OT) and anterior (MTG and ITG) components of the ventral system. For example, it has been demonstrated that IFG is sensitive to spelling-to-sound consistency effects

(Fiez et al., 1999; Frost et al., 2005) and is differentially influenced by repetition in lexical decision and naming, whereas SMG exhibits equivalent repetition-related reductions in lexical decision and naming (Katz et al., 2005). In addition, it has been shown that the angular gyrus (within the temporoparietal system) and the middle/inferior temporal gyri (within the ventral system) appear to have more abstract lexico-semantic functions: Activation in these areas is greater for words than for pseudowords, and for words that have highly image-able referents than for words that do not (Binder et al., 2005b; Frost et al., 2005; Price et al., 1997; Sabsevitz et al., 2005; Sandak et al., 2004); it has also been suggested that the angular gyrus is involved in mapping between auditory, visual, and semantic representational systems during lexical processing (Booth et al., 2004).

Whereas MTG and ITG appear to be semantically tuned, OT is the putative visual word form area (VWFA) or "skill zone": Activation in this region during reading tasks has been shown to be reliably correlated with reading skill in children and adolescents (Paulesu et al., 2001; Shaywitz et al., 2002, 2003, and developmental dyslexics do not engage this region during reading (Paulesu et al., 2001; Shaywitz et al., 1998, 2002). The functional specificity of this region develops later than the dorsal and anterior systems; however, in adults it responds faster than these other systems (Shaywitz et al., 2002; Tarkiainen et al., 1999). Additionally, recent studies (e.g., Sandak et al., 2004; Xu et al., 2001) indicate that OT is phonologically tuned, that is, activated by phonological as well as other types of lexical information (Devlin et al., 2004). It makes good sense that this region should be so structured given the failure to develop this system in reading disability when phonological deficits are one of the core features of this population. Thus, it is now clear that many of the claims we initially made about the ventral system as a whole are understood more

properly as claims about OT in particular. (It is worth noting that the anatomical center of the area we refer to OT/VWFA is located at Talairach coordinates: x: -47; y: -52; z: -5, and thus is slightly superior to, but overlaps with, the putative visual word-form area described by Cohen et al., 2002).

2. *Findings concerning the roles of the dorsal and ventral pathways in the transition to skilled reading.* The dual-route perspective is consistent with many recent neuroimaging findings (see Jobard et al., 2003; Price, 2000 for summaries). However this account is not easily reconciled with the finding that word repetition yields similar effects (reduced activation) in OT, SMG, and IFG (parts of the ventral, dorsal, and anterior systems, respectively, in our original terminology), which differs from the effect of repetition on the more anterior ventral region MTG (increased activation) (Katz et al., 2005; Sandak et al., 2004). This is not what one would expect if learning results in both the progressive engagement of the ventral (lexical) system and a corresponding disengagement of the dorsal and anterior (sublexical) subsystems. Interpreting the reduced activation in SMG and IFG as reflecting disengagement of these systems with repetition creates a paradox if the same logic is applied to the reduced activation observed in OT, given its crucial role in skilled reading. A more plausible interpretation is that the repetition-related reduction of activation in OT is associated with an item-specific increase in processing efficiency (Poldrack and Gabrieli, 2001; Poldrack et al., 1999). Thus the associated reduction of activation in SMG and IFG with repetition is also due to increased processing efficiency (e.g., in phonological recoding) rather than disengagement.

3. *Cooperative and competitive interactions between components rather than independent "routes."* Demonstrations of interactions among the cortical subsystems

are not easily reconciled with the hypothesis that the two routes operate independently of one another. One example of such evidence concerns the interaction of imageability and regularity. Behavioral experiments by Strain et al. (1996) and Strain and Herdman (1999) reveal that the deleterious effects of irregular spelling–sound correspondences on visual word naming are attenuated when words are highly imageable, suggesting a coordination of semantics and phonology such that the semantic characteristics of a word can influence phonological assembly. In a recent fMRI study, Frost et al. 2005 observed complementary evidence: Activation in regions associated with phonological (inferior frontal gyrus) and semantic (middle temporal and angular gyri) processes interacted such that decreases in consistency-related activation in IFG for high imageability words were associated with corresponding increases in activation in MTG and AG. These findings provide evidence that skilled performance results from complementary, cooperative processing involving different components of the cortical reading system (see also Mechelli et al., 2005).

5.3 *Revising the model*

From these findings, we speculate that subregions within SMG and IFG operate in a yoked fashion to bind orthographic and phonological features of words during learning; these systems also operate in conjunction with the AG where these features are further yoked to semantic knowledge systems distributed across several cortical regions. Adequate binding, specifically adequate orthographic/phonological integration, enables the development of the presemantic OT skill zone into a functional pattern identification system. As words become better learned, this area becomes capable of efficiently activating lexico-semantic subsystems in MTG/ITG, further enabling the development of a rapid ventral word

identification system. RD individuals, with demonstrable anomalies in temporoparietal function (and associated difficulties with phonologically analytic processing on behavioral tests), fail to adequately "train" ventral subsystems (particularly the OT skill zone), and thus develop compensatory responses in frontal and RH systems.

In our original model (Pugh et al., 2000a), the ventral system was characterized as a unitary system responsible for the rapid access of word-specific information. Recent studies suggest that the ventral system includes two functionally distinct components. The posterior aspect of the ventral system (OT) is a "visual word form area" or "skill zone" that transforms visual patterns into codes that are maximally efficient for activating the phonological and semantic information associated with printed words (see also McCandliss et al., 2003). Anterior aspects of the ventral system (MTG; inferior temporal gyrus, ITG) are semantically tuned regions that bind semantic features that are widely distributed across the brain.

We continue to assume that the dorsal system (SMG in particular) is critically involved in sublexical phonological decoding, and that the anterior system (IFG in particular) is active in the recoding of print into articulatory-phonetic information. However, rather than emphasizing differences in processing speed in the various component systems (with ventral = fast and dorsal = slow), the constituents of the reading system are now distinguished primarily in terms of the types of information they process. In our developing framework, the dorsal and anterior systems, together with OT, form a closely coupled circuit specialized for extracting phonological information from written words and supporting phonologically mediated activation of semantics.

5.4 *Considering a connectionist framework*

Whereas our preliminary model assumed the dorsal and ventral systems were independent, parallel subsystems (similar to dual-route models of reading), our current view emphasizes the interdependence of these systems and the way they jointly and cooperatively achieve an efficient solution in the course of learning to read, consistent with both computational and neurobiological evidence. These assumptions are readily aligned with those made by connectionist models of reading (collectively referred to as the *triangle model*; Harm and Seidenberg, 1999, 2004; Plaut et al., 1996; Seidenberg and McClelland, 1989). To illustrate the computational principles embodied by the triangle framework, we briefly describe one implementation of the triangle model.

Harm and Seidenberg (2004) implemented a large-scale version of the triangle model that incorporated computations from both orthography to semantics (analogous to the direct, visual route to meaning; henceforth O→S) and orthography to phonology to semantics (the phonologically mediated route to meaning; henceforth O→P→S). Previous theories assumed that one or the other of these pathways would "win" the race to meaning as a function of factors such as type of word (regular, irregular), reader skill, and type of orthography (opaque, transparent). In the Harm and Seidenberg model, however, distributed representations of meaning are partially activated by input from both pathways simultaneously. Moreover, the pathways do not develop independently; the computational properties of each pathway depend on those of the other pathway. The main theoretical issue then concerns the division of labor between the components of the system, rather than which pathway wins the race. The model simulated behavioral data that have provided strong evidence for the role of phonological information in skilled reading (e.g., Van Orden et al., 1988) and showed how pressure to read rapidly and the need to disambiguate homophones (e.g., *plane–plain*) promotes development of the O→S pathway. Early in training the model relied more on O→P→S, consistent with evidence about the importance of phonological recoding in early reading (National Reading Panel, 2000). Learning also occurred

in the O→S pathway, but more slowly. In its skilled state the model relied on both pathways in reading almost all words. Moreover, it has been shown that lesioning the O→P and O→S pathways resulted in models that behaved as if they had either phonological or surface dyslexia, respectively (Plaut and Shallice, 1993; Plaut et al.,1996).

Like the triangle model, our current working model emphasizes the role of statistical learning in reading acquisition. Thus, a primary determinant of the way the brain solves the reading problem is the statistical structure of the mappings from written forms to phonology and semantics. The relative ease of the O→P mapping is central to our explanation of both reading acquisition (behavioral and neuroimaging evidence that beginning readers rely heavily on phonological decoding) and skilled reading performance (the prominent role of phonological information early in the time course of visual word recognition). Similar to the triangle model, our theory assumes that as the brain learns to read, the properties of each of the subsystems are shaped by the mappings in which it participates. For example, representations in OT capture both orthographic *and* phonological structure (Sandak et al., 2004; Xu et al., 2001), just as the hidden representations in connectionist models are shaped by their participation in different tasks (Harm and Seidenberg, 2004; Plaut and Kello, 1999).

Earlier findings from neuroimaging studies are also consistent with a connectionist approach to reading: Like the O→P→S subsystem in the triangle model, the dorsal-anterior pathway develops earlier in reading acquisition, is more strongly implicated in phonological processing, and operates less efficiently in less skilled readers (Pugh et al., 2000a; Turkeltaub et al., 2003). Like O→S in the model, the ventral system develops more slowly but is more strongly implicated in skilled performance. Empirical results (e.g., Frost et al., 2005; Katz et al., 2005; Sandak et al., 2004; described earlier) that suggest cooperative interactions between the dorsal and ventral systems are readily understood in terms of how the components of the triangle model mutually develop and jointly determine word recognition.

6 Conclusions

In this chapter, we have reviewed how our knowledge of how the brain reads words has been informed by patient lesion studies and neuroimaging studies of skilled, disabled, and developing readers. Theoretical models of reading serve to facilitate and constrain the interpretation of neurobiological evidence and to generate testable hypotheses. Conversely, the results of neurobiological studies should motivate revisions of computational theories. Moving forward, acquiring neuroimaging data with a systems-level focus will be critical if we are to begin to construct neurobiological models of skilled word identification that can speak to the complexities and dynamics of reading performance. Indeed, computational models of reading in the behavioral domain stand or fall, not by their capacity to account for main effects of isolated variables (e.g., lexicality, frequency, consistency, concreteness, and the like), but rather by whether they can seamlessly account for complex interactions among them (Harm and Seidenberg, 1999). Ultimately, the same criteria must be applied to neurobiologically grounded models as well. Thus, it is critical that we begin to look beyond simply more and more fine-tuned localization and consider also a systems-level approach. This type of research is a realistic possibility at this stage, given (a) evidence that extant neurophysiological measures are amenable to sophisticated psycholinguistic designs (Dehaene et al., 2004; Frost et al., 2005; Sandak et al., 2004), and (b) new advances in assessing functional connectivity (Hampson et al., 2002) and dynamic causal modeling (Friston et al., 2003) techniques. When we add to all this the clinically oriented goal of better understanding what differences in activation patterns between skilled and struggling readers imply about core deficits and optimal remediation, the need to develop dynamic accounts becomes all the more pressing.

References

Beauvois, M. F. & Derouesne, J. (1979). Phonological alexia: three dissociations. *Journal of Neurology, Neurosurgery and Psychiatry, 42*, 1115–24.

Black, S. E. & Behrmann, M. (1994). Localization in alexia. In Kertesz, A. (Ed.) *Localization and neuroimaging in neuropsychology*. New York: Academic Press.

Binder, J. R., Medler, D. A., Desai, R., Conant, L. L., & Liebenthal, E. (2005a). Some neurophysiological constraints on models of word naming. *Neuroimage, 27*, 677–93.

Binder, J. R., Westbury, C. F., McKiernan, K. A., Possing E. T., & Medler, D. A. (2005b). Distinct brain systems for processing concrete and abstract concepts. *Journal of Cognitive Neuroscience, 17*, 905–17.

Bookheimer, S. (2002). Functional MRI of language: New approaches to understanding the cortical organization of semantic processing. *Annual Review of Neuroscience, 25*, 151–88.

Booth, J. R., Burman, D. D., Meyer, J. R., Gitelman, D. R., Parrish, T. B., & Mesulam, M. (2004). Development of brain mechanisms for processing orthographic and phonologic representations. *Journal of Cognitive Neuroscience, 16*, 1234–49.

Booth, J. R., Burman, D. D., Van Santen, F. W., Harasaki, Y., Gitelman, D. R., Parrish, T. B., & Mesulam, M. M. (2001). The development of specialized brain systems in reading and oral-language. *Neuropsychol Dev Cogn Sect C Child Neuropsychol, 7*, 119–41.

Brunswick, N., McCrory, E., Price C., Frith, C. D., & Frith, U. (1999). Explicit and implicit processing of words and pseudowords by adult developmental dyslexics: A search for Wernicke's Wortschatz. *Brain, 122*, 1901–17.

Bruck, M. (1992). Persistence of dyslexicsÕ phonological awareness deficits. *Development Psychology, 28*, 874–86.

Castles, A. & Coltheart, M. (1993). Varieties of developmental dyslexia. *Cognition, 47*, 149–80.

Chee, M. W. L., O'Craven, K. M., Bergida, R., Rosen, B. R., & Savoy, R. L., (1999). Auditory and visual word processing studied with fMRI. *Hum. Brain Mapp, 7*, 15–28.

Coltheart, M. (1978). Lexical access in simple reading tasks. In Underwood, G. (Ed.) *Strategies of information processing* (pp. 151–216). New York: Academic Press.

Coltheart, M., Curtis, B., Atkins, P., & Haller, M. (1993). Models of reading aloud: Dual-route and parallel-distributed-processing approaches. *Psychological Review, 100,* 589–608.

Coltheart, M., Patterson, K., & Marshall, J. C. (1987). (Eds.) *Deep Dyslexia.* London: Routledge and Kegan Paul.

Cohen, L., Martinaud, O., Lemer, C., Lehericy, S., Samson, Y., & Obadia, M., et al. (2003). Visual word recognition in the left and right hemispheres: anatomical and functional correlates of peripheral alexias. *Cerebral Cortex, 13,* 1313–33.

Cohen, L., Lehericy, S., Chochon, F., Lemer, C., Rivaud, S., & Dehaene, S. (2002). Language-specific tuning of visual cortex? Functional properties of the Visual Word Form Area. *Brain, 125,* 1054–69.

Cornelissen, P. L. & Hansen, P. C. (1998). Motion detection, letter position encoding, and single word reading. *Annals of Dyslexia, 48,* 155–88.

Dehaene, S., Jobert, A., Naccache, L., Ciuciu, P., Poline, J. B., Le Bihan, D., et al. (2004). Letter binding and invariant recognition of masked words: Behavioral and neuroimaging evidence. *Psychological Science, 15,* 307–13.

Dejerine, J. (1891). Sur un cas de cecite verbale avec agraphie, suivi d'autopsie. *Memoires de la Societe Biologique, 3,* 197–201.

(1892). Contribution a l'etude anatomoclinique et clinique des differentes varietes de cecite verbal. *Compte Rendu Hebdomadaire des Seances et Memoires de la Societe de Biologie, 4,* 61–90.

Devlin, J. T., Jamison, H. L., Matthews, P. M., & Gonnerman, L. M. (2004). Morphology and the internal structure of words. *Proceedings of the National Academy of Science, 101,* 14984–8.

Eden, G. & Moats, L. (2002). The role of neuroscience in the remediation of students with dyslexia. *Nature Neuroscience supplement, 5,* 1080–4.

Fiebach, C. J., Friederici, A. D., Mueller, K., & von Cramon, D. Y. (2002). fMRI evidence for dual routes to the mental lexicon in visual word recognition. *Journal of Cognitive Neuroscience, 14,* 11–23.

Fiez, J. A., Balota, D. A., Raichle, M. E., & Petersen, S. E. (1999). Effects of lexicality, frequency, and spelling-to-sound consistency on the functional anatomy of reading. *Neuron, 24,* 205–18.

Fiez, J. A. & Peterson, S. E. (1998). Neuroimaging studies of word reading. *Proceedings of the National Academy Sciences, 95,* 914–21.

Fletcher, J., Shaywitz, S. E., Shankweiler, D. P., Katz, L., Liberman, I. Y., Stuebing, K. K., Francis, D. J., Fowler, A. E., & Shaywitz, B. A. (1994). Cognitive profiles of reading disability: Comparisons of discrepancy and low achievement definitions. *Journal of Educational Psychology, 86,* 6–23.

Friston, K. (1994). Functional and effective connectivity: A synthesis. *Human Brain Mapping, 2,* 56–78.

Friston, K. J., Harrison, L., & Penny, W. (2003). Dynamic causal modeling. *Neuroimage, 19,* 1273–1302.

Frost, S. J., Mencl, W. E., Sandak, R., Moore, D. L., Rueckl, J., Katz, L., Fulbright, R. K., & Pugh, K. R. (2005). An fMRI study of the trade-off between semantics and phonology in reading aloud. *Neuroreport, 16,* 621–4.

Galaburda, A. M. (1994). Developmental dyslexia and animal studies: At the interface between cognition and neurology. *Cognition, 50,* 133–49.

Grigorenko, E. L., Wood, F. B., Meyer, M. S., Hart, L. A., Speed, W. C., Shuster, A., & Pauls, D. L. (1997). Susceptibility loci for distinct components of developmental dyslexia on chromosomes 6 and 15. *American Journal of Human Genetics, 60,* 27–39.

Habib, M. (2000). The neurological basis of developmental dyslexia: An overview and working hypothesis. *Brain, 123,* 2372–99.

Hampson, M., Peterson, B. S., Skudlarski, P., Gatenby, J. C., & Gore, J. C. (2002). Detection of functional connectivity using temporal correlations in MR images. *Human Brain Mapping, 15,* 247–62.

Harm, M. W. & Seidenberg, M. S. (2004). Computing the meanings of words in reading: Cooperative division of labor between visual and phonological processes. *Psychological Review, 111,* 662–720.

(1999). Computing the meanings of words in reading: Cooperative division of labor between visual and phonological processes. *Psychological Review, 106,* 491–528.

Hodges, J. R., Patterson, K., Oxbury, S., & Funnell, E. (1992) Semantic dementia. *Brain, 115,* 1783–1806.

Horwitz, B., Rumsey, J. M., & Donohue, B. C. (1998). Functional connectivity of the angular gyrus in normal reading and dyslexia. *Proceedings of the National Academy Sciences, 95,* 8939–44.

Jobard, G., Crivello, F., & Tzourio-Mazoyer, N. (2003). Evaluation of the dual route theory of reading: a metanalysis of 35 neuroimaging studies. *NeuroImage, 20,* 693–712.

Katz, L., Lee, C. H., Tabor, W., Frost, S. J, Mencl, W. E., Sandak, R., Rueckl, J., & Pugh, K. R.

(2005). Behavioral and neurobiological effects of printed word repetition in lexical decision and naming. *Neuropsychologia*, *43*, 2068–83.

Kuo, W. J., Yeh, T. C., Lee, C. Y., Wu, Y. T., Chou, C. C., Ho, L. T., Hung, D. L., Tzeng, OJL, & Hsieh, J. C. (2003). Frequency effects of Chinese character processing in the brain: an event-related fMRI study. *NeuroImage*, *18*, 720–30.

Kuo, W. J., Yeh, T. C., Lee, J. R., Chen, L. F., Lee, P. L., Chen, S. S., Ho, L. T., Hung, D. L., Tzeng, OJL, & Hsieh, J. C. (2004). Orthographic and phonological processing of Chinese characters: An fMRI study. *NeuroImage*, *21*, 1721–31.

Lambon, RMA & Graham, N. L. (2000). Acquired phonological and deep dyslexia. *Neurocase*, *6*, 141–78.

Liberman, A. M. (1992). The relation of speech to reading and writing. In Frost, R. & Katz, L. (Eds.) *Orthography, phonology, morphology, and meaning*. Amsterdam: Elsevier.

Liberman, I. Y., Shankweiler, D., Fischer, W., & Carter, B. (1974). Explicit syllable and phoneme segmentation in the young child. *Journal of Child Psychology*, *18*, 201–12.

Lukatela, G. & Turvey, M. T. (1994). Visual lexical access is initially phonological: 1. Evidence from associative priming by words, homophones, and pseudohomophones. *Journal of Experimental Psychology: General*, *123*, 107–28.

Marshall, J. C. & Newcombe, F. (1973). Patterns of paralexia: A psycholinguistic approach. *Journal of Psycholinguistic Research*, *2*, 175–99.

McCandliss, B. D., Cohen, L., & Dehaene, S. (2003). The visual word form area: expertise for reading in the fusiform gyrus. *Trends in Cognitive Sciences*, *7*, 293–9.

Mechelli, A., Crinion, J. T., Long, S., Friston, K. J., Lambon Ralph, M. A., Patterson, K., McClelland, J. L., & Price, C. J. (2005). Dissociating reading processes on the basis of neuronal interactions. *Journal of Cognitive Neuroscience*, *17*, 1753–95.

Montant, M. & Behrmann, M. (2000). Pure alexia. *Neurocase*, *6*, 265– 94.

National Reading Panel (2000). Teaching children to read. Available from www.nationalreading-panel.org.

Patterson, K. E. (1982). The relation between reading and phonological coding, A.W. Ellis, Editor, *Normality and pathology on cognitive functions*, (pp. 77–112). London: Academic Press.

Patterson, K. & Hodges, J. (1992). Deterioration of word meaning: implications for reading. *Neuropsychologia*, *30*, 1025–40.

Patterson, K., Marshall, J. C., & Coltheart, M. (1985). (Eds.) *Surface Dyslexia: Cognitive and Neuropsychological Studies of Phonological Reading*. London: Lawrence Erlbaum Associates.

Paulesu, E., Demonet, J. F., Fazio, F., McCrory, E., Chanoine, V., Brunswick, N., Cappa, S. F., Cossu, G., Habib, M., Frith, C. D., & Frith, U. (2001). Dyslexia: Cultural diversity and biological unity. *Science*, *291*, 2165–7.

Perfetti, C. A. (1985). *Reading Ability*. New York: Oxford University Press.

Perfetti, C.A., Bell, L., & Delaney, S. (1988). Automatic phonetic activation in silent word reading: Evidence from backward masking. *Journal of Memory and Language*, *27*, 59–70.

Plaut, D. C., McClelland, J. L., Seidenberg, M. S., & Patterson, K. (1996). Understanding normal and impaired reading: computational principles in quasi-regular domains. *Psychological Review*, *103*, 56–105.

Plaut, D. C. & Kello, C. T. (1999). The emergence of phonology from the interplay of speech comprehension and production: A distributed connectionist approach. In MacWhinney, B. (Ed.) *The Emergence of Language* (pp. 381–415). Mahwah, NJ: Erlbaum.

Plaut, D. C. & Shallice, T. (1993). Deep dyslexia: a case study of connectionist neuropsychology. *Cognitive Neuropsychology*, *10*, 377–500.

Poldrack, R. A., & Gabrieli, JDE (2001). Characterizing the neural mechanisms of skill learning and repetition priming. Evidence from mirror-reading. *Brain: A Journal of Neurology*, *124*, 67–82.

Poldrack, R. A., Wagner, A. D., Prull, M. W., Desmond, J. E., Glover, G. H., & Gabrieli, J. D. (1999). Functional specialization for semantic and phonological processing in the left inferior prefrontal cortex. *NeuroImage*, *10*, 15–35.

Price, C. J. (2000). The anatomy of language: contributions from functional neuroimaging. *Journal of Anatomy*, *197*, 335–59.

Price, C. J., More, C. J., Humphreys, G. W., & Wise, R. J. S. (1997). Segregating semantic from phonological processes during reading. *Journal of Cognitive Neuroscience*, *9*, 727–33.

Price, C. J., Gorno-Tempini, M. L., Graham, K. S., Biggio, N., Mechelli, A., Patterson, K., & Nopenny, U. (2003a). Normal and pathological reading: converging data from lesion and imaging studies. *NeuroImage*, *20*, S30-S41.

Price, C. J., Winterburn, D., Giraud, A. L., Moore, C. J., & Noppeney, U. (2003b). Cortical localization of the visual and auditory word form areas: A reconsideration of the evidence. *Brain and Language*, 86, 272–86.

Price, C. J., Wise, R. J. S., & Frackowiak, R. S. J. (1996). Demonstrating the implicit processing of visually presented words and pseudowords. *Cerebral Cortex*, 6, 62–70.

Pugh, K. R., Mencl, W. E., Jenner, A. R., Katz, L., Frost, S. J., Lee, J. R., Shaywitz, S. E., & Shaywitz, B. A. (2000a). Functional neuroimaging studies of reading and reading disability (developmental dyslexia). *Mental Retardation & Developmental Disabilities Research Reviews*, 6, 207–13.

Pugh, K. R., Mencl, W. E., Shaywitz, B. A., Shaywitz, S. E., Fulbright, R. K., Skudlarski, P., Constable, R. T., Marchione, K., Jenner A. R., Shankweiler, D. P., Katz, L., Fletcher, J., Lacadie, C., & Gore, J. C. (2000b). The angular gyrus in developmental dyslexia: Task-specific differences in functional connectivity in posterior cortex. *Psychological Science*, 11, 51–6.

Pugh, K. R., Shaywitz, B. A., Shaywitz, S. A., Shankweiler, D. P., Katz, L., Fletcher, J. M., Skudlarski, P., Fulbright, R. K., Constable, R. T., Bronen, R. A., Lacadie, C., & Gore, J. C. (1997). Predicting reading performance from neuroimaging profiles: The cerebral basis of phonological effects in printed word identification. *Journal of Experimental Psychology: Human Perception and Performance*, 2, 1–20.

Rumsey, J. M., Horwitz B., Donohue B. C., Nace K. L., Maisog J. M., & Andreason P. A. (1999). Functional lesion in developmental dyslexia: left angular gyral blood flow predicts severity. *Brain & Language*, 70, 187–204.

Rumsey, J. M., Nace, K., Donohue, B., Wise, D., Maisog, J. M., & Andreason, P. (1997). A positron emission tomographic study of impaired word recognition and phonological processing in dyslexic men. *Archives of Neurology*, 54, 562–73.

Sabsevitz, D. S., Medler, D. A., Seidenberg, M., & Binder, J. R. (2005). Modulation of the semantic system by word imageability. *NeuroImage*, 27, 188–200.

Salmelin, R., Service, E., Kiesila, P., Uutela, K., & Salonen, O. (1996). Impaired visual word processing in dyslexia revealed with magnetoencephalography. *Annals of Neurology*, 40, 157–62.

Sandak, R., Mencl, W. E., Frost, S. J., Mason, S. A., Rueckl, J. G., Katz, L., Moore, D. L., Mason, S. A., Fulbright, R., Constable, R. T., & Pugh, K. R. (2004). The neurobiology of adaptive learning in reading: A contrast of differ-

ent training conditions. *Cognitive Affective and Behavioral Neuroscience*, 4, 67–88.

Sarkari, S., Simos, P. G., Fletcher, J. M., Castillo, E. M., Breier, J. I., & Papanicolaou, A. C. (2002). The emergence and treatment of developmental reading disability: Contributions of functional brain imaging. *Seminars in Pediatric Neurology*, 9, 227–36.

Scarborough, H. & Dobrich, W. (1990). Development of children with early language delay. *Journal of Speech and Hearing Research*, 33, 70–83.

Seidenberg, M. S. (this volume). Computational models of reading: Connectionist and dual-route approaches.

Seidenberg, M. & McClelland, J. (1989). A distributed, developmental model of word recognition and naming. *Psychological Review*, 96, 523–68.

Shallice, T., Warrington, E. K., & McCarthy, R. (1983). Reading without semantics. *Quarterly Journal of Experimental Psychology*, 35A, 111–38.

Shallice, T. & Warrington, E. K. (1980). Single and multiple component central dyslexic syndromes. In Coltheart, M., Patterson, K., & Marshall, J. C. (Eds.) *Deep Dyslexia*. London: Routledge and Kegan Paul.

Shaywitz, S. E., Shaywitz, B. A., Fulbright, R. K., Skudlarski, P., Mencl, W. E., Constable, R. T., Pugh, K. R., Holahan, J. M., Marchione, K. E., Fletcher, J. M., Lyon, G. R., & Gore, J. C. (2002). Disruption of posterior brain systems for reading in children with developmental dyslexia. *Biological Psychiatry*, 52,101–10.

Shaywitz, S. E., Shaywitz, B. A., Fulbright, R. K., Skudlarski, P., Mencl, W. E., Constable, R. T., Pugh, K. R., Holahan, J. M., Marchione, K. E., Fletcher, J. M., Lyon, G. R., & Gore, J. C. (2003). Neural systems for compensation and persistence: young adult outcome of childhood reading disability. *Biological Psychiatry*, 54, 25–33.

Shaywitz, S. E., Shaywitz, B. A., Pugh, K. R., Fulbright, R. K., Constable, R. T., Mencl, W. E., Shankweiler, D. P., Liberman, A. M., Skudlarski, P., Fletcher, J. M., Katz, L., Marchione, K. E., Lacadie, C., Gatenby, C., & Gore, J. C. (1998). Functional disruption in the organization of the brain for reading in dyslexia. *Proceedings of the National Academy of Sciences*, 95, 2636–41.

Simos, P. G., Breier, J. I., Fletcher, J. M., Foorman, B. R., Castillo, E. M., & Papanicolaou, A. C. (2002). Brain mechanisms for reading words and pseudowords: an integrated approach. *Cerebral Cortex*, 12, 297–305.

Simos, P. G., Fletcher, J. M., Bergman, E., Breier, J. I., Foorman, B. R., Castillo, E. M., Davis, R. N., Fitzgerald, M., & Papanicolaou, A. C. (2002). Dyslexia-specific brain activation profile becomes normal following successful remedial training. *Neurology*, 58, 1203–13.

Siok, W. T., Perfetti, C. A., Jin, Z., & Tan, L. H. (2004). Biological abnormality of impaired reading is constrained by culture. *Nature*, 431, 71–6.

Strain, E., Patterson, K., & Seidenberg, M. S. (1996). Semantic effects in single-word naming. *Journal of Experimental Psychology: Learning, Memory, and Cognition*, 21, 1140–54.

Strain, E. & Herdman, C. (1999). Imageability effects in word naming: An individual differences analysis. *Canadian Journal of Experimental Psychology*, 53, 347–59.

Tagamets, M. A., Novick, J. M., Chalmers, M. L., & Friedman, R. B. (2000). A parametric approach of orthographic processing in the brain: an fMRI study. *Journal of Cognitive Neuroscience*, 1, 281–97.

Tallal, P. (1980). Auditory temporal perception, phonics, and reading disabilities in children. *Brain & Language*, 9, 182–98.

Tan, L. H., Spinks, J. A., Gao, J. H., Liu, H. L., Perfetti, C. A., Xiong, J., Stofer, K. A., Pu, Y., Liu, Y., & Fox, P. T. (2000). Brain activation in the processing of Chinese characters and words: A functional MRI study. *Human Brain Mapping*, 10, 16–27.

Tarkiainen, A., Cornelissen, P. L., & Salmelin, R. (2003). Dynamics of visual feature analysis and object-level processing in face versus letter-string perception. *Brain*, 125, 1125–36.

Tarkiainen A., Helenius P., Hansen P. C., Cornelissen P.L., Salmelin R. (1999). Dynamics of letter string perception in the human occipitotemporal cortex. *Brain*, 122, 2119–32.

Temple, E., Deutsch, G. K., Poldrack, R. A., Miller, S. L., Tallal, P., Merzenich, M. M., & Gabrieli, JDE (2003). Neural deficits in children with dyslexia ameliorated by behavioral remediation: Evidence from functional MRI. *Proceedings of the National Academy of Sciences*, 100, 2860–5.

Temple, E., Poldrack, R. A., Salidis, J., Deutsch, G. K., Tallal, P., Merzenich, M. M. & Gabrieli, J. D. (2001) Disrupted neural responses to phonological and orthographic processing in dyslexic children: An fMRI study. *NeuroReport* 12, 299–307.

Turkeltaub, P. E., Gareau, L., Flowers, D. L., Zeffiro, T. A., & Eden, G. F. (2003). Development of neural mechanisms for reading. *Nature Neuroscience*, 6, 767–73.

Van Orden, G. C. (1987). A ROWS is a ROSE: Spelling, sound, and reading. *Memory and Cognition*, 10, 434–42.

Van Orden, G. C., Johnston, J. C., & Hale, B. L. (1988). Word identification in reading proceeds from the spelling to sound to meaning. *Journal of Experimental Psychology: Memory, Language and Cognition*, 14, 371–86.

Van Orden, G. C. & Kloos, H. (2003). The module mistake. *Cortex*, 39, 164–6.

Wolf, M. & Bowers, Greig, P. (1999). The double-deficit hypothesis for the developmental dyslexias. *Journal of Educational Psychology*, 91, 415–38.

Xu, B., Grafman, J., Gaillard, W. D., Ishii, K., Vega-Bermudez, F., Pietrini, P., Reeves-Tyer, P., DiCamillo, P., & Theodore, W. (2001). Conjoint and extended neural networks for the computation of speech codes: The neural basis of selective impairment in reading words and pseudowords. *Cerebral Cortex*, 11, 267–77.

Ziegler, J. C. & Goswami, U. (2005). Reading Acquisition, Developmental Dyslexia, and Skilled Reading Across Languages: A Psycholinguistic Grain Size Theory. *Psychological Bulletin*, 131, 3–29.

Section 4

SEMANTIC MEMORY

CHAPTER 12

The Human Conceptual System

Lawrence W. Barsalou

The human conceptual system contains people's knowledge about the world. Rather than containing holistic images of experience, the conceptual system represents components of experience, including knowledge about settings, objects, people, actions, events, mental states, properties, and relations. Componential knowledge in the conceptual system supports a wide variety of basic cognitive operations, including categorization, inference, the representation of propositions, and the productive creation of novel conceptualizations. In turn, these basic operations support the spectrum of complex cognitive activities, including high-level perception, attention, memory, language, thought, and socio-cultural cognition. Traditional theories of Good-Old-Fashioned Artificial Intelligence (GOFAI), such as semantic memory, constitute the dominant approach to the conceptual system. More recently, researchers have developed alternative approaches, including connectionist theories and simulation/embodied/situated theories.

1 Recording versus interpretative systems

The distinction between a recording system and an interpretive system is central to characterizing conceptual systems (e.g., Barsalou, 1999b; Dretske, 1995; Haugeland, 1991; Pylyshyn, 1973). A recording system captures information about a situation by creating attenuated (not exact) copies of it. Cameras, video recorders, and audio recorders constitute good examples of recording systems, each capturing records of experience (e.g., photos, videos, audiotapes). A recording system does not interpret what each component of a recording contains – it simply creates an attenuated copy. For example, a photo of a wedding records the light present at each point in the scene without interpreting the types of entities and events present.

Conversely, a conceptual system interprets the entities perceived in an experience or in a recording of one. To interpret a wedding, the human conceptual system might construe perceived individuals as instances of *bride, chair, cake,* and so forth.[1] To achieve interpretation, the conceptual system binds specific individuals in perception to knowledge about components of experience in memory. This is essentially the process of categorization. A system that only records perceptual experience does not categorize individuals in this manner. Instead, it simply records them in the holistic context of an undifferentiated scene.

Interpretation supports other powerful computational abilities besides categorization. Interpretation supports the production of inferences, allowing the cognitive system to go beyond perceptual input. Interpretation supports the formulation of propositions, where a proposition is a representational structure that binds a concept (type) to an individual (token) in a manner that is true or false. Interpretation is productive, supporting the construction of complex conceptual representations from simpler ones. Because the conceptual system supports these basic functions, it provides the larger cognitive system with computational abilities not possible in recording systems. Cameras and other recording devices have limited, if any, ability to implement categorization, inference, propositions, and productivity.

1.1 *Perceptual versus conceptual representations*

Because recent theories propose that category knowledge is grounded in the brain's modality-specific systems, it is useful to establish a distinction between representations that are perceptual versus those that are conceptual. Much work suggests that the brain produces mental images that are much like recordings (e.g., Kosslyn, 1980; 1994). Furthermore, perceptual experience can also be viewed as being at least

somewhat like a recording, based both on experiential qualities and also on the numerous feature areas in the brain that are mapped topographically, tonotopically, and somatotopically (e.g., Bear, Connors, and Paradiso, 2001). Although imagery and perception depart significantly from recordings in important ways (e.g., Chambers and Reisberg, 1992; Hochberg, 1998), they nevertheless appear to have image-like qualities such as orientation, extent, resolution, vividness, and so forth. Thus, the argument here is not that the brain lacks anything like recording systems. To the extent that the brain represents images in perception and imagery, it appears to utilize recording-like representations. Instead, the argument is that the brain also contains conceptual representations used to interpret image-like representations, thereby implementing powerful computational functions such as categorization, inference, propositions, and productivity.

Selective attention and memory integration are central to creating the conceptual knowledge that underlies interpretive processing (Barsalou, 1999b; 2003a). Whenever selective attention focuses consistently on some component of experience, conceptual knowledge about the component develops (cf. Schyns, Goldstone, and Thibaut, 1998). Each time the component is attended, the information extracted becomes integrated with past information about the same component in memory. When attention focuses on a green patch of color, for example, the information extracted is stored with previous memories of *green,* thereby establishing conceptual knowledge for this component. Over time, myriad components of experience accumulate memories in a similar manner, including objects, events, locations, times, introspective states, relations, roles, properties, and so forth. As conceptual knowledge about these components develops, it can be used to interpret regions of perception and imagery, as described in greater detail later. Thus, perceptual and conceptual representations work together to achieve cognitive processing.

---

1   Italics will be used to indicate concepts, and quotes will be used to indicate linguistic forms (words, sentences). Thus, *bride* indicates a concept, and "bride" indicates the corresponding word.

2 Basic operations in a conceptual system

Once a system of conceptual knowledge develops for components of experience, it supports basic conceptual operations, which in turn support more complex cognitive activities. As just described, these basic operations include categorization, inference, propositions, and productivity. Each is described in further detail here. Their roles in complex cognitive activities are addressed later.

2.1 *Categorization*

During the process of categorization, the cognitive system assigns perceived individuals in perception and imagery to units of conceptual knowledge. While perceiving a soccer match, for example, individual settings (field), people (goalie), objects (ball), actions (kick), mental states (elation), and so forth are assigned to categories. While imagining a soccer match, imagined individuals in the simulated perception can be categorized similarly.

Categorization not only occurs in vision but in all modalities of experience. Thus, auditory events can be categorized (beep), as can actions (walk), tactile sensations (soft), tastes (sweet), smells (pungent), affect (boredom), motivation (hunger), cognitive states (disbelief), and cognitive operations (comparison). Furthermore, categorization is central to processing all units of linguistic analysis, including phonemes ("ba"), verbalized words ("hello"), and written words ("exit"). In each case, a linguistic entity is categorized as an instance of a phoneme or word. Categorization is similarly central to identifying syntactic units (noun phrase) and speech acts (question). Thus, categorization is not only central to processing the meaning of language but also to processing its structure.

The semantic and structural aspects of language are aligned (Langacker, 1986). For example, categorizing nonlinguistic aspects of the world typically (but not always)

produces naming. On perceiving a robin, for example, conceptual knowledge for *robin* becomes active to categorize it. In turn, the word "robin" becomes active to name both the perceived individual and the conceptual knowledge activated, where the actual word produced is an individual instance of the word category. Even when naming is implicit (i.e., subvocal), this can be viewed as the production of a word instance, grounded in a motor and auditory simulation.

Finally, recent work suggests that mental simulations are central to linguistic processing (e.g., Glenberg et al., 2005; Spivey, Richardson, and Gonzalez-Marquez, 2005; Zwaan and Madden, 2005). To the extent that meaning is represented this way, categorizing components of mental simulations is central to linguistic processing. For example, examining a simulation and categorizing its components would be central to the process of language production. Categorizing the components of simulation activates associated words, which are produced in utterances to describe the simulation. Analogously, categorizing components of a perceived scene similarly underlies the production of an utterance to describe an actual perception. In addition, categorizing regions of a simulated or perceived scene not mentioned explicitly produces inferences (e.g., inferring *knife* from an unlabeled region of the simulation produced by the sentence, "Jeffrey cut the sandwich in half.").

2.2 *Inference*

An important theme in categorization research is that categorization is not an end itself (e.g., Markman and Ross, 2003). Simply knowing the category to which a perceived individual belongs is not particularly useful. What *is* useful are the inferential capabilities that result.

Once an individual has been assigned correctly to a category, a multitude of useful inferences follow from associated conceptual knowledge that go beyond what has been perceived thus far for the individual. Imagine perceiving and categorizing an unfamiliar individual as a *cat*. Useful inferences about the individual's structure, behavior, and internal states include that the cat has teeth and claws, that it can purr and scratch, and that it could be hungry and grateful. Useful inferences about relevant actions that the perceiver could perform follow as well, such as being cautious toward the cat, petting it, and feeding it. Many other potentially useful inferences also follow, including that the cat had a mother and father (potentially relevant for breeding purposes), that it could carry disease (relevant for health purposes), and so on. Once integrated conceptual knowledge about *cat* becomes active during categorization, a variety of associated inferences follow.

2.3 *Propositions*

Theories of psycholinguistics typically assume that propositional representations underlie the meanings of comprehended texts (e.g., Kintsch and van Dijk, 1978). Most simply, a proposition can be viewed as a type–token relation that becomes established between an individual and a concept. Thus, the process of categorization described earlier produces propositions. Categorizing an individual chicken, for example, creates a proposition that consists of the individual chicken (a token) being bound to the concept for *chicken* (a type). In text comprehension, similar type–token propositions arise as the meanings of words are combined. Hearing "Ralph is a chicken," for example, produces the proposition, *chicken (Ralph)*, where the notation used is *type (token)*. As this example illustrates, *chicken* is a predicate that takes individuals as arguments, such as *Ralph*. Other concepts take multiple arguments, in particular, verbs and prepositions. For example, the verb *eat* can take arguments for *agent, patient,* and *instrument*, as in *eat (John, soup, spoon)*. While comprehending phrases, sentences, and texts, many elemental propositions like these are constructed, which are then assembled hierarchically into larger and more complex propositional structures. Because the types in propositions are concepts, the conceptual

system plays a central role in constructing the meaning of a text.

The conceptualizations that underlie language production are similarly assumed to rely on systems of propositions. As people conceptualize what they want to describe, they categorize individuals related to the topic under discussion, which produces type–token propositions (e.g., Bock, 1987). In turn, larger propositions, constructed from conceptual predicates, result from combining simpler ones. As the propositional representation develops, concepts in it activate associated words and syntactic structures, which then surface in utterances. The conceptual system provides a fundamental link between the specific situation being described and the words used to describe it.

2.4 *Productivity*

The human cognitive system can produce an infinite number of linguistic and conceptual structures that go far beyond those experienced. No one ever experienced a real Cheshire cat, but it is easy to imagine and then describe "a cat whose body fades and reappears while its human smile remains." Similarly, it is possible to begin with the conceptualization of a familiar object and then to imagine it in nonexperienced forms, such as conceptualizing a *gray cat* and then conceptualizing it as a *purple cat* or as a *purple cat with green polka dots*.

Productivity underlies people's creative abilities to combine words and concepts into complex linguistic and conceptual structures compositionally (e.g., Fodor and Pylyshyn, 1988; also see Barsalou, 1999b; 2003a). Productivity generally appears to result from combinatorial and recursive mechanisms. Combinatorial mechanisms allow people to take a word (or concept), and then rotate other words (or concepts) through a particular relation associated with it. Beginning with the noun "cat," for example, noun phrases can be constructed combinatorially by rotating other words through a modifier relation, thereby creating "gray cat," "orange cat," "purple cat," "pink cat," and so forth. Similarly, nouns can be combinatorially rotated through the thematic roles associated a particular verb, such as rotating "cake," "pizza," and "tamale" through the patient role of "eat" (other nouns could similarly be rotated through other roles for "eat," such as "fork" and "fingers," for the instrument).

In recursion, complex conceptual and linguistic structures are nested within existing linguistic and conceptual structures. When conceptualizing a face, for example, people could first conceptualize a head. Nested within the conceptualization of the head, people could then conceptualize the eyes, then the eyeballs, then the irises, and so forth. Analogously, people can describe this embedded conceptual structure linguistically, as in "the head contains the eyes, which contain eyeballs, which contain irises, and so forth." Embedding conceptual and linguistic structures within other structures allows people to construct novel conceptualizations and verbalizations not encountered previously.

In summary, using combinatoric and recursive mechanisms, people construct an unlimited number of complex representations from finite numbers of words and concepts. This ability appears to result from a productive system for language that is closely coupled to a productive system for conceptualization. It is generally assumed that these two systems have parallel structure (e.g., Langacker, 1986). As a result, constructing linguistic expressions productively produces corresponding conceptual structures. Conversely, constructing conceptualizations productively produces corresponding linguistic descriptions.

3 The conceptual system supports the spectrum of complex cognitive activities

Researchers often assume that the conceptual system resides in the province of higher cognition along with language and thought. Conversely, researchers often assume that the conceptual system is irrelevant to lower cognitive processes such as perception and attention. As we will see, however, conceptual knowledge permeates every aspect of cognition from high to low. Without knowledge, any cognitive process would stumble into ineffectiveness. There is no such thing as a knowledge-free cognitive process. To understand cognition, it is essential to understand the conceptual system and its ubiquitous presence across the spectrum of cognitive activities.

3.1 *High-level perception*

As people interact with the environment and attempt to achieve goals, the conceptual system supports the construction of perceptions. For example, conceptual knowledge contributes to the mechanisms that separate figure from ground (e.g., Peterson and Gibson, 1994), and also to processes that fill in missing regions of incomplete perceptual experiences (e.g., Palmer, 1999; Samuel, 1997). Conceptual knowledge produces anticipation inferences about what is likely to happen next (e.g., Reed and Vinson, 1996), and also the specific forms that these anticipations take (e.g., Shiffrar and Freyd, 1993; Stevens et al., 2000). Finally, conceptual knowledge helps to predict entities and events likely to be present in the current scene, thereby speeding their categorization (e.g., Biederman, 1981; Palmer, 1975; Yeh and Barsalou, 2006).

3.2 *Selective attention*

Once a concept becomes active to construe a situation, it controls the distribution of attention across it. For example, when the concept for a spatial preposition becomes active (e.g., *above*), it directs attention to a likely region where a focal figure will appear relative to the ground below. Specifically, the ideal position is for the figure to be aligned geometrically above the center of the ground, not too far away. On hearing "the square is above the circle," for example, people generally infer that the square is center aligned above the circle, not too far away. Much work demonstrates that spatial concepts direct attention to prototypical locations in this manner (e.g., Carlson-Radvansky and Logan, 1997; Hayward and Tarr, 1995; Logan and Compton, 1996). After reading the word for a spatial location, the activated spatial concept directs attention to the most likely position in the display.

Additional research shows that inferences about function modify these attentional inferences (e.g., Carlson-Radvansky, Covey, and Lattanzi, 1999; Conventry, 1998). Consider the statement "the toothpaste tube is above the toothbrush." If spatial geometry were the only factor affecting attentional inferences, then a picture of a toothpaste tube centered geometrically over a toothbrush should be verified faster than when the two objects are not centered geometrically. Verification is fastest, however, when the toothpaste tube is positioned functionally (not geometrically) over the end of the toothbrush having the bristles. Thus, the concept *above* does not trigger a single attentional inference based on idealized geometry. Instead, the noun concepts combined with *above* during the construction of propositions jointly determine the inference.

3.3 *Episodic memory*

Besides being central to online processing of the environment, the conceptual system is central to offline processing in memory, language, and thought. In each of these complex cognitive activities, processing a nonpresent situation is often of primary importance, with perception of the current environment being suppressed to facilitate processing the imagined situation (Glenberg, Schroeder, and Robertson, 1998). Humans are much more adept at representing nonpresent situations than other species, with the control of conceptual representations via language appearing central to this ability (e.g., Donald, 1993).

The conceptual system enters into all three classic phases of memory activity: encoding, storage, and retrieval. During encoding, the conceptual system provides diverse forms of elaboration (e.g.,

Carmichael, Hogan, and Walter, 1932; Craik and Lockhart, 1972; Huttenlocher, Hedges, and Duncan, 1991). Rather than solely capturing perceptual images as does a camera or video recorder, the brain encodes images together with concepts that interpret them. As a result, the memory of a stimulus contains both perceptual and conceptual information. Once a stimulus is encoded, it becomes stored together with other memories encoded previously with similar conceptual structures. Much work shows that as the number of memories stored with a concept increases (i.e., *fan*), interference between the memories becomes more severe (e.g., Anderson, 1976; Postman and Underwood, 1973). Finally, concepts further become active during memory retrieval to produce classic reconstruction effects (e.g., Bartlett, 1932; Brewer and Treyens, 1981). Thus, concepts enter ubiquitously into all phases of memory processing.

3.4 *Language*

The semantics of natural language are closely related to the human conceptual system. Although lexical meanings are not identical to concepts, the two have much in common and influence each other extensively (e.g., Barsalou et al., 1993; Marslen-Wilson, 1992; Schwanenflugel, 1991). The access of word meaning can be viewed as an inferential process. On perceiving a word such as "bird," retrieving semantic information constitutes inferences about the word's meaning. American readers are more likely, for example, to infer that "bird" means something having the properties of *small*, *flies*, and *sings*, rather than something having the properties of *large*, *runs*, and *squawks*. Typically, these meanings are highly context dependent, reflecting both the surrounding text and the pragmatics of the communicative situation (e.g., Barsalou, 1999a; Yeh and Barsalou, 2006).

As the meanings of words become combined during the construction of propositions, background conceptual knowledge is used extensively. In particular, knowledge of conceptual relations is often central to integrating word meanings (e.g., Gagné and Shoben, 1997; Wisniewski, 1997). For example, integrating the meanings of *lake* and *trout* to understand "lake trout" requires activating knowledge about the relation *LOCATION (X, Y)*, whereas integrating the meanings of *swinging* and *vine* to understand "swinging vine" requires activating knowledge about the relation *MOTION (X, Y)*.

Inference production beyond individual words is a well-established aspect of language comprehension (e.g., Bransford and Johnson, 1973; Schank and Abelson, 1977). As people comprehend a text, they infer considerable amounts of background knowledge not stated explicitly. For example, comprehenders infer a variety of thematic roles, such as hearing "Mary pounded a nail into the wall" and inferring that a hammer was used (e.g., McRae, Spivey-Knowlton, and Tanenhaus, 1998). Similarly, when people hear the sentence "The surgeon put on gloves before beginning the operation," they are surprised when the next sentence begins "She was tired from the previous operation," because they make default gender inferences (e.g., Carreiras et al., 1996). In general, the more deeply people comprehend a text, the richer the inferences they produce, not only about thematic roles but about explanations and a wide variety of other conceptual structures (e.g., Graesser, Singer, and Trabasso, 1994). Researchers typically assume that these rich comprehension inferences arise via the conceptual system as relevant conceptual knowledge becomes active.

3.5 *Thought*

Thought requires extensive use of conceptual representations. As people perform decision making, reasoning, and problem solving, conceptual representations become activated as the objects of thought. During decision making, the choice objects under consideration are represented conceptually (e.g., Markman and Medin, 2002). As possible choice objects are evaluated, features, relations, values, and diverse forms of background knowledge are retrieved and incorporated into the decision making process. Loken, Barsalou, and Joiner (2008) document a wide variety of roles that conceptual processes play in consumer decision making.

The conceptual system is also central to reasoning. While performing deductive reasoning, people do not simply manipulate abstract logical expressions. Instead, they appear to manipulate conceptual representations about the reasoning domain, thereby exhibiting widespread content effects (e.g., Cheng and Holyoak, 1985; Johnson-Laird, 1983). Conceptual representations are also central to inductive reasoning, especially when it concerns categories (e.g., Medin et al., 2003). Finally, conceptual representations are central to causal reasoning across a wide variety of domains, including clinical diagnosis (e.g., Kim and Ahn, 2002) and artifact function (e.g., Barsalou, Sloman, and Chaigneau, 2005).

Problem solving also relies extensively on conceptual processes. Similar to reasoning, widespread effects of domain-specific knowledge occur (e.g., Newell and Simon, 1972). The same abstract problem can be difficult to solve when grounded in one domain but easy when grounded in another, depending on the availability of relevant knowledge. Ross (1996) argues further that knowing how to use artifacts for solving problems constitutes a significant aspect of category knowledge. Rather than simply containing physical features that identify category members, a category representation contains extensive knowledge about how to use its exemplars for achieving goals (also see Barsalou, 1991).

3.6 *Social and cultural cognition*

The conceptual system plays extensive roles in social cognition (e.g., Fiske and Taylor, 1991; Kunda, 1999). During social interaction, people use social knowledge to categorize perceived individuals into social groups. Stereotypes for these groups can be viewed as conceptual representations that have been distorted by various sources of background knowledge. Once a perceived individual has been assigned to a social category, rich inferences (attributions) result about the causes of the person's behavior, their mental state, and likely actions. Self-concepts constitute another central form of conceptual knowledge in the social domain.

Although the basis of a culture can be localized in its artifacts, activities, organizations, and institutions to a considerable extent, it can also be localized in conceptual knowledge of these external entities (e.g., Shore, 1996). Cultural transmission can be viewed, in part, as the propagation of conceptual knowledge from generation to generation, along with the transmission of other things, such as skills. Much recent work illustrates that different conceptual knowledge produces major cognitive and behavioral differences among cultures (e.g., Atran, Medin, and Ross, 2005).

4 Theories of the conceptual system

Three approaches to theorizing about the conceptual system enjoy varying degrees of acceptance in psychology, cognitive science, and cognitive neuroscience. The most traditional theories, and perhaps still the most dominant, originated in what Haugeland (1985) dubbed "GOFAI" for Good Old Fashioned Artificial Intelligence. In particular, the theory of semantic memory constitutes perhaps the best known and most widely accepted view of the conceptual system. Connectionist theories constitute a second major class of theories. This approach reflects an increasing appreciation of neural mechanisms and statistical processing, both relatively absent in GOFAI theories. Simulation, embodied, and situated theories constitute the most recent class. While incorporating neural and statistical mechanisms, they further emphasize the brain's modality-specific systems, the body, and the environment.

Each of these three approaches is described next. Within each approach, a wide variety of models exists, and an even wider variety is possible. A relatively generic description of each approach will serve to illustrate it.

4.1 *GOFAI theories*

GOFAI theories of the conceptual system originated in artificial intelligence during the cognitive revolution (e.g., Haugeland, 1985). To represent knowledge in computers, artificial intelligence researchers developed new representation languages based on predicate calculus (e.g., Charniak and McDermott, 1985; Newell and Simon, 1972). Typically, these representation languages included predicates to represent conceptual relations, arguments that become bound to values, and recursive nesting that embeds predicates within predicates (e.g., Barsalou, 1992). Reflecting the goals of knowledge engineering, the GOFAI representation of a concept typically contains an extensive amount of information, such that a given concept contains many propositions. If a computer is to have sufficient knowledge for understanding language, answering questions, and solving problems, its knowledge must be extensive.

In contrast, psychological versions of GOFAI theories are typically much sparser, reflecting the goal of testing psychological models in a controlled and rigorous manner. Thus, psychological versions likely considerably underestimate the complexity of naturally occurring conceptual representations (e.g., Barsalou and Hale, 1993). Two general subclasses of the GOFAI approach have dominated theories of the conceptual system and continue to do so: semantic memory and exemplar models. The semantic memory view, in particular, continues to constitute the primary way that researchers in many communities think about the conceptual system. Researchers across psychology, cognitive science, and cognitive neuroscience implicitly adopt the semantic memory framework when they must address knowledge in their respective research areas. Semantic memory and exemplar models are each addressed in turn.

4.1.1 SEMANTIC MEMORY

The construct of semantic memory arose from a proposed distinction between semantic and episodic memory (Tulving, 1972). Specific examples include the network models of Collins and Quillian (1969), Collins and Loftus (1975), and Glass and Holyoak (1975). As Hollan (1975) notes, prototype and other feature set models (e.g., Reed, 1972; Rosch and Mervis, 1975) are roughly equivalent to their network counterparts, together forming a more general class of semantic memory models. Thus, semantic network, feature list, and prototype models will be subsumed here under the larger rubric of semantic memory. For further review of these models, see Smith (1978).

Following Tulving's classic proposal, semantic memory is widely viewed as modular, that is, as an autonomous system separate from the episodic memory system. Less explicitly, but equally true, semantic memory is also viewed widely as separate from the brain's modality-specific systems. It is generally assumed that semantic memory does not share representation and processing mechanisms with perception, action, and interoception,[2] but is instead a relatively independent system with its own principles of representation and processing.

One of these distinguishing principles is representational format, namely, representations in semantic memory are widely viewed as amodal. Rather than being representations in modality-specific systems, semantic memory representations are typically viewed as *redescriptions* of modality-specific states in an amodal representation language, namely, one that lacks modality-specific qualities. For example, the conceptual representation of the visual property *red* is an amodal symbol that stands for perceptual states of *red* in the visual system and their physical counterparts in the world. In general, amodal representations in semantic memory stand for representations in the modalities and for the environmental entities they represent.

Representations in semantic memory are also generally assumed to be relatively abstract and decontextualized. In the typical theory, the representation of a category is a prototype or rule that distills relatively invariant properties from exemplars. Lost in the distillation are idiosyncratic properties of exemplars and background situations. Thus the representation of *chair* might be a decontextualized prototype that includes *seat, back,* and *legs,* with idiosyncratic properties and background situations filtered out. Although functional properties may be extracted and stored, they typically tend to be decontextualized invariants, not detailed information about specific situations. The resulting representations have the flavor of detached encyclopedia descriptions in a database of categorical knowledge about the world.

Similar to being decontextualized, semantic memory representations are typically viewed as relatively stable. For a given category, these theories assume that different people share roughly the same representation, and that the same person uses the same representation on different occasions.

Finally, semantic memory models excel in implementing the basic operations of propositions and productivity described earlier. Because the representations in these models typically include predicates whose arguments become bound to values, with the potential for predicates to embed recursively, they naturally implement propositions and productivity. Although semantic memory models can implement categorization and inference using prototypes and definitions, they have been widely criticized as being too abstract and rigid in how they perform these basic operations. Typically, semantic memory models are not sensitive to the details of exemplars and situations and do not contain adaptive mechanisms that implement learning.

4.1.2 EXEMPLAR MODELS

Since Medin and Schaffer's (1978) context model, exemplar models have provided

---

2 *Interoception* here will refer to the perception of internal states, namely, states of motivation, emotion, and cognition that are accessible to consciousness.

a strong competitor to semantic memory models. Many important variants of the basic exemplar model have been developed, including Nosofsky (1984), Heit (1998), and Lamberts (1998). Exemplar models are included within the broader class of GOFAI models because they tend to use standard symbolic notation for expressing the properties of exemplars, unlike connectionist theories and simulation/embodied/situated theories, which use statistical and neural representation languages.

Architecturally, exemplar models tend to be modular in that exemplar knowledge is again assumed implicitly to reside in memory stores outside the brain's modality-specific systems. Similar to semantic memory models, redescriptions in an amodal representation language typically capture the content of exemplar memories, standing in for the modality-specific states experienced originally.

Notably, however, some exemplar models view exemplar representations as implicit memories in modality-specific systems (e.g., Brooks, 1978; Jacoby and Brooks, 1984; cf. Roediger and McDermott, 1993). According to this approach, for example, an exemplar for a visual category is stored as a visual memory in the visual system, not as an amodal description outside it. Exemplar models that store exemplars in modality-specific systems can be construed as nonmodular, given that common representations underlie both conceptual and modality-specific processing.

Where exemplar models differ most from semantic memory models is on abstraction and decontextualization. Whereas semantic memory models distill properties across exemplars and store them as abstractions (e.g., prototypes and rules), exemplar models simply store exemplar memories, thereby capturing idiosyncratic information about category instances along with details about the situations in which they occur.

Perhaps counterintuitively, exemplar models tend to assume that category representations are relatively stable, much like semantic memory models. Stability exists in most exemplar models because they tend to assume that all exemplar memories for a category are accessed every time the category is processed. Although an exemplar set can be very large, its constant application across different occasions is relatively stable, with all exemplars being applied. Exemplar models that sample small subsets of exemplars, on the other hand, are dynamic (e.g., Barsalou, Huttenlocher, and Lamberts, 1999; Nosofsky and Palmeri, 1997).

Where exemplar models excel is in categorization. Because extensive detail about a category is stored – both in terms of idiosyncratic exemplar properties and background situations – these models are highly accurate during categorization and can adapt quickly to changing category information. Although exemplar models have not been developed to explain inference, they can in principle produce highly accurate inferences following categorization, again because of the large amounts of information stored and the context-specificity of retrieval processes that operate on it. Where exemplar models are weakest is on symbolic operations. Thus far, this approach has not attempted to implement predicates, arguments, and recursion, and therefore does not implement the basic operations of propositions and productivity.

4.2 Connectionist theories

Feedforward connectionist networks constitute a relatively recent but increasingly influential theory of the conceptual system. For general accounts of feedforward nets, see Rumelhart, Hinton, and Williams (1986) and Bechtel and Abrahamsen (2002). For specific applications of the feedforward architecture to representing conceptual knowledge, see Hinton (1989), Kruschke (1992), Rumelhart and Todd (1993), Tyler et al., (2000), and Rogers and McClelland (2004). A variety of other connectionist architectures have also been used to model the conceptual system, which are not addressed here (e.g., Cree, McRae, and McNorgan, 1999; Farah and McClelland, 1991; Humphreys and Forde, 2001; McClelland and Rumelhart, 1985; Rumelhart et al., 1986).

Perhaps surprisingly, feedforward nets, like GOFAI theories, implement a modular conceptual system. Whereas the input layer of a feedforward net is interpreted as a perceptual system, its hidden layer is viewed as implementing conceptual representations. Thus one "module" of units underlies perception, and a second module underlies conception, thereby establishing a modular distinction between them. Because complex interactions can arise between these two systems, they are not modular in the sense of being impenetrable (cf. Fodor, 1983; Pylyshyn, 1984). Nevertheless different representational systems underlie perception and cognition, such that modularity exists in a somewhat nonstandard sense. As will be seen shortly, it is possible to formulate a conceptual system in which shared neural units represent information in perception and conception. It is also worth noting that some of the alternative connectionist architectures mentioned earlier operate in this latter manner. Thus, modularity only applies to connectionist nets that have feedforward architectures, along with other architectures that use separate pools of units for perception and conception.

Because of this modular architecture, internal representations in feedforward nets are amodal. Before learning begins, connections between the input and hidden layers are set initially to small random values so that learning is possible. As a result, the particular units in the hidden layer that become positively (or negatively) associated with particular units in the input layer are determined arbitrarily. The surprising implication is that statistical patterns on the hidden units associated with particular categories function as "fuzzy" amodal symbols, standing in for their perceptual counterparts. With each new set of random starting weights, a different mapping develops.[3] The arbitrariness that results is much in the spirit of semantic memory representations. In both approaches,

modality-specific and conceptual representations reside in different modular systems, with arbitrary mappings between them. No doubt, other significant aspects of the representations differ, with connectionist representations being statistical, and semantic memory representations being discrete. Nevertheless both approaches contain amodal redescriptions of perceptual input at a general level of analysis.

Where feedforward nets depart most notably from semantic memory models is on abstraction and stability (similar to exemplar models). Rather than establishing decontextualized representations of categories, feedforward nets store situated representations in two ways. First, these nets acquire much idiosyncratic information about exemplars (as in exemplar models), rather than discarding this information during the abstraction of category invariants. Although invariants may be abstracted implicitly, much idiosyncratic information is maintained that plays central roles in processing. Second, feedforward nets store extensive information about the situations in which exemplars occur. Rather than extracting focal knowledge of a particular category instance from a background situation, much correlated information about the situation is stored as well (e.g., Rumelhart et al., 1986). As a consequence, activating an exemplar typically retrieves situational information and vice versa.

Feedforward nets are also highly dynamic. Rather than representing a category with a stable representation, as in semantic memory and exemplar models, a feedforward net uses a space of representations. Specifically, a category's representation is an attractor within the possible activation states of the hidden units, with an infinitely many states around the attractor providing possible representations. On a given occasion, the representation activated to represent the category is a function of the network's current state, input, and learning history. Thus a concept in a feedforward net is a dynamic system that produces a family of representational states, depending on current conditions.

Like exemplar models, feedforward nets excel in categorization and inference.

3   It is worth noting that invariants exist across the different mappings. Regardless, each mapping is a redescription of the input in a separate modular system.

Because extensive detail about a category is stored – both in terms of idiosyncratic exemplar properties and background situations – feedforward nets are highly accurate during categorization, and can adapt quickly to changing category information. For the same reason, feedforward nets produce highly accurate inferences following categorization. Where connectionist models are weakest (like exemplar models) is on symbolic operations (Fodor and Pylyshyn, 1988). Although some attempts have been made to implement predicates, arguments, and recursion (e.g., Pollack, 1990; Smolensky, 1990), these approaches have not been widely accepted as plausible psychological or neural accounts of the conceptual system. So far, connectionism has not succeeded in convincing the cognitive psychology, cognitive science, and cognitive neuroscience communities that this approach explains the basic conceptual operations of propositions and productivity.

4.3 Simulation, embodiment, and situated theories

Recent theories have focused on the roles of modality-specific simulation, embodiment, and situations in conceptual processing. Damasio (1989), Martin (2001), Barsalou (1999b; 2003a), and Simmons and Barsalou (2003) focus on modality-specific simulation. Glenberg (1997) and Barsalou et al. (2003) focus on embodiment. Barsalou (1999a; 2003b; 2005) and Barsalou, Niedenthal et al. (2003) focus on situations. Although these approaches differ somewhat in emphasis, they all assume that the conceptual system specifically and cognition in general are grounded in the brain's modality-specific systems, in the body, and in the environment. According to these approaches, the cognitive system is not self-sufficient but depends in important ways on its groundings. Indeed, these approaches assume that grounding mechanisms are central parts of the cognitive system, not merely a peripheral interface. For a recent collection of papers on this approach, see Pecher and Zwaan (2005). Much additional work in

cognitive linguistics adopts similar views (e.g., Fauconnier, 1985; Lakoff and Johnson, 1980, 1999; Langacker, 1986; Talmy, 1983), but have not yet typically drawn strong connections to cognitive and neural mechanisms (although see Gallese and Lakoff, 2005).

All of these approaches assume that the conceptual system is nonmodular. Rather than having separate systems for modality-specific and conceptual processing, a common representational system is assumed to underlie both. According to this view, conceptual processing relies heavily on modality-specific simulations to represent categories (for more detail on the simulation process, see Barsalou, 1999b; 2003a).

A consequence of this nonmodular architecture is that conceptual representations are modal, not amodal. The same types of representations underlie perception and conception. When the conceptual system represents an object's visual properties, it uses representations in the visual system; when it represents the actions performed on an object, it uses motor representations. Depending on the distribution of modalities on which people experience a category, a particular distribution of modality-specific information becomes established for it (e.g., vision and taste for *fruit* versus vision and action for *tools*; Cree and McRae, 2003).

Although perception and conception are similar in this framework, they are not identical. Whereas bottom-up mechanisms dominate the activation of modality-specific systems during perception, top-down mechanisms dominate during conception. Furthermore, the representations activated in conception are *partial* reenactments of modality-specific states, and may often exhibit bias and reconstructive error. Nevertheless, perception and conception are far from being modular autonomous systems.

The claim is not that modal reenactments constitute the sole form of conceptual representation. As Simmons and Barsalou (2003) suggest, representations in the brain's association areas also play a role, perhaps somewhat analogous to the hidden unit representations in connectionist nets. This is consistent with the widespread finding that other factors influence conceptual processing besides the modalities (e.g., statistical strength, correlation, and uniqueness; Cree and McRae, 2003; Tyler et al., 2000). Thus, the claim is simply that modal simulations are one important and widely utilized form of representation during conceptual processing.

Regarding abstraction and stability, this approach assumes that conceptual representations are dynamic and situated. Rather than being a single abstracted representation for a category, a concept is a skill for constructing idiosyncratic representations tailored to the current needs of situated action (Barsalou, 2003b). Actually, Barsalou, et al. (2003) advocate discarding the use of *concept* altogether and replacing it with accounts of the specific mechanisms that represent categories. In this spirit, Barsalou (1999b; 2003a) proposes the construct of a *simulator* as a distributed neural mechanism that constructs an infinite set of specific simulations to represent a category, property, or relation dynamically. Thus, the simulator for *chair* can construct many simulations of different chairs, from different perspectives, used for different purposes, reflecting the agent's current goal and situation.

A given simulation is assumed to represent more than the focal category of interest. Additional information about background settings, goal-directed actions, and introspective states is also assumed to be included, making simulations situated (e.g., Barsalou, 1999a, 2003b, 2005; Barsalou, Niedenthal, et al., 2003). On a given occasion, a specific simulation is tailored to the computational and pragmatic demands of the current situation. Thus, the conceptual system is dynamic and situated, similar to feedforward nets, but with modal representations instead of amodal ones.

A related theme is that the conceptual system is organized around situated action (cf. Glenberg, 1997). A fundamental problem in situated action is mapping action effectively into the world, and one possibility is that the conceptual system develops to facilitate this process. According to Barsalou (1991; 2003b), ad hoc and goal-derived categories develop to bind roles in action schemata with their instantiations in the environment. As systems of these mappings develop, the conceptual system becomes organized around the action–environment interface.

4.3.1 COMMON MISCONCEPTIONS

Three common misconceptions arise frequently about simulation/embodied/situated views. One is that they are purely empiricist with no nativist contributions. Although extreme empiricist views are possible and sometimes taken, there is no a priori reason why strong genetic constraints could not underlie a system that relies heavily on simulation, embodiment, and situatedness. For example, specific simulations could in principle be determined genetically. More plausibly, however, strong genetic constraints may exist on the mechanisms that capture and implement simulations. In this spirit, Simmons and Barsalou (2003) propose that the association and feature areas underlying simulations reflect constraints on categories that developed over the course of evolution (also see Caramazza and Shelton, 1998).

A second common misconception about simulation/embodied/situated approaches is that they necessarily implement recording systems and cannot implement conceptual systems for interpreting the world. As Barsalou (1999b; 2003a) proposes, however, modality-specific systems can implement basic conceptual operations, such as categorization, inference, propositions, and productivity. The essential idea is that selective attention extracts information about the components of experience to establish simulators for these components. Once these simulators exist for object, events, mental states, relations, properties, and so forth, the argument is that they naturally implement basic conceptual operations.

A third common misconception is that abstract concepts cannot be represented in simulation/embodied/situated approaches. Various researchers, however, have argued that mechanisms within this approach are capable of representing these concepts.

For example, Lakoff and Johnson (1980; 1999) propose that abstract concepts are grounded metaphorically in concrete concepts (but see Murphy, 1996 for a critique). Alternatively, Barsalou (1999b) and Barsalou and Wiemer-Hastings (2005) propose that abstract concepts are grounded in situated simulations, just like concrete concepts, but focus on different situational content, especially on interoceptions and events.

4.3.2 COMPUTATIONAL IMPLEMENTATION

One major limitation of the simulation/embodied/situated approach to date is the relative lack of computational frameworks for implementing it. Increasingly, however, implementations are being developed. For example, Cangelosi and his colleagues have recently begun implementing the grounding mechanisms in simulation/embodied/situated theories (e.g., Cangelosi, Greco, and Harnad, 2000; Cangelosi et al., 2005; Cangelosi and Riga, 2005; Joyce et al., 2003). Also, the top-down mechanisms in O'Reilly's neural net architectures have significant potential for implementing simulations (e.g., O'Reilly, 1998, 2006). Other recent attempts to ground computational accounts of cognition in modality-specific processing include Roy (2005) and Clark and Mendez (2005). Acceptance of the simulation/embodied/situated approach clearly depends on increasing formalization, but there appears to be no a priori reason why formalization is not possible. Given the relative recency of this approach, together with the complexity of the mechanisms that must be implemented, it is not surprising that mature formal accounts do not yet exist (for discussion of these complexities, see Barsalou, 1999b, pp. 651–2). Of interest will be whether viable computational accounts can be constructed in the coming years.

4.3.3 RELATIONS BETWEEN LANGUAGE AND SIMULATION

Finally, several lines of research propose that the linguistic system is closely coupled with the simulation system. As mentioned earlier, a central tenet of Langacker's (1986) approach to cognitive linguistics rests on this assumption, namely, the linguistic system serves as an instrument for controlling the conceptual system.

Increasing empirical research suggests that both the linguistic and conceptual systems are active as people perform conceptual tasks (see Glaser, 1992 for a provocative review). Depending on task materials (e.g., words versus pictures) and task conditions (e.g., superficial versus deep processing), conceptual processing relies on varying mixtures of the linguistic and conceptual systems. Further evidence for this view comes from Solomon and Barsalou (2004) and Kan et al., (2003). In these experiments, subjects used different mixtures of linguistic processing and simulation while verifying the conceptual properties of objects under different task conditions. Barsalou et al., (2005) offer further behavioral and neural evidence that conceptual processing utilizes varying mixtures of linguistic processing and simulation.

5 Conclusion

As reviewed here, three basic accounts of the conceptual system exist in modern cognitive psychology, cognitive science, and cognitive neuroscience: (1) classic GOFAI approaches, such as semantic memory and exemplar models, that utilize amodal symbols in a modular conceptual system; (2) statistical approaches, such as connectionism and neural nets, that implement dynamic and situated conceptual representations; (3) simulation/embodied/situated approaches that ground conceptual knowledge in modality-specific systems, in the body, and in the environment.

Claiming that significant value exists in all three approaches might seem unduly diplomatic. To the contrary, however, each of these approaches has discovered something fundamentally important about the human conceptual system. Classic GOFAI approaches have established the importance of propositional representations and productivity in conceptual processing.

Statistical approaches have highlighted the importance of adaptation, generalization, partial matching, frequency effects, and pattern completion. Simulation/embodied/situated approaches have drawn attention to the importance of grounding knowledge in the brain's modality-specific systems, in the body, and in the environment.

Barsalou (1999b) ends with the following conjecture: Successful theories in the future are likely to integrate all three frameworks into a single system (p. 652). It is unlikely that theories implementing only one or even two of these approaches will succeed. What each approach offers appears essential to the human conceptual system.

It is probably fair to say that GOFAI and connectionist theories have generally attempted to incorporate only one, or occasionally two, of these approaches. In contrast, simulation/embodied/situated views have typically attempted to incorporate two and sometimes three approaches, not only emphasizing grounding, but also emphasizing statistical processing and symbolic operations. Again, however, we have yet to see fully developed computational accounts that integrate all three approaches. Nevertheless, this seems like a potentially productive direction for theory development, and it will be interesting to see what form theories of the conceptual system take in coming years.

References

Anderson, J. R. (1976). *Language, memory, and thought*. Hillsdale, NJ: Lawrence Erlbaum Associates.

Atran, S., Medin, D. L., & Ross, N. O. (2005). The cultural mind: Environmental decision making and cultural modeling within and across populations. *Psychological Review, 112*, 744–76.

Barsalou, L. W. (1991). Deriving categories to achieve goals. In Bower, G. H. (Ed.) *The psychology of learning and motivation: Advances in research and theory* (Vol. 27, pp. 1–64). San Diego, CA: Academic Press.

(1992). Frames, concepts, and conceptual fields. In Lehrer, A. & Kittay, E. F. (Eds.) *Frames, fields, and contrasts: New essays in lexical and semantic organization* (pp. 21–74). Hillsdale, NJ: Lawrence Erlbaum Associates.

(1999a). Language comprehension: Archival memory or preparation for situated action. *Discourse Processes, 28*, 61–80.

(1999b). Perceptual symbol systems. *Behavioral and Brain Sciences, 22*, 577–660.

(2003a). Abstraction in perceptual symbol systems. *Philosophical Transactions of the Royal Society of London: Biological Sciences, 358*, 1177–87.

(2003b). Situated simulation in the human conceptual system. *Language and Cognitive Processes, 18*, 513–62.

(2005). Continuity of the conceptual system across species. *Trends in Cognitive Sciences, 9*, 309–11.

Barsalou, L. W. & Hale, C. R. (1993). Components of conceptual representation: From feature lists to recursive frames. In Van Mechelen, I., Hampton, J., Michalski, R., & Theuns, P. (Eds.) *Categories and concepts: Theoretical views and inductive data analysis* (pp. 97–144). San Diego, CA: Academic Press.

Barsalou, L. W., Huttenlocher, J., & Lamberts, K. (1998). Basing categorization on individuals and events. *Cognitive Psychology, 36*, 203–72.

Barsalou, L. W., Niedenthal, P. M., Barbey, A., & Ruppert, J. (2003). Social embodiment. In Ross, B. (Ed.) *The Psychology of Learning and Motivation* (Vol. 43, pp. 43–92). San Diego: Academic Press.

Barsalou, L. W., Sloman, S. A, & Chaigneau, S. E. (2005). The HIPE theory of function. In Carlson, L. & van der Zee, E. (Eds.) *Representing functional features for language and space: Insights from perception, categorization and development* (pp. 131–47). Oxford: Oxford University Press.

Barsalou, L. W., Simmons, W. K., Barbey, A. K., & Wilson, C. D. (2003). Grounding conceptual knowledge in modality-specific systems. *Trends in Cognitive Sciences, 7*, 84–91.

Barsalou, L. W., Simmons, W. K., Santos, A., Hamann, S. B., & Harenski, C. L. (2005). Word association and situated simulation in conceptual processing. Manuscript in preparation.

Barsalou, L. W. & Wiemer-Hastings, K. (2005). Situating abstract concepts. In Pecher, D. & Zwaan, R. (Eds.) *Grounding cognition: The role of perception and action in memory, language, and thought* (pp. 129–63). New York: Cambridge University Press.

Barsalou, L. W., Yeh, W., Luka, B. J., Olseth, K. L., Mix, K. S., & Wu, L. (1993). Concepts and meaning. In Beals, K., Cooke, G., Kathman, D., McCullough, K. E., Kita, S., & Testen, D. (Eds.) *Chicago Linguistics Society 29: Papers from the parasession on conceptual representations* (pp. 23–61). University of Chicago: Chicago Linguistics Society.

Bartlett, F. C. (1932). *Remembering: A study in experimental and social psychology.* New York: Cambridge University Press.

Bechtel, W. & Abrahamsen, A. (2002). *Connectionism and the Mind: Parallel processing, dynamics, and evolution in networks.* Cambridge, MA: Basil Blackwell.

Bear, M. F., Connors, B. W., & Paradiso, M. A. (2001). *Neuroscience: Exploring the brain* (2nd ed.). Baltimore: Williams & Wilkins.

Biederman, I. (1981). On the semantics of a glance at a scene. In Kubovy, M. & Pomerantz, J. R. (Eds.) *Perceptual organization* (pp. 213–53). Hillsdale, NJ: Lawrence Erlbaum Associates.

Bock, J. K. (1987). Co-ordinating words and syntax in speech plans. In Ellis, A. W. (Ed.) *Progress in the psychology of language* (Vol. 3, pp. 337–90). Hillsdale, NJ: Lawrence Erlbaum Associates.

Bransford, J. D. & Johnson, M. K. (1973). Considerations of some problems of comprehension. In Chase, W. G. (Ed.) *Visual information processing.* New York: Academic Press.

Brewer, W. F. & Treyens, J. C. (1981). Role of schemata in memory for places. *Cognitive Psychology, 13,* 207–30.

Brooks, L. R. (1978). Nonanalytic concept formation and memory for instances. In Rosch, E. & Lloyd, B. B. (Eds.) *Cognition and categorization* (pp. 169–211). Hillsdale, NJ: Lawrence Erlbaum Associates.

Caramazza, A. & Shelton, J. R. (1998). Domain-specific knowledge systems in the brain: The animate-inanimate distinction. *Journal of Cognitive Neuroscience, 10,* 1–34.

Carlson-Radvansky, L. A., Covey, E. S., & Lattanzi, K. M. (1999). "What" effects on "where": Functional influences on spatial relations. *Psychological Science, 10,* 516–21.

Carlson-Radvansky, L. A. & Logan, G. D. (1997). The influence of reference frame selection on spatial template construction. *Journal of Memory and Language, 37,* 411–37.

Carmichael, L., Hogan, H. P., & Walter, A. A. (1932). An experimental study of language on the reproduction of visually perceived form. *Journal of Experimental Psychology, 15,* 73–86.

Cangelosi, A., Greco, A., & Harnad, S. (2000). From robotic toil to symbolic theft: Grounding transfer from entry-level to higher-level categories. *Connection Science, 12,* 143–62.

Cangelosi, A., Coventry, K., Rajapakse, R., Joyce, D., Bacon, A., Richards, L., & Newstead, S. (2005). Grounding language in perception: A connectionist model of spatial terms and vague quantifiers. In Cangelosi, A., Bugmann, G., & Borisyuk, R. (Eds.) *Modeling language, cognition and action: Proceedings of the 9th Neural Computation and Psychology Workshop* (pp. 47–56). Singapore: World Scientific.

Cangelosi, A. & Riga, T. (2005). An epigenetic robotic model for sensorimotor grounding and grounding transfer. Under review.

Carreiras, M., Garnham, A., Oakhill, J. V., & Cain, K. (1996). The use of stereotypical gender information in constructing a mental model: Evidence from English and Spanish. *Quarterly Journal of Experimental Psychology, 49A,* 639–63.

Chambers, D. & Reisberg, D. (1992). What an image depicts depends on what an image means. *Cognitive Psychology, 24,* 145–74.

Charniak, E. & McDermott, D. (1985). *Introduction to artificial intelligence.* Reading, MA: Addison-Wesley.

Cheng, P. W. & Holyoak, K. J. (1985). Pragmatic reasoning schemas. *Cognitive Psychology, 17,* 391–416.

Clark, D. G. & Mendez, M. F. (2005). Topographic dissociation of "concepts" in a self-organizing neural network. Under review.

Collins, A. M. & Loftus, E. F. (1975). A spreading activation theory of semantic processing. *Psychological Review, 82,* 407–28.

Collins, A. M. & Quillian, M. R. (1969). Retrieval time from semantic memory. *Journal of Verbal Learning and Verbal Behavior, 8,* 240–8.

Coventry, K. R. (1998). Spatial prepositions, functional relations, and lexical specification. In Oliver, P. & Gapp, K. P. (Eds.) *Representation and processing of spatial expressions* (pp. 247–62). Mahwah, NJ: Erlbaum.

Craik, F. I. M. & Lockhart, R. S. (1972). Levels of processing: A framework for memory research. *Journal of Verbal Learning and Verbal Behavior, 11,* 671–84.

Cree, G. S. & McRae, K. (2003). Analyzing the factors underlying the structure and computation of the meaning of chipmunk, cherry, chisel, cheese, and cello (and many other such concrete nouns). *Journal of Experimental Psychology: General, 132,* 163–201.

Cree, G. S., McRae, K., & McNorgan, C. (1999). An attractor model of lexical conceptual processing: Simulating semantic priming. *Cognitive Science, 23,* 371–414.

Damasio, A. R. (1989). Time-locked multiregional retroactivation: A systems-level proposal for the neural substrates of recall and recognition. *Cognition, 33,* 25–62.

Donald, M. (1993). Precis of "Origins of the modern mind: Three stages in the evolution of culture and cognition." *Behavioral and Brain Sciences, 16,* 739–91.

Dretske, F. (1995). *Naturalizing the mind.* Cambridge, MA: MIT Press.

Farah, M. J. & McClelland, J. L. (1991). A computational model of semantic memory impairment: Modality specificity and emergent category specificity. *Journal of Experimental Psychology: General, 120,* 339–57.

Fauconnier, G. (1985). *Mental spaces.* Cambridge, MA: MIT Press.

Fiske, S. T. & Taylor, S. E. (1991). *Social cognition* (2nd ed.). New York: McGraw-Hill.

Fodor, J. A. (1983). *The modularity of mind: An essay on faculty psychology.* Cambridge, MA: Bradford Books, MIT Press.

Fodor, J. A. & Pylyshyn, Z. W. (1988). Connectionism and cognitive architecture: A critical analysis. *Cognition, 28,* 3–71.

Gagné, C. L. & Shoben, E. J. (1997). The influence of thematic relations on the comprehension of modifier-noun combinations. *Journal of Experimental Psychology: Learning, Memory, and Cognition, 23,* 71–87.

Gallese, V. & Lakoff, G. (2005). The brain's concepts: The role of the sensory-motor system in reason and language. *Cognitive Neuropsychology, 22,* 455–79.

Glaser, W. R. (1992). Picture naming. *Cognition, 42,* 61–105.

Glass, A. L. & Holyoak, K. J. (1975). Alternative conceptions of semantic memory. *Cognition, 3,* 313–39.

Glenberg, A. M. (1997). What memory is for. *Behavioral and Brain Sciences, 20,* 1–55.

Glenberg, A. M., Havas, D., Becker, R., & Rinck, M. (2005). Grounding language in bodily states: The case for emotion. In Pecher, D. & Zwaan, R. (Eds.) *Grounding cognition: The role of perception and action in memory, language, and thought* (pp. 115–28). New York: Cambridge University Press.

Glenberg, A. M., Schroeder, J. L., & Robertson, D. A. (1998). Averting the gaze disengages the environment and facilitates remembering. *Memory & Cognition, 26,* 651–8.

Graesser, A. C., Singer, M., & Trabasso, T. (1994). Constructing inferences during narrative text comprehension. *Psychological Review, 101,* 371–95.

Haugeland, J. (1985). *Artificial intelligence: The very idea of it.* Cambridge, MA: MIT Press.

(1991). Representational genera. In Ramsey, W., Stitch, S.P., & Rumelhart, D. E. (Eds.) *Philosophy and connectionist theory* (pp. 61–89). Hillsdale, NJ: Lawrence Erlbaum Associates.

Hayward, W. G. & Tarr, M. J. (1995). Spatial language and spatial representation. *Cognition, 55,* 39–84.

Heit, E. (1998). Influences of prior knowledge on selective weighting of category members. *Journal of Experimental Psychology: Learning, Memory, and Cognition, 24,* 712–31.

Hinton, G. E. (1989). Learning distributed representations of concepts. In. Morris, RGM (Ed) *Parallel distributed processing: Implications for psychology and neurobiology.* (pp. 46–61). New York: Oxford University Press.

Hochberg, J. (Ed.) (1998). *Perception and cognition at century's end: Handbook of perception and cognition* (2nd ed.). San Diego, CA: Academic Press.

Hollan, J. D. (1975). Features and semantic memory: Set-theoretic or network model? *Psychological Review, 82,* 154–5.

Humphreys, G. W. & Forde, EME (2001). Hierarchies, similarity, and interactivity in object recognition: "Category-specific" neuropsychological deficits. *Behavioral & Brain Sciences, 24,* 453–509.

Huttenlocher, J., Hedges, L. V., & Duncan, S. (1991). Categories and particulars: Prototype effects in estimating spatial location. *Psychological Review, 98,* 352–76.

Jacoby, L. L. & Brooks, L. R. (1984). Nonanalytic cognition: Memory, perception, and concept learning. In Bower, G. H. (Ed.) *The psychology of learning and motivation: Advances in research and theory* (Vol. 18, pp. 1–47). New York: Academic Press.

Johnson-Laird, P. N. (1983). *Mental models.* Cambridge, MA: Harvard University Press.

Joyce, D., Richards, L., Cangelosi, A., & Coventry K. R. (2003). On the foundations of perceptual symbol systems: Specifying embodied representations via connectionism. In Detje, F., Dörner, D., & Schaub, H. (Eds.) *The logic of cognitive systems. Proceedings of the Fifth International Conference on Cognitive Modeling* (pp. 147–52). Universitätsverlag Bamberg.

Kan, I. P., Barsalou, L. W., Solomon, K. O., Minor, J. K., & Thompson-Schill, S. L. (2003). Role of mental imagery in a property verification task: fMRI evidence for perceptual representations of conceptual knowledge. *Cognitive Neuropsychology*, 20, 525–40.

Kim, N. & Ahn, W. (2002). Clinical psychologists' theory-based representations of mental disorders predict their diagnostic reasoning and memory. *Journal of Experimental Psychology: General*, 131, 451–76.

Kintsch, W. & van Dijk, T. A. (1978). Toward a model of text comprehension and production. *Psychological Review*, 85, 363–94.

Kosslyn, S. M. (1980). *Image and mind*. Cambridge, MA: Harvard University Press.

(1994). *Image and brain*. Cambridge, MA: MIT Press.

Kruschke, J. K. (1992). ALCOVE: An exemplar-based connectionist model of category learning. *Psychological Review*, 99, 22–44.

Kunda, Z. (1999). *Social cognition: Making sense of people*. Cambridge, MA: MIT Press.

Lakoff, G. & Johnson, M. (1980). *Metaphors we live by*. Chicago: University of Chicago Press.

(1999). *Philosophy in the flesh: The embodied mind and its challenge to western thought*. Basic Books: New York.

Lamberts, K. (1998). The time course of categorization. *Journal of Experimental Psychology: Learning, Memory, and Cognition*, 24, 695–711.

Langacker, R. W. (1986). An introduction to cognitive grammar. *Cognitive Science*, 10, 1–40.

Logan, G. D. & Compton, B. J. (1996). Distance and distraction effects in the apprehension of spatial relations. *Journal of Experimental Psychology: Human Perception and Performance*, 22, 159–72.

Loken, B., Barsalou, L. W., & Joiner, C. (2008). Concepts and categorization in consumer psychology. In Haugtvedt, C. P., Herr, P., & Kardes, F. (Eds.). *Handbook of Consumer Psychology*. Mahwah, NJ: Lawrence Erlbaum Associates.

Markman, A. & Medin, D. L. (2002). Decision making. In Pashler, H. (Ed.) *Steven's Handbook*. New York: J. Wiley and Sons.

Markman, A. B. & Ross, B. H. (2003). Category use and category learning. *Psychological Bulletin*, 129, 592–613.

Marslen-Wilson, W. D. (Ed.) (1992). Special issue on Lexical Semantics. *Cognition*, 42.

Martin, A. (2001). Functional neuroimaging of semantic memory. In Cabeza, R. & Kingstone, A. (Eds.) *Handbook of functional neuroimaging of cognition* (pp. 153–86). Cambridge, MA: MIT Press.

McClelland, J. L. & Rumelhart, D. E. (1985). Distributed memory and the representation of general and specific information. *Journal of Experimental Psychology: General*, 114, 159–88.

McRae, K., Spivey-Knowlton, M. J., & Tanenhaus, M. K. (1998). Modeling the influence of thematic fit (and other constraints) in on-line sentence comprehension. *Journal of Memory and Language*, 38, 283–312.

Medin, D., Coley, J. D., Storms, G., & Hayes, B. (2003). A relevance theory of induction. *Psychonomic Bulletin and Review*, 10, 517–32.

Medin, D. L. & Schaffer, M. (1978). A context theory of classification learning. *Psychological Review*, 85, 207–38.

Murphy, G. L. (1996). On metaphoric representation. *Cognition*, 60, 173–204.

Newell, A. & Simon, H. A. (1972). *Human problem solving*. Englewood Cliffs, NJ: Prentice-Hall.

Nosofsky, R. M. (1984). Choice, similarity, and the context theory of classification. *Journal of Experimental Psychology: Learning, Memory, and Cognition*, 10, 104–14.

Nosofsky, R. M. & Palmeri, T. J. (1997). An exemplar-based random walk model of speeded classification. *Psychological Review*, 104, 266–300.

O'Reilly, R. C. (1998). Six principles for biologically-based computational models of cortical cognition. *Trends in Cognitive Sciences*, 2, 455–62.

(2006). Modeling integration and dissociation in brain and cognitive development. In Munakata, Y. & Johnson, M. H. (Eds.) *Processes of change in brain and cognitive development: Attention and performance XXI*. Oxford: Oxford University Press.

Palmer, S. E. (1975). The effects of contextual scenes on the identification of objects. *Memory & Cognition*, 3, 519–26.

(1999). *Vision science: Photons to phenomenology*. Cambridge, MA: MIT Press.

Pecher, D. & Zwaan, R. (Eds.) (2005). *Grounding cognition: The role of perception and action in memory, language, and thought*. New York: Cambridge University Press.

Peterson, M. A. & Gibson, B. S. (1994). Must figure-ground organization precede object recognition? *Psychological Science*, 5, 253–9.

Pollack, J. (1990). Recursive distributed representations. *Artificial Intelligence*, 46, 77–105.

Postman, L. & Underwood, B. J. (1973). Critical issues in interference theory. *Memory & Cognition*, 1, 19–40.

Pylyshyn, Z. W. (1973). What the mind's eye tells the mind's brain: A critique of mental imagery. *Psychological Bulletin*, 80, 1–24.

(1984). *Computation and cognition*. Cambridge, MA: MIT Press.

Reed, C. L. & Vinson, N. G. (1996). Conceptual effects on representational momentum. *Journal of Experimental Psychology: Human Perception and Performance*, 22, 839–50.

Reed, S. K. (1972). Pattern recognition and categorization. *Cognitive Psychology*, 3, 382–407.

Roediger, H. L. III & McDermott, K. B. (1993). Implicit memory in normal human subjects. In Boller, F. & Grafman, J. (Eds.) *Handbook of Neuropsychology* (Vol. 8, 63–131). Elsevier Science Publishers B.V.

Rogers, T. T. & McClelland, J. L. (2004). *Semantic cognition: A parallel distributed processing approach*. Cambridge, MA: MIT Press.

Rosch, E. & Mervis, C. B. (1975). Family resemblances: Studies in the internal structure of categories. *Cognitive Psychology*, 7, 573–605.

Ross, B. H. (1996). Category learning as problem solving. In Medin, D. L. (Ed.) *The Psychology of Learning and Motivation: Advances in Research and Theory* (Vol. 35, pp. 165–92). San Diego, CA: Academic Press.

Roy, D. (2005). Grounding words in perception and action: Insights from computational models. *Trends in Cognitive Science*, 9, 389–96.

Rumelhart, D. E., Hinton, G. E., & Williams, R. J. (1986). Learning internal representations by error propagation. In Rumelhart, D. E., McClelland, J. L., & the PDP Research Group (Eds.) *Parallel distributed processing: Explorations in the microstructure of cognition, Vol. 1: Foundations* (pp. 318–62). Cambridge, MA: MIT Press.

Rumelhart, D. E., Smolensky, P., McClelland, J. L., & Hinton, G. E. (1986). Schemata and sequential thought processes in PDP models. In McClelland, J.L., Rumelhart, D.E., & the PDP Research Group (Eds.) *Parallel distributed processing: Explorations in the microstructure of cognition. Vol. 2: Psychological and biological models*. Cambridge, MA: MIT Press.

Rumelhart, D. E. & Todd, P. M. (1993). Learning and connectionist representations. In D.E. Meyer, D. E. & Kornblum, S. (Eds.) *Attention and performance 14: Synergies in experimental psychology, artificial intelligence, and cognitive neuroscience* (pp. 3–30). Cambridge, MA: MIT Press.

Samuel, A. G. (1997). Lexical activation produces potent phonemic percepts. *Cognitive Psychology*, 32, 97–127.

Schwanenflugel, P. J. (Ed.) (1991). *The psychology of word meaning*. Mahwah, NJ: Erlbaum.

Schank, R. C. & Abelson, R. P. (1977). *Scripts, plans, goals, and understanding: An inquiry into human knowledge structures*. Hillsdale, NJ: Lawrence Erlbaum Associates.

Schyns, P. G., Goldstone, R. L., & Thibaut, J. P. (1998). The development of features in object concepts. *Behavioral and Brain Sciences*, 21, 1–54.

Shiffrar, M. & Freyd, J. J. (1993). Timing and apparent motion path choice with human body photographs. *Psychological Science*, 6, 379–84.

Shore, B. (1996). *Culture in mind: cognition, culture, and the problem of meaning*. Oxford: Oxford University Press.

Simmons, W. K. & Barsalou, L. W. (2003). The similarity-in-topography principle: Reconciling theories of conceptual deficits. *Cognitive Neuropsychology*, 20, 451–86.

Smith, E. E. (1978). Theories of semantic memory. In Estes, W. K. (Ed.) *Handbook of learning and cognitive processes* (Vol. 6, pp. 1–56). Hillsdale, NJ: Lawrence Erlbaum Associates.

Smolensky, P. (1990). Tensor product variable binding and the representation of symbolic structures in connectionist systems. *Artificial Intelligence*, 46, 159–216.

Solomon, K. O. & Barsalou, L. W. (2004). Perceptual simulation in property verification. *Memory & Cognition*, 32, 244–59.

Spivey, M. J., Richardson, D. C., & Gonzalez-Marquez, M. (2005). On the perceptual-motor and image-schematic infrastructure of language. In Pecher, D. & Zwaan, R. (Eds.) *Grounding cognition: The role of perception and action in memory, language, and thought* (pp. 246–81). New York: Cambridge University Press.

Stevens, J. A., Fonlupt, P., Shiffrar, M., & Decety, J. (2000). New aspects of motion perception: Selective neural encoding of apparent human movements. *NeuroReport*, 111, 109–15.

Talmy, L. (1983). How language structures space. In Pick, H. & Acredelo, L. (Eds.) *Spatial orientation: Theory, research, and application* (pp. 225–82). New York: Plenum Press.

Tulving, E. (1972). Episodic and semantic memory. In Tulving, E. & Donaldson, W. (Eds.) *Organization and memory* (pp. 381–403). New York: Academic Press.

Tyler, L. K., Moss, H. E., Durrant-Peatfield, M. R., & Levy, J. P. (2000). Conceptual structure and the structure of concepts: A distributed account of category-specific deficits. *Brain and Language*, 75, 195–231.

Wisniewski, E. J. (1997). When concepts combine. *Psychonomic Bulletin & Review*, 4, 167–83.

Yeh, W. & Barsalou, L. W. (2006). The situated nature of concepts. *American Journal of Psychology*, 119, 349–384.

Zwaan, R. A. & Madden, C. J. (2005). Embodied sentence comprehension. In Pecher, D. & Zwaan, R. (Eds.) *Grounding cognition: The role of perception and action in memory, language, and thought* (pp. 224–45). New York: Cambridge University Press.

Author Notes

This work was supported by National Science Foundation Grants SBR-9421326, SBR-9796200, and BCS-0212134 and by DARPA contracts BICA FA8650–05-C-7256 and BICA FA8650–05-C-7255 to Lawrence W. Barsalou. Address correspondence to Lawrence W. Barsalou, Department of Psychology, Emory University, Atlanta, GA 30322 (barsalou@emory.edu) http://www.psychology.emory.edu/cognition/barsalou/index.html).

CHAPTER 13

Computational Models of Semantic Memory

George S. Cree and Blair C. Armstrong

Computational models of semantic memory provide controlled environments for studying the complex, interactive nature of knowledge representation and processing. They range in scope from dealing with the components of meaning activated immediately when a word is encountered, to theories of how our complete storehouse of general world knowledge may be represented and accessed. They typically outline the format in which knowledge is stored and/or the mechanisms and time course of how that knowledge becomes available as we read, listen, or think. In this chapter we outline the contributions of three classes of computational models which have had the greatest influence on our understanding of semantic memory: semantic network theory, parallel distributed processing (PDP) networks, and word co-occurrence models.

Scientists who study semantic memory are usually concerned with word meaning and how the meanings of multiple words can be combined to understand longer text segments. They have also been concerned with how people acquire word meanings, how they use them to draw appropriate

inferences, how they can efficiently store and search vast amounts of information, why some systems of categorization seem better and more natural than others, what components of meaning become active immediately when we encounter words, and why various kinds of brain damage can lead to specific patterns of loss of word meanings. Most research has been conducted using tasks that present simple statements (e.g., "A dog is an animal.") or combinations of words in temporal sequence (e.g., dog -> cat) and ask people to make judgments about the stimuli. To help understand how people perform these tasks, researchers have designed computer models that embody the assumptions they theorize are important about how knowledge is stored and computed.

The advantages of computer models over descriptive theories are well known (Hintzman, 1991). Modeling forces researchers to be explicit about their assumptions and the components that make up their theories. Implemented models allow researchers to test predictions and to derive new ones by running simulations. They also allow researchers to create "artificial patients" by removing or altering components of the model and examining the effect on behavior. Implemented models can serve as existence proofs that a theory is logically coherent and behaves as advertised.

The goal of this chapter is to summarize the important insights that have come from each of the three main approaches to modeling semantic memory. We will outline the important contributions of each and point the interested reader to more detailed explanations when available.

1 Semantic network theory

Semantic networks are collections of nodes linked together by labeled relational links. Each node typically represents a single concept, and hence these models are referred to as having localist representation schemes. The meaning of a concept is represented through a set of pointers to other nodes. A goal of this type of modeling is to determine how to link up the nodes such that the resultant knowledge structures can be used to produce realistic semantic inferences. The implementations that have best stood the test of time are those of Ross Quillian (e.g., Quillian, 1962; 1967; 1968; 1969), who was concerned with understanding both natural language and memory. Quillian's early models worked by instantiating specially coded dictionary definitions into networks of nodes and examining how inferences could be drawn from the intersections of paths emanating from target nodes.

Collins and Quillian (1969) realized that if they included assumptions about efficiency of storage and the length of time it should take to move between nodes, it would be possible to derive predictions about how humans retrieve information. They suggested that conceptual information was stored in a hierarchy, with more general concepts (e.g., animal) at the top, and more specific concepts (e.g., canary) at the bottom (see Figure 13.1). *Concepts* were defined in two ways: as a set of features held within each concept node, and in the set of pointers to other nodes. Properties of concepts were stored at the highest node in the hierarchy for which the property held true for all concepts below (e.g., <has wings> was stored at the bird node, but not the animal or canary node), thus implementing a form of cognitive economy.

Predictions regarding the length of time it should take participants to verify statements could be generated directly from the model. These were tested most thoroughly through use of the sentence verification task in which participants were asked to verify the truth/falsity of simple sentences (e.g., "A canary is a bird."). This task could be simulated in the Collins and Quillian framework by starting at a node and searching properties in nodes and along relational links to other nodes until the information necessary to evaluate the statement had been found. Collins and Quillian found, as predicted, that it took longer for people to verify statements that required longer searches (e.g., traveling two nodes) than statements that required shorter searches (e.g., traveling one node).

The Collins and Quillian framework also provided a mechanism through which information could be inherited. If the system needed to learn about a new concept, then a node for that concept could be attached at the appropriate level of the hierarchy, and the concept would automatically inherit all of the appropriate information about members of that category that were stored at higher nodes.

Initial behavioral evidence appeared to support both the ideas of hierarchical organization and inheritance through cognitive economy (e.g., Collins and Quillian, 1969), but hierarchical network theory did not hold up well to further investigation. A series of findings convincingly demonstrated that the strength of relation between a concept and property, or concept and concept, was more important in determining verification latency than was distance in the hierarchy (e.g., Conrad, 1972). Furthermore, the model could not explain typicality effects, such as why people are faster to verify that a robin is a bird than that a chicken is a

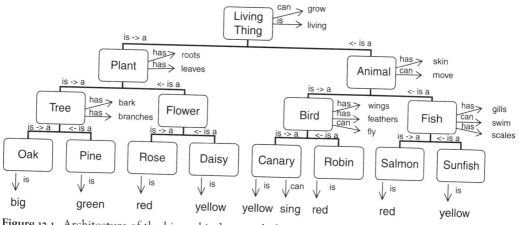

Figure 13.1. Architecture of the hierarchical network theory as proposed by Collins and Quillian (1969).

bird (Rosch and Mervis, 1975). Additionally, it was not clear how one would decide where in the taxonomy to store concepts that belonged to more than one category (e.g., knife), or when to add a new node for items that were similar, but not identical, to those already represented. These observations, along with others, were used to argue against semantic memory as a strict taxonomic hierarchy.

Spreading activation theory (Collins and Loftus, 1975) was proposed as an alternative and was framed as a semantic network without hierarchical organization. It was used to account for a number of behavioral phenomena that posed problems for hierarchical network theory. But this power came at a cost, as it was ultimately determined that the model was too flexible and could be used to account for just about any pattern of data (Johnson-Laird, Herrmann, and Chaffin, 1984). This flexibility came mainly from the fact that there were no constraints on which nodes could be connected to which other nodes, and more importantly, no manner for determining the strengths of weights between nodes.

Semantic network theory was the first major computational approach designed to investigate semantic memory. It succeeded in inspiring over a decade of behavioral research and in promoting the need for future models to account for inheritance and typicality effects. The modeling framework itself is quite simple and provides a language with which one can easily discuss predictions. Yet despite this, the framework is unsatisfying, because the concessions needed to allow it to account for the known behavioral data leave the approach too unconstrained, and hence unviable as a research framework within which to study human cognition. A small number of theories were proposed as alternative explanations of the sentence verification data (e.g., McCloskey and Glucksberg, 1979; Smith, Shoben, and Rips, 1974), but none were proposed as grand theories of semantic memory on the scale of hierarchical network theory or spreading activation theory. Despite the limitations, semantic network models are still under development, although more as a means to implement an efficient knowledge system than for generating novel predictions. The various instantiations of ACT, for example, include a spreading activation-like semantic component (Anderson, 1983). A second example, although not exactly a semantic network, is CYC, a very large database of common sense assertions linked together by relations and designed to produce coherent inferences (Lenat and Guha, 1990). CYC is being developed with the hopes of producing a common sense reasoning component for a full artificial intelligence system (see http://www.cyc.com/).

2 Parallel distributed processing models

PDP models, also known as *connectionist networks*, have grown in popularity since the early 1980s as an alternative to semantic network theory. In PDP models, concepts are typically represented as distributed patterns of activity across sets of representational units. The units often represent features of concepts (e.g., <has four legs>), but not necessarily nameable features. Units are organized into layers and are connected by weighted links, which are usually set through use of either an error-correcting, or Hebbian, learning algorithm.

There are several important differences between PDP and semantic network models. First, a form of cognitive economy is implemented through the fact that multiple concepts can be represented as distributed patterns across the same set of units. Second, they offer mechanisms for determining weights on connections. Third, by combining the use of distributed patterns and discovering weight strengths algorithmically, similarity among items emerges as an implicit result. Finally, PDP models are said to degrade gracefully, in that when they are damaged (e.g., by removing weights), knowledge about concepts is lost gradually and not in an all-or-none manner as in localist theories.

Hinton (1981) proposed one of the first PDP alternatives to semantic network theory. He was interested in understanding the rich microstructure of semantic representations, arguing that a single relational link in a semantic network would in reality be represented by multiple units and connections in a distributed system like the brain. He designed a model in which propositional information (e.g., the moose is brown) was represented as distributed patterns of activity across sets of processing units (e.g., *role 1*: moose, *relation*: color, *role 2*: brown). These three banks of units interacted with one another through a set of hidden *prop* (proposition) units that encoded conjunctions of roles and relations (see Figure 13.2). When a pattern of activation was enacted across a

layer, the system was designed to settle to a stable state (i.e., represent a correct association) by updating its activation states over time.

PDP networks that update unit states over time and settle to stable states are known as *connectionist attractor networks*. Hinton noted that attractor networks are appropriate for simulating semantic memory because not all points in semantic space correspond to lexical concepts (Hinton and Shallice, 1991). Semantic space can be thought of as a multidimensional space in which each dimension corresponds to a unit and a location corresponds to a pattern of activation across those units. To borrow Hinton's example, the point in semantic space exactly halfway between rhinoceros and unicorn is not likely to correspond to anything that exists in the real world, and certainly not anything for which we have a name. It therefore makes sense to have a system that moves towards a valid semantic representation, known as an *attractor*, when a word is presented. Regions surrounding attractors are called *attractor basins*, and once the network computes a semantic state that is within one of these basins, then as long as the input to the network does not change, the network will settle into the attractor. Hinton used the properties of the attractor network to show how a distributed system could exhibit pattern completion, cognitive economy, generalization, and property inheritance.

The model was capable of completing partial propositions. One way to understand how it accomplished this is to think of the *relation* layer as encoding contexts within which specific roles occur. A context would then interact with a pattern of activity in the *role 1* units to produce an appropriate pattern across the *role 2* units. An efficient way to represent the regularities that exist in the role–relation contexts is to determine which specific units are active together across many patterns and to assign a hidden *prop* unit to represent those conjunctions of unit activations. Subsequently, whenever a role and relation are presented together that activate that *prop* unit, the *prop* unit would partially activate units across the *role 2* layer,

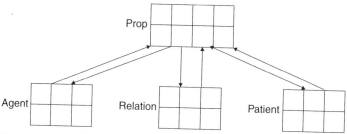

Figure 13.2. Architecture of Hinton's (1981) PDP model designed to encode propositional information. Note that the number of units in each layer is meant to be illustrative and does not reflect the number used in Hinton's simulations.

which would ultimately settle to one of the concepts stored in the system, completing the pattern.

A second important property was that multiple propositions could be stored in the same set of weights. This provided a second form of cognitive economy, again different from that proposed by Collins and Quillian.

Third, the model could generalize in an intelligent manner based on the similarity of representations at the role layers. Imagine, for example, that a novel concept (e.g., deer) was instantiated across the *role 1* units, and it had a representation similar to another concept stored in the network (e.g., moose). If it was activated along with an appropriate relation pattern (e.g., color), the network was capable of completing the proposition with an appropriate *role 2* due to the fact that the pattern instantiated across the *role 1* units would sufficiently activate suitable *prop* units.

Finally, property inheritance, an important feature built into Collins and Quillian's semantic network theory, arises naturally in Hinton's model, assuming that appropriate representations are chosen. Collins and Quillian are said to have built in property inheritance because they did not provide an account of why or how knowledge would be stored at only the highest concept node for which the feature applied. Hinton's representational scheme provided an elegant alternative. Membership in a superordinate category could be represented as the subset of role units common to each of the

relevant subordinate concepts. That subset of units could then activate *prop* units fitting for the category. A new concept that shared that subset of features would automatically activate *prop* representations true of the category, and hence provide correct inferences through pattern completion in the *role 2* layer.

Hinton's work did not, however, solve satisfactorily the problem of how to determine the strengths of the weights between units (Hinton set his weights by hand). By the mid-eighties, methods had been discovered for training sets of weights in networks that included hidden layers, sometimes referred to as *deep networks*. One of the most effective was backpropagation (Rumelhart, Hinton, and Williams, 1986).

Hinton (1986) showed that a system trained with backpropagation could discover implicit semantic features and represent them across a hidden layer by picking up on the regularities that existed in the inputs and the outputs of the training patterns. Specifically, he demonstrated how propositions about personal relationships, typically represented in family trees, could be coded efficiently in a distributed system. For example, a hidden unit could come to code for an aspect of a relation (represented in the *relation* units) corresponding to the idea that if the person in *role 1* is young, then the person that appears in *role 2* must also be young. This hidden unit could then take part in representing this relation across multiple propositions, not just a single instance. This was an advance over Hinton (1981) because the implicit features were not built in by the experimenter, but rather were an emergent property of the use of the learning algorithm.

David Rumelhart extended Hinton's models with a demonstration that a PDP system trained with backpropagation and exposed to a set of concepts and features taken from an independent source would exhibit properties consistent with human semantic memory (Rumelhart, 1990; Rumelhart and Todd, 1993). Rumelhart used the exact set of concepts, features, and relations depicted by Collins and Quillian in the figure that illustrated their hierarchical semantic network. Rumelhart's model was a feedforward system (i.e., not an attractor network), in which activation flowed in one direction, from inputs to outputs (see Figure 13.3). The model had five layers of units, with two input layers and one output layer. Concept name input units (e.g., canary) passed activation to representation units, and representation units passed activation to relational units, which also accepted inputs from the other input bank, known as relation units (e.g., can, is, etc.). The relational units ultimately passed activation to a set of output units that coded for features of each concept (e.g., <fly>, <sing>, etc.). Localist representations were used for both concepts and relations. Output representations were distributed patterns of features.

Rumelhart was interested primarily in the representations that would develop across the hidden units through repeated exposure to items in the training set. By using a localist representation at the input layer he had stripped out of the input all of the similarity among concepts (e.g., canary was as similar to salmon as it was to robin). Therefore, if similarities were encoded at the hidden layers during training it must be because the system was making use of similarities that existed at the output layer and encoding them in the representation layer. This was interesting for two reasons. First, the network would be developing its own internal representations as a means of solving the mapping problem. Second, the internal representations could be examined

using statistical analyses to determine which aspects of semantic knowledge were being encoded. This was an advance over Hinton's work because it used an independent yet penetrable training set in which the implicit semantic features encoded at the hidden representation layer could be interpreted in terms of concepts, categories, and features of common objects.

Rumelhart used the model to illustrate three points, the most novel of which was that the patterns of activity developed at the representation unit hidden layer captured the featural similarities of concepts that existed at the output layer. The representation of canary, for example, was more similar to the representation of robin than it was to the representation of any of the fish, flowers, or trees. He went on to demonstrate that the activity in the representation units could be interpreted as coding for the major conceptual distinctions that existed in the training set (e.g., in one simulation representation unit 3 might be active consistently for animals but not plants). He also showed, like Hinton (1981), that the system displayed property inheritance and that it also displayed the "cancellation principle," or in other words, that it could learn that there are members of a category that do not have a property that is common to most other members of the category (e.g., an ostrich is a bird but does not fly).

Hinton and Rumelhart demonstrated that PDP systems could produce patterns of behavior consistent with the human conceptual system. The models were able to generalize appropriately, demonstrate property inheritance, and develop internal representations that reflected the structure inherent in the training patterns. Although these models did not provide a full account of the behavioral phenomena associated with semantic memory and had not been used to closely simulate any behavioral tasks, they were viewed as a promising new approach to studying semantic representation and processing.

Rogers and McClelland (2004) have significantly extended the Rumelhart framework to account for a large body of findings.

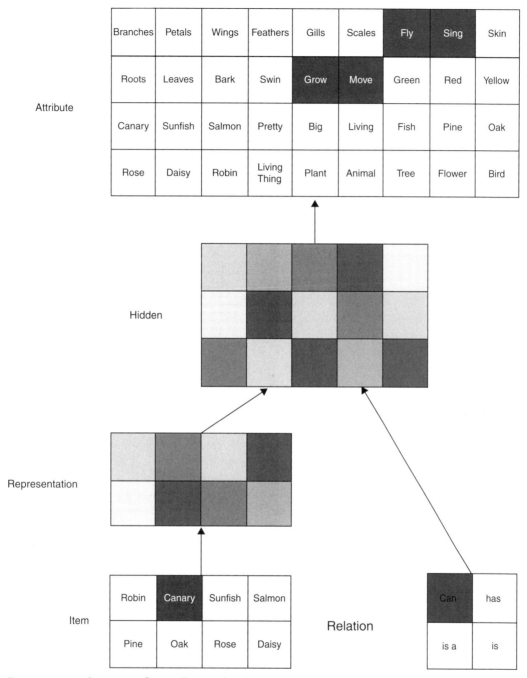

Figure 13.3. Architecture of Rumelhart and Todd's (1991) PDP network designed to encode the information present in Collins and Quillian's (1969) hierarchical network theory. In this illustration, *canary* and *can* have been activated at the input layer and the network has produced the correct output pattern across the attribute layer.

An important explanatory principle in their work is that of coherent covariation of properties. This refers to the fact that some sets of features tend to co-occur together more often than others, and that these sets tend to occur more often within than across category boundaries. Many concepts, for example, <have wings>, <have beaks>, and

<lay eggs>. Furthermore, those that <have wings> tend not to be <used for carpentry>. Learning in a PDP network can benefit from these regularities because a set of weight changes that benefits one concept will benefit all of the other concepts that share that same set of features. This principle is important in explaining why children first learn to differentiate concepts at the superordinate level yet prefer to name at the basic level, why some categories are more coherent than others, how different kinds of properties can become more central to one category than another, and why causal properties appear to be more central to determining category membership than others. We will consider one example.

Theory theorists propose that knowledge is structured around naïve, domain-specific, causal theories (e.g., Murphy and Medin, 1985). An issue discussed within this domain of study is why some concepts seem to be better and more coherent (e.g., birds), than others (e.g., large blue things found outdoors). Rogers and McClelland suggest that this can be explained, at least partially, through the fact that causal structure, as it exists in the world, leads to the coherent covariation of object properties in the environment. For example, having bird DNA tends to cause a creature to have wings, a beak, and to be able to fly. Coherent covariation of such sets of properties across objects makes these objects easier to learn due to mutually beneficial weight changes across concepts, and when combined with the fact that we need to refer to these clusters of objects more often than to others (e.g., clusters of large blue things found outdoors), we can see why we will tend to find the category of birds to be a more satisfying, natural category.

Rogers and McClelland make an ambitious attempt to provide a mechanistic account of several other phenomena studied by theory theorists. The issues are complex, and are beyond the scope of discussion in this chapter, but if one is interested in reading an excellent summary of the issues, with pointers to important directions that future work should address, then this book is highly recommended (or see McClelland and Rogers, 2003 for a brief overview).

Semantic computation unfolds over time. When we read or hear a word, different components of the meaning become active at different rates over the first several hundred milliseconds. Feedforward connectionist networks are not well-suited for studying these computations because activation is computed across entire layers in a single sweep. Attractor networks, however, in which units update their states continuously based on both their prior states and input from other units, are well-suited for this work. The networks usually have at least one set of recurrent connections in which there can be feedback activation from top-down influences (see, e.g., Figure 13.4). These models have been used primarily to study semantic priming, feature verification, and semantic impairments in cases of brain damage and disease.

Semantic priming refers to the finding that participants are faster to respond to a target word (e.g., eagle) if it is preceded by a semantically related word (e.g., hawk) than by an unrelated word (e.g., hook; see McNamara, 2005 for a highly readable review). Priming was originally thought to reveal the structure of semantic memory on the assumption that if priming occurred, it was evidence that two concept nodes must be closely linked in a semantic network. PDP simulations of priming have offered alternative interpretations of why and how priming arises (Masson, 1991, 1995; Plaut, 1995; Sharkey, 1989). We will consider one example.

Plaut (1995) offered a clear demonstration of how two different kinds of priming effects could be instantiated in a single PDP system. *Semantic similarity priming* is due to similarity in meaning of two concepts. One way of formalizing similarity is to talk in terms of shared features: the more shared features, the stronger the priming. *Associative priming*, on the other hand, has traditionally been discussed as priming that occurs due to associative relations between two concepts, as indexed through association norms, in which a large number of

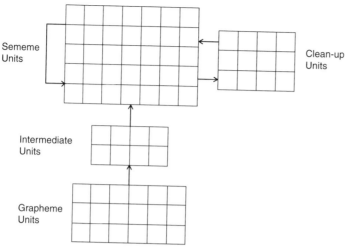

Figure 13.4. Architecture of Hinton and Shallice's (1991) attractor network. Note the connections leading back from the clean-up units to the sememe units. Also, note that the self-connections at the sememe layer represent the fact that small sets of sememe units were interconnected, each set representing values on one attribute dimension, and that not all sememe units were fully interconnected.

participants are asked to respond to a word with the first word that comes to mind (e.g., ham -> sandwich). Association almost certainly reflects semantic relations, including featural similarity, and so it is difficult to nail down exactly what association is, besides a grab bag of relations. One important type of relation that we can agree is included, that is relatively distinct from featural similarity, is co-occurrence in time and/or space. For example the words *tennis* and *elbow* share few, if any, semantic features, but they do tend to occur together in language more often than chance. We can refer to this as *word co-occurrence*, and it has been demonstrated to produce reliable priming effects. Plaut discussed two different mechanisms in PDP attractor networks that may give rise to these two different kinds of priming.

Priming due to semantic overlap arises naturally in PDP networks because concepts that share features are typically represented by similar patterns of distributed activity. Computing the meaning of the prime will therefore put the network into a state in which both the prime and target are simultaneously active. Hence the system will be

faster to process the meaning of the target when it is presented at the input layer after the prime, allowing for faster responding.

Plaut suggested that associative (or word co-occurrence) priming could be realized through the ability of the system to move from one attractor state to another. He manipulated the ability of the network to perform these mappings by varying the likelihood that one word followed another during training, and importantly, not resetting the activation values between training trials. This forced the network to develop weights that allowed it to move easily between attractors for words that co-occurred frequently during training, producing a priming effect when compared to non co-occurring words.

Several other models of priming have been reported, providing further insight into factors such as the role of similarity and correlational strength in predicting priming effects (McRae, de Sa, and Siedenberg, 1997), the degree of similarity required to observe priming (Cree, McRae, and McNorgan, 1999), long-term semantic priming (Becker et al., 1997), and individual and developmental differences in priming (Plaut and Booth, 2000). An important area for future work is to unpack the different relations that drive semantic and associative priming through carefully designed experiments and simulations that demonstrate the proposed mechanism(s) at work.

3 Feature verification

The feature verification task involves asking participants to verify whether or not a feature is reasonably true of a concept (e.g., cat – <meows>). It can be used to reveal the time course of activation of features of a concept. McRae and colleagues have used it to examine how statistical concept–feature and feature–feature relations influence semantic computation, and have simulated the findings using a two-layer attractor network framework in which word forms map to semantic features (see McRae, 2004 for a review).

Two aspects of the approach taken by McRae and colleagues deserve note. First, the semantic representations are empirically derived, being taken from a set of semantic feature production norms in which participants were asked to list the features they thought were part of a concept (McRae et al., 2005). This has the benefits of reducing degrees of freedom in modeling, allows statistics to be computed from the norms regarding the occurrence of features across concepts and categories, and permits the use of exactly the same items in both experiments and simulations. Second, because they have been interested in how attractor networks encode feature–feature statistics, they have been less concerned with the internal representations developed across hidden layers. The modeling framework used in their simulations has therefore typically involved a set of word form units that maps to a set of fully interconnected semantic units, with perhaps a set of hidden units connected to the semantic units that can encode higher-order correlations of features across the semantic layer (sometimes called a clean-up layer). This framework allows

for feature–feature relations to be directly encoded in the weights. Using this framework, McRae and colleagues have uncovered two relationships that govern speeded computation of semantic meaning in both humans and the model: correlations among features, and the distinctiveness of features.

Features are said to be correlated if they tend to occur together across concepts. Strength of correlation can be measured by computing how often feature pairs occur together across all the concepts in a set of semantic feature production norms. In a feature verification task, McRae et al. (1999) found that features with high intercorrelational strength, a measure of how correlated a target feature is with the other features in the concept, were verified faster than control features. The accompanying attractor network simulation revealed the same effect. Analysis of the network showed that this was because the high intercorrelational strength features received strong support from other correlated features, with strong connection weights that were also activated by the concept's word form and thus reached higher states of activation than did control features during the early stages of processing.

Distinguishing features have been defined as features that are true of only one, or at most a few, concepts (e.g., cow – <moos>). Cree, McNorgan, and McRae (2006) demonstrated that distinguishing features are verified faster than control features by human participants, and provided a simulation that reflected this pattern of responding. Analysis of the network revealed that distinguishing features reached higher levels of activation faster than did control features because strong weights had formed during training between the word form units that represented each concept name and the distinguishing features of that concept. This makes sense, given that the goal of the network during training was to learn to settle into the correct attractor as fast as possible. Distinctive features are an excellent source of information about which attractor basin to enter, because, by definition, they occur in only a few concepts. The network can then fully settle to the correct representation by filling in the rest of the semantic representation around the distinguishing features.

The attractor network framework used by McRae and colleagues has been used more recently to explore how superordinate concepts are learned and to simulate speeded tasks that include superordinate concepts as items. O'Connor, Cree, and McRae (2007) proposed that superordinate concepts are learned, at least partially, over many learning trials, with each trial instantiating a mapping from the word form for a superordinate concept to the semantic features of a specific category member (e.g., animal -> moose). They found that when these learning trials are interspersed with basic-level learning trials (e.g., moose -> moose), the system is able to extract the regularities with which features occur across the various category members to form superordinate attractor states. Once trained, the model produces superordinate representations that intuitively make sense (e.g., tool: <used for carpentry>, <made of metal>, <has a handle>, etc.) that capture general information about the category and yet are not the same as any individual concept. The network has been used successfully to simulate a typicality rating task in which participants are asked to rate how good a concept is as an example of a category. The model outperformed family resemblance, the gold standard for simulating typicality ratings, on a large number of the categories on which the network was trained.

Finally, the superordinate network has been used to provide insight into some findings that are counterintuitive in terms of both semantic network theory and the standard PDP explanation of semantic priming. There have been several reports of priming studies in which high and low typicality targets produce equivalent priming effects when preceded by a superordinate word as prime (e.g., Schwanenflugel and Rey, 1986). According to the standard PDP explanation of semantic similarity priming, priming should be larger for high typicality items because they should share more features with the superordinate term. O'Connor

et al. (2007) have replicated this behavioral effect and explained why this occurs in terms of the ability of the system to move out of a superordinate versus basic-level attractor. This serves as an example of how the dynamics of processing in an attractor network can explain patterns of human performance that do not make sense in terms of traditional semantic network modeling frameworks.

4 Constraints on structure: Semantic impairments

The patterns of semantic impairment observed in patients with brain damage and disease have served as constraints on the structure of computational models of semantic memory. Several distinct patterns of impairment have been reported. Semantic dementia, for example, tends to lead to a general impairment that first produces an inability to recall specific facts about concepts and later influences general knowledge about concepts. Alzheimer's dementia, on the other hand, tends to produce a general semantic deficit as the disease progresses, but with a more severe impairment for living thing knowledge during the moderate to severe stages. Other complex patterns of category-specific impairments have been observed as a result of herpes simplex encephalitis, closed head injury, and stroke (see Capitani et al., 2003 for a review). Computational models offer a powerful tool for creating "artificial patients" in which researchers can induce damage that mimics either focal damage or diffuse brain damage due to various diseases and injuries.

Semantic network theory was the first framework used to try to interpret the patterns of impairment (Warrington, 1975). The progression from loss of specific to general knowledge in semantic dementia can be thought of as loss of the bottom levels of a hierarchical semantic network. Category-specific semantic deficits can be interpreted as loss of branches in a hierarchical network. These explanations are ultimately unsatisfying, however, because they fail to explain why the bottom levels should be more susceptible to damage than others, or why the reported patterns of impairment do not always follow category boundaries. Thus researchers have turned to other modeling frameworks.

Tim Rogers and colleagues have used PDP networks to provide detailed accounts of what might be occurring in cases of semantic dementia (Rogers et al., 2004; Rogers and McClelland, 2004). Rogers et al. (2004) used an attractor network that mapped from verbal and visual input/output layers through a set of hidden units, labeled semantic units, that functioned much like the *prop* units in Hinton's (1981) model. When damaged, the system mimicked patient performance in confrontation naming, word and picture sorting, word to picture matching, and drawing tasks. Analyses of the network revealed that specific information was lost before general information due to the nature in which regularities across the visual and verbal patterns were stored in the semantic hidden units. Features that occurred together across numerous concepts tended to be represented in larger, more contiguous regions of the semantic space defined by those units than were distinguishing features. Therefore distinguishing features were more likely to be affected by damage, causing the system to lose the ability to discriminate among similar concepts. Another way of thinking of this is in terms of the boundaries of the attractor basins for each concept. Damage shifts the boundaries, due to loss of distinguishing dimensions, such that a pattern of activation that would have once led into the attractor basin of one concept may subsequently lead into the attractor basin of a similar concept.

Hinton and Shallice (1991) were the first to describe semantic impairments in terms of shifts in the boundaries of attractor basins in their work on acquired dyslexia. Some dyslexics, when asked to read aloud a printed word (e.g., peach), will produce a word that is related in meaning (e.g., apricot). Interestingly, many of the errors reveal a visual component, and the combination of mixed visual and semantic errors (e.g.,

rat – cat) is much higher than would be expected from the prevalence of independent visual or semantic errors alone. They noted that two aspects of attractor networks are important for explaining these effects. First, even if the input to the system is noisy, the system will still move towards one of its known states. Second, attractor networks are able to map similar inputs to similar regions of semantic space, something that feedforward connectionist networks do naturally, yet still settle to distant points in semantic space, as the attractor network settles into a basin of attraction. The production of *apricot* when the system had read *peach* was an example of the system settling into a nearby attractor due to a shift in the boundary resulting from damage.

Counter to intuition, Hinton and Shallice learned that it didn't matter which set of weights they damaged, be they early in the system or late, the network still produced visual, semantic, and mixed errors. This was not what they had expected to observe, and is not what would be predicted from traditional models used in cognitive neuropsychology, which would predict that damage to weights between the input and semantic layer would be the most likely to produce visual errors. They discovered that this was because damage anywhere in the system would lead to shifts in the boundaries of the attractors, and so based on the set of concepts represented close in the semantic space, damage anywhere could lead to errors that would be classified as visual, semantic, or mixed, depending on which incorrect attractor the system now mapped into. Plaut and Shallice (1993) provided an extended investigation of these issues.

Attractor networks have also been applied to interpreting category-specific semantic deficits. Four factors have been found to be important in explaining the observed patterns of deficits. The first is that different modalities of information may be differentially important for discriminating among objects from various categories (Warrington and McCarthy, 1987; Warrington and Shallice, 1984). Functional information is important for discriminating among tools, for example, and hence damage to regions that code functional information could differentially disrupt the ability to discriminate tools. The second is that living and nonliving things differ in the ratio of perceptual to functional features (Farah and McClelland, 1991). Farah and McClelland instantiated these principles in a PDP network and demonstrated how they can give rise to category-specific semantic deficits in a system in which living and nonliving thing concepts are both represented over a set of semantic processing units with specialization by modality. Hence they demonstrated that a category-level behavioral deficit could emerge from a system in which knowledge was stored by modality of knowledge, not category.

The most counterintuitive simulation reported by Farah and McClelland was one in which damage to perceptual properties gave rise to an inability to activate functional information for living things. Analysis of the model revealed that this occurred because activation of the functional features was reliant on the mass of activation they got from perceptual properties, and thus when the perceptual properties were impaired, there was not enough activation in the system to push the functional features above threshold. This finding ran counter to the (still) generally held prediction that if damage to perceptual features was the cause of living things deficits, then patients with living things deficits should still be able to answer questions about the functional properties of living things.

The second two factors were highlighted by Devlin et al. (1998) in a model they used to explain how severity of impairment can interact with the structure of the semantic system to produce different patterns of impairment as damage progresses. Devlin et al. noted that concepts from different domains vary in terms of the average degree of correlation among features, with living things features tending to be more correlated. They also differ in terms of proportion of distinctive features, with nonliving things tending to have more informative features.

As a result, when mild damage impairs the ability to activate features, knowledge about nonliving things will be most likely to be lost, because there are relatively more distinctive features in the representations of nonliving things and because the correlations among shared features of living things will mutually reinforce one another and preserve their ability to become activated. As the damage progresses, more of the correlated features will become impaired, and they will eventually lose the ability, en masse, to reinforce one another. Because correlated features tend to be the ones that help discriminate living things, there will be a shift from a trend for nonliving things deficits to clear deficits for living things. Subsequent patient data has confirmed the living things deficit in moderate to severe AD, but not the predicted initial nonliving things impairment in mild AD. It remains to be seen whether models that use more realistic semantic representations would produce the same predictions for mild AD.

Recent theories and simulations have focused on the role of topographic representation schemes in explaining patterns of deficits (Jankowicz, Becker, and Howell, 2003; Miikkulainen, 1997; Vinson et al., 2003). Plaut (2002), for example, has brought attention to the idea that the brain's natural tendency to prefer short over long neural connections can lead the system to develop graded topographic, modality-specific knowledge representations when mapping between visual and tactile inputs to verbal and action-based outputs. Simmons and Barsalou (2003) have presented a potential modeling framework based on Damasio's (1989) idea of topographically organized convergence zones that appears to explain many of the trends in impairment observed in cases of category-specific semantic deficits, but their theory remains to be implemented. In contrast, Tyler and colleagues have argued for a single semantic system that has internal structure based on patterns of shared and distinctive properties across concepts and categories, and have implemented a number of their claims in PDP networks (Durrant-Peatfield et al., 1997; Greer et al., 2001).

Despite success in explaining aspects of patient performance, no single model has yet been able to explain all of the patterns of impairment observed in the various cases of brain damage and disease that have been reported. PDP models have clearly provided explanations of how these deficits might arise that go far beyond what was possible to explain with traditional semantic network theories. All of these explanations appeal to the regularities with which specific features pattern across concepts and categories. It is therefore imperative that researchers derive large-scale, realistic representations for each input and output modality if they hope to be able to simulate the complete spectrum of deficits that have been reported. We turn next to state of the art methods that are being used to derive such representations.

5 Deriving representations and exploring structure: Word co-occurrence models

A major problem in modeling semantic memory has been how best to derive realistic semantic representations. Solutions have involved using handcrafted features (Hinton, 1981), randomly generated features (e.g., Plaut, 1995), and semantic feature production norms (McRae et al., 2005). There are positives and negatives with each approach, relating to how many concepts are included, how realistic the representations need to be in structure both at the level of an individual concept and in terms of how concepts cluster into different categories, the word classes for which representations are required (e.g., noun, verb, adjective, etc.), and the resources required/available to derive the representations (see Harm, 1998 for extended discussion). As a result researchers have been searching for methods that will produce representations that are all-encompassing, richly structured, realistic, and can be generated fairly effortlessly via simple learning rules applied to rich data sources.

Two solutions to the problem of generating large-scale representations have emerged. The first is to mine relational information from a large lexical database such as WordNet (Fellbaum, 1998; see Harm, 1998 for a computational implementation of feature mining). The second, which has generated much more research interest, has been to mine large text corpora for information about how words tend to co-occur around one another. The resultant models have become known as *word co-occurrence models*. The two most prevalent are Latent Semantic Analysis (LSA; Deerwester et al., 1990; Landauer and Dumais, 1997), and the Hyperspace Analogue to Language (HAL; Lund and Burgess, 1996), but there are several newcomers, including Correlated Occurrence Analogue to Lexical Semantics (COALS; Rohde, Gonnerman, and Plaut, 2007), Bound Encoding of the Aggregate Language Environment (BEAGLE; Jones and Mewhort, 2007), and the Topic model (Griffiths, Steyvers, and Tenenbaum, 2007), that seek to improve on early methods.

LSA learns word meaning from a text corpus by examining the patterns of word co-occurrence across discrete passages of text (e.g., segmented documents). The first stage of LSA consists of constructing a global co-occurrence matrix in which each row represents a word, each column represents a document, and each cell represents the frequency with which a given word occurs in a given document. This procedure is illustrated in Table 13.1.

The matrix produced during the first stage of LSA is usually subjected to a normalization procedure designed to control for word frequency (see Landauer and Dumais, 1997 for details) and is compressed using singular value decomposition (SVD), a process which serves to emphasize the contexts in which words do and do not occur, and thus a specific word's meaning. Conceptually, this process can be likened to a factor analysis, in which a large number of items are reduced to a small number of latent factors. Consequently, words which may not have been strongly related in the text itself could share a common latent factor and thus be related to one another. It should be noted, however, that the resulting dimensions of

Table: 13.1 LSA representation for eight sentences

A1: *Divert more power from the warp engines.*
A2: *Can the engines sustain warp five given their current state?*
A3: *Captain, the impulse engines are buckling under the stress.*
A4: *Drop out of warp and switch to impulse engines.*
B1: *Captain to transporter room, five to beam up.*
B2: *I tried to beam them down, but the transporter beam is destabilizing.*
B3: *The transporter is ready to beam you down, Captain.*
B4: *Lock on the transporter and beam them up.*

	A1	A2	A3	A4	B1	B2	B3	B4
the	1	1	2					1
Warp	1	1		1		1		
Engines	1	1	1	1				
Captain			1		1		1	
To				1	2	1		
Transporter					1	1	1	1
Beam					1	2	1	1
Up					1	1		1

Each column represents a sentence, and each row represents how frequently each word occurred in that sentence. In this example, words which did not occur at least three times across all sentences have been removed from the table.

each word vector, although related to the original vectors, no longer directly correspond to any of the words from the corpus on which the model was trained.

Given the fact that LSA focuses on a word's co-occurrence within a general context (e.g., a document), LSA is particularly well-suited to capture the general contextual associations and similarities that exist between words (e.g., bread and butter). However, LSA overlooks the importance of positional information in deriving word meaning (e.g., butter is spread on bread, bread is not spread on butter), and thus fails to capture the positional similarities that exist between words.

LSA has been used to model a wide variety of tasks, including: improving a child's ability to summarize via LSA-based feedback (Kintsch et al., 2000), assessing the importance of word order in the meaning of a document (Landauer et al., 1997), metaphor comprehension (Kintsch, 2000; Kintsch and Bowles, 2002), and modeling performance on the Test of English as a Foreign Language (TOEFL). Additional information and publications related to LSA can be found at http://lsa.colorado.edu/.

Representation vectors in the HAL model are built from information about the proximal co-occurrence of words within a large body of text. In HAL, the initial co-occurrence matrix is defined such that there is a row and a column for each word in the corpus. A moving window, usually ten words in size, is passed over the entire text corpus. As the window passes across the text, information is computed regarding the distance of other words within the moving window, relative to the target word at the center of the window. A context word immediately beside the target word receives a value of ten, whereas if there are three words between the context word and the target word, the context word receives a six. Each row denotes the co-occurrence of a context word before the target word, and each column denotes the co-occurrence of a context word after the target word. This procedure is illustrated in Table 13.2.

Once the entire corpus has been processed, meaning vectors are extracted by

Table: 13.2: HAL representation matrix for the sentence "Captain to transporter room, five to beam up."

	captain	to	transporter	room	five	beam	Up
captain							
to	6	2	3	4	5		
transporter	4	5					
room	3	4	5				
five	2	3	4	5			
beam		1	2	3	4		
up			1	2	3	5	

Each row denotes the co-occurrence of context words (column labels) *before* the key word (the row label). Cells with a co-occurrence value of zero were left blank. Each column denotes the co-occurrence of context words (row labels) *after* the key word (the column label). In this example, a window of five words was used to record co-occurrence for illustrative purposes.

concatenating the row and column for a given word. The first half of this vector then represents the frequency with which context words "x" tend to occur preceding "y" in the corpus, whereas the row vectors represent the frequencies with which the context words "y" tend to follow "x" in the corpus. Thus, the vector representations of each word in the HAL model preserve some positional information. To reduce the size of the vectors, which at this stage of processing contain two dimensions for each word encountered in the corpus, the variance of each word vector is computed, and only the word dimensions corresponding to the word vectors with the greatest variance are conserved. Trimming words based on the overall variance in their meaning vectors makes sense because the words with the largest variance contribute the most to the calculation of the overall similarity between vectors.

As with LSA, the similarity of the vectors generated by the HAL model can be compared to one another by calculating the distance between vectors in the semantic space. Given that these word vectors represent the positional context within which each word occurs, HAL is well-suited to capturing the positional similarities between words. For example, *pen* and *pencil* will tend to have similar word vectors because these words tend to occur in the same position surrounded by the same set of context words. However, in capturing positional information, the HAL model is largely insensitive to the types of contextual information to which LSA is sensitive (e.g., the strong association between *bread* and *butter*, despite the fact that bread and butter represent very different objects).

The HAL model has been used to successfully account for a variety of phenomena, including: resolving semantic ambiguity (Burgess, 2001), modeling verb morphology (Burgess and Lund, 1997a), representing abstract words and concrete words (Audet and Burgess, 1999), emotional connotations (Burgess and Lund, 1997b), and how word meaning is learned (Li, Burgess, and Lund, 2000). Additional information related to HAL can be found at http://hal.ucr.edu/.

COALS is one of the more recent co-occurrence models and represents an attempt at improving HAL both via theoretically motivated improvements to the algorithmic procedures used to derive a word's representation, and in the case of the COALS-SVD model, via the use of SVD to reduce the dimensionality of the meaning vectors and emphasize latent information in word representations as in LSA.

The process of creating the co-occurrence matrix for COALS is much the same as that for HAL, with a few notable exceptions.

COALS disregards whether a context word occurs before or after a key word, and uses a ramped four-word window instead of ten. Additionally, the initial sparse matrix that COALS generates is reduced by discarding all but the columns representing the words with the highest word frequency.

Rohde et al. (2007) argue that the most interesting data contained in the norms is not the raw co-occurrence patterns of words (i.e., do words x and y tend to co-occur in general), but rather the conditional co-occurrence patterns (i.e., does x tend to occur around y more or less often than it does in general). They determine the conditional co-occurrence by computing Pearson's correlation coefficients between the different word pairs in the matrix, and replace the individual cell values in the co-occurrence matrix with these correlation values. To simplify the matrix, the negative correlations are set to zero, as they likely do not have a large impact on determining a word's meaning (e.g., it is easier to guess a word from a small number of positively correlated words, such as *wings* and *beak*, than a small number of negatively correlated words, such as *cement* and *chair*; although see Griffiths et al., 2007 for a discussion on the importance of small negative associations). As a final step, the correlation coefficients are square rooted to magnify the differences between the different correlations. Optionally, the final COALS matrix can be compressed using a special form of SVD, as in LSA, to produce low dimensionality binary-valued vectors which may be better suited for use in connectionist models.

The COALS model, and especially the COALS-SVD variant, has been shown to be approximately equal or superior to other co-occurrence models (e.g., HAL, LSA) and other WordNet-based models on a variety of word pair similarity ratings (e.g., Miller Charles Ratings, Miller and Charles, 1991; Finkelstein et al. ratings, Finkelstein et al., 2002), and on multiple-choice vocabulary tests (e.g., the TOEFL as first used by Landauer and Dumais, 1997; *The Reader's Digest* Word Power quizzes as used by Jarmasz and Szpakowicz, 2003). Additionally,

Rohde et al. (2007) have provided a thorough analysis of how different model parameters (e.g., number of dimensions conserved after trimming based on frequency, size of text corpus, size of ramped window) influence results. This has provided researchers with a valuable tool in understanding how the different model parameters interact and how to optimize the model's efficacy in a specific situation. Additional information related to COALS can be found at http://dlt4.mit.edu/~dr/COALS/.

BEAGLE is a fourth approach to deriving meaning from text, and takes inspiration from Murdock's (1982) work on associative memory theory. The main benefits of BEAGLE are that it incorporates a mechanism through which both context and transitional information can be encoded within the same vector representation, it learns continuously, and its representations develop and can be accessed throughout learning.

Words are represented as holographic vectors. Each unique word in the corpus is assigned an environmental vector of normally distributed random values that stands for the word form. Each word is also assigned a memory vector, which is updated each time that word appears in text to reflect information about the context in which the word appears. As the model processes a sentence (this model's unit of processing), a context vector is computed which reflects the sum of the environmental vectors for the other words in the sentence. This context vector is then added to the memory vector for the word and represents the associative component of the word's representation. Transitional information is encoded by adding to the memory vector via noncommutative circular convolution (Plate, 1995). Conceptually, this process corresponds to creating additional position vectors which reflect the order with which individual words, pairs of words, and groups of words are associated (i.e., co-occur) with the word of interest.

Word vectors thus come to represent both context and positional information. Similar vectors are produced for words with similar meanings that may not have occurred in the same contexts. For example, *kerosene* and *paraffin* may not co-occur frequently in sentences, but could still come to have similar memory vectors. These memory vectors differ from those produced by the other word co-occurrence models because contextual or positional information (or both) can be extracted from a single memory representation. BEAGLE has been shown to perform well on a variety of cognitive tasks including: semantic priming, associative priming, mediated priming (Jones, Kintsch, and Mewhort, 2006), and modeling the developmental trajectories of language acquisition (Riordan and Jones, 2007). Additionally, BEAGLE has been shown to be largely insensitive to the dimensionality of a word's memory vectors, so long as they are sufficiently large to represent all of the learned information. This is an important distinction between this model and the other three models which have been discussed (particularly LSA), as the dimensionality of the word representations have been shown to significantly modulate the model's performance (Landauer and Dumais, 1997; Rohde et al., 2007).

The Topic model (Griffiths et al., 2007) is a fifth approach to extracting meaning from text, and is based on earlier models (Blei, Ng, and Jordan, 2003) developed to generate documents based on the underlying topics under discussion. Recent work has expanded the application of the Topic model to invert this inference, such that this model can now be used to infer the general topic(s) of a document dynamically based on the contributions of each word's meanings to different topics.

Many variants of the Topic model have been proposed, but the most interesting cases for our purposes are the recent variants able to represent both the positional and associative information in text (Griffiths et al., 2005), and which are able to dynamically adjust the number of topics required to adequately capture the structure of meanings in words (Griffiths and Steyvers, 2004; Griffiths et al., 2007). To accomplish these goals, the topic model uses various Bayesian statistical procedures (e.g., Marcov Chain Monte Carlo algorithms, Latent

Dirichlet Allocation) to generate distributed representations of latent topics and words as the probabilities that particular words will occur in particular contexts.

The Topic model has several advantages relative to previous word co-occurrence models, primarily because it does not represent words as locations in a semantic space (BEAGLE's holographic representations may also possess these advantages, but to date this has not been explicitly tested). One of the most important of these differences is the ability to represent the different meanings of semantically ambiguous words (i.e., homonymous and polysemous words), which tap different semantic representations depending on the context in which they are encountered (e.g., *bank* can refer to either a financial institution or the border of a river, depending on the context). This is an important step forward relative to previous models, which conflated the meanings of semantically ambiguous words to produce representations in which the different meanings were averaged into a single representation. For example, in the previously discussed accounts, words such as *bank* are represented as an average of the points in semantic space representing each different interpretation of the word. Thus, the location in semantic space in which these words are represented does not capture the fact that these words are strongly associated with two different clusters of knowledge. In contrast, the Topic model can represent each meaning of a word as occurrences in two distinct latent topics, thus conserving a representation of each particular interpretation.

A second major advantage of the Topic model is that it does not suffer from the disadvantages of purely spatial representations of memory, as outlined by Tversky (1977). Tversky originally criticized spatial accounts of memory because they failed to fully capture human similarity judgments. To borrow Tversky's examples, semantic space accounts fail to capture the fact that similarity can be asymmetric (e.g., North Korea is judged to be more like China than China is to North Korea), and that similarity does not always obey the triangle equality, in which meaning "x" can resemble meaning "y," meaning "y" can resemble meaning "z," but meaning "x" does not resemble meaning "z" (e.g., Jamaica is similar to Cuba, Cuba is similar to Soviet Russia, but Jamaica is not similar to Soviet Russia). To account for these trends, Tversky argued that specific features must be defined so that the total number of shared and nonshared features can be contrasted to one another to assess similarity. The Topic model provides solutions to both of these issues because each topic within which a word occurs with a high probability can be interpreted as a feature, and these features can be used as the basis for similarity judgments which are not subject to the problems of pure semantic space accounts.

The Topic model has been successfully employed in many tasks including dynamically selecting a correct meaning of an ambiguous word (Griffiths et al., 2007); word association; document classification (Blei et al., 2003), including identifying scientific topics which are rising in popularity based on abstracts from the Proceedings of the National Academy of Sciences (Griffiths and Steyvers, 2004); document modeling; and collaborative filtering (Blei et al., 2003). Tools for implementing the topic model are available at http://psiexp.ss.uci.edu/research/programs_data/toolbox.htm.

Although the recent development of COALS, BEAGLE, and Topic has precluded a direct comparison of these models to date, it is interesting to note that an important component of these models' success is the fact that they attempt to integrate the contextual and positional information which is captured by LSA and HAL respectively. Given the substantially different approaches to representing association employed by these techniques, a direct comparison of these models will undoubtedly provide useful insights into the finer details of semantic representations and the mechanisms used to derive them. Furthermore, the combination of the components responsible for each model's particular successes within a single framework promises to be an interesting research avenue in future years.

There are two important limitations to current versions of word co-occurrence models that should be noted. First, representations are not sufficiently grounded in perception and action (Glenberg and Robertson, 2000). Word meanings are generated from the co-occurrence of a word with other words. This is certainly one important mechanism through which humans learn word meaning, but humans are also exposed to other sources. For example, they learn co-occurrences between words and sounds, tastes, smells, physical objects in the environment, and actions that can be performed on those objects. This is why some speak of language as being grounded in the environment – something current models are missing. Second, the vectors created by co-occurrence models can be compared to one another to assess their similarity, but there is more to meaning than the simple fact that two words *are* related – we also know *how* they are related. For example, the vectors for *dog* and *bark* may be more similar to one another than *dog* and *meow*, but there is no obvious way of determining why they are similar. The Topic model begins to assess this issue, but has yet to map the particular representations of topics onto a knowledge source other than word/context co-occurrence, nor has it provided a deep understanding of the representational structure and processes underlying semantic memory. These issues are ripe for future research, and the solutions will be major contributions to the study of semantic memory.

6 Conclusions

We have reviewed the three major approaches to modeling semantic memory. Emphasis has been placed on highlighting findings that run counter to semantic network theory, the oldest, and probably still most widely accepted framework outside of the field for thinking about semantic memory. These novel findings include new ways of thinking about cognitive economy and property inheritance, explanations of differences in the speeded computation of components of meaning during word reading, insight into the often puzzling patterns of deficits observed in cases of damage, and new methods for thinking about and deriving word meaning. We are far from a complete understanding of semantic memory, but hopefully it is clear how computational models have contributed to our current understanding and will play an important role in future research.

It is interesting to consider why semantic network theory remains the dominant model used to think about semantic memory despite the fact that its flaws have been well publicized. Several reasons are likely. First, many believe that the new alternatives produce the same old predictions. This is clearly not true. We have reviewed several cases where the predictions that would be derived from semantic network theory are at odds with the accounts provided by PDP models. Second, the alternative theories are more difficult to understand due to the inclusion of formulae, and the perceived impenetrability of the representations derived from the simulations. This may be partially true, but it is clearly not a good reason to avoid the approaches, and new techniques are being developed for visualizing the knowledge stored in PDP networks. Finally, there was a clear shift in the early 1980s away from the study of semantic memory and towards the new and emerging field of concepts and categorization (see Rips and Medin, 2005 for a review). Researchers in the new field articulated the flaws with the old ways of thinking about knowledge representation, and provided successful new alternatives in their place. However, computational models of semantic memory continued to be developed within the field of PDP modeling, and as we hope we have outlined clearly, many exciting advances have been made. Indeed, as some have argued, the two fields are now ready for reintegration, with PDP modeling perhaps providing a rigorous framework within which to incorporate the descriptive proposals of theory theory (Rehder and Murphy, 2003; Rogers and McClelland, 2004), a process which may be

facilitated and enhanced by the use of rich knowledge representations from word co-occurrence models. Regardless of the labels used to describe the work, it is the meaning of the work that is important, and there are clearly still many issues that need to be explored. Computational modeling will play an important role in providing a descriptive language for that work.

References

Anderson, J. A. (1983). *The Architecture of Cognition*. Cambridge, MA: Harvard University Press.

Audet, C. & Burgess, C. (1999). Using a high-dimensional memory model to evaluate the properties of abstract and concrete words. *Proceedings of the Cognitive Science Society* (pp. 37–42). Hillsdale, NJ: Lawrence Erlbaum Associates.

Becker, S., Moscovitch, M., Behrmann, M., & Joordens, S. (1997). Long-term semantic priming: A computational account and empirical evidence. *Journal of Experimental Psychology: Learning, Memory and Cognition*, 23, 1059–82.

Blei, D. M., Ng, A. Y., & Jordan, M. I. (2003). Latent Dirichlet Allocation. *Journal of Machine Learning Research*, 3, 993–1022.

Burgess, C. (2001). Representing and resolving semantic ambiguity: A contribution from high-dimensional memory modeling. In Gorfein, D.S. (Ed.) *On the Consequences of Meaning Selection: Perspectives on Resolving Lexical Ambiguity*. APA Press.

Burgess, C. & Lund, K. (1997a). Modeling parsing constraints with high-dimensional context space. *Language and Cognitive Processes*, 12, 177–210.

(1997b). Representing abstract words and emotional connotation in high-dimensional memory space. *Proceedings of the Cognitive Science Society* (pp. 61–6). Hillsdale, NJ: Lawrence Erlbaum Associates.

Capitani, E., Laiacona, M., Mahon, B., & Caramazza, A. (2003). What are the facts of semantic category-specific deficits? A critical review of the clinical evidence. *Cognitive Neuropsychology*, 20(3/4/5/6), 213–61.

Collins, A. M. & Quillian, M. R. (1969). Retrieval time from semantic memory. *Journal of Verbal Learning and Verbal Behavior*, 8, 240–7.

Collins, A. M. & Loftus, E. F. (1975). A spreading-activation theory of semantic processing. *Psychological Review*, 82(6), 407–28.

Conrad, C. (1972). Cognitive economy in semantic memory. *Journal of Experimental Psychology*, 92(2), 149–54.

Cree, G. S., McRae, K., & McNorgan, C. (1999). An attractor network model of lexical conceptual processing: Simulating semantic priming. *Cognitive Science*, 23(4), 371–414.

Cree, G. S., McNorgan, C., & McRae, K. (2006). Distinctive features hold a privileged status in the computation of word meaning: Implications for theories of semantic memory. *Journal of Experimental Psychology: Learning, Memory, and Cognition*, 32(4), 643–58.

Damasio, A. R. (1989). The brain binds entities and events by multiregional activation from convergence zones. *Neural Computation*, 1, 123–32.

Deerwester, S., Dumais, S. T., Furnas, G. W., Landauer, T. K., & Harshman, R. (1990). Indexing By Latent Semantic Analysis. *Journal of the American Society for Information Science*, 41, 391–407.

Devlin, J. T., Gonnerman, L. M., Anderson, E. S., & Seidenberg, M. S. (1998). Category-specific semantic deficits in focal and widespread brain damage: A computational account. *Journal of Cognitive Neuroscience*, 10(1), 77–94.

Durrant-Peatfield, M. R., Tyler, L. K., Moss, H. E., & Levy, J. P. (1997). The distinctiveness of form and function in category structure: A connectionist model. In Shafto, M. G. & Langley, P. (Eds.) *Proceedings of the 19th Annual Conference of the Cognitive Science Society*. Mahwah, NJ: Erlbaum.

Farah, M. & McClelland, J. L. (1991). A computational model of semantic memory impairment: Modality-specificity and emergent category-specificity. *Journal of Experimental Psychology: General*, 120, 339–57.

Fellbaum, C. (1998). *Wordnet: An electronic lexical database*. Cambridge, MA: MIT Press.

Finkelstein, L., Gabrilovish, E., Matias, Y., Rivlin, E., Solan, Z., Wolfman, G., & Ruppin, E. (2002). Placing search in context: The concept revisited. *ACM Transactions on Information Systems*, 20(1), 116–31.

Glenberg, A. M. & Robertson, D. A. (2000). Symbol grounding and meaning: A comparison of high-dimensional and embodied theories of meaning. *Journal of Memory & Language*, 43(3), 379–401.

Greer, M. J., van Casteren, M., McLellan, S. A., Moss, H. E., Rodd, J., Rogers, T. T., & Tyler, L. K. (2001). The emergence of semantic categories from distributed featural representations. In Moore, J. D. & Stenning, K. (Eds.) *Proceedings of the 23rd Annual Conference of the Cognitive Science Society* (pp. 358–63). London, UK: Lawrence Erlbaum Associates.

Griffiths, T. L. & Steyvers, M. (2003). Prediction and semantic association. *Advances in Neural Information Processing Systems 15*.

Griffiths, T. L. & Steyvers, M. (2004). Finding scientific topics. *Proceedings of the National Academy of Sciences*, 101, 5228–35.

Griffiths, T. L., Steyvers, M., Blei, D. M., & Tenenbaum, J. B. (2005). Integrating topics and syntax. *Advances in Neural Information Processing Systems 17*.

Griffiths, T. L., Steyvers, M., & Tenenbaum, J. B. (2007). Topics in semantic representation. *Psychological Review*, 114, 211–44.

Harm, M. W. (1998). Division of Labor in a Computational Model of Visual Word Recognition Doctoral Dissertation. University of Southern California.

Hinton, G. E. (1981). Implementing semantic networks in parallel hardware. In Hinton, G. E. & Anderson, J. A. (Eds.) *Parallel Models of Associative Memory* (pp. 161–87). Hillsdale, NJ: Erlbaum.

(1986). Learning distributed representations of concepts. In *Proceedings of the Eighth Annual Conference of the Cognitive Science Society* (pp. 1–12). Hillsdale, NJ: Erlbaum.

(1990). Mapping part-whole hierarchies into connectionist networks. *Artificial Intelligence*, 46, 47–75.

Hinton, G. E. & Shallice, T. (1991). Lesioning an attractor network: Investigations of acquired dyslexia. *Psychological Review*, 98(1), 74–95.

Hintzman, D. L. (1991). Why are formal models useful in psychology? In Hockley, W. E. & Lewandowsky, S. (Eds.) *Relating Theory and Data: Essays on Human Memory in Honor of Bennet B. Murdock*. Hillsdale, NJ: Lawrence Erlbaum Associates.

Jankowicz, D., Becker, S., & Howell, S. R. (2003). Modelling Category-Specific Deficits using Topographic, Corpus-Derived Representations. *Poster presented at the 44th annual meeting of the Psychonomic Society, Vancouver, B.C.*.

Jarmasz, M. & Szpakowicz, S. (2003). Roget's thesaurus and semantic similarity. In *Proceedings of the Conference on Recent Advances in Natural Language Processing* (pp. 212–19). Borovets, Bulgaria.

Johnson-Laird, P. N., Herrmann, D. J., & Chaffin, R. (1984). Only connections: A critique of semantic networks. *Psychological Bulletin*, 96, 292–315.

Jones, M. N., Kintsch, W., & Mewhort, D. J. K. (2006). High-dimensional semantic space accounts of priming. *Journal of Memory and Language, 55,* 534–52.

Jones, M. N. & Mewhort, D. J. K. (2007). Representing word meaning and order information in a composite holographic lexicon. *Psychological Review, 114(1),* 1–37.

Kintsch, W. (2000). Metaphor comprehension: A computational theory. *Psychonomic Bulletin and Review, 7,* 257–66.

Kintsch, W. & Bowles, A. (2002) Metaphor comprehension: What makes a metaphor difficult to understand? *Metaphor and Symbol, 17,* 249–62.

Kintsch, E., Steinhart, D., Stahl, G., & LSA Research Group (2000). Developing Summarization Skills through the use of LSA-based feedback. *Interactive Learning Environments, 8,* 87–109.

Landauer, T. K. & Dumais, S. T. (1997). A solution to Plato's problem: The latent semantic analysis theory of acquisition, induction, and representation of knowledge. *Psychological Review, 104(2),* 211–40.

Landauer, T. K., Foltz, P. W., & Laham, D. (1998). An introduction to latent semantic analysis. *Discourse Processes, 25,* 259–84.

Landauer, T. K., Laham, D., Rehder, B., & Schreiner, M. E. (1997). How well can passage meaning be derived without using word order? A comparison of latent Semantic Analysis and humans. In Shafto, M. G. & Langley, P. (Eds.) *Proceedings of the 19th Annual Meeting of the Cognitive Science Society* (pp. 214–417). Mahwah, NJ: Erlbaum.

Lenat, D. & Guha, R. V. (1990). *Building Large Knowledge-Based Systems: Representation and Inference in the CYC Project.* Reading, Mass: Addison-Wesley Publishing Co.

Li, B., & Lund, K. (2000). The acquisition of word meaning through global lexical co-occurrences. In *Proceedings of the 30th Child Language Research Forum* (pp. 167–78). Stanford, CA: CSLI, 2000.

Lund, K. & Burgess, C. (1996). Producing high-dimensional semantic spaces form lexical co-occurrence. *Behavioral Research Methods, Instruments, & Computers, 28(2),* 203–8.

McClelland, J. L. & Rogers, T. T. (2003). The parallel distributed processing approach to semantic cognition. *Nature Reviews Neuroscience, 4,* 310–22.

McCloskey, M. & Glucksberg, S. (1979). Decision processes in verifying category membership statements: Implications for models of semantic memory. *Cognitive Psychology, 11,* 1–37.

McNamara, T. P. (2005). *Semantic priming.* New York, NY: Psychology Press.

McRae, K. (2004). Semantic memory: Some insights from feature-based connectionist attractor networks. In Ross, B. H. (Ed.) *The Psychology of Learning and Motivation: Advances in Research and Theory* (Vol. 45, pp. 41–86). San Diego, CA: Academic Press.

McRae, K., Cree, G. S., Seidenberg, M. S., & McNorgan, C. (2005). Semantic feature production norms for a large set of living and nonliving things. *Behavioral Research Methods, Instruments, and Computers, 37,* 547–59.

McRae, K., Cree, G. S., Westmacott, R., & de Sa, V. R. (1999). Further evidence for feature correlations in semantic memory. *Canadian Journal of Experimental Psychology, 53,* 360–73.

McRae, K., de Sa, V., & Seidenberg, M. (1997). On the nature and scope of featural representations of word meaning. *Journal of Experimental Psychology: General, 126(2),* 99–130.

Masson, M. E. J. (1991). A distributed memory model of context effects in word identification. In Besner, D. & Humphreys, G. W. (Eds.) *Basic Processes in Reading: Visual word recognition* (pp. 233–63). Hillsdale, NJ: Erlbaum.

(1995). A distributed memory model of semantic priming. *Journal of Experimental Psychology: Learning, Memory, and Cognition, 21(1),* 3–23.

McClelland, J. L. & Rogers, T. T. (2003). The parallel distributed processing approach to semantic cognition. *Nature Reviews Neuroscience, 4(4),* 310–22.

Miikkulainen, R. (1997). Dyslexic and category-specific aphasic impairments in a self-organizing feature map model of the lexicon. *Brain and Language, 59,* 334–66.

Miller, G. A. & Charles, W. G. (1991). Contextual correlates of semantic similarity. *Language and Cognitive Processes, 6(1),* 1–28.

Murdock, B. B. (1982). A theory for the storage and retrieval of item and associative information. *Psychological Review, 89,* 609–26.

Murphy, G. L. & Medin, D. L. (1985). The role of theories in conceptual coherence. *Psychological Review, 92,* 289–316.

O'Connor, C., Cree, G. S., & McRae, K. (2007). *Conceptual hierarchies arise from the dynamics of learning and processing: Insights from a flat attractor network.* In prep.

Plaut, D. C. (1995). Semantic and associative priming in a distributed attractor network. In *Proceedings of the Seventeenth Annual Conference of the Cognitive Science Society* (pp. 37–42). Pittsburgh, PA; Hillsdale, NJ: Lawrence Erlbaum Associates.

(2002). Graded modality-specific specialization in semantics: A computational account of optic aphasia. *Cognitive Neuropsychology*, 19(7), 603–39.

Plaut, D. C. & Booth, J. R. (2000). Individual and developmental differences in semantic priming: Empirical and computational support for a single-mechanism account of lexical processing. *Psychological Review*, 107, 786–823.

Plaut, D. C. & Shallice, T. (1993). Deep dyslexia: A case study of connectionist neuropsychology. *Cognitive Neuropsychology*, 10(5), 377–500.

Plate, T. A. (1995). Holographic reduced representations. *IEEE Transactions on Neural Networks*, 6, 623–41.

Quillian, M. R. (1962). A revised design for an understanding machine, *Mechanical Translation*, 7, 17–29.

(1968). Semantic Memory. In Minsky, M. (Ed.) *Semantic Information Processing* (pp. 227–70). Cambridge, MA: MIT Press.

(1967). Word Concepts: A theory and simulation of some basic semantic capabilities. *Behavioral Science*, 12(5), 410–30.

(1969). The teachable language comprehender. *Communications of the Association for Computing Machinery*, 12, 459–75.

Rehder, B. & Murphy, G. L. (2003). A knowledge-resonance (KRES) model of category learning. *Psychonomic Bulletin & Review*, 10(4), 759–84.

Riordan, B. & Jones, M. N. (2007). Comparing semantic space models using child-directed speech. In MacNamara, D. S. & Trafton J. G. (Eds.) *Proceedings of the 29th Annual Cognitive Science Society*, 599–604.

Rips, L. J. & Medin, D.L. (2005). Concepts, Categories, and Semantic Memory. In Holyoak, K. & Morrison, R. (Eds.) *Cambridge Handbook of Thinking and Reasoning* (pp. 37–72). Cambridge, UK: Cambridge University Press.

Rogers, T. T., Lambon Ralph, M. A., Garrard, P., Bozeat, S., McClelland, J. L., Hodges, J. R., & Patterson, K. (2004). The structure and deterioration of semantic memory: A neuropsychological and computational investigation. *Psychological Review*, 111, 205–35.

Rogers, T. T. & McClelland, J. L. (2004). *Semantic Cognition: A parallel distributed processing approach*. MIT Press.

Rogers, T. T. & Plaut, D. (2002). Connectionist perspectives on category specific deficits. In Forde, E. & Humphreys, G. (Eds.) *Category Specificity in Mind and Brain* (pp. 251–89). Hove, East Sussex, UK: Psychology Press.

Rohde, D. L., Gonnerman, L. M., & Plaut, D. C. (2007). An improved method for deriving word meaning from lexical co-occurrence. *Cognitive Science*, Submitted.

Rosch, E. & Mervis, C. B. (1975). Family resemblances: Studies in the internal structure of categories. *Cognitive Psychology*, 7, 573–605.

Rumelhart, D. E. (1990). Brain style computation: Learning and generalization. In Zornetzer, S. F., Davis, J. L., & Lau, C. (Eds.) *An Introduction to Neural and Electronic Networks* (pp. 405–20). San Diego, CA: Academic Press.

Rumelhart, D. E., Hinton, G. E., & Williams, R. J. (1986). Learning internal representations by error propagation. In Rumelhart, D. E., McClelland, J. L., & the PDP Research Group, (Eds.) *Parallel Distributed Processing: Explorations in the Microstructure of Cognition* (Vol. 1, pp. 318–62). Cambridge, MA: MIT Press.

Rumelhart, D. E. & Todd, P. M. (1993). Learning and connectionist representations. In Meyer, D. E. & Kornblum, S. (Eds.) *Attention and Performance XIV: Synergies in Experimental Psychology, Artificial Intelligence, and Cognitive Neuroscience* (pp. 3–30). Cambridge, MA: MIT Press.

Schwanenflugel, P. J. & Rey, M. (1986). Interlingual semantic facilitation: Evidence for a common representational system in the bilingual lexicon. *Journal of Memory and Language*, 25, 605–18.

Sharkey, N. E. (1989). The lexical distance model and word priming. *Journal of Memory and Language*, 31, 543–72.

Simmons, W. K. & Barsalou, L. W. (2003). The similarity-in-topography principle: Reconciling theories of conceptual deficits. *Cognitive Neuropsychology*, 20(3/4/5/6), 451–86.

Smith, E. E., Shoben, E. J., & Rips, L. J. (1974). Structure and process in semantic memory: A featural model for semantic decisions. *Psychological Review*, 81, 214–41.

Tversky, A. (1977). Features of similarity. *Psychological Review*, 84, 327–52.

Vinson, D. P., Vigliocco, G., Cappa, S., & Siri, S. (2003). The breakdown of semantic knowledge along semantic field boundaries: Insights from an empirically-driven statistical model of meaning representation. *Brain & Language*, 86, 347–65.

Warrington, E. K. (1975). The selective impairment of semantic memory. *Quarterly Journal of Experimental Psychology*, 27, 635–58.

Warrington, E. K. & McCarthy, R. (1987). Categories of knowledge: Further fractionation and an attempted integration. *Brain*, 110, 1273–96.

Warrington, E. K. & Shalice, T., (1984). Category specific semantic impairments. *Brain*, 107, 829–54.

Author Notes

The authors would like to acknowledge the insightful comments and discussion on previous versions of this manuscript provided by D. C. Plaut, DJK Mewhort, M. Jones, K. Simmons, S. Gotts, and A. Martin. The creation of this manuscript was supported in part by a Natural Sciences and Engineering Research Council Discovery Grant to G. S. C. and a Canada Graduate Scholarship to B. C. A.

CHAPTER 14

Developing Categories and Concepts

Linda B. Smith and Eliana Colunga

The literature on concept development is highly contentious because there is a lot at stake. The processes that give rise to categories are at the very core of how we understand human cognition. In broad strokes, the debate is about whether categories reflect internal representations that are highly stable symbolic proposition-like and manipulated via logical operators, or whether they are probabilistic, context dependent, and derived from bundles of correlated features and ordinary processes of perceiving and remembering (for reviews, see, Komatsu, 1992; Murphy and Medin, 1985; E. Smith, 1989; E. Smith and Medin, 1981). The literature appears to cycle through these two classes of accounts, advancing with each pass through but never quite leaving these two general points of view. Many of the contentious issues in the developmental literature on concepts and categories are variants of this debate. Accordingly, this review begins with a brief history of theories of categories. This is a history of back-and-forth transitions between a focus on the more stable and the more probabilistic aspects of categories, and it is a debate that is not resolved.

However, by either view, categories result from internal representations that capture the structure in the world. Accordingly, this review of the developmental literature is organized with respect to recent advances in understanding outside-the-mind factors that organize and recruit the cognitive processes that create categories: the statistical regularities in the learning environment, the cognitive tasks and the nested time scales of the internal processes they recruit, and the body which is the interface between the external world and cognition.

1 Back – and – forth theories

Traditionally, categories have been viewed as discrete bounded things that are stable over time and context. In this view, categories are enduringly real, object-like, truly out there in the world and also in our heads. Thus, theorists in this tradition write about categories being acquired, discovered, and possessed. The boundedness and stability expected of categories is well exemplified in the following quote from Keil (1994):

Shared mental structures are assumed to be constant across repeated categorizations of the same set of instances and different from other categorizations. When I think about the category of dogs, a specific mental representation is assumed to be responsible for that category and roughly the same representation for a later categorization of dogs by myself or by another (p. 169).

Within this framework, the central question about categories concerns the structure of the internal representations that give rise to this stability. The classic approach is derived from the logic of classes and distinguishes between the extension of a class and its intension. The extension is all the possible instances. Thus the extension of the class "triangle" is all possible triangles. The intension is the rule that picks out all and only members of the class, for example, the intensional definition of a triangle might be a "closed figure having three sides." Traditional theories assume both the extension and intension of a category to be fixed.

In the 1960s, theories of categorization attempted to explain the assumed fixed category extensions by internally represented definitions that were lists of necessary and sufficient features. This approach came to be rejected on both theoretical and empirical grounds. First, there is no psychological basis for determining the features that form the primitives for concepts (Murphy and Medin, 1985). Second, no successful version of the theory was ever formulated; no one could find the defining properties of such everyday categories as dog, cow, or game (see Rosch and Mervis, 1975). Third, there were data that directly contradicted the idea of necessary and sufficient features. Necessary and sufficient defining features imply all instances of a category should be equally good members. But the data say otherwise; people reliably judge some members of a category to be better than others. For example, a robin is a better example of a bird than is a penguin (Rosch, 1973). As a consequence, in the 1970s, the field turned to probabilistic theories (Rosch, 1973; E. Smith and Medin, 1981).

These theories by their very nature weakened the idea of fixed category representations by focusing on dynamic and context dependent general cognitive processes of memory, attention, association, and generalization by similarity (see E. Smith and Medin, 1981 for review). By the 1980s there were two versions of these probabilistic accounts and arguments that the two versions were empirically and formally indistinguishable (Estes, 1986). By one account, *prototype theory*, concepts are lists of characteristic rather than defining features, a move that readily elevates robins over penguins as examples of birds (see E. Smith and Medin, 1981). In the second, more radical version known as *exemplar theory*, concepts do not really exist in the sense of intensional definitions that determine category membership. Instead, people remember instances and associated properties (including associated language), and then general processes of memory retrieval, association, and generalization by similarity give rise to in-task category judgments (Nosofsky, 1984; see also E. Smith and Medin, 1981), a move that opens the way for shifting and context dependent categories and also for ad hoc categories such as "things on my desk with which I can pound in a nail" (Barsalou, 1983). These accounts also readily explain typicality and other effects that suggest probabilistic decision making in determining category membership. These theories also explain a wide array of experimental results on category learning, recognition, recall, and generalization (Nosofsky, 1984; Zaki and Nosofsky, 2001). Despite the success of these approaches in explaining adult category learning in the laboratory, they have had relatively little impact in the developmental literature. This is primarily because prototype and exemplar theories were not readily extendable as explanations of people's knowledge of natural categories such as dog and chair and animal and furniture. This inability to explain reasoning about natural categories (and the acquisition of natural categories) constitutes a significant failure.

The fundamental problem with probabilistic feature theories as theories of the real categories that people use and that children learn is in specifying the relevant features. There is, at present, no principled basis for feature selection. Moreover, different categories are structured in different ways. For example, colors are relevant to categorizing foods but not to categorizing trucks (Macario, Shipley and Billman, 1990; Murphy and Medin, 1985). This is a fact about natural categories that has attracted considerable attention from developmental researchers because children seem to acquire these regularities as young as two or three years of age, as we review in a later section. Further, some categories are decidedly incoherent and not the sort of category that people might form. For example, people do not form categories that include fish and elephants but not lions (Keil, 1991; Murphy and Medin, 1985; Sloman, 1997). A complete theory of human categorization must explain how different kinds of categories, and how some categories but not others, are selected. Feature selection and category coherence are deeply related and core *unresolved* issues in theories of categorization.

Feature theories also have difficulty accounting for how people reason about categories. Specifically, people often make category judgments that seem more in accord with a defining feature view than a probabilistic view. For example, people will maintain that an organism that has no bird-like properties – other than bird DNA – is, nonetheless, a bird (Keil, 1994; Rips, 1989). In light of these results, a number of researchers in the 1990s suggested that people's concepts were more like naïve theories with causally related systems of features rather than mere lists of characteristic features. (Keil, 1994; Murphy and Medin, 1985; Sloman, 1997). Sometimes called the "theory-theory" of concepts and categories, the main idea is that feature relevance is determined by the causal relatedness of different kinds of properties, both observable and nonobservable, across systems of categories and features. For example, such a theory might include the following: Birds have wings and are lightweight because they fly and these behavioral and physical properties arise because of the genetic structure of birds. Accordingly, researchers began studying people's beliefs about feature relevance, that is, how a feature "really makes something what it is," and their reasoning about the causal relatedness of properties relevant to category membership (Carey, 1985; Gelman and Bloom, 2000; Gelman and Markman, 1987; Malt 1994). The results of these studies suggest a distinction between the core characteristics of things (and often not directly observable properties such as DNA) and the surface characteristics of things (for example, being bird-shaped). That is, within intuitive theories, some features are more important and have more causal force than others.

One version of the intuitive theory account posits that people's theories about kinds are *essentialist* (see Gelman, 2003). The idea here is that people believe there is an essence that determines whether or not an instance is a member of a category. In this account, the reason that an organism that looks and acts nothing like a bird might still be judged to "really be a bird" is because the subject believes the organism possesses the essential but nonobvious properties that are true of all and only birds. These essentialist ideas thus resurrect the criterial property concepts of the 1960s and the idea that a believed intension (a belief in an essential property) determines the extension (the belief in what really is a bird). However, in the modern-day essentialist perspective, it is not that instances actually share these properties or that these essential properties are even useful in recognizing instances in the world, but rather that fixed beliefs in the existence of these essential properties govern how people reason about category members. That is, people believe an instance to have some necessary and sufficient property that determines its membership in a category (that distinguishes *real* water, for example, from a substance that looks like but is not water; see Malt, 1994). Moreover, these essentialist beliefs appear stronger for natural kinds than for artifacts (Gelman and Coley, 1990).

Much contemporary research has been devoted to the study of intuitive theories and their development, opening up new domains of inquiry such as induction, conceptual combination, and causal reasoning (Carey, 1985; Gelman and Coley, 1990; Keil, 2003, 2006; Medin, 1989; E. Smith, 1989). Research on intuitive theories has also led to interesting insights about how reasoning differs in different domains (e.g., for biological versus nonbiological kinds, see Gelman, 2003). The theory-theory of concepts also makes the significant advance in highlighting the importance of *systems* of properties interconnected to each other and systems of categories.

Still, the naïve theory view has its own problems. First, there is no consensus as to what a naïve theory is, the formal nature of the representations, or the kinds of knowledge included (see Ahn et al., 2000 for a discussion). In general, naïve theory theories have not been as formalized as the probabilistic feature sort, and the rigorous testing of predictions has been difficult. Second, naïve theories clearly do not explain the full range of data traditionally viewed as the province of a theory of categorization. Instead, certain phenomena (induction, conceptual change, conceptual combination, and judgments of causal relatedness) are singled out as theoretically more important than phenomena concerning the recognition of instances. Thus, naïve theory accounts do not explain how one knows a bird when one sees (or hears) one, nor do they explain why robins are judged by people psychologically to be better birds than penguins. Indeed, the fact that people readily make these judgments is seen as pretty much irrelevant to the naïve theory account of human categories (Armstrong, Gleitman, and Gleitman, 1983). Third, naïve theories may not be able to explain the very data they take to be their core phenomena. Keil (2006) and Rozenblit and Keil (2002) have presented compelling data that adults' naïve theories are typically explanatorily inadequate and incoherent. People believe they understand a phenomenon when they do not. Keil (2003) suggested that people have at best coarse, not quite right, and gap-filled understandings of the causal structure of even basic things, such as how electricity or gravity work. His experiments suggest that adults' seemingly causally

based reasoning in the laboratory may not reflect well-formed theories but rather a few bits of (not necessarily correct) knowledge coupled with in-the-moment reasoning. That is, causal reasoning in experimental tasks appears much like Barsalou's (1983) ad hoc categories. Nonetheless, these bits and pieces of knowledge, assembled in the service of some specific task, do reasonably well.

Now, not quite a decade into the twenty-first century, accounts of categories based on general processes and probabilistic feature correlations are again on the ascendancy, but this time, borrowing on advances from theory-theory, they are focused on natural categories and systems of feature, category, and language correlations (Colunga and L. Smith, 2006; Cree, McNorgan, and McRae, 2006; Rogers and McClelland, 2005; Xu and Tenenbaum, 2007), with new emphases on how tasks recruit cognitive processes over nested time scales to soft-assemble concepts online (Colunga and L. Smith, 2008a; Samuelson and Horst, 2007), and on the role of bodily action in organizing concepts (Maouene, Hidaka, and Smith, 2008; Richardson et al., 2003). As a backdrop to reviewing these new domains of research, we first consider a distinction concerning kinds of features and categories that has figured prominently in the study of category development.

2 Perceptual or conceptual categories

In the developmental literature, the back-and-forth battle between the two views of concepts is typically couched in terms of whether young children's concepts are fundamentally different from older children's and adults' in being based on static perceptual properties (such as shape or having wheels), whereas more mature concepts are based on conceptual properties or relational roles (such as being edible or growing). One way of putting the developmental debate is whether there is a developmental transition from probabilistic feature accounts (immature concepts) to theory-theory accounts for more fully developed concepts. Perceptual features such as having wheels or having a mouth are generally seen as more relevant to the first kind of theory, and relational roles (carries people places or eats) as more central to the causal relatedness of properties.

Although there are many confusions in this literature about just what should count as perceptual or conceptual (see Colunga and L. Smith, 2008a; Samuelson and Horst, 2007), there is clearly something to the distinction. A large set of findings suggests a developmental shift from more perceptually based to more conceptually based categories (Carey, 1985; Jones and L. Smith, 1993; Keil and Batterman, 1984; Sheya and Smith, 2010). The developmental literature is replete with experiments pitting perceptual versus conceptual properties with perhaps the main conclusion emerging being that both static perceptual properties and relational roles matter in children's early category learning (Booth and Waxman, 2002a; Gelman and Bloom, 2000; Kemler Nelson et al., 2000; Madole and Oakes, 1999; Mandler and McDonough, 1996; Nelson and Ware, 2002; Rakison and Butterworth, 1998b; L. Smith et al., 1996).

Certainly, mature knowledge would seem to include many different but interrelated components. For example, our understanding of dogs must include knowledge that dogs have a characteristic shape, four legs, two eyes, and a mouth, but also knowledge of the roles in which dogs participate, like fetching, playing, sleeping, and eating. Thus the better developmental question may be how children build such a system of knowledge. Figure 14.1 illustrates three kinds of relations relevant to such a system that have been studied in children's categories.

2.1 Property–property correlations

The first relation is among perceptual properties; that is, children's knowledge about categories might include not just perceptual properties but also knowledge about the co-occurrence of properties, for example, knowledge that things with eyes typically have mouths, and things with mouths typically have feet. Knowledge about associations

among properties has been hypothesized to underlie basic level and superordinate level categories (McRae et al., 1999). Knowledge about such co-occurring clusters of properties could help children recognize novel instances, as in recognizing a novel animal as an animal because it contains the relevant cluster of properties (Jones and L. Smith, 2002).

Considerable evidence shows that infants readily learn about the properties typical of category members and that they also learn which properties regularly co-occur (Mareschal et al., 2002; Quinn and Eimas, 1996; Rakison, 2003; Rakison and Butterworth, 1998a, 1998b; Younger, 2003). For example, Quinn and Eimas (1996) showed that three- and four-month-old infants classify cats versus dogs on the basis of features such as head shape. Using methods in which eighteen- and thirty-month-olds were presented with small (and randomly selected) portions of pictures, Colunga (2003) found they discriminated cows versus cars primarily on the basis of properties such as eyes, ears, and head shape versus wheels, windshields, and doors. Rakison and Butterworth (1998b) showed that in at least some tasks, fourteen- to twenty-two-month-old children partition objects into the superordinate categories of animals versus vehicles primarily on the basis of the properties of legs versus wheels. From these results, Rakison (2003) has hypothesized that children may organize superordinate categories around a very small set of salient features.

Other studies show that infants readily learn about correlated properties. In one study, Younger (1990) presented ten- to fourteen-month-old infants with an array of objects in which the features were perfectly correlated. For example, animals with feathered tails had ears and animals with furry tails had antlers. After familiarization, the infants detected changes in feature combinations, treating an instance with a feathered tail and antlers as novel even though both features were highly familiar (see also Younger and Cohen, 1983; 1986). Other evidence suggests that preschool children may make inferences from one perceptual

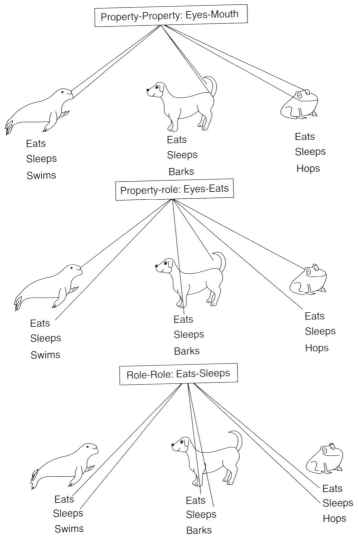

Figure 14.1. Three kinds of correlations among perceptual features and relational roles.

property to another. For example, Gelman (1990) reports that three-year-olds assume that objects with eyes and other animacy properties also have feet (Jones and L. Smith, 1993; Macario et al., 1990). Property–property co-occurrences thus appear readily learnable and an early part of children's developing category knowledge.

2.2 *Property–role correlations*

The second relation is among perceptual properties and roles. That is, children's knowledge about categories could also

include knowledge about the co-occurrence of physical properties and roles, for example, that mouths are used for eating, eyes for seeing, or that things with eyes typically also have some manner of eating. Knowledge about these relations seems crucial to making inferences about the behavior and function of things and to building causal theories about why entities have the properties they do (Ahn et al., 2000).

Research by Mervis and Mervis (1988) and Bates et al. (1991), among others, shows that parents actively provide young children with information about the meaningful roles of objects in play. For example, parents make toy animals walk, eat, sleep, and drink but they drive, zoom, and give rides with toy cars and planes. This kind of play – and the contingencies present in the everyday world – provide an opportunity for children to learn how the perceptual properties of things correlate with the roles of those things in meaningful events. Studies of young children's play suggest that they are aware of these property–role contingencies (Mandler and McDonough, 1998). For example, children appear to know that eyes enable seeing (McCarrell and Callanan, 1995), that wings enable flying (Gelman and Coley, 1990; Goodman, McDonough, and Brown, 1998), that things with feet can move (Massey and Gelman, 1988), that round things can roll, that nonrigid materials can be folded (Samuelson and L. Smith, 2000), and that things with brushes on them can be used for painting (Kemler Nelson et al., 2000a). Goodman et al. (1998) even showed that very young word learners could use these relations to learn new words. For example, when told that "a wug eats…" children chose a picture of a novel animal over pictures of other novel kinds as the referent of *wug*. Further, Madole and Cohen (1995) have shown that when functions such as twisting or rolling are linked to particular parts of objects, eighteen-month-old children attend to those parts more than to others (see also Gerskoff-Stowe, 2005; Rakison and Cohen, 1999).

Other evidence shows that infants also readily learn property–role correlations in experimental tasks. For example, Rakison and Poulin-Dubois (2002) found that four-teen-month-old infants learned how the parts of objects (e.g., arm-like projections) predicted their motion. Rakison (2003) hypothesized that predictive relations between features and roles play a causative role in children's parsing of objects into features, and in their selective attention to some features over others in forming a category. Thus, the extant evidence indicates that young children learn a link between roles and the characteristic properties of things that participate in those roles and that these links strongly influence their category decisions.

2.3 *Role–role correlations*

A third relation that should be important to children's developing category knowledge is among roles. This includes the knowledge, for example, that things that eat also sleep, and that they drink and grow, and so forth. Direct associations among roles that do not depend on links to the perceptual properties of things might be particularly crucial for reasoning about abstract and hypothetical categories. For example, such knowledge would enable one to reason – in a conceptually coherent way – about possible life forms, and to make inferences about entities from their roles in events despite unusual perceptual properties. Knowledge of role–role correlations would also seem crucial to developing a higher-level (and causal) understanding about different kinds (Carey, 1985; Gelman and Coley, 1990; Keil, 1979).

There is less direct evidence on what young children might know about role–role correlations that is not linked through the perceptual properties of the participating entities. One relevant set of studies by Mandler and McDonough (1996; 1998; 2000) examined young children's imitations of category relevant roles across a diverse set of entities. For example, Mandler and McDonough (1996) presented fourteen-month-old children with a toy dog, demonstrated the action of giving it a drink from a cup, and then asked children to do the same thing with similar and prototypical instances that drink (e.g., a cat), with dissimilar animals that one does not usually think of as drinking (e.g., a fish), and entities of a different superordinate category (e.g., a car). Children generalized the action broadly to items in the same superordinate category (cats and fish), but not to items in a different superordinate category. In addition, children only extended actions that were appropriate to the category (e.g., when the experimenter gave a vehicle a drink, children did not imitate the action on the vehicle match). These results show that very young children's generalizations of roles are not based solely on overall similarity, but these results do not unambiguously show direct knowledge, unmediated by perceptual properties, of role–role correlations either.

Indeed, Rakison and Poulin-Dubois (2001) suggest that Mandler and McDonough's results could reflect children's use of a single prominent feature such as having a mouth or having eyes that are predictive of entities that engage in the role of drinking. Thus, Mandler and McDonough's results could reflect knowledge about how roles link to features rather than knowledge about roles that can be accessed independently of the perceptual features that co-occur with those roles. Mandler (2003) countered that a feature–role explanation cannot explain all her results because in several experiments, they included a "Flying Tiger" toy airplane that had a mouth painted on its nose cone. She notes that children never offered a drink to the airplane but did generalize the action to models of animals that had the barest hint of a mouth. If this observation is generally true, it might indicate that young children have knowledge of category roles – and perhaps their relations to each other – that is not dependent on, and can be accessed independently of, their knowledge about the characteristic properties of things. Alternatively, children's nongeneralization of the drinking action to the airplane could reflect their use of predictive properties other than mouths (e.g., eyes), or could be due to idiosyncratic aspects of the particular airplane used in the Mandler and McDonough studies. Clearly, these are issues that merit further empirical study.

Other evidence in the literature on children's knowledge about role–role correlations derives mostly from verbal reasoning tasks, and these suggest a protracted developmental course. For example, Keil (1979) showed that older preschoolers could systematically judge which predicates could sensibly apply to nouns and in this way showed that they know that things that eat also sleep, and so forth. However, the children in this task were not asked to directly link roles to each other but did so through familiar nouns. In her studies on conceptual change, Carey (1985) also found that four-year-olds generalize nonvisible properties

such as breathes, sleeps, and eats collectively (that is, generalizing *breathes* in the same way that they generalize *sleeps*) to unfamiliar animal categories. However, four-year-olds' judgments depended more than did older children's and adults' on the similarity of the target category to people, a result consistent with the idea that these generalizations go through the object and its surface properties.

Two other lines of research – although not directly asking whether young children form and use role–role connections – suggest that they might. These studies show that preschool children can treat the very same perceptual object as a different kind – as an artifact versus a material, or as an animate versus an inanimate – if given information about its relational roles. For example, Gelman and Bloom (2000) found that when three-year-old children were told that an object was intentionally created (e.g., folded, cut, sawed), they labeled it as an artifact (e.g., hat, knife, belt), but when told the very same object was accidentally created (e.g., dropped, ripped, knocked), they labeled it with a material term (e.g., newspaper, plastic, metal). Similarly, Booth and Waxman (2002b) showed that three-year-old children could interpret the very same object as animate if told it had a mommy and daddy, was happy, slept, and was hungry, but as inanimate if told it was made, was fixed, got worn, and was bought. Both of these results suggest that three-year-olds have knowledge about co-occurring and kind-defining relations that may not depend on direct links to the perceptual properties of the objects that take part in those relations.

Recently, Sheya and Smith (2010) directly asked if children could make an inference from one role to another. For example, when children were told that an object like that in Figure 14.2a eats, could children infer that it also sleeps? Four-year-old but not three-year-old children could do this. However, if shown an object like in Figure 14.2b, with a defining feature of animacy, three-year-olds judged that it would sleep. Two-year-olds required a cluster of features

Figure 14.2. Three stimulus types used in Sheya and Smith (2007). **a.** No defining features. **b.** One defining feature. **c.** Clusters of correlated features.

like that in Figure 14.2c to make the inference. Sheya and Smith suggested that static object features serve as the glue that holds and aggregates information in this developing system. This may be because specific features (e.g., mouths) are causally tied to specific roles (e.g., eating). Alternatively, it could also be because statistically, static perceptual cues may simply be better predictors of roles than roles are of other roles. After all, the static surface properties of an object are regularly available to the learner whenever an instance is. In contrast, different roles (say drinking and hugging) are evident only in specific contexts and two roles relevant to the same kind may rarely occur together. Thus, the perceptual to conceptual trend could reflect – not intrinsic differences about different kinds of properties – but merely their statistical properties in the data available to learners.

This developmental distinction between perceptual and conceptual features is also related to one made in the cognitive neuroscience literature between perceptual and functional features. In the literature on category-specific deficits as a function of brain impairment, perceptual features in the form of visual properties have been contrasted with functional features in the form of actions as a basis for distinguishing animals versus artifacts (and more specifically, tools, see Moss and Tyler, 2003; Pilgrim, Moss, and Tyler, 2005). The proposal that different kinds of ontological categories derive primarily from the fact that different kinds of features and thus different brain regions (e.g., perceptual features for animals and functional ones for artifacts) matter for different kinds of categories is controversial

(see Moss and Tyler, 2003 for discussion). One criticism is that there are patients with specific deficits involving categories of living thing deficits who do not have the expected perceptual deficits. One possibility is that although perceptual and functional features characterize all kinds of categories, functional/semantic information is particularly important to conceptual representations, is more robust, and is more resistant to damage. If one accepts the developmental evidence, functional features would also be later acquired. The function of artifacts is also strongly linked to properties such as shape. Furthermore, biological functions (eating, sleeping) are crucial for categories of living things, and these biological functional features link to specific perceptual properties and to modes of interacting with the environment. These ideas again reinforce the potential importance of understanding how perceptual and conceptual (or functional) features may be correlated and mutually support the developmental of a system of features and categories.

3 Development as data mining

Data mining is a process through which implicit but previously unknown regularities can be extracted from large volumes of data. This still developing interdisciplinary field uses techniques drawn from statistics, database technology, pattern recognition, and machine learning, and has proven to be highly effective and of significant practical value. Can human concepts be understood as a form of data mining? Young children – as they observe their world and as they learn language – amass a large data set. Do their cognitive systems, in a sense, mine that data, discovering latent regularities that constitute what we call concepts and categories?

Perhaps the most promising new work on category development uses data mining techniques to examine how learning about *many* categories with *many* overlapping and correlated properties may enable higher-order structural patterns (or categories) to be formed. The approaches that seek to understand the latent structure in feature, instance, and category correlations include connectionist approaches (see, especially, Rogers and McClelland, 2005) and also Bayesian approaches (see, especially, Xu and Tenenbaum, 2007). Both concentrate on the statistical feature structure of natural categories and the emergent higher-order relations in that structure.

One phenomenon that suggests the developmental potency of such latent structure is children's early noun learning. Although children initially learn words slowly, by the time they are two to three years old, they seem to be expert learners. Indeed, many studies have shown that two- and three-year-old children need to hear only a *single* object named to correctly generalize that name to the whole category (Golinkoff, Mervis, and Hirsh-Pasek, 1994; Markman, 1989; L. Smith, 1995; Waxman and Markow, 1995). Young children's facility in mapping nouns to categories is particularly remarkable because, as noted earlier, not all categories are organized in the same way. Instead, there are different kinds of categories – animals, objects, and substances – with fundamentally different organizational structures. The ease with which two- and three-year-old children learn names for these different kinds suggests that they understand the different organizations at a very early age.

The key experimental results derive from what is known as Novel Noun Generalization (NNG). This task was originally designed to measure the one-trial category learning that two- to three-year-old children seem to naturally show (see Katz, Baker, and Macnamara, 1974; Markman, 1989). In this task, the child is shown a single novel object, told its name (e.g., *This is a toma*) and then asked what other things have the same name (e.g., *Where is the toma here?*) With no more information than this – a novel name applied to a single novel thing – two- and three-year-olds extend the name in systematic ways that seem right to adults. Experimenters have studied three kinds of entities (as shown in Figure 14.3) and found three different patterns of generalization. Given objects with features typical

Figure 14.3. Three different kinds of stimulus types commonly used in Novel Noun Generalization tasks: rigid solid things, things with eyes or other characteristic features of animates, nonsolid things.

of animates (e.g., eyes), children extend the name narrowly to things that are similar in multiple properties. Given a solid inanimate thing, children extend the name broadly to all things that match in shape. Given a nonsolid substance, children extend the name by material. These are highly reliable and replicable results – obtained by many researchers – and in their broad outline characteristic of children learning a variety of languages (Booth and Waxman, 2002b; Gathercole and Min, 1997; Imai and Gentner, 1997; Jones and L. Smith, 2002; Jones, L. Smith, and Landau, 1991; Kobayashi, 1998; Landau, L. Smith, and Jones, 1988, 1992, 1998; Markman, 1989; Soja, Carey, and Spelke, 1991; Yoshida and L. Smith, 2001; see also Gelman and Coley, 1990; Keil, 1994). However, children's specific patterns of performances in this task are also highly dependent on the task, the stimuli, and specific language cues.

Children's use of different features to form new categories in these tasks appears to directly reflect the category likelihoods of those features for categories children already know. Samuelson and L. Smith (see also Colunga and L. Smith, 2005; L. Smith, Colunga, and Yoshida, 2003) examined the category structure of the first 312 nouns typically known by children learning English (and in other studies the first 300 nouns learned by children learning Japanese). They measured category structure by asking adults to judge the shared properties of typical instances of individual noun categories on four dimensions – shape, color, texture, and material. They found that individual artifact categories (chairs, forks, spoons, cups) were judged to have instances that were highly

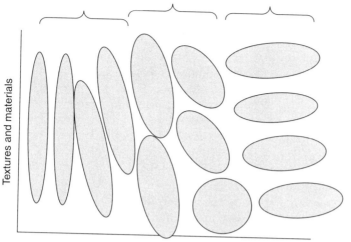

Textures and materials

Shape–from constructed to animal like to simple

Figure 14.4. A theoretical representation of a gradient of generalization patterns (or category shapes) for categories in a feature space defined by aspects of shape and solidity and material substance.

similar in shape but variable in other properties, that animal categories were judged to have instances that were similar in all properties, and that substance categories were judged have instances that were similar in material (and color). Thus, the importance of features to different kinds of categories may reflect the expected distributions of those features *for nearby categories*, a point we expand on later in this chapter.

Several recent studies further indicate that children's different patterns of category generalization for different kinds of features may be geometrically organized in some larger feature space (Colunga and L. Smith, 2005, 2008a Imai and Gentner, 1997; Yoshida and L. Smith, 2003). For example, Colunga and L. Smith (2005) showed that children's generalizations of novel names by shape versus material shifted gradually as the presented novel instances varied incrementally from shapes typical of artifacts (complex, lots of angles) to shapes typical of substances (simple rounded shapes). Similarly, Colunga and L. Smith (2008a see also Yoshida and L. Smith, 2005) showed that children's generalization by shape versus material shifted systematically as (identically shaped) instances were incrementally varied from solid (brick-

like), to perturbable (play dough-like), to nonsolid (applesauce-like). We illustrate this idea in Figure 14.4. Individual categories of instances are represented as areas in a two-dimensional feature space. The shape of the categories – that is, the distribution of features across the two dimensions of shape and texture/material – varies systematically as a function of location in that space.

This idealized representation illustrates the structure that appears to characterize the nouns that are learned early by young children and also to characterize children's generalizations of a newly learned noun to new instances. That is, instances of categories with highly constructed and angular shapes vary little in shape but vary greatly in texture and material. In contrast, categories of animal-like shapes vary little in shape but are also constrained in their variation in texture/material. Finally, the unconstructed simple shapes of substances are correlated with category distributions of relatively variable shapes but limited texture/materials. This is a very interesting structure: Similar categories, that is categories close in the feature space, have similar patterns of category likelihoods for different features. Put another way, the categories in the same region of feature space have similar shapes (their generalization patterns), and there is a gradient of category shapes (range of generalizations across different features) across the space as a whole. They show the mathematical property of *smoothness* (Hidaka and Smith, 2010): near (or categories with similar instances) have similar generalization patterns and far (or categories with dissimilar instances) have dissimilar generalization patterns. Understanding the developmental emergence of this structure seems key to solving the feature selection problem more generally. In brief, *kinds* may be defined by a higher-order property of the geometry of categories in feature space, an idea related to the proposals in the cognitive neuroscience literature that different kinds of categories emerge as a consequence of the relevance of different kinds of properties (Moss and Tyler, 2003).

The fact that children's novel noun generalizations – by shape for angular solid things, by multiple similarities for animals, by material for nonsolid things – follow the statistical regularities that characterize early learned nouns (Samuelson and L. Smith, 1999; L. Smith, Colunga and Yoshida, 2003) suggests that this smooth structure is learned. Two additional facts about children's novel noun generalizations suggest that these generalizations are, in fact, a learned consequence of learning object names.

First, experiments have included control tasks that are identical to the NNG task, except the object is not named. Instead, children are shown the exemplar and then are asked what other objects are "like" or "go with" the exemplar. With these cues, children do not systematically attend to the different properties of different kinds (Imai and Gentner, 1997; Landau et al., 1988, 1992; Jones, L. Smith and Landau, 1991; Soja et al., 1991). This fact suggests a link between naming and knowledge about category-specific organizations (see Deisendruck and Bloom and also Colunga and L. Smith, 2008a for a further discussion).

Second, kind-specific name generalizations emerge *with* vocabulary growth (Landau et al., 1988; Soja et al., 1991; Jones

et al., 1991; Samuelson and L. Smith, 1999, 2000; L. Smith, 1995). The evidence indicates that the tendency to attend to shape in the context of naming emerges only after children already know some fifty to 150 nouns. For children learning English, a bias to extend names for animates by multiple similarities and a bias to extend names for nonsolid substances by material emerge even later (see, especially, Jones et al., 1991; Samuelson and Smith, 2000). Thus, biases to attend to different properties when extending names for different kinds codevelops with increasing vocabulary, a fact consistent with the idea that children's word learning helps create these generalized expectations about different kinds.

Indeed, language learning may play the crucial role in enabling children to build the systems of generalizations that enable the rapid selection of just the right features for different kind of categories. In particular, kind-specific name generalizations are modulated by linguistic cues. One result is the influence of count and mass syntactic frames on English-speaking children's interpretations of novel objects and substances. Count nouns are those that take the plural and can be preceded by words such as *a*, *another*, *several*, and *few*, as well as numerals. Count nouns thus label things we think of as discrete individuals, such as chairs, trucks, shirts, studies, and wishes. Mass nouns, in contrast, cannot be pluralized but instead are preceded by words such as *some*, *much*, and *little*. Mass nouns thus label things that are conceptualized as unbounded continuous masses, such as water, sand, applesauce, research, and justice. Past research shows that count syntactic frames (e.g., *a mel*, *another mel*) push children's attention to the shape of the named thing whereas mass syntactic frames (e.g., *some mel*, *more mel*) push attention to material (Gathercole et al., 1995; McPherson, 1991; Soja, 1994). Other studies show that linguistic cues associated with animacy (descriptors such as *happy* or the personal pronouns *he* and *she*) push attention to multiple similarities even when the objects do not possess perceptual cues such as eyes that are diagnostic of animacy (Booth and Waxman, 2002a; Yoshida and L. Smith, 2001, 2005), and even when these words do not refer to the object in question (Colunga and L. Smith, 2004; Colunga, 2006). In brief, the evidence shows that language exerts an online influence on children's category formation in the NNG task.

The particular language a child learns also influences the child's novel noun generalizations. Although there are overarching universals in the name generalizations of children learning different languages, there are differences as well (Colunga and L. Smith, 2005; Gathercole, Thomas, and Evans, 2000; Imai and Gentner, 1997; Kobayashi, 1998; Yoshida and L. Smith, 2005). For example, Japanese-speaking children are more sensitive to animacy cues than are English-speaking children (Yoshida and L. Smith, 2003), Spanish-speaking children are more sensitive to count mass syntactic cues than English-speaking children (Gathercole, 1997), and Japanese- and English-speaking children place the boundaries between animals and objects and between objects and substances in different places (Colunga and L. Smith, 2005; Yoshida and L. Smith, 2003b).

Colunga and L. Smith (2008a) hypothesized that children's knowledge of different kinds – and their ability to systematically generalize a name to new instances – emerged as a consequence of the higher-order correlations among words, features, and categories. In a series of simulations in which they fed a connectionist network the statistical regularities of the first 300 nouns learned by children learning English or Japanese, they showed that the network could discover the latent structure across these words and categories, and systematically form and generalize new categories in ways that fit the specific task performances of English- and Japanese-speaking children.

Two- and three-year-olds' generalization of names for different kinds of things in different ways is so robust that some have tried to explain this knowledge with fixed propositional representations, "over hypotheses," or theories about the causal structure of different kinds (Booth and Waxman, 2002b;

Deisendruck and Bloom, 2003; Hall, 1996; Soja et al., 1991). Others have suggested that forms of Bayesian statistical learning applied to symbolic representations may be used to explain the evidence that children learn these generalizations as they learn the noun categories (and related syntactic structures in their language), and that their knowledge reflects the statistical structure of their language (see Xu and Tenenbaum, 2007). These proposals thus present an alternative view to the connectionist accounts of Colunga and L. Smith (2005; or relatedly, Rogers and McClelland, 2005). Again, we see the standard contrast in theories – propositions versus general processes of association and generalization by similarity. However, both of these new kinds of accounts have moved forward by concentrating on systems of statistical regularities and how the child might be data mining those regularities for latent structure.

4 Nested time scales in tasks

Categories are evident to experimenters, theorists, and naïve observers only across large stretches in time. It is only when an individual labels, for example, one thing as a "dog," and then sometime later labels something else as a "dog," and then sometime later recognizes another thing as a "dog," and so on that we have evidence of a category. *Categories* are demonstrated and *acquired* in real time, in moment-by-moment encounters with specific things in specific task contexts. This is one fundamental problem with thinking of categories in terms of fixed and stable representations (Samuelson and L. Smith, 2000). A second problem is the idea that category decisions are simply repeated without variation. Instead, responses and judgments are bent, adapted, and fine-tuned to the context. For example, we think about (and classify) frogs differently when we are next to a pond than when we are in a fine restaurant. Experimental studies of adult categorization also show that adults make systematically different category decisions when asked to name things, when asked to judge their functional utility, when asked about typicality, when asked to predict certain properties, and when asked to make similarity judgments (Malt, 1995; Malt and Sloman, 2004; Rips and Collins, 1993). Such context effects are also seen in children's categorizations.

The smartness of children's noun learning is not just due to data mining the regularities, but also to their inventive extension of those regularities in novel contexts. A number of experiments have shown that very small changes in the stimuli, task context, and words *systematically* shift children's novel noun generalizations. As noted earlier, children form categories by different properties – even given the very same instance (e.g., a solid, irregularly shaped thing), if the novel name occurs in the context of "a" (e.g., " a dax") versus "some" ("some dax"), if it has eyes versus if it does not, or if it is labeled as "happy" versus "bought in a store" (Booth, Waxman, and Huang, 2005; Gathercole et al., 1995; McPherson, 1991; Soja, 1994). Such results suggest that children's category generalizations are the product of the integration of past knowledge with current input.

Colunga and L. Smith (2008b; Colunga, 2006), building on the Attentional Learning Account first proposed by L. Smith et al. (2002), have proposed that this inventiveness may be understood as a product of the nested dynamics of attentional learning.

The original Attentional Learning Account (ALA) (L. Smith et al., 2002 Colunga and L. Smith, 2005) was concerned with children's learning of statistical regularities among features, category organization, and words, but not with the adaptive generalization of that knowledge across tasks. More specifically, ALA explains children's novel noun generalizations through learned cues that shift dimension weights among potentially relevant dimensions. Previous versions of the attentional learning account of children's novel noun generalizations have concentrated on changes on one time scale (the time scale of development and learning, see Colunga and Smith, 2005; L. Smith et al., 2002). Nonetheless,

part of this account is that attention is dynamically tied to contextual cues that activate learned associations, an d through these processes, attention selects some similarities over others as relevant to the task at hand. Viewed in this way, attention is a powerful process because it is inherently multicausal, integrating influences over multiple time scales. Further, attention in the moment will strongly constrain the future – and acquired statistical regularities – by determining what is learned at that moment. In brief, attention is one important mechanism through which prior knowledge is brought into the present and through which the past constrains learning and thus future knowledge.

The Dynamic-Attentional Learning Account (D-ALA) extends this idea by integrating experience at three time scales. Figure 14.5 illustrates the three nested processes. The larger box represents learned correlations between properties, words, and categories. These feed into an attention map in which some areas of the feature space may be more highly weighted than others. The building of these representations operates over the slowest time scale. The next box represents processes that operate at the time scale of tasks. Relevant inputs include the attention map, the perceptual properties of the object, and what is actually being said in the task. These shift attention weights in the moment – integrating various forces on attention, including the attention map which reflects statistical regularities in experienced categories and any attention-grabbing aspects of the current input such as glowing surfaces (Samuelson and Horst, 2007), surprising properties (L. Smith, Jones, and Landau, 1992), or opening or closing (Kemler Nelson et al., 2000b). Finally, these attentional processes operate within the specific task, in, for example, the comparison of a test object with an exemplar in the NNG task. Critically, as shown in the right side of Figure 14.5, these nested processes do not interact in just one direction, but also feedback on each other. Each decision – a mapping of a word to an object and to its attended property – feeds back into the

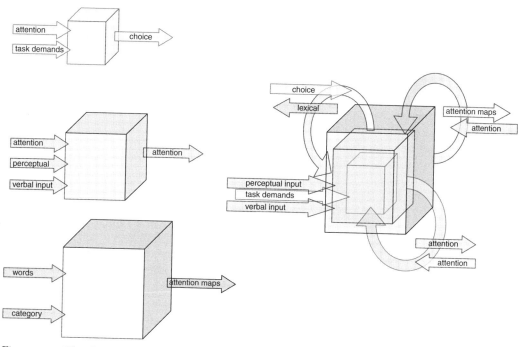

Figure 14.5. The three nested time scales of the Dynamic-Attentional Learning Account: developmental time, task time, and decision/action time, shown separately on the left and in terms of their nested influences on each other on the right.

accumulating correlations as does the task contexts and associated words.

The beauty of such nested processes is that they integrate these processes and inputs over different time scales, generating behaviors that are optimal, stable, and generalizable – the behaviors that seem so essential to higher cognition – but also generating category decisions that are flexible and inventive. Through such multilayered and nested processes, the child's noun learning can effectively adapt to different environments (say, English-speaking or Japanese-speaking), a changing world (moving from one activity to the next or one place to the next), and changing inputs and task goals (biting the cookie, but rolling the ball). Thus, this soft-assembly of attention out of unthinking and nested processes may lead to robust knowledge-based behavior and also to smart, flexible adaptability.

Colunga and L. Smith (2008b) tested the model in two tasks designed to examine two kinds of inventiveness – interpolation and extrapolation. In the interpolation task,

the objects fell between solids and nonsolids (doughs and goops), whereas in the extrapolation task, the objects had extra animacy features (e.g., five eyes). Children categorized the objects within the task contexts in new and inventive ways that were highly systematic, suggesting the integrative finding of new solutions through nested forces on attention. Samuelson, Schutte, and Horst (2009) tested a related model in a series of tasks that altered the current attention-grabbing properties – making solid things with glowing colors, for example, or changing aspects of the task (e.g., forced choice versus other kinds of category responses). Both sets of results support the conceptualization of categorization, not as specific knowledge about fixed categories, but as momentary events that collect and integrate information over multiple processes and time scales.

Such dynamic systems accounts of categorization may be particularly important for understanding category development, its accelerating pace in the early preschool years, and findings of cross-linguistic differences in feature selection and ontological categories (see Imai and Gentner, 1997; Lucy and Gaskins, 2001; Yoshida and L. Smith, 2003, 2005). Self-organizing nested attentional processes build moment-to-moment knowledge that makes for stable categorization patterns and also dynamically finds new solutions to tasks never encountered, as in Colunga and Smith (2008b). Understanding the interactions among these nested time scales may also benefit the translation of these basic research findings into ways to help children with developmental delays in language learning. The front end of the system is attention in the moment; this is what provides the data upon which category relevant shifts in attention and rapid word learning depend. Manipulating attention in the moment in ways relevant to those statistics may give delayed learners a leg up (see Smith et al., 2002) for relevant data on these issues.

5 Embodiment

A growing movement in cognitive science suggests that the body creates higher-order concepts through perception and action (Clark, 1997; Gallese and Lakoff, 2005; Glenberg and Kaschak, 2003; Núñez and Lakoff, 2005; Varela, Thompson, and Rosch, 1993; Yeh and Barsalou, 2006; Zwaan, 2004). *Nothing* gets into or out of the cognitive system (or the brain) except through the surface structure of the body. Parts of the body – head, hands, legs, and feet – play a role in every experience, every second, every minute from birth to death.

How much of the human semantic system, then – and children's understanding about categories – depends on the body and bodily action? There are reasons to believe that the influence is considerable. G. Holmes (1922/1979) documented the representational role of the body early in the history of neuroscience, discovering the organizational system known as the "neural map." This is a topographic array of nerve cells across which there is systematic variation in the value of some sensory-motor parameter. Maps organized by the body's surface are a particularly common form of cortical representation (Graziano, Cohen, and Botvinick, 2002; N. P. Holmes et al., 2004; Penfield and Rasmussen, 1950). Studies of neurological disorders and functional brain imaging demonstrate important roles for these body maps in the perception of one's body (N. P. Holmes et al., 2004), in the production of action (Gallese et al., 1999), in understanding others' actions, and in the categorization of objects such as tools strongly linked to action by a particular body part (Hauk, Johnsrude, and Pulvermüller, 2004).

Studies of the world's languages also point to body parts as a universal representational medium (Heine, 1997; Svorou, 1993). Words derived from body parts are remarkably common in semantic domains of space, number, measurement, and emotion (de Leon, 1994; Lakoff and Johnson, 1980; Sakuragi and Fuller, 2003; Saxe, 1981; Yu, 2004). Indeed, researchers have proposed a universal semiotics of body parts to interpret and translate images and texts from ancient cultures (Bron, Corfu-Bratschi, and Maouene, 1989; see also Lakoff and Johnson, 1980). All this suggests that the body may be more than a mere interface between mind and world; rather, it may be central to the origin and representational basis of meaning.

Bodily actions make things happen in the world, and in so doing create meaning. The body part most intimately involved in this meaning creation is the hands. As such, hands are near constants in children's visual fields as they learn about the world, a fact recently documented by experiments that placed a head camera on young children as they interacted with objects and others in naturalistic settings (Yoshida and L. Smith, 2008). Early category learning – prior to words – may well be constrained and shaped by action in general and by hand actions on objects in particular (Ruff and Rothbart, 1996). The constraints on meaning from the body may be fundamentally of two different kinds, each worthy of investigation. First are constraints from bodily actions themselves; for example, the trajectory, starting point, and goal point of reaching may provide the grounded meaning for the whole set of concepts related to "retrieval" (see Richardson et al., 2003). Second, the body also constrains the input by placing real physical limitations as to what can be perceived, known, and made to happen in the world (Clark, 1997).

Multimodal interactions between action and perceptual experience may even play a role in defining relevant properties for categories. For example, in one experiment, Smith (2005) presented children with the object shown in Panel A of Figure 14.4. The child was told it was a "wug" and was then given the object to hold and shown how to move it up and down on a vertical path. The child then repeated this action three times. The experimental question was this: What other kinds of objects are also *wugs*? Children chose from new instances that were either elongated vertically or horizontally relative to the exemplar, as shown in Panel B. Smith's conjecture was that children would be more likely to categorize the exemplar with the vertically rather than the horizontally extended alternative *because* of the experience of *manually* moving the object vertically. This conjecture was right, at least for two- to three-year-old children. Children who *acted* on an object by moving it up and down extended the name to vertically – but not horizontally – elongated objects. Children who acted on an object by moving it horizontally extended the name to horizontally but not vertically elongated objects. Children who only watched the experimenter perform the action did not prefer test objects elongated in the direction of the watched action.

These results are reminiscent of an earlier adult experiment by Freyd (1983), who showed an effect of action on the perception of letter-like figures. Freyd taught adults to recognize new letter-like characters by having them watch a letter being drawn. Subjects watched characters drawn by one of two methods. Figure 14.6 illustrates a character and the two drawing methods. Although the drawing methods differed, the final static characters were identical. After

(a)

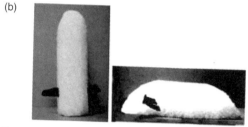
(b)

Figure 14.6. The exemplar (A) and two choice objects (B) used in Smith (2005).

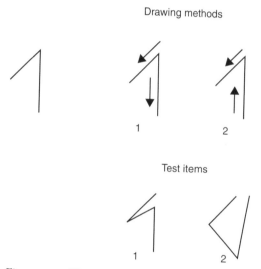

Drawing methods

1   2

Test items

1   2

Figure 14.7. Illustration of two drawing techniques and two test items used in the Freyd (1983) experiment.

training with one drawing method, subjects were presented with static representations and asked whether they were instances of the modeled character. Some of these test characters were "sloppily" drawn versions of the modeled character. Freyd found that subjects were reliably faster at recognizing static characters distorted in a manner consistent with the drawing method they observed during training than they were at recognizing equally distorted characters inconsistent

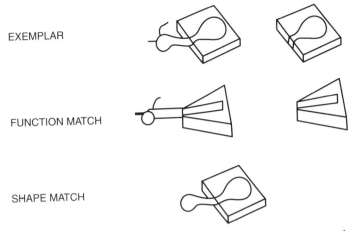

EXEMPLAR

FUNCTION MATCH

SHAPE MATCH

Figure 14.8. Illustration of the objects used by Kemler Nelson et al. (2000). Shown are the exemplar in its closed and open form and the "function" matching test object that closes and opens and the "shape" matching test object than cannot be opened.

with the observed drawing method. In brief, the static visual features that mattered for category membership were influenced by dynamic information about how those features were made in real time. Again, the coupling of vision and manual action yields visual percepts that are a blend, a joint product, of the multimodal experience.

One unexplored area is how the multimodal interaction of vision and action may lead to higher-order and more abstract concepts. One potential example of how this might work is suggested by Kemler-Nelson's programmatic series of experiments on young children's attention to function in forming categories. This research also illustrates the potential power of the hands and action in category formation. In Kemler-Nelson et al. (2000b), two-year-old children were presented with novel complex objects with multiple parts like those shown in Figure 14.8. One object, the exemplar, was given a novel name. In addition, the children were shown a function that depended on one of those parts. For example, they were shown how the hinged shape could open, close, and latch. They then manipulated the part causing the box to open and close. After seeing and manipulating the hinge, the children were more likely to extend the object name to the test objects that also had

hinged parts rather than to those that were similar in global shape but lacked the hinge. How the children acted on the objects – and the outcomes generated by their actions – seems likely to have drawn their attention to some aspects of the visual information over others, potentially changing how object shape itself was perceived. Multimodal regularities emergent in the coupling of vision and manual action may, in this way, create such abstract meanings as "open." If so, then much meaning may reside in the hands – in their actions on objects and in the dynamic visual trajectories they create.

In the adult literature, the evidence for a role for action and specific body parts is in action categories and verb meanings (Glenberg and Kaschak, 2005; Pulvermüller, 1999; Pulvermüller et al., 2005; Richardson et al., 2003). One relevant developmental result is a study by Huttenlocher, Smiley, and Charney (1983) of young children's early comprehension and production of action words. These researchers found that young children were more likely to comprehend and produce words when they were about their own actions than about the actions of others. For example, children would say "kick" more frequently when they themselves were kicking than when they were watching someone else kick.

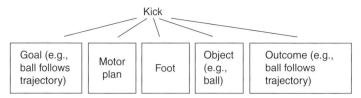

Figure 14.9. Verbs are linked to momentary events that include goals, motor plans, body parts, objects, and outcomes.

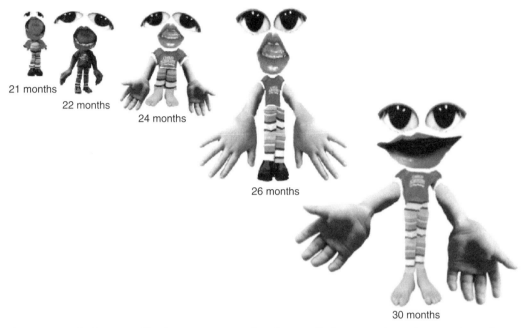

Figure 14.10. Body maps of body parts associated with typically known verbs at five ages. Size of figure illustrates number of known verbs at each age; area of body part region indicates percentage of associations (across all verbs known at that age).

Self-action provides a richly interrelated set of immediate experiences out of which one might build meanings. As illustrated in Figure 14.9, these include the agent's goal, the motor plan for a specific bodily action by a specific body part, the objects one acts on, as well as information about the effects of the action. Critically, it may be the action *by a body part* that links these components, physically connecting goals to outcomes and realizing causes, effects, manners, and paths. Yet the role of the body in verb learning has rarely been considered.

A recent finding by Maouene et al. (2008) demonstrates the potential importance of body parts that perform actions to early learning of verb meanings. They examined the body part associations of a corpus of the first 100 verbs learned in English. The main data derive from a free association task in which adults were asked to indicate the single body part (at any level of scale) most associated with each verb. The results indicate strong and consistent body part associations. Overall, early learned verbs are organized into four major bodily areas: the mouth, eyes, legs and feet, and hands. Further, many of these individual verbs – and particularly those acquired at the youngest age levels – are systematically and strongly associated with a *single* region of the body.

Further analyses suggested a relation among verbs, body parts, and age of acquisition as illustrated by the body maps in Figure 14.10.

These were generated such that the overall size of the homunculus indicates the total number of verbs normatively known at a given age and the size of the body part indicates the association strength (by adult judgment) of those verbs to specific body parts. These maps illustrate the strong association of early learned verbs with body parts, the initial dominance of mouth verbs and subsequent growth of eye and hand verbs, and the overall dominance among these early learned verbs of associations to hands.

Traditional theories of cognition segregate the mind from the body, from perception, and from action. Sensory systems are seen only as input devices and motor systems as output devices. Some have argued against this conceptualization of the cognitive system (Barsalou, 2003; Clark, 1997; Thelen and Smith, 1994); however, even within this traditional conceptualization, it seems highly likely that the body and its structure would leave its mark on internal cognitive processes and representations (Clark, 1997; Shepard, 2001). Our own body – how it moves, the location of its parts and sensors, how those parts interact with the physical world and create change in the physical world – is the most pervasive regularity in experience.

6 What next in the study of category development?

Categories, be they fixed or momentary creations, are the very stuff of cognition. This review has attempted to place the study of category development in its larger context and to highlight several areas of contemporary research. The review is far from exhaustive and complete. It would be especially hopeful if one could point to this moment in the history of the study of categories as special, or particularly promising, or about to break away in new directions. But progress happens incrementally and nonmonotonically. Theories of the very nature of categories and the underlying processes and representations that give rise to them seem to oscillate between two general views – one that focuses on representations and on stability, as

if categories were fixed things (in heads or worlds) to be discovered and acquired, and another that focuses on process and associations and the more probabilistic and context dependent nature of categories. Perhaps this is not surprising; categories fundamentally have both properties – providing stability, generalization, and compositionality to human cognition, but also being formed through one's real-time interaction in a statistically data-rich world and inventively adaptive to the local statistics. Each cycle through – from a perhaps overemphasis on one side of this duality to the other – seems to bring gains, both empirically and theoretically. Currently, there is a renewed interest in probabilistic feature accounts that includes a new emphasis on the structure available in a large system of natural categories with many overlapping feature correlations, in integrating processes at multiple time scales, and in broadening the range of features and processes to include multimodal integrations across perception and action. These seem to be appropriate – perhaps even essential – steps forward in the developmental trajectory toward a complete understanding of categories.

References

Ahn, W. K., Gelman, S. A., Amsterlaw, J. A., Hohenstein, J., & Kalish, C. W. (2000). Causal status effect in children's categorization. *Cognition*, 76, B35-B43.

Armstrong, S. L., Gleitman, L. R., & Gleitman, H. (1983). What some concepts might not be. *Cognition*, 13, 263–308.

Bates, E., Bretherton, I., Snyder, L., Beeghly, M., Shore, C., & McNew, S. et al. (1991). *From first words to grammar: Individual differences and dissociable mechanisms*. New York, NY, US: Cambridge University Press.

Barsalou, L. W. (1983) Ad hoc categories. *Memory and Cognition*, 11, 211–27.

(2003). Abstraction in perceptual symbol systems. Philosophical Transactions of the Royal Society of London: *Biological Sciences*, 358, 1177–87.

Booth, A. E. & Waxman, S. (2002a). Object names and object functions serve as cues to categories for infants. *Developmental Psychology*, 38, 948–57.

(2002b). Word learning is 'smart': Evidence that conceptual information affects preschoolers' extension of novel words. *Cognition, 84*, B11-B22.

Booth, A. E., Waxman, S. R., & Huang, Y. T. (2005). Conceptual information permeates word learning in infancy. *Developmental psychology, 41*, 491–505.

Bron, C., Corfu-Bratschi, P., & Maouene, M. (1989). "Hephaistos bacchant ou le cavalier comaste: simulation de raisonnement qualitatif par le langage informatique LISP" *Annali Istituto Universitario Orientale (Archeologia e Storia Antica). vol. XII*, 155–72.

Carey, S. (1985). *Conceptual Change in Childhood*. Cambridge, MA: MIT Press.

Clark, A. (1997). *Being There: Putting Brain, Body And World Together Again*. Cambridge, MA: MIT Press.

Colunga, E. (2003). *Where is the cow hiding? A new method for studying the development of features*. Presented at the biennial meeting of the Society for Research on Child Development, Tampa, FL.

(2006). The effect of priming on preschoolers' extensions of novel words: How far can "dumb" processes go? In *Proceedings of the 30th Annual Boston University Conference on Language Development*.

Colunga, E. & Smith, L. B. (2004). Dumb Mechanisms make Smart Concepts. *Proceedings of the Annual Conference of the Cognitive Science Society, 26*, 239–44.

(2005). From the Lexicon to Expectations About Kinds: A Role for Associative Learning. *Psychological Review, 112*, 347–82.

(2008a). Knowledge embedded in process: The self-organization of skilled noun learning. *Developmental Science, 11*, 195–203

(2008b). Flexibility and variability: Essential to human cognition and the study of human cognition. *New Ideas in Psychology. 26*, 174–92.

Cree, G. S., McNorgan, C., & McRae, K. (2006). Distinctive features hold a privileged status in the computation of word meaning: Implications for theories of semantic memory. *Journal of Experimental Psychology: Learning, Memory, and Cognition, 32*, 643–58.

de León, L. (1994). Exploration in the acquisition of geocentric location by tzotzil children.. *Linguistics, 32*, 857–84.

Diesendruck, G. & Bloom, P. (2003). How specific is the shape bias? *Child Development, 74*, 168–78.

Estes, W. (1986). Memory storage and retrieval processes in category learning. *Journal of Experimental Psychology: General, 115*, 161–74.

Freyd, J. J. (1983). Representing the dynamics of a static form. *Memory & Cognition, 11*, 342–6.

Gallese, V. & Lakoff, G. (2005). The brain's concepts: The role of the sensory-motor system in conceptual knowledge. *Cognitive Neuropsychology, 22*, 455–79.

Gallese, V., Craighero, L., Fadiga, L., & Fogassi, L. (1999). Perception through action. *Psyche: An Interdisciplinary Journal of Research on Consciousness, 5*, NP.

Gathercole, V. C. M. (1997). The linguistic mass/count distinction as an indicator of referent categorization in monolingual and bilingual children. *Child development, 68*, 832–42.

Gathercole, V. C. M. & Min, H. (1997). Word meaning biases or language-specific effects? Evidence from English, Spanish and Korean. *First Language, 17*(49 Pt 1), 31–56.

Gathercole, V. C. M., Cramer, L., Somerville, S. C., Haar, M. J. O. D. (1995). Ontological categories and function: acquisition of new names. *Cognitive Development, 10*, 225–51.

Gathercole, V. C. M., Thomas, E. M., & Ecans, D. (2000). What's in a noun? Welsh-, English-, and Spanish-speaking children see it differently. *First Language, 20*(58 Pt 1), 55–90.

Gelman, R. (1990). First principles organize attention to and learning about relevant data: Number and the animate- inanimate distinction as examples. *Cognitive Science, 14*, 79–106.

Gelman, S. (2003) *The Essential Child*. London: Oxford University Press.

Gelman, S. A. & Bloom, P. (2000). Young children are sensitive to how an object was created when deciding what to name it. *Cognition, 76*, 91–103.

Gelman, S. A. & Coley, J. D. (1990). The importance of knowing a dodo is a bird: Categories and inferences in 2-year-old children. *Developmental Psychology, 26*, 796–804.

Gelman, S. A. & Koenig, M. A. (2001). The role of animacy in children's understanding of "move." *Journal of Child Language, 28*, 683–701.

Gelman, S. A. & Markman, E. M. (1986). Categories and induction in young children. *Cognition, 23*, 183–209.

(1987). Young children's inductions from natural kinds: The role of categories and appearances. *Child Development, 58*, 1532–41.

Gershkoff-Stowe, L. (2005). Imposing equivalence on things in the world: A dynamic systems perspective. Mahwah, NJ: Erlbaum.

Glenberg, A. M. & Kaschak, M. P. (2005). *Language is grounded in action*. New York, NY: Oxford University Press.

——— (2003). The body's contribution to language. In Ross, B. H. (Ed.) *The Psychology of Learning and Motivation: Advances in Research and Theory* (Vol. 43, pp. 93–126). New York: Elsevier Science.

Goodman, J. C., McDonough, L., & Brown, N. B. (1998). The role of semantic context and memory in the acquisition of novel nouns. *Child development*, 69, 1330–44.

Golinkoff, R. M., Hirsh-Pasek, K., Bloom, L., Smith, L. B., Woodward, A., Akhtar, N., Tomasello, M., & Hollich, G. (2000). *Becoming a word learner: A debate on lexical acquisition*. London: Oxford University Press.

Golinkoff, R. M., Mervis, C. B., & Hirsh-Pasek, K. (1994). Early object labels: The case for a developmental lexical principles framework. *Journal of Child Language*, 21, 125–55.

Graziano, M., Cohen, J. D., & Botvinick, M. (2002). How the brain represents the body. In Prinz, W. & Hommel, B. (Eds.) *Attention and Performance XIX: Common Mechanisms in Perception and Action* (pp. 136–57). Oxford, UK: Oxford University Press.

Hall, D. G. (1996). Preschoolers default assumptions about word meaning: proper names designate unique individuals. *Developmental Psychology*, 32, 177–86.

Hauk, O., Johnsrude, I., & Pulvermüller, F. (2004). Somatotopic representation of action words in human motor and premotor cortex. *Neuron*, 41, 301–7.

Heine, B., (1997). *Cognitive Foundations of Grammar*. Oxford University Press, Oxford.

Hidaka, S. & Smith, L. B. (2010). A single word in a population of words. *Language Learning and Development*, 6, 206–22.

Holmes, G. (1922). The Croonian Lectures on the clinical symptoms of cerebellar disease and their interpretation. Lancet. Reprinted in Phillips, C. G. (Ed.) (1979). *Selected papers of Gordon Holmes* (pp. 186–247). Oxford University Press, Oxford.

Holmes, N. P., Spence, C., Giard, M., & Wallace, M. (2004). The body schema and multisensory representation(s) of peripersonal space. *Cognitive Processing*, 5, 94–105.

Huttenlocher, J., Smiley, P., & Charney, R. (1983). Emergence of action categories in the child: Evidence from verb meanings. *Psychological Review*, 90, 72–93.

Imai, M. & Gentner, D. (1997). A cross-linguistic study of early word meaning: Universal ontology and linguistic influence. *Cognition*, 62, 169–200.

Jones, S. S. & Smith, L. B. (1993). The place of perception in children's concepts. *Cognitive Development*, 8, 113–39.

——— (2002). How children know the relevant properties for generalizing object names. *Developmental Science*, 5, 219–32.

Jones, S. S., Smith, L. B., & Landau, B. (1991). Object properties and knowledge in early lexical learning. *Child Development*, 62, 499–516.

Katz, N., Baker, E., & Macnamara, J. (1974). What's in a name? A study of how children learn common and proper names. *Child Development*, 45, 469–73.

Keil, F. C. (1989). *Concepts, kinds, and cognitive development*. Cambridge, MA: MIT Press.

——— (1994). The birth and nurturance of concepts by domains: The origins of concepts of living things. In Hischfeld, L. & Gelman, S. (Eds.) *Mapping the mind: Domain specificity in cognition and culture* (pp. 234–54). New York, NY: Cambridge University Press.

——— (1991). The emergence of theoretical beliefs as constraints on concepts. In Carey, S. & Gelman, R. (Eds.) *The epigenesis of mind: Essays on biology and cognition. The Jean Piaget Symposiumn Series*. Hillsdale, NJ: LEA.

——— (1979). *Semantic and conceptual development: An ontological perspective*. Cambridge, MA: Harvard University Press.

——— (2003). Folkscience: coarse interpretations of a complex reality. *Trends in Cognitive Sciences*, 7, 368–73.

——— (2006). Explanation and understanding. *Annual Review of Psychology*, 57, 227–54.

Keil, F. C. & Batterman, N. (1984). A characteristic-to-defining shift in the development of word meaning. *Journal of Verbal Learning & Verbal Behavior*, 23, 221–36.

Kemler Nelson, D. G., Frankenfield, A., Morris, C., & Blair, E. (2000a). Young children's use of functional information to categorize artifacts: Three factors that matter. *Cognition*, 77, 133–68.

Kemler Nelson, D. G., Russell, R., Duke, N., & Jones, K. (2000b). Two-year-olds will name artifacts by their functions. *Child Development*, 18, 1271–88.

Kobayashi, H. (1998). How 2-year-olds learn novel part names of unfamiliar objects. *Cognition*, 68, B41-B51.

Komatsu, L. K. (1992). Recent views of conceptual structure. *Psychological bulletin*, 112, 500–26.

Lakoff, G. & Johnson, M. (1980). The metaphorical structure of the human conceptual system. *Cognitive Science*, 4, 195–208.

Landau, B., Smith, L. B., & Jones, S. S. (1988). The importance of shape in early lexical learning. *Cognitive Development*, 3, 299–321.

(1992). Syntactic context and the shape bias in children's and adults' lexical learning. *Journal of Memory and Language*, 31, 807–25.

(1998). Object perception and object naming in early development. *Trends in Cognitive Science*, 2, 19–24.

Lucy, J., & Gaskins, S. (2000). Grammatical categories and the development of classification preferences: A comparative approach. In M. Bowerman & S. C. Levinson (Eds.), Language acquisition and conceptual development (pp. 257–83). Cambridge: Cambridge University Press.

Macario, J. F. (1991). Young children's use of color in classification: Foods and canonically colored objects. *Cognitive Development*, 6, 17–46.

Macario, J. F., Shipley, E. F., & Billman, D. O. (1990). Induction from a single instance: Formation of a novel category. *Journal of Experimental Child Psychology*, 50, 179–99.

Madole, K. L., & Cohen, L. B. (1995). The role of object parts in infants' attention to form-function correlations. *Developmental Psychology*, 31, 637–48.

Malt, B. C. (1994). Water is not H2O. *Cognitive Psychology*, 27, 41–70.

(1995). Category coherence in cross-cultural perspective. *Cognitive Psychology*, 29, 85–148.

Malt, B. C. & Sloman, S. A. (2004). Conversation and convention: Enduring influences on name choice for common objects. *Memory & Cognition*, 32, 1346–54.

Madole, K. L. & Oakes, L. M. (1999). Making sense of infant categorization: Stable processes and changing representations. *Developmental Review*, 19, 263–96.

Madole, K. L., Oakes, L. M., & Cohen, L. B. (1993). Developmental changes in infants' attention to function and form-function correlations. *Cognitive Development*, 8, 189–209.

Mandler, J. M. (2003). Conceptual categorization. In Rakison, D. H. & Oakes, L. M. (Eds.) *Early category and concept development: Making sense of the blooming, buzzing confusion* (pp. 103–31). London: Oxford University Press.

Mandler, J. M. & McDonough, L. (1996). Drinking and driving don't mix: Inductive generalization in infancy. *Cognition*, 59, 307–35.

(1998). Studies in inductive inference in infancy. *Cognitive Psychology*, 37, 60–96.

(2000). Advancing downward to the basic level. *Journal of Cognition & Development*, 1, 379–403.

Maouene, J., Hidaka, S., & Smith, L. B. (2008). Body parts and early learned verbs. *Cognitive Science*, 32, 1200–16.

Mareschal, D., Quinn, P. C., & French, R. M. (2002). Asymmetric interference in 3- to 4-month olds' sequential category learning. *Cognitive Science*, 26, 377–89.

Markman, E. M. (1989). *Categorization and naming in children: Problems of induction*. MIT Series in learning, development, and conceptual change. Cambridge, MA: MIT Press.

Massey, C. M. & Gelman, R. (1988). Preschoolers' ability to decide whether a photographed unfamiliar object can move itself. *Developmental Psychology*, 24, 307–17.

McCarrell, N. S. & Callanan, M. A. (1995). Form-function correspondences in children's inference. *Child Development*, 66, 532–46.

McPherson, L. (1991). A little goes a long way: Evidence for a perceptual basis of learning for the noun categories COUNT and MASS. *Journal of Child Language*, 18, 315–38.

McRae, K., Cree, G. S., Westmacott, R., & de Sa, V. R. (1999). Further evidence for feature correlations in semantic memory. *Canadian Journal of Experimental Psychology*, 53, 360–73.

Medin, D. (1989). Concepts and conceptual structure. *American Psychologist*, 44, 1469–81.

Mervis, C. B. & Mervis, C. A. (1988). Role of adult input in young children's category evolution: I. An observational study. *Journal of Child Language*, 15, 257–72.

Moss, H. E. & Tyler, L. K. (2003). Weighing up the facts of category-specific semantic deficits. *Trends in Cognitive Sciences*, 7, 480–1.

Murphy, G. & Medin, D. L. (1985). The role of theories in conceptual coherence. *Psychological Review*, 92, 289–316.

Nelson, K. & Ware, A. (2002). The reemergence of function. In Stein, N. L. & Bauer, P. J. (Eds.) *Representation, memory, and development: Essays in honor of Jean Mandler* (pp. 161–84). Mahwah, NJ: Erlbaum.

Nosofsky, R. (1984). Choice, similarity, and the context theory of classification. *Journal of Experimental Psychology: Learning, Memory, & Cognition*, 10, 104–14.

Núñez, R. & Lakoff, G. (2005). The cognitive foundations of mathematics: The role of conceptual metaphor. In Campbell, JID (Ed.) *Handbook of mathematical cognition* (pp. 109–24). New York: Psychology Press.

Penfield, W. & Rasmussen, T. (1950). The Cerebral Cortex of Man: A Clinical Study of Localization of Function. New York: Macmillan.

Pilgrim, L. K., Moss, H. E., & Tyler, L. K. (2005). Semantic processing of living and nonliving concepts across the cerebral hemispheres. *Brain and language*, 94, 86–93.

Pulvermüller, F. (1999). Words in the brain's language. *Behavioral and Brain Sciences*, 22, 253–336.

Pulvermüller, F., Hauk, O., Nikulin, V. V., & llmoniemi, R. J. (2005). Functional links between motor and language systems. *European Journal of Neuroscience*, 21, 793–7.

Quinn, P. C. & Eimas, P. D. (1996). Perceptual organization and categorization in young infants. In Rovee-Collier, C. & Lipsitt, L. P. (Eds.) *Advances in infancy research* (Vol. 10, pp. 1–36). Stamford, CT: Ablex Publishing Corp.

Rakison, D. H. (2003). Parts, motion, and the development of the animate-inanimate distinction in infancy. In Rakison, D. H. & Oakes, L. M. (Eds.) *Early category and concept development: Making sense of the blooming, buzzing confusion* (pp. 159–92). London: Oxford University Press.

(2005). The perceptual to conceptual shift in infancy and early childhood: A surface to deep distinction? In Gershkoff-Stowe, L. & Rakison, D. H. (Eds.) *Building object categories in developmental time*. Hillsdale, NJ: Erlbaum.

Rakison, D. H. & Butterworth, G. E. (1998a). Infants' attention to object structure in early categorization. *Developmental Psychology*, 34, 1310–25.

(1998b). Infants' use of object parts in early categorization. *Developmental Psychology*, 34, 49–62.

Rakison, D. H. & Cohen, L. B. (1999). Infants' use of functional parts in basic-like categorization. *Developmental Science*, 2, 423–31.

Rakison, D. H. & Poulin-Dubois, D. (2001). The developmental origin of the animate-inanimate distinction. *Psychological Bulletin*, 127, 209–28.

(2002). You go this way and I'll go that way: Developmental changes in infants' detection of correlations among static and dynamic features in motion events. *Child development*, 73, 682–99.

Richardson, D. C., Spivey, M. J., Barsalou, L. W., & McRae, K. (2003). Spatial representations activated during real-time comprehension of verbs. *Cognitive Science*, 27, 767–80.

Rips, L. (1989) Similarity, typicality, and categorization. In Vosniadou, S. & Ortony, A. (Eds.) *Similarity and Anological Reasoning* (pp. 21–59). New York: Cambridge University Press.

Rips, L. J. & Collins, A. (1993). Categories and resemblance. *Journal of Experimental Psychology: General*, 122, 468–86.

Rogers, T. T. & McClelland, J. L. (2005). A parallel distributed processing approach to semantic cognition: Applications to conceptual development. Mahwah, NJ: Erlbaum.

Rosch, E. H. (1973). Natural categories. *Cognitive Psychology*, 4, 328–50.

Rosch, E. H. & Mervis, C. (1975). Family resemblances: Studies in the internal structure of categories. *Cognitive Psychology*, 7, 573–605.

Rozenblit, L. & Keil, F. C. (2002). The misunderstood limits of folk science: An illusion of explanatory depth. *Cognitive Science*, 26, 521–62.

Ruff, H. A. & Rothbart, M. K. (1996). *Attention in early development: Themes and variations*. New York, NY: Erlbaum.

Sakuragi, T. & Fuller, J. W. (2003). Body-part metaphors: A cross-cultural survey of the perception of translatability among Americans and Japanese. *Journal of Psycholinguistic Research*, 32, 381–95.

Samuelson, L. K. & Smith, L. B. (2000b). Grounding development in cognitive processes. *Child Development*, 71, 98–106.

(1999). Early noun vocabularies: Do ontology, category structure and syntax correspond? *Cognition*, 73, 1–33.

(2000). Children's attention to rigid and deformable shape in naming and non-naming tasks. *Child Development*, 71, 1555–70.

Samuelson, L. K. & Horst, J. S. (2007). Dynamic noun generalization: Moment-to-moment interactions shape children's naming biases. *Infancy*, 11, 97–110.

Samuelson L. K., Schutte A. R., & Horst, J. S. (2009). The dynamic nature of knowledge: Insights from a dynamic field model of children's novel noun generalizations. *Cognition*, 110, 322–45.

Saxe, G. B. (1981). Body parts as numerals: A developmental analysis of numeration among the oksapmin in papua new guinea. *Child Development*, 52, 306–16.

Shepard, R. (2001). Perceptual and cognitive universals as reflections of the world. *Behavioral and Brain Sciences*, 24, 581–601.

Sheya, A. & Smith, L. B. (2010). Changing priority maps in 12- to 18-month-olds: An emerging role for object properties. *Psychonomic Bulletin & Review*, 17, 22–8.

Sloman, S. A. (1997). Explanatory coherence and the induction of properties. *Thinking and Reasoning*, 3, 81–110.

Smith, E. E. (1989). Concepts and induction. In Posner, M. I. (Ed.) *Foundations of cognitive science* (pp. 501–26). Cambridge, MA: MIT Press.

Smith, E. E. & Medin, D. L. (1981). *Concepts and categories*. Cambridge, MA: Harvard University Press.

Smith, L. B. (1995). Self-organizing processes in learning to learn words: Development is not induction. In Nelson, C. (Ed.) *Basic and applied perspectives on learning, cognition, and development* (pp. 1–32). Marwah, NJ: Lawrence Erlbaum Associates.

(2005). Action alters shape categories. *Cognitive Science*, 29, 665–79.

Smith, L. B., Colunga, E., & Yoshida, H. (2003). Making an ontology: Cross-linguistic evidence. In Rakison, D. & Oakes, L. (Eds.) *Early category and concept development: Making sense of the blooming, buzzing confusion* (pp. 275–302). London: Oxford University Press.

Smith, L. B., Jones, S. S., & Landau, B. (1992). Count nouns, adjectives, and perceptual properties in children's novel word interpretations. *Developmental psychology*, 28, 273–86.

(1996). Naming in young children: A dumb attentional mechanism? *Cognition*, 60, 143–71.

Smith, L. B., Jones, S. S., Landau, B., Gershkoff-Stowe, L., & Samuelson, L., (2002). Object name learning provides on-the-job training for attention. *Psychological Science*, 13, 13–9.

Smith, L. B. & Samuelson, L. K. (2006). An attentional learning account of the shape bias: Reply to Cimpian and Markman (2005) and Booth, Waxman, and Huang (2005). *Developmental Psychology*, 42, 1339–43.

Soja, N. N. (1994). Evidence for a distinct kind of noun. *Cognition*, 51, 267–84.

Soja, N. N., Carey, S. & Spelke, E. S. (1991). Ontological categories guide young children's inductions of word meaning:object terms and substance terms. *Cognition*, 38, 179–211.

Svorou, S., (1993). *The Grammar of Space*. Amsterdam: John Benjamins.

Thelen, E. & Smith, L. B. (1994). A Dynamic Systems Approach to the Development of Cognition and Action. MIT Press.

Varela, F. J., Thompson, E., & Rosch, E. (1993). *The embodied mind: Cognitive science and human experience*. Cambridge, MA: MIT Press.

Waxman, S. R. & Markow, D. B. (1995). Words as invitations to form categories. *Cognitive Psychology*, 29, 257–302.

Xu, F. & Tenenbaum, J. B. (2007). Sensitivity to sampling in bayesian word learning. *Developmental Science*, 10, 288–97.

Yeh, W. & Barsalou, L. W. (2006). The situated nature of concepts. *American Journal of Psychology*, 119, 349–84.

Yoshida, H. & Smith, L. B. (2003). Known and novel noun extensions: Attention at two levels of abstraction. *Child Development*, 74, 564–77.

(2008). What's in view for toddlers? Using a head camera to study visual experience. *Infancy*, 13, 229–248.

(2001). Early noun lexicons in English and Japanese. *Cognition*, 82, B63-B74.

(2003b). Correlations, concepts and cross-linguistic differences. *Developmental Science*, 6, 30–4.

(2003). Known and novel noun extensions: Attention at two levels of abstraction. *Child Development*, 564–77.

(2005). Linguistic cues enhance the learning of perceptual cues. *Psychological Science*, 16, 90–5.

Youer, B. (1990). Infants' detection of correlations among feature categories. *Child Development*, 61, 614–21.

Younger, B. A. (2003). Parsing objects into categories: Infants' perception and use of correlated attributes. In Rakison, D. H. & Oakes, L. M. (Eds.) *Early category and concept development: Making sense of the blooming, buzzing confusion* (pp. 77–102). London: Oxford University Press.

Younger, B. A. & Cohen, L. B. (1983). Infant perception of correlations among attributes. *Child Development*, 54, 858–69.

(1986). Developmental change in infants' perception of correlations among attributes. *Child Development*, 57, 803–15.

Yu, N. (2004). The eyes for sight and mind. *Journal of Pragmatics*, 36, 663–86.

Zaki, S. R. & Nosofsky, R. M. (2001). Exemplar accounts of blending and distinctiveness effects in perceptual old-new recognition. *Journal of Experimental Psychology: Learning, Memory & Cognition*, 27, 1022–41.

Zwaan, R. A. (2004). The immersed experiencer: Toward an embodied theory of language comprehension. In Ross, B. H. (Ed.) *The psychology of learning and motivation: Advances in research and theory* (Vol. 44, pp. 35–62). New York: Elsevier Science.

MORPHOLOGICAL PROCESSING

CHAPTER 15

Derivational Morphology and Skilled Reading

An Empirical Overview

Kevin Diependaele, Jonathan Grainger and Dominiek Sandra

1 Introduction

The present chapter aims at providing an overview of approximately thirty years of experimental research on morphological processing within the context of the larger goal of specifying the mental representations and processes involved in normal word recognition. As this issue has been approached with a broad variety of techniques and paradigms, an exhaustive review is beyond the scope of a single chapter. Instead we aim to provide readers with an overview of the main theoretical questions and empirical results that form the cornerstones for current psycholinguistic theories of morphological processing, with a focus on derivational morphology. We start by clarifying the basic linguistic terminology that will be used in the remainder of this chapter.

In linguistics, *morphology* is defined as the study of internal word structure. *Morphemes* are the elementary units in this structure, given that they are the smallest units in language that bear at least some meaning. Depending on whether a word consists of one or several morphemes, it is called

morphologically *simple* or *complex*. Hence, a word like *viewer* is complex because it is built from the morphemes *view* and *-er*. This example shows that morphemes differ a lot in the nature of the meaning they carry: The morpheme *view* determines the word's core meaning, whereas the morpheme *-er* modifies this meaning (i.e., by adding an agentive component). Morphemes of the former type are called *root morphemes*. When complex words contain more than one root morpheme (as in *milkman*), they are called *compound* words.

Morphemes other than root morphemes are called *affixes*. Affixes are known as *bound morphemes*[1] because they must be tied to a root morpheme or a set of morphemes (at least one root plus affixes). They can be categorized, depending on the place where they are inserted. In English *prefixes* and *suffixes* are most common; a prefix is attached to the beginning of a root

---

1 Note that although most root morphemes can occur as words in isolation, they can also occur as bound morphemes. This is for instance the case for the root *-mit* in forms like *permit, submit, admit*, and so forth.

or an already complex word, whereas a suffix is added at the end. In other languages *interfixes* (in between two roots or complex words), *circumfixes* (around a root or complex word), and *infixes* (inside a root or complex word) can also occur commonly.[2] Circumfixation and infixation are cases of *nonconcatenative* (or *nonlinear*) word formation, as they induce a nonserial morpheme alignment.

Affixes can further be classified on the basis of their linguistic function. A *derivational affix* produces a new word from another one. Compared to the original word, this new word expresses a different, but often closely related, meaning and often belongs to a different lexical category (noun, verb, etc.). Conversely, an *inflectional affix* does not produce a new word. Its function is to make a word's form compatible with the grammatical context. Returning to our example, we can thus describe the noun *viewer* as a complex word containing the root morpheme *view* and the derivational suffix *-er*. In the appropriate grammatical context we can inflect *viewer* to its plural form by adding the inflectional suffix *-s*. The word part to which an inflectional affix is added is referred to as the *stem*. Thus, the stem of the inflection *viewers* is *viewer*, whereas the stem of *views* is *view*.

In order to understand why researchers have been interested in morphology ever since the very early days of psycholinguistics, we need to consider the key question that was guiding research at that time: "How is the adult mind able to learn, use, and understand a vocabulary of well over sixty thousand words?" In those early days, the computer metaphor dominated the way researchers thought about this question. More specifically, our language processor was thought of as an information processing device with a highly efficient retrieval procedure. Central to this device is a word store, referred to as the *mental lexicon*, a sort of mental dictionary. The challenge then was to find dimensions along which storage and retrieval were organized to account for the remarkable efficiency of human performance. Since, theoretically speaking, morphemes capture the recurrence of formal and semantic patterns in our vocabulary, they were seen as potential units to increase efficiency in storage and/or processing. Figure 15.1 shows six different architectures for word recognition, with and without morphology. These have each been considered in the psycholinguistic literature and will guide our theoretical and empirical overview.

From the perspective of storage, morphemes offer a way for an economic organization of the lexicon. As they are the building blocks of novel words and grammatical variants of existing words, they form bundles of orthographic, phonological, semantic, and syntactic information that tend to be constant across the different word forms they appear in. Therefore, morpheme storage provides a means to store information about orthography, phonology, semantics, and/or syntax in units shared by a large number of different words. The extreme application of this principle is illustrated in panel B in Figure 15.1. Here we see that sublexical form information (e.g., letters, phonemes) is mapped onto meaning information via morphemic representations. In this view the lexicon thus only contains morphemes. This stands in sharp contrast with the architecture depicted in panel A, where there are lexical representations for each known word and no morphemic representations. Although this so-called *full-listing hypothesis* has been entertained in the literature (e.g., Butterworth, 1983), it is clear that

2 An interfix is often present in Dutch and German compounds (e.g., "bruid-*s*-taart" [*wedding cake*]). Dutch and German have many cases of circumfixation (e.g., "*ge*-berg-*te*" [*mountain range*]). Examples of infixes can be found in Semitic languages like Arabic and Hebrew. The words in these languages can generally be decomposed into two abstract morphemes: a root (**R**) and a *word pattern* (**P**). The root usually consists of three consonants that convey the core meaning of the word. The word pattern consists of vowels or vowels and consonants and usually only carries syntactic information. Importantly, the letters of the word pattern are often interwoven with those of the root (e.g., $R_1R_2R_3 + P_1P_2 = R_1P_1R_2P_2R_3$).

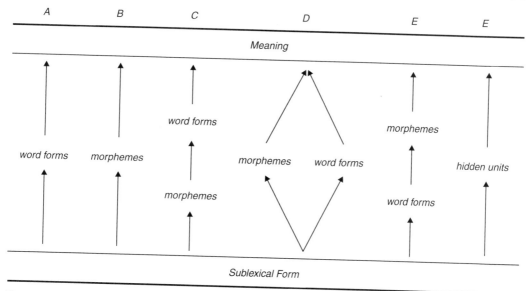

Figure 15.1. Six architectures for word recognition with or without morphology. Each of the architectures (A-F) places whole-word representations (word forms) and/or morphological representations (morphemes) at different points on the processing pathway that leads from sublexical form representations (e.g., letters / phonemes) to meaning. The hidden units in architecture F represent word forms and morphemes at the same level(s).

information storage is highly redundant in this case.[3]

Despite the attractiveness of a pure morpheme-based lexicon, it rapidly became obvious that this could not work in most

languages (at least not for all words). The main reason for this is the unpredictability of morphologically complex words (see Sandra, 1994). There are two sides to this unpredictability: a formal and a semantic one. On the one hand, not all possible morphologically complex forms actually exist (i.e., not all morphemes that can formally combine do so, unlike in the hypothetical situation described in endnote iii). So in order to know that the form *respeak* does not exist, we need to have some knowledge about which combinations exist. On the other hand, the meaning of existing complex forms cannot always be predicted from the morphemic meanings (a *cooker* is not someone who cooks, and a *corner* is certainly not someone who *corns*). It thus seems that we need to have access to information about the form and meaning of words and not just to information about the form and meaning of morphemes.

The implausibility of a purely morpheme-based lexicon did not, however, shift the attention away from morphology. In the context of derivational morphology, attention

---

3 To illustrate this point, one can imagine a hypothetical language in which there only exists words consisting of two out of six possible morphemes. If all these morphemes can combine with each other, it follows that there exist fifteen words in this language. If we suppose that (a) the information carried by each word equals the sum of the information carried by each of its morphemes and that (b) each morpheme has an information value equal to one, it follows that a full storage of all words implies the storage of fifteen times two – thirty pieces of information. If the storage would instead be based on the morphemes, there would only be a need to store six pieces of information. Needless to say, the savings due to morphemic storage (here expressed by the ratio of six to thirty) grow as the amount of morphemes and possible combinations increases. So a mental lexicon that only stores the morphemes in a language would achieve a maximum of storage efficiency. However, this increase in storage efficiency is accompanied by an increased processing cost in the form of two extra processes: (1) a recoding process between a word form and its morphemic forms and (2) a recoding process between the morpheme meanings and their integrated meaning.

shifted more towards morphology as a means for enhancing processing instead of economizing on storage. One way to enhance processing is to use morphemic representations to access whole-word representations. This is illustrated in panel C in Figure 15.1. An example of such a model is the one of Taft and Forster (1975). The emphasis on processing efficiency in this model is already clear from its basic distinction between access representations and central representations (also referred to as *lexical entries*). The word recognition process is thought of as a serial search mechanism that searches through modality-specific (i.e., phonological or orthographic) representations, which provide *access* to central a-modal (i.e., form independent) lexical information. It is hypothesized that access representations are organized along dimensions that optimize this serial search process.

Taft and Forster proposed that one such dimension is the root, which functions as the access code for morphologically complex words. Designed initially to account for the recognition of prefixed derivations, their model includes a *prelexical* left-to-right parsing mechanism, which detects possible prefixes in the input and strips them away. Hence, this decomposition mechanism is often referred to as *prefix stripping*. After the root has been freed from its prefix, the lexicon is searched for an access representation that matches the root. After successful access, the lexical entry is searched for the specific prefix–root combination at hand. In this model the processing efficiency results from a considerable reduction in the search space when the search is for the root of a prefixed word rather than for the word itself. For instance, a word-based search for a word like *remind* would include the massive number of items starting with the orthographic string *re* (including all prefixed words with *re*-), whereas a root-based search would only include items starting with *mi*, a considerably smaller number.

However, a number of researchers have pointed out that this approach is not viable on purely computational grounds, at least for languages like French (Colé et al.,

1986) and English (Schreuder and Baayen, 1994) which contain prohibitively large numbers of pseudoprefixes (e.g., *re-* in *repertoire*). In such languages, prefix stripping would cause many mis-parsings and thus lead to an overall decrease in processing efficiency rather than the hypothesized increase. In general, the problem that arises with models such as Taft and Forster's is that morphemic units only represent form information and that their activation is not mediated by lexical information about the whole input. As such, these models cannot distinguish pseudomorphemes from real ones. This problem led to the development of several theoretical alternatives that can be categorized into three types. The first is the *dual-route* approach to morphology and word recognition, illustrated in panel D of Figure 15.1. Here, morpheme representations are situated at the same level as whole-word representations. As in Taft and Forster's model, these representations are activated via a prelexical morphological parsing mechanism. However, contrary to the situation in Taft and Forster's model, morphemic representations do not provide *access* to whole-word representations (the latter are activated directly through a full-form processing route), but are used by a compositional process to derive the word's meaning and syntactic function. Instances of dual-route models are the Augmented Addressed Morphology model (AAM) (Caramazza, Laudana, and Romani, 1988) and the Morphological Race model (MR) (Schreuder and Baayen, 1995). Both models assume that when a derivation is encountered, the input is simultaneously mapped onto corresponding whole-word and morphemic form (access) representations. The AAM model assumes that for known derivations whole-word form access is the default procedure. The MR model, however, maintains that derivations can either be recognized via full-form or morphemic processing, depending on variables such as whole-word versus morphemic frequency. The general proposal is that full-form and morphemic processing race against each other. The architecture found in the MR model is also known as the *parallel* dual-route architecture.

According to a radically different view, illustrated in panel E of Figure 15.1, morphological representations are superimposed on whole-word form representations. Hence, this approach is commonly referred to as the *supralexical* view. In this approach, morphemes are identified at a hypothesized processing level that captures the systematic correspondence of form and meaning in sets of morphologically related words (Giraudo and Grainger, 2000; Grainger, Colé, and Segui, 1991). As such, morphological representations impose a morpho-semantic clustering on word form representations. As opposed to the two previous architectures, morphemic representations are not used to access whole-word representations. Rather, they reflect interword relationships (i.e., they represent so-called *morphological families*; e.g., Lukatela et al., 1980) and aim for a straightforward process of semantic integration. This aspect of the supralexical architecture resembles the addressed morphology component of the AAM model mentioned previously. Still, morphological representations can influence the accessibility of word form representations. In the model proposed by Giraudo and Grainger, for instance, morphemic representations can provide positive feedback to all compatible word form representations.

Up to this point, all architectures we have discussed (that included morphology) contained a separate representational level and/or a separate access procedure for morphemes. A final model type rejects the presence of such specialized representational levels and access procedures, while acknowledging that morphological relationships among words do affect lexical processing. This theoretical approach is illustrated in panel F of Figure 15.1. It was proposed in the context of *connectionist* models. These models are artificial *neural networks* that learn to associate activity patterns across input and output units (*neuron pools*) via gradual adjustments to internal connection weights. An important outcome of the learning process is that the weight structure comes to represent the frequency and consistency of input–output mappings. For a network with mappings between (sublexical) form units and semantic units, this implies that morphemes can naturally acquire a special status in the representational structure. In particular, the network will capture the typically high form–meaning consistency across morphologically related words in its internal weight structure. Importantly, morphemic representations can emerge at the same level(s) as other form–meaning representations (including whole-word representations of complex words), and they are also activated via the same principles. Perhaps the most important feature of the connectionist approach is that it explicitly rejects the idea that morphological representation and processing is an all or none issue. The presence of morphological representations and morphological effects in experimental data is considered a continuous function of statistical regularities in the form and meaning of different words and is hence predicted to be a graded phenomenon (e.g., Plaut and Gonnerman, 2000; Rueckl and Raveh, 1999; see also Hay and Baayen, 2005).

Given the different theoretical perspectives that have been proposed over the last thirty years, it appears that empirical research on morphology and word recognition has been guided by two main questions. The first is: "Does morphemic information influence word recognition?" Perhaps the major goal of empirical research on derivational morphology has been to demonstrate morphological influences on word recognition that cannot be reduced to purely form-based effects (orthographic and/or phonological), purely semantic effects, or some combination of these. The second question is: "How does morphemic information influence word recognition?" Given evidence for morphological influences on word recognition, what are the mechanisms that best capture such influences within a general model of language comprehension? Here the debate revolves around issues such as the precise locus of morphological representation (e.g., prelexical versus supralexical), and whether or not the observed influences of morphological variables can be captured by subtle variations in the statistical regularities linking form and meaning.

We now turn to our empirical overview. As noted earlier, the present overview will be limited to summarizing psycholinguistic research on derivational morphology (see the chapter by Woollams and Patterson in this volume for research on inflectional morphology). Our attention will also be primarily focused on the largest body of evidence in this context: *single* word recognition. Our presentation will be guided by the main questions presented previously, with an effort to link key results to the different theoretical alternatives. The overview is structured around the main types of experimental manipulations used in the literature: frequency manipulations and priming manipulations.

2 Morphological frequency effects

The observation that high-frequency words are recognized faster than low-frequency words is one of the earliest and most reported findings in the psycholinguistic literature (e.g., Howes and Solomon, 1951). At a theoretical level, researchers largely agree that the frequency of a word influences the speed of its lexical processing (Broadbent, 1967).[4] Given this interpretation, frequency effects can serve as a diagnostic tool for investigating the nature and organization of lexical representations. Frequency manipulations have been widely adopted to investigate the role of morphology in word recognition. In general, linguistic units allow for two frequency counts: the number of times a unit is observed in a corpus (called a *token* frequency) and the number of different contexts in which this unit occurs (called a *type* frequency). For morphemes

the *type* frequency is obtained by counting the number of different words in which they occur as constituents (e.g., view+ viewer + reviewer + ...). Their *token* frequency then corresponds to the total number of times each of these words is realized. Separating effects of type and token frequency is theoretically important, as these effects potentially highlight different aspects of the underlying representational architecture. A positive effect of a root's token frequency, for instance, generally supports the idea that each time a word containing this root is processed, the same representation(s) is (are) activated at some level(s).[5] A positive effect of a root's type frequency, on the other hand, indicates that its recurrence across different words (i.e., its productivity) is captured by the representational architecture. Nevertheless, due to the high degree of correlation between the two frequency counts, it is often not evident to empirically distinguish token frequency effects from type frequency effects and many studies have failed to do so. As a consequence, the interpretation of the reported frequency effects is not always straightforward.

2.1 *Token frequency effects*

Two kinds of token frequency have received most attention in the case of derivations: their *surface frequency* (i.e., their word token frequency), and the token frequency of their constituent morphemes. Since all models in Figure 15.1, except the one in panel B, need to store whole-word information at some level (see Introduction), they each

---

4 In models of word recognition, word frequency can affect ease of word recognition either via a frequency-ordered search mechanism, or because high-frequency words reach criterion levels (or stable patterns) of activation faster than low-frequency words via greater activation input and/or lower thresholds.

5 In quite a few influential word recognition models it is assumed that token frequency effects arise at a level of form-dependent lexical (access) representations (e.g. Forster, 1976; McClelland and Rumelhart, 1981). Hence, positive effects of a root's token frequency have often been considered as evidence for root-based lexical access in the case of derived words, which implies some form of prelexical decomposition (e.g., Taft, 1979). Several authors have pointed out, however, that a pure form-based interpretation of token frequency effects is too narrow in the light of a number of empirical findings. Baayen, Feldman, and Schreuder (2006), for instance, argue that token frequency primarily reflects conceptual familiarity, rather than form familiarity.

predict an effect of surface frequency. This is indeed what has typically been found in a wide range of studies. The surface frequency effect has been demonstrated in different tasks: visual lexical decision (e.g., Burani and Caramazza, 1987; Colé, Beauvillain, and Segui, 1989; Taft, 1979), auditory lexical decision (e.g., Meunier and Segui, 1999; Wurm, 1997), and eye fixation durations on derived words that are embedded in sentences (e.g., Niswander, Pollatsek, and Rayner, 2000). It was also shown across different languages: English (e.g., Niswander et al., 2000; Taft, 1979; Wurm, 1997), French (e.g., Colé et al., 1989; Meunier and Segui, 1999) and Italian (e.g., Burani and Caramazza, 1987). Furthermore, the effect was found with prefix derivations (e.g., Colé et al., 1989; Taft, 1979; Wurm, 1997) as well as with suffix derivations (e.g., Burani and Caramazza, 1987; Colé et al., 1989; Meunier and Segui, 1999; Niswander et al., 2000). Nevertheless, recent eye movement studies found different effects of surface frequency with different word lengths, more specifically, larger surface frequency effects appeared with shorter derivations (Bertram and Hyönä, 2003; Niswander-Klement and Pollatsek, 2006).

If the recognition of a derivation involves the activation of morphemic representations, as predicted by all models, except model A in Figure 15.1, the token frequency of the constituent morphemes can be expected to have an additional effect. Effects of root frequency are indeed quite robust. They have been established in visual lexical decision (e.g., Andrews, 1986; Burani and Caramazza, 1987; Burani and Thornton, 2003; Colé et al., 1989; Schreuder, Burani, and Baayen, 2003; Taft, 1979), auditory lexical decision (Meunier and Segui, 1999) and eye movement research (e.g., Beauvillain, 1996; Holmes and O'Regan, 1992; Niswander et al., 2000). Root frequency effects have also been reported for different languages: English (e.g., Andrews, 1986, Niswander et al., 2000; Taft, 1979), Dutch (Schreuder et al., 2003), French (e.g., Beauvillain, 1996; Colé et al., 1989; Holmes and O'Regan, 1992; Meunier and Segui, 1999), and Italian (e.g.,

Burani and Caramazza, 1987; Burani and Thornton, 2003). Several findings indicate, however, that the effect of root frequency depends on the root's position in the derived word. Whereas consistent effects have been found with suffix-derivations, root frequency effects were not always evident with prefix-derivations (Colé et al., 1989; Holmes and O'Regan, 1992; Taft, 1979). This may reflect a beginning-to-end directionality in the processing of complex words: Only in the case of suffixed derivations would the root be encountered before the whole word. Evidence from eye movement recordings is compatible with this idea: A root frequency effect is found for both types of derivations but the effect occurs later for prefixed derivations (Beauvillain, 1996; Niswander-Klement and Pollatsek, 2006). Eye monitoring studies further suggest that, like surface frequency effects, root frequency effects interact with the length of the input.[6] The relation with word length is, however, opposite to the one involving surface frequency; larger root frequency effects are found for longer derivations (Bertram and Hyönä, 2003; Niswander-Klement and Pollatsek, 2006).

Apart from surface frequency and root frequency, the token frequency of affixes has also been examined. However, since most studies addressing this issue used morphologically complex pseudowords, they do not provide direct evidence as to whether affix frequency affects the processing of real derived words. These studies do show, however, that readers can quickly apply some form of morphological decomposition on novel items. A basic finding is that it is more difficult to reject pseudowords that combine a genuine root and a genuine affix (e.g., Caramazza, Laudanna, and Romani, 1988; Taft and Forster, 1975; Wurm, 2000). It has also been shown that this interference effect grows with increasing affix frequency. Burani and Thornton (2003), for instance,

6 Unlike the other studies reported here, these studies manipulated the surface frequency of roots (i.e., their token frequency as words). This measure is, however, correlated with the morpheme token frequency of the root.

found significant negative effects of suffix frequency in visual lexical decision. Wurm (2000) found comparable negative effects of prefix frequency in an auditory lexical decision task. Wurm also found a negative effect of so-called *prefix likelihood*, that is, the proportion of times that a phoneme string is a true prefix across all occurrences of this string in word-initial position. The scant evidence on real words is less clear. In the visual domain Burani and Thornton (2003) have shown that lexical decision latencies to Italian suffix-derived words are not affected by suffix frequency. In the auditory domain Wurm (1997) showed a negative effect of prefix frequency on lexical decision latencies to English prefix derivations. He also reported a negative effect of prefix likelihood.

In summary, the data regarding token frequency effects indicate that both the frequency of the derived word itself and the frequency of its component morphemes play an important role. The latter finding is especially true for root morphemes. This generally supports the idea that the recognition of derivations can involve the activation of both whole-word representations and morphemic (root) representations.[7] Since all models in Figure 15.1 (except type A) incorporate this idea, it seems that the data regarding token frequency effects are not particularly constraining. The finding of differential root frequency effects for suffixed and prefixed derivations could indicate, however, that the effect depends on form characteristics (i.e., the position of the root) and thus arises during pure form-based processing. This is compatible with the idea of a prelexical morphological decomposition process (models C and D in Figure 15.1). Combined with the effects of prefix likelihood, which suggest that morphological decomposition is sensitive to

form–meaning consistency, this would point towards a parallel dual-route view in which prelexical decomposition is not obligatory (model D). Parallel dual-route models are also supported by results showing an interaction between root frequency and surface frequency, with root frequency effects being strongest in derived words with a low surface frequency (e.g., Burani and Caramazza, 1987; see also Hay, 2001).

These models could even provide a plausible framework for understanding the interactions of surface frequency and root frequency with word length. As words get longer, the integration of the whole input could indeed become more difficult and it could become more important (to maintain adequate processing) to try to recognize the input through its morphemes. Nevertheless, it is important to note that the effects of prefix likelihood can also be taken to support the view in which morphology is represented at the interface between form and meaning (models E and F), as prefix likelihood captures the consistency with which a given letter or phoneme string (corresponding to a prefix) is mapped onto the same meaning across all the words in which it appears.

The strong correlation between token and type frequencies makes it possible, however, that the reported morpheme token frequency effects are (at least partially) determined by type frequency. If so, these effects might reflect an architecture in which morphemic representations capture interword relationships, or more generally, an architecture that emphasizes the recurrence of morphemes across different words (see models E and F). A number of recent studies have indeed pointed out the importance of controlling type frequency when considering morpheme token frequency effects. Baayen, Tweedie, and Schreuder (2002), for instance, found that after controlling for type frequency, the recognition of isolated roots is not positively, but negatively influenced by the so-called *family frequency* (i.e., a root's morpheme token frequency minus its surface frequency). The finding that token frequency does not facilitate

---

7   Some authors have questioned the interpretation of the effect of root token frequency as an index of morphemic representation. They point out that the effect is induced by the proportion of morphologically complex words in the experimental materials, and thus reflects response strategies. For instance, Andrews (1986) only found an effect of root frequency for suffixed derivations when many compound words appeared in the list.

recognition independently from type frequency is problematic for models assuming that each time a morpheme is detected in the input, an attempt is made to activate a corresponding representation (see models C and D). In such models the accessibility of morphemic representations should (also) be determined by the plain recurrence of morphemes. It remains unclear, however, whether Baayen et al.'s findings generalize to the root token frequency effects observed in the recognition of derivations (see e.g., de Jong et al., 2002).

2.2 Type frequency effects

Type frequency has only recently been considered in the morphological literature. This is due to a phenomenon discovered quite recently: the *morphological family size effect* (Schreuder and Baayen, 1997). The *morphological family* of a root comprises all derived and compound words containing that root and excludes all inflectional variants. Whereas the token count of a root's morphological family appears to have a negative effect on word recognition (at least in the case of isolated roots; see previous), its *family size*, that is, the number of family members, has been shown to have an independent positive effect in a large number of recent studies.

Simple nouns and verbs (e.g., Baayen et al., 2002; de Jong, Schreuder, and Baayen, 2000; Schreuder and Baayen, 1997) and derived and inflected words (e.g., Bertram, Baayen, and Schreuder, 2000; de Jong, et al, 2000; Moscoso del Prado Martín et al., 2004) are recognized faster if the root has a large morphological family. Although the effect was first discovered in Dutch (e.g., de Jong et al., 2000; Dijkstra et al., 2005; Schreuder and Baayen, 1997), it has also been established in English (e.g., Dijkstra et al., 2005; Pylkkänen et al., 2004), German (Lüdeling and de Jong, 2002), Hebrew (Moscoso del Prado Martín et al., 2005) and Finnish (Moscoso del Prado Martín et al., 2004). In most of these studies, visual lexical decision latencies were investigated. However, recently Pylkkänen et al. (2004) demonstrated that the effect

also shows up in a measure of brain activity. The effect of family size is considered to be semantic in nature, rather than being mediated by form characteristics. This interpretation especially follows from the finding that only the semantically related family members of a given word exert a positive effect on its recognition (e.g., Bertram et al., 2000; Dijkstra et al., 2005; Moscoso del Prado Martín et al., 2004; Schreuder and Baayen, 1997).

It appears that the morphological family size effect stands out as the empirically best grounded and theoretically most relevant morpheme type frequency effect.[8] In light of the models depicted in Figure 15.1, the effect aligns with the predictions of models E and F. In both models the representation of a morpheme and its influence during processing is a function of the number of different words that are related in both form and meaning with respect to that morpheme. This not only predicts the effect of morphological family size, but also that this effect should only be determined by semantically related family members.

2.3 Conclusion

The previous review illustrates that different frequency variables jointly determine the speed with which skilled readers can recognize derived words during reading. Recently, Moscoso del Prado Martín, Kostic, and Baayen (2004) argued that this joint effect can effectively be captured by a single measure, the so-called *information residual* of a word. This measure combines several frequency counts, including a word's surface frequency and the type and token count of its morphological family. Note that the possibility of collapsing these effects into a single measure does not imply a single locus of morpheme frequency effects in a

---

8 Few studies have addressed the effect of affix type frequency. Laudanna, Burani, and Cermele (1994) report a negative effect of prefix likelihood (calculated as described earlier, but now using type counts) on pseudoword decisions in a visual lexical decision task. They also show that this prefix likelihood is a better predictor of decision times than the token frequency of the prefix.

representational model. However, Moscoso del Prado Martín et àl.'s study clearly illustrates the large amount of variance in recognition times that can be explained by a word's frequency properties, which emphasizes the importance of considering these properties when modeling lexical processing.

The studies reviewed in this section support a model of complex word recognition in which both whole-word representations and morphemic representations are active during the recognition process. Existence of the former follows from the surface frequency effect of derived words. Evidence for the latter is indicated by the token and type frequency effects of the root (and, although studied less extensively, the affixes). The locus of these morpheme frequency effects is not entirely clear, however. Although the reported root token frequency effects can be explained by models with a prelexical decomposition routine (models B and C in Figure 15.1), it is less obvious how the morphological family size effect can be accommodated by these models (but see Schreuder and Baayen, 1997). The morphological family size effect and its reliance on semantic variables hint towards a more abstract (form independent) locus of morphological representation. At the same time this type frequency effect highlights the key role of morphological productivity and form–meaning consistency in morphological processing. Models that situate morphology at the interface between form and meaning representations (see panel E and F in Figure 15.1) readily account for such a state of affairs.

3 Morphological priming effects

Priming can be defined as the technique that investigates the influence of one stimulus (the *prime*) on the processing of another stimulus that is presented subsequently (the *target*). Priming effects have been used extensively to explore the different types of representations involved in word recognition. The typical rationale is that if prime and target share a given type of information (e.g., letters, phonemes, morphemes), and if target processing is facilitated by the prior presentation of the prime, then that shared information must be represented in the processing architecture. Target facilitation is taken to reflect residual activation in representations that were accessed before by the prime. A classic example of a morphological priming study is the one by Murrell and Morton (1974). These authors showed that participants were better at identifying very briefly presented visual targets (e.g., *numb*) when a word with the same root (e.g., *numbing*) had previously appeared in a study list. As the effect of a morphologically related prime was much larger than that of a formally related one (e.g., *number*), they argued that this effect was due to the existence of shared morphemic representations between primes and targets.

Priming methodologies can generally be distinguished on the basis of whether targets follow primes immediately (*immediate priming*) or only after a number of intervening items or lag (*long-lag priming*). The first morphological priming studies were of the long-lag type (e.g., Murrell and Morton, 1974; Stanners, Neiser, and Painton, 1979). However, it soon became clear that long-lag priming effects might not reflect residual activation in a lexical representation but rather be driven by some form of representation of the prime in episodic memory. As an episodic memory representation not only encodes word properties but also the situation in which the word was encountered, any perceived similarity between the prime situation and the target situation (e.g., experimenter, task, response type, etc.) could cause target facilitation.

One of the first hints of episodic memory involvement came from the observation that long-lag priming effects with identical primes and targets are found with lags as long as two days (Scarborough, Cortese, and Scarborough, 1977). The most compelling evidence, however, was provided in a seminal study by Forster and Davis (1984). They showed that whereas identity priming in the long-lag priming paradigm has a much larger effect on low-frequency words than on high-frequency ones (see Scarborough et al., 1977), identity priming in a *masked priming paradigm* (i.e., immediate priming with primes that are presented so briefly that they cannot be consciously perceived) produces equal priming effects for both word types. Given that in the latter technique primes are presented too briefly to enable the formation of episodic memory traces, Forster and Davis argued that this differential outcome demonstrates that long-lag priming is highly contaminated by episodic memory effects.

As a result of these difficulties with long-lag priming, the method has only been used in a minority of the more recent morphological priming studies (e.g., Feldman 2000; Rueckl and Galantucci, 2005). In contrast, immediate priming experiments have become more popular, as they are assumed to reflect online lexical processing. In our review of morphological priming we will distinguish studies that allowed for conscious prime perception (so-called *overt priming* studies) and then consider the data from masked priming studies.

3.1 *Overt morphological priming effects*

In *overt priming*, facilitation from morphologically related primes has been established across a variety of experimental settings. First, the effects are observable in a large number of different languages. Apart from English, overt morphological priming has been shown in German (e.g., Drews and Zwitserlood, 1995), Dutch (e.g., Drews and Zwitserlood, 1995), French (e.g., Longtin, Segui, and Hallé, 2003; Meunier and Segui, 2002), Spanish (Sánchez-Casas, Igoa, and García-Albea, 2003), Serbian (e.g., Feldman, Barac-Cikoja, and Kostic, 2002), Polish (Reid and Marslen-Wilson, 2003), Hebrew (e.g., Frost et al., 2000), and Arabic (e.g., Boudelaa and Marslen-Wilson, 2004).

Second, although there are considerable differences in the morphological systems of these languages, facilitatory effects were consistently found across a wide variety of prime–target configurations. The most extensively used configuration is a suffix-derived

prime with a root target (i.e., *suffixed-root*; *payment-pay*; e.g., Feldman, 2000; Longtin et al., 2003; Marslen-Wilson et al., 1994; Meunier and Segui, 2002; Rastle, et al., 2000; Reid and Marslen Wilson, 2003). However, there are also reports of *prefixed-root priming* (*repay-pay*; e.g., Marslen-Wilson et al., 1994; Meunier and Segui, 2002), *root-suffixed priming* (*pay-payment*; e.g., Marslen-Wilson, et al., 1994), *root-prefixed priming* (*pay-repay*; e.g., Marslen-Wilson et al., 1994), *suffixed-suffixed priming* (*payment-payable*; e.g., Feldman, et al., 2004; Meunier and Segui, 2002; Pastizzo and Feldman, 2002; Sánchez-Casas et al., 2003), *prefixed-prefixed priming* (*repay-prepay*; e.g., Marslen-Wilson et al., 1994; Meunier and Segui, 2002), *prefixed-suffixed priming* (repay-*payment*; e.g., Marslen-Wilson et al., 1994), and *suffixed-prefixed priming* (*payment-repay*; e.g., Marslen-Wilson et al., 1994). For Arabic and Hebrew, priming was also consistently found across the two main elements of the morphological structure (see endnote ii): the *root* (Boudelaa and Marslen-Wilson, 2004; Frost et al., 2000) and the *word-pattern* (Boudelaa and Marslen-Wilson, 2004; Frost et al., 2000).

Overt morphological priming also shows up robustly in different presentation modalities. The effects were not only found with visually presented stimuli, but also with auditory stimuli (e.g., Reid and Marslen-Wilson, 2003), and also in a cross-modal (auditory prime/visual target) situation (e.g., Boudelaa and Marslen-Wilson, 2004; Frost et al., 2000; Longtin et al., 2003; Marslen-Wilson et al., 1994; Meunier and Segui, 2002; Pastizzo and Feldman, 2002; Reid and Marslen-Wilson, 2003; Rueckl and Galantucci, 2005). Finally, whereas most studies used lexical decision, the effects are also robust in tasks such as naming (e.g., Drews and Zwitserlood, 1995; Pastizzo and Feldman, 2002) and fragment completion (e.g., Rueckl and Galantucci, 2005).

A theoretically important finding in overt morphological priming is that it is difficult to reduce the observed priming patterns to effects of orthographic/phonological and/or semantic similarity. Items that match the form or meaning similarity

of morphologically related primes and targets (e.g., *freeze-free* and *task-job* for *viewer-
view*) typically elicit smaller and less robust
priming effects. Even after summing the
effects for these two item types the size and
robustness of morphological priming tends
to be superior (e.g., Boudelaa and Marslen-
Wilson, 2004; Drews and Zwitserlood,
1995; Feldman, 2000; Frost et al., 2000;
Gonnerman, Seidenberg, and Andersen,
2007; Longtin et al., 2003; Marslen-Wilson
et al., 1994; Meunier and Segui, 2002; Napps,
1989; Pastizzo and Feldman, 2002; Sánchez-
Casas et al., 2003).

Even though overt morphological priming cannot be reduced to separate effects of
form and meaning it is influenced by semantic variables and also by form characteristics.
The role of semantics is most clearly demonstrated by effects of semantic transparency,
that is, the degree to which the meaning of
a derivation is related to its constituents. In
general, when prime and target are morphologically related, but are only weakly or not
semantically related (e.g., *department-depart*),
significantly less or even no morphological facilitation is found (e.g., Feldman et al.,
2002; Feldman et al., 2004; Frost et al., 2000;
Gonnerman et al., 2007; Longtin et al, 2003;
Marslen-Wilson et al., 1994; Reid and Marslen-
Wilson, 2003; Sánchez-Casas et al., 2003). This
is also evident in studies looking at priming effects with compound words (Sandra,
1990; Zwitserlood, 1994). Feldman, Basnight-
Brown, and Pastizzo (2006) found that overt
morphological priming is also positively influenced by other semantic factors, more particularly, family size and semantic concreteness.
Although investigated to a lesser extent,
form variables seem to play a role as well. A
number of recent studies revealed positive
effects of form similarity on overt morphological priming (with stronger facilitation for
items like *acceptable-accept* than for items like
introduction-introduce; e.g., Gonnerman et al.,
2007; Meunier and Segui, 2002).

Taken together, the results of overt priming studies again demonstrate the robustness
of morphological effects in language processing. The observation that these effects
cannot be explained on the basis of pure

form and/or semantic prime–target overlap, has led many researchers to argue that
morphology has a special representational
status in the lexicon (i.e., models C–F).
The influence of semantic variables seems
most in line with models in which morphological representations indeed capture
semantic relationships between morphological relatives (i.e., models E and F). These
effects could also be explained, however, as
the result of semantic feedback in models
with form-dependent morpheme representations that are activated via prelexical
decomposition (models C and E). The latter models could also predict the observed
influence of form similarity (see Meunier
and Segui, 2002). Nevertheless, the latter
influence also readily aligns with the predictions of the connectionist view (model
F; see Gonnerman et al., 2007), where morphological effects are a (graded) function of
their consistency in both form and meaning across their morphological family. Such
an approach also finds support in the finding that *phonaesthemes* (i.e., words sharing
both form and meaning, in the absence of
a compositional morphological relationship;
e.g., *screech* and *scream*) behave quite similar
to morphological relatives in overt priming
(Bergen, 2004, see also Rastle et al., 2000).

The overt priming results need to be
treated with caution, however. Although
immediate priming has been promoted as a
better technique than long-lag priming on
the basis of reduced contamination from
episodic factors, in the overt variant, influences extraneous to the processes of normal word recognition cannot be excluded.
Since prime stimuli are clearly visible in
these experiments, participants can become
aware of the prime–target relation that is
being manipulated. It is therefore possible
that they develop strategies to help them
perform the task they are required to do
(e.g., classify as rapidly as possible the target
stimulus as a word or a nonword).

3.2 *Masked morphological priming effects*

A solution to the problem just raised is
to compare the results of overt priming

with those of masked priming (Forster and Davis, 1984). In masked priming, participants are typically unaware of the presence of primes. It is therefore argued that it is impossible to develop strategies that depend on awareness of the type of prime–target relation that is manipulated in an experiment. Unconscious prime presentations are accomplished by presenting primes very briefly (usually around thirty to eighty ms) and by pattern masking. The typical sequence of events is (1) a forward pattern mask (e.g., #######), (2) the prime and (3) the target. In most cases the target is used as a backward mask for the prime, although an extra pattern mask is sometimes inserted between prime and target. It is also common practice to present primes and targets in different cases to minimize the purely visual overlap that occurs when the two overlap orthographically.

Morphological priming has also been consistently found in the masked priming paradigm, and again there has been a lot of cross-language validation. Apart from English, the effects have been shown in Dutch (Diependaele, Sandra, and Grainger, 2005; Drews and Zwitserlood, 1995), French (Diependaele et al., 2005; Giraudo and Grainger, 2000, 2001, 2003; Grainger et al., 1991; Longtin et al., 2003; Longtin and Meunier, 2005), Spanish (e.g., Sánchez-Casas et al., 2003), Bulgarian (Nikolova and Jarema, 2002), Serbian (Feldman et al., 2002), Greek (Voga and Grainger, 2004), Hebrew (e.g., Deutsch, Frost, and Forster, 1998; Frost, Deutsch, and Forster, 2000; Velan et al., 2005), and Arabic (e.g., Boudelaa and Marslen-Wilson, 2005). Again, the most documented prime–target configuration is *suffixed-root priming* (e.g., Diependaele et al., 2005; Drews and Zwitserlood, 1995; Feldman, 2000; Giraudo and Grainger, 2000, 2001; Longtin et al., 2003; Longtin and Meunier, 2005; Rastle et al., 2000; Rastle, Davis, and New, 2004), but there are also reports of *root-prefixed priming* (e.g., Grainger et al., 1991; Nikolova and Jarema, 2002), *prefixed-root priming* (Nikolova and Jarema, 2002), *suffixed-suffixed priming* (Feldman et al., 2004; Giraudo and Grainger, 2001; Grainger et al., 1991; Sánchez-Casas

et al., 2003), and *prefixed-prefixed priming* (e.g., Grainger et al., 1991).

Apart from these root-mediated priming effects, affix priming has also been found (primes and targets have a common affix and different roots), but only in the case of prefixes (Chateau, Knudsen, and Jared, 2002; Giraudo and Grainger, 2003). The failure to observe suffix priming has been regarded as further evidence for the influence of left-to-right processing in morphological processing (Beauvillain, 1996; Giraudo and Grainger, 2003). Finally, for Arabic and Hebrew there are also masked priming data showing both root priming (Boudelaa and Marslen-Wilson, 2005; Deutsch et al., 1998; Velan et al., 2005) and word pattern priming (e.g., Boudelaa and Marslen-Wilson, 2005; Deutsch et al., 1998; Frost et al., 2000).

Although most of these studies have used visual primes and targets in a lexical decision task, priming was also found in naming (e.g., Deutsch et al., 1998) and recently also in a cross-modal context, using masked visual primes and auditory targets (Diependaele et al., 2005). Comparable results have been reported in studies that monitor eye movements while participants read sentences (e.g., Deutsch et al., 2005). In these studies the prime is parafoveally presented (i.e., immediately to the right of the currently fixated word), and is replaced by the target as soon as the eyes move to the target position (this technique is referred to as the *boundary paradigm*, Rayner, 1975). The obtained facilitation shows that morphological priming also appears in these arguably more natural reading conditions.

It should be clear at this point that morphological priming is certainly not restricted to overt priming and that, hence, prime awareness does not cause entirely different effects. Furthermore, as is the case in overt priming, masked morphological priming effects have also been clearly distinguished from orthographic/phonological effects (e.g., Boudelaa and Marslen-Wilson, 2005; Deutsch et al., 1998; Diependaele et al., 2005; Drews and Zwitserlood, 1995; Feldman, 2000; Frost et al., 2000; Giraudo and Grainger, 2000, 2001, 2003; Grainger et al., 1991; Longtin et al.,

2003; Rastle et al., 2000, 2004; Sánchez-Casas et al., 2003; Voga and Grainger, 2004) and from semantic effects (e.g., Boudelaa and Marslen-Wilson, 2005; Feldman, 2000; Rastle et al., 2000; Sánchez-Casas et al., 2003). This again suggests that information about the morphological structure of complex words has a special status in long-term memory.

Despite the apparent commonality between the effects obtained with overt and masked morphological priming, a growing body of evidence suggests a clear difference regarding the role of semantic transparency. Recall that morphologically complex primes only seem to elicit an overt priming effect if there is (at least some degree of) semantic relatedness to the targets. In masked priming it appears, however, that transparent and opaque prime–target pairs (e.g., *involvement-involve* versus *department-depart*) produce similar levels of facilitation relative to form controls (e.g., Feldman et al., 2002, 2004; Lavric, Clapp, and Rastle, 2007; Longtin et al., 2003; Rastle et al., 2000, 2004; Sánchez-Casas et al., 2003). This pattern is commonly interpreted as evidence for a so-called *morpho-orthographic* decomposition mechanism that operates within the very first stages of word recognition. This mechanism is assumed to activate morpheme representations whenever a letter input is *exhaustively* decomposable into morphemic forms, independently of the item's semantic transparency. Morpho-orthographic decomposition can thus be considered to instantiate the concept of prelexical morphological decomposition (see models C and D in Figure 15.1). Its prelexical locus is indeed supported by studies showing equivalent priming effects with transparent word primes and pseudoword primes that are fully decomposable into morphemes (e.g., *cornity-corn*; Deutsch et al., 1998; Longtin and Meunier, 2005).

The data thus suggest that there is a level of morphological processing at which only the sublexical form characteristics of morphologically complex words determine activation in the mental lexicon. It might seem puzzling that, as noted above, models incorporating this idea (i.e., models C and D) can also predict semantic transparency

effects. However, this prediction hinges on the effect of later processing stages, that is, when feedback from semantic representations to form representations can be established. The data of Rastle et al. (2000) are in line with this prediction. As soon as priming was found with semantic relatives (from seventy-two ms of prime exposure onwards; e.g., *task-work*), transparent primes started to show stronger priming than opaque primes. This pattern seems to suggest that, for (fully) opaque items, initial morphological activation due to morpho-orthographic decomposition disappears once semantics enters the stage.

The data from masked priming thus seem to make a strong case for models of type C and D in Figure 15.1. According to the supralexical view (model E), fully opaque morphologically structured words like *corner* should always behave in the same way as form control items like *freeze*, as their lexical form representation is not connected to supralexical morphemic representations. A connectionist model mapping sublexical form onto meaning (model F) also runs into problems when confronted with the above data. Such a model can in principle predict morphological activation in the case of fully opaque complex words. However, as demonstrated by Plaut and Gonnerman (2000), this activation only seems to occur when extremely productive morphemes are involved (which arguably only occurs in morphologically rich languages like Arabic and Hebrew) and it seems to be considerably smaller than that observed with transparent items.

Nevertheless, there remain a number of masked priming results that offer a challenge for a pure prelexical account. First, the effect of transparent primes appeared at shorter prime durations than the effect of opaque primes in an incremental priming study reported by Diependaele et al. (2005). If the transparency effect were indeed purely semantic, that is, does not reflect morphological processing, it could never turn up before the effect of purely formal morphological decomposition. The fact that it does seems to indicate that, at least under some circumstances, morpho-semantically defined representations can influence early phases of word recognition. Diependaele et al. argued that a parallel dual-route model in which there are also morphological representations at a supralexical level (i.e., models D+E) could account for such a pattern in the effects: Although both transparent and opaque derivational primes may (at some point) activate the lexical form representations of their root (via prelexical decomposition), the parallel mapping of the whole input on a corresponding lexical form representation allows for a fast and independent supralexical activation of these root representations only in the case of transparent primes. Morris et al. (2007) provided further evidence in this direction by combining masked priming with the recording of event-related brain potentials (ERPs). A relatively early ERP component (N250), thought to reflect prelexical processing, was found to be sensitive to the semantic transparency of masked morphologically related primes.

A pure prelexical model is also questioned by the data of Giraudo and Grainger (2000, 2001). These authors showed that suffixed–root priming is insensitive to cumulative root frequency but sensitive to the surface frequency of the primes (Giraudo and Grainger, 2000). They concluded that the absence of a cumulative root frequency effect questions a prelexical decomposition mechanism, whereas the influence of surface frequency indicates that morphological effects originate beyond the level of whole-word representations. Furthermore, Giraudo and Grainger (2001) showed that root–suffixed priming is not larger than suffixed–suffixed priming, which questions the existence of a time-consuming prelexical decomposition mechanism for suffix-derived primes.

The prelexical account may also be also questioned by data showing that masked priming is affected by form–meaning consistency. Chateau et al. (2002, Experiment 2) found priming between pseudoprefixed words and truly prefixed words (sharing the prefix letter string) when the prefix likelihood

(calculated as a type count) was high (as for *un-* in *uncle-unable*), but not when it was low (as for *be-* in *behold-beloved*). Since prefix likelihood reflects how consistently a given letter or phoneme string maps onto a given meaning (see previous), they argued that morphological processing is already sensitive to the statistical nature of form–meaning relations in a language during the first stages of word recognition. Taft and Kougious (2004) recently came to a similar conclusion. They demonstrated that masked priming in pairs like *virus-viral* could not be reduced to the form priming found in pairs like *future-futile*. Although, linguistically, words like *virus* and *viral* are not considered complex, they certainly share a form unit that relates them semantically (*vir*). Taft and Kougious explain their result by assuming a representational level that captures form–meaning consistency during the very first stages of word processing. Note, however, that the results of Chateau et al. (2002) and Taft and Kougious (2004) could still be brought in line with the idea of morpho-orthographic decomposition in the context of a dual route model (model D), as the speed/success of prelexical decomposition is assumed to rely on variables such as the form–meaning consistency of the involved units.

3.3 Conclusion

To summarize, it appears from the large amount of empirical data presented in this section that morphological priming effects in overt and masked priming are quite robust. Moreover, these effects appear to be genuinely morphological. That is, they cannot be explained as due to independent effects of form and/or meaning similarity, suggesting that morphological information is indeed encoded in lexical memory. Hence, as with the results of morphological frequency, the critical theoretical debate seems not to revolve around the question of whether morphology is represented or not. Rather, the precise locus/nature of these representations forms the key theoretical issue.

The finding that fully semantically opaque derivations and morphologically fully parsable nonwords can facilitate the recognition of root target words more than form controls in masked priming strongly suggests that there is a prelexical form-driven component to morphological priming (as in models C and D). However, the exact functional description of morpho-orthographic decomposition remains unclear. What seems to be critical is that an input corresponds to an exhaustive set of possible morphemes in the language. One might quite rightly remark that this implies a full-form processing of the letter input. It should also be kept in mind that thus far the evidence for morpho-orthographic decomposition only comes from items with a root+suffix structure. In order to gain full insight into the functional properties of morpho-orthographic decomposition, future research will have to consider different structures as well.

On the other hand, the observed effects of semantic transparency in masked priming seem to question the idea that all morphological activation in word recognition originates from morpho-orthographic decomposition. They could indicate a double (i.e., a prelexical and a supralexical) locus of morphological processing as proposed by Diependaele et al. (2005). Still, one might want to argue that effects of semantic transparency in masked priming are compatible with the notion of a morpho-orthographic mechanism as well. This is possible (a) if morpho-orthographic decomposition is sensitive to form–meaning consistency, which would be the case if the representations activated by morpho-orthographic decomposition only involve units with a high form–meaning consistency (e.g., in the context of a dual-route account, model D) and (b) if it turned out that there was a mismatch in the form–meaning consistency of roots in the transparent and opaque derived priming conditions in the reported experiments (with more consistent mappings for transparent roots). Although none of the studies reported above explicitly controlled form–meaning consistency in the comparison of transparent and opaque masked priming conditions, Feldman et al. (2004) found no positive

correlation between opaque priming and root family size, a measure that at least partially captures form–meaning consistency. This does not reject the presence of a fast morpho-semantic effect, though. Before we can conclude that the transparency effect is an artifact of a difference in form–meaning consistency, analyses are needed that use a direct quantification of this variable.

4 General conclusions and future directions

The last thirty years has seen an increase in the number of empirical studies on word recognition in general, and morphological processing in particular. The present chapter has summarized this empirical research and tried to link it to different accounts of the role of morphological information in language comprehension. We argued that the initial fascination with morphology was probably the result of the predominance of the computer metaphor in early theories of human language processing. Within that particular approach, morphemic units, given their unique linguistic properties, provided an ideal means to economize on storage and increase processing efficiency. Our overview of the empirical data was guided by the different models that grew out of this initial approach and were modified by subsequent theoretical developments in psycholinguistics. These models describe precisely how morphological information is taken into account during lexical processing (see Figure 15.1). Although our overview is limited to frequency and priming manipulations in the context of derivational morphology and single word recognition, we have tried to illustrate how the observed data patterns constrain the different theoretical possibilities. In this final section we will recapitulate the main conclusions and discuss some possible directions for future research.

The positive influence of morpheme frequency and morphologically related primes on the fluency (speed and accuracy) with which words are recognized points to a key role for morphological information in the recognition process. These facilitation effects are highly consistent across experimental settings, that is, languages, tasks, type of morphological relationship, and presentation modality. Priming studies further demonstrate the special status of morphological structure, given that the observed effects cannot simply be explained as due to independent effects of form and/or meaning overlap between primes and targets. This leaves little or no doubt that morphology is indeed encoded and hence, a model that denies this (see model A in Figure 15.1) can be rejected. When considering the different models that do include morphology (explicitly or implicitly), it is clear that the alternative in which *only* morphemes are stored (model B) is not viable. As we discussed in the Introduction, such a model can only work if all possible morpheme combinations actually exist in the language and are semantically predictable. In that hypothetical situation whole-word storage would, of course, be totally redundant. The typical absence of predictability at the levels of form and meaning makes it possible to reject model B on purely logical grounds.

However, difficulties arise in attempting to select among the remaining theoretical alternatives (C, D, E, and F) in light of the empirical evidence. These models can be distinguished on the basis of whether they exploit the fact that morphemes tend to have consistent form–form mappings (model C) or consistent form–meaning mappings at the level of sublexical form (model D), whole-word form (model E), or both (model F). Models C and D postulate a prelexical morphological decomposition mechanism in order to enhance access to whole-word information (model C) or to enhance the computation of meaning (model D). This mechanism only takes into account form information (orthographic and/or phonological) derived from the stimulus. The observation that root token frequency effects are more elusive for prefix derivations than for suffix derivations seems to align with this characteristic, as it suggests that morpheme activation is sensitive to the position of a morpheme in an input, that is, a word form property. The data from masked priming provide more direct evidence for prelexical decomposition, however. In particular, they support the prediction that morpheme activation emerges without reference to whole-word semantic information, as they show equivalent facilitation effects with transparent, opaque, and even nonexistent derivations as primes.

At the same time, however, the data from these experiments also seem to impose a nontrivial restriction on the operation of a prelexical decomposition process: A prerequisite for successful prelexical decomposition seems to be that the input can be exhaustively segmented into morphemic forms. As we already pointed out, this latter property poses a great challenge if one wants to incorporate an algorithm that reflects prelexical morphological decomposition into a computational model. The idea of a pure left-to-right parsing of the input that activates morphemes as soon as they are encountered (Taft and Forster, 1975) is difficult to maintain in the light of the evidence. In that case, equivalent root priming would be expected with any prime that carries that root at its beginning, regardless of whether it is fully decomposable or not. It should be kept in mind, however, that the prerequisite of a fully decomposable surface structure remains an issue for further research itself. It might well be that it is merely the presence of a suffix (or any highly recurrent morpheme) that triggers a prelexical segmentation attempt.

Despite the evidence from masked priming, it is less obvious to see how the data concerning morphological family size (more particularly, its semantic nature) can be accommodated within a prelexical view. The same seems to hold for the effects of semantic transparency in masked priming. Both findings are instead readily accounted for by the supralexical and connectionist view (models E and F) where morphological processing, situated at the interface between form and meaning processing, is crucially sensitive to productivity and form–meaning consistency.

An interesting direction for future research seems therefore to investigate the possibility of a hybrid model in which morphology affects pure formal processing as well as form–meaning processing. In a localist connectionist framework (e.g., Giraudo and Grainger, 2000), this could be accomplished by combining the prelexical and supralexical ingredients of models C/D and E. It is also possible, however, that the evidence for morpho-orthographic processing can be explained within the orthography-phonology mapping of a distributed connectionist model, in which there is no room for dedicated morpheme representations (e.g., Harm and Seidenberg, 2004). A connectionist network trained to map orthography onto phonology will naturally capture the frequency and consistency with which a given letter combination maps onto a certain phonological pattern. Given that this frequency and/or consistency is typically higher for units within morphemes (e.g., *art* in *department*) than for units across morphemes (e.g., *rtm* in *department*; see Seidenberg, 1987), the activity patterns evoked by fully decomposable words (e.g., *involvement, department*) or even nonwords (e.g., *departness*) would often virtually fall apart into patterns corresponding to the (pseudo-) morphemes. As such, the evidence for morpho-orthographic decomposition could be explained without the requirement of a specialized processing algorithm for morphological structure.

Along the same lines, it can be considered that letter clusters within and across morphemes will also show significant differences in the frequency and consistency with which they mark a particular stress pattern, syllable boundary, and so forth. The general hypothesis is that morphological effects might be explained through the correlation of morphological structure with not only the frequency and consistency of form–meaning mappings, but also with the frequency and consistency of orthography-phonology mappings (see e.g., Gonnerman et al., 2007). We believe that one way of approaching this hypothesis is to develop probabilistic measures that predict how *decompositional* the processing of an input

will be, based on the distribution of both form–meaning and orthography-phonology mappings in the language.

In conclusion, although there is at present a large database on the processing of morphologically complex words covering many different languages (see e.g., Frost, Grainger, and Rastle, 2005), there is still no consensus on the way the human brain might encode this particular type of information during language acquisition and exploit it during skilled language comprehension. The methods and models described in this chapter – together with other methodological approaches, such as electrophysiological measurements (e.g., Lavric et al., 2007; Morris et al., 2007; Pylkkänen et al., 2004), neuroimaging (e.g., Devlin et al., 2004), and alternative modeling approaches – should continue to help researchers make progress in this critical area of psycholinguistics.

References

Andrews, S. (1986). Morphological influences on lexical access: Lexical or nonlexical effects? *Journal of Memory and Language*, 25, 726–40.

Baayen, R. H., Feldman, L. B., & Schreuder, R. (2006). Morphological influences on the recognition of monosyllabic monomorphemic words. *Journal of Memory and Language*, 55, 290–313.

Baayen, R. H., Tweedie, F. J., & Schreuder, R. (2002). The subjects as a simple random effect fallacy: Subject variability and morphological family effects in the mental lexicon. *Brain and Language*, 81, 55–65.

Beauvillain, C. (1996). The integration of morphological and whole-word form information during eye fixations on prefixed and suffixed words. *Journal of Memory and Language*, 35, 801–20.

Bergen, B. K. (2004). The psychological reality of phonaesthemes. *Language*, 80(2), 290–311.

Bertram, R., Baayen, R. H., & Schreuder, R. (2000). Effects of family size for complex words. *Journal of Memory and Language*, 42, 390–405.

Bertram, R., & Hyönä, J. (2003). The length of a complex word modifies the role of morphological structure: Evidence from eye movements when reading short and long Finnish compounds. *Journal of Memory and Language, 48*, 615–34.

Boudelaa, S. & Marslen-Wilson, W. D. (2004). Allomorphic variation in Arabic: Implications for lexical processing and representation. *Brain and Language, 90*, 106–16.

(2005). Discontinuous morphology in time: Incremental masked priming in Arabic. *Language and Cognitive Processes, 20(1/2)*, 207–60.

Broadbent, D. (1967). Word-frequency effect and response bias. *Psychological Review, 74(1)*, 1–15.

Burani, C. & Caramazza, A. (1987). Representation and processing of derived words. *Language and Cognitive Processes, 2(3–4)*, 217–27.

Burani, C. & Thornton, A. M. (2003). The interplay of root, suffix and whole-word frequency in processing derived words. In Baayen, R. H. & Schreuder, R. (Eds.) *Morphological structure in language processing* (pp. 157–208). Mouton de Gruyter.

Butterworth, B. (1983). Lexical representation. In Butterworth, B. (Ed.) *Language production* (Vol. 2, pp. 257–94). London: Academic Press.

Caramazza, A., Laudanna, A., & Romani, C. (1988). Lexical access and inflectional morphology. *Cognition, 28*, 297–332.

Chateau, D., Knudsen, E. V., & Jared, D. (2002). Masked priming of prefixes and the influence of spelling-meaning consistency. *Brain and Language, 81*, 587–600.

Colé, P., Beauvillain, C., Pavard, B., & Segui, J. (1986). Organisation morphologique et accès au lexique. *L'Année Psychologique, 86*, 349–65.

Colé, P., Beauvillain, C., & Segui, J. (1989). On the representation and processing of prefixed and suffixed derived words: A differential frequency effect. *Journal of Memory and Language, 28*, 1–13.

de Jong, N. H., Feldman, L. B., Schreuder, R., Pastizzo, M., & Baayen, R. H. (2002). The processing and representation of Dutch and English compounds: Peripheral morphological and central orthographic effects. *Brain and Language, 81*, 555–67.

de Jong, N. H., Schreuder, R., & Baayen, R. H. (2000). The morphological family size effect and morphology. *Language and Cognitive Processes, 15(4/5)*, 329–65.

Deutsch, A., Frost, R., & Forster, K. I. (1998). Verbs and nouns are organized and accessed differently in the mental lexicon: Evidence from Hebrew. *Journal of Experimental Psychology: Learning, Memory, and Cognition, 24(5)*, 1238–55.

Deutsch, A., Frost, R., Pollatsek, A., & Rayner, K. (2005). Morphological parafoveal preview benefit effects in reading: Evidence from Hebrew. *Language and Cognitive Processes, 20(1/2)*, 341–71.

Devlin, J. T., Jamison, H. L., Matthews, P. M., & Gonnerman, L. M. (2004). Morphology and the internal structure of words. *Proceedings of the National Academy of Sciences, 101(41)*, 14984–8.

Diependaele, K., Sandra, D., & Grainger, J. (2005). Masked cross-modal morphological priming: Unravelling morpho-orthographic and morpho-semantic influences in early word recognition. *Language and Cognitive Processes, 20(1–2)*, 75–114.

Dijkstra, T., Moscoso del Prado Martín, F., Schulpen, B., Schreuder, R., & Baayen, R. H. (2005). A roommate in cream: Morphological family size effects on interlingual homograph recognition. *Language and Cognitive Processes, 20(1/2)*, 7–41.

Drews, E. & Zwitserlood, P. (1995). Morphological and orthograpihc similarity in visual word recognition. *Journal of Experimental Psychology: Human Perception and Performance, 21(5)*, 1098–1116.

Feldman, L. B. (2000). Are morphological effects distinguishable from effects of shared meaning and shared form? *Journal of Experimental Psychology: Learning, Memory, and Cognition, 26(6)*, 1431–44.

Feldman, L. B., Barac-Cikoja, D., & Kostic, A. (2002). Semantic aspects of morphological processing: Transparency effects in Serbian. *Memory & Cognition, 30(4)*, 629–36.

Feldman, L. B., Basnight-Brown, D., & Pastizzo, M. J. (2006). Semantic influences on morphological facilitation: Concreteness and family size. *The Mental Lexicon, 1(1)*, 59–84.

Feldman, L. B., Soltano, E. G., Pastizzo, M. J., & Francis, S. E. (2004). What do graded effects of semantic transparency reveal about morphological processing. *Brain and Language, 90*, 17–30.

Forster, K. I. (1976). Accessing the mental lexicon. In Wales, R. J. & Walker, E. (Eds.) *New approaches to language mechanisms* (pp. 257–87). Amsterdam: North-Holland.

Forster, K. I. & Davis, C. (1984). Repetition priming and frequency attenuation in lexical access. *Journal of Experimental Psychology: Learning, Memory, and Cognition, 10(4)*, 680–98.

Frost, R., Deutsch, A., & Forster, K. I. (2000). Decomposing morphologically complex words in a nonlinear morphology. *Journal of*

Experimental Psychology: Learning, Memory, and Cognition, 26(3), 751–65.

Frost, R., Deutsch, A., Gilboa, O., Tannenbaum, M., & Marslen-Wilson, W. D. (2000). Morphological priming: Dissociation of phonological, semantic, and morphological factors. *Memory & Cognition, 28(8)*, 1277–88.

Frost, R., Grainger, J., & Rastle, K. (2005). Current issues in morphological processing: An introduction. *Language and Cognitive Processes, 20(1)*, 1–5.

Giraudo, H. & Grainger, J. (2000). Effects of prime word frequency and cumulative root frequency in masked morphological priming. *Language and Cognitive Processes, 15(4/5)*, 421–44.

(2001). Priming complex words: Evidence for supralexical representation of morphology. *Psychonomic Bulletin & Review, 8(1)*, 127–31.

(2003). On the role of derivational affixes in recognizing complex words: Evidence from masked priming. In Baayen, R. H. & Schreuder, R. (Eds.) *Morphological structure in language processing* (pp. 209–32). Mouton de Gruyter.

Gonnerman, L. M., Seidenberg, M. S., & Andersen E. S. (2007). Graded semantic and phonological similarity effects in priming: Evidence for a distributed connectionist approach to morphology. *Journal of Experimental Psychology: General, 136(2)*, 323–45.

Grainger, J., Colé, P., & Segui, J. (1991). Masked morphological priming in visual word recognition. *Journal of Memory and Language, 30*, 370–84.

Harm, M. W. & Seidenberg, M. S. (2004). Computing the meanings of words in reading: Cooperative division of labor between visual and phonological processes. *Psychological Review, 111*, 662–720.

Hay, J. B. (2001). Lexical frequency in morphology: Is everything relative? *Linguistics, 39(6)*, 1041–70.

Hay, J. B. & Baayen, R. H. (2005). Shifting Paradigms: Gradient structure in morphology. *Trends in Cognitive Sciences, 9(7)*, 342–8.

Holmes, V. M. & O'Regan, J. (1992). Reading derivationally affixed French words. *Language and Cognitive Processes, 7(2)*, 163–92.

Howes, D. H. & Solomon, R. L. (1951). Visual duration threshold as a function of word-probability. *Journal of Experimental Psychology, 41*, 401–10.

Laudanna, A., Burani, C., & Cermele, A. (1994). Prefixes as processing units. *Language and Cognitive Processes, 9(3)*, 295–316.

Lavric, A., Clapp, A., & Rastle, K. (2007). ERP evidence of morphological analysis from

orthography: a masked priming study. *Journal of Cognitive Neuroscience, 19*, 866–77.

Longtin, C. M. & Meunier, F. (2005). Morphological decomposition in early visual word processing. *Journal of Memory and Language, 53*, 26–41.

Longtin, C. M., Segui, J., & Hallé, P. A. (2003). Morphological priming without morphological relationship. *Language and Cognitive Processes, 18(3)*, 313–34.

Lüdeling, A. & de Jong, N. H. (2002). German particle verbs and word formation. In Dehé, N., Jackendoff, R., McIntyre, A., & Urban, S. (Eds.) *Explorations in Verb-Particle Constructions* (pp. 315–33). Berlin: Mouton de Gruyter.

Lukatela, G., Gligorijevic, B., Kostic, A., & Turvey, M. T. (1980). Representation of inflected nouns in the internal lexicon. *Memory & Cognition, 8(5)*, 415–23.

Marslen-Wilson, W. D., Tyler, L. K., Waksler, R., & Older, L. (1994). Morphology and meaning in the English mental lexicon. *Psychological Review, 101(1)*, 3–33.

McClelland, J. L. & Rumelhart, D. E. (1981). An interactive activation model of context effects in letter perception: Part 1. An account of basic findings. *Psychological Review, 88*, 375–405.

Meunier, F. & Segui, J. (1999). Frequency effects in auditory word recognition: The case of suffixed words. *Journal of Memory and Language, 41*, 327–44.

(2002). Cross-modal morphological priming in French. *Brain and Language, 81*, 89–102.

Morris, J., Frank, T., Grainger, J., & Holcomb, P. J. (2007). Semantic transparency and masked morphological priming: An ERP investigation. *Psychophysiology, 44*, 506–21.

Moscoso del Prado Martín, F., Bertram, R., Häikiö, T., Schreuder, R., & Baayen, R. H. (2004). Morphological family size in a morphologically rich language: The case of Finnish compared with Dutch and Hebrew. *Journal of Experimental Psychology: Learning, Memory, and Cognition, 30(6)*, 1271–8.

Moscoso del Prado Martín, F., Deutsch, A., Frost, R., Schreuder, R., de Jong, N. H., & Baayen, R. H. (2005). Changing places: A cross-language perspective on frequency and family size in Dutch and Hebrew. *Journal of Memory and Language, 53*, 496–512.

Moscoso del Prado Martín, F., Kostic, A., & Baayen, R. H. (2004). Putting the bits together: An information theoretical perspective on morphological processing. *Cognition, 94*, 1–18.

Murrell, G. A. & Morton, J. (1974). Word recognition and morphemic structure. *Journal of Experimental Psychology, 102(6)*, 963–8.

Napps, S. E. (1989). Morphemic relationships in the lexicon: Are they distinct from semantic and formal relationships? *Memory & Cognition*, 17(6), 729–39.

Nikolova, R. & Jarema, G. (2002). Interaction of morphological structure and prefix transparency in the processing of Bulgarian aspectual verb forms. *Brain and Language*, 81, 649–65.

Niswander, E., Pollatsek, A., & Rayner, K. (2000). The processing of derived and inflected suffixed words during reading. *Language and Cognitive Processes*, 15(4/5), 389–420.

Niswander-Klement, E. & Pollatsek, A. (2006). The effects of root frequency, word frequency, and length on the processing of prefixed English words during reading. *Memory and Cognition*, 34, 685–702.

Pastizzo, M. J. & Feldman, L. B. (2002). Does prime modality influence morphological processing? *Brain and Language*, 81, 28–41.

Plaut, D. C. & Gonnerman, L. M. (2000). Are non-semantic morphological effects incompatible with a distributed connectionist approach to lexical processing? *Language and Cognitive Processes*, 15(4/5), 445–85.

Pylkkänen, L., Feintuch, S., Hopkins, E., & Marantz, A. (2004). Neural correlates of the effects of morphological family frequency and size: An meg study. *Cognition*, 91(3), B35–B45.

Rastle, K., Davis, M. H., Marslen-Wilson, W. D., & Tyler, L. K. (2000). Morphological & semantic effects in visual word recognition: A time-course study. *Language and Cognitive Processes*, 15(4/5), 507–37.

Rastle, K., Davis, M. H., & New, B. (2004). The broth in my brother's brothel: Morpho-orthographic segmentation in visual word recognition. *Psychonomic Bulletin & Review*, 11(6), 1090–8.

Rayner, K. (1975). The perceptual span and peripheral cues in reading. *Cognitive Psychology*, 7, 65–81.

Reid, A. A. & Marslen-Wilson, W. D. (2003). Lexical representation of morphologically complex words: Evidence from Polish. In Baayen, R. H. & Schreuder, R. (Eds.) *Morphological structure in language processing* (pp. 287–336). Mouton de Gruyter.

Rueckl, J. G. & Galantucci, B. (2005). The locus and time course of long-term morphological priming. *Language and Cognitive Processes*, 20(1/2), 115–38.

Rueckl, J. G. & Raveh, M. (1999). The influence of morphological regularities on the dynamics of a connectionist network. *Brain and Language*, 68, 110–17.

Sánchez-Casas, R., Igoa, J. M., & García-Albea, J. E. (2003). On the representation of inflections and derivations: Data from Spanish. *Journal of Psycholinguistic Research*, 32(6), 621–68.

Sandra, D. (1990). On the representation and processing of compound words: Automatic access to constituent morphemes does not occur. *The Quarterly Journal of Experimental Psychology*, 42A(3), 529–67.

(1994). The morphology of the mental lexicon: Internal word structure viewed from a psycholinguistic perspective. *Language and Cognitive Processes*, 9(3), 227–69.

Scarborough, D., Cortese, C., & Scarborough, H. (1977). Frequency and repetition effects in lexical memory. *Journal of Experimental Psychology: Human Perception and Performance*, 3, 1–17.

Schreuder, R. & Baayen, R. H. (1994). Prefix stripping re-revisited. *Journal of Memory and Language*, 33, 357–75.

(1995). Modeling morphological processing. In Feldman, L. B. (Ed.) *Morphological aspects of language processing* (pp. 131–56). Hillsdale, NJ: Erlbaum.

(1997). How complex simple words can be. *Journal of Memory and Language*, 37, 118–39.

Schreuder, R., Burani, C., & Baayen, R. H. (2003). Parsing and semantic opacity. In Assink, EMH & Sandra, D. (Eds.) *Neuropsychology and cognition: Vol. 22 Reading complex words: Cross-language studies* (pp. 159–90). Kluwer Academic Publishers.

Seidenberg, M. S. (1987). Sublexical structures in visual word recognition: Access units or orthographic redundancy? In Coltheart, M. (Ed.) *Attention and Performance XII: The Psychology of Reading* (pp. 245–63). London: Erlbaum.

Stanners, R., Neiser, J., & Painton, S. (1979). Memory representation for prefixed words. *Journal of Verbal Learning and Verbal Behavior*, 18, 733–43.

Taft, M. (1979). Recognition of affixed words & the word frequency effect. *Memory & Cognition*, 7(4), 263–72.

Taft, M. & Forster, K. I. (1975). Lexical storage and retrieval of prefixed words. *Journal of Verbal Learning and Verbal Behavior*, 14, 638–47.

Taft, M. & Kougious, P. (2004). The processing of morpheme-like units in monomorphemic words. *Brain & Language*, 90, 9–16.

Velan, H., Frost, R., & Deutsch, A. (2005). The processing of root morphemes in Hebrew: Contrasting localist and distributed accounts. *Language and Cognitive Processes*, 20(1/2), 169–206.

Voga, M. & Grainger, J. (2004). Masked morphological priming with varying levels of form overlap: Evidence from Greek verbs. *Current Psychology Letters: Behaviour, Brain, & Cognition, 13(2)*.

Woollams, A. & Patterson, K. (this volume). The neural basis of morphology: A tale of two mechanisms?

Wurm, L. H. (1997). Auditory processing of prefixed English words is both continuous and decompositional. *Journal of Memory and Language, 37,* 438–61.

—— (2000). Auditory processing of polymorphemic pseudowords. *Journal of Memory and Language, 42,* 255–71.

Zwitserlood, P. (1994). The role of semantic transparency in the processing and representation of Dutch compounds. *Language and Cognitive Processes, 9(3),* 341–68.

CHAPTER 16

The Neural Basis of Morphology

A Tale of Two Mechanisms?

Anna Woollams and Karalyn Patterson

1 Introduction

Our ability to combine various morphemes in principled ways to express different concepts is one of the factors underlying the amazing productivity of human language. Explication of the mechanisms involved is therefore of great relevance to cognitive neuroscience. In broad terms, morphology may be divided into two types: derivational and inflectional. *Derivational morphology* refers to the creation of new words from the concatenation of existing morphemes, resulting in a change in part of speech (*comfort-comfortable; admire-admiration*). *Inflectional morphology* refers to the modification of words within one part of speech to fit a grammatical role, such as past tense for verbs (*walk-walked; teach-taught*) or plural for nouns (*book-books; woman-women*). Although English derivation is a fairly complex morphological system, English inflectional morphology – in contrast to that of many other languages – is relatively simple. It may therefore appear somewhat ironic that consideration of alternative theoretical approaches to inflectional morphology

has been based so largely on the case of the English past tense (PT). As will become apparent, however, the English PT debate has broader implications for an understanding of linguistic processing.

The transformations involved in English PT inflection exemplify a quasi-regular domain: The relationship between a stem and its PT form is on the whole systematic (the regular part), but a number of exceptional instances also exist (the quasi part). The overwhelming majority of verbs are regular (Plunkett and Nakisa, 1997) in that they involve only the application of the *-ed* suffix to the stem form (*walk-walked; blink-blinked*). Phonologically, this process translates to the addition of one of three allophones depending upon the stem-final phoneme: the voiced [d] for voiced stem-final verbs (*stab, love*), the unvoiced [t] for unvoiced stem-final verbs (*stop, race*) or the syllable [Id] for voiced or unvoiced alveolar stop stem-final verbs (*fade, hate*). The remaining verbs are considered irregular by virtue of the fact that they do not take the *-ed* suffix and involve a variety of types of PT transformations, namely: no change (*cut-cut*, *hit-hit*), vowel change (*bleed-bled*, *come-came*), consonant addition (*spell-spelt*, *burn-burnt*), vowel change and consonant addition (*sleep-slept*, *say-said*), consonant change (*build-built*, *have-had*), and complete change (*be-was*, *go-went*) in the case of a few very common suppletive forms. The debate surrounding formation of the English PT primarily concerns the question of whether inflecting a verb for tense is a fundamentally different process for regular versus irregular verbs; this is the *raison d'etre* for the title of our chapter. Other issues pale in significance beside this central one, but there are others and some are germane to the central one; these include the potential relevance of (a) differences within either the regular or the irregular subset, and (b) differences between regular and irregular verbs other than their morphological regularity.

1.1 *Accounts of inflectional morphology based on normal processing*

Dual-mechanism models of inflectional morphology, such as the Words and Rules Theory (Pinker 1991; 1994; Pinker and Prince, 1988), derive from traditional linguistic theory, in which a lexicon and a grammar are independent cognitive subsystems. In this framework, all monomorphemic words, including verb stems, have entries in the lexicon. If a verb is irregular (*think*), then its PT form (*thought*) will also be listed in the lexicon; but if it is regular (*blink*), then its PT form (*blinked*) has no independent existence but instead is created online every time it is needed through application of the generalised grammar that encodes the regular PT rule. The existence of the PT rule is inferred in part through its application to novel forms (*wug-wugged*), irrespective of their phonological properties. An irregular verb escapes regularisation (*thinked*) by virtue of the presence in the lexicon of its PT form, retrieval of which blocks application of the rule. This blocking process takes time, which provides the dual-mechanism framework with an explanation for the response

time (RT) advantage observed for regular verbs when English speakers are asked to turn verb stems into their PT forms as rapidly as possible. The principle that efficiency of retrieval from the lexicon is modulated by word frequency further explains the strong frequency effect on RT in this task for irregular but not regular verbs (Pinker, 1999; Prasada, Pinker, and Snyder, 1990; Seidenberg, 1992; Seidenberg and Bruck, 1990).

Single-mechanism models of inflectional morphology (Joanisse and Seidenberg, 1999; McClelland and Patterson, 2002; Rumelhart and McClelland, 1986) derive from a broader connectionist approach to human information processing, in which transformations between forms are accomplished according to multiple probabilistic mappings learnt from exposure during training. In terms of the English PT, this framework proposes that inflection proceeds with reference to semantic and phonological knowledge for all verbs, irrespective of their regularity, and that these same processes are also applied to new verbs that enter the language (*fax-faxed*) and to the nonce verbs beloved of psycholinguists (*wug-wugged*). The single-mechanism approach is based in part on the observation that the mappings between stem and PT irregular forms are neither entirely arbitrary nor, in many cases, so dissimilar to regular forms. Apart from the small vowel change in the irregular *sleep-slept*, for example (for which there are other reasons or pressures: Burzio, 2002), this pairing strongly resembles regular verb inflections like *step-stepped* and *peep-peeped*. These observations suggest that a strict separation of the two classes may not be the most appropriate manner in which to characterise the problem domain (McClelland and Patterson, 2002). Within computational models that implement this single mechanism, the general connectionist factor of similarity-based weightings means that inflection of regular verbs receives substantial support, as this mapping is overwhelmingly the most prevalent within the training corpus. The other major factor that determines the weights between processing units within a connectionist network is an individual item's frequency of occurrence. Common irregular verbs, with which the speaker/network has so much experience, overcome interference from the regular mapping efficiently; but less common ones are more susceptible to this interference and rely more on other sources of word information to achieve the correct outcome. Thus, the single-mechanism approach, like the dual-mechanism framework, can also explain the regularity by frequency interaction observed in RT during inflection from stem amongst normal adults (Daugherty and Seidenberg, 1992).

What about other features of performance when normal speakers are asked to transform verb stems into PT forms? Take, for example, the facts (a) that regular verbs whose stems rhyme with many irregular verbs (e.g., *ping-pinged* cf. *sing-sang* and *ring-rang*) are inflected more slowly than their regular counterparts from consistently regular neighbourhoods (like *rushed-rushed*, *hush-hushed*, *gush-gushed*, etc.) (Seidenberg, 1992); and (b) that nonce verbs of this irregular rhyme type (e.g., *spling*) are occasionally inflected in accordance with their irregular lexical neighbours (*spling*→"splang" rather than "splinged") (Bybee and Moder, 1983). These facts are compatible with, indeed even a direct prediction from, the single-mechanism approach in which processing – both its outcome and its speed – is determined largely by the degree of consistency of a particular verb with its phonological (rhyming) neighbourhood and, though to a lesser extent, with the whole verb vocabulary. At least some versions of the dual-mechanism approach have, however, accommodated such findings via one or more modifications (Ullman, 2001; 2004). One is the idea that the PT forms of regular verbs with many irregular neighbours, such as *pinged*, may in fact be lexically listed to prevent them from being "captured" by the gang of *ring-rang/sing-sang* irregular verbs. This would account for fact (a) discussed previously. Another is the proposal (in keeping with modifications to other dual-mechanism approaches, like the

dual-route model of reading by Coltheart et al., 2001) that a nonce form like *spling* might produce partial activation of phonologically similar lexical neighbours like *ring-rang/sing-sang*. This would account for fact (b) mentioned earlier.

Given the difficulties of adjudicating between dual- and single-mechanism theories of PT inflection on the basis of behavioural data from normal participants alone, in recent years the English PT debate has to a large extent shifted to two other sorts of evidence that will constitute the focus of this chapter: (a) behavioural and lesion data from neurological patients with deficits in PT processing; (b) patterns of regional brain activation observed using a variety of recording techniques when normal individuals perform PT tasks. Major credit for attention to these new forms of evidence goes to Ullman and colleagues (1997; 2005), whose dual-mechanism Declarative Procedural Model is effectively an extension of the Words and Rules Theory designed to encompass the neural basis for PT inflection. Ullman et al. (1997) reported a neuropsychological double dissociation in success in inflecting regular versus irregular verbs. Double dissociations are traditionally regarded as demonstrating the neural and functional independence of two cognitive processes (Shallice, 1988), and thus these data were interpreted as strong support for the dual-mechanism perspective on inflectional morphology.

We turn now to a summary of the predictions of dual- and single-mechanism models with respect to, first, neuropsychological data, and then, functional imaging or electrophysiological data, combined with an evaluation of the existing evidence. It would perhaps be clearer for expository purposes to separate these two components, predictions and data, but that would be difficult given the nature of the research process: Models make predictions but are also revised in response to data (usually the data published by researchers with contrasting theories!). As a result, our explication of the state of this research field will necessarily intertwine theory and evidence.

2 Neuropsychological investigations of inflectional morphology

We begin with predictions about and evidence for the double dissociation originally reported by Ullman et al. (1997). The main task used by Ullman and many others is called either generation (by the participant) or elicitation (by the experimenter) of PT forms embedded in sentence contexts. The participant (patient or normal control) hears a set of sentence pairs; in each pair, the first sentence contains the present tense form of a verb (which in English, though not in many other languages, is always the same as the stem of the verb, at least in the first person); the second sentence contains a gap into which the PT form of the same verb is meant to be inserted: for example, "Every day I dig a hole. Yesterday I ___ a hole." Studies employing this paradigm that are based on a dual-mechanism view (e.g. Tyler et al., 2004; Ullman et al., 1997) chiefly manipulate the regularity of the target verbs, because the underlying theory predicts a sharp distinction between regular and irregular. Studies inspired by a connectionist perspective, particularly when concentrating on deficits for irregular verbs (e.g. Nation, Snowling, and Clarke, 2005; Patterson et al., 2001), also manipulate the frequency of the target verbs, because frequency is such a major determinant of processing in a connectionist network, especially for items like irregular verbs that are not typical of their domain.

It should be noted that the commonly used elicitation task is not the only form of evidence used in this debate. First of all, most of the cases in one of the main patient groups of interest in the original Ullman et al. study (1997; see also Ullman et al., 2005), the so-called anterior aphasic group, were unable to perform the elicitation task. For these patients, the main evidence came from the simpler task of reading aloud regular and irregular PT forms like *washed* and *thought*. Secondly, although the elicitation task is recommended by Pinker (1999, p.129) as a good analogy to the natural process of inflection in spontaneous speech,

other researchers regard primed lexical decision RTs as providing a better window into the processing of inflectional morphology (Marslen-Wilson and Tyler, 1998; Tyler, Marslen-Wilson, and Stamatakis, 2005). In this task, a participant hears one item (the prime) followed immediately by another item (the target) to which he or she makes a lexical decision ("Is this a real word?"). On critical trials, the target is a verb stem morphologically related to the inflected regular or irregular PT prime (*jumped-jump; slept-sleep*). Facilitation (faster lexical decision RTs) on these critical trials relative to various control conditions is taken to reflect efficient processing of the inflected prime word. Such facilitation is consistently observed in normal individuals and therefore, if facilitation does not characterise a patient's performance, he or she is assumed to have a deficit in inflectional processing (see Tyler et al., 2002a; 2004 for more details).

In any of these tasks (though to begin with, we focus on the elicitation task), dual-mechanism frameworks predict a neuropsychological double dissociation. The Declarative Procedural Model, for example, proposes that the lexicon responsible for processing irregular verbs is part of the declarative memory system located in the left temporal lobe, and that the rule-based grammatical system responsible for processing regular and novel verbs is part of the procedural memory system located in the left frontal lobe. Brain damage or disease in the left temporal lobe is expected to disrupt lexical processing and therefore to yield a pattern of regular > irregular PT production; lesions in the left frontal lobe are predicted to disrupt rule-based processing and therefore to have the opposite effect, namely irregular > regular PT production.

The single-mechanism framework, as already indicated, has no separate procedures for inflecting the two subsets of verbs; but it proposes that learnt mappings between phonological forms of the stem and PT, while mostly sufficient for processing of regular and/or high-frequency verbs, leave lower frequency irregular verbs at risk of interference from the strong vocabulary bias towards +-*ed*. The normal speaker, it is argued, achieves correct inflection of these items because additional support is available from word-specific semantic information. When a person is asked to produce the PT of *teach*, activation of *taught* suffers phonological competition not only from general prevalence of the +-*ed* PT form, but also from the speaker's specific knowledge of *teach*'s regular neighbours *reach-reached* and *beach-beached*; but the semantic representation of *teach* + PT – which is, after all, the usual starting point for saying *taught* in spontaneous speech – pushes the outcome of the process away from *teached* and towards *taught*. Brain damage or disease affecting semantic processing is therefore predicted, in this account, to yield a (frequency-sensitive) pattern of regular > irregular PT production. Apart from the substitution of "semantics" for "lexicon" and the added emphasis on frequency-modulated success for irregular verbs, this is not so different from the dual-mechanism account, and the predictions become even more similar by virtue of evidence that the left temporal lobe regions argued to house the lexicon in the Declarative Procedural Model are vital to semantic knowledge (Hodges et al., 1992). The distinction between the two approaches remains, however, because the single-mechanism model predicts that there will only be a single, not a double, dissociation in PT processing of familiar forms. A semantic deficit (from left-temporal lesions) will produce the regular > irregular pattern, but, with the caveat of appropriate control of other characteristics of the regular and irregular verbs used as stimuli (explained further later in this chapter), no kind of brain damage should ever produce an advantage for production of the irregular relative to the regular PT. So what is the evidence for the two sides of this putative double dissociation?

2.1 *Regular > Irregular: Lexicon or semantics?*

Ullman et al. (1997) reported a significant regular > irregular pattern in the elicitation task for individuals with either (a) fluent aphasia due to posterior left temporal lesions, or (b) Alzheimer's disease, which produces widespread brain atrophy but always affects medial-temporal lobe structures bilaterally. Regularisation responses to the irregular verbs (yesterday I *digged* instead of *dug* a hole) were the most common form of error observed. As indicated above, this pattern could be – and is – interpreted in two different ways. According to the dual-mechanism view, problems with the irregular PT result from a lexical deficit; according to the single-mechanism view, they result from a semantic deficit. What further evidence might help to choose between these views? The Ullman et al. study did not include a direct measure of the patients' comprehension of the verbs that they were asked to inflect, but both of these patient groups do often have semantic deficits, so that does not solve the conflict. Ullman et al. reported that the extent of the irregular verb deficit correlated with the patients' degree of anomia (a deficit in object naming); and, in line with this pattern, a case of left temporal damage with severe anomia but no apparent semantic impairment has been reported to show a marked deficit in the production of irregular past tenses, past participles, and plural forms (Miozzo, 2003; Miozzo and Gordon, 2005). This would seem to favour the lexical interpretation. Yet these results are also compatible with the single-mechanism view, in that object naming requires adequate activation of phonological representations by the semantic system – exactly the activation proposed, in this framework, to be required as additional support for correct inflection of (lower frequency) irregular verbs.

Patterson and colleagues (2001) argued for the role of semantic information in the inflection of irregular verbs on the basis of an investigation of patients with semantic dementia (Hodges et al., 1992; Snowden, Goulding, and Neary, 1989), a condition characterised by the selective deterioration of semantic memory due to focal atrophy of the anterior temporal lobes (see Figure 16.1a). A marked deficit in irregular verb inflection was observed for a group of eleven patients

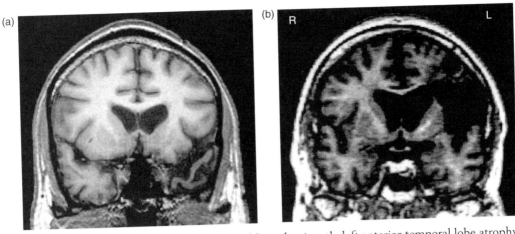

Figure 16.1. Representative MRI scans showing (a) predominantly left anterior temporal lobe atrophy in semantic dementia (taken from Figure 3a of Hodges, Davies, and Patterson, 2006) and (b) a left inferior frontal lesion in Broca's aphasia (reprinted from Figure 6 of Bird et al., 2003, with permission from Elsevier).

of this type in both the standard elicitation task and a forced choice version of the task ("Today I *grind* the coffee; yesterday I *ground* or *grinded* the coffee?"). Two additional features of the patients' performance were claimed to support the single-mechanism view. First, although the majority of errors to irregular verbs were regularisations like those reported by Ullman et al., a smaller but still substantial number suggested partially retained knowledge of irregular PT forms rather than reliance on a completely separate rule-governed mechanism. For example, errors like freeze→"frozed" incorporate both regular and irregular PT components, and an error like slit→"slat" seems more like an analogy to *sit-sat* than a rule-based response, which should be slit→"slitted." Such analogy-based errors have also been observed when patients with semantic dementia are required to generate the PT of regular verbs with a stem similar to many irregular verbs (e.g. *beep-beeped* cf. *sleep-slept* and *sweep-swept*) (Cortese et al., 2006). Second, the magnitude of the irregular PT deficit observed in both versions of the task was highly correlated with success on a separate task assessing the patients' comprehension of the same verbs: They were asked to select one of two words with approximately the same meaning as the verb stem (e.g. "grind – does that mean to

crush or to sip?"). The association between semantic deficits and accuracy of irregular verb inflection has since been replicated both in semantic dementia (Bird et al., 2003; Patterson et al., 2006; Saffran et al., 2003) and in patients with left temporal lobe damage due to Herpes Simplex Virus Encephalitis (Tyler et al. 2002a).

Despite a fair bit of evidence in line with the conclusion that degraded semantic knowledge (or degraded communication from semantics to phonology) might explain the irregular PT deficit, there are challenges to this perspective. Primed lexical decision studies that have considered the amount of facilitation from the irregular PT (*taught-teach*) relative to that from semantically related nouns (*swan-goose*) have yielded mixed results. An association between reduced irregular morphological and semantic priming was observed in one case of semantic dementia (Marslen-Wilson and Tyler, 1997; 1998), but intact morphological priming in the presence of impaired semantic priming has been observed in three others (Tyler et al., 2004). It is not, however, clear that this outcome runs convincingly counter to the single-mechanism view, given the far greater semantic similarity between *teach* and *taught* than between *swan* and *goose*. More problematic is the report of three semantic dementia patients who did not show the regular > irregular pattern in the standard elicitation task (Tyler et al., 2004). As this experiment did not manipulate verb frequency and in fact only included a small number of less common irregular verbs, it is possible that failure to detect an irregular deficit resulted, at least in part, from lack of sensitivity of the task/stimulus set (see Patterson et al., 2006 for further discussion).

In summary, the majority of patients with damage to left temporal lobe regions and a regular > irregular pattern for verb inflection have also had semantic impairments, with the exception of one case with only anomia (Miozzo, 2003; Miozzo and Gordon, 2005). Within the dual-mechanism approach, these results reflect damage to the lexical aspect of declarative memory necessary for correct irregular verb inflection. According to the single-mechanism model, this pattern arises from degraded semantic information, thus reducing the semantic support proposed to be more influential in activating the correct phonology of irregular PT forms. This side of the putative double dissociation could therefore be judged a stand-off in the debate between the two basic approaches to inflectional morphology.

2.2 Irregular > Regular: Grammar or phonology?

As already indicated, dual-mechanism theory incorporates a special rule-governed procedure for regular and nonce verbs as part of the grammar system in the left-frontal lobe. For single-mechanism theory, there is no such special procedure that could be selectively disrupted by a focal brain lesion; thus any brain injury yielding difficulty in inflecting regular verbs should also affect irregulars. On initial glance, then, the report of patients with an irregular > regular advantage in comprehending or producing PT forms (Tyler et al., 2002a; Tyler, Randall, and Marslen-Wilson, 2002b; Ullman et al., 1997, 2005) might seem to be "curtains" for the single-mechanism framework – though note that all such reports are only of relatively better performance on irregulars, never

normal. But there is another factor to consider. Recall our earlier remarks about "differences between regular and irregular verbs other than their morphological regularity" and "appropriate control of other characteristics of the regular and irregular verbs used as stimuli"? Forgive us, but a short lesson in linguistics/phonetics is required here.

Two features of regular PT forms in English have the consequence that they are, on average, more phonologically complex than their irregular mates. The first and more obvious feature is that they are longer, because an alveolar phoneme (voiceless /t/ or voiced /d/) is always added to a regular stem to form the PT. The alveolar is voiced if the final phoneme of the stem is voiced (*stem-stemmed*, *pray-prayed*); it is voiceless if the final phoneme of the stem is voiceless (*stop-stopped*, *laugh-laughed*); and it is preceded by a schwa to form an extra syllable if the stem already ends in either a voiceless or voiced alveolar (*want-wanted*, *load-loaded*). In contrast to these obligatory added phonemes for the regular PT, most irregular PT forms are no longer than their stems (e.g., *make-made*, *come-came*, *think-thought*: Remember that we are talking about phonological, not orthographic length, although this is not universally true (e.g., *sleep-slept*). The second and less recognised feature is that the combinations of phonemes at the end of many regular PT forms occur only in these inflected words and never in a monomorphemic English word. The voiced consonant plus voiced alveolar at the end of *robbed, loved, dragged*, or *breathed* is unique to PT regular verbs; and although voiceless consonants followed by voiceless alveolars are found in uninflected words, this is only true after short vowels as in *apt* or *duct*. The same voiceless consonants followed by voiceless alveolars, when preceded by long vowels (e.g., *heaped* or *faked*), are once again unique to PT forms. Irregular PT forms never contain these phonologically unique patterns. Why is this important? The fact that regular PT forms are, on average, both longer and characterised by atypical sound combinations could very plausibly make them harder either to perceive or to pronounce (or both) relative to irregular PT forms. Is this pertinent to an understanding of the neuropsychological pattern of irregular > regular PT production reported by Ullman et al. (1997) and others? It is, because the patients who show this pattern are non-fluent aphasic patients with a striking deficit in phonological (as well as syntactic) processing. Of particular note, they find it difficult to utter phonologically complex words and make errors of simplification when they attempt to produce such words (e.g., omitting either the /k/ or the /t/ from the consonant cluster at the end of *duct*). This is not very different from omitting the inflection on a regular PT form like *packed*, which is the most typical error reported by Ullman et al. for patients of this type (in the elicitation task for the one or two patients who could manage to perform it; in the reading task for the others). Ullman et al., of course, attributed such errors to an impaired grammatical rule system, but if regular PT forms tend to be longer and composed of more unusual combinations of phonemes than their irregular mates, this nonmorphological factor might contribute to, or even constitute the primary basis for, the nonfluent aphasic patients' irregular > regular PT pattern.

This question has been addressed empirically in several ways. Bird and colleagues (2003) first established a significant irregular > regular pattern in ten patients with nonfluent aphasia due to left frontal lesions (see Figure 16.1b). Note first of all that they screened fifty patients to find these ten, indicating that the advantage for irregular verbs is not a consistent consequence of this condition; and note secondly, as emphasised earlier, that the dissociation in all ten cases was relative: The patients were poor at generating, reading, or repeating irregular PT forms, but even worse with the regulars. This pattern was obtained using the materials from Ullman et al. and an additional set of words, both of which had the typical confounding of greater phonological complexity in the regular PT forms. Bird et al. then constructed a list of regular and irregular verbs whose PT forms were matched pair by pair for consonant/vowel structure, including pairs like *train-trained/grind-ground*, in which both PT forms have a CCVCC structure, and *tie-tied/bite-bit*, where both PT forms have a CVC pronunciation. For this matched set, the success rate was still low for both regular and irregular verbs, but the important finding was a complete abolition of the irregular advantage for both PT elicitation and PT repetition. An advantage remained in the reading task, which Bird et al. explained on the basis that many irregular PT forms (as in *grind-ground* and *rise-rose*) are homophones of concrete nouns, which is never true of the regular PT. These patients have a reading deficit that strongly favours imageable/concrete nouns and, when asked to read single words like *rose*, there is no way for the patients to know that the experimenter meant the PT of *rise* rather than the flower! Results from these production tasks suggest that the irregular > regular PT pattern observed in many nonfluent aphasic patients is attributable to differences in phonological complexity rather than morphological class. If the cause were morphological, as claimed by dual-mechanism theory, the irregular advantage should not be erased by phonological matching between regular and irregular PT forms.

A second way in which the phonological hypothesis has been addressed is with a receptive task in which nonfluent aphasic patients hear two spoken words and are asked to judge whether the two are the same or different. Necessarily, a reasonable proportion of the trials present the same word twice and are of little interest to the experimenter other than to establish that the patients are performing above chance. The different trials are the important ones, and the critically different pairs are words like *press-pressed* and *chess-chest*; the phonological relationship between the members of each of these two pairs is the same, but only the former pair is morphologically related. Dual-mechanism theory predicts that the patients will be impaired in detecting the difference between *press* and *pressed*, but not (or at least significantly less so) between *chess* and *chest*; single-mechanism theory, with its emphasis on the phonological characteristics of the regular PT, predicts no difference between the morphological and nonmorphological conditions. Two studies have assessed this prediction, with outcomes that were (alas for resolution of the debate) somewhat different. Bird et al. (2003), testing the same ten patients who participated in the production tasks described previously, measured accuracy only and obtained virtually identical (and very impaired) performance in the two conditions; this fits the prediction of the single-mechanism model. Tyler et al. (2002b), testing four nonfluent aphasic patients, measured both accuracy and reaction times; the results revealed an advantage for the nonmorphological condition that was not significant for accuracy but was reliable for speed of response; this fits the dual-mechanism account. In addition, the same four nonfluent aphasic patients demonstrated reduced regular morphological priming (*baked-bake*) in the presence of intact irregular morphological priming (*bent-bend*) (Tyler et al., 2002a). Both single- and dual-mechanism theories therefore remain on the table when considering evidence from receptive tasks.

Some other evidence could probably also currently be deemed to constitute a "draw" between the two theories. For example, Tyler et al. (2002b) have emphasised two findings as further argument against the single mechanism's phonological interpretation of the irregular > regular pattern in nonfluent aphasia: Neither the time to judge regular stem/PT pairs as different, nor the size of the regular verb morphological priming effect, bears any systematic relation to the patients' scores on standardised tests of phonological ability (such as phoneme segmentation or blending). In fact this particular lack of relationship has been seconded by researchers holding a single-mechanism view. Lambon Ralph et al. (2005), testing eight nonfluent aphasic patients, found no correlation between the size of the irregular > regular verb deficit in production tasks (with materials that "encourage" this discrepancy, i.e. those not matched for phonological complexity of their PT forms) and scores on standardised phonological tests. There was, however, a significant correlation between the magnitude of the irregular > regular pattern and two other phonological measures: (a) the extent to which the patients showed an advantage for repeating monomorphemic words with phonologically simple relative to complex structure (indexed by the presence/number of consonant clusters, as in *lick* versus *blink*); (b) the extent to which they were better at naming pictures (or repeating the same picture names) with typical as opposed to atypical syllabic stress: In English, two-syllable words, first-syllable stress (as in *rocket*) is overwhelmingly more common than second-syllable stress (as in *balloon*). The resolution of this debate awaits new forms of evidence.

To recap, all English-speaking patients with nonfluent aphasia reported to show an irregular > regular pattern for verb inflection have also had marked phonological impairments. Within the dual-mechanism approach, these results reflect damage to the grammatical rule system necessary for correct regular verb inflection. According to the single-mechanism model, this pattern arises from the impact of phonological impairment upon inflection of the more complex regular PT forms. Although the rule-based morphological interpretation seems more compatible with RT results from the receptive tasks (same–different judgements and primed lexical decision) of Tyler et al. (2002a; 2002b), the phonological complexity interpretation is favoured by results from the expressive tasks of Bird et al. (2003) and Lambon Ralph et al. (2005). An additional complication is that German-speaking patients with the same aphasic syndrome apparently show a dissociation in the opposite direction, with better performance at inflecting regular verbs and nouns (Penke, Janssen, and Krause, 1999; Penke and Krause, 2002). Further research into the precise nature of the phonological deficit associated with the left frontal damage seen in nonfluent aphasia is clearly required in order to advance our understanding of this side of the putative double dissociation.

3 Neuroimaging and electrophysiological investigations of inflectional morphology

The patterns of neural activity observed in normal individuals while engaged in the task of PT generation provides another important line of evidence relevant to assessment of the relative adequacy of dual- and single-mechanism models of inflectional morphology. The dual-mechanism Declarative Procedural Model predicts that a double dissociation according to verb regularity – comparable to that claimed to exist in the neuropsychological data – should also be observed amongst normal adults in terms of differences in neural activation (Ullman et al., 1997, 2005; Ullman, 2001, 2004). Irregular verb inflection would be expected to produce greater activation in left temporal regions as this is the location of the declarative memory system that contains the lexicon. Regular verb inflection should result in greater activity in left frontal regions as this is the area of the procedural memory system responsible for application of the grammar. Although reports of double dissociations in neural activity during normal inflection have often been interpreted as evidence for the dual-mechanism model, the areas involved have not consistently corresponded to those predicted within the Declarative Procedural Model. Further, as will become apparent, methodological concerns limit the theoretical conclusions that may be drawn from many of the neuroimaging studies conducted to date.

As outlined earlier, the single-mechanism model of inflectional morphology (Joanisse and Seidenberg, 1999) attributes the irregular verb deficit accompanying left temporal damage to a semantic impairment and the regular verb deficit when seen in cases of left frontal damage to a phonological impairment. However, the single-mechanism view does not necessarily entail a prediction of more activation in left temporal regions for irregular verbs in normal speakers. This is because, given the nature of the task, one would always expect access to semantic information – and its corresponding neural activity – for regular

as well as irregular verbs. Nevertheless, as reviewed later, a number of neuroimaging studies have reported higher activation for irregular than regular verb inflection in a variety of brain regions; yet such single dissociations alone do not provide strong evidence of functional independence as they may be explained in terms of differential task difficulty (Shallice, 1988). Although reports of higher activation for regular than irregular verb inflection provide the putative double dissociation central to the dual-mechanism model, such findings are also compatible with a single-mechanism account framed in terms of phonological complexity. In fact, as for the patient data, the single-mechanism model makes the strong prediction that when phonological complexity is carefully matched, there should not be any areas of higher activation for regular than irregular inflection, and recent imaging evidence seems compatible with this claim.

3.1 *Time course of inflectional morphology*

Many investigations of inflectional morphological processing amongst normal individuals have considered evidence of any difference in the neural response to regular and irregular verbs to provide support for the dual-mechanism model over the single-mechanism model. One such study recorded electrical activity at the scalp during PT generation from visually presented verb stems in order to derive Event Related Potentials (ERPs) for regular and irregular verbs (Lavric et al., 2001). Although RTs were not acquired in this task due to the need to delay response in order to avoid head movement artefacts, the accuracy data showed a robust regularity effect. A double dissociation was observed at around 300 milliseconds after stem presentation, with greater activity for irregular verbs in left temporal regions and the bilateral anterior cingulate, and for regular verbs in right prefrontal and temporal areas. The greater left temporal activity for the irregulars may be regarded as compatible with either theory, but the greater frontal activity in the right hemisphere for the regulars frankly fits neither: Both the

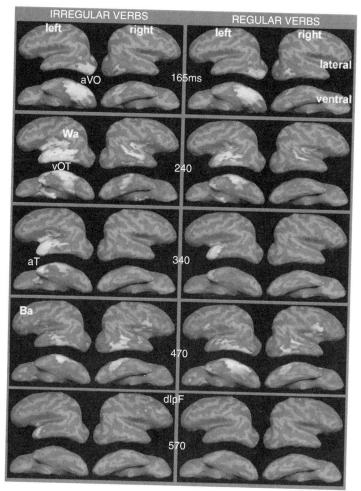

Figure 16.2. Spatiotemporal maps of neural activity during silent inflection of regular and irregular English verbs (reprinted from Figure 1 of Dhond et al., 2003, with permission from Elsevier). Note: avO = anteroventral occipital cortex; Wa = Wernicke's area; vOT = ventral occipitotemporal areas; aT = anterior temporal lobe; Ba = Broca's area; dlpF=dorsolateral prefrontal cortex.

rule-based procedure of the dual-mechanism account and the phonological processing of the single-mechanism account are supposed to depend on left-frontal regions. Nonetheless, it must be kept in mind that while electrophysiological techniques offer excellent temporal resolution, their spatial resolution is relatively poor as the anatomical locus of differences in electrical activity depends on source estimation techniques rather than direct observation.

More recently, Magnetoencephalography (MEG), a technique measuring the magnetic fields generated by electrical activity at the scalp, has been used to investigate silent English PT inflection from visually presented stems (Dhond et al., 2003). The most striking result of this study is the large areas of overlapping neural activity apparent for both regular and irregular inflection, as can be seen in a comparison of the spatiotemporal activation maps for each verb type (see Figure 16.2). Small dissociations between regular and irregular verb inflection were, however, also obtained. Around 340 milliseconds after stem presentation, greater activation was seen for irregular verbs in left occipitotemporal cortex, followed at around 470 milliseconds by greater activity for regular verbs in left inferior prefrontal areas, and then at around 570 milliseconds by greater activity for irregular verbs in the right dorsolateral prefrontal cortex. The greater left temporal activity observed in this study for irregular verbs converges with the results of Lavric et al. (2001) and is compatible with either a dual- or single-mechanism view. Although the finding of greater activity for the regular verbs in left inferior frontal regions may be regarded as support for the dual-mechanism model, it may also be accounted for within the single-mechanism model given that phonological complexity of the PT forms was not explicitly controlled. Hence, although electrophysiological investigations of English PT inflection have yielded double dissociations according to verb regularity, these results have not been consistent across methodologies and the results obtained cannot be regarded as strong support for either the dual- or single-mechanism view.[1]

3.2 *Spatial localisation of inflectional morphology*

One of the first neuroimaging investigations of English inflectional morphology employed Positron Emission Tomography (PET) to index changes in regional cerebral blood flow during overt production of the PT of irregular, regular, and nonce verbs from visually presented stems (Jaeger et al., 1996). When activity associated with reading aloud verb stems was subtracted from activity associated with their inflection, the left mid-temporal gyrus showed higher activation for irregular verbs than regular and nonce verbs, a finding in accord with both the dual- and single-mechanism models. The double dissociation

provided by the observation of higher activity for regular and nonce verbs than irregular verbs in the left dorsolateral prefrontal cortex was interpreted as providing evidence for the dual-mechanism model – but once again, this occurred in the absence of any matching for phonological complexity. Moreover, activity in the left lateral orbito-frontal cortex was found to be higher for irregular and nonce forms than regular verbs, a pattern not expected within the dual-mechanism framework and possibly suggesting an explanation in terms of difficulty: though for different reasons, both irregular and nonce forms are somewhat more difficult to inflect than regular forms. In addition, although PET methodology allows excellent spatial resolution, the relatively low temporal resolution requires blocked presentation of each verb type. As there was evidence to suggest that the blocked presentation functioned to magnify the regularity effect obtained in RTs, this raises questions regarding interpretation of the observed differences in neural activation (Seidenberg and Hoeffner, 1998).

In a recent PET study of German verb inflection, Sach, Seitz, and Indefrey (2004) attempted to counter the limitations of blocked presentation by demonstrating that comparable behavioural results were obtained in a pretest involving mixed blocks. The similarity of performance seen irrespective of blocking was likely to have arisen from the requirement to insert either the past tense or past participle of a visually presented verb stem into a neutral sentence frame, thereby reducing the predictability of the transformations required in the regular block. Despite the observation of a significant regularity effect that was most pronounced for low frequency verbs in the behavioural data, when the neural responses during regular and irregular verb inflection were directly compared, no significant differences were apparent. Neural activity observed during inflection of regular and irregular verbs was also compared to a baseline condition in which the inflected form of the verb was provided for insertion into the neutral sentence frame. This contrast revealed common areas of activation for

---

1   Other electrophysiological studies have considered ERP correlates of delayed morphological priming in visual or auditory lexical decision (e.g. Marslen-Wilson and Tyler, 1998; Munte et al., 1999; Rodriguez-Fornells, Munte, and Clahsen, 2002; Weyerts et al., 1996) and of inflectional violations to verbs presented in context (Bartke et al., 2005; Gross et al., 1998; Morris and Holocomb, 2005; Penke et al., 1997; Weyerts et al., 1997), however these are not considered in detail here given that the processes involved in such tasks are not directly comparable to those that underlie overt past tense generation.

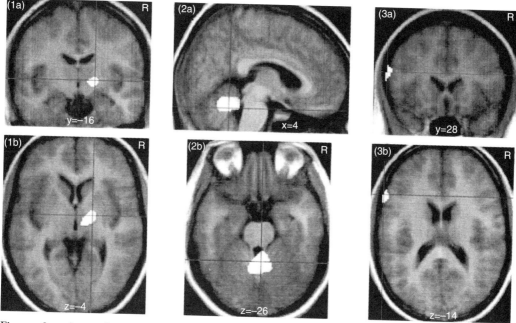

Figure 16.3. Areas of common activation for overt inflection of regular and irregular German verbs as revealed by PET (reprinted from Figure 2 of Sach et al., 2004), namely (1a,b) right nucleus lentiformis and thalamus; (2a,b) superior medial cerebellum; (3a,b) left inferior frontal gyrus.

regular and irregular inflection in the right lentiform nucleus, thalamus, medial cerebellum, and left inferior frontal gyrus (see Figure 16.3), all areas associated with phonological and articulatory processing. The pattern of results obtained in this study would therefore seem to support a single- rather than dual-mechanism account of the neural basis of German inflection.

The neural mechanisms involved in German inflection have also been assessed by Beretta and colleagues (2003) using event-related functional Magnetic Resonance Imaging (fMRI). This technique allows assessment of changes in the blood oxygenation level dependent (BOLD) signal of neural tissues during cognitive tasks and has sufficient temporal resolution to permit analysis of brain responses to single trials, thus eliminating the need for blocked presentation. During silent generation of the past participle or plural form of relatively low frequency verbs and nouns, greater activation was observed for irregular than regular forms over both frontal and temporal areas bilaterally. Critically, no areas were preferentially activated by the inflection of regular relative

to irregular forms. As noted by Seidenberg and Arnoldussen (2003), the pattern of greater bilateral frontal activation for irregular than regular verbs observed in this study suggests an interpretation framed in terms of general task difficulty. In the absence of any behavioural data to index the relative difficulty of conditions, this possibility cannot be excluded, and hence the results of this study do not effectively discriminate between dual- and single-mechanism models.

Support for a task difficulty based interpretation of higher neural activation for irregular relative to regular verbs has been provided by the results of an fMRI study of overt English PT inflection from visually presented stems. Desai et al. (2006) found significantly greater activity for irregulars than regulars in bilateral inferior frontal and parietal regions, but these differences were substantially reduced when analysis of covariance was used to control for variations in reaction time assumed to index task difficulty. The areas of greater activation for irregular inflection seen in this study were therefore taken as reflecting differential attentional or response selection demands.

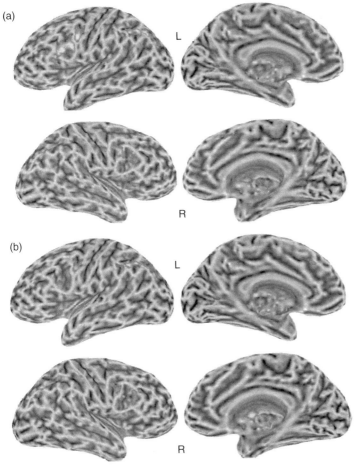

Figure 16.4. Activation map for overt inflection when regular and irregular English verbs are (a) phonologically mismatched and (b) phonologically matched (taken from Figures 1f and 1d of Desai et al., 2006).

Although one small region in the left dorsal superior temporal gyrus did show higher activation for regular than irregular verb inflection (see Figure 16.4a), this was only the case when considering stimuli in which the regular verbs were more phonologically complex than the irregular verbs. A subset of the items matched in terms of phonological complexity yielded no areas more strongly activated for regular than irregular inflection (see Figure 16.4b). This outcome is more in line with the predictions of the single- than the dual-mechanism model.

A similar interpretation may apply to the results of a recent fMRI study of silent inflection of regular and irregular verbs and nouns from visual presentation of the stem (Sahin, Pinker, and Halgren, 2006). For both verbs and nouns, greater activity for irregular than regular forms was observed in inferior frontal regions bilaterally. This pattern is concordant with a task difficulty account, although once again this cannot be conclusively established in the absence of behavioural data. No areas were found to be more active for inflection of regular forms than irregular forms. This result would be expected according to the single-mechanism model given that phonological similarity across regularity was deliberately controlled in this study. Further testament to the importance of phonological factors in determining neural activation during inflection has been provided by Joanisse and Seidenberg (2005) in an fMRI study of overt PT generation from aurally presented stems. Although no areas were more active during inflection of irregular relative to regular and nonce verbs, greater activation for regular and nonce relative to irregular verbs was observed in the inferior frontal gyrus bilaterally. This difference disappeared, however, when regular and nonce verbs were compared to irregular verbs of equivalent phonological complexity.

Overall, then, existing neuroimaging data concerning the production of inflectional morphology amongst English- and German-speaking normal participants seem difficult to align with the predictions of the Declarative Procedural Model. This particular model, however, represents only one instantiation of the dual-mechanism approach and hence inconsistent localization of dissociations in neural activation according to verb type does not invalidate the dual-mechanism framework per se. What is critical for the continued viability of the dual-mechanism approach is the presence of a genuine double dissociation in the patterns of neural activation seen during normal inflection. Although a number of studies have reported greater activation for inflection of irregular than regular forms, it is not clear whether this outcome reflects differential lexical/semantic reliance or merely variations in relative task difficulty. More theoretically informative is the fact that, as yet, no regions of greater activation have been reported for regular than irregular inflection once the phonological complexity of the materials is controlled. Thus the single-mechanism account appears to have a slight edge here.

4 Derivations: A tale of two morphologies?

As mentioned earlier, the English PT debate represents only one instance of a broader conflict between dual- and single-mechanism models of linguistic processing. Given that neuropsychological dissociations between inflectional and derivational morphological processing have been observed (Tyler and Marslen-Wilson, 1997), it is of interest briefly

to consider whether the conclusions drawn from studies of impaired and intact inflection may extend to the more complex processes involved in derivation. In one of the few neuropsychological studies of derivational morphology to date, the nominal suffixation performance of a number of Japanese-speaking fluent aphasics with left temporal lobe damage and nonfluent aphasics with left frontal lobe damage was assessed using a forced choice paradigm (Hagiwara et al., 1999). As predicted by both dual- and single-mechanism models, a deficit in selection of the appropriate irregular -mi suffixed familiar and novel forms was apparent amongst the fluent aphasics. In contrast, while the non-fluent aphasics did not show any evidence of impairment in selection of the appropriate regular -sa suffix to familiar forms, such a deficit was apparent for novel forms. The results obtained in this study for the nonfluent aphasic patients therefore pose a challenge to both theories and more research into the impact of neurological damage upon derivational morphological processing is clearly required in order to resolve this issue.

With reference to normal adult language comprehension, the dual-mechanism model of morphological processing proposes that derived words must be decomposed by the grammar in order to access the lexical entries associated with the meanings of their stems (Tyler et al., 2005; Vannest, Polk, and Lewis, 2005). In contrast, single-mechanism models of visual word recognition do not incorporate any explicit decompositional component (Plaut and Gonnerman, 2000; Rueckl and Raveh, 1999). As would be expected according to the single-mechanism view, an fMRI study of masked priming in visual lexical decision has demonstrated that although reductions in neural activation were obtained as the result of priming by derived words (*darkness-dark*), the areas involved overlapped entirely with those showing orthographic priming (*tenable-ten*) in the left occipitotemporal cortex and semantic priming (*idea-notion*) in the left middle temporal gyrus (Devlin et al., 2004). Similar conclusions can be drawn from an fMRI study considering the visual recognition of both inflected and derived forms using a synonym detection task (Davis, Meunier, and Marslen-Wilson, 2004). Contrary to the predictions of the dual-mechanism model, there were not any areas of higher activation for suffixed words (*prancing, lawful*) relative to matched monomorphemic words (*pursue, menace*). It would therefore appear that the existing neuroimaging data concerning derivational morphological processing are more compatible with the single-mechanism account.

5 Conclusion

The widespread observation of selective deficits of irregular inflection under conditions of semantic impairment resulting from left temporal lobe damage is compatible with both the dual- and single-mechanism models. Similarly, the finding of greater neural activation for irregular than regular verb inflection amongst normal participants may be accommodated within either framework, although it must be kept in mind that such a pattern of activation may also be attributed to differential task difficulty. Turning to the other side of the putative double dissociation that provides the rationale for the dual-mechanism model, the neuropsychological evidence is somewhat mixed. The fact that the self-same nonfluent aphasic patients who showed an irregular > regular pattern in generation and repetition no longer did so when the two verb sets were matched for phonological complexity seems more in line with a phonological than a rule-based deficit, and hence with the single-mechanism theory. Proponents of the dual-mechanism view, on the other hand, would argue that this account cannot explain the irregular > regular pattern observed in RTs for receptive tasks. Nonetheless, unequivocal support for a separate rule-governed mechanism has not been obtained in any neuroimaging study to date. The great PT debate therefore continues almost unabated, but our assessment is that the current evidence does not provide a compelling demonstration of the need to postulate two fundamentally different linguistic mechanisms for processing of regular and irregular forms.

References

Bartke, S., Rosler, F., Streb, J., & Wiese, R. (2005). An ERP-study of German "irregular" morphology. *Journal of Neurolinguistics*, 18(1), 29–55.

Beretta, A., Campbell, C., Carr, T. H., Huang, J., Schmitt, L. M., Christianson, K., & Cao, Y. (2003). An ER-fMRI investigation of morphological inflection in German reveals that the brain makes a distinction between regular and irregular forms. *Brain and Language*, 85(1), 67–92.

Bird, H., Lambon Ralph, M. A., Seidenberg, M. S., McClelland, J. L., & Patterson, K. (2003). Deficits in phonology and past-tense morphology: What's the connection? *Journal of Memory and Language*, 48(3), 502–26.

Burzio, L. (2002). Missing players: Phonology and the past tense debate. *Lingua*, 112, 157–99.

Bybee, J. L. & Moder, C. L. (1983). Morphological classes as natural categories. *Language*, 59, 251–70.

Coltheart, M., Rastle, K., Perry, C., Langdon, R., & Ziegler, J. (2001). DRC: A dual route cascaded model of visual word recognition and reading aloud. *Psychological Review*, 108(1), 204–56.

Cortese, M. J., Balota, D. A., Sergent-Marshall, S. D., Buckner, R. L., & Gold, B. T. (2006). Consistency and regularity in past tense verb generation in healthy aging, Alzheimer's disease and semantic dementia. *Cognitive Neuropsychology*, 23(6), 856–76.

Daugherty, K. & Seidenberg, M. S. (1992). The past tense revisited. *Proceedings of the Fourteenth Annual Conference of the Cognitive Science Society* (pp. 259–64). Hillsdale, NJ: Lawrence Erlbaum.

Davis, M. H., Meunier, F., & Marslen-Wilson, W. D. (2004). Neural responses to morphological, syntactic, and semantic properties of single words: an fMRI study. *Brain and Language*, 89(3), 439–49.

Desai, R., Conant, L. L., Waldron, E., & Binder, J. R. (2006). fMRI of past tense processing: The effects of phonological complexity and task difficulty. *Journal of Cognitive Neuroscience*, 18(2), 278–97.

Devlin, J. T., Jamison, H. L., Matthews, P. M., & Gonnerman, L. M. (2004). Is morphology a fundamental component of language? *Proceedings of the National Academy of Sciences of the United States of America*, 101(41), 14984–8.

Dhond, R. P., Marinkovic, K., Dale, A. M., Witzel, T., & Halgren, E. (2003). Spatiotemporal maps of past-tense verb inflection. *Neuroimage*, 19(1), 91–100.

Gross, M., Say, T., Kleingers, M., Clahsen, H., & Munte, T. F. (1998). Human brain potentials to violations in morphologically complex Italian words. *Neuroscience Letters*, 241(2–3), 83–6.

Hagiwara, H., Ito, T., Sugioka, Y., Kawamura, M., & Shiota, J. (1999). Neurolinguistic evidence for rule-based nominal suffixation. *Language*, 75(4), 739–63.

Hodges, J. R., Davies, R., & Patterson, K. (2006). Semantic dementia, or, a little knowledge is a dangerous thing. In Miller, B. & Boeve, B. (Eds.) *The Behavioural Neurology of Dementia*. Cambridge: Cambridge University Press.

Hodges, J. R., Patterson, K., Oxbury, S., & Funnell, E. (1992). Semantic dementia. Progressive fluent aphasia with temporal lobe atrophy. *Brain*, 115(6), 1783–806.

Jaeger, J. J., Lockwood, A. H., Kemmerer, D. L., van Valin, R. D., Murphy, B. W., & Khalak, H. G. (1996). A positron emission tomography study of regular and irregular verb morphology in English. *Language*, 72, 451–97.

Joanisse, M. F. & Seidenberg, M. S. (1999). Impairments in verb morphology after brain injury: a connectionist model. *Proceedings of the National Academy of Sciences of the United States of America*, 96(13), 7592–7.

(2005). Imaging the past: Neural activation in frontal and temporal regions during regular and irregular past-tense processing. *Cognitive, Affective and Behavioral Neuroscience*, 5(3), 282–96.

Lambon Ralph, M. A., Braber, N., McClelland, J. L., & Patterson, K. (2005). What underlies the neuropsychological pattern of irregular > regular past-tense verb production? *Brain and Language*, 93(1), 106–19.

Lavric, A., Pizzagalli, D., Forstmeier, S., & Rippon, G. (2001). A double-dissociation of English past-tense production revealed by event-related potentials and low-resolution electromagnetic tomography (LORETA). *Clinical Neurophysiology*, 112(10), 1833–49.

Marslen-Wilson, W. D. & Tyler, L. K. (1997). Dissociating types of mental computation. *Nature*, 387, 592–4.

(1998). Rules, representations and the English past tense. *Trends in Cognitive Sciences*, 2(11), 428–35.

McClelland, J. L. & Patterson, K. (2002). Rules or connections in past-tense inflections: What does the evidence rule out? *Trends in Cognitive Sciences*, 6(11), 465–72.

Miozzo, M. (2003). On the processing of regular and irregular forms of verbs and nouns: Evidence from neuropsychology. *Cognition*, 87(2), 101–27.

Miozzo, M., & Gordon, P. (2005). Facts, events and inflexction: When language and memory

dissociate. *Journal of Cognitive Neuroscience*, 17(7), 1074–86.

Morris, J., & Holcomb, P. J. (2005). Event-related potentials to violations of inflectional verb morphology in English. *Cognitive Brain Research*, 25(3), 963–81.

Munte, T. F., Say, T., Clahsen, H., Schiltz, K., & Kutas, M. (1999). Decomposition of morphologically complex words in English: Evidence from event-related brain potentials. *Cognitive Brain Research*, 7(3), 241–53.

Nation, K., Snowling, M. J., & Clarke, P. (2005). Production of the English past tense by children with language comprehension impairments. *Journal of Child Language*, 32(1), 117–37.

Patterson, K., Lambon Ralph, M. A., Hodges, J. R., & McClelland, J. L. (2001). Deficits in irregular past-tense verb morphology associated with degraded semantic knowledge. *Neuropsychologia*, 39(7), 709–24.

Patterson, K., Lambon Ralph, M. A., Jeffries, E., Woollams, A., Jones, R., Hodges, J. R., & Rogers, T. T. (2006). "Pre-semantic" cognition in semantic dementia: Six deficits in search of an explanation. *Journal of Cognitive Neuroscience*, 18(6), 169–83.

Penke, M., Janssen, U., & Krause, M. (1999). The representation of inflectional morphology: Evidence from Broca's aphasia. *Brain and Language*, 68(1–2), 225–32.

Penke, M. & Krause, M. (2002). German noun plurals: A challenge to the dual-mechanism model. *Brain and Language*, 81(1–3), 303–11.

Penke, M., Weyerts, H., Gross, M., Zander, E., Munte, T. F., & Clahsen, H. (1997). How the brain processes complex words: An event-related potential study of German verb inflections. *Cognitive Brain Research*, 6(1), 37–52.

Pinker, S. (1991). Rules of language. *Science*, 253, 530–5.

(1994). *The language instinct*. New York, NY: William Morrow & Co.

(1999). *Words and rules: The ingredients of language*. New York, NY: Basic Books.

(1988). On language and connectionism: Analysis of a parallel distributed processing model of language acquisition. *Cognition*, 28, 73–193.

Plaut, D. C. & Gonnerman, L. M. (2000). Are non-semantic morphological effects incompatible with a distributed connectionist approach to lexical processing? *Language and Cognitive Processes*, 15(4–5), 445–85.

Plunkett, K. & Nakisa, R. C. (1997). A connectionist model of the Arabic plural system. *Language and Cognitive Processes*, 12(5–6), 807–36.

Prasada, S., Pinker, S., & Snyder, W. (1990). Some evidence that irregular forms are retrieved from memory but regular forms are rule generated: Paper presented at the 31st annual meeting of the Psychonomic Society, Chicago.

Rodriguez Fornells, A., Munte, T. F., & Clahsen, H. (2002). Morphological priming in Spanish verb forms: An ERP repetition priming study. *Journal of Cognitive Neuroscience*, 14(3), 443–54.

Rueckl, J. G. & Raveh, M. (1999). The influence of morphological regularities on the dynamics of a connectionist network. *Brain and Language*, 68(1–2), 110–17.

Rumelhart, D. & McClelland, J. L. (1986). On learning the past tenses of English verbs. In McClelland, J. L. & Rumelhart D. E. (Eds.) *Parallel distributed processing (Volume 2): Psychological and biological models* (pp. 216–71). Cambridge, MA: MIT Press.

Sach, M., Seitz, R. J., & Indefrey, P. (2004). Unified inflectional processing of regular and irregular verbs: A PET study. *Neuroreport*, 15(3), 533–7.

Saffran, E. M., Coslett, H., Martin, N., & Boronat, C. B. (2003). Access to knowledge from pictures but not words in a patient with progressive fluent aphasia. *Language and Cognitive Processes*, 18(5–6), 725–57.

Sahin, N. T., Pinker, S., & Halgren, E. (2006). Abstract grammatical processing of nouns and verbs in Broca's area. *Cortex*, 42(4), 540–62.

Seidenberg, M. S. (1992). Connectionism without tears. In Davis, S. (Ed.) *Connectionism: Theory and practice* (pp. 84–122). London: Oxford University Press.

Seidenberg, M. S. (2003). The brain makes a distinction between hard and easy stimuli: Comments on Beretta et al. *Brain and Language*, 85(3), 527–30.

Seidenberg, M. S. (1990). Consistency effects in the generation of past-tense morphology. Paper presented at the 31st annual meeting of the Psychonomic Society, Chicago.

Seidenberg, M. S. (1998). Evaluating behavioral and neuroimaging data on past tense production. *Language*, 74, 104–22.

Shallice, T. (1988). *From neuropsychology to mental structure*. Cambridge: Cambridge University Press.

Snowden, J. S., Goulding, P. J., & Neary, D. (1989). Semantic dementia: A form of circumscribed cerebral atrophy. *Behavioural Neurology*, 2(3), 167–82.

Tyler, L. K., deMornay Davies, P., Anokhina, R., Longworth, C., Randall, B., & Marslen-Wilson, W. D. (2002a). Dissociations in processing past tense morphology: Neuropathology and behavioral studies. *Journal of Cognitive Neuroscience*, 14(1), 79–94.

Tyler, L. K. & Marslen-Wilson, W. D. (1997). Disorders of combination: Processing complex words. *Brain and Language*, 60, 48–50.

Tyler, L. K., Marslen-Wilson, W. D., & Stamatakis, E. A. (2005). Differentiating lexical form, meaning and structure in the neural language system. *Proceedings of the National Academy of Sciences of the United States of America*, 102(23), 8375–80.

Tyler, L. K., Randall, B., & Marslen-Wilson, W. D. (2002b). Phonology and neuropsychology of the English past tense. *Neuropsychologia*, 40(8), 1154–66.

Tyler, L. K., Stamatakis, E. A., Jones, R. W., Bright, P., Acres, K., & Marslen-Wilson, W. D. (2004). Deficits for semantics and the irregular past tense: A causal relationship? *Journal of Cognitive Neuroscience*, 16(7), 1159–72.

Tyler, L. K., Stamatakis, E. A., Post, B., Randall, B., & Marslen-Wilson, W. D. (2005). Temporal and frontal systems in speech comprehension: An fMRI study of past tense processing. *Neuropsychologia*, 43(13), 1963–74.

Ullman, M. T. (2001). The declarative/procedural model of lexicon and grammar. *Journal of Psycholinguistic Research*, 30(1), 37–69.

(2004). Contributions of memory circuits to language: The declarative/procedural model. *Cognition*, 92(1–2), 231–70.

Ullman, M. T., Corkin, S., Coppola, M., Hickok, G., & et al. (1997). A neural dissociation within language: Evidence that the mental dictionary is part of declarative memory, and that grammatical rules are processed by the procedural system. *Journal of Cognitive Neuroscience*, 9(2), 266–76.

Ullman, M. T., Pancheva, R., Love, T., Yee, E., Swinney, D., & Hickok, G. (2005). Neural correlates of lexicon and grammar: Evidence from the production, reading, and judgment of inflection in aphasia. *Brain and Language*, 93(2), 185–238.

Vannest, J., Polk, T. A., & Lewis, R. L. (2005). Dual-route processing of complex words: New fMRI evidence from derivational suffixation. *Cognitive, Affective and Behavioral Neuroscience*, 5(1), 67–76.

Weyerts, H., Munte, T. F., Smid, H. G., & Heinze, H. J. (1996). Mental representations of morphologically complex words: An event-related potential study with adult humans. *Neuroscience Letters*, 206(2–3), 125–8.

Weyerts, H., Penke, M., Dohrn, U., Clahsen, H., & Munte, T. F. (1997). Brain potentials indicate differences between regular and irregular German plurals. *Neuroreport*, 8(4), 957–62.

SENTENCE COMPREHENSION

CHAPTER 17

Individual Differences in Sentence Processing

Thomas A. Farmer, Jennifer B. Misyak
and Morten H. Christiansen

1 Introduction

Language comprehension is a complex task that involves constructing an incremental interpretation of a rapid sequence of incoming words before they fade from immediate memory, and yet the task is typically carried out efficiently and with little conscious effort. Given the complexity associated with extracting intended meaning from an incoming linguistic signal, it is perhaps not surprising that multiple cognitive and perceptual systems are simultaneously engaged during the process. One ramification of the multifarious nature of online language comprehension is that individuals tend to vary greatly in terms of their processing skill. Indeed, considerable by-subject variability in performance on syntactic processing tasks has been observed in numerous studies over the past two decades (e.g., King and Just, 1991; MacDonald, Just, and Carpenter, 1992; Novick, Trueswell, and Thompson-Schill, 2005; Pearlmutter and MacDonald, 1995; Swets et al., 2007), and yet debate still exists in regard to both the sources and the nature of this documented variability.

This chapter explores some potential sources of variability in online comprehension skill. First, we briefly discuss the proposed role that verbal working memory plays during syntactic processing, followed by the exploration of an alternative hypothesis that reassesses the effects of verbal working memory in terms of individual differences in learning-based, experiential factors. Subsequently, we consider the degree to which variability in "cognitive control" has the potential to account for variability in syntactic processing tasks, and then we touch on, briefly, the influence of variability of perceptual systems on processes related to language comprehension. The literature on individual differences in syntactic processing is vast, and it is not possible to cover all of it in the small number of pages allotted to this chapter. Instead, we hope that the information contained here will help guide those with burgeoning interests in the area of individual differences research toward some of the current topics and debates within the field.

Before discussing factors that may account for variability in online syntactic processing, however, it must be noted that the information provided here is presented largely under a framework heavily influenced by constraint-based theories of online language comprehension, which have been the dominant mainstream theories since the mid 1990s (e.g., MacDonald, Pearlmutter, and Seidenberg, 1994; Tanenhaus and Trueswell, 1995; Whitney, 1998). Under these accounts, comprehenders use all salient and reliable sources of information, as soon as possible, to guide their interpretation of an incoming linguistic signal. Indeed, many factors, including (but not limited to) referential context (e.g., Altmann and Steedman, 1988; Tanenhaus et al., 1995), frequency (e.g., Trueswell, 1996), phonological regularities (e.g., Farmer, Christiansen, and Monaghan, 2006), and plausibility (e.g., Garnsey et al., 1997) may influence how an incoming string of words is processed.

One key phenomenon within the domain of sentence processing that these theories help explain is the so-called *garden-path effect*. Sentences such as, "The horse raced past the barn fell" are difficult to process because, at least temporarily, multiple possible structural representations exist (see Bever, 1970). In this example, *raced* could either signal the onset of a reduced relative clause, equivalent in meaning to *The horse that was raced past the barn...*, or *raced* could be interpreted as the main verb of the sentence, such that the horse is the entity that was willfully racing. If *raced* is initially interpreted as the main verb, then processing difficulty is experienced upon encountering the word *fell* because it requires the less- or nonactive reduced relative clause interpretation. It is this kind of processing difficulty that is classically referred to as the garden-path effect. Constraint-based theories argue that in the face of such ambiguity, each of the possible syntactic interpretations of the sentence is partially active. The multiple sources of information integrate *immediately* to determine the amount of activation provided to each of the competing alternatives. In this framework, garden-path effects arise because the incorrect syntactic alternative wins much of the competition during the early portion of the sentence, and then nonconforming information from the latter portion of the sentence induces a laborious reversal of that activation pattern. The degree to which the incorrect alternative had been winning the competition early on affects the degree to which the reversal of that activation pattern will be protracted and difficult.

The competition-based resolution of temporarily ambiguous sentences is highlighted here due to the fact that it is the model of ambiguity resolution that is most amenable to explaining individual differences in performance on processing tasks. Indeed, some of the earliest instantiations of a competition-based approach to language learning were designed in order to account for the fact that both languages, and the people who process them, are highly variable (e.g., Bates and MacWhinney, 1989), and thus can help explain why people seem to exhibit such high levels of variability in online comprehension tasks. These accounts propose that the availability and reliability of relevant cues drives the analysis of incoming linguistic input, and indeed, more formally specified competition-based models have been proposed to account for the manner in which multiple cues (or constraints) can integrate over time to influence, for example, competition between syntactic alternatives in the face of ambiguity (McRae, Spivey-Knowlton, and Tanenhaus, 1998; Spivey and Tanenhaus, 1998). Crucially, however, the degree to which cues are reliable, and thus useful, for individuals during language processing is determined by an individual's unique experience with those cues over time, thus emphasizing a strong continuity between language acquisition and processing in adulthood (Seidenberg, 1997; Seidenberg and MacDonald, 2001). Implicit in such claims is the fact that an individual's linguistic experience may be shaped not just by exposure to the regularities of a language over time, but also by the unique nature of the cognitive systems specific to that individual. That is, individual variability in factors such as memory, attention, perceptual systems, reading skill, and so forth may interact with a person's experience with language to produce vastly different patterns of performance on syntactic processing tasks. Flexible frameworks such as the functionalist multiple constraint-based approaches detailed previously provide a unified account of how variability in cognitive skill and linguistic experience influence language acquisition and processing. Accordingly, it is for this reason that we approach the topic of individual differences in language comprehension from this perspective.

2 Verbal working memory versus the role of linguistic experience

A longstanding account of variability in online syntactic processing is that performance on language comprehension tasks varies primarily as a function of verbal working memory capacity (Caplan and Waters, 1999; Just and Carpenter, 1992; Waters and Caplan, 1996). However, a thorough review of research on the relationship between language processing and verbal working memory capacity is beyond the scope of this present paper (but see Chipere, 2003; Daneman and Merikle, 1996; Friedman and Miyake, 2004; MacDonald and Christiansen, 2002 for summaries of relevant literature). What therefore follows is an abbreviated and highlighted treatment of findings relevant to key accounts in the literature.

Within a capacity-based approach to individual differences in online syntactic processing, Just and Carpenter (1992) argued that the systems supporting syntactic processing are reliant upon a single pool of working memory resources, and that such a resource pool exists independent of linguistic knowledge (viz., the hypothesized working memory resource pool exists outside of the systems that are directly responsible for syntactic processing). Just and Carpenter also argued, in accordance with many more recent constraint-based accounts of syntactic processing (MacDonald et al., 1994; McRae et al., 1998), for a highly interactive processing system whereby the many processes

related to language comprehension occur in parallel.

Given the large number of demands placed on the highly interactive processing architecture, it perhaps makes sense to propose the existence of a system-external pool of memory resources. Such a resource pool can serve as a sort of support mechanism for the comprehension system when processing becomes too cumbersome for the system to support on its own. Accordingly, Just and Carpenter argued for a systematic trade-off between processing and working memory resources in such a way that as memory resource demands increase, processing becomes more difficult, and vice versa. The impact of verbal working memory capacity on language processing tasks can be evidenced through patterns of Reading Times (RTs) on syntactically complex sentences, compared to their simpler counterparts (see example [1]).

(1A) The reporter that attacked the senator admitted the error. (subject relative)
(1B) The reporter that the senator attacked admitted the error. (object relative)

In example (1), sentences with a head noun (*the reporter*) that is the object of the embedded verb (*attacked*), as in (1B), are famously more difficult to process than sentences in which the head noun is the subject of the embedded verb, as in (1A), as evidenced by increased RTs on the main verb (*admitted*) of the object – as opposed to the subject-embedded relative clauses sentences (e.g., King and Just, 1991 – though see Reali and Christiansen, 2007).

When encountering syntactically complex sentences such as those containing object-embedded relative clauses, King and Just (1991) found that subjects with low scores on a test of verbal working memory ability produced longer RTs on the difficult regions of these sentences and were also less accurate on related comprehension questions than their high-span counterparts. Purportedly, the smaller amount of working memory resources available to low-span subjects became more quickly taxed, given the object-subject ordering of the object-embedded relative clause, making these subjects subsequently more sensitive to the increased processing demands of syntactically complex sentences. It is necessary to note, however, that the Just and Carpenter view does not exist unchallenged. Indeed, Caplan and Waters (1999) argue against the existence of a single pool of working memory resources responsible for language comprehension in favor of a multiresource theory. They assert that one pool of working memory resources is accessed during online interpretive processing whereas a separate pool of resources is accessed during offline postinterpretive processing. What is important about this and the other memory-based account cited, however, is that they both rely on access to working memory resources hypothesized to exist outside of the systems responsible for language processing.

Based on the data detailed earlier, MacDonald and Christiansen (2002) proposed that reading span tasks – the tasks used to measure verbal working memory, as in the Just and Carpenter studies – are actually better conceptualized as measuring language comprehension skill. Indeed, over the past two decades, the Daneman and Carpenter (1980) reading span task has been the most frequently used measure of "verbal working memory resources." The task requires individuals to read out loud progressively longer sets of sentences while simultaneously retaining the final word of the sentences for later recall. So, although memory is one component of the task, its main component requires lower-level reading skills and the ability to process phonological, syntactic, and semantic information. In light of this fact, it is not unreasonable to argue that tasks of this nature measure, to some degree, language processing skill (which is presumably, although imperfectly, correlated with linguistic experience).

To evaluate an experience-based hypothesis whereby accrued linguistic experience over time substantially influences sentence processing, MacDonald and Christiansen trained a series of neural networks to predict the next word in syntactically simple versus syntactically complex sentences. They trained ten simple recurrent networks (SRNs; Elman, 1990) on sentences from a context-free grammar with grammatical properties inherent to English such as subject-verb agreement, present and past tense verbs, and so forth. Importantly, many of the training sentences contained simple transitive and intransitive constructions, and a small number of the training sentences contained subject- (1A) or object- (1B) embedded relative clause constructions. To assess the role of experience on the network's ability to learn, they examined the networks after one, two, and three training epochs. After each epoch, the networks were tested on novel training sentences containing object- and subject-embedded relative clause constructions in order to examine average performance as a function of experience.

After each of the three epochs, average performance of the networks was the same across all regions of the simpler subject-embedded relative clause sentences. However, on the more difficult object-embedded relative clause sentences, an effect of experience was elicited. Early in training, the network produced more errors on the main verb of the object-embedded relative clause constructions than it did after three epochs of training. The initial disparity in the processing of embedded object- and subject-relative clauses occurred due to the fact that the syntactic structure of the subject-embedded relative clauses was very similar to that of many of the other simple training sentences. Thus, whereas the networks quickly learned to process subject-embedded relative clauses via generalization from the subject-object ordering common to simple transitive sentences, direct experience with the object relative clauses was needed to deal with the reverse ordering of subjects and objects. Such a demonstration can be seen as an example of the accumulated effects that linguistic experience can exert on phenomena such as the frequency x regularity interaction.

Indeed, when comparing the performance of the SRNs presented by MacDonald and Christiansen to the working memory data presented by King and Just, a striking pattern emerges. The networks that were examined after the first epoch in training strongly matched the performance of individuals measured to have low verbal memory span in King and Just, with higher error rates (commensurate to higher RTs at the critical region of the sentence) on the object- than on the subject-embedded relative clause sentences. After training, however, the networks exhibited a decrease in the error rate difference between the two sentence conditions, and such a pattern maps onto the decreased difficulty exhibited by high-span individuals in the King and Just study. The simulations provided by MacDonald and Christiansen, then, provide computational support for the role that linguistic experience may play in capturing variability in online syntactic processing, while calling into question whether verbal working memory span tasks measure a system-external working memory capacity. Instead, given the strong language-related task demands, these tasks very well may be an index of an individual's overall processing skill, driven by interactions between the cognitive architectures and linguistic experiences of an individual.

The emphasis placed on linguistic experience is in line with a relatively large literature on the degree to which variables that may logically correlate with linguistic experience can account for variability in language comprehension skill. For example, Stanovich and West (1989) operationally defined reading experience in terms of the coarse-grained variable they called "print exposure." As a measure of print exposure, the authors created the Author Recognition Test (ART), in which participants are presented with a list of names – some which are the names of real authors and some which are not – and are asked to place a checkmark next to the names they believe to be real authors. The overarching idea motivating the creation of this task, obviously, was that people who spent more time reading would also be more likely to have a better knowledge of the set of popular authors spanning multiple genres. Indeed, scores on this task significantly correlated with scores on measures of

various reading-related processes. Likewise, education level, another probable correlate of reading experience, has also been shown to influence overall comprehension ability. Dabrowska (1997) found, for example, that those with higher education levels were better able to accurately identify the meaning of sentences with complex syntactic structures (see also Chipere, 2003; Dabrowska and Street, 2006).

Although it is the case that individual differences in variables that might act as "proxies" to linguistic experience do seem to account for some of the variability in language comprehension, such an approach is naturally limited due to the fact that such variables are not direct indicators of linguistic experience. In a more direct test of the effects of accrued experience over time, a training study by Wells et al. (2009) systematically manipulated participants' exposure to relative clause constructions over the course of three thirty- to sixty-minute experimental sessions spanning nearly a month. During the three training sessions, an experimental group of participants was exposed to equal amounts of subject and object relatives. A control group, however, received an equivalent amount of reading, but without the inclusion of embedded relatives (i.e., they read complex sentential complements and conjoined sentences). Both groups were matched beforehand on reading span (i.e., verbal working memory) scores (which were fairly low). Importantly, after training, the two groups' processing of relative clauses diverged such that the RTs of the experimental group resembled the pattern for high-span individuals noted before, whereas the control group showed the kind of RT profile associated with low-span individuals. Together, these two studies argue for a crucial role of experience in relative clause processing and against the notion of verbal working memory as a parameter varying independently from processing skills.

While Wells et al. hypothesized that statistical learning may be an underlying mechanism for mediating these effects of experience, a further study by Misyak,

Christiansen, and Tomblin (2009) empirically investigated this idea, using a within-subjects design to assess syntactic processing performance for subject-object relatives in relation to statistical learning ability. Statistical learning (see Gómez and Gerken, 2000; Saffran, 2003, for reviews) has been a proposed mechanism for acquiring probabilistic knowledge of the distributional regularities governing language structure, and is theoretically compatible with the constraint-based framework assumed herein regarding the rapid online application of learned, statistical constraints in linguistic processing. Misyak et al. found that individual differences in the statistical learning of artificial nonadjacent dependencies were associated with variations in individuals' processing for the same types of embedded relative clause sentences discussed earlier in the chapter. Specifically, better statistical learning skill correlated with reduced processing difficulty at the main verb regions of these sentence types. Additionally, when participants were classified into "high" and "low" statistical learning groups based on performance on the statistical learning task, the language performance of these two groups reproduced the key reading time patterns documented in the literature for those characterized as having "high" or "low" verbal working memory spans, respectively. That is, "low"-performing statistical learners (compared to "high"-performing statistical learners) exhibited slower overall reading times as well as substantially greater difficulty for processing object relatives versus subject relatives at the main verb. These results suggest that individual differences in statistical learning may be a largely overlooked contributor to language processing variation, and moreover, may mediate experience-based effects on relative clause performance that had been traditionally attributed to working memory differences.

Despite disputes regarding interpretation, scores on verbal working memory tasks sometimes account for a statistically significant amount of variance in dependent measures thought to index syntactic processing skill. However, it is worth pointing out that even recent studies employing rigorous psychometric approaches while exploring a constellation of traits involving working memory leave a substantial amount of variance unaccounted for (e.g., Swets et al., 2007). Next, we therefore consider what other factors might contribute to differential language performance at the level of the individual.

3 The role of cognitive control

Another factor that likely influences language comprehension-related phenomena, such as syntactic ambiguity resolution, is that of attentional/control mechanisms. In the broader cognitive literature, several terminological and descriptive variations of cognitive control have been postulated. Accordingly, it has also been called *suppression ability*, *cognitive inhibition*, *executive function*, and *attentional control*. In some cases, these labels connote potentially broader or narrower categories of operation (e.g., executive function and suppression ability, respectively), or have somewhat different emphases (e.g., "inhibitory control" as the suppression of irrelevant information, versus "selective attention" as the sustained focus on relevant information). Such skills could theoretically specify a unitary architectural component, although in other cases, researchers have posited distinct subcomponents or component processes (behaviorally and/or neurally; e.g., Dreher and Berman, 2002), and in other accounts, the conflict resolution processes corresponding to cognitive control are subsumed under the activities of one among other anatomically distinct attentional networks (Fan et al., 2005; Fan et al., 2002; see also the overview by Raz and Buhle, 2006).

However, analogous to the discussion of working memory, the more idiosyncratic details for these hypothetical formulations do not concern us here. Central to all these conceptualizations is the notion of effectively resolving competing or conflicting internal representations, especially under conditions requiring one to override a biased response pattern or otherwise maintain task-relevant information online. Further, despite a wide literature on this construct, current work has only begun to explore more rigorously its contribution to normal online language processing. As standard tasks for assessing cognitive control are mutually employed throughout these studies (i.e., the Eriksen flanker task, the Go/No-go task, the Stroop interference task, and related variants of these such as the item/letter recognition task used by Novick et al., 2005), we will more conservatively reference the skills tapped by the aforementioned tasks and the basic concept of internal conflict resolution as constituting our provisional notion of cognitive control.

Within the adult language comprehension literature, the notion of "suppression mechanisms" figures prominently in Gernsbacher's (1993, 1997; Gernsbacher and Faust, 1991) work on discourse processing. Gernsbacher identified *suppression* as attenuated or dampened activation of a mental representation, which she distinguished from either inhibition (as akin to blocking activation at the onset) or to interference (an activated but irrelevant representation). Differential performance of more-skilled and less-skilled readers in language comprehension was attributed to the latter's weaker suppressive skills. Gernsbacher reported experiments in which less-skilled readers had greater difficulty rejecting isolated test words (e.g., *ace*) as unrelated to a previously presented sentence in those cases where the meaning of the test word was consistent with the inappropriate, alternate meaning suggested by the final polysemous word of the sentence (e.g., *He dug with the spade*, where *spade* on its own could ambiguously refer to either a garden tool or a playing card). Specifically, for less-skilled readers, on probes where a test word's meaning was related to the irrelevant meaning of the sentence-final word, the contextually inappropriate meaning still remained activated a second later, in contrast to the performance of more-skilled readers who did not retain activation of the inappropriate meaning. (Activation is inferred as the difference in response latencies from

test probes after sentence-final homographs versus after sentence-final nonhomographs.) Analogous findings were also obtained for: a) homophones; b) when sentences were replaced with scenic arrays (in which the test probe described an item that was either present *or* that was absent but prototypical of the scenic array); c) and when sentences were replaced with a word superimposed over a picture (and test probes consisted of either related item pictures or words).

More recently, Novick et al. (2005) proposed that individual differences (and developmental differences) in cognitive control may influence syntactic parsing commitments, particularly with regard to garden-path recovery abilities. By their account (in line with constraint-based and interactive theories), multiple levels of information continuously conspire towards an interpretation as one processes a garden-path sentence – that is, when disambiguating, countervailing information is encountered, cognitive control mechanisms are required to suppress the inappropriate analysis and to recharacterize the input towards settling appropriately into a new correct analysis. They supported their view by presenting neuroscience evidence implicating the posterior left inferior frontal gyrus (LIFG), including Broca's area (Brodmann Areas 44 and 45) specifically, in the detection and recruitment of control mechanisms for resolving incompatible information that conflicts with situational demands. They predicated involvement of the LIFG for only ambiguous constructions that activated conflicting information (or generated indeterminacy among multiple interpretations), and *not* for ambiguous or complex constructions more generally (in cases where information nonetheless reliably converges towards the correct analysis). The attentional shifts required for biasing against a competing inappropriate representation and for maintaining attentional focus were thus hypothesized by definition to occur at an internal/representational level, rather than a more response-based level of conflict.

Following these claims, January, Trueswell, and Thompon-Schill (2009), in a functional magnetic resonance imaging (fMRI) study, reported colocalization of conflict resolution with BA 44/45 within each participant on a sentence comprehension task and a modified Stroop task. In the sentence comprehension task, participants heard ambiguous and unambiguous sentences describing actions to be carried out upon objects in photographs, and were instructed to vividly imagine performing the action. Ambiguous sentences contained a prepositional phrase (e.g., *Clean the pig* **with the leaf**), and were accompanied with a visual reference scene that parametrically varied in composition so as to modulate the amount of contextual support for either the instrument or modifier interpretation of the verb. That is, the visual scenes afforded weaker or stronger conflict for interpreting the sentences, and thus trials varied in their cognitive control demands. Additionally, two different types of parametric series were used whereby the scene was appropriately altered so as to manipulate the degree of either *syntactic* or *referential* conflict.

Results of January et al.'s (2009) study showed that activation in LIFG (BA 44/45) increased for trials where greater cognitive control was hypothesized to be required (stronger conflict trials) in the syntactic conflict condition. This activation was also in the same area as for trials generating representational conflict in the nonsyntactic Stroop task. Increased activation in LIFG was not observed, however, for the referential conflict condition. As they reasoned, either the ambiguity manipulation here was potentially too weak/transient, or LIFG may be involved in representational conflict that is linguistic in nature (though not syntactically specific, given that Stroop task performance also generated activation in this area). These results appear compatible with constraint-based sentence processing theories, rather than serial modular accounts in which an initial representational structure is constructed from a syntactic parse alone. This claim cannot be conclusively based from the fMRI time-signal data, but is supported from previous eyetracking studies investigating syntactic ambiguity phenomena

with the same or similar contextual factors and demonstrating rapid contextual influences modulating sentence interpretation (see Spivey and Tanenhaus, 1998; Tanenhaus et al., 1995).

The studies briefly detailed here seem to implicate cognitive control as a potential source of variability in online comprehension skill, with the underlying assumption being that those with more control ability may learn language and process language differently than those with less cognitive control. The influence of cognitive control on sentence processing skill, and the development of it is, with few exceptions, a burgeoning area of interest. It is likely that future research on the relationship between cognitive control and language processing will more explicitly pin down the role that cognitive control plays in sentence processing-related phenomena such as syntactic ambiguity resolution.

4 Perceptual and perceptuo-motor related factors

In this final section, we briefly consider the degree to which variability in lower-level perceptual processes can account for variability in online language processing skill. This class of individual difference sources is vast, and could include basically any faculty that plays a role in any type of perception. Here, we consider a small number of studies that have aimed to illuminate the effects of various perceptual processes, and variability associated with them, on language comprehension skill and the development of it.

Competing speech demands are typical in real-world environments, but the effect of such noise is rarely investigated in standard language processing experiments conducted under well-controlled laboratory settings. However, there is some evidence suggesting that not only are such influences on language performance substantial, but that individual differences may also exist here in this regard. Thus, Leech et al. (2007) surveyed a wide body of evidence in atypical and developmental literatures indicating that the influence of perceptual processing deficits (or underdeveloped perceptual skills) on language processing is substantial. For example, young children are more greatly affected by both attentional and perceptual distractors in processing speech, and follow a protracted developmental trajectory towards adult-like performance. More generally, under conditions when two or more perceptual and attentional stressors are present, normal individuals display linguistic performance patterns mirroring those observed in developmental or acquired language disorders.

In line with these observations, Dick and colleagues (2001) have reported that under situations of "cognitive stress" induced by perceptually degraded speech *and* increased attentional demands, normal adults have greater difficulty comprehending object-cleft and passive sentences, but that simpler constructions, namely subject-cleft and active sentences, are not affected. They hypothesize that the greater robustness of the simpler constructions in these cases might be due to regularity and frequency properties. That is, object-clefts (e.g., *It's the cow that the dog is biting*) and passives (e.g., *The cow is bitten by the dog*) are sentence types with low microstructural (and absolute) frequency in English, whereas subject-clefts (e.g., *It's the dog that is biting the cow*) contain microstructurally more frequent properties, despite being less frequent in absolute occurrence. Additionally, active sentences (e.g., *The dog is biting the cow*) are highly common in type and instantiate canonical word order.

In a study systematically manipulating perceptual, attentional, and external semantic demands on language processing, Leech et al. (2007) administered a spoken sentence comprehension task to 348 normally hearing children and sixty-one normally hearing adults, spanning a continuous age range from five to fifty-one years. Perceptual, attentional, and semantic interference were modulated by combinations of distractors (energetic perceptual masking, speech-like noise applied to one ear, and competing semantic content, respectively) across four speech conditions: different ear/backward speech (attentional interference), different ear/forward speech (attentional and semantic interference), same ear/backward speech (perceptual and attentional interference), and same ear/forward speech (perceptual, attentional, and semantic interference). Sentence types comprised actives, passives, and subject- and object- clefts.

Overall, a gradual, nonlinear, and protracted developmental trajectory towards adult performance levels was observed. Perceptual (but not attentional or semantic) interference significantly reduced comprehension for the more difficult constructions in adults relative to a baseline no-competition speech condition, whereas comprehension of simple sentence types was impervious to this form of interference. Inspection of the provided scatterplots indicates considerably larger individual differences in adults for comprehending passives under the perceptual interference conditions. Lexical production efficiency (word reading efficiency), general speed of processing (reaction time to auditory nonlinguistic sound signals), and chronological age were significantly associated with language comprehension, and predicted the most variance for the difficult constructions (object-clefts and passives).

Related work has additionally shown that perceptual efficiency is related to reading proficiency (cf. Plaut and Booth, 2000), the latter of which encompasses both accuracy and speed (Geva, Wade-Woolley, and Shany, 1997). And in young adult readers (ages sixteen to twenty-four) who were administered a comprehensive battery of tasks, individual differences in reading speed and literal comprehension correlate strongly and positively (Braze et al., 2007). In a study investigating individual differences in speed of processing on spoken idiom comprehension, Cacciari, Padovani, and Corradini (2007) split participants into fast/slow groups on the basis of processing speed and assessed responses to idiomatic targets embedded in sentential contexts that either biased interpretation towards the idiom's literal or idiomatic meaning. They observed differences among the participants such that those with slow speed of processing also required more perceptual information from the sentence before identifying the idiomatic meaning. Thus, individual differences in perceptual processing have been linked to both reading ability and spoken language comprehension.

In these aforementioned cases, perceptual interference and sentence comprehension appear interrelated through the recruitment of phonological representations. Indeed, within MacDonald and Christiansen's (2002) proposal that observed variations in language processing among individuals were attributable to both differential experiential and biological factors, they discussed evidence suggesting that there may be intrinsic differences in the precision of phonological representations formed by individuals. Consistent as well with MacDonald and Christiansen's proposal then, perceptually related processes (e.g., integrity of phonological representations and robustness to noise) and "efficiency" (faster/slower activation in transmitting informational signals) could be encompassed more or less within the computational resources/processes of a singular system, and thus be an interwoven part of the language architecture.

5 Conclusion

Performance on measures of language comprehension skill is notoriously variable, a fact that is not terribly surprising once one considers the large number of perceptual and cognitive systems engaged during linguistic processing. In order to account for such variability, working memory and other memory-related principles have traditionally received the largest amount of attention within the language processing literature. Although we have no doubt that memory plays an important role in online language processing, studies that find links between variability in verbal working memory capacity and variability in processing skill only account for a small proportion of the variance. Accordingly, we additionally discussed other factors that may help account for

the variance left unexplained by studies of verbal working memory effects, such as by-individual variation in cognitive control/attentional mechanisms and perceptual processes, along with the interaction of those factors with variability in the linguistic experiences of individuals and the ability of individuals to learn from these experiences via statistical learning. More generally, individual differences research can aid in advancing the architectural specification of the systems responsible for language, thus fostering more mechanistic explanations of the processes underlying language comprehension. Such an advantage is not to be taken lightly, for it has large repercussions for many theories spanning the entire spectrum of the language sciences, from domains such as online language processing, to acquisition processes, to the understanding of language-related disorders and the development of interventions to attenuate them.

References

Altmann, GTM & Steedman, M. J. (1988). Interaction with context during human sentence processing. *Cognition*, 30, 191–238.

Bates, E. & MacWhinney, B. (1989). Functionalism and the competition model. In MacWhinney, B. & Bates, E. (Eds.) *The crosslinguistic study of sentence processing* (pp. 3–73). Cambridge, UK: Cambridge University Press.

Bever, T. G. (1970). The cognitive basis for linguistic structures. In Hayes, J. R. (Ed.) *Cognition and the growth of cognition* (pp. 279–362). New York, NY: Wiley.

Braze, D., Tabor, W., Shankweiler, D. P., & Mencl, W. E. (2007). Speaking up for vocabulary: Reading skill differences in young adults. *Journal of Learning Disabilities*, 40, 226–43.

Cacciari, C., Padovani, R., & Corradini, P. (2007). Exploring the relationship between individuals' speed of processing and their comprehension of spoken idioms. *European Journal of Cognitive Psychology*, 19, 417–45.

Caplan, D. & Waters, G. S. (1999). Verbal working memory and sentence comprehension. *Behavioral and Brain Science*, 22, 77–126.

Chipere, N. (2003). *Understanding complex sentences: Native speaker variation in syntactic competence.* New York, NY: Palgrave Macmillian.

Dabrowska, E. (1997). The LAD goes to school: A cautionary tale for nativists. *Linguistics*, 35, 735–66.

Dabrowska, E. & Street, J. (2006). Individual differences in language attainment: Comprehension of passive sentences by native and non-native English speakers. *Language Sciences*, 28, 604–15.

Daneman, M. & Carpenter, P. A. (1980). Individual differences in working memory and reading. *Journal of Verbal Learning and Verbal Behavior*, 19, 450–66.

Daneman, M. & Merikle, P. M. (1996). Working memory and language comprehension: A meta-analysis. *Psychonomic Bulletin and Review*, 3, 422–33.

Dick, F., Bates, E., Wulfeck, B., Utman, J. A., Dronkers, N., & Gernsbacher, M. A. (2001). Language deficits, localization, and grammar: Evidence for a distributive model of language breakdown in aphasic patients and neurologically intact individuals. *Psychological Review*, 108, 759–88.

Dreher, J. C. & Berman, K. F. (2002). Fractionating the neural substrate of cognitive control processes. *Proceedings of the National Academy of Sciences*, 99, 14595–600.

Elman, J. L. (1990). Finding structure in time. *Cognitive Science*, 14, 179–211.

Fan, J., McCandliss, B. D., Fossella, J., Flombaum, J. I., & Posner, M. I. (2005). The activation of attentional networks. *NeuroImage*, 26, 471–79.

Fan, J., McCandliss, B. D., Sommer, T., Raz, A., & Posner, M. I. (2002). Testing the efficiency and independence of attentional networks. *Journal of Cognitive Neuroscience*, 14, 340–7.

Farmer, T. A., Christiansen, M. H., & Monaghan, P. (2006). Phonological typicality influences online sentence comprehension. *Proceedings of the Nation Academy of Sciences*, 103, 12203–8.

Friedman, N. P. & Miyake, A. (2004). The reading span test and its predictive power for reading comprehension ability. *Journal of Memory and Language*, 51, 136–58.

Garnsey, S. M., Pearlmutter, N. J., Myers, E., & Lotocky, M. A. (1997). The contributions of verb bias and plausibility to the comprehension of temporarily ambiguous sentences. *Journal of Memory and Language*, 37, 58–93.

Gernsbacher, M. A. (1993). Less skilled readers have less efficient suppression mechanisms. *Psychological Science*, 4, 294–8.

(1997). Group differences in suppression skill. *Aging, Neuropsychology, and Cognition*, 4, 175–84.

Gernsbacher, M. A. & Faust, M. E. (1991). The mechanism of suppression: A component of general comprehension skill. *Journal of Experimental Psychology: Learning, Memory, and Cognition*, 17, 245–62.

Geva, E., Wade-Wooley, L., & Shany, M. (1997). Development of reading efficiency in first and second language. *Scientific Studies of Reading*, 1, 119–44.

Gómez, R. L. & Gerken, L. A. (2000). Infant artificial language learning and language acquisition. *Trends in Cognitive Sciences*, 4, 178–86.

January, D., Trueswell, J. C., & Thompson-Schill, S. L. (2009). Co-localization of stroop and syntactic ambiguity resolution in Broca's area: Implications for the neural basis of sentence processing. *Journal of Cognitive Neuroscience*, 21, 2434–2444.

Just, M. A. & Carpenter, P. A. (1992). A capacity theory of comprehension: Individual differences in working memory. *Psychological Review*, 99, 122–49.

King, J. & Just, M. A. (1991). Individual differences in syntactic processing: The role of working memory. *Journal of Memory and Language*, 30, 580–602.

Leech, R., Aydelott, J., Symons, G., Carnevale, J., & Dick, F. (2007). The development of sentence interpretation: Effects of perceptual, attentional and semantic interference. *Developmental Science*, 10, 794–813.

MacDonald, M. C. & Christiansen, M. H. (2002). Reassessing working memory: A comment on Just & Carpenter (1992) and Waters & Caplan (1996). *Psychological Review*, 109, 35–54.

MacDonald, M. C., Just, M. A., & Carpenter, P. A. (1992). Working memory constraints on the processing of syntactic ambiguity. *Cognitive Psychology*, 24, 56–98.

MacDonald, M. C., Pearlmutter, N. J., & Seidenberg, M. S. (1994). The lexical nature of syntactic ambiguity resolution. *Psychological Review*, 101, 676–703.

McRae, K., Spivey-Knowlton, M., & Tanenhaus, M. (1998). Modeling the effects of thematic fit (and other constraints) in on-line sentence comprehension. *Journal of Memory and Language*, 37, 283–312.

Misyak, J. B., Christiansen, M. H. & Tomblin, J. B. (2009). Statistical learning of nonadjacencies predicts on-line processing of long-distance dependencies in natural language. In Taatgen, N. A. & van Rijn, H., Nerbonne, J., & Schomaker, L. (Eds.) *Proceedings of the 31st Annual Cognitive Science Society Conference* (pp. 177–82). Austin, TX: Cognitive Science Society.

Novick, J. M., Trueswell, J. C., & Thompson-Schill, S. L. (2005). Cognitive control and parsing: Reexamining the role of Broca's area in sentence comprehension. *Cognitive, Affective, & Behavioral Neuroscience, 5*, 263–81.

Pearlmutter, N. J. & MacDonald, M. C. (1995). Individual differences and probabilistic constraints in syntactic ambiguity resolution. *Journal of Memory and Language, 34*, 521–42.

Plaut, D. C. & Booth, J. R. (2000). Individual and developmental differences in semantic priming: Empirical and computational support for a single-mechanism account of lexical processing. *Psychological Review, 107*, 786–823.

Raz, A. & Buhle, J. (2006). Typologies of attentional networks. *Nature Reviews Neuroscience, 7*, 367–79.

Reali, F. & Christiansen, M. H. (2007). Processing of relative clauses is made easier by frequency of occurrence. *Journal of Memory and Language, 57*, 1–23.

Saffran, J. R. (2003). Statistical language learning: Mechanisms and constraints. *Current Directions in Psychological Science, 12*, 110–14.

Seidenberg, M. S. (1997). Language acquisition and use: Learning and applying probabilistic constraints. *Science, 275*, 1599–1603.

Seidenberg, M. S., & MacDonald, M. C. (2001). Constraint satisfaction in language acquisition and processing. In Christiansen, M. H. & Chater, N. (Eds.) *Connectionist psycholinguistics* (pp. 281–318). Westport, CT: Ablex Publishing.

Spivey, M. J. & Tanenhaus, M. (1998). Syntactic ambiguity resolution in discourse: Modeling the effects of referential context and lexical frequency. *Journal of Experimental Psychology: Learning, Memory, and Cognition, 24*, 1521–43.

Stanovich, K. E., West, R. F. (1989). Exposure to print and orthographic processing. *Reading Research Quarterly, 24*, 402–33.

Swets, B., Desmet, T., Hambrick, D. Z., & Ferreira, F. (2007). The role of working memory in syntactic ambiguity resolution: A psychometric approach. *Journal of Experimental Psychology: General, 136*, 64–81.

Tanenhaus, M. K., Spivey-Knowlton, M. J., Eberhard, K. M., & Sedivy, J. C. (1995). Integration of visual and linguistic information in spoken language comprehension. *Science, 268*, 1632–4.

Tanenhaus, M. K. & Trueswell, J. C. (1995). Sentence comprehension. In Miller, J. L. & Eimas, P. D. (Eds.) *Handbook of perception and cognition* (Vol. 11, pp. 217–62). San Diego: Academic Press.

Trueswell, J. C. (1996). The role of lexical frequency in syntactic ambiguity resolution. *Journal of Memory and Language, 35*, 566–85.

Waters, G. S. & Caplan, D. (1996). The measurement of verbal working memory capacity and its relation to reading comprehension. *Quarterly Journal of Experimental Psychology, 49*, 51–79.

Wells, J. B., Christiansen, M. H., Race, D. S., Acheson, D. J., & MacDonald, M. C. (2009). Experience and sentence processing: Statistical learning and relative clause comprehension. *Cognitive Psychology, 58*, 250–71.

Whitney, P. (1998). *Psychology of language.* Houghton Mifflin.

CHAPTER 18

The Neurobiology of Sentence Comprehension

Lee Osterhout, Albert Kim, and Gina R. Kuperberg

1 Introduction

On the surface, a sentence (for example, *I am writing this chapter on an aging Sony notebook computer with a sticky Q key that I bought six years ago.*) is a linear sequence of words. But in order to extract the intended meaning, a reader must combine the words in just the right way. That much is obvious. What is not obvious is how we do that in real time, as we read or listen to a sentence. The standard answer to that question, which derives from generative linguistic theories (Chomsky, 1986), is that we combine words at two levels: a level of structure (*syntax*) and a level of meaning (*semantics*). In our example sentence, syntactic combination entails assigning the grammatical subject role to *I*, the direct object role to *this chapter*, the object of the preposition role to *aging Sony notebook computer*, and so on. Semantic combination entails identifying who is doing the writing (the *Agent*) and what is being written (the *Theme*). Furthermore, the standard view claims that syntactic combination involves application of phrase structure rules that

are abstracted away from individual words. For example, the rule S → NP VP stipulates that every sentence in English is composed of a noun phrase and a verb phrase, in that order, regardless of the individual words in the sentence. These rules define hierarchical relationships within each sentence, in which some phrases or clauses modify others (e.g., the prepositional phrase *with a sticky Q key* modifies the noun phrase *aging Sony notebook computer*). The phrase structure rules are also claimed to contain recursive elements that permit sentences to be glued together (*I am writing this chapter on an aging Sony notebook computer* and *I bought [the Sony notebook computer] six years ago*) to form even longer sentences. One result of recursion is the existence of "long-distance dependencies," which can obscure aspects of semantic combination. The clause *that I bought six years ago* does not explicitly provide any indication of what was purchased; nonetheless, every fluent speaker of English immediately recognizes that the purchased item was a Sony computer (or perhaps a sticky Q key). Another claim of the standard model is that syntactic combination precedes and prepares the way for semantic combination. Correspondingly, the syntax tells the semantics that the item being purchased was in fact either the Sony computer or the sticky Q key referred to in the main clause. In other words, syntactic combination is claimed to always come first, followed by semantic combination. Finally, because the recursive, hierarchical nature of human syntax seems to be so unique (with respect to other natural communication systems and other aspects of human cognition), syntax is presumed to involve language-specific neural circuits that evolved in humans.

This view of how words are combined has dominated thinking for a long time. The longevity of the standard view is a testament to its elegant explanatory power in terms of linguistic and cognitive modeling. We will argue here, however, that many aspects of this model are very likely wrong, and that its inadequacies become clear when one tries to relate the model to neurobiology. Much of the extant work on language and brain has assumed some variant of the standard model. We review this work here and conclude that these efforts have met with limited success (for similar conclusions, see Kaan and Swaab, 2002; Stowe, Haverkort, and Zwarts, 2005; for a more optimistic opinion, see Friederici, 2002 or Friederici and Kotz, 2003). In our review, we will attempt to describe which aspects of the model seem to be supported by the neurobiological evidence, and which aspects do not.

We will conclude our chapter by advocating for a research paradigm that is grounded as much in the principles of evolution, genetics, and neurobiological design as it is in the principles of linguistic and psycholinguistic modeling. In his engaging introduction to *Neurobiology*, Gordon Shepherd (1994) comments that "nothing in neurobiology makes sense except in the light of behavior" (p. 9). His point is that no matter how complex a neural circuit might seem, one can always be confident that it is designed to mediate some specific naturally occurring behavior. Generally, the neural circuit becomes more understandable once the relevant behavior

is known. It seems reasonable to suggest that the converse is equally true: No matter how complex a naturally occurring behavior might seem, one can always be confident that there is a neural circuit designed to mediate it. The complex behavior will become more understandable once the relevant neural circuits are known. This is because neural circuits (that is, "functional units" of neurobiological organization; Shepherd, 1994) are the likely basis of neurobiological evolution (Jacob, 1974). Knowledge of the relevant neural circuits therefore links the behavior to its evolutionary history and to relevant genetic mechanisms, and will almost certainly lead to a more accurate vision of the behavior. Conversely, a theoretical perspective that imposes a priori assumptions concerning language and linguistic structure onto the brain, without due consideration of known neurobiological principles, might lead to a biased and ultimately inaccurate view of human language, language processing, and the evolutionary history of this important behavior.

We believe that a serious effort to understand the neurobiology of language should adopt a neurobiological perspective right from the start. One reasonable assumption is that some principles of neurobiological design are conserved across different functions. If so, then useful analogies might be made between language processing and functions better understood at the neural circuit level. One potentially useful concept is the notion of "streams of processing." Visual information, for example, is segregated at the cortical level into multiple parallel streams of processing (e.g., dorsal and ventral streams that process object and spatial aspects of the stimulus, respectively; Ungerleider and Haxby, 1994). These processing streams are thought to be independent in some respects (each stream processes a distinct aspect of the visual world) but highly interactive in others (crosstalk between the streams occurs constantly). Analogously, aspects of sentence comprehension might be segregated into distinct but interacting processing streams (Hickok and Poeppel, 2000; Kim and Osterhout, 2005;

Osterhout et al., 2004; Trueswell, Tanenhaus, and Garnsey, 1994).[1] If so, then the primary task would be to identify the processing streams and characterize their interactions. Eventually, we would want to identify the neural circuits that mediate these processing streams and learn something about their evolutionary histories and genetic influences. Ultimately, the goal would be to link the neurobiological evidence with a psycholinguistic theory of language processing.

2 Some commentary on methods of investigation

Progress in this area, as in any other, depends on the appropriateness and utility of the available methods of investigation. The primary methods include the study of brain-damaged patients who have language impairments (the "deficit" approach); noninvasive hemodynamic-based neuroimaging methods such as functional magnetic resonance imaging (fMRI) and positron emission tomography (PET) (Cabeza and Kingstone, 2001); and methods for recording the brain's electromagnetic activity from the scalp, such as event-related brain potentials (ERPs) (Handy, 2005) and magnetoencephalography (MEG) (Hämäläinen et al., 1993). Another less frequently used method, transcranial magnetic stimulation (TMS) (Walsh and Cowey, 2000), can be used to induce "reversible lesions" in restricted parts of the human brain.[2] Inevitably, none of these methods perfectly reflects the neural processes involved in language comprehension; each method comes with strengths and

limitations. We discuss some of the more important ones here.

Deficit studies have been the most important method historically. However, they are complicated by the fact that the lesions are "accidents of nature" and are therefore not controlled in terms of the lesion's location and extent. It is also not at all trivial to properly characterize the behavioral/cognitive deficit resulting from a lesion, or to ascertain the exact type and degree of neurobiological damage.[3] For example, a deficit could result due to damage to the cortical tissue, or to damage to the fiber tracts that lie underneath the gray matter; different conclusions would follow concerning the neural circuits underlying the deficit, depending on what type of damage is assumed. As a consequence, lesion studies can tell us whether an area is essential for some function, but cannot tell us much about the whole circuitry that is involved in the task (cf. Price et al., 1999). Furthermore, compensatory processes can improve the patient's functioning. This is useful for the patient, but obscures the relationship between neural circuits and specific functions. Each lesion and the resulting deficit tends to be unique to the patient, making it difficult to appropriately group individual patients into larger groups. Some researchers have therefore advocated for single-subject designs (Shallice, 1979). Studies of single subjects are often designed to identify *dissocations* between functions or, even better, *double dissociations*. A dissociation of functions A and B is found if, for Patient Y, A is damaged while B is preserved. A double dissociation exists if, for Patient Z, function B is damaged while function A is preserved (Shallice, 1988). The inferred dissociability of the functions would be supported even if the neural substrates of those functions are not clear. However, single-subject studies also come with caveats, most notably the inability to

---

1 Streams of processing operate differently from the "modules" proposed within influential "syntax-first" psycholinguistic models (Frazier and Clifton, 1986). These modules are serially ordered rather than parallel (grammatical analysis precedes semantic interpretation) and informationally encapsulated rather than interactive (grammatical analysis is not influenced by meaning). As we will see, modular and streams-based approaches can lead to very different ways of predicting and explaining brain-based data.

2 To date, MEG and TMS have not been used extensively to study sentence comprehension. We therefore focus on other methods in this review.

3 The difficulty associated with characterizing the functional loss that results from brain lesions is due, in part, to the fact that we do not yet know the neural or cognitive architecture of language in neurologically intact people.

statistically generalize to larger groups of people. Finally, the location of neurological damage is generally assessed using computerized tomography (CT) or structural magnetic resonance imaging (MRI). These methods identify areas of necrosis, but are less sensitive to the presence of hyperfusion and hypofusion. Hypometabolic cortical areas might not sustain normal function (Caplan, Hildebrandt, and Makris, 1996).

Neuroimaging methods such as PET and fMRI provide relatively good spatial resolution and do not suffer from the caveats associated with deficit studies. However, these methods do not directly measure brain activity but instead index changes in blood flow and blood oxygenation, which are assumed to be useful proxies of neural activity. Although there is some evidence to support this assumption (Mukamel et al., 2005), much is unknown about the precise coupling between neural activity and blood flow (Logothetis and Pfeuffer, 2004). Furthermore, changes in blood flow that result from increased activity in the brain are quite sluggish compared to the dynamics of cortical activity. Consequently, these tools suffer from a temporal resolution that is probably at least an order of magnitude worse than the presumed temporal resolution of the processes of interest (tens and hundreds of milliseconds). The hemodynamic response measured with fMRI (BOLD) is delayed several seconds (relative to the event eliciting it) and evolves over ten to fifteen seconds. This contrasts starkly with the fact that in normal fluent conversation, speakers produce (on average) three word, four syllables, and twelve phonemes per second (Levelt, 1999). Furthermore, the processing of a single linguistic unit, such as a word, most likely involves a constellation of processes, each having temporal durations considerably less than one second. In other words, under conditions that approximate normal speaking and reading, it is difficult to isolate the hemodynamic response to a particular word embedded within a sentence, much less the (phonological, syntactic, semantic, etc.) steps that occur in processing that word. Furthermore,

because sentence comprehension is inherently an integrative process, one cannot reasonably assume that successive words and sentences are processed independently. This complicates efforts to isolate the response to particular words in a sentence by using event-related fMRI designs (e.g., Burock et al., 1998). Event-related designs measure the BOLD response to rapidly sequenced individual events and assume that temporally overlapping BOLD responses summate linearly. Although the independence of overlapping hemodynamic functions has been demonstrated for simple visual stimuli (Dale and Buckner, 1997), the same cannot be said for words in sentences.

Assumptions of linearity and additivity play a crucial role in much of the deficit and neuroimaging literature. Researchers have generally assumed that language processing consists of activation of abstract linguistic codes (e.g., phonological, semantic, and syntactic codes) and computational processes that manipulate these codes (Caplan, 1994; Saffran, 2006). The component processes are assumed to be sufficiently independent (both functionally and neuroanatomically) such that they can be disrupted independently (with brain damage) or methodologically isolated from other components (in neuroimaging studies). If these assumptions are valid, then it should be possible to find patients with deficits that reflect breakdown in a particular component of the model (Saffran, 2006), or brain activations in neuroimaging experiments that reflect the engagement of that particular component (Caplan, 1994).

Unfortunately, these crucial assumptions are difficult to validate, and the invalidity of any one of them would be highly problematic for much of the deficit and neuroimaging literature. Consider, for example, a neuroimaging study designed to isolate the brain areas involved in sentence comprehension. Each subject participates in two conditions, one in which lists of isolated words are presented, and another in which sentences are presented. To isolate the sentence comprehension processes, activations observed in the word list condition are subtracted from activations observed in the sentence comprehension condition. But what function, exactly, does the subtractive method isolate? Many neuroimagers assume that the subtractive method successfully isolated the process of interest, and conclude that the residual activations reflect that process. But this conclusion assumes that the component processes of interest are independent. If that assumption is not valid, then it becomes very difficult to ascertain the function reflected in the residual activations. Because most subtractions are likely to result in some residual activation, this approach suffers from a powerful confirmation bias, in the absence of independent evidence to support the assumption of additivity. There are neuroimaging research designs that mitigate this problem, including conjunction analysis (Price and Friston, 1997; see also Caplan and Moo, 2004) and parametric designs that look for graded activity (Buchel et al., 1998; Penny et al., 2004; for a general account of fMRI designs, see Petersson et al., 1999). However, these designs are only now being adopted for use in sentence comprehension studies. It seems likely that these designs will turn out to be more constructive.

Neuroimaging methods based on hemodynamic measures provide a static image of language comprehension, in which the time dimension is collapsed into one image of brain activity. Language comprehension, however, is a highly dynamic process. It would be advantageous to have methods that measure the process of comprehension as it unfolds over time. One such method involves recording ERPs from the scalp. ERPs reflect changes in electrical activity that occur in response to a sensory, cognitive, or motor event. They are thought to reflect the summed, simultaneously occurring postsynaptic activity within neocortical pyramidal neurons. Topographical features of the ERP are referred to as components and can be described in terms of polarity (positive and negative), amplitude, peak latency, and scalp distribution. Because ERPs are multidimensional, they are more likely to be differentially sensitive to different aspects of processing than are other measures. And unlike other methods, ERPs provide a nearly continuous sampling of the brain's electrical activity during the process of sentence comprehension.

However, ERPs are not without disadvantages. All methods for localizing the neural source(s) of a scalp-recorded effect provide relatively low spatial resolution, much worse than the resolution of hemodynamic neuroimaging methods (Slotnick, 2005). Furthermore, the so-called inverse solution (computing the neural source from the scalp activity) is a mathematically ill-posed problem, as any distribution across the scalp can be accounted for by a large number of possible source configurations. Unique solutions are possible given certain limiting assumptions (Michel et al., 2004). The traditional approach to source localization has been to search for point dipole sources (Michel et al., 2004). In general, this entails assuming a small number of dipole sources and iterating through all possible combinations of dipole location, orientation, and strength, looking for the best match between the source model and the observed scalp distribution. This method brings with it numerous limitations and caveats (Halgren et al., 2002). More recently developed "distributed source" methods provide a true tomographic analysis analogous to that provided by hemodynamic neuroimaging methods, but with much greater temporal resolution (Dale et al., 2000; Dale and Sereno, 1993; for a review, see Michel et al., 2004). For example, Low Resolution Electromagnetic Tomography (LORETA) (Pascual-Marqui, Michel, and Lehmann, 1994) estimates the current distribution throughout the entire three-dimensional cortex. The primary assumption is that dramatic changes do not occur across contiguous areas of cortex (i.e., in adjacent voxels). The primary advantage is that LORETA can provide an estimate of current distribution for each sample of brain activity (i.e., every few ms). The primary disadvantage is a reduced spatial resolution, relative to hemodynamic-based methods.

Clearly, then, each method for relating language to brain brings with it significant limitations. Some of the limitations can be minimized by combining methods. For example, fMRI activations can be used to constrain the inverse solution for ERP or MEG effects (Dale and Halgren, 2001; Dale et al., 2000). Unfortunately, one fundamental limitation cannot be minimized: All of these methods are correlational in nature. Although the antecedent conditions that elicit or modulate some ERP component (or produce some change in hemodynamic response) are relatively easy to determine, the specific cognitive process manifested by the component (or activation) is not. Similarly, although one can assess the correlation between some lesion site and some behavioral deficit, one can never be certain that that lesion site is the "neural home" of that behavior.

3 Segregating language into streams of processing

3.1 *Deficit studies*

The initial evidence of separable processing streams derived from studies of aphasic patients, in particular the syndromes known as Broca's and Wernicke's aphasia. Broca's aphasics typically produce slow, labored speech; the speech is generally coherent in meaning but very disordered in terms of sentence structure. Many syntactically important words are omitted (e.g., *the, is*), as are the inflectional morphemes involved in morphosyntax (e.g., *-ing, -ed, -s*). Wernicke's aphasics, by contrast, typically produce fluent, grammatical sentences that tend to be incoherent. Initially, these disorders were assumed to reflect deficits in sensorimotor function; Broca's aphasia was claimed to result from a motoric deficit, whereas Wernicke's aphasia was claimed to reflect a sensory deficit. This interpretation was motivated by the proximity of the damaged areas to the left hemisphere motor and auditory cortices, respectively. Thus, Broca's aphasia was thought to reflect a problem in production and Wernicke's aphasia was thought to reflect a problem in comprehension, perhaps reflecting two processing streams, one for production and one for comprehension.

The model was centered around the use of words and had nothing to say about how words are combined to produce or understand sentences.

The standard assumptions about aphasia changed radically in the 1970s. Theorists began to stress the ungrammatical aspects of Broca's aphasics' speech; the term *agrammatism* became synonymous with Broca's aphasia. Particularly important in motivating this shift was evidence that some Broca's aphasics have a language comprehension problem that mirrors their speech production problems. Specifically, some Broca's aphasics have trouble understanding syntactically complex sentences (e.g., *John was finally kissed by Louise.*) in which the intended meaning is crucially dependent on syntactic cues – in this case the grammatical words *was* and *by* (Caramazza and Zurif, 1976). This evidence seemed to rule out a purely motor explanation for the disorder; instead, Broca's aphasia was viewed as fundamentally a problem in using the rules of syntax (or, alternatively, problems in using the function word vocabulary) to produce or understand sentences. Furthermore, it was assumed that Broca's aphasia resulted from lesions to the left inferior frontal gyrus (Brodmann's Area [BA] 44, 45) and that this area was a neural center for syntax. Accounts of agrammatism were very explicitly linked to models of syntactic structure and language processing that derived from linguistic theory and psycholinguistic models (Caplan, 1994; 1995). By contrast, Wernicke's aphasia was assumed to reflect a problem in accessing the meanings of words, and to result from damage to the left posterior temporoparietal region, including the angular gyrus and parts of the inferior parietal lobe (roughly, the posterior part of BA 22, and BA 39 and 40). The standard claim thus became one in which the left inferior frontal gyrus was a center for syntactic aspects of word combination (for both production and comprehension), whereas the left posterior temporoparietal cortex was a center for retrieving semantic knowledge associated with individual words, and perhaps for combinations of words as well. Thus, like the classical model, this model also posits two processing streams: one for dealing with syntactic aspects of word combination, and another for dealing with semantics (meaning).

These claims about the nature of the aphasic disorders are still quite influential. Closer consideration, however, raises many questions (Mohr et al., 1978; Vanier and Caplan, 1990). Caplan (1995), for example, notes many inadequacies in the agrammatism literature, including inadequate stimuli, overly specific interpretations of data combined with too little testing of the patients, and problems with subject grouping. Many of the problems stem from the difficulty of ascertaining in a precise way what is wrong (if anything) with the patients' ability to comprehend sentences (in contrast to speech production, in which the grammatical problems are overt). More generally, there is now a greater appreciation of the variability in symptoms and of the underlying anatomical complexities. Symptoms often vary considerably across patients, over time within a single patient, and across different tasks (Alexander, 2006; Kolk and Hescheen, 1992; McNeil and Doyle, 2000). "Pure" functional deficits affecting a single linguistically defined function are rare; most patients have a mixture of problems, some of which seem linguistic but others of which seem to involve motor or sensory processing, such as dysarthria or disprosody (Alexander, 2006). Many of the Broca's patients who produce asyntactic output are relatively good at making explicit grammaticality judgments (Linebarger, Schwartz, and Saffran, 1983), suggesting that their knowledge of syntax is largely intact. Similarly, it is not uncommon for Broca's aphasics to have asyntactic output but (seemingly) intact comprehension, bringing into question the claim that Broca's aphasia reflects damage to an abstract "syntax" area used in production and comprehension (Miceli et al., 1983; see also Caramazza et al., 2005).

With respect to the anatomical correlates of the aphasic syndromes, lesions in the left inferior frontal gyrus are neither necessary nor sufficient to produce problems with syntactic comprehension (Alexander, 2006; Caplan et al., 1996; Dick et al., 2001; Dronkers et al., 2004). Instead, lesions to almost any area around the left (and in some cases even the right) sylvian fissure can produce problems with syntactic aspects of sentence comprehension. Controversy continues to exist concerning the lesion sites most likely to produce Broca's aphasia. Some researchers claim that damage to subcortical structures such as the basal ganglia are essential for producing lasting asyntactic symptoms (Alexander, Naeser, and Palumbo, 1990; Ullman et al., 1997; see also Friederici et al., 2003). Other researchers have argued that cortical structures are critical and that subcortical structures play no role in the disorder (Nadeau and Crosson, 1995), or that lesions affecting both cortical and subcortical structures (and underlying white matter) are needed (Alexander, 2006). Lesions that produce classic Wernicke's aphasia are generally located in the posterior half of the left temporal lobe, sometimes involving the angular gyrus (Dronkers, Redfern, and Knight, 2000; Dronkers et al., 2004). More recently, Bates et al. (2003) and Dronkers et al. (2004) have used voxel-based lesion-symptom mapping (VBLSM) to evaluate the relationships between areas of injury and performance on language-related behavioral tasks, on a voxel-by-voxel basis, in a wide variety of patients with left-hemisphere strokes. Lesion locations that degraded the ability to combine words at the sentence level included the anterior (BA 22) and posterior superior temporal and angular gyrus (BA 39), and frontal areas BA 46 and 47.

In summary, it is clear that damage to the perisylvian cortex of the left hemisphere (the area surrounding the sylvian fissure), perhaps requiring additional damage to underlying white matter and subcortical structures such as the basal ganglia, is needed to produce a deficit in sentence comprehension. Anterior lesions do seem more likely to produce agrammatic symptoms whereas posterior lesions seem more likely to produce the comprehension problems typical of Wernicke's aphasia; furthermore, large lesions are necessary to produce lasting symptoms. What remains unclear are the exact correspondences between lesion site and dysfunction, and also the proper functional characterizations of the observed dysfunctions. On this last point, several theorists have proposed alternative explanations of the asyntactic behavior of Broca's aphasics. For example, in order to account for preserved grammaticality judgments in combination with asyntactic comprehension, several researchers have suggested that patients have limited processing resources insufficient for parsing purposes (Kolk and Heeschen, 1990; 1992). This notion is quite different from the claim that specifically syntactic knowledge or processes are lost. Another idea is that patients are able to parse sentences (that is, construct their grammatical structures) but cannot carry out additional operations on the computed structure (for example, mapping from a syntactic representation to thematic roles) (Schwartz, Saffran, and Fink, 1994). Grodzinsky (2000) has proposed that the agrammatism associated with damage to Broca's area reflects a very specific set of syntactic phenomena, specifically the processing of long-distance dependencies in sentences. Many of these ideas are supported (to varying degrees) by the published literature. Nonetheless, the actual nature of "asyntactic" comprehension (and indeed of the aphasias more generally) remains highly controversial (Saffran, 2006), and the problems noted by Caplan (1995) continue to plague the field. Progress has been limited by other factors as well. Many studies have simply summarized radiological reports and/or have displayed lesions on a single transverse section of the brain. Studies reporting more comprehensive radiological investigations have examined relatively few patients (Caplan et al., 1996; Tramo, Baynes, and Volpe, 1988), have not adopted a psycholinguistic approach to defining syntactic deficits (Karbe et al., 1989), or have not specified the boundaries of regions of interest that were analyzed (Dronkers et al., 2004).

Taken collectively, the deficit literature provides a confusing picture for those attempting to infer the normal neural organization of language. This confusion is reflected in the disparate and mutually exclusive proposals deriving from the deficit work. Influential proposals include the following:

1) Localizationist models; e.g., Grodzinsky (2000), who claims that Chomskian traces are coindexed in Broca's area.
2) Variable localization models, in which different small areas of the brain support the same function in different individuals (Caplan, 1994).
3) Evenly distributed models; e.g., Damasio and Damasio (1992) and Dick et al. (2001), who hypothesize that large regions of the brain support a function and usually assume that all parts of the region contribute equally to the function.
4) Unevenly distributed models, in which particular functions are unevenly distributed throughout a region (Mesulam, 1990).

It is not clear how, or even if, the deficit literature will provide the constraints needed to arbitrate between these and other competing ideas.

3.2 Hemodynamic neuroimaging studies

Noninvasive neuroimaging seems, at first glance, to be an excellent tool for identifying separate streams of syntactic and semantic processing, if they exist in the brain. Reassuringly, tasks involving sentence comprehension tend to activate the left perisylvian areas classically associated with aphasic sentence comprehension, including the left inferior frontal gyrus (LIFG) and left posterior superior and middle temporal gyri (Bavelier et al., 1997; Caplan, Alpert, and Waters, 1998, 1999; Just et el., 1996; Keller, Carpenter, and Just, 2003; Mazoyer et al., 1993; Price, 2000; Stowe et al., 1999; Stromswold et al., 1996). The left inferior parietal region is also frequently activated in sentence comprehension tasks (Awh et al., 1996; Paulesu et al., 1993), as are a number of right-hemisphere sites. In some reports, subcortical structures, most notably the basal ganglia, are activated. An important caveat is that many of these same areas are also activated by lists of words, although the activations are often larger in magnitude for the sentence comprehension tasks (Stowe et al., 1998). Whether or not there are activations that are specific to word combination at the sentence level, for either syntactic or semantic aspects of combination, remains unclear.

One clear implication of the neuroimaging work is that the classic model of aphasia, in which Broca's area subserves language production whereas Wernicke's area subserves language comprehension, seems to be wrong (cf. Stowe et al., 2005). Sentence comprehension often produces frontal as well as posterior activations, and activity in both regions increases when sentences are complex (Caplan et al., 1998, 1999; Stowe et al., 1998).

Less easy to evaluate are implications of neuroimaging work for the revised model of aphasia, in which syntax is mediated by the frontal cortex and semantics is mediated by the posterior cortex. In order to evaluate this claim, stimulus or task manipulations are needed that isolate these two putative streams of processing. Some of the strategies used to isolate syntactic processing in sentence comprehension experiments have included the following contrasts: (1) syntactically complex sentences *versus* syntactically simple ones (Caplan et al., 1998; Caplan et al., 1999; Caplan et al., 2001; Stowe et al., 1998); (2) sentences which contain syntactic structure *versus* word lists (Kuperberg et al., 2000; Stowe et al, 1998; Stowe et al., 1999); (3) sentences that contain "pseudowords" (e.g., "The blives semble on the plim.") *versus* normal sentences (Friederici et al., 2000; Mazoyer et al., 1993; Moro et al., 2001); and (4) sentences that contain a syntactic anomaly *versus* sentences that are syntactically well-formed (Friederici et al., 2003; Kuperberg et al., 2000; Kuperberg et al., 2003; Ni et al., 2000; Newman et al., 2001). The assumptions underlying these contrasts are roughly as follows: (1) syntactically more complex sentences induce more syntactic

processing relative to syntactically simple sentences; (2) sentences but not word lists engage syntactic processes; (3) sentences with pseudowords minimize semantic processing but not syntactic processing; and (4) sentences with syntactic anomalies require more syntactic "work." Unfortunately, the reported patterns of activation vary widely across these different contrasts (Kaan and Swaab, 2002; Stowe et al., 2005). For example, in most studies complex sentences elicit more activation in or near Broca's area than do simple sentences, although angular gyrus activations have been reported instead in at least one report (Caplan et al., 2001). Sentences sometimes but not always activate Broca's area more than word lists do; in fact, the converse is sometimes reported (cf. Stowe et al., 2005). Syntactically anomalous sentences usually activate regions in the temporal lobe more than do well-formed sentences, although frontal activations (generally anterior to Broca's area) have occasionally been reported.

Semantic processing has been isolated in sentence processing experiments by comparing sentences with real words to sentences containing pseudowords (i.e., word-like stimuli with no semantic representations) (Röder et al., 2002), and well-formed sentences to sentences with semantic anomalies (Friederici et al., 2000; Hagoort et al., 2004; Kiel, Laurens, and Liddle, 2002; Kuperberg et al., 2000, 2003). The assumption seems to be that real words will activate semantic processes to a greater extent than pseudowords, and that semantic anomalies will lead to more semantic processing than semantically plausible words. Several of these studies have indicated that sentences containing semantic anomalies evoke more activation in the posterior or middle temporal lobe than do sentences that do not contain anomalies, which is consistent with the revised model of aphasia. However, Kuperberg et al. (2003), Kiel et al. (2002), and Hagoort et al. (2004) report inferior frontal activations to the semantically anomalous sentences either in addition to or in the absence of temporal activation, which is not consistent with the model.

It may be worth pointing out again that fMRI does not isolate online processing at the point of the critical word itself but also images everything that comes before or after that point. While what comes before may wash out in the counterbalancing, what comes afterward may not. So, in imaging a syntactic anomaly, one is not just imaging what happens at the anomaly itself but all the other consequences of encountering the anomaly, as well as task and decision-related activity (if subjects are required to carry out a task). Such consequences after encountering the anomaly may range from syntactic to semantic to attentional. One cannot necessarily assume that these processes cancel out in comparing different types of anomalies because the consequences of the anomalies after the word may differ depending on the nature of the anomaly (Kuperberg et al., 2003).

Recently, alternatives to the revised model of aphasia have been proposed, based on neuroimaging results (Bookheimer, 2002; Dapretto and Bookheimer, 1999; Gabrieli, Poldrack, and Desmond, 1998; Hagoort, 2005; Poldrack et al., 1999; Thompson-Schill et al., 1997). For example, Hagoort (2005) proposes that different areas of the left inferior frontal gyrus mediate different levels of combinatory analysis (integration in Hagoort's terminology), for both sentence production and sentence comprehension. Specifically, the claim is that more posterior regions of the left inferior prefrontal cortex (BA 44 and the ventral portion of BA 6) integrate phonological units, middle regions of the inferior prefrontal gyrus (BA 45) integrate syntactic units, and the most anterior and ventral regions (BA 47) integrate semantic units. Lexical semantics and structural frames associated with each word are claimed to be retrieved in the posterior superior temporal lobe. This is an interesting model, but the relevant imaging evidence motivating the LIFG claims is mixed (e.g., Barde and Thompson-Schill, 2002; Gold and Buckner, 2002; Thompson-Schill, 2002). One important caveat is that the relevant evidence is comprised mostly of studies involving presentation of individual words rather than sentences. Another is that damage to the relevant LIFG areas does not necessarily disrupt semantic processing (Price et al., 1999), suggesting that the LIFG is not essential for semantic processing (cf. Thompson-Schill, 2002). Furthermore, other neuroimaging evidence seems to indicate that semantic knowledge (and relevant processing) is represented within a widely distributed network encompassing large swathes of the frontal, temporal, parietal, and occipital lobes, rather than in discrete cortical locations (Tyler et al., 2003).

Taken as a whole, then, the imaging literature does not provide clear evidence of anatomically distinct syntactic and semantic processing streams, and does not definitively locate these streams in the brain. This conclusion is reinforced by a recent meta-analysis of PET and fMRI studies designed to isolate phonological, syntactic, and semantic processes in the brain (Vigneau et al., 2006). The meta-analysis shows that (across studies) all three types of processes have been localized to posterior portions of the left frontal lobe, much of the temporal lobe, and the inferior parietal lobe (see figure 1 in Vigneau et al.). The authors gamely attempt to infer distinct neural circuits for each of the three types of processes based on this evidence. It seems to us, however, that the collective data do not provide compelling evidence of separate processing streams.

A related and very important issue concerns the language specificity of these activations. Interestingly, listening to or mentally rehearsing music activates many of the same regions activated during sentence comprehension, including the LIFG and left posterior temporal lobe (Halpern and Zatorre, 1999; Hickok et al., 2003; Koelsch, 2005; Koelsch et al., 2002). Nonverbal and nonmusical motor planning also activates the LIFG (Binkofski et al., 2000; Lacquaniti et al., 1997). Tasks that require manipulation of sequences over time (Barde and Thompson-Schill, 2002; Gelfand and Bookheimer, 2003) and stimuli that deviate from a familiar patterned sequence (Huettel, Mack, and McCarthy, 2002) produce activation in many frontal areas (including the inferior frontal gyrus) and in the basal ganglia. With respect to the temporoparietal areas, the temporal cortices are often activated in tasks that are not linguistic but that require conceptual processing (e.g., Bar and Aminoff, 2003; Chao et al., 1999; Martin and Chao, 2001). More generally, several reviewers of the neuroimaging-and-language literature conclude that there is little evidence of any truly language-specific neural centers (Kaan and Swaab, 2002; Patel, 2003; Price, Thierry, and Griffiths, 2005; Stowe et al., 2005). Instead, these reviewers propose that language might take advantage of a number of domain-general neural circuits. Indeed, a number of proposals associate LIFG and surrounding prefrontal cortex with functions that extend beyond grammar and language, including working memory (Smith and Jonides, 1998), selection (Thompson-Schill et al., 1997), and cognitive control (Miller and Cohen, 2001).

3.3 *Event-related potential studies*

Unlike hemodynamic-based methods, ERPs allow one to track changes in brain activity over time with great temporal resolution, as a person is reading or listening to a sentence. ERPs might therefore be ideal for isolating the neural responses to particular critical words in sentences. A particularly fruitful approach has involved the presentation of linguistic anomalies. If syntactic and semantic aspects of sentence comprehension are segregated into distinct streams of processing, then syntactic and semantic anomalies might affect the comprehension system in distinct ways. ERPs (unlike hemodynamic methods) have the temporal resolution necessary to isolate the neural response to the anomalous words. A large body of evidence suggests that syntactic and semantic anomalies do in fact elicit qualitatively distinct ERP effects, and that these effects are characterized by distinct and consistent temporal properties. Semantic anomalies (e.g., *The cat will bake the food...*) elicit a negative wave that peaks at about 400 ms after the anomalous word appears (the *N400 effect*) (Kutas and Hillyard, 1980, 1984; Osterhout and Nicol, 1999). By contrast,

syntactic anomalies (e.g., *The cat will eating the food...*) elicit a large positive wave that onsets at about 500 ms after presentation of the anomalous word and persists for at least half a second (the *P600 effect*) (McKinnon and Osterhout, 1996; Osterhout, 1997; Osterhout and Holcomb, 1992, 1993; Osterhout and Mobley, 1995; Osterhout and Nicol, 1999; Osterhout et al., 1996; Osterhout et al., 2002). These results generalize well across types of anomaly (with anomalies involving phrase structure, agreement, verb subcategorization, and constituent-movement all eliciting P600-like effects), types of languages (including word-order languages such as English, Dutch, and French, and case-marked languages such as Italian and Japanese; Angrilli et al., 2002; Inoue and Osterhout, in preparation), and various methodological factors (including modality of the input, rate of word presentation, and presenting isolated sentences and natural prose; Allen, Badecker, and Osterhout, 2003; McKinnon and Osterhout, 1996; Osterhout and Holcomb, 1993; Osterhout et al., 2002). In some studies, syntactic anomalies have also elicited a negativity over anterior regions of the scalp, with onsets ranging from 100 to 300 ms (the so-called *left anterior negativity*, or LAN, effect; Friederici, 1995; Neville et al., 1991; Osterhout and Holcomb, 1992; Osterhout and Mobley, 1995).

These results seem to indicate that the human brain does in fact honor the distinction between the form and the meaning of a sentence. However, as we note below, there are exceptions to this generalization, and the exceptions tell us quite a bit about how the syntactic and semantic "processing streams" interact with each other during sentence comprehension (Kim and Osterhout, 2005; Kuperberg et al., 2003).

The sensitivity of the N400 and LAN/P600 effects to semantic and syntactic manipulations, respectively, does not necessarily imply that these effects are direct manifestations of semantic and syntactic processing (Osterhout et al., 2004); nor does it indicate that they are in any sense language-specific. The available evidence suggests that they are not, in fact, direct manifestations of neural circuits specific to syntactic or semantic aspects of language processing. For example, some types of misspelled words elicit a positive wave indistinguishable from the P600 elicited by syntactic anomalies (Van de Meerendonk et al., 2011), suggesting that the P600 effect is not specific to syntax. Furthermore, deviations from expected musical forms (e.g., deviant notes in well-known musical pieces) elicit P600-like effects (Besson et al., 1998; Koelsch, 2005; Patel, 2003; Patel et al., 1998), suggesting that the P600 effect is not specific to language. It is also conceivable that the P600 effect is a member of the P300 family of positive waves elicited by a wide variety of "oddball" stimuli, that is, stimuli that deviate from a preceding sequence (Donchin, 1981; for commentary on this possibility, see Coulson and Kutas, 1998; Osterhout et al., 1996; Osterhout and Hagoort, 1999). What do these categories of anomaly all have in common? One reasonable generalization is that they all deviate from some expected pattern or sequence. That is, the P600 effect conceivably reflects the operation of a neural circuit that mediates "patterned sequence processing." Consistent with this possibility, Dominey and colleagues have shown that violations of syntax-like patterns that are implicitly learned in the laboratory elicit a P600-like positivity (Hoen and Dominey, 2004).

Similarly, the N400 component is sensitive to manipulations not explicitly linguistic in nature. In semantic priming studies, smaller N400s are evoked by pictures preceded by related compared to unrelated picture primes (Barrett and Rugg, 1990; Holcomb and McPherson, 1994; McPherson and Holcomb, 1999), and objects that are congruous with their surrounding visual scene evoke a smaller N400 than objects that are incongruous with their surrounding visual scenes (Ganis and Kutas, 2003). Scenes preceded by congruous contexts – written sentence contexts (Federmeier and Kutas, 2001), successively presented static visual scenes conveying stories (West and Holcomb, 2002), or movie clips – evoke a smaller N400 than pictures preceded by

incongruous contexts (Sitnikova, Kuperberg, and Holcomb, 2003). All of these experiments involved manipulations of meanings that are not explicitly presented in linguistic codes.[4] Intriguingly, Sitnikova et al. (2003) have shown that events in short silent movies of everyday activities (e.g., a movie clip of a man preparing to shave and then shaving with a rolling pin rather than a razor) that deviate from relevant "event schemas" elicit both N400 and P600 effects. Sitnikova (personal communication) has proposed that the N400 effect reflects the implausibility of the unexpected scene, whereas the P600 effect reflects the deviation from the expected sequence of events within the event schema. If so, then both of these processing streams may be involved in real-world visual comprehension as well as in sentence comprehension.

Ideally, one would like to locate these two processing streams in the brain. Lesion studies have attempted to identify the sites that eliminate or reduce the N400 and P600 effects. The lesion evidence seems to indicate that the N400 semantic context effect is affected by damage to the left temporal lobe and the temporoparietal junction. Importantly, damage to these areas tends to also produce aphasic syndromes characterized by a semantic processing deficit (for a review, see Friederici, Hahne, and von Cramon, 1998; Hagoort et al., 1996; Swaab et al., 1997; Van Petten and Luka, 2006). Conversely, damage to the frontal lobe does not typically affect the N400 effect to semantically inappropriate words (Hagoort, Wassenaar, and Brown, 2003). Dipole and distributed source modeling of the magnetic equivalent of the N400 effect (the voltage difference between the semantically anomalous and well-formed conditions) has generally implicated the posterior halves of the left superior and middle temporal gyri and the temporoparietal junction (Helenius

---

4 More recently, Koelsch (2005) and colleagues report that unexpected switches from one musical piece to another also elicit an N400-like effect. This result stretches the set of antecedent conditions known to modulate the N400, although the theoretical implications are uncertain at the moment.

et al., 1999; Simos, Basile, and Papanicolaou, 1997).[5] With respect to the P600 effect, Kotz and colleagues have reported that damage to the basal ganglia can eliminate the P600 effect while leaving the N400 effect intact (Kotz et al., 2003).

Inoue and Osterhout (in preparation) used LORETA to estimate the current distribution associated with *normal* sentence processing (rather than anomalous sentences, which has been the strategy in previously published work) within two critical time windows: the window associated with the N400 component (during which the brain is most robustly sensitive to conceptual aspects of the stimulus) and the window associated with the P600 effect (during which the brain is most robustly sensitive to syntax or, more generally, patterned sequences). The LORETA solutions indicated a posterior distribution for the N400 window (the temporoparietal region, BA 39 and 40), and an anterior distribution for the P600 window (the left inferior frontal gyrus, BA 45 and 47). If the posterior and anterior streams really do mediate certain crucial conceptual and syntactic aspects of word combination, then we would expect to see differences in how words from different grammatical classes engage these streams. Both nouns and verbs should engage the conceptual processing stream, as both types of word are conceptually rich. However, because verbs (in configurational languages like English) specify the structure for the clauses in which they appear, one should expect verbs to engage the anterior processing stream to a greater extent. This prediction was verified: During the N400 window, nouns and verbs both strongly engaged the posterior stream. During the P600 window,

however, verbs engaged the anterior stream to a much greater degree than did nouns.

4 Interactions between the processing streams

Assuming that separable processing streams mediate syntactic and conceptual aspects of word combination, the question arises as to how these streams interact during sentence comprehension. This interaction must occur in real time, as a person is reading or listening to a sentence. A priori, it seems likely that ERPs will be the most useful tool for studying interactions between the streams. This follows because ERPs (unlike hemodynamic neuroimaging methods) provide dynamic measurement of a dynamic process, and are also differentially sensitive to events occurring within the two streams.

Language processing models have been deeply influenced by the "syntax-first" assumptions of generative linguistics (Chomsky, 1986). A standard assumption has been that comprehension is controlled by an initial stage of purely syntactic processing (Ferreira and Clifton, 1986; Fodor and Ferreira, 1998). As words arrive in the linguistic input, they are rapidly organized into a structural analysis by a process that is not influenced by semantic knowledge. The output of this syntactic process then guides semantic interpretation. This model has been given a neurobiological instantiation by Friederici and her colleagues (Friederici, 2002). They claim that the LAN effect reflects the operation of a rapid, reflexive syntactic processor that precedes semantic analysis (reflected in the N400 component). The P600 effect is claimed to reflect a "reanalysis" of a syntactic string when the sentence is ungrammatical, or when the comprehender chooses the wrong parsing option when confronted with syntactic ambiguity (for a critical assessment of these claims, see Osterhout et al., 2004).

However, the syntax-first processing theory seems at odds with the massively parallel and highly interactive nature of computation in the brain (Fuster, 1995). This general

5   Although we and other recent reviewers (Van Petten and Luka, 2006) conclude that the primary sources of the "semantic integration" N400 effect are located in the left temporal lobe, another reviewer (Marinković, 2004) concludes that the primary sources are bilaterally present in temporal and prefrontal areas. We tend to agree with Van Petten and Kutas that the extant literature strongly supports a temporal source but not significant frontal involvement. For further comment on this debate, see Osterhout et al., 2004.

principle of neurobiological design fits better with a second class of psycholinguistic models, a diverse family of models often referred to as *constraint-based models*. These models posit a probabilistic constraint satisfaction process in which syntactic knowledge is only one of a number of constraints on interpretation (Trueswell et al., 1994). But the implicit assumption in these models (as for the syntax-first models) is that unless syntactic cues are indeterminate, syntax always controls the direction of processing.

In one of the few studies to dynamically study the real-time interaction of the two processing streams, Kim and Osterhout (2005) presented anomalous sentences that began with a passive structure, for example, *The mysterious crime had been solving*.... The syntactic cues in the sentence require that the noun *crime* be the agent of the verb *solving*. If syntax drives sentence processing, then the verb *solving* would be perceived to be *semantically anomalous*, as crime is a poor agent for the verb *solve*, and therefore should elicit an N400 effect. However, although *crime* is a poor agent, it is an excellent theme (as in *solved the crime*). The theme role can be accommodated simply by changing the inflectional morpheme at the end of the verb to an active form ("The mysterious crime had been *solved*..."). Therefore, if meaning drives sentence processing in this situation, then the verb *solving* would be perceived to be in the wrong syntactic form, and should therefore elicit a P600 effect. Kim and Osterhout observed that verbs like *solving* elicited a P600 effect, showing that a strong "semantic attraction" between a predicate and an argument can determine how words are combined, even when the semantic attraction contradicts unambiguous syntactic cues. Conversely, in anomalous sentences with an identical structure but with no semantic attraction between the subject noun and the verb (e.g., *The envelope was devouring*..."), the critical verb elicited an N400 effect rather than a P600 effect. These results show quite clearly that semantics, rather than syntax, can drive word combination during sentence comprehension (for related work see Hoeks et al.,

2004; Kolk et al., 2003; and Kuperberg et al., 2003).

This method permits detailed investigation of interactions between the two processing streams. For example, because semantic attraction is almost certainly a continuous variable, there must be a "tipping point" (i.e., some amount of semantic attraction) at which the semantics "wins" and the syntax "loses." For example, the introduction of syntactic complexity or ambiguity may weaken the syntactic processing stream, thereby increasing the impact of semantic-thematic factors (Kuperberg et al., 2007; Weckerly and Kutas, 1999; see also Ferreira, 2003). Similarly, it might be possible to strengthen the syntactic stream to make it impervious to the effects of semantic attraction. We are currently examining this possibility using a "syntactic priming" paradigm, in which we precede the critical sentence (e.g., *The mysterious crime had been solving*...) with sentences unrelated in meaning to the critical sentence but which have the same syntactic form. Preliminary data suggest that the syntactic stream can in fact be sufficiently strengthened to make it resistant to even strong doses of semantic attraction.

5 Neural circuits, evolution, and genetics

Let's assume for the moment that the combinatorial properties of sentence comprehension are in fact enabled by two processing streams: An anterior stream processes patterns of sequences that occur over time, with the patterned sequences that comprise the syntax of a human language representing just one particularly salient manifestation of this stream. A posterior stream is crucial for combining words at a conceptual level.[6] These streams run in parallel and are,

---

6   Our idea here is that the posterior stream might be particularly important for aspects of sentence processing that involve the combination of meanings. We recognize that conceptual processing in its entirety is much more than this and probably engages a large and widely distributed network of neural circuits.

under some circumstances at least, highly interactive. A truly satisfying understanding of the combinatorial aspects of language would provide answers to questions such as these: Exactly where in the brain are the neural circuits that mediate these processing streams, and how are they organized? How and when did they evolve? What genetic mechanisms might account for the species-specific aspects of human language, in particular its combinatory power? We will argue here that compelling (albeit speculative) answers to each of these questions are readily available, and that the answers are grounded in comparative analyses.

Do we know of an anterior neural circuit that mediates patterned sequence processing in a communicative system? The answer is yes. Songbirds rely on a specialized cortical-basal ganglia-cortical loop to learn, produce, and perceive birdsong (Brenowitz and Beecher, 2005). Disruptions to this circuit disrupt the sensorimotor learning needed to acquire song, and also the sequencing skills needed to produce and properly perceive it. Recent advances in understanding the anatomical, physiological, and histochemical characteristics of this circuitry have revealed a remarkable homology between birds and mammals (Doupe et al., 2005). The homologous circuit in human and non-human primates involves loops connecting many regions in the frontal cortex to the basal ganglia. Afferents from the frontal cortex densely innervate the striatum of the basal ganglia, which also receives inputs from many other areas of the cortex. The striatal output then travels back to the same areas of the frontal cortex via the thalamus, forming a closed loop. The striatum seems to control behavioral sequencing in many species (Aldridge and Berridge, 1998; Graybiel, 1997, 1998). Spiny neurons, the principal cells of the striatum, have properties that make them ideal for recognizing patterned sequences across time (Beiser, Hua, and Houk, 1997). Damage to this loop in primates produces problems with motor and cognitive skills that require planning and manipulating patterns of sequences over time (Fuster, 1995). The striatum is also

a major site for adaptive plasticity (Graybiel, 2004). All of these observations lend plausibility to the notion that the basal ganglia play a role in the syntax of human language (see also Lieberman, 2000).

Given the striking homologies between birds and mammals with respect to the cortical-basal ganglia circuitry, it is probably not coincidental that the acquisition of human language and birdsong have compelling parallels (Bolhuis and Gahr, 2006; Doupe and Kuhl, 1999). Humans and songbirds learn their complex, sequenced vocalizations in early life. They similarly internalize sensory experience and use it to shape vocal outputs through sensorimotor learning and integration. They show similar innate dispositions for learning the correct sounds and sequences; as a result, humans and some species of songbird have similar critical periods for vocal learning, with a much greater ability to learn early in life (Brenowitz and Beecher, 2005). These behavioral parallels are what one would expect if both species rely on a similar neural substrate for learning and using their communicative systems.

Relevant genetic evidence is also available. The much-discussed *FOXP2* gene is similarly expressed in the basal ganglia of humans and songbirds (Teramitsu et al., 2004; Vargha-Khadem et al., 2005). *FOXP2* mutation in humans results in deficits in language production and comprehension, especially aspects of (morpho)syntax that involve combining and sequencing linguistic units (Vargha-Khadem et al., 2005). One of the neurobiological effects of the mutation is a fifty percent reduction in the gray matter of the striatum (Vargha-Khadem et al., 2005). Perhaps, then, the combinatorial aspects of human language were enabled by the preadaptation of an anterior neural circuit that has been highly conserved over evolutionary time and across species and by a genetic mutation in this circuit that doubled its computational space.

Comparative analyses might also be useful when attempting to identify the neural circuits underlying the posterior stream and for understanding the nature of the interactions between the two streams. The temporoparietal cortex in humans appears to correspond to polymodal association areas in the monkey, which could plausibly act as the neural substrate of relevant polymodal conceptual representations and processes (Fuster, 1995). Furthermore, the temporoparietal polymodal areas are directly connected to the frontal areas putatively involved in sequence processing by long fibers that are part of the uncinate fasciculus (Fuster, 1995). These connections are robust and reciprocal and provide an obvious mechanism for interaction between the two streams. Of course, this characterization is highly speculative.

6 Conclusions

How are words combined during sentence comprehension? The evidence we reviewed here suggests several conclusions. Different sets of processes combine words syntactically and semantically. The two processing streams operate in parallel but independently most of the time; this enables each stream to pursue an internally attractive analysis even when it is inconsistent with the output of other processes (although usually the two streams converge on the same result). But under certain conditions, either stream can take charge of word combination, forcing the other stream to do its bidding. More speculatively, we have suggested that the syntactic processing stream depends on the preadaptation of a highly conserved anterior cortical-basal ganglia circuit for processing patterns of sequences, rather than on language-specific neural circuits that evolved in humans. The relevant conceptual processing may depend on a highly conserved posterior circuit that evolved for representing some aspects of conceptual knowledge.[7]

This account is consistent with several known principles of neurobiological design.

Neural circuits tend to be organized hierarchically along the nerve axis, from spinal cord to cortex. They are massively parallel and interactive. They act as the functional unit of evolution; one would therefore expect them to be conserved across species rather than invented out of thin air in humans. "Learning" in neural circuits is generally associative. The model we are proposing here has all of these elements. By contrast, the standard models described throughout this chapter have none of them: These models assume a purely cortical representation for language, serial and modular processes, species-specificity of relevant neural circuits, and a strong belief that associative processes cannot account for language. All of which might be true. But if so, then the neurobiology and evolution of human language remain deeply mysterious.

An advocate of the standard story is likely to object to these conclusions. Surely the syntax of human language is too complex (too highly structured, too recursive, too creative) to be modeled as a simple patterned sequence processor that relies on associative learning mechanisms. In fact, the explanatory burden placed on rule-based, recursive syntax has diminished over recent decades. Modern grammars tend to be lexicalist in nature; that is, much of the knowledge relevant to sentence structure is stored in the lexicon with individual words, rather than being computed by abstract phrase structure rules. Recursion, while clearly a characteristic of human language, is much more limited in actual language usage than would be predicted given the standard model. And, because conceptual knowledge has its own structure (Jackendoff, 1990), it seems plausible that some of the burden for structuring the input rests with the conceptual stream (Jackendoff, 2002). Indeed, this type of influence is precisely what we have recently demonstrated (Kim and Osterhout, 2005; Kuperberg et al., 2003). Thus, multiple theoretical developments converge neatly with the idea that human syntax is processed by a sequence processor relying on associative learning, and indeed sequence learning

---

7   We should explicitly note that other theorists have proposed that the basal ganglia-frontal cortex loops subserve semantic aspects of language comprehension, rather than or in addition to syntactic aspects (Copland, 2003; Crosson, 1985; Longworth et al., 2005; Wallesch and Papagno, 1988).

mechanisms such as hidden markov models and simple recurrent networks are shown to acquire grammatical knowledge and simulate human grammatical behavior (Kim, Srinivas, and Trueswell, 2002). The computational properties of the basal ganglia-frontal cortex circuit are well-suited for implementing that type of computational model (Dominey, 1997). The seemingly unique characteristics of human syntax might be partly due to the effects of the human version of the *FOXP2* gene, which drastically increased the computational space in this circuit.

We are not claiming that all of the available evidence (or even all of that reviewed in this chapter) is consistent with our conclusions. That is clearly not the case. For example, not all patients with agrammatism have obvious damage to the basal ganglia, and functions other than conceptual processing activate the polymodal areas in temporoparietal cortex. Even so, we think it is essential to try to construct a neurobiologically grounded explanation of sentence comprehension. Part of the problem, as we see it, is that the standard procedure in the deficit and neuroimaging fields (at least as it relates to language studies) has been to take a detailed functional model as a given, and to attempt to use the resulting deficit or imaging data to construct a neurobiological model that can implement the functional model. In our opinion, this strategy has not led to many genuine advances in our understanding. We believe that the data from these methods needs to be put in a larger context, one that includes consideration of the principles of neurobiology, genetics, and evolution. For example, neuroimaging work has generated many conflicting functional hypotheses concerning the roles of various regions of the frontal cortex during language processing. These hypotheses are usually motivated and evaluated in the context of other neuroimaging studies on language or related cognitive functions. Only occasionally are they discussed in the larger context of cortical-basal ganglia neural circuits. But a careful consideration of the neural circuits is

absolutely central to discerning the function of some patch of cortical tissue.

Finally, this account of the neurobiology of sentence comprehension is not new. In an amazingly prescient paper, Karl Lashley (1951) proposed a similar model even though much of the evidence favoring it had yet to be discovered. More recently, a number of theorists have advocated for these or related claims (Aldridge and Berridge, 1998; Dominey, 1997; Fuster, 1995; Grossman, 1999; Jackendoff, 2002; Lieberman, 2000; Ullman, 2001).[8] What has changed, in our view, is the quantity and quality of evidence, from diverse fields, that converges on the same explanation for the remarkable combinatorial powers of human language.

Acknowledgments

This chapter is dedicated to the memory of David A. Swinney. We thank Ann Graybiel, David Perkel, Eliot Brenowitz, and Tatiana Sitnikova. Any errors or misconceptions in this chapter are the fault of the authors. Preparation of this chapter was supported by Grants R01DC01947, F32DC05756, and P30DC04661 from the National Institute on Deafness and Other Communication Disorders, and Grant RO1-MH071635 from the National Institute of Mental Health.

8 Our proposal differs a bit from some similar proposals. For example, Ullman (2001) makes a distinction between an anterior "procedural" rule-based system mediated by cortico-basal ganglia circuits and a posterior "declarative memory" system mediated by hippocampal-temporal lobe circuits. One difference is that in Ullman's model the anterior circuit mediates language-specific rules of combination. In our model, the anterior circuit is a general patterned sequence processor that learns via associative processes. Furthermore, Ullman focuses specifically on the distinction between regular and irregular past tense forms of verbs, and claims that the anterior circuit computes the rule-governed form of regular verbs, whereas the posterior circuit retrieves the irregular form from memory. The evidence to support this specific claim is mixed (cf. Longworth et al., 2005). We are suggesting here that some (or many) of the combinatorial aspects of sentence comprehension rely on the putative anterior circuit but do not have specific suggestions about which aspects those might be, given the paucity of relevant evidence.

References

Aldridge, J. W. & Berridge, K. C. (1998). Coding serial order by neostriatal neurons: A "natural action" approach to movement sequence. *The Journal of Neuroscience*, *18*, 2777–87.

Alexander, M. P. (2006). Aphasia I: Clinical and anatomical issues. In Farah, M. J. & Feinberg, T. E. (Eds.) *Patient-based approaches to cognitive neuroscience* (2nd edition). Cambridge, MA: MIT Press.

Alexander, M. P., Naeser, M. A., & Palumbo, C. (1990). Broca's area aphasia. *Neurology*, *40*, 353–62.

Allen, M. D., Badecker, W., & Osterhout, L. (2003). Morphological analysis during sentence processing. *Language and Cognitive Processes*, *18*, 405–30.

Angrilli, A., Penolazzi, B., Vespignani, F., De Vincenzi, M., Job, R., Ciccarelli, L., Palomba, D., & Stegagno, L. (2002). Cortical brain responses to semantic incongruity and syntactic violation in Italian language: An event-related potential study. *NeuroscienceLetters*, *322*, 5–8.

Awh, E., Jonides, J., Smith E. E., Schumacher, E. H., Koeppe, R. A., & Katz, S. (1996). Dissociation of storage and rehearsal in verbal working memory: Evidence from positron emission tomography. *Psychological Science*, *7*, 25–31.

Barrett, S. E. & Rugg, M. D. (1990). Event-related potentials and the semantic matching of pictures. *Brain and Cognition*, *14*, 201–12.

Bates, E., Wilson, S. M., Saygin, A. P., Dick, F., Sereno, M. I., Knight, R. T., & Dronkers, N. F. (2003). Voxel-based lesion-symptom mapping. *Nature Neuroscience*, *6*, 448–50.

Bar, M. & Aminoff, E. (2003). Cortical analysis of visual context. *Neuron*, *38*, 347–58.

Barde, L. H. & Thompson-Schill, S. L. (2002). Models of functional organization of the lateral prefrontal cortex in working memory: evidence in favor of a process model. *Journal of Cognitive Neuroscience*, *14*, 1054–63.

Bavelier, D., Corina, D., Jezzard, P., Padmanabhan, S., Clark, V. P., Karni, A., Prinster, A., Braun, A., Lalwanim, A., Rauschecker, J. P., Turner, R., & Neville, H. (1997). Sentence reading: A functional MRI study at 4 Tesla. *Journal of Cognitive Neuroscience*, *9*, 664–86.

Beiser, D. G., Hua, S. E., & Houk, J. C. (1997). Network models of the basal ganglia. *Current Opinion in Neurobiology*, *7*, 185–90.

Besson, M., Faita, F., Peretz, I., Bonnel, A., & Requin, J. (1998). Singing in the brain: Independence of lyrics and tunes. *Psychological Science*, *9*, 494–8.

Binkofski, F., Amunts, K., Stephan, K. M., Posse, S., Schormann, T., Freund, H.-J., Zilles, K., & Seitz, R. J. (2000). Broca's region subserves imagery of motion: a combined cytoarchitectonic and fMRI study. *Human Brain Mapping*, *11*, 273–285.

Bolhuis, J. J. & Gahr, M. (2006). Neural mechanisms of birdsong memory. *Nature Reviews. Neuroscience*, *7*, 347–57.

Bookheimer, S. (2002). Functional MRI of Language: New Approaches to Understanding the Cortical Organization of Semantic Processing. *Annual Review of Neuroscience*, *25*, 151–88.

Brenowitz, E. & Beecher, M. D. (2005). Song learning in birds: diversity and plasticity, opportunities and challenges. *Trends in Neurosciences*, *28*, 127–32.

Buchel, C., Holmes, A. P., Rees, G., & Friston, K. J. (1998). Characterizing stimulus-response functions using nonlinear regressors in parametric fMRI experiments. *Neuroimage*, *8*, 140–8.

Burock, M. A., Buckner, R. L., Woldorff, M. G., Rosen, B. R., & Dale, A. M. (1998). Randomized event-related experimental designs allow for extremely rapid presentation rates using functional MRI. *NeuroReport*, *9*, 3735–9.

Cabeza, R. & Kingstone, A. (2001). *Handbook of functional neuroimaging of cognition*. Cambridge, MA: MIT Press.

Caplan, D. (1994). Language and the brain. In Gernsbacher, M. (Ed.) *Handbook of Psycholinguistics*. Cambridge, UK: Cambridge University Press.

(1995). Issues arising in contemporary studies of disorders of syntactic processing in sentence comprehension in agrammatic patients. *Brain and Language*, *50*, 325–38.

Caplan, D., Alpert, N., & Waters, G. (1998). Effects of syntactic structure and propositional number on patterns of regional cerebral blood flow. *Journal of Cognitive Neuroscience*, *10*, 541–52.

(1999). PET studies of syntactic processing with auditory sentence presentation. *NeuroImage*, *9*, 343–51.

Caplan, D., Hildebrandt, N., & Makris, N. (1996). Location of lesions in stroke patients with deficits in syntactic processing in sentence comprehension. *Brain*, *119*, 933–49.

Caplan, D. & Moo, L. (2004). Cognitive conjunction and cognitive functions. *NeuroImage*, *21*, 751–6.

Caplan, D., Vijayan, S., Kuperberg, G., West, C., Waters, G., Greve, D., & Dale, A. M. (2001). Vascular responses to syntactic processing: Event-related fMRI study of relative clauses. *Human Brain Mapping*, 15, 26–8.

Carammaza, A., Capasso, R., Capitani, E., & Miceli, G. (2005). Patterns of comprehension performance in agrammatic Broca's aphasia: A test of the Trace Deletion Hypothesis. *Brain and Language*, 94, 43–53.

Caramazza, A. & Zuriff, E. (1976). Dissociations of algorithmic and heuristic processes in language comprehension: Evidence from aphasia. *Brain and Language*, 3, 572–82.

Chao, L. L., Haxby, J. V., & Martin, A. (1999). Attribute-based neural substrates in temporal cortex for perceiving and knowing about objects. *Nature Neuroscience*, 2, 913–19.

Chomsky, N. (1986). *Knowledge of language*. New York: Praeger.

Copland, D. (2003). The basal ganglia and semantic engagement: potential insights from semantic priming in individuals with subcortical vascular lesions, Parkinson's disease, and cortical lesions. *Journal of the International Neuropsychological Society*, 9, 1041–1052

Coulson, S. & Kutas, M. (1998). Expect the unexpected: Event-related brain responses to morphosyntactic violations. *Language and Cognitive Processes*, 13, 21–58.

Crosson, B. (1985). Subcortical functions in language: a working model. *Brain and Language*, 25, 257–92.

Dale, A. M. & Buckner, R. L. (1997). Selective averaging of individual trials using fMRI. *Human Brain Mapping*, 5, 329–40.

Dale, A. M. & Halgren, E. (2001). Spatiotemporal mapping of brain activity by integration of multiple imaging modalities. *Current Opinion in Neurobiology*, 11, 202–8.

Dale, A. M., Liu, A. K., Fischl, B. R., Buckner, R. L., Belliveau, J. W., Lewine, J. D., et al. (2000). Dynamic statistical parametric mapping: Combining fMRI and MEG for high-resolution imaging of cortical activity. *Neuron*, 26, 55–67.

Dale, A. M. & Sereno, M. I. (1993). Improved localization of cortical activity by combining EEG and MEG with MRI cortical surface reconstruction: A linear approach. *Journal of Cognitive Neuroscience*, 5, 162–76.

Dapretto, M. & Bookheimer, S. Y. (1999). Form and content: dissociating syntax and semantics in sentence comprehension. *Neuron*, 24, 427–32.

Damasio, A. R. & Damasio, H. (1992). Brain and language. *Scientific American*, 63–71.

Dick, F., Bates, E., Wulfeck, B., Utman, J. A., & Dronkers, N. (2001). Language deficits, localization, and grammar: Evidence for a distributive model of language breakdown in aphasic patients and neurologically intact individuals. *Psychological Review*, 108, 759–88.

Dominey, P. F. (1997). An anatomically structured sensory-motor sequence learning system displays some general linguistic capacities. *Brain and Language*, 59, 50–75.

Donchin, E. (1981). Surprise!…Surprise? *Psychophysiology*, 30, 90–7.

Doupe, A. & Kuhl, P. (1999). Birdsong and human speech: Common Themes and Mechanisms. *Annual Review of Neuroscience*, 22, 567–631.

Doupe, A., Perkel, D., Reiner, A., & Stern, E. (2005). Birdbrains could teach basal ganglia research a new song. *Trends in Neurosciences*, 28, 353–63.

Dronkers, N. F., Redfern, B. B., & Knight, R. T. (2000). The neural architecture of language disorders. In Gazzaniga, M. (Ed.) *The new cognitive neurosciences* (pp. 949–58). Cambridge, MA: MIT Press.

Dronkers, N. F., Wilkins, D. P., Van Valin, R., Redfern, B., & Jaeger, J. J. (2004). Lesion analysis of the brain areas involved in language comprehension. *Cognition*, 92, 145–77.

Federmeier, K. D. & Kutas, M. (2001). Meaning and modality: Influences of context, semantic memory organization, and perceptual predictability on picture processing. *Journal of Experimental Psychology: Learning, Memory, and Cognition*, 27, 202–24.

Ferreira, F. (2003). The misinterpretation of non-canonical sentences. *Cognitive Psychology*, 47, 164–203.

Ferreira, F. & Clifton, C. Jr. (1986). The independence of syntactic processing. *Journal of Memory and Language*, 25, 348–68.

Fodor, J. D. & Ferreira, F. (1998). *Reanalysis in sentence processing*. Boston: Kluwer Academic Publishers.

Friederici, A. F. (1995). The time course of syntactic activation during language processing: A model based on neuropsychological and neurophysiological data. *Brain and Language*, 50, 259–84.

(2002). Towards a neural basis of auditory sentence processing. *Trends in Cognitive Sciences*, 6, 78–84.

Friederici, A. D., Hahne, A., & von Cramon, D. Y. (1998). First-pass versus second-pass parsing processes in a Wernicke's and a Broca's aphasic: electrophysiological evidence for a double dissociation. *Brain and Language*, 62, 311–41.

Friederici, A. F. & Kotz, S. A. (2003). The brain basis of syntactic processes: Functional imaging and lesion studies. *NeuroImage*, 20, S8–17.

Friederici, A. F., Kotz, S. A., Werheid, K., Hein, G., & von Cramon, D. Y. (2003). Syntactic comprehension in Parkinson's disease: Investigating early and late integrational processes using event-related brain potentials. *Neuropsychology*, 17, 133–42.

Friederici, A. F., Optiz, B., & von Cramon, D. Y. (2000). Segregating semantic and syntactic aspects of processing in the human brain. *Cerebral Cortex*, 10, 698–705.

Friederici, A. F., Ruschemeyer, S. A., Hahne, A., & Fiebach, C. J. (2003). The role of the left inferior frontal and superior temporal cortex in sentence comprehension: localizing syntactic and semantic processes. *Cerebral Cortex*, 13, 170–7.

Fuster, J. M. (1995). *Memory in the cerebral cortex*. Cambridge, MA: MIT Press.

Gabrieli, J. D., Poldrack, R. A., & Desmond, J. E. (1998). The role of left prefrontal cortex in language and memory. *Proceedings of the National Acadamy of Sciences*, 95, 906–13.

Ganis, G. & Kutas, M. (2003). An electrophysiological study of scene effects on object identification. *Brain Reserch: Cognitive Brain Research*, 16, 123–44.

Gelfund, J. R. & Bookheimer, S. Y. (2003). Dissociating neural mechanisms of temporal sequencing and processing phonemes. *Neuron*, 38, 831–42.

Gold, B. T. & Buckner, R. L. (2002). Common prefrontal regions coactivate with dissociable posterior regions during controlled semantic and phonological tasks. *Neuron*, 35, 803–12.

Graybiel, A. (1997). The basal ganglia and cognitive pattern generators. *Schizophrenia Bulletin*, 23, 459–69.

(1998). The basal ganglia and chunking of action repertoires. *Neurobiology of Learning and Memory*, 70, 119–36.

(2004). Network-level neuroplasticity in cortico-basal ganglia pathways. *Parkinsonism and Related Disorders*, 10, 293–6.

Grodzinsky, Y. (2000). The neurology of syntax: Language use without Broca's area. *Behavioral and Brain Sciences*, 23, 1–71.

Grossman, M. (1999). Sentence processing in Parkinson's disease. *Brain and Cognition*, 40, 387–413.

Grossman, M., Glosser, G., Kalamanson, J., Morris, J., Stern, M. B., & Hurtig, H. I. (2001).

Dopamine supports sentence comprehension in Parkinson's Disease. *Journal of the Neurological Sciences*, 184, 123–30.

Hagoort, P. (2005). On Broca, brain, and binding: a new framework. *Trends in Cognitive Sciences*, 9, 416–23.

Hagoort, P., Brown, C. M., & Swaab, T. Y. (1996). Lexical-semantic event-related potential effects in patients with left hemisphere lesions and aphasia, and patients with right hemisphere lesions without aphasia. *Brain*, 119, 627–49.

Hagoort, P., Hald, L., Bastiaansen, M., & Petersson, K. M. (2004). Integration of word meaning and world knowledge in language comprehension. *Science*, 304, 438–41.

Hagoort, P., Wassenaar, M., & Brown, C. (2003). Real-time semantic compensation in patients with agrammatic comprehension: Electrophysiological evidence for multiple-route plasticity. *Proceedings of the National Academy of Sciences*, 100, 4340–5.

Halgren, E., Dhond, R. P., Christensen, N., Van Petten, C., Marinkovic, K., Lewine, J. D., et al. (2002). N400-like magnetoencephalography responses modulated by semantic context, word frequency, and lexical class in sentences. *NeuroImage*, 17, 1101–16.

Halpern, A. R. & Zatorre, R. J. (1999). When the tune runs through your head: a PET investigation of auditory imagery for familiar melodies. *Cerebral Cortex*, 9, 697–704.

Hämäläinen, M., Hari, R., Ilmoniemi, P. J., Uutila, J. K., & Lounasmaa, O. V. (1993). Magnetoencephalography theory, instrumentation, and applications to noninvasive studies of the working human brain. *Reviews of Modern Physics*, 65, 413–97.

Handy, T. (2005). *Event-related potentials: A methods handbook*. Cambridge, MA: MIT Press.

Helenius, P., Salmelin, R., Service, E., & Connolly, J. F. (1999). Semantic cortical activation in dyslexic readers. *Journal of Cognitive Neuroscience*, 11, 535–50.

Hickok, G., Buchsbaum, B., Humphries, C., Muftuler, T. (2003). Auditory–motor interaction revealed by fMRI: speech, music, and working memory in area SPT. *Journal of Cognitive Neuroscience*, 15, 673–82.

Hickok, G. & Poeppel, D. (2000). Towards a functional neuroanatomy of speech perception. *Trends in Cognitive Sciences*, 4, 131–8.

Hoeks, C. J., Stowe, L. A., & Doedens, G. (2004). Seeing words in context: the interaction of lexical and sentence level information during reading. *Cognitive Brain Research*, 19, 59–73.

Hoen, M. & Dominey, P. (2004). Evidence for a shared mechanism in linguistic and nonlinguistic sequence processing? ERP recordings of on-line function- and content- information integration. In Carreiras, M. & Clifton, C. Jr. (Eds.) *The on-line study of sentence comprehension: Eyetracking, ERPs, and beyond*. New York: Psychology Press.

Holcomb, P. J. & McPherson, W. B. (1994). Event-related brain potentials reflect semantic priming in an object decision task. *Brain and Cognition*, 24, 259–76.

Huettel, S. A., Mack, P. B., & McCarthy, G. (2002). Perceiving patterns in random series: dynamic processing of sequence in prefrontal cortex. *Nature Neuroscience*, 5, 485–90.

Inoue, K., & Osterhout, L. (in preparation). *Sentence processing as a neural tug-of-war.*

Jackendoff, R. (1990). *Semantic structures*. Cambridge, MA: MIT Press.

(2002). *Foundations of language: Brain, meaning, grammar, evolution*. New York: Oxford University Press.

Jacob, F. (1974). *The logic of life*. New York: Vintage.

Just, M., Carpenter, P. A., Keller, T. A., Eddy, W. F., & Thulborn, K. R. (1996). Brain activation modulated by sentence comprehension. *Science*, 274, 114–16.

Kaan, E. & Swaab, T. (2002). The brain circuitry of syntactic comprehension. *Trends in Cognitive Sciences*, 6, 350–5.

Karbe, H., Herholz, K., Szelies, B., Pawlik, G., Wienhard, K., & Heiss, W. D. (1989). Regional metabolic correlates of token test results in cortical and subcortical left hemispheric infarction. *Neurology*, 39, 1083–8.

Keller, T. A., Carpenter, P. A., Just, M. A. (2003). Brain imaging and tongue twister sentence comprehension: twisting the tongue and the brain. *Brain and Language*, 84, 189–203.

Kiehl, K. A., Laurens, K. R., & Liddle, P. F. (2002). Reading anomalous sentences: An event-related fmri study of semantic processing. *Neuroimage*, 17, 842–50.

Kim, A. & Osterhout, L. (2005). The independence of combinatory semantic processing: Evidence from event-related potentials. *Journal of Memory and Language*, 52, 205–25.

Kim, A. E., Srinivas, B., & Trueswell, J. C. (2002). The convergence of lexicalist perspectives in psycholinguistics and computational linguistics. In Stevenson, S. & Merlo, P. (Eds.) *The Lexical Basis of Sentence Processing*. John Benjamins.

Koelsch, S. (2005). Neural substrates of processing syntax and semantics in music. *Current Opinion in Neurobiology*, 15, 207–12.

Koelsch, S., Gunter, T. C., von Cramen, D. Y., Zusset, S., Lohmann, G., & Friederici, A. F. (2002). Bach speaks: a cortical language-network serves the processing of music. *Neuroimage*, 17, 956–66.

Kolk, HHJ, Chwilla, D. J., van Herten, M., & Oor, PJW (2003). Structure and limited capacity in verbal working memory: A study with event-related potentials. *Brain and Language*, 85, 1–36.

Kolk, HHJ & Heeschen, C. (1990). Adaptation symptoms and impairment in Broca's aphasia. *Aphasiology*, 4, 221–31.

(1992). Agrammatism, paragrammatism, and the management of language. *Language and Cognitive Processes*, 7, 89–129.

Kotz, S. A., Frisch, S., von Cramon, D. Y., & Friederici, A. D. (2003). Syntactic language processing: ERP lesion data on the role of the basal ganglia. *Journal of the International Neuropsychological Society*, 9, 1053–60.

Kuperberg, G. R., McGuire, P. K., Bullmore, E. T., Brammer, M. J., Rabe-Hesketh, S., Wright, I. C., Lythgoe, D. J., Williams, S. C., & David, A. S. (2000). Common and distinct neural substrates for pragmatic, semantic, and syntactic processing of spoken sentences: an fMRI study. *Journal of Cognitive Neuroscience*, 12, 321–41.

Kuperberg, G. R., Holcomb, P. J., Sitnikova, T., Greve, D., Dale, A. M., & Caplan, D. (2003). Distinct patterns of neural modulation during the processing of conceptual and syntactic anomalies. *Journal of Cognitive Neuroscience*, 15, 272–93.

Kuperberg, G., Kreher, D. A., Sitnikova, T., Caplan, D., & Holcomb, P. J. (2007). The role of animacy and thematic relationships in processing active English sentences: Evidence from event-related potentials. *Brain and Language*, 100, 223–237.

Kuperberg, G., Sitnikova, T., Caplan, D., Holcomb, P. (2003). Eletrophysiological distinctions in processing conceptual relationships within simple sentences. *Cognitive Brain Research*, 17, 117–29.

Kutas, M. & Hillyard, S. A. (1980). Reading senseless sentences: brain potentials reflect semantic incongruity. *Science*, 207, 203–5.

(1984). Brain potentials during reading reflect word expectancy and semantic association. *Nature*, 307, 161–3.

Lashley, K. (1951). The problem of serial order in behavior. In Jeffress, L. A. (Ed.) *Cerebral mechanisms in behavior*. New York: Wiley.

Lieberman, P. (2000). *Human Language and our Reptilian Brain*. Cambridge, MA: Harvard University Press.

Linebarger, M., Schwartz, M., & Saffran, E. (1983). Sensitivity to grammatical structure in so-called agrammatic aphasics. *Cognition*, 13, 361–93.

Levelt, WJM (1999). *Producing spoken language: A blueprint of the speaker*. Oxford: Oxford University Press.

Logothetis, N. K., & Pfeuffer, J. (2004). On the nature of the BOLD fMRI contrast mechanism. *Magnetic Resonance Imaging*, 22, 1517–31.

Longworth, C. E., Keenan, S. E., Barker, R. A., Marslen-Wilson, W. D., & Tyler, L. K. (2005). The basal ganglia and rule-governed language use: evidence from vascular and degenerative conditions. *Brain*, 128, 584–96.

Marinković K., (2004). Saptiotemporal dynamics of word processing in human cortex. *The Neuroscientist*, 10, 142–52.

Martin, R. C. (2003). Language processing: Functional organization and neuroanatomical basis. *Annual Review of Psychology*, 54, 55–89.

Martin, A. & Chao, L. L. (2001). Semantic memory and the brain: Structure and processes. *Current Opinion in Neurobiolology*, 11, 194–201.

Mazoyer, B. M., Tzourio, N., Frak, V., Syrota, A., Murayama, N., Levrier, O., Salamon, G., Dehaene, S., Cohen, L., & Mehler, J. (1993). The cortical representation of speech. *Journal of Cognitive Neuroscience*, 5, 467–79.

McKinnon, R. & Osterhout, L. (1996). Constraints on movement phenomena in sentence processing: Evidence from event-related brain potentials. *Language and Cognitive Processes*, 11, 495–523.

McNeil, M. & Doyle, P. J. (2000). Reconsidering the hegemony of linguistic explanations in aphasia: The challenge for the beginning of the millenium. *Brain and Language*, 71, 154–6.

McPherson, W. B. & Holcomb, P. J. (1999). An electrophysiological investigation of semantic priming with pictures of real objects. *Psychophysiology*, 36, 53–65.

Mesulam, M. (1990). Large-scale neurocognitive networks and distributed processing for attention, language, and memory. *Annals of Neurology*, 28, 597–613.

Miceli, G., Mazzuchi, A., Menn, L., & Goodglass, H. (1983). Contrasting cases of Italian agrammatic aphasia without comprehension disorder. *Brain and Language*, 19, 65–97.

Michel, C. M., Murray, M. M., Lantz, G., Gonzalez, S., Spinelli, L., & Peralt, R. (2004). EEG source imaging. *Clinical Neurphysiology*, 115, 2195–2222.

Miller, E. K., & Cohen, J. D. (2001). An integrative theory of prefrontal cortex function. *Annual Review of Neuroscience*, 24, 167–202.

Mohr, J. P., Pessin, M. S., Finkelstein, S., Funkenstein, H., Duncan, G. W., & Davis, K. R. (1978). Broca aphasia: Pathologic and clinical. *Neurology*, 28, 311–24.

Moro, A., Tettamanti, M., Perani, D., Donati, C., Cappa, S. F., & Faxio, F. (2001). Syntax and the brain: Disentangling grammar by selective anomalies. *NeuroImage*, 13, 110–18.

Muente, T. F., Heinze, H. J., Matzke, M., Wieringa, B. M., & Johannes, S. (1998). Brain potentials and syntactic violations revisited: No evidence for specificity of the syntactic positice shift. *Neuropsychologia*, 36, 217–26.

Mukamel, R., Gelbard, H., Arieli, A., Hasson, U., Fried, I., & Malach, R. (2005). Coupling between neuronal firing, field potentials, and fMRI in human auditory cortex. *Science*, 309, 951–4.

Nadeau, S. E. & Crosson, B. (1995). Subcortical aphasia. *Brain and Language*, 58, 355–402.

Neville, H. J., Nicol, J. L., Barss, A., Forster, K. I., & Garret, M. (1991). Syntactically based sentence processing classes: Evidence from event-related brain potentials. *Journal of Cognitive Neuroscience*, 3, 151–65.

Newman, A. J., Pancheva, R., Ozawa, K., Neville, H. J., & Ullman, M. T. (2001). An event-related fMRI study of syntactic and semantic violations. *Journal of Psycholinguistic Research*, 30, 339–64.

Ni, W., Constable, R. T., Mencl, W. E., Pugh, K. R., Fullbright, R. K., Schaywitz, B. A., & Gore, J. (2000). An event-related neuroimaging study distinguishing form and content in sentence processing. *Journal of Cognitive Neuroscience*, 12, 120–33.

Osterhout, L. (1997). On the brain response to syntactic anomalies: Manipulations of word position and word class reveal individual differences. *Brain and Language*, 59, 494–522.

(2000). On space, time and language: For the next century, timing is (almost) everything. *Brain and Language*, 71, 175–7.

(1999). A superficial resemblance does not necessarily mean you are part of the family: Counterarguments to Coulson, King, and Kutas (1998) in the P600/SPS-P300 debate. *Language and Cognitive Processes*, 14, 1–14.

Osterhout, L. & Holcomb, P. J. (1992). Event-related brain potentials elicited by syntactic anomaly. *Journal of Memory and Language*, 31, 785–806.

(1993). Event-related potentials and syntactic anomaly: Evidence of anomaly detection during the perception of continuous speech. *Language and Cognitive Processes*, 8, 413–38.

Osterhout, L., McKinnon, R., Bersick, M., & Corey, V. (1996). On the language-specificity of the brain response to syntactic anomalies: Is the syntactic positive shift a member of the P300 family? *Journal of Cognitive Neuroscience*, 8, 507–26.

Osterhout, L., McLaughlin, J., Allen, M., & Inoue, K. (2002). Brain potentials elicited by prose-embedded linguistic anomalies. *Memory and Cognition*, 30, 1304–12.

Osterhout, L., McLaughlin, J., & Bersick, M. (1997). Event-related brain potentials and human language. *Trends in Cognitive Sciences*, 1, 203–9.

Osterhout, L., McLaughlin, J., Kim, A., Greenwald, R., & Inoue, K. (2004). Sentences in the brain: Event-related potentials as real-time reflections of sentence comprehension and language learning. In Carreiras, M. & Clifton, C. Jr. (Eds.) *The on-line study of sentence comprehension: Eyetracking, ERP, and beyond*. Psychology Press.

Osterhout, L. & Mobley, L. A. (1995). Event-related brain potentials elicited by failure to agree. *Journal of Memory and Language*, 34, 739–73.

Osterhout, L. & Nicol, J. (1999). On the distinctiveness, independence, and time course of the brain responses to syntactic and semantic anomalies. *Language and Cognitive Processes*, 14, 283–317.

Pascual-Marqui, R. D., Michel, C. M., & Lehmann, D. (1994). Low resolution electromagnetic tomography: A new method for localizing electrical activity in the brain. *International Journal of Psychophysiology*, 18, 49–65.

Patel, A. (2003). Language, music, syntax and the brain. *Nature Reviews Neuroscience*, 6, 674–9.

Patel, A., Gibson, E., Ratner Besson, M., & Holcomb, P. J. (1998). Processing syntactic relations in language and music: An ERP study. *Journal of Cognitive Neuroscience*, 10, 717–33.

Paulesu, E., Firth, C. D., and Frackowiak, RSJ (1993). The neural correlates of the verbal component of working memory. *Nature*, 362, 342–5.

Paulesu, E., Goldacre, B., Scifo, P., Cappa, S. F., Gilardi, M. C., Castiglioni, I., Perani, D., &

Fazio, F. (1997). Functional heterogeneity of left inferior frontal cortex as revealed by fMRI. *NeuroReport*, 8, 2011–17.

Penny, W. D., Stephan, K. E., Mechelli, A., & Friston, K. J. (2004). Modelling functional integration: A comparison of structural equation and dynamic causal models. *NeuroImage*, 23, Suppl 1, S264–274.

Petersson, K. M., Nichols, T. E., Poline, J. B., & Holmes, A. P. (1999). Statistical limitations in functional neuroimaging. I. Non-inferential methods and statistical models. *Philosophical Transactions of the Royal Society of London B Biological Science*, 354, 1239–60.

Poldrack, R. A., Sabb, F. W., Foerde, K., Tom, S. M., Asarnow, R. F., Bookheimer, S. Y., & Knowlton, B. J. (2005). The neural correlates of motor skill automaticity. *The Journal of Neuroscience*, 25, 5356–64.

Poldrack, R. A., Wagner, A. D., Prull, M. W., Desmond, J. E., Glover, G. H., & Gabrieli, J. D. (1999). Functional specialization for semantic and phonological processing in the left inferior prefrontal cortex. *NeuroImage*, 10, 15–35.

Price, C. J. (2000). The anatomy of language: Contributions from functional neuroimaging. *Journal of Anatomy*, 197, 335–59.

Price, C. J. & Friston, K. J. (1997). Cognitive conjunction: A new approach to brain activation experiments. *NeuroImage*, 5, 261–70.

Price, C., Mummery, C. J., Moore, C. J., Frakowiak, RSJ, & Friston, K. J. (1999). Delineating necessary and sufficient neural systems with functional imaging studies of neuropsychological patients. *Journal of Cognitive Neuroscience*, 11, 371–82.

Price, C., Thierry, G., & Griffiths, T. (2005). Speech-specific auditory processing: Where is it? *Trends in Cognitive Sciences*, 9, 271–6.

Röder, B., Stock, O., Neville, H. J., Bien, S., & Rösler, F. (2002). Brain activation modulated by the comprehension of normal and pseudo-word sentences of different processing demands: a functional magnetic resonance imaging study. *NeuroImage*, 15, 1003–14.

Saffran, E. (2006). Aphasia II: Cognitive Issues. In Farah, M. J. & Feinberg, T. (Eds.) *Patient-based approaches to cognitive neuroscience* (2nd edition). Cambridge, MA: MIT Press.

Schwartz, M., Saffran, E. M., & Fink, R. B. (1994). Mapping therapy: A treatment program for agrammatism. *Aphasiology*, 8, 19–54.

Shallice, T. (1979). Case-study approach in neuropsychological research. *Journal of Clinical Neuropsychology*, 1, 183–211.

(1988). *From neuropsychology to mental structure*. Cambridge, UK: Cambridge University Press.

Shepherd, G. (1994). *Neurobiology*. Oxford: Oxford University Press.

Simos, P. G., Basile, L. F., & Papanicolaou, A. C. (1997). Source localization of the N400 response in a sentence-reading paradigm using evoked magnetic fields and magnetic resonance imaging. *Brain Research*, 762, 29–39.

Sitnikova, T., Kuperberg, G. R., & Holcomb, P. (2003). Semantic integration in videos of real-world events: An electrophysiological investigation. *Psychophysiology*, 40, 160–4.

Slotnick, S. (2005). Source localization of ERP generators. In Handy, T. C. (Ed.) *Event-related potentials: A methods handbook*. Cambridge, MA: MIT Press.

Smith, E. E., & Jonides, J. (1998). Neuroimaging analyses of human working memory. *Proceedings of the National Academy of Sciences*, 95, 12061–68.

Stowe, L. A., Broere, CAJ, Paans, AMJ, Wijers, A. A., Mulder, G., Vaalburg, W., & Zwarts, F. (1998). Localizing cognitive components of a complex task: sentence processing and working memory. *NeuroReport*, 9, 2995–9.

Stowe, L. A., Haverkort, M., & Zwarts, F. (2005). Rethinking the neurological basis of language. *Lingua*, 115, 997–1042.

Stowe, L. A., Paans, AMJ, Wijers, A. A., Zwarts, F., Wijers, A. A., Mulder, G., & Vaalburg, W. (1999). Sentence comprehension and word repetition: a positron emission tomography investigation. *Psychophysiology*, 36, 786–801.

Stromswold, K., Caplan, D., Albert, N., & Rauch, S. (1996). Localization of syntactic comprehension by positron emission tomography. *Brain and Language*, 52, 452–73.

Swaab, T., Brown, C., & Hagoort, P. (1997). Spoken sentence comprehension in aphasia: Event-related potential evidence for a lexical integration deficit. *Journal of Cognitive Neuroscience*, 9, 39–66.

Teramitsu, I., Kudo, L. C., London, S. E., Geschwind, D., & White, S. A. (2004). Parallel *FOXP1* and *FOXP2* expression in songbirds and human brain predicts functional interaction. *Journal of Neuroscience*, 24, 3152–63.

Thompson-Schill, S. L. (2002). Neuroimaging sstudies of semantic memory: inferring "how" from "where." *Neuropsychologia*, 41, 280–92.

Thompson-Schill, S. L., D'Esposito, M., Aguirre, G. K., & Farah, M. J. (1997). Role of left inferior prefrontal cortex in retrieval of semantic knowledge: A reevaluation. *Proceedings of the National Academy of Sciences*, 94, 14792–7.

Tramo, M. J., Baynes, K., & Volpe, B. T. (1988). Impaired syntactic comprehension and production in broca's aphasia: Ct lesion localization and recovery patterns. *Neurology*, 95–8.

Trueswell, J. C., Tanenhaus, M. K., & Garnsey, S. M. (1994). Semantic influences on parsing: Use of thematic role information in syntactic ambiguity resolution. *Journal of Memory and Language*, 33, 285–318.

Tyler, L. K., Bright, P., Dick, E., Tavares, L., Pilgrim, L., Fletcher, P., Greer, M., & Moss, H. (2003). Do semantic categories activate distinct cortical regions? Evidence for a distributed neural semantic system. *Cognitive Neuropsychology*, 20, 541–59.

Ullman, M. T. (2001). A neurocognitive perspective on language: The declarative/procedural model. *Nature Reviews Neuroscience*, 2, 717–26.

Ullman, M. T., Corkin, S., Coppola, M., Hickok, G., Growdon, J. H., Koroshetz, W. J., et al. (1997). A neural dissociation within language: Evidence that the mental dictionary is part of declarative memory, and that grammatical rules are processed by the procedural system. *Journal of Cognitive Neuroscience*, 9, 266–76.

Ungerleider, L. G. & Haxby, J. V. (1994). "What" and "where" in the human brain. *Current Opinion in Neurobiology*, 4, 157–65.

Van de Meerendonk, N., Indefrey, P., Chwilla, D.J., & Kolk, HHJ (2011). Monitoring in language perception: Electrophysiological and hemodynamic responses to spelling violations. *NeuroImage*, 54, 2350–63.

Vanier, M. & Caplan, D. (1990). Ct-scan correlates of agrammatism. In Menn, L. & Obler, L. K. (Eds.) *Agrammatic aphasia* (pp. 97–114). Amsterdam: Benjamins.

Van Petten, C. & Luka, B. J. (2006). Neural localization of semantic context effects in electromagnetic and hemodynamic studies. *Brain and Language*, 97, 279–93

Vargha-Khadem, F., Gadian, D., Copp, A., & Mishkin, M. (2005). FOXP2 and the neuroanatomy of speech and language. *Nature Reviews Neuroscience*, 6, 131–8.

Vigneau, M., Beaucousin, V., Hervé, P. Y., Duffau, H., Crivello, F., Houdé, O., Mazoyer, B., & Tzourio-Mazoyer, N. (2006). Meta-analyzing left hemisphere language areas: Phonology, semantics, and sentence processing. *NeuroImage*, 30:1414–32

Wagner, A. D., Pare-Blagoev, E. J., Clark, J., & Poldrack, R. A. (2001). Recovering meaning:

Left prefrontal cortex guides controlled semantic retrieval. *Neuron, 31,* 329–38.

Wallesch, C. W. & Papagno, C. (1988). Subcortical aphasia. In Rose F. C., Whurr, R., & Wyke, M. (Eds.), *Aphasia.* London: Whurr Publishers.

Walsh, V. & Cowey, A. (2000). Transcranial magnetic stimulation and cognitive neuroscience. *Nature reviews: Neuroscience, 1,* 73–80.

Weckerly, J. & Kutas, M. (1999). An electro-physiological analysis of animacy effects in the processing of object relative sentences. *Psychophysiology, 36,* 559–70.

West, W. C. & Holcomb, P. J. (2002). Event-related potentials during discourse-level semantic integration of complex pictures. *Brain Research: Cognitive Brain Research, 13,* 363–75.

CHAPTER 19

Computational and Corpus Models of Human Sentence Comprehension

Douglas Roland and Mary Hare

1 Introduction

Computational and corpus-based modeling plays an increasingly important role in the study of human sentence comprehension. There are at least two reasons for this. As probabilistic accounts of language comprehension have become increasingly dominant, there has been a corresponding interest in explicit models of the assumed processes. The modeling effort has also been aided by the rapid increases in the size and variety of available corpora, and in the increasing availability of tools to manipulate the resulting corpus data.

Building a complete model of human sentence comprehension is a very complex task. Research has shown that understanding even a simple sentence involves the integration of a large number of possible sources of information, ranging from knowledge of the meaning of different words, and the frequency with which they have been encountered, to the comprehender's awareness of objects present in the environment. A complete model of this process would include the appropriate knowledge and

use; it would arrive at the same interpretations as a human, with similar reading times and errors. Ideally, this model would verify researchers' hypotheses about the types of information used during language comprehension, the time course over which information becomes available, and how reliable that information is.

In reality, there are no models of the entire comprehension process, and current representations are much less rich than those used by human comprehenders. Despite this, computational models have yielded a wide variety of valuable results. These will be discussed throughout this chapter; here we simply highlight two points: First, it has become apparent that fairly simple models, relying on only a subset of the information known to matter to comprehension, can account for a large share of the experimental data. This representational simplicity makes the models tractable, but in the end makes them difficult to judge: When a model fails to capture the full range of data, it is often impossible to determine whether this is because it adopts the wrong architectural or computational approach, or simply because it does not incorporate the necessary information.

The second, and related, point is that in the current state of modeling, models with apparently very different architectures appear to account for the same psycholinguistic data. In some cases this indicates that their architectures, although very different on the surface, still capture the same underlying process. In other cases, however, different architectures do make the same predictions, for different reasons. Finally, there are cases where different models fail to capture different subsets of apparently unified data, as we will discuss later in this chapter.

In the remainder of this chapter we provide an overview of several current computational models of sentence processing, considering the phenomena they cover, the information they use, the manner in which they combine different sources of information, and claims each makes about the causes of processing difficulty/reading time delays in the experimental data. We restrict our coverage to the class of models which use, in one form or another, corpus data as a means of representing the effects of how long-term exposure to language influences the processing of that language. While we believe that language processing is influenced by both long-term exposure to language and memory limitations, we will not be discussing models of short term memory of such as Gibson (1998; 2000) and Lewis and Vasishth (2006).

2 Corpus data as a model of language

2.1 Background

Many computational models rely on corpus data to determine the statistical probabilities that account for processing difficulty. This presupposes, of course, that the relevant probabilities exist. However, different corpora can yield very different probabilities for the same structures (see, for example, Merlo, 1994; Roland and Jurafsky, 1998, 2002; Roland et al., 2000). On the face of it this appears to negate the corpus approach, because if statistics compiled in one genre differ significantly from those in another, it would be impossible to determine which are most appropriate for modeling human behavior. Recent evidence, however, suggests that this is less of a concern: Language is highly constrained by the context in which it is used, and the contexts in which a particular structure is appropriate occur with different frequencies across genres. Thus the question is not which genre or corpus provides the best estimate of language use, but which interpretation is most likely in a given context.

Corpus-based modeling complements the experimental study of sentence comprehension for a number of reasons. For one, it allows researchers to look at more complex interactions of factors than would be feasible to include in an experiment. For another, by studying naturally occurring language samples we can determine, to some extent, the ecological validity of experimental results. That is, while experimental work allows us to demonstrate that a particular factor can influence comprehension, it does not tell us how often that factor would be useful in the daily life of the comprehender. Corpus data, on the other hand, can potentially show that.

It has also been pointed out that low-frequency structures are difficult to process. One explanation has been that the difficulty is due to inherent structural complexity, which in turn leads to the low frequency. However, as discussed later in this chapter, discourse or contextual explanations for low frequency can be found as well, and thus reduce the need to appeal to explanations based on structural complexity alone.

Finally, a better understanding of the full wealth of probabilistic information available during comprehension will help us understand the true point at which an ambiguous utterance is disambiguated (or at least can potentially be disambiguated) by the comprehender. Results such as those in Roland, Elman, and Ferreira (2006), described later, suggest that such early disambiguating information is available.

2.2 Specific models

A variety of work has been done in recent years using corpus data to look at how multiple factors combine to govern the use of various linguistic structures. Below we summarize a number of recent models, all of which suggest that language is highly constrained by the context in which it is used, and that a correspondingly rich set of information is available to guide the comprehension process.

Jaeger and colleagues (Jaeger, 2005, 2006; Wasow, Jaeger, and Orr, 2005) examine the use of the relativizer *that* in object relative clauses (*the book I bought* versus *the book that I bought*). Using data from the Switchboard corpus, they demonstrate that the presence/absence of the complementizer is predictable from a complex set of contextual factors ranging from discourse-level factors to phonological factors.

Bresnan et al. (2005) model the dative alternation in English (*gave the book to Bill* versus *gave Bill the book*). The model includes 2,360 examples from the Switchboard corpus (Godfrey, Holliman, and McDaniel, 1992) and additional data from the Penn Treebank version of the Wall Street Journal Corpus. The authors find that the alternation is highly predictable – relying only on contextual evidence, the model predicts the correct alternative ninety-four percent of the time. Additionally, the model performs well on both Switchboard and Wall Street Journal data (based on the same factors), despite the differences in the distribution of the alternation between the corpora.

Roland et al. (2006) look at the direct object/sentential complement ambiguity (*the athlete realized* [*her goals*]_{Direct Object} versus *the athlete realized* [*her goals would be difficult to achieve*]_{Sentential Complement}) and the presence/absence of the complementizer *that* in sentential complements. The authors labeled approximately two hundred and fifty thousand examples from the British National Corpus for a variety of relatively simple factors such as length, frequency, and automatically generated semantic properties.

These were used as predictors in a regression model that predicted whether the sentence would continue as a DO or SC structure. The model was able to correctly predict the DO/SC ambiguity resolution for 86.4 percent of the examples, given information available at a point before which the examples were structurally disambiguated. In addition, a similar model correctly predicted the presence/absence of the complementizer *that* in sentential complements 78.2 percent of the time. It is likely that humans, who are presumably sensitive to much richer information than the model had available, would be even more successful at these tasks.

Gries (2001) investigates the verb–particle word order alternation in English (*pick up the book* versus *pick the book up*). His analysis relies on 403 examples from the British National Corpus (Burnard, 1995), and finds that more than eighty-four percent of the examples can be predicted based on a variety of factors ranging from the length of the direct object to degree of idiomaticity of the verb phrase.

Models such as these demonstrate that contextual factors clearly govern the use and distribution of a wide variety of structures. However, these models do not make direct predictions about processing difficulty during comprehension or reading times in experiments. In the next section, we will discuss models that do make such predictions.

3 Modeling reading time results

3.1 Background

Many of the models of sentence comprehension rely on probabilistic context free grammars (PCFGs) to derive at least part of the information used. These are simply context free grammars with a probability associated with each rule. One question that arises immediately is where the rules and associated probabilities come from. For the purposes of computational modeling, one commonly used source of this information for English is the Penn Treebank

(Marcus et al., 1994; Marcus, Santorini, and Marcinkiewicz, 1993) parsed version of the Brown Corpus (Francis and Kučera, 1982; Kučera and Francis, 1967). The Penn Treebank corpora have the advantage of hand-corrected parse structures, but also have two potential downsides – one relating to the sample size and the other to the limitations of current corpus data. The approximately one million words Brown Corpus provides give good frequency estimates for individual words and for common structures, but the sample size is not large enough to generate good estimates of lexical item-specific structural frequencies. For example, of the 100 verbs used in the Garnsey, et al. (1997) study of the effects of subcategorization bias in structural ambiguity resolution, sixty-three verbs occurred fewer than 100 times in the Brown Corpus. As a result, many of the verbs occurred rarely, if at all, in most of their possible subcategorizations, leading to uncertainty about the actual distribution of their possible uses.

One alternative is to use larger corpora, such as the 100-million-word British National Corpus (Burnard, 1995). But these have their own drawbacks. First, they must be used in conjunction with an automatic parser (e.g., Charniak, 1995, 1997; Collins, 1997), and the results will be less accurate than the hand-corrected Treebank data. Roland, Dick, and Elman (2007) provide estimated accuracy rates ranging from as high as ninety-seven percent to lower than sixty-seven percent, depending upon the target structure and the corpus being parsed. Second, even if the accuracy problem were resolved, limits would remain on the information available from parsed corpora. Although large corpora are an excellent source of lexical and structural probabilities, other data, such as animacy, semantic roles, or the thematic fit of an argument to a verb, must be coded by hand. Ongoing projects like Framenet (Baker, Fillmore, and Lowe, 1998) or Propbank (Palmer, Kingsbury, and Gildea, 2005) have begun to provide some of this information, so these limits might be less strict in the future.

3.2 Using probabilistic context free grammars to predict parsing decisions and garden path difficulties

Much of the experimental literature in sentence processing over the past ten years has focused on ambiguity resolution. As a result, a number of computational models do the same, looking in particular at the verb/reduced relative ambiguity found in sentences such as example (1), from Bever (1970).

(1) The horse raced past the barn fell.

In this sentence, *raced* is initially interpreted as the verb of the main clause *The horse raced past the barn*. The comprehender then faces substantial difficulty at the word *fell*, and must reanalyze *raced past the barn* as a reduced relative clause.

Jurafsky (1996) uses probabilistic context free grammars to model this so-called garden-path effect, as well as a number of other psycholinguistic phenomenon. The model uses a Bayesian (or evidential) access algorithm, which predicts how likely a structure is given the context to that point. As actually implemented, the model relies on two sources of contextual information – overall structural probabilities from a probabilistic context free grammar, and verb valence probabilities, or structural probabilities given a specific verb. Both are based on data from the Penn Treebank.

The Bayesian aspect of the model accounts for how parsing decisions are made, but does not directly predict which structures would result in comprehension difficulties or garden-path effects. These predictions come from a second component of the model, a beam search, which is used to determine the correct interpretation: As each new piece of information is encountered, new predictions are made, and only the most likely are maintained. Less likely predictions are dropped from consideration, leading to difficulty if they turn out to be correct. For example, in the grammar used by Jurafsky, there is a twelve to one bias toward the main verb over the reduced relative reading of *the horse raced*. Hence this reading does not meet the criteria for likely predictions, and is dropped from consideration, leading to an eventual garden-path effect.

The same aspect of the model also allows it to explain why some reduced relative sentences are easier to comprehend. In an example like *The bird found in the room died*, the probability difference between the main verb and reduced relative interpretation of *the bird found* is relatively small, and so the reduced relative parse is not dropped. That interpretation is still available to the model at the point where *died* is encountered, and the model correctly predicts that the sentence will not lead to a severe garden path. Thus the model's predictions match the human data in both cases.

There are other cases, however, that this model is unable to handle. One factor known to mitigate the difficulty of reduced relative clauses is the thematic fit between the subject noun phrase and the subsequent verb (McRae, Spivey-Knowlton, and Tanenhaus, 1998; Rayner, Carlson, and Frazier, 1983). Because the initial verb must be interpreted as a passive, sentences like (2) below, in which the initial noun phrase is a good agent of the initial verb, result in more disambiguation difficulty than those like (3), in which the initial noun is a good patient of that verb.

(2) The cop arrested by the detective was guilty of taking bribes.
(3) The crook arrested by the detective was guilty of taking bribes.

Because the Jurafsky model lacks information about thematic roles, it is not able to capture this difference, but models that combine structural probabilities with information from other sources are able to do so. The first to successfully address these data was the competition-integration model of Spivey and Tanenhaus (1998) and McRae et al. (1998). This model simulates the time course of sentence processing by adding information in steps corresponding to the information gained at each word or region in a reading time experiment. In the model, shown in Figure 19.1, alternative syntactic structures are represented by interpretation nodes, whose activity levels indicate the strength of the corresponding interpretation. Interpretations compete for activation in the following way: As a word is encountered, nodes representing relevant information (or constraints) feed activation to one interpretation or the other. The interpretation nodes then feed activation back to these input nodes, strengthening those associated with the most active interpretation. At this point a new cycle of competition begins, and the process continues until one interpretation reaches criterion. At this point the competition ends and the model moves on to process the next word. The model's reading time prediction is based on the number of cycles it takes for the activation of one of the two interpretations to reach that criterion. Because competition is resolved quickly when all the evidence favors one alternative, the model predicts reading times will be shorter compared to cases in which the evidence is conflicting.

McRae et al. tested the model's performance on temporarily ambiguous sentences like (2) and (3) shown previously. In this implementation of the model, a number of constraints were either structural or based on the probability of specific verbs occurring in particular tense–aspect combinations. Probabilities on these biases were derived from corpus data. In addition, thematic fit probabilities, used to determine the goodness of agents or patients for specific verbs, were determined through norms with human subjects.

The model closely mimicked the self-paced reading data with these sentences, with more competition with good patient than good agent sentences at the verb *(arrested by)* but subsequently more competition for the good agent sentences at the disambiguation and beyond. The same model, with slightly different constraints, was subsequently used to model the effects of semantic context and verb sense on the

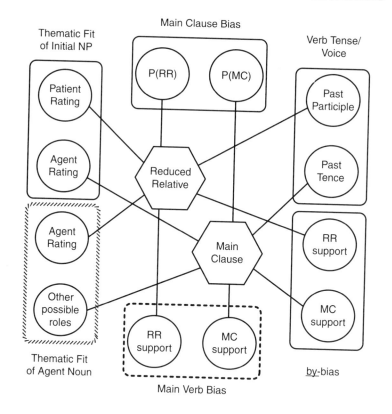

Figure 19.1. Diagram of the competition-integration model showing which information is added to at each stage while processing *The cop/crook arrested by the detective was guilty*. Reprinted from McRae, K., Spivey-Knowlton, M. J., and Tanenhaus, M. K. (1998), with permission from Elsevier.

resolution of the Direct Object/Sentential Complement ambiguity (Elman, Hare, and McRae, 2004).

Green and Mitchell (2006) ran a careful exploration of the dynamics of the competition-integration model, and found that contrary to earlier expectations (e.g., Traxler, Pickering, and Clifton, 1998; van Gompel, et al., 2005), competition takes longest to resolve when new evidence conflicts with the interpretation at the previous state. Thus the heaviest processing load occurs when the model must switch from one interpretation to another. They further noted that the ability to incorporate such bias reversals appears to be required for a model to account for the so-called ambiguity advantage, or cases in which reading times for ambiguous materials are faster than for those that have been disambiguated (Traxler et al., 1998; van Gompel et al., 2005).

A number of other models, among them Narayanan and Jurafsky (2002; 2005), Hale (2001), and Levy (2008) share this property, despite having different architectures or processing mechanisms. Here, and in the

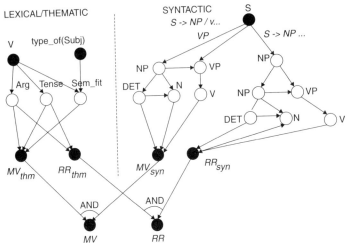

Figure 19.2. Bayesian belief network for Main Verb/Reduced
Relative ambiguity resolution combining semantic and syntactic
information (Figure 5 from Narayanan & Jurafsky, 1998).

next section, we will describe their different
approaches to the issue.

Narayanan and Jurafsky (1998; 2002; 2005)
progressively extend the Bayesian model of
Jurafsky in a series of more complex models that include both semantic and corpus-
based structural information. In particular,
these models include information on thematic fit, and therefore can also capture
the *cop/crook arrested...* contrast addressed
by McRae et al. In Narayanan and Jurafsky
(1998; 2002), the models predict the main
verb/reduced relative preference of the comprehender at each point during the comprehension process by combining syntactic and
lexical/thematic information as illustrated
in Figure 19.2. While Green and Mitchell
show that the McRae et al. model predicts
the most difficulty when the prediction bias
reverses, the Narayanan and Jurafsky (2002)
model gives such changes in bias a special
status by assigning an extra processing cost
to these, which are referred to as "flips."
Thus, the model not only predicts difficulty
whenever there is a large change in expectation, but provides a special penalty when
the change results in a reversal in bias.

However, neither of these instantiations
of the model predicts explicit word-by-word
reading times. This is added in Narayanan
and Jurafsky (2005), which eliminates the

beam search mechanism as an explanation for garden-path effects, and replaces it
with the more general notion of *surprisal.*
Surprisal, which will be discussed in more
detail in the next section, is a measure of the
information conveyed by a word. Following
Hale (2001), Narayanan and Jurafsky take
the surprisal of a word as a measure of its
reading time. Their model also carries over
the notion of flips from Narayanan and
Jurafsky (2002). Reading time predictions
improve when such interpretation reversals
are taken into account. This model, when
tested on the McRae et al. (1998) experimental data, achieves as good a fit as that
of the competition-integration model (see
Figure 19.3).

3.3 *Using probabilistic context free grammars to predict word reading times*

3.3.1 SURPRISAL
Many current models of sentence processing rely on the intuition that the more predictable or expected a word or phrase is in a
given context, the easier it is to process, and
the faster it is read. At one extreme, a word
or phrase that is completely predictable
from the context should require the minimal amount of processing effort, because
any information that it might provide is

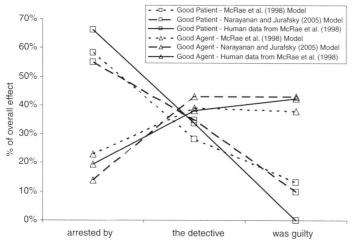

Figure 19.3. Results from McRae et al. and Narayanan and Jurafsky, mapped to the same unit of measure.

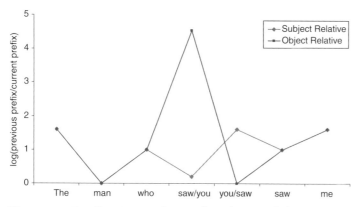

Figure 19.4. Reading time predictions for subject and object relative clauses (data from Figures 7 and 8 in J. Hale, 2001).

already known. At the other extreme, a word or phrase that is entirely unexpected would require more processing effort and time to read – possibly resulting in a severe garden-path effect. While this intuition forms the basis of much research in sentence processing, it has proven difficult to formalize. In the models described here, the difficulty in processing a word or phrase is taken to be proportional to that word's negative log-probability, given the context in which it appears. This is also known as the word's *surprisal*. As Levy (2008) points out, surprisal predictions are independent of the representational formalism used to make the predictions: Models based on different

grammatical formalisms would be equivalent as long as they predicted the same probability distributions over the same strings of words. In this chapter, however, we will concentrate on models that rely at least in part on probabilistic context free grammars to estimate the relevant probabilities.

The first model to use a probabilistic context free grammar to directly predict reading times was Hale (2001). He demonstrates that reading time predictions based on a probabilistic context free grammar (generated from the Penn Treebank) predicted both difficulty on reduced relatives (e.g., *the horse raced past the barn fell*; see Figure 19.5) and on object relative clauses in comparison with subject relative clauses (see Figure 19.4). The difficulty faced at *fell* in Figure 19.5 is the result of the high degree of surprisal in discovering that the very probable main verb interpretation was incorrect, and that the much less probable reduced relative interpretation of the verb *raced* is correct. Similarly, the differences in reading time predictions in Figure 19.4 reflect the fact that the subject relative is more expected than the object relative clause.

Levy further shows that surprisal models can account for a variety of experimental results: reading times for German verb final constructions, the reading time advantage for ambiguous structures over equivalent nonambiguous structures (e.g., Traxler et al., 1998), and the subject preference in German *welches* questions. However, he also points out cases in which surprisal models make incorrect predictions. For example, while the models do predict an advantage for subject relative clauses over object relative clauses, the difficulty is predicted to occur earlier than it actually occurs in reading time experiments. Levy also suggests that surprisal models would have difficulty accounting for local coherence effects such as those found in Ferreira and Henderson (1991).

We note that the difficulties that surprisal models face in accounting for relative clause reading time data go beyond simply predicting the difficulties at the wrong place. However, the shortcomings may be a reflection of problems with the data used in the model, rather than a problem with the notion of surprisal per se. The grammars used by Hale (2001) and Levy (2008) predict that object relative clauses are always more difficult than subject relative clauses – and thus cannot account for a variety of factors that have been shown to affect the processing of relative clauses, including whether the modified noun is animate or inanimate (Traxler, Morris, and Seely, 2002; Traxler et al., 2005), whether the embedded NP is a full NP or pronominal (Reali and Christiansen, 2005; Warren and Gibson, 2002), whether the embedded NP is a proper noun (Gordon, Hendrick,

and Johnson, 2001), or the quantified pronoun *everyone* (Gordon et al., 2004). This does not necessarily reflect a shortcoming in surprisal, since corpus data (e.g., Fox and Thompson, 1990; Reali and Christiansen, 2007; Roland et al., 2007) shows that these factors are reflected in the corpus distributions of subject and object relative clauses, and thus would be reflected in a probabilistic model that took these factors into account. Nonetheless, because of the lack of a complete probabilistic model of all of the factors involved in relative clause processing, one cannot yet tell whether a surprisal-based model can account for the full set of experimental data.

3.3.2 ENTROPY REDUCTION

An alternative approach to calculating the processing effort associated with each word or phrase was subsequently employed by Hale (2003; 2004; 2006). Rather than base reading times on surprisal of each word, these more recent papers by Hale rely on the intuition that over the course of processing a sentence, the parser moves from a state of comparative uncertainty to one of relative certainty. That is, before the first word is processed, any sentence in the language is possible. But by the end of the sentence the correct parse is known – or, even if the sentence is ambiguous, only a limited number of options remain. Hale's Entropy Reduction Hypothesis posits that the change in the conditional entropy (see *Equation 1*) of the complete analysis of the sentence as the parser goes from a state of uncertainty (entropy is high) to a state of certainty (entropy is low) is the best measure of the amount of work done by the processor (see *Equation 2*). *Equation 1* shows that the entropy (uncertainty) of a state is the (negative) sum of probabilities of each possible outcome $p(x)$ multiplied by the logarithm (base 2) of the probability $\log_2 p(x)$. Thus the reduction in entropy is simply the difference in entropy between the current state and the previous state, with the proviso that the reduction is zero (rather than a negative number) when entropy actually increases instead of decreasing.

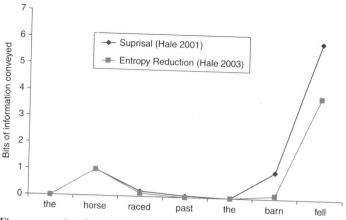

Figure 19.5. Reading time predictions based on Surprisal (data taken from Figure 3 in J. Hale, 2001) and Entropy Reduction (data taken from Figure 11 in J. Hale, 2003).

$$H(X) = -\sum_{x \in X} p(x) \log_2 p(x)$$

Equation 1: Calculating the entropy of a distribution of probabilities.

$$ER(w_i) = \max(0, H_{i-1} - H_i)$$

Equation 2: Entropy reduction at word i.

While the entropy reduction model and the surprisal model can make quite different predictions, in many cases their predictions are very similar. One such case involves the main verb/reduced relative ambiguity. Figure 19.5 shows the nearly identical surprisal and entropy reduction predictions for the main verb/reduced relative ambiguity, taken from Hale (2001) and Hale (2003).

Like the surprisal model, the entropy reduction model can also capture the difference between subject and object relative clauses. Furthermore, as Figure 19.6 shows, processing difficulty is found at a later region than predicted by the surprisal model – thus better matching the human reading time results. The entropy reduction model can also model human subject difficulty with center embedding, without resorting to an explicit appeal to memory limitations. Finally, because the model is sensitive to the details of each grammar, and not just the string probabilities, Hale (2004; 2006) was able to use the relationship

between the model's predictions and human reading time results to distinguish between different possible structural analyses for the same string.

Like the surprisal model, the entropy reduction model is faced with difficulties in accounting for the full range of data on relative clause comprehension. The grammar used to make the successful predictions shown in Figure 19.6 also generates relative clauses where the embedded NP is either pronominal or a proper noun – both situations that have been shown to reduce the difficulties faced in processing object relatives. In this situation (illustrated in Figure 19.7), subject relatives are slightly more difficult than object relatives – which is not inconsistent with the human reading time results (e.g., Reali and Christiansen, 2007) and (Gordon et al., 2001). However, for both object and subject relatives, the full NP is predicted to be easier to process than the pronominal or proper noun. This prediction is counter to the actual experimental results, and is a direct result of a property of the entropy reduction model. NPs which can still be recursively expanded (which is the case for any nonpronominal, nonproper noun NP in the grammar by the model, up until the point where a word that cannot be part of a recursive expansion of the NP is processed) have a large degree of uncertainty associated with them, and thus tend

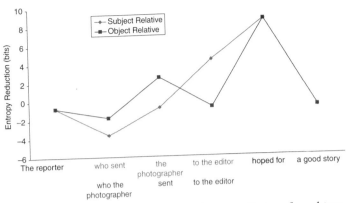

Figure 19.6. Entropy Reduction Hypothesis predictions for subject and object relative clauses, based on the grammar provided in Hale (2003). The Entropy Reduction Hypothesis, as presented in Hale (2006) and as represented by Equation 2 does not allow negative values for entropy reduction. Our graphs represent these values as negative rather than as zeros for comparison with Figure 14 and 15 from Hale (2003).

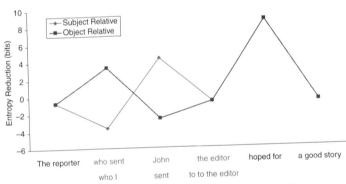

Figure 19.7. Entropy Reduction Hypothesis predictions for pronominal/proper noun subject and object relative clauses, based on the grammar provided in Hale (2003).

to not be associated with large drops in uncertainty. Alternatively, *I* and *John* cannot be expanded according to the grammar, and thus always result in the reduction of all uncertainty originally associated with the NP. Additionally, because the entropy reduction hypothesis is only concerned with the net change in entropy with each new word or phrase, a situation in which the parser eliminates a large number of possibilities but opens up a similar number of new possibilities shows the same lack of change in entropy (and associated lack of processing

difficulty) as a situation in which nothing changes at all. Thus although entropy reduction is a promising approach, there are issues that remain to be resolved.

3.4 *Connectionist approaches*

In the final section we will review a number of sentence comprehension models that use connectionist architectures. The McRae et al. (1998) model described earlier was one, although this model did not involve learning to approximate experimental results, as more recent models often do. As one example, MacDonald and Christiansen (2002) use a measure based on learning error in a simple recurrent network (SRN) (Elman, 1990) to predict reading times for subject and object relative clauses. Their network successfully captured the interaction between reading span and relative clause type found in the human subject data (King and Just, 1991). Rohde (2002), using a more complex architecture, also made a number of interesting predictions about the processing of an artificial language with properties of English grammar. In this model, reading time predictions were also related to network prediction error, although here the reading time measure also considered the change in the internal representation at the current word.

Tabor and colleagues (Tabor, Juliano, and Tanenhaus, 1997; Tabor and Tanenhaus, 2001) suggested a dynamical systems account to relate network prediction error to reading times. Their Visitation Set Gravitation model had two components. The first was an SRN whose task was to learn to predict the next word in a sentence. As Elman (1990; 1991) had shown, this task leads the network to develop internal representations that capture key elements of linguistic structure. In the gravitation model, these representations developed over the course of learning into attractor basins representing distinct parse states.

These internal representations were then used in a second processor, which operated by analogy to gravitational systems. In this module, each learned hidden-unit vector exerted a gravitational influence in the multidimensional representational space. Sentences with similar grammatical structures formed attractors in this space, as noted earlier, while those with different structures developed into competing attractors. The predicted reading time of a word in a given context was then measured by treating its hidden unit representation as a point in attractor space, and counting the number of processing iterations required for that representation to gravitate to an attractor.

The model shows a good fit to the reading time data in the McRae et al. (1998) study on reduced relative disambiguation.

Furthermore, analysis of the model dynamics found that given the distributional properties of the training data, the gravitational system developed the same two-attractor account argued for in the earlier study.

Stevenson (1994) developed a hybrid symbolic/connectionist model in which the potential parses of an incoming sentence are represented in a connectionist network of interconnected nodes. These are of two types: *phrasal nodes*, corresponding to the X-bar category of the current word, and *attachment nodes*, which represent how the phrasal node is attached into the parse tree.

In this model, as a word is read the corresponding phrasal node is activated. For words such as *raced*, which are ambiguous as to their phrasal category, all potential phrasal nodes are activated in proportion to their relative frequencies. These new phrasal nodes establish potential attachments with all allowable attachment sites. Both attachment nodes and phrasal nodes then compete for activation. Attachment nodes accrue activation based on their relative frequency and their current activation levels – this is a "rich get richer" system, in which structural attachments with more initial activation have an advantage in the competition. At the lexical level, competition also determines which phrasal node will be activated when the input is ambiguous. Here the competition favors the candidate that best fits the current assessment of what the overall structure is.

Competition continues until a stable state is reached. At this point, the most highly activated phrasal and attachment nodes are taken to have won, and represent the current structural configuration. Note that it is possible to reanalyze such established attachments, but only along the right side of the tree. If the evidence shows that an earlier structural hypothesis was incorrect, it cannot be changed. Thus certain misanalyses lead to severe garden paths.

Stevenson and Merlo (1997) use this competitive attachment parser to account for the difficulty of reduced relatives with manner of motion verbs like *The horse raced past the barn fell*. In their account the transitive verb, as in *Willie Shoemaker raced Ferdinand to victory in the Kentucky Derby*, is a syntactic causative. This has a different phrasal structure than the lexical causative found with change of state verbs like *melt* in *The cook melted the butter in the pan* (cf. Hale and Keyser, 1993). As a result, the competitive parser is unable to activate the attachments required for the reduced relative interpretation of the *raced* example. Note that this interpretation does not simply lose the competition – it cannot be parsed.

This model captures the fact that reduced relative clauses with manner of motion verbs tend to be rare and more difficult, compared to those with verbs expressing a change of state. However, one weakness of the model is that the prediction of severe difficulty with *The horse raced past the barn fell* is not predicted just of that sentence. Instead, it must hold for all reduced relatives with manner of motion verbs. This is inconsistent with the fact that acceptable reduced relatives with manner of motion verbs are attested both experimentally and in corpora (Hare, Tanenhaus, and McRae, 2007; McKoon and Ratcliff, 2003).

A more recent model, which makes somewhat overlapping claims, is the self-organizing parser of Tabor and colleagues (Tabor, Galantucci, and Richardson, 2004; Tabor and Hutchins, 2004). This model involves a set of parse tree fragments, which in turn consist of sets of feature vectors specifying syntactic and semantic information. As in Stevenson's competitive parser, a tree fragment becomes activated when the corresponding word is encountered and, once active, attempts to attach to other tree fragments. The link between two fragments increases in activation based on goodness of fit, the fragments' own current activation, and the activation of the link itself, in a rich-get-richer feedback process.

This model presupposes a grammar rather than allowing structure to emerge from distributional properties of the data, as Tabor's earlier gravitational system did. However, attachments are local, rather than imposed top-down by the grammar. This leads the model to make rather novel predictions.

As one example, the self-organizing parser allows local parses to be computed even if they are unacceptable given the parse so far, suggesting that, for example, comprehenders might continue to have difficulty with reduced relatives even though context should rule out the main verb interpretation. Tabor et al. (2004) found experimental evidence for this claim. In a self-paced reading task, participants showed interference from the locally coherent string *the player tossed a Frisbee*, even though the main verb reading of this string was incompatible with its context, *The coach smiled at the player tossed a frisbee*. It remains to be shown whether other models might also account for such results.

4 Conclusion

While it may be widely accepted that probabilistic expectations influence sentence processing, and the models discussed in this chapter clearly demonstrate the viability of this notion, they also demonstrate that there is still much work to be done in formalizing exactly what factors drive these expectations and exactly how these factors interact to yield the reading time and eyetracking data that we observe in experimental research. More complete accounts of sentence processing will clearly require more complex models, but fortunately, advances in the computational resources available allow for increasingly realistic computational models.

Acknowledgments

We would like to thank John Hale and Roger Levy for helpful discussion. We would also like to thank the members of the computational psycholinguistics seminar at the University at Buffalo for helpful discussion.

References

Baker, C. F., Fillmore, C. J., & Lowe, J. B. (1998). The Berkeley FrameNet Project. Paper presented at the Proceedings of the 36th Annual Meeting of the Association for Computational Linguistics and the 17th International Conference on Computational Linguistics (COLING-ACL '98), Montreal, Canada.

Bever, T. G. (1970). The cognitive basis for linguistic structure. In Hayes, J. R. (Ed.) *Cognitive development of language* (pp. 279–362). New York: John Wiley.

Bresnan, J., Cueni, A., Nikitina, T., & Baayen, H. (2005). Predicting the Dative Alternation. To appear in Royal Netherlands Academy of Science Workshop on Foundations of Interpretation proceedings.

Burnard, L. (1995). *Users Reference Guide for the British National Corpus*. Oxford: Oxford University Computing Services.

Charniak, E. (1995). *Parsing with context free grammars and word statistics* (No. CS-95-28). Providence, Rhode Island: Brown University.

(1997). Statistical parsing with a context-free grammar and word statistics. In *Proceedings of the Fourteenth National Conference on Artificial Intelligence* (pp. 598–603). Menlo Park: AAAI Press/MIT Press.

Collins, M. J. (1997). Three generative, lexicalised models for statistical parsing. In *Proceedings of the 35th annual meeting on Association for Computational Linguistics* (pp. 16–23). Madrid, Spain.

Elman, J. L. (1990). Finding structure in time. *Cognitive Science, 14*, 179–211.

(1991). Distributed representations, simple recurrent networks, and grammatical structure. *Machine Learning, 7*, 195–224.

Elman, J. L., Hare, M., & McRae, K. (2004). Cues, constraints, and competition in sentence processing. In Tomasello, M. & Slobin, D. (Eds.) *Beyond Nature-Nurture: Essays in Honor of Elizabeth Bates* (pp. 111–38). Mahwah, NJ: Lawrence Erlbaum Associates.

Ferreira, F. & Henderson, J. M. (1991). Recovery from misanalyses of garden-path sentences. *Journal of Memory & Language, 30(6)*, 725–45.

Fox, B. A. & Thompson, S. A. (1990). A discourse explanation of the grammar of relative clauses in English conversation. *Language, 66(2)*, 297–316.

Francis, W. N. & Kučera, H. (1982). *Frequency analysis of English usage: Lexicon and grammar*. Boston: Houghton Mifflin.

Garnsey, S. M., Pearlmutter, N. J., Myers, E., & Lotocky, M. A. (1997). The contributions of verb bias and plausibility to the comprehension of temporarily ambiguous sentences. *Journal of Memory & Language, 37(1)*, 58–93.

Gibson, E. (1998). Linguistic complexity: Locality of syntactic dependencies. *Cognition, 68(1)*, 1–76.

(2000). The dependency locality theory: A distance-based theory of linguistic complexity. In Miyashita, Y., Marantz, A. & O'Neil, W. (Eds.) *Image, Language, Brain* (pp. 95–126). Cambridge, MA: MIT Press.

Godfrey, J., Holliman, E., & McDaniel, J. (1992). SWITCHBOARD: Telephone speech corpus for research and development. *In Proceedings of ICASSP-92* (pp. 517–20). San Francisco.

Gordon, P. C., Hendrick, R., & Johnson, M. (2001). Memory interference during language processing. *Journal of Experimental Psychology: Learning, Memory, and Cognition, 27(6)*, 1411–23.

(2004). Effects of noun phrase type on sentence complexity. *Journal of Memory and Language, 51(1)*, 97–114.

Green, M. J. & Mitchell, D. C. (2006). Absence of real evidence against competition during syntactic ambiguity resolution. *Journal of Memory and Language, 55*, 1–17.

Gries, S. T. (2001). A multifactorial anaylsis of syntactic variation: particle movement revisited. *Journal of Quantitative Linguistics, 8(1)*, 33–50.

Hale, J. (2001). A Probabilistic Earley Parser as a Psycholinguistic Model. In *Proceedings of the Second Meeting of the North American Chapter of the Asssociation for Computational Linguistics*.

(2003). The Information Conveyed by Words in Sentences. *Journal of Psycholinguistic Research, 32(2)*, 101–23.

(2004). The Information-Processing Difficulty of Incremental Parsing. In Keller, F., Clark, S., Crocker, M. W., & Steedman, M. (Eds.) *Proceedings of the ACL Workshop Incremental Parsing: Bringing Engineering and Cognition Together* (pp. 58–65).

(2006). Uncertainty about the rest of the sentence. *Cognitive Science, 30(4)*, 643–72.

Hale, J. & Keyser, S. J. (1993). On argument structure and the lexical expression of syntactic relations. In Hale, J. & Keyser, S. J. (Eds.) *The view from Building 20* (pp. 53–109). Cambridge, MA: MIT Press.

Hare, M., Tanenhaus, M. K., & McRae, K. (2007). Understanding and producing the reduced relative construction: Evidence from ratings, editing and corpora. *Journal of Memory and Language, 56(3)*, 410–35.

Jaeger, T. F. (2005). Optional that indicates production difficulty: Evidence from disfluencies. In *Proceedings of DiSS'05, Disfluency in*

Spontaneous Speech Workshop (pp. 103–109). Aix-en-Provence, France.

(2006). Phonological optimization and syntactic variation: The case of optional that. In *Proceedings of the 32nd annual meeting of the Berkeley Linguistics Society.*

Jurafsky, D. (1996). A probabilistic model of lexical and syntactic access and disambiguation. *Cognitive Science,* 20(2), 137–94.

King, J. & Just, M. A. (1991). Individual differences in syntactic processing: the role of working memory. *Journal of Memory and Language* 30(5), 580–602.

Kučera, H. & Francis, W. N. (1967). *Computational analysis of present-day American English.* Providence: Brown University Press.

Levy, R. (2008). Expectation-based syntactic comprehension. *Cognition,* 106, 1126–1177.

MacDonald, M. C. & Christiansen, M. H. (2002). Reassessing Working Memory: Comment on Just and Carpenter (1992) and Waters and Caplan (1996). *Psychological Review,* 109(1), 35–54.

Marcus, M. P., Kim, G., Marcinkiewicz, M. A., MacIntyre, R., Bies, A., Ferguson, M., et al. (1994). The Penn Treebank: Annotating predicate argument structure. In *Human Language Technology: Proceedings of a workshop held at Plainsboro, New Jersey, March 8–11, 1994* (pp. 114–19). Plainsboro, N.J.

Marcus, M. P., Santorini, B., & Marcinkiewicz, M. A. (1993). Building a large annotated corpus of English: The Penn Treebank. *Computational Linguistics,* 19(2), 313–30.

McKoon, G. & Ratcliff, R. (2003). Meaning through syntax: Language comprehension and the reduced relative clause construction. *Psychological Review,* 110, 490–525.

McRae, K., Spivey-Knowlton, M. J., & Tanenhaus, M. K. (1998). Modeling the influence of thematic fit (and other constraints) in on-line sentence comprehension. *Journal of Memory & Language,* 38(3), 283–312.

Merlo, P. (1994). A corpus-based analysis of verb continuation frequencies for syntactic processing. *Journal of Psycholinguistic Research,* 23(6), 435–47.

Narayanan, S. & Jurafsky, D. (1998). Bayesian models of human sentence processing. In *Proceedings of the Twentieth Annual Meeting of the Cognitive Science Society COGSCI-98* (pp. 752–7).

(2002). A Bayesian Model Predicts Human Parse Preference and Reading Time in Sentence Processing. In Dietterich, T. G., Becker, S., &

Ghahramani, Z. (Eds.) *Advances in Neural Information Processing Systems* (Vol. 14, pp. 59–65). Cambridge, MA: MIT Press.

(2005). *A Bayesian Model of Human Sentence Processing.* Unpublished manuscript.

Palmer, M., Kingsbury, P., & Gildea, D. (2005). The Proposition Bank: An Annotated Corpus of Semantic Roles. *Computational Linguistics,* 31(1), 71–106.

Rayner, K., Carlson, M., & Frazier, L. (1983). The interaction of syntax and semantics during sentence processing: Eye movements in the analysis of semantically biased sentences. *Journal of Verbal Learning & Verbal Behavior,* 22(3), 358–74.

Reali, F. & Christiansen, M. H. (2005). Word-chunk frequency affects the processing of relative clauses. Poster presented at the 2005 CUNY Sentence Processing Conference, March 31-April 2, Tucson, Arizona.

Reali, F., & Christiansen, M. H. (2007). Processing of relative clauses is made easier by frequency of occurrence. *Journal of Memory and Language,* 57(1), 1–23.

Rohde, DLT (2002). A Connectionist Model of Sentence Comprehension and Production. Unpublished doctoral dissertation, Carnegie Mellon University, Pittsburgh, PA.

Roland, D., Dick, F., & Elman, J. (2007). Frequency of basic English grammatical structures: A corpus analysis. *Journal of Memory & Language,* 57, 348–379.

Roland, D., Elman, J. L., & Ferreira, V. S. (2006). Why is that? Structural prediction and ambiguity resolution in a very large corpus of English sentences. *Cognition* 98(3), 245–72.

Roland, D. & Jurafsky, D. (1998). How verb subcategorization frequencies are affected by corpus choice. In *Proceedings of COLING-ACL 1998* (pp. 1117–21). Montreal, Canada.

(2002). Verb sense and verb subcategorization probabilities. In Merlo, P. & Stevenson, S. (Eds.) *The Lexical Basis of Sentence Processing: Formal, Computational, and Experimental Issues.* John Benjamins.

Roland, D., Jurafsky, D., Menn, L., Gahl, S., Elder, E., & Riddoch, C. (2000). Verb subcategorization frequency differences between business-news and balanced corpora: The role of verb sense. In *Proceedings of the Workshop on Comparing Corpora* (pp. 28–34). Hong Kong, October 2000.

Spivey, M. J. & Tanenhaus, M. K. (1998). Syntactic ambiguity resolution in discourse: Modeling the effects of referential context and lexical frequency. *Journal of Experimental Psychology: Learning, Memory, & Cognition, 24*(6), 1521–43.

Stevenson, S. (1994). A Unified Model of Preference and Recovery Mechanisms in Human Parsing. In *Proceedings of the Sixteenth Annual Conference of the Cognitive Science Society* (pp. 824–9). Atlanta, Georgia.

Stevenson, S., & Merlo, P. (1997). Lexical structure and parsing complexity. *Language & Cognitive Processes, 12(2&3)*, 349–99.

Tabor, W., Galantucci, B., & Richardson, D. (2004). Effects of Merely Local Syntactic Coherence on Sentence Processing. *Journal of Memory and Language, 50*(4), 355–70.

Tabor, W., & Hutchins, S. (2004). Evidence for Self-Organized Sentence Processing: Digging In Effects. *Journal of Experimental Psychology: Learning, Memory, and Cognition, 30*(2), 431–50.

Tabor, W., Juliano, C., & Tanenhaus, M. K. (1997). Parsing in a dynamical system: An attractor-based account of the interaction of lexical and structural constraints in sentence processing. *Language & Cognitive Processes, 12(2&3)*, 211–71.

Tabor, W., & Tanenhaus, M. K. (2001). Dynamical systems for sentence processing. In Christiansen, M. H. & Chater, N. (Eds.) *Connectionist Psycholinguistics: Capturing the empirical data*, Westport, CT: Ablex.

Traxler, M. J., Morris, R. K., & Seely, R. E. (2002). Processing subject and object relative clauses: Evidence from eye movements. *Journal of Memory and Language, 47*(1), 69–90.

Traxler, M. J., Pickering, M. J., & Clifton, C. Jr. (1998). Adjunct attachment is not a form of lexical ambiguity resolution. *Journal of Memory and Language, 39*(4), 558–92.

Traxler, M. J., Williams, R. S., Blozis, S. A., & Morris, R. K. (2005). Working memory, animacy, and verb class in the processing of relative clauses. *Journal of Memory and Language, 53*(2), 204–24.

van Gompel, RPG, Pickering, M. J., Pearson, J., & Liversedge, S. P. (2005). Evidence against competition during syntactic ambiguity resolution. *Journal of Memory and Language, 52*(2), 284–307.

Vasishth, S. & Lewis, R. L. (2006). Argument-Head Distance and Processing Complexity: Explaining Both Locality and Antilocality Effects. *Language: Journal of the Linguistic Society of America, 82*(4), 767–94.

Warren, T. & Gibson, E. (2002). The influence of referential processing on sentence complexity. *Cognition, 85*(1), 79–112.

Wasow, T., Jaeger, T. F., & Orr, D. (2005). Lexical variation in relativizer frequency. Paper presented at the workshop on expecting the unexpected: Exceptions in grammar at the 27th annual meeting of the German Linguistic Association, University of Cologne, Germany.

Section 7

SENTENCE PRODUCTION

CHAPTER 20

Research in Language Production

Zenzi M. Griffin and Christopher M. Crew

The aim of this chapter is to provide an overview of developments in language production research over the past decade or so, primarily in the spoken modality with an emphasis on the production of utterances and words by adults speaking their native languages. For introductions to this area of research, we refer the reader to reviews such as Bock and Levelt (1994), Griffin and V. S. Ferreira (2006), and Meyer and Belke (2007). The reader wishing an in-depth analysis of spoken language production should read Levelt's (1989) book *Speaking*, in which he summarized existing research while bridging numerous disciplines and providing a theoretical framework that has guided subsequent research. Here we begin with a brief, relatively theory-neutral description of the computational steps involved in speaking, before addressing recent advances, trends, and the major controversies surrounding them.

1 An overview of language production processes

Ideally, language production research covers all of the processes from deciding what to say to the actions used to say it. However, how speakers communicate over the course of a conversation to achieve their goals is typically left to social psychologists and specialists in discourse processing. This process of *macroplanning* (e.g., Butterworth, 1980) is intertwined with the behavior of the speaker's conversational partner or audience, making it desirable to consider multiple individuals who act as both speakers and listeners over time. In contrast, language production researchers typically consider speaking across smaller units of discourse: individual utterances or spurts of speech. A rough time course of these processes is illustrated in Figure 20.1. When a speaker selects content to express in a single utterance, the process is referred to as *microplanning* or *message planning*. The result of microplanning is seen as a set of semantic and pragmatic specifications of the content to be expressed, which is called a *message* (e.g., Garrett, 1975). These semantic specifications can be conceptualized as propositions or other unordered conceptual representations. Pragmatic specifications take into account the particulars of the referents (the actual things being talked about), what has already been expressed in the discourse, as well as the knowledge, status, and assumed

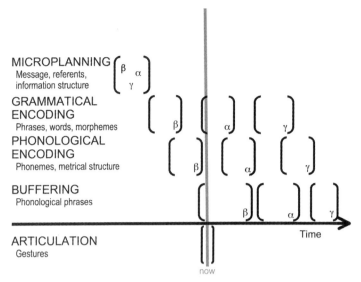

Figure 20.1. Language production processes for producing a simple utterance. Message elements are denoted by Greek letters and the duration of a grammatical and phonological encoding associated with each element is indicated by subscripted brackets. The brackets associated with buffering note the approximate amount of buffered phonetic material. So, while articulating the beginning of the words expressing β, the speaker is grammatically encoding α, and has done no formulation of γ although it is part of the message representation and could therefore affect processing. Relative timing here assumes that message elements are encoded one at a time (but see Meyer et al., 2008).

linguistic and cognitive abilities of the addressee.

The first part of formulating a way to express a message is called *grammatical encoding* and it has two aspects (e.g., Bock and Levelt, 1994). One aspect of grammatical encoding is syntactic processing: deciding the order in which message elements will be encoded and which grammatical markings are needed to convey the relationships between concepts (such as who did what to whom and what modifies what). The result can be seen in different syntactic structures such as actives (1) and passives (2).

(1) *Millions watched the competition.*
(2) *The competition was watched by millions.*

Message elements that are highly available because they have previously been discussed or semantically primed tend to be placed earlier in an utterance than less available elements (see Bock, Irwin, and Davidson, 2004). So previous discussion of large audiences would bias speakers to produce (1) and previous mention of racing would favor (2).

The other aspect of grammatical encoding is selecting a single- or multiword expression to convey a message element, such as deciding whether to call the old device used to stream video a *TV*, *TV set*, *idiot box*, or *television*. Converging evidence suggests that speakers access knowledge about a word's meaning and grammatical use before they fully access knowledge of the sounds that form the word. The representation associated with word meaning and grammatical use is often called a *lemma* rather than a *word*, because the lay definition of a *word* includes its orthographic or phonological forms.[1]

[1] In the Vigliocco chapter, the term *lexico-semantic/ syntactic representation* is used. We will try to use the term *word*.

The most intuitively appealing evidence for separating semantic and syntactic word information from phonological forms comes from the *tip-of-the-tongue* phenomenon. Speakers experience tip-of-the-tongue (TOT) states when they have a strong feeling of knowing a word that they wish to say but feel frustratingly unable to summon its component sounds (see Brown, 1991; Gollan and Brown, 2006). Speakers have TOTs most often for proper names, making it hard to get through a discussion of movies without at least one person experiencing a TOT. When this occurs for a movie star, for example, the speaker can often rattle off a list of movies the actor has appeared in, his or her current and former lovers, as well as a detailed description of the actor's physical appearance. Clearly, a lack of individuating information to guide word selection is not the problem. Other knowledge that speakers can report suggests that they have successfully accessed a word representation (the lemma) in addition to a wealth of nonlinguistic information. For example, nouns in several Indo-European languages bear grammatical gender that is unpredictable from their meanings. While the French word for *flower* is feminine, its Italian translation is masculine (Miozzo and Caramazza, 1999). Nonetheless, speakers in a TOT state can indicate grammatical gender with greater-than-chance accuracy (Miozzo and Caramazza, 1997; Vigliocco, Garrett, and Antonini, 1997). At the same time, speakers only have limited access to phonological information during TOTs. For example, when English speakers have TOTs for common words (e.g., the word defined as "inscription on a tomb"), they can often report the first sound or letter in the word (e) and its number of syllables (three). Sometimes they report words that sound very similar but differ significantly in meaning (such as *epithet*). When presented with the sought-for word, speakers gratefully identify it as the one that was on the tip of their tongues (*epitaph*).

Additional evidence that access typically fails in form retrieval, subsequent to lemma selection, comes from phonological priming studies. For example, hearing words with overlapping sounds that occupy the same syllable positions as the sought-for word promotes resolution of TOT states (James and Burke, 2000). Likewise, having recently generated a homonym (producing *pit* as in a cherry before naming Brad Pitt) significantly reduces the likelihood of a TOT (Burke et al., 2004).

As the literature on TOTs suggests, information about the sounds of a word is built up piecemeal. Even when phonological encoding occurs without problems, converging evidence suggests that speakers sequence a word's sounds each time they use it rather than retrieving a whole word form from memory (see Meyer and Belke, 2007). For example, when generating words as object names or repeating them, the effect of hearing and ignoring a phonologically related word increases with the number of initial sounds shared. So with an overlap of two sounds the word *cab* would have a greater effect on producing *cat* than the word *cog* would. Also, phonological overlap at the start of a word has a different or earlier effect than overlap at the end of the word (e.g., *cab* and *mat* would have different effects on *cat*).

The form of a word often differs when it is spoken in isolation as opposed to part of a multiword utterance (see Wheeldon, 2000 and F. Ferreira, 2007 for review). For example, the sound /d/ in *hand* may end up in the same syllable as *it* in the utterance *Hand it to me* rather than taking its canonical position in the syllable after /n/ (or it may be dropped completely). Each pair of words (*hand + it, to + me*) combine to form a separate *phonological word*, each with a single stressed syllable (*HAN-di tuh-ME*). Speakers seem to organize the sounds for at least one phonological word before beginning to articulate an utterance. The time needed to retrieve information from a phonological memory buffer is a function of the number of phonological words it contains rather than the number of words or their length (Sternberg et al., 1988). An additional process is required to convert phonologically specified syllables into articulatory gestures (see Meyer and Belke, 2007). Research on the details of articulation is typically left to laboratory phonologists and experts on motor movement (see Fowler, 2007).

Although these stages of production are described separately and as a sequence, they may overlap in time. Furthermore, while speakers articulate one part of an utterance, they simultaneously prepare other parts of it. More on this later in the chapter.

2 Developments and controversies

We begin with methodological changes within language production research over the past decade or so. Next we consider changes in topics studied and views, before working our way through several new findings in language production.

2.1 Methods and tools

Consistent with the view of cognitive processing as symbol manipulation (see Clark, 2001), the dominant experimental method for studying language production in the late twentieth century involved individual participants responding to stimuli presented by a computer screen (see Bock, 1996). Along with the shift in cognitive sciences to embodied and situated cognition, experiments in language production are increasingly designed to have participants communicate with other people to achieve goals rather than talk to computer monitors or tape recorders. These addressees may be confederates (e.g., Branigan, Pickering, and Cleland, 2000) or other participants (e.g., V. S. Ferreira and Dell, 2000). Happily, many factors that influence the individual speakers have identical effects (e.g., V. S. Ferreira, Slevc, and Rogers, 2005) or even greater effects in the context of a dialog (Branigan et al., 2000). At the same time as interactions are more natural in these studies, experimental control is maintained via carefully crafted stimuli and clever tasks. Moving away from prime–target sequences and decontextualized language, researchers construct *targeted language games* to elicit particular utterances under different conditions as part of a continuous dialog (Brown-Schmidt and Tanenhaus, 2008).

Also increasing the external validity of language production research are developments in corpus linguistics and the increasing availability of large spoken corpora. These allow production researchers to test hypotheses about processing with natural, spontaneously generated speech (e.g., Wasow, 1997) and determine whether variables that influence production in carefully controlled laboratory experiments also impact speech in the wild (e.g., Gennari and MacDonald, 2009; Gries, 2005; Slevc and V. S. Ferreira, 2006).

Following the work of Tanenhaus and colleagues (1995) in using advances in eye-tracking to study spoken language comprehension, language production researchers have begun to track speakers' eye movements as another reflection of language processing (for review, see Griffin, 2004 and Meyer and Lethaus, 2004). When describing visually presented scenes or telling stories about pictured characters, speakers tend to look at referents for about a second before articulating their names. The amount of time spent looking at each referent is very similar to the amount of time it would take to name it in isolation. Moreover, speakers look at the things that they intend to talk about rather than the object that most closely resembles the word that they say (e.g., a speaker who decides to call a dog *cat* looks at the dog instead of looking at a cat). Thus, a speaker's eye movements often provide a good measure of what the speaker intends to talk about and how difficult it is to retrieve the referring expression. More important, eye movement measures can approximate the timing of word production processes during error-free and fluent speech without adding a second task, which is difficult if not impossible with other measures. However, under some circumstances, speakers may process more than what they are currently gazing at (e.g., Meyer, Ouellet, and Häcker, 2008).

Unlike the rest of cognitive psychology, advances in neuroimaging have had relatively little impact on language production research (see Vigliocco et al. chapter in this volume). Some of this is due to concern with motion artifacts from articulation. At the same time, language production research has always been influenced by studies of brain-damaged individuals, particularly aphasics (see Martin, 2003). Nonetheless, the links between research in normal adult production and aphasia appear to be growing stronger, with more researchers contributing to both literatures (see Dell and Cholin chapter in this volume).

Finally, the tools for collecting and processing samples of spoken language have improved significantly over the last decade. It is becoming commonplace for researchers to digitally record responses directly onto computers, eliminating the need for analog or digital audiotapes. Recordings can be synchronized with the presentation of stimuli on a trial, and simple programs can extract time measurements based on amplitude (i.e., like a digital voice key) or more sophisticated variations in the signal. Unfortunately, speech recognition systems still lack the flexibility and accuracy desired to use them for transcribing a small number of isolated sentences from different speakers. However, they are advanced enough to allow researchers to perform forced alignments. That is, software outputs the timing of words in a recording using speech recognition routines and a transcription (as in Bock et al., 2003; Spieler and Griffin, 2006). Such programs are very accurate and significantly reduce the time needed to process speech data before analyzing it.

2.2 Processing differences across languages

Initially, language production experiments were conducted almost exclusively with native speakers of Germanic languages such as Dutch, English, or German. The tacit assumption was that processing principles that held for one language would naturally hold for others since humans come into this world prepared to learn any human language. However, inconsistencies became apparent. For example, slips of the tongue in Spanish stubbornly failed to show the same tendency to disproportionately involve word initial sounds as in English and Dutch (see Berg, 1998 for comprehensive review). Several theories held that the first sound in a word played a special role in retrieval, making this deviation a thorny theoretical problem. Similarly, syllables were seen as odd units in language production in that syllable position severely constrained phoneme slips but at the same time, syllables rarely slipped as wholes in speech errors (Fromkin, 1971). Eventually, data from Semitic languages (Berg, 1998) and Mandarin Chinese (see Chen, Chen, and Dell, 2002) were found to flagrantly violate generalizations based on Germanic languages about syllables and speech errors.

Instead of the processing principles suggested by considering Germanic languages alone, more general processing principles appear to interact with differences between languages in word formation and the distribution of sounds. In general, the transitional probabilities between sounds in a language's lexicon determine where slips occur. Languages have surprisingly large differences in the transitional probabilities for sounds within words. For example, in English, unlike in Spanish, word endings (e.g. -able part of cable) occur with many different initial consonants (table, label, fable, Mabel). Such differences in transitional probabilities across languages also affect the forms used in poetry and language games such as Pig Latin (Ig-pay Atin-lay). Spanish lacks this distributional difference for word-initial sounds and therefore word-initial consonants in Spanish do not disproportionately participate in slips of the tongue. Similarly, sounds in Mandarin are combined to form a smaller set of syllables than sounds in English do, and each Mandarin syllable is used much more frequently than each English syllable is. This difference in vocabulary makes sounds within a syllable less likely to separate from each other and speech errors more likely to involve whole syllables in Mandarin than in Germanic languages. In Semitic languages, in which consonants in morphemes alternate between syllable initial and final positions (e.g., Hebrew roots *xšv* in *xošev* [*think* present tense] and *yaxšov* [*think* future tense] from Prunet, Béland, and Idrissi, 2000), slips of the tongue do not show a tendency to maintain syllable position although they nearly always do in languages like English (see Berg, 1998).

Cross-linguistic studies have also been important in constraining models of sentence production. In English (and other languages in which verbs tend to precede their arguments), there is a strong tendency for short phrases to precede long ones. So *Pat brought [to the party] [a box with a ribbon around it]* is preferred over *Pat brought [a box with a ribbon around it] [to the party]* (from Wasow, 1997). The opposite holds in languages like Japanese where verbs and other important content words appear at the ends of phrases. This is a challenge for theories that hold that shorter units are more accessible than longer ones and should therefore be produced earlier due to universal constraints on processing (Chang, 2009).

In addition, it is very difficult in English to disentangle the grammatical function of being the subject of a sentence from the property of being the first noun phrase in a sentence and its topic (i.e., the thing the sentence is predicating something about; Levelt, 1989). For example, when *Professors relish sabbaticals* is paraphrased as *Sabbaticals are relished by professors*, the word *sabbaticals* changes both its grammatical role from direct object to subject as well as its position in the sentence, taking the initial, topic position. In many other languages, it is much easier to alter the linear order of phrases without altering their grammatical roles. Several studies have tested the relationships between being the agent of an action, being the most human participant in an event, and being the topic of a response on the form of sentences and found distinct effects of each of these on how a sentence is constructed (see e.g., Christianson and F. Ferreira, 2005).

Even when producing simple noun phrases such as *a lovely bicycle*, speakers engage in syntactic processing although there is often little flexibility in word order.

In English, grammatical agreement within a noun phrase is limited to number (e.g., plural: *some lovely bicycles*). Other languages require determiners (e.g., *a*) and adjectives (e.g., *lovely*) to agree with the grammatical gender of the nouns they modify within noun phrases. Furthermore, the way in which grammatical gender affects processing varies by language. For example, the phonological properties of a noun affect the form of its gender-marked morphemes in Romance language like Italian (e.g., *il tavolo* [masc; *the table*] and *lo scoiattolo* [masc; *the squirrel*], but not in Germanic languages with grammatical gender such as Dutch. This has consequences for processing. Dutch speakers are slower to produce a noun phrase to refer to an object (e.g., *de flas* [*the bottle*]) in the presence of a written word of a different gender (e.g., *glas* [*glass*] which takes *het*) than one of the same gender (*tafel* [*table*]), but Italian speakers are not affected by the same type of manipulation (see Miozzo and Caramazza, 1999). Initially, such gender congruency effects were attributed to competition between abstract gender representations (e.g., common versus neuter genders in Dutch; Schriefers, 1993). Further research indicated that gender-marked forms such as determiners (e.g., *de* versus *het*) rather than abstract gender nodes (common versus neuter) interfere with one another to produce such gender congruency effects. For example, latencies are slower for nouns that appear with different determiner forms (e.g., *het* in singular but *de* in plural) than for nouns that consistently appear with the same form (e.g., *de* for both plural and singular; see e.g., Spalek and Schriefers, 2005). Furthermore, grammatical gender only appears to affect production when speakers produce noun phrases rather than bare nouns (Vigliocco et al., 2004).

2.3 *Bilingualism*

Most humans are effective communicators in more than one language. This proficiency has consequences for processing. For example, bilinguals are significantly more likely to experience word retrieval failures

(TOTs) than monolinguals (see Gollan and Brown, 2006). However, this does not hold for words that are shared between languages (cognates such as English *microphone* and Spanish *microfóno*) and proper names (e.g., *Doctor Who*). Gollan and colleagues have considered a number of potential causes of monolingual–bilingual differences in TOT rates. Assuming words are only retrieved or strengthened in one language at a time, words in bilinguals' vocabularies will tend to be used less often than the same words for monolinguals. TOTs occur more often for infrequently used words. Similarly, when words in all languages are considered, multilinguals may have larger overall vocabularies than monolinguals, which could affect word retrieval via several mechanisms. Under such hypotheses, there is nothing special about multilingual word production aside from vocabulary use across speakers. Other theories of bilingual production posit competition or other complex interactions between representations in each language or that processing resources may not be used or available to the same extent in bilinguals and monolinguals. Indeed, some research suggests that bilinguals show advantages over monolinguals in nonlinguistic tasks that require inhibition of irrelevant information (e.g., Bialystok et al., 2004). However, work with infants suggests that such benefits may be due to learning to comprehend two different languages rather than, or at least prior to, speaking two languages (Kovács and Mehler, 2009).

Multilinguals differ from monolinguals not only in their word knowledge, but also in their ability to construct sentences that conform to different grammatical rules. Researchers have tested the extent to which experiencing a sentence in one language affects syntactic processing in another language (e.g., Hartsuiker, Pickering, and Veltkamp, 2004; Loebell and Bock, 2003). These studies suggest that the syntactic structures for different languages in a bilingual are not fully independent, at least when the constructions express similar semantic and pragmatic content.

2.4 *Production in different modalities*

Language production includes communication via multiple modalities. Although spoken language is the typical modality studied in production, many people can also write or sign words (see Kellogg, 1994, and Emmorey, 2002, respectively). For this reason, *language production* cannot be synonymous with *speech production*. Furthermore, the term *speech* is associated with more peripheral language processes such as perceiving and articulating speech sounds rather than communication more generally. Historically, research on the articulation of speech has been conducted by people interested in motor behavior in general or laboratory phonologists (see Fowler, 2007) rather than psycholinguists. Researchers in language and speech production come from different backgrounds, use different methods, rarely communicate with one another, and do not consider one area to be a subset of the other.

As with all specializations, researchers interested in similar processes often end up communicating primarily with others within their narrowly defined area. However, it has become more common to see researchers not only considering other production modalities in developing theories, but conducting research in more than one modality and explicitly comparing processes across modalities. For example, the factors that affect the time to produce a spoken word have similar effects on the production of written words (see Bonin et al., 2002). Although tip-of-the-fingers states when signing resemble tip-of-the-tongue states when speaking, the components of signs appear to be retrieved together more often than the sounds of words (Thompson, Emmorey, and Gollan, 2005), at least when compared to TOTs in Indo-European languages. This suggests that the components of signs are more tightly linked than sounds are (although given the cross-linguistic work on speech errors, this may be a vocabulary difference rather than a true modality difference). Like crosslinguistic work, research on modality similarities and differences provides invaluable insight about the generality of proposed processing principles in language production.

In addition, researchers have increasingly attended to the relationship between language production and nonverbal communication (see contents of Goldin-Meadow, 2003; Kita, 2003; and McNeill, 2000). Of particular concern has been the relationship between production processes and the gestures that frequently accompany them. Because gestures often reflect speakers' conceptualizations of events, this work has strong implications for message planning.

2.5 Learning in language production

Producing an utterance subtly alters the efficiency of processes involved in producing subsequent utterances. That is, experience results in learning. For example, English-speaking participants in one study read aloud English-like sound sequences over several days (Dell et al., 2000). The sequences contained sequencing rules that are not present in English, like the *f* sound only appearing at the end of a syllable as in *mef* and never at the start of a syllable as in *fem* (or vice versa). After experience with vocabulary conforming to these novel rules, participants' slips of the tongue showed the same patterns. As one would expect given a lifetime of experience with English rules, speech errors also obeyed strong English constraints on word formation such as the *ng* sound never occurring at the start of a syllable. In word selection, long-lasting effects can be seen in faster word production latencies over minutes or longer despite differences in the eliciting stimuli (see Griffin and V. S. Ferreira, 2006).

In producing sentences, speakers tend to reuse syntactic structures that they have recently experienced, even in the absence of overlapping words (see V. S. Ferreira and Bock, 2006; Pickering and V. S. Ferreira, 2008). So, having heard a sentence with a prepositional dative structure such as *The governess made a pot of tea for the princess* rather than the double object dative *The governess made the princess a pot of tea*, a speaker is more likely to describe a picture using a prepositional dative structure, as in *A boy is handing a guitar to a musician*. The effect of such a priming sentence lasts at least over ten structurally unrelated sentences (e.g., *Strawberries and whipped cream are delicious*; Bock and Griffin, 2000). Structural priming also accrues over the course of an experimental session. With all this evidence of learning, it is perhaps not surprising that researchers who have studied language production in adults have been looking toward child language research to see if the same learning principles apply. Thus, models have begun to address learning mechanisms and results from child language acquisition (e.g., Chang, Dell, and Bock, 2006; Gennari and MacDonald, 2009; see Dell and Cholin in this volume).

2.6 Audience design and referring expressions

In tandem with increasing interest in language production during real communication, researchers have considered the extent to which speakers tailor their utterances for the people they speak to. Although it sounds like a straightforward question, it has been complicated by the fact that listeners probably make use of cues that speakers might rather not produce such as *um* (e.g., Arnold, Fagnano, and Tanenhaus, 2003). One vein of this research in production has looked at situations in which listeners typically experience at least temporary processing difficulty and whether speakers do anything to avoid or reduce such difficulty.

Sentences like *The coach knew you missed practice* may cause comprehenders mild difficulty because they expect *you* to be the direct object of the verb (as in *The coach knew you for a long time*) rather than an embedded subject. There are two easy ways in which speakers could eliminate uncertainty in how to interpret the noun phrase (*you*) after the verb (*knew*) and prevent processing difficulty for listeners. One method is to add the optional complementizer *that* to the sentence (e.g., *The coach knew that you missed practice*). Despite instructions to make utterances understandable for a listener with whom they interacted, speakers were no more likely to include *that* when the following word would be ambiguous (e.g., *you*) rather than unambiguous due to case marking (e.g., *I*; V. S. Ferreira and Dell, 2000). Instead, the use of *that* varied with the difficulty speakers had in retrieving the following word (e.g., how recently they had retrieved it). Another way to make interpretation of such sentences clearer is through variations in prosody. Although many studies have investigated whether speakers use prosody in this way, their results conflict and the processing constraints on speakers may prove to be a better predictor of prosody (e.g., Watson, Breen, and Gibson, 2006).

In contrast to syntactic ambiguities, there is good evidence that speakers are somewhat sensitive to how difficult it is for listeners to identify the referents they talk about. For example, how a speaker refers to an object depends on the presence of other similar objects that could be mistaken for the intended referent (see Olson, 1970). To investigate what types of referential ambiguity speakers can be sensitive to, V. S. Ferreira and colleagues (2005) asked participants to describe particular objects in a display that either contained objects of the same type (e.g., two mammalian bats), objects with the same name (a mammalian bat and a baseball bat), or completely unrelated objects. They found that speakers consistently avoided producing ambiguous labels by saying something like *the big bat* when a potential ambiguity (e.g., two mammalian bats) could be detected by just looking at the display and noticing the physical similarity between objects. Although it might confuse their listeners, participants called a mammalian bat *bat* in the presence of a baseball bat quite often, only about ten percent less often than when there was no other bat in the display (i.e., when the referent was unambiguous). Once speakers called one bat *bat*, they tended to be much more specific in referring to the other kind of bat (e.g., saying *a bat and a baseball bat*). So, it seems easiest for speakers to avoid confusing their listeners when they can see that there are multiple objects of the same kind and when they have already said a label that could apply to more than one object.

Once a speaker uses a label with a particular listener, the speaker is more likely to use the label later with the same listener than with another. This could be due to the speaker intentionally making life easier for the listener. Alternatively, it could be due to basic context-sensitive memory processes (Horton and Gerrig, 2005). That is, the presence of a particular person may make a recently used label for an object more available than another recently used label, regardless of any intention to communicate with the person. Thus, another trend in production research is testing the extent to which basic cognitive processes and the demands of language production processes within speakers can account for the variations in speech that listeners find useful without invoking processes that only exist to aid listener comprehension (see also Fowler, Levy, and Brown, 1997 on word duration).

So speakers can take listeners into account in forming messages by doing things like including extra information to make intended referents clearer and by simplifying the content of messages (e.g., when talking to children or the elderly). However, speakers are far less likely to alter the linguistic forms of their utterances such as their syntactic structures and prosody to ease interpretation. Instead variations in these seem more sensitive to what is easier for the speaker.

2.7 *Stages of creation of syntactic structure*

Linguists and psycholinguists identify two different properties in the surface structure of sentences. Take for example the sentence *A cat is among the flowers*. The grammatical function of *a cat* is subject and *the flowers* is the object of a prepositional phrase. These grammatical functions remain the same if the sentence is restated as *Among the flowers is a cat*, although the ordering of the phrases (or constituents) is different. The distinction is even clear in languages other than English in which the two properties are relatively more independent (see e.g., Christianson and F. Ferreira, 2005). Initial theories of language production posited that the assignment of grammatical functions preceded the ordering of constituents. Early studies of sentence production supported this theoretical point (see Bock and Levelt, 1994). Although grammatical functions and linear order are clearly separable concepts, increasing evidence suggests that they are determined concurrently during language production.

Speakers are more likely to produce a passive sentence following a passive rather than active sentence (see Pickering and V. S. Ferreira, 2008). Noun phrases in actives and passives differ in their functional assignments, suggesting that syntactic priming affects the process of function assignment or it could more specifically be called function assignment priming. It is also possible to prime constituent ordering. After participants were primed with sentences such as the cat–flowers ones in Dutch, their picture descriptions tended to show similar word orders (Hartsuiker, Kolk, and Huiskamp, 1999). That is, hearing a prepositional phrase before a subject noun phrase led speakers to create sentences in which prepositional phrases preceded subject noun phrases. So there appears to be constituent order priming in addition to functional assignment priming.

If the process of function assignment precedes constituent assignment, it should be possible to demonstrate it experimentally. Specifically, sentences that preserve grammatical functions should produce the same priming effects regardless of the order of their constituents (Pickering, Branigan, and McLean, 2002). Instead, functional assignment was not primed independent of constituent ordering (but see Shin and Christianson, 2009). Further evidence for a single stage in which words are grammatically sequenced comes from experimental studies of speech errors (V. S. Ferreira and Humphreys, 2001). Recent models of sentence production have function and position determined simultaneously (e.g., Chang et al., 2006).

2.8 *Older theoretical issues*

Traditionally, there have been three major theoretical issues within language production. The foremost was interactivity, that is, the extent to which later processing stages or representations could influence earlier ones. In particular, the concern was whether the availability of sounds could influence the selection of words. While it is still possible to argue about whether interactivity is most elegantly accounted for by mechanisms contained within initial language production processes as opposed to an independently motivated postproduction monitor (see Dell and Cholin chapter in this volume), word production is functionally interactive. That is, via whatever mechanism, the availability of sounds affects word choice in ways that make, for example, a speaker more likely to mistakenly call a cat *rat* rather than *dog*, all else being equal (see V. S. Ferreira and Griffin, 2003).

Similarly, in the spirit of symbolic cognitive science, early models of production often assumed that processing was discrete in that only minimal information was passed from one processing stage to the next and that processing was completed at one stage for a unit before output was passed onto the next state (see Vigliocco and Hartsuiker, 2002). Such processing systems conformed to the serial processing assumption that less information made processing easier and that redundancy was not only inelegant but also detrimental. Interactivity presupposes a lack of discreteness, so evidence of interactivity argues against discrete processing. Furthermore, experiments suggest that the sounds of multiple words become available although only one word is ultimately selected and uttered (see Vigliocco and Hartsuiker, 2002 for review). However, a current unresolved issue is under what circumstances a viewed object that a speaker does not intend to name will activate word and sound representations (e.g., V. S. Ferreira et al., 2005; Meyer and Damian, 2007; Navarete and Costa, 2005; Oppermann, Jescheniak, and Schriefers, 2008).

The third issue has been the degree of incrementality in production. That is, how much of an utterance do speakers prepare in advance of speaking as opposed to concurrent with its articulation? Because there are not enormous pauses between utterances, it has long been thought that processing of some parts of an utterance must occur during articulation of other parts. At the very least, phonological processes were thought to occur shortly before words were articulated (see Levelt, 1989). The time course is less clear for processing at higher levels such as word selection and message planning, particularly during fluent error-free sentences. Congruent with evidence from other experimental methods, eyetracking studies strongly suggest that words and message content for an utterance can be processed while other parts of the utterance are being articulated (see Brown-Schmidt and Tanenhaus, 2006 and Griffin, 2004). The relative timing of these processes and their difficulty affect the fluency of the associated words. However, the details of the time course for production are quite unclear, particularly the degree to which different parts of utterances may be processed simultaneously and under what circumstances and constraints.

2.9 *Recent issues*

So the modern version of the incrementality issue concerns how and when speakers vary the amount of preparation they engage in. For example, what representations do people buffer and how? Messages and phonological phrases are clearly important units (e.g., Wheeldon and Lahiri, 1997), with less evidence for buffering of intermediate representations (but see Martin and Freedman, 2001). Another question is what sorts of factors affect the degree to which people prepare different units prior to articulation and how does this vary across situations and individuals? Within the lab, large differences in the degree of preparation are observed with variations in stimulus availability and instructions (e.g., F. Ferreira and Swets,

2002; Griffin and Bock, 2000; Griffin, 2003; Wheeldon and Lahiri, 1997), while smaller changes in the scope have been seen with changes in stimulus properties (e.g., Meyer et al., 2008; Oppermann et al., 2008).

Usually theories assume that speakers plan in terms of units such as grammatical phrases (e.g., Martin and Freedman, 2001) or phonological words (Wheeldon and Lahiri, 1997). These theories tend to implicitly assume that speakers begin to articulate these units as soon as they are ready (termed *radical incrementality* in F. Ferreira and Swets, 2002). However, speakers do not necessarily articulate words as soon as the words (or some other unit) are prepared during connected speech (see Griffin, 2003). Speakers may coordinate the articulation and preparation of words based on the time available and estimated to complete the processes rather than units. Evidence comes from variation in the degree of preparation for upcoming words with factors such as word length for preceding words and speech rate.

Most of the experimental data addressing preparation and timing is based on uttering sentences based on novel visual stimuli without a discourse context. Of course, this is not representative of naturally occurring speech. So far though, the tendency for speakers to prepare words immediately before uttering them (even when fluent) appears to hold for dialogs (e.g., Brown-Schmidt and Tanenhaus, 2006) and narration without picture description (Richardson and Dale, 2005). Because the time course of processing is a strong constraint on theories of production, much more work remains to be done on these questions. In particular, recent theories differ considerably in when speakers commit to using particular syntactic structures (cf. Chang et al., 2006; F. Ferreira, 2000), and there is relatively little empirical evidence for when such commitments are made (but see Wasow, 1997).

Occasionally complicating matters of interpretation of empirical results are theoretical differences among researchers in considering the source of differences in sentence structure and processing. Some approaches assume that because message planning precedes grammatical encoding, differences in syntactic structure that express (or are strongly related to) differences in meaning should be attributed to differences in the underlying messages that then have syntactic consequences (see e.g., Chang et al., 2006; Dell et al., 2000; Griffin and Weinstein-Tull, 2003; Levelt, 1989; Solomon and Perlmutter, 2004). For example, in such views, differences in syntactic complexity usually follow from differences in message complexity; word repetition presupposes an intention to express a similar meaning (except in perseverative speech errors); verb subcategorization differences follow largely from properties of the meanings they express; and structural priming starts with some overlap in conceptual structure between the messages in prime and target sentences.

In contrast, other researchers place a greater emphasis on the role linguistic units themselves play in shaping utterances (e.g., Bock and Levelt, 1994; F. Ferreira, 2000; Levelt, 1989; Pickering and Branigan, 1998). Initially, this tendency was motivated by the need for the field to establish that the realization of a message as a spoken utterance is not a trivial transformation. An emphasis on the role of verbs in planning sentences followed the move toward lexically based grammars in linguistics and studies showing strong verb effects in comprehension. This bias may also be due to the greater ease of defining linguistic units rather than message units or the precedence of sentence comprehension research, where identification of linguistic units may often precede interpretation of messages. In any case, there is sometimes a bias to look toward linguistic forms before communicative intentions for processing explanations. In some cases, the availability of syntactic structures and words is seen as shaping not only the form of an utterance, but also its content (e.g., Scheepers, 2003). From this perspective, differences in syntactic complexity are attributed to difficulty building syntactic structures; word repetition is attributed to word (lemma) availability; verb preferences constrain the syntactic coding of messages; and the availability of a

syntactic structure can result in differences in the information expressed.

As with many theoretical dichotomies, both views have empirical motivation and the tension is likely to be resolved with more theoretically intermediate positions. That is, while messages shape and largely precede the formulation of utterances, the availability of forms and syntactic constraints within a language must also shape the forms messages take. Indeed, even at present, researchers with either attribution bias are unlikely to reject such a statement. The real issue is not which of these is primary but rather how they jointly interact using well-specified and plausible models that capture these interactions and generate testable predictions.

2.10 *Complex sentence structures*

Several experimental studies addressing the production of complex sentences have been published over the past few years, marking a move away from the extremely simple utterances of earlier work (e.g., Table: 20.1, a-c). The clause (roughly a sentence structure involving a single verb) or the proposition that corresponds to a clause has long been considered a critical unit of planning in production (e.g., Garrett, 1975). However, this conclusion was based on speech errors, disfluencies, and dual task paradigms, which may not be representative of speech more generally. Studying sentences that contain more than one clause is important for establishing the generality of sentence processing principles that operate for simple clauses. The conceptual and grammatical relationships between phrases and across clauses makes the production of complex sentences more difficult than, say, the production of two simple clauses connected by a conjunction like *and*. The most popular structures of study so far have been relative clauses (Table: 20.1d; e.g., Gennari and MacDonald, 2009; Solomon and Perlmutter, 2004) and sentence complements (Table: 20.1e; e.g., V. S. Ferreira and Dell, 2000). The production of various subject- and object-raising and control structures have also been studied experimentally (Table: 20.1f-

Table 20.1. Example sentences with varying complexity

	Structure	Example
a	conjoined noun phrase	*a chair and a bicycle*
b	locative clause	*The chair is next to the bicycle.*
c	double-object dative clause	*Santa gave the productive professor a shiny new bicycle.*
d	cleft sentence with relative clause	*That is the bicycle that I like best.*
e	sentence with sentence complement	*The mechanic said that he repaired the bicycle.*
f	object-raising construction	*John believed Mary to have stolen the bicycle.*
g	object-control construction	*John persuaded Mary to steal the bicycle.*
h	subject-verb agreement over a prepositional phrase	*The cyclist with the lovely bicycles was happy.*
i	subject-verb agreement over a relative clause	*The cyclist who owned the lovely bicycles was happy.*
j	subject-verb agreement over a less semantically integrated prepositional phrase	*The cyclist near the lovely bicycles was happy.*
k	pronoun-antecedent agreement	*The cyclists in the Tour were fast, weren't they?*

g; e.g., Griffin and Weinstein-Tull, 2003), as have clefts (Table: 20.d; e.g., Martin and Freedman, 2001). These studies suggest that relationships between words in different clauses or propositions have complex effects on production.

A related issue is how speakers create agreement between subjects and verbs (Table: 20.1h-j) and pronouns and referents (Table: 20.1k; see Eberhard, Cutting, and Bock, 2005 for review and theory). Although the plural word *bicycles* is the closest noun to the verb *was* in sentences (h-j), the verb agrees (i.e., has the same number) with the singular word *cyclist*, which is the subject of each sentence. Although speakers rarely make agreement errors, they are more likely to when there is a nearby noun like *bicycles* that has a different number than the subject noun. Furthermore, such agreement errors occur more often when the interfering noun is expressed in the same clause (or proposition) as the subject noun (e.g., h) rather than a different clause (i). Interference is also modulated by how closely tied together the two nouns are in meaning (Solomon and Perlmutter, 2004). When the intervening prepositional phrase expresses an attribute of the referent of the subject noun (i), speakers make more agreement errors than when the phrase expresses a location (j). In (j), if the cyclist moves away, she will no longer be near the bicycles, whereas the attribute of owning (*with*) many bicycles is a more enduring property of the cyclist. The likelihood of agreement errors varies across languages, such that languages with more clearly marked case, number, and gender are less prone to errors than less morphologically rich languages (see Lorimor et al., 2008). Like syntactic priming studies, agreement studies provide insight into the way messages are represented and the consequences of subtle meaning differences for syntactic processes. In addition, the area of agreement highlights interplay between message features and word properties in syntactic processes.

2.11 *Prearticulatory monitoring of speech*

Over twenty-five years ago, extremely clever speech error studies showed strong evidence that speakers were at least occasionally able to prevent themselves from articulating errors that arose while preparing speech (see Motley, Camden, and Baars, 1982). Although prearticulatory monitoring formed a critical part of production theories (e.g., Levelt, 1989), relatively little empirical work directly assessed what speakers were able to monitor and how before this millennium. As consciousness became a respectable topic of study in cognitive neuroscience, the empirical study of prearticulatory speech monitoring has increasingly been seen as tractable and theoretical accounts more testable (see contents of Hartsuiker et al., 2005).

3 Conclusions

Research in language production is growing exponentially as members of one cohort of researchers in turn train larger numbers of new researchers. The degree of growth will hopefully make this one of the last handbooks to subsume all of language production under one heading while aspects of language comprehension receive separate headings. That is, future psycholinguistic handbooks are likely to devote separate chapters to spoken word production, spoken sentence production, written language production, signed language production, self-monitoring of speech, production in multilingual speakers, and so on (see Gaskell, 2007).

   In addition to the increase in the number of researchers working on production, growth in the field has been spurred by new methods that ease data collection, increase external validity, and provide insights into processing without adding secondary tasks or distracting stimuli. These new methods as well as older ones from within language production and borrowed from other fields are being used to explore the production of a wider range of utterances and production under a wider range of situations. Indeed, in many areas, the empirical results are rapidly

outstripping the ability of existing theories to even begin to address them. It is a truly exciting time to study the processes that allow people to achieve goals through language.

References

Arnold, J. E., Fagnano, M., & Tanenhaus, M. K. (2003). Disfluencies signal thee, um, new information. *Journal of Psycholinguistic Research*, 32, 25–36.

Berg, T. (1998). *Linguistic structure and change: An explanation from language processing*. Oxford: Oxford University Press.

Bialystok, E., Craik, FIM, Klein, R., & Viswanathan, M. (2004). Bilingualism, aging, and cognitive control: Evidence from the Simon task. *Psychology and Aging*, 19, 290–303.

Bock, J. K. (1996). Language production: Methods and methodologies. *Psychonomic Bulletin and Review*, 34, 395–421.

Bock, J. K. & Griffin, Z. M. (2000). The persistence of structural priming: Transient activation or implicit learning? *Journal of Experimental Psychology: General*, 129(2), 177–92.

Bock, J. K., Irwin, D. E., & Davidson, D. J. (2004). Putting First Things First. In Henderson, J. M. & Ferreira, F. (Eds.) *The Interface of Language, Vision, and Action: Eye Movements and the Visual World* (pp. 249–78). New York: Psychology Press.

Bock, J. K., Irwin, D. E., Davidson, D. J., & Levelt, WJM (2003). Minding the clock. *Journal of Memory and Language*, 48, 653–85.

Bock, J. K. & Levelt, WJM (1994). Language production: Grammatical encoding. In Gernsbacher, M. A. (Ed.) *Handbook of psycholinguistics* (pp. 945–84). San Diego: Academic Press.

Bonin, P., Chalard, M., Meot, A., & Fayol, M. (2002). The determinants of spoken and written picture naming latencies. *British Journal of Psychology*, 93, 89–114.

Branigan, H. P., Pickering, M. J., & Cleland, A. A. (2000). Syntactic co-ordination in dialogue. *Cognition*, 75, B13–25.

Brown, A. S. (1991). A review of the tip-of-the-tongue experience. *Psychological Review*, 109, 204–23.

Brown-Schmidt, S. & Tanenhaus, M. K. (2006). Watching the eyes when talking about size: An investigation of message formulation and utterance planning. *Journal of Memory and Language*, 54, 592–609.

Brown-Schmidt, S. & Tanenhaus, M. K. (2008). Real-time investigation of referential domains in unscripted conversation: A targeted language game approach. *Cognitive Science*, 32(4), 643–84.

Burke, D. M., Locantore, J. K., Austin, A. A., & Chae, B. (2004). Cherry pit primes Brad Pitt: Homophone priming effects on young and older adults' production of proper names. *Psychological Science*, 15, 164–70.

Butterworth, B. (1980). Evidence from pauses in speech. In Butterworth, B. (Ed.) *Language production (vol. 1): Speech and talk* (pp. 155–76). London: Academic Press.

Chang, F. (2009). Learning to order words: A connectionist model of heavy NP shift and accessibility effects in Japanese and English. *Journal of Memory and Language*, 61(3), 374–97.

Chang, F., Dell, G. S., & Bock, K. (2006). Becoming syntactic. *Psychological Review*, 113, 234–72.

Chen, J. Y., Chen, T. M., & Dell, G. S. (2002). Word-form encoding in mandarin Chinese as assessed by the implicit priming task. *Journal of Memory and Language*, 46, 751–81.

Christianson, K. & Ferreira, F. (2005). Conceptual accessibility and sentence production in a free word order language (Odawa). *Cognition*, 98, 105–35.

Clark, A. (2001). *Mindware: An introduction to the philosophy of cognitive science*. New York: Oxford University Press.

Dell, G. S., & Cholin, J. (this volume). Language production: Computational models.

Dell, G. S., Reed, K. D., Adams, D. R., & Meyer, A. S. (2000). Speech errors, phonotactic constraints, and implicit learning: A study of the role of experience in language production. *Journal of Experimental Psychology: Learning Memory and Cognition*, 26, 1355–67.

Eberhard, K. M., Cutting, J. C., & Bock, K. (2005). Making syntax of sense: Number agreement in sentence production. *Psychological Review*, 112, 531–59.

Emmorey, K. (2002). *Language, cognition, and the brain: Insights from sign language research*. Lawrence Erlbaum.

Ferreira, F. (2000). Syntax in language production: An approach using tree-adjoining grammars. In Wheeldon, L. (Ed.) *Aspects of language production* (pp. 291–330). Philadelphia, PA: Psychology Press.

(2007). Prosody and performance in language production. *Language and Cognitive Processes*, 22(8), 1151–77.

Ferreira, F. & Swets, B. (2002). How incremental is language production? Evidence from the production of utterances requiring the computation of arithmetic sums. *Journal of Memory and Language*, 46, 57–84.

Ferreira, V. S. & Bock, J. K. (2006). The functions of structural priming. *Language and Cognitive Processes*, 21(7–8), 1011–29.

Ferreira, V. S. & Dell, G. S. (2000). Effect of ambiguity and lexical availability on syntactic and lexical production. *Cognitive Psychology*, 40, 296–340.

Ferreira, V. S. & Griffin, Z. M. (2003). Phonological influences on lexical (mis)selection. *Psychological Science*, 14, 86–90.

Ferreira, V. S. & Humphreys, K. R. (2001). Syntactic influences on lexical and morphological processing in language production. *Journal of Memory and Language*, 44, 52–80.

Ferreira, V. S., Slevc, L. R., & Rogers, E. S. (2005). How do speakers avoid ambiguous linguistic expressions? *Cognition*, 96, 263–84.

Fowler, C. A. (2007). Speech production. In Gaskell, M. G. (Ed.) *Oxford Handbook of Psycholinguistics* (pp. 489–501). Oxford: Oxford University Press.

Fowler, C. A., Levy, E. T., & Brown, J. M. (1997). Reductions of spoken words in certain discourse contexts. *Journal of Memory and Language*, 37, 24–40.

Fromkin, V. A. (1971). The non-anomalous nature of anomalous utterances. *Language*, 47, 27–52.

Garrett, M. F. (1975). The analysis of sentence production. In Bower, G. H. (Ed.) *The psychology of learning and motivation* (pp. 133–77). New York: Academic Press.

Gaskell, M. G. (Ed.) (2007). *Oxford Handbook of Psycholinguistics*. Oxford: Oxford University Press.

Gennari, S. P. & MacDonald, M. C. (2009). Linking production and comprehension processes: The case of relative clauses. *Cognition*, 111, 1–23.

Goldin-Meadow, S. (2003). *Hearing gesture: How our hands help us think*. Cambridge MA: Harvard University Press.

Gollan, T. H., & Brown, A. S. (2006). From tip-of-the-tongue (TOT) data to theoretical implications: When more TOTs means better retrieval. *Journal of Experimental Psychology: General*, 135, 462–83.

Gries, S. T. (2005). Syntactic Priming: A Corpus-based Approach. *Journal of Psycholinguistic Research*, 34, 365–99.

Griffin, Z. M. (2003). A reversed word length effect in coordinating the preparation and articulation of words in speaking. *Psychonomic Bulletin and Review*, 10, 603–9.

(2004). Why look? Reasons for eye movements related to language production. In Henderson,

J. M. & Ferreira, F. (Eds.) *The interface of language, vision, and action: Eye movements and the visual world* (pp. 213–47). New York: Psychology Press.

Griffin, Z. M. & Bock, K. (2000). What the eyes say about speaking. *Psychological Science, 11,* 274–9.

Griffin, Z. M. & Ferreira, V. S. (2006). Properties of Spoken Language Production. In Traxler, M. J. & Gernsbacher, M. A. (Eds.) *Handbook of Psycholinguistics* (2nd ed., pp. 21–59). London, England: Elsevier.

Griffin, Z. M. & Weinstein-Tull, J. (2003). Conceptual structure modulates structural priming in the production of complex sentences. *Journal of Memory & Language, 49,* 537–55.

Hartsuiker, R. J., Bastiaanse, R., Postma, A., & Wijnen, F. (Eds.) (2005). *Phonological encoding and monitoring in normal and pathological speech.* Hove, UK: Psychology Press.

Hartsuiker, R. J., Kolk, HHJ, & Huiskamp, P. (1999). Priming word order in sentence production. *Quarterly Journal of Experimental Psychology, 52A,* 129–47.

Hartsuiker, R. J., Pickering, M. J., & Veltkamp, E. (2004). Is syntax separate or shared between languages? Cross-linguistic syntactic priming in Spanish-English bilinguals. *Psychological Science, 15,* 409–14.

Horton, W. S. & Gerrig, R. J. (2005). The impact of memory demands on audience design during language production. *Cognition, 96,* 127–42.

James, L. E. & Burke, D. M. (2000). Phonological priming effects on word retrieval and tip-of-the-tongue experiences in young and older adults. *Journal of Experimental Psychology: Learning, Memory, and Cognition, 26,* 1378–91.

Kellogg, R. T. (1994). *The psychology of writing.* London: Oxford University Press.

Kita, S. (Ed.) (2003). *Pointing: Where language, culture, and cognition meet.* Mahwah, NJ: Lawrence Erlbaum Associates.

Kovács, Á. M. & Mehler, J. (2009). Cognitive gains in 7-month-old bilingual infants. *Proceedings of the National Academy of Sciences, 106(16),* 6556–60.

Levelt, WJM (1989). *Speaking: From intention to articulation.* Cambridge, MA: MIT Press.

Loebell, H. & Bock, K. (2003). Structural priming across languages. *Linguistics, 41,* 791–824.

Lorimor, H., Bock, K., Zalkind, E., Sheyman, A., & Beard, R. (2008). Agreement and attraction in Russian. *Language and Cognitive Processes, 23(6),* 769–99.

Martin, R. C. (2003). Language processing: Functional organization and neuroanatomical basis. *Annual Review of Psychology, 54,* 55–89.

Martin, R. C. & Freedman, M. L. (2001). Short-term retention of lexical-semantic representations: Implications for speech production. *Memory, 9,* 261–80.

McNeill, D. (Ed.). (2000). *Language and gesture.* Cambridge: Cambridge University Press.

Meyer, A. S. & Belke, E. (2007). Word form retrieval in language production. In Gaskell, M. G. (Ed.) *Oxford Handbook of Psycholinguistics* (pp. 471–87). Oxford: Oxford University Press.

Meyer, A. S. & Damian, M. F. (2007). Activation of distractor names in the picture-picture interference paradigm. *Memory & Cognition, 35(3),* 494–503.

Meyer, A. S. & Lethaus, F. (2004). The use of eye tracking in studies of sentence generation. In Henderson, J. M. & Ferreira, F. (Eds.) *The interface of language, vision, and action: Eye movements and the visual world* (pp. 191–211). New York: Psychology Press.

Meyer, A. S., Ouellet, M., & Häcker, C. (2008). Parallel Processing of Objects in a Naming Task. *Journal of Experimental Psychology: Learning, Memory, and Cognition, 34(4),* 982–7.

Meyer, A. S., Roelofs, A., & Levelt, WJM (2003). Word length effects in object naming: The role of a response criterion. *Journal of Memory and Language, 48,* 131–47.

Miozzo, M. & Caramazza, A. (1997). Retrieval of lexical-syntactic features in tip-of-the-tongue states. *Journal of Experimental Psychology: Learning, Memory, and Cognition, 23,* 1410–23.

(1999). The selection of determiners in noun phrase production. *Journal of Experimental Psychology: Learning, Memory, and Cognition, 25,* 907–22.

Motley, M. T., Camden, C. T., & Baars, B. J. (1982). Covert formulation and editing of anomalies in speech production: Evidence from experimentally elicited slips of the tongue. *Journal of Verbal Learning and Verbal Behavior, 21,* 578–94.

Navarrete, E. & Costa, A. (2005). Phonological activation of ignored pictures: Further evidence for a cascade model of lexical access. *Journal of Memory and Language, 53,* 359–77.

Olson, D. R. (1970). Language and thought: Aspects of a cognitive theory of semantics. *Psychological Review, 77,* 257–73.

Oppermann, F., Jescheniak, J. D., & Schriefers, H. (2008). Conceptual coherence affects phonological activation of context objects during object naming. *Journal of Experimental Psychology: Learning, Memory, and Cognition, 34(3),* 587–601.

Pickering, M. J. & Branigan, H. P. (1998). The representation of verbs: Evidence from syntactic priming in language production. *Journal of Memory and Language*, 39, 633–51.

Pickering, M. J. & Ferreira, V. S. (2008). Structural Priming: A Critical Review. *Psychological Bulletin*, 134(3), 427–59.

Pickering, M. J., Branigan, H. P., & McLean, J. F. (2002). Constituent structure is formulated in one stage. *Journal of Memory and Language*, 46, 586–605.

Prunet, J. F., Béland, R., & Idrissi, A. (2000). The mental representation of Semitic words. *Linguistic Inquiry*, 31, 609–48.

Richardson, D. C. & Dale, R. (2005). Looking to understand: The coupling between speakers' and listeners' eye movements and its relationship to discourse comprehension. *Cognitive Science*, 29, 1045–60.

Scheepers, C. (2003). Syntactic priming of relative clause attachments: Persistence of structural configuration in sentence production. *Cognition*, 89, 179–205.

Schriefers, H. (1993). Syntactic processes in the production of noun phrases. *Journal of Experimental Psychology: Learning, Memory, and Cognition*, 19, 841–50.

Shin, J. A. & Christianson, K. (2009). Syntactic processing in Korean-English bilingual production: Evidence from cross-linguistic structural priming. *Cognition*, 112(1), 175–80.

Slevc, L. R. & Ferreira, V. S. (2006). Halting in single word production: A test of the perceptual loop theory of speech monitoring. *Journal of Memory and Language*, 54, 15–540.

Solomon, E. S. & Perlmutter, N. J. (2004). Semantic integration and syntactic planning in language production. *Cognitive Psychology*, 49, 1–46.

Spieler, D. H. & Griffin, Z. M. (2006). The influence of age on the time course of word preparation in multiword utterances. *Language and Cognitive Processes*, 21, 291–321.

Sternberg, S., Knoll, R. L., Monsell, S., & Wright, C. E. (1988). Motor programs and hierarchical organization in the control of rapid speech. *Phonetica*, 45, 175–97.

Spalek, K. & Schriefers, H. J. (2005). Dominance affects determiner selection in language production. *Journal of Memory and Language*, 52, 103–19.

Tanenhaus, M. K., Spivey-Knowlton, M. J., Eberhard, K. M., & Sedivy, J. C. (1995). Integration of visual and linguistic information in spoken language comprehension. *Science*, 268, 1632–4.

Thompson, R., Emmorey, K., & Gollan, T. H. (2005). "Tip of the fingers" experiences by deaf signers. *Psychological Science*, 16, 856–60.

Vigliocco, G. & Hartsuiker, R. J. (2002). The interplay of meaning, sound, and syntax in sentence production. *Psychological Bulletin*, 128, 442–72.

Vigliocco, G., Garrett, M. F., & Antonini, T. (1997). Grammatical gender is on the tip of Italian tongues. *Psychological Science*, 8, 314–17.

Vigliocco, G., Tranel, D. & Druks, J. (this volume). Language production: Patient and imaging research.

Vigliocco, G., Vinson, D. P., Indefrey, P., Levelt, WJM, & Hellwig, F. (2004). Role of grammatical gender and semantics in German word production. *Journal of Experimental Psychology: Learning, Memory, and Cognition*, 30, 483–97.

Wasow, T. (1997). End-weight from the speaker's perspective. *Journal of Psycholinguistic Research*, 20, 347–61.

Watson, D., Breen, M., & Gibson, E. A. (2006). The role of syntactic obligatoriness in the production of intonational boundaries. *Journal of Experimental Psychology: Learning, Memory and Cognition*, 32, 1045–56.

Wheeldon, L. (2000). Generating prosodic structures. In Wheeldon, L. R. (Ed.) *Aspects of Language Production* (pp. 249–74). Philadelphia, PA: Psychology Press.

Wheeldon, L. & Lahiri, A. (1997). Prosodic units in speech production. *Journal of Memory and Language*, 37, 356–81.

Author Note

Thanks to Sid Horton and Gary Dell for comments on drafts of this chapter. This material is based upon work supported by the National Science Foundation under Grant No. 0318456. The original draft of this text was completed in 2006 and has been revised.

CHAPTER 21

Language Production

Computational Models

Gary S. Dell and Joana Cholin

Theories of language production are, more often than not, expressed as computational models. There are dozens of published production models covering everything from representations of intended meanings (e.g., Vigliocco, Vinson, Lewis, & Garrett, 2004) to the detailed movements of articulators (e.g., Guenther, 1995). The models attempt to explain the speed of error-free production (e.g., Roelofs, 1997), production choices (e.g. Ferreira, 1996), and the speech errors made by normal adults (e.g., Dell, 1986; Harley, 1993), children (e.g., Berg & Schade, 1992), and aphasic speakers (e.g., Rapp & Goldrick, 2000).

In this chapter, we review four implemented production models, the *interactive two-step model* of aphasia (Dell, Schwartz, Martin, Saffran, & Gagnon, 1997), the *WEAVER++ model* of lexical access (Levelt, Roelofs & Meyer, 1999), the *marking and morphing model* of number agreement (Eberhard, Cutting, & Bock, 2005), and the *dual-path model* of sentence production and structural priming (Chang, Dell, & Bock, 2006). Our choices include models that have been highly influential for years such as been highly influential for years such as

WEAVER++, along with some more recent developments. As a group, these models are diverse with regard to the kind of data they cover and their computational assumptions. We shall see, however, that there are core similarities as well. All of the models are, in one form or another, based on a parallel spread of activation within networks representing linguistic knowledge. In this sense, models of production are as attuned to the connectionist Zeitgeist as any other psycholinguistic models (see, e.g., Magnuson et al., this volume; Seidenberg, this volume).

What makes a good production model? The simplest answer is that good production models, like all models, clarify theory. They flesh out vague theoretical mechanisms and reveal the hidden consequences of a complicated theory for data. Of course, a successful model also accounts for data. In production, this means mimicking quantitative or qualitative patterns of production errors, response times, or choices (e.g., whether to say "a black cat" or "a cat that's black"). Two of the models that we present account for errors, one for response times, and one for production choices. The phrase *accounts for data*, though, is deceptively simple. Intuitively, we think that models succeed when they match the observations, or at least match better than alternative models do. More important than matching the data, though, is *explaining* the data. A model offers an explanation for a finding when the finding emerges from independently motivated model properties. The clearest examples of this occur when a model's predictions are verified, that is, when it matches previously unknown data, ideally data of a different sort than any data that may have inspired the model. Two of the models that we describe deliberately use this prediction strategy. More commonly, though, modelers achieve explanatory power just by being stingy about model assumptions, including only those with solid independent motivation. In production, these motivations often come from functionality (e.g., production processes must allow for novel utterances), linguistic theory (e.g., inflectional versus derivational morphology), and cognitive theory (e.g., maintenance in working memory versus storage in long-term memory).

1 Models of Lexical Access

We begin with models of the simplest speaking task, the production of single-word utterances. For example, when given a picture of a tree to name, how do people retrieve the form /tri/? Two of our models are concerned with lexical access, Levelt et al.'s (1999) WEAVER++, and the interactive two-step model (Dell et al., 1997; 2007). The latter model is simpler and so we present it first.

2 Interactive two-step model

The interactive two-step model is designed to account for errors in lexical access by normal and aphasic speakers. For example, in a picture naming task, a picture of a cat can elicit *semantic* errors (DOG), formally related words, or *formal* errors (CAP or MAT), *mixed* semantic-formal errors (RAT), *unrelated* word errors (LOG), and *nonword* errors (CAG). Unimpaired speakers rarely err when naming

pictures and, when they do, errors are typically semantic. Aphasic speakers make many errors, exhibiting a variety of patterns.

The model identifies mechanisms of lexical access and how these lead to error. Lexical knowledge resides in a network of semantic, word, and phonological units (Figure 21.1). Connections between layers are excitatory and bidirectional and serve to translate a pattern of activation across semantic units to a set of phoneme units. The two most important characteristics of the two-step interactive model are given in its name. There are two steps in the retrieval process, and both are carried out through the interactive or bidirectional spread of activation. Let us walk through an example using CAT as the target word.

The first step is *word retrieval*. The semantic units of the target are activated and this activation spreads through the network for a fixed period of time. This activates the target word unit, CAT, and potential error units (semantic – DOG, formal – MAT, and mixed – RAT). DOG and RAT get activation from semantic units shared with CAT, and MAT and RAT get it from the bottom-up spread of activation from phoneme units (e.g., /æ/ and /t/) in common with the target. The word retrieval step is concluded by the selection of the most activated word unit of the proper grammatical category. In a task in which one names pictured objects (implicitly saying "This is a(n)____"), the proper category is noun. Because there is noise in the activations there is some chance that a semantic, mixed, formal, or in extreme cases, an unrelated word may be selected instead of the target, setting the stage for the production of a lexical error.

The second step is phonological retrieval. The selected word unit is given a boost in activation, and another phase of spreading activation is initiated. After a period of time, the most activated phoneme units are selected, thus completing lexical access. Errors in this step typically lead to nonwords (CAG) or formal errors (MAT).

The central assumption of the model's application to aphasia is that aphasic errors are not qualitatively different from everyday

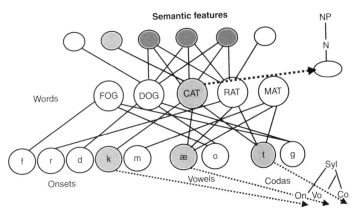

Figure 21.1. An example of the interactive two-step model activating the word CAT.

speech errors. This assumption, called the *continuity thesis*, was first proposed by Freud (1901). To implement the continuity thesis, Dell et al. (1997; see also Dell et al., 2007) first created a normal version of the model that simulated the error proportions made by unimpaired speakers in a picture naming task consisting of 175 pictured objects. Next, they defined a "random pattern" of errors; the random pattern is the hypothesized error-category proportions that would occur in the naming task if lexical knowledge contributed nothing to the speaker's output. In such a situation, speech would be phonologically legal gibberish, and the random pattern thus consists largely of nonwords, any words being chance events. And finally, they identified a set of processing parameters such that, by varying these parameters, they created a continuum of models with the normal version of the model at one end, and a broken down version that produces the random pattern at the other end. Varying these processing parameters is thus how the model can be "lesioned" to simulate aphasia, and the hypothesized continuum of models is supposed to represent the range of aphasic error patterns on the naming task.

The most successful characterization of this aphasic error–pattern continuum came from a version of the two-step interactive model that assumes two lesionable parameters, the weight of the bidirectional connections between the semantic and lexical units (parameter s), and the weight of the connections between the phonological and lexical units (parameter p) (Foygel & Dell, 2000). Reducing these parameters leads to aphasic-like error patterns because low weights impede the transmission of activation required for successful lexical access. A recent study of ninety-four representative aphasic subjects (Schwartz, Dell, Martin, Gahl, & Sobel, 2006) showed that this version of the model, called the semantic-phonological model, could give a good account of the variability of the patients' errors in the naming task. The model explained 94.4 percent of the variance among the patterns. An example using a single patient illustrates how it works.

Patient NAC's naming-error pattern consisted of .74 correct, .07 semantic errors, .08 formal errors, .05 mixed errors, .06 unrelated errors, and .01 nonword errors. The model accurately mimics this pattern with s = .0165, and p = .0382 (.73 correct, .10 semantic, .08 formal, .03 mixed, .06 unrelated, .00 nonwords). Normal values of the s and p parameters are around .05 or greater, and so the model's account of NAC is that the lexical–semantic connections (parameter s) are considerably weaker than normal and that there is a mild phonological deficit as well (parameter p). The similarity of the model and patient proportions can be quantified as the uncorrected root mean squared deviation (*rmsd*) between the two sets of numbers. Here it is .018, meaning that, on average, each patient and model proportion differs by about .018. Patient NAC's fit in this respect was slightly better than the average *rmsd* of the ninety-four patients, which was .024.

The fact that the model can behave like NAC and the other patients with respect to their naming error proportions is good, but it is not a strong test of the model. As we noted previously, a model's explanations can be verified from tests of its predictions. In this case, can the lesioned parameters assigned by the model predict other aspects of patient behavior? One such prediction concerns formal errors, such as MAT for CAT. In the model, these errors can occur either at the word retrieval step or the phonological retrieval step. Lexical-level formals happen when the wrong word (e.g., MAT) is selected during word retrieval, and that word is then correctly encoded at phonological retrieval. Phonological-level formals occur when the correctly chosen target (CAT) is encoded as a similar word (MAT) during phonological retrieval.

The model's propensity to produce lexical as opposed to phonological formals varies with its parameters. A formal error requires that a formal neighbor of the target (e.g., MAT) be more active than the target and the target's semantic neighbors. This is most likely to happen when p is large and s is small. A large p allows activation to flow from the target's phonemes to the word unit for the potential formal error (e.g., from /ae/ and /t/ to MAT). A small s means that the activation of the target word and its semantic neighbors will be low. So a large p and a small s are conducive to formal errors at the lexical level. Specifically, the model predicts that, if $p > s$, the patient's formal errors will occur mostly at the lexical level. But how can we tell whether these errors are lexical or not? Recall that at the word retrieval step selected words are required to be nouns. Thus, according to the model, lexical formals should be nouns, unlike formals that result from phonological errors, which would be nouns by chance. Now we can state the prediction precisely: The extent

to which a patient's formal errors are nouns can be predicted by the extent to which p is greater than s. NAC's p is much greater than s, and consequently, this patient's formal errors should tend to be nouns. In support of the prediction, ninety-two percent of NAC's formals were nouns. (Most English words are nouns, so chance is sixty-four percent). More generally, the formal errors from patients in the study in which p was not greater than s were nouns only sixty-six percent of the time; when p was greater than s by .02 or more (like NAC), the formal errors were nouns ninety-one percent of the time. This successful test of a prediction supports the model's treatment of formal errors as both lexical and phonological (the two-step assumption) and that lexical formals are promoted by feedback from the phonological to the lexical level (the interactive assumption).

Another example of a prediction concerns the task of word repetition, in which the patient listens to a word and then repeats it. Many of the patients in Schwartz et al. (2006) did a repetition test in addition to the picture naming test. On the assumption that word repetition entails the recognition of the word, followed by the production of that word using the phonological retrieval step, one can use the model to predict repetition from naming, provided that one has previously determined that the patient has no difficulty recognizing the word. Successful repetition predictions would support the two-step nature of the model, and the assumption that repetition and naming share the phonological retrieval step. Consider NAC again. NAC's predicted performance on repetition can be determined by running the model using only the phonological retrieval step, using the values for s and p that were already determined from picture naming (s=.0165, p = .0382). Because NAC has a relatively large phonological parameter, predicted repetition is quite good (.98 correct, .00 semantic, .01 formal, .00 mixed, .00 unrelated, .01 nonwords). This predicted pattern can then be compared to NAC's actual repetition (.86 correct, .00 semantic, .10 formal, .00

mixed, .00 unrelated, .04 nonwords). Here, the model correctly predicts the general form of the pattern (only formal and non-word errors) and the fact that repetition is more accurate than naming for NAC, but it overpredicts performance somewhat (the *rmsd* is .062). Across the fifty-nine patients in the study who had good word recognition abilities, the model's predictions were fairly accurate with a mean *rmsd* of .052. So NAC is actually one of the more poorly predicted patients. Although an average *rmsd* of .052 for the repetition predictions is larger than that for the fits of the model to picture naming (.024), it must be noted that in fitting the model to the naming data, the model had the freedom to choose the best fitting values of *s* and *p*. That is, *s* and *p* were *free parameters*. When the model was applied to repetition, however, the values of *s* and *p* were those determined from the naming data. The repetition predictions are thus absolute, or zero-parameter, predictions. The strategy of fixing model parameters based on some aspects of the data and then seeing if those parameters can explain the rest of the data is a time-honored method of testing a quantitative model.

In summary, the interactive two-step model views aphasic error patterns as a consequence of lowered connection weights in a network of words, their sounds, and their meanings. The model can mimic much of the variability of aphasic naming and repetition deficits, and can generate testable predictions. Its successes stem largely from its two-step and interactive assumptions, and the continuity thesis, the proposal that aphasic errors are akin to normal speech errors. Its ability to generate quantitative predictions arises from its modest empirical goals – it only deals with a small set of error categories – and its simplicity – the variety of aphasic syndromes is reduced to a two-dimensional continuum. As we move onto the next model, which also deals with lexical access, we will see that the simplicity of the aphasia model is a drawback because important linguistic and psycholinguistic phenomena were not considered.

3 WEAVER++

WEAVER++ (Word-Encoding by Activation and VERification) is the spreading activation-based network model developed by Roelofs (1992, 1997, 1998, 1999), which is based on Levelt's (1989, 1992) and Levelt, Roelofs, and Meyer's (1999) theory of speech production. WEAVER++ integrates stages from conceptual preparation, lemma retrieval, and word form encoding, with the encoding of word forms further divided into morphological, phonological, and phonetic encoding. It adopts Dell's (1986) assumption of word retrieval by the spread of activation and Levelt's (1992) online syllabification and access to a syllabary (Cholin, Levelt, & Schiller, 2006; Levelt & Wheeldon, 1994). In these respects, WEAVER++'s properties are well motivated by previously existing linguistic and psycholinguistic theory.

WEAVER++ aims to describe how words are produced. It explains facts about language performance such as how information is computed and/or stored in memory and how stored items are accessed by the speaker during speech planning. Contrary to the interactive two-step model (Dell et al., 1997; 2007) that we just described, the WEAVER++ model has been primarily designed to account for latency data from error-free speech.

As in the previously described model, lexical access happens in two steps, but, and herein lies the major difference to the interactive two-step model, there is no bidirectional spread of activation between the levels of lemma and word form retrieval. In WEAVER++, the retrieval of the *lemma*, comprising the lexical item's syntactic features and the retrieval of this item's sound form, its *word form*, are strictly serial processes performing different functions. While a lemma has to be selected under competition with other coactivated lemmas, the activation of a word form is not subject to competition, as only the word form of the selected lemma will be activated. Word forms do not receive activation unless their corresponding lemmas have been selected

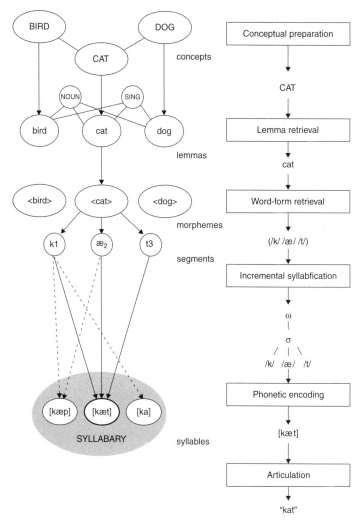

Figure 21.2. An example of the WEAVER++ model activating the word CAT.

and there is no feedback from the lower, word form level to the upper, lemma level.

In the following, the stages from conceptualization to syllabary access will be described in more detail with a focus on lexical access. Evidence from chronometric data will be mentioned at relevant places and a discussion of how WEAVER++ can account for these data will be provided after the model has been outlined.

WEAVER++ implements the mental lexicon as an associative network with nodes, links, and link labels, all accessed by the spread of activation (see Figure 21.2).

Imagine the same picture naming situation described for the previous model: A speaker is presented a picture of a cat that he or she is instructed to name. The conceptual preparation of the word *cat* consists of activating the corresponding lexical concept node for CAT in the conceptual network (Lexical concepts will be denoted in capitals).

Related concepts such as DOG or BIRD will also be activated in the network, but only CAT is flagged as goal concept. Each active lexical concept spreads activation to its lemma, the lexical item's syntactic description. For instance, the lemma for CAT,

cat (italics will be used to denote lemmas) specifies that it is a count noun and it has a variable diacritic for number (singular versus plural). In languages that encode gender, such as French or German, the equivalent (*chat*, *Katze*) would also be specified for gender (masculine, feminine, respectively). Verbs would also be specified for word class and for their morphosyntactic parameters such as PERSON, NUMBER, TENSE, and ASPECT.

In WEAVER++, the spread of activation follows a linear rule with a decay factor, the same as in the interactive two-step model. Each node sends a proportion of its activation to the nodes it is connected to. In our example, the concept CAT sends activation to other related concepts such as DOG, BIRD, and ANIMAL and also to its lemma node *cat*. The lemma *cat* will be the most activated lemma as it receives the full proportion of CAT whereas the other activated lemmas of DOG, BIRD, and ANIMAL will only receive a proportion of a proportion of the activation of CAT. It is important to note that in WEAVER++, as in the interactive two-step model, there are no inhibitory links in the network. All activated lemmas will compete for selection. The actual selection of lemma nodes (and all other nodes in the model) is accomplished by production rules. A production rule is a condition–action pair that specifies a condition to be fulfilled and an action to be taken when the condition is met. For example, *IF the lemma,* cat, *is linked to the concept CAT, and the activation of the lemma exceeds threshold, THEN select* cat *as target lemma*. The production rule is stored within a specific node and is triggered when this lemma node exceeds activation threshold. The production rule itself then verifies the link between this lemma node and the selected node one level up, the active concept node. The actual moment of firing of the production rule is determined by the ratio of activation of the lemma node and the sum of the activation of all the other lemmas (Luce's Choice rule, 1959). Hence, the selection latency of a specific lemma is dependent on the activation of the other nodes. Given the choice ratio, the expected selection latency can be computed.

In short, the selection of the target lemma *cat* depends on two things: First, on the activation of *cat* that has to compete with the other coactivated lemmas such as *dog* and *bird*, and second on the verification procedure that is implemented by the production rule, which checks the link between the activated node cat with the appropriate active conceptual node one level up, CAT.

The output of lemma retrieval is input to the second step in lexical access, the level of *word form retrieval*. A crucial feature of WEAVER++ is that *only* the selected lemma (e.g., *cat*) will activate its corresponding word form in the mental lexicon (e.g., /kæt/). Activation of the word form only takes place after the lemma has been selected; that is, no other lemma than the previously selected lemma *cat* will pass activation onto this next encoding level, word form encoding. Specifically, WEAVER ++ does not allow phonological coactivation of semantic competitors. For example, while preparing the target utterance "cat," the word forms of coactivated lemmas like *dog* and *bird* remain unactivated.

The word form encoding level contains morphemes, segments, and syllable program nodes, and links between these nodes: The morphemes are connected to a lemma and its morphosyntactic parameters (e.g., NUMBER, PERSON) (Janssen, Roelofs, & Levelt, 2002). The links between morphemes and segments indicate the serial order of the segments within the lemma's morphemes. The first step during word form encoding is the retrieval of the single phonemic segments the morpheme(s) consist of. In our *cat* example, the segments /k/, /æ/, and /t/ will be spelled out. In the WEAVER++ model, segments in the retrieved phonological code are only specified for their serial order within a word, but not for their syllable positions (onset, nucleus, and coda) or the C(onsonant)–V(owel) structure (Roelofs & Meyer, 1998). The segments contain labeled links for their ordering within the word form. The actual syllabic position of a segment is determined by the online syllabification process. The justification for not predetermining syllable positions in the phonological codes stored in the lexicon comes from the phenomenon of *resyllabification*. In connected speech, syllable boundaries often differ from a word's or morpheme's canonical syllabification. If, for instance, the stored phonological code for the verb *defend* would be syllabified as de–fend, then the speaker must "resyllabify" the word when used in a different context, such as the past tense (de-fen-ded) or cliticization ("defend it" as de – fen – dit). Therefore, WEAVER ++ implements an online syllabification process, also called *prosodification*, that incrementally computes successive syllables (Cholin, Schiller, & Levelt, 2004; Meyer, 1990; Wheeldon & Levelt, 1995). The prosodification proceeds from left to right, assigning segments to syllable positions following the syllabification rules of the language. Next, these constructed syllables are input to a final encoding step, phonetic encoding. A crucial assumption of this final step is that speakers have access to a store of ready-made syllable motor programs, a *mental syllabary*. Each segment in the phonological code is linked to all syllable program nodes in which it partakes, that is, the segments /k/, /æ/, and /t/ spread activation to all syllable program nodes that contain these segments in the particular positions. Essentially the same selection criteria that were described for lemma selection are implemented for syllable node selection as well. When one of the coactivated syllables exceeds threshold, a production rule has to verify the link between the segments of the syllable in the syllabary and the phonological syllable that was incrementally composed one level up. When the target syllable node has been selected, it will be executed by the articulatory network to perform overt speech. The picture will thus successfully be named as [kæt].

In sum, we saw how the concept CAT is first transformed into the lexicalized item cat. The selection of cat is subject to competition and once the lemma *cat* has been selected as target lemma, this will trigger the activation of its corresponding word form /kæt/. The morpheme node of cat activates the segments connected to it. During syllabification, the segments are bundled together to form a phonological syllable. The segments will activate multiple syllable program nodes in the syllabary. The selected syllable program node will then guide articulation.

Let us now turn to the question of how the WEAVER ++ model fits chronometric data and how the crucial claim that lemma selection and word form activation are qualitatively different can be found in these data. One of the most prominent experimental paradigms in production research is the *picture-word interference paradigm* (MacLeod, 1991). The standard findings in this paradigm are the *semantic interference* and *phonological facilitation* effects (Damian & Martin, 1999; Glaser & Düngelhoff, 1984; Jescheniak, Schriefers, & Hantsch, 2001; Jescheniak, Schriefers, & Hantsch, 2003; Meyer & Schriefers, 1991; Schriefers, Meyer, & Levelt, 1990; Starreveld, & La Heij, 1995). The semantic interference effect is thought to reflect lexical competition during lemma selection. The phonological facilitation effect on the other hand, is thought to reflect enhanced activation of the activated word form. In this paradigm, participants are instructed to name a displayed picture (e.g., of a cat) while ignoring a distractor word presented before, with, or after picture onset (Stimulus Onset Asynchrony, SOA). The distractor word can either be semantically (e.g., dog, bird, horse) or phonologically related (e.g., cap), or unrelated (e.g., bed) to the target utterance (e.g., cat). WEAVER ++ simulates the standard findings of the semantic interference effect (Glaser & Düngelhoff, 1984; Roelofs, 1992) for picture naming and the phonological facilitation effect by implementing the following parameters: (1) a real-time value in milliseconds for the smallest time interval (time step) in the model, (2) values for the general spreading rate at the conceptual level, (3) values for the general spreading rate at the lemma level, (4) decay rate, (5) strength of the distractor input to the network, (6) time interval during which this input was provided, and (7) a selection threshold (see Roelofs, 1992; Levelt et al, 1999).

Semantically related distractor words are assumed to affect the activation of competing lemmas, while phonologically related distractor words affect the activation of the target's word form. Semantically related distractor words add activation to coactivated lemmas and make them even stronger competitors for lemma selection, thereby delaying the selection process. In our example, semantic interference results from the fact that additional activation is given to a nontarget lemma (e.g., *dog*, because CAT sends activation to DOG). Thus, the semantically related nontarget lemma becomes a stronger competitor than any nontarget lemma that is activated by the distractor only (e.g., bed), and thus the selection of the target lemma will be slowed, causing longer naming latencies for semantically related distractor words compared to unrelated distractors. Contrary to the enhanced lemma competition resulting in semantic interference, a phonologically related distractor word *shortens* naming latencies compared to unrelated distractors. This effect arises in the model by *adding* activation to the shared phonological segments of the target word form. (Remember that there is no competition during the word form retrieval. Only the selected lemma will be phonologically activated.) A phonologically related distractor (e.g., initial segments are identical as in *ca*p–*ca*t) will add activation to the shared segments and thereby *speed up* segmental retrieval. Thus, the qualitatively different effects of semantic interference, due to enhanced lemma competition, and phonological facilitation, due to the additional part-activation of the shared segments, indicate that the processes of lemma and word form retrieval are distinct.

In summary, WEAVER++ successfully simulates standard findings in the latency data. It explains how concepts are transformed into lexical entries and how a speaker will get from there to abstract articulatory units. Although we have only described how WEAVER++ explains data from the picture-word interference paradigm, it also accounts for findings from other paradigms, such as the syllable priming (e.g., Schiller,

1998) and the implicit priming paradigms (e.g., Meyer, 1990) used to investigate specific mechanisms in word form encoding (see Levelt et al. for review). More generally, WEAVER++'s considerable success is owed to its ability to apply to chronometric data from a variety of tasks, tasks concerned with multiple levels in the lexical access process. In this respect, it contrasts with the simpler interactive two-step model, which is limited to explaining specific error categories.

4 Models of sentence production

Describing a picture of a cat running from some dogs as, "The cat is chased by the dogs," is orders of magnitude more complex than naming a picture of a cat (see Griffin & Crew, this volume). Not only are there several words to access, but their order must also be determined. On top of this, each decision about what word to say and when to say it is constrained by the overall meaning of the sentence, the grammar of the language, and the other words that have been, or are about to be, spoken. For example, if "the cat" is the subject of the sentence, the main verb must appear as *chased*, not *chase*, and a singular form of the verb *to be* (e.g., *is*) must precede it to agree with the singular *cat*. These constraints, however, would not apply if the speaker chose to describe the picture as "The dogs are chasing the cat." The implemented models of sentence production confront this complexity. They tackle the knotty issue of the representation of meaning, and the relation between meaning and sentence structure. In the case of the marking and morphing (or M&M) model, which we turn to next, the focus is on agreement: How speakers say "the cat IS…" but "the dogs ARE…"

4.1 *Marking and morphing model of agreement*

Agreement is a common feature of language. In English, for example, verbs agree with subject noun phrases in number (*The key to the cabinet* is *lost*), and pronouns agree with their antecedents in number and gender (*Mary's here, isn't she?*). We can learn how speakers implement agreement by looking at utterances with agreement errors, such as "The key to the cabinets *are* lost." Bock and Miller (1991) elicited such errors in experiments by giving subjects a sentence preamble, "the key to the cabinets" and asking them to repeat it and complete the sentence. The task requires the speaker to supply a verb and, hence, the factors that contribute to agreement errors can be assessed.

An important source of agreement errors is *attraction*: Nearby phrases with different feature values can interfere. Bock and Miller (1991) showed that a *local noun* that mismatches the *head noun* in number greatly increases the chance of an agreement error. So the plural local noun *cabinets* in *the key to the cabinets* would lead to the erroneous production of plural verbs as much as twenty percent of the time. When the local noun is singular, such errors are rare.

There are two particularly important properties of attraction. First is the singular–plural asymmetry. As illustrated with the "key to the cabinets" example, when the head noun is singular, a plural local noun will often lead to the erroneous production of a plural verb. Attraction from singular local nouns, however, is much weaker. In fact, sometimes the rate with which "keys to the cabinet" will lead to a singular verb is not reliably different from that of "keys to the cabinets" (Bock, et al., 2001). This empirical asymmetry can be attributed to a representational one. Plural nouns are specified as plural, but singular ones are not specified in any particular way (e.g., Eberhard, 1997). As we will see, the M&M model's implementation makes this claim concrete. The other property concerns the effects of notional or conceptual influences on agreement. Collective nouns such as *choir* and *army* are notionally plural, but are often singular, particularly in American English. Nonetheless, their notional plurality can affect agreement. Singular collective head nouns (*choir*), regardless of whether their local nouns are singular or plural, lead to more plural verb agreement than do individual head nouns

(e.g., *singer*). This notional influence is limited, however. Collectives in the local noun position ("The picture of the choir") have no power to promote attraction, unlike plural individual nouns ("The picture of the singers"), which create considerable attraction.

Eberhard et al. (2005) present both a general theory and an implemented model. The theory identifies three key processes in number agreement: the valuation of notional number, number *marking*, and number *morphing*. *Notional number* is a property of the message to be conveyed and depends on how entities are conceived. This number is transmitted to the linguistic system through the marking process. *Marking* constrains the subject noun phrase to carry a number consistent with the notional number of its referent, regardless of any particular singular or plural specification on nouns that are retrieved for realizing the noun phrase. For example, the phrase *the dog and cat* will be marked as plural even though each retrieved noun is singular. Of course, lexical specifications can sometimes dominate this marking. The phrase *the scissors* is notionally singular, but lexically plural. *Morphing* reconciles the constraints imposed from the lexicon with the marking of the subject noun phrase, thus determining whether a verb is singular or plural.

The implemented component of the model focuses on two sources of number information and how they are reconciled during morphing. These are the initial marking of notional number on the subject noun phrase, and the lexical number specifications of the head and local nouns. In the model, this number information corresponds to activation values, or "SAP," (standing for "singular and plural") running from zero (singular) to one (plural).[1] Let us illustrate the model's operations using *the key to the cabinets* as the subject noun phrase (Figure 21.3). First, the marking process assigns a SAP value to the subject noun phrase based on its notional number. Assuming that the phrase

---

[1] The model also allows for negative activations standing for specific individuation via quantifiers, such as "one girl," but we will not consider this here.

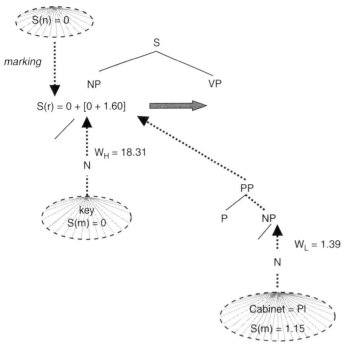

Figure 21.3. The Marking and Morphing model assigning singular and plural (SAP) values to constituents to determine verb agreement.

refers to a single key, the SAP from marking, S(n), is zero. Had the subject NP been *the keys*, S(n) would have been one, and had it been something like *the choir*, it would have been some value between zero and one. Next, lexical specification SAPs, or S(m)s, are determined for *key* (zero) and *cabinets* (one, which is transformed to 1.15 by a factor reflecting the relative frequency of singulars and plurals for plural count nouns). The S(n) and the S(m) values are then reconciled through the "flow" of SAP from the lexical items at the bottom of the subject noun phrase tree to the root of the tree. This results in the determination of S(r), the total SAP at the root. S(r) is then transmitted to the verb phrase, determining the number of the verb; the higher S(r) is, the greater the probability that the verb is plural.

The model does an excellent job of simulating the probabilities of singular and plural verbs in experimental studies of agreement (*rmsd* = .032 across seventeen experimental conditions). Crucially, the model exhibits plural attraction. *The key to the cabinets*

leads to plural verbs thirteen percent of the time in both the model and in Eberhard's et al.'s (2005) average data from seventeen studies. In contrast, the model generates a plural verb for *the key to the cabinet* only one percent of the time, also in agreement with the data. Attraction in the model happens because the SAP of the local noun contributes to reconciliation. It flows into the root just as the head noun's SAP does, albeit more weakly. The model also explains the singular–plural asymmetry. Although *the key to the cabinets* creates plural attraction errors, *the keys to the cabinet* exhibits no singular attraction in the model or the data. In the model this is because a singular count noun such as *cabinet* has a SAP of zero and hence has no influence on S(r). The model's attraction asymmetry arises from the numeric asymmetry inherent in zero (singulars) and one (plurals), thus implementing Eberhard's (1997) proposal about the lack of specification for singulars. The model also accounts for the differing effects of notional number on head and local nouns. Singular collectives such as *choir* will create some plural agreement when they are heads, but have no influence in the local noun position. In the model, this property of the data is reflected in the SAP contributions; local nouns get their SAP from lexical specifications only, not from notional number.

One particularly valuable feature of the M&M model is that it can also apply to errors in pronoun agreement with minimal changes ("The key to the cabinets fell, didn't it/they?"). In fact, Eberhard et al. estimated model parameters from verb agreement data and then used these to predict pronoun agreement error rates (*rmsd* = .089 across eleven conditions). This demonstration of predictive validity is like that shown by the interactive two-step model, which used parameters derived from picture naming to predict word repetition.

The M&M model achieves its successes because of three properties. First, it is derived from a motivated theory of production, specifically one that distinguishes meaning from the grammar, the lexicon from the syntax, and grammatical functions (e.g., subjecthood) from surface phrase structures. Second, the database is considerable. Since Bock and Miller (1991), there have been well over thirty published experimental studies of agreement. Finally, the model's focus on a specific measure, number agreement error probability, allows for quantitative predictions of the data. The final model that we consider, the dual-path model, differs from the M&M model on this last point. It deals with a broad array of phenomena, but qualitatively rather than quantitatively.

4.2 *Dual-path model of syntactic acquisition and sentence production*

The dual-path model (Chang, Dell, & Bock, 2006) attempts to integrate three research domains: structural priming studies of sentence production, the acquisition of syntax, and connectionist models of sequence learning.

Structural priming is the tendency for speakers to use the syntactic structure of recently spoken or heard utterances. In a

typical experiment, participants describe pictured events that can be described by either of two alternate structures, such as actives ("Lightning strikes the church.") or passives ("The church is struck by lightning."). In a trial, a *prime* sentence exhibiting one of the forms (e.g., passive) is presented to the participant, who performs some task with it such as repeating it or judging whether it was heard before. Subsequently, a target picture is presented, and the participant describes it in a sentence. Structural priming is obtained when manipulation of the prime structure boosts target descriptions whose structure matches the prime. The key finding is that priming can be quite abstract. It is obtained when the prime and target do not share meaning or lexical items (Bock, 1986). Even more dramatically, priming occurs in the absence of similarity of thematic structure (e.g., agent, patient) between the prime and target. For example, a prime that is not passive, but nonetheless has the phrase structure of a passive ("The 747 was landing by the tower."), will stimulate passives in descriptions of unrelated target pictures (Bock & Loebell, 1990).

The dual-path model holds that structural priming is a form of learning. Specifically, priming results from the same mechanisms that are responsible for language acquisition. Consequently, the model first needs to explain how the ability to produce sentences is acquired. Figure 21.4 illustrates the major components of the model. Specifically, it is a multilayered connectionist network with learnable connections between most of its layers. To produce a sentence, the model must learn to map from a message to a word sequence that expresses the message. For example, assume that the model's message is this proposition [X=DOG, DEF, .25; Y=CAT, DEF, .50; A=CHASE, .50], where X and Y are agent and patient thematic roles for the action A, DEF is a definite marker, and the numbers reflect the relative prominence of the roles. The model then must output an appropriate sentence one word at a time. Here, either *the dog chase s the cat* or *the cat is chase pastpart by the dog* would be appropriate, although the latter would

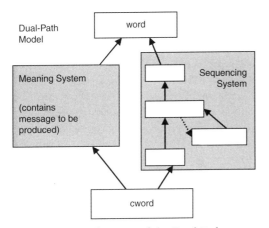

Figure 21.4. A schematic of the Dual Path model (see text for details).

be better given this message because CAT is more prominent than DOG. The model learns to produce sentences by experiencing sentences in context. That is, it hears sentences in situations in which it can infer the meaning. As it hears each word (the input labeled *cword* in Figure 21.4), it uses the inferred message, which is stored in temporary weights that bind concepts to roles, to predict what the next word will be. That is, it outputs a set of activations across vocabulary units (the model component labeled *word* in Figure 21.4). To the extent that its predictions are in error, which is determined when each next word is heard, the model changes its connection weights so as to reduce the chance of that error in the future. Because the model learns to predict heard word sequences under the guidance of an inferred message, it can seamlessly transfer this knowledge to production, which also involves the generation of word sequences constrained by a message. Thus, word-sequence prediction and sentence production are construed as related tasks.

The touchstone for a production model is the ability to create appropriate sequences that it has never experienced before. The dual-path model has good generalization abilities. If, for example, it has never experienced a particular concept as a direct object, it can nonetheless produce such as sentence when its message demands it. The model's ability to generalize arises from the two

pathways that inspire its name. As Figure 21.4 illustrates, the model separates the lexical concepts and roles of the message (the *meaning system*) from a mostly independent network that learns to sequence these roles and provide morphosyntactic markers (the *sequencing system*). Because it is largely isolated from the meaning system, the sequencing system learns abstract syntactic patterns. Thus, it will learn that whatever lexical concept is associated with its X role (typically the agent) will tend to appear in certain syntactic slots. This knowledge is fully functional regardless of what concept is assigned to the X role.

The model's learning and sequencing assumptions are borrowed from *simple recurrent networks* or SRNs (Elman, 1990, see Roland and Hare, this volume). An SRN is a feedforward layered network that also contains a layer of units called the *context* that stores the network's activation pattern from the previous sequential step (each step corresponding to a word in the dual-path model). The changing context enables an SRN to use its memory of the past to anticipate the future of a sequence. The model's sequencing system uses such a context and is thus a kind of SRN. SRNs have explained how people extract generalizations in nonlinguistic sequence learning tasks (e.g., Cleeremans & McClelland, 1991) and how syntactic categories might be acquired from the distributions of words in sentences (Christiansen & Chater, 1999; Elman, 1993). Learning in an SRN involves changing connection weights in response to prediction error, and this is exactly how the dual-path model acquires the weights that represent its knowledge of sentence structures.

The dual-path model explains three kinds of data: structural priming in adults, elicited productions of children, and preferential-looking studies of syntax acquisition in very young children (e.g., Naigles, 1990). All of these phenomena are explained through learning. As the model is exposed to sentences in context, it changes its weights, and thus learns the structures of its English-like training language and how they map onto meaning. Early in training, it simulates acquisition data. For example, both children and the model respond to transitive sentences better than to intransitive ones. In the model, transitives are experienced relatively more often than intransitives and they have a more consistent mapping between their roles and structural positions.

After the model has reached "adulthood," learning does not stop, though. Each experienced sentence changes connection weights, albeit less dramatically. This is how structural priming arises. When a prime sentence is experienced, there are small weight changes. These then bias the model to assemble a structurally similar sentence when it is given the target's message to produce, in such a manner as to simulate the results of structural priming experiments. For example, because priming is weight change, rather than temporary activation, the model accounts for the fact that structural priming is undiminished when up to ten unrelated sentences are interspersed between prime and target (Bock & Griffin, 2000). Moreover, it can explain when priming occurs and does not occur. Chang et al. (2006, Table 13) summarize eight different priming phenomena that the model simulates. One example: Because the model's representations within the sequencing system are somewhat isolated from meaning, the model can explain why locative sentences such as "The 747 was landing by the tower" can prime for the production of thematically unrelated, but structurally similar, passives such as "A church is struck by lightning" as effectively as passives can. Both in the model and the data, locative and passive primes boost the production of passive targets by approximately five percent (Bock & Loebell 1990).

The principal strength of the dual-path model is its use of learning as an explanation for production data. Not only is the model's learning algorithm directly responsible for the priming itself by changing the weights during prime processing, but this algorithm also plays a key role in the acquisition of the abstract structural representations that underlie the priming. This focus on learning is unique in models of sentence production.

The model's most important limitations concern its simplifications. Although the model acquires its knowledge by trying to predict words as it listens to sentences in context, it does not actually *comprehend* the sentences, that is, extract meaning from the input sequence. Comprehension presents its own challenges to modelers (Roland and Hare, this volume). A second key simplification is the model's restriction to simple single-clause sentences. Consequently, it does not address issues associated with the production of sentences with coordination, recursion, and "moved" constituents. Because many linguistic and psycholinguistic theories concern the nature and processing of such complex sentences, the model is not informative in this regard.

5 Summary and conclusions

We have presented four models of production, two dealing with lexical access (the interactive two-step model, and WEAVER++) and two with sentence production (the M&M model and the dual-path model). Within each of these domains, one model emphasizes data fitting and zero-parameter quantitative predictions using a single data type (the interactive two-step model's six aphasic error categories, and the M&M model's probabilities of singular versus plural agreement), while the other (WEAVER++ and the dual-path model) is more complex and broad in scope, and applies to diverse data types.

What kind of computational model is best suited for expressing and testing theoretical claims about production? Clearly models that implement a fairly complete picture, such as WEAVER++ or the dual-path model, are desirable. Production is an extraordinarily complex process and it is now examined through a variety of experimental paradigms (Griffin & Crew, this volume). Models that respect this complexity and provide insight about data from multiple tasks are thus essential. Such models are quite difficult to understand, though. It is particularly hard to generate true predictions from them, that is, precise claims about new data. Thus, the more focused models that generate quantitative predictions are important. Predictions provide uniquely powerful support when upheld and unambiguously signal that something is amiss when they are not.

We anticipate two future developments in models of production. For one, we expect that models will increasingly seek motivation from psycholinguistic data outside of production's typical database, studies of production errors and latencies in simple description tasks. For example, the dual-path model attempts to account for acquisition as well as adult production data, and recent instantiations of WEAVER++ (e.g., Roelofs, 2004) have been applied to the perception and monitoring of speech, as well as production. Because production, comprehension, and acquisition are mutually constraining, these extensions are essential. The other likely development will consist in the linkage of model components and parameters to the brain. Although all four of the models that we reviewed employ quasi-neural spreading activation processes, they have, thus far, made no specific claims about actual neural mechanisms and brain regions. For example, one can ask whether the semantic and phonological parameters of the interactive two-step model of lexical access correspond to distinct brain regions by correlating across patients, parameter values, and lesion locations. In general, as findings from neuropsychological and neuroimaging studies of production become more extensive and systematic (e.g., Vigliocco, Tranel & Drucks, this volume), computational models will, no doubt, follow their lead.

References

Berg, T. & Schade, U. (1992). The role of inhibition in a spreading activation model of language production, Part 1: The psycholinguistic perspective. *Journal of Psycholinguistic Research*, 22, 405–34.

Bock, J. K. (1986). Syntactic persistence in language production. *Cognitive Psychology*, 18, 355–87.

Bock, J. K. & Miller, C. A. (1991). Broken agreement. *Cognitive Psychology*, 23, 45–93.

Bock, K. & Griffin, Z. M. (2000). The persistence of structural priming: Transient activation or implicit learning? *Journal of Experimental Psychology: General*, 129, 177–92.

Bock, K. & Loebell, H. (1990). Framing sentences. *Cognition*, 35, 1–39.

Bock, K. Eberhard, K. M., Cutting, J. C., Meyer, A. S., & Schriefers, H. (2001). Some attractions of verb agreement. *Cognitive Psychology*, 43, 83–128.

Chang, F. (2002). Symbolically speaking: A connectionist model of sentence production. *Cognitive Science*, 26, 609–51.

Chang, F., Dell, G. S., & Bock, K. (2006). Becoming syntactic. *Psychological Review*, 113, 234–272.

Cholin, J, Levelt, W. J. M., & Schiller, N. (2006). Effects of syllable frequency in speech production. *Cognition*, 99, 205–235.

Cholin, J., Schiller, N. O., & Levelt, W. J. M. (2004). The preparation of syllables in speech production. *Journal of Memory and Language*, 50, 47–60.

Christiansen, M. H. & Chater, N. (1999). Toward a connectionist model of recursion in human linguistic performance. *Cognitive Science*, 23(2), 157–205.

Cleeremans, A. & McClelland, J. L. (1991). Learning the structure of event sequences. *Journal of Experimental Psychology: General*, 120, 235–253.

Damian, M. F. & Martin, R. C. (1999). Semantic and phonological codes interact in single word production. *Journal of Experimental Psychology: Learning, Memory, and Cognition*, 25, 345–361.

Dell, G. S. (1986). A spreading activation theory of retrieval in language production. *Psychological Review*, 93, 283–321.

Dell, G. S., Schwartz, M. F., Martin, N., Saffran, E. M, & Gagnon, D. A. (1997). Lexical access in aphasic and nonaphasic speakers. *Psychological Review*, 104, 801–838.

Dell, G. S., Martin, N., & Schwartz, M. F. (2007). A case-series test of the interactive two-step model of lexical access: Predicting word repetition from picture naming. *Journal of Memory and Language*, 56, 490–520.

Eberhard, K. M. (1997). The marked effect of number on subject-verb agreement. *Journal of Memory and Language*, 36, 147–164.

Eberhard, K. M., Cutting, J. C., & Bock, K. (2005). Making syntax of sense: Number agreement in sentence production. *Psychological Review*, 112, 531–559.

Elman, J. L. (1990). Finding structure in time. *Cognitive Science*, 14, 179–211.

(1993). Learning and development in neural networks: The importance of starting small. *Cognition*, 48, 71–99.

Ferreira, V. S. (1996). Is it better to give than to donate? Syntactic flexibility in language production. *Journal of Memory and Language*, 35, 724–755.

Foygel, D. & Dell, G. S. (2000). Models of impaired lexical access in speech production. *Journal of Memory and Language*, 43, 182–216.

Freud, S. (1901). Psychopathology of everyday life (Zur Psychopathologie des Alltagslebens). *Monatschrift für Psychiatrie und Neurologie*, 10, 1–13.

Glaser, W. R. & Düngelhoff, F. J. (1984). The time course of picture-word interference. *Journal of Experimental Psychology: Human Perception and Performance*, 10, 640–654.

Griffin, Z. M. & Crew, C. M. (this volume). Research in language production.

Guenther, F. H. (1995). Speech sound acquisition, co-articulation, and rate effects in a neural network model of speech production. *Psychological Review*, 102, 594–621.

Harley, T. A. (1993). Phonological activation of semantic competitors during lexical access in speech production. *Language and Cognitive Processes*, 8, 291–310.

Janssen, D. P., Roelofs, A., & Levelt, W. J. M. (2002). Inflectional frames in language production. *Language and Cognitive Processes*, 17, 209–236.

Jescheniak, J. D., Schriefers, H., & Hantsch, A. (2001). Semantic and phonological activation in noun and pronoun production. *Journal of Experimental Psychology: Learning, Memory, and Cognition*, 27, 1058–1078.

(2003). Utterance format affects phonological priming in the picture-word task: Implications for models of phonological encoding in speech production. *Journal of Experimental Psychology: Human Perception & Performance*, 29, 441–454.

Levelt, W. J. M. (1989). *Speaking: From intention to articulation*. Cambridge, MA: MIT Press.

(1992). Accessing words in speech production: Stages, processes and representations. *Cognition*, 42, 1–22.

Levelt, W. J. M., Roelofs, A., & Meyer, A. S. (1999). A theory of lexical access in speech production. *Behavioral and Brain Sciences*, 22, 1–75.

Levelt, W. J. M. & Wheeldon, L. (1994). Do speakers have access to a mental syllabary? *Cognition*, 50, 239–269.

Luce, R. A. (1959). Individual choice behavior. New York: Wiley.

MacLeod, C. M. (1991). Half a century of research on the stroop effect: An integrative review. *Psychological Bulletin*, 109, 163–203.

Magnuson, J. S., Mirman, D., & Harris, H. D. (this volume). Computational models of spoken word recognition.

Meyer, A. S. (1990). The time course of phonological encoding in language production: The encoding of successive syllables of a word. *Journal of Memory and Language*, 29, 524–545.

(1991). The time course of phonological encoding in language production: Phonological encoding inside a syllable. *Journal of Memory and Language*, 30, 69–89.

Meyer, A. S., Schriefers, H. (1991). Phonological facilitation in picture-word interference experiments: Effects of stimulus onset asynchrony and types of interfering stimuli. *Journal of Experimental Psychology: Learning, Memory, & Cognition*, 17, 1146–1160.

Naigles, L. R. (1990). Children use syntax to learn verb meanings. *Journal of Child Language*, 17, 357–374.

Roelofs, A. (1992). A spreading-activation theory of lemma retrieval in speaking. *Cognition*, 42, 107–142.

(1997). The WEAVER model of word-form encoding in speech production. *Cognition*, 64, 249–284.

(1998). Rightward incrementality in encoding simple phrasal forms in speech production: Verbparticle combinations. *Journal of Experimental Psychology: Learning, Memory, and Cognition*, 24, 904–921.

(1999). Phonological segments and features as planning units in speech production. *Language and Cognitive Processes*, 14, 173–200.

(2004). Error biases in spoken word planning and monitoring by aphasic and nonaphasic speakers: Comment on Rapp and Goldrick (2000). *Psychological Review*, 111, 561–572.

Roelofs, A. & Meyer, A. S. (1998). Metrical structure in planning the production of spoken words. *Journal of Experimental Psychology: Learning, Memory and Cognition*, 24, 922–939.

Roland, D. & Hare, M. (this volume). Computational and corpus models of human sentence comprehension.

Schiller, N. O. (1998). The effect of visually masked syllable primes on the naming latencies of words and pictures. *Journal of Memory and Language*, 39, 484–507.

Schriefers, H., Meyer, A. S., & Levelt, W. J. M. (1990). Exploring the time course of lexical access in production: Picture-word interference studies. *Journal of Memory & Language*, 29, 86–102.

Schwartz, M. F., Dell, G.S., Martin, N., Gahl, S., & Sobel, P. (2006). A case-series test of the interactive two-step model of lexical access: Evidence from picture naming. *Journal of Memory and Language*, 54. 228–264.

Seidenberg, M. S. (this volume). Computational models of reading: Connectionist and dual-route approaches.

Starreveld, P. A. & La Heij W. (1995). Semantic interference, orthographic facilitation, and their interaction in naming tasks. *Journal of Experimental Psychology: Learning, Memory, & Cognition*, 21, 686–698.

Vigliocco, G., Tranel, D., & Druks, J. (this volume). Language production: Patient and imaging research.

Vigliocco, G., Vinson, D. P., Lewis, W., & Garrett, M. F. (2004). The meanings of object and action words. *Cognitive Psychology*, 48, 422–488.

Wheeldon, L. R., & Levelt, W. J. M. (1995). Monitoring the time course of phonological encoding. *Journal of Memory and Language*, 34, 311–334.

Author Notes

This work was supported by NIH DC-00191, HD-44458, and a TALENT stipend (S 29–1) from the Netherlands Organization for Scientific Research (NWO) to the second author. We thank Gabriella Vigliocco and Kay Bock for valuable comments.

CHAPTER 22

Language Production

Patient and Imaging Research

Gabriella Vigliocco, Daniel Tranel, and Judit Druks

1 Introduction

In this chapter we review recent research on language production from a cognitive neuroscience perspective, considering both studies involving neuropsychological populations and imaging. We will focus on language production as entailed by two principal aspects: single word production and sentence production. Because we believe that an understanding of the neural substrate underpinning a cognitive function (language production in our case) is a central ingredient to theory development, our review will draw from those patient studies in which cognitive–anatomical correlations are discussed, and we will not be much concerned with debates based on the implications of specific type of deficit for cognitive-only models (an approach that has been also referred to as *ultra* cognitive neuropsychology, Shallice, 1988).

Establishing clear connections between neuroanatomical data and cognitive models of language production to date is at a far more advanced state for single word production than for sentence production.

The imaging literature for single word production is very rich, and we can go as far as developing clear hypotheses of the workings of the neural networks engaged in concept and word retrieval. The matter is different in the case of sentence production. Less than a handful of imaging studies have investigated the neural systems engaged. Moreover, the vast majority of neuropsychological investigations aimed at explaining patterns of sentence production deficits in aphasia have focused on impairments of the cognitive systems, independent of the specific brain systems implementing those processes. Thus, because of this asymmetry in the available evidence concerning word and sentence production, our discussion of the theoretical implications will necessarily also be asymmetrical: detailed for word production; sketchy and speculative for sentence production.

The chapter is structured in the following manner. In line with a longstanding tradition in psycholinguistic and neurolinguistic research, we discuss word and sentence production separately and for each topic, we start by outlining the main processing steps, as assumed in psycholinguistic models. Because current models of lexical retrieval and of sentence production are discussed elsewhere in this volume (see chapters by Griffin and Crew, and Dell and Cholin), our discussion of the models will be limited to sketching the main (generally agreed upon) processing steps in going from intention to articulation, with a special emphasis on those processes that have received neuroscientific attention. We discuss then relevant patient and imaging work. We conclude, in the case of sentence production, with suggesting speculative ideas and, in the case of single word production, with an explicit model of how the different processing steps may be linked to specific neural systems in the brain.

2 Word production

2.1 *Psycholinguistic theories of lexicalisation*

It is generally agreed upon that lexicalisation requires the retrieval of different types of information (conceptual, lexico-semantic, and phonological) and there is agreement in assuming at least three different types of processes underlying lexicalisation. First, conceptual representations would be activated, second, intermediate lexico-semantic representations would be selected, and finally, phonological word forms would be retrieved and articulated (Dell, 1986; Garrett, 1984; Levelt et al., 1999). The distinction between conceptual and lexical-semantic representations is crucial here as it marks the divide between cognition and language (and thus, between the processes involved in retrieving concepts from "semantic memory" versus retrieving words from "lexical memory").

Models of lexical retrieval differ with respect to whether they assume that concepts guiding production should be conceived as unitary or decomposable (see Vigliocco and Vinson, 2007 for a discussion). As we will see in the next section, neuropsychological and imaging investigations have provided extremely valuable

insights on this matter, leading to favouring a decompositional view, more precisely a decompositional embodied view of conceptual representation in which conceptual representations are directly grounded in our sensorial and motoric experiences of the world (Barsalou et al., 2001; Damasio et al., 2004; Gallese and Lakoff, 2005; Glenberg and Robertson, 2000; Vigliocco et al, 2004).

Lexico-semantic representations are said to provide an interface between modality-related conceptual representations and linguistic information relevant at the word level. The latter, in turn, encompasses syntactic information (e.g., word class) and the phonological specification of the word. While conceptual and lexico-semantic representations are considered to be separate levels of representation in models of language production developed within psycholinguistics, they are considered to be referring to the same level of representation in many models developed within a concept and categorization tradition and in neurocognitive models. As we have discussed elsewhere (e.g., Vigliocco et al, 2004), the assumption that concepts and lexico-semantic representations are indistinguishable incurs a number of problems among which are the following. First, in the neuropsychological literature we can find cases of category-related deficits limited to the verbal domain (Cappa et al., 1998e.g., Hart et al., 1985). If concepts and lexico-semantic representations were to be the same thing, the observed deficits should span both verbal and nonverbal tasks. Second, this view runs into difficulties in explaining why different languages lexicalize a given conceptual domain in somewhat different manners (e.g., Slobin, 1996; Vigliocco and Filipovic Kleiner, 2004).

The process of retrieving lexico-semantic representations is characterized as a competitive process in which multiple semantically related candidates are considered (Levelt et al., 1999; Vigliocco et al., 2004). Failure during this retrieval step gives rise to semantically related substitution errors (e.g., saying *nose* instead of *mouth*; Dell, 1986; Garrett, 1984). It is further assumed that along with the retrieval of lexico-semantic representations, syntactic information also becomes available to the system. In some models, this syntactic information is strictly lexically represented (e.g., Levelt et al., 1999), in others it is associated with the processes engaged in building sentences (Chang et al., 2006; Vigliocco et al., 2004). The retrieval/encoding of the phonological form of words occurs in a subsequent step. Failures during this step in the retrieval process give rise to phonologically related substitution errors (e.g., saying *mushroom* instead of *mustache*) (Dell, 1986; Garrett, 1984).

2.2 *Neural systems subserving naming*

Naming has been used in a large number of neuropsychological and imaging studies as a tool to gain insight into the neural representation of linguistic and semantic knowledge. Naming difficulties are the hallmark of all aphasia types, whether due to cerebral insults (e.g., stroke, head injury) or to cerebral atrophy (as in Primary Progressive Aphasias, Mesulam, 2001). In addition to (overt and covert) picture naming, PET and fMRI studies have also used tasks such as verb generation (speakers are asked to produce a verb semantically associated to a noun being presented, e.g., given *apple*, say *eat*) and word generation (speakers are asked to generate as many words as they can in a given period of time (e.g., sixty seconds) that belong to a given semantic category or that start with a given letter). There are important differences between the tasks. While picture naming can be considered a relatively ecologically valid task that should not engage decision and control processes to any high extent, decision and control processes are central to verb generation and fluency tasks. This inevitably leads to additional activations (especially in prefrontal cortices) that may be associated to processes involved in selecting among alternatives and other executive functions, more than production processes per se.

In the next section we review some of this literature focusing primarily on the two main areas in which neuroscientific work

has led to clear progress: the neural underpinning of representing concepts and words from different domains of knowledge and the neural separability of semantic and phonological lexical retrieval.

2.2.1 RETRIEVING WORDS FROM DIFFERENT DOMAINS OF KNOWLEDGE

2.2.1.1 Concrete objects In regard to the retrieval of words for various categories of concrete objects, work by H. Damasio, Tranel, and collaborators has led to several general conclusions (H. Damasio et al., 2004; Grabowski et al., 2003; Tranel, 2006; Tranel et al., 2005). First, there is strong left-hemisphere specialization, as would be expected for word retrieval processes (although category-related word retrieval deficits have been reported in connection with right-hemisphere lesions, e.g., Neininger and Pulvermüller, 2003). Second, there is consistent evidence for category-relatedness in the arrangement of systems that support word retrieval for different categories of concrete entities (although some of this evidence has been criticized on methodological grounds, e.g., Laws, 2005). Lesion studies have shown that defective naming of unique persons and unique landmarks is associated with lesions in the left temporal pole. Defective naming of animals is associated with lesions in left anterior inferior temporal (IT) areas, anterior insula, and dorsal temporo-occipital junction. Defective naming of tools is associated primarily with lesions in the left posterior lateral temporo-occipito-parietal junction, and with lesions in the inferior pre- and post-central gyri and the insula. Defective naming of fruits/vegetables is associated with lesions in left inferior pre- and post-central gyri and anterior insula. Defective naming of musical instruments is associated with lesions in the left temporal polar region and anterior IT, the posterolateral temporal region (close to MT), the insula, and the inferior pre- and post-central gyri. The degree of segregation for different categories varies, and is more or less defined, depending on the categories being contrasted. For example, the association between retrieval of proper names (persons, landmarks) and the left temporal polar region has been particularly strong, as has been the association between retrieval of tool names and the left posterior lateral temporo-occipito-parietal junction. However, categories such as musical instruments and fruits/vegetables have not revealed highly localized and reliable neural correlates. Converging findings have been reported by a number of other laboratories (e.g., Crutch and Warrington, 2003; Gorno-Tempini et al., 2000; Hillis and Caramazza, 1991; Martin et al., 1996; Ojemann, 1991).

2.2.1.2 *Actions versus objects* Tranel and colleagues have completed several studies focused on the neural correlates of retrieving words referring to actions (H. Damasio et al., 2001; Tranel et al., 2001; Tranel et al., 2005). Two specific anatomical hypotheses were tested in these studies: (1) The neural systems subserving naming of actions and naming of concrete objects are segregated. (2) Naming of actions depends not only on the classical implementation structures of the left inferior frontal gyrus (IFG), in particular the frontal operculum (Brodmann Area, BA, 44), but also on intermediary structures located in left premotor/prefrontal areas (BA 6, 45 and 47). The Tranel et al. (2001) study used the lesion method and involved seventy-five subjects with focal, stable lesions in the left or right hemispheres. The experimental tasks were standardized procedures for measuring action and object naming. The findings offered partial support for the hypotheses, in that: (1) Lesions of the left anterior temporal and inferotemporal regions, which produce impairments in naming of concrete entities, did not cause action naming deficits. (2) Lesions related to impaired action naming overlapped maximally in the left frontal operculum and in the underlying white matter and anterior insula. A follow-up analysis indicated that action naming impairments, especially when they were disproportionate relative to concrete entity naming impairments, were not only associated with premotor/prefrontal lesions, but also with lesions of the left mesial occipital cortex and of the paraventricular white

matter underneath the supramarginal and posterior temporal regions.

The finding that action naming might depend in part on mesial occipital cortex and the posterior temporal region (Tranel et al., 2001) may relate to the task demands of the experiment (picture naming), which probably require different degrees of mental reconstruction of the action image that is implied in the stimulus. This idea has been hinted at in other studies, which have shown dissociations between naming of action pictures versus naming of real (dynamic) actions (Druks and Shallice, 2000), and has received some initial support in preliminary studies using a dynamic action naming test that uses video clips of a large number of actions (Tranel et al., 2005).

The dissociation between deficits in naming objects and deficits in naming actions is also confirmed in studies of patients with degenerative conditions, variants of Primary Progressive Aphasia (PPA) (Mesulam, 2001). Patients with Semantic Dementia (SD) are impaired in their semantic knowledge concerning objects (e.g., Breedin et al., 1994). SD is characterized by prominent atrophy in anterolateral temporal cortex (and relative sparing of medial temporal regions such as hippocampus and associated structures) limited to the left or involving both hemispheres (Galton, 2000; Grossman, 2002; Knibb et al., 2006; Lambon Ralph et al., 2001; Levy et al., 2004). The speech of patients with SD is fluent, but dramatically marked by anomia.

Greater difficulties in action versus object naming have been reported in another variant of PPA: Progressive Non Fluent Aphasia (PNFA). PNFA is characterized by neuronal loss most prominent in inferior frontal and superior temporal regions (Grossman, 2002). The production of patients suffering from PNFA is nonfluent and effortful, characterized by grammatical and phonological errors (e.g., Grossman, 2002). Cappa et al. (2002) reported that patients with PPA and atrophy in left frontal cortex were more impaired in action than object naming. These findings have general agreement with the findings from focal lesion patients, as noted earlier.

The association between object naming <-> left inferior temporal areas and action naming <-> left IFG is discussed in the literature also in terms of a dissociation between noun and verb naming, with the implication that there is a syntactic, rather than semantic, distinction (e.g., Bernt et al., 1997; Daniele et al., 1994).[1] One version of this hypothesis is that grammatical class determines how and where (roughly, left IT versus left IFG for nouns and verbs, respectively) lexical representations are stored in the brain. According to this view, the syntactic distinction between nouns and verbs, in addition to the semantic distinction between objects and actions, determines the neural systems engaged by these different types of words (Caramazza and Hillis, 1991; Laiacona and Caramazza, 2004). Another version of the grammatical hypothesis argues that neural separability between nouns and verbs is determined by differences in the morphological and sentential processes engaged by words of different grammatical class (Shapiro and Caramazza, 2003). This second hypothesis predicts that verb impairments are associated to deficits in syntactic encoding at the sentence level and is discussed in more detail below in Section 3.2.1.

In the literature concerning nouns and verbs, the finding of grammatical category deficits limited to either spoken or written naming has been argued to provide strong evidence against a purely semantic (e.g., objects versus actions) account of the dissociation (e.g., Rapp and Caramazza, 2002). However, there is clear evidence that argues against a purely grammatical nature of the deficit in the domain of language production. In an er-fMRI study in which Italian speakers were asked to name the same pictures of events either as a verb (e.g., *distruggere* [to destroy]) or as a noun (e.g., *distruzione* [destruction]), it was found that both nouns and verbs engaged a common neural system (Siri et al., 2008). Crucially, however, nouns engaged the left IFG to a greater extent than verbs. This latter finding, opposite to what has been observed in previous imaging studies that have shown verb specific activations in left IFG (e.g., Perani et al., 1999), can be interpreted in terms of greater effort in choosing and producing morphologically complex forms, regardless of whether they are nouns or verbs. In the Siri et al. study, the nouns used were morphologically derived from the verbs, thus plausibly more morphologically complex than the verbs. In most previous studies, the verb forms could be considered as more morphologically complex than the nouns (the nouns used, referring to objects, are usually morphologically simple).

Second, in a recent review of thirty-nine studies (encompassing 279 stroke patients), Maetzig et al. (submitted) reported a clear asymmetry in the number of patients with relative better performance with nouns than verbs (N = 208) and relative better performance with verbs than nouns (N = 30).[2] This asymmetric distribution of selective noun and verb impairments suggests a role for additional factors that likely have little or no relation to grammatical class per se. Stronger activations in left IFG for verbs, and verb-specific impairments after left IFG lesions could, therefore, be linked to the role of this area in dealing with the processing of more complex forms. Verbs would be in general more complex to produce than nouns referring to concrete objects (hence the asymmetry in the distribution of selective impairments of nouns versus verbs); however, nouns referring to events would be more complex than verbs referring to the same events (hence, greater activations in left IFG for nouns such as *distruzione* [destruction] than for the corresponding verbs).

2.2.1.3 *Spatial relationships* Very little research has explored which neural systems may be important for retrieving the meanings of locative prepositions (e.g., *in*, *on*,

---

1 Note that in the vast majority of studies the two dimensions: syntactic (nouns/verbs) or semantic (objects/actions) are confounded since pictures of objects and pictures of actions are usually contrasted.

2 The remaining cases did not show any relative difference between noun and verb production.

around). Tranel and colleagues (H. Damasio et al., 2001; Kemmerer, 2005; Kemmerer and Tranel, 2003; Tranel and Kemmerer, 2004) have carried out exploratory work in this domain. In one lesion study, the hypothesis that processing the meanings of locative prepositions depends on neural structures in the left inferior prefrontal cortex and left inferior parietal cortex was tested. Seventy-eight subjects with focal, stable lesions to various parts of the telencephalon and a comparison group of sixty normal participants were studied with tasks that required production, comprehension, and semantic analysis of locative prepositions. In support of the hypothesis, it was found that in subjects with impaired knowledge of locative prepositions, the highest region of lesion overlap was in the left frontal operculum and the left supramarginal gyrus, and in the white matter subjacent to these two areas (Tranel and Kemmerer, 2004).

A second study focused on six patients who had pervasive defects for locative prepositions confirmed that such defects were associated specifically with damage to the posterior left frontal operculum, white matter subjacent to this region, and white matter underneath the inferior parietal operculum. These patients did not have basic impairments in spatial processing or working memory, and they had relatively well-preserved conceptual knowledge for actions and various categories of concrete entities (e.g., persons, animals, tools). All six patients, however, had defects in naming actions, and some of them also had defective naming of some categories of concrete entities. Overall, the findings converge nicely with recent results from functional imaging, and with classic cases from the aphasia-based literature, and suggest that the left inferior prefrontal and left inferior parietal regions have crucial – albeit not exclusive – roles in processing knowledge associated with locative prepositions.

2.2.2 THE NEURAL SEPARABILITY OF RETRIEVING CONCEPTS AND WORDS

The majority of imaging studies concerning word naming do not allow one to distinguish between the neural systems engaged in retrieving a concept corresponding to a given object/action in the world, and the neural systems engaged in retrieving the corresponding name (due to the fact that both of these processes unfold, more or less obligatorily, in normal people). There are, however, neuropsychological studies that suggest that the two processes can be separated, and that they may be subserved by partially distinct brain networks. Some evidence for the separability of retrieving a concept, and a lexical representation specified for meaning corresponding to the concept, comes from category-related deficits limited to the verbal modality. For example, Cappa et al. (1998) reported the performance of patient CP (with a left IT lesion) who was selectively impaired in the naming of artifacts. He could, however, recognize the objects he could not name, indicating a lexical rather than conceptual deficit, and he could recognize and name objects from other categories.

Evidence compatible with the separability between conceptual and lexical retrieval also comes from the finding reported by Lambon Ralph et al. (2001) that patients suffering from SD and bilateral temporal lesions are impaired both in naming and recognition, whereas patients with left temporal damage tend to be impaired only in naming but not in recognition. In a lesion study including a large cohort of patients, Damasio et al. (2004) found some evidence for neural separation between retrieval of conceptual object knowledge and the retrieval of lexical labels by examining lesion overlap in patients who showed only naming problems and patients who showed both naming and recognition problems.

An interesting observation that warrants further empirical scrutiny is the fact that retrieving concepts/words from different domains seems to engage both modality-related cortices and supramodal cortices. In the anatomical model proposed by H. Damasio, Tranel, and colleagues that is discussed in Section 2.3), the modality-related areas may be engaged during conceptual retrieval, whereas the supramodal areas would be engaged in lexical retrieval, with these areas serving as *converging zones* of various sensory and motor information (for different and provocative views on the involvement of modality-related versus supramodal integration areas in conceptual/lexical representation see Gallese and Lakoff, 2005). These convergence zones are assumed to respect category and domain distinctions in order to account for the finding that naming deficits, in the absence of recognition and comprehension problems, can be category-related (Cappa et al., 1998; Damasio et al., 1996).

2.2.3 THE NEURAL SEPARABILITY OF RETRIEVING MEANING AND FORM

Errors made by patients in naming are often classified according to whether they are errors of commission (i.e., saying another word rather than the target) or omission (saying, for example, "I don't know."). Both types of error can occur as a failure in lexico-semantic retrieval (e.g., semantic substitution errors) and as a failure in word form retrieval (e.g., phonologically related substitution errors). In addition, patients' erroneous responses can be nonwords (Caplan et al., 1986) or a mixture of these different types of errors. Dell and Cholin (this volume) provide an in depth discussion of how the relative distributions of different types of errors made by patients provides important constraints on the architecture and information flow assumed within models of lexical retrieval in production (for discussions of how these errors have been used to argue for different word production models see Dell et al., 2004; Rapp and Goldrik, 2000; 2005).

Indefrey and Levelt (2004) provide a meta-analysis of eighty-two imaging studies of word production. On the basis of a component analysis of the tasks used, they distinguish between areas engaged by the core processes of lexicalization and those areas engaged by lead-in processes (i.e., task-specific cognitive processes such as visual object recognition in picture naming that take place before the core production processes are engaged).

The studies considered in the meta-analysis included picture naming, word generation (both verb and noun generation), and word and pseudoword reading. The authors reasoned that picture naming and verb generation engage all systems involved in lexicalization (i.e., from conceptually driven lexical retrieval to articulation). Word reading would not involve the system engaged in retrieving a lexical word form from its conceptual specification, and pseudoword reading would solely involve output phonology and articulation. Thus, areas activated in both picture naming and word generation but not in word reading would underpin the processes of conceptually driven lexical retrieval; areas activated in picture naming, word generation, and word reading but not pseudoword reading would underpin the processes engaged in lexicalization but not sublexical and articulatory processes.

Only one area, the midsection of the left middle temporal gyrus was found to be active in both picture naming and word generation but not in the other tasks. Thus, this area must be engaged during lexico-semantic retrieval. It is unclear, however, what the role of this area in the retrieval process is, given that it is not necessarily linked to semantic retrieval. This is because, as we discussed earlier, imaging and patient studies provide strong evidence for category and domain-related neural segregation (with different regions within left IT being implicated to a different extent in retrieving words referring to different concrete entities). The studies included in the meta-analysis included words from a variety of different object categories, thus common areas of activation must reflect only semantic or lexical processes shared by all these different categories.

Areas activated in picture naming, word generation, and word reading but not in pseudoword reading, and therefore, areas involved in the phonological encoding of real words, included the right supplementary motor area (SMA), the left inferior insula, and the left posterior superior and middle temporal gyri (BA areas 21 and 42 – Wernicke's area). Results of lesion studies converge to some extent in highlighting the importance of these areas in phonological and phonetic encoding (although not necessarily limited to real words). For example, lesions of the left insula have been associated with apraxia of speech in lesion overlap studies (Dronkers, 1996). Lesions of Wernicke's area have long been associated to production problems (in addition to comprehension problems). Individuals with Wernicke's aphasia may speak in long sentences that have no meaning, add unnecessary words, produce phonemic paraphasias (phonological errors), and produce neologisms. Moreover, they usually have great difficulty understanding speech and are therefore often unaware of their mistakes in production.

The importance of the SMA in speech production (especially in phonetic encoding) is supported by the finding that spontaneous (Pai et al., 1999; Ziegler et al., 1997) or surgical (e.g., Krainik et al., 2003) lesions of the SMA, as well as intracerebral electrical stimulation (Chauvel et al., 1996), yield a variety of speech disorders. These range in severity from speech reduction and slowing to the production of repetitive vocalization patterns or complete mutism. On the other hand, it is well known that the SMA plays an important role in motor control. Speech production requires, just as motor control, choices and planning at different levels. A number of the aspects of motor control that are known to modulate the activation of the SMA are likely to have equivalents in the planning and execution of speech output (MacNeilage et al., 2001).

2.3 A neurocognitive theory of lexicalization in word production

We have characterized word production as a process that involves three main types of information: conceptual, lexical-semantic, and phonological, we have then reviewed neuropsychological and imaging studies of word naming that suggest that: (a) partially distinct neural networks underlie the retrieval of words from different semantic categories; (b) retrieving concepts and retrieving words may require partially distinct networks; and (c) meaning and phonology can break down separately and are processed in (partially) distinct networks.

The theoretical framework recently put forward by H. Damasio, A. Damasio, and Tranel provides us with a very promising attempt to integrate the patient and imaging data described previously with the basic assumptions underlying the cognitive models of lexicalization outlined earlier. Let us describe this hypothesis in some detail (H. Damasio et al., 2004; see also Simmons and Barsalou, 2003).

The input to the system are *images*, which are explicit, online mental patterns of any sensory type (e.g., visual, auditory, somatosensory), some of which constitute the manifest mental contents that are experienced consciously, and some of which remain nonconscious. The principal neural substrates for images are the explicit neural patterns (or maps) formed in areas of cerebral cortex located in and around the points of entry of sensory signals in the cerebral cortex (the early sensory cortices). These neural patterns continuously change under the influence of external and internal inputs (for example, as in perception or recall). The factual knowledge base of the system, as well as the know-how mechanisms for image and action processing, are contained in dispositions, with which (a) images can be constructed from recall, (b) processing of images can be facilitated, (c) movements can be generated, and (d) biological processes can be regulated. The contents of dispositions are implicit, that is, they exist in latent form and are nonconscious.

As far as neural substrates are concerned, structures subserving dispositions are distributed in higher order cortices, parts of the limbic cortices, and numerous subcortical nuclei (e.g., basal ganglia, amygdala). When disposition circuits are activated, they signal to other circuits and cause either images or actions to be generated elsewhere in the brain. The framework posits that dispositions are held in neuron ensembles called *convergence zones*. Convergence zones are made of microcircuits, which cannot be resolved individually by current neuroimaging techniques, although it is presumed that aggregates of many activated convergence zones constitute, temporarily, anatomically macroscopic sets that can be visualized by current techniques. Convergence zones of comparable functional level are distributed within *convergence regions* that correspond to large-scale sectors of the brain, for example, temporal pole; anterior inferotemporal region; frontal operculum.

Because of the constraints of the anatomical design of the brain, convergence zones involved in certain classes of tasks are likely to be found, in most individuals, in the same large-scale convergence region of the brain, for example, posterior inferotemporal region, frontal operculum. The process of anatomical selection of convergence zones, both during learning and during subsequent operation, is probability driven, flexible, and individualized. It is only at the large scale that the spatial placement of convergence zones should be predictable in single subjects and across individuals.

Concept and lexical retrieval in this framework would occur in the following manner. When a stimulus depicting a concrete entity is shown to a subject, the visual properties of the stimulus prompt activity in primary and early visual association cortices of both hemispheres. Next, engagement of intermediary regions occurs in higher order association cortices, which are the basis for dispositions necessary for concept retrieval. In this example, the engagement of dispositions results in a reconstruction of explicit sensorimotor patterns pertaining to the object, which occur in the appropriate early sensory cortices and motor structures. The evocation of some parts of the large number of such patterns and in varied sensorimotor cortices, over a brief lapse of time, constitutes conceptual retrieval. When a concept from another category is evoked, for example, that of a familiar person, different intermediary regions are engaged .

Naming a stimulus from a particular conceptual category is dependent on three kinds of neural structures: (1) structures which support conceptual knowledge that were just mentioned; (2) structures which support the implementation of word forms (the classical language areas located in the left perisylvian region, including Broca's and Wernicke's areas). These structures would correspond to the neural substrate of phonological word forms and the processes engaged in their retrieval. Finally, (3) intermediary structures for "words." These intermediary structures would correspond to the neural substrate of lexico-semantic representations in the cognitive model outlined in Section 2.1. In naming, the intermediary structures are engaged by the structures in (1) to trigger and guide the implementation process executed by the structures in (2).

When a subject is shown a picture of a cup or a picture of a familiar person and is asked to name the item, there will be activation of the appropriate "concept" intermediary regions, which will promote concept retrieval as outlined earlier in this chapter. Activation in the concept intermediary regions leads to activation in the corresponding "word" intermediary region, which in turn promotes the retrieval of lexical knowledge required for word production This is likely to require auditory structures (areas 41/42; 22), which overlap in part with the classic Wernicke's area. This step can be considered to closely correspond to the retrieval of word form information again in cognitive models of lexicalizations. Finally, somatomotor (Brodmann areas 3/1/2; 40; 44/45) structures are engaged for the phonetic sequencing and production of the actual spoken name; these structures overlap in part with the classical Broca's area.

Thus, this theoretical framework provides us with a clear anatomical interpretation of the cognitive processes engaged in concept and lexical retrieval compatible with the large body of evidence we reviewed earlier. Let us now turn to sentence production.

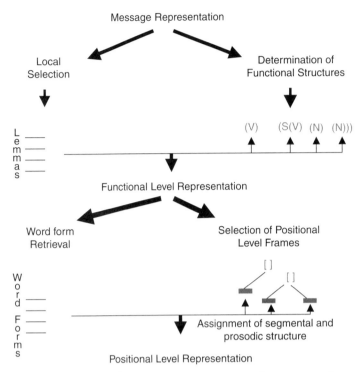

Figure 22.1. Levels of integration in sentence production according to Garrett (1984). The figure does not include the processes of phonetic encoding. From Vigliocco, G. and Hartsuiker, R. J. (2002). Reprinted with permission.

3 Sentence Production

3.1 *Psycholinguistic theories of sentence production*

The general architecture of sentence-level processes we use here to organize the discussion of neuropsychological and imaging data is the framework detailed in Vigliocco and Hartsuiker (2002), which follows closely from Garrett (1984). Figure 22.1 presents a sketch of the levels of integration that we assume between an intention that a speaker wants to express and articulation. Let us briefly describe these different levels and the main processing characteristics of each of them. The *message level* representation is conceived as a level at which nonlinguistic cognitive processes (e.g., information about the visual environment, encyclopedic knowledge, the discourse record, and a person's intentions) converge in preparation for verbal expression. At this level many of the details present in our perceptual/

conceptual experience of the world are stripped, leaving a much impoverished representation that, because impoverished, can effectively interface with language (e.g., Druks and Shallice, 2000; Levelt, 1989). A second important property of this level of representation is that it is tuned to the specific language used by the speakers. The message guides both lexical retrieval as well as phrasal integration. The distinct lexical representations retrieved during a semantically based and a phonologically based lexical retrieval process would be closely involved in phrasal integration processes: Lexico-semantic representations would be involved in the unfolding of frames for sentences at the functional level of processing, and word form representations would be involved in positional level processes. *Functional level* processes can be conceived as realizing the mapping between the message and a bound-sentence level frame that corresponds to that message. The domain on which functional level processes operate is semantic and syntactic. Representations at this level honor hierarchical syntactic relationships among words. *Positional level* processes are concerned with the mapping between a hierarchically specified representation to a linearly ordered frame that is phonologically spelled out. Such a mapping involves two steps: First, word forms would be inserted in slots that correspond to linear positions; second, phonological segments would be linearized within phonological words. The domain of frames at this level is prosodic. Thus, for both lexical retrieval and phrasal integration, the main distinction is between a level guided by a message in which semantic and syntactic relationships determine the structure of the representation and a level in which representations are specified for linear word order (sequentiality) and phonological content.

3.2 *The neural system(s) subserving sentence production*

3.2.1 EVIDENCE FROM APHASIC PRODUCTION

A general distinction drawn in the patient literature is between the consequences for sentence production of anterior versus posterior lesions. In broad strokes, associated with posterior temporal or temporo-parietal lesions are anomia and Wernicke's aphasia. In the cognitive model, these aphasia syndromes have been associated with deficits in retrieving stored representations specifying semantic or phonological information (in addition to comprehension deficits) rather than in building sentences. Associated with anterior lesions (in particular BA 44/45, Broca's area) are: (i) dynamic aphasia; and (ii) Broca's aphasia. Let us describe them in some detail.

Dynamic aphasia is characterized by severely reduced spontaneous speech in the context of preserved naming and sentence production in constrained contexts (e.g., answering questions), repetition, and well-preserved comprehension (e.g., Costello and Warrington, 1989; Luria, 1970; Robinson

et al., 1998; Robinson et al., 2005). Dynamic aphasia has been documented both in the context of neurodegenerative conditions and focal lesions. Patients reported in the literature with a diagnosis of dynamic aphasia presented consistently with focal lesions or atrophy involving left IFG, in particular BA44 and BA45. For example, Robinson et al. (2005) describe a case of dynamic aphasia in a patient with progressive nonfluent aphasia (PNFA) with focal atrophy in the left frontal lobe primarily involving BA44 (with BA45 being only mildly atrophic). The patient (CH) showed a form of mixed dynamic aphasia (Luria, 1970) in which the severe limitations in spontaneous speech production were accompanied by some grammatical errors in all speech output.[3] The impairment in CH encompassed a number of tasks in which a specific response had to be selected among a number of competitors while he had no comparable problems of selection in nonverbal tasks, and no problems in language tasks not involving selection. For example, CH could produce single sentences to describe a pictorial stimulus, but was severely impaired in more open-ended tasks such as having to produce a short story in response to a picture, or completing a sentence with a phrase in a low predictability context (in a high predictability context he was flawless). Indeed, the role of left IFG in the process of selecting among (semantic) alternatives has been confirmed in imaging studies, albeit only for word-level processes (Thompson-Schill, et al., 1997; Thompson-Schill, et al., 2002). In the cognitive model of sentence production we have outlined in Section 3.1, dynamic aphasia could arise as a consequence of deficit in encoding a message, and/or going from a message to a functional-level representation for the sentence.

Language deficits in Broca's aphasia are different. *Broca's aphasia* is characterized by halting, fragmentary, and effortful speech

---

3 "Pure" dynamic aphasia would, instead, be characterized by severe limitation in spontaneous speech with no accompanying grammatical, phonological, or articulatory problems.

production. Many patients with Broca's aphasia are also *agrammatic*. Their speech is dependent on the production of content words (mainly nouns) with difficulties in computing the syntactic/hierarchical representation for the sentence and in the realization of grammatical morphemes. In terms of the cognitive model, these deficits have been associated to problems in developing either a functional- or positional-level representation (with different authors emphasizing one over the other, see Bernt, 2001 for a discussion).

While these syntactic problems are typical symptoms of agrammatism, there is no clear evidence of association between specific problems in sentence construction (i.e., reduced sentence complexity or omission of function words) and lesion in Broca's area or in any other specific brain region. The lesions of Broca's aphasic patients are variable and are, usually, not confined to Broca's area, and, similarly, the patterns of syntactic and morphological deficits of the patients considered under the diagnostic umbrella of agrammatic Broca's aphasia are extremely varied. As a consequence, the literature is abundant in yet unexplained links between different constellations of grammatical deficits in speech, on the one hand, and specific lesions, on the other. For example, two patients with impaired ability to assign thematic roles, thus showing a deficit in developing the hierarchical/syntactic structure of a sentence, and preserved production of function words had parietal (Caramazza and Miceli, 1991) and temporoparietal (Martin and Blossom-Stach, 1986) lesions. The patients with relatively spared structural ability but impaired production of function words described by Miceli et al. (1983), Kolk et al. (1985), and Nespolous et al. (1988) also had temporal or parietal lesions. This suggests that we are still unable to identify the anatomical substrate of the different aspects of sentence production, and that lesions to Broca's area may be neither sufficient nor perhaps necessary to give rise to such problems.

As we have already mentioned in Section 2.2.1.2, an association has also been observed between lesions in Broca's area and verb naming impairments. Moreover, action naming impairments can correlate with syntactic problems in sentence production. In a study by Berndt (1997), it was found that Broca's aphasics with an action naming impairment were also impaired in sentence construction. The correlation between verb retrieval problems and syntactic encoding can, possibly, be accounted for by the impossibility of developing a functional-level representation in the absence of a verb. In lexicalist views (e.g., Levelt, 1989), if the verb cannot be retrieved, then its argument structure and subcategorization information also cannot be retrieved. Thus a correlation should be seen between problems in retrieving lexical representations for verbs and agrammatic sentence production. Such a correlation, however, is not always present (e.g., Druks and Carroll, 2005; Maetzig et al., submitted). This was particularly striking in the case of DOR (Druks and Carroll, 2005) who had a moderate action naming deficit, but whose speech contained almost no lexical verbs.

The difficulty of associating problems in developing a hierarchical structure for a sentence (functional-level processes), or problems in producing function words (possibly linked to positional-level processes) to Broca's area may be related to a number of factors. Most evidence for the role of left IFG so far comes from focal lesion studies. These have the inherent problem of vascular lesions not respecting cognitive boundaries but following the distribution of blood vessels. Converging evidence from studies with patients suffering neurodegenerative disease, such as PNFA, therefore, could allow us to derive a clearer picture. Second, sentence production engages resources beyond the linguistic processes required for word production. It is, therefore, more complicated to establish whether a given deficit is the consequence of an impairment of linguistic processes, or cognitive processes, or a combination of the two. Kolk and colleagues (e.g., Kolk, 1995) have argued that the asyntactic speech production of agrammatic patients arises due to a combination of linguistic impairments and limitations of general resources and the use of strategies. Finally, in contrast to research carried out on single word production, when it comes to sentences, there is no wealth of converging results from imaging studies. As far as we are aware, only four imaging studies have investigated the processes involved in sentence production. These studies are described in Section 3.2.2.

To summarize the lesion studies, while the involvement of left IFG in functional- or positional-level processing is questionable, its role in the initial stages of language production (the generation of a message and the selection of lexico-semantic representations necessary to express that message seems more clearly established (at least on the basis of only a handful of cases of dynamic aphasia described in the literature). Moreover, a role for left IFG in sequencing processes in the development of a phonologically specified representation for a word or sentence, such as the processes engaged in syllabification and more generally in phonological encoding, also seem well supported (Indefrey and Levelt, 2004).

3.2.2 THE NEURAL SYSTEMS UNDERLYING UNIMPAIRED PRODUCTION

To our knowledge, only four studies have investigated unimpaired sentence production processes using imaging techniques (Haller et al., 2005; Indefrey et al., 2001, 2004; Kircher et al., 2000). This limited number of studies is due to difficulties of investigating overt production using tools such as fMRI that are particularly affected by motion artifacts.[4] This problem is often resolved in word production studies requiring speakers to produce the words only covertly (while measures such as naming latencies are obtained outside the scanner). Covert production of sentences is more problematic because of the increased difficulties in controlling whether participants are carrying

out the task as required (see the discussion of "exuberant responding" in Bock, 1995). There is recent evidence, however, that suggests that motion artifacts can be avoided by limiting volume acquisition to pauses in speaking (Gracco et al., 2005) or by image correction techniques (Haller et al., 2005). Moreover, motion artifacts are less of an issue if PET rather than fMRI is used.

In the study by Kircher et al. (2000), spontaneous production was elicited by presenting Rorschach inkblots. Of interest, the authors reported that speech rate was positively correlated with signal change in left STG and left supramarginal gyrus. Speaking rate, however, is correlated with a number of different production processes: lexical retrieval, syntactic phonological and prosodic planning; it is therefore difficult to attribute the reported activations to a specific process. More relevant to our goals are the studies by Indefrey et al. (2001; 2004) and by Haller et al. (2005). In the experiments reported by Indefrey and colleagues (2001; 2004), speakers of German were presented with displays showing animated scenes and asked to describe them using full sentences (e.g., "The red square launches the blue ellipse."), sequences of phrases with local-, but not sentence-level syntactic structure (e.g., "red square," "blue ellipse," etc.) or sequences of words without any syntactic structure (e.g., "square," "red," "ellipse," etc.). It was found that a left IFG region, overlapping in part with Broca's area (BA44), although mainly posterior to Broca's area (most likely in BA6), was most activated in the sentence condition, less active in the phrasal condition, and least active in the word condition. The authors concluded that the left IFG activations correspond to syntactic encoding. Activations in left IFG, greater in BA45 than in BA44, were also reported in the study by Haller et al. (2005) in which German speakers were asked to produce sentences aloud (e.g., "The child throws the ball.") in response to syntactically incomplete stimuli (e.g., "throws," "ball," "child"), relative to the condition in which they were asked to read aloud the same words or in which they were asked to read aloud

---

4 The impossibility to avoid motion during production is also a clear reason for why, in contrast to comprehension, the time course of sentence production processes have not been investigated using ERPs (but see van Turrenaut et al., 1998 for a study concerning single words).

corresponding sentences. However, in both studies the degree of prosodic planning, the amount of phonological material, and the engagement of working memory were not equated across conditions.

Thus, imaging studies provide evidence that left IFG is playing an important role in sentence generation. The involvement of left IFG in these studies, however, cannot be linked exclusively to language production per se as the engagement of other cognitive processes cannot be excluded. Furthermore, even if we assume that sentence generation processes are engaged, it is not obvious that the activations reflect solely syntactic encoding. Finally, just as in comprehension studies (see Vigliocco, 2000), the lack of consistency in the activations reported, even in very similar experiments (as in the Indefrey and Haller studies), presents a clear challenge to the interpretation.

3.3 *Future directions: Toward a neurocognitive theory of sentence production*

In Section 2.3 we presented a relatively detailed hypothesis of the anatomical substrate of lexical retrieval. Here, because of the lack of studies and clear evidence when it comes to sentence production, we can only offer speculations. In particular in the next section we present a discussion of the possible role of Broca's area in producing sentences.

3.3.1 LEFT IFG AND SENTENCE INTEGRATION

The imaging and patients studies reviewed earlier suggest that left IFG, in particular Broca's area, plays a crucial role in sentence integration, although it appears not to serve a single function in production. For example, we cannot exclude that activations in this area were linked to working memory rather than syntactic encoding processes in the Indefrey et al. (2001; 2004) studies, and we have seen how this area plays a crucial role in dynamic aphasia, which in its pure form does not include agrammatism among its symptoms. Finally, a role of this area (in

particular BA44) in syllabification and phonological encoding has also been shown (Indefrey and Levelt, 2004).

Broca's area (comprising BA44 and 45, that is the pars opercularis and pars triangularis of the third frontal convolution) is anatomically heterogeneous and there is no strong motivation for why BA44 and BA45 should be considered as having the same functions (Amunts et al., 1999; Hagoort, 2005). In particular, whereas BA45 (along with BA47 which is sometimes considered also to be part of the language network) is considered as prefrontal cortex, BA44 is classically seen as part of premotor cortex (along with BA6, which might also be involved in language processing, see Indefrey et al., 2001). Important, for comprehension, imaging evidence suggests some degree of segregation within Broca's area (Bookheimer, 2002; Devlin et al., 2003; Gough et al., 2005).[5] Roughly, when we consider language comprehension, BA45 and BA47 would be involved in semantic processing, BA45, 44, and 46 would contribute to syntactic processing, and BA44 and BA6 would play a role in phonological processing. This segregation (which is far from being absolute as the overlap revealed in imaging studies is larger than the degree of separation, Bookheimer, 2002) suggests that this area of the brain is involved in at least three different domains of language processing. Given that integration of information has been argued to be an important property of prefrontal cortex functions, in the literature concerning language comprehension, the role of left IFG is discussed in terms of recruiting and integrating lexical information that would be stored in left temporal areas (both lexico-semantic and phonological information) (Hagoort, 2005; Price, 1998).

Under the assumption that production and comprehension must be organized according to similar criteria given their complementarity, and the possible sharing of, at least, some level of representation and

---

5 The role of Broca's area has been largely addressed in studies of language comprehension in addition to language production.

processes at the neural level, it is plausible to speculate that a similar organization is relevant to production processes. At present, however, it is impossible to identify any clear segregation within left IFG as related to sentence production. Nonetheless, the findings we have reviewed concerning a role for this area in semantic processes (e.g., Robinson et al., 2005; Thompson-Schill et al., 1997), syntactic encoding (e.g., Indefrey et al., 2001; 2004), and processes of syllabification and phonological encoding (Indefrey and Levelt, 2004) strongly suggest that left IFG is implicated in processes (both processes related to selection among alternative information as well as processes involved in sequencing information) that are crucial for the integration of conceptual, lexico-semantic, and phonological information about words at the message, functional and positional level of representation for sentences.

Hagoort (2005), when discussing the role of Broca's area in sentence comprehension, considers this area as a "unification space" (for details of unification as a syntactic process, see Vosse and Kempen, 2000), namely, binding together lexical information stored in the lexicon. Unification as a general syntactic operation has also been proposed in the domain of sentence production (Vigliocco and Hartsuiker, 2002). It is therefore plausible to speculate that the left IFG underlies processes shared between production and comprehension that integrate stored information: conceptual, lexical-semantic, and phonological.

4 Conclusions

Language production is often characterized as the Cinderella of psycholinguistics given that traditionally it has received far less attention than language acquisition and language comprehension. When we move from behavioral studies to patient and imaging studies, we see again that research concerning the neural anatomy of language is far more developed for language comprehension than language production. Nonetheless, the presence and type of speech errors made by aphasic patients have played and continue to play a central role in the diagnosis and rehabilitation of aphasia, even more than comprehension errors. The importance of production measures (e.g., fluency in addition to errors) in aphasia, however, does not readily translate into insight on the neural system(s) affected by different lesion type, size, and location, especially when we consider sentence rather than word production.

In this chapter we have taken up the challenge of trying to bring together the available evidence concerning the neural substrate of word naming and sentence production and to present a theoretical discussion of this evidence guided by models of production developed within cognitive psychology and neuroscience. This approach led us to the discussion of an explicit hypothesis concerning word naming, but only to speculations concerning sentence production. It is a challenge for future research to develop experimental tools that allow us to investigate the neural systems involved in sentence production in healthy individuals using imaging techniques (tools that are not affected by motion artifacts). A further challenge for future research is to determine the extent of segregation/overlap in the neural substrate of language production and comprehension. We have speculated that there may be many similarities in the organization of the system for comprehension and production, at least when it comes to syntactic and semantic processes. However, the degree of overlap between the two systems is unclear, especially if we consider that independence of production versus comprehension have been argued for in the neuropsychological literature on the basis of the existence of double dissociations between production and comprehension deficits (e.g., Miceli et al., 1983).

References

Amunts, K., Schleicher, A., Burgel, U., Mohlberg, H., Uylings, H. B., & Zilles, K. (1999). Broca's region revisited: Cytoarchitecture and intersubject variability. *Journal of Comparative Neurology*, 412, 319–41.

Barsalou, L. W., Simmons, W. K., Barbey, A. K., & Wilson, C. D. (2003). Grounding conceptual knowledge in the modality specific systems. *Trends in Cognitive Sciences*, 7, 84–91.

Bleasel, A., Comair, Y., & Lüders, H. (1996). Surgical ablations of the mesial frontal lobe in humans. In Lüders, H. (Ed.) *Supplementary sensorimotor area* (pp. 217–35). Philadelphia: Lippincott-Raven.

Bernt R. S. (2001). Sentence Production. In Rapp, B. (Ed.) *The handbook of cognitive neuropsychology* (p. 375–96). Taylor & Francis.

Berndt, R. S., Mitchum, C. C., Haendiges, A. N., & Sandson, J. (1997). Verb retrieval in aphasia. I. Characterizing single word impairments. *Brain and Language*, 56, 68–106.

Bock, K. J. (1995). Language production, methods and methodologies. *Psychonomic Bulletin and Review*, 2, 3–15.

Bookheimer S. (2002). Functional MRI of language: New approaches to understanding the cortical organization of semantic processing. *Annual Review of Neuroscience*, 25, 151–88.

Breedin, S. D., Saffran, E. M., & Coslett, H. B. (1994). Reversal of the concreteness effect in a patient with semantic dementia. *Cognitive Neuropsychology*, 11, 617–60.

Caplan, D., Vanier, M., & Baker, C. (1986). A case study of reproduction conduction aphasia. 1. Word production. *Cognitive Neuropsychology*, 3, 99–128.

Cappa, S. F., Sandrini, M., Rossini, P. M., Sosta, K., & Miniussi, C. (2002). The role of the left frontal lobe in action naming: rTMS evidence. *Neurology* 59, 720–723.

Cappa, S. F., Frugoni, M., Pasquali, P., Perani, D., & Zorat, F. (1998). Category-specific naming impairment for artefacts: A new case. *Neurocase*, 4, 391–7.

Carammaza, A. & Hillis, A. (1991). Lexical organization of nouns and verbs in the brain. *Nature*, 349, 788–90.

Caramazza, A. & Miceli, G. (1991). Selective impairment of thematic role assignment in sentence processing. *Brain and Language*, 41, 402–36.

Chang, F., Dell, G. S., & Bock, K. (2006). Becoming syntactic. *Psychological Review*.

Chauvel, P. Y., Rey, M., Buser, P., & Bancaud, J. (1996). What stimulation of the supplementary motor area in humans tells about its functional organization. *Advances in Neurology*, 70, 199–209.

Costello de Lacy, A. & Warrington, E. K. (1989). Dynamic aphasia. The selective impairment of verbal planning. *Cortex*, 25, 103–14.

Crutch, S. J. & Warrington, E. K. (2003). The selective impairment of fruit and vegetable knowledge: A multiple processing channels account of fine-grain category specificity. *Cognitive Neuropsychology*, 20, 355–72.

Damasio, A. R., & Tranel, D. (1993). Nouns and verbs are retrieved with differently distributed neural systems. *Proceedings of the National Academy of Sciences of the United States of America*, 90, 4957–60.

Damasio, H., Tranel, D., Grabowsky, T. J., Adolphs, R., & Damasio, A. R. (2004). Neural systems behind word and concept retrieval. *Cognition*, 92, 179–229.

Damasio, H. Grabowski, T. J., Tranel, D., Hichwa R. D., & Damasio, A.R. (1996). A neural basis for lexical retrieval. *Nature*, 380, 499–505.

Damasio, H., Grabowski, T. J., Tranel, D., Ponto, L. L., Hichwa, R. D., & Damasio, A. R. (2001). Neural correlates of naming actions and of naming spatial relations. *Neuroimage*, 13, 1053–64.

Daniele, A., Giustolisi, L., Silveri, M. C., Colosimo, C., & Gainotti, G. (1994). Evidence for a possible neuroanatomical basis for lexical processing of nouns and verbs. *Neuropsychologia*, 32, 1325–41.

Dell, G. S. (1986). A spreading activation theory of retrieval in sentence production. *Psychological Review*, 93, 283–321.

Dell, G. S. & Cholin, J. (this volume). Language production: Computational models.

Dell, G. S., Lawler, E. N., Harris, H. D., et al. (2004). Models of errors of omission in aphasic naming. *Cognitive Neuropsychology*, 21, 125–45.

Devlin, J. T., Matthews, P. M., & Rushworth, M. F. S. (2003). Semantic processing in the left inferior prefrontal cortex: A combined functional magnetic resonance imaging and transcranial magnetic stimulation study. *Journal of Cognitive Neuroscience*, 15, 71–84.

Dronkers, N. F. (1996). A new brain area for coordinating speech articulation. *Nature*, 384, 159–161.

Druks, J. & Carroll, E. (2005). The crucial role of tense for verb production. *Brain and Language*, 94, 1–18.

Druks, J. & Shallice, T. (2000). Selective preservation of naming from description and the "restricted preverbal message." *Brain and Language*, 72, 100–28.

Garrett, M. F. (1984). The organization of processing structure for language production:

Application to aphasic speech. In Caplan, D., Lecours, A. R., & Smith, A. (Eds.) *Biological perspectives on language* (pp. 172–93). Cambridge, MA: MIT Press.

Gallese, V. & Lakoff, G. (2005). The brain's concepts: the role of the sensory-motor system in conceptual knowledge. *Cognitive Neuropsychology*, 22, 455–79.

Galton, C. J., Patterson, K., Xuereb, J. H., et al. (2000). Atypical and typical presentations of Alzheimer's disease: a clinical, neuropsychological, neuroimaging and pathological study of 13 cases. *Brain*, 123, 484–98.

Glenberg, A. M. & Robertson, D. A. (2000). Symbol grounding and meaning: A comparison of high-dimensional and embodied theories of meaning. *Journal of Memory & Language*, 43, 379–401.

Gorno-Tempini, M. L., Cipolotti, L., & Price, C. J. (2000). Category differences in brain activation studies: where do they come from? *Proceedings of the Royal Society of London B*, 267, 1253–8.

Gough, P. M., Nobre, A. C., & Devlin, J. T. (2005). Dissociating linguistic processes in the left inferior frontal cortex with transcranial magnetic stimulation. *Journal of Neuroscience*, 25, 8010–16.

Grabowski, T. J., Damasio, H., Tranel, D., Cooper, G. E., Ponto, L. L. B., Watkins, G. L., & Hichwa, R. D. (2003). Residual naming after damage to the left temporal pole: a PET activation study. *NeuroImage*, 19, 846–60.

Gracco V. L., Tremblay P., Pike B. (2005). Imaging speech production using fMRI. *NeuroImage*, 26, 294–301.

Griffin, Z. M. & Crew, C. M. (this volume). Research in language production.

Grossman, M. (2002). Progressive aphasic syndromes: clinical and theoretical advances. *Current Opinion in Neurology*, 15, 409–13.

Hagoort, P. (2005). On Broca, brain, and binding: a new framework. *Trends in Cognitive Sciences*, 9, 416–23.

Haller, S., Radue, E. W., Erb, M., Grodd, W., & Kircher, T. (2005). Overt sentence production in event-related fMRI. *Neuropsychologia*, 43, 807–14.

Hart, J., Berndt, R. S., & Caramazza, A. (1985). Category-specific naming deficit following cerebral infarction. *Nature*, 316, 439–40.

Heim, S. & Friderici, A. D. (2003). Phonological processing in language production: time course of brain activity. *NeuroReport*, 14, 2031–3.

Hillis, A. E. & Caramazza, A. (1991). Category-specific naming and comprehension impairment: A double dissociation. *Brain*, 114, 2081–94.

Indefrey, P., Brown, C. M., Hellwig, F., Amunts, K., Herzog, H., Seitz, R. J., & Hagoort, P. (2001). A neural correlate of syntactic encoding during speech production. *Proceedings of the National Academy of Sciences*, 98, 5933–36.

Indefrey, P., Hellwig, F., Herzog, H., Seitz, R. J., & Hagoort, P. (2004). Neural responses to the production and comprehension of syntax in identical utterances. *Brain & Language*, 89, 312–19.

Indefrey, P., & Levelt, W. J. M. (2004). The spatial and temporal signatures of word production components, *Cognition*, 92, 101–44.

Krainik, A., Lehericy, S., Duffau, H., Capelle, L., Chainay, H., Cornu, P., Cohen, L., Boch, A. L., Mangin, J. F., Le Bihan, D., & Marsault, C. (2003). Postoperative speech disorder after medial frontal surgery – Role of the supplementary motor area, *Neurology*, 60, 587–94.

Kemmerer, D. (2005). The spatial and temporal meanings of English prepositions can be independently impaired. *Neuropsychologia*, 43, 797–806.

Kemmerer, D. & Tranel, D. (2003). A double dissociation between the meanings of action verbs and locative prepositions. *Neurocase*, 9, 421–35.

Kempen, G. & Vosse, T. (1989). Incremental syntactic tree formation in human sentence processing: A cognitive architecture based on activation decay and simulated annealing. *Connection Science*, 1, 273–90.

Kircher, T. T. J., Brammer, M. J., Williams, S. C. R., & McGuire, P. K. (2000). Lexical retrieval during fluent speech production: an fMRI study. *NeuroReport*, 11, 4093–6.

Knibb, J. A., Xuereb, J. H., Patterson, K., et al. (2006). Clinical and pathological characterization of progressive aphasia. *Annals of Neurology*, 59, 156–65.

Kolk, H. H. J. (1995). A time-based approach to agrammatic production. *Brain and Language*, 50, 282–303.

Kolk, H. H. J., van Grunsven, M. J. F., & Keyser, A. (1985). On parallelism between production and comprehension in agrammatism. In Kean, M. L. (Ed.) *Agrammatism* (pp. 165–206). Orlando, FL: Academic.

Laiacona, M. & Caramazza, A. (2004). The noun/verb dissociation in language production: Varieties of causes. *Cognitive Neuropsychology*, 21, 103–23.

Lambon Ralph, M. A., McClelland, J. L., Patterson, K. E., Galton, C. J., & Hodges, J. R.

(2001). No right to speak? The relationship between object naming and semantic impairment: Neuropsychological evidence and a computational model. *Journal of Cognitive Neuroscience*, 13, 341–56.

Laws, K. R. (2005). "Illusions of normality": A methodological critique of category-specific naming. *Cortex*, 41, 842–51.

Levelt, W. J. M. (1989). *Speaking: From Intention to Articulation*. Cambridge, MA: MIT Press.

Levelt, W. J. M., Roelofs, A., & Meyer, A. S. (1999). A theory of lexical access in speech production. *Behavioral and Brain Sciences*, 22, 1–75.

Levy, D. A., Bayley, P. J., & Squire, L. R. (2004). The anatomy of semantic knowledge: Medial vs. lateral temporal lobe. *Proceedings of the National Academy of Sciences of the United States of America*, 101, 6710–15.

Luria, A. R. (1970). *Traumatic aphasia*. The Hague: Mouton.

MacNeilage, P. F. & Davis, B. L. (2001). Motor mechanisms in speech ontogeny: phylogenetic, neurobiological and linguistic implications. *Current Opinion in Neurobiology*, 11, 696–700.

Maetzig, S., Druks, J., Mastedrson, J., & Vigliocco, G. (submitted). Object and action naming: A double dissociation?

Martin, A. & Chao, L.L. (2001). Semantic memory and the brain: Structure and processes. *Current Opinion in Neurobiology*, 11, 194–201.

Martin, A., Wiggs, C. L., Ungerleider, L. G., & Haxby, J. V. (1996). Neural correlates of category-specific knowledge. *Nature*, 379, 649–52.

Martin, R. C. (2003). Language Processing: Functional organization and neuroanatomical basis. *Annual Review of Psychology*, 54, 55–89.

Martin, R. C. & Blossom-Stach, C. (1986). Evidence of syntactic deficits in fluent aphasia. *Brain and Language*, 28, 196–234.

Mesulam, M. M. (2001). Primary progressive aphasia. *Annals of Neurology*, 49, 425–32.

Miceli, G., Mazzucchi, A., Menn, L., & Goodglass, H. (1983). Contrasting cases of Italian agrammatic aphasia without comprehension disorders. *Brain and Language*, 19, 65–97.

Nickels (2001). Spoken word production. In Rapp, B. (Ed.) *The handbook of Cognitive Neuropsychology* (pp. 291–320). Taylor & Francis.

Neininger, B. & Pulvermüller, F. (2003). Word-category specific deficits after lesions in the right hemisphere. *Neuropsychologia*, 41, 53–70.

Nespolous, J. D., Dordain, M., Perron, C., et al. (1988). Agrammatism in sentence production without comprehension deficits: reduced availability of syntactic structures and/or of grammatical morphemes? A case study. *Brain and Language*, 33, 273–5.

Ojemann, G. A. (1991). Cortical organization of language. *Journal of Neuroscience*, 11, 2281–7.

Pai, M. C. (1999). Supplementary motor area aphasia: a case report. *Clin Neurol Neurosurg*, 101, 29–32.

Perani, D., Cappa, S. F., Schnur, T., Tettamanti, M., Collina, S., Rosa, M. M., & Fazio, F. (1999). The neural correlates of verb and noun processing: A PET study. *Brain*, 122, 2337–44.

Price, C. J. (1998). The functional anatomy of word comprehension and production. *Trends in Cognitive Science*, 2, 281–8.

Rapp, B. & Caramazza, A. (2002). Selective difficulties with spoken nouns and written verbs: A single case study. *Journal of Neurolinguistics*, 15, 373–402.

Rapp, B. & Goldrick, M. (2005). Speaking words: Contributions of cognitive neuropsychological research. *Cognitive Neuropsychology*, 23, 1–35.

Rapp, B. & Goldrick, M. (2000). Discreteness and interactivity in spoken word production. *Psychological Review*, 107, 460–99.

Robinson, G., Blair, J., & Cipolotti, L. (1998). Dynamic aphasia: An inability to select between competing verbal responses? *Brain*, 121, 77–89.

Robinson, G., Shallice, T., & Cipollotti, L. (2005). A failure of high level verbal response selection in progressive dynamic aphasia. *Cognitive Neuropsychology*, 22, 661–94.

Shallice, T. (1988). *From neuropsychology to mental structure*. Cambridge: Cambridge University Press.

Shapiro, K. & Caramazza, A. (2003). The representation of grammatical categories in the brain. *Trends in Cognitive Science*, 7, 201–6.

Simmons, W. K. & Barsalou, L. W. (2003). The similarity-in-typography principle: Reconciling theories of conceptual deficits. *Cognitive Neuropsychology*, 20, 451–86.

Siri, S., Tettamanti, M., Cappa, S.F., Della Rosa, P., Saccuman, C., Scifo, P., Vigliocco, G. (2008). The neural substrate of naming events: Effects of processing demands but not of grammatical class. *Cerebral Cortex* 18, 171–7.

Slobin, D. I. (1996). From "thought and language" to "thinking for speaking." In Gumperz, J. J. & Levinson, S. C. (Eds.) *Studies in the social and cultural foundations of language: No. 17. Rethinking linguistic relativity* (pp. 70–96). New York, NY: Cambridge University Press.

Thompson-Schill, S. L., D'Esposito, M., Aguirre, G. K., & Farah, M. J. (1997). Role of left inferior prefrontal cortex in retrieval of semantic knowledge: A reevaluation. *Proceedings of the National Academy of Sciences USA*, *94*, 14792–7.

Thompson-Schill, S. L., Jonides, J., Marshuetz, C., Smith, E. E., D'Esposito, M., Kan, I. P., & Swick, D. (2002). Effects of frontal lobe damage on interference effects in working memory. *Cognitive, Affective, and Behavioural Neuroscience*, *2*, 109–120.

Tranel, D. (2006). Impaired naming of unique landmarks is associated with left temporal polar damage. *Neuropsychology*, *20*, 1–10.

Tranel, D., Adolphs, R., Damasio, H., & Damasio, A. R. (2001). A neural basis for the retrieval of words for actions. *Cognitive Neuropsychology*, *18*, 655–70.

Tranel, D., Damasio, H., & Damasio, A. R. (1997). A neural basis for the retrieval of conceptual knowledge. *Neuropsychologia*, *35*, 1319–27.

Tranel, D., Damasio, H., Eichhorn, G. R., Grabowski, T. J., Ponto, L. L. B., & Hichwa, R. D. (2003). Neural correlates of naming animals from their characteristic sounds. *Neuropsychologia*, *41*, 847–54.

Tranel, D., Enekwechi, N., & Manzel, K. (2005). A test for measuring recognition and naming of landmarks. *Journal of Clinical and Experimental Neuropsychology*, *27*, 102–26.

Tranel, D., Grabowski, T. J., Lyon, J., & Damasio, H. (2005). Naming the same entities from visual or from auditory stimulation engages similar regions of left inferotemporal cortices. *Journal of Cognitive Neuroscience*, *17*, 1293–305.

Tranel, D. & Kemmerer, D. (2004). Neuroanatomical correlates of locative prepositions. *Cognitive Neuropsychology*, *21*, 719–49.

Tranel, D., Kemmerer, D., Damasio, H., Adolphs, R., & Damasio, A. R. (2003). Neural correlates of conceptual knowledge for actions. *Cognitive Neuropsychology*, *20*, 409–32.

Tranel, D., Logan, C. G., Frank, R. J., & Damasio, A. R. (1997). Explaining category-related effects in the retrieval of conceptual and lexical knowledge for concrete entities: Operationalization and analysis of factors. *Neuropsychologia*, *35*, 1329–39.

Tranel, D., Martin, C., Damasio, H., Grabowski, T., & Hichwa, R. (2005). Effects of noun-verb homonymy on the neural correlates of naming concrete entities and actions. *Brain and Language*, *92*, 288–99.

van Turennout, M., Hagoort, P., & Brown, C. M. (1998). Brain activity during speaking: From syntax to phonology in 40 milliseconds. *Science*, *280*, 572–4.

Vigliocco, G. (2000). Language processes: the anatomy of meaning and syntax. *Current Biology*, *10*, R78–R80.

Vigliocco, G. & Filopovic Kleiner, L. (2004). From mind in the mouth to language in mind. *Trends in Cognitive Science*, *8*, 5–7.

Vigliocco, G. & Hartsuiker, R. J. (2002). The interplay of meaning, sound & syntax in language production. *Psychological Bulletin*, *128*, 442–72.

Vigliocco G. & Vinson, D. (2007). Semantic Representation. In Gaskell, G. (Ed.) *Oxford Handbook of Psycholinguistics*, Oxford: Oxford University Press.

Vigliocco, G., Vinson, D. P, Lewis, W., & Garrett, M. F. (2004). Representing the meaning of objects and actions words: The featural and unitary semantic space hypothesis. *Cognitive Psychology*, *48*, 422–88.

Vosse, T. & Kempen, G. (2000). Syntactic structure assembly in human parsing: A computational model based on competitive inhibition and lexicalist grammar. *Cognition*, *75*, 105–43.

Ziegler, W., Kilian, B., & Deger, K. (1997). The role of the left mesial frontal cortex in fluent speech: Evidence from a case of left supplementary motor area hemorrhage. *Neuropsychologia*, *35*, 1197–208.

Section 8

FIGURATIVE LANGUAGE

CHAPTER 23

Figurative Language

Normal Adult Cognitive Research

Raymond W. Gibbs, Jr., Nicole L. Wilson,
and Gregory A. Bryant

1 Figurative language: Normal adult cognitive research

Experimental research on figurative language use has reached maturity within psycholinguistics and is surely deserving of its own special section in this handbook. But one difficulty with separating figurative language from other aspects of language use, such as sentence comprehension and discourse and conversation, is that it gives the impression that one can study sentence comprehension or discourse processing without attending to figurative language. In fact, figurative language permeates all spoken and written discourse. It is hard to conceive of any adequate theory of sentence comprehension, for instance, that does not directly address the ways that people readily use and understand figurative meaning.

Consider as a random example the opening lines of a typical newspaper article on the front page of the *San Francisco Chronicle* (March 12, 2006) titled "GOP is in 'deep funk' over Bush spending." The title alone is figurative in several ways given the metonymic use of GOP to stand for people who are Republicans, the use of "deep funk" metaphorically referring to a generalized depressed state of mind, and the metaphorical use of the preposition "over' to talk about a relation that is clearly nonphysical. But now read the first two lines of the story:

> *The Republican rebellion that President Bush smacked into with the Dubai ports deal was the tip of the iceberg of Republican discontent that is much deeper and more dangerous to the White House than a talk radio tempest over Arabs running U.S. ports.*
>
> *A Republican pushback on Capitol Hill and smoldering conservative dissatisfaction have already killed not just the ports deal but key elements of Bush's domestic agenda, and threatens GOP control of Congress if unhappy conservatives sit out the November midterm election.*

These two long sentences are full of metaphors (e.g., "smacked into," "tip of the iceberg," "much deeper," "tempest," "running," "pushback," "smoldering," "killed," and "sit out") and metonymies (e.g., "The Republican," "The White House," "Capitol Hill") that most people can easily interpret. Psycholinguists face the challenge of describing how readers comprehend phrases like "smacked into," "tip of the iceberg," "pushback," and "The White House" as conveying figurative meanings that differ from talk about physical actions like smacking into something, pushing back something, and entities like icebergs in the ocean and large buildings in Washington, DC. We now know a good deal about how people comprehend some of these words/ phrases, and more generally recognize that the frequency of these figurative forms reveals important insights into the ways people ordinarily conceive of those concepts to which this language refers. It is fair to say that psycholinguistic research has not yet addressed how people combine their understandings of various figurative phrases to achieve more global interpretations of speakers' complex utterances or discourse, such as seen in the newspaper excerpts we quoted earlier. But psycholinguists are slowly beginning to addresses this issue in their experimental and theoretical work on the mental processes employed during spoken and written figurative language use.

This chapter describes some of this important research, raises several criticisms of contemporary theories and research, highlights the need to include corpus data in constructing psycholinguistic experiments, and even suggests that there is no unified concept of "figurative" language that is necessarily distinct from some other unified concept known as "literal" speech. Finally, we offer several suggestions for future research by specifically calling for more empirical work on the integration of multiple tropes (i.e., rhetorical figures of speech) in discourse understanding and for greater attention to the later meaning products of figurative language use and not just earlier comprehension processes.

2 Literal versus figurative language distinction?

There remains a longstanding division in psycholinguistics between work addressing ordinary sentence and discourse processes and research on figurative language use. This divide is motivated, in our view, by an enduring belief in a fundamental distinction between literal and figurative meaning with work on sentence comprehension focusing on literal processing and work on figurative language focusing on processing of metaphors, metonymies, ironies, and so on, all of which fall under the umbrella of "nonliteral" language use. But there are several problems with this belief that has hindered development of a greater appreciation of the prominence of figurative language in psycholinguistic studies of linguistic processing.

First, there exists no single common feature that unites all the variety of tropes that typically make up the category of figurative language (e.g., metaphor, metonymy, idioms, proverbs, irony, oxymora) (Gibbs, 1994). Metaphor and metonymy, for instance, reflect very different kinds of mental mappings (i.e., metaphor involves the mapping of information between different conceptual domains, and metonymy involves the highlighting of a salient part of a single domain), while irony is composed of many different forms of contrast (e.g., sarcasm, jocularity, understatement, hyperbole), all of which differ considerably from the cognitive mappings seen in metaphor and metonymy. Nothing unites these diverse forms of talk, and as we demonstrate later, there is no single mental process or strategy that can account for the production and processing of figurative language. This conclusion greatly weakens any argument that figurative language/meaning represents one side of a psychologically valid literal–figurative distinction.

On the other hand, a significant part of the interdisciplinary literature on figurative language is devoted to defining metaphor, metonymy, irony, and so on in opposition to literal meaning with the hidden assumption that the concept "literal" is well understood and in no need of further clarification. Psycholinguists rarely attempt to provide an operational definition of literal meaning when constructing their studies and experimental stimuli. Figurative language experiments individually contrast metaphoric versus literal meaning, ironic versus literal meaning, idiomatic versus literal meaning, metonymic versus literal meaning, and so on. But across the vast number of empirical studies that have compared literal and figurative meanings, the variety of forms for literal utterances is as great as are the differences between metaphors, metonymies, ironies, and so on. Yet scholars continue to assume that the literal meaning they examine empirically is the same variable, reflecting the same type of meaning that other researchers investigate in their respective experiments.

In fact, studies demonstrate that people have varying intuitions about what literal meaning is depending on what aspects of literality are being emphasized (e.g., subject-matter literality, conventional literality, context-free literality, truth-conditional literality) (Gibbs, 1994). Moreover, as we describe later in this chapter, people's ideas about both literal and figurative meanings often vary considerably from corpus analyses of the ways various words and phrases are actually used. These observations also damage any claim that "literal" is a well-formed concept that differs in principled ways from "figurative" meaning and language. More recent appeals to the idea that literal and figurative language/meaning exist on a continuum (Coulson and Lewandowska-Tomaszcyk, 2005) also lack theoretical weight, precisely because both ends are far too heterogeneous in the forms/meanings of language they presumably represent (Gibbs, 2005).

A related problem for psycholinguistic accounts of figurative language use is the belief that we already know how literal language is processed. Psycholinguists have made a huge effort over the past forty years to create adequate accounts of sentence parsing and discourse processing. Although there has been significant progress in our understanding of different aspects of online sentence processing in regard to specific topics (e.g., the interaction of syntax and semantic in sentence parsing, reference assignment, ambiguity resolution,

establishing coherence relations in text), there is no single agreed upon position as to what people ordinarily do as they encounter language word-by-word in speech and reading. Thus, there is not a single position on literal meaning processing that can be readily used to compare understanding of different forms of figurative language.

We raise these critical issues about defining literal and figurative language because the failure to attend to these problems has shaped the progress of figurative language research over the years. First, psycholinguists will often posit the existence of figurative language processing models without acknowledging the diversity of forms making up so-called figurative speech and incorrectly assume that such models stand in contrast to some well-understood idea of how literal language is understood. Second, the belief in the literal and figurative distinction has relieved psycholinguists studying sentence comprehension from the challenge of examining how figuration is dealt with in online models of linguistic processing, precisely because figurative language is seen as something different and special. Finally, the emphasis on the ways processing of figurative language, as a whole, is similar to or differs from, according to one's perspective, processing of literal speech, distracts psycholinguists from exploring the neglected topic of what listeners and readers actually understand (i.e., the products of comprehension) when figurative language is encountered.

3 Figurative language understanding: Is it relatively difficult?

Much of the attention given to figurative language throughout the past thirty years has centered on the relative difficulty of understanding figurative language compared to literal speech. Following several proposals in the philosophy of language (Grice, 1989; Searle, 1979), many early studies in psycholinguistics examined whether people must analyze the complete literal meaning of a figurative utterance, finding that meaning inappropriate, before deriving its contextually relevant nonliteral interpretation. This hypothesis implied that figurative utterances must necessarily be more difficult to understand than corresponding literal speech, an idea consistent with the belief that figurative language is ornamental or unusual.

But various experimental studies demonstrated that people do not always require additional mental effort to comprehend many kinds of figurative utterances compared to so-called literal speech (Gibbs, 1994; 2001). One conclusion drawn from these studies is that similar psychological mechanisms appear to drive the understanding of both literal and figurative speech, at least insofar as very early cognitive processes are concerned. Appropriate contextual information provides a pragmatic framework for people to understand many types of figurative utterances without any recognition that these utterances violate conversational norms.

Some studies have found evidence that people sometimes take longer to process certain figurative utterances than corresponding literal speech, exactly as would be predicted by the traditional view (Giora, 2002; Schwoebel et al., 2000). But there may be various reasons for why people take longer to interpret particular figurative expressions that have little to do with processing of an expression's complete literal meaning. In some cases, the experimental contexts in which figurative words or expressions are encountered may be relatively weak in setting up a framework for interpreting figurative meaning (Gibbs, 2001). In other cases, such as when people interpret novel poetic metaphors, such as "Death is the coal-black milk of morning," the processing difficulty lies in integrating the figurative meaning with the context and not with an obligatory first step in which literal meanings are analyzed and then rejected. These alternative possibilities are all plausible ways of explaining the long time needed to comprehend certain novel metaphors, ironies, or proverbs, to take a few notable examples. One problem in empirically distinguishing between the different theories is that most

early studies looking at figurative language processing have examined reading time to interpret an entire utterance. Findings showing that many kinds of figurative language need not take longer overall to process than corresponding nonfigurative speech clearly falsify any claim that figurative language must always be more difficult to understand (Gibbs, 1994; Giora, 2001). Yet the overall reading time for individual sentences masks many fast-occurring linguistic processes that may be key to explaining how figurative language is understood.

These debates over literal meaning in figurative language processing have primarily focused on early aspects of comprehension rather than on later stages of utterance and discourse interpretation. Scholars from other disciplines often view psycholinguists' fascination with processing time as irrelevant to broader concerns about the interpretation and appreciation of figurative language, especially as seen in literary texts. But psycholinguists have maintained an enduring interest in the speed with which figurative utterances are initially understood because of longstanding theoretical debates between modular and interactive models of language processing.

For example, many psycholinguists have argued that even if much figurative language does not necessarily demand extra cognitive effort to understand, people may still analyze literal, conventional, or salient aspects of word meaning during immediate figurative comprehension regardless of context (i.e., a modular account) (Blasko and Connine, 1993; Giora, 2001). Some studies, which measured the meanings activated during each part of the moment-by-moment process of linguistic comprehension, indeed suggest that understanding familiar (e.g., "The belief that hard work is a ladder is common to this generation.") and less familiar (e.g., "The thought that a good professor is an oasis was clung to by the entire class.") metaphors, for example, engage different interpretation processes. Analysis of literal word meaning (e.g., *oasis* as an actual place in the desert) still precedes metaphorical meaning (*oasis* referring to a rare, valuable resource) during novel metaphor understanding with both types of meaning arising in parallel during familiar metaphor processing. Gibbs (2001) suggested, however, that these studies often conflate analysis of literal word meaning with figurative phrasal meaning, thus offering an unfair comparison of so-called literal and figurative meaning processes. Other studies that assessed people's speeded judgments about the sensibility of different word strings at different moments find no difference in the comprehension speed for literal (e.g., "Some temples are stone.") and figurative (e.g., "Some hearts are stone.") strings (McElree and Nordlie, 1999). This lack of time course differences is inconsistent with the claim that metaphoric interpretations are computed after a literal meaning has been analyzed, and suggest to some that literal and metaphoric interpretations are computed in parallel.

Yet even if some linguistic meanings (e.g., literal or metaphoric) are created sooner during figurative language processing does not imply that entirely different mental processes operate to produce these different meanings (Gibbs, 2002). Different kinds of meaning may arise from a single comprehension process. The fact that scholars label one kind of meaning "literal" and another "metaphoric," for example, does not necessarily indicate that different processes operate (i.e., a literal processing mode and a metaphoric processing mode) as people create these meanings (either in a serial or parallel manner) during online interpretation.

4 Figurative language understanding: Recent theories and data

The continuing debates over the relative difficulty of figurative language understanding have led to the development of several alternative theories. These new models describe the influence of context on figurative language processing at a more fine-grained level than earlier proposals. Thus, the newer models suggest when and how context prompts figurative meanings during word-by-word linguistic processing, and not just by looking at the interaction of context and sentence meaning. These newer models also attempt to offer general accounts that may apply to all aspects of figurative language, compared to most theories that aim to describe individual tropes (e.g., metaphor, irony, proverbs). Although these models recognize that trope-specific types of processing might be necessary, they suggest that obligatory linguistic processes operate early on, mostly at the lexical level, with all types of figurative language.

Consider first the graded salience hypothesis (Giora, 2002). This view claims that context constrains figurative meanings only after salient word or phrase meanings have already been accessed. Salient word or phrase meanings are not necessarily literal meanings, but reflect the most common, conventional use of a word or phrase, including those that may be figurative. Various empirical studies lend support for this model. For example, one set of studies examined people's understanding of familiar (e.g., "Very funny") and less familiar (e.g., "Thanks for your help") ironies in comparison to literal uses of the same expressions in appropriate contexts (Giora and Fein, 1999). Participants read stories ending with either literal or ironic remarks. After reading the final sentence, participants were presented with a letter string and had to quickly respond whether that string was a meaningful word. For example, after reading the statement "Thanks for your help," participants were presented with either an ironic test word (e.g., "angry") or a literal test word (e.g., "useful"). These test words were presented either 150 ms or 1,000 ms after participants read the final statements.

The results showed that when people read less familiar ironies they responded faster to the literal test words than to the ironic test words in the 150 ms condition, but there were no differences in the lexical decision times to the literal and ironic test words after 1,000 ms. In contrast, the literal and ironic test words were responded to equally fast after both 150 and 1,000 ms when people read familiar ironies. This pattern of data suggests that when people read familiar ironies both literal and ironic meanings are quickly accessed, but only literal meanings are initially activated when people read less familiar ironic statements. Salient meanings of both words and sentences are always accessed first regardless of context, which is consistent with modular theories of linguistic interpretation.

One difficulty with the graded salience view is that it is unclear what defines the salient meaning for any given word or expression. Salient meanings are thought to be those immediately active apart from context, which assumes that a clear distinction exists between semantically rich mental lexicons and real-world and contextual knowledge, an idea that is open to criticism (Elman, 2004; Gibbs and Lonergan, 2006). Moreover, there are times when the salient meaning of an entire phrase should be immediately activated (e.g., for "kick the bucket") and override the access of salient word meanings (e.g., "kick"). Yet it is unclear how this conflict is resolved or whether context comes into play to determine contextually appropriate word meanings before conventionalized phrasal meanings are accessed. Despite these problems, the graded salience model is sensitive to the fact that figurative meanings for both words and some phrases are sometimes highly salient and most easily accessed during online language processing. This view is also unique within general theories of figurative language use in suggesting that the immediate activation of salient meanings is not always eventually suppressed, but can play some role in how different forms of figurative language are ultimately interpreted (i.e., the "retention hypothesis").

Another general theory of figurative language processing claims that the language processor initially accesses an interpretation that is compatible with both a word's literal and figurative meanings before context comes in to sharpen the intended meaning (Frisson and Pickering, 2001). Consider the verb *disarmed* in "Mrs. Graham is quite certain that they disarmed about every critic who was opposed to spending more money on art." The underspecification model assumes that the initial

meaning recovered when reading the verb *disarmed* in any context is underspecified as to whether it refers to removing literal or figurative arms. Further downstream, as the reader continues, context operates to hone in on the appropriate meaning of *disarmed*, with the honing process working faster when the preceding context is strong, and slower when the preceding context is neutral. Context does not operate to judge between different word meanings (i.e., literal or figurative), but functions to change an underspecified or highly general meaning into a specific interpretation.

Support for the underspecification model comes from several eye movement studies. In one study, Frisson and Pickering (2001) examined people's processing of ambiguous verbs, such as *disarmed*. The eye movement data showed that the processing difficulty with the subordinate sense of *disarmed*, relative to when the word was used in a literal, dominant sense (e.g., "After the capture of the village, we disarmed about every rebel and sent them to prison."), did not emerge until *after* the critical verb was read. Thus, context reduced processing difficulty, but the difference did not emerge until much after the verb was seen. Frisson and Pickering suggested that people did not initially access either a specific sense or several senses for an ambiguous verb. Instead, readers initially recovered a general, underspecified meaning for the verb and then created a further concrete instantiation of its meaning later on given contextual information (also see Frisson and Pickering, 1999 for an application of the underspecification view to metonymy).

Similar to the graded salience view, the underspecification model embraces a modular account of linguistic processing, at least in the sense that lexical access is encapsulated from contextual effects. But the underspecification model also suffers from the problem of not being able to specify what constitutes the initial, underspecified meaning accessed when a word is first encountered. Although some linguists and psychologists contend that highly abstract, even semantically unspecifiable, aspects of word meaning are initially accessed during ordinary language processing (Groesfema, 1995; Ruhl, 1989), others are skeptical of whether people actually encode such abstract, vague meanings for words and phrases (Gibbs, 2001).

A very different general model of figurative language understanding that is more in line with interactive views of linguistic processing embraces the notion of constraint satisfaction, an idea that has gained much support in psycholinguistics and cognitive science (Katz and Ferretti, 2001; Katz, 2005). When people comprehend a text or a figurative utterance, they must construct an interpretation that fits the available information (including context) better than alternative interpretations. The best interpretation is one that offers the most coherent account of what people are communicating, which includes information that best fits with certain other information and excludes information that does not. Under this view, understanding a figurative utterance requires people to consider different linguistic and nonlinguistic information that best fits together to make sense of what a speaker or writer is saying. Constraint satisfaction models are computationally efficient, and perhaps represent psychologically plausible ways of showing how different information is considered and integrated in everyday cognition.

Katz and Ferretti (2001) argued that a constraint satisfaction model provides the best explanation for experimental data on proverb understanding. They employed a self-paced moving window paradigm to show that context affects people's immediate reading of familiar (e.g., "Lightning never strikes the same place twice.") and unfamiliar proverbs (e.g., "Straight trees have crooked roots.") that have both well-formed literal and figurative meanings. Familiar proverbs were understood more easily than unfamiliar ones, and the speed up in processing for familiar proverbs occurred as soon as the second word of the expression was read. But the first words of unfamiliar proverbs were read more quickly in contexts supporting their figurative, rather than literal, interpretations. Yet the analysis of an unfamiliar

proverb's figurative meaning was not always complete when the last word was read.

These findings support a constraint satisfaction model by positing how different sources of information (e.g., syntactic, lexical, conceptual) compete for activation over time in parallel. Constraints interact to provide probabilistic evidence in support of various alternatives with the competition ending when one alternative fits best. For example, when reading an unfamiliar proverb, people immediately focus on a literal interpretation because there is less competition from other sources of information supporting a figurative meaning. Similarly, familiar proverbs are easier to process than unfamiliar expressions because there is more information available from the context and the words in familiar proverbs to support a figurative interpretation.

Another test of the constraint satisfaction view examined people's immediate understanding of expressions like "Children are precious gems" as having metaphoric (children are valuable) or ironic (children are burdens) meaning (Pexman, Ferretti, and Katz, 2000; see also Ivanko and Pexman, 2003). Several sources of information could induce either the metaphoric or ironic meaning, including the occupation of the speaker, whether the statement was counterfactual to information in the previous discourse, and the familiarity of the expression. Results from an online reading task (i.e., moving window) demonstrated that the "A is B" statements were initially read as metaphors, but that the speaker's occupation and counterfactuality of the statement given the previous context play an early role in processing, thus slowing processing at the space following the statement or by the time the first word of the next statement is read. Furthermore, knowing that a speaker is often associated with irony slows down reading of the first word in the following statement if the context leads one to expect a metaphoric reading, yet acts immediately to speed up processing right after the target statement if the context induces an ironic meaning. The complex interaction between the three sources of information is consistent with the idea that understanding whether an expression is meant metaphorically or ironically depends, similar to other aspects of language, on multiple sources of information being examined and interpreted continuously during online reading (McRae, Spivey-Knowlton, and Tanenhaus, 1998).

Finally, an encouraging new trend in the field is the development of computational models of figurative language processing based on experimental data that also aim to provide more comprehensive theories of linguistic processing. Budiu and Anderson's (2004) INP (interpretation-based processing) model emphasizes the different roles that sentence context (i.e., context can both precede or follow a metaphor) and similarity-based reasoning can play in metaphor understanding. The model is a single production system that employs a similarity-based mechanism of spreading activation to provide the correct combination of bottom-up and top-down processes leading to the most plausible contextual interpretations of metaphors. Degree of comprehensibility depends on how similar words are to their referents (e.g., the metaphor word *hens* to the idea of a group of women talking noisily), and how similar an expression is to the preceding text. INP is nicely able to explain contradictory results in the metaphor literature, such as those showing different patterns of reading times for predicative (e.g., "Muhammad Ali floats like a butterfly.") and anaphoric (e.g., "The butcher was sued for malpractice.") metaphors compared to literal statements. Most generally, INP offers important insights into a plausible unified model of literal and metaphoric language processing, as well as the interpretation of sentences containing semantic illusions (e.g., "How many animals of each kind did Moses take on the ark?"). A related computational model of metaphor, using Latent Semantic Analysis to predict human participants' judgments, also provides interesting insights into when certain metaphors are likely to be easy or difficult to understand (Kintsch and Bowles, 2002).

5 Corpus linguistics and figurative language research

When psycholinguists design their experiments, they make various assumptions about whether a word or phrase is typically used in a literal or figurative manner, and the extent to which any context biases its literal or figurative meaning or is even neutral as to which meaning is intended. But these assumptions are often incorrect. Consider first the problem of deciding whether a metaphorically used word is conventional or novel by examining two texts used in a series of psycholinguistic experiments looking at people's understanding of conventional and novel metaphors (Keysar et al., 2000).

1. As a scientist, Tina thinks of her theories as her children. She is a prolific researcher, conceiving an enormous number of new findings each year. Tina is currently weaning her latest child.
2. As a scientist, Tina thinks of her theories as her children. She is a fertile researcher, giving birth to an enormous number of new findings each year. Tina is currently weaning her latest child.

Keysar et al. argued that the opening sentence of both stories established an explicit metaphorical mapping. But the second line in both stories differs in that the first contains conventional words (e.g., *prolific* and *conceiving*), while the second contains novel metaphors (e.g., *fertile* and *giving birth*). The final sentence of both stories presents the same novel metaphor (e.g., *weaning her latest child*). Keysar et al. claimed that their assumption about the conventionality of each phrase was supported by a rating study in which undergraduate students were asked to judge the conventionality of each phrase.

However, it is not clear that assessing people's intuitive judgments best reflects natural language patterns (a lesson psychologists already know from the different data on people's familiarity with words and actual word frequency from corpora studies). In fact, Deignan (2005) performed a corpus analysis, using the British National Corpus, of the different items in the above texts and discovered something different from what Keysar et al. claimed to be the case. For instance, there were 365 cases of *fertile* in the corpora, 210 referring to lands that bear crops, and ninety-seven referring to people, animals, and plants. However, sixty-one of the ninety-seven citations of *fertile* referring to people were metaphorical, such as "For me, the artist's fertile imagination failed him." These data suggest, then, that *fertile* is not a novel metaphor, contrary to what was claimed by Keysar et al.

An analysis of *wean*, in reference to *weaning* in the last sentence of both texts, showed that it and its affiliates appeared 188 times in the corpus. But only five citations had *weaning* followed by a direct object (e.g., *weaning her latest child*). All of these were used specifically in discussing the feeding of children (e.g., "She didn't experience any trouble weaning her daughter."). In this way, Keysar et al. are correct that *weaning* in this context was a novel metaphor, at least in terms of this exact lexico-grammatical form. But *wean* like fertile has various metaphorical meanings closely related to the meaning conveyed in the experimental texts, such as "wean people away from exclusive reliance on the automobile." As suggested by research on processing polysemy during online text comprehension (Williams, 1992), it is quite likely that these closely related metaphorical senses may be accessed during reading. This fact could have led experimental participants in Keysar et al.'s reading time studies to treat *weaning* as a conventional metaphor and not a novel one (as claimed by Keysar et al., based on the results of an independent norming study using undergraduate psychology students).

Finally the term *latest child* in the texts' final sentence appears on the surface to be ambiguous between a literal and metaphorical reading. Yet a corpus analysis shows that a metaphorical interpretation is strongly favored because the collocation "latest + child" almost never occurs (compared to words like *youngest* which appears frequently with *child*). This result suggests that the collocation *latest child* would convey a novel meaning of *child*, because it reflects an atypical language pattern, regardless of the previous context.

This corpus analysis raises questions about the stimuli employed by Keysar et al., especially in the way they classified different phrases as having literal or metaphorical, and conventional or novel metaphorical, meanings. Thus, people's raw intuitions about whether a given word or expression has metaphorical meaning, and the extent of its metaphoricity, may differ from how words are actually employed in real discourse.

Consider now a different corpus analysis that examined the context in which metaphorically used words appeared. Recall the use of the word *disarmed* in the metaphorical sentence from the Frisson and Pickering study: "Mrs. Graham is quite certain that they disarmed about every critic who was opposed to spending more money on art." An independent corpus analysis of *disarmed* showed that the majority of its uses were indeed literal, as claimed by Frisson and Pickering (Deignan, 2005). But further examination of the actual contexts in which *disarmed* is found showed that there is rarely any ambiguity between the literal and metaphorical senses of the word, such as "The enemy crews were disarmed and handcuffed." (literal) and "Her smile and pretty face disarmed the expectation of everyone." (metaphor). None of the contexts in which *disarmed* was found in the corpus analysis came close to the neutral context sentences created by Frisson and Pickering.

These observations from corpus linguistic research have important consequences for the conduct of work in experimental psycholinguistics on figurative language. First, both researcher and participant-elicited intuitions about the nature of meanings are highly variable and may not be accurate reflections of the ways words are really used in context. Second, attempts to investigate context effects in immediate figurative language processing by positing neutral contexts for experimental study may create an unrealistic situation for readers/listeners that have little to do with language processing in natural conditions. We suggest that figurative language scholars closely examine their experimental stimuli in comparison to real speech and written language patterns to ensure that experimental conditions truly match what goes on in the real world of language use. Corpus research has become increasingly visible in linguistic studies of metaphor and metonymy, for example, and we anticipate that corpus work will need to play an integral part in what psycholinguists do in their own experimental work.

6 Metaphor understanding

Beyond the questions related to general models of figurative language processing, the topic of metaphor has garnered the most interest among experimental psycholinguists studying figurative language. Numerous studies have explicitly examined the ways that the A, or target, and B, or vehicle, terms interact to produce metaphorical meaning for expressions like "My job is a jail" and "Lawyers are sharks." A longstanding assumption in many academic fields is that metaphors are understood by recognizing the ways that topic and vehicle terms are similar. Thus, in understanding the metaphor "My job is a jail," listeners are presumed to figure out the properties of jobs and jails that are similar.

But psycholinguistic experiments indicate that metaphor comprehension does not demand that the topic and vehicle terms must share properties or associations (Glucksberg, 2001). This claim is supported by many studies showing that metaphors have directional meaning. If metaphorical meaning arises from the overlap of the topic and vehicle's semantic features, expressions such as "The surgeon is a butcher" and "The butcher is a surgeon" should have similar metaphoric meanings; however, this is clearly not the case (but see Campbell and Katz, 2006 and Wolff and Gentner, 2000

for evidence showing how this effect can be diminished). The similarity that arises from the comparison of a topic and vehicle does not produce metaphorical meaning. Instead, similarity is created as an emergent property of metaphor understanding. Thus, many psychological studies demonstrate that the novel features emerging from metaphor comprehension are not salient in one's separate understanding of the topic or vehicle (Gineste, Indurkhya, and Scart, 2000; Utsumi, 2005).

Psychologists disagree, however, about the cognitive mechanisms involved in feature emergence during metaphor understanding. The two main proposals state that metaphorical mappings between concepts from dissimilar domains can be accomplished by either comparison or categorization processes. Traditional comparison theories posit that metaphor understanding demands a mapping of low-salient features from the source domain with high-salient features of the target domain (Miller, 1979). But understanding many metaphors, such as "Men are wolves," seems to involve features not typically associated with either the source or target domain until after the metaphor has been understood (Ortony, 1979). Gentner's structure mapping theory of analogy and metaphor avoids this problem by suggesting that people begin processing a metaphor by first aligning the representations of the source and target domain concepts (Gentner, 1983; Gentner et al., 2001). Once these two domains are aligned, further inferences are directionally projected from the source to the target domain. Finally, new inferences arise within the target domain reflecting relational, and not just feature-specific, aspects of the metaphor comprehension processes.

Experimental evidence in support of this comparison view shows, for instance, that people infer relational, but not feature-specific meanings when interpreting metaphors (Gentner et al., 2001). For instance, when people read "Plant stems are drinking straws," they infer that both plants and straws convey liquid to nourish living things and not just that both plants and straws are long and thin (i.e., object commonalities). Other research indicates that metaphors expressing relational information (e.g., "Plant stems are drinking straws.") are judged to be far more apt than those that only map object features ("Her arms were like twin swans.") (Tourangeau and Rips, 1991).

An alternative view claims that metaphors are better understood via categorization processes as class inclusion, and not comparison statements (Glucksberg, 2001). For example, the statement "Yeltsin was a walking time bomb" asserts that the former Russian president is a member of a category best exemplified by time bombs. Of course, *time bombs* can belong to several other categories, such as the weapons used by terrorists. But in the context of talking about people, *time bombs* best exemplifies the abstract category of "things that explode at some unpredictable time in the future and cause a lot of damage." In this way, metaphors reflect ad hoc categories and refer at two levels: the concrete level (i.e., an explosive device) and a superordinate level (i.e., the properties of time bombs).

One implication of the class inclusion view, now called the interactive property attribution model, is that it suggests that the topics and vehicles, or target and source domains, in metaphors play different but interactive roles in metaphor comprehension (Glucksberg, McGlone, and Manfredi, 1997; Jones and Estes, 2005). For example, the word *snake* evokes different meanings in the phrases "my lawyer is a snake" and "the road was a snake." In this way, metaphor topics provide dimensions for attribution, while vehicles provide properties to be attributed to the topic. Psychological evidence supporting this position was found in a reading time study (McGlone and Manfredi, 2001). Participants were first presented with a topic (*lawyer*) or vehicle (*sharks*) term or one of two property attribution statements that either described a metaphor-relevant property or a metaphor-irrelevant property for the topic ("lawyers can be ruthless" and "lawyers can be married") and vehicle ("sharks can be ruthless" and "sharks can swim"). Following this,

people read a metaphorical statement (e.g., "Lawyers are sharks."). The results showed that all prime types facilitated metaphor comprehension except irrelevant-property primes. This suggests that people do not consider the literal referents of metaphor vehicles (e.g., real sharks) when reading metaphorical statements (e.g., "Lawyers are sharks."), because this irrelevant information is suppressed during comprehension (also see Gernsbacher et al., 2001).

These patterns of data illustrate how level of constraint is an important feature of metaphor topics, while degree of ambiguity is an important characteristic of metaphor vehicles. Comparison models of metaphor understanding cannot explain the importance of constraint and ambiguity because they assume that metaphor comprehension always begins with an exhaustive extraction of the properties associated with both topics and vehicles. Having advanced knowledge about either the topic or vehicle should presumably, then, prime metaphor processing. However, the categorization view correctly predicts that only advanced knowledge about highly constrained topics and unambiguous vehicles facilitates metaphor comprehension, a finding that is most consistent with the claim that metaphor understanding involves creating a new, ad hoc category and not merely comparing one's knowledge about topic and vehicle domains.

A very recent proposal, titled the career of metaphor theory, combines aspects of both the comparison and categorization views (Bowdle and Gentner, 2005; Gentner and Bowdle, 2001). This theory claims that there is a shift in the mode of mappings from comparison to categorization processes as metaphors become conventionalized. For instance, novel metaphors such as "Science is a glacier" involve base terms like *glacier* with a literal source (i.e., "a large body of ice spreading outward over a land surface"), but no relational metaphoric sense (i.e., "anything that progresses slowly but steadily"). People comprehend novel metaphors as comparisons, in which the target concept (e.g., *science*) must be structurally aligned with the literal base concept (e.g., *glacier*). In some instances, the comparison process may lead to the induction of a novel metaphor category. On the other hand, conventional metaphors can be understood either by comparison or categorization processes. For example, the metaphor "A gene is a blueprint" has two closely related senses (e.g., "a blue and white photographic print detailing an architect's plans" and "anything that provides a plan"). The relations between these two senses make the conventional base term polysemous (i.e., semantically related literal and metaphoric meanings). As such, conventional metaphors may be understood by matching the target concept with the literal base concept (a comparison process) or by viewing the target concept as a member of the superordinate metaphoric category named by the base term (a categorization process).

Evidence favoring the career of metaphor view comes from studies comparing comprehension of similes, which evoke comparison processes (e.g., "Faith is like an anchor"), and metaphors, which evoke categorization processes (e.g., "Faith is an anchor") (Bowdle and Gentner, 2005). People preferred the metaphors to the similes when these statements increased from being novel to conventional. Novel similes (e.g., "Friendship is like wine") were read more quickly than metaphors, while the metaphors (e.g., "Alcohol is a crutch") were read more quickly than similes when these statements were conventional. Finally, giving people repeated exposures to novel similes using the same base term over time provoked individuals to shift to using the metaphor form in subsequent statements, indicating a shift from comparison to categorization aspects of metaphorical language use within the course of a single study.

Most generally, the career of metaphor view argues that whether a metaphorical statement is processed as a comparison or categorization, and whether it may be understood directly or indirectly, depends on the conventionality of the base term and the grammatical form (i.e., simile or metaphor) of the statement.

7 Metaphoric thought in language processing

Much of the psychological research on metaphor has focused on how metaphorical meaning is created de novo by linguistic statements (e.g., "Friendship is wine."). But in the past twenty years, various linguists, philosophers, and psychologists have argued that metaphor is not merely a figure of speech, but is a specific mental and neural mapping that influences a good deal of how people think, reason, and imagine in everyday life (Lakoff and Johnson, 1999). Evidence supporting this claim about conceptual metaphor comes from linguistic research on the historical evolution of what words and expressions mean, the systematicity of conventional expressions within and across languages, novel extensions of conventional metaphors, studies on polysemous word meaning, and nonverbal behaviors such as gesture (Gibbs, 1994; Lakoff and Johnson, 1980; 1999). To a large extent, this perspective on metaphor has focused on correlational metaphors (metaphors arising from recurring correlations in embodied experience such as between life and journeys), such as "Our marriage is on the rocks" rather than the resemblance, or A is B metaphors (e.g., "My lawyer is a shark") typically studied within the psycholinguistic literature.

However, many psychologists have been critical of much of the work on conceptual metaphors and its possible implications for theories about conceptual structure and metaphor understanding. They argue that most of the evidence for metaphorical thought, or conceptual metaphor, comes from purely linguistic analyses and is based on linguists' heavy reliance on their own linguistic intuitions (Murphy, 1996). Several psychologists further claim that conceptual metaphor theory is unfalsifiable if the only data in its favor is the systematic grouping of metaphors linked by a common theme, such as ARGUMENT IS WAR or LIFE IS A JOURNEY (Verveake and Kennedy, 1996). Finally, some psychologists argue that many conventional expressions (e.g., "Our marriage is on the rocks") viewed as metaphorical by cognitive linguists are really not metaphorical at all and are treated by ordinary speakers/listeners as literal speech (Glucksberg, 2001). Even if people seem able to think metaphorically about various domains, many psychologists find it difficult to believe that conceptual metaphors play much of a role in how people interpret verbal metaphors such as "Surgeons are butchers" or "Lawyers are sharks."

Despite the skeptical reaction of some psychologists to the idea of metaphorical thought or conceptual metaphor, a large body of evidence from psychological studies, employing different methods, clearly demonstrates that (a) people conceptualize certain topics via metaphor, (b) conceptual metaphors assist people in tacitly understanding why metaphorical words and expressions mean what they do, and (c) that people access conceptual metaphors during their immediate, online production and comprehension of much conventional and novel metaphoric language. This work includes studies investigating people's mental imagery for metaphorical action statements (e.g., "grasp the concept") (Gibbs, Gould, and Andric, 2006; Wilson and Gibbs, 2007), people's immediate processing of idiomatic phrases (Gibbs et al., 1997), several kinds of conventional and novel metaphors (Pfaff, Gibbs, and Johnson, 1997), readers' understanding of metaphorical time expressions (McGlone and Harding, 1998), and people's responses to questions about metaphorical expressions about time (Boroditsky and Ramscar, 2002; Gentner, Imai, and Boroditsky, 2002). This work does not imply that conceptual metaphors are accessed when processing all kinds of metaphoric language, such as classic A is B statements. But the frequency of correlational metaphors (i.e., those arising from correlations in people's bodily experiences) in speech and writing suggests that knowledge of conceptual metaphors is key to people's interpretations of much metaphoric language.

A final emerging trend in the metaphor literature is the growth of studies examining the role of embodied experience in people's use and understanding of metaphoric language (Gibbs, 2006). For example, research shows that people's previous bodily experiences of hunger partly predicts their use and understanding of metaphorical expressions about different forms of desire, as seen in statements like "I hunger for fame" or "I craved her affection" (Gibbs, Lima, and Francuzo, 2004). Other studies demonstrate that having people make, or imagine making, relevant body movements, such as grasping, facilitates people's processing of metaphorical expressions referring to those motions, such as "grasp the concept" (Wilson and Gibbs, 2007). Thus, people need not necessarily inhibit the physical meanings of certain metaphorically used words, like *grasp*, because these meanings are recruited during the online construction of metaphorical meanings as when concepts are metaphorically understood as things that can be grasped.

Bodily experience and current bodily positioning also appear to shape the way people respond to questions about the time, which is often characterized by two different versions of the TIME IS SPACE metaphor (e.g., time is moving while the ego is still, and time is still while the ego is moving). In one series of studies, students waiting in line at a café were given the statement "Next Wednesday's meeting has been moved forward two days" and then asked "What day is the meeting that has been rescheduled?" (Boroditsky and Ramscar, 2002). Students who were farther along in the line (i.e., who had thus very recently experienced more forward spatial motion) were more likely to say that the meeting had been moved to Friday. Similarly, people riding a train were presented the same ambiguous statement and asked about the rescheduled meeting. Passengers who were at the end of their journeys reported that the meeting was moved to Friday significantly more than did people in the middle of their journeys. Although both groups of passengers were experiencing the same physical experience of sitting in a moving train, they thought differently about the journey and consequently responded differently to the rescheduled meeting question.

In another version of this same experiment, participants studied a drawing that depicted a chair with a rope attached (Boroditsky and Ramscar, 2002). Half of the participants imagined that they were pulling the chair toward them with the rope. The other half imagined being seated in the chair, pulling themselves forward along the rope. Following the imagination activity, the participants were asked the same question as before about the rescheduled meeting. Participants who imagined pulling the chair toward themselves were more likely to answer that the meeting had been moved to Monday, consistent with a metaphorical idea of time moving. Conversely, the participants who imagined pulling themselves along the rope more typically adopted an ego-moving metaphorical perspective, and answered that the meeting had been rescheduled for Friday. These results also suggest how ongoing sensorimotor experience can strongly influence people's comprehension of metaphorical statements about time.

Debate over the role of metaphoric thought and its possible embodied basis will surely continue within experimental psycholinguistics. But it is clear that a comprehensive theory of metaphor will have to be broad enough to deal with the multiple types of metaphoric language that people ordinarily use, including both resemblance and correlational metaphors.

8 Irony

Many of the experimental studies investigating the relative difficulty of processing figurative language have focused on irony comprehension, as noted earlier in this chapter. But irony has several distinct characteristics that make it an important topic of research on its own. Consider some excerpts from a newspaper column titled "The loving arms of arms lovers" in the business section of the *San Francisco Chronicle* (February 5, 2006: J1):

I have joined the NRA.

Some well-meaning reader has paid $35 to buy me a one-year membership in the National Rifle Association, no doubt as a remedy for all the misguided, pro-consumer sentiment that's come to characterize this column.

So now I can proudly say my name is attached to safeguarding an industry with about $2 billion in annual sales and 150,000 employees, according to the Professional Gun Retailers Association.

That means I enjoy a connection to the main product of this industry (guns) and to what researchers say is this product's undeniable economic impact on the United States – a price tag of at least $100 billion annually in medical, legal, and judicial costs.

At last, I can boast that I'm part of efforts to protect people's access to a product that the federal government says is responsible for more than 30,000 deaths each year, including murders, suicides, and accidents.

Yes, my name is now associated with a commercial good that's responsible for the killing of at least eight children and teenagers every day (a record of product efficacy, as far as young people go, that not even the tobacco industry can touch).

Best of all, I can enjoy the full power and prestige of being one of the 4 million members of what lawmakers surveyed by the National Journal call the most powerful lobbying organization in Washington.

The author of this column is using irony to achieve particular communicative goals, such as being humorous, creating solidarity with his readers, appearing clever, indirectly mocking the victim (i.e., NRA supporters), and evoking specific emotional reactions in his readers. Recognizing the intended irony in this piece is not terribly difficult, as the author clearly signals his dissociation from his words when he notes how his previous columns were "misguided" for being "pro-consumer," and when he explicitly contrasts his own pretended proud, boastful enjoyment at being associated with the NRA and the fact that this organization is partly responsible for the deaths of thirty thousand people in the United States each year.

Many contemporary theories of irony discussed in the psycholinguistic literature claim that irony is based on speakers pretending to be certain people or have certain views (a kind of "staged communicative act," see Clark, 1996), achieving ironic effects by echoing or alluding to previous statements or beliefs associated with other individuals (Kumon-Nakamura, Glucksberg, and Brown, 1995; Sperber and Wilson, 1995), or offering an implicit display of an ironic environment (Utsumi, 2000). These different theories share the common idea that irony involves layers of meaning that require metarepresentational reasoning to be produced and understood. For instance, when the author above says "my name is now associated with a commercial good that's responsible for the killing of at least eight children and teenagers every day," he is taking action at two levels. First, he is making an assertion. Second, he is pretending to embrace the idea expressed in his assertion. By highlighting the contrast between these two levels of meaning, the author can efficiently communicate a variety of social and affective meanings. Layering reflects metarepresentational reasoning because a speaker is, once more, alluding to or echoing some attributed utterance or thought of another person (i.e., people who embrace the NRA), thus creating a representation of a representation (i.e., a second-order belief). Understanding ironic utterances, therefore, requires people to recognize the second-order nature of the speaker's beliefs if they are to correctly infer that individual's intended meaning (Sperber and Wilson, 1995).

The fact that understanding irony involves metarepresentational reasoning suggests that it differs significantly from metaphor use. One set of studies showed that ironic utterances took longer to read than the same utterances presented in a context making them metaphorical (Colston and Gibbs, 2002). For example, the sentence "This one's really sharp" could be understood metaphorically when in reference to a particularly smart student, or ironically if used to describe the quality of a bad pair of scissors. Metaphor understanding does not require second-order metarepresentational reasoning as does verbal irony, and so utterances that differ in only that regard should take longer to read when they are ironic. Moreover, different participants associated the ironic versions of the same utterances much more with pretense, attributed beliefs, and attitudes toward those beliefs than they did metaphorical uses of the same utterances. These findings illustrate the importance of metarepresentational reasoning in understanding irony. They also demonstrate the profound differences between various types of figurative expressions, enough so that it often makes little sense to suppose that a single theory can account for all aspects of figurative language compared to a different theory needed to explain literal language processing.

Other analyses of verbal irony in psycholinguistic research indicate that irony is not a unified form of talk, but instead represents a global term for different forms of ironic language, including sarcasm (e.g., "A fine friend you are"), jocularity (e.g., "I just love it when you spread your clothes all over the living room"), hyperbole (e.g., "I have absolutely nothing to wear"), rhetorical questions (e.g., "Isn't it lovely weather?" in the midst of a rainstorm), and understatement (e.g., "John seems to be a tad bit tipsy" when John is extremely intoxicated) (Gibbs, 2000). People employ these different forms of talk on varying occasions to communicate different, complex pragmatic goals (Colston, 2005) and to evoke different emotional reactions in listeners (Leggitt and Gibbs, 2000). For instance, Leggitt and Gibbs found that sarcasm, rhetorical questions, and hyperbole all evoked similar negative emotional reactions in listeners, whereas understatement and satire evoked relatively neutral reactions. Listeners also attributed different intentions to speakers depending on which form of irony they used. Furthermore, people tended to experience greater degrees of emotional involvement having heard different forms of irony than when they encountered literal statements, a finding that contradicts the idea that irony mutes speakers' intended messages (e.g., Dews and Winner, 1995).

Irony's capacity to convey different emotions and evoke various affective states in listeners, depending on the exact form of irony used, illustrates irony's important role in helping speakers negotiate social relationships, including who is, and who is not, a friend (Gibbs, 2000). Studies also show that speakers with different occupations (Katz and Pexman, 1997) and different genders (Colston and Lee, 2004) are expected to speak ironically with varying degrees, information that listeners use to draw ironic inferences in some situations but not others. Many other factors affect normal adults' recognition and understanding of verbal irony, including the perceived personality characteristics of the conversationalists (Pexman and Olineck, 2002), the degree of contrast between situational factors and ironic statements (Colston, 2002; Kreuz and Glucksberg, 1989; Kreuz and Roberts, 1995), and whether the contrast is a matter of kind or magnitude (Colston and O'Brien, 2000).

Psycholinguistic research has also addressed the issue of how nonverbal vocal and body cues relate to the communication of verbal irony (e.g., Anolli, Ciceri, and Infantino, 2000; Attardo et al., 2003; Bryant and Fox Tree, 2002, 2005; Rockwell, 2000). Speakers and listeners often rely on nonverbal information when using verbal irony, but not in such a systematic fashion as once thought. Instead of using some particular "ironic tone of voice" to help listeners derive proper inferences, spontaneous speakers tend to contrast prosodic features of ironic utterances with speech immediately proceeding them (Bryant, 2006). For instance, a sarcastic speaker might lower his pitch, speak louder, and slow down his speech rate relative to his baseline speech. These particular adjustments are often found with actors (e.g., Rockwell, 2000). But in spontaneous conversations, the acoustic patterns are not at all consistent, except that speakers quite often slow down (Bryant, 2006).

This slowdown in irony production could be done implicitly to allow listeners more time to process the metarepresentational information by recognizing the contrast in speech rate. Speakers also tend to contrast other nonverbal cues such as facial expressions and body movements with their baseline movements when speaking ironically (Attardo et al., 2003).

Somewhat surprising, studies also show that people are more likely to speak sarcastically during computer than face-to-face communications when they are interacting with strangers, although computer users are less likely to offer feedback to their interlocutors when comprehension problems arise (Hancock, 2004). In computer interactions, speakers use punctuation to mark aspects of their ironic intentions, comparable to the paralinguistic cues used in spoken discourse. One possible reason people use more irony in computer-mediated discourse is that strangers feel safer to risk offending their audience by speaking sarcastically, for example, when there is little chance they will meet the person, compared to face-to-face conversations where a misused irony can create immediate interpersonal problems.

9 Conclusions and future challenges

Our discussion of some, but by no means all, of the recent psycholinguistic work on figurative language use and understanding leads us to draw certain conclusions and raise several challenges for future experimental research.

First, much of the research on figurative language has focused on early aspects of linguistic processing, conducted with the aim of discriminating between different theories and models of the human language processor. Thus, the debates over the exact role that context has on figurative interpretations and whether the literal meanings of entire expressions or individual words are automatically accessed, is directed toward supporting either modular or more interactive models of language processing. One challenge is that theories favoring some automatic access of literal, salient, or unde-termined word meanings must provide a fuller account of what these meaning representations actually look like as psychological entities. Another issue is that researchers tend to trust their own intuitions, or those of undergraduate students, in creating experimental stimuli and labeling these as exhibiting specific types of meaning. But corpus studies suggest that these intuitions are often incorrect and that psycholinguists should place greater reliance on available evidence on the actual ways that words and phrases are used.

Second, psycholinguists' primary interest with early aspects of processing leads them to quickly posit general models of figurative language processing that might be quite misleading. People may not process all figurative language in the same way, precisely because the kinds and forms of different tropes are sufficiently varied as to resist classification within a single theoretical framework. In a similar manner, psycholinguists must resist suggestions that there are different processing modes for literal and figurative language or that parallel processes operate to produce literal and figurative meanings for utterances. Single linguistic processes may be sufficient to produce a variety of meanings without the need to postulate distinct processing modes for individual types of linguistic meaning.

Third, as important as the larger theoretical debates are on the architecture of the language processor, and the recognition that studies on figurative language use can contribute important data to these debates, it seems evident that the concerns with early processing ignore the critical problem of how people eventually get to figurative meanings. Right now, there is surprisingly little attention given to the actual meaning products that people infer when they understand different kinds of figurative language. There is great effort toward showing how people infer that something may have a metaphoric as opposed to a literal meaning in some contexts, but we still do not know enough about the complex metaphorical meanings people create during rich

pragmatic processing of figurative speech and writing. We know a good deal about the social and affective effects of irony understanding, for instance, but still do not have a clear idea as to the nature of what ironic meanings arise during irony comprehension. Of course, the exact meanings people infer in discourse depend on many individual, linguistic, and situational factors. But the time is ripe for greater exploration of these influences, with the long-term aim of showing how different meaning products relate to different types of cognitive effort during language production and understanding.

One concrete example of research related to the challenge just discussed investigated the pragmatic uses of metaphor (Gibbs and Tendahl, 2006). When people hear an expression such as "Lawyers are sharks" in discourse, their aim is to not just understand the metaphoric meaning of this phrase, but to understand what pragmatic effect the speaker wishes to communicate by using this metaphor. For instance, in a conversation between two people, one may state a number of negative images about lawyers with a second person supporting this argument by saying "Lawyers are sharks." In this case, the metaphor simply strengthens the existing set of beliefs held by the conversational participants. But in a slightly different situation, one person may say several negative things about lawyers, to which the second speaker adds an additional negative assertion by uttering, "Lawyers are sharks." Finally, in a third situation, one speaker may utter many positive features of lawyers to which the second person says "Lawyers are sharks" in order to contradict the first person. Thus, the same metaphor can achieve three different pragmatic effects (i.e., strengthening an existing idea, adding new information consistent with an existing idea, and contradicting an existing idea) depending on the context. Not surprising, people take more time to comprehend the metaphor "Lawyers are sharks" in the contradictory situation than in the other two.

One implication of this work is that understanding what any figurative utterance means is not simply a matter of getting to a particular figurative meaning, but also understanding what a speaker pragmatically intends to achieve by use of that trope. Most reading time studies, for example, fail to consider these pragmatic effects by focusing exclusively, and simplistically, on crude distinctions between literal and figurative meanings, and incorrectly attributing variations in processing time to constructions of those meanings as opposed to the pragmatic roles that speakers' utterances play in real discourse. In general, much greater attention is needed on the precise pragmatic effects achieved by different tropes and how particular figurative expressions may lead to very different pragmatic effects in varying contexts.

Finally, the work on figurative language use has almost exclusively focused on people's understanding of single instances of figurative words or utterances. Research has not yet examined how people comprehend very typical but still complex expressions such as seen in the opening newspaper excerpts (e.g., "The Republican rebellion that President Bush smacked into with the Dubai ports deal was the tip of the iceberg of Republican discontent that is much deeper and more dangerous to the White House than a talk radio tempest over Arabs running U.S. ports."). People seem to understand *something* when they read sentences like this. How they do so, and what they actually understand are two questions that should also be the focus of future research, with the overarching goal of integrating such findings into related theories of sentence comprehension and discourse processing.

References

Anolli, L., Ciceri, R., & Infantino, M. G. (2000). Irony as a game of implicitness: Acoustic profiles of ironic communication. *Journal of Psycholinguistic Research, 29(3)*, 275–311.

Attardo, S., Eisterhold, J., Hay, J., & Poggi, I. (2003). Multimodal markers of irony and sarcasm. *Humor, 16(2)*, 243–60.

Blasko, D. & Connine, C. (1993). Effects of familiarity and aptness on metaphor processing.

Journal of Experimental Psychology: Learning, Memory, and Cognition, 19, 295–308.

Boroditsky, L. & Ramscar, M. (2002). The roles of body and mind in abstract thought. *Psychological Science, 13*, 185–9.

Bowdle, B. & Gentner, D. (2005). The career of metaphor. *Psychological Review, 112*, 193–216.

Bryant, G. A. (2006). *Prosodic contrasts in ironic speech.* Manuscript under review.

Bryant, G. A. & Fox Tree, J. E. (2002). Recognizing verbal irony in spontaneous speech. *Metaphor and Symbol, 17(2)*, 99–117.

(2005). Is there an ironic tone of voice? *Language and Speech, 48(3)*, 257–77.

Budiu, R. & Anderson, J. (2004). Interpretation-based processing: A united theory of semantic sentence processing. *Cognitive Science, 28*, 1–44.

Campbell, J. & Katz, A. (2006). On reversing the topics and vehicles of metaphors. *Metaphor and Symbol, 21*, 1–22.

Clark, H. H. (1996). *Using language.* Cambridge: Cambridge University Press.

Colston, H. L. (2002). Contrast and assimilation in verbal irony. *Journal of Pragmatics, 34*, 111–42.

(2005). Social and cultural influences on figurative and indirect language. In Colston, H. & Katz, A. (Eds.) *Figurative language comprehension: Social and cultural influences* (pp. 99–130). Mahwah, NJ: Erlbaum.

Colston, H. L. & Gibbs, R. W. (2002). Are irony and metaphor understood differently? *Metaphor and Symbol, 17*, 57–80.

Colston, H. L. & Lee, S. Y. (2004). Gender differences on verbal irony use. *Metaphor and Symbol, 19*, 289–306.

Colston, H. L. & O'Brien, J. (2000). Contrast of kind versus contrast of magnitude: the pragmatic accomplishments of irony and hyperbole. *Discourse Processes, 30*, 179–99.

Coulson, S. & Lewandowska-Tomaszcyk, B. (Eds.) (2005). *The literal and nonliteral in language and thought.* Frankfurt: Peter Lang.

Deignan, A. (2005). *Metaphor and corpus linguistics.* Amsterdam: Benjamins.

Dews, S. & Winner, E. (1995). Muting the meaning: A social function of irony. *Metaphor and Symbolic Activity, 10*, 3–19.

Elman, J. (2004). An alternative view of the mental lexicon. *Trends in Cognitive Sciences, 8*, 301–6.

Frisson, S. & Pickering, M. (1999). The processing of metonymy: Evidence from eye-movements. *Journal of Experimental Psychology: Learning, Memory and Cognition, 25*, 1366–83.

(2001). Obtaining a figurative interpretation of a word: Support for underspecification. *Metaphor and Symbol, 16*, 149–72.

Gentner, D. (1983). Structure-mapping: A theoretical framework for analogy. *Cognitive Science, 7*, 155–70.

Gentner, D. & Bowdle, B. (2001). Convention, form, and figurative language processing. *Metaphor and Symbol, 16*, 223–48.

Gentner, D., Bowdle, B., Wolff, P., & Boronat, C. (2001). Metaphor is like analogy. In Gentner, D., Holyoak, K., & Kokinov, B. (Eds.) *The analogical mind: Perspectives from cognitive science* (pp. 199–253). Cambridge, MA: MIT Press.

Gentner, D., Imai, M., & Boroditsky, L. (2002). As time goes by: Evidence for two systems in processing space time metaphors. *Language and Cognitive Processes, 17*, 537–65.

Gernsbacher, M. A., Keysar, B., Robertson, R. R. W., & Werner, N. K. (2001). The role of suppression and enhancement in understanding metaphors. *Journal of Memory and Language, 45*, 433–50.

Gibbs, R. (1994). *The poetics of mind: Figurative thought, language, and understanding*. New York: Cambridge University Press.

(2000). Irony in talk among friends. *Metaphor and Symbol, 15*, 5–27.

(2001). Evaluating contemporary models of figurative language understanding. *Metaphor and Symbol, 16*, 317–33.

(2002). A new look at literal meaning in understanding what speakers say and implicate. *Journal of Pragmatics, 34*, 457–86.

(2005). Literal and nonliteral meanings are corrupt ideas: A view from psycholinguistics. In Coulson, S. & Lewandowska-Tomaszcyk, B. (Eds.) *The literal and nonliteral in language and thought* (pp. 121–39). Frankfurt: Peter Lang.

(2006). *Embodiment and cognitive science*. New York: Cambridge University Press.

Gibbs, R. & Lonergan, J. (2006). Identifying, specifying, and processing metaphorical word meanings. In Rakova, M. (Ed.) *Cognitive aspects of polysemy* (pp. 101–19). Franfurt: Peter Lang.

Gibbs, R. & Tendahl, M. (2006). Cognitive effort and effects in metaphor comprehension: Relevance theory and psycholinguistics. *Mind & Language, 21*, 379–403.

Gibbs, R., Bogdonovich, J., Sykes, J., & Barr, D. (1997). Metaphor in idiom comprehension. *Journal of Memory and Language, 37*, 141–54.

Gibbs, R., Lima, P., & Francuzo, E. (2004). Metaphor is grounded in embodied experience. *Journal of Pragmatics, 36*, 1189–210.

Gibbs, R., Gould, J., & Andric, M. (2006). Imagining metaphorical actions: Embodied simulation makes the impossible real. *Imagination, Cognition, & Personality, 25*, 221–38.

Gineste, M. D., Indurkhya, B., & Scart, V. (2000). Emergence of features in metaphor comprehension. *Metaphor and Symbol, 15*, 117–36.

Giora, R. (2001). *On our minds: Salience and context in figurative language understanding*. New York: Oxford University Press.

(2002). Literal vs. figurative language: Different or equal? *Journal of Pragmatics, 34*, 487–506.

Giora, R. & Fein, O. (1999). Irony: Context and salience. *Metaphor and Symbol, 14*, 241–58.

Glucksberg, S. (2001). *Understanding figurative language*. New York: Oxford University Press.

Glucksberg, S., McGlone, M. S., & Manfredi, D. A. (1997). Property attribution in metaphor comprehension. *Journal of Memory and Language, 36*, 50–67.

Grice, H. (1989). *Studies in the ways of words*. Cambridge, MA: Harvard University Press.

Groesfema, M. (1995). Can, may, must, and should: A relevance-theoretic account. *Journal of Linguistics, 31*, 53–79.

Hancock, J. T. (2004). Verbal irony use in computer-mediated and face-to-face conversations. *Journal of Language and Social Psychology, 23*, 447–63.

Ivanko, S. & Pexman, P. (2003). Context incongruity and irony processing. *Discourse Processes, 35*, 241–79.

Jones, L. L. & Estes, Z. (2005). Metaphor comprehension as attributive categorization. *Journal of Memory and Language, 53(1)*, 110–24.

Katz, A. N. (2005). Discourse and sociocultural factors in understanding nonliteral language. In Colston, H. L. & Katz, A. N. (Eds.) *Figurative language comprehension: Social and cultural influences* (pp. 183–208). Mahwah, NJ: Erlbaum.

Katz, A. N. & Ferretti, T. (2001). Moment-by-moment reading of proverbs in literal and nonliteral contexts. *Metaphor and Symbol, 16*, 193–222.

Katz, A. N. & Pexman, P. M. (1997). Interpreting figurative statements: Speaker occupation can change metaphor to irony. *Metaphor and Symbol, 12*, 19–41.

Keysar, B., Shen, Y., Glucksberg, S., & Horton, W. (2000). Conventional language: How metaphoric is it? *Journal of Memory and Language, 43*, 576–93.

Kintsch, W. & Bowles, A. (2002). Metaphor comprehension: What makes a metaphor difficult to understand? *Metaphor and Symbol, 17*, 249–62.

Kreuz, R. J. & Glucksberg, S. (1989). How to be sarcastic: The echoic reminder theory of verbal irony. *Journal of Experimental Psychology: General, 118*, 374–86.

Kreuz, R. J. & Roberts, R. M. (1995). Two cues for verbal irony: Hyperbole and the ironic tone of voice. *Metaphor and Symbolic Activity, 10*, 21–31.

Kumon-Nakamura, S., Glucksberg, S., & Brown, M. (1995). How about another piece of pie: The allusional pretense theory of discourse irony. *Journal of Experimental Psychology: General, 124*, 3–21.

Lakoff, G. & Johnson, M. (1980). *Metaphors we live by*. Chicago: Chicago University Press.

(1999). *Philosophy in the flesh*. New York: Basic Books.

Leggit, J. & Gibbs, R. (2000). Emotional reactions to verbal irony. *Discourse Processes, 29*, 1–24.

McElree, B. & Nordlie, J. (1999). Literal and figurative interpretations are computed in equal time. *Psychonomic Bulletin and Review, 6*, 486–94.

McGlone, M. & Harding, J. (1998). Back (or forward) to the future: The role of perspective in temporal language comprehension. *Journal of Experimental Psychology: Learning, Memory, and Cognition, 24*, 1211–23.

McGlone, M. & Manfredi, D. (2001). Topic-vehicle interaction in metaphor comprehension. *Memory and Cognition, 29*, 1209–19.

McRae, K., Spivey-Knowlton, M. J., & Tanenhaus, M. K. (1998). Modeling the influence of thematic fit (and other constraints) in on-line sentence comprehension. *Journal of Memory and Language, 38*, 283–312.

Miller, G. (1979). Images and models, similes and metaphors. In Ortony, A. (Ed.) *Metaphor and thought* (pp. 203–253). New York: Cambridge University Press.

Murphy, G. (1996). On metaphoric representation. *Cognition, 60*, 173–86.

Pexman, P. & Olineck, K. (2002). Understanding irony: How do stereotypes cue speaker intent? *Journal of Language and Social Psychology, 21*, 245–74.

Pexman, P., Ferratti, T., & Katz, A. N. (2000). Discourse factors that influence on-line reading of metaphor and irony. *Discourse Processes, 29*, 201–22.

Pfaff, K., Gibbs, R., & Johnson, M. (1997). Metaphor in using and understanding euphemism and dysphemism. *Applied Psycholinguistics, 18*, 59–83.

Ortony, A. (1979). Beyond literal similarity. *Psychological Review, 86*, 161–80.

Rockwell, P. (2000). Lower, slower, louder: Vocal cues of sarcasm. *Journal of Psycholinguistic Research, 29*, 483–95.

Ruhl, C. (1989). *Monosemy: A study in linguistic semantics*. Stony Brook, NY: SUNY Press.

Schwoebel, J., Dews, S., Winner, E., & Srinivas, K. (2000). Obligatory processing of the literal meaning of ironic utterances: Further evidence. *Metaphor and Symbol, 15*, 47–61.

Searle, J. (1979). Metaphor. In Ortony, A. (Ed.) *Metaphor and thought* (pp. 92–123). New York: Cambridge University Press.

Sperber, D. & Wilson, D. (1995). *Relevance: Communication and cognition*. Cambridge: Harvard University Press.

Utsumi, A. (2000). Verbal irony as implicit display of ironic environment: Distinguishing ironic utterances from nonirony, *Journal of Pragmatics, 32*, 1777–806.

(2005). The role of feature emergence in metaphor appreciation. *Metaphor and Symbol, 20*, 151–72.

Tourangeau, R. & Rips, L. (1991). Interpreting and evaluating metaphors. *Journal of Memory and Language, 30*, 452–72.

Verveake, J. & Kennedy, J. (1996). Metaphor in language and thought: Falsification and multiple meanings. *Metaphor and Symbolic Activity, 11*, 273–84.

Williams, J. N. (1992). Processing polysemous words in context: Evidence for interrelated meanings. *Journal of Psycholinguistic Research, 21*, 193–218.

Wilson, N. & Gibbs, R. (2007). Real and imagined body movement primes metaphor comprehension. *Cognitive Science, 31*, 721–731.

Wolff, P. & Gentner, D. (2000). Evidence for role-neutral initial processing of metaphors. *Journal of Experimental Psychology: Learning, Memory, and Cognition, 26*, 529–41.

CHAPTER 24

Computational Approaches
to Figurative Language

Birte Loenneker-Rodman and Srini Narayanan

1 Introduction

Several phenomena can be subsumed under the heading of *figurative language*. Figurative language can be used to perform most linguistic functions including predication, modification, and reference. Figurative language can tap into conceptual and linguistic knowledge (as in the case of idioms, metaphor, and some metonymies) as well as evoke pragmatic factors in interpretation (as in humor, irony, or sarcasm). Indeed, the distinction between the terms *literal* and *figurative* is far from clear cut. While there is a continuum or scale from literal to figurative, certain kinds of language including metaphor and metonymy are considered prototypical instances of figurative language.

To date, no comprehensive computational system addressing all of figurative language has been implemented or even designed. Most computational work has focused on the conceptual and linguistic underpinnings of figurative language. Our discussion will focus on the two types of figurative language phenomena that have been studied computationally: metonymy (2) and metaphor (3).

Each section introduces the phenomenon by way of examples and provides an overview of computational approaches that deal with it. Section 4 mentions some attempts at computationally processing further subtypes of figurative language and draws conclusions.

2 Metonymy

Metonymy is by far the most studied type of figurative language from a computational point of view. The discussion to follow situates the computational work on metonymy along several dimensions. Section 2.1 presents the phenomenon from a linguistics point of view, introducing some of the problems computational approaches have to face. Corpus annotation gives some insights into subtypes and frequency of metonymy (Section 2.2); annotated data can also be further exploited by automatic systems, although some systems do not need such training data. Examples of computational methods and systems are discussed in Section 2.3.

2.1 *Metonymy in linguistics*

In metonymy, one entity stands for another entity, and this is reflected in language. In these examples, metonymical expressions are emphasized in variants (a.); variants (b.) are literal paraphrases spelling out what the metonymically used expression stands for.

(1) a. I am reading *Shakespeare.*
   b. I am reading *one of Shakespeare's works.*
(2) a. America doesn't want another *Pearl Harbor.*
   b. America doesn't want another *defeat in war.*
(3) a. *Washington* is negotiating with *Moscow.*
   b. *The American government* is negotiating with *the Russian government.*
(4) a. We need a better *glove* at third base.
   b. We need a better *baseball player* at third base.

According to commonly agreed upon views in cognitive linguistics (e.g., Kövecses, 2002, pp. 143–4), the metonymically used word refers to an entity that *provides mental access* to another entity (the one that is referred to in the literal paraphrase). The access-providing entity has been called *vehicle*; the one to which mental access is provided is the *target entity* (cf. Kövecses, 2002).

Entities participating in metonymy must be *related* to one another. Rather than belonging to different conceptual domains, as in metaphor, metonymically related entities are members of the same domain. For example, both an author (such as *Shakespeare*) and written works belong to the artistic production domain. The coherence of a domain is brought about by the repeated co-occurrence of its component entities in the world, where we experience them as being (closely) together (Kövecses, 2002, pp. 145–6); thus, the relation underlying metonymy has been called *contiguity*.

Although belonging to the same experiential domain, metonymical vehicle and target are usually different types of entities; they are *ontologically different*. For example, in (1), the example given earlier, a human stands for a physical object. In (5), the example given here, a physical object stands for a process.

(5) a. Mary finished *the cigarette.*
   b. Mary finished *smoking the cigarette.*

As with metaphor, metonymy is common in spoken and written communication. The relation between some entities is in fact so *salient* (Hobbs, 2001) or *noteworthy* (Nunberg, 1995) that it is more natural to use metonymy than a literal paraphrase. This has been confirmed by corpus studies, as we will discuss in Section 2.2. While there are obviously many relations between entities that are rarely or never exploited for metonymy, other relations between some types of entities tend to entail widespread, regular metonymic patterns.

2.1.1 REGULAR METONYMY

Certain systematically exploited relations between entities give rise to larger clusters of metonymic expressions: Thanks to these relations, many members of an entity class can stand for members of a different class. The regularity of some of the metonymic patterns has been noted by Apresjan (1973) and Nunberg (1995), who discusses them under the label of *systematic polysemy*. Examples including some of the following can also be found in Lakoff and Johnson (1980, pp. 38–9):

(6) the place for the event
   a. Let's not let *Thailand* become another *Vietnam.*
   b. *Watergate* changed our politics.
(7) object used for user
   a. The *sax* has the flu today.
   b. The *gun* he hired wanted fifty grand.
   c. The *buses* are on strike.
   d. [flight attendant on a plane]: Ask *seat 19* whether he wants to swap. (Nissim and Markert, 2003, p. 56)

(8) the tree for the wood (Nunberg, 1995)
    a. The table is made of *oak*.

Nunberg (1995) notes that languages differ with respect to the set of regular metonymies available.

The grouping of metonymies into clusters presumably facilitates their understanding and makes language use more economic. However, a correct and detailed interpretation of metonymies always requires the activation of world knowledge. For example, the reader or listener has to figure out to which target entity the vehicle entity is related, or among a set of related entities, select the one that is intended by the writer/speaker. To illustrate, in object used for user metonymies, this interpretation involves accessing knowledge on the *function* of the user: *player* of the sax, *killer* (using a gun), *driver* (but not passenger) of the bus, *passenger currently occupying* a numbered seat. Probably because of the relative unpredictability of the function of the user, Nissim and Markert (2003, p. 57) call Example (7d) "unconventional." In some cases, the meaning of metonymies is indeed underspecified, especially when they are presented out of context.

2.1.2 CHALLENGES

A prominent discussion of certain complex cases of metonymy is presented by Nunberg. Examples (9) and (10) illustrate the phenomenon.

(9) *Roth* is Jewish and widely read.
(10) *The newspaper* Mary works for was featured in a Madonna video.

The theoretical question invited by these examples is whether it is correct to consider the noun phrases as metonymical expressions, or whether one of the verb phrases (predicates) is not used literally. The difference can be exemplified by the respective paraphrases.

(11) a. *Roth* is Jewish and widely read.
    b. *Roth* is Jewish and *the works by Roth* [are] widely read.

(12) a. Roth is Jewish and *widely read*.
    b. Roth is Jewish and *the works by Roth are widely read*.

The second solution (12) is known as *predicate transfer*. If *widely read* can mean "the works by X are widely read," then *widely read* can be predicated of a human. This interpretation is motivated by the idea that a noun phrase should not have two meanings concurrently: *Roth* should only refer to an entity of type human; the interpretation in (11b), where *Roth* means both *Roth* and *the works by Roth* should be avoided. Predicate transfer also brings metonymy closer to syntactic phenomena (Copestake and Briscoe, 1995; Hobbs, 2001; Nunberg, 1995; Warren, 2002).

This discussion might seem theoretic and the examples constructed, had they not been confirmed by recent corpus studies. When annotating a corpus for metonymically used place names, Markert and Nissim (2003) found examples in which two predicates are involved, each of them triggering a different reading of the predicated noun. For instance, (13) invokes both a literal reading of *Nigeria* (triggered by *arrived in*) and a place-for-people reading (triggered by *leading critic*).

(13) [T]hey arrived in *Nigeria*, hitherto a leading critic of the South African regime... (Nissim and Markert, 2003, p. 57).

Markert and Nissim call this phenomenon a "mixed reading" of the noun. In their corpus study, it occurs especially often with coordinations and appositions.

Despite the challenge presented by the mixed reading phenomenon, most computational approaches to metonymy still consider the nouns to be used metonymically (and, if necessary, to be the bearer of two interpretations simultaneously); this solution is also known as *type coercion*. Others explicitly model the verb as having a metonymical meaning, following the *predicate transfer view*. Finally, computational approaches can also be constructed in such a way that they are compatible with either theoretical interpretation.

2.2 Computationally oriented corpus studies on metonymy

Example (14) is another instance of the physical object for process metonymy.

(14) Mary began her coffee.

Several corpus studies have addressed the issue whether the supposedly most likely interpretation, *Mary began to drink her coffee*, could be derived from corpus texts. In general, the question is: Given the pattern *begin V NP*, what are likely values of *V*? Briscoe et al. (1990) investigate this in a corpus study on the Lancaster-Oslo/Bergen corpus (one million words). However, they find that *begin V NP* is very rare when the value of *V* corresponds to a highly plausible interpretation of *begin VP*. This finding has been confirmed by Lapata and Lascarides (2003) on the British National Corpus (BNC) (100 million words). Summarizing the output of a partial parser on the BCN data, Lapata and Lascarides find that *begin to pour coffee* is the most frequent instantiation of *begin V (DET) coffee*; but the corpus fails to provide attestations of *begin to drink coffee*.

Some regular metonymies, especially those involving place names and other proper names, seem to be widespread among different languages. As proper names are at the same time relevant to practical tasks, such as summarization or information extraction, recent efforts on corpus annotation for metonymy focus on metonymies involving named entities.

Markert and Nissim (2003) report on an English corpus study concerning *country names* as vehicle entities. The study reveals that the following three mapping patterns account for most of the metonymical instances encountered:

1 PLACE FOR PEOPLE: This is often labeled *place for institution* in cognitive linguistics. The annotation scheme of Markert and Nissim (2003) distinguishes different subclasses. Examples include: America *did try to ban alcohol* and a *29th-minute own goal from* San Marino *defender Claudio Canti*. A country name can indeed also stand for (almost) the entire population of the country, which makes place for institution too narrow a category;

2 PLACE FOR EVENT as in Example (2a), given earlier;

3 PLACE FOR PRODUCT: the place for a product manufactured there (e.g., *Bordeaux*).

One thousand occurrences of country names were extracted from the BNC together with a three-sentence context and manually labeled according to eleven categories. The categories included the three metonymic patterns given above, but also literal and mixed (for mixed readings). Nine hundred and twenty-five examples could be labeled clearly and unambiguously. Among those, 737 or 79.7 percent, are literal. Among the metonymic usages, the largest subgroup is place-for-people, attested by 161 examples. With three members, place-for-event metonymies constitute the smallest group in the corpus study.

Markert and Nissim (2006) report on the annotation of organization names. Nine hundred and eighty-four instances of organization names were manually labeled. The largest portion of the organization name instances was literal (64.3 percent). Among the five metonymic categories defined by Markert and Nissim, organisation-for-members (15) was the most frequent one (188 instances).

(15) Last February *NASA* announced [...].

In organisation-for-members metonymies, the concrete referents are often underspecified. Possible target entities include, for example, *spokesperson*, (certain classes of) *employees*, or *all members*.

Another corpus annotated for some types of metonymy (among other things) is the ACE corpus (LDC, 2005), created for purposes of information extraction and related tasks.

2.3 Computational approaches to metonymy

As opposed to most approaches to metaphor (Section 3) or idioms (Section 4), computational approaches to metonymy are usually not limited to a literal–non-literal distinction. Rather than attempting to detect whether a given linguistic expression is used metonymically or not, approaches to metonymy try to interpret metonymical expressions in some way. In what follows, we will present some examples, ranging from symbolic/logic systems over paraphrasing approaches, presupposing metonymic input and thus assigning a specific metonymic interpretation to each instance they process to methods combining detection and interpretation, given as the classification according to a regular metonymic pattern.

2.3.1 METONYMY AND INFERENCE

In symbolic applications using handcrafted knowledge bases, metonymy is one of the phenomena that hampers user interaction. Queries to the knowledge base would have to match the encoded knowledge exactly, if no further processing or interpretation of the query were undertaken. Metonymical expressions in user-formulated queries can usually not be resolved directly against the contents of a knowledge base, given that (a) axioms in knowledge bases define entity types on their participant entities as hard constraints, and (b) in metonymy, one type of entity stands for another one.

Hobbs (2001) discusses different varieties of metonymic transfer. He designs additional axioms to deal with (noun) type coercion and predicate transfer and illustrates them with sample parses of metonymical input. The axioms facilitate the correct parsing of sentences such as (16) and (17) against a knowledge base of axioms and assertions.

(16) John read Proust.
(17) She lost her first tooth. (*First* really modifies the loss, not the tooth: "She had her first loss of a tooth.")

Fan and Porter (2004) address phenomena close to metonymy under the heading of *loose speak*. As expressions produced by humans are less precise than the axioms in a knowledge base (a chemistry knowledge base, in their case), the aim of their work is to find the right axiom given an imperfect query, so that an answer can be given to "loosely encoded" questions.

2.3.2 PARAPHRASING METONYMY

The aim of the approach presented by Lapata and Lascarides (2003) is to provide an interpretation of submitted metonymic expressions in the form of the most likely paraphrase. The expressions studied are derived from the literature on metonymy of the type physical object for process, as illustrated by Example (5) given earlier. The starting point is to draw a list of illustrative examples of this type of metonymy, where each example takes the abstract form *V-NP* or *V-N*, with *N* being the head noun of *NP*. The list of examples contains expressions such as *begin cigarette* or *enjoy book*.

The task of the computational model is to automatically acquire possible interpretations of these metonymic verb–noun combinations from corpora, where an interpretation is given in the form of a verb referring to the process that is left implicit in the metonymic expression. For example, given the input *enjoy book*, the system generates *read*. This ultimately facilitates the paraphrasing of (18a) by (18b).

(18) a. John enjoyed the book.
     b. John enjoyed reading the book.

The model usually finds several possible interpretations for each submitted *V-N* pair and ranks them.

The method is unsupervised insofar as it requires a part-of-speech tagged and lemmatized corpus and a partial parser, but no lexical-semantic resources or annotations. It uses distributional information in the form of co-occurrence frequencies in the corpus; Lapata and Lascarides work with the BNC. Probabilities for the implicit process, such as *reading* in (18), are estimated on the basis of corpus frequencies. In particular, the method looks at verbs referring to this process (p) appearing as a complement to the verb in the submitted V-N pair (e.g., *enjoy*) and at instances of the verb p taking the submitted noun (e.g., *book*) as the head of its object.

More specifically, the model combines the probabilities of

- seeing a reference to the implicit process (p) in the corpus (the number of times a given verb referring to p is attested, divided by the sum of all verbs in the corpus);
- seeing the verb v with an explicit reference to the process p (the number of times v takes p as its complement, as obtained from the output of the parser, divided by the number of the times p is attested)
- seeing a noun o as the object of p: the number of times a noun o is the object of the process-denoting verb p, divided by the number of times p is attested.

The last parameter is an approximation of the actual paraphrase that does not take into account the contribution of the verb v to the paraphrase itself. This is so because it would be problematic to model the entire paraphrase that is being searched for: Corpus studies show that in many cases, the likelihood of uttering the metonymic construction is higher than that of uttering its full interpretation. In fact, as we have seen in Section 2.2, many likely interpretations are not at all attested in the form of the explicit paraphrase.

The intersection of the most frequent process verbs p related with the verb v and the most frequent process verbs p which take noun as their object, as attested in the corpus, is the set of interpretations of the V-N metonymy. For example, for *enjoy film*, the set is constituted by the verbs *see*, *watch*, and *make*. These are ranked by probability.

Finally, an extended version of the model also takes into account the contribution of the sentential subject. It thus prefers different paraphrases for (19) and (20), among others.

(19) The composer began the symphony.

(20) The pianist began the symphony.

Lapata and Lascarides evaluate the performance of their model by measuring the agreement with human paraphrase ratings. This is done by selecting some metonymic constructions, deriving their paraphrase interpretations using the model, eliciting human judgments on these paraphrases, and then looking at how well the human ratings correlate with the model probabilities for the same paraphrases. The comparison yields a reliable correlation of .64 with an upper bound (provided by intersubject agreement) of .74.

The paraphrase approach is compatible with either theoretical account of metonymy (i.e., coercion of the noun or predicate transfer; see Section 2.1.2).

2.3.3 METONYMY RECOGNITION AS WORD SENSE DISAMBIGUATION

The aim of the approach presented by Nissim and Markert (2003) is to distinguish between literally and metonymically used country names, and to further label metonymic instances with one of five predefined patterns: 1. place for event, 2. place for people, 3. place for product, 4. other metonymy (rare for country names), and 5. mixed metonymy.

Nissim and Markert model the task as a word sense disambiguation (WSD) problem: Each of the six labels (*literal* plus the five metonymy labels) represents one of the possible interpretations ("senses") of a country name. The approach can be further characterized as *supervised*, presupposing an annotated corpus of country name attestations, and *class based*. Aims and methods of traditional WSD versus class-based metonymy recognition can be summarized as follows. A WSD algorithm assigns a word sense label from a predefined set (e.g., *bank#1*, *bank#2*) to occurrences of a given word (e.g., *bank*) in an unseen test corpus, after having been trained on correctly sense-labeled occurrences of that word. Class-based metonymy recognition assigns either the label *literal* or that of the relevant metonymic pattern to words of a given semantic class (e.g., the words *U.S.*, *Japan*, *Malta* from the country name class), after having seen the same *or* different words from the same class (e.g., *England*, *Scotland*, *Hungary*) in a manually labeled training corpus.

The class-based approach is supposed to take advantage of the regularities of metonymic mappings, even if exemplified by different lexical material. The model exploits several similarities that follow from the regular mapping:

1. *semantic class similarity* of the possibly metonymic noun (e.g., *Japan* in the test data is similar to *England* in the training data),
2. *grammatical function similarity* (e.g., whether the possibly metonymic noun appears in subject position),
3. *head word (verb) similarity*: In Examples (21) and (22), similar events are denoted by the verbs that are the semantic heads of the possibly metonymic word, in a dependency grammar framework.

(21) Pakistan had *won* the World Cup.

(22) Scotland *loses* in the semifinal.

Nissim and Markert (2003) train a decision list classifier on the manually annotated corpus of 925 instances of country names (Section 2.2) and estimate probabilities via maximum likelihood with smoothing. Performance is evaluated by ten-fold cross-validation, where different subsets of the training data are withheld for testing and the results averaged.

The basic feature – Algorithm I. The training feature of the basic version of the decision list classifier is called *role-of-head*. This is *one feature*, composed of:

1. the grammatical role (grammatical function) of the possibly metonymic word with respect to its head; Nissim and Markert use a set of seven functions, including *active subject* (subj), *subject* of a *passive sentence*, and *modifier in* a *prenominal genitive*;
2. the lemmatized lexical head of the possibly metonymic word.

For example, the value of the role-of-head feature for (21) with the possibly metonymic word *Pakistan* is subj-of-win.

The feature is manually annotated on the training corpus. Accuracy of the classifier, defined as the number of correct decisions divided by the number of decisions made, is high (.902). However, due to data sparseness, the classifier has not always seen the exact value of the role-of-head feature in the training data, and thus makes decisions in only sixty-three percent of the cases. The remaining instances are submitted to a backoff procedure, always assigning the majority reading *literal*. This results in a low recall for metonymies: Only 18.6 percent of the metonymies are identified.

Low coverage is the main problem of this algorithm. Therefore, two methods are used to generalize the role-of-head feature, *in those cases where a decision cannot be made* based on the full feature. This means that data already classified by the basic algorithm remains untouched, and generalization applies only to those examples that would otherwise be sent to the simple backoff procedure.

Generalization – Algorithm II. To generalize from a test data value of role-of-head to a value seen in the training data, this method replaces the actual lexical head by similar words, obtained from the thesaurus developed by Lin (1998). For example, suppose the feature value subj-of-lose has not been seen during training; the basic algorithm would thus not be able to classify sentence (23).

(23) **Scotland** *lost* in the semifinal.

The thesaurus suggests a generalization from *win* to *lose*, which facilitates a decision for test sentence (23) based on information from training sentence (24).

(24) **England** *won* the World Cup.

For each submitted content word, the thesaurus returns a ranked list of similar words. The generalization algorithm first tries a substitution by the most similar word, and then works down the list. It stops as soon as a decision can be made; less similar words are thus less likely to influence the decision. The maximum number of similar words examined is fifty.

Thesaurus generalization raises recall of metonymies to forty-one percent. Accuracy before backoff drops to 0.877, but accuracy after backoff increases. Whereas the basic algorithm sends almost seventy percent of the metonymies to backoff or generalization, the thesaurus-based method deals with a much higher proportion of metonymies: The generalization method is applied to 147 instances, among which sixty-eight (forty-six percent) are metonymies.

Generalization – Algorithm III. The second generalization method is to rely on grammatical role as the only feature. A separate decision list classifier is trained for this parameter. The authors observe that country names with the grammatical roles *subject* or *subject of a passive sentence* are predominantly metonymic, whereas all other roles are biased toward a literal reading. The algorithm thus assigns all target words in subject position to the nonliteral group. It performs slightly better than thesaurus-based generalization.

Combination. Performance is best when the two generalization methods are combined such that grammatical role information is used only when the possibly metonymic word is a subject, and thesaurus information otherwise. This method yields a metonymy recall of fifty-one percent; accuracy is 0.894 before backoff and 0.87 after backoff.

Discussion and extensions. The data used for this experiment is very clean. First, all instances of names that were not country names were removed manually. Second, only those instances that are decidable for a human annotator were retained. Finally, the manual annotation of the training feature role-of-head ensures high quality of the data. Deriving the feature value from the output of an automatic parser reduces performance (as reflected by the f-measure for metonymies) by about ten percent. Nissim

and Markert do not break down their evaluation to different classes of metonymies; results are thus averaged over all metonymic patterns.

Other approaches to proper name metonymies include Peirsman (2006), experimenting with an unsupervised approach, based on a WSD algorithm proposed by Schütze (1998) and reminding of LSA (Latent Semantic Analysis, [Landauer and Dumais, 1997]). Though failing to achieve the majority baseline for accuracy, this unsupervised WSD algorithm finds two clusters that significantly *correlate* with the manually assigned literal/nonliteral labels (as measured with the χ_2 test). Finally, Markert and Nissim (2007) report on the SemEval-2007 task on Metonymy Resolution, in which five systems participated in the country name task. The best performing systems exploited syntactic features and made heavy use of feature generalization, integrating knowledge from lexical databases. With respect to the individual classes of metonymies, only those covered by a larger number of examples in the training data could be recognized with reasonable success; for country names, this is the place for people class.

All of these approaches consider the noun (the country name) as metonymic, as opposed to the predicate.

2.4 *Summary*

Different subtypes of metonymy have been identified, clustered around the basic notion of relatedness or contiguity of two entities, and giving raise to linguistic shortcuts, where one entity stands for another. From a theoretical point of view, the ensuing semantic incompatibilities have been treated as coercion of either the noun (altering its semantic type) or the predicate of the involved expression, with the aim of reconciling their semantics. Computational approaches reflect either view, and some have found ways to avoid this theoretical decision altogether, still coming up with a practical solution. Recently, a concentration of computational approaches on regular metonymy involving proper nouns can be observed. Although immediately relevant to applications such as information retrieval or information extraction, where named entities play a central role, this concentration narrows down the phenomenon and might make it seem overly regular. Some types of metonymy, partly discussed against the background of earlier inference systems, are more creative and irregular, presupposing larger amounts of world knowledge and connections to be resolved. In fact, even named entities can participate in more creative metonymic expressions, and when they do, current statistical approaches fail to interpret them.

3 Metaphor

In linguistics and in philosophy, there is rich continuing theoretical debate on the definition and use of metaphor. On the other hand, computational approaches usually make reference to a conceptual model of metaphor based on empirical findings in cognitive science.

Several decades of research in cognitive science suggest that there are powerful primary schemas underlying much of human language and thought (Feldman, 2006; Johnson, 1987; Lakoff, 1987; Lakoff and Johnson, 1980; Langacker, 1987; Slobin, 1997 Talmy, 1988, 1999). These schemas arise from embodied interaction with the natural world in a socio-cultural setting and are extended via conceptual metaphor to structure the acquisition and use of complex concepts. Specifically, cross-cultural and cross-linguistic research has revealed that the structure of abstract actions (such as states, causes, purposes, means) is characterized cognitively in terms of *image schemas* which are *schematized* recurring patterns from the embodied domains of force, motion, and space.

Section 3.1 introduces the theory of metaphor that forms the basis of the existing computational models. Section 3.2 describes computational implementations of the theory. A discussion of ongoing research and an outlook are provided in Section 3.3.

3.1 *Conceptual metaphor*

A *conceptual metaphor* is the systematic set of correspondences that exist between constituent elements of experientially based schemas and abstract concepts. Many conceptual metaphors are cross-cultural and highly productive. An example is the Event Structure Metaphor (ESM) which has been found in all cultures studied to date. ESM projects our understanding of spatial motion (movement, energy, force patterns, temporal aspects) onto abstract actions (such as psychological, social, political acts, or economic policies).

A primary tenet of conceptual metaphor theory is that metaphors are matter of thought and not merely of language: hence, the term *conceptual metaphor*. The metaphor does not just consist of words or other linguistic expressions that come from the terminology of the more concrete conceptual domain, but conceptual metaphors underlie a system of related metaphorical expressions that appear on the linguistic surface. Similarly, the mappings of a conceptual metaphor are themselves motivated by image schemas which are prelinguistic schemas concerning space, time, moving, controlling, and other core elements of embodied human experience.

Conceptual metaphors typically employ a more abstract concept as target and a more concrete or physical concept as their source. For instance, metaphors such as "the days [the more abstract or target concept] ahead" or "giving my time" rely on more concrete concepts, thus expressing time as a path into physical space, or as a substance that can be handled and offered as a gift. Different conceptual metaphors tend to be invoked when the speaker is trying to make a case for a certain point of view or course of action. For instance, one might associate "the days ahead" with leadership, whereas the phrase "giving my time" carries stronger connotations of bargaining.

3.1.1 A CROSS-LINGUISTIC MAPPING: THE STRUCTURE OF EVENTS

1. Consider our conceptualization of events as exemplified in the mapping called The Event Structure Metaphor (ESM).
2. States are locations (bounded regions in space).
3. Changes are movements (into or out of bounded regions).
4. Causes are forces.
5. Actions are self-propelled movements.
6. Purposes are destinations.
7. Means are paths (to destinations).
8. Difficulties are impediments to motion.
9. Expected progress is a travel schedule; a schedule is a virtual traveler who reaches prearranged destinations at prearranged times.
10. External events are large, moving objects.
11. Long term, purposeful activities are journeys.

This mapping generalizes over an extremely wide range of expressions for one or more aspects of event structure. For example, take states and changes. We speak of *being in* or *out of* a state, of *going into* or *out of* it, of *entering* or *leaving* it, of *getting* to a *state* or *emerging from* it. This is a rich and complex metaphor whose parts interact in complex ways. To get an idea of how it works, consider the submapping difficulties are impediments to motion. In the metaphor, purposeful action is self-propelled motion toward a destination. A difficulty is something that impedes motion to such a destination. Metaphorical difficulties of this sort come in five types: blockages; features of the terrain; burdens; counterforces; lack of an energy source. Here are examples of each:

Blockages: *He got over his divorce. He's trying to get around the regulations. He went through the trial. We ran into a brick wall. We've got him boxed into a corner.*

Features of the terrain: *He's between a rock and a hard place. It's been uphill all the way. We've been bogged down. We've been hacking our way through a jungle of regulations.*

Burdens: *He's carrying quite a load. He's weighed down by lot of assignments. He's been trying to shoulder all the responsibility. Get off my back!*

Counterforces: *Quit pushing me around. She's leading him around by the nose. She's holding him back.*

Lack of an energy source: *I'm out of gas. We're running out of steam.*

Many abstract and contested concepts in politics, economics, and even mathematics may be metaphoric (Lakoff, 1994; Lakoff and Nuñez, 2000). As an example, consider the concept of freedom. Lakoff argues that metaphor is central to the core concept of freedom, and that this abstract concept is actually grounded in bodily experience. Physical freedom is freedom to move – to go places, to reach for and get objects, and to perform actions. Physical freedom is defined in a frame in which there are potential impediments to freedom to move: blockages, being weighed down, being held back, being imprisoned, lack of energy or other resources, absence of a path providing access, being physically restrained from movement, and so on. Freedom of physical motion occurs when none of these potential impediments is present.

Various metaphors turn freedom of physical motion into freedom to achieve one's goals. The Event Structure Metaphor, for instance, characterizes achieving a purpose as reaching a desired destination or getting a desired object. Freedom to achieve one's purposes then becomes, via the Event Structure Metaphor, the absence of any metaphorical impediments to motion. Other ideas, like political freedom and freedom of the will build on that concept. The concept of political freedom is characterized via a network of concepts that necessarily includes the Event Structure Metaphor and the inferences that arise via that metaphor.

3.2 *Computational models of metaphor*

Computational models have focused on one or more of the following issues.

1. Metaphor recognition in text and discourse (Section 3.2.1),
2. Acquisition and representation of metaphors (Section 3.2.2),
3. Metaphor and inference (Section 3.2.3).

3.2.1 METAPHOR RECOGNITION FROM TEXT

Linguistic realizations of conceptual metaphors are ubiquitous in everyday speech and text. In a text experiment, (Gedigian et al., 2006) report that over ninety percent of the uses of motion terms (*fall, move, stumble, slide*) in the *Wall Street Journal* were abstract usages (about stock market activity, international economics, political acts). While this staggering figure may partly be explained by the high priority on articles about politics or the stock market in the selected sections, a more balanced corpus (the BNC) yielded abstract uses in sixty-one percent of the instances in which motion terms were used. Semantically oriented language analyzers that are trained on carefully selected, gold standard resources such as FrameNet (Fillmore et al., 2003) often perform poorly when applied to newspaper text because of their inability to handle metaphoric uses.

Automated work on metaphor recognition, including Mason (2004), Gedigian et al. (2006), and Birke and Sarkar (2006), focuses on *verbs* as parts of speech. A further recent approach to metaphor recognition is Krishnakumaran and Zhu, 2007.

Birke and Sarkar implemented a clustering approach for separating literal from nonliteral language use, with verbs as targets. The algorithm is a modification of the similarity-based word-sense disambiguation algorithm developed by Karov and Edelman (1998).

Similarities are calculated between sentences containing the word to be disambiguated (target word), and collections of seed sentences for each word sense (feedback sets). In this particular case, there are only two feedback sets for each verb: literal or nonliteral. The authors do not make reference to any particular theory of metaphor or of figurative language in general. Accordingly, their literal–nonliteral distinction (important for building and cleaning feedback sets and for annotating a test set) is relatively vague and based mainly on examples. "[W]e will take the simplified view that *literal* is anything that falls within accepted selectional restrictions [...] or our knowledge of the world [...]. *Nonliteral* is then anything that is "not literal" [...]." (Birke and Sarkar, 2006, p. 330) The modified WSD algorithm achieves an average f-score[1] of 53.8 percent over the twenty-five words in the manually annotated test set. Precision and recall are not provided individually. A baseline using the original WSD algorithm with attraction to the set containing the most similar sentence achieves an f-score of 36.9 percent. Active learning, where some examples are given back to a human annotator for decision during the classification, achieves an f-score of 64.9 percent.

Gedigian et al. (2006) used a maximum entropy classifier to identify metaphors. The examples to train the classifier were chosen from concrete frames likely to yield metaphors, especially motion-related frames, but also placing and cure. The example words were collected from the FrameNet frames as lexical units and sentences from the PropBank (Kingsbury and Palmer, 2002) Wall Street Journal corpus containing these words were extracted and annotated. As described earlier, more than ninety percent of the 4,186 occurrences of these verbs in the corpus data are metaphors.

A classifier was trained on the annotated corpus to discriminate between literal and metaphorical usages of the verbs in unseen utterances. The features used by the classifier included information about the arguments of the verbs, which are believed to be an important factor for determining whether

---

1 (2 x precision x recall) / (precision + recall).

a verb is being used metaphorically (see Subsection 3.2.3 on selectional restrictions):

1. Argument information was extracted from PropBank.
2. The head word of each argument was extracted using a method proposed by Collins (1999).
3. A "semantic type" was assigned to the head word of each argument. How this is done depends on the type of head word:
   - If the head was a pronoun, a pronoun type (human/nonhuman/ambiguous) was assigned.
   - If the head was a named entity, the tag assigned by a named entity recognizer was used as the type of the argument.
   - Otherwise, the name of the head's WordNet (Fellbaum, 1998) synset was used as the type of the argument.

Another feature used for the classifier was the bias of the target verb itself. The authors used this feature because they noticed that most verbs show a clear tendency toward literal or metaphorical uses. The classifier was trained on the hand-discriminated data with different combinations of features. On a validation set, the best results were obtained when a combination of the following features were used:

1. verb bias;
2. semantic type of argument 1 (ARG1), typically realized as the direct object in active English sentences such as *Traders threw* stocks *out of the windows*;
3. (optionally,) semantic type of argument 3 (ARG3), the semantics and syntactic form of which is difficult to generalize due to verb-specific interpretations in PropBank.

On a test set of 861 targets, the classifier result (trained with features 1 and 2) over all verbs in all frames was an accuracy of 95.12. This is above the baseline of 92.9 overall, achieved by selecting the majority class of the training set, or above the alternative

baseline of 94.89, achieved by selecting the majority class of each verb specifically.

Accuracy varied a little over frames. It is equal or higher than the baselines in all frames, with the exception of the Cure frame. It remains open whether this is due to verbs with strong biases in the training data (*treat* had no metaphorical uses in the training data) or whether a different feature set might be more successful with this frame. The classifier has been ported to a different maximum entropy implementation and similar methods have been applied to metonymy by Schneider (2007).

3.2.2 ACQUISITION AND REPRESENTATION OF METAPHORS

As Martin (1994) points out, one of the problems for systems that deal with metaphor is the acquisition of sufficient and suitable knowledge (Barnden et al., 2002; Hobbs, 1992; Martin, 1994; Narayanan, 1997a). It would thus be useful to provide more knowledge about metaphor in lexical resources, which could be either directly used in Natural Language Processing (NLP) systems, or as a basis for building rules and networks in systems designed especially for metaphor handling. If well-studied linguistic knowledge supported by attestations in corpora was encoded in lexical resources, they could also be regarded as a common starting point for different systems, and the results of the systems would become more directly comparable.

Current general-domain lexical semantic resources (WordNet, PropBank, FrameNet) are of restricted usefulness for systems that aim at understanding or creating metaphorical expressions. One reason for this state of affairs is that metaphor captures generalizations across word senses and frames not represented in any of the popular linguistic resources. In English, there are specialized lists of metaphors, the most notable of which is the venerable Berkeley Master Metaphor list (Lakoff et al., 1991), which is quite unsuitable for computational use; we will discuss some of its shortcomings later in this chapter. For specialized use, there is a Mental Metaphor databank created by John Barnden at the University of Birmingham (http://www.cs.bham.ac.uk/~jab/ATT-Meta/Databank/) that deals with metaphors of the mind. Another ongoing effort is the *Metaphor in discourse* project (Steen, 2007), where subsets of the BNC are annotated for metaphors at word level, as opposed to the level of conceptual mappings. As far as we know, these databases and annotations have not been linked directly to any general purpose linguistic resource such as WordNet or FrameNet.

There have also been efforts in other languages which could inform representation and annotation efforts. To our knowledge, the most advanced such effort is the Hamburg Metaphor Database (Lönneker, 2004; Lönneker and Eilts, 2004) which combines data from corpora, EuroWordNet, and the Berkeley Master Metaphor List. For example, Reining and Lönneker-Rodman (2007) annotated more than one thousand instances of lexical metaphors from the motion and building domains in a French newspaper corpus centered on the European Union and integrated them into the Hamburg Metaphor Database.

The Berkeley Master Metaphor List, while useful in the efforts described previously, has fundamental flaws that severely restrict its wider applicability. The list was built almost two decades ago and subsequent research has made significant advances that directly bear on metaphor representation and annotation. A central problem with the Berkeley Master Metaphor List is that the mapping ontology is noncompositional in that there is no easy way to combine the existing mappings to create more complex ones. The main reason for this shortcoming is that projections from specific source to target domains are only partial (many aspects of the source are not mapped, many attributes of the target are not projected onto) making it very hard to generalize from existing mappings to find shared structure, or for composition of existing maps.

There has been research in cognitive linguistics on *primary metaphors* that directly bears on the issue of compositionality. Also, Gedigian et al. (2006) have done some preliminary work that suggests that linking to semantic frames such as those provided by the FrameNet project could significantly help in metaphor representation and they provide a connection via FrameNet frames to linguistic realizations of metaphor.

Primary Metaphors. The Berkeley Master Metaphor list and all other efforts to date are noncompositional. At the time of the construction of the resource, there was not enough known about either the developmental aspects of metaphor acquisition or of the kind of basic metaphors that could provide a basis set for more complex compositions. This results in mappings being ad hoc and no principled way to compose two maps into a more complex metaphor.

Joseph Grady, in his 1997 Berkeley dissertation research (Grady 1997) addressed this state of affairs. Grady looked at developmental and cross-linguistic evidence and hypothesized that the conceptual metaphor system is grounded in the body in terms of "primary metaphors." Primary metaphors are acquired earlier than other metaphors and can be composed to form more complex mappings. Primary metaphors bring together subjective judgments correlated with sensory-motor experience. An example of a primary metaphor is affection (subjective experience) is warmth (sensory-motor experience of temperature). Such correlations are picked up in language where affection is often described in terms of warmth. Here are some examples of primary metaphors found by Grady. We leave it to the reader to attest to the frequent linguistic realizations of these conceptual mappings.

Affection Is Warmth

Important Is Big

Happy Is Up

Intimacy Is Closeness

Bad Is Stinky

Difficulties Are Burdens

More Is Up

Categories Are Containers

Similarity Is Closeness

Linear Scales Are Paths

Organization Is Physical Structure

Help Is Support

Time Is Motion

States Are Locations

Change Is Motion

Actions Are Self-Propelled Motions

Purposes Are Destinations

Purposes Are Desired Objects

Causes Are Physical Forces

Relationships Are Enclosures

Control Is Up

Knowing Is Seeing

Understanding Is Grasping

Seeing Is Touching

Grady argues from developmental and linguistic evidence that the primary metaphor system forms the developmentally early mappings from which are composed more complex metaphors such as the ESM. For instance, the primary metaphors states are locations, causes are physical forces, change is motion, purposes are destinations and others when composed result in our conceptualization of abstract action as physical motion.

3.2.3 METAPHOR AND INFERENCE

Conventionalized metaphor is an everyday issue. Most systems dealing with NLP have to face it sooner or later. A successful handling of conventional metaphor is also the first step toward the processing of novel metaphor.

Obvious problems for NLP systems caused by metaphorical expressions consist in the incompatibility of metaphorically used nouns as arguments of verbs. In systems which constrain the type of arguments for every verb by semantic features like human, living, concrete, or abstract (selectional restrictions), metaphors can cause inconsistencies that will have to be solved.

For example, if the grammatical subject of the English verb *go* was restricted to entities classified as living in a given system, the following sentence (25) taken from Hobbs (1992) could not be parsed.

(25) The variable N goes from 1 to 100.

Obviously, there is an open-ended number of such sentences. In fact, there have been attempts to increase the ability of systems to deal with incompatibilities of this kind, caused by instantiations of conceptual metaphors (or metonymies).

Systems explicitly aimed at metaphor processing encode a representation of at least a part of the conventionalized mapping. Those systems can be called *knowledge-based* systems; they "leverage knowledge of systematic language conventions in an attempt to avoid resorting to more computationally expensive methods" (Martin, 1994). The systems generally perform most of the necessary knowledge-based *reasoning* in the source domain and transfer the results back to the target domain using the provided mapping; this procedure is applied, for example, in KARMA's networks (Feldman and Narayanan, 2004; Narayanan, 1999) or in the rules of TACITUS (Hobbs, 1992) and ATT-Meta (Barnden and Lee, 2001).

Systems designed explicitly for reasoning with metaphors and explicit reference to conceptual metaphors are KARMA (Narayanan, 1999) and ATT-Meta (Barnden and Lee, 2001). These two systems, at least in their current state, offer a slightly different functionality. KARMA can be seen as a *story understanding system*, producing a time-sliced representation of the development of (features in) the target domain, and/or an output of the end state in terms of feature structures; ATT-Meta can be seen as a *question-answering system* that verifies whether a fact (submitted as a user query) holds, given a possibly metaphorical representation of the current state of the world.

There are some fundamental differences in the computational design and particular abilities of the two systems. For example, at design and implementation level, KARMA uses x-schemas ("executing schemas" [Feldman and Narayanan, 2004, p. 387]) implemented as extended Stochastic Petri Nets for the source domain and Belief networks for the target domain. On the other hand, ATT-Meta uses situation-based or episode-based first-order logic throughout (Barnden and Lee, 2001, p. 34).

KARMA demonstrated the beginnings of the ability to detect interpreter's bias in metaphorical utterances; for example, (26) implies that the speaker or writer in general opposes government control of economy, whereas (27) does not imply this. KARMA detects this difference in speaker attitude because it can draw source domain inferences of "stranglehold," which has a detrimental effect on business (in the target domain); see Narayanan (1999).

(26) Government loosened stranglehold on business.
(27) Government deregulated business.

ATT-Meta is supposed to handle uncertainty and to be able to cope with a minimal set of interdomain mappings, emphasizing the importance of reasoning within domains, especially within the source domain; see Barnden and Lee (2001).

A commonality between the systems is that both have three main components, or representational domains, which reflect the influence of central ideas from metaphor theory:

1. Knowledge (common sense knowledge, facts, default inferences) about the source domain, including relations in the form of (pre-)conditions.
2. Knowledge about the target domain. This is usually less elaborate than source domain knowledge.
3. Mapping information (KARMA) or conversion rules (ATT-Meta), which can be of different types and can also include information about features or facts not to be varied or changed, such as aspect (e.g., ongoing versus completed action).

Both systems rely on extensive domain knowledge which has to be hand-coded, i.e., manually entered by the designer or user. The computational "engines" of the systems (x-schemas in KARMA or back-chaining/backward reasoning of rules in ATT-Meta, starting from the user query) then derive new facts or consequences within the domains–usually within the source domain.[2]

3.3 *The road ahead*

Existing systems have only scratched the surface of the information being communicated by metaphor. An early evaluation of the KARMA system (Narayanan, 1997a) revealed the following types of inferences that were encoded in conceptual metaphor.

3.3.1 MANNER AND METAPHOR
Distances, speeds, force values, sizes, and *energy levels* are obviously important perceptual and motor control parameters, but with metaphor projections, they become important descriptive features of events in abstract domains, including impacting early parsing decisions of inferring semantic role assignments. Examples abound in ordinary discourse (economies crawl, goals remain far or near, we take giant steps, recoveries are anemic, etc.).

3.3.2 ASPECTUAL INFERENCES
Narayanan (1997b) outlined a model of *aspect* (the internal temporal structure of events) which is able to detect and model subtle interactions between grammatical devices (such as morphological modifiers like *be +* *V-ing* (progressive aspect) versus *has V-ed* (perfect aspect) and the inherent aspect of events (such as the inherent iterativity of *tap* or *rub*, or the punctuality of *cough* or *hit*). In examining the KARMA metaphor database, Narayanan (1997a) found aspectual distinctions to be *invariantly projected* across domains. Furthermore, the high frequency of aspectual references in describing events

---

2   (Barnden et al., 2002, p. 1190) explain why it is sometimes necessary to reason in the target domain.

makes it important to model the relevant semantic distinctions.

3.3.3 GOALS, RESOURCES

It is well known (Schank and Abelson, 1977; Wilensky, 1983) that narratives are generally about *goals* (their accomplishment, abandonment, etc.) and *resources*. KARMA pilot experiments showed that metaphors such as the ESM may in fact be *compactly coding* for these features. Narratives are able to exploit aspects of spatial motion, forces, and energy expenditure to assert information about changing goals and resources. For instance, the amount of *energy* usually maps to *resource* levels as in *slog, anemic, sluggish* or *bruised and bloodied*, or *stagger to their feet*. Similarly *slippery slopes, slipperiest stones, slide into recessions*, get projected as the possible thwarting of goals due to unanticipated circumstances. In general, stories in the abstract domain are often about the complex notion of controllability, monitoring problems, and policy adjustments. Again, monitoring, changing directions, rates, and so forth are obviously common in sensory-motor activity, and so using these features and appropriate projections allows the speaker to communicate monitoring and control problems in abstract plans.

3.3.4 NOVEL EXPRESSIONS AND BLENDS

As Lakoff (1994), Gibbs (1994), Fauconnier and Turner (2002), and other researchers point out, a variety of novel expressions in ordinary discourse as well as in poetry make use of highly conventionalized mappings such as the ones described here. The expressions *slippery slope, crossroads*, or *rushing headlong on the freeway of love* are all immediately interpretable even if one has no previous exposure to these expressions in the abstract domains of their usage. Indeed, these expressions are interpretable due to the event structure metaphor that maps motion to action.

It appears that even in the cases where there are blends from multiple source domains, as long as they are interpretable and coherent in the *target*, these expressions are interpretable by humans. As far as

we know, there has been no model that can scalably deal with such blends (Fauconnier and Turner).

3.3.5 AGENT ATTITUDES AND AFFECTS

Agent attitudes often encode anticipatory conditions, motivation, and determination of agents involved. Some of this is implemented in the KARMA system and annotating and studying performance on a larger dataset could be productive for computational approaches. For instance, the expression *taking bold steps* encodes determination in the face of anticipated obstacles/counterforces ahead.

3.3.6 COMMUNICATIVE INTENT AND METAPHOR

One of the important aspects of communication involves evaluative judgments of situations to communicate speaker intentions and attitudes. While the KARMA system showed some ability to handle this phenomenon, we hypothesize that the crosslinguistic prevalence of the use of embodied notions of force and motion to communicate aspects of situations and events is linked to the ease with which evaluative aspects can be communicated in experiential terms. This is likely to be an extremely productive area for computational research in natural language understanding.

3.4 *Summary*

Metaphor is an important aspect of everyday language which provides a great deal of information about both the content and pragmatic aspects of communication. There is now a body of theory within cognitive science and a set of empirical data that can support a systematic analysis of the information content of metaphors. To perform such an analysis would require a scalable version of existing metaphor systems that is applied to a significantly enhanced inference task. To accomplish this would also require adapting and/or the building of a new set of semantic resources to identify, represent, and annotate metaphors. The pieces are there and the time is ripe for these enhancements.

4 Other figurative language

Metaphor and metonymy have received considerable attention in philosophy, linguistics, media science, and similar fields. These two phenomena are clearly central types of figurative language, and have been shown to be frequent in everyday language as well as in more specialized texts. Against this background, it is surprising how relatively little attention has been paid to them from a computational point of view, unless we hypothesize that they have been considered as "too difficult," and constantly postponed to later research. The individual approaches and systems we have discussed in this chapter are selected examples, but we can safely state that the pool we drew them from does not offer a wealth of additional material.

Many further phenomena can be treated under the heading of figurative language. In particular, idioms such as (28) are another important subcategory.

(28) a. It's been a while since we last *shot the breeze*.
b. It's been a while since we last *had a relaxed conversation*.

Idioms extend over a stretch of words. These can be treated as one linguistic entity, a relatively fixed expression with a meaning of its own that cannot be compositionally derived from its constituents. Again, several corpus studies have confirmed that idioms are widespread (e.g. Fellbaum et al., 2006; Villavicencio et al., 2004). As their *form* is more constrained, detection of idioms might be easier than that of other nonliteral language phenomena. Consequently, idiom extraction (Degand and Bestgen, 2003; Fazly and Stevenson, 2006) exploits lexical and syntactic fixedness of idioms. However, some questions remain open. In particular, the results of corpus investigations (Fellbaum et al., 2006, pg. 350) show that lexical and syntactic variants of idioms are far from rare. For example, a noun participating in an idiom can have lexical variants that *conserve* idiom meaning, and those nouns are likely to be just among the most similar ones in a semantic resource. It is thus not clear whether the usage of a thesaurus to extract similar words when creating variants of a possible idiom (Fazly and Stevenson, 2006) is helpful at all in idiom detection. What is more important, the crucial step from idiom recognition to idiom interpretation has not yet been attempted.

As opposed to the previously discussed phenomena, nonliteralness can also arise from the context. In those cases, the figurative meaning of an expression cannot be ascribed to the usage of single words or fixed phrases any more. Rather, we are dealing with *pragmatic* phenomena, including indirect speech acts (29a), irony (30a), and certain types of humor (31).

(29) a. Do you have a watch?
b. Please tell me what time it is.
(30) a. I just love spending time waiting in line.
b. I hate spending time waiting in line.
(31) Why did the elephant sit on the marshmallow? – Because he didn't want to fall into the hot chocolate.

The joke in (31) does not have a literal paraphrase because its communicative effect relies on the fact that the situation it describes is absurd, that is, against the laws of nature, logic, or common sense. Absurdness is one of the factors that have been exploited in computational approaches to humor. Such approaches almost unanimously come along as *humor generation* (as opposed to detection). Humor generation has long been restricted to puns, largely influenced by Binsted's (1996) seminal work on JAPE, a *Joke Analysis and Production Engine*, generating question-answer punning riddles. Recently, two new lines of computational humor generation have appeared: word play reinterpretation of acronyms (Stock and Strapparava, 2005) and jokes based on the ambiguity of pronouns (Njiholt, 2006; Tinholt, 2007). Sample outputs are presented in (32) to (34).

(32) What do you call a gruesome investor?
A *grisly bear*. (Binsted, 1996, p. 96)

(33) FBI – Federal Bureau of Investigation
-*Fantastic Bureau of Intimidation* (Stock
and Strapparava, 2005, p. 115)

(34) The members of the band watched
their fans as they went crazy. *The members of the band went crazy? Or their
fans?* (Tinholt, 2007, p. 66)

As with other approaches to figurative language, the strategy of humor generation systems is to reduce the complexity of the task.
First, each of them focuses on a particular
type of humor. Second, the problem is formulated in terms of certain *patterns* at different levels:

1. a more or less flexible syntactic pattern;
2. an inventory of lexical entities and
   semantico-conceptual relations between
   them;
3. in the case of pun generation and acro-
   nym deformation, phonologic aspects.

Humor generation involves not only knowledge about language. World knowledge and
common sense, and the representation of
beliefs, attitudes, and emotional states play-
san equally important role. Njiholt (2006, p.
63) states: "We won't be able to solve this
problem until we've solved all AI problems."
Whether or not this is true, and whether or
not it applies to all figurative language phenomena, remains to be seen.

References

Apresjan, J. D. (1973). Regular polysemy.
Linguistics, 142, 5–32.

Barnden, J., Glasbey, S., Lee, M., & Wallington,
A. (2002). Reasoning in metaphor understanding: The ATT-Meta approach and system.
*Proceedings of the 19th International Conference
on Computational Linguistics (COLING-2002)*
(pp. 1188–92). San Francisco, CA. Morgan
Kaufman.

Barnden, J. A. & Lee, M. G. (2001). Understanding
open-ended usages of familiar conceptual metaphors: an approach and artificial intelligence

system. *CSRP 01–05*, School of Computer
Science, University of Birmingham.

Binsted, K. (1996). *Machine humour: An implemented model of puns*. Unpublished doctoral dissertation, University of Edinburgh,
Edinburgh, Scotland.

Birke, J. & Sarkar, A. (2006). A clustering
approach for the nearly unsupervised recognition of nonliteral language. *Proceedings of the
11th Conference of the European Chapter of the
Association for Computational Linguistics* (pp
329–36). Trento, Italy.

Briscoe, E., Copestake, A., & Boguraev, B. (1990).
Enjoy the paper: lexical semantics via lex-
icology. *Proceedings of the 13th International
Conference on Computational Linguistics
(COLING-90)* (pp. 42–7). Helsinki.

Collins, M. (1999). *Head-Driven Statistical Models
of Natural Language Parsing*. Unpublished doctoral dissertation, University of Pennsylvania.

Copestake, A. & Briscoe, E. J. (1995). Semi-
productive polysemy and sense extension.
Journal of Semantics, 1(12), 15–67.

Degand, L. & Bestgen, Y. (2003). Towards automatic retrieval of idioms in French newspaper
corpora. *Literary and Linguistic Computing,
18(3)*, 249–59.

Fan, J. & Porter, B. (2004). Interpreting loosely
encoded questions. *Proceedings of the
Nineteenth National Conference on Artificial
Intelligence (AAAI 2004)* (pp. 399–405). San
Jose, California.

Fauconnier, G. & Turner, M. (2002). *The way we
think: Conceptual blending and the mind's hidden complexities*. New York: Basic Books.

Fazly, A. & Stevenson, S. (2006). Automatically
constructing a lexicon of verb phrase idio-
matic combinations. *Proceedings of the 11th
Conference of the European Chapter of the
Association for Computational Linguistics
(EACL-2006)* (pp. 337–44). Trento, Italy.

Feldman, J. (2006). *From Molecule to Metaphor*.
Cambridge, MA: MIT Press.

Feldman, J. & Narayanan, S. (2004). Embodied
meaning in a neural theory of language. *Brain
and Language, 89*, 385–92.

Fellbaum, C. (Ed.) (1998). *WordNet: An Electronic
Lexical Database*. Cambridge, MA: MIT Press.

Fellbaum, C., Geyken, A., Herold, A., Koerner, F.,
& Neumann, G. (2006). Corpus-based studies
of German idioms and light verbs. *International
Journal of Lexicography, 19(4)*, 349–60.

Fillmore, C. J., Johnson, C. R., & Petruck, MRL
(2003). Background to FrameNet. *International
Journal of Lexicography, 16(3)*, 235–50.

Gedigian, M., Bryant, J., Narayanan, S., & Ciric, B. (2006). Catching metaphors. *Proceedings of the 3rd Workshop on Scalable Natural Language Understanding* (pp. 41–8). New York City.

Gibbs, R. (1994). *The Poetics of mind: Figurative thought, language, and understanding.* Cambridge, UK: Cambridge University Press.

Grady, J., (1997). *Foundations of meaning: Primary metaphors and primary scenes.* Ph.D. dissertation, University of California, Berkeley.

Hobbs, J. R. (1992). Metaphor and abduction. In Ortony, A., Salck, J., & Stock, O. (Eds.) *Communication from an Artificial Intelligence Perspective: Theoretical and Applied Issues* (pp. 35–8). Springer, Berlin.

(2001). Syntax and metonymy. In Bouillon, P. & Busa, F. (Eds.) *The Language of Word Meaning* (pp. 290–311). Cambridge, UK: Cambridge University Press.

Johnson, M. (1987). *The Body in the Mind.* Chicago, IL: University of Chicago Press.

Karov, Y. & Edelman, S. (1998). Similarity-based word sense disambiguation. *Computational Linguistics, 24(1)*, 41–59.

Kingsbury, P. & Palmer, M. (2002). From Treebank to PropBank. *Proceedings of the 3rd International Conference on Language Resources and Evaluation (LREC-2002)*, Las Palmas, Canary Islands, Spain.

Kövecses, Z. (2002). *Metaphor: a practical introduction.* New York: Oxford University Press.

Krishnakumaran, S. & Zhu, X. (2007). Hunting elusive metaphors using lexical resources. *Proceedings of the Workshop on Computational Approaches to Figurative Language* (pp. 13–20). Rochester, New York.

Lakoff, G. (1987). *Women, Fire, and Dangerous Things: What Categories Reveal about the Mind.* Chicago, IL: University of Chicago Press.

(1994). What is metaphor? In Barnden, J. A. & Holyoak, K. J. (Eds.) *Advances in connectionist and neural computation theory (Vol. 3).* New York: Ablex Publishing Corporation.

Lakoff, G. & Johnson, M. (1980). *Metaphors we live by.* Chicago, IL: University of Chicago Press.

Lakoff, G. and Núñez, R. E. (2000). *Where Mathematics Comes From: How the Embodied Mind Brings Mathematics into Being.* New York: Basic Books.

Lakoff, G., Espenson, J., & Schwartz, A. (1991). Master metaphor list. Second draft copy. Technical report, Cognitive Linguistics Group, University of California Berkeley. http://cogsci.berkeley.edu.

Landauer, T. K. & Dumais, S. T. (1997). A solution to Plato's problem: The latent semantic analysis theory of acquisition, induction and representation of knowledge. *Psychological Review, 104*, 211–40.

Langacker, R. W. (1987). *Foundations of Cognitive Grammar, (Vol. 1).* Palo Alto, CA: Stanford University Press.

Lapata, M. & Lascarides, A. (2003). A probabilistic account of logical metonymy. *Computational Linguistics, 29(2)*, 261–315.

Linguistic Data Consortium. (2005). ACE (Automatic Content Extraction) English Annotation Guidelines for Entities.

Lin, D. (1998). An information-theoretic definition of similarity. In *Proceeding of the 15th International Conference on Machine Learning* (pp. 296–304). San Francisco, CA: Morgan Kaufmann.

Lönneker, B. (2004). Lexical databases as resources for linguistic creativity: Focus on metaphor. *Proceedings of the LREC 2004 Satellite Workshop on Language Resources and Evaluation: Language Resources for Linguistic Creativity* (pp. 9–16). Lisbon, Portugal.

Lönneker, B. & Eilts, C. (2004). A current resource and future perspectives for enriching Word-Nets with metaphor information. *Proceedings of the Second International WordNet Conference – GWC 2004* (pp. 157–62). Brno, Czech Republic.

Markert, K. & Nissim, M. (2003). Corpus-based metonymy analysis. *Metaphor and Symbol, 18(3)*, 175–88.

(2006). Metonymic proper names: A corpus-based account. In Stefanowitsch, A. & Gries, S. T. (Eds.) *Corpus-based approaches to metaphor and metonymy* (pp. 152–74). New York: Mouton de Gruyter.

(2007). Semeval-2007 task 08: Metonymy resolution at SemEval-2007. *Proceedings of the 4th International Workshop on Semantic Evaluations (SemEval-2007)* (p. 3641). Prague.

Martin, J. H. (1994). MetaBank: A knowledge-base of metaphoric language conventions. *Computational Intelligence, 10(2)*, 134–49.

Mason, Z. J. (2004). CorMet: A computational, corpus-based conventional metaphor extraction system. *Computational Linguistics, 30(1)*, 23–44.

Narayanan, S. (1997a). *Knowledge-based Action Representations for Metaphor and Aspect (KARMA).* Unpublished doctoral dissertation, University of California – Berkeley.

(1997b). Talking the talk is like walking the walk: A computational model of verbal aspect. *Proc. 19th Cognitive Science Society Conference* (pp. 548–53). Palo Alto, CA.

(1999). Moving right along: A computational model of metaphoric reasoning about events. *Proceedings of the National Conference on Artificial Intelligence (AAAI '99)* (pp. 121–9). Orlando, Florida: AAAI Press.

Nissim, M. & Markert, K. (2003). Syntactic features and word similarity for supervised metonymy resolution. *Proceedings of the 41st Annual Meeting of the Association for Computational Linguistics* (pp. 56–63).

Njiholt, A. (2006). Embodied conversational agents: "a little humor too." *IEEE Intelligent Systems, 21(2)*, 62–4.

Nunberg, G. (1995). Transfers of meaning. *Journal of Semantics, 1(12)*, 109–132.

Peirsman, Y. (2006). What's in a name? The automatic recognition of metonymical location names. *Proceedings of the EACL-2006 workshop on Making Sense of Sense: Bringing Psycholinguistics and Computational Linguistics Together* (pp. 25–32). Trento, Italy.

Reining, A. & Lönneker-Rodman, B. (2007). Corpus-driven metaphor harvesting. *Proceedings of the HLT/NAACL-07 Workshop on Computational Approaches to Figurative Language* (pp. 5–12). Rochester, NY.

Schank, R. C. & Abelson, R. P. (1977). *Script, Plans, Goals and Understanding. An Inquiry into Human Knowledge Structures.* Hilldale, NJ: Lawrence Erlbaum Associates.

Schneider, N. (2007). *A metonymy classifier.* Unpublished manuscript.

Schütze, H. (1998). Automatic word sense discrimination. *Computational Linguistics, 24(1)*, 97–123.

Slobin, D. I. (1997). The origins of grammaticizable notions: Beyond the individual mind. In Slobin D. I. (Ed.) *The Crosslinguistic Study of Language Acquisition: Vol 5. Expanding the Contexts.* Mahwah, NJ: Lawrence Erlbaum Associates.

Steen, G. J. (2007). Finding metaphor in discourse: Pragglejaz and beyond. Cultura, Lenguaje y Representación / *Culture, Language and Representation (CLR), Revista de Estudios Culturales de la Universitat Jaume I*, 5, (pp. 9–26).

Stock, O. & Strapparava, C. (2005). HAHAcronym: A computational humor system. In *Proceedings of the ACL Interactive Poster and Demonstration Sessions* (pp. 113–16). Ann Arbor.

Talmy, L. (1988). Force dynamics in language and cognition. *Cognitive Science*, 12, 49–100.

(1999, April). *Spatial schematization in language.* Paper presented at Spatial Cognition Conference, University of California – Berkely, Palo Alto, CA.

Tinholt, J. W. (2007). *Computational Humour. Utilizing cross-reference ambiguity for conversational jokes.* Unpublished master's thesis, University of Twente, Enschede, the Netherlands.

Villavicencio, A., Copestake, A., Waldron, B., & Lambeau, F. (2004). Lexical encoding of MWEs. In Tanaka, T., Villavicencio, A., Bond, F., & Korhonen, A. (Eds.) *Second ACL Workshop on Multiword Expressions: Integrating Processing* (pp. 80–7). Barcelona, Spain.

Warren, B. (2002). An alternative account of the interpretation of referential metonymy and metaphor. In Dirven, R. & Pörings, R. (Eds.) *Metaphor and Metonymy in Comparison and Contrast* (pp. 113–30). New York: Mouton de Gruyter.

Wilensky, R. (1983). *Planning and Understanding.* Cambridge, MA: Addison-Wesley.

CHAPTER 25

The Development of Figurative Language

Cristina Cacciari and Roberto Padovani

1 Introduction

Figurative language is formed by a variety of expressions that might remarkably differ from a semantic and syntactic point of view: metaphor, similes, idioms, oxymora, proverbs, and for some authors sarcasm and irony as well. The search for a satisfactory inclusion criterion has led many researchers to a tautology that roughly states that the essential aspect of figurative language is that no one can take it literally (Pollio and Pollio, 1974). Figurative strings occur very frequently in spoken and written language as revealed by simple frequency counts that estimate that people use about six nonliteral expressions (metaphors, idioms, proverbs, and so forth) per minute of discourse (Glucksberg, 1989). The same pervasiveness holds also in the language directed to children: for instance, 6.7 percent of the sentences of the reading programs for the primary schools in the United States contain an idiomatic expression (Nippold, 1991).

However, not all types of figurative expression are equally frequent in written and spoken language. This imbalance also surfaces in the theoretical and experimental attention devoted to the different types of figurative expression in the psycholinguistic literature. This literature has primarily addressed how children process idiomatic expressions (e.g., Abkarian, Jones, and West, 1992; Cacciari and Levorato, 1989; Gibbs, 1987, 1991; Levorato, 1993; Levorato and Cacciari, 1992, 1995; Nippold, 1988) and much less metaphors (e.g., Gentner, 1988; Vosniadou et al., 1984; Winer et al., 2001), leaving the study of other types of figurative expression (i.e., ironic and sarcastic speech acts, speech formulas, proverbs, clichés) mostly to theorists of social communication and of the pragmatics of language.

In this chapter we concentrate our attention on the two types of figurative expression that have been most investigated in the developmental literature, that is, idiomatic expressions and metaphors. Specifically, we concentrate on the evidence concerning idiom and metaphor comprehension in monolingual normally and abnormally developing school-aged children.

2 The acquisition of a figurative competence

The acquisition of the ability to comprehend and use figurative language – namely the acquisition of *figurative competence* (Levorato, 1993) – plays a crucial role in becoming a literate adult. Such acquisition is based on a long-lasting process that begins in early childhood and gradually improves throughout the school years, adolescence, and adulthood. Moderate age-related improvements in figurative language acquisition were in fact reported for participants aged between nineteen and fifty-five years (Nippold and Duthie, 2003).

In this chapter, we consider idiomatic expressions and metaphors separately. These two instances of figurative language are in fact different in many linguistic and conceptual respects (it is however surprising how often they are confused in the literature!).

3 How are idiomatic expressions acquired?

We examine the evidence on the acquisition of idioms in children with normal cognitive/linguistic profiles and in children with good versus poor reading comprehension skills. Then we review the evidence on children with developmental disorders and/or brain damages

3.1 *Factors influencing the acquisition of an idiomatic expression*

Many but not all idiomatic expressions have both a literal and a figurative meaning. Even when an expression has two meanings (e.g., *break the ice*), there is almost always a meaning dominant over the other (in most cases the figurative one). In general, the figurative interpretation of an expression is based on a conventional meaning shared by the native speakers of a linguistic community. The extent to which an idiom has a well-formed literal interpretation or is literally defective and the extent to which the meaning of the constituent words contributes to the overall

interpretation of the idiom string have constituted important research problems, as we will see. Extreme variability exists in the linguistic realization of idioms. The linguistic and lexical properties that have been shown to contribute to the acquisition of idioms are: a) an idiom's semantic analyzability or transparency; b) an idiom's familiarity; and c) an idiom's syntactic frozenness. In the following paragraphs each of these elements is briefly presented.

3.1.1 SEMANTIC TRANSPARENCY

The problem of the mapping between the constituent word meanings and the global figurative meaning of an idiom string (i.e., its *semantic transparency*) was first raised in the linguistic literature (Wasow, Sag, and Nunberg, 1983). Compositionality, transparency, analyzability, and decomposability are the labels that, since the seminal studies of Nunberg and colleagues, have been used to describe the notion that some parts of an idiom can carry a meaning perceived by the listener as related to the global figurative meaning of the string. The Idiom Decomposition Hypothesis (Gibbs, Nayak, and Cutting, 1989) was proposed to account for the comprehension of idioms by adults: According to such an influential hypothesis, the semantic compositionality of idiomatic expressions, that is, whether their constituents carry identifiable parts of the idiomatic meaning, influences the time it takes to understand them. In *spill the beans*, for example, *spill* and *beans* correspond to relevant parts of the figurative meaning "divulge information," whereas in *kick the bucket* there is no correspondence between *kick* and *bucket* and "die suddenly." For compositional expressions, the mapping between literal and figurative constituents is consistent and this facilitates their comprehension. However, for noncompositional idioms, the result of the linguistic analysis conflicts with the idiomatic meaning, making idiom comprehension more difficult. It should be noted, however, that since the Idiom Decomposition Hypothesis was first proposed, the evidence accumulated on the role of the semantic transparency of the idiom string in adults' online comprehension is substantially scarce and inconclusive.

The specific role of the information conveyed by the words forming an idiom has been investigated in a developmental framework as well (Cacciari and Levorato, 1998; Gibbs, 1987, 1991; Levorato and Cacciari, 1999; Nippold and Rudzinski, 1993). Cacciari and Levorato (1998) investigated children's ability to explain the rationale for the meaning of semantically transparent and opaque idioms. In semantically transparent idioms there is a discernable relationship between the idiom's component words and the idiom's stipulated meaning (e.g., *cry over spilt milk*). In semantically opaque idioms no apparent relationship is perceivable between the literal and the idiomatic meaning of the string (e.g., *break the ice*). Cacciari and Levorato found that second and fifth graders were more successful in explaining and providing a motivation for the meaning of transparent idioms than for opaque ones. Children were able to reason about the semantic similarity between literal and figurative meanings only from ten to eleven years of age.

Gibbs (1987; 1991) investigated the comprehension of transparent and opaque idioms in children whose age ranged from kindergarten to fourth grade. He found that idiom analyzability accounted for the ease with which children comprehended idioms, with younger children understanding transparent idioms better than opaque ones. Older children understood both kinds of idioms equally well in supporting contexts, but they were better at interpreting idioms out of context only for transparent idioms. Gibbs's results showed an interesting task effect: Semantic analyzability facilitated comprehension when children were asked to *explain* the expression (a result replicated later in other studies) but it had no effect when children had to choose the idiom meaning in a multiple choice task (see Table: 25.1 for an example of these tasks). If semantic transparency indeed facilitated idiom comprehension, this should have emerged in a clearer way in a task designed to test comprehension like the multiple choice task.

In fact, later studies reported effects of the semantic transparency of the idiom string with tasks tapping on idiom comprehension. Nippold and Rudzinski (1993) found that semantic analyzability did not affect the ability to explain the idiomatic meaning for fifth graders, but it did affect eighth and eleventh graders' performance, suggesting that the ability to use the meaning of constituent words is acquired at a later stage.

Levorato and Cacciari (1999) investigated second and fourth graders' ability to comprehend transparent and opaque familiar idioms presented either in supporting contexts or out of context using a multiple choice task. Semantic transparency affected the ease with which children of both age groups chose the idiomatic answer. However, the effect was stronger for fourth graders that chose the idiomatic answer in and out of context. In contrast, the younger children were more sensitive to the conjoint effects of contextual bias and semantic analyzability: They mostly chose an idiomatic answer for transparent idioms and a literal answer for opaque idioms in the out of context condition.

3.1.2 FAMILIARITY

The *familiarity* of an idiom string is considered to reflect the degree of exposure of a speaker/reader to an idiom. Although it is often recognized as an important factor in modulating idiom acquisition, the evidence supporting this claim is somewhat contradictory: Some authors (e.g., Levorato and Cacciari, 1992) reported that idiom familiarity is an important cue at age seven but less so at age nine, and is particularly relevant for explaining production processes rather than comprehension ones. However, other investigators reported that the role of familiarity increased with age (between ten and seventeen years) regardless of the task (Nippold and Martin, 1989; Nippold and Rudzinski, 1993; Nippold and Taylor, 2002). Differences in the age of the participants, in the experimental materials, and in the tasks might easily explain these contradictory findings: for instance, some studies used metalinguistic tasks, such as the verbal explanation task (e.g., Nippold and Martin, 1989; Nippold and Rudzinski, 1993), that are more difficult than the multiple-choice task (Cacciari and Levorato, 1989; Levorato and Cacciari, 1992, 1995).

3.1.3 SYNTACTIC FROZENNESS
Some verbal idiom strings tolerate morphological and syntactic modifications without loss of the figurative meaning but other strings do not. This high degree of internal cohesion was defined as *idiom frozenness*. For example, *The bucket was kicked by John* is syntactically well-formed, but the passivization destroys the idiomatic meaning of the string. In contrast, in other idioms, adjectival or adverbial modifications, as in *When drugs are involved, its time to speak your parental mind*, or in *Did he finally speak his mind?* (Glucksberg, 1993), preserve the idiomatic interpretation. But what is the scope of the adjectival or adverbial modification? *He kicked the proverbial bucket* clearly exemplifies a metalinguistic comment on the idiom as a unit, and not a modification on the constituent over the right of the adjective, but in *He left no legal stone unturned* (Wasow et al., 1983) or in the parental mind example the scope seems to be local. Thus, idioms can be classified on the basis of their degree of frozenness ranging from the very frozen ones (i.e., those that lose the figurative meaning if transformed by any syntactic operation) to the very flexible ones (i.e., those that can be transformed into many syntactic forms still maintaining their figurative meaning).

The problem of idiom frozenness was addressed in the 1970s in the adult literature in the theoretical climate of generative grammar, but it was left almost unresolved (Gibbs, Nayak, and Cutting, 1989). Recently, Abrahamsen and Burke-Williams (2004) investigated idiom frozenness effects using a multiple choice task and a verbal explanation task in third and fifth grade children. Frozen idioms were as easily understood as flexible ones when inserted in short stories that biased the children toward the figurative interpretation of the idiom string.

3.2 *Idiom processing in typically developing children*

One of the first investigations on idiom comprehension in children was carried out by Lodge and Leach (1975), who asked English children between the ages of six and twelve years to choose which of two pictures matched the content of a short story containing an ambiguous idiom. Children's responses showed that younger children interpreted idioms literally and older children figuratively. Since then, this result has been systematically replicated in English children (Abkarian et al., 1992; Ackerman, 1982; Nippold, 1988; Nippold and Martin, 1989; Prinz, 1983), Italian children (Cacciari and Levorato, 1989; Levorato and Cacciari, 1992, 1995, 1999), and French children (Laval, 2003). Box 25.1 shows the main experimental tasks used for investigating idiom acquisition.

Box 25.1 Examples of the experimental tasks used for investigating idiom and metaphor acquisition.

*Multiple-choice task** (adapted from Qualls and Harris, 1999)

Saturday afternoon is a special time for the Peabody family. This is when the two youngest children get to decide what the family outing will be. So when the twins, Johnny and Joseph, came out of their room, they announced: "We put our heads together and decided the family should have a picnic." What does it mean to put their heads together?

1. to come up with your own idea
2. to plan things together (correct response)
3. to call a friend
4. to listen to the other person

* The number of responses might vary from two to four.

Verbal explanation task (adapted from Gibbs, 1987)

Box 25.1 cont'd.

When Betty got home from school early for disrupting the class, she knew that her mother would be angry. When her mother asked her why she was home so early, Betty started to ask her mother what was for dinner that night. Finally her mother said, "Stop beating around the bush."

What did Betty's mother mean when she said, "Stop beating around the bush"?

Idiom fragment completion task (adapted from Levorato and Cacciari, 1995)

A naval captain had to reach the United States but was very upset. In fact he calculated the wrong course and directed the ship toward Africa instead of toward the United States. As soon as his assistant made him note this mistake, the captain fell from the ....*.

* In Italian, *to fall from the clouds* (*cadere dalle nuvole*) means to be dumbfounded.

Comparison task (adapted from Vosniadou and Ortony, 1983)

A nose is like a

Metaphorical/literal word pair: mountain/ mouth

Literal/anomalous word pair: mouth/bed

Metaphorical/anomalous word pair: mountain/bed

Multiple sentences task (adapted from Pollio and Pollio, 1974)

Words can be used in many different ways. Try to give as many meanings as you can from the following words. Use them in sentences for each meaning.

For example: *runs*

1. The boy runs along the street.
2. The rain runs down the windowpane.
3. The year runs its course through the seasons.

*Metaphorical enactment task** (adapted from Vosniadou et al., 1984)

Box 25.1 cont'd.

Metaphorical sentences:

1. Billy was a squirrel burying the nuts.
2. Mary was a car being taken to the repair shop.
3. Sally was a tiger walking toward the jungle.

Literal sentences:

1. Billy was a child hiding the cookies.
2. Mary was a girl being taken to the hospital.
3. Sally was a girl walking toward the school.

*The child acts out the action described in the story manipulating some objects in a specially constructed "toy world."

Sally-Anne task (adapted from Baron-Cohen et al., 1985)

Sally has a box and Anne has a basket. Sally puts her marble into the box. Then she goes out for a walk. While she is out, naughty Anne takes the marble from the box and puts it into her own basket. Now Sally comes back and wants to play with her marble. Where will she look for the marble – where does she think the marble is?

The effect of contextual information was first tested by Ackerman (1982). Children aged from six to ten years were required to explain and identify the meaning of an idiom inserted in short narratives biased toward an idiomatic, a literal, or a neutral interpretation of the idiom. Children aged six were the most literal (i.e., they interpreted idioms in a literal way); at age eight children were able to interpret the idiom figuratively only when the contextual information supported such interpretation. At age ten children explained and understood the idiom figuratively regardless of context (but see Nippold and Martin, 1989 for contrasting evidence). Prinz (1983) found that age and contextual information interacted: Children younger than nine interpreted idioms literally more frequently than older children. Interestingly, a dissociation emerged between the comprehension and the production of idioms: Children were able to comprehend idioms in context earlier than they were able to explain the idiom's meaning. This result was subsequently replicated with children aged from six to nine in studies that used a completion task to assess idiom production processes (Cacciari and Levorato, 1989; Levorato and Cacciari, 1995).

Based on evidence collected in a number of studies, Levorato and Cacciari proposed the Global Elaboration Model (GEM) (Levorato and Cacciari, 1992, 1995, 1999, 2002; Levorato, 1993; Levorato, Nesi, and Cacciari, 2004; Levorato et al., 2006) according to which the development of the figurative competence can be explained within the general linguistic and cognitive development of the child. The same strategies, processes, and background knowledge at work in the understanding of language *tout court*, be it literal, metaphorical, indirect, and so forth, can account for idiom acquisition. This does not imply that all idioms are acquired in the same way: Semantically opaque expressions, for instance, might be acquired in a rote manner. The GEM identifies five developmental phases along which the figurative competence develops (Levorato and Cacciari, 1992; 1995; 1999; 2002). These phases are not necessarily sequential and can sometimes overlap depending upon factors such as the knowledge of the semantic domain to which the figurative expression belongs, the linguistic complexity (e.g., the semantic transparency) of the expression, and so forth. The phases along which figurative competence develops can be summarized as follows: In Phase 1 language processing is based on a word-by-word strategy that leads children to comprehend all language in a literal way. This strategy is prevalent up to approximately the age of seven. In Phase 2 children start searching for the clues that could lead to a nonliteral interpretation of the linguistic input. In this phase of *suspended literalness* (that goes up to nine or ten years of age), children are able to perceive the incongruency of the literal interpretation of an idiom string when the contextual information instead supports the idiomatic

interpretation. Phase 3 is characterized by the child's awareness that a communicative intention can be realized by means of different linguistic formats (e.g., literally, idiomatically, ironically). This phase characterizes children approximately aged from ten to twelve. A gap between the almost reached ability to comprehend idioms and a still incomplete ability to produce them is evident in this phase (e.g., Levorato and Cacciari, 1995; Prinz, 1983). In Phase 4 (up to fifteen years of age) the ability to use the conventional repertoire of figurative expressions is almost achieved and the developmental gap between idiom comprehension and production is reduced. Finally, at Phase 5 an adult-like figurative competence is achieved that includes the ability to use figurative language creatively and with a full-fledged metalinguistic awareness.

The extent to which idioms can be acquired via simple exposure to the adult language and to other sources of information (e.g., TV programs, textbooks) was especially investigated by Nippold and colleagues, who proposed the acquisition via exposure hypothesis. According to this hypothesis, the child acquires idioms in a rote manner by simply being exposed to them in his\her everyday discourse environment (Nippold and Martin, 1989; Nippold and Rudzinski, 1993; Nippold and Taylor, 2002). However, as previously noted, the effect of idiom familiarity is less clear than the acquisition via exposure hypothesis claims. Recently, Nippold and colleagues redefined this hypothesis, stressing the role of lexical development and mental imagery in learning the meaning of idioms. Their metasemantic hypothesis (Nippold and Duthie, 2003) is reminiscent of the conceptual metaphor approach (Lakoff and Johnson, 1980), and claims that idioms may be learned through a variety of strategies depending on the availability of contextual information, degree of semantic transparency, and the learner's past exposure.

The figurative meaning of idioms is linked to underlying conceptual metaphors reflected in the images that people supposedly associate to idioms (e.g., *The mind is a container, Life is a journey*). Nippold and Duthie provided experimental support to this hypothesis by presenting adults and twelve-year-old children with a multiple-choice task and a mental imagery task (in which participants were asked to form a mental image for an idiom meaning and describe it). Adults outperformed the children both in the idiom comprehension task and in the mental imagery task, suggesting an association between idiom comprehension and mental imagery (but see Cacciari and Glucksberg, 1995, for contrasting evidence on adults).

3.3 *Online versus offline techniques in idiom acquisition studies*

A still underdeveloped field in the developmental literature concerns the online processing of figurative language. In general, the use of online techniques to track the time course of language processing in children is unfortunately still infrequent (e.g., Nation, Marshall, and Altmann, 2003; Padovani, 2005) and almost all the studies conducted on idiom acquisition used experimental techniques that are silent as to moment-by-moment comprehension processes. To our knowledge only one study (Padovani, 2005; Padovani et al., 2005) investigated idiom comprehension using an eyetracking technique. This paradigm is particularly useful for an online assessment of comprehension processes since it has been established that the point at which a person is looking is closely linked with sentential meaning activation and integration processes. In Padovani (2005), the eye movements of second or fourth graders were monitored while the children were auditorily presented with an idiomatically biased short story that ended with a familiar ambiguous idiom (the idiomatic interpretation was always the dominant one). At the beginning of the idiom string, the child was presented with four pictures on a computer screen (see Figure 25.1 for an example) that alternatively depicted: a) the idiomatic interpretation of the idiom string; b) the literal interpretation of the idiom string; c) a contextual distractor, namely a contextually plausible but idiom-unrelated content; d) a literal distractor, namely an object referred to in the idiom but unrelated to the story. The child was asked to choose the picture that had the best match with the story just heard.

The eyetracking data were recorded from the idiom onset to the choice of the picture (the total observation time, the fixations and their latency, and the regressions were measured). The results showed that the online comprehension of ambiguous idioms qualitatively differed according to the children's age and also to their general cognitive skills (syntactic comprehension, lexical access, reading comprehension, and inference making). The way in which the children explored the visual scene provided a source of information more revealing than their final choice of the story-appropriate picture since it reflected online comprehension processes. In fact in many cases the visual exploration of the pictures and the final choice dissociated: For instance, younger children preferentially chose the literal picture but their eyes extensively explored the contextually appropriate but idiom-unrelated picture. This picture was explored much more than both the idiomatic picture (almost ignored) and the literal picture, despite the final choice. This suggests that children did not recognize the string as idiomatic and tried to resolve the incongruency between the literal interpretation assigned to the idiom string and the story context exploring the picture that depicted the story context. On the contrary, older children preferentially interpreted the story idiomatically and consistently explored the picture corresponding to the idiomatic meaning of the string much more than any other picture. The cognitive competence of children clearly influenced the strategy with which the idioms were processed. At the age of nine all children were equally capable of interpreting the idiom strings figuratively. However, the children with weaker linguistic and cognitive skills were more visually locked to the pictures that were contextually appropriate but unrelated to the meaning of the idiom string.

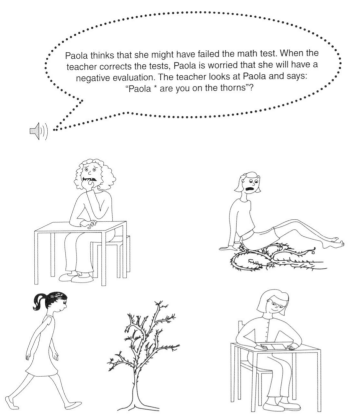

Figure 25.1. Example of the auditorily presented story context for the idiom *to be on the thorns* (namely *to be very worried*) (Padovani, 2005). The child's eye movements were recorded from the auditory onset of the idiom string (marked by an asterisk) to the choice of the picture.

How does the recognition of the idiomatic nature of the idiom string occur in children? Padovani (2005) adapted to children a hypothesis originally proposed to account for spoken idiom recognition in adults, the configuration hypothesis (Cacciari and Tabossi, 1988). According to this hypothesis, an idiomatic string is processed word by word, as any other piece of language, until enough information accumulates to render the string identifiable (or highly expected) as a memorized idiom. Only at this moment is the idiomatic meaning retrieved. For understanding an idiom, the children, as the adults, proceed incrementally integrating the word-by-word information into the representation of the sentential meaning. Once sufficient input is accumulated to allow the subject to recognize that what is currently at

issue is an idiom, the subject has to retrieve the appropriate figurative meaning from semantic memory and instantiate it into the sentential representation.

Recognition can of course be facilitated by contextual information for both adults and children: An appropriate context can for instance anticipate the point in time at which the listener/reader recognizes the idiomatic nature of the string. For children, especially the younger ones, idiom recognition can primarily be guided by the incongruity of the idiom with the contextual information that surrounds the idiom. This would explain why even when younger children chose the picture corresponding to the literal interpretation, they still explored the contextually appropriate but idiom-unrelated picture much more than the other pictures. More online research is needed in order to definitively clarify the role of idiom recognition mechanisms in the online understanding of idioms in children.

3.4 What is the relationship between reading comprehension skills and idiom acquisition?

Children with poor reading comprehension skills are typically developing children with no specific learning disabilities but poor reading comprehension skills and almost preserved reading decoding abilities. Recent studies of Italian and English children with reduced reading comprehension skills showed that a child's text comprehension level predicts his/her ability to understand an idiomatic expression and to produce it (Cain, Oakhill, and Lemmon, 2005; Levorato et al., 2004, 2006. In Levorato et al., children with poor reading comprehension skills aged from seven to ten years provided a literal interpretation for idioms inserted in short stories even when the narratives biased toward the idiomatic meaning. On the contrary, children with good reading comprehension skills were able to go beyond a word-by-word comprehension strategy and to integrate the figurative meaning into context. Interestingly, in a follow-up experiment Levorato et al. (2004) found that the children whose general reading comprehension skills improved also improved in idiom comprehension. Similar results were obtained with an idiom fragment completion task (Levorato et al., 2006).

3.5 Idiom processing in atypically developing children

If comprehending and producing idiomatic expressions takes normally developing children a long time to achieve, it takes children with language and/or brain deficits even longer. To our knowledge, no developmental disorder selectively affecting idiom acquisition has ever been reported. Many studies reported that children with developmental disorders that disrupt the ability to use language and/or communicative abilities often have deficits in understanding some forms of figurative expression as well. Figurative language impairments have been reported for children characterized by: a. autism spectrum disorders (Adachi et al., 2004; Dennis, Lazenby, and Lockyer, 2001; Happè, 1995; Nikolaenko, 2004; Norbury, 2004); b. specific language impairments (Kerbel and Grunwell, 1998a, 1998b; Norbury, 2004; Qualls et al., 2004); c. learning disabilities (Abrahamsen and Burke-Williams, 2004; Lee and Khami, 1990); d. mental retardation (Ezell and Goldstein, 1991); and e. a variety of brain-based disorders, including unilateral brain damages (Kempler et al., 1999), corpus callosum agenesis (Huber-Okramec, Blaser, and Dennis, 2005), and hydrocephalus (Barnes and Dennis, 1998).

However, the results emerging from these studies are not yet conclusive. For instance, Rinaldi (2000) reported impaired understanding of ambiguous language (including idioms) in children with specific language impairments aged from eleven to fourteen years. In contrast, Vance and Wells (1994) observed no deficit in idiom comprehension for children with the same diagnosis. Kerbell and Grunwell (1998a; 1998b) reported that when children with language and communication impairments (particularly, children with semantic pragmatic disorder and children with autism or Asperger's syndrome) were required to act out the meaning of idiomatic phrases in a play-based setting, they were more *literal* than both typically developing age-matched children and children with other language disorders (not primarily semantic or pragmatic).

Part of the inconsistent results emerging from these studies is again due to methodological factors: Often the authors used a mélange of different types of figurative expression; when they used idioms, they did not systematically consider some crucial characteristics of the experimental materials (e.g., familiarity, semantic transparency), nor did they consistently assess and/or report the linguistic and cognitive skills of the children.

Beyond these methodological problems, a still open question on figurative language impairments in atypically developing children concerns what causes them: specifically, whether it is a language-based deficit that does not permit children to reach a linguistically mature competence that includes figurative language acquisition (a bottom-up approach) or whether the deficit is language-aspecific and originates, for instance, from an inability to understand the speaker's mind and intentions (a top-down approach).

An influential perspective on figurative language impairments comes from the studies on autism, a biologically based disorder characterized by deficits relating to socialization, communication, and imagination. Irrespective of the autistic's general cognitive level (that can be either retarded or normal) and of his/her linguistic competence (that can be either totally absent or intact), autistic individuals tend to interpret language literally with a clear difficulty in going beyond a word-by-word interpretation of the message. This was anecdotally shown in a recent novel that has gained some popularity, *The curious incident of the dog in the night-time* (Haddon, 2003). Unfortunately, as already noted by Norbury (2004), there is a paucity of experimental research investigating idiom understanding in individuals with autism. Happé (1995) studied autistic children with normal intelligent quotients (i.e., high-functioning autistics) and found unimpaired understanding of stories containing idioms. On the contrary, Dennis et al. (2001) reported lower scores on the *Figurative Language Subtest* of the *Test of Language Competence* (Wiig and Secord, 1989) for high-functioning autistic children with respect to age-matched controls.

An influential theory first proposed by Baron-Cohen, Leslie, and Frith (1985) claims that autism springs from a deficient ability to attribute mental states and predict behavior accordingly. In other words, autistics would be characterized by an inability to read minds during normal communication. According to Happé, the understanding of figurative language is dependent upon the level of Theory of Mind (TOM) possessed by an individual, that is his/her ability to

attribute thoughts and feelings in order to predict and explain actions. Autistic children would have trouble understanding figurative language because of their inability to mentalize, namely to comprehend someone else's intentions in everyday communication, a crucial capacity for the acquisition of figurative language.

A different point of view has been recently proposed by Norbury (2004), who investigated idiom comprehension in typically developing children and in children with autism and specific language impairments. When required to define the meaning of an unfamiliar idiom (semantically transparent or opaque), all children significantly benefited from context. Interestingly, children with lexical and syntactic comprehension deficits did not benefit from context as much as both typically developing peers and children with autism but preserved language competence. These findings are not easily accommodated by a TOM approach. Furthermore, evidence of figurative language comprehension impairments was reported for children with learning disabilities (dyslexia) and with hydrocephalus (Barnes and Dennis, 1998), two pathologies not characterized by communication/socialization problems. This suggests that the figurative competence may be impaired even when the child is able to mentalize (i.e., when he/she possesses a TOM). In sum, the evidence on what causes figurative language impairments in children seem to be more consistent with a language-based deficit account rather than with a defective theory of mind account.

A topic that has been extensively, and controversially, discussed is whether and to what extent cerebral asymmetries are involved in figurative language acquisition. The picture emerging from the few existing studies on children suffering from brain injury seems to favor a developmental plasticity viewpoint: Kempler et al. (1999) tested idiom comprehension (using a picture-pointing procedure) in children between seven and ten years of age with perinatal focal brain damage either in the right hemisphere (RH) or in the left one (LH). The authors found no difference between children with LH versus RH lesions, nor did they find any difference between brain-injured children and normally developing controls: Children with focal brain injury did not display any double dissociation between the comprehension of literal and idiomatic expressions. It should be noted that this dissociation was reported in the first studies on figurative language comprehension in adults but has been recently questioned by several authors.

To sum up, overall these results suggest a composite picture of idiom comprehension impairments in children: Sometimes these deficits are specific to the clinical population investigated, sometimes they are not. Often in fact idiom acquisition in special populations occurs in the same time course and with the same cognitive prerequisites of normally developing children. Also what causes such figurative language acquisition impairments – whether they are due to language-specific deficits or to a defective theory of mind – is still an open issue.

4 How are metaphors acquired?

A *metaphor*, according to the still most influential definition that comes from Aristotle, is a form of transfer of a name from one entity to another. In more modern terms, a metaphor is a cognitive/linguistic device used to describe something new by reference to something familiar. As we already noted for figurative language, the task of defining a metaphor is so complex to discourage the most: as noted by Eco (1984, p. 88), *The chronicle of the discussion on metaphor is the chronicle of a series of variations on a few tautologies, perhaps on a single one: A metaphor is that artifice which permits one to speak metaphorically.*

How can we define the meaning of a metaphor? The *ground* of a metaphor can be represented by the set of properties that two concepts share (e.g., in *Dew is a veil* both are transparent, covering, shimmering), by a superordinate category that subsumes both concepts (e.g., in *the tooth of the mountain* the mountain peak and the

tooth partake of the category *sharpened forms*), or by an ad hoc category (e.g., in *my lawyer is a shark* both terms partake of the category of *vicious, aggressive, and dangerous beings*). In other cases, it may be necessary to reconstruct the underlying analogy (e.g., in Virginia Woolf's *She allowed life to waste as a tap left running*) (Cacciari and Glucksberg, 1994). According to the terminology used to describe a metaphor, the subject is the metaphor's *topic* (e.g., *lawyer*) and the predicate its *vehicle* (e.g., *shark*).

Metaphors can be characterized on the basis of different elements: a. the nature of the relationship between the topic and the vehicle (e.g., a perceptual one in *The train is a snake*, a functional one in *The mushroom is an umbrella*); b. the number and type of properties transferred from vehicle to topic; c. the linguistic/conceptual complexity of the vehicle and of the concept to which the metaphor belongs. Quite often, the term *metaphor* has been used for referring to different linguistic structures: attributive/nominal metaphors (i.e., of the form *An A is a B*), relational metaphors (i.e., of the form *A:B::C:D*), single word metaphor (i.e., a verb or an adjective used metaphorically). Recently it has been used to refer also to conceptual structures that are considered to be metaphorical in nature (Lakoff and Johnson, 1980).

4.1 *Early onset of metaphorical language?*

The vast majority of the developmental literature on metaphors has concerned their possible emergence in early age, that is, in preschool children (Winner, 1988), and much less their comprehension and production in school-aged children. There is ample evidence arguing that very young children (i.e., at the beginning of the third year of life) are able to exploit perceptual features of objects (shape, color, texture, and size) and to make what are often, but not uncontroversially, considered to be metaphorical associations (e.g., Winner, McCarthy, and Gardner, 1980). For example, Gentner (1988) reported about a two-year old boy who said that a crescent moon was *bent like a banana*. In general, early nonconventional language in children might be very creative (e.g., *comb* for *galleyworm, ball* for *apple*). However, Winner and colleagues (Winner, 1988; Winner et al., 1980), following Piaget, argued that these early linguistic creations can easily be overextensions that fill lexical gaps (e.g., *ball* for any round object) rather than true metaphors. These overextensions might provide the developmental basis for future metaphorical productions.

Hence, a critical aspect in studying metaphor production in very young children is the status of the child's lexical and conceptual knowledge. According to Winner and to Eve Clark (1993), children's lexical creativity is a resource they use in order to fill a gap in their lexicon, a linguistic strategy employed when the appropriate word is not available. The very young children tested in many studies on the emergence of metaphorical language did not yet certainly possess the metalinguistic awareness necessary to intentionally produce a metaphor. Some studies have shown that children as young as three or four years produced new metaphors, but since they did not possess an extended lexicon or the ability to recognize that a single linguistic expression might convey several different meanings, how can we label these expressions as metaphors? (Winner, 1988).

Winner et al. (1980) proposed a model of the developmental steps through which a child acquires the ability to understand and produce a metaphor. In the first step two- and three-year old children produce action-based metaphors during sessions of symbolic play when children pretend to use an object as if it was another one. From age three children are more apt to produce perceptually-based metaphors: The production of action-based metaphors sharply declines, giving rise to metaphors based on the perceptual properties of objects (e.g., a child describes a plate of spaghetti as a *bunch of worms*). Finally, during the third step, a decline in the amount of spontaneous metaphors is observed in school-aged children as a consequence of the general augmented literacy. Vosniadou and Ortony (1983) reported that by the age of four children might already have some rudimental metaphorical competence: Children were asked to verbally complete statements such as *A river is like a* _____ (Comparison task, see Box: 25.1) or *A river is the same kind of thing as* _____ (Categorization task) choosing one of three alternatives (i.e., a literal completion word as *lake*, a metaphorical completion as *snake*, or an anomalous one as *cat*). By age three, children distinguished meaningful comparisons from anomalous ones, while four-year-old and older children provided completions that suggest that they were aware that the terms forming the metaphorical comparison, unlike the literal one, belonged to different conventional categories. Similarly, in a study on the comprehension of synaesthetic metaphors in nearly 500 children, Marks, Hammeal, and Bornstein (1987) reported that children at age four showed some capacity to metaphorically translate a term from one perceptual modality to another (e.g., judging *low-pitched* as *dim* and *high-pitched* as *bright*).

Other studies revealed that children develop the ability to comprehend metaphorical statements much later than initially assumed (e.g., Vosniadou and Ortony, 1983; Waggoner and Palermo, 1989). For instance, children younger than seven were not able to rephrase or correctly choose the meaning of a metaphorical statement that involved an implicit comparison (Winner et al., 1980) and to provide appropriate metaphorical completions for sentence fragments (Gardner et al., 1975; Winner, Engel, and Gardner, 1980). Similar results came from studies on metaphors involving systematic analogical mappings between psychological traits and physical sensations (e.g., *cold water*: *cold person*). Overall, the vast majority of the authors found a lack of comprehension of metaphorical meaning until seven to ten years of age (Cicone, Gardner, and Winner, 1981; Winner, Rosenstiel, and Gardner, 1976). Pioneer studies by Asch (Asch and Nerlove, 1960) reported that children were not able to comprehend the psychological meaning of *double function* terms (e.g., *hard, soft, warm*) until age twelve.

The assumption of an early capacity to produce metaphors would lead to the contradictory prediction that young children would produce metaphors that they cannot comprehend. As the case of idioms shows, comprehension abilities typically precede production abilities. This further questions the *true* metaphorical nature of early spontaneous productions.

Some authors investigated the role of contextual information in metaphor acquisition (e.g., Levorato and Donati, 1998; Ozcaliskan, 2005; Vosniadou et al., 1984; Winner, 1988). For instance, Levorato and Donati (1998) investigated the role of context in comprehending and producing perceptually and functionally based metaphors in Italian children aged from four to seven years. The results showed that the ability to comprehend a metaphor was absent at age four, irrespective of contextual information, and progressively increased for children aged from five to seven. In the production task, children were not able to metaphorically complete a sentence until the age of seven. Recently, Ozcaliskan (2005) further investigated how contextual information helps metaphor understanding in children aged from three to five. Turkish-speaking children listened to a brief story containing a metaphor while seeing a visual illustration sequence of the same story. Children were requested to choose between the metaphorical interpretation of the story and an incorrect version. The results showed a lack of metaphorical comprehension at age three, a partial comprehension in a contextually supported situation at age four, and finally the onset of a verbal reasoning on metaphorical mappings at age five. Similar results were obtained in another study that investigated English children's understanding of metaphorical motion events (e.g., *time flies by*) (Ozcaliskan, 2003). Vosniadou et al. (1984) showed that both the predictability of the story ending and the complexity of the sentence that contained the metaphor affected the ease of metaphor comprehension.

4.2 Experimental methods in metaphor testing in children

The experimental methods used to test metaphor acquisition (see Box: 25.1) differ to a great extent and range from simple matching tasks (e.g., children are asked to match a target object, *a cone shaped block*, to either a categorically relevant object, *a block*, to an unrelated object, *a fire engine*, or to a perceptually similar object considered as the metaphorical match, *a toy rocked ship*; Winner et al., 1980), to verbal rephrasing of metaphorical statements based on perceptually driven comparisons among multiple choice alternatives (e.g., children are asked to either describe or choose the best match for a metaphorical statement such as *Jenny is a soft piece of silk*; Nippold, Leonard, and Kail, 1984).

In general, the greater the reliance only on linguistic measures, the more likely the experiment is to underestimate children's ability to master metaphorical language. The use of a multiple choice task or of nonverbal matching measures like the metaphorical enactment task (i.e., listening to a story containing a metaphor and acting its meaning out with toys, see Box: 25.1 for an example) has in fact revealed metaphorical comprehension skills in children at a very early stage of language acquisition (i.e., at age three) (Vosniadou et al., 1984). The domain from which metaphorical experimental materials are extracted also plays a crucial role: Children in fact understand perceptually based metaphors before nonperceptual ones because of the well-known salience of perceptual similarities for young children (Winner, 1988). In general, the ability to comprehend a metaphor develops on a domain-by-domain basis and is a function of the richness of knowledge of the topic and vehicle domains (Keil, 1986).

4.3 Metaphorical language, intentionality, and theory of mind

Marschark and Nall (1985) claimed that one critical aspect in deciding whether the expressions produced by young children are metaphorical lies in the concept of *intentionality*. The production of spontaneous metaphors requires the awareness that the topic and the vehicle belong to different semantic domains. Thus, the child has to be conscious that the linguistic expression he/she produced is literally false because it contains an intentional violation of the relationship between elements belonging to different conceptual domains. This problem has gained a renewed interest since TOM theorists investigated children's understanding of the distinction between communicative intention and literal meaning (Beal and Flavell, 1984). According to the TOM, the ability to understand intentions can be assessed with tasks that involve attribution of false beliefs. The false believe task was first proposed by Baron-Cohen et al. (1985) (see the Sally-Anne task in Box: 25.1.). Children with autism, even those with mental ages well above four years, failed in the Sally-Anne false-believe task. Four-year-old normally developing children can instead predict the correct location but not the younger ones. According to TOM theorists, intentionality derives from the general ability of children to understand the mental states of others. Leslie (1987) proposed that the understanding of pretence in infancy demonstrates the availability of a special computational form of representation for mental states. This would be consistent with the observation that the first metaphorical expressions are usually produced during spontaneous symbolic play.

4.4 *Metaphor comprehension and production in school-age children*

The ability to comprehend metaphors improves throughout the school years and also adolescence and adulthood (e.g., Gentner, 1988). Chronological age, verbal ability, and cognition interact to produce metaphor comprehension, as noted by Vosniadou (1987, p. 880): *The development of metaphor comprehension is constrained primarily by limitations on children's conceptual knowledge, linguistic skill, and information-processing ability.*

Is there any domain-specific effect on metaphor comprehension also for school-age children? Winner et al. (1976) compared the ability of children of the ages of ten, twelve, and fourteen to understand psychological–physical metaphors (e.g., *After many years of working at the jail, the prison guard had become a hard rock that could not be moved*) and cross-sensory metaphors (e.g., *The smell of my mother's perfume was bright sunshine*). The comprehension steadily improved through the age of fourteen with cross-sensory metaphors easier to understand than psychological–physical ones, particularly for ten-year-olds. However, contrasting evidence was obtained by Nippold et al. (1984) with nine-year-olds.

The development of metaphoric production in school-age children has been frequently investigated with a multiple sentences task in which a child is required to produce a narrative or a sentence according to a given topic (see Box: 25.1 for an example). For instance, Pollio and Pollio (1974) examined third, fourth, and fifth graders, asking them to write stories about imaginative topics (e.g., *a talking goldfish, adventures in space*). The results showed that children produced more conventionalized metaphors (e.g., *I went into the kitchen and ate up a storm*) than novel ones (e.g., *I saw a coffin and was scared. I walked slowly toward it. I was amazed my feet were brave enough to take me there*). The metaphorical productions overall decreased as grade level increased, suggesting a decline in metaphoric production during formal teaching (Winner et al., 1980), but this interpretation raised some controversy. The coinage of new figurative expressions was investigated by Levorato and Cacciari (2002) who asked third, fourth, fifth graders, teenagers, and adults to coin new linguistic expressions for labeling a set of emotion targets (e.g., *being happy, being ashamed, being sad*) and action targets (e.g., *telling a lie, revealing a secret, sleeping too much*). The task did not explicitly ask participants to use a figurative expression. Despite this, more than half of the productions contained figurative expressions (e.g., *being a speaking letter, being like the days that change*). Even children produced a remarkably high percentage of new figurative expressions (thirty-seven percent and 42.4 percent in nine- and eleven-year olds, respectively) that increased in adolescents (67.5 percent) but, interestingly, not in adults (61.3 percent). The comprehensibility, novelty, and aptness of the figurative productions increased as the producers' age increased and depended on the domain: The figurative expressions coined for emotions were rated as more comprehensible, novel, and apt than those created for actions.

Unsurprisingly, school-aged children were in any case more locked to literal understanding than adults (Winer et al., 2001), as shown in a study where children and college students were presented with questions that included unusual ones such as *Do you see with your ears?* or *Do you touch with your eyes?* Nine-year-olds gave more "no" responses than college students that were instead able to consider the metaphorical similarities between touch and vision.

4.5 *Metaphor comprehension in atypically developing children*

The literature on the comprehension of metaphor in atypically developing children is very scarce and almost only devoted to children with autistic spectrum disorders (Adachi et al., 2004; Happé, 1995; Nikolaenko, 2004). Dennis et al. (2001) recently compared high-functioning autistic children aged ten with typically developing children. Children were asked to perform different tasks, including one in which the children were presented with lexical ambiguities and figurative expressions (including idioms and metaphors) and were required to select a picture that corresponded to the figurative meaning. Despite the fact that autistic children were able to identify the multiple meanings of an ambiguous word as much as typically developing children, they did not understand metaphors.

As we said, the deficits in metaphor understanding in autistic children and adults have been explained on the basis of their deficient TOM. Leslie (1987) proposed that mental state representations are special forms of representation that permit people to interpret the intentionality of others and, consequently, to have a TOM. These metarepresentations capture the attitude an agent takes toward a representation of an aspect of reality. For example, the metarepresentation corresponding to *Mother – pretends – of this banana – it is a telephone* is formed by a four-parts relation among agent (*Mother*), propositional attitude (*pretends*), target in the concrete world (*banana*), and proposition (*it is a telephone*).

Despite the fascinating idea of a relationship between metaphorical language and TOM, further research is needed before we might definitively conclude that it accounts for figurative language comprehension impairments in abnormally developing children. Adachi et al. (2004), for instance, showed that children with autistic spectrum disorders and children with attention deficit/hyperactivity disorder (ADHD: a disorder primarily related to attention and executive function deficits rather than communication and socialization deficits) were similarly impaired in understanding metaphors inserted in brief metaphorical stories. But ADHD children had no deficits in the TOM task questioning the link between TOM and metaphorical language comprehension.

5 Conclusions and future directions

In this chapter we reviewed the models and experimental evidence on the comprehension and production of the two types of figurative expression that attracted most of the attention of developmental researchers: idioms and metaphors. An unbalance certainly exists between them, with idiomatic expressions acquisition investigated much more than that of metaphors, at least in recent years. Despite the consistent and rich bulk of evidence accumulated in the field, many questions are still unanswered that relate to methodological as well as to theoretical aspects. The relationships between language and intentionality and between behavioral and brain-related data are some of the promising venues that might characterize the research on the acquisition of figurative language in the near future.

References

Abkarian, G., Jones, A. & West, G. (1992). Young children's idiom comprehension: Trying to get the picture. *Journal of Speech and Hearing Research*, 35, 580–7.

Abrahamsen, E. P. & Burke-Williams, D. (2004). Comprehension of idioms by children with learning disabilities: Metaphoric transparency and syntactic frozenness. *Journal of Psycholinguistic Research*, 33, 203–15.

Ackerman, B. P. (1982). On comprehending idioms: Do children get the picture? *Journal of Experimental Child Psychology*, 33, 439–54.

Adachi, T., Koeda, T., Hirabayashi, S., Maeoka, Y., Shiota, M., Wright, E. C. & Wada, A. (2004). The metaphor and sarcasm scenario test: A new instrument to help differentiate high functioning pervasive developmental disorder from attention deficit/hyperactivity disorder. *Brain & Development*, 26, 301–6.

Asch, S. & Nerlove, H. (1960). The development of double function terms in children. An exploratory investigation. In Kaplan, B. & Wapner, S. (Eds.) *Perspectives in psychological theory: Essays in honor of Heinz Werner*. New York: International University Press.

Barnes, M. A. & Dennis, M. (1998). Discourse after hydrocephalus: Core deficits in children of average intelligence. *Brain & Language*, 61, 309–34.

Baron-Cohen, S., Leslie, A. M., & Frith, U. (1985). Does the autistic child have a "theory of mind"? *Cognition*, 21, 37–46.

Beal, C. R. & Flavell, J. H. (1984). Development of the ability to distinguish communicative intention and literal message meaning. *Child Development*, 55, 920–8.

Cacciari, C. & Glucksberg, S. (1994). *Understanding figurative language*. In Gernsbacher, M. A. (Ed.) *Handbook of psycholinguistics* (447–77). San Diego: Academic Press.

(1995). Understanding idioms: Do visual images reflect figurative meanings? *European Journal of Cognitive Psychology*, 7, 283–305.

Cacciari, C. & Levorato, M. C. (1989). How children understand idioms in discourse. *Journal of Child Language*, 16, 387–405.

(1998). The effect of semantic analyzability of idioms in metalinguistic tasks. *Metaphor & Symbol*, 13, 159–77.

Cacciari, C. & Tabossi, P. (1988). The comprehension of idioms. *Journal of Memory and Language*, 27, 668–83.

Cain, K., Oakhill, J., & Lemmon, K. (2005). The relation between children's reading comprehension level and their comprehension of idioms. *Journal of Experimental Child Psychology*, 90, 65–87.

Cicone, M., Gardner, H. & Winner, E. (1981). Understanding the psychology in psychological metaphors. *Journal of Child Language*, 8, 213–16.

Clark, E. V. (1993). *The lexicon in acquisition*. Cambridge: Cambridge University Press.

Dennis, M., Lazenby, A. L., & Lockyer, L. (2001). Inferential language in high-functioning children with autism. *Journal of Autism and Developmental Disorders*, 31, 47–54.

Eco, U. (1984). *Semiotics and the philosophy of language*. Bloomington: Indiana University Press.

Ezell, H. K. & Goldstein, H. (1991). Observational learning of comprehension monitoring skills in children who exhibit mental retardation. *Journal of Speech and Hearing Research*, 34, 141–54.

Gardner, H., Kircher, M., Winner, E., & Perkins, D. (1975). Children's metaphoric productions and preferences. *Journal of Child Language*, 2, 125–41.

Gentner, D. (1988). Metaphor as structure mapping: The relational shift. *Child Development*, 59, 47–59.

Gibbs, R. W. (1987). Linguistic factors in children's understanding of idioms. *Journal of Child Language*, 14, 569–86.

(1991). Semantic analyzability in children's understanding of idioms. *Journal of Speech and Hearing Research*, 34, 613–20.

Gibbs, R. W., Nayak, N. P., & Cutting, J. C. (1989). How to kick the bucket and not decompose: Analyzability and idiom processing. *Journal of Memory and Language*, 28, 576–93.

Glucksberg, S. (1989). Metaphors in conversation: How are they understood? Why are they used? *Metaphor and Symbolic Activity*, 4, 125–43.

(1993). Idiom meaning and allusional content. In Cacciari, C. & Tabossi, P. (Eds.) *Idioms. Processing, structure and interpretation* (pp. 3–26). Hillsdale, NJ: Laurence Erlbaum.

Haddon, M. (2003) *The curious incident of the dog in the night time*. London: Jonathan Cape.

Happé, FGE (1995). Understanding minds and metaphors: Insights from the study of figurative language and autism. *Metaphor and Symbolic Activity*, 10, 275–95.

Huber-Okramec, J., Blaser, S. E. & Dennis, M. (2005). Idiom comprehension deficits in relation to corpus callosum agenesis and hypoplasia in children with spina bifida meningomyelocele. *Brain & Language*, 93, 349–68.

Keil, F. C. (1986). Conceptual domains and the acquisition of metaphor. *Cognitive Development*, 1, 73–96.

Kempler, D., Van Lancker, D., Marchman, V., & Bates, E. (1999). Idiom comprehension in children and adults with unilateral brain damage. *Developmental Neuropsychology*, 15, 327–49.

Kerbel, D. & Grunwell, P. (1998a). A study of idiom comprehension in children with semantic-pragmatic difficulties. Part I: Between-groups results and discussion. *International Journal of Language and Communication Disorders*, 35, 1–22.

(1998b). A study of idiom comprehension in children with semantic-pragmatic difficulties. Part II: Task effects on the assessment of idioms comprehension in children. *International Journal of Language and Communication Disorders*, 35, 23–44.

Lakoff, G. & Johnson, M. (1980). *Metaphors we live by*. Chicago: University of Chicago.

Laval, V. (2003). Idiom comprehension and metapragmatic knowledge in French children. *Journal of Pragmatics*, 35, 723–39.

Lee, R. F. & Khami, A. G. (1990). Metaphoric competence in children with learning disabilities. *Journal of Learning Disabilities*, 23, 476–52.

Leslie, A. M. (1987). Pretence and representation: The origin of "theory of mind." *Psychological Review*, 94, 412–26.

Levorato, M. C. (1993). The acquisition of idioms and the development of figurative competence. In Cacciari, C. & Tabossi, P. (Eds.) *Idioms. Processing, structure and interpretation* (pp. 105–28). Hillsdale, NJ: Laurence Erlbaum.

Levorato, M. C. & Cacciari, C. (1992). Children's comprehension and production of idioms: The role of context and familiarity. *Journal of Child Language*, 19, 415–33.

(1995). The effects of different tasks on the comprehension and production of idioms in children. *Journal of Experimental Child Psychology*, 60, 261–83.

(1999). Idiom comprehension in children: Are the effects of semantic analyzability and context separable? *European Journal of Cognitive Psychology*, 11, 51–66.

(2002). The creation of new figurative expressions: Psycholinguistic evidence on children, adolescents and adults. *Journal of Child Language*, 29, 127–50.

Levorato, M. C. & Donati, V. (1998). La farfalla è solo un insetto o è anche un arcobaleno? *Età Evolutiva*, 59, 98–107.

Levorato, M. C., Nesi, B. & Cacciari, C. (2004). Reading comprehension and understanding idiomatic expressions: A developmental study. *Brain & Language*, 91, 303–14.

Levorato, M. C., Nesi, B., Roch, M., & Cacciari, C. (2006). To break the embarrassment: Text comprehension skills and figurative competence in skilled and less-skilled text comprehenders. *European Psychologist*, 11, 128–36.

Lodge, L. & Leach, E. (1975). Children's acquisition of idioms in the English language. *Journal of Speech and Hearing Research*, 18, 521–9.

Marks, L. E., Hammeal, R. J., & Bornstein, M. H. (1987). Perceiving similarity and comprehending metaphor. *Monograph of the Society for Research in Child Development*, 52, 1–102.

Marschark, M. & Nall, L. (1985). Metaphoric competence in cognitive and language development. In Reese, H. W. (Ed.) *Advances in child development and behavior, Vol. 19*. New York: Academic Press.

Nation, K., Marshall, C. M. & Altmann, G. T. M. (2003). Investigating individual differences in children's real-time sentence comprehension using language-mediated eye movements. *Journal of Experimental Child Psychology*, 86, 314–29.

Nikolaenko, N. N. (2004). Metaphorical and associative thinking in healthy children and in children with Asperger's syndrome at different ages. *Human Physiology*, 30, 532–6.

Nippold, M. A. (1988). Figurative language. In Nippold, M. A. (Eds.) *Later language development. Ages 9 through 19* (pp. 179–211). Boston: A College-Hill Publication.

(1991). Evaluating and enhancing idiom comprehension in language disordered students. *Language, Speech and Hearing Services in the Schools*, 22, 100–6.

Nippold, M. A. & Duthie, J. K. (2003). Mental imagery and idiom comprehension. A comparison of school-age children and adults. *Journal of Speech and Hearing Research*, 46, 788–99.

Nippold, M. A., Leonard, L. B. & Kail, R. (1984). Syntactic and conceptual factors in children's understanding of metaphors. *Journal of Speech and Hearing Research*, 27, 197–205.

Nippold, M. A. & Martin, S. T. (1989). Idiom interpretation in isolation vs. context. A developmental study with adolescents. *Journal of Speech and Hearing Research*, 32, 59–66.

Nippold, M. A. & Rudzinski, M. (1993). Familiarity and transparency in idiom explanations: A developmental study of children and adolescents. *Journal of Speech, Language and Hearing Research*, 36, 728–37.

Nippold, M. A. & Taylor, C. L. (2002). Judgments of idiom familiarity and transparency: A comparison of children and adolescents. *Journal of Speech and Hearing Research*, 45, 384–91.

Norbury, C. F. (2004). Factors supporting idiom comprehension in children with communication disorders. *Journal of Speech, Language and Hearing Research*, 47, 1179–93.

Ozcaliskan, S. (2003). Metaphorical motion in crosslinguistic perspective: A comparison of English and Turkish. *Metaphor & Symbol*, 18, 189–228.

(2005). On learning to draw the distinction between physical and metaphorical motion: Is metaphor an early emerging cognitive and linguistic capacity? *Journal of Child Language*, 32, 291–318.

Padovani, R. (2005). Difficoltà di comprensione del testo e acquisizione delle espressioni idiomatiche: profili cognitivi e movimenti oculari in bambini di età scolare [Text comprehension problems and idiom acquisition: cognitive profiles and eyetracking measurement in school-age children]. Ph.D. dissertation, University of Modena, Italy.

Padovani, R., Cacciari, C., Levorato, M. C., Corradini, M., Bulf, L., Rubichi, S., & Fonda, S. (2005). L'elaborazione del linguaggio nei bambini con difficoltà di comprensione del testo. Cosa rivelano i loro movimenti oculari? [Language processing in children with reading comprehension difficulties. What do eye movements reveal?] *Proceedings of the Conference Neurolinguistics and Language Disorders*. Modena (Italy).

Pollio, M. & Pollio, H. (1974) The development of figurative language in school children. *Journal of Psycholinguistic Research*, 3, 185–201.

Prinz, P. M. (1983). The development of idiomatic meaning in children. *Language & Speech*, 26, 263–72.

Qualls, C. D. & Harris, J. L. (1999). Effects of familiarity on idiom comprehension in African American and European Americans fifth graders. *Language, Speech, and Hearing Services in Schools*, 30, 141–51.

Qualls, C. D., Lantz, J. M., Pietrzyk, R. M., Blood, G. W., & Scheffner Hammer, C. S. (2004). Comprehension of idioms in adolescents with language-based learning disabilities compared with their typically developing peers. *Journal of Communication Disorders*, 37, 295–311.

Rinaldi, W. (2000). Pragmatic comprehension in secondary school-aged students with specific developmental language disorder. *International Journal of Language and Communication Disorders*, 35, 1–29.

Vance, M. & Wells, B. (1994). The wrong end of the stick: Language-impaired children's understanding of non-literal language. *Child Language Teaching and Therapy*, 10, 23–46.

Vosniadou, S. (1987). Children and metaphors. *Child Development*, 58, 870–85.

Vosniadou, S. & Ortony, A. (1983). The emergence of the literal-metaphorical-anomalous distinction in young children. *Child Development*, 54, 154–61.

Vosniadou, S., Ortony, A., Reynolds, R. E. & Wilson, P. T. (1984). Sources of difficulty in the young child's understanding of metaphorical language. *Child Development*, 55, 1588–1606.

Waggoner, J. E. & Palermo, D. S. (1989). Betty is a bouncing bubble: Children's comprehension of emotion-descriptive metaphors. *Developmental Psychology*, 25, 152–63.

Wasow, T., Sag, I., & Nunberg, G. (1983). Idioms: An interim report. In Hattori, S. & Inoue, K. (Eds.) *Proceedings of the XIIIth International Congress of Linguistics* (pp.102–5). Tokyo: CIPL.

Wiig, E. & Secord, W. (1989). *Test of language competence*. San Antonio, TX: The Psychological Corporation.

Winer, G. A., Cottrell, J. E., Mott, T., Cohen, M., & Fournier, J. (2001). Are children more accurate than adults? Spontaneous use of metaphor by children and adults. *Journal of Psycholinguistic Research*, 30, 485–96.

Winner, E. (1988). *The point of words: Children's understanding of metaphor and irony*. Cambridge, MA: Harvard University Press.

Winner, E., Engel, M. & Gardner, H. (1980). Misunderstanding metaphor: What's the problem? *Journal of Experimental Child Psychology*, 30, 22–32.

Winner, E., McCarthy, M. & Gardner, H. (1980). The ontogenesis of metaphor. In Honeck, R. P. & Hoffman, R. R. (Eds.) *Cognition and figurative language* (pp. 341–61). Hillsdale, NJ: Erlbaum.

Winner, E., Rosenstiel, A. & Gardner, H. (1976). The developmental of metaphoric understanding. *Developmental Psychology*, 12, 289–97.

CHAPTER 26

Cognitive Neuroscience of Figurative Language

Seana Coulson

1 Introduction

On pornography, U.S. Supreme Court Justice Potter Stewart famously wrote, "I shall not today attempt further to define the kinds of material I understand to be embraced within that shorthand description; and perhaps I could never succeed in intelligibly doing so. But I know it when I see it…" (cited in Gewirtz, 1996). The same might be said for figurative language. Usually defined in opposition to literal language, figurative language encompasses a variety of rhetorical techniques, such as metaphor, personification, hyperbole, and many others, all used to increase the affective and inferential impact of one's statements. Though most scholars have rejected a dichotomous division between literal and figurative language (Coulson and Lewandowska-Tomaszczyk, 2005), it remains a useful heuristic for talking about particular figures of speech.

Figurative language is an important topic in psycholinguistics for a number of reasons. First, while many people think of figurative language as confined to artistic venues, it is in fact far more common than many people

realize (Gibbs, Wilson, and Bryant, this volume). Second, the diversity of figurative language highlights the range of different cognitive processes people bring to bear on language production and comprehension. Finally, the study of figurative language has led to an important locus of generativity in language, namely the human ability to map within and between concepts, frames, and scenarios (Coulson, 2001).

Despite the importance of figurative language, to date it has attracted relatively little attention from cognitive neuroscientists. This is changing, however, both because of advances in our understanding of the neural underpinnings of basic word and sentence processing, and because researchers in the field have begun to understand the importance of figurative language in everyday communication (see, e.g., the special issue of *Brain & Language* devoted to the neural correlates of nonliteral language [Giora, 2007]). One area of particular interest stems from the observation of brain-injured patients, namely the role of the nondominant right hemisphere (RH) in the production and comprehension of figurative language.

Whereas left hemisphere (LH) lesions are frequently associated with deficits in core language ability, such as the production of fluent, grammatical speech, or the comprehension of spoken words and sentences, the incidence of such aphasic deficits is far less common in patients with lesions in the RH (Hecaen and Consoli, 1973). Instead, patients with RH damage present with more subtle deficits involving the relationship between an utterance and its context. Besides socially inappropriate remarks and digressions of topic, such deficits have been argued to include various kinds of figurative language (Joanette, Goulet, and Hannequin, 1990). For example, RH damaged patients have been shown to have difficulty understanding jokes (Bihrle, Brownell, and Gardner, 1986; Brownell et al., 1983), interpreting sarcastic utterances (Giora, 2003; Rehak, Kaplan, and Gardner, 1992), and have been characterized as deriving overly literal interpretations of metaphoric language (Winner and Gardner, 1977).

One consequence of these observations of the disparate effects of LH and RH damage is that traditional (problematic) distinctions between literal and nonliteral meaning have been invoked to explain them. Thus the left hemisphere is often associated with language processing commonly construed as literal, while the right hemisphere has been associated with nonliteral processing, including figurative language as well as other sorts of pragmatic phenomena that depend upon extra-linguistic knowledge for their interpretation. In a selective review of research on the cognitive neuroscience of figurative language, we address the veracity of classic assumptions about lateralization and the distinction between literal and nonliteral language. Moreover, we address how the methods of cognitive neuroscience have been used to test models of figurative language comprehension.

The chapter focuses on two well-studied examples of figurative language: jokes and metaphors. We begin each section with a review of cognitive neuroscience research used to test and develop models of the comprehension of these phenomena, and follow with a review of evidence for the importance of the RH in each. We conclude with some speculations about how the potential relevance of recent advances in other areas of cognitive neuroscience impacts the study of figurative language, and general issues relevant to meaning in language.

2 Joke comprehension

Though language researchers have traditionally looked to syntax as the chief source of our productive language capacity, another important source of productivity in language arises from the interdependence of the meaning of a word and the contextual assumptions that surround its use. For example, it is impossible to understand the meaning of *weekend* without an understanding of the structure of the week, as well as the cultural knowledge that many people in industrialized countries work Monday through Friday, and not on Saturday and Sunday (Fillmore, 1976). This context dependence in meaning has been explored in frame semantics, a research program in cognitive linguistics in which a word's semantic properties are described with respect to how they highlight aspects of an associated frame or a structured set of background assumptions. Langacker argues that while *roe* and *caviar* refer to the same thing, their meanings differ because *roe* presumes a biological frame while *caviar* presumes a culinary one (Langacker, 1987). Conversely, Lakoff argues that the different meanings of *mother*, as in my *birth mother* versus my *adopted mother*, rely on different frames for parenthood (Lakoff, 1987).

The study of joke comprehension addresses the importance of frames for language comprehension, since many jokes are funny because they deceive the listener into using the wrong frame to help interpret the information presented in the first part of the joke. For example, consider the following joke: "I let my accountant do my taxes because it saves time; last spring it saved me ten years." Initially, the listener activates a busy-professional frame. However, at the punch line "saved me ten years," it becomes apparent that a crooked-businessman frame is more appropriate. Although lexical reinterpretation plays an important part in joke comprehension, to truly appreciate this joke it is necessary to recruit background knowledge about particular sorts of relationships that can obtain between business people and their accountants so that the initial busy professional interpretation can be mapped into the crooked businessman frame. The semantic and pragmatic reanalysis to understand jokes like this is known as *frame shifting* (Coulson, 2001).

2.1 *Cognitive electrophysiology of joke comprehension*

The neurophysiology of language processes can be investigated in healthy people via the noninvasive recording of event-related brain potentials (ERPs). ERPs are small voltage fluctuations in the electroencephalogram (EEG) that are timelocked to perceptual, motor, or cognitive events collected by recording EEG while participants perform a cognitive task such as reading (Rugg and Coles, 1995). By averaging the EEG timelocked to multiple tokens of a given type (e.g., the onset of a word used metaphorically), it is possible to isolate aspects of the electrical signal that are temporally associated with the processing of that type of event (such as understanding a metaphoric meaning). The result of averaging is a waveform with a series of positive and negative peaks, known as components, and labeled by reference to their polarity ("P" for positive-going and "N" for negative-going), and when they occur relative to the onset of the stimulus event, or relative to other ERP components.

Over the last twenty-five years, cognitive neuroscientists have identified ERP components associated with processing different sorts of linguistic information, such as the link between the N400 and semantic integration processes. The N400 component of the ERPs was first noted in experiments contrasting sentences that ended sensibly and predictably with others that ended with an incongruous word. Congruous words elicited a late positive wave, while incongruous endings elicited a negative wave beginning about 200 ms after word onset and peaking at 400 ms (Kutas and Hillyard, 1980). Subsequent experiments have shown that finer gradations of semantic context also modulate N400 amplitude. For example, amplitude shows a strong inverse correlation with the predictability of the eliciting word within a given sentence context (Kutas, Lindamood, and Hillyard, 1984). In general, experimental manipulations that make semantic integration more difficult result in larger amplitude N400, while those that facilitate it result in smaller N400 (see also Van Berkum, this volume).

Given the impact of frame shifting on the interpretation of one-line jokes, one might expect the underlying processes to be reflected in the brain's real-time response. Coulson and Kutas compared ERPs elicited by sentences that ended as jokes that required frame shifting with nonfunny "straight" endings consistent with the contextually evoked frame (Coulson and Kutas, 2001). Two types of jokes were tested, high constraint jokes such as (1) which elicited at least one response on a sentence completion task with a cloze probability of greater than forty percent, and low constraint jokes like (2) which elicited responses with cloze probabilities lower than forty percent. For both (1) and (2) the word in parentheses was the most popular response on the cloze task.

(1) I asked the woman at the party if she remembered me from last year and she said she never forgets a (*face*: eighty-one percent).
(2) My husband took all the money we were saving to buy a new car and blew it all at the (*casino*: eighteen percent).

To control for the fact that the joke endings are (by definition) unexpected, the straight controls were chosen so that they matched the joke endings for cloze probability, but were consistent with the frame evoked by context. For example, the straight ending for (1) was *name* (the joke ending was *dress*), while the straight ending for (2) was *tables* (the joke ending was *movies*). The cloze probability of all four ending types (high and low constraint joke and straight endings) was equal, and ranged from zero to five percent.

Coulson and Kutas (2001) found that ERPs to joke endings differed in several respects from those to the straight endings, depending on contextual constraint as well as participants' ability to get the jokes. In good joke comprehenders, high but not low constraint joke endings elicited a larger N400 than the straight endings. This effect may result because the activation of the relevant frame facilitated lexical integration of the high constraint straight endings relative to the jokes. Similar effects may have been absent from the low constraint stimuli, because those sentences led to the activation of a diverse set of frames less likely to be consistent with the straight ending.

However, both sorts of jokes (high and low constraint) elicited a late positivity in the ERP (500–900 ms post onset), as well as a slow sustained negativity (300–900 ms post onset), evident over left frontal sites. The effect at left frontal sites has been suggested to reflect the manipulation of information in working memory (Coulson and Kutas, 2001; Coulson and Lovett, 2004). The late positivity is an ERP effect often associated with the activation of information in memory (i.e., retrieval), consistent with the suggestion that joke comprehension requires the activation of a novel frame.

In poor joke comprehenders, jokes elicited a negativity between 300 and 700 ms after the onset of the sentence final word. The absence of the late positivity and the left frontal negativity in the poor comprehenders' ERPs suggests that these effects index cognitive operations important for actually getting the joke. The poor joke comprehenders apparently searched for a coherent interpretation of the joke endings, but because they were unable to retrieve the frame necessary to get the joke, neither the late positivity nor the left frontal effect was evident in their ERPs.

These demonstrations of the brain's relatively early sensitivity to discourse-level manipulations are consistent with the dynamic inferencing mechanisms assumed in many frame-based models of comprehension. Based on computational considerations, Shastri proposed that frame-based inferences necessary for language comprehension occur in a time frame on the order of hundreds of milliseconds (Shastri, 1999), consistent with our observation that high-level manipulations begin to affect the ERPs 300 ms after the onset of a critical word (Coulson and Kutas, 2001; Coulson and Lovett, 2004). In such models, comprehension is achieved by binding elements of the discourse representation to frames in long-term memory (Coulson, 2001; Lange, 1989). Such models help explain how speakers can rapidly and routinely compute predictions, explanations, and speaker intentions (DeLong, Urbach, and Kutas, 2005; Shastri and Ajjanagadde, 1993).

2.2 *RH and joke comprehension*

Researchers in neuropsychology have long noted that joke comprehension is compromised in patients with RH lesions, especially when there is damage to the anterior portion of the frontal lobe (Brownell et al., 1983; Shammi and Stuss, 1999). In one classic study, right hemisphere-damaged (RHD) patients were given the set-up part for a number of jokes and asked to pick the punch line from an array of three choices: straightforward endings, non sequitur endings, and the correct punch line. While age-matched controls had no trouble choosing the punch lines, RHD patients tended to choose the non sequitur endings, suggesting the patients understood that jokes involve a surprise ending, but were impaired on the frame-shifting process required to reestablish coherence (Brownell et al., 1983).

The pattern of deficits in RHD patients differs dramatically from those evidenced by LHD patients whose communicative difficulties are seemingly more severe. To compare the performance of LHD and RHD patients on joke comprehension, Bihrle and colleagues used both verbal (jokes) and nonverbal (cartoons) materials with the same narrative structure (Bihrle et al., 1986). Whether patients received verbal or non-verbal materials, they were asked to pick the punch line (or punch frame) from an array of four choices: a straightforward ending, a neutral non sequitur, a humorous non sequitur, or the correct punch line. Though both patient groups were impaired on this task, their errors were qualitatively different. In both verbal and nonverbal materials, RHD patients showed a consistent preference for non sequitur endings over straightforward endings and correct punch lines (Bihrle et al., 1986). In contrast, LHD patients (who participated only in the nonverbal task) more often chose the straightforward endings than either of the non sequitur endings (Bihrle et al., 1986). These data suggest the deficits RHD patients experience in the comprehension and production of humor is not attributable to the emotional problems associated with some kinds of RHD, as the RHD patients displayed preserved appreciation of the slapstick depicted in the humorous non sequitur endings.

One attempt to link the deficits observed in RHD patients to hemispheric asymmetries evident in healthy adults is Beeman's coarse coding hypothesis (Beeman and Chiarello, 1998; Beeman et al., 1994). According to this hypothesis, words in the RH are represented by means of wide semantic fields, while words in the LH are represented via a narrow range of features relevant to the immediate discourse context. Although coarse RH semantic activations would predictably include contextually irrelevant information, they might nonetheless be important for the comprehension of figurative language such as that needed to understand jokes. Because jokes frequently require the integration of novel information, the reinterpretation of a word or phrase, and the reinterpretation of the scenario depicted by the preceding context, diffuse RH activation might provide additional information that makes joke processing easier. Similarly, reduced access

to these diffuse semantic activations in RH damaged patients could result in joke comprehension deficits.

Several studies in our laboratory have addressed whether hemispheric differences in semantic activation are relevant for joke comprehension. In one study, we recorded ERPs as healthy adults read laterally presented "punch words" to one-line jokes (Coulson and Williams, 2005). Parafoveal presentation of critical words was intended to affect which cerebral hemisphere received the initial information from the stimulus, and to increase the participation of that hemisphere in the processing of the stimulus. The N400 component was of particular interest, as its amplitude can be interpreted as an index of how hard it is to integrate the meaning of a given word into one's model of the discourse context (Kutas and Hillyard, 1980; Kutas and Van Petten, 1994). As noted above, the critical word in a joke often elicits a larger N400 than a similarly unexpected "straight" ending for the same sentence: the N400 joke effect (Coulson and Kutas, 2001).

We reasoned that if hemispheric differences in semantic activation are relevant for joke comprehension, lateral presentation of joke (GIRL) versus straight (BALL) endings for sentences such as "A replacement player hit a home run with my" would result in different N400 joke effects as a function of visual field of presentation. In this sentence comprehension paradigm, the difficulty of joke comprehension is indexed by the size of the N400 joke effect with larger effects pointing to relatively more processing difficulty. In fact, N400 joke effects were smaller when the critical words were presented to the LVF/RH than the RVF/LH, suggesting joke comprehension was easier with LVF presentation and consistent with the claim that coarse coding in the RH facilitates joke comprehension (Coulson and Williams, 2005).

In a similarly motivated study, we measured ERPs elicited by laterally presented probe words preceded either by a joke or by a non-funny control (Coulson and Wu, 2005). Since all jokes turned on the last word of the sentence, control sentences were formed by replacing the sentence final word with a "straight" ending. For example, the straight ending for "Everyone had so much fun diving from the tree into the swimming pool, we decided to put in a little water," was *platform*. Probes (such as CRAZY) were designed to be related to the meaning of the joke, but unrelated to the meaning of the straight control. In this sentence prime paradigm, the activation of information relevant to joke comprehension was signaled by differences in the size of the N400 elicited by related versus unrelated probes. The more active the joke-related information was, the larger the N400 relatedness effect could be expected to be. Consistent with the coarse coding hypothesis, we found larger N400 relatedness effects with LVF/RH presentation suggesting joke-related information was more active in the RH (see also Hull et al., 2005) for comparable evidence using behavioral measures).

However, it is important not to construe jokes as a monolithic language phenomenon. The word play in puns, for example, is different from that in the more semantically based jokes discussed earlier. This difference lies chiefly in its reliance on the retrieval of word meanings over the more inferential demands of semantic jokes. While semantic jokes begin by suggesting one interpretation of the discourse situation only to replace it with another at the punch line (Giora, 1991; 2003), the point of puns is simply to promote both meanings of an ambiguous word or phrase.

Coulson and Severens addressed hemispheric sensitivity to the different meanings of a pun using a sentence prime paradigm with puns and pun-related probe words (Coulson and Severens, 2007). We recorded ERPs as healthy adults listened to puns and read probe words presented in either participants' left or right visual hemifields. Probe words were *highly related* to the pun that preceded them, *moderately related* to the pun that preceded them, or *unrelated* to the pun that preceded them. For example, the highly related probe for "During branding cowboys have sore calves," was *cow* and the moderately related probe was *leg*.

The activation of pun-related information was assessed by the presence of relatedness effects on the N400 component of the ERP and on positive waveforms that frequently follow the N400 such as the late positive complex (LPC). With an ISI of zero ms, we observed similarly sized priming effects for both the highly and moderately related probes with RVF (LH) presentation; with LVF (RH) presentation, we observed priming for the highly but not the moderately related probes. With an ISI of 500 ms, we observed similarly sized N400 relatedness effects for highly and moderately related probes with presentation to the RVF (LH) as well as the LVF (RH). In addition, RVF (LH), but not LVF (RH) presentation, resulted in a larger centro-parietally distributed LPC for related probes. In sum, these results suggest that initially both meanings of a pun were equally active in the LH while only the highly related probes were active in the RH. By 500 ms after the offset of the pun, both meanings were available in both hemispheres.

The LH advantage observed (Coulson and Severens, 2007) may reflect the importance of this hemisphere (especially the left frontal lobe) in coding the association between a word's form and its meaning. In fact, a neuroimaging study that compared semantic jokes with non-funny controls revealed bilateral temporal lobe activations, while an analogous comparison using puns revealed left frontal activations (Goel and Dolan, 2001). Whereas the temporal lobe activation presumably reflects memory processes necessary for the inferential demands of jokes, the frontal activations to puns were consistent with the need to retrieve word meanings.

3 Metaphor

A speaker uses a metaphor whenever he or she refers to one domain with vocabulary more generally associated with another. For example, in "I made some good arguments, but he crushed me with statistics," the speaker uses a term of physical combat, (*crushed*), to discuss the outcome of a verbal argument. Linguistic accounts of metaphor propose that metaphors reflect the output of a cognitive process by which we understand one domain in terms of another (Lakoff and Johnson, 1980). Because classical accounts of metaphor comprehension (Grice, 1975; Searle, 1979) depict a two-stage model in which literal processing is followed by metaphorical processing, many empirical studies have addressed the time course of metaphor processing. Because ERPs provide a real-time index of brain activity related to language comprehension, they have been used to test various models of metaphor comprehension.

3.1 *Electrophysiological studies of metaphor comprehension*

Pynte and colleagues (1996), for example, used ERPs to address the validity of three hypotheses about metaphor comprehension: the standard model, the parallel hypothesis, and the context-dependent hypothesis. First, the *standard pragmatic model* posits two discrete stages of metaphor processing, as metaphorical meanings are accessed only after the literal meaning has been rejected. This model predicts an initial effect of metaphoricity on the N400, reflecting the literal incongruity, followed by a later ERP effect, reflecting the access of the metaphorical meaning. However, although metaphors (*Those fighters are* lions) elicited slightly larger N400s than literal controls (*Those animals are* lions) there were no reliable ERP effects after the N400, viz. between 600 and 1200 ms after the onset of the sentence final word. Pynte and colleagues thus suggested that the enhanced N400 to the metaphors reflected participants' apprehension of the literal incongruity of these sentences, as predicted by the model. However, the absence of late ERP effects is contrary to the predictions of the standard model.

In contrast to the standard model, the *parallel hypothesis* is that literal and metaphorical meanings are processed in parallel. According to the parallel model, if N400 amplitude reflects the difficulty of comprehending literal meanings, it should also reflect the difficulty of comprehending metaphorical meanings. The parallel model thus entails that differences in the comprehensibility of familiar versus unfamiliar metaphors should be reflected in N400 amplitude. However, when presented out of context, Pynte et al. found no differences in ERPs elicited by familiar metaphors such as "*Those fighters are* lions," and unfamiliar metaphors such as "*Those apprentices are* lions."

The *context-dependent hypothesis* is the idea that the metaphorical meaning is directly accessed when it is relevant to the preceding context. To test this hypothesis, Pynte and colleagues recorded ERPs as participants read sentences with familiar and unfamiliar metaphors placed in either relevant (e.g., for the lion example, "*They are not cowardly*,") or irrelevant (e.g., "*They are not idiotic*,") contexts. The context-dependent hypothesis predicts that regardless of the familiarity of the metaphor, the relevance of the context should modulate N400 amplitude. Accordingly, Pynte et al. found that while metaphor familiarity did not affect the ERPs, the relevance of the context did. Compared to the relevant contexts, metaphors in irrelevant contexts elicited more negative ERPs in both the N400 window and the subsequent 600–100 ms interval, suggesting irrelevant metaphors were more difficult to process.

Further evidence that metaphorical meanings are activated very early in the processing stream comes from an ERP study of the metaphor interference effect (MIE). The MIE is elicited in a sentence verification paradigm in which the subject is given literally true, literally false, and metaphorically true (but literally false) sentences. The MIE refers to the increased response times to reject metaphorically true sentences such as "*The divorce is a nightmare*," compared to literally false sentences such as "*The divorce is a table*" (Glucksberg, Gildea, and Bookin, 1982). Because the task demands that the participant attend only to the literal meaning of these sentences, the MIE is interpreted as reflecting the automatic activation of metaphoric meanings.

Kazmerski and colleagues recorded ERPs as healthy participants judged the literal truth of sentences such as "*Tulips grow from a bulb*," "*The beaver is a lumberjack*," and "*The rumor is a lumberjack*." They observed an MIE in participants' reaction times, as it took participants longer to respond "no" to the metaphorical sentences than their literal counterparts (Kazmerski, Blasko, and Dessalegn, 2003). Interestingly, the MIE was only eleven ms in participants with low IQ (<100), but was thirty-five ms in participants with high IQ (>115). The ERP correlates of the MIE included a smaller N400 for the metaphorically true sentences than the literally false sentences, suggesting participants found metaphorical words easier to process than the anomalous endings, as well as a larger late positivity for the metaphors, perhaps reflecting the greater difficulty in responding "no" to these items. Moreover, these ERP effects were marked and robust in the high IQ group, but largely absent in the low IQ group whose behavioral MIE was also negligible.

Research to date thus suggests that, contrary to the standard model of metaphor comprehension, metaphoric meanings are available quite early in processing, affecting the ERPs beginning 250–300 ms after the onset of a metaphorical word (Kazmerski et al., 2003; Pynte, 1996). Decontextualized metaphors elicit slightly larger N400s than plausible literal controls such as "*Those animals are lions*," (Pynte, 1996), suggesting they place more demands on semantic integration processes. However, metaphors elicit smaller N400s than implausible literal controls such as "*The rumor is a lumberjack*," (Kazmerski et al., 2003), suggesting they are easier to process than incongruous sentence completions. This latter finding casts doubt on the suggestion that the enhanced N400 (relative to plausible literal endings) elicited by metaphors indexes their literal incongruity.

Coulson and Van Petten have suggested that N400 amplitude to metaphors is driven by the complexity of mapping and blending operations involved in the comprehension of metaphors, but also in the comprehension of literal language (Coulson and Van Petten,

2002). In our model, metaphor comprehension involves coordinating various conceptual domains in a *blend*, a hybrid model that consists of structure from multiple conceptual domains, and that often develops emergent structure of its own. Metaphor comprehension involves the temporary construction of simple cognitive models along with the establishment of mappings, or systematic correspondences among objects and relationships represented in various models. Mappings are based on relationships such as identity, similarity, or analogy. Consequently, metaphoric meanings – that use analogy to link objects in different spaces – do not fundamentally differ from meanings that employ other sorts of mappings.

For instance, understanding the metaphor in "*All the nurses at the hospital say that surgeon is a butcher*," requires coordinating conceptual structures associated with surgery, butchery, and a blend of the two. To understand this metaphor it is necessary to apprehend mappings between surgeon and butcher, patient and dead animal (e.g., cow), as well as scalpel and cleaver. However, it also involves construction of a blended model that integrates some information from each of the two domains. In this example, the blend inherits the goals of the surgeon, and the means and manner of the butcher. The inference that the surgeon is incompetent arises when these structures are integrated to create a hypothetical agent with both characteristics.

Similar conceptual operations are involved in understanding literal language. For example, understanding *butcher* in "*During the war, that surgeon had to work as a butcher*," also requires the comprehender to establish mappings and integrate information about a surgeon's training and skill with general information about butchers, and other aspects of the context (Coulson and Matlock, 2001). One might for instance, infer that the surgeon in question was over-qualified for his job, or that he was forced to work as a butcher in a labor camp. Differences in the comprehensibility of these *butcher* sentences, then, might be less a matter of their figurativity than the extent to which they require the comprehender to activate additional information to establish mappings and elaborate the blend.

To test these ideas, Coulson and Van Petten (2002) compared ERPs elicited by words in three different contexts on a continuum from literal to figurative, as suggested by conceptual integration theory (Fauconnier and Turner, 1998). For the literal end of the continuum, they used sentences that prompted a literal reading of the last term, as in *"He knows that whiskey is a strong intoxicant."* At the metaphoric end of the continuum, they used sentences such as *"He knows that power is a strong intoxicant."* The literal mapping condition, hypothesized to fall somewhere between the literal and the metaphoric uses, involved sentences such as, *"He has used cough syrup as an intoxicant."* Literal mapping stimuli employed fully literal uses of words in ways hypothesized to include some of the same conceptual operations as in metaphor comprehension. These sentences described cases in which one object was substituted for another, one object was mistaken for another, or one object was used to represent another – all contexts that require the comprehender to set up a mapping, that is, understand a correspondence, between the two objects in question and the domains in which they typically occur.

In the time window in which the N400 is observed (300–500 ms post onset), ERPs in all three conditions were qualitatively similar, displaying similar waveshape and scalp topography, suggesting that processing was similar for all three sorts of contexts. Moreover, as predicted, N400 amplitude differed as a function of the metaphoricity, with literals eliciting the least N400, literal mappings the next most, and metaphors the most N400, suggesting a concomitant gradient of processing difficulty. The graded N400 difference argues against the literal/figurative dichotomy inherent in the standard model, and suggests processing difficulty associated with figurative language is related to the complexity of mapping and conceptual integration.

Although the comprehension of metaphoric meanings poses a challenge that is greater than that associated with literal language of comparable syntactic complexity, there does not seem to be much evidence to support a view of metaphor comprehension as involving a qualitatively distinct processing mode. ERP studies of metaphor comprehension suggest metaphoric meanings are active during the same temporal interval as literal meanings (Kazmerski et al., 2003). As in the case of literal language, semantic integration difficulty of metaphoric language is largely a function of contextual support (Pynte, 1996), and may also be attributable to demands of conceptual mapping and blending operations (Coulson and Van Petten, 2002).

3.2 *RH in metaphor comprehension*

The early theory that the comprehension abilities of the right hemisphere were especially suited for metaphor was based on sparse data, and may have also suffered from the assumption that all forms of "nonstandard" language use – metaphor, humor, sarcasm, and so forth – had the same neural bases. Although there is some evidence from the patient literature for greater right than left hemisphere involvement in metaphor processing, use of the hemifield priming paradigm has yielded mixed findings on hemispheric asymmetries in metaphor comprehension (see Kacinik and Chiarello, 2007 for review).

In the first such study, Anaki and colleagues had healthy adult participants read centrally presented words with literal and metaphoric meanings and then make lexical decisions to target words presented peripherally (Anaki, Faust, and Kravets, 1998). If the prime was *stinging*, for example, the target might be a word (such as *bee*) related to the literal meaning of the prime, or a word (such as *insult*) related to the prime's metaphorical meaning. When the stimulus onset asynchrony (SOA) was short (200 ms), both meanings were primed with RVF presentation, but only the metaphoric meaning was primed with LVF presentation. When the SOA was long enough to index controlled processes (800 ms), only the literal meaning was primed with RVF presentation, and only the metaphorical meaning was primed with LVF presentation. Anaki and colleagues argued that these findings suggest metaphoric meanings are initially activated in both cerebral hemispheres, but decay rapidly in the LH while being maintained in the RH.

Unfortunately, subsequent attempts to replicate results reported by Anaki and colleagues have failed. Using English materials, Kacinik found literal (stinging BEE) and metaphoric (stinging INSULT) priming with RVF/LH presentation at short SOAs, but only literal priming with an 800 ms SOA. With LVF/RH presentation, literal priming was observed at SOAs of 100, 200, and 800 ms, while metaphor priming was evident only in accuracy scores, suggesting the activation of the metaphoric meaning in the RH was weak at best (Kacinik, 2003). Further, hemifield priming studies using sentential stimuli have revealed priming for both literal and metaphorical meanings with presentation to both visual fields (Kacinik and Chiarello, 2007), and even shown more pronounced metaphor priming with presentation to the RVF (Faust and Weisper, 2000).

In Coulson and Van Petten (2007), participants read centrally presented sentence contexts that promoted either a literal or a metaphorical meaning of the sentence-final word, which was presented in either the left or the right visual field. Despite other indications that hemifield presentation shifted the balance of activity between the two hemispheres during both early (N1) and later (post-N400 positivity) stages of processing, the ERP differences between metaphoric and matched literal sentence completions were essentially identical after RVF and LVF presentation.

In a PET study of neurologically intact adults, Bottini and colleagues observed greater blood flow increase in the right hemisphere when participants read blocks of sentences containing metaphors than when they read literal control sentences (Bottini et al., 1994). However, a more recent functional magnetic resonance imaging (fMRI) study in which task difficulty was well-matched for literal and metaphorical sentences revealed additional LH activation for metaphors (Rapp et al., 2004). Other studies in which investigators have made significant efforts to control for task difficulty have revealed LH activations in comparisons of literal versus metaphorical meanings (Lee and Dapretto, 2006; Rapp et al., 2005, submitted). Right hemisphere recruitment may depend on overall task difficulty rather than the figurativity of the meanings (Coulson and Van Petten, 2002).

A systematic review of frontal hemodynamic activity reveals that, as a wide variety of tasks becomes more difficult, bilateral increases in restricted areas of frontal cortex are observed, as well as additional RH activation in mid-ventrolateral areas (Duncan and Owen, 2000). Other fMRI studies in healthy adults indicate that when literal sentence comprehension places increased demands upon lexical and syntactic processes, increased activation in both classic LH language areas and in their RH homologues are observed (Keller, Carpenter, and Just, 2001). In general, RH activation is associated with complex sentences and discourse-level processing (Bookheimer, 2002; Kircher et al., 2001; St. George et al., 1999), suggesting that semantic complexity triggers the recruitment of RH areas.

The hemifield presentation paradigm employed in Coulson and Van Petten (2007) had measurable effects both on participants' behavior and their event-related brain response. However, hemifield presentation did not modulate the size of the N400 metaphoricity effect, suggesting that both hemispheres are sensitive to the processing difficulty engendered by metaphorically used nouns in sentence contexts. These data are consistent with other recent studies that argue against a privileged role for the RH in metaphor comprehension, and are in keeping with the claim that the brain does not treat literal and metaphoric language as qualitatively distinct categories.

Interestingly, Coulson and Van Petten's results contrast with those discussed earlier that indicate the RH *does* play an important role in joke comprehension (Coulson and Lovett, 2004; Coulson and Williams, 2005; Coulson and Wu, 2005). This may reflect the fact that appreciation of a joke requires listeners to suppress previously computed inferences and to exploit nonsalient aspects of contextual knowledge that may be more prominent in the right hemisphere. Because there are many different ways that linguistic utterances can diverge from literality, we should expect to observe a similar diversity in networks of brain areas recruited to comprehend them. We suggest that just as the brain areas activated in the comprehension of literal language differ as a function of the degree to which visual imagery or emotions are evoked (Ferstl, Rinck, and Cramon, 2005; Just et al., 2003), the comprehension of nonliteral language is likely to recruit different brain areas depending on the cognitive processes it engenders. Neural resources recruited for metaphor comprehension have been found to vary as a function of factors such as the novelty and complexity of the mapping that also impact the comprehension of literal language (Coulson and Van Petten, 2002; Mashal et al., 2007). Given that metaphoric mapping is a basic mechanism of meaning extension, perhaps it is not surprising that both hemispheres are similarly sensitive to metaphoric meaning.

4 Cognitive neuroscience of figurative language

As we progress through the twenty-first century, it will be important to move beyond the traditional question of the right hemisphere's role in metaphor comprehension to address the particular cognitive and neural underpinnings of this complex process. By combining information from the study of brain-injured patients with behavioral, electrophysiological, and imaging data from healthy participants, it is possible to learn a great deal about the neural substrate of particular cognitive processes. In particular, research on the sensorimotor grounding of concepts and research on the neural instantiation of cross-domain mappings are areas of great promise in the study of metaphor, and potentially for other varieties of figurative language as well.

4.1 *Sensorimotor grounding of concepts*

An exciting development in neuroimaging research is the finding that the neural substrate of action and perception is often exploited in higher cognitive activities, including conceptualization that may be important for language comprehension. Sensory regions, for example, are active during sensory processing as well as during sensory imagery (Kosslyn et al., 1995). Motor regions are active during the execution of action, but also during motor imagery, as well as during the perception of the motor actions of others (Decety et al., 1997; Deiber et al., 1998; Jeannerod and Decety, 1995; Jeannerod and Frak, 1999).

A series of studies suggests further that modality-specific areas become active in conceptual tasks; for example, color processing regions (i.e., V4) are active for color concepts, motion processing areas (MT/MST) are active for conceptualizing motion, and shape (infero-temporal) versus motor (premotor cortex) processing regions for animals versus tools, respectively (Martin, 2001; Martin and Chao, 2001). One issue for future research is whether modality-specific activation occurs in the comprehension of metaphors, idioms, or other sorts of figurative language.

Reasoning on the basis of neural learning mechanisms, Pulvermuller and colleagues have long argued that the neural representation of word meaning must differ as a function of our experience with what those words represent (Braitenberg and Pulvermuller, 1992; Pulvermuller, 1996, 1999). Hebbian learning, for example, is a mechanism by which connection strength between two neurons increases as a function of correlated firing. Because we might expect that words for objects would tend to co-occur with the visual experience of those objects, correlated firing patterns between the neural representations of the word forms and the associated visual experiences would result in the establishment of permanent connections between their neural substrates. Similarly, because words for actions would tend to co-occur with motor activity, simple Hebbian learning would result in connections between activity in motor cortex and the neural representation of action words (Pulvermuller, 2003).

Similarly, in the neural theory of language (NTL), it has been proposed that language comprehension involves simulating the situation being described (Feldman and Narayanan, 2004). For example, the simulation semantics of NTL suggests that cortical networks that subserve the action of grasping also serve as the neural substrate of the meaning of *grasp*. Because metaphor involves exploiting concepts from a concrete domain to understand a more abstract one, this framework suggests that networks that subserve the action of grasping are also activated to understand the metaphorical meaning of *grasp*. Conceptual blending theory, which suggests that "grasping an idea" involves the parallel activation of an abstract and a concrete meaning of grasp, also makes this prediction (Coulson and Matlock, 2001).

Recent findings suggest the representation of word meaning extends beyond the classic language areas identified by neuropsychologists (Damasio et al., 1996; Tranel et al., 1997), and raise the possibility that the neural substrate of metaphor comprehension depends on the particular source (vehicle) and target (topic) domains of the metaphor. In this framework, one would not expect metaphorical meanings to be processed in a single brain area, or even a particular network of brain areas. Rather, action metaphors would be expected to recruit brain areas underlying the comprehension of action, while spatial metaphors would be expected to recruit brain areas that subserve spatial cognition.

The idea that conceptual knowledge is grounded in sensorimotor experience is closely related to the claim in cognitive linguistics that metaphoric understandings of abstract domains recruit concepts from more experientially basic ones (Lakoff and Nunez, 2000). One example for which there is some empirical support is that the abstract concept of numbers is understood by recruiting spatial concepts in the metaphor of numbers as points on a spatially extended line. Inherent in the concept of a number line, this metaphor posits a mapping or correspondence between particular numbers and particular regions in space, such that quantity goes from left to right, with the largest numbers mapping onto the right-most regions of the line.

This predicts that neural structures that support spatial reasoning will be systematically recruited in numerical operations, and that damage to brain structures involved in spatial reasoning will also have a detrimental effect on numerical calculations that recruit the mental number line. In fact, neuroimaging studies show that right intraparietal areas important for visuospatial processing are consistently activated by number comparison tasks (Chochon et al., 1999; Pinel et al., 2001). Further, the prediction of damage to the underlying substrate of visuospatial processing is borne out by the fact that hemineglect impacts various arithmetic tasks.

Hemineglect is a neurological condition resulting from lesions to the RH parietal lobe in which the patient has difficulty attending to objects on the left side of space. Consistent with a mapping between numbers and regions of space, hemineglect patients have been shown to be impaired when making judgments about numbers to the left of a reference number on a linear number line. For example, when asked to judge whether numeric stimuli were greater or less than five, patients with neglect were slower to respond to four than to six; when asked to judge whether numeric stimuli were greater or less than seven, patients with neglect were slower to respond to six than eight (Vuilleumier, Ortigue, and Brugger, 2004). These findings argue strongly for the reality of a mapping between the domains of space and number.

5 Conclusion

Cognitive neuroscience data argue for a dynamic, context-sensitive language processor capable of handling a diverse array of figurative language phenomena. Indeed, this context sensitivity may arise naturally out of the way in which information is stored in the brain. Modern neuroscientists understand memory as experience-driven changes in the brain that affect subsequent behavior (e.g., Fuster, 1997). The fundamental mechanism for memory formation is Hebbian learning, in which synaptic connections between neurons are strengthened as a result of temporally coincident firing ("cells that fire together wire together"). Associations result in the formation of cell assemblies that serve as the functional units of memory, and "retrieval" is the transient activation of a cell assembly.

As memory is stored in overlapping and distributed networks of neurons, spatial metaphors for memory are not particularly apt. Information in memory does not exist in a particular place, but rather is inherent in the connections between the neurons in a cell assembly that facilitates their synchronous activity. The same neurons that mediate experience – perception and action in the world – also mediate memory for that experience. Further, because of the transient nature of cell assemblies, semantic memory representations are not constant, but change as a function of experience and context. The idea of language comprehension as a process of activating and linking information in memory follows naturally from neural processing mechanisms that are fundamentally constructive. Indeed, the commonplace nature of figurative language may reflect the fact that meaning construction processes are fundamentally imaginative.

References

Anaki, D., Faust, M., & Kravets, S. (1998). Cerebral hemispheric asymmetries in processing lexical metaphors. *Neuropsychologia, 36*, 353–62.

Beeman, M. J. & Chiarello, C. (1998). Complementary right- and left-hemisphere language comprehension. *Current Directions in Psychological Science, 7(1)*, 2–8.

Beeman, M. J., Friedman, R., Grafman, J., Perez, E., Diamond, S., & Lindsay, M. (1994). Summation priming and coarse coding in the right hemisphere. *Journal of Cognitive Neuroscience, 6*, 26–45.

Bihrle, A., Brownell, H., & Gardner, H. (1986). Comprehension of humorous and nonhumorous materials by left- and right- brain damaged patients. *Brain & Cognition, 5*, 399–411.

Bookheimer, S. (2002). Functional MRI of language: new approaches to understanding the cortical organization of semantic processing. *Annu Rev Neurosci, 25*, 151–88.

Bottini, G., Corcoran, R., Sterzi, R., Paulesu, E., Schenone, P., Scarpa, P., et al. (1994). The role of the right hemisphere in the interpretation of figurative aspects of language: A positron emission tomography activation study. *Brain, 117*, 1241–53.

Braitenberg, V. & Pulvermuller, F. (1992). Entwurf einer neurologischen Theorie der Sprache. *Naturwissenschaften, 79*, 103–17.

Brownell, H., Michel, D., Powelson, J., & Gardner, H. (1983). Surprise but not coherence: Sensitivity to verbal humor in right-hemisphere patients. *Brain & Language, 18*, 20–7.

Chochon, F., Cohen, L., van de Moortele, P., & Dehaene, S. (1999). Differential contributions of the left and right inferior parietal lobules to number processing. *Journal of Cognitive Neuroscience, 11(6)*, 617–30.

Coulson, S. (2001). *Semantic Leaps: Frame-shifting and Conceptual Blending in Meaning Construction*. Cambridge, UK: Cambridge University Press.

Coulson, S. & Kutas, M. (2001). Getting it: Human event-related brain response in good and poor comprehenders. *Neuroscience Letters, 316*, 71–4.

Coulson, S. & Lewandowska-Tomaszczyk, B. (Eds.). (2005). *The Literal and Nonliteral in Language and Thought*. Frankfurt: Peter Lang.

Coulson, S. & Lovett, C. (2004). Handedness, hemispheric asymmetries, and joke comprehension. *Cognitive Brain Research, 19*, 275–88.

Coulson, S. & Matlock, T. (2001). Metaphor and the space structuring model. *Metaphor & Symbol, 16*, 295–316.

Coulson, S. & Severens, E. (2007). Hemispheric asymmetry and pun comprehension: When cowboys have sore calves. *Brain and Language, 100*, 172–87.

Coulson, S. & Van Petten, C. (2002). Conceptual integration and metaphor: An ERP study. *Memory & Cognition, 30(6)*, 958–68.

(2007). A special role for the right hemisphere in metaphor comprehension? ERP evidence from hemifield presentation. *Brain Research, 1146*, 128–45.

Coulson, S. & Williams, R. W. (2005). Hemispheric asymmetries and joke comprehension. *Neuropsychologia, 43*, 128–41.

Coulson, S. & Wu, Y. C. (2005). Right hemisphere activation of joke-related information: An event-related potential study. *Journal of Cognitive Neuroscience, 17(3)*, 494–506.

Damasio, H., Grabowski, T. J., Tranel, D., Hichwa, R. D., & Damasio, A. R. (1996). A neural basis for lexical retrieval. *Nature, 380(6574)*, 499–505.

Decety, J., Grezes, J., Costes, N., Parani, D., Jeannerod, M., Procyk, E., et al. (1997). Brain activity during observation of actions: Influence of action content and subject's strategy. *Brain, 120*, 1763–77.

Deiber, M. P., Ibanez, V., Honda, M., Sadato, N., Raman, R., & Hallett, M. (1998). Cerebral processes related to visuomotor imagery and generation of simple finger movements studied with positron emission tomography. *Neuroimage, 7(2)*, 73–85.

DeLong, K., Urbach, T., & Kutas, M. (2005). Probabilistic word pre-activation during language comprehension inferred from electrical brain activity. *Nature Neuroscience, 3*, 1117–21.

Duncan, J. & Owen, A. (2000). Common regions of the human frontal lobe recruited by diverse cognitive demands. *Trends Neurosci, 23*, 475–83.

Fauconnier, G. & Turner, M. (1998). Conceptual integration networks. *Cognitive Science, 22*, 133–87.

Faust, M. & Weisper, S. (2000). Understanding metaphoric sentences in the two cerebral hemispheres. *Brain & Cognition, 43(1–3)*, 186–91.

Feldman, J. & Narayanan, S. (2004). Embodied meaning in a neural theory of language. *Brain and Language, 89(2)*, 385–92.

Ferstl, E., Rinck, M., & Cramon, D. V. (2005). Emotional and temporal aspects of situation model processing during text comprehension: An event-related fMRI study. *Journal of Cognitive Neuroscience, 17*, 724–39.

Fillmore, C. J. (1976). The need for frame semantics within linguistics. *Statistical Methods in Linguistics, 12(5)*, 5–29.

Fuster, J. (1997). Network memory. *Trends in Neurosciences, 20*, 451–9.

Gewirtz, P. (1996). On "I know it when I see it." *Yale Law Journal, 105*, 1023–47.

Gibbs, R., Wilson, N., & Bryant, G. (this volume). Figurative language: Normal adult cognitive research.

Giora, R. (1991). On the cognitive aspects of the joke. *Journal of Pragmatics, 16*, 465–85.

——— (2003). *On Our Mind: Salience, Context, and Figurative Language*. New York: Oxford University Press.

——— (2007). Is metaphor special? *Brain & Language, 100(2)*, 111–14.

Glucksberg, S., Gildea, P., & Bookin, H. B. (1982). On understanding nonliteral speech: Can people ignore metaphors? *Journal of Verbal Learning & Verbal Behavior, 21(1)*, 85–98.

Goel, V. & Dolan, R. J. (2001). The functional anatomy of humor: Segregating cognitive and affective components. *Nature Neuroscience, 4*, 237–8.

Grice, H. (1975). Logic and conversation. In Morgan, PCJ (Ed.) *Syntax and Semantics: Vol. 3, Speech Acts*. New York: Academic Press.

Hecaen, H. & Consoli, S. (1973). Analyse des troubles de language au cours del lesions de l'aire de Broca. *Neuropsychologia, 11*, 377–88.

Hull, R., Chen, H. C., Vaid, J., & Martinez, F. (2005). Great expectations: Humor comprehension across hemispheres. *Brain & Cognition, 57*, 281–2.

Jeannerod, M. & Decety, J. (1995). Mental motor imagery: A window into the representational stages of action. *Current Opinion in Neurology, 5(6)*, 727–32.

Jeannerod, M. & Frak, V. (1999). Mental imaging of motor activity in humans. *Current Opinion in Neurobiology, 5(6)*, 735–9.

Joanette, Y., Goulet, P., & Hannequin, D. (1990). *Right hemisphere and verbal communication*. New York: Springer-Verlag.

Just, M. A., Newman, S., Keller, T. A., McEleny, A., & Carpenter, P. A. (2003). Imagery in sentence comprehension: An fMRI study. *NeuroImage, 21*, 112–24.

Kacinik, N. A. (2003). *Hemispheric Processing of Literal and Metaphoric Language*. Unpublished doctoral dissertation. University of California, Riverside.

Kacinik, N. A. & Chiarello, C. (2007). Understanding metaphors: Is the right hemisphere uniquely involved? *Brain and Language, 100*, 188–207.

Kazmerski, V., Blasko, D., & Dessalegn, B. (2003). ERP and behavioral evidence of individual differences in metaphor comprehension. *Memory and Cognition, 31(5)*, 673–89.

Keller, T. A., Carpenter, P. A., & Just, M. A. (2001). The neural bases of sentence comprehension: a fMRI examination of syntactic and lexical processing. *Cereb Cortex, 11(3)*, 223–37.

Kircher, T., Brammer, M. J., Andreu, N., Williams, S., & McGuire, P. K. (2001). Engagement of right temporal cortex during processing of linguistic context. *Neuropsychologia, 39*, 798–809.

Kosslyn, S. M., Thompson, W. L., Kim, I. J., & Alpert, N. M. (1995). Topographic representations of mental images in primary visual cortex. *Nature*, 378, 6556.

Kutas, M. & Hillyard, S. A. (1980). Reading senseless sentences: Brain potentials reflect semantic incongruity. *Science*, 207, 203–5.

Kutas, M., Lindamood, T., & Hillyard, S. A. (1984). Word expectancy and event-related brain potentials during sentence processing. In Requin, SKJ (Ed.) *Preparatory States and Processes* (pp. 217–37). Hillsdale, NJ: Erlbaum.

Kutas, M. & Van Petten, C. (1994). Psycholinguistics electrified. In Gernsbacher, M. (Ed.), *Handbook of Psycholinguistics* (pp. 83–143). San Diego, CA: Academic Press.

Lakoff, G. (1987). *Women, Fire, and Dangerous Things: What Categories Reveal about the Mind*. Chicago: University of Chicago Press.

Lakoff, G. & Johnson, M. (1980). *Metaphors We Live By*. Chicago: University of Chicago Press.

Lakoff, G. & Nunez, R. (2000). *Where mathematics comes from: How the embodied mind brings mathematics into being*. New York: Basic Books.

Langacker, R. W. (1987). *Foundations of Cognitive Grammar: Theoretical Prerequisites*. Stanford, CA: Stanford University Press.

Lange, T. E. & Dyer, M. G. (1989). High-level inferencing in a connectionist network. *Connection Science*, 1, 181–217.

Lee, S. & Dapretto, M. (2006). Metaphorical vs. literal word meanings: fMRI evidence against a selective role of the right hemisphere. *NeuroImage*, 29, 536–44.

Martin, A. (2001). Functional neuroimaging of semantic memory. In Cabeza, A. (Ed.) *Handbook of Functional Neuroimaging of Cognition* (pp. 153–86). Cambridge: MIT Press.

Martin, A. & Chao, L. (2001). Semantic memory and the brain: Structure and processes. *Current Opinion in Neurobiology*, 11(2), 194–201.

Mashal, N., Faust, M., Hendler, T., & Jung-Beeman, M. (2007). An fMRI investigation of the neural correlates underlying the processing of novel metaphoric expressions. *Brain and Language*, 100, 115–26.

Pinel, P., Dehaene, S., Riviere, D., & Le Bihan, D. (2001). Modulation of parietal activation by semantic distance in a number comparison task. *NeuroImage*, 14, 1013–26.

Pulvermuller, F. (1996). Hebb's concept of cell assemblies and the psychophysiology of word processing. *Psychophysiology*, 33, 317–33.

(1999). Words in the brain's language. *Behavioral and Brain Sciences*, 22, 253–336.

(2003). *The Neuroscience of Language*. Cambridge: Cambridge University Press.

Pynte, J., Besson, M., Robichon, F., & Poli, J. (1996). The time-course of metaphor comprehension: An event-related potential study. *Brain & Language*, 55, 293–316.

Rapp, A., Leube, D., Erb, M., Grodd, W., & Kircher, T. (2004). Neural correlates of metaphor processing. *Cognitive Brain Research*, 20, 395–402.

(2005, submitted). Laterality in metaphor processing: Lack of evidence from Functional Magnetic Resonance Imaging for the right hemisphere theory. *Brain & Language*.

Rehak, A., Kaplan, J., & Gardner, H. (1992). Sensitivity to conversational deviance in right-hemisphere damaged patients. *Brain & Language*, 42, 203–17.

Rugg, M. D. & Coles, M. (Eds.). (1995). *Electrophysiology of Mind: Event-Related Brain Potentials and Cognition*. Oxford, UK: Oxford University Press.

Searle, J. (1979). *Expression and Meaning: Studies in the Theory of Speech Acts*. Cambridge, UK: Cambridge University Press.

Shammi, P., & Stuss, D. T. (1999). Humour appreciation: A role of the right frontal lobe. *Brain*, 122, 657–66.

Shastri, L. (1999). Advances in SHRUTI: A neurally motivated model of relational knowledge representation and inference using temporal synchrony. *Applied Intelligence*, 11, 79–108.

Shastri, L. & Ajjanagadde, V. (1993). From simple associations to systematic reasoning: A connectionist representation of rules, variables, and dynamic bindings using temporal asynchrony. *Behavioral & Brain Sciences*, 16(3), 417–94.

St. George, M., Kutas, M., Martinez, A., & Sereno, M. I. (1999). Semantic integration in reading: engagement of the right hemisphere during discourse processing. *Brain*, 122 (Pt 7), 1317–25.

Tranel, D., Logan, C. G., Frank, R. J., & Damasio, A. R. (1997). Explaining category-related effects in the retrieval of conceptual and lexical knowledge for concrete entities: operationalization and analysis of factors. *Neuropsychologia*, 35(10), 1329–39.

Van Berkum, J. J. A. (this volume). The electrophysiology of discourse and conversation.

Vuilleumier, P., Ortigue, S., & Brugger, P. (2004). The number space and neglect. *Cortex*, 40, 399–410.

Winner, E., & Gardner, H. (1977). The comprehension of metaphor in brain-damaged patients. *Brain*, 100, 719–27.

Section 9

DISCOURSE AND CONVERSATION

CHAPTER 27

Spoken Discourse and Its Emergence

Herbert H. Clark

Language arises when people do things together – buy and sell goods to each other, build things together, entertain each other, sing in groups, or play games. It arises even when people do things together at a distance with books, newspapers, magazines, email, television, or films. Language is an instrument by which people coordinate with each other.

But how? For two people to do anything together – from hugging to negotiating contracts – they must share certain information, including who is participating, in what roles, when, where, and on what. It takes communication to establish this information as shared. To communicate is, as the Latin root suggests, to *make common* – to establish ideas as common among two or more people. One way to communicate is with a language such as English, Japanese, or Lakota. Languages like these are repertoires of techniques for communicating.

Spoken discourse is really the utterances used as two or more people coordinate on an extended joint enterprise. The two prototypical forms of discourse are *dialogue* and *narrative*. I will take up these two forms and show how they emerge as the participants try to coordinate with each other.

1 Dialogue

People communicate in order to carry out *joint activities*. A joint activity is any activity in which two or more participants coordinate with each other to reach what they take to be a common set of goals. Joint activities range from hugging and walking on crowded sidewalks to consulting with doctors and gossiping. Some joint activities (such as gossiping) are coordinated almost entirely with *linguistic* signals, and others (such as walking on crowded sidewalks) almost entirely with *nonlinguistic* signals. Most everyday joint activities are coordinated with a combination of the two – speech as well as gestures of the hands, head, face, eyes, and torso, along with placement and orientation of the body (Clark, 1996, 2003; Kendon, 1990, 2004).

I thank Eve V. Clark, Michelle Gumbrecht, Deborah Hendersen, and Michael Spivey for suggestions on this chapter.

The primary form these take in daily affairs is dialogue – two or more people talking in interaction. When a person named Ken buys a loaf of bread in a bakery, or plans a meeting with a colleague, or gets directions to City Hall, he engages his interlocutor in a dialogue both to establish a common set of goals (buying bread, planning a meeting, or getting directions) and to accomplish these goals. What is remarkable is that the two of them proceed without any prior agenda, reaching their goals one turn at a time. How do they do that?

1.1 *Dialogues in joint activities*

People don't just *happen* to do things together. When Ken and Julia greet as old friends, he cannot proceed to hug her without some sense, belief, or trust that she will do her part of the hug – and do it here and now – and the same goes for her. They coordinate their parts of such joint activities by means of joint commitments. But what joint commitments do they need, and how do they establish them? To illustrate, I will begin with the cooperative assembly of a TV stand.

Two people I will call Ann and Burton were brought into a small room, given the parts of a commercial kit for a wooden TV stand, and asked to assemble the stand from its parts.[1] They took about fifteen minutes and were videotaped as they worked. In one twenty-second segment, they attached a crosspiece onto a sidepiece in a sequence of five paired actions:

	Ann's action	Burton's action
1	A gets crosspiece	B holds sidepiece
2	A holds crosspiece	B inserts peg
3	A affixes crosspiece	B holds sidepiece
4	A inserts peg	B holds side-, crosspiece
5	A affixes sidepiece	B holds side-, crosspiece

In line 3, for example, Burton holds a side-piece steady while Ann affixes the cross-piece onto it. This is a simple joint action. The two coordinate their individual actions (Ann affixes one board while Burton holds the other one steady) in order to reach a common goal (the attachment of the two boards). Ann does what she does contingent on what Burton is doing, and he does what *he* does contingent on what *she* is doing. Viewed together, these five joint actions constitute a joint action at a higher level, "attaching the two sidepieces to the crosspiece," which is one segment of a still higher-level joint action, "assembling the TV stand." Like most joint activities, assembling the TV stand emerges as a *hierarchy* of joint actions (Bangerter and Clark 2003).

But joint activities take more than these joint actions. If we look again at the twenty-second segment, we discover Ann and Burton in a dialogue about what they are doing:[2]

(1)	Ann	Should we put this in, this, this little like kinda cross bar, like the T? like the I bar?
	Burton	Yeah ([we can do that]).
	Ann	So, you wanna stick the ([screws in])? Or wait is, is, are these these things, or?
	Burton	That's these things I bet. Because there's no screws.
	Ann	Yeah, you're right. Yeah, probably. If they'll stay in.
	Burton	I don't know how they'll stay in ([but]).
	Ann	Right there.
	Burton	Is this one big enough?
	Ann	Oh ([xxx]) I guess cause like there's no other side for it to come out.
	Burton	M-hm. [8.15 sec]
	Burton	([Now let's do this one]).
	Ann	Okay.

---

1 I am indebted to Julie Heiser and Barbara Tversky for videotapes of this example (see Heiser and Tversky, 2005).

2 Double parentheses mark uncertain transcriptions and "xxx" marks untranscribable speech.

Ann and Burton's dialogue has a clear purpose: It allows them to arrange, agree on, or coordinate who is to do what, when, and where. Here, too, Ann and Burton carry out paired actions, but the pairs are sequences of turns like this:

(2) Ann   Should we put this in, this, this little like kinda cross bar, like the T? like the I bar?
    Burton   Yeah ([we can do that]).

In the first turn, Ann proposes that they attach the crosspiece, and in the second, Burton takes up her proposal and agrees to it. In these two turns, they establish at least five elements:

a. Participants (Ann, Burton)
b. Roles (Ann, Burton as equal partners)
c. Content (Ann controls crosspiece, Burton controls sidepiece)
d. Place (here)
e. Time (beginning now)

The two of them proceed this way throughout the TV stand assembly, making agreement after agreement about which pieces to connect when, how to orient each piece, who is to hold, and who is to attach.

Most joint activities can be partitioned into two types of actions: a *basic* joint activity, and *coordinating* joint actions. This point is illustrated in Ann and Burton's assembly of the TV stand:

> Basic joint activity. *This is the joint activity proper, or what Ann and Burton are* basically *doing – assembling a TV stand. It consists of the actions and positions they consider essential to their basic goal – assembling the TV stand.*

> Coordinating joint actions. *These are the actions by which Ann and Burton coordinate their basic activity. They consist of* communicative acts *about the basic activity, acts that generally come in pairs.*

It takes both sets of actions to assemble the TV stand. The first set brings about the assembly proper, and the second coordinates the joint actions needed to bring about the assembly proper. Ann and Burton surely see these two activities as different. What they were asked to do was "assemble a TV stand." If asked, "But weren't you talking?" they might have replied, "Oh yes. That was to figure out who was to do what."

1.2 *Projective pairs*

It takes joint commitments for people to do things together. When Ken and Julia hug, he commits himself to taking part in the hug just so long as she does too – at the right time and in the right way – and the same goes for her. If he were to go ahead without the right joint commitments, he might bump her nose, knock her over, or offend her. One way to reach joint commitments is with communicative acts in pairs.

Two people in joint activities pass through *choice points*: What to do next? For example, after Ann and Burton had attached the crosspiece to the two sidepieces, they were at a choice point. They needed to establish a joint commitment to the next course of action. They couldn't count on such a commitment arising spontaneously and simultaneously. They had to *make* it happen:

(3) Burton   ([Now let's do this one.])
           [picking up the toppiece]
    Ann   Okay.

Burton proposed to Ann that the two of them ("let's") assemble the toppiece ("do this one") next ("now"). Ann took up his proposal by agreeing to it ("Okay."). In just two turns, they established a joint commitment to assemble the toppiece next. They specified the participants ("us") and goal ("do this one") as well as the commitments to do their parts in reaching the goal.

The pair of turns in (3) is what Schegloff and Sacks (1973) called an *adjacency pair*. In such pairs, one person produces the first part and another person the second part. The first part is of a type for which it is conditionally relevant for the second part to be of a type *projected* by the first part.

Burton produced a *suggestion*; that projected Ann's *consent* to go ahead as the second part, and Ann immediately gave her consent with "Okay." (see Bangerter and Clark, 2003).

But what is needed here is the more general notion of *projective pair* (Clark, 2004). In Schegloff and Sacks's adjacency pairs, both parts must be spoken turns at talk, yet in many situations, one or both parts of analogous pairs are gestural. Later in assembling the TV stand, Ann and Burton produced this sequence of actions:

(4) Ann   [Extends hand with screw] So
             you want to stick the screws in?
     Burton [Extends hand to take screw]

In line 1, Ann proposed that Burton stick the screws in. In line 2, Burton could take her up with "Okay." Instead, he extended his hand to take the screw. She construed that move as signaling consent roughly as if he had said "Okay." The term *projective pair* is intended to cover adjacency pairs as well as analogous pairs with gestures.

A projective pair consists of a *proposal* plus an *uptake*. By proposal, I mean any signal that raises the possibility, at any strength, of a joint action or position by the initiator and addressee or addressees. By uptake, I mean any action that deals with that possibility. So when Ann makes her proposal to Burton, she is simply initiating a process. Burton has the options of accepting, altering, rejecting, or even disregarding her proposal. Here are examples of these four options.

Full acceptance of proposal. In (4), Ann proposes, "So you want to stick the screws in [extending her hand with a screw]?" Burton could have replied, "No, you do it" or "Hold on. I've got a better idea." Instead, he takes hold of the screw, accepting her proposal *in full*. With this act, they are jointly committed to transferring the screw from her to him.

Altered acceptance of proposal. In (5), Burton asks a question that projects "Yes, it is" or "No, it isn't" as uptake:

(5) Burton Is this one big enough?
     Ann   Oh. ([xxx]) I guess cause like
             there's no other side for it to
             come out.
     Burton M-hm.

In line 2, instead of saying yes or no, Ann formulates an *altered* version of Burton's proposal and accepts that version. He accepts her altered version with "M-hm."

Rejection of proposal. In (6), from another corpus, we find yet another pattern:[3]

(6) Grace Do you think it's a reasonable
            thing to do, – -
     Helen Well. I don't know an awful lot
            about it really, Grace.

Grace's question projects a yes or no answer, but because Helen is unable to provide one, she turns down, or *rejects*, the proposal that she provide one. Although Helen rejects the proposal, she does give her reasons for rejecting it: She doesn't "know an awful lot about it really."

Disregard of proposal. In (7), Ann asks Burton a question, which projects a yes or no in agreement:

(7) Ann   They snap in? [said as she
             snaps the rollers in]
     Burton [Silence, no visible gesture or
             response]

Although Burton presumably has heard Ann, he appears to *disregard* her proposal by going on without addressing it. He appears unwilling to let her engage him in the potential projective pair. He opts out.

Projective pairs are efficient ways of creating joint commitments. When Burton realizes he and Ann need to plan their next joint action, he initiates a projective pair, "Now let's do this one," and Ann completes it, "Okay." With projective pairs people are

---

3 All the remaining examples, except where noted, are from a corpus of British conversation (Svartvik and Quirk, 1980). Brief silences are marked with a period (.), and silences of "one beat" with a dash (-).

really *negotiating* joint commitments. No matter what the first person proposes, the second person has options in taking it up. The joint commitments that emerge are shaped by them both.

1.3 *Types of joint commitments*

What do people make joint commitments about? The answer can be found in the actions in the first and second parts of projective pairs. These actions, traditionally called *illocutionary acts*, fall into four main types (if we exclude certain institutional uses of language) (Austin, 1962; Bach and Harnish, 1979; Searle, 1969, 1975):

a. *Assertives*, such as assertions, claims, statements, denials
b. *Directives*, such as orders, requests, suggestions, questions
c. *Commissives*, such as promises, threats, offers
d. *Expressives*, such as thanks, condolences, apologies, greetings

Illocutionary acts have usually been treated as autonomous. For Searle (1969), a question "counts as an attempt to elicit [certain information] from [the hearer] H." But in (5), when Burton asks, "Is this one big enough?" he isn't trying simply to elicit "yes" or "no." He is proposing that Ann join him in establishing whether or not a particular peg is big enough. In her uptake, she offers useful information, but without saying yes or no. Together, they establish a joint commitment to the proposition, roughly stated, that "the peg is probably big enough because there's no other side for it to come out." This proposition isn't either Ann's or Burton's alone. It is their *joint position* – an amalgam of contributions from them both.

Projective pairs can also be used to establish *joint courses of action*. Recall this exchange from the TV stand assembly:

(3) Burton ([Now let's do this one])
     [picking up the toppiece]
     Ann   Okay.

Burton suggests a course of action with one illocutionary act (a directive), and Ann consents to it with another (a commissive). The result is a joint commitment to a course of action – doing the toppiece next.

In dialogue, then, the participants use projective pairs for establishing both joint positions and joint actions. Here are four major patterns:

Illocutionary act	Projective pair	Commitment
Assertives, expressives	Ann: This is the toppiece. Burton: Yes.	joint position
Questions	Burton: Is this one big enough? Ann: Oh, I guess....	joint position
Action directives	Burton: Now let's do this one. Ann: Okay.	joint action
Commissives	Ann: I'll get that for you. Burton: Okay.	joint action

The joint positions people negotiate include greetings ("Hi," "Hi"), farewells ("Bye," "Bye"), apologies ("Sorry," "Oh, that's okay"), and other information ("Where is your office?" "In the Strand"). The joint actions include both conditional actions ("Have a beer," "Thanks") and coerced actions ("Sit down," "Yes, sir").

1.4 *Sections of dialogues*

If dialogues proceed one turn at a time, how do participants establish commitments to broader joint activities? One way is by projecting entire sections of dialogues. One of these techniques is illustrated here:

(8) Duncan   Edgar, I I . may I ask you a question? [*pre-question*]
    Edgar   Surely. [*uptake of pre-question*] [Duncan and Edgar exchange fifteen turns as Duncan describes an author's claim about Danish usage.]

| Duncan | It is really so, that that is the common usage in Denmark? I don't know if you've heard, of that. [*question proper*] |
| Edgar | - – umm. I'm. I would be surprised if it was accepted usage. [*answer to question proper*] |

Duncan's first turn is what Schegloff (1980) called a *pre-question*. With it Duncan proposes to ask Edgar a question, and Edgar agrees. Duncan now has the freedom to take up preliminaries to his question, and it takes the two of them fifteen turns to do that. Only then does Duncan ask his question and Edgar answer it. Pre-questions project not just the eventual question, but preliminaries to that question.

Pre-questions and their responses belong to a large family of so-called *pre-sequences*. Here are a few more examples (from various sources):

Pre-request	Customer	Do you have hot chocolate?
	Waitress	Yes, we do.
Pre-invitation	Man	What are you doing?
	Woman	Nothing. What's up?
Pre-narrative	June	Did I tell you I'm going to Scotland?
	Kenneth	No.
Pre-conversation	Caller	[rings telephone]
	Recipient	Miss Pink's office.

Each pre-sequence prepares the way for another joint action. The pre-request sets up a request ("I'll have one"); the pre-invitation sets up an invitation ("Would you like…"); the pre-narrative sets up a narrative; and the pre-conversation sets up an entire telephone conversation.

With techniques like this, conversations often emerge as a sequence of topics, or sections. Each section reflects a different phase in the overall joint activity – the next bit of gossip, the next segment of the vacation being planned, the next issue of the contract being negotiated. The participants must agree on the opening and closing of each section, and that is where pre-sequences are useful.

Sections consisting of narratives (jokes, anecdotes, stories) are often introduced by a pre-narrative and its response (Sacks, 1975), as here:

(9)	Nancy	I acquired an absolutely magnificent sewing machine by foul means. Did I tell you about that? [*pre-narrative*]
	Kate	No. [*response*]
	Nancy	Well, when I was . doing freelance advertising – [proceeds to give a five-minute narrative]

Nancy proposes to tell Kate a story ("Did I tell you about that?"), and Kate accepts ("No"). That allows Nancy to embark on her narrative – an extended section of the conversation. It takes both parties to agree, because the recipient can always decline, as in this example:

(10)	Connie	Did I tell you, when we were in this African village, and [- they were all out in the fields, – the]
	Irene	[yes you did, yes, – yes]
	Connie	babies left alone, -
	Irene	yes.

Irene interrupts Connie (the speech in brackets is overlapping) to say that she *has* heard the story, and the two of them then go down a different path. Dialogue is opportunistic: The paths people take depend on the opportunities that become available with each agreement. Nancy and Connie use their pre-narratives to find the best way to proceed and, receiving different replies, go different directions. People often signal which opportunities they are taking by using *discourse markers* (Schiffrin, 1987). For example, Nancy used "well" to signal that she was introducing a change in perspective as she began her story. Other discourse markers indicate the start of a new topic (e.g., "so," "then," "speaking of that"), the start of a digression ("incidentally," "by the way"), or the return from a digression ("anyway," "so"). All help coordinate what happens next.

Opening a conversation takes special coordination as two or more people move from not being in a conversation to being in one (Schegloff, 1968; 1979). The following is the opening of a conversation between acquaintances:

(11) Karen   (rings Charlie's telephone)
      Charlie Wintermere speaking. -
      Karen   Hello?
      Charlie Hello.
      Karen   Charlie?
      Charlie Yes.
      Karen   Actually it's…
      Charlie Hello, Karen.
      Karen   It's me.
      Charlie M-hm.
      Karen   I (- laughs) I couldn't get back
               last night. [continues]

Karen and Charlie first coordinate mere contact through a proposal to have a conversation (the telephone ring) and its uptake ("Wintermere speaking."). Next, they mutually establish their identities. Karen tells Charlie that she recognizes him in turn five, but Karen has to say "Hello?" "Charlie?" and "Actually it's…" before he identifies her in turn eight. Only then does Karen introduce the first topic. It took ten turns for them to coordinate on the participants, roles, and initial content of the conversation.

Conversations are no easier to close (Schegloff and Sacks, 1973), as illustrated in this ending to a telephone conversation:

(12) June And I'll . I'll ring again, as soon as I
            can on the tenth, uhh to definitely
            confirm it.
      Kay   Right.
      Kay   Okay.
      June Right.
      June Thanks a lot.
      Kay   R . Right.
      June Bye bye.
      Kay   Bye.

Although June and Kay finish a topic in turns one and two, they cannot hang up without agreeing to hang up. So in turn three, Kay proposes to close the conversation ("Okay"), and although June could introduce a new topic, she agrees to Kay's proposal ("Right"). That opens up the closing in which the two exchange thanks ("Thanks a lot," "Right") and then good byes. The two must *agree* to close the conversation before they actually close it.

1.5 *Grounding what is said*

People carry out joint activities against their *common ground* – their mutual knowledge, mutual beliefs, and mutual assumptions (Clark and Marshall, 1981; Lewis, 1969; Stalnaker, 1978). They infer their common ground from past conversation, joint perceptual experiences, and joint membership in cultural communities. When Karen tells Charlie in (11) "I couldn't get back last night," she *presupposes* certain common ground – for example, that Charlie knows where she should have been "last night." And with the assertion itself, she *adds to* their common ground that she couldn't get back. Dialogues proceed by orderly increments to the part of common ground relevant to the current joint activities.

So, if dialogues are to succeed, the participants must *ground* what they say. To ground what is said is to establish the mutual belief that the addressees have attended, identified what is said, and understood what is meant well enough for current purposes (Clark, 1996, 2004; Clark and Brennan, 1991; Clark and Schaefer, 1989; Clark and Wilkes-Gibbs, 1986).

One technique for grounding is to use the projective pair itself, as illustrated in this exchange:

(13) Susan Where, where is your office?
      Tom   In the Strand.
      Susan I- oh well, yes.

When Tom said "In the Strand," he displayed to Susan how he had interpreted her question. If Susan hadn't been satisfied with that interpretation, she could have corrected it by replying "No, I meant…" or something similar (Schegloff, Jefferson, and Sacks, 1977). By following up Tom's reply with "oh well, yes," she implied her acceptance of his interpretation.

Another technique is the *back-channel response, acknowledgment,* or *continuer* (Schegloff, 1982). In two-party dialogues, addressees are expected to add "uh huh" or "m-hm" or "yeah" at or near the ends of certain phrases. With these, they signal that they understand well enough for the speaker to continue.

Grounding is sometimes achieved through *side sequences* (Jefferson, 1972), as in this spontaneous example:

(14)	Roger	Well there's no general agreement on it, I should think.
	Sam	On what?.
	Roger	On uhm – – on the uhm – the mixed-up bits in the play, the… [uhm]
	Sam	[yes]

When Sam didn't understand Roger's "it," he initiated an embedded projective pair in turns two and three, a side sequence, to clear up the problem. Only when Roger had cleared it up did Sam agree with "yes." Side sequences can be initiated to clear up not only mishearings and misunderstandings, but other pre-conditions to taking up the first part (e.g., "Why do you want to know?").

Grounding is also sometimes accomplished with overlapping speech. When Irene interrupted Connie's offer "Did I tell you…" to say, "yes you did, yes, – yes," it was to signal that she already understood and Connie didn't need to go on. And in (14), Sam overlapped Roger's "uhm" with "yes" to signal to Roger that he didn't need further explanation. Grounding often occurs mid-utterance (Clark and Krych, 2004).

The point is that speaking and listening is itself a joint activity. In (14), when Roger speaks, Sam must try to attend, identify Roger's words, and understand what Roger means *at the same time*, or all may be lost. It takes the two of them to synchronize Roger's speaking with Sam's listening. In doing so, they may exploit techniques that range from gestures, body placement, and eye gaze to the use of *uh* and *um*, repeated words, and prolonged syllables (Clark, 2004; Kendon, 1990). As a result, people in dialogue gaze at things in close synchrony, and they even sway their bodies in synchrony (Richardson and Dale, 2005; Richardson, Dale, and Kirkham, 2007; Shockley, Santana, and Fowler, 2003).

Dialogues, in short, emerge step by step as people coordinate on each new move in their joint activities. People need to coordinate on the participants, roles, content, place, and time of each joint action, and they do that in a sequence of local, opportunistic agreements. These techniques give dialogues their emergent structure.

2 Narratives

The second prototypical form of spoken discourse is narratives – extended descriptions of chains of events. In this type of discourse there is a traditional distinction between the story someone tells and the telling of that story. As Chatman (1978) put it:

> [E]ach narrative has two parts: a story (histoire), the content or chain of events (actions, happenings), plus what may be called the existents (characters, items of setting); and a discourse (discours), that is, the expression, the means by which the content is communicated. In simple terms, the story is the what in a narrative that is depicted, discourse the how.

With Chatman, I will distinguish between the *story* and the *narrative* (or *telling*). Stories may be fact or fiction, but it is narratives that are in the first or third person, fresh creations, or retellings. Narratives may be introduced into dialogues as jokes, anecdotes, route directions, or parables, or they may be told in rounds of storytelling (Bauman, 1975; Kirshenblatt-Gimblett, 1989).

Why tell stories? The primary goal is to amuse, shock, or educate. But to accomplish that, narrators must engage their audiences in the joint activity of *imagining* the characters and events of the story world – Chatman's existents and chains of events. As novelist John Gardner (1983) said about novels, "The writer's intent is that the reader fall through the printed page into the scene represented" (p. 132). That, in turn, takes imagination coordinated by narrator and audience, what Gardner called "controlled dreaming." So as with dialogues, people are engaged in a joint activity – jointly imagining the events of a story world – and they coordinate their imaginings by means of language – the narrative.

2.1 *Narrative structure*

Among the earliest modern work on spoken narratives is William Labov's work on *narratives of personal experience* (Labov, 1972; Labov and Waletzky, 1967). In one study, Philadelphia preadolescents, teenagers, and adults were asked such questions as (Labov, 1972, p. 354): "Were you ever in a situation where you were in serious danger of being killed, where you said to yourself – 'This is it'?" or "Were you ever in a fight with a guy bigger than you?" When the respondents said "yes," they were asked "What happened?" and out came a narrative. Indeed, Labov spoke of these narrators becoming "deeply involved in rehearsing or even reliving events of [their] past" (p. 354).

Labov's narrators engaged the imagination of their audiences by the way they structured their narratives. They tended to divide their tellings in six parts (which I will illustrate with Nancy's anecdote about the sewing machine in (9):

1. *Abstract* (a brief summary of the whole story). Nancy begins, "I acquired an absolutely magnificent sewing machine by foul means."
2. *Orientation* (a stage setting about the who, when, what, and where of the story). In some narratives, the orientation is a separate sentence or section,

as in this Philadelphia teenager's story: "It was on Sunday and we didn't have nothin' to do after I – after we came from church. Then we ain't had nothing to do" (Labov, 1972). In other narratives, the orientation is incorporated in the first part of the complicating action, as in the italicized phrases here (the narrative is divided line by line into so-called intonation units):

> well *when I was . doing freelance advertising -*
> *the advertising agency*
> *that I . sometimes did some work for.*
> rang me

3. *Complicating action* (what happened). Nancy continues with what Labov called *narrative clauses* (in italics) that raise the point to be resolved in her narrative:

> *and said um – we've got a client*
> who wants um – – a leaflet designed
> .
> to go to s- uh instructions how to use a sewing machine
> *and I said I haven't used a sewing machine for years -*
> *and uh he said well . go along and talk to them*
> *and I went along and tal-*
> and I was quite honest about it
> *I said you know I . I haven't used one for years*
> Nancy then continues describing what happened.

4. *Evaluation* ("the point of the narrative, its *raison d'être*: why it was told, what the narrator is getting at") (Labov, 1972, p. 266). The evaluation is normally expressed in background clauses set in among the complicating actions and resolution. In Nancy's complicating action, the evaluation is expressed in the intonation units not in italics – "who wants um – – a leaflet designed,. to go to s- uh instructions how to use a sewing machine" and "and I was quite honest about it."

5. *Result or resolution* (how the complicating action got resolved). Nancy completes her narrative by returning to her original point, how she "acquired an

absolutely magnificent sewing machine by foul means," adding a twist about her ignorance of sewing machines:

> so I've got this fabulous machine
> which I – in fact and in order to use it
> I have to read my instruction booklet
> cos it's so complicated

6. *Coda* (a signal that the narrative is finished). Nancy's resolution signals the end of her narrative, but in other narratives, there is a separate coda such as "And that's what happened" or "That's it." Codas "bring the narrator and the listener back to the point at which they entered the narrative" (Labov, 1972, p. 365).

Narrators are really guides into, through, and back out of the story being imagined. Narrators must distinguish between: (1) the *current world*, which they share with their audience in the here and now; and (2) the *story world*, which they are trying to get their addressees to imagine. In her abstract, Nancy identifies Kate and herself as the participants in the current world (with "did *I* tell *you...*") and then leads Kate from the current world to the story world (with "I acquired..." in the past tense). Next, with her orientation, she gets Kate to zoom in on the story world, which she populates with the needed players (herself, the advertising agency) and other props. She then leads Kate from one story event to the next until she reaches the resolving event. Finally, with her coda, she guides Kate back into the current world (with "so I've got this fabulous machine" in the present tense). Nancy seems to have designed her narrative for precisely this tour.

2.2 Story spaces

Narrators guiding audiences through a story world need to get them to imagine *where* the protagonists and other "existents" are. There is much evidence, mostly from research on written narratives, that audiences create visual or spatial models of these entities. In a study by Glenberg, Meyer, and Lindem (1987), people were asked to read very brief narratives one sentence at a time. Some read one of the two versions of (15):

(15) Warren spent the afternoon shopping at the store.
      He picked up [*or:* set down] his bag and went over to look at some scarves.
      He had been shopping all day.
      He thought it was getting too heavy to carry.

The pronoun *it* in the last sentence refers to the bag mentioned in line two. When the verb in line two is *picked up*, Warren keeps the bag with him in looking at the scarves, but when the verb is *set down*, he leaves it behind. The bag's location is important in interpreting the pronoun. People read the final sentence a full .6 sec faster when the verb was *picked up* than when it was *set down*. It was easy to locate the bag in the imagined scene when it was still with Warren, but not when it was not. Readers must be imagining a spatial model of the scene to determine the referent (see also Graesser, Millis, and Zwaan, 1997; Zwaan, 1999, 2004).

Narrators and their audiences keep especially close track of the protagonists. In an experiment by Morrow (1985), people were shown a small model house and asked to memorize its layout. They then read brief narratives that ended like this with a question at the end:

(16) She walked from the study into the bedroom.
      She didn't find the glasses in the room.
      Which room is referred to?

For different people, line one had different prepositions (*from* versus *through* versus *past the study* and *into* versus *to the bedroom*) and different verb modalities (*walked* versus *was walking*). All these differences influenced which room people took to be the referent of *the room* in line two. Here are two of the variants (with percent of choices by the participants):

(17) She walked from the study into the bedroom.
      The room referred to: the bedroom, seventy-seven percent; the study, twenty-one percent; other rooms, two percent.

(18) She walked past the study to the
bedroom
The room referred to: the bedroom
twenty-one percent; the study seventy-
three percent; other rooms, six percent.

In (17), most people took the woman to be
in the bedroom, but in (18), most took her to
be near the study. Hence, people must have
imagined where the protagonist was as she
traveled through the story world (see also
Bower and Morrow, 1990; Morrow, Bower, and
Greenspan, 1990 Rinck and Bower, 1995).

People need such spatial representations
to interpret even single words. Take *approach*
in these three descriptions:

(19) I am standing on the porch of a farm
house looking across the yard at a
picket fence. A tractor [*or:* mouse] is
just approaching it.
(20) I am standing across the street from
a post office with a mailbox in front
of it. A man crossing the street is
just approaching the post office [*or:*
mailbox].
(21) I am standing at the entrance to an
exhibition hall looking at a slab of
marble. A man is just approaching it
with a camera [*or:* chisel].

In one experiment (Morrow and Clark,
1988), people were given one of the two
alternatives of these and other descriptions
and asked to estimate the distance of, say,
the tractor, or mouse, from the picket fence.
The average estimates were as follows:

(19') tractor to fence, thirty-nine feet;
mouse to fence, two feet
(20') man to post office, twenty-eight feet;
man to mailbox, thirteen feet
(21') man with camera to marble slab,
eighteen feet; man with chisel to
marble slab, five feet

Apparently, people arrived at a denotation
for *approach* by considering how near one
object must be to a landmark in order to be in
"interaction with it" for its assumed purpose.

Tractors come into interaction with a fence
at thirty-nine feet, whereas mice do so only
at two feet. These judgments depended on
the size of the referent object (19), the size
of the landmark (20), and the approacher's
purpose (21).

Tracking the narrator, or the protagonist,
requires following a *deictic center* – the narrator's *I*, *here*, and *now* in the story world.
This is especially important for interpreting
deictic expressions like *come* and *go*, *this* and
that, and *here* and *there* (see Bühler, 1982;
Duchan, Bruder, and Hewitt, 1995; Fillmore,
1997). In Hemingway's *The Killers*, the narrator opens his story this way:

(22) The door to Henry's lunchroom
opened and two men came in.

As Fillmore (1981) noted, the narrator must be
inside the lunchroom, because he describes
the door as opening by unseen forces and
the men as "coming" in, not "going" in. The
deictic center is inside the room. Point of
view is essential to many of the narrator's
choices, and imagining the scene from the
narrator's or protagonist's vantage point is
crucial to getting that point of view right.

Changes in point of view lead to changes
in the imagined representation. In a demonstration by Black, Turner, and Bower (1979),
people were asked to read simple descriptions such as these:

(23) Bill was sitting in the living room
reading the paper, when John came
[*or:* went] into the living room.
(24) Alan hated to lose at tennis. Alan
played a game of tennis with Liz.
After winning, she came [*or:* went] up
and shook his hand.

As Black et al. suggested, we can think of
point of view in (23) and (24) by setting up
a camera to view the scenes. For the first
clause in (23), we would set it up in the living
room and leave it there when John "comes"
in. But for John "goes" in, the camera would
need to be moved out of the living room.
In (24), the camera would be near Alan for

the first two sentences, so it wouldn't need to be moved when Liz "comes" up to him. It *would* need to be moved when she "goes" up to him. Changing points of view, as with "went" in (23) and (24), should be disruptive to understanding, and it was. People took reliably longer to read the passages with the changed points of view, and they were also more likely to misrecall them (see also Bruder, 1995).

2.3 *Showing and telling*

Another distinction in narratives, dating back to Plato, is between *diegesis* and *mimesis*. With diegesis, narrators *describe* things, and with mimesis, they *depict* things, as in direct quotation. As novelist David Lodge (1990) put it, "Roughly speaking, mimesis gives us the sense of reality in fiction, the illusion of access to the reality of personal experience, and diegesis conveys the contextualising information and framework of values which provide thematic unity and coherence" (p. 144). Lodge noted that both devices are common in *written* narratives: "[The] alternation of authorial description and characters' verbal interaction remains the woof and warp of literary narration to this day." But both devices are also common in spoken narratives. Descriptions *tell* us what to imagine, whereas depictions *show* us what to imagine (see Clark and Van Der Wege, 2001).

Showing, in its everyday sense, includes both *indicating* and *demonstrating*. I can show you my car by pointing at it, *indicating* it *as my car*. And I can show you how my brother walks by doing a limp across the floor, by *demonstrating* the limp. Indicating, demonstrating, and describing also come in combinations.

In spoken narratives, showing often takes the form of gestures (Goodwin, 1981; Kendon, 1980, 2004; McNeill, 1992; Schegloff, 1984). *Iconic* gestures, which depict things, are particularly common. In a narrative analyzed by Kendon (1980), Fran is telling a joke based on the film *Some Like it Hot*. Her speech is on the left, divided into four intonation units, and her gestures are on the right:

(25)	Speech	Gestures
	they wheel a big table in	Fran sweeps her left arm inward in a horizontal motion.
	with a big with a big [1.08 sec] cake on it	During pause Fran makes series of circular motions with forearm pointing downward and index finger extended.
	and the girl	Fran raises her arm until it is fully extended vertically above her.
	jumps up	

While describing the scene in words, Fran uses her hands and arms to depict selective pieces of it.

Iconic gestures rely crucially on imagination. In line one, Fran depicts the motion of big table, and in line two, a large birthday cake on it. Her audience is to put the gestures together with her description ("wheel a big table in" and "with a big with a big cake on it") and *visualize* a moving table and a cake the size and shape of her outline. In line two, the vantage point of Fran's gesture is outside the cake, but in line three, as she depicts the girl jumping out of the cake, it is inside the cake on the table. Fran changes her point of view in an instant, and her audience follows.

Deictic gestures, which indicate things, also rely on imagination when they are used in narratives. Consider two such gestures in a Tzetal narrative recorded by Haviland (1996), presented here in translation:

(26)   There were indeed people living there [pointing to a fence in the imaginary space of the narrative]. Beside the path [vertical hand moving up and down, representing an imaginary gate]. (That house) was the same size as this house here [pointing at actual house nearby].

The narrator first points at an *imaginary* fence in the space in which he has situated the story around him, and with an iconic gesture, he adds an *imaginary* gate. But then he points at an actual house nearby, saying, in effect, "That house [whose gate I can point to in the imaginary narrative space] is the same size as this house [which I can point to here]." As Haviland noted, narrators and their audience must keep track of the imaginary and the current spaces separately and in relation to each other.

Another form of depiction is direct quotations, which enable audiences to imagine the voices and gestures of the protagonists. The depiction of voices goes well beyond quotations, as illustrated in the first lines of a joke told by Sam to Reynard:

(27)   let me tell you a story, – – -
       a girl went into a chemist's shop, and
       asked for, . contraceptive tablets, – -
       so he said "well I've got . all kinds,
       and . all prices, what do you want,"
       she said "well what have you got,"

Here we find four voices. The first (in line one) is Sam in the current world telling Reynard that he has a story. The second (in lines two, three, and four) already belongs to the narrator in the story world, who reports on the girl's and the chemist's actions. With the quotation in line three, we add the chemist's voice, and in line four, the girl's voice. Although Sam explicitly identifies the chemist's and the girl's voices with "he said" and "she said," he expects Reynard to recognize his own voice and the voice of the fictional narrator without marking.

Quotations, like gestures, are depictive aids to imagination. Narrators use them to help their audiences imagine characters, what they say, and how they speak. Narrators often dramatize the voices for gender, emotion, dialect, and much more (Clark and Gerrig, 1990; Tannen, 1989; Wade and Clark, 1993). For one recorded narrative, Tannen (1989) observed "at least five different voices animated in this narrative, and each of these voices is realized in a paralinguistically distinct acoustic representation:

literally, a different voice." She described various voices as sobbing, innocent, upset, hysterically pleading, and bored. Still other quotations include the protagonist's gestures, as in this narrative about a woman in a hospital (Polanyi, 1989):

(28)   I went out of my mind and I just
       screamed. I said, "Take that out!
       that's not for me!" ... And I shook
       this IV and I said "I'm on an IV, I
       can't eat. Take it out of here!"

As part of her quotations, the woman "shakes her arm as if shaking the IV and shouts in the conversational setting as she shouts in the story" (p. 92), helping the audience imagine the physical actions accompanying her speech.

2.4 *Emotion*

Imagining a story usually includes experiencing emotions. Take what Walton (1978) called *quasi-fear*. When people listen to a ghost story, they are afraid of what the crazed killer will do as he stalks the young couple on Lovers Lane. If the story is told well, the audience's hearts beat faster, muscles tighten, and breathing shortens as the killer approaches the couple. But does the audience yell out to warn the couple as they would if the actual couple were in front of them? Not at all. They may experience most of the physical sensations of genuine fear, but not all of them. They realize that the stalker and couple don't exist in the current world – that the object of their fear is imaginary.

Put differently, people *compartmentalize* their cognitive, emotional, and volitional experiences in the current and story worlds. They construe certain beliefs, emotions, and desires as belonging to the story world, and others as belonging to the current world. Take what Gerrig (1989a; 1989b; 1993) called *anomalous suspense*. Ordinarily, suspense is a state in which we "lack knowledge about some sufficiently important target outcome (p. 79)." Yet, as Gerrig showed, when people read suspense stories, they often feel suspense even when they know how the stories turn out. In a narrative about Lincoln's assassination, they may experience surprise when Lincoln gets shot and want him to survive the shooting even though, in the current world, they know what actually happened. Apparently, people can separate their knowledge, emotions, and desires about a story world from their knowledge, emotions, and desires about the current world.

Most narratives are designed to elicit emotion. Novels, movies, and short stories sort into genres largely by the emotions they evoke. Mysteries lead to suspense and fear; adventures to excitement, fear, and elation; horror stories to horror, loathing, and fear; light romances to sexual excitement; heavier romances to erotic arousal; satires to amusement or anger; and so on. Narratives evoke these emotions by getting us to imagine the stories in part *as if* we were experiencing them before our very eyes.

2.5 *Joint imagination*

In the view taken here, narratives engage narrator and audience in joint imagining. Such a view accounts for four properties of spoken narratives:

1. *Experience*. People experience certain features of the story world partly *as if* they were actual, current experiences. These include: visual appearances; spatial relations; points of view; voices; and emotions.
2. *Imaginal support*. The experience of imagining is supported by narrative techniques that range from the descriptions of events and existents (*diegesis*) to depictions with gestures and quotation (*mimesis*).
3. *Participation*. Narrators may design what they say to encourage certain forms of imagination, but to succeed they must get their audiences to join them.
4. *Compartmentalization*. In participating in narratives, people are able more or less to separate off experiences in the story world from experiences in the current world.

But what conception of imagination accounts for these features?

In the early 1900s, people were assumed to understand and remember narratives in terms of schemas – sets of cultural preconceptions about causal or other relationships. In a classic experiment by Bartlett (1932), people read and then retold a Native American folk story called "The War of the Ghosts." These narrators often distorted their retellings to fit Western cultural expectations, changing "hunting seals," for example, into "fishing," a more likely pastime in their schema. The notion of schema was later refined into such notions as *story grammar* (Rumelhart, 1975), *scripts* (Schank and Abelson, 1977), and *mental models* (Johnson-Laird, 1983). And yet none of these characterize how people imagine a story – seeing events, experiencing emotions, and having desires.

An alternative account is that imagining is a type of *mental simulation*. In a proposal by Kahneman and Tversky (1982), mental simulations are representations in which people simulate a process, perhaps modify its initial settings, and compare outcomes. People might simulate a process: (1) to predict its outcome; (2) to assess its probability; (3) to assess counterfactual alternatives ("if only..."); and (4) to project the effects of causality. When people simulate alternative endings to a story, for example, they tend to make "downhill" changes to the stories – they remove unusual or unexpected aspects of the situation. They rarely make "uphill" changes, which introduce unusual aspects, and they never make "horizontal" changes, which alter arbitrary aspects. So mental simulations represent *imagining* working through a process.

Mental simulations are well-suited for imagining emotions (see Davies and Stone, 1995). When people go back over fatal accidents of loved ones, they often experience guilt, anger, or regret as they mentally simulate alternatives for those accidents – as they think "if only she hadn't driven down that street" or "what if he had left two minutes earlier" (Kahneman and Tversky, 1982). To allow these comparisons, mental simulations separate the simulation from reality (taking the system "offline" and feeding it *as-if* inputs).

Participating in narratives can therefore be viewed as creating joint mental simulations (Bruce, 1981; Clark, 1996; Currie, 1990; Goffman, 1974; Walton, 1978, 1983, 1990). When Sam narrates the joke in (27), he says to Reynard, "A girl went into a chemist's shop and asked for contraceptive tablets." He intends Reynard to join him in mentally simulating a scene in which he, Sam, is a reporter, Reynard is a reportee, and the reporter is telling the reportee about an actual girl in an actual chemist's shop. And with "I've got all kinds and all prices," Sam intends Reynard to join him in simulating the chemist producing "I've got all kinds and all prices." Treating imagining as mental simulation comports well with all four features of narratives.

3 Coda

Speaking and listening in discourse is a profoundly social activity. People use language – indeed, all forms of communication – to coordinate with each other. They participate in dialogues to establish hierarchical sets of joint commitments to joint activities (such as building TV stands, gossiping, exchanging information). They participate in spoken narratives to coordinate imagining events in a story world (for amusement, shock, or education). Speaking and listening is itself a social process. People in spoken discourse must establish *as they go along* that the listeners have attended to the speakers, heard what they said, and understood them well enough for current purposes.

References

Austin, J. L. (1962). *How to do things with words.* Oxford: Oxford University Press.

Bach, K. & Harnish, R. M. (1979). *Linguistic communication and speech acts.* Cambridge: MIT Press.

Bangerter, A. & Clark, H. H. (2003). Navigating joint projects with dialogue. *Cognitive Science, 27,* 195–225.

Bartlett, F. C. (1932). *Remembering.* Cambridge: Cambridge University Press.

Bauman, R. (1975). Verbal art as performance. *American Anthropologist, 77,* 2, 290–311.

Black, J. B., Turner, T. J., & Bower, G. H. (1979). Point of view in narrative comprehension. *Journal of Verbal Learning and Verbal Behavior, 18,* 187–98.

Bower, G. H. & Morrow, D. G. (1990). Mental models in narrative comprehension. *Science, 247(4938),* 44–8.

Bruce, B. (1981). A social interaction model of reading. *Discourse Processes, 4,* 273–311.

Bruder, G. A. (1995). Psychological evidence that linguistic devices are used by readers to understand spatial deixis in narrative text. In Duchan, J. F., Bruder, G. A., & Hewitt, L. E. (Eds.) *Deixis in narrative: A cognitive science perspective* (pp. 243–60). Hillsdale, NJ: Lawrence Erlbaum Associates.

Bühler, K. (1982). The deictic field of language and deictic words. In Jarvella, R. J. & Klein, W. (Eds.) *Speech, place, and action.* New York: John Wiley.

Chatman, S. (1978). *Story and discourse: Narrative structure in fiction and film.* Ithaca, NY: Cornell University Press.

Clark, H. H. (1996). *Using language.* Cambridge: Cambridge University Press.

 (2003). Pointing and placing. In Kita, S. (Ed.) *Pointing. Where language, culture, and cognition meet* (pp. 243–68). Hillsdale, NJ: Erlbaum.

 (2004). Pragmatics of language performance. In Horn, L. R. & Ward, G. (Eds.) *Handbook of pragmatics* (pp. 365–82). Oxford: Blackwell.

 (2006). Social actions, social commitments. In Levinson, S. C. & Enfield, N. J. (Eds.) *Roots of human sociality: Culture, cognition, and human interaction.* Oxford: Berg Press.

Clark, H. H. & Brennan, S. A. (1991). Grounding in communication. In Resnick, L. B., Levine, J. M., & Teasley, S. D. (Eds.) *Perspective on socially shared cognition* (pp. 127–49). Washington, DC: APA Books.

Clark, H. H. & Gerrig, R. J. (1990). Quotations as demonstrations. *Language, 66,* 764–805.

Clark, H. H. & Krych, M. A. (2004). Speaking while monitoring addressees for understanding. *Journal of Memory and Language, 50(1),* 62–81.

Clark, H. H. & Marshall, C. R. (1981). Definite reference and mutual knowledge. In Joshi, A. K., Webber, B. L., & Sag, I. A. (Eds.) *Elements of discourse understanding* (pp. 10–63). Cambridge: Cambridge University Press.

Clark, H. H. & Schaefer, E. R. (1989). Contributing to discourse. *Cognitive Science*, 13, 259–94.

Clark, H. H.& Van Der Wege, M. (2001). Imagination in discourse. In Schiffrin, D. Tannen, D., & Hamilton, H. E. (Eds.) *Handbook of discourse analysis*. Oxford: Basil Blackwell.

Clark, H. H.& Wilkes-Gibbs, D. (1986). Referring as a collaborative process. *Cognition*, 22, 1–39.

Currie, G. (1990). *The nature of fiction*. Cambridge: Cambridge University Press.

Davies, M. & Stone, T. (Eds.). (1995). *Mental simulation*. Oxford: Blackwell.

Duchan, J. F. Bruder, G. A., & Hewitt, L. E. (Eds.) (1995). *Deixis in narrative: A cognitive science perspective*. Hillsdale NJ: Lawrence Erlbaum Associates.

Fillmore, C. (1981). Pragmatics and the description of discourse. In Cole, P. (Ed.) *Radical pragmatics* (pp. 143–66). New York: Academic Press.

(1997). *Lectures on deixis*. Stanford CA: CSLI Publications.

Gardner, J. (1983). *The art of fiction: Notes on craft for young writers*. New York: Alfred Knopf.

Gerrig, R. J. (1989a). Re-experiencing fiction and non-fiction. *Journal of Aesthetics and Art Criticism*, 47, 277–80.

(1989b). Suspense in the absence of uncertainty. *Journal of Memory and Language*, 28, 633–48.

(1993). *Experiencing narrative worlds: On the psychological activities of reading*. New Haven, CN: Yale University Press.

Glenberg, A. M., Meyer, M., & Lindem, K. (1987). Mental models contribute to foregrounding during text comprehension. *Journal of Memory and Language*, 26(1), 69–83.

Goffman, E. (1974). *Frame analysis*. New York: Harper and Row.

Goodwin, C. (1981). *Conversational organization: Interaction between speakers and hearers*. New York: Academic Press.

Graesser, A. C., Millis, K. K., & Zwaan, R. A. (1997). Discourse comprehension. *Annual Review of Psychology*, 48, 163–89.

Haviland, J. B. (1996). Projections, transpositions, and relativity. In Gumperz, J. J. & Levinson, S. C. (Eds.) *Rethinking linguistic relativity* (pp. 271–323). Cambridge: Cambridge University Press.

Jefferson, G. (1972). Side sequences. In Sudnow, D. (Ed.) *Studies in social interaction*, (pp. 294–338). New York, NY: Free Press.

Johnson-Laird, P. N. (1983). *Mental models*. Cambridge: Cambridge University Press.

Kahneman, D. & Tversky, A. (1982). The simulation heuristic. In Slovic, P., Kahneman, D., & Tversky, A. (Eds.) *Judgment under uncertainty: Heuristics and biases* (pp. 201–8). Cambridge: Cambridge University Press.

Kendon, A. (1980). Gesticulation and speech: Two aspects of the process of utterance. In Key, M. R. (Ed.) *Relationship of verbal and nonverbal communication* (pp. 207–27). Amsterdam: Mouton de Gruyter.

(1990) *Conducting Interaction: Patterns of behavior in focused encounters*. Cambridge: Cambridge University Press

(2004). *Gesture: Visible action as utterance*. Cambridge: Cambridge University Press.

Kirshenblatt-Gimblett, B. (1989). The concept and varieties of narrative performance in East European Jewish culture. In Bauman, R. & Sherzer, J. (Eds.) *Explorations in the ethnography of speaking* (pp. 283–308). Cambridge: Cambridge University Press.

Labov, W. (1972). The transformation of experience in narrative syntax. In Labov, W. (Ed.) *Language in the inner city: Studies in the Black English vernacular* (pp. 354–96). Philadelphia, PA: University of Pennsylvania Press.

Labov, W. & Waletzky, J. (1967). Narrative analysis: Oral versions of personal experience. In Helms, J. (Ed.), *Essays on the verbal and visual arts*. Seattle, WA: University of Washington Press.

Lewis, D. K. (1969). *Convention: A philosophical study*. Cambridge, MA: Harvard University Press.

Lodge, D. (1990). Narration with words. In Barlow, H., Blakemore, C., & Weston-Smith, M. (Eds.) *Images and understanding* (pp. 141–53). Cambridge: Cambridge University Press.

McNeill, D. (1992). *Hand and mind*. Chicago: University of Chicago Press.

Morrow, D. G. (1985). Prepositions and verb aspect in narrative understanding. *Journal of Memory and Language*, 24, 390–404.

Morrow, D. G., Bower, G. H., & Greenspan, S. E. (1990). Situation-based inferences during narrative comprehension. In Graesser, A. C. & Bower, G. H. (Eds.) *Inferences and text comprehension: The psychology of learning and motivation* (Vol. 25). New York: Academic.

Morrow, D. G. & Clark, H. H. (1988). Interpreting words in spatial descriptions. *Language and Cognitive Processes*, 3, 275–91.

Polanyi, L. (1989). *Telling the American story*. Cambridge, MA: MIT Press.

Richardson, D. C. & Dale, R. (2005). Looking To Understand: The Coupling Between Speakers' and Listeners' Eye Movements and its Relationship to Discourse Comprehension. *Cognitive Science*, 29, 1045–60.

Richardson, D. C., Dale, R., & Kirkham, N. Z. (2007). The art of conversation is coordination: Common ground and the coupling of eye movements during dialogue. *Psychological Science*.

Rinck, M. & Bower, G. H. (1995). Anaphora resolution and the focus of attention in mental models. *Journal of Memory and Language, 34*, 110–31.

Rinck, M. & Bower, G. H. (2000). Temporal and spatial distance in situation models. *Memory and Cognition, 28 (8)*, 1310–20.

Rumelhart, D. E. (1975). Notes on schemas for stories. In Bobrow, D. G. & Collins, A. M. (Eds.) *Representation and understanding: Studies in cognitive science* (pp. 211–36). New York: Academic Press.

Sacks, H. (1975). Everyone has to lie. In Sanches, M. & Blount B. (Eds.) *Sociocultural dimensions of language use* (pp. 57–80). New York: Academic Press.

Schank, R. C. & Abelson, R. P. (1975). *Scripts, plans, goals, and understanding*. Hillsdale, NJ: Erlbaum.

Schegloff, E. A. (1968). Sequencing in conversational openings. *American Anthropologist, 70(4)*, 1075–95.

(1979). Identification and recognition in telephone conversational openings. In Psathas, G. (Ed.) *Everyday language: studies in ethnomethodology* (pp. 23–78). New York: Irvington.

(1980). Preliminaries to preliminaries: "Can I ask you a question?" *Sociological Inquiry, 50*, 104–52.

(1982). Discourse as an interactional achievement: Some uses of "uh huh" and other things that come between sentences. In Tannen, D. (Ed.) *Analyzing discourse: Text and talk. Georgetown University Roundtable on Languages and Linguistics 1981* (pp. 71–93). Washington, DC: Georgetown University Press.

(1984). On some gestures' relation to talk. In Atkinson, J. M. & Heritage, J. (Eds.) *Structures of social action: Studies in conversation analysis* (pp. 262–96). Cambridge: Cambridge University Press.

Schegloff, E. A., Jefferson, G., & Sacks, H. (1977). The preference for self-correction in the organization of repair in conversation. *Language, 53*, 361–82.

Schegloff, E. A. & Sacks, H. (1973). Opening up closings. *Semiotica, 8*, 289–327.

Schiffrin, D. (1987). *Discourse markers*. Cambridge: Cambridge University Press.

Searle, J. R. (1969). *Speech acts*. Cambridge: Cambridge University Press.

(1975). A taxonomy of illocutionary acts. In Gunderson, K. (Ed.) *Minnesota studies in the philosophy of language* (pp. 344–69). Minneapolis: University of Minnesota Press.

Shockley, K., Santana, M. V., & Fowler, C. A. (2003). Mutual interpersonal postural constraints are involved in cooperative conversation. *Journal of Experimental Psychology: Human Perception and Performance, 29*, 326–32.

Stalnaker, R. C. (1978). Assertion. In Cole, P. (Ed.) *Syntax and semantics 9: Pragmatics* (pp. 315–32). New York: Academic Press.

Svartvik, J. & Quirk, R. (Eds.). (1980). *A corpus of English conversation*. Lund, Sweden: Gleerup.

Tannen, D. (1989). *Talking voices: Repetition, dialogue and imagery in conversational discourse*. Cambridge: Cambridge University Press.

Wade, E. & Clark, H. H. (1993). Reproduction and demonstration in quotations. *Journal of Memory and Language, 32*, 805–19.

Walton, K. L. (1978). Fearing fictions. *Journal of Philosophy, 75*, 5–27.

(1983). Fiction, fiction-making, and styles of fictionality. *Philosophy and Literature, 8*, 78–88.

(1990). *Mimesis as make-believe: On the foundations of the representational arts*. Cambridge, MA: Harvard University Press.

Zwaan, R. A. (1999). Situation models: the mental leap into imagined worlds. *Current Directions in Psychological Science, 8*, 15–18.

(2004). The immersed experiencer: toward an embodied theory of language comprehension. In Ross, B. H. (Ed.) *The psychology of learning and motivation* (pp. 35–62). Academic Press, New York.

CHAPTER 28

Computational Modeling of Discourse and Conversation

Arthur C. Graesser, Danielle S. MacNamara, and Vasile Rus

Sentences and spoken utterances are nearly always expressed in the context of a text or conversation. It is therefore important to understand the mechanisms that drive the comprehension and production of connected discourse. In this chapter we will use the term *discourse* as a covering term for text, monologues, dialogues, and multiparty conversations. Our goal is to understand the structures, representations, strategies, and processes that underlie the comprehension and production of discourse. There is a field, called *discourse processes*, devoted to scientific investigations of these mechanisms. It has its own journal (*Discourse Processes*), affiliated society (Society for Text and Discourse), and its own *Handbook of Discourse Processes* (Graesser, Gernsbacher, and Goldman, 2003).

This chapter focuses on computational models of discourse processing. There are two senses of computation, both relevant to this chapter. The first sense refers to the architectures and algorithms in models of human discourse processing. The second sense refers to computer implementations of components of these psychological

models. Some psychological components can be programmed in computers, whereas others are currently beyond the immediate technological horizon. We hope to clarify the boundaries of what is technically feasible on computers, knowing full well that the boundaries change yearly.

There are many types of discourse, or what some researchers call *genre* (category in French), *registers*, or simply discourse categories. Discourse typologies vary in grain size and theoretical slant, with some researchers viewing the discourse landscape as a set of fuzzy categories, others a structured ontological hierarchy, and yet others viewing it as a multidimensional space (Biber, 1988). There are prototypical discourse categories in the American culture, such as folktales, scientific journal articles, jokes told in stand-up comedy, and one-on-one tutoring. These four examples would funnel into more superordinate classes that might be labeled as narrative, exposition, monologue, and dialogue, respectively. Of course, there will always be blends, hybrids, and borderline cases, such as a faculty member chatting with a student about a funny story involving an experiment that failed. Whether there is a set of prototypical discourse categories is a lively topic of debate.

This chapter will concentrate on two forms of discourse: text comprehension and two-party dialogue. We acknowledge that there are other important forms of discourse, such as text production, comprehension and production of spoken monologues, and multiparty conversations with three or more participants. However, most research has been conducted on text comprehension and two-party dialogue.

1 Computational models of text comprehension

1.1 *Levels of representation*

Multiple levels of representation are constructed when a text is comprehended. Five of these levels are the surface code, the propositional textbase, the situation model, the text genre, and the pragmatic communicative context (Graesser, Singer, and Trabasso, 1994; Kintsch, 1998; van Dijk and Kintsch, 1983). Suppose, for illustration, that the following excerpt about a corporation was read in a newspaper:

> When the board met on Friday, they discovered they were bankrupt. They needed to take some action, so they fired the president.

The *surface code* preserves the exact wording and syntax of the sentences. The *textbase* contains explicit propositions in the text in a stripped down, logical form that preserves the meaning but not the surface code. The first sentence would have the following propositions, a theoretical construct that will be elaborated shortly:

> PROP 1: meet (board, TIME = Friday)
> PROP 2: discover (board, PROP 3)
> PROP 3: bankrupt (corporation)
> PROP 4: when (PROP 1, PROP 2)

The *situation model* (sometimes called *mental model*) is the referential content or microworld that the text describes. This would include the people, objects, spatial setting, actions, events, plans, thoughts, and emotions of people and other referential content in a news story, as well as the world knowledge recruited to interpret this contextually specific content. The *text genre* is the type of discourse, in this case a news story about a corporation. The pragmatic *communicative context* is the implicit dialogue between the author (story writer, editor) and the reader (a public citizen). The story was presumably written to convey some point to the reader, such as the particular corporation is on the brink of collapse. The public, of course, loves disaster stories.

Discourse context and world knowledge are extremely important in guiding the construction of these levels of representation. The referents and propositional content of the textbase would not be composed correctly if one relied on the local sentence context. For example, *they* in the phrase *they were bankrupt* refers to the corporation rather than the board, yet models that assign referents to pronoun anaphors on the basis of sentence syntax would make just the opposite assignment. The *president* refers to the president of the board, not the president of the United States, even though the U.S. president is shared knowledge among U.S. citizens and the modifying determiner is definite (*the*). These assignments are rather subtle and require a fine-grained analysis of context and world knowledge. This subtlety and complexity become more salient as soon as a researcher tries to get computers to perform these computations.

Researchers are not entirely in agreement that the explicit discourse can be segmented into a structured set of propositions. One problem with the construct of a proposition is that researchers from different fields (i.e., artificial intelligence, logic, linguistics, and psychology) do not entirely agree on the format and formal constraints of propositions. In the field of discourse psychology, a proposition refers to a state, event, or action that may or may not have a truth value with respect to the referential situation model; this contrasts with propositional calculus theories of traditional logic where a truth value must be assigned and the meaning of the proposition is unimportant. In psychology, each proposition contains a predicate (e.g., main verb, adjective, connective) and one or more arguments (e.g., nouns, embedded propositions). In most notational systems, the arguments are placed within the parentheses, whereas the predicates are outside of the parentheses. Each argument has a functional role, such as agent, patient, object, time, or location, although the theoretical set of functional roles differs somewhat among the fields of psychology, linguistics, artificial intelligence, and computational linguistics (Allen, 1995; Kintsch, 1998; van Dijk and Kintsch, 1983). Discourse psychologists sometimes ignore the role of quantifiers (one, some, all) when propositional representations are constructed, whereas quantifiers are explicitly captured in the predicate calculus representations (called first order logic) of artificial intelligence, computational linguistics, and formal logic. There are yet other differences among fields that pertain to structural composition and the epistemological status of propositions (e.g., facts, beliefs, wants), far too many to enumerate here.

There would be tremendous advantages to having a computational model that translates the language of discourse into the logical forms in logic or AI (such as first-order predicate calculus) or the deep structures in standard linguistics. One advantage of a logical form is that well-established computational procedures can execute theorem proving and inference generation in an elegant manner. Another advantage is that discourse structures and world knowledge structures would have a uniform representation that could be systematically aligned, compared, and integrated. Unfortunately, there are two serious challenges that beset this neat and tidy picture. The first challenge is that researchers in AI and computational linguistics have not been able to develop a computer program that can reliably translate discourse constituents into a logical form or deep structure representations, even in large-scale evaluations that aspire to such a goal (Rus, 2004) and even when there

is an attempt to loosen the constraints with logical entailment (Rus et al., 2008). The vast majority of today's syntactic parsers, such as Apple Pie (Sekine and Grishman, 1995) and the Charniak parser (2000), construct tree structures that capture surface structure composition rather than deep structures or logical forms. The second challenge is that propositional representations and logical form may not be the most psychologically plausible forms of representing meaning. Instead, a direct route to the situation model and other meaning representations may be guided by words, syntactic frames, and various discourse signals that interact jointly with world knowledge. Of course, those who dismiss the construct of a proposition need to have a principled way of specifying meaning representations and how they systematically get constructed. As yet, an alternative to propositions has not been developed in compositional theories of meaning, apart from a few proposals that can handle only a small corpus of examples.

1.2 *World knowledge*

A computational model of discourse comprehension must make some commitments to the representation of world knowledge. World knowledge is needed to guide the interpretation of explicit information and also to furnish plausible inferences (Graesser et al., 1994; Kintsch, 1998). Three theoretical frameworks for handling world knowledge are conceptual graph structures (Lehmann, 1992; Schank and Reisbeck, 1981; Sowa, 1983), high dimensional semantic spaces (Landauer, Foltz, and Laham, 1998; Landauer et al., 2007), and embodied representations (de Vega, Glenberg, and Graesser, 2008). Conceptual graph structures (CGSs) contain a set of nodes (referring to noun-like concepts or propositions) that are interrelated by labeled, directed arcs such as Is-a, Has-as-parts, Cause, and Reason. The referent of a CGS may include a family of related concepts (such as a semantic network for animals), a package of nodes that capture a specific experience (e.g., a previous experience or text that is read), or a generic package of knowledge, such as a script on how people dine in restaurants, a stereotype about professors, or a schema about corporate bankruptcy (Schank and Reisbeck, 1981). During the course of comprehending a particular text, a family of these background CGSs gets activated and guides the interpretation of sentences and the generation of inferences. The CGS approach was the dominant approach to representing world knowledge between the late 1970s and the late 1990s.

One salient limitation of the CGSs is that the researcher has to construct the content and relations by hand. Progress on automatic construction of these structures through machine learning algorithms and theoretical formal systems has not scaled up to handling a large corpus of texts, although there were some notable successes in inducing noun concept taxonomies in semantic networks (Hearst, 1992; Stevenson, 2002) and case hierarchies in case-based reasoning (Veloso and Carbonell, 1993).

In the mid-1990s the zeitgeist shifted from handcrafted structures to high-dimensional conceptual spaces that accommodate the constraints of a large corpus of texts. Notable examples of statistical, corpus-based approaches to analyzing the world knowledge that underlies discourse are the Hyperspace Analog to Language (Burgess, Livesay, and Lund, 1998), the Latent Semantic Analysis (Kintsch, 1998; Landauer, Foltz, and Laham, 1998; Landauder et al., 2007), and the Linguistic Inquiry Word Count (Pennebaker and Francis, 1999). LSA uses a statistical method called "singular value decomposition" (SVD) to reduce a large Word-by-Document co-occurrence matrix to approximately 100–500 functional dimensions. The Word-by-Document co-occurrence matrix is simply a record of the number of times word W_i occurs in document D_j. A document may be defined as a sentence, paragraph, or section of an article. Each word, sentence, or text ends up a weighted vector on the K dimensions. The "match" (i.e., similarity in meaning, conceptual relatedness) between two unordered bags of words (single words, sentences, or texts) is computed as a geometric cosine between the two vectors, with values ranging from negative one to one. LSA-based technology is currently used within a number of applications, such as essay graders that grade essays as reliably as experts in English composition and automated tutors that give feedback equivalent to human tutors (see chapters in Landauer et al., 2007).

One limitation in both CGSs and LSA is that they gloss over many of the fine details of perceptual experiences and motor activity. CGSs are symbolic and LSA is a statistical representation. In contrast, the embodied framework grounds discourse in sensorimotor experience and constraints of the body as the body interacts with a particular world (see chapters in de Vega et al., 2008). It should be acknowledged that some structural theories ground the symbolic nodes (concepts, propositions) in perception and action, and there are LSA-based models capable of representing sensorimotor procedures with a suitable corpus. However, an embodied framework is arguably needed to go the full distance in handling references to perception, action, deixis, and experiences that ground symbols. Unfortunately, no one has built a model on a computer that is capable of generating fully embodied representations from naturalistic text and of inducing embodied representations of world knowledge from experiences. There are robotic systems that ground words and simple spoken utterances in perception and action (Roy, 2005), but there are no systems that take text input and automatically produce a representation that is even close to an embodied representation. This is one direction for future computational research.

1.3 Cohesion and coherence

Sentences and clauses in connected discourse need to be coherently related in order to convey the desired message to the reader. A distinction is often made between *cohesion* and *coherence* (Graesser et al., 2004; van Dijk and Kintsch, 1983). Cohesion is an objective property of the explicit text. Explicit words, phrases, sentences, and linguistic features guide the reader in interpreting the substantive ideas in the text, in connecting ideas with other ideas, and in connecting ideas to higher-level global units (e.g., topics, themes). Coherence refers to the quality of the mental representation constructed by the comprehender. Cohesive devices cue the reader how to construct a coherent representation in the mind; how and whether this happens, however, depends on the skills and knowledge the reader brings to the situation (Graesser et al., 1994; McNamara and Kintsch, 1996). For example, if the reader has adequate world knowledge about the subject matter or if there are adequate linguistic and discourse cues, then the reader is likely to form a coherent mental representation of the text. Readers follow an underlying pragmatic assumption that texts are coherent and expend effort to construct coherent representations while reading well-constructed texts. However, if text is very poorly composed, their efforts fail so they give up trying and attribute problems to either the text or their own deficits in world knowledge.

Coh-Metrix is a computer tool available on the Web that analyzes texts on multiple levels of cohesion, as well as other levels of language (http://cohmetrix.memphis.edu, Graesser et al., 2004). Coh-Metrix has the potential to replace standard readability formulas, such as Flesch-Kincaid Grade Level (Klare, 1974–5), which rely exclusively on word length and sentence length to scale texts on readability. The user of Coh-Metrix enters a text into the Web site and it prints out measures of the text on over sixty metrics that span different levels of discourse and language. The public version of Coh-Metrix on the Web (version 1.3) has measures in the following categories: (1) co-referential cohesion, such as nouns referring to other nouns and phrases; (2) causal cohesion; (3) density of different categories of connectives and logical operators; (4) LSA-based conceptual cohesion; (5) type-token ratio; (6) readability measures; (7) word frequency measures; (8) density of words in different parts of speech; (9) other word characteristics, such as concreteness,

polysemy, and age of acquisition; (10) density of noun phrases; and (11) syntactic complexity. Coh-Metrix integrates lexicons, pattern classifiers, part-of-speech taggers, syntactic parsers, shallow semantic interpreters, LSA, and other components that have been developed in the field of computational linguistics (Allen, 1995; Jurafsky and Martin, 2008). For example, Coh-Metrix incorporates several lexicons, including CELEX (Baayen, Piepenbrock, and Van Rijn, 1995), WordNet (Fellbaum, 1998), and the MRC Psycholinguistic Database (Coltheart, 1981). These lexicons allow us to measure each word on number of syllables, abstractness, imagery, ambiguity, frequency of usage, age of acquisition, number of senses (meanings), and dozens of other dimensions. There is a part-of-speech "tagger" (Brill, 1995) that assigns each word to one of fifty-six syntactic classes; it uses context to assign the most likely class when a word can be assigned more than one part of speech. A syntactic parser assigns syntactic tree structures to sentences and measures them on syntactic complexity (Charniak, 2000). The LSA module (Landauer et al., 2007) measures the conceptual similarity between sentences, paragraphs, and texts on the basis of world knowledge.

Coh-Metrix 2.0 has been expanded to incorporate more levels of cohesion in discourse. It computes the referents of pronouns on the basis of syntactic rules, semantic fit, and discourse pragmatics by existing algorithms proposed by Mitkov (1998) and Lappin and Lease (1994); however, the accuracy of automated pronoun referent resolution is quite limited so this was not a module that was shared on the public Web site. Coh-Metrix segregates different dimensions of the situation model, including those of agency, temporal, spatial, causal, intentional, and logical cohesion. These dimensions of the situation model were included in Zwaan and Radvansky's (1998) event indexing model. Zwaan and Radvansky's review of the psychological literature has confirmed that incoming sentences take more time to read to the extent there are coherence gaps in agency, temporality, spatiality, intentionality (i.e., goals, plans, actions of agents), and causality.

Coh-Metrix identifies intentional actions and goals by combining syntactic information with information from the WordNet database (Fellbaum, 1998). Intentional actions and goals have main verbs that are either causal or intentional (as defined by a cluster of lexicographical categories in WordNet) and *animate* or *human* subject nouns (e.g., in *the girl bought a car*, the verb *buy* is intentional and the subject noun *girl* is human). A text is cohesive on the intentional dimension to the extent that there are more intentional linguistic particles that link actions and goals, such as conjunctions and other forms of connectives (e.g., *in order to, so that*).

The Coh-Metrix research team has developed software to compute measures of structural cohesion, including syntactic similarity of sentences, ease of identifying topic sentences, genre uniformity, document headings, and given-new information contrasts. One of the most influential analyses of genre has been that of Biber (1988), who used factor analysis to classify a large corpus of texts on the basis of sixty-seven features of language and discourse. These sixty-seven features have been automated so we can compute the extent to which a text fits different genres (such as narrative, science, history texts). Associated with each genre is a diagnostic set of connectives, discourse markers, and other signaling devices. Discriminant function analyses identify the features that diagnostically predict whether text *T* is in genre/class G. Texts can thereby be scaled on global genre cohesion in at least two ways. First, a text has higher genre cohesion when it cleanly fits into one prototypical genre/class G (as measured by an inverse of the classification entropy score). Second, there is higher global cohesion when there is a higher density of diagnostic features associated with the dominant genre/class G. One interesting finding is that the genre/class of a text can be identified very quickly as a text is received, possibly as soon as the first few words (McCarthy et al., 2009).

Another analysis of structure contrasts *new* from *given* information by segregating constituents that are introduced for the first time in the text from references to previous text constituents and from information that is in the common ground (shared knowledge) of discourse participants (Clark, 1996; Prince, 1981). Whereas previous analytical treatments of the given-new distinction have been compositional and symbolic, the Coh-Metrix research team uses an LSA algorithm to segregate *new* versus *given* information as sentences are comprehended, one by one (Hempelmann et al., 2005). The LSA algorithm is both automated and is highly correlated with a Prince-based continuum of given versus new.

1.4 *Computational models of text comprehension in humans*

Discourse psychologists have developed a number of models that simulate how humans comprehend text. Among these are the Collaborative Action-based Production System (CAPS) Reader model (Just and Carpenter, 1992), the Construction-Integration model (Kintsch, 1998), the constructivist model (Graesser et al., 1994), and the landscape model (Van den Broek et al., 2002). The architectures of these models go beyond simple finite state automata that have a small finite set of states (categories) and a small set of transition matrices (one per process) that specify the likelihood that a theoretical entity will change states. Rather, they are complex dynamical models with a very large or infinite state space that can evolve in complex and sometimes chaotic trajectories. It is impossible to sufficiently capture these models with a set of linear equations or with a set of simple rules. This subsection will describe the CAPS/Reader and Construction-Integration (CI) model.

Just and Carpenter's (1992) CAPS/Reader model directs comprehension with a large set of production rules. The CAPS/Reader model is a hybrid between a production system and a connectionist computational architecture. Each of the production rules

(a) scans explicit text input, (b) governs the operation of working memory, (c) changes activation values of information in working memory, and long-term memory, and (d) performs other cognitive or behavioral actions. Production rules have an "If <state>, then <action>" form, but these rules are probabilistic, with activation values and thresholds, rather than brittle. If the contents of working memory have some state S activated to a degree that meets or exceeds some threshold T, then action A is executed by spreading activation to one or more information units in working memory, long-term memory, or response output. A state slot may be arbitrarily complex, often consisting of several substates that capture a pattern of language or discourse. For example, consider a possible rule that would identify intentional actions: If the subject noun is animate and the main verb is causal or intentional, then activation is spread to the proposition category of intentional action. The proposition would be classified as intentional only probabilistically, because other activated production rules may spread activation in a fashion that does not converge on the category of intentional action. All of the production rules are evaluated in parallel within each cycle of the production system, and multiple rules may get activated within each cycle. The researcher can therefore trace the activation of information units (nodes) in the text, working memory, and long-term memory as a function of the cycles of production rules that get activated. Just and Carpenter have reported that these profiles of nodal activation can predict patterns of reading times for individual words, eyetracking behavior, and memory for text constituents.

Kintsch's (1998) CI model directs comprehension with a connectionist network. As text is read, sentence by sentence (or alternatively, clauses by clause), a set of word concept and proposition nodes is activated (constructed). Some nodes match constituents in the explicit text whereas others are activated inferentially by world knowledge. The activation of each node fluctuates systematically during the course of comprehension, sentence by sentence.

When any given sentence S (or clause) is comprehended, the set of activated nodes include (a) N explicit and inference nodes affiliated with S and (b) M nodes held over in working memory from the previous sentence S-1 by virtue of meeting some threshold of activation. As a consequence, there are N+M nodes to reckon with while comprehending sentence S. These N+M nodes are fully connected to each other in a weight space. The set of weights in the resulting (N+M) by (N+M) *connectivity matrix* specifies the extent to which each node activates or inhibits the activation of each of the other N+M nodes. The values of the weights in the connectivity matrix are theoretically motivated by multiple levels of language and discourse. For example, if two word nodes (A and B) are closely related in a syntactic parse, they would have a high positive weight, whereas if two propositions contradict each other, they would have a high negative weight.

The dynamic process of comprehending sentence S has a two-stage process, namely *construction* and *integration*. During construction, the N+M nodes are activated and there is an initial activation vector for the set of nodes (a_1, a_2, ... a_{N+M}). The connectivity matrix then operates on this initial node activation vector in multiple activation cycles until there is a settling of the node activations to a new final stable activation profile for the N+M nodes. At that point, integration of the nodes has been achieved. Mathematically, this is accomplished by the initial activation vector being multiplied by the same connectivity matrix in multiple iterations until the N+M output vector of two successive interactions shows extremely small differences (signifying a stable settling of the integration phase). Sentences that are more difficult to comprehend would presumably require more cycles to settle. These dynamic processes have testable implications for psychological data. Reading times should be correlated with the number of cycles during integration. Recall of a node should be correlated with the number of relevant sentences and cycles of activation. Inferences should be encoded to the extent that they are activated and survive the integration phase. Kintsch summarizes substantial empirical evidence that supports these and other predictions from the CI model.

One weakness of the CI model has concerned the connectivity matrix, which captures the core of the language and discourse constraints. In the early days of CI modeling, the researchers had to compose the weights in the connectivity matrix by hand. This approach falls prey to the criticism that the researchers finagled the weights to fit the data in an ad hoc fashion. The obvious exit out of this loop is to generate the weights in a principled fashion computationally, ideally by a computer. The field of computational linguistics is close to achieving such a goal. Kintsch has used LSA to automatically activate concepts (near neighbors) from long-term memory associated with explicit words and to generate weights that connect the N+M nodes. Syntactic parsers can be used to compute weights by virtue of structural proximity. One technical limitation that researchers are facing is that there is no reliable mechanism for translating language to propositions, an important functional unit in the CI model. The new frontier of the CI model is to identify principled automated mechanisms for generating the weights in the connectivity matrices and initial activation values of nodes during sentence comprehension.

2 Two-party dialogue

Discourse analysts have identified dialogue patterns in different types (registers) of two-party dialogue. Some patterns are context-free in the sense that they occur in most conversational registers. Context-free patterns include the adjacency pairs in two-party dialogue identified by Schegloff and Sachs (1973), such as [question → answer] and [offer → {acceptance/refusal}]. Another ubiquitous pattern is an embedded counter-clarification question (Schober and Conrad, 1997), as illustrated in the context of a survey interview:

Person 1 (survey interviewer): How many pets are in your home?
Person 2 (interviewee): Should I include fish?
Person 1: Only include mammals and birds.
Person 2: Okay, I have four pets.

The embedded question is of course constrained by the knowledge state of Person 2, namely the uncertainty about what constitutes a pet. Another dialogue pattern that is frequent in classrooms is the [Initiate → Response → Evaluation] sequence (Sinclair and Coulthard, 1975), or more specifically the [Question → Answer → Feedback] sequence.

Teacher: What's 6 X 9? (Initiation, Question)
Student: 54 (Response, Answer)
Teach: Very good. (Evaluation, Feedback)

In tutorial dialogue, this sequence is expanded into the five-step tutoring frame introduced by Graesser and Person (1994).

Teacher: Why is it warmer in the summer than the winter here? (Question)
Student: The earth is closer to the sun? (Answer)
Teacher: I don't think so. (Short Feedback)
Teacher&Student: <Collaborative multiturn exchange to improve answer>
Teacher: Do you understand? (Comprehension gauging question)
Student: Yeah.

One reason why tutoring is better than classroom instruction is attributable to step four, in which the student and teacher have a collaborative exchange that scaffolds explanatory reasoning

2.1 *Representing regularities in dialogue*

Discourse analysts have documented discourse patterns such as these that occur in different discourse registers. In order to make some progress, they typically segment the conversations into speech act units and assign each unit to a speech act category. For example, D'Andrade and Wish (1985) have developed a system that is both theoretically grounded and that trained judges can reliably use. Their categories include: question (Q), reply to question (RQ), assertion (A), directive (D), indirect directive (ID), expressive evaluation (E), short verbal response (R, including back channel feedback, e.g., *uh huh*), and nonverbal response (N, such as head nod). There has been an ongoing effort to improve the categorization (tagging) of dialogue acts in the Discourse Resource Initiative (Core et al., 1999). Once the speech acts are tagged, sequences of these categories can be analyzed to test theoretical claims about discourse or to discover new patterns through machine learning inductive procedures.

It is convenient to represent the dialogue regularities by a set of production rules, a finite state automata, or a state transition network. The number of constraints in the condition slots of the production rules is a rough index of the extent to which the rules are context-sensitive versus context-free. Some researchers believe there are a large number of conceptual and pragmatic constraints that must be in place before a speech act can be classified in a particular category. A smooth dialogue with a conversational partner may be unlikely without the system having internal representations of the knowledge, beliefs, goals, intentions, plans, norms, values, and other cognitive representations of speech participants (Allen, 1995). Consider, for example, a symbolic structure of the speech act that is functionally a *request*.

REQUEST (S, H, ACT)

[Meaning the speaker requests the hearer to perform an action]

Constraints: **Speaker(S)** $\wedge$ **Hearer (H)** $\wedge$ **ACT(A)** $\wedge$

H is agent of ACT

Precondition: **WANT (S, ACT [H])**

[Meaning the speaker wants the hearer to do the action]

Effect: **WANT (H, ACT [H])**

[Meaning the hearer wants to do the action after the request]

BELIEVE (H, WANT S ACT [H])

[The hearer believes the speaker wants the hearer to do the action]

A speech act allegedly does not function as a request if the speaker does not want action A to occur, and is ineffective if the listener does not realize the speaker wants A.

The process of reliably reconstructing these knowledge states is of course a challenge computationally. Some progress is being made by statistical algorithms that induce patterns from large corpora of speech samples in particular applications, such as dialogues about train or airline schedules, but a general purpose pattern recognizer of knowledge, goals, and plans is not in the immediate technological horizon (Jurafsky and Martin, 2008). There must be a close alignment in the common ground (shared knowledge) between the two participants in the dialogue before there can be a reliable recognition of the other's knowledge, goals, and plans, but the process of achieving such an alignment is under debate (Clark, 1996; Pickering and Garrod, 2004).

2.2 *Computer simulation of dialogue*

Weizenbaum's (1966) Eliza program was the first conversational system that was reasonably successful, popular, and widely used. Eliza simulated a Rogerian client-centered psychotherapist, as illustrated in the conversation below.

> *Patient: You are like my father in some ways.*
> *ELIZA: How am I like your father?*
> *Patient: You are very aggressive but I think you don't want me to notice that.*
> *ELIZA: What makes you think I am aggressive?*
> *Patient: You always argue with me.*
> *ELIZA: Why do you think I argue with you?*

Like a typical Rogerian therapist, Eliza tried to get the patient to do the talking by asking the patient questions about the patient's verbal contributions. Eliza turned the patient's assertions into therapist's questions by simple syntactic transformational rules. That is, Eliza detected keywords and word combinations that matched production rules, which in turn generated Eliza's responses. The only intelligence in Eliza was the stimulus-response knowledge captured in production rules that operate on keywords and that perform syntactic transformations. What was so remarkable about Eliza is that 100–200 simple production rules could very often create an illusion of comprehension, even though Eliza had minimal depth and common ground with the user.

Efforts to build conversational systems continued in the 1970s and early 1980s. Schank and his colleagues built computer models of natural language understanding and rudimentary dialogue about scripted activities (Schank and Reisbeck, 1981). SHRDLU manipulated simple objects in a blocks world in response to a user's command (Winograd, 1972). By the mid-1980s, however, researchers were convinced that the prospect of building a good conversational system was implausible. The chief challenges were (a) the inherent complexities of natural language processing, (b) the unconstrained, open-ended nature of world knowledge, and (c) the lack of research on lengthy threads of connected discourse. This pessimistic picture was arguably premature because there have been a sufficient number of technical advances in the last decade for researchers to revisit the vision of building dialogue systems. The current conversational systems are not perfect, but they go a long way in creating the impression that the system is comprehending the user and responding appropriately.

A plan-based architecture is routinely adopted in current systems with dialogue modeling in computational linguistics, such as TRINDI (Larsson and Traum, 2000) and COLLAGEN (Rich, Sidner, and Lesh, 2001). The TRINDI project assumes the existence of an information state, that is, a rather detailed record of the current state of the dialogue. The information state is sufficiently detailed at multiple levels of language and planning to make the particular dialogue

distinct and to support the successful continuation of the dialogue. The information state approach is general enough to accommodate dialogue systems that range from the simplest finite-state script to the most complex Belief-Desire-Intention (BDI) model. The information state theory of dialogue modeling requires: (1) a description of the components of the information state, (2) formal representations of these components, (3) external dialogue from the human/other which triggers the update of the information state, (4) internal update rules which select dialogue moves and update the information state, and (5) a control strategy for selecting update rules to apply, given a particular information state. The COLLAGEN project (Rich et al., 2001) is very similar but contrasts three kinds of structure: linguistic, intentional, and attentional. Linguistic structure captures the sequence of utterances, whereas intentional structure captures the conversation goals and the attentional state is the focus of attention on salient elements of the discourse at a particular point. Existing implementations of COLLAGEN are an approximation of an underlying discourse theory of Grosz and Sidner (1986).

Natural language dialogue (NLD) facilities are expected to do a reasonable job in some conversational contexts, but not others. It depends on the subject matter, the knowledge of the learner, the expected depth of comprehension, and the expected sophistication of the dialogue strategies. A NLD facility is progressively more feasible when more of the following conditions are met.

1) An imperfect system is useful.
2) Expected precision of the information is modest.
3) Content is verbal content rather than mathematical.
4) The user has low or modest subject matter knowledge.
5) Idiomatic expressions are rare.
6) The computer doesn't need to construct a novel mental model.
7) The computer anticipates what users will say.

8) There are simple pragmatic ground rules.

9) The computer has many options and a license to redirect the dialogue by changing topics, asking questions, expressing generic dialogue moves (*Uh huh, Anything else?, I don't follow, That's interesting*).

2.3 *Tutorial dialogue systems*

Tutoring environments are feasible NLD applications because they meet most or all of the above nine conditions, particularly when the subject matter is verbal. It is noteworthy that even human tutors are not able to monitor the knowledge of students at a precise fine-grained level because much of what students express is vague, underspecified, ambiguous, fragmentary, and error-ridden (Fox, 1993; Graesser and Person, 1994). There are potential costs if a tutor attempted to do so. For example, it is often more worthwhile for the tutor to help build new correct knowledge than to become bogged down in dissecting and correcting each of the learner's knowledge deficits. Tutors do have an approximate sense of what a student knows and this appears sufficient to provide productive dialogue moves that lead to significant learning gains in the student (Chi et al., 2001; Graesser and Person, 1994).

Researchers have developed approximately a half dozen intelligent tutoring systems with dialogue in natural language. These systems help college students generate cognitive explanations and patterns of knowledge-based reasoning when solving particular problems (Moore, 1995). *AutoTutor* (Graesser, Jeon, and Dufty, 2008; Graesser et al., 2005) was developed for introductory computer literacy and Newtonian physics. *Why/Atlas* (Van Lehn et al., 2007) also has students learn about conceptual physics via a coach that helps them build explanations. The *Mission Rehearsal* system (Gratch et al., 2002) helps Army personnel interact in a virtual war scenario. *iSTART* helps students learn reading strategies by providing students with feedback concerning their explanations of sentences in text (McNamara, Levinstein, and Boonthum, 2004).

Tutorial NLD appears to be more feasible to the extent that the tutoring strategies follow what most human tutors do, as opposed to strategies that are highly sophisticated (Graesser and Person, 1994). Most human tutors anticipate particular correct answers (called *expectations*) and particular misunderstandings (*misconceptions*) when they ask learners questions and trace the learners' reasoning. As a learner articulates the answer or solves the problem, this content is constantly compared with the expectations and misconceptions. The tutor responds adaptively and appropriately when particular expectations or misconceptions are expressed. This tutoring mechanism is called *expectation and misconception tailored dialogue* (EMT dialogue), the mechanism incorporated in AutoTutor (Graesser et al., 2005; 2008). The EMT dialogue moves of most human tutors are not particularly sophisticated from the standpoint of ideal tutoring strategies that have been proposed in the fields of education and artificial intelligence. For example, analyses of human tutoring have revealed that tutors rarely implement intelligent pedagogical techniques such as bona fide Socratic tutoring strategies, modeling-scaffolding-fading, reciprocal teaching, building on prerequisites, and diagnosis/remediation of deep misconceptions. Instead, tutors tend to coach students in constructing explanations according to the EMT dialogue patterns. Fortunately, the EMT dialogue strategy is substantially easier to implement computationally than are the sophisticated tutoring strategies.

AutoTutor (Graesser et al., 2005, 2008; Van Lehn et al., 2007) attempts to hold a mixed-initiative dialogue with the student during tutoring. AutoTutor segments the student's turns into speech act units and then assigns these units into categories, such as Assertion, Short Answer, Metacognition (*I don't follow?*), Metacommunication (*What did you say?*), Definition Question (*What does X mean?*), and so on. There are approximately twenty categories of student speech acts; sixteen of these are different categories of student questions. AutoTutor attempts to accommodate any student question, assertion, comment, or extraneous speech act. AutoTutor needs to produce language in addition to comprehending language. Each turn of AutoTutor requires the generation of one or more dialogue moves that either adaptively respond to what the student just expressed or advance the conversation in a constructive fashion that answers the main question or problem. The dialogue moves within a turn are connected by dialogue markers (*Okay, Next consider* …). Some dialogue moves are very responsive to the student's preceding turn, such as the short feedback (positive, neutral, negative), the answers to student questions, and corrections of student misconceptions. Other dialogue moves push the dialogue forward in an attempt to cover the expectations in an answer to the main question. These forward-directed dialogue moves include Pumps (e.g., *Tell me more, What else?*), Hints, Prompts for specific words or phrases, and Assertions. The responsive and forward-directed dialogue moves together provide a mixed-initiative dialogue in which both parties of the conversation exert an influence over the conversation. These are not scripted conversations, but rather are dynamically emerging exchanges.

AutoTutor and human tutors attempt to get the learner to fill in words and propositions in the expectations. For example, suppose an answer requires the expectation: *The force of impact will cause the car to experience a large forward acceleration.* The following family of prompts is available to encourage the student to articulate particular content words in the expectation:

1. The impact will cause the car to experience a forward _____?
2. The impact will cause the car to experience a large acceleration in what direction?
3. The impact will cause the car to experience a forward acceleration with a magnitude that is very _____?
4. The car will experience a large forward acceleration after the force of _____?
5. The car will experience a large forward acceleration from the impact's _____?

6. What experiences a large forward acceleration?

The particular prompts selected are those that fill in missing information if answered successfully. That is, the dialogue management component adaptively selects hints and prompts in an attempt to achieve pattern completion. The expectation is covered when enough of the ideas underlying the content words in the expectation are articulated by the student so that the expectation is sufficiently covered. LSA and other semantic analyzers determine whether the student has sufficiently articulated each particular expectation.

Evaluations of AutoTutor have been encouraging in several respects. First, AutoTutor is useful because students learn about computer literacy and physics much better than by reading a textbook for an equivalent amount of time, and nearly as well as when studying with an expert human tutor. Second, the conversations of AutoTutor are surprisingly smooth because bystanders in a bystander Turing test cannot tell whether a randomly selected turn was generated by AutoTutor or a human tutor. Third, the LSA based judgments of whether a sentence-like expectation was covered in the dialogue is approximately as accurate as a graduate research assistant. These successes are surprising because AutoTutor does not really understand the learner at a deep level, with a fine-grained alignment of knowledge states in a common ground. This raises questions about the notion of common ground. That is, do participants in a dialogue really need to know a great deal of what each other knows for successful conversation to proceed? Perhaps not in tutoring environments in which there is a large gulf between the knowledge of a student and a tutor.

3 Closing Comments

This chapter has reviewed progress that has been made in developing computational models of text comprehension and two-party dialogue. Sufficient progress has been made in the fields of discourse processes, cognitive science, and computational linguistics to build detailed models of how discourse is comprehended and produced at multiple levels. Many of these levels are sufficiently well-specified to automate them on computer. Unlike ten or twenty years ago, we have reasonable solutions to handling problems of world knowledge, the vagueness and underspecification of natural language, and the management of longer threads of discourse. The computational models have evolved to the point of building useful computer technologies, such as essay graders, automated conversational tutors, question answering systems, and text analyzers that go well beyond readability formulae. It is hard to imagine what breakthroughs will emerge during the next ten years. Some of the difficult challenges for the future, which we could not cover in this chapter, will be computational models that perform automatic text generation, discourse-sensitive speech recognition, speech generation with appropriate intonation, and management of dialogue among three or more discourse participants.

References

Allen, J. (1995). *Natural language understanding*. Redwood City, CA: Benjamin/Cummings.

Baayen, R. H., Piepenbrock, R., & Gulikers. L. (1995). *The CELEX lexical database* (CD-ROM). Philadelphia, PA: Linguistic Data Consortium, University of Pennsylvania.

Biber, D. (1988). *Variations across speech and writing*. Cambridge, MA: Cambridge University Press.

Brill, E. (1995). Transformation-based error-driven learning and natural language processing: A case study in part-of-speech tagging. *Computational Linguistics*, 21, 543–66.

Burgess, C., Livesay, K., & Lund, K. (1998). Explorations in context space: Words, sentences, and discourse. *Discourse Processes*, 25, 211–57.

Charniak, E. (2000). A maximum-entropy-inspired parser. *Proceedings of the First Conference on North American Chapter of the Association for Computational Linguistics* (pp. 132–39). San Francisco, CA: Morgan Kaufmann Publishers.

Chi, M. T. H., Siler, S. A., Jeong, H., Yamauchi, T., & Hausmann, R. G. (2001). Learning from human tutoring. *Cognitive Science*, 25, 471–533.

Clark, H.H. (1996). *Using language*. Cambridge: Cambridge University Press.

Core, M., Ishizaki, M., Moore, J. D., Nakatani, C., Reithinger, N., Traum, D., & Tutiya, S. (1999). The report of the third workshop of the Discourse Resource Initiative, Chiba University and Kazusa Academia Hall. Technical Report No. 3, Chiba Corpus Project, Chiba, Japan.

Coltheart, M. (1981). The MRC Psycholinguistic Database. *Quarterly Journal of Experimental Psychology*, 33A, 497–505.

D'Andrade, R. G. & Wish, M. (1985). Speech act theory in quantitative research on interpersonal behavior. *Discourse Processes*, 8, 229–59.

De Vega, M., Glenberg, A. M., & Graesser, A. C. (Eds.) (2008). *Symbols, embodiment, and meaning*. Oxford, UK: Oxford University Press.

Fellbaum, C. (Ed.) (1998). *WordNet: An electronic lexical database*. Cambridge, MA: MIT Press.

Fox, B. (1993). *The human tutorial dialogue project*. Hillsdale: Erlbaum.

Graesser, A. C., Jeon, M., & Dufty, D. (2008). Agent technologies designed to facilitate interactive knowledge construction. *Discourse Processes*, 45, 298–322.

Graesser, A. C., Gernsbacher, M. A., & Goldman, S.R. (Eds.) (2003). *Handbook of discourse processes*. Mahwah, NJ: Erlbaum.

Graesser, A. C., McNamara, D. S., Louwerse, M. M., & Cai, Z. (2004). Coh-Metrix: Analysis of text on cohesion and language. *Behavioral Research Methods, Instruments, and Computers*, 36, 193–202.

Graesser, A. C., Olney, A., Haynes, B. C., & Chipman, P. (2005). AutoTutor: A cognitive system that simulates a tutor that facilitates learning through mixed-initiative dialogue. In Forsythe, C., Bernard, M. L., & Goldsmith, T. E. (Eds.) *Cognitive systems: Human cognitive models in systems design*. Mahwah, NJ: Erlbaum.

Graesser, A. C., & Person, N. K. (1994). Question asking during tutoring. *American Educational Research Journal*, 31, 104–37.

Graesser, A. C., Singer, M., & Trabasso, T. (1994). Constructing inferences during narrative text comprehension. *Psychological Review*, 101, 371–95.

Gratch, J., Rickel, J., Andre, E., Cassell, J., Petajan, E., & Badler, N. (2002). Creating interactive virtual humans: Some assembly required. *IEEE Intelligent Systems*, 17, 54–63.

Grosz, B. J. & Sidner, C. L. (1986). Attention, intentions, and the structure of discourse. *Computational Linguistics*, 12 (3), 175–204.

Hearst, M. (1992). Automatic acquisition of hyponyms from large text corpora, *Proceedings of the Fourteenth International Conference on Computational Linguistics*. Nantes, France: ACL.

Hempelmann, C. F., Dufty, D., McCarthy, P., Graesser, A. C., Cai, Z., & McNamara, D. S. (2005). Using LSA to automatically identify givenness and newness of noun-phrases in written discourse. In Bara, B. (Ed.) *Proceedings of the 27th Annual Meeting of the Cognitive Science Society* (pp. 941–6). Mahwah, NJ: Erlbaum.

Jurafsky, D. & Martin, J. H. (2008). *Speech and language processing: An introduction to natural language processing, computational linguistics, and speech recognition* (Edition 2). Upper Saddle River, NJ: Prentice-Hall.

Just, M. A. & Carpenter, P. A. (1992). A capacity theory of comprehension: Individual differences in working memory. *Psychological Review*, 99, 122–49.

Kintsch, W. (1998). *Comprehension: A paradigm for cognition*. Cambridge, UK: Cambridge University Press.

Klare, G.R. (1974–1975). Assessing readability. *Reading Research Quarterly*, 10, 62–102.

Landauer, T. K., Foltz, P. W., & Laham, D. (1998). An introduction to latent semantic analysis. *Discourse Processes*, 25, 259–84.

Landauer, T, McNamara, D. S., Dennis, S., Kintsch, W. (Eds.) (2007). *Handbook of Latent Semantic Analysis*. Mahwah, NJ: Erlbaum

Lappin, S. & Leass, H. J. (1994). An algorithm for pronominal coreference resolution. *Computational Linguistics*, 20, 535–61.

Larsson, S. & Traum, D. (2000). Information state and dialogue management in the TRINDI dialogue move engine toolkit. *Natural Language Engineering*, 6 (3–4), 323–40.

Lehmann, F. (Ed.) (1992). *Semantic networks in artificial intelligence*. Oxford, England: Pergamon Press.

Louwerse, M. M. & Mitchell, H. H. (2003). Toward a taxonomy of a set of discourse markers in dialog: A theoretical and computational linguistic account. *Discourse Processes*, 35, 199–239.

McCarthy, P. M., Myers, J. C., Briner, S. W., Graesser, A. C., & McNamara, D. S. (2009). Are three words all we need? A psychological and computational study of genre recognition. *Journal for Computational Linguistics and Language Technology*, 24, 23–55.

McNamara, D. S. & Kintsch, W. (1996). Learning from text: Effects of prior knowledge and text coherence. *Discourse Processes*, 22, 247–87.

McNamara, D. S., Levinstein, I. B., & Boonthum, C. (2004). iSTART: Interactive strategy trainer for active reading and thinking. *Behavioral Research Methods, Instruments, and Computers*, 36, 222–33.

Mitkov, R. (1998). Robust pronoun resolution with limited knowledge. *Proceedings of the 18th International Conference on Computational Linguistics* (pp. 869–75). Montreal, Canada.

Moore, J. D. (1995). *Participating in explanatory dialogues*. Cambridge: MIT Press.

Pennebaker, J. W. & Francis, M. E. (1999). Linguistic inquiry and word count (LIWC). Mahwah, NJ: Erlbaum.

Pickering, M. J. & Garrod, S. (2004). Toward a mechanistic psychology of dialogue. *Brain and Behavioral Sciences*, 27, 169–90.

Prince, E. F. (1981). Toward a taxonomy of given-new information. In Cole, P. (Ed.) *Radical pragmatics* (pp. 223–55). New York: Academic Press.

Rich, C., Sidner, C.L., & Lesh, N. (2001). COLLAGEN: Applying collaborative discourse theory to human-computer interaction. *AI Magazine*, 22(4), 15–25.

Roy, D. (2005). Grounding words in perception and action: Computational insights. *Trends in Cognitive Sciences*, 9, 389–96.

Rus, V. (2004). A first exercise for evaluating logic form identification systems, *Proceedings Third International Workshop on the Evaluation of Systems for the Semantic Analysis of Text (SENSEVAL-3)*, at the Association of Computational Linguistics Annual Meeting, July 2004. Barcelona, Spain: ACL.

Rus, V., McCarthy, P. M., McNamara, D. S., & Graesser, A. C. (2008). A study of textual entailment. *International Journal on Artificial Intelligence Tools*, 17, 659–85.

Schank, R. & Riesbeck, C. (1981). *Inside computer understanding*. Hillsdale, NJ: Lawrence Erlbaum.

Schegloff, E. A. & Sacks, H. (1973). Opening up closings. *Semiotica*, 8, 289–327.

Schober, M. F. & Conrad, F. G. (1997). Does conversational interviewing reduce survey measurement error? *Public Opinion Quarterly*, 60, 576–602.

Sekine, S. & Grishman, R. (1995). A corpus-based probabilistic grammar with only two nonterminals. *Fourth International Workshop on Parsing Technologies* (pp. 260–70). Prague/Karlovy Vary, Czech Republic.

Sinclair, J. M. & Coulthard, R. M. (1975). *Towards an analysis of discourse: The English used by teachers and their pupils.* London: Oxford University Press.

Sowa, J. F. (1983). *Conceptual structures: Information processing in mind and machines.* Reading, MA: Addison-Wesley.

Stevenson, M. (2002). Augmenting noun taxonomies by combining lexical similarity metrics. *Proceedings of The 17th International Conference on Computational Linguistics.* Taipei, Taiwan: ACL.

Van den Broek, P., Virtue, S., Everson, M. G., & Tzeng, Y., & Sung, Y. (2002). Comprehension and memory of science texts: Inferential processes and the construction of a mental representation. In Otero, J., Leon, J., & Graesser, A. C. (Eds.) *The psychology of science text comprehension* (pp. 131–54). Mahwah, NJ: Erlbaum.

van Dijk, T.A. & Kintsch, W. (1983). *Strategies of discourse comprehension.* New York: Academic Press.

Van Lehn, K., Graesser, A. C., Jackson, G. T., Jordan, P., Olney, A., & Rose, C. P. (2007). When are tutorial dialogues more effective than reading? *Cognitive Science, 31,* 3–62.

Veloso, M. M., & Carbonell, J. G. (1993). Derivational analogy in PRODIGY: Automating case acquisition, storage, and utilization. *Machine Learning, 10,* 249–78.

Weizenbaum, J. (1966). ELIZA – A computer program for the study of natural language communication between man and machine. *Communications of the ACM, 9,* 36–45.

Winograd, T. (1972). *Understanding natural language.* New York: Academic Press.

Zwaan, R.A. & Radvansky, G.A. (1998). Situation models in language comprehension and memory. *Psychological Bulletin, 123,* 162–85.

CHAPTER 29

Children, Conversation, and Acquisition

Eve V. Clark

Conversation is central to first language acquisition in children: They learn language from participating in conversation. Adults talk to babies from the start, and, through all kinds of interchange – looking, talking versus babbling, exchange games like peek-a-boo – start them on the road to language use. And children learn what is needed to use language for communication by taking part in conversational exchanges.

When speaking to young children, adults adjust how they say things because children know so little. To catch and hold young children's attention, they use shorter utterances than for adults, pause between utterances rather than within them, often rely on higher pitch, and use a lot of repetition and reformulation (e.g., Cameron-Falkner et al., 2003; Chouinard and E. V. Clark, 2003; Gallaway and Richards, 1994). They tend to introduce new words in formulaic frames and anchor them to words that are already familiar (e.g., Callanan, 1989; E. V. Clark and Wong, 2002). Children attend to such cues, and use statistical frequency during acquisition from the earliest stages on (e.g., Saffran, Aslin, and Newport, 1996; Pine and Lieven, 1997).

The two main issues I address here are (a) what young children need to know in order to participate in conversation, and (b) how conversation itself affects the process of acquisition. To start with, children must grasp the fact that language offers a means for communicating, that adults use words, phrases, and utterances to carry conventional meanings for talking about what's going on, what they want, and what they'd like others to do. Adult usage plays a critical role in exposing children to language and its uses for specific purposes in conversation (E. V. Clark, 2003; Tomasello, 2003).

1 Preliminaries to conversation

In talking, adults impose turns on children. They talk, then pause until the young child does something that can count as a contribution before they continue. With preverbal infants, adults may count a smile, a kick, or a burp as child-turns. Once infants begin to babble, adults up the ante and wait for a babble before they continue themselves; and after children begin to produce their first words, adults will wait for a word (e.g., Snow, 1977). This social reciprocity imposed prior to language use by children presents them with a social structure for later taking real turns in conversation.

1.1 *Intentions*

Critical to participation in any exchange is the interpretation of intentions. Why did A say that? What does A want? Is A offering or ordering? What is A warning B about? Children need to learn from their speech and actions what others intend. They also need to learn how to convey their own intentions, to indicate what they want, what they find interesting, what they intend to do. At the earliest stages, they tend to rely on gesture. By the age of twelve months, children use gestures to mark what they appear to want (reaching, leaning toward) versus what attracts their interest (pointing, staring intently) (Werner and Kaplan, 1963). These contrasting gestures are used for making requests and drawing attention to items of interest respectively, and so could be considered proto-speech acts of requesting and asserting (see Bates, Camaioni, and Volterra. 1975; Bruner, 1975). Some infants this age make use of gestures before words for objects and actions more generally (e.g., Kelly, 2006; Ozcaliskan and Goldin-Meadow, 2005). And, prior to speech, children can be very persistent in trying to get their meaning across nonverbally. For instance, they will go on reaching toward something they want until the adult hits on just what it is. Only at that point will they relax and wait for it to be handed to them (e.g., Golinkoff, 1983). In summary, by twelve months, infants make determined efforts to convey their own intentions.

Infants by this age construe adult actions, including speaking, as intentional. They attend to another's gaze at objects, and to actions on objects (e.g., Moll and Tomasello, 2004; Woodward, 2003). They attend to how adults carry out actions and take account of the circumstances. For example, if an adult touches something with her forehead while holding something else in her hands,

infants take that into account in copying the adult action and use their hands instead (Gergely, Bekkering, and Király, 2002; see also Carpenter, Call, and Tomasello, 2002). This suggests that they have identified the intended action, not just the means originally used to produce it. Children this age also distinguish intentional from unintentional actions (e.g., Carpenter, Akhtar, and Tomasello, 1998), and, when appropriate, ignore the unintentional ones.

Infants also seem to recognize that when adults speak, their intentions differ with the words used (E. V. Clark, 1987; 1990). They respond differently to familiar words (find known referents in the locus of joint attention) and unfamiliar ones (look for other possible referents in the focus of joint attention). They even infer that a hidden object is more likely to be the intended referent of an unfamiliar word than a familiar, visible object is (Baldwin, 1993a; 1993b). And when adults utter a command or request, young children consistently respond with actions linked to the content of what the adult just said (Shatz, 1978).

Children who are just two years old can track repairs that reflect intentions. When an adult names something and then corrects himself, using another new term instead, children discard the first term and learn the second. So when tested on both terms, they correctly identify referents of the second term and say they don't know what the first one means (E. V. Clark and Grossman, 1998). In short, by age two, children are already quite skilled at discerning intentions in others.

1.2 *Speech acts*

Language and conversational skill emerge in tandem. As children learn their first words, they also learn how to use them. But building up a vocabulary takes time, so children may at first use just one word at a time, continuing to rely on gestures to distinguish requests from assertions. They name the object desired, for example, while reaching toward where it is kept, as in the hypothetical example in (1):

(1) Small boy, looking toward the kitchen counter: *Cookie* + REACH

Or they will point at something they are interested in, as in (2):

(2) Small girl, looking at two birds on the grass: *Bird* + POINT

Gestures are occasionally combined with gestures, but more often with words as children make the transition from one word at a time to combinations of words (e.g., Iverson, Capirci, and Caselli 1994; Ozcaliskan and Goldin-Meadow, 2006). In (1), the child makes a request, a request that could later be expressed with *Want cookie* at first, then *I want a cookie* or *Can I have a cookie?* as the child adds increasing complexity. In much the same way, the assertion of interest in (2) will also be elaborated, perhaps *There bird*, then *Look at the birds*, as the child learns about how to express such intentions in words (E. V. Clark, 2003).

One task, then, is to work out which forms in a language can be used for which speech acts. What kind of utterance counts as a request? An assertion? A prohibition? Or a promise? Because there is no one-to-one assignment of sentences to speech act types, children can only draw on what they have observed about adult usage, along with any information in the current context. That is, they can take account of what is physically co-present – the context – and conversationally co-present – the words uttered by the speaker on that occasion (E. V. Clark, 2001; H. Clark, 1996, this volume).

Several studies have looked at whether children can identify speech acts in context. Three-year-olds, for instance, are quite good at distinguishing offers from requests when they hear variants of "Would you like to do A?" and then have to judge, in context, whether this utterance is equivalent to either "I want you to do A" (a request), or "I'll let you do A" (an offer) (Reeder, 1980). For instance, children might hear the sentence to be judged, followed by possible interpretations in context, as in (3):

(3) *Would you like to play on the train?*
　　(a) I want you to play on the train.
　　(b) I'll let you play on the train.

Children's judgments were elicited for settings with a Speaker (S), an Addressee (H), and the target toy. With offers, H stood near the toy with S at a neutral distance. With requests, S was near the toy with H at a neutral distance. Reeder argued that these scenarios licensed the pragmatic inferences needed to distinguish offers (4) from requests (5):

(4) OFFER Inference 1: H wants to do act A
　　　　　　Inference 2: No indication that S wants H to do A
　　　　　　Inference 3: No indication that S objects to H doing A
(5) REQU Inference 1: S wants H to do A
　　　　　　Inference 2: No indication that H wants to do A
　　　　　　Inference 3: No indication that H objects to doing A

At age two and a half (2;6), children chose the "let" variant in (3b) for offers sixty-nine percent of the time, but showed no preference yet for the "want" variant in (3a) for requests. By age three, they usually chose the appropriate variants for both offers and requests. How did they identify the speech acts? They could have been using simple inferences like the following: When the Hearer is closer to the toy, he wants to play with it; and when the Speaker is closer, he can let the Hearer play. In both cases, though, children must keep track of where the speaker is and draw the appropriate inference.

Older children produce more speech act types and more forms for each type. By age five, they can draw on a variety of forms to ask, order, forbid, and allow, for example (Grimm, 1975), even though what counts as a promise remains rather ill-defined even at age seven (Chomsky, 1969). Hannelore Grimm elicited speech acts from children by having them participate in scenarios like that in (6):

(6) To get a child to <u>ask</u> for something: "You're at the playground with Felix [a

large toy cat]. He's sitting on the swing and you're on the slide. Now you'd like Felix to let you swing too. What do you say to him?"

The adult doing the voice for Felix routinely refused to cooperate at least three times, compelling the child to reiterate the targeted speech act several times. The kind of exchange this elicited is illustrated in (7):

(7) *Child:* Felix, will you let me swing too, just once, please?
  Felix: I don't want you to swing. [refusal 1]
  Child: But then you can slide down the slide.
  Felix: I'd rather not let you swing. [refusal 2]
  Child: I'd like to swing just once, not you all the time.
  Felix: I'd still rather not let you swing. [refusal 3]
  Child: But you must!

Five-year-olds found it easier to ask, order, and forbid than to allow or promise. Seven-year-olds did well on all four directives, but still had difficulty with promising. Overall, children found it easier to produce speech acts that required addressees to act than speech acts in which the obligation remained with the speaker (see also Bernicot, 1992). Notice, though, that in these studies, children are either making a judgment about a speech act or taking on a specific role; they are not expressing their own intentions directly.

1.3 *Adding to common ground*

With each turn, the participants in a conversation accumulate common ground, information they both have, and know that the other has, for purposes of the current exchange. Consider the following episode in which a child first tries to initiate a conversation with an adult observer, fails, and then reinitiates it, this time successfully, when her mother enters the room (Snow, 1978, 254–5):

(8) *Meredith* (1;6), to an unfamiliar observer: Band-aid.
  Observer: Where's your band-aid?
  Meredith: Band-aid.
  Observer: Do you have a band-aid?
  Meredith: Band-aid.
  Observer: Did you fall down and hurt yourself?

(9) Meredith (after her mother enters the room): Band-aid.
  Mother: Who gave you the band-aid?
  Meredith: Nurse.
  Mother: Where did she put it?
  Meredith: Arm.

There are two points to note here. First, the difference between (8) and (9) turns on the absence versus presence of common ground. The observer doesn't know the circumstances under which Meredith acquired a band-aid, while Meredith's mother does and so can offer appropriate scaffolding for her daughter's one-word contributions. Second, the child's turns consist of just one word at a time so she still depends heavily on getting the relevant adult support (Bruner, 1983). As children learn to express more of what they know, they become less dependent on having events framed by adult speakers.

Just what children say depends in part on how well they can update the common ground they share with the addressee. By age two, they can keep rather careful track of what others know. For instance, in tasks where children aged 2;7 had to enlist parental help to retrieve a toy placed out of reach, O'Neill (1996) found that children provided significantly more information about where a toy was when the parent did *not* know its location (parents who had been outside or had had their eyes closed) than when the parent *did* know (parents who watched while the toy was put into one of two containers).

In another game with younger children (2;3), O'Neill again had them ask for parental help in retrieving stickers dropped into one of two identical opaque containers, again out of reach. In some trials the parent watched; in others, the parent sat with eyes closed and ears covered. These children also took into account what their parents knew, and mentioned the location more often when parents had *not* seen which container was used than when they had. In short, both one- and two-year-olds can add information to common ground. Meredith, at 1;6, needed considerable help in setting up the event she wanted to talk about. But at 2;0 to 2;6, children are considerably less dependent on such scaffolding, and can also judge what their parents do and don't know in context.

1.4 *Participating in conversation*

Young children, it turns out, initiate up to two-thirds of the exchanges between adult and child (Bloom et al., 1996). One-year-olds readily respond to adult questions and prompts, and also initiate conversations themselves, even though they may contribute just one word at a time, as in Meredith's exchange with her mother. However, some aspects of turn taking take longer than others to learn.

What one- and two-year-olds actually say on most occasions tends to be pertinent to what's happening. But their timing often goes awry: they often come in late, perhaps because they are less skilled than older speakers in planning for language production. As a result, their contributions can get misplaced. Making one's contribution depends not only on *what* one says but also on just *when* one says it. Children need to learn how to time their turns.

One measure of this is how good children are at taking over from the current speaker. In a study of two- and four-year-olds, Ervin-Tripp (1979) observed that when the younger children interrupted during another's turn, they then delayed in starting their own utterances between twenty-seven percent and fifty-five percent of the time. In the same situation, four-year-olds delayed their follow-up utterances only nine percent to twenty percent of the time.

Children get better at placing their interruptions as they get older. In another study of interruptions, Ervin-Tripp found that children under four and a half managed to enter at syntactic or prosodic boundaries twenty-five percent of the time with one other speaker, but only twelve percent of the time with two other speakers. Because they were slow in starting their contribution, they tended to overlap with or even follow another speaker's next turn, so what they said was often no longer relevant. Older children (ages 4;6 to 6;0) did better, and got the timing right more often (twenty-seven percent) even when they were interrupting two other speakers.

One reason children may be slow in their turn taking could be that they take longer than adults to plan what they want to say. Garvey (1984) looked at how long it took children in dyadic peer conversations to switch speakers. This "switching pause" was measured as children switched from one speaker to the next by using a question or some other turn transfer device. For the simplest exchanges (greetings, requests for repetition), three-year-olds had just under one second (0.9 sec) for their median switching pause duration. In more complicated exchanges (e.g., answering a *wh*-question, as in *What's that noise? – Maybe it's a typewriter*), the median duration for their switching pause was one and a half seconds. For five-year-olds, switching pauses were significantly shorter overall, at 0.7 second in simpler turn transfers and 1.1 seconds in more complex ones. As children get more skilled at planning and producing what they want to say, their turn taking becomes more adept.

1.5 *Attention*

Conversations require contributions appropriate to the occasion. Participants in a conversation need to come up with appropriate information when they take a turn. This ability has been studied in several ways. Researchers have looked at how well children can answer questions, how well they can join in ongoing conversations with family members, and how well they can contribute to conversations between a parent and an older sibling.

Children appear to track what others are saying from an early age. For instance, when two-and-a-half-year-olds hear their own names used by others, they consistently look at that speaker, presumably expecting to be addressed in the next turn (Forrester, 1988). And their intrusions at age two to three into conversations between parents and older siblings offer further evidence that they are attending to what is being said. In their analysis of family interactions, Dunn and Shatz (1989) found that intrusions were quite frequent, even when the younger children were just two, and became more so over the course of a year of observations. Take the exchanges in (10) and (11) (Dunn and Shatz, 1989, 402–3):

(10) Sibling to mother (about a picture): *I don't know where to stick it.*
     Mother to sibling: On your door. Stick it on your door.
     Child (2;9): ***I'll stick it for her***.

(11) Older sibling is playing a game with mother about a pretend shopping trip; she gets confused about where she has put her bag down.

     Sibling-to-mother: Did I leave my bag there? [i.e., at the "shop"]

     Mother-to-sibling: You didn't leave your bag at Sainsbury's, did you?

     *Child-to-sibling(pointing out bag at pretend" home"): **No! At home!***

These typical intrusions contain information immediately pertinent to the preceding adult or sibling utterances. This strongly suggests that the younger child is both attending to and understanding the ongoing conversation.

Over the course of a year, Dunn and Shatz found no change in the overall rate of child intrusions. But the number of intrusions addressed to others doubled, suggesting that the younger children understood more of each conversation as they got older (see also Barton and Tomasello, 1991). The degree of pertinence was greater when the topic concerned the child, with ninety-seven percent of intrusions counted as relevant at age two. For other topics, the relevance was lower (ranging from thirty-six percent to sixty-one percent). But the number of irrelevant intrusions also declined steadily with age, from twenty-nine percent at age two down to only ten percent at three. Lastly, young children's intrusions became more likely to include new information as they got older, with a rise from forty-one percent at age two to sixty-eight percent at age three. This evidence of understanding also shows that, with their intrusions, young children are already learning to add to common ground.

2 Social roles

People speak in different ways in different roles – as parent, teacher, clarinetist, rock climber, and plumber. Their speech also differs with the topic, and with the addressee – from siblings and other close family members, to more distant relatives, to friends, to strangers. Their choice of forms in language in each setting also reflects their relative power, status, and gender. In short, speakers deploy a variety of registers for use on different occasions, with different addressees, for different purposes. As Gumperz (1982) noted, every speaker belongs to myriad speech communities – groups that share rules and norms for using language.

Languages come not in just one variety, but in many. In each community, speakers must learn the conventional practices for specific roles on different occasions. Their choices and practices reflect the current role they are projecting – as sibling, friend, parent, or tutor, say – together with how that role is marked as male or female, in talking to specific addressees. Even adults are continually adding to the communities they participate in and so have to pick up on yet other practices (Eckert and McConnell-Ginet, 1992). The roles in each case are those assigned by society – in the family, in specialized groups (a classroom, a choir, a lacrosse team), and in the larger society. Effectively, these roles involve a construction of identity through an interaction of biology (one's age and sex) and social setting (the language viewed as appropriate for male versus female children, for adolescents, and for adults in different social positions).

Learning different registers, and the features that characterize them, requires that children attend to who uses what (a) in different types of interaction (e.g., playing, instructing, teasing, narrating), (b) in each setting (e.g., playground, home, classroom, clinic, train station), (c) for each subgroup, and (d) for each type of addressee (e.g., another child, an adult, a family member, a friend, a stranger). The range of roles children can use in specific settings shifts with age, as do the skills at their disposal for marking the appropriate register (e.g., Andersen, 1990; Sachs and Devin, 1976).

Preschool children have already gleaned some knowledge of the dimensions at work in marking certain roles and the relative power associated with them. When asked to enact different roles by doing the voices for puppets in settings such as the home, the clinic, or the classroom, for instance, one can identify the features children make use of and assess how skilled they are at distinguishing one role from another (Andersen, 1990). Four- to seven-year-olds are sensitive to relative power, for example, associating it with fathers over mothers and children, teachers over pupils, and doctors over nurses and patients. When doing puppet voices in powerful roles, they are less likely to make polite requests, and instead issue more imperatives than when they speak in less powerful roles. In the role of children in the family, for example, they favor indirect requests and hints to fathers (*Ice cream tastes nice, doesn't it?*) over direct requests (*I need some ice cream*).

As children get older, they become better at differentiating roles through language. At age two to three, they use a high pitch for baby dolls and small toy animals, and continue to do this to distinguish child roles from adult ones (Sachs and Devin 1976). By age four, they will try to lower their pitch for adult male voices but find this hard to maintain (Andersen, 1990). They can also supply appropriate vocabulary in a familiar setting like the home, but have minimal knowledge of the relevant vocabulary for doctors or visits to a doctor. There, for instance, the terms they produced included *temperature* and *thermometer* (often confused), *cast, broken, cut* (meaning *operate*), *damage* (in the throat), *medical* (for medicine), *shot things* (for syringes), *stitches, X-ray,* and *aspirin*. How much they still have to learn is nicely illustrated by one six-year-old doing the voice for the role of doctor, in (12):

(12) *I'll have to operate – scalpel, screwdriver, and uh, what else can we use?*

Children aged six and seven are beginning to acquire specialized vocabulary for this domain, but adult-like mastery can take many years (Andersen, 1990). How to talk in a role, then, takes understanding of status and power in a group and in the larger community. It also takes understanding of who has power and the extent to which it stems from gender, age, and status. Children must also learn what kinds of speech are considered appropriate in their society and their community by sex and age. In short, speaker choices are often used to signal social allegiances as well as communicative intentions.

3 Acquisition in conversation

In conversation adults expose children to how to use language in the community, how to tailor it to specific addressees, and how to talk about particular topics. In displaying a language to young children, adults frequently present them with new words and constructions they've not met before. Everyday use provides extensive information about how a language works – its grammatical rules – and how it is used. But adults do even more with young children. They rely on frequent formulaic utterances to introduce new words, for example, and thereby flag new words as new for their young children. And they make frequent use of basic constructions using general-purpose verbs like *go, make,* and *put* (e.g., Cameron-Falkner et al., 2003; Goldberg, 1995; Sethuraman, Goldberg, and Goodman, 1997). Children are sensitive to frequency in usage and also to cues that they are being offered new or special information. This can be seen in their uptake of new words at age two to three and in their responses to adult side-sequences and embedded corrections after they have made an error (e.g., Chouinard and E. V. Clark, 2003; E. V. Clark, 2007; E. V. Clark and Wong, 2002).

3.1 *Getting words*

Adults make use of a small number of formulaic frames when they offer young children unfamiliar words (E. V. Clark and Wong, 2002). These nearly always take one of the forms in (13):

(13) This/That is a ——.
      These/Those are ——.
      This is called a ——.
      See/Look at the ——.

Children show that they are attending to new words by responding to offers like these with repeats and incorporations of the new words, as in (14) and (15):

(14) M (1;10, picking up a toy walrus and putting her finger on a tusk): *Big nose.*
      Father: *No. Those are tusks.*
      M: *Tusks.*
      Father: *They're like big teeth. (E. V. Clark, unpublished observations)*

(15) D (3;9.18, at the airport; watching as a mechanic put two chocks by the plane wheels): *Why did he put two loggers?*
      Mother: *Oh, they're called chocks and they keep the wheels from moving.*
      D: *Why did he put the chocks? (E. V. Clark, diary data)*

In (14), M immediately picks up on the new word *tusks* and repeats it, as a single-word utterance, in her next turn; in (15), D does

the same but instead of repeating the new word on its own, he incorporates it into his next utterance as the direct object of *put* (E. V. Clark, 2007; Réger 1986).

Children on occasion acknowledge new words with forms like *yeah, uh-huh,* and *mmh* in their next utterance, sometimes as a preface to saying something further about the current topic. On other occasions, they continue on, in their next turn, to talk about the referent of a new word even if they do not use the word itself. By responding in these ways, young children show that they are *attending to* new words and, in repeating or acknowledging them, *ratifying* the adult's use on that occasion.

Once adults have offered a new word, they typically go on to provide further information about properties of the referent. They give information about class or set membership (*a spaniel is a dog, ivy is a kind of plant*), about parts such as paws, teeth, and tails (*here's his nose; a thumb is part of your hand*); about texture, color, and material (*the boat is made of wood, fish have scales*); about characteristic sounds and motion (*cats go "meow," rabbits hop around*), and about function (*this whisk is used for stirring, the knife is for cutting, the strainer lets water through and holds the tea leaves*) (e.g., Callanan, 1989; E. V. Clark and Wong, 2002; Masur, 1997; Saylor and Sabbagh, 2004). In assigning new words to semantic fields and setting up semantic relations that link new words to familiar ones, adults license a range of inferences in context, for children, about the probable meanings of the new words (e.g., E. V. Clark, 2002).

Adult offers of words and relations help children start to set up semantic domains as they add to their vocabulary. The information adults offer about objects and actions allow children to begin specifying the networks of relations that link word meanings within and across domains (e.g., Bowerman, 2005; Ebeling and Gelman, 1994; Goodman, McDonough, and Brown, 1998; Rogers, 1978). But this happens, not as language lessons, but in the course of conversation. Building up domains takes a long time.

3.2 *Getting language – sound, morpheme, word, construction*

In talking to them, adults offer children extensive information about how language works. They make use of the conventional expressions and idioms in that language; they offer terms for objects, actions, relations, and events that are the focus of joint attention; and they use language appropriate to the speech acts relevant for conveying their intentions on each occasion. They are also intent on making sure their children understand them, given that children know very little language when they start out. So adults keep track of what their children are trying to say and check up when their children can't understand them. This happens when children make errors of omission or of commission. Adults then often reformulate what the children wanted to say, using conventional language to restate the children's apparent intentions, as in (16) and (17):

(16) Abe (2;5.0): *playing game.*
     Father: *Okay, Abe let's play a game.*

(17) Abe (2;5.7): *baker!*
     Father: *You're a baker?*

Notice that the adult reformulations offered in (15) and (16) offer specific alternatives to the child's initial wording, but they are designed to express the same intention, the same meaning as the child. The child therefore has two forms, his own and the adult's, apparently expressing the same meaning. But since differences in form mark differences in meaning, only one of the forms conventionally expresses the intended meaning, namely the adult one. In short, children use contrast here, along with priority to adult speech, to eliminate errors in the course of development (Chouinard and E. V. Clark, 2003; E. V. Clark, 1987, 1990).

Adult reformulations often come in the form of side sequences, follow-up questions that check on just what the child means, where the child's next turn often includes some correction of the original child error, as in (18):

(18) Abe (2;5.10): *I want butter mine.*
     Father: *Okay. Give it here and I'll put butter on it.*
     Abe: *I need butter on it.*

Adults use such side sequences, along with embedded corrections, to reformulate errors of pronunciation, of morphology (noun and verb inflections), of lexicon (the right words for the occasion), and of syntax (the appropriate construction for the intended meaning). Through comparisons with the forms adults offer for all kinds of errors, children get extensive corrections indirectly, especially during early acquisition (Chouinard and E. V. Clark, 2003; Saxton, Backley, and Gallaway, 2005; Saxton, Houston-Price, and Dawson, 2005; see also Pullum and Scholz, 2002; Legate and Yang, 2002).

Adult speech, replete with side sequences and embedded corrections, plays a critical role in presenting children with conventional ways to express meanings. Because the conventional versions are immediately juxtaposed to erroneous child forms in conversation, adults draw children's attention to conventional compared to nonconventional uses, and thereby license children's opting for the conventional forms for their intended meanings.

Yet whether adults talk to children, and how much they do so, differs with social class and cultural norms. Social groups have different expectations about how children should behave in talking to adults and about what is appropriate. Children may be encouraged, for example, to display what they know in response to questions, but not to participate in conversation otherwise. They may be encouraged to deal with teasing and to tease back, but not to argue (e.g., Heath, 1983; Miller, 1986). They may be given extensive directions about how to act and use speech, yet at age two or three rarely be regarded by an adult as a conversational partner (e.g., Ochs and Schieffelin, 1984).

4 Genres of talk in conversation

As children learn more about language, they also learn more about how to use it. They learn how and when to be polite, how to be persuasive, how to resolve conflicts and negotiate. They learn how to give stage directions for pretend play they are planning, and how to tell stories.

4.1 *Politeness*

What counts as polite? And when is politeness called for? What is the gain in being polite? Some aspects of politeness are imposed by adults who demand that young children say *please* and *thank you*, ask before getting down from the table, and greet newcomers to the house. But in their requests, four-year-olds rely mostly on direct questions and imperatives. At age five or six, children can produce some polite requests, and, at seven, command a larger range of polite options.

What do children know about politeness? By age three, they identify *please*, question intonation, and questions as politer than absence of *please*, assertive intonation, and imperatives. But even at six, children judge uses of the conditional and of formal pronouns in Italian as politer than uses of the indicative and of informal pronouns only sixty percent of the time (Bates, 1976).

When somewhat older children are introduced to a game where they have to get the adult in charge to give them enough of the right color pegs to complete a design, the first requests from nine-year-olds are just as abrupt as those from five-year-olds. All the children relied on imperatives. But nine-year-olds then modulated their requests to draw on politer forms when they were turned down. Five- and seven-year-olds had difficulty doing this (Axia and Baroni, 1985). They also had difficulty judging who the recipient of a polite versus impolite request was. By age nine, though, they identified polite forms as directed to adults and impolite ones to children. Yet at all three ages (five, seven, nine), they found it hard to identify the features that made an utterance polite or not.

Politeness appears to demand rather detailed pragmatic analysis of the relations between speaker and addressee, along with identification of the speaker's goal in trying to obtain something from the addressee (Brown and Levinson, 1987). This in turn requires assessing benefits versus costs to the participants, which may require quite a sophisticated grasp of how social groups work.

4.2 *Persuasion*

Persuading someone else to act, to give up a toy, or to take a different perspective takes skill. The speaker must minimize the cost to the addressee while maximizing the benefit of what's being asked for. Adults often use polite forms for this purpose in their negotiations, and this can also be observed in children.

In one study of role playing, three- to six-year-olds were asked to persuade a mother to buy a toy or a playmate to share one. The addressee in each case refused to accede to the children's requests five times in succession, following a set script. In their efforts to persuade, the children relied mainly on bargains and guarantees. As they got older, they used a greater number of positive elements (offers, bargains, politeness) and fewer assertions of their own rights. In doing this, older children emphasized benefits for the addressee over any costs. Finally, all the children made some appeal to norms and notions of fairness, but boys were slightly more likely to do so than girls (Weiss and Sachs, 1991).

Do children's spontaneous attempts at persuasion parallel those in role play? In one study, an observer recorded adult–child pairs as they shopped in a store where they had to pass through the toy department on their way to the food section. None of the adults entered intending to buy their children a toy. Axia (1996) looked at children's attempts to persuade their parents, predicting that six- to eight-year-olds would be egocentric in perspective while ten-year-olds would be better negotiators, able to take the adult's perspective as well, and likely to use politer requests. As predicted, the older children were more strategic in trying to persuade parents to buy a toy, and were willing to negotiate, conceding adult points, then bringing up new reasons for buying anyway.

Effective persuasion takes a long time to master. Even fifteen-year-olds are not always good at persuading a parent, teacher, best friend, or unfamiliar peer to buy a school newspaper (Piché, Rubin, and Michlin, 1978). Both eleven- and fifteen-year-olds used more imperatives to lower-status addressees (friends and peers). Their imperatives included commands, threats (*If you don't subscribe …*), and bribes (*If you get it, I'll …*). They also used more imperatives to parents and best friends than to teachers and unfamiliar peers. But fifteen-year-olds were better at coming up with appeals based on norms, status in the school class, and attitude toward the school, as in (19) and (20):

(19) *Well, you're my friend and if you're my friend you'll buy one.*

(20) *Your whole class oughta do it. They owe it to the school.*

As children get older, they rely more on politeness to persuade. They also adopt a negotiating stance where they take account of the other's objections and propose alternatives as they try to achieve their goal.

4.3 *Resolving conflicts*

Children appeal to negotiation quite early when faced with conflicts. This is apparent even for three-year-olds, as in (21) when the first speaker, Ken, announces his intention of playing with a truck that belongs to the other child, Dan:

(21) (Ken goes to the truck as Dan plays with blocks)

> *Ken: I'm drive on truck.*
> *Dan: But this is my truck.*
> *Ken: Can I drive on it?*
> *Dan (joins Ken at truck): No, you can ride on the back.*

When Dan objects, Ken asks permission. And although Dan refuses, he offers Ken an alternative. By three, then, children

can cooperate in dealing with a conflict (Eisenberg and Garvey 1981).

Conflicts occur whenever one person refuses a request, blocks an action, or disagrees with an assertion. To resolve such encounters, children – like adults – appeal to reasons and justifications for their positions, as in (22) (Eisenberg and Garvey 1981):

(22) (Anna and Ben are playing with plastic dishes)
> *Anna: I need a knife.*
> *Ben. You have a knife. [refusal]*
> *Anna: No, I don't. This is a spoon. [justification for request]*
> *Ben: Well, I've got all the knifes.*

Appeals to reasons and justifications show that children understand the general conditions of requests: The first speaker wants the addressee to do something. Offers of alternatives underline this understanding, as in the exchange between four-year-olds in (23):

(23) (Annie has taken the ladder away from Rachel.)

> *Rachel: Annie, gimme that ladder.*
> *Annie: No, I don't have to.*
> *Rachel: I wanna play with it. [justification]*
> *Annie: Well, I got it first. [counter-justification]*
> *Rachel: I gotta put it on here. Now you gimme it. [reason; reiteration]*
> *Annie (offer struck): You can have this. [alternative offer]*
> *Rachel: No, if you gimme ladder, I'll give you this (offers flashlight) if you gimme ladder. [counter to alternative]*
> (Annie drops ladder and picks up flashlight.)

Children who offer compromises are the most successful in getting what they want. Use of conditional proposals, counteroffers, and reasons also lead to successful resolutions. But children who simply reiterate their requests and ignore refusals meet with little success.

The resolution of conflicts can differ by community. Local assumptions about socialization and appropriate behavior enter here, even where the causes of disputes – possession of a toy, say – appear similar (see Corsaro and Rizzo, 1990; Goodwin, 1993).

4.4 *Stage directions*

When children play together, they often plan their play ahead of time, in the form of quite elaborate stage directions. Take this exchange observed by Sawyer (1997: 65), between two boys, in (24).

(24) [John and Muhammad playing with legos]
> John (5;2): *My flying saucer comes up.*
> *He's a bad guy.*
> *Pretend they were my guy's friend,*
> *and=*
> Muhammed (4;0): *=but they were still*
> *good guys.*
> John: *Unhuh, and they, he– And they*
> *din't know what's in it.*
> *And they were very curious. And so they*
> *opened it.*
> *Now come on. Let's play.*

The first speaker, John, lays out an elaborate set of directions and then, with *Let's play*, they launch into the enactment. Sometimes stage directions and enactment are intermingled, as in (25), with two children playing Cinderella (Lodge, 1979:365).

(25) A: *Where are you going tonight?*
> *You said you were going to the ball.*
> B: *I'm going to the ball.*
> A: *Is the Prince going too?*
> B: *Yes, and I'm going with him.*
> *You got cross and argued about it.*
> A: *Oh no you're not – I am.*
> B: *We'll see about that. Mother!*
> *You were mother and she didn't*
> *want you to go.*
> A (as mother):*You're not going to the*
> *ball tonight!*
> B: *There you are, see.*
> A: *I'll never speak to you again!*

The stage directions suggest that children as young as three and a half to four are capable of planning elaborate sequences of events while keeping track of what each character is to do and say.

Children consistently put stage directions into the past tense, possibly to mark them as unreal with respect to the present moment (Lodge, 1979). This distinguishes them from utterances used in the enactments of the directions. Children do this not only in English, but also in other languages – Dutch, French, German, and Italian – at around the same age (Kaper, 1980). After such planning, children remember and carry out the anticipated events in their play. Stage directions offer an interesting domain in which to track children's ability to jointly plan characters and events, and then act out those plans, all the while coordinating with at least one other child.

4.5 *Telling stories*

What do children need to know to tell a story? They need to be able to coordinate a setting, some characters, and a series of events. (This, of course, resembles their stage directions for playing.) They need to be able to link characters' motives to goals and a final outcome for the sequence of events. They must keep track of the main story and of subplots. And they must use the appropriate linguistic options, including any relevant rhetorical devices (*Once upon a time …*) in telling the story. This list, though, gives only the barest idea of what one needs to know. Tellers of tales are also expected to entertain, maintain suspense, take different perspectives in the course of the telling, and keep track of both main and subsidiary characters.

Children's storytelling skills have been studied by eliciting narratives for a picture book without words, at different ages and for different languages (Berman and Slobin, 1994; Hickmann and Hendricks, 1999). Their success depends both on their emerging skill in tracking the various elements crucial to maintaining the plot of a story, and on their available linguistic knowledge. At four, children do quite poorly on both counts. By nine, they are beginning to do quite well.

Children take some time to develop the discursive skills demanded here: they have to manage a complex story line, with both main and subsidiary events, main and minor characters, and at the same time keep track of what the listener does and doesn't know. And they need to identify the relevant linguistic devices to do all this. They need to know how to use aspect marking, if this is available in their language; how to use pronouns after first references; how to distinguish main from subsidiary events; and how to start and end stories (Slobin, 1996).

While storytelling is not central to conversation, it is a skill often deployed within conversation, but it makes use of planning and organization over larger domains than are usually called for in conversational exchanges. It stretches children's linguistic skills still further, and reveals how they integrate linguistic knowledge, rhetorical devices, and planning over large domains of discourse.

5 Summary

Children's conversational skills emerge along with their language. In effect, they learn what to say and how to say it from conversations. Adults not only offer models of the conventional way to say things, they check up when they're not sure they have understood their children, and, in doing so, they present conventional ways to say what they think was intended. Children in their turn add more linguistic options and exhibit growing skill in their uses for conversational purposes: They learn to instruct and persuade, to negotiate their way out of conflict, to use politeness to gain what they want with requests, and to entertain with stories.

References

Andersen, E. S. (1990). *Speaking with style: The sociolinguistic skills of children*. London: Routledge.

Axia, G. (1996). How to persuade mum to buy a toy. *First Language*, 16, 301–17.

Axia, G. & Baroni, M. R. (1985). Linguistic politeness at different ages. *Child Development*, 56, 918–27.

Baldwin, D. A. (1993a). Early referential understanding: Infants' ability to recognize referential acts for what they are. *Developmental Psychology*, 29, 832–43.

(1993b). Infants' ability to consult the speaker for clues to word reference. *Journal of Child Language*, 20, 395–418.

Barton, M. E. & Tomasello, M. (1991). Joint attention and conversation in mother-infant-sibling triads. *Child Development*, 62, 517–29.

Bates, E. (1976). *Language and context: the acquisition of pragmatics*. New York: Academic Press.

Bates, E., Camaioni, L., & Volterra, V. (1975). The acquisition of performatives prior to speech. *Merrill-Palmer Quarterly*, 21, 205–26.

Berman, R. A. & Slobin, D. I. (1994). *Relating events in narrative: A cross-linguistic developmental study*. Hillsdale, NJ: Lawrence Erlbaum.

Bernicot, J. (1992). *Les actes de langage chez l'enfant*. Paris: Presses Universitaires de France.

Bloom, L., Margulis, C., Tinker, E., & Fujita, N. (1996). Early conversations and word learning: contributions from child and adult. *Child Development*, 67, 3154–75.

Bowerman, M. (2005). Why can't you "open" a nut or "break" a cooked noodle? Learning covert object categories in action word meanings. In Gershkoff-Stowe, L. & Rakison, D. (Eds.) *Building object categories in developmental time* (pp. 209–43). Mahwah, NJ: Lawrence Erlbaum.

Brown, P. & Levinson, S. C. (1987). *Politeness: some universals in language usage*. Cambridge: Cambridge University Press.

Bruner, J. S. (1975). The ontogenesis of speech acts. *Journal of Child Language*, 2, 1–20.

(1983). *Child's talk: Learning to use language*. New York: Norton.

Callanan, M. A. (1989). Maternal speech strategies and children's acquisition of hierarchical category labels. *Genetic Psychology*, 17, 3–12.

Cameron-Falkner, T., Lieven, E., & Tomasello, M. (2003). A construction based analysis of child directed speech. *Cognitive Science*, 27, 843–73.

Carpenter, M., Akhtar, N., & Tomasello, M. (1998). Fourteen-through 18-month-old infants differentially imitate intentional and accidental actions. *Infant Behavior & Development*, 21, 315–30.

Carpenter, M., Call, J., & Tomasello, M. (2002). Understanding others' prior intentions enables 2-year-olds to imitatively learn a complex task. *Child Development*, 73, 1431–42.

Chomsky, C. S. (1969). *The acquisition of syntax in children from 5 to 10*. Cambridge, MA: MIT.

Chouinard, M. M., & Clark, E. V. (2003). Adult reformulations of child errors as negative evidence. *Journal of Child Language, 31*, 637–69.

Clark, E. V. (1987). The principle of contrast: a constraint on language acquisition. In MacWhinney, B. (Ed.) *Mechanisms of language acquisition* (pp. 1–33). Hillsdale, NJ: Lawrence Erlbaum.

(1990). The pragmatics of contrast. *Journal of Child Language, 17*, 417–31.

(2001). Grounding and attention in the acquisition of language. In Andronis, M., Ball, C., Elston, H., & Neuvel, S. (Eds.) *Papers from the 37th meeting of the Chicago Linguistic Society* (Vol.1, pp. 95–116). Chicago: Chicago Linguistic Society.

(2002). Making use of pragmatic inferences in the acquisition of meaning. In Beaver, D. Kaufmann, S., Clark, B. Z., & Casillas, L. (Eds.) *The construction of meaning* (pp. 45–58). Stanford, CA: CSLI Publications.

(2003). *First language acquisition*. Cambridge: Cambridge University Press.

(2007). Young children's uptake of new words in conversation. *Language in Society, 36*, 157–82.

Clark, E. V. & Grossman, J. B. (1998). Pragmatic directions and children's word learning. *Journal of Child Language, 25*, 1–18.

Clark, E. V. & Wong, ADW (2002). Pragmatic directions about language use: words and word meanings. *Language in Society, 31*, 181–212.

Clark, H. H. (1996). *Using language*. Cambridge: Cambridge University Press.

(this volume). Spoken discourse and its emergence.

Corsaro, W. A. & Rizzo, T. A. (1990). Disputes in the peer culture of American and Italian nursery-school children. In Grimshaw, A D. (Ed.) *Conflict talk: Sociolinguistic investigations of arguments in conversations* (pp. 21–66). Cambridge: Cambridge University Press.

Dunn, J. & Shatz, M. (1989). Becoming a conversationalist despite (or because of) having an older sibling. *Child Development, 60*, 399–410.

Ebeling, K. S. & Gelman, S. A. (1994). Children's use of context in interpreting "big" and "small." *Child Development, 65*, 1178–92.

Eckert, P. & McConnell-Ginet, S. (1992). Think practically and look locally: Language and gender as community-based practice. *Annual Review of Anthropology, 21*, 461–90.

Eisenberg, A. R. & Garvey, C. (1981). Children's use of verbal strategies in resolving conflicts. *Discourse Processes, 4*, 149–70.

Ervin-Tripp, S. (1979). Children's verbal turn-taking. In Ochs, E. & Schieffelin, B. B. (Eds.) *Developmental pragmatics* (pp. 391–414). New York: Academic Press.

Forrester, M. A. (1988). Young children's polyadic conversation monitoring skills. *First Language, 7*, 145–58.

Gallaway, C. & Richards, B. J. (Eds.) (1994). *Input and interaction in language acquisition*. Cambridge: Cambridge University Press.

Gergely, G., Bekkering, H., & Király, I. (2002). Rational imitation in preverbal infants. *Nature, 415 (6873)*, 755.

Goldberg, Adele E. 1995. *Constructions: A construction grammar approach to argument structure*. Chicago: University of Chicago Press.

Golinkoff, R. M. (1983). The preverbal negotiation of failed messages: insights into the transition period. In Golinkoff, R. M. (Ed.) *The transition from prelinguistic to linguistic communication* (pp. 57–78). Hillsdale, NJ: Lawrence Erlbaum.

Goodman, J. C., McDonough, L., & Brown, N. B. (1998). The role of semantic context and memory in the acquisition of novel nouns. *Child Development, 69*, 1330–44.

Goodwin, M. H. (1993). Tactical uses of stories: Participation frameworks within boys' and girls' disputes. In Tannen, D. (Ed.) *Gender and conversational interaction* (pp. 110–43). Oxford: Oxford University Press.

Grimm, H. (1975). Analysis of short-term dialogues in 5–7 year olds: Encoding of intentions and modifications of speech acts as a function of negative feedback. Paper presented at the Third International Child Language Symposium, London.

Gumperz, J. J. (1982). *Discourse strategies*. Cambridge: Cambridge University Press.

Heath, S. B. (1983). *Ways with words*. Cambridge: Cambridge University Press.

Hickmann, M. & Hendriks, H. (1999). Cohesion and anaphora in children's narratives: a comparison of English, French, German, and Mandarin Chinese. *Journal of Child Language, 26*, 419–52.

Iverson, J. M., Capirci, O., & Caselli, M. C. (1994). From communication to language in two modalities. *Cognitive Development, 9*, 23–43.

Kaper, W. (1980). The use of the past tense in games of pretend. *Journal of Child Language, 7*, 213–15.

Kelly, B. F. (2006). The development of constructions through early gesture use. In Clark, E. V.

& Kelly, B. F. (Eds.) *Constructions in acquisition* (00–00). Stanford, CA: CSLI Publications.

Legate, J. A. & Yang, C. D. (2002). Empirical reassessment of stimulus poverty arguments. *Linguistic Review*, 19, 151–62.

Lodge, K. R. (1979). The use of the past tense in games of pretend. *Journal of Child Language*, 6, 365–9.

Masur, E. F. (1997). Maternal labeling of novel and familiar objects: Implications for children's development of lexical constraints. *Journal of Child Language*, 24, 427–39.

Miller, P. (1986). Teasing as language socialization in a white working-class community. In Schieffelin, B. B. & Ochs, E. (Eds.) *Language socialization across cultures* (pp. 199–212). Cambridge: Cambridge University Press.

Moll, H., & Tomasello, M. (2004). 12- and 18-month-olds follow gaze to hidden locations. *Developmental Science*, 7, F1–F9.

Ochs, E. & Schieffelin, B. B. (1984). Language acquisition and socialization: Three developmental stories. In Schweder, R. & Levin, R. (Eds.) *Culture theory: Essays in mind, self and emotion* (pp. 276–320). Cambridge: Cambridge University Press.

O'Neill, D. K. (1996). Two-year-olds' sensitivity to the parent's knowledge when making requests. *Child Development*, 67, 659–77.

Ozcaliskan, S. & Goldin-Meadow, S. (2005). Gesture is at the cutting edge of early language development. *Cognition*, 96, B101–B113.

(2006). How gesture helps children construct language. In Clark, E. V. & Kelly, B. F. (Eds.) *Constructions in acquisition* (00–00). Stanford, CA: CSLI Publications.

Piché, G. L., Rubin, D. L., & Michlin, M. L. (1978). Age and social class in children's use of persuasive communicative appeals. *Child Development*, 49, 773–80.

Pine, J. M. & Lieven, EVM (1997). Slot and frame patterns and the development of the determiner category. *Applied Psycholinguistics*, 18, 123–38.

Pullum, G. & Scholz, B. (2002). Empirical assessments of stimulus poverty arguments. *Linguistic Review*, 19, 8–50.

Reeder, K. (1980). The emergence of illocutionary skills. *Journal of Child Language*, 7, 13–28.

Réger, Z. (1986). The functions of imitation in child language. *Applied Psycholinguistics*, 7, 323–52.

Rogers, D. (1978). Information about word-meaning in the speech of parents to young children.

In Campbell, R. N. & Smith, P. T (Eds.) *Recent advances in the psychology of language* (pp. 187–98). London: Plenum.

Sachs, J. & Devin, J. (1976). Young children's use of age-appropriate speech styles in social interaction and role playing. *Journal of Child Language*, 3, 81–98.

Saffran, J. R., Aslin, R. N., & Newport, E. L. (1996). Statistical learning by 8-month-old infants. *Science*, 274, 1926–8.

Sawyer, R. K. (1997). *Pretend play as improvisation*. Mahwah, NJ: Lawrence Erlbaum.

Saxton, M., Backley, P., & Gallaway, C. (2005). Negative input for grammatical errors: effects after a lag of 12 weeks. *Journal of Child Language*, 32, 643–72.

Saxton, M., Houston-Price, C., & Dawson, N. (2005). The prompt hypothesis: Clarification requests as corrective input for grammatical errors. *Applied Psycholinguistics*, 26, 393–414.

Saylor, M. M. & Sabbagh, M. A. (2004). Different kinds of information affect word learning in the preschool years: The case of part-term learning. *Child Development*, 75, 395–408.

Sethuraman, N., Goldberg, A. E., & Goodman, J. C. (1997). Using the semantics associated with syntactic frames for interpretation without the aid of context. In Clark, E. V. (Ed.) *Proceedings of the 28th Child Language Research Forum* (pp. 283–93). Stanford, CA: CSLI Publications.

Shatz, M. (1978). On the development of communicative understanding: An early strategy for interpreting and responding to messages. *Cognitive Psychology*, 10, 271–301.

Slobin, D. I. (1996). From "thought and language" to "thinking for speaking." In Gumperz, J. J. & Levinson, S. C. (Eds.) *Rethinking linguistic relativity* (pp. 70–96). Cambridge: Cambridge University Press.

Snow, C. (1977). The development of conversation between mothers and babies. *Journal of Child Language*, 4, 1–22.

Snow, C. (1978). The conversational context of language acquisition. In Campbell, R. N. & Smith, P. T. (Eds.) *Recent advances in the psychology of language* (pp. 253–69). London: Plenum.

Tomasello, M. (2003). *Constructing a language: A usage-based theory of language acquisition*. Cambridge, MA: Harvard University Press.

Weiss, D. M. & Sachs, J. (1991). Persuasive strategies used by preschool children. *Discourse Processes*, 14, 55–72.

Werner, H. & Kaplan, B. (1963). *Symbol formation: An organismic-developmental approach to language and the expression of thought*. New York: Wiley.

Woodward, A. L. (2003). Infants' developing understanding of the link between looker and object. *Developmental Science*, 6, 297–311.

Woodward, A. L. & Guajardo, J. J. (2002). Infants' understanding of the point gesture as an object-directed action. *Cognitive Development*, 17, 1061–84.

CHAPTER 30

The Electrophysiology of Discourse and Conversation

Jos J. A. Van Berkum

1 Introduction

What's happening in the brains of two people having a conversation? One reasonable
guess is that in the fMRI scanner we'd see
most of their brains light up. Another is that
their EEG would be a total mess, reflecting dozens of interacting neuronal systems.
Conversation recruits *all* of the basic language systems reviewed in this book. It
also heavily taxes cognitive systems more
likely to be found in handbooks of memory, attention and control, or social cognition (Brownell and Friedman, 2001). With
most conversations going beyond the single
utterance, for instance, they place a heavy
load on episodic memory as well as on the
systems that allow us to reallocate cognitive
resources to meet the demands of a dynamically changing situation. Furthermore,
conversation is a deeply social and collaborative enterprise (Clark, 1996; this volume)
in which interlocutors have to keep track of
each other's state of mind and coordinate
on such things as taking turns, establishing common ground, and the goals of the
conversation.

For somebody invited to review the neurocognition of discourse and conversation
in a handful of pages, this doesn't sound
too good. Fortunately, others have already
recently surveyed the implications of patient
research (Brownell and Friedman, 2001; Marr,
2004), as well as those of fMRI and PET (Ferstl,
2007; Ferstl et al., 2008). Here, I review the
EEG research on discourse and conversation
to date, to see what electrophysiology tells
us about the systems involved. EEG studies
on discourse and conversation have thus far
practically all focused on the *comprehension
of multi-sentence text*, and as such they provide a convenient operational definition of
the domain. However, an important theme
developed in this review is that for the processes that extract meaning from language,
the classic separation between a single sentence and a whole bunch of them may not
be all that relevant.

2 Why bother with EEG?

The term *neuroimaging* has come to stand
for functional magnetic resonance imaging

(fMRI) or positron emission tomography (PET). Images obtained with fMRI or PET can be extremely informative, and they strongly resonate with our desire to look into our working brains. However, in the end, these are images of blood, and, for that matter, slowly responding blood. Neurons do need it, but the real work for which the brain has become famous – computation – is carried by electricity (and, at synapses, electro-chemical transduction). This is precisely what the EEG taps in to. The EEG or electro-encephalogram is a record of tiny voltage fluctuations over time, usually recorded at the scalp. Roughly speaking, these fluctuations arise when large populations of similarly oriented neurons are simultaneously (de-) activated. Because a great many such ensembles are at work at any one time, the EEG is usually a bit of a mess. However, there are ways to extract useful information from this signal. In the most common method, the EEG is recorded to many instances of some critical event (say, a word), and the associated bits of EEG are averaged to create an event-related brain potential or ERP.

Now, to a psycholinguist, this probably doesn't sound too exciting so far. However, in the late 1970s, researchers discovered that words that were semantically anomalous in their local sentence context, as in "He spread the warm bread with socks," elicited a negative ERP deflection that peaked at about 400 ms after the offending word (Kutas and Hillyard, 1980). Because this so-called N400 effect was not elicited by a typographic anomaly, it was taken to reflect some aspect of how words are related to their semantic context. Follow-up experiments soon confirmed this, and made clear that N400 effects actually reflected graded modulations of an underlying N400 *component*, elicited by every content word, with an amplitude that increased to the extent that the word was harder to relate to its sentence–semantic context (see Kutas and Federmeier, 2000; Kutas, Van Petten, and Kluender, 2006 for review).

The significance of all this was enhanced when syntactically anomalous or unexpected words were found to elicit a very different ERP effect, the so-called P600 effect (Hagoort, Brown, and Groothusen, 1993; Osterhout and Holcomb, 1992; see Osterhout, Kim, and Kuperberg, this volume; Kuperberg, 2007 for review). The discovery of two very different ERP "signatures" associated with sentence-level language comprehension not only raised interesting theoretical questions about the architecture of the comprehension system and the types of representations it computed, but also implied that ERPs could be used to *selectively* keep track of specific aspects of comprehension, as a sentence unfolded in time. Of course, a process as complex as this was bound to generate more than just two ERP effects, and many other language-relevant ERP phenomena have been discovered since (cf. Newman et al., this volume; Coulson, this volume, Osterhout et al., this volume). With a steadily growing repertoire of ERP effects in hand, researchers are now examining the processes involved in comprehending single sentences.

Until quite recently, however, psycholinguists have been reluctant to use EEG to examine the comprehension of larger units of language. One reason is that psycholinguistic ERP research is for historical reasons strongly rooted in the sentence processing community. This means that (at the time of writing) most of the people with EEG expertise and easy access to EEG labs have sentence processing issues in mind, whereas those most interested in discourse and conversation are short of expertise and labs. Furthermore, combining EEG with single sentences is already difficult enough as it is, and with a text or conversation in each trial, things are just getting worse.

As testified by the work reviewed here, though, it is not impossible to use EEG to track discourse comprehension (see Van Berkum, 2004 for a methodological tutorial). Moreover, the additional work does sometimes really pay off. Later in this chapter, I take stock of the discourse-oriented EEG studies conducted so far. I begin with studies that used the N400 to address the construction of discourse-level meaning (Section 3), then turn to research on how people find out to what or whom certain expressions refer (Section 4), and subsequently review the evidence for discourse-based anticipation (Section 5). After this review of exclusively text-oriented research, I briefly look at initial attempts to draw the speaker into the picture (Section 6), and discuss the challenge of combining electrode caps with conversation (Section 7). Finally, I extract several general implications (Section 8), and end with where I think the field should be heading (Section 9). For related research on figurative processing, I refer to Coulson (this volume).

3 Making sense of discourse

3.1 *Initial observations*

Although prose passages had in fact already featured in several of the early landmark ERP experiments on language comprehension (Kutas and Hillyard, 1983; Van Petten et al., 1991), ERP research specifically aimed at *discourse*-level comprehension took off in 1994, with a pioneering study by St. George et al. (1994). Building on classic work in cognitive psychology, St. George et al. asked their subjects to read short stories with or without a title, such as:

(1) The procedure is actually quite simple. First you arrange things into different groups depending on their makeup. Of course, one pile may be sufficient depending on how much there is to do. If you have to go somewhere else due to lack of facilities that is the next step, otherwise you are pretty well set. It is important not to overdo any particular endeavor. That is, it is better to do too few things at once than too many. In the shorter run this may not seem important, but complications from doing too many can easily arise. A mistake can be expensive as well. The manipulation of the appropriate mechanisms should be self-explanatory, and we need not dwell on it here. At first the whole procedure will seem complicated. Soon, however,

it will become just another facet of life. It is difficult to foresee any end to the necessity of this task in the immediate future, but then one can never tell.

Whereas each story was locally coherent in that individual sentences were interconnected and related to a single topic, it was difficult to find out what that topic actually was without a story title (e.g., *Procedure for washing clothes*). Content words in stories without a title elicited larger N400 deflections than the same words in titled stories, clearly indicating that the N400 is not only sensitive to local lexical or sentential context.

In follow-up research, Van Berkum and colleagues (Van Berkum, Hagoort, and Brown, 1999; Van Berkum et al., 2003) examined the brain's response to words that were equally acceptable in their local carrier sentence but differed radically in how well they fit the wider discourse (e.g., "The dean told the lecturer that there was ample reason to promote him" in a context in which the lecturer had just been found out to be a fraud). Words not supported by the wider discourse elicited a much larger N400 deflection than discourse-supported words, in readers and listeners alike. Furthermore, this N400 effect collapsed when the same carrier sentences were presented in isolation. Because the discourse-dependent N400 effect emerged for clause-final as well as clause-medial words, these findings suggested that *every* incoming word is immediately related to the wider discourse. Furthermore, with spoken words, the discourse-dependent N400 effect had its onset as early as 150 ms after acoustic word onset, that is, only some *two to three phonemes into the word* (such early onsets are quite common for spoken-language N400 effects). Spoken words are thus related to the wider discourse extremely rapidly, well before they have been fully pronounced, and possibly even before they have become acoustically unique. Finally, the timing, shape, and scalp distribution of the N400 effect elicited by discourse-dependent anomalies did not differ from that of the "classic" sentence-dependent N400 effect, indicating that

discourse- and sentence-dependent semantic constraints have a comparable impact on
some aspect of semantic processing.

Three additional observations ruled out
relatively trivial accounts of discourse-
dependent N400 effects. First, like its sentence-dependent counterpart, it does not
depend on anomaly but can also be elicited
by somewhat less expected coherent words
like *lance* in (2) (Otten and Van Berkum,
2007; see also Burkhard, 2006, 2007; Ditman
and Kuperberg, 2007; St. George, Mannes,
and Hoffman, 1997; Van Berkum et al.,
2005).

(2) The brave knight saw that the dragon
    threatened the benevolent sorcerer.
    He quickly reached for a *sword/lance*
    and... (story continues).

Thus we can take these ERP modulations to
reflect something about the normal computations involved in understanding sentences
in context. Second, discourse-dependent
N400 effects also emerge at story positions
where no *particular* word is highly expected
(Camblin, Gordon, and Swaab, 2007; Van
Berkum et al., 2003), and thus do not critically depend on disconfirming a specific
lexical prediction. Third, experiments that
controlled for potential confounding effects
from lexical priming have shown that at
least *some* discourse-dependent N400 effects
hinge on the precise message-level representation established for the discourse at that
point. For example, whereas *lance* elicited a
large standard N400 effect relative to *sword*
in (2), it did not do so in (3), in which the
message was altered while keeping the same
prime words (Otten and Van Berkum, 2007;
see also Ditman and Kuperberg, 2007).

(3) The benevolent sorcerer saw that the
    dragon threatened the brave knight.
    He quickly reached for a *sword/lance*
    and... (story continues).

In all, the N400 findings so far consistently
indicate that words are related to a message-
level representation of the wider discourse
very rapidly, in a way that is no different
from how they are related to local sentence-
level context.

3.2 *What is going on here?*

Because these are message-level discourse
effects, it is tempting to take them to *directly*
reflect some aspect of high-level conceptual
structure building, such as (contextually
modulated) sentence-level semantic composition (e.g., Jackendoff, 2007) or the incremental expansion of a discourse model (e.g.,
along the lines of Discourse Representation
Theory; Kamp and Reyle, 1993; Geurts,
1999). This *integration account* of the N400
is implicitly or explicitly behind much discourse-level N400 research (including e.g.,
Van Berkum, Hagoort, and Brown, 1999),
and discourse-dependent N400 effects are
sometimes taken as strong evidence *for* the
integration view. However, these effects are
also fully compatible with a *memory retrieval
account* (Kutas and Federmeier, 2000; Kutas
et al., 2006), in which "N400 amplitude is
a general index of the ease or difficulty of
retrieving stored conceptual knowledge
associated with a word (or other meaningful stimuli), which is dependent on both the
stored representation itself, and the retrieval
cues provided by the preceding context"
(Kutas et al., 2006, p. 669). After all, prior
discourse can make for a fine retrieval cue.

These alternative accounts of discourse-
level N400 effects are difficult to disentangle. However, as argued in detail elsewhere
(Van Berkum, 2009), a long-term memory
retrieval account of discourse-dependent
N400 effects allows these findings to be
much more parsimoniously unified with a
wide range of other N400 phenomena. For
example, N400 effects can also be obtained
by semantically odd combinations that are
nonlinguistic, such as an unexpected turn of
events in a film clip (e.g., a guy in front of
the bathroom mirror putting shaving cream
on his chin, and then picking up a rolling
pin; Sitnikova, Kuperberg, and Holcomb,
2003) or a cartoon-like picture sequence
(West and Holcomb, 2002). Furthermore,
lexical or lexico-conceptual factors such
as repetition, word frequency, associative

or semantic word-word priming, the number of orthographically similar words, and concreteness also modulate the N400 (see Kutas et al., 2006 for review, or Van Berkum, 2009, for references). Although the impact of such factors is often attenuated in richer contexts, the fact that they modulate the N400 speaks against an account in which the N400 *directly* reflects sophisticated conceptual structure building. Although the N400 might be sensitive to the latter, it clearly reflects a more general mechanism.

A central idea in the so-called memory-based text processing tradition (e.g., Gerrig and McKoon, 1998; Gerrig and O'Brien, 2005) is *readiness*, the timely availability of plausibly relevant information. Firmly based in general models of human memory (e.g., Ratcliff and McKoon, 1988; Anderson, 1990), research in this tradition has shown that as we read though a text, potentially relevant additional information waxes and wanes without cost, as a function of how our content-addressable long-term memory passively resonates to currently active representations (Myers and O'Brien, 1998). What is being anticipated here is not necessarily upcoming communication – our long-term memory is simply trying to predict information that might soon be needed (cf. Anderson, 1990). However, to the extent that such cost-free memory-based anticipation is also sensitive to complex *message-level* cues, this automatic resonance may well be a critical ingredient in how discourse-dependent N400 effects emerge. In the St. George et al. (1994) study, for instance, the presence of a story title can help retrieve the relevant meaning of content words in the story. In the Otten and Van Berkum (2007) study, the precise message-level representation of "The brave knight saw that the dragon threatened the benevolent sorcerer. He quickly reached for a…" should facilitate retrieval from memory of a relevant meaning for *sword*, more so than for *lance*. And in a story about a swindling lecturer (Van Berkum et al., 1999), the exact meaning of "The dean told the lecturer that there was ample reason to…" presumably increases the readiness of concepts involving grave consequences

(being reprimanded or fired), at the expense of happier concepts (e.g., being praised or promoted).

Like the integration account, the memory retrieval account of N400 effects is as yet far from explicit. It also has one distinct and experimentally nasty drawback: If a message-level representation of the prior discourse is but one of a mixed bag of memory cues that can facilitate the retrieval of this word's meaning from conceptual long-term memory, next to, say, associatively and semantically related prime words, scenario-based world knowledge activated the preceding text, and aspects of the visual and auditory scene (Kutas and Federmeier, 2000; Van Berkum, 2009); scientific prediction doesn't get any easier. After all, the net N400 amplitudes observed are then a function of some unknown (and possibly weighed) balance of high- and lower-level retrieval cues. But then again, perhaps nature just isn't any more accommodating. Below, we'll encounter several cases in which exactly this mixing of higher- and lower-level cues seems to be at hand.

3.3 *Inferencing*

The word-elicited N400 is clearly sensitive to the level of contextual support from prior text. In principle, this makes it an attractive tool with which to study the mechanisms below various types of text-based inferences. Again, St. George et al. were the first to do so, in an experiment on bridging and elaborative inferences in text. Unfortunately, with only few texts per condition (fifteen), the ERPs were relatively noisy and hence difficult to interpret. Also, because not every item had been designed to elicit an N400 effect at a single critical word, ERPs were pooled across *all* words in the critical sentence, a procedure that must inevitably have attenuated critical differences between conditions.

Two more recent studies on inferences avoided both of these problems. In the first (Ditman and Kuperberg, 2007), participants read sentences like (7) in the context of an explicitly supportive discourse context

(4), an inferentially supportive discourse context (5), or a nonsupportive discourse context (6):

(4) Mark and John were having an argument. Mark began to hit John hard.
(5) Mark and John were having an argument. Mark got more and more upset.
(6) Mark and John were gambling at the casino. They won every game of blackjack.
(7) The next morning John had many *bruises*.

As might be expected, a critical word like *bruises* elicited a smaller N400 effect in an explicitly supportive discourse context than in a nonsupportive one. However, such words also elicited a smaller N400 effect in the inferentially supportive discourse context, indicating that readers can rapidly work out how the sentences of an unfolding discourse are connected.

Results from the second study (Yang, Perfetti, and Schmalhofer, 2007) seem to be at odds with this conclusion. Here, participants read sentences like (12) in the context of a referentially explicit discourse context (8), a referentially paraphrased context (9), an inferentially supportive context (10), or a nonsupportive context (11):

(8) After being dropped from the plane, the bomb hit the ground and exploded.
(9) After being dropped from the plane, the bomb hit the ground and blew up.
(10) After being dropped from the plane, the bomb hit the ground.
(11) Once the bomb was stored safely on the ground, the plane dropped off its passengers and left.
(12) The *explosion* was quickly reported to the commander.

The referentially explicit and referentially paraphrased contexts attenuated the N400 on critical words (e.g., *explosion*), relative to the nonsupportive context. But inferentially supportive context did *not*, suggesting that the critical word was as unexpected there as it was in the nonsupportive control context.

This could be taken to reflect that readers were not making the needed inference (i.e., a bomb hitting the ground will explode), at least not sufficiently rapidly.

Although it is not immediately clear how to reconcile these findings, the Ditman and Kuperberg study does provide an existence proof that inferences *can* be made sufficiently rapidly to support the processing of a subsequent critical word in a text. Research discussed in Sections 4 and 5 below (e.g., Burkhardt, 2006; Burkhardt and Roehm, 2007; Otten and Van Berkum, 2007; Van Berkum et al., 2005) points in the same direction. In line with the memory retrieval perspective outlined in Section 3.2, as well as with behavioral evidence for automatic memory-based inferences (Gerrig and O'Brien, 2005), I suspect that these inference-dependent N400 attenuations are the result of automatic anticipatory processing before the critical word comes along, afforded by how our long-term memory works (see also Section 5).

3.4 *World knowledge, counterfactuals, and negation*

Several recent studies use the N400 to explore the interaction between a dynamically configured discourse context and stable, default background knowledge about the world. In a first study (Nieuwland and Van Berkum, 2006a), a cartoon-like discourse context was pitted against default knowledge about what animate and inanimate entities tend to be like in the real world:

(13) A woman saw a dancing peanut who had a big smile on his face. The peanut was singing about a girl he had just met. And judging from the song, the peanut was totally crazy about her. The woman thought it was really cute to see the peanut singing and dancing like that. The peanut was *salted/in love*, and by the sound of it, this was definitively mutual. He was seeing a little almond.

In texts such as (13), discourse-supported but animacy violating predicates (*in love*) elicited a smaller N400 effect than animacy respecting but discourse-inappropriate alternatives (*salted*), showing that in this case, discourse-contextual fit completely overruled local animacy requirements in driving the N400. A recent follow-up (Filik and Leuthold, 2008) confirmed these results and showed that such fiction-dependent overrides of default world knowledge can be brought about with a single sentence (e.g., "The Incredible Hulk was annoyed that there was a lot of traffic in his way. He picked up the *lorry* and…"). Under some models, such results might be very surprising. However, I suspect that even the first few words of a single sentence ("The Incredible Hulk picked up the *lorry*") can do the trick. Note that sentences are *always* interpreted against a background. In the absence of specific prior information, the interpretive background defaults to our conceptual knowledge of the real world. A prior discourse context simply customizes the interpretive background. Either way, it will always be the case that some bits of information are more expected than others (cf. Section 3.2).

This is not to say that well-known, real-world constraints cannot "leak through" and have their own independent effect on N400 amplitude over and above what might be expected on the basis of a dynamically configured message-level representation of the discourse (e.g., see Federmeier and Kutas, 1999; Ferguson, Sanford, and Leuthold, 2008; Hald, Steenbeek-Planting, and Hagoort, 2007). In fact, if a message-level representation is but one of a mixed bag of memory cues that can facilitate the retrieval of the next word's meaning from memory (Kutas and Federmeier, 2000; Van Berkum, 2009), this is exactly what one can expect. As discussed before, the net balance between message-level and other cues should then depend on the relative strengths of the cues. And indeed, lexical primes such as *arms* and *legs* or *moon* and *stars*, which instantiate default world knowledge in a simple associative or category-dependent way, seem to have a bigger effect on the N400 in moderately constraining contexts (Camblin et al.,

2007) than in strongly constraining ones (Van Petten, 1993).

The balance between the dynamically configured message and simpler word- or scenario-based memory cues may also be relevant to a recent ERP study on negation in counterfactuals (Ferguson et al., 2008).

(14) If cats were not carnivores, they would be cheaper for owners to look after. Families could feed their cat a bowl of *carrots/fish* and listen to it purr happily.

In stories such as (14), discourse-supported words like *carrots* elicited a larger N400 effect than words like *fish*, a result taken to index the failure of discourse context to immediately affect language comprehension. However, in items like these, the precise message-level representation faces rather tough competition from other cues that reinforce real-world contingencies, such as convergent or scenario mediated priming from nearby words like *feed*, *cat*, and possibly *bowl*. In addition, the effectiveness of the message-level cue depends on how well (and how rapidly) readers have been able to incorporate the negator. At odds with early N400 observations (Fischler et al., 1983; Kounios and Holcomb, 1992), everyday language experience suggests that people can in principle interpret negations very effectively ("I'm afraid your paper is not suitable for publication in *Science*"), and recent evidence (Nieuwland and Kuperberg, 2008) suggests that what may matter is how pragmatically felicitous the negation is. With negation "coming out of the blue" ("if cats were not carnivores," "a robin is not a bird"), it is probably much more difficult to rapidly construct an adequate message-level representation.

In all, it seems that in pragmatically felicitous narratives, the N400 is highly sensitive to how things fit what is being talked about right now, even if it happens to be some imaginary world or negated microworld. Whether real-world knowledge leaks through in the amplitude of a word-elicited N400 may well depend on how effective the discourse is as a cue to long-term memory, relative to the (possibly convergent and/or scenario-mediated) word cues that provide access to default knowledge.

3.5 *Semantic illusions and information structure*

Behavioral research has shown that people sometimes overlook quite severe semantic anomalies in language, even when asked to look for them (see Sanford and Sturt, 2002 for review). For example, after having been told about a plane crash right on the border between France and Italy, many people miss the anomaly in "The authorities were trying to decide where to bury the survivors" (Barton and Sanford, 1993). What seems critical here is that (a) the context activates a strong scenario, (b) the impostor word – *survivors* – fits the scenario, (c) the impostor word is semantically related to the acceptable word – *victims* – it replaces, and (d) the impostor word is not marked as particularly noteworthy by linguistic focus, such as prosodic stress, italics, or cleft constructions ("It was the survivors that…"). The ERP studies reviewed before all indicate that semantically unexpected or anomalous words immediately generate an N400 effect. However, when embedded in spoken stories that obeyed the previously mentioned illusion-inducing conditions, such as (15), the severe anomaly at *suitcase* did *not* elicit an N400 effect (Nieuwland and Van Berkum, 2005; see Bohan, 2008 for a similar finding).

(15) A tourist wanted to bring his huge suitcase onto the airplane. However, because the suitcase was so heavy, the woman behind the check-in counter decided to charge the tourist extra. In response, the tourist opened his suitcase and threw some stuff out. So now the suitcase of the resourceful tourist weighed less than the maximum twenty kilos. Next, the woman told the *tourist/ suitcase* that… (story continues).

The precise interpretation of this remains to be established, and again depends in part on what the N400 can be assumed to reflect. On the integration assumption, the absence of an N400 effect to anomalous words suggests that the comprehension system suffers from a temporary semantic illusion (Nieuwland and Van Berkum, 2005; cf. Hoeks, Stowe, and Doedens, 2004 for a similar result in sentences). However, the memory retrieval account of the N400 pursued in this review may open up other possibilities. In the Nieuwland and Van Berkum study, for example, a relevant factor might be that *suitcase* has been mentioned several times before and is highly salient, eliminating the need for long-term memory retrieval. For both studies, the impostor word's strong association to the scenario as well as to the coherent word may also facilitate retrieval.

The behavioral literature on semantic illusions has revealed that they are more likely to occur in situations in which the word is deaccented or otherwise marked as business as usual (e.g., Sanford et al., 2006). This predicts that if the anomaly is brought into focus, an N400 effect should resurface, and studies investigating this are currently underway. Also, there is initial evidence that words brought into focus by accentuation elicit a larger N400 component than a deaccented word, irrespective of anomaly (Li, Hagoort, and Yang, 2008). The story for how such phenomena mesh with the memory retrieval account is far from complete (but see Van Berkum, 2009 for an attempt in terms of attention controlled intensified memory retrieval, along lines suggested by Sanford and Garrod, 2005). But I suspect that a closer examination of these surprising phenomena will help us make important progress in unraveling the architecture of interpretation and its link to the N400.

In all, I have argued (see Van Berkum, 2009, for details) that the many discourse-dependent modulations of a word-elicited N400 probably do *not directly* reflect the ease or difficulty with which the word's meaning is integrated in a structured (e.g., Jackendoffian or DRT-style) conceptual representation of the unfolding message. In the face of many other N400 phenomena, a more parsimonious account is that the N400 directly reflects whatever sense making is achieved through a more primitive resonance-based "analysis-by-retrieval" in long-term memory (i.e., pattern recognition and pattern completion). Message-dependent N400 effects can then simply come about because the structured conceptual representations involved – if sufficiently rapidly computed – can act as retrieval cues (or primes) to semantic long-term memory. Of course, parsimony only takes you that far. But if the proposal holds up, more direct ERP reflections of message-level structure building must be sought elsewhere.

4 Establishing reference in discourse

In "The deadline for my chapter was ten days ago. If I don't finish it soon, the editor will start bugging me," determining the referent of *it* seems quite trivial. However, in "The deadline for my chapter was ten days ago. If I keep on ignoring it, the editor will start bugging me," things are not so clear, for *it* can now refer to the chapter or the deadline. Moreover, upon closer examination, in the original example the neuter pronoun *it* can formally also refer to either, and the ambiguity is removed by the meaning of other words in its vicinity. These examples reveal that establishing reference in discourse is a nontrivial job.

4.1 *Ambiguous referential expressions*

In an ERP study that examined the nature and time course of such discourse-level referential analysis (Van Berkum, Brown, and Hagoort, 1999a), participants were presented with short passages that contained a referentially unambiguous or ambiguous expression in the last sentence, such as *the lecturer* in (16).

(16) In dismay, the faculty dean called the lecturer and the professor (the two lecturers) to his office. This was because the lecturer (one of the lecturers) had committed plagiarism, and the professor (the other one) had faked some of his research data. The dean told the lecturer that there was ample reason to sack him.

Relative to their referentially successful counterparts, referentially ambiguous expressions elicited a sustained negative ERP shift right at the ambiguous written noun, emerging at about 300–400 ms over the front of the head. A similar effect was obtained with spoken nouns (Van Berkum et al., 2003), as well as with spoken and written pronouns in single sentences ("David shot at Michael as he jumped over the fence"; Nieuwland and Van Berkum, 2006b; see Van Berkum et al., 2007, for review and Hammer et al., 2005 for a possible exception). Also, the mechanism involved is relatively smart: In a context in which, say, one of the two lecturers has just fled from the building, "The dean told the lecturer" does not elicit the effect, even though the episodic memory of the discourse does contain *two* lecturers (Nieuwland, Otten, and Van Berkum, 2007).

Thus, based on the unfolding sentence as well as prior text, people rapidly work out which are the conceptually *suitable* referents. Also, because the effect of referential ambiguity is largest over the front of the head, clearly different from the N400 effect, we can infer that different aspects of interpretation are handled by at least partly different networks in the brain (see Nieuwland, Petersson, and Van Berkum, 2007 for convergent evidence from fMRI). What the network at hand is doing exactly remains to be established, but plausible options include computationally intensive inferencing as people are trying to resolve the ambiguity and, possibly related, a higher load on frontal working memory systems (cf. Baggio, Van Lambalgen, and Hagoort, 2008; Müller, King, and Kutas, 1997; Münte, Schiltz, and Kutas, 1998; Pylkkänen, 2008; Streb, Rösler, and Hennighausen, 1999; see Van Berkum, 2009; Van Berkum et al., 2007; Nieuwland and Van Berkum, 2008a for discussion).

Interestingly, if people do not know who or what is being referred to, this can immediately affect their word-by-word *syntactic* analysis of the sentence (Van Berkum et al., 1999a). For instance, when *the lecturer* in "The dean told the lecturer that…" is referentially ambiguous, people are lured into analyzing the subsequent word *that* as starting a relative clause that will tell them which lecturer was meant (e.g., "…the lecturer that had committed plagiarism") rather than as starting some other syntactic structure (e.g., "…that there was ample reason to sack him"). If the sentence then continues with the latter after all, we see a P600 effect, an effect reliably elicited by words at which the currently pursued syntactic analysis runs into problems (Osterhout et al., this volume). Thus, referential factors can lead readers to momentarily perceive a syntactic error when there is none (see Van Berkum et al., 2007 for a comparable phenomenon in single sentences; and Bornkessel, Schlesewsky, and Friederici, 2003 for related findings with question–answer pairs).

Even more striking, the conceptual pull of referential ambiguity can sometimes briefly lure people into pursuing a syntactic analysis that is *ungrammatical*. In a Dutch version of "The dean told the lecturer that…" for example, referential ambiguity can lead people to momentarily read *that* as a relative pronoun *even if* a relative pronoun of this form does not agree in gender marking with the gender of the preceding noun (Van Berkum et al., 1999b). Such observations are important, because they suggest that when interpreting language, people don't just slavishly follow the syntax. Other recent ERP findings also suggest that good sense can sometimes outweigh good syntax (Kuperberg, 2007). Against so-called syntax-first or "syntactocentric" models of processing, this indicates that comprehenders are trying to deal with multiple levels of linguistic structure simultaneously, without giving one of them absolute priority.

In a recent ERP study on how referential processing interacts with semantic composition (Nieuwland and Van Berkum, 2008b), nouns embedded in a short story could be semantically anomalous, referentially ambiguous, or both (e.g., "The dean ate the lecturer" in a story about two equally salient lecturers). These doubly problematic nouns elicited a clear N400 effect, indicating a problem with how the words' meaning fit the story context. However, they did not elicit the sustained frontal negativity typically observed with referentially ambiguous nouns, presumably indicating that people did not engage in additional work to disambiguate reference. This is in line with a standard story in which sense-dependent processing precedes – and sometimes preempts – referential computations (but see Nieuwland and Van Berkum, 2008b for a catch involving P600 effects in a subset of the participants).

4.2 *Unambiguous referential expressions*

Referential ambiguity is not the only way to tap into aspects of establishing reference. Several studies have compared the effects of using a repeated, inferable, or new nominal NP in text. In one of these (Anderson and Holcomb, 2005), participants read ministories like:

(17) In dismay, Kathy sat nervously in the *cab/taxi* on her way to the airport. *The/A cab* came very close to hitting a car.

Relative to newly introduced nouns (e.g., *cab* in the first sentence), synonyms in the second sentence (*cab* after *taxi*) elicited a smaller N400 effect, and literally repeated nouns (e.g., *cab* after *cab*) elicited the smallest N400 effect. Although now crossing a sentence boundary, these effects echo other N400 repetition and semantic priming effects, and are easily explained as a result of facilitated long-term memory retrieval (literally repeated NPs do sometimes elicit a *larger* N400 effect than newly introduced NPs but this has been shown to depend on whether the discourse status of the antecedent makes repeated reference felicitous or not; Camblin et al., 2007; Ledoux et al., 2007; Swaab, Camblin and Gordon, 2004).

The N400 effects in the Anderson and Holcomb study did not depend on whether the article suggested a previously introduced ("The...") or new ("A...") discourse entity, a null result that was speculatively explained as resulting from weak information structure effects of definiteness being washed out by much stronger effects of repetition and (synonym-)semantic priming in this particular set of materials. Such an explanation is in line with the memory retrieval account of the N400 discussed before. However, and this is important, this should *not* be taken as evidence that readers entirely failed to pick up on the semantic and pragmatic difference between *The cab* and *A cab* – on the memory retrieval account, all one can infer here is that the distinction did not differentially affect memory retrieval at the subsequent noun. The stronger inference that the distinction was somehow not represented in conceptual structure only follows from the stronger assumption that the N400 directly reflects core semantic and pragmatic integration operations.

A second study on repeated, inferable, and new nominal NPs (Burkhardt, 2006; see also Burkhardt, 2007; Burkhardt and Roehm, 2007) examined ERPs to the NP in the second sentence in:

(18) Tobias was having a chat with Nina. He said that the *conductor* was very impressive.
(19) Tobias visited a concert in Berlin. He said that the *conductor* was very impressive.
(20) Tobias visited a conductor in Berlin. He said that the *conductor* was very impressive.

Relative to newly introduced nouns (e.g., *conductor* in [18]), repeated nouns ("*conductor*" in [20]) elicited a smaller N400 effect. "Bridged" nouns that were inferentially related to the antecedent (e.g., *conductor* after *concert* in [19]) also elicited a smaller N400 effect, of equal amplitude as that to the repeated noun. The latter is interesting, as it seems to suggest that in coherent discourse, words like *concert* prepare the reader for *conductor* to the same extent as *conductor* itself does.

Relative to repeated nouns, new and bridged nouns also both elicited an enhanced positivity between 600 and 900 ms, which was interpreted as a P600 effect indexing anaphoric integration cost due to the establishment of an independent, new discourse referent (see Burkhardt, 2007 for a related result). Whether this positivity is indeed an instance of the P600 effect elicited by unexpected structure remains to be established. However, the findings do suggest that late positivities can sometimes index discourse-referential operations. A possibly related finding involving bare quantifiers (Kaan, Dallas, and Barkley, 2007) was obtained in a very repetitive and possibly quite transparent design, and should therefore be interpreted with caution.

Two ERP studies have examined the implications of changing the referential status of pronouns across the sentence boundary. One of them (Streb, Hennighausen, and Rösler, 2004) systematically varied the distance between a pronoun and its antecedent:

(21) Beate has a small "boardy home" for animals.
Everywhere in the house are animals.
Tom is an old cat.
Today *it* scratched the door of the woman. [near]
(22) The weather is beautiful today.
Gerhart is an experienced mountaineer.
Anna wants to go on a walking tour.
Then *he* shows the ascent to the tourist. [intermediate]
(23) *Lisa* strolls across a bazaar.
Peter sells gems to tourists.
The gems are cut excellently.
Then *she* will buy a diamond from the trader. [far]

In line with the notion that pronouns tend to prefer highly salient antecedents (Garnham, 2001), more distant pronouns elicited larger N400 components. Because pronouns have relatively shallow semantic content, this could be taken as a challenge to the memory retrieval account of the N400. However, they do have *some* meaning, and retrieving this can still be more difficult. A conceptual mismatch between context and word might also lead to intensified retrieval of information related to the *context*. Why such mismatch results in an N400 effect here and in a P600 effect in other studies (e.g., Hammer et al., 2005; Osterhout and Mobley, 1995; Van Berkum et al., 2007) is not yet clear.

Elevated N400 components have also been observed to text-embedded singular definite pronouns *he* or *she* as compared to plural *they* (Filik, Sanford, and Leuthold, 2008):

(24) The in-flight meal I got was more impressive than usual.
     In fact, *she/they* courteously presented the food as well.
(25) The in-flight meal I got from the stewardess was more impressive than usual.
     In fact, *she/they* courteously presented the food as well.

Because *they* can more easily be used without an explicit antecedent (e.g., "They're digging up the road again"), this N400 effect has been proposed to reflect a difference in the referential demands structurally imposed by *he* or *she*, as compared to *they*. However, note that it is not the case that *they* can *always* leave its referent relatively unspecified (e.g., "At the UN meeting, the Chinese felt increasingly uncomfortable because of the human rights issues continuously raised by other delegates. So they left."). Important, the pronoun *itself* does not signal which situation is at hand. This N400 effect may thus be in need of another explanation.

In the same study, singular definite pronouns without an explicit antecedent, like *she* in (24), also elicited a frontocentral positivity that peaked around 750 ms, relative to all other three conditions. Analogous to the late positivity to new and bridged nominals (Burkhardt, 2006; 2007), this – more anterior – late positivity was taken to reflect the discourse complexity involved in inferring and adding an additional entity to the discourse

model. Of course, this convergence does not imply that *all* referentially induced late positivities reflect discourse-model expansion. For example, the P600 effect to the pronoun in sentences like "David praised Linda because *he*…" (in which verb meaning sets up a referential expectation; Van Berkum et al., 2007) is difficult to explain in terms of the need to set up a new discourse entity, as in this case, the required entity is already there. Whether this means that we're dealing with a single late positivity with an as yet ill-understood functional interpretation, or with two distinct positivities that happen to look the same, remains to be established (and may require other techniques, e.g., MEG).

So what does all this tell us? Although the diverse ERP findings on establishing reference in discourse resist a simple interpretation, several general observations can be made. First, these findings testify to the speed with which comprehenders try to bind incoming words to entities in the discourse or situation model. Furthermore, although contingent upon some form of compositional semantics, referential processing is not fully constrained by the syntax. Third, whereas the processing consequences of referential ambiguity consistently show up as sustained frontal negativities, the various computations that occur in the absence of such ambiguity show up in several very different ERP effects. The late positivity reported by Burkhardt (2006) and Filik et al. (2008) may genuinely reflect the establishing of a new discourse entity. Other late positivities (Van Berkum et al., 1999b; Van Berkum et al., 2007) are more plausibly explained by a strong referential attractor leading the system to at least momentarily put the blame on syntax. And many of the N400 effects to referring nouns and pronouns (Anderson and Holcomb, 2005; Burkhardt, 2006; possibly Streb et al., 2004) may well reflect simple (word priming) or complex (information-structural) modulations of the ease with which the critical word's meaning is retrieved from memory, making these effects rather indirect – possibly sometimes even poor – indices of establishing a referential dependency. In all, there is clearly no unique ERP signature of referential processing, and the signatures that we get need not all *directly* reflect the processes that link an expression to its discourse-model referent.

5 Anticipation in discourse

To what extent does the speed with which readers and listeners relate the syntactic, semantic, and referential implications of incoming words to their knowledge of the wider discourse depend on expectations? This is a difficult question to answer, and we won't get very far unless we ask an additional question: expectations of *what*? After all, language users are continuously analyzing the unfolding discourse at many different levels (such as phonology, syntax, semantics, and reference). Furthermore, listeners and readers not only keep a record of *what is being talked about*, that is, the "situation model" (Kintsch, 1998; Zwaan and Singer, 2003) or "situational representation" (Clark, 1996), but they also keep track of *how the communicative enterprise itself is getting along*, encompassing the "textbase" (Kintsch, 1998) or "discourse record" (Clark, 1996) as well as, for example, inferences about what the speaker may or may not know, and about why this conversation is being held in the first place. In discourse, people might in principle develop expectations at *any* of these levels, based on information supplied by any other level.

Some of the first N400 experiments on interpretation in language comprehension were already framed as revealing the effects of word expectancy, in a way not deemed limited to single sentences (e.g., Kutas and Hillyard, 1984). The attenuated N400 elicited by discourse-predictable words (e.g., *sword* in example [2]) relative to coherent but somewhat less predictable control words (*lance*; Otten and Van Berkum, 2007) is compatible with the idea that readers and listeners actually anticipate such predictable words as the discourse unfolds. More ERP evidence for discourse-based anticipation

of features has come from studies (e.g., Federmeier and Kutas, 1999; see Federmeier, 2007 for review) in which highly predictive stories were continued with the expected critical word, a semantically related but anomalous alternative, or an unrelated anomalous alternative, as in (26):

(26) They wanted to make the hotel look more like a tropical resort.
So, along the driveway, they planted rows of *palms/pines/tulips*.

Relative to unrelated anomalous words like *tulips*, expected words like *palms* elicited an attenuated N400. However, anomalous words like *pines* that were semantically related to the expected word *also* elicited an attenuated N400. Based on several control results, the most plausible interpretation is that people were preactivating *palms* to such an extent that semantically related concepts were also preactivated. Note that the attenuated N400 to anomalous *pines* relative to equally anomalous *tulips* is not easy to account for if the N400 directly indexes high-level conceptual integration. But it is readily interpreted under a memory-based account of the N400; in fact, one can see this as another case of undesirable real-world knowledge leaking through (cf. Section 3.4).

Stronger evidence that people predict upcoming words was obtained in an ERP study that probed for traces of lexical anticipation *before* the discourse-predictable word came along (Van Berkum et al., 2005). Participants listened to (Dutch) mini-stories such as (27), which in a paper-and-pencil cloze test were predominantly completed with one particular critical noun (in this case, *painting*, the Dutch translation of which is a neuter-gender word). To test whether such discourse-based lexical prediction would also occur online as part of real-time language comprehension, the EEG participants at this point first heard a gender-inflected adjective, whose syntactic gender either agreed with the anticipated noun, as in (28), or did not agree with this expected noun, as in (29).

(27) The burglar had no trouble locating the secret family safe.
Of course, it was situated behind a…

(28) …big$_{neu}$ but rather unobtrusive painting$_{neu}$

(29) …big$_{com}$ but rather unobtrusive bookcase$_{com}$.

Relative to the gender-congruent prenominal adjective in (28), the gender-incongruent adjective in (29) elicited a small but reliable ERP effect right at the inflection. Because this prediction effect hinged on the idiosyncratic (hence memorized) syntactic gender of an expected but not yet presented noun, and because the effect collapsed when the prior context sentence was removed, it suggested that discourse-level information can indeed lead people to anticipate specific upcoming words as the text unfolds. In addition, the fact that such prediction could be probed via syntactic gender agreement suggested that the syntactic properties of those anticipated "ghost" words can immediately begin to interact with locally unfolding syntactic constraints, such as the gender inflection on a prenominal adjective. Follow-up experiments have revealed that, at least when probed in this gender-sensitive paradigm, such discourse-based lexical predictions cannot be reduced to the effects of simple or convergent lexical priming (Otten and Van Berkum, 2008; Otten, Nieuwland, and Van Berkum, 2007). Also, comparable prediction has been observed in constraining single sentences (e.g., Wicha, Moreno, and Kutas, 2004).

These findings suggest that people predict specific upcoming words as syntactic entities (lemmas), that is, a representation of the word in terms of its syntactic category and the associated syntactic features (e.g., gender). However, consistent with the idea that opportunities for discourse-based prediction exist at many levels of analysis, there is also ERP evidence for the anticipation of upcoming referents (Nieuwland and Van Berkum, 2006a; Van Berkum et al., 2007) and, in a sentence paradigm, upcoming phonological word forms (DeLong, Urbach, and Kutas, 2005). The mechanisms behind all

this anticipation remain to be established. One currently debated idea is that comprehenders need to run a sophisticated forward model at various levels of analysis as part of their basic comprehension strategy (see e.g., Pickering and Garrod, 2007). However, as argued elsewhere (Van Berkum, 2009), much of it may actually come for free as a function of how human memory works (Gerrig and O'Brien, 2005).

6 Getting the speaker into the picture

In EEG research with spoken language materials, the need for a speaker is often seen as an unavoidable complication, the price to be paid for having naturally unfolding spoken input instead of word-by-word presentation on the screen. In line with this, speakers are usually chosen on how well they produce text without drawing any attention to themselves (by, say, hesitations, or a highly salient accent). However, pragmatic analyses of language meaning (e.g., Carston, 2002; Clark, 1996; Grice, 1957; Kempson, 2001; Levinson, 1983; Sperber and Wilson, 1995; Wilson and Sperber, 2004) reveal that listeners can only really make sense of language if they take the speaker and his or her perspective into account. Thus, to understand the neurocognition of interpretation in full, we need to bring the speaker into the picture.

One immediate reminder of the speaker's existence is when he or she hesitates in delivering a message. In a refreshing ERP study (Corley, MacGregor, and Donaldson, 2007), the impact of such hesitations on the listener has recently been examined with materials such as:

(30) Everyone's got bad habits, and mine is biting my *nails/tongue*.

(31) Everyone's got bad habits, and mine is biting my…er…*nails/tongue*.

In a fluently delivered utterance like (30), highly expected words elicited a much reduced N400 effect relative to their less expected counterparts, in line with other observations of predictability effects (e.g.,

Federmeier and Kutas, 1999; Hagoort and Brown, 1994; Otten and Van Berkum, 2007). But after a disfluency such as in (31), predictable words were much less effective in attenuating the N400. On an N400 integration account, this suggests that hesitation can interfere with integrating the meaning of a subsequent word. On a memory retrieval account, it suggests that implicit text-based anticipation is sensitive to speaker performance, possibly mediated by implicit knowledge about when (and when not) to expect fluent delivery. Either way, a marked delivery matters. More generally, the study is a good example of how to address at least some issues relevant to conversation without actually having one.

Another ERP study (Van Berkum et al., 2008), recently examined when and how listeners make use of voice-based inferences about who the speaker is. As revealed by the fact that "I need to see my gynecologist" is really odd for a man to say (unless he's Arnold Schwarzenegger in that absurd Hollywood product), inferences about the speaker are directly relevant to interpretation. There is debate, however, on how and precisely when such knowledge is used (cf. Lattner and Friederici, 2003). In the EEG experiment, people heard utterances whose content did or did not match probabilistic inferences supported by the speaker's voice, as in (32) delivered with a male or female voice, (33) with the voice of a young kid or an adult, and (34) delivered with a stereotypically "common" or "upper class" accent.

(32) I always rent movies with lots of *violence* in them.
(33) On Saturday I spent the whole afternoon playing *marbles* on the street.
(34) I have a big *tattoo* on my back.

Speaker-inconsistent critical words elicited a small but reliable N400 effect, beginning at 200–300 ms from acoustic word onset. This reveals that listeners rapidly classify speakers on the basis of their voices and anchor the utterance to the speaker immediately, somehow using their knowledge of the speaker's probable sex, age, and social

stratum to evaluate the plausibility of what is being asserted. Again, the most parsimonious account for this is that, after, for example, having heard "I have a big" in a stereotypically "upper class" accent (instead of a more "common" accent), listeners find it more difficult to retrieve the meaning of *tattoo* from long-term memory.

Finally, recent work on concurrent speech–gesture comprehension (Özyürek et al., 2007) has shown that a mismatch between a spoken word (e.g., "He slips on the roof and *rolls* down") and a simultaneous iconic co-speech gesture (e.g., finger-gestured *walking*) also elicits an increased N400. Because such gestures probably have little to no context-independent meaning stored in long-term memory, this result is sometimes taken as strong evidence for an integration account of the N400. However, because mismatching gestures can hinder the retrieval of a relevant meaning for concurrently presented words, this result is also easily accommodated in a memory retrieval account of that component. Either way, the findings testify to the speed with which extra-sentential information picked up from the speaker can affect the processes involved in making sense of an utterance.

7 How about conversation?

Whereas the electrophysiology of text comprehension is now gradually picking up speed, the electrophysiology of conversation is as yet nonexistent. To some extent, this simply echoes the fact that most psycholinguistic theories and experiments are, implicitly or explicitly, about monologue. Furthermore, the various reasons that have caused many EEG experimenters to think twice before entering the domain of text comprehension will surely also have caused them to stay away from conversation. In addition, real two-person conversation brings with it an entirely new set of methodological problems. One of them is that in contrast to text, conversation cannot be fully predesigned. As in eyetracking research on conversation (see Trueswell and Tanenhaus,

2005), probably the best way to make sure that EEG participants encounter the critical input at the right time is to have them interact with a confederate of the experimenter in a collaborative setting that can be scripted in relatively natural ways. Unfortunately, fitting many lengthy conversational trials into an EEG experiment is not easy. Also, people tend to speak, gesture, and otherwise move a lot in conversation, which gives rise to large EEG artifacts. In all, we're currently facing the enormous challenge to come up with conversational settings that minimize movement, supply lots of critical trials, and are yet sufficiently natural to be worth our while. Whether a virtual reality setup can help attenuate some of these problems is currently being explored.

Some researchers have recently turned to other ways to get a handle on conversationally relevant phenomena. One, as we have seen, is to modify the classic monologue paradigm in ways that bring the speaker into the picture. Another promising avenue is to use an "overhearing" paradigm, in which the participant listens to predesigned conversational exchanges (e.g., Magne et al., 2005; Toepel, Pannekamp, and Alter, 2007). In an ERP experiment on the role of prosody in discourse context (Magne et al., 2005), participants listened to relatively natural question–answer exchanges between male and female speakers, designed such that a contrastive accent in the answer did or did not match expectations raised by the question, as in (35) versus (36):

(35) Q: Did he give his fiancée a ring or a bracelet? A: He gave a *RING* to his fiancée.

(36) Q: Did he give a ring to his fiancée or his sister? A: He gave a *RING* to his fiancée.

Surprisingly, whether a noun did or did not carry a contrastive accent by itself did not affect the ERPs, in spite of the fact that accent substantially altered the physical realization of the spoken noun (contra Li et al., 2008). The only thing that mattered was whether the prosody matched expectations raised by the question: Relative to pragmatically congruous counterparts, the pragmatically incongruous NPs consistently elicited very rapid differential ERP effects. However, the results of this innovative experiment may have been compromised by the fact that at every trial, participants were asked to decide whether the intonation of the answer was coherent or not in relation to the question. Because secondary tasks recruit their own brain activity, and because the instruction to only respond after the linguistic input does not guarantee that the task-related *evaluation* will also be delayed that long, an additional task like this carries the risk that language-related ERP effects become confounded with task-related ERP effects (see also Van Berkum, 2004).

The possibility of task-related confounds should not in general deter people from studying language comprehension (and production) in a task environment. Most EEG research to date falls squarely within the *language-as-product* tradition (Clark, 1996; 1997), in which readers and listeners are faced with bits of text they essentially don't care about (but see Van Berkum et al., 2009, for an exception). Of course, to the extent that the processes under study do their job in the same way regardless of what the linguistic input is for – as is commonly and perhaps reasonably assumed for syntactic parsing – this isn't too much of a problem. However, with *interpretation*, things are not so clear. Again, some processes may well turn out to do their job regardless of whether the input serves a bigger purpose. Also, if the stimuli themselves are sufficiently engaging, the experiment will be relevant to what language users do when they pick up a novel, or, say, a tabloid in a commuter train. Nevertheless, it seems critical to also record EEG in experiments where language truly matters to *getting things done* (*language-as-action*; Clark, 1996), such as building a Lego construction or baking a cake (see Trueswell and Tanenhaus, 2005, for examples). Such paradigms can help examine the generality of results obtained with snippets of text, as well as address specific issues associated with goal-oriented conversation. Moreover,

Discourse-dependent referential, syntactic, and semantic ERP effects

In dismay, the faculty dean called the lecturer and the professor (the two lecturers) to his office. This was because the lecturer (one of the lecturers) had committed plagiarism, and the professor (the other one) had faked some of his research data. The dean told the **lecturer** *that* **there** *was ample reason to* **sack/promote** *him.*

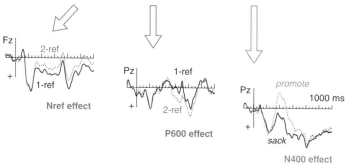

Figure 30.1. From left to right: A sustained frontal negative shift or "Nref effect" to a discourse-induced referential problem (in the two-referent version of the story, *lecturer* is ambiguous), a P600 effect to a discourse-induced syntactic problem (the provisional relative-clause analysis temporarily pursued at *that* in the two-referent context is subsequently ruled out by *there*), and an N400 effect to a discourse-induced semantic problem (*promote* does not fit the wider story context). The example item is shown here in several variants (one- and two-referent contexts, coherent/ anomalous ending), but any one participant saw just a single version. ERP waveforms are time-locked to the presentation of the written critical word (zero ms) and are shown for 1200 ms each. Negative voltage is up. All data were obtained in a single reading experiment.

and particularly relevant here, they would have the enormous advantage of getting *naturally motivated* language comprehension for free.[1]

8 So what kind of system is this?

Stepping back from all the details, we can discern several general operating principles at work in discourse comprehension.

(1) *Rapidly contextualized processing.* First of all, the words of an unfolding spoken or written sentence are very rapidly related to what the wider discourse is about, as soon as they come in. Because

words encode information at various levels of linguistic analysis (phonology, syntax, meaning, and reference, Jackendoff, 2002), such discourse-sensitive incremental processing can show up in various ways, some of which have been summarized in Figure 30.1.

Illustrated here is, from left to right, the harvest of a *single* EEG experiment, designed to obtain three different discourse-relevant effects in the same participants: a rapid ERP effect of discourse-level referential ambiguity, a downstream P600 garden-path effect associated with the discourse-dependent modulation of how the parser analyzes a subsequent syntactic ambiguity, and the N400 effect elicited by a discourse-dependent semantic anomaly. The impact of discourse-level factors does not only show up at the first relevant word in each of the three

[1] Note that what matters is not so much whether the collaborative task at hand is a natural one, but whether the relevant utterances are a natural part of whatever is needed to get the job done.

cases, but also shows up extremely rapidly *at that particular word*. Furthermore, studies that contrasted discourse-level factors with convergent lexical priming or other more superficial mechanisms confirm that what is at work here is more than just a lexical priming or repetition confound. Unfolding words make very rapid contact with a deep representation of the wider discourse, at the level of *what's being talked about*, as well as *how* and *by whom*.

(2) *Discourse-based "presonance" at multiple levels.* The evidence discussed in Section 5 suggests that readers and listeners go beyond incremental processing and can use discourse-level information to make predictions about what information might be needed soon, as well as about upcoming communication. Such predictions need not involve costly conscious deliberation. Instead, many of them may virtually come for free, as a result of how information in our content-addressable long-term memory resonates with low- and high-level aspects of currently processed information. This idea of predictive resonance has nicely been captured in the term *presonance* coined by Zwaan and Kaschak (2009). What the EEG records suggest is that such presonance can be driven by simple primes in prior discourse as well as by much more complex message-level representations of that prior discourse. Furthermore, the targets of anticipation can involve such things as the semantic, syntactic, and phonological features of specific upcoming words, whom or what will be referred to soon, and upcoming syntactic structure. In all, it seems that people can extrapolate unfolding discourse at a variety of levels in a relatively cost-free way. Of course, that doesn't make presonance (or more sophisticated forward modeling) a complete model of discourse comprehension – much of the work there *must* be about building precisely structured and dynamically evolving representations of what is said and meant, as well

as of the situation being talked about. However, such complex representations do also drive simple long-term memory retrieval, and thereby prepare the system to a greater or lesser extent for the next bit of linguistic information coming up.

(3) *Simultaneous multiple constraint satisfaction.* In line with evidence from other methodologies, the ERP data are not in line with a classic feedforward model of comprehension in which different levels of language analysis – phonology/orthography, syntax, compositional sentence semantics, reference, and other discourse-level pragmatics – only constrain each other in an ordered left-to-right fashion. Syntax does constrain interpretation, and specific combinations of word meanings do help define a referential target. But at the same time, the evidence that discourse-level constraints can briefly override locally unambiguous syntactic information, and that a suitable cartoon-like wider discourse can completely override a severe real-world anomaly, attests to the power that discourse-level representations can have over more local lower-level constraints. In all, the picture painted here is that of a system trying to simultaneously satisfy constraints at multiple levels of representation (Trueswell and Tanenhaus, 2005; Jackendoff, 2002, 2007), without giving strict priority to any one level.

(4) *Discourse is not so special.* Nothing in the ERP evidence reviewed here supports the idea that the processes involved in discourse-dependent conceptual interpretation are any different from those involved in sentence-internal conceptual interpretation. For example, discourse- and sentence-dependent N400 effects are identical for anomalies, for more subtle manipulations of contextual fit, and, as a special case of absence, for semantic illusions. The ERP effect of referential ambiguity reported in Section 4 can be elicited in texts and single sentences alike. And people predict

upcoming words in discourse and single sentences alike. The sentence domain is of course highly relevant for syntax, as well as for the compositional semantics involved in determining *sentence* meaning. However, for much of the interpretation beyond that, the sentence boundary is irrelevant. Interpretation is fundamentally contextualized, and it doesn't seem to matter to the brain whether this context is defined by, say, the first few words of a single unfolding sentence, a 500-page Russian novel, or who the speaker is.

9 Where to go next?

9.1 *From discourse-unit to discourse-level processing*

To get this review started, I provisionally defined *discourse comprehension* as the processes involved in digesting *units of language* bigger than a single sentence, that is, a fragment of text or conversation. Within neurocognitive research on language comprehension, this reflects current practice in thinking about discourse. But *discourse* has an important second meaning, that of a *level of mental representation and processing*. This is evident in psycholinguistic research on situation models (e.g., Garnham, 2001; Johnson-Laird, 1983; Kintsch, 1998; Zwaan, 2004; Zwaan and Radvansky, 1998; see Clark, this volume), and in linguistic research on discourse-level representations (e.g., DRT; Geurts and Beaver, 2007; Kamp and Reyle, 1993). Discourse-*level* representation and processing is in principle orthogonal to whether the exchange consists of a single sentence or more, because even a single isolated sentence is analyzed at the discourse level (hence explaining the similarity of sentence- and discourse-dependent ERP effects). It just happens to be the case that prior discourse context is often a convenient way to modulate discourse-level processing.

This has three important implications. First, we need not *always* go beyond the single sentence to study interpretive

phenomena associated with discourse and conversation. Research on, say, discourse connectives or turn taking obviously requires a bigger unit. But research on establishing reference or updating situation models can in principle be conducted with texts, conversations, and single sentences alike – good news for the cognitive neuroscientist. An important second implication, and the other side of the coin, is that "the neural substrate of discourse and conversation" cannot simply be isolated by comparing the processing of connected text to that of single sentences (a relatively standard working assumption in fMRI research on text comprehension). The comparison may well reveal various systems that are being taxed *more* by a long piece of discourse, as well as some of the processes that by necessity require text (e.g., those sensitive to discourse connectives). But if much of the really interesting discourse-level stuff occurs in *every* sentence regardless of whether or not it is embedded in a larger text, the subtraction is going to partial out the very stuff that one is after. The third and related implication is that in developing new research on the electrophysiology of discourse and conversation, researchers may want to think twice about what they are really after. Studying the neurocognition of discourse and conversation by examining language comprehension embedded in a big and rich *unit* of language use looks immediately relevant (and for a reason discussed later, it is). At the same time, I think the deeper thing we should be after is the neurocognition of discourse-*level* processing, as formalized in pragmatics and some corners of semantics (cf. Van Berkum, 2009). If a big unit helps, that's fine. But in this particular enterprise, size is not the issue.

9.2 *Other directions*

One of the strengths of ERPs is that their multidimensional nature (polarity, distribution, shape, and timing) can inform us about the identity of the processes engaged. However, this is difficult to benefit from when, instead of having two crisp ERP effects (say, N400 and P600) with clearly separable descriptions and well-understood functional significance, our inferential benchmark in the literature is a large set of many rather similar and many very different ERP effects, with multiple competing functional accounts for each. Unfortunately, it looks like we are steadily moving towards the latter situation. This doesn't mean that the electrophysiology of discourse and conversation is doomed. It does suggest that whenever one can design ERP experiments such that the logic does not solely rely on the *nature* of the effect, this is the safer way to go (Van Berkum, 2004). It also points to the growing importance of linking specific ERP effects to their neural sources, by whatever available means (constrained source modeling, using evidence from hemifield studies, MEG, and fMRI, etc.)

Another way out of the increasing mess of ERP effects is to make a serious start with relating ERP research to detailed linguistic (e.g., DRT-style) and computational (Graesser, McNamara, and Rus, this volume) models of discourse-level interpretation, and to derive further studies from that (see Baggio et al., 2008 for a good example). Neuroimagers are sometimes inclined to think that, now that we can "look under the hood of the car," we can pin down the architecture of comprehension by simply running more EEG, fMRI, and TMS experiments. I think this is a mistake. Language interpretation is complex business, and we can only seriously move forward if we ground our neural research in more precise theories that also take the relevant semantic, pragmatic, and behavioral findings into account.

Finally, we must take EEG, MEG, and other neuroimaging measures a little further into the arena of real language use (Clark, 1996). As mentioned before, not all discourse-level issues necessarily require a big chunk of language to be investigated. However, language is first and foremost an instrument by which people coordinate with each other (Clark, this volume). Thus, as with any system designed for a purpose, it is not unlikely that at least some of the features of our language comprehension and production system will be customized to operate in this particular cognitive and social niche. Ignoring that niche in our neurocognitive research would be a capital mistake. In the words of Small and Nussbaum (2004, p. 301; see also Clark, 1997; Kutas, 2006), it is high time to "examine cortical activity during language behavior that most closely matches conditions of evolution: language use by people at a time and place, aiming to understand and to be understood, fulfilling a purpose."

References

Anderson, J. E. & Holcomb, P. J. (2005). An electrophysiological investigation of the effects of coreference on word repetition and synonymy. *Brain and Language*, 94(2), 200–16.

Anderson, J. R. (1990). *The Adaptive Character of Thought*. Hillsdale, NJ: Erlbaum.

Baggio, G., van Lambalgen, M., & Hagoort, P. (2008). Computing and recomputing discourse models: An ERP study. *Journal of Memory and Language*, 59, 36–53.

Barton, S. B. & Sanford, A. J. (1993). A case study of anomaly detection: Shallow semantic processing and cohesion establishment. *Memory & Cognition*, 21(4), 477–87.

Bohan, J. T. (2008). *Depth of Processing and Semantic Anomalies*. Unpublished dissertation.

Bornkessel, I., Schlesewsky, M., & Friederici, A. D. (2003). Contextual information modulates initial processes of syntactic integration: The role of inter- versus intrasentential predictions. *Journal of Experimental Psychology: Learning, Memory, and Cognition*, 29(5), 871–82.

Brownell, H, & Friedman, O. (2001). *Discourse ability in patients with unilateral left and right hemisphere brain damage*. In Berndt, R. S. (Ed.) *Language and aphasia* (Handbook of neuropsychology, 2nd edition, volume 3) pp. 189–204. Amsterdam: Elsevier.

Burkhardt, P. (2006). Inferential bridging relations reveal distinct neural mechanisms: Evidence from event-related brain potentials. *Brain and Language*, 98(2), 159–68.

Burkhardt, P. (2007). The P600 reflects cost of new information in discourse memory. *NeuroReport*, 18(17), 1851–4.

Burkhardt, P. & Roehm, D. (2007). Differential effects of saliency: An event-related brain potential study. *Neuroscience Letters*, 413(2), 115–20.

Camblin, C. C., Gordon, P. C., & Swaab, T. Y. (2007). The interplay of discourse congruence and lexical association during sentence processing: Evidence from ERPs and eye tracking. *Journal of Memory and Language*, *56(1)*, 103–28.

Camblin, C. C., Ledoux, K., Boudewijn, M., Gordon, P. C., & Swaab, T. Y. (2007). Processing new and repeated names: Effects of coreference on repetition priming with speech and fast RSVPs. *Brain Research*, *1146*, 172–84.

Carston, R. (2002). *Thoughts and Utterances: The Pragmatics of Explicit Communication*. Oxford: Blackwell.

Clark, H. H. (1996). *Using language*. Cambridge: Cambridge University Press.

(1997). Dogmas of understanding. *Discourse Processes*, *23*, 567–98.

(this volume). Spoken discourse and its emergence.

Corley, M., MacGregor, L. J., & Donaldson, D. I. (2007). It's the way that you, er, say it: Hesitations in speech affect language comprehension. *Cognition*, *105(3)*, 658–68.

Coulson, S. (this volume). Cognitive neuroscience of figurative language.

Delong, K. A., Urbach, T. P., & Kutas, M. (2005). Probabilistic word pre-activation during language comprehension inferred from electrical brain activity. *Nature Neuroscience*, *8(8)*, 1117–21.

Ditman, T. & Kuperberg, G. R. (2007). The time course of building discourse coherence in schizophrenia: An ERP investigation. *Psychophysiology*, *44(6)*, 991–1001.

Federmeier, K. D. (2007). Thinking ahead: The role and roots of prediction in language comprehension. *Psychophysiology*, *44(4)*, 491–505.

Federmeier, K. D. & Kutas, M. (1999). A rose by any other name: Long-term memory structure and sentence processing. *Journal of Memory and Language*, *41(4)*, 469–95.

Ferguson, H. J., Sanford, A. J., & Leuthold, H. (2008). Eye-movements and ERPs reveal the time-course of processing negation and remitting counterfactual worlds. *Brain Research*, *1236*, 113–25.

Ferstl, E. C. (2007). The functional neuroanatomy of text comprehension: What's the story so far? In Schmalhofer, F. & Perfetti, C. (Eds.) Higher Level Language Processes in the Brain: Inference and Comprehension Processes (pp. 53–102). Mahwah: NJ, Lawrence Erlbaum.

Ferstl, E. C., Neumann, J., Bogler, C., & von Cramon, D. Y. (2008). The extended language network: A meta-analysis of neuroimaging studies on text comprehension. *Human Brain Mapping*, *29(5)*, 581–93.

Filik, R. & Leuthold, H. (2008). Processing local pragmatic anomalies in fictional contexts: Evidence from the N400. *Psychophysiology*, *45(4)*, 554–8.

Filik, R., Sanford, A. J., & Leuthold, H. (2008). Processing pronouns without antecedents: Evidence from event-related brain potentials *Journal of Cognitive Neuroscience*, *20(7)*, 1315–26.

Fischler, I., Bloom, P. A., Childers, D. G., Roucos, S. E., & Perry, N. W. (1983). Brain potentials related to stages of sentence verification. *Psychophysiology*, *20(4)*, 400–9.

Garnham, A. (2001). Mental models and the interpretation of anaphora. Hove, UK: Psychology Press.

Gerrig, R. J. & O'Brien, E. J. (2005). The scope of memory-based processing. *Discourse Processes*, *39(2–3)*, 225–42.

Gerrig, R. J. & McKoon, G. (1998). The readiness is all: The functionality of memory-based text processing. *Discourse Processes*, *26(2–3)*, 67–86.

Geurts, B. (1999). *Presuppositions and pronouns*. Oxford: Elsevier.

Geurts, B. & Beaver, D. (2007). Discourse representation theory. *Stanford encyclopedia*.

Graesser, A. C., McNamara, D. S., & Rus, V. (this volume). Computational modeling of discourse and conversation.

Grice, P. (1957). Meaning. *The Philosophical Review*, *66*, 377–88.

Hagoort, P. & Brown, C. M. (1994). Brain responses to lexical ambiguity resolution and parsing. In C. Clifton Jr., L. Frazier, & K. Rayner (Eds.) *Perspectives on sentence processing* (pp. 45–80). Hillsdale, NJ: Erlbaum.

Hagoort, P., Brown, C. M., & Groothusen, J. (1993). The syntactic positive shift (SPS) as an ERP measure of syntactic processing. *Language and Cognitive Processes*, *8(4)*, 439–83.

Hagoort, P., Hald, L. A., Bastiaansen, M., & Petersson, K. M. (2004). Integration of word meaning and world knowledge in language comprehension. *Science*, *304*, 438–41.

Hald, L. A., Steenbeek-Planting, E. G., & Hagoort, P. (2007). The interaction of discourse context and world knowledge in online sentence comprehension. Evidence from the N400. *Brain Research*, *1146*, 210–18.

Hammer, A., Jansma, B. M., Lamers, M., & Münte, T. F. (2005). Pronominal reference in sentences about persons or things: An electrophysiological approach. *Journal of Cognitive Neuroscience*, *17(2)*, 227–39.

Hoeks, JCJ, Stowe, L. A., & Doedens, G. (2004). Seeing words in context: The interaction of lexical and sentence level information during reading. *Cognitive Brain Research, 19(1)*, 59–73.

Jackendoff, R. (2002). *Foundations of Language: Brain, Meaning, Grammar, Evolution.* Oxford University Press.

(2007). A Parallel Architecture perspective on language processing. *Brain Research, 1146, 2–22.*

Johnson-Laird, P. N. (1983). *Mental Models.* Harvard University Press.

Kaan, E., Dallas, A. C., & Barkley, C. M. (2007). Dealing with new discourse referents: An ERP study. *Brain Research, 1146, 199–209.*

Kamp, H. & Reyle, U. (1993). *From discourse to logic.* Dordrecht: Kluwer.

Kempson, R. (2001). *Pragmatics: Language and communication.* In Aronoff, M. & Rees-Miller, J. (Eds.) *Handbook of linguistics.* Malden, Massachusetts: Blackwell.

Kintsch, W. (1998). *Comprehension: A paradigm for cognition.* New York: Cambridge University Press.

Kounios, J. & Holcomb, P. J. (1992). Structure and process in semantic memory: Evidence from event-related brain potentials and reaction times. *Journal of Experimental Psychology: General, 121(4), 459–79.*

Kuperberg, G. R. (2007). Neural mechanisms of language comprehension: Challenges to syntax. *Brain Research, 1146, 23–49.*

Kutas, M. (2006). One lesson learned: Frame language processing – literal and figurative – as a human brain function. *Metaphor and Symbol, 21(4), 285–325.*

& Federmeier, K. D. (2000). Electrophysiology reveals semantic memory use in language comprehension. *Trends in Cognitive Sciences, 4(12), 463–70.*

Kutas, M. & Hillyard, S. A. (1980). Reading senseless sentences: Brain potentials reflect semantic incongruity. *Science, 207, 203–5.*

(1983). Event-related brain potentials to grammatical errors and semantic anomalies. *Memory and Cognition, 11(5), 539–50.*

(1984). Brain potentials during reading reflect word expectancy and semantic association. *Nature, 307, 161–3.*

Kutas, M., Van Petten, C., & Kluender, R. (2006). *Psycholinguistics electrified II: 1994–2005.* In Traxler, M. & Gernsbacher, M. A. (Eds.) *Handbook of Psycholinguistics, 2nd Edition* (pp. 659–724). New York: Elsevier.

Lattner, S. & Friederici, A. D. (2003). Talker's voice and gender stereotype in human auditory sentence processing – evidence from event-related brain potentials. *Neuroscience Letters, 339(3), 191–4.*

Ledoux, K., Gordon, P. C., & Swaab, T. Y. (2007). Coreference and lexical repetition: Mechanisms of discourse integration. *Memory & Cognition, 35(4), 801–15.*

Levinson, S. C. (1983). *Pragmatics.* Cambridge University Press.

Li, X., Hagoort, P., & Yang, Y. (2008). Event-related Potential Evidence on the Influence of Accentuation in Spoken Discourse Comprehension in Chinese. *Journal of Cognitive Neuroscience, 20(5), 906–15.*

Magne, C., Astésano, C., Lacheret-Dujour, A., Morel, M., Alter, K., & Besson, M. (2005). On-line Processing of "Pop-Out" words in spoken french dialogues. *Journal of Cognitive Neuroscience, 17(5), 740–56.*

Marr, R. A. (2004). The neuropsychology of narrative: Story comprehension, story production and their interrelation. *Neuropsychologia, 42(10), 1414–34.*

Müller, H. M., King, J. W., & Kutas, M. (1997) Event-related potentials elicited by spoken relative clauses. *Cognitive Brain Research, 5(3), 193–203.*

Münte, T. F., Schiltz, K., & Kutas, M. (1998). When temporal terms belie conceptual order. *Nature, 395, 71–3.*

Myers, J. L. & O'Brien, E. J. (1998). Accessing the discourse representation during reading. *Discourse Processes, 26(2–3), 131–57.*

Newman, R., Forbes, K., & Connolly, J. F. (this volume). Event-related potentials and magnetic fields associated with spoken word recognition.

Nieuwland, M. S. & Kuperberg, G. R. (2008). When the truth isn't too hard to handle: An event-related potential study on the pragmatics of negation. *Psychological Science, 19 (12), 1213–18.*

Nieuwland, M. S.& Van Berkum, JJA (2005). Testing the limits of the semantic illusion phenomenon: ERPs reveal temporary semantic change deafness in discourse comprehension. *Cognitive Brain Research, 24(3), 691–701.*

(2006a). When peanuts fall in love: N400 evidence for the power of discourse. *Journal of Cognitive Neuroscience, 18(7), 1098–111.*

(2006b). Individual differences and contextual bias in pronoun resolution: Evidence from ERPs. *Brain Research, 1118(1), 155–67.*

(2008a). The neurocognition of referential ambiguity in language comprehension. *Language and Linguistics Compass, 2(4), 603–30.*

(2008b). The interplay between semantic and referential aspects of anaphoric noun phrase resolution: Evidence from ERPs. *Brain and Language*, 106(2), 119–31.

Nieuwland, M. S., Otten, M., & Van Berkum, JJA (2007). Who are you talking about? Tracking discourse-level referential processing with ERPs. *Journal of Cognitive Neuroscience*, 19(2), 228–36.

Nieuwland, M. S., Petersson, K. M., & Van Berkum, J. J. A. (2007). On sense and reference: Examining the functional neuroanatomy of referential processing. *NeuroImage*, 37, 993–1004.

Osterhout, L. & Holcomb, P. J. (1992). Event-related brain potentials elicited by syntactic anomaly. *Journal of Memory and Language*, 31(6), 785–806.

Osterhout, L. & Mobley, L. A. (1995). Event-related brain potentials elicited by failure to agree. *Journal of Memory and Language*, 34(6), 739–73.

Osterhout, L., Kim. A., & Kuperberg, G. (this volume). The neurobiology of sentence comprehension.

Otten, M. & Van Berkum, JJA (2007). What makes a discourse constraining? Comparing the effects of discourse message and scenario fit on the discourse-dependent N400 effect. *Brain Research*, 1153, 166–77.

(2008). Discourse-based anticipation during language processing: Prediction or priming? *Discourse Processes* 45(6), 464–96.

Otten, M., Nieuwland, M. S., & Van Berkum, JJA (2007). Great expectations: Specific lexical anticipation influences the processing of spoken language. *BMC Neuroscience*, 8(89), 1–9.

Özyürek, A., Willems, R. M., Kita, S., & Hagoort, P. (2007). On-line integration of semantic information from speech and gesture: Insights from event-related brain potentials. *Journal of Cognitive Neuroscience*, 19(4), 605–16.

Pickering, M. J. & Garrod, S. (2007). Do people use language production to make predictions during comprehension? *Trends in Cognitive Sciences*, 11(3), 105–10.

Pylkkänen, L. (2008). Mismatching Meanings in Brain and Behavior. *Language and Linguistics Compass* 2(4), 712–38.

Ratcliff, R. & McKoon, G. (1988). A retrieval theory of priming in memory. *Psychological Review*, 95(3), 285–408.

Sanford, A. J. & Garrod, S. C. (2005). Memory-based approaches and beyond. *Discourse Processes*, 39(2–3), 205–24.

Sanford, A. J. & Sturt, P. (2002). Depth of processing in language comprehension: Not noticing the evidence. *Trends in Cognitive Sciences*, 6(9), 382–6.

Sanford, AJS, Sanford, A. J., Molle, J., & Emmott, C. (2006). Shallow processing and attention capture in written and spoken discourse. *Discourse Processes*, 42 (2), 109–30.

Sitnikova, T., Kuperberg, G. R., & Holcomb, P. J. (2003). Semantic integration in videos of real-world events: An electrophysiological investigation. *Psychophysiology*, 40(1), 160–4.

Small, S. L. & Nusbaum, H. C. (2004). On the neurobiological investigation of language understanding in context. *Brain & Language*, 89(2), 300–11.

Sperber, D. & Wilson, D. (1995). *Relevance: Communication and Cognition*. Oxford: Blackwell

St. George, M., Mannes, S., & Hoffman, J. E. (1994). Global semantic expectancy and language comprehension. *Journal of Cognitive Neuroscience*, 6(1), 70–83.

(1997). Individual differences in inference generation: An ERP analysis. *Journal of Cognitive Neuroscience*, 9(6), 776–87.

Streb, J., Rösler, F., & Hennighausen, E. (1999). Event-related responses to pronoun and proper name anaphors in parallel and nonparallel discourse structures. *Brain and Language*, 70(2), 273–86.

(2004). Different anaphoric expressions are investigated by event-related brain potentials. *Journal of Psycholinguistic Research*, 33(3), 175–201.

Swaab, T. Y., Camblin, C. C., & Gordon, P. C. (2004). Electrophysiological evidence for reversed lexical repetition effects in language processing. *Journal of Cognitive Neuroscience*, 16(5), 715–26.

Toepel, U., Pannekamp, A., & Alter, K. (2007). Catching the news: Processing strategies in listening to dialogs as measured by ERPs. *Behavioral and Brain Functions*, 3(53).

Trueswell, J. & Tanenhaus, M. (Eds). (2005). Approaches to studying world-situated language use: Bridging the language-as-product and language-action traditions. Cambridge, MA: MIT Press.

Van Berkum, JJA (2004). Sentence comprehension in a wider discourse: Can we use ERPs to keep track of things? In Carreiras, M. & Clifton, C. Jr. (Eds.) The on-line study of sentence comprehension: Eyetracking, ERPs and beyond (pp. 229–70). New York: Psychology Press.

(2009). The neuropragmatics of "simple" utterance comprehension: An ERP review. To appear in Sauerland, U. & Yatsushiro, K. (Eds.)

Semantic and pragmatics: From experiment to theory. Palgrave.

Van Berkum, JJA, Brown, C. M., & Hagoort, P. (1999a). Early referential context effects in sentence processing: Evidence from event-related brain potentials. *Journal of Memory and Language*, 41(2), 147–82.

(1999b). When does gender constrain parsing? Evidence from ERPs. *Journal of Psycholinguistic Research*, 28(5), 555–71.

Van Berkum, JJA, Brown, C. M., Hagoort, P., & Zwitserlood, P. (2003). Event-related brain potentials reflect discourse-referential ambiguity in spoken-language comprehension. *Psychophysiology*, 40(2), 235–48.

Van Berkum, JJA, Brown, C. M., Zwitserlood, P., Kooijman, V., & Hagoort, P. (2005). Anticipating upcoming words in discourse: Evidence from ERPs and reading times. *Journal of Experimental Psychology: Learning, Memory, & Cognition*, 31(3), 443–67.

Van Berkum, JJA, Hagoort, P., & Brown, C.M. (1999). Semantic integration in sentences and discourse: Evidence from the N400. *Journal of Cognitive Neuroscience*, 11(6), 657–71.

Van Berkum, JJA, Holleman, B., Nieuwland, M. S., Otten, M., & Murre, J. (2009). Right or wrong? The brain's fast response to morally objectionable statements. *Psychological Science*, 20, 1092–1099.

Van Berkum, JJA, Koornneef, A. W., Otten, M., & Nieuwland, M. S. (2007). Establishing reference in language comprehension: An electrophysiological perspective. *Brain Research*, 1146, 158–71.

Van Berkum, JJA, Van den Brink, D., Tesink, CMJY, Kos, M., & Hagoort, P. (2008). The neural integration of speaker and message. *Journal of Cognitive Neuroscience*, 20(4), 580–91.

Van Berkum, JJA, Zwitserlood, P., Brown, C. M., & Hagoort, P. (2003) When and how do listeners relate a sentence to the wider discourse? Evidence from the N400 effect. *Cognitive Brain Research*, 17(3), 701–18.

Van Petten, C. (1993). A comparison of lexical and sentence-level context effects in event-related potentials. *Language and Cognitive Processes*, 8(4), 485–531.

Van Petten, C., Kutas, M., Kluender, R., Mitchiner, M., & McIsaac, H. (1991). Fractionating the word repetition effect with event-related potentials. *Journal of Cognitive Neuroscience*, 3(2), 131–50.

West, W. C. & Holcomb, P. J. (2002). Event-related potentials during discourse-level semantic integration of complex pictures. *Cognitive Brain Research*, 13(3), 363–75.

Wicha, NYY, Moreno, E. M., & Kutas, M. (2004). Anticipating words and their gender: An event-related brain potential study of semantic integration, gender expectancy, and gender agreement in Spanish sentence reading. *Journal of Cognitive Neuroscience*, 16(7), 1272–88.

Wilson, D. & Sperber, D. (2004). *Relevance Theory*. In Ward, G. & Horn, L. (Eds.) *Handbook of Pragmatics* (pp. 607–32). Oxford: Blackwell.

Yang, C. L., Perfetti, C. A., & Schmalhofer, F. (2007). Event-related potential indicators of text integration across sentence boundaries. *Journal of Experimental Psychology: Learning, Memory, and Cognition*, 33(1), 55–89.

Zwaan, R. A. (2004). The immersed experiencer: Toward an embodied theory of language comprehension. To appear in B. H. Ross (Ed.), The Psychology of Learning and Motivation. Vol. 44 (pp. 35–62). New York: Academic Press.

Zwaan, R. A. & Kaschak, M. P. (2009). Language comprehension as a means of "re-situating" oneself. In Robbins, P. & Aydede, M. (Eds.) *The Cambridge Handbook of Situated Cognition*. Cambridge, UK: Cambridge University Press.

Zwaan, R. A. & Radvansky, G. A. (1998). Situation models in language comprehension and memory. *Psychological Bulletin*, 123(2), 162–85.

Zwaan, R. A. & Singer, M. (2003). *Text comprehension*. In Graesser, A. C., Gernsbacher, M. A., & Goldman, S. R. (Eds.) *Handbook of discourse processes* (pp. 83–121). Mahwah, NJ: Lawrence Erlbaum.

LANGUAGE AND THOUGHT

CHAPTER 31

How the Languages We Speak Shape the Ways We Think

The FAQs

Lera Boroditsky

Do people who speak different languages think differently? Does learning new languages change the way you think? Do polyglots think differently when speaking different languages? Are some thoughts unthinkable without language? The topic of the interactions between language and thought invariably brings up a host of fascinating interrelated questions. In recent years, research on linguistic relativity has enjoyed a remarkable resurgence, and much new evidence regarding the effects of language on thought has become available. In this chapter, I provide answers to some of the most frequently asked questions (to the best of our knowledge to date).

1 Why might the languages we speak shape the ways we think?

Humans communicate with one another using a dazzling array of languages, and each language differs from the next in innumerable ways (from obvious differences in pronunciation and vocabulary to more subtle differences in grammar). For example, I can tell you in English that "my brother and his seven children live in the blue house to the left of the big tree." In some languages it would be impossible for me to tell you about my brother without revealing whether he is older or younger than me (because there are only words for older brother and younger brother, not a generic word for brother). In other languages it would be most natural to specify simply that the person is a sibling, without revealing gender. In many languages there is no word meaning exactly seven, so instead one might say several or many. Some languages don't have a color word for blue: Some distinguish only between dark and light; some have a color word that includes both blue and green, and others would require one to specify necessarily whether the house was dark blue or light blue. Many languages don't have words like *left*, and instead might require you to locate the house as southwest or volcano-ward or uphill from the tree. And some languages don't have a generic superordinate word like *tree*, instead requiring speakers to specify the type of tree in each instance. And on and on.

In addition to these kinds of wide differences in vocabulary, languages differ in what kind of information is grammatically required. Let's take a (very) hypothetical example. Suppose you want to say, "Bush read Chomsky's latest book." Let's focus on just the verb, *read*. To say this sentence in English, we have to mark the verb for tense; in this case, we have to pronounce it like *red* and not like *reed*. In Indonesian you need not (in fact, you can't) alter the verb to mark tense. In Russian, you would have to alter the verb to indicate tense and gender. So, if it was Laura Bush who did the reading, you'd use a different form of the verb than if it was George. In Russian, you would also have to include in the verb information about completion. If George read only part of the book, you would use a different form of the verb than if he had diligently plowed through the whole thing. In Turkish, you would have to include in the verb how you acquired this information. For example, if you had witnessed this unlikely event with your own two eyes, you'd use one form of the verb, but if you had simply read or heard about it, or inferred it from something Bush said, you'd use a different form of the verb.

Observations like these have led scholars to wonder whether speakers of different languages have to attend to and encode strikingly different aspects of the world in order to use their language properly (Sapir, 1921; Slobin, 1996). Do these quirks of languages affect the way their speakers think about the world? Do English, Mandarin, Russian, and Turkish speakers end up attending to, partitioning, and remembering their experiences differently simply because they speak different languages?

The idea that thought is shaped by language is most commonly associated with the writings of Benjamin Lee Whorf (Whorf, 1956). Whorf, impressed by linguistic diversity, proposed that the categories and distinctions of each language enshrine a way of perceiving, analyzing, and acting in the world. Whorf asked, "Are our own concepts of time, space, and matter given in substantially the same form by experience to all men, or are they partly conditioned by the structure of particular languages?" (Whorf, 1956). This question, often called the Whorfian question, has attracted much attention and controversy throughout the years. Some scholars have found the idea that different languages encapsulate different world views intuitive and compelling and have been happy to accept it without need of empirical evidence. Long before Whorf, Charlemagne the Holy Roman Emperor proclaimed that "to have a second language is to have a second soul." One of his successors, Frederick the Great of Prussia, quipped, "I speak French to my ambassadors, English to my accountant, Italian to my mistress, Latin to my God and German to my horse." Others, however, have been much less enthusiastic about the idea of linguistic relativity. As Jerry Fodor colorfully put it, "I hate relativism more than I hate anything else, excepting, maybe, fiberglass powerboats" (Fodor, 1985).

There are, of course, many powerful and noncontroversial ways in which language acts on our thoughts and actions. With a few well-chosen syllables, it is possible to make a complete stranger laugh, blush, or give one a good solid sock on the nose (I leave the exact syllables required as an exercise for the reader). In its perfected form language can uplift, educate, and inspire. In more turbulent times, poignant words can incite revolutions and loose lips can sink ships. Other times we may just want to say "pass the salt." In all of these cases, language causes real conceptual and physical outcomes, be they revolutions, broken noses, soggy ships, or seasoning. Further, an overwhelming proportion of what we know about the world outside of our direct physical experience we learn through the medium of language. The importance of these rather obvious influences of language on thought is generally overlooked in the literature, so it is worth spelling them out at least briefly.

Consider an analogy with visual perception. Our experience of aspects of the visual world like color and motion are fundamentally constrained by the physiology of the visual system. For example, humans generally have only three types of cones for perceiving color. This means that many physically different surfaces in the world will reflect light in a way that produces the same relative levels of excitation in our three cone types, and so will look the same to us (they will be perceptual metamers). If our knowledge of these surfaces is limited to our visual experience with them, then our knowledge of their reflective properties will be fundamentally limited by the physiology of the color perception system.

The same is true in the case of language. Language, like the physiological underpinnings of visual perception, is a limited input channel. A very large proportion of what we know is communicated to us through language. Language is the main way in which contents of individual minds are transmitted across individuals, between groups and cultures, and through time. What information gets transmitted (or even what information can be transmitted) is necessarily constrained by the particular properties of the language being used.

As we saw in the examples cited earlier, different languages will incidentally communicate very different information about the world. In some languages, you would often learn more about the birth order of siblings, in others more specifics about numbers, colors, gender, local arborous species, or locations with respect to nearby volcanoes. Because so much of our knowledge of the world is learned through language (and often only through language), the particular aspects of the languages we use for communication can potentially exert a tremendous influence over the contents of our minds.

Of course, language is not the only source of information we have. We also receive tremendously rich streams of information from the physical world, through our perceptual and motor systems, and we come to the learning problem equipped with some important skills and predispositions. Still, accompanying this rich stream of perceptual information is an ever-present stream of language. By the time infants are born, they have already learned a great deal about the sound properties and regularities of their language from the sound patterns that reached them in the womb (e.g., Mehler et al., 1988). From the very beginning of life, linguistic and other perceptual information occurs concurrently and children are avidly learning and processing both at the same time.

Further, though the information we receive from the physical world is incredibly rich, we are able to attend to and process only a small fraction of that information (e.g., Simons and Rensink, 2005). While we have the feeling of always having a complete and clear picture of the visual world, decades of research on attention have shown that this feeling is a grand illusion. We are really able to attend to only a very small number of elements at any given time. One way to think about language in this context is as an attentional guide. The aspects of the world encoded by language are those that generations of people before us have found useful to pay attention to. On this conception, each language functions as a culturally created guide to attention, a way of highlighting certain aspects of the world important within a culture. This suggests that if languages differ in interesting ways, then speakers of different languages may learn to attend to and encode different aspects of the world, even when confronted with the same physical stimuli.

There is, of course, an alternative view. Just because speakers of different languages talk differently, doesn't necessarily mean they think differently. It is possible for example, that speakers of all languages attend to and encode all the same things. Then, each language chooses some subset of those universally attended things to talk about. After all, just because speakers don't habitually encode some aspect of the world in their linguistic utterances doesn't mean that they don't attend to it nonlinguistically. In this view, speakers of all languages attend to all the same things (logically, this would mean that all people attend to the set of all distinctions made by all the world's languages), and differ only in how they talk. This leads us to the second question: Do speakers of different languages actually perceive, attend to, encode, and represent their worlds differently?

2 Do people who speak different languages think differently?

In recent years, research on linguistic relativity has enjoyed a remarkable resurgence, and much new evidence regarding the effects of language on thought has become available. Some studies have been successful in finding cross-linguistic differences in thought (e.g., Boroditsky, 2001; Bowerman, 1996; Davidoff, Davies, and Roberson, 1999; Gentner and Imai, 1997; Kay and Kempton, 1984; Levinson, 1996; Lucy, 1992; Winawer et al, 2007), while others have failed to find differences (e.g., Heider, 1972; Li and Gleitman, 2002; Papafragou, Massey, and Gleitman, 2002). Cross-linguistic differences have been found in many of the most fundamental domains of thought including color perception, object categories, conceptions of shape, substance, events, and people's representations of motion, space, causality, time, and number.

I will draw on examples from space, color, and grammatical gender to illustrate three important ways in which languages shape thinking. First, I will describe work on spatial reference frames. This work reveals a remarkably deep set of cross-linguistic differences in spatial thinking, showing that practice with a particular language can equip one with cognitive abilities that seem amazing to speakers of other languages. Then I will describe work on the role of language in color discrimination. This work reveals that patterns in language are involved not only in very complex or high-level domains of thought, but also meddle in the very nuts and bolts of perceptual experience. Finally, I will describe work showing the influence of grammatical gender on representations of objects and other entities. This work demonstrates that

grammatical features, even the seemingly arbitrary mandatory mechanics of language like grammatical gender, also have the power to shape people's thinking.

2.1 *Do speakers of different languages really think all that differently?*

One example of really striking cross-linguistic differences comes from the domain of spatial reference. Languages differ dramatically in how they describe spatial relations. For example, in English, terms like *left* and *right* that define space relative to an observer are common (e.g., "the salad fork is to the left of the dinner fork"). Unlike English, some languages do not make use of terms like *left* and *right*, and instead rely on an absolute reference frame system to describe such relations (e.g., Levinson, 2003; Levinson and Wilkins, 2006). For example, Guugu Yimithirr (an Australian Aboriginal language), uses cardinal direction terms – roughly aligned with north, south, east, and west – to define space. While English speakers also sometimes use cardinal direction terms, our use of them is restricted to large spatial scales. For example, English speakers do not say "the salad fork is to the east of the dinner fork." In languages like Guugu Yimithirr, no words like *left* and *right* are available, and absolute spatial reference is used at all scales. This means that Guugu Yimithirr speakers say things like "There's an ant on your southeast leg" or "The boy standing to the south of Mary is my brother" (e.g., Majid et al, 2004). One obvious consequence of speaking such a language is that you have to stay oriented at all times, else you cannot speak the language properly. For example, the normal greeting in Kuuk Thaayorre (an Australian Aboriginal language with a roughly N/S/E/W absolute direction system) is "Where are you going?" and the answer ought to be something like "South-southeast, in the middle distance." If you don't know which way you're facing at all times, you can't even get past "Hello."

Not only is it important to stay oriented in the moment, all experiences must be coded in memory with respect to these absolute bearings if you wish to be able to talk about them later (e.g., "I must have left my keys to the north of the coffee maker" or "They set the salad forks southeast of the dinner forks. The philistines!"). Further, you must be able to dead reckon your own position and have your mental maps correctly oriented so that you can calculate the bearing between any two locations that you may wish to talk about or the direction to any location from where you are at the moment. And all of this has to happen quickly and automatically, which means it has to be attended to and updated all the time.

To demonstrate the big difference between this way of being oriented in space and what English speakers usually do, I often have the whole English-speaking audience in a lecture hall close its eyes. I then give the audience members a surprise quiz: Point southeast. People's responses are informative on many levels. First, many people laugh because they think it's a ridiculous and unfair question. How are they supposed to know which way southeast is? Then, it takes people a while to start pointing. There is an effortful computation to be done: This isn't information that is readily available for most English speakers. Finally, when people do point, they point in all possible directions. I don't generally know which way southeast is myself, so I cannot tell who is right and who is wrong, but given that in any group of English speakers most directions are pointed to about equally often, I infer that the accuracy is not very high. A task like this is trivial for speakers of absolute languages. A few summers ago I had the chance to ask some Kuuk Thaayorre five-year-olds the same question. They were able to point in the right direction (I had to check with a compass) and without hesitation. Asking the same question of Kuuk Thaayorre adults is vaguely insulting. How could anyone not know which way southeast is?

Another striking observation comes from people's spontaneous cospeech gestures. When speakers of absolute languages like Guugu Yimithirr make spontaneous gestures to accompany a description of motion, their gestures preserve the absolute direction of the motion being described. For example, if telling a story about a boat that was observed moving north (and left to right in the field of view), a Guugu Yimithirr speaker would make a gesture from left to right if facing west at the time of telling, but from right to left if facing east, toward the body if facing south, and so on. Speakers of relative languages like English tend to gesture the relative direction of motion, so would gesture the motion from left to right, regardless of their facing direction at the time of telling (Majid et al, 2004).

Because space is such a fundamental domain of thought, differences in how people think about space don't end there. People rely on their spatial knowledge to build other, more abstract representations. Representations of such things as time, number, musical pitch, kinship relations, morality, and emotions have been shown to depend on how we think about space. So if speakers of different languages think differently about space, do they also think differently about other things, like time?

To test this idea, Boroditsky and Gaby (2006) compared speakers of English and Kuuk Thaayorre. Participants received sets of pictures that showed some kind of temporal progression (e.g., pictures of a man aging, or a crocodile growing, or a banana being eaten). Their job was to arrange the shuffled photos on the ground to show the correct temporal order. Each person was tested in two separate sittings, each time facing in a different cardinal direction. When English speakers are asked to do this, they arrange the cards so that time proceeds from left to right. Hebrew speakers tend to lay out the cards from right to left, showing that writing direction in a language plays a role (Fuhrman and Boroditsky, 2007; Tversky, Kugelmass, and Winter, 1991). So what about folks like the Kuuk Thaayorre, who don't use words like *left* and *right*? What do they do?

The Kuuk Thaayorre did not arrange the cards more often from left to right than from right to left, or more toward or away from the body. But their arrangements were not random: There was a beautiful pattern, just a different one from that of English speakers. Instead of arranging time from left to right, they arranged it from east to west. That is, when they were seated facing south, the cards went left to right. When they faced north, the cards went from right to left. When they faced east, the cards came toward the body, and so on. This was true even though participants were never told which direction they were facing. The Kuuk Thaayorre not only knew that already, they also spontaneously used this spatial information to construct their representations of time. Important, these results demonstrate that cross-linguistic differences, at least in some cases, are not simply a matter of degree – they can constitute qualitatively different ways of organizing the world. Most of the English speakers tested on these tasks simply could not have done what the Kuuk Thaayorre did, because they did not know which way they were facing (even in a highly familiar environment). And even those English speakers who could figure out which way was which would never have thought to use that information to organize time.

To summarize, there are profound differences in navigational ability and spatial knowledge between speakers of languages that rely primarily on absolute reference frames (like Guugu Yimithirr) and languages that rely on relative reference frames (like English) (e.g., Majid et al, 2004). Simply put, speakers of languages like Guugu Yimithirr are much better than English speakers at staying oriented and keeping track of where they are, even in unfamiliar landscapes (or inside unfamiliar buildings). The constant practice of paying attention to and tracking orientation in order to speak their language enables them (in fact, forces them) to be able to perform navigational feats once thought beyond human capabilities. Further, cross-linguistic differences in spatial reference frames profoundly shape not only people's reasoning about space, but also their representations of other domains that are typically scaffolded on top of spatial representations (e.g., time).

2.2 Does language just shape the way we construe or remember our experiences or does it shape how we actually perceive things?

Language divides the continuous spectrum of color into discrete categories (e.g., in English: yellow, green, blue, etc.). Different languages divide up the color continuum differently: Some make many more distinctions between colors than others, and the boundaries often don't line up across languages. Do these linguistic categories play a role in how people perceptually experience colors? Can language play a role in even such low-level perceptual decisions as judging whether two squares of color are exactly the same? Recent research on color language and color perception has demonstrated that languages meddle even in surprisingly basic perceptual tasks (e.g., Davidoff et al., 1999; Kay and Kempton, 1984; Winawer et al, 2007).

For example, in Russian, there is no single word that covers all the colors English speakers call *blue*. Russian makes an obligatory distinction between light blue (*goluboy*) and dark blue (*siniy*). Does having to make a distinction between lighter and darker blues in language cause Russian speakers to perceive lighter and darker blues as being more different from one another than they would appear to an English speaker?

To test this, (Winawer et al, 2007) compared Russian and English speakers' ability to discriminate shades of blue. On each trial of the task, English and Russian speakers were shown three color chips on the screen at the same time: one above, and two below. One of the bottom color chips was identical to the top chip. The subjects' task was to indicate which of the bottom two chips was the same as the chip on top (they did so by pressing a button on the right or left side of the keyboard). All of the color chips in the study fell into the English category *blue*, spanning the *goluboy/siniy* border in Russian.

The results showed a clear cross-linguistic difference. Russian speakers were faster to respond when the two bottom color chips they had to distinguish between were from different linguistic categories in Russian (one would be called *siniy* and one *goluboy* in Russian) than if they were from the same linguistic category (both were *siniy* or both were *goluboy*). For English speakers, of course, all of these colors are called by the same basic color term – *blue* – so there should be no such differences. And indeed, English speakers tested on the same stimuli showed no such differences: They were not faster when the two colors to compare crossed the Russian *goluboy/siniy* boundary than when they didn't. Both in language and in perception, these colors were all *blue* to English speakers.

Further, the Russian linguistic boundary effect disappeared when subjects were asked to perform a verbal interference task (verbally rehearsing a string of digits), while making color judgments – but not when they were asked to perform an equally difficult spatial interference task (keeping a novel visual pattern in memory). Neither verbal interference nor spatial interference had any effect on the English speakers' pattern of results. The fact that verbal (and not spatial) interference had an effect and only on the language group that makes the relevant linguistic distinction demonstrates that it is language per se that creates this difference in perception between Russian and English speakers. It appears that under normal viewing conditions (without verbal interference) linguistic processes meddle in Russian speakers' perceptual decisions. When Russian speakers are blocked from their normal access to language by a verbal interference task, the differences between Russian speakers and English speakers disappear.

These results demonstrate that language is involved in even surprisingly basic perceptual judgments. Importantly, these cross-linguistic differences were observed in an objective perceptual discrimination task. All stimuli were present on the screen and available to perception while people were making their judgments: They did not need to be retrieved from long-term memory. There was no ambiguity in how to interpret the task. On all trials there was an objective correct answer (one of the bottom chips was identical to the chip on top and the other chip was different), and subjects knew the correct answer and performed the task with high accuracy. Further, the task was entirely nonlinguistic: Subjects were not asked to name the colors or to produce or understand language at all. Still, the amount of time people required to arrive at these simple perceptual decisions (even in the presence of all the necessary perceptual stimuli) depended on their native language. The fact that cross-linguistic differences can be found even in such basic perceptual tasks suggests that linguistic processes get involved not just in higher-level cognition, but in relatively low-level perceptual processes as well.

An ingenious study by Gilbert et al (2006) has shed light on some of the neural bases of the effects of language on color discrimination. Gilbert et al tested English speakers in a speeded visual search task with colors spanning the blue/green border. Just as in the previous studies, they found effects specific to linguistic boundaries – English-speaking subjects were faster to find a blue among greens than a blue among blues and these effects were reduced with verbal interference. Importantly, Gilbert et al. showed that this effect was only obtained when the target was presented in the right visual field (and thus available primarily to the left – language-dominant hemisphere), and not when the target was presented on the left (and thus primarily available to the right hemisphere which is less involved in language). This finding once again reinforces the idea that linguistic processing is involved in simple perceptual judgments (at least in one half of the brain).

2.3 *Do aspects of grammar shape thinking?*

One important aspect of the debate on language and thought centers on the question of what to count as language. On some views of language, only aspects of grammar, the very mechanics of constructing utterances, are at the very core of language. Correspondingly, some scholars wonder whether grammatical differences (i.e., not what you say, but how you have to say it) play any role in shaping people's thinking.

Aspects of grammar make for a very exciting test case of linguistic relativity because grammatical markers can be so pervasive in language. For example in some languages grammatical markers like tense or aspect will need to be attached to all verbs, and categories like grammatical gender may affect all nouns. If it can be shown that grammatical markers that attach to all verbs or all nouns have an effect on how people think about objects or events, then that means language might affect how people think about anything that can be named by a noun or a verb. This would indeed be a very pervasive effect of language on thought.

It turns out that even what might be deemed frivolous aspects of grammar can have far-reaching subconscious effects on how we see the world. Take grammatical gender. In Spanish and other Romance languages, all nouns are either masculine or feminine. In many other languages, nouns are divided into many more genders (*gender* in this context meaning class or kind). For example, some Australian Aboriginal languages have up to sixteen genders, including grammatical classes for hunting weapons, canines, things that are shiny, or, as George Lakoff (1987) made famous, "Women, Fire, and Dangerous Things."

What it means for a language to have grammatical gender is that words belonging to different genders get treated differently grammatically and words that belong to the same grammatical gender get treated the same grammatically. Languages can require speakers to change pronouns, adjective and verb endings, possessives, numerals, and so on, depending on the noun's gender. For example, to say something like "my chair was old" in Russian (*moy stul bil stariy*), you would need to make every word in the

sentence agree in gender with *chair* (*stul*), which is masculine in Russian. So you'd use the masculine form of *my*, the masculine form of *was*, and the masculine form of *old*. These are the same forms that you would use if speaking about a biological male, for example to say "my grandfather was old." If, instead of speaking of a chair, you were speaking of a bed (*krovat*), which is feminine in Russian, you would use the feminine form of *my*, the feminine form of *was*, and the feminine form of *old*. These are the same feminine forms that you would use if speaking of a biological female (e.g., "my grandmother was old").

Does treating chairs similarly to biological males and beds similarly to biological females in grammar make Russian speakers think of chairs as being more like men and beds as more like women in some way?

To find out, Boroditsky, Schmidt, and Phillips (2003) asked German and Spanish speakers to describe objects that have opposite grammatical gender assignment in the two languages. The descriptions people gave differed in a way predicted by grammatical gender. For example, when asked to describe a *key* – a word that is masculine in German and feminine in Spanish – German speakers were more likely to use words like "hard," "heavy," "jagged," "metal," "serrated," and "useful," whereas Spanish speakers were more likely to say "golden," "intricate," "little," "lovely," "shiny," and "tiny." To describe a *bridge*, a word that is feminine in German and masculine in Spanish, German speakers said "beautiful," "elegant," "fragile," "peaceful," "pretty," and "slender," and Spanish speakers said "big," "dangerous," "long," "strong," "sturdy," and "towering." This was true even though all testing was done in English (a language without grammatical gender).

The same pattern of results also emerged in entirely nonlinguistic tasks. For example, Spanish and German speakers were asked to rate similarities between pictures of people (males or females) and pictures of objects (the names of which had opposite genders in Spanish and German). Both groups rated grammatically feminine objects to be more similar to females and grammatically masculine objects more similar to males. This was true even though all objects had opposite genders in Spanish and German, the test was completely non-linguistic (conducted entirely in pictures with instructions given in English), and even when subjects performed the task during a verbal suppression manipulation (which would interfere with their ability to sub-vocally name the objects in any language).

Further studies showed that aspects of language per se can create these kinds of cognitive differences. For example, teaching English speakers new grammatical gender categories in a novel language produced the same kinds of biases in their mental representations of objects as were observed with German and Spanish speakers. It appears that even small flukes of grammar, like the seemingly arbitrary assignment of gender to a noun, can have an effect on people's conceptions of concrete objects.

In fact, one doesn't even need to go into the lab to see these kinds of effects of grammar; it is possible to literally see them at an art gallery. Consider the case of personification in art: the ways that abstract entities such as death, sin, victory, or time are given human form. How does an artist decide whether death, say, or time should be painted as a man or a woman? It turns out that in eighty-five percent of such personifications, whether a male or female figure is chosen is predicted by the grammatical gender of the word in the artist's native language. So, for example, German painters are more likely to paint death as a man, while Russian painters are more likely to paint death as a woman.

The fact that even seeming flukes of grammar like grammatical gender can have an effect on our thinking is exciting because grammatical features can be so pervasive in language. A small quirk of grammar like grammatical gender for example applies to all nouns. That means that this quirk of grammar can subtly shape how we think about anything that can be named by a noun. And that of course is a lot of stuff!

3 Does language really play a causal role in shaping thought? Or how do you know that it's language shaping thought and not the other way around? Or how do you know it's not culture or some other aspects of the environment that create these differences?

The question of causality, whether it is language per se that causes speakers of different languages to think differently, is a crucial one for the study of linguistic relativity. This question comes up so often because it is difficult to establish causality in studies that compare performance across populations or groups. What allows us to establish causal power in the majority of psychology experiments is the basic structure of the experimental method: randomly assign subjects to conditions, and see if manipulating the independent variable produces differences in outcomes. So a perfect cross-linguistic experiment would invite participants into the study, randomly assign them to be Russian, German, or Indonesian speakers and then test whether the languages subjects were assigned affected their thinking. Of course, this design is difficult to apply in practice. By the time subjects arrive in the lab they are already Russian or German or Indonesian speakers, and they bring with them not just this difference in the languages they speak, but also a myriad of other uncontrolled differences in their life experiences.

So if we find a difference on some cognitive task between Russian and English speakers, for example, how do we know this difference stems from differences in language per se, and not from all the other possible differences between the groups? Further, how do we establish the direction of causality? How do we know that it is language that shaped thought, and not the other way around? A priori it is equally plausible that the two groups ended up talking differently because they think differently (perhaps because they live in different physical environments or simply through some series of historical accidents).

This question has been taken very seriously by researchers in this field and a number of different approaches have been developed specifically to try to establish causality.

3.1 How do you know if it's language or just the physical environment in which people live?

One approach has been to make comparisons not between just two language groups, but across a wide range of languages. For example, the work on spatial reference frames described earlier has been done across a wide range of languages spoken in many different types of environments. This approach allows one to control for different aspects of culture or physical environment (e.g., literacy, climate, geography, natural resources, etc.) and rule these factors out as potential confounds. For example, it has been found that languages that rely primarily on absolute reference frames exist all over the world. They are not restricted to a particular type of landscape, geographical location, natural environment, or style of living. Absolute reference frame languages are found in large deserts, on small islands, in the steppes, and in tropical rainforests. They are found in cultures that move around and in cultures that stay put, in cultures that use written language and those that do not.

Nor is it the case that a particular type of environment necessitates absolute spatial reference. While absolute reference frames are more commonly found in rural than in urban environments, people do not end up thinking in terms of absolute reference frames simply by virtue of living in a rural environment: Plenty of rural dwellers speak and think in relative terms. What seems to matter most for predicting people's patterns of spatial reasoning are the reference frames most commonly used in the language and gesture systems (Majid et al., 2004). Looking across a broad range of languages in this way is one way to test and rule out other plausible explanations for cross-linguistic differences in thought.

3.2 What if you teach people a new way of talking; does that change the way they think?

Another way to address the question of whether experience with language really causes differences in thinking is to teach people new ways of talking and see if that changes the way they think. In the studies on grammatical gender described earlier, for example, it was shown that teaching English speakers different ways of talking changes their mental representations. Similar results have been obtained in the domain of color perception. For example, Ozgen and Davies (2002) showed that teaching subjects new color categories resulted in the same kinds of categorical perception effects observed across languages. Altogether these results suggest that patterns in a language can indeed play a causal role in constructing how we think.

3.3 Does learning new languages change the way one thinks?

Many of us endeavor to learn languages other than our native tongue. When we try to learn a new language, are we simply learning a new way of talking, or are we also learning a new way of thinking? Results from language training studies discussed above show that learning to talk in a new way does also lead one to think in a new way. Studies with bilinguals also support this idea. For example, studies comparing Indonesian speakers who have and have not learned English as a second language show that those who have learned English at some point in their lives show more English-like attentional patterns in nonlinguistic tasks than Indonesian speakers who have not learned English (Boroditsky, Ham, and Ramscar, 2002). This is true even though both groups are tested in Indonesian in Indonesia, by a native Indonesian speaker, and are never asked about their proficiency in English until after the end of the experiment. This pattern of findings signals that in addition to online effects of language (as found in the case of color), language can also have a long-term effect on thinking. Even when a particular language is not being used, simply having learned that language at some point in life has created an attentional habit, tuned one's attentional system to the distinctions encoded in that language. It appears that when we learn a new language, we're not simply learning a new way of talking; we are also inadvertently learning a new way of thinking, a new way of partitioning, organizing, and construing the world.

3.4 *What if you disable language in some way, how does that affect thought?*

Another way to address the question of whether language shapes thought is to see what happens when language is disabled in some way. One noninvasive way to interrupt people's fluent access to their linguistic resources is to engage them in some kind of verbal interference task, like repeating digits or syllables, or shadowing speech. One can then see if disrupting normal access to linguistic processing in this way causes changes in cognitive performance (compared to when people perform some other equally difficult secondary task that is not verbal). It turns out that in some cases verbal interference does change people's cognitive performance. For example, in the color discrimination studies comparing Russian and English speakers described earlier, verbal interference changed the Russian speakers' pattern of responses erasing the effect of the Russian *goluboy/siniy* linguistic boundary on their color discrimination. Important, the same was not found when Russian speakers were tested in a control spatial interference condition. Nor was there any effect of verbal interference on the behavior of English speakers for whom no obligatory linguistic boundary exists in the range of stimuli being tested. This pattern of results demonstrates that language is responsible for the cross-linguistic difference observed under natural testing conditions. More generally, findings showing effects of verbal interference on cognitive performance demonstrate that linguistic processes are normally recruited

for many seemingly nonlinguistic cognitive tasks (see also Lupyan, Rakison, and McClelland, 2007).

It is important to point out that while in some studies verbal interference wipes out or diminishes cross-linguistic differences (e.g., color), in other studies, cross-linguistic differences seem unaffected by verbal interference (e.g., grammatical gender). This suggests that language affects performance differently in different cases. In the case of color discrimination, language appears to be having an acute effect; it is involved online, meddling in perceptual decisions as they are made. In the case of grammatical gender, language appears to be more of a chronic affliction; it has had a long-term effect on the underlying conceptual representations such that even if language is disabled, its effects in the conceptual system remain. This means that verbal interference cannot be used as a general test of whether language shapes thought; it's a test of whether language shapes thought in a particular way. Specifically, it is a good technique for testing whether language is involved online during a task.

3.5 *Do bilinguals think differently when speaking different languages?*

Another approach to establishing the causal role that language plays in cognition is to study bilingual populations. For example, in a group of bilinguals, it is possible to randomly assign subjects to be tested in one language or another, and then see whether the linguistic context in which the test is conducted has an effect on the results. In one such study, Boroditsky et al. (2002) tested a group of Indonesian–English bilinguals on a set of nonlinguistic tasks designed to assess attention to temporal frames in events (an aspect that English cares more about than Indonesian). Half of the participants were greeted and given instructions in Indonesian, and half in English. Being tested in an English or an Indonesian linguistic context had an influence on how people performed the tasks. Bilinguals who were tested in the English linguistic context showed attentional patterns that were more like those of English speakers, while bilinguals tested in the Indonesian linguistic context showed a more Indonesian attentional pattern. This was true even though the tasks themselves were nonlinguistic (e.g., remembering sets of photographs, or rating photographs for similarity), and the linguistic context was established simply by the language that the experimenter used to give instructions.

Studies on bilingual autobiographical memory have shown a similar contextual effect of language. For example, in one study Russian–English bilinguals were prompted with either English or Russian words and asked to recall an event from their past. The autobiographical memories they generated tended to be from the times in their life when they were predominantly speakers of the prompted language (Marian and Neisser, 2000).

It appears that bilinguals do sometimes show different cognitive patterns when tested in one language versus another. However it is also the case that the patterns one has learned in a language are somewhat active even when that particular language is not being spoken (see Section 3C). The extent to which two languages are integrated in daily use will undoubtedly serve to shift these results. For example, if a person is a perfectly balanced bilingual and both languages are used in very similar and interrelated contexts, then one might expect more integration in cognitive patterns as well: less difference as a function of language of test and a stronger effect of the language not currently being used on the patterns in behavior. If the two languages are not well integrated in daily use, then there may be a bigger difference in behavior when tested in different languages. And of course, as languages go into disuse and start to fade from memory, so may their cognitive influence.

Many other approaches to establishing the causal power of language in shaping thought are possible. For example, one can study the effects of language deprivation in development, one can present stimuli in a way that "hides" them from the language-dominant left hemisphere (e.g., Gilbert, 2006), one can disrupt linguistic processes using TMS, one can create longitudinal language training programs, or one can look at people who have lost the ability to speak due to injury. These different techniques get at slightly different ways in which language might be involved in thinking. Using the full complement of methods available will yield a more refined understanding of how language interacts with and shapes thinking in different cases.

Does language only shape thinking when you're speaking or does it also shape non-linguistic thought? We have already seen that languages can exert influence even when people are not being tested in the language of interest. For example, Spanish and German speakers show effects of grammatical gender categories in their native language even when tested in English, a language without grammatical gender. We have also seen that cross-linguistic differences surface even when people are tested in tasks that do not require them to produce or understand language. In some cases these cross-linguistic differences in behavior persist despite verbal interference, suggesting that language has influenced the underlying representations and is not involved online.

In all of these cases, however, it is possible that people do somehow rely on language in the task. They may not be asked to speak out loud, or they may even be somewhat inhibited by verbal interference, but it is possible that they still manage to bring up some information from the linguistic system. What does this mean for the claim that language is shaping nonlinguistic thought?

The question of whether experience with a language affects nonlinguistic thought is central to the Whorfian debate. But what should be counted as nonlinguistic thought? The argument that language and thought are entirely separate (such that language doesn't affect thought) is only meaningful if a sufficiently large number of cognitive tasks are normally accomplished without the involvement of language. A good candidate for this set of tasks would be tasks that do not require participants to produce or understand language.

But what then of all the cross-linguistic differences found even in such tasks? It could be argued that the tasks were not truly non-linguistic, that language is automatically or involuntarily recruited for these tasks even though subjects are not overtly required to use language (and even overtly discouraged from using language by a concurrent verbal suppression task). For example, one might argue that people implicitly name pictures as soon as they see them and this cannot be wiped out entirely by verbal suppression. However, taking this line of argument runs counter to the original premise one would be trying to defend – namely that language and thought are entirely separate (such that language does not affect thought).

If language is indeed involuntarily recruited for most cognitive tasks (even ones that do not overtly require language use), then language *is* having a profound effect on thought by being an involuntary component of the processes we call thinking. In fact, if this is the case, then what we colloquially call "thought" is indeed a complex set of collaborations between linguistic and nonlinguistic representations and processes. The evidence available so far suggests that language affects thought both by being involved in a variety of cognitive processes online and by effecting long-term change in nonlinguistic representations.

4 Are some thoughts unthinkable without language?

In 1984, George Orwell describes a dystopian society in which the Party meticulously controls and manipulates language to create a new dialect – Newspeak. The purpose of Newspeak is to make thoughts of freedom and rebellion impossible by removing any words or phrases that could express these ideas. The suggestion is that thoughts that are impossible to express in language become unthinkable.

The question of whether some thoughts are unthinkable without language is a popular topic of debate. Is this the case? Are some thoughts unthinkable without the right words to express them? Is language necessary for certain types of thinking? Is language a straitjacket for thought?

4.1 *Are some thoughts unthinkable without the right words to express them? Is language necessary for thought?*

Language, of course, is not our sole source of information. We can learn about the world in many other ways. Just because some information or some distinction is missing from language doesn't mean it will be impossible to discover it or acquire it in some other way. It may take much longer to discover that particular feature of the world, and many people may never come across it at all, but that doesn't mean it's impossible. Language, after all, is developed by humans. We are constantly inventing new words and expressions, adjusting the structures, and staking out new uses for elements in our language. We use our languages as tools to achieve many goals, and as our goals develop and change, we often develop and change the tools of language. This is a laborious process, but through cultural time humans are clearly developing new knowledge as well as new ways of talking about it.

Language is also not the sole cognitive tool we have. Language is extremely useful for many types of thinking and in practical terms greatly expands our repertoire of cognitive skills. Language can act as a crutch in memory, serve as an external placeholder, and encourage us to schematize, categorize, abstract, and build knowledge through analogical inferences. But is it the only way we can possibly achieve these things? Could other forms of representation that share some of the virtues of language also do the job?

Let's take this question up in a particular example domain: number. The domain of number has recently been championed as the star case in which language, and in particular the system of exact number words (e.g., *one, two, three, four, five, six, seven*, etc.) is necessary to be able to keep track of exact quantities above three (e.g., Gordon, 2004). If there was really no other way to keep track of exact quantities except by learning exact number words, then this would indeed be a very strong case for the idea that some thoughts are unthinkable without language.

However, there are other ways of keeping track of exact quantities. For example, the Arrernte (Central Australia) do not have exact number words above two, but are still able to keep track of large exact quantities (Wilkins, 2002). Arrernte, like many Australian languages, has terms roughly corresponding to *one*, *two*, *few*, and *many*. There are no everyday language terms for *three*, *four*, *five*, and so on. However, there is a term which means *thus many*. This term shifts the expression of number quantification out of the language system and into other external representation systems, like gestures (holding up the correct number of fingers for example) or to a form of conventional tallying in the sand (e.g., with dots). The Arrernte use these two external systems to keep track of exact quantities far beyond the number words available in their language.

In one demonstration, David Wilkins presented Arrernte elders with two groupings of pebbles of about the same size (e.g., one with sixty-three and one with sixty pebbles). When he asked (in Arrernte) how many pebbles there were, he would get the Arrernte word for *many* as the answer for both piles. Then he would say, in Arrernte, "Oh, so are they the same." The elders would think and say no, and that one pile had more (or was bigger). When asked more or bigger by how many, they would answer by showing three more in the sand, or by gesture (or both) while saying *urrpetye*, the Arrernte word for *few*.

It appears that people's number vocabulary is neither a direct reflection of their numerical abilities nor does it impose a hard limit on numerical cognition. While number words are undoubtedly extremely useful for keeping track of exact quantities, other systems of external placeholders (in this case gestures, sand drawings, etc.) can also be used to accomplish the job.

That said, languages have built into them thousands of years of cultural knowledge and invention. Each language is an incredibly useful guidebook to the world: It comes with ways of categorizing, differentiating, organizing, and making sense of objects, actions, events, internal states, dimensions of perceptual experience, useful analogies for conceiving of entities that are beyond perception, and so on. The process of learning a language and becoming enculturated in a particular society teaches us a way of understanding, compartmentalizing, and managing the very rich and complicated physical world we inhabit. While it is not technically impossible to create and think thoughts for which there are not ready linguistic forms in one's language, without the benefit of cultural learning, a great many of the thoughts we take for granted would go unthunk. How many of us would independently invent a system for keeping track of exact quantities if number words were not already available in our language? While it may not be strictly impossible, the probability of any given individual independently arriving at such an idea is vanishingly small.

4.2 Is language a straitjacket for thought?

The Whorfian hypothesis has often been either misrepresented or misunderstood as claiming that language is a straitjacket for thought. In this construal, language binds us into a particular way of viewing the world, and we cannot conceive of things outside of the bounds of our language. This construal of the role that language plays in cognition is problematic because it is self-contradictory. On the one hand, it states that language importantly shapes thinking, which suggests that thinking is something pliable, something that can be changed with experience. On the other hand, it claims that language locks us into a particular way of thinking, and nothing can be done to change it. If language is indeed a powerful tool for shaping thought, and (by implication) thought is a shapeable entity, then why couldn't we learn a new way of thinking simply by learning a new way of talking?

Rather than conceiving of language as a straitjacket, let us consider experience with language as simply part of the history of the human organism. Experiences with a particular language, just as all other experiences, leave a trace. Each experience subtly tweaks and nudges the complex internal state of the organism. The full history of these changes over time leads us to our current state, our current set of ideas and dispositions. We can no more unlearn the effects of the structures and patterns of our languages than we can willfully unexperience any other event from our past (or return our bodies to the exact state they were the day we turned seventeen for that matter). While language is not a straitjacket, it is an ever-present part of the fabric of human experience. To the extent that we cannot fully escape the effects that any other experiences have had on us, we also cannot fully escape the effects of our experiences with language. Important, this does not mean that we can't learn things that are outside of the bounds of our language. What it does mean is that whenever we do endeavor to learn something new, we are doing so from a particular point of view. We are not starting from a blank or a neutral state; our starting point is the place we have arrived as a result of all of our life experiences, including those with language.

For example, by the time I started learning English, I had already spent twelve years speaking Russian. There is no way for me to erase that experience. When I started learning English, I did so from the point of view of a twelve-year-old Russian speaker. While my English passes for native most of the time, my mind is certainly not the same as that of a monolingual English speaker (nor as that of a monolingual Russian speaker). I include more aspectual information in my English speech than native English speakers generally do, because this is an element required in Russian. I learned and so mentally represent English morphology as a function of its similarities and differences with Russian morphology. Needless to say, this is not how monolingual English speakers think about English morphology. When

later in life I started learning French, I was doing it from the point of view of someone who had learned Russian and then English. Had I learned English first and Russian second, my starting point for learning French would have been somewhat different. When later in life I started learning Indonesian, I again analyzed this new language in terms of its similarities and differences to Russian, English, and French: spatial prepositions more like Russian, word order more like English, and so on. I used a Russian-based mneumonic to remember the Indonesian words for hundred (*ratus*) and thousand (*ribu*), which has to do with the happiness of fish (*radost' ribi* in Russian). As a result, whether I am negotiating a ride on a motorcycle in Jakarta or bargaining for rambutan at a market in Sumatra, I inadvertently end up thinking about the happiness of fish. It would be a rare Indonesian speaker who routinely thinks about the happiness of fish when bargaining for rambutan, and even then they probably would have a rather different fish in mind, not to mention our notions of what makes fish happy.

Each of us has an idiosyncratic set of experiences, and through these we collect a vast idiosyncratic knowledge base. We certainly manage to use language to achieve cooperative goals with each other, some of the time. But this does not mean that the underlying representations we have (either linguistic or conceptual) are identical or even very similar. While it is not impossible to learn things outside of the bounds of one's language, what is highly improbable is being able to achieve the same mental states as the monolingual speaker of another language. For example, it is extremely unlikely that I can arrive at a conception of time that is exactly the same as that of a monolingual Indonesian speaker because my starting point for learning Indonesian is that of a Russian, English, and sort-of French speaker. I cannot unlearn the conceptions of time that I have learned through my experiences with these other languages. At best I may arrive at an idea of time that may *include* the way monolingual Indonesian speakers conceive of time, but even this would be very different from really seeing the world as a monolingual Indonesian speaker does.

To summarize, structures that exist in languages serve many useful functions both in individual cognition and in communication. Languages do not place a hard limit on what is learnable, but they do exert profound influences on the contents of our minds, making some ideas tremendously easier and some harder to use and acquire.

5 Summary

In this chapter I have provided evidence that languages are not simply tools for expressing our thoughts. Instead, the very thoughts we wish to express are fundamentally shaped by the structures of the languages we use to express them. I have described how languages shape the way we think about space, colors, and objects. Beyond the differences I have described, other studies have found effects of language on how we construe events, reason about causality, keep track of numbers, understand material substance, perceive and experience emotion, reason about other people's minds, choose to take risks, and even in the way we choose professions and spouses (Barrett, Lindquist, and Gendron, 2007; Boroditsky, 2003; de Villiers and de Villiers, 2000; Gentner and Goldin-Meadow, 2003; Lucy and Gaskins, 2001; Pelham, Mirinberg, and Jones, 2007; Pica et al., 2004; Tversky and Kahneman, 1981).

Beyond showing that speakers of different languages think differently, these results suggest that linguistic processes are pervasive in most fundamental domains of thought. That is, it appears that what we normally call "thinking" is in fact a complex set of collaborations between linguistic and nonlinguistic representations and processes. Unbeknownst to us, linguistic processes meddle in and subconsciously influence our thinking from the very basics of perception to the loftiest abstract notions and the most major life decisions. Language is central to our experience of being human and the languages we speak profoundly shape the way we think, the way we see the world, and the way we live our lives.

References

Barrett, L. F., Lindquist, K., & Gendron, M. (2007). Language as a context for emotion perception. *Trends in Cognitive Sciences*, 11, 327–32.

Boroditsky, L. (2001). Does Language Shape Thought? Mandarin and English speakers' conceptions of time. *Cognitive Psychology*, 43(1), 1–22.

Boroditsky, L., Ham, W. & Ramscar, M. (2002). What is universal about event perception? Comparing English and Indonesian speakers. *Proceedings of the 24th Annual Meeting of the Cognitive Science Society.*

Boroditsky, L. (2003). Linguistic Relativity. In Nadel, L. (Ed.) *Encyclopedia of Cognitive Science* (pp. 917–21). MacMillan Press: London, UK.

Boroditsky, L., Schmidt, L. S., & Phillips, W. (2003). In Gentner, D. & Goldin-Meadow, S. (Eds.) *Language in Mind: Advances in the study of language and thought.* Cambridge, MA: MIT Press.

Boroditsky, L. & Gaby, A. (2006). East of Tuesday: Representing time in absolute space. *Proceedings of the 28th Annual Meeting of the Cognitive Science Society*, 2657.

Bowerman, M. (1996). The origins of children's spatial semantic categories: cognitive versus linguistic determinants. In Gumperz, J. & Levinson, S. (Eds.) *Rethinking linguistic relativity* (pp. 145–76). Cambridge, MA: Cambridge University Press.

Davidoff, J., Davies, I., & Roberson, D. (1999). Colour categories of a stone-age tribe. *Nature*, 398, 203–4.

Dehaene, S., Spelke, E., Pinel, P., Stanescu, R., & Tsivkin, S. (1999). Sources of mathematical thinking: Behavioral and brain-imaging evidence. *Science*, 284, 970–4.

de Villiers, J. G. & de Villiers, P. A. (2000) Linguistic determinism and false belief. In Mitchell, P. & Riggs, K. (Eds.) *Children's Reasoning and the Mind.* Hove, U.K.: Psychology Press.

Fodor, J. A. (1985). Precis of the modularity of mind. *Behavioral and Brain Sciences*, 8(11), 1–42.

Fuhrman, O. & Boroditsky, L. (2007). Mental timelines follow writing direction: Comparing English and Hebrew speakers. *Proceedings of the 29th Annual Meeting of the Cognitive Science Society*, Nashville, TN.

Gentner, D. & Imai, M. (1997). A cross-linguistic study of early word meaning: Universal ontology and linguistic influence. *Cognition 62(2)*, 169–200.

Gentner, D. & Goldin-Meadow, S. (Eds.) (2003). *Language in Mind. Advances in the Study of Language and Thought*. Cambridge MA: MIT Press.

Gilbert, A. Regier, T., Kay, P., & Ivry, R. (2006). Whorf hypothesis is supported in the right visual field but not the left. *Proceedings of the National Academy of Sciences, 103(2)*, 489–94.

Gordon, P. (2004). Numerical Cognition without Words: Evidence from Amazonia. *Science, 306,* 496–9.

Heider, E. (1972). Universals in color naming and memory. *Journal of Experimental Psychology,* 93, 10–20.

Kay, P., & Kempton, W. (1984). What is the Sapir–Whorf hypothesis? *American Anthropolo- gist,* 86, 65–79.

Lakoff, G. (1987). *Women, Fire & Dangerous Things*. Chicago: University of Chicago Press.

Levinson, S. (1996). Frames of reference and Molyneux's question: Crosslinguistic evidence. In Bloom, P. & Peterson, M. (Eds.) *Language and Space* (pp. 109–69). Cambridge, MA: MIT Press.

(2003). *Space in language and cognition.* Cambridge, MA: Cambridge University Press.

Levinson, S. & Wilkins, D. (2006). *Grammars of space*. Cambridge, MA: Cambridge University Press.

Li, P. & Gleitman, L. (2002). Turning the tables: language and spatial reasoning. *Cognition,* 83, 265–94.

Lucy, J. (1992). *Grammatical categories and cognition: A case study of the linguistic relativity hypothesis*. Cambridge, UK: Cambridge Univ. Press.

Lucy, J. & Gaskins, S. (2001). Grammatical categories and the development of classification preferences: a comparative approach. In Bowerman, M. & Levinson, S. C. (Eds.) *Language acquisition and conceptual development* (pp. 257–83). Cambridge, UK: Camridge University Press.

Lupyan, G., Rakison, D. H., McClelland, J. L. (2007). Language is not just for talking: Redundant labels facilitate learning of novel categories. *Psychological Science*, 18, 1077–83.

Majid, A., Bowerman, M., Kita, S., Haun, DBM, & Levinson, S. C. (2004). Can language restructure cognition? The case for space. *Trends in Cognitive Sciences*, 8, 108–14.

Malt, B., Sloman, S., Gennari, S., Shi, M., & Wang, Y. (1999). Knowing versus naming: Similarity and the linguistic categorization of artifacts. *Journal of Memory and Language,* 40, 230–62.

Marian, V. & Neisser, U. (2000). Language-dependent recall of autobiographical memories. *Journal of Experimental Psychology: General,* 129, 361–8.

McDonough, L., Choi, S., & Mandler, J. (2000). Development of language-specific categorization of spatial relations from prelinguistic to linguistic stage: a preliminary study. Paper presented at the Finding the Words conference at Stanford University.

Mehler, J. et al. (1988). A precursor of language acquisition in young infants. *Cognition* 29, 144–78.

Ozgen, E. & Davies, I. (2002). Acquisition of categorical color perception: A perceptual learning approach to the linguistic relativity hypothesis. *Journal of Experimental Psychology-General*, 131(4), 477–93.

Papafragou, A., Massey C., & Gleitman, L. (2002). Shake, rattle, 'n' roll: The representation of motion in language and cognition. *Cognition,* 84, 189–219.

Pelham, B. W., Mirenberg M. C., & Jones, J. T. (2007). Why Susie Sells Seashells by the Seashore: Implicit Egotism and Major Life Decisions. *Journal of Personality and Social Psychology,* 82, 469–87.

Pica, P., Lemer, C., Izard, V., & Dehaene, S. (2004). Exact and Approximate Arithmetic in an Amazonian Indigene Group. *Science,* 306(5695), 499–503.

Sapir, E. (1921). *Language*. New York, NY: Harcourt, Brace, and World.

Simons D. & Rensink R. (2005). Change blindness: Past, present, and future. *Trends in Cognitive Sciences,* 9, 16–20.

Slobin, D. (1996). From "thought and language" to "thinking for speaking." In Gumperz, J. & Levinson, S. C. (Eds.) *Rethinking linguistic relativity* (pp. 70–96). Cambridge, MA: Cambridge University Press.

Tversky, B., Kugelmass, S., & Winter, A. (1991). Crosscultural and developmental-trends in graphic productions. *Cognitive Psychology,* 23, 515–57.

Tversky, A. & Kahneman, D. (1981). The Framing of Decisions and the Psychology of Choice. *Science,* 211, 453–8.

Whorf, B. (1956). *Language, Thought, and Reality: selected writings of Benjamin Lee Whorf* Carroll, J. B. (Ed.) Cambridge, MA: MIT Press.

Wilkins, D. (2002). Integrating speech, gesture and sand drawings: How external representation systems both influence and reflect spatial thinking. Invited talk delivered at interdisciplinary workshop on Spatial Thinking in the Humanities and Sciences: From perception to meaning. Stanford University.

Winawer, J., Witthoft, N., Frank, M., Wu, L., Wade, A., & Boroditsky, L. (2007). Russian blues reveal effects of language on color discrimination. *Proceedings of the National Academy of Science* 104(9), 7780–5.

CHAPTER 32

Computational Approaches to Language and Thought

Terry Regier

1 Introduction

Does language shape thought, such that speakers of different languages apprehend the world differently? Or do universals of thought shape language, giving rise to linguistic universals? This "language and thought" debate is a classic nature-versus-nurture controversy in cognitive science. The polarized framing of the debate just presented can be misleading, since current evidence suggests *both* that language can shape thought and that thought can shape language. But this framing is also useful for conceptually organizing the field: for quickly conveying the central questions at issue and their connection to broader questions of the malleability or universality of human nature.

When speaking of "language and thought," I will use the word *thought* in a broad sense that also includes perception (cf. Talmy's (1996) coinage *'ception* – an abstraction over *per*ception and *con*ception). I take the language and thought debate to concern influences between language on the hand, and thought broadly construed on the other.

The goal of this chapter is to familiarize the reader with computational approaches to the language and thought question, with an emphasis on relatively recent work. The coverage is meant to be representative rather than complete, and no single unified approach is advanced here. Having read the chapter, the reader should know which sorts of computational methods have been applied to this and closely related questions – and should also know which papers to read for further detail on any given subtopic.

The chapter contains three main sections. The first section briefly reviews the standard theoretical framing of the debate over language and thought, centered on the Whorf hypothesis. The second section treats computational models of how language shapes thought, while the third treats models of how thought shapes language. Throughout, the emphasis is on general concepts rather than formal presentation – the latter may be found in the works cited. An overarching theme of the chapter is that computational models can be helpful in resolving this and other nature/nurture debates, by transcending the polarized framing of the debate and specifying in detail how universal and language-specific forces may interact.

2 Theoretical framing and the Whorf hypothesis

A classic view of the relation between language and thought holds that there is a universal repertoire of thought to which speakers of all languages have access. In this *universalist* view, thought shapes language: Our universal cognitive repertoire leaves its imprint on the languages of the world, such that the same linguistic categories appear in unrelated languages worldwide, yielding semantic universals.

In contrast, Benjamin Lee Whorf (1956) argued that the language you speak affects the way you think and the way you apprehend reality – such that there is no universal cognitive repertoire. For example, Whorf pointed out that English uses the same word *ten* for either ten men or ten days, although there is a fundamental difference in meaning: One may see ten men all together at the same time, but not ten days. Whorf argued that by applying the same cardinal numbers to objects (men) and time periods (days), English invites its speakers to think of objects and time periods as conceptually similar. In contrast, he argued that speakers of languages that did not apply the same linguistic forms to objects and time periods would be more likely to view these as dissimilar entities. In this sense, he argued, we see the world filtered through the semantic categories of our native language. Often bundled with this idea is the notion that semantic categories are themselves determined largely by linguistic convention, such that there is nothing privileged about the particular semantic categories any language happens to exhibit – for instance, in this view the applicability of *ten* to both men and days is an arbitrary feature of English and is not determined by any universal cognitive force. Taken as a whole, the Whorf hypothesis, or *linguistic relativity*, holds that we view the world through the lens of categories defined

by linguistic convention – such that there are potentially as many different views of the world as there are languages. This position constitutes a wholesale rejection of the universalist view.

Empirical findings have been mixed. Some experiments appear to support the Whorf hypothesis – in some respects, in some circumstances (Davidoff, Davies, and Roberson, 1999; Gordon, 2004; Lupyan, Rakison, and McClelland, 2007; Pica et al., 2004) – while others instead support the universalist position – in other respects and circumstances (Malt et al., 1999; Munnich, Landau, and Dosher, 2001; Papafragou, Massey, and Gleitman, 2002). Thus, neither pole of the standard universalist-versus-relativist framing is fully empirically supported. Instead, it appears that Whorf may have been half right in complex and interesting ways. For example, several recent studies suggest that language affects perception primarily in the right half of the visual field, and less in the left half (Drivonikou et al., 2007; Gilbert et al., 2006; Gilbert et al., 2008) – a pattern predicted by the functional organization of the brain. More generally, these mixed empirical findings strongly suggest some sort of interaction between universal aspects of cognition on the one hand and linguistic convention on the other (Regier et al., 2010) – an interaction that computational models can help to clarify.

3 How does language shape thought?

The question of how language affects thought has not attracted a great deal of computational work (but see Dilkina, McClelland, and Boroditsky, 2007, discussed at the end of this section). However, a substantial amount of computational work has treated *categorical perception* (e.g., Harnad, 1987) – a phenomenon directly relevant to this question. Categorical perception (CP) is enhanced perceptual discrimination for stimuli that straddle a category boundary, and decreased discrimination for stimuli that fall within the same category. CP is well-established in the perception of some speech sounds.[1] Much of the current debate over whether language affects thought and perception asks whether this idea can be extended to the way we perceive other aspects of the world – such as objects, events, and people: Do we perceive them categorically, according to the semantic categories of our native language? Since languages differ in the semantic categories they use to partition the world, this would lead speakers of different languages to perceive the world differently: a Whorfian finding.

I first briefly discuss how CP has been analyzed and then how it has been explained.

3.1 *Analysis*

CP is generally assessed empirically, without computational tools. A typical Whorfian experiment testing for CP will compare perceptual discrimination in speakers of two languages, one of which makes a semantic distinction that the other does not. For example, Kay and Kempton (1984) showed various colors, ranging from green to blue, to speakers of English, in which *green* and *blue* are separate categories, and to speakers of Tarahumara, a language that uses a single color term to cover both green and blue. English speakers found colors straddling the English green/blue category boundary more dissimilar than they did analogously spaced colors within these categories. In contrast, speakers of Tarahumara did not show this pattern. Thus, in English speakers, the enhanced distinctiveness at the category boundary may be driven by language. This conclusion was reinforced by the further finding that CP in English speakers was eliminated under a condition designed to interfere with verbal processing: In this case at least, language appears to affect perception through the online use of verbal codes. More recent studies have replicated

the finding of color CP consistent with the color categories of the speaker's native language (e.g. Roberson, Davies, and Davidoff, 2000), as well as the elimination of that CP under verbal interference (Gilbert et al., 2006; Roberson and Davidoff, 2000; Winawer et al., 2007).

3.2 *Explanation*

In computational models of categorical perception (see Damper and Harnad, 2000; Pastore, 1987 for reviews), perceived stimuli are often thought of as points in a perceptual space, and the distance between two stimuli generally corresponds to their dissimilarity or discriminability: The greater the distance, the more dissimilar or discriminable the stimuli. Given this framework, CP consists of increasing the distance between points that straddle a category boundary and decreasing within-category distances. There are two broad classes of CP model, corresponding to two very general ways of achieving this end. One class explicitly warps perceptual space in a manner that yields greater discrimination for stimuli near category boundaries. This warping is usually long-term and changes only very slowly under continued training. The other class does not warp perceptual space, but instead moves points (percepts) themselves away from category boundaries and toward category centers in an unwarped space. These adjustments move apart stimuli that fall in different categories and move together those that fall in the same category, resulting in CP. This adjustment happens rapidly and online, as the stimulus is perceived. The distinction between these two classes of model echoes Gentner and Goldin-Meadow's (2003) distinction between two views of Whorfian effects: "language as lens," in which the world is invariably viewed through the categories of our native language (corresponding to long-term warping), and "language as tool kit," in which language augments our representational repertoire – and these additional representational resources may either be deployed or not (corresponding roughly

---

1 Specifically, syllable-initial stop consonants (Liberman et al., 1957). See also the related "perceptual magnet effect" in vowel perception (Kuhl, et al., 1992).

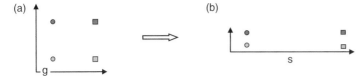

Figure 32.1 Attentional stretching. Four exemplars in a 2-dimensional psychological space of possible objects (a) without categorization, and (b) with attention allocated so as to categorize these four objects as "balls" and "boxes", highlighting shape at the expense of color. The resulting warped space exhibits CP.

to rapid, online adjustments that do not permanently warp perception itself).

3.2.1 LONG-TERM WARPING OF PERCEPTUAL SPACE

Some models of categorization capture the Whorfian intuition that naming (categorizing) can draw *attention* to category-relevant aspects of experience at the expense of other aspects. An example is Kruschke's (1992) ALCOVE model. ALCOVE is an exemplar-based model of category learning: It represents categories in terms of individual exemplars of those categories. Each exemplar is represented as a point in a multidimensional psychological space,[2] and each dimension of the space receives a certain amount of selective attention. ALCOVE learns to gradually deploy attention to category-relevant dimensions as it learns the categories. Thus, when a dimension is important for categorization, it will receive more attention, which will cause the space to be "stretched" along that dimension. As a result, exemplars that differ along that dimension become more distant – and in principle more easily discriminable.[3] And when a dimension loses attention, it

"shrinks", causing exemplars that differ along that dimension to become closer – and in principle less discriminable.

For example, Figure 32.1(a) shows a two-dimensional space of possible objects: The two dimensions are object shape (sphere versus. cube) and object color (green versus. red). The space is shown populated by four exemplars: a red ball, a red box, a green ball, and a green box. In Figure 32.1(a) the shape and color dimensions are equally weighted, while in Figure 32.1(b) the shape dimension receives selective attention and is therefore stretched, while the color dimension loses attention and shrinks. This warping of the space supports the categorization of the four objects into the shape-based categories *ball* and *box*. At the same time, it can cause CP: cross-category discrimination is easier than within-category discrimination, since the attentionally weighted distances are greater across than within categories. This attentional warping idea has accounted for findings in category learning, in perceptual classification in children and adults (Smith, 1989), and in early word learning (Merriman, 1999; Regier, 2005; Smith, 2000; Smith et al., 2002). It can also potentially explain some Whorfian findings. For instance, Lucy (1992) has argued that the Yucatec Mayan language highlights the *substance* of which an object is made, while English highlights object shape – and has shown that speakers of these two languages group objects together nonlinguistically in accordance with their native language. This can be explained in terms of Yucatec speakers allocating selective attention to

---

2   Of the sort produced by multidimensional scaling (see later note).

3   "In principle" since Kruschke's focus was category learning rather than CP; moreover, the tradition out of which this work springs (e.g., Nosofsky, 1986) considers attentional weighting to affect categorization and not discrimination. However, the idea could also in principle be applied to CP, as sketched here, if one assumes an effect on discrimination as well. This idea also serves as stage-setting for related and more explicitly CP-oriented work, discussed later.

the dimension of substance, and English speakers attending to shape, so that differences along the linguistically highlighted dimension become particularly salient.

This idea has a serious limitation, however: It cannot account for CP that occurs at only one position along a dimension. For instance, recall the finding of language-driven (Whorfian) CP of color at the boundary between green and blue (Kay and Kempton, 1984). Both of these color categories contain exemplars at many different positions along the single psychological dimension of hue. If the hue dimension as a whole receives greater attention, then on the above idea *all* hue discrimination should be enhanced, whether within or across categories. This prediction is not empirically supported.

Goldstone, Steyvers, and Larimer (1996) present a model of CP similar to those just mentioned but that avoids this limitation. Their model is also exemplar based, but does not stretch or shrink entire dimensions of space. Instead, it learns to gradually shift the positions of its exemplar representations in space so that regions near a category boundary are densely populated by exemplars – yielding greater discrimination there than at other points. This can be loosely thought of as paying more attention to particular areas of space (boundaries), rather than to a dimension as a whole. After learning to categorize a set of stimuli that vary along a dimension, the model exhibits categorical perception.

Harnad, Hanson, and Lubin (1995) accounted for learned CP using connectionist networks trained under back-propagation (Rumelhart, Hinton, and Williams, 1986). When such networks are trained to categorize a set of stimuli, their internal (hidden unit) spatial representations of the stimuli adjust so that cross-category distances are increased while within-category distances are decreased relative to those found after training on a noncategorical task. As in the other models discussed above, this work casts learned CP in terms of a gradually learned and enduring distortion of representational space.

3.2.2 ON-LINE ADJUSTMENT OF PERCEPTS IN UNWARPED SPACE

Another class of models suggests a qualitatively different way of accounting for CP, and thus for effects of language on perception. In these models, an online process pulls the representation of the stimulus away from category boundaries and toward category prototypes during perception. This process yields CP, since pairs of stimuli that straddle a category boundary will be pulled apart, making them more discriminable.

Anderson et al.'s (1977) neural network model of categorical perception is an example. Like the other models we have considered, it represents a stimulus as a point in a psychological space. It operates as an associative memory: When presented with a stimulus, it retrieves the stored pattern most similar to that stimulus (Hopfield, 1982). It does this by incrementally adjusting its internal representation of the stimulus until it matches the nearest stored pattern. The stimulus representation is constrained to lie within a hypercube in psychological space, and the stored pattern to which it is attracted is always at one of the hypercube's corners; for this reason, the network is referred to as a "brain state in a box" model. If we take the set of stimuli that get pulled to a given stored pattern to be a category, we can see that this model exhibits CP by pulling apart stimuli from different categories and pulling together stimuli from the same category. The TRACE model of speech perception (McClelland and Elman, 1986), while different in many specifics from Anderson et al.'s model, also exhibits CP for the same general reason: In this connectionist network as well, the representation of the input stimulus is adjusted toward values prototypical of a category. The TRACE model is a member of a large class of *interactive-activation* connectionist models. In a typical model of this class (e.g. McClelland and Rumelhart, 1981), low-level feature detector nodes receive perceptual input and these both feed activation to, and receive activation from, higher-level category nodes (hence the name "interactive activation"). Over time, the pattern of activation in the low-level feature detectors is influenced by category-level knowledge through this process of interactive activation. This leads to input stimuli being pulled toward category prototypes, yielding CP and related category effects (Lupyan and Spivey, 2008).

Similar behavior is also exhibited – and explained as rational – by Huttenlocher, Hedges, and Duncan's (1991) model of category effects on memory. They wished to account for a memory phenomenon similar to CP that could underlie some effects of language on thought and perception. People's memories of particular experiences are often systematically biased away from category boundaries and toward prototypes. For instance, when asked when a particular film was shown on campus, college students tended to respond with dates biased away from the true date and toward the middle of the academic quarter in which the film was shown (Huttenlocher, Hedges, and Prohaska, 1988) – here, the academic quarter is a temporal category. Similar effects are obtained for visual stimuli. If a dot appears somewhere in a circle and then vanishes, and people are asked a few seconds later just where it appeared, their responses tend to be biased toward the centers of the four quadrants of the circle, which apparently serve as spatial categories. Huttenlocher et al. (1991) explain this phenomenon in terms of Bayesian combination of two sources of evidence: the memory of the particular experience, which is taken to be veridical but uncertain (this is the likelihood), and the broader category in which it falls (this is the prior). Both are modeled as probability distributions, with uncertainty about the exact location of the particular experience captured by the variance of its distribution. The combination of these two sources of evidence produces responses biased toward the category prototype. Feldman and Griffiths (2007) account for the "perceptual magnet effect" in vowel perception in very similar terms. Interestingly, if applied to the Whorf hypothesis, such a model may be able to naturally account for the mixed pattern of results sketched earlier, suggesting that "Whorf was half right" – that is, it may be able to account for the fact that language appears to sometimes affect perception and sometimes not. How? In this model, a strong category effect is predicted when the memory (or perception) of the particular experience is uncertain, but not when it is certain. A useful question for future research is how well this idea and related ones can account for the mixed pattern of results found in the literature.

3.2.3 EVIDENCE

What is the evidence for and against these classes of models, and what are the implications for the Whorf hypothesis? The picture is mixed. As mentioned earlier, some studies show that language-driven CP may be experimentally eliminated through a verbal interference task (Gilbert et al., 2006; Roberson and Davidoff, 2000; Winawer et al., 2007). This suggests that CP is mediated not by long-term warping of space, which would presumably be unaffected by a brief interference task, but rather by online verbal codes, which could potentially adjust the percept itself. When verbal codes are incapacitated by verbal interference, the influence of named categories is removed, and the percepts are not adjusted – yielding no CP.

The Huttenlocher et al. model was originally intended to account for category effects on memory, but it is in principle applicable to any situation in which there is uncertainty about a stimulus – whether from memory or from perception. This model could potentially account for some Whorfian effects, as it fits the "brief adjustment, not long-term warping" criterion. However, there is some initial evidence against this account (Pilling et al., 2003). Further investigation of this model, and others, in the context of language-driven CP, is needed.

There is also some evidence that may actually suggest perceptual warping, after all. In an experiment probing learned categorical perception, Goldstone et al. (1996) found heightened discrimination not just for stimulus pairs that straddle a category boundary, but also for stimulus pairs that are near a boundary but on the same side.

They took this as support for their view that perceptual space itself has been stretched in the vicinity of the boundary. In sum, there is currently no single clear picture that emerges, and it is of course possible that no single account will cover all phenomena.

The models we have reviewed here were proposed to account for CP and related phenomena, but not specifically for effects of language on thought. However there is at least one existing model that directly concerns the effect of language on thought and that has been brought into contact with empirical data. Boroditsky, Schmidt, and Phillips (2003) asked speakers of Spanish and German to produce adjectives in English describing a set of inanimate objects. Half of the objects were of feminine gender in Spanish and masculine gender in German, and half were the other way around. It was found that subjects tended to assign more "masculine" adjectives (e.g., *sturdy*) to objects that their native language marked as masculine, and more "feminine" adjectives (e.g., *pretty*) to objects that their native language marked as feminine. Dilkina et al. (2007) modeled these results and related ones using a recurrent connectionist network. The structure of the model makes it in essence a variant of an interactive activation model, trained under back-propagation. The authors argue that the model captures these empirical findings because of general features of connectionist networks: sensitivity to coherent covariation in the input, and distributed overlapping representations. Further work along these lines can help establish which classes of models readily accommodate which classes of phenomena concerning effects of language on thought.

4 How does thought shape language?

The Whorf hypothesis holds not only that the semantic categories of our native language affect the way we think, but also that these categories are themselves determined by language – that is, by largely arbitrary linguistic convention, rather than universal forces.

This cannot be true in its strongest form, since there are many *universal tendencies* of linguistic meaning. These are semantic generalizations that appear to hold across languages, and thus presumably reveal something broad about language as a human capacity, and about the thought processes that underlie it. In some cases, universal semantic tendencies have been traced to domain-general aspects of cognition. In such cases, we can speak of thought shaping language – specifically, of nonlinguistic aspects of human thought molding linguistic structure, and causing human languages to appear as they do. Still, it is important to emphasize the "tendency" in "universal tendency" – languages often share some aspects of semantic structure, and differ in others (see Romney et al. (2000) for statistical techniques that can parcel out how much of semantic structure is shared versus language-specific). Since there are significant cross-language differences in semantic structure, Whorf may have been half right in this respect as well: It may be that semantic categories are formed by an interaction of universal and language-specific forces and that computational models can help in pinning down the nature of this interaction.

Analyses that attribute linguistic universal tendencies to universal cognitive structure represent that cognitive structure either discretely or continuously. Later in this chapter, I discuss these two forms of representation, together with some applications of these ideas, and their interaction with language-specific forces. I include an extended discussion of color naming and cognition, an area that has long been central to the broader language-and-thought debate, and that has attracted some recent computational work. I conclude with a discussion of the role of socio-historical forces in shaping semantic universals.

4.1 *Discrete representations of meaning*

Discrete representation of universal cognitive structure generally takes the form of a graph of nodes, each of which stands for a concept or meaning, with the nodes

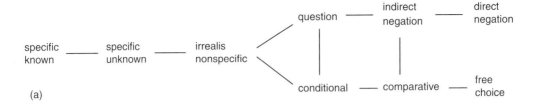

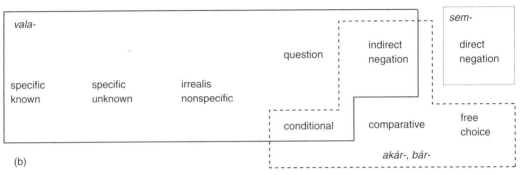

Figure 32.2 Senses for indefinite pronouns, arranged to show (a) a semantic map, and (b) the regions in the map expressed by the four Hungarian indefinite pronoun prefixes vala-, sem-, akár-, and bár-. Other languages partition the same semantic space differently. Based on Croft (2003), citing Haspelmath (1997).

connected by links. This graph-based representation is sometimes referred to as a *semantic map*.

The idea can be illustrated by Haspelmath's (1997, cited in Croft, 2003) cross-linguistic analysis of indefinite pronouns (e.g., *someone, anywhere*). Indefinite pronouns express a range of different meanings across languages.[4] The three critical points for our purposes are: (1) that these meanings differ, (2) that indefinite pronouns in different languages group these meanings together in different ways, and (3) that this variation is constrained: Not all possible groupings are attested. Figure 32.2(a) shows a semantic map of these meanings, linked together so that any attested category from a specific language will pick out

a *connected region* in the map. For example, Figure 32.2(b) shows how these meanings are grouped in Hungarian; other languages group them differently, but always selecting connected regions of the graph. Thus, the graph implicitly represents a hypothesis concerning the universal conceptual structure that constrains semantic variation – a "geography of the human mind" (Croft, 2003, p. 139).

This structure allows one to derive *implicational universals*: statements of the form "if a language has feature X, it will also have feature Y." For instance, if a newly encountered language has a form that may be used for either of two meanings A and B in the graph, we expect that same form to also be used for all intervening meanings on a chain connecting A to B in the graph – since otherwise this form's subgraph would not be connected.

Semantic maps can be viewed synchronically, as snapshots of the conceptual terrain that a given language carves up in some

4   For instance, "specific known": a specific referent whose identity is known to the speaker but not the hearer; "specific unknown": a specific referent whose identity is unknown to both speaker and hearer. The remaining senses are defined in Haspelmath's (1997) work, and Croft's (2003) which cites it.

manner at any given time. They can also be viewed diachronically, as routes showing the semantic changes that particular linguistic forms can be expected to undergo over historical time (e.g. Bybee, Perkins, and Pagliuca, 1994; Hopper and Traugott, 1993). Historically, grammatical markers in language are often derived from lexical forms – this process is termed *grammaticalization*. For instance, the future tense expressed by English *will* as in I *will* go derives from the word *will* in the sense of intending or wanting – presumably since the intention to go often leads to going in the near future. This sort of semantic shift, from a concrete meaning (intention, wanting) to a more abstract grammatical one (futurity), is found across different linguistic forms. This shift can be seen as a sort of semantic "reduction," since the grammatical meaning generally requires fewer semantic features to specify, compared with the original concrete meaning. Interesting, there is often a parallel reduction in linguistic form: As forms become grammatical, they lose phonological as well as semantic substance (e.g., the form '*ll* as in I'*ll go*).

Semantic maps are generally constructed by hand rather than computationally. However, they provide a useful backdrop to computational analyses, treated later, in that they highlight the idea of a universal conceptual space, which is partitioned in different ways by different languages.

4.2 *Continuous representations of meaning*

The other major form of conceptual representation is a continuous conceptual space, with concepts represented as points in that space, and interpoint distance representing conceptual dissimilarity – as in our discussion of categorical perception. Multidimensional scaling (abbreviated MDS: Shepard, Romney, and Nerlove, 1972; see Steyvers, 2002 for a brief and accessible review) is a widely used family of techniques that falls in this class. MDS accepts measures of similarity among objects and then represents those objects as points in a psychological

space that it creates: Interpoint distances in the space bear a monotonic relation to the observed similarities. The measures of similarity can come from any of a variety of sources, including overt similarity ratings, identification errors, or how a given language names different objects.

4.2.1 UNIVERSAL SPACE

MDS is sometimes used to construct a universal conceptual/semantic space, based on data from many languages. Levinson and Meira (2003) used MDS in exploring the meanings expressed by spatial adpositions across nine languages. They constructed a psychological space based on the naming of spatial relations in all languages they studied – an approximation to universal conceptual space. They found near-universal "focal" spatial meanings, corresponding roughly to the concepts IN, ATTACHMENT, NEAR/ UNDER, ON TOP, and ON/OVER. They argue that this suggests an analogy with the focal colors commonly held to underlie universals of color naming (Berlin and Kay, 1969; but see later in the chapter for work questioning this view of color naming). Croft and Poole (2008) provide an MDS reanalysis of Haspelmath's cross-language data on indefinite pronouns, originally analyzed using semantic maps (see previous). Again, since their space is based on cross-language data, they suggest that it captures universal conceptual structure, much as a semantic map does – however this time there are distances, rather than discrete links, between meanings. As a result, the inferences one can draw are graded (based on distance), rather than absolute (based on connectedness). Forms from different languages carve off different sections of this universal conceptual space,[5] much as they would pick out different regions of a universal semantic map.

5 In the version of MDS they use, each form expresses all meanings on one side of a linear decision boundary, which may be placed anywhere in the shared space. The position of meanings in the space is adjusted so that form meanings are linearly separable. The same concept also governs the working of individual units in standard multilayer connectionist networks (Rumelhart et al., 1986).

4.2.2 LANGUAGE-SPECIFIC SPACES

The use of MDS to construct a universal space *assumes* that conceptual structure is universal and that languages vary only in how they carve up this universal structure. But the universality of thought is precisely what is at question for much of the language and thought debate – so it cannot always be simply assumed. MDS is also often used to analyze data from individual languages separately, in order to explore cross-language similarities and differences in the resulting spaces (Heider and Olivier, 1972; Malt, Sloman, and Gennari, 2003; Roberson et al., 2000). One such use of MDS in the language-and-thought debate is classic but has recently been contested: the use of MDS to analyze and compare color naming and cognition in different languages, discussed later in the context of the debate over language, thought, and color.

4.3 *Color*

The naming and perception of color is a classic testing ground of the language-and-thought debate, and it has been recently recontested. Color is naturally represented as a continuous space, one that could in principle be partitioned or categorized arbitrarily. However, color naming across languages appears constrained by universals of color cognition (Berlin and Kay, 1969; Kay and Maffi, 1999). Specifically, it has been held that there are universal "focal" colors, or prototypes, in color space, corresponding to the best examples of English black, white, red, green, yellow, and blue. In this view, these focal colors are privileged *linguistically*, in that they are selected as the best examples of color terms across languages (Berlin and Kay, 1969). They have also appeared to be privileged *cognitively*: Speakers of Dani, a Papua New Guinea language with a color naming system very different from that of English, were found to recognize focal colors better than nonfocal colors – and this was also the case for English speakers (Heider, 1972). The universalist message of this study was confirmed by Heider and Olivier (1972): They constructed four MDS spaces, one based on color naming

responses and one based on color memory, from English speakers and Dani speakers. They found the memory spaces for the two languages to be similar, although the naming spaces were dissimilar – suggesting that color memory is unaffected by differences in naming: an anti-Whorfian, universalist finding. Thus, in the standard universalist account, color cognition is universal and structured around focal colors, which are taken to be the cognitive underpinning of color naming universals. This view has been very influential, and several models of color naming have been proposed that ground universals in focal colors (e.g., Kay and McDaniel, 1978; Lammens, 1994).

4.3.1 THE RELATIVIST CHALLENGE

Recently, however, this universalist understanding has been challenged on several fronts. Lucy (1997) argued – correctly at the time – that universals in color naming had never been objectively demonstrated: Prior analyses had relied on subjective interpretation of the data. A further weakness was that the languages directly investigated by these prior analyses were almost all from industrialized societies; thus any commonalities may have resulted from cultural contact rather than genuinely universal forces. Roberson et al. (2000) investigated the language of a nonindustrialized Papua New Guinea society, Berinmo, and found a color naming pattern that they asserted did not match proposed universal patterns. Critically, they also failed to replicate the earlier finding of universal color memory structured around foci. They argued on this basis that there are no universal foci, and that therefore categories are not organized around them. They argued instead that color categories are defined at their boundaries by local linguistic convention, and are only loosely constrained by general principles of categorization; they cite one such principle, *grouping by similarity*, which holds that categories must constitute connected regions in color space (cf. semantic maps). The implication is that apart from this rather loose constraint, language-defined boundaries are free to vary largely arbitrarily across languages. In support of the importance of boundaries, they found categorical perception (or possibly categorical memory) at language-specific boundaries.

4.3.2 RESOLVING THE MATTER

Given this, are there genuine universals of color naming or not? Kay and Regier (2003) provided the first objective test of this question. They based the test on a large database of color naming data from languages of both nonindustrialized and industrialized societies. This was done computationally through a Monte Carlo test. They measured the extent to which named color categories cluster across languages in the actual data, and compared that quantity with the clustering found in a series of randomized hypothetical datasets of comparable complexity. They found significantly more clustering in the actual data set than would be expected by chance. Regier, Kay, and Cook (2005) used related techniques to show that best examples of color terms across these languages cluster near the proposed foci. Moreover, this clustering occurred in a manner incompatible with Roberson et al.'s proposal that categories are defined at their boundaries by linguistic convention. Finally, they showed that best examples in Berinmo, the proposed counterexample to universal tendencies, in fact also cluster near these universal foci. Kay and Regier (2007) showed – again by considering computationally created hypothetical color naming systems – that category boundaries in Berinmo align with those in other languages more closely than would be predicted if grouping by similarity were the only major constraint on color naming. Thus, there is firm evidence for universal tendencies of color naming and for the importance of focal colors in naming – although their centrality to color memory remains in question.

However there is also recent evidence that supports the relativist view that boundaries are determined by language. Roberson et al. (2005) found that Himba, a language of Namibia, has a color naming system similar to that of Berinmo: In a universal foci account the two languages would receive the same analysis. Yet category boundaries

fall in measurably different places in the two languages, and speakers of both languages show categorical perception of color at their native language's boundaries. This finding suggests strongly that color naming is determined by more than just universal foci and that linguistic convention may play some role in determining where boundaries are placed. Overall, the empirical picture is decidedly mixed: There is evidence both for universal foci and for linguistic relativity. This is a situation in which Whorf indeed appears to have been half right and half wrong.

4.3.3 MODELS OF COLOR NAMING

Interestingly, this empirically mixed situation can be accounted for in computationally simple terms. Jameson and D'Andrade (1997) proposed that named color categories carve up perceptual color space so as to maximize the information conveyed by a category name. They noted that the outermost surface of the perceptual color solid (the space of realizable colors) has irregularities or "bumps" on it – places that protrude away from the rest of the color solid since these colors are exceptionally saturated. They suggested that information maximization over such an irregular space causes certain colors to be linguistically privileged across languages, and may account for the general pattern of universal tendencies observed empirically. This is a natural generalization of the focal color account, one in which every color is focal to some extent: the extent to which it protrudes from the color solid. Regier, Kay, and Khetarpal (2007) formalized this idea and tested it against existing empirical data. They considered a categorical partition of irregularly shaped color space to be *well-formed* to the extent that it maximized similarity within categories, and minimized it across categories (Garner, 1974). They then used computer simulation to create theoretically optimal color naming systems – that is, naming systems that maximize well-formedness – with three, four, five, and six categories. The results are shown in Figure 32.3, compared with actual color naming systems that resemble them.

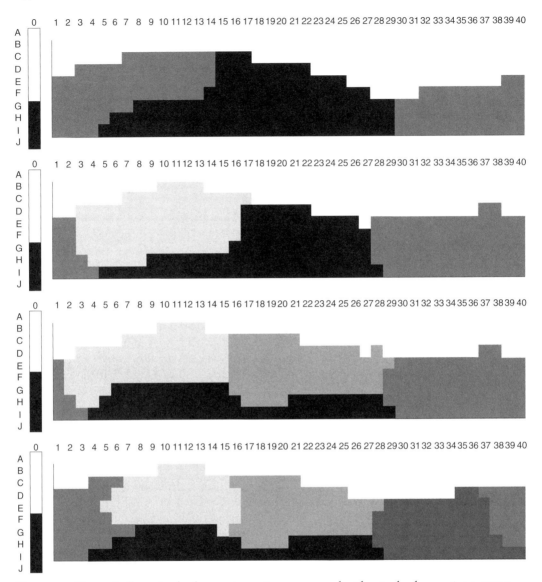

Figure 32.3 Theoretically optimal color naming systems compared with actual color naming systems.

These findings suggest that some color naming systems are near optimal in this sense (see also Griffin, 2006; Komarova, Jameson, and Narens, 2007 for related arguments). While other languages deviate, sometimes considerably, from these patterns, across all 110 languages examined there was a strong tendency for color naming to be shaped at least in part by well-formedness – providing an explanation for universal tendencies in color naming. At the same time, this model suggests a role for language in determining category boundaries. There are often several similar systems that are roughly equally well-formed – if linguistic convention selects from among such highly ranked systems, that could potentially account for the subtle but real differences we see empirically, such as those between Berinmo and Himba. This account thus helps to specify an empirically supported middle ground between universalist and relativist views of color naming.

Yendrikhovskij (2001) argued, in contrast, that universals of color naming reflect the distribution of colors in the world, rather than the structure of perceptual color space

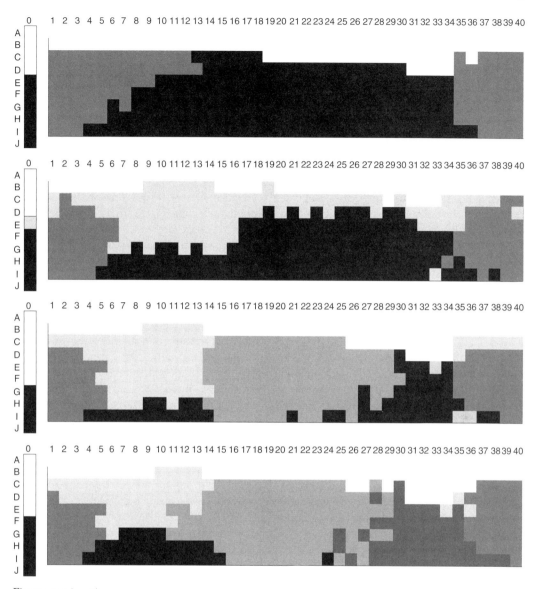

Figure 32.3 *(cont.)*

in our minds. He gathered a set of images of natural scenes, from which he sampled colored pixels. Each of these was represented as a point in a color space that was designed so that interpoint distance roughly corresponds to perceptual dissimilarity. This collection of points, in this space, was his approximation to the distribution of perceived colors in the world. He showed that k-means clustering of these data, with k = eleven, yielded clusters that were centered near the foci for the eleven color terms of English. He showed further that k-means clustering with lower values for k yielded results comparable to the categories observed by Berlin and Kay (1969) for languages with the corresponding number of color categories. He argued on this basis that color naming reflects our color diet. While this explanation is superficially quite different from explanations grounded in the structure of perceptual color space, a possible resolution of these two views is suggested by Shepard's (1992; 2001) argument that cognitive universals may be traceable to regularities in the world around us. Specifically, he argued that over the course of evolution, our perceptual systems have internalized perceptual invariants in the environment, and that this internalization causes cognitive universals – including those concerning color. Thus, color naming universals may be explained in terms of the structure of perceptual color space – which may itself be explained in terms of the distribution of colors in the environment.

Models have also been advanced to support the argument that color naming reflects not just color space, or the distribution of colors in the world, but also the social process of communicating about colors (Dowman, 2007; Steels and Belpaeme, 2005). These models are treated later, when we turn to the general issue of how social and historical forces may shape semantic universals.

4.4 *Spatial motion*

Computational modeling has also been applied to semantic universals of spatial motion. Regier (1996) presented a connectionist model that learned to name spatial motion events in several different languages. The search for a simple model that could perform this task led to one with a constraint on its operation, a constraint that suggested a universal tendency in spatial language. Specifically, in this model, people attend preferentially to event endpoints, compared to event beginnings. This endpoint emphasis allows languages to make finer semantic distinctions at event endpoints than at comparatively under-attended event beginnings. For example, consider hanging a picture on a wall versus placing it flat on a desk. The endpoints of these two events differ – vertical versus horizontal contact – and German marks this distinction by using two different spatial prepositions to describe the two events (*an* and *auf* respectively). However, German uses a single preposition (*von*) to describe removing the picture from the wall and from the desk. The model predicts that this pattern of greater semantic detail at endpoints should appear across languages. Empirical work with speakers of Arabic, English, and Mandarin has supported this idea directly (Regier and Zheng, 2007), while

other findings provide independent evidence of endpoint emphasis (Lakusta and Landau, 2005; Zheng and Goldin-Meadow, 2002).

A related example is Narayanan's (1997) model of motor control and grammatical *aspect*. Aspect describes the internal structure of an event described by a verb. It is distinct from *tense*, which describes how the event is located in time relative to other events. For instance, the English form "X-ing," as in "She is (or was or will be) running," expresses *progressive* aspect: the view of the action as being in progress, regardless of whether it is in the past, present, or future. There are many aspectual meanings marked in the world's languages, marking whether an event is performed habitually, repetitively, continuously, punctually, and so on (Comrie, 1976). Narayanan proposed that aspect reflects schematic processes of *sensory-motor control* – processes such as inception, interruption, enabling, and completion – necessary for controlling and monitoring the spatial motion of oneself or others in the world. He presented a computational model – a variant of a finite automaton – and showed that it could account both for simulated motor control (e.g., walking to a destination), and for a range of different aspectual distinctions. Narayanan's work thus suggests that universals of aspect may spring from shared structure that is ultimately concerned with governing the spatial movement of one's body (see Loenneker-Rodman and Narayanan, this volume, for further discussion).

4.5 *Social and historical forces*

We have sought to explain semantic universals in terms of universal conceptual (or perceptual or motor) structure. However, there is an apparently missing link in this line of argument. The semantic systems of the world's languages are the product of a long history of people communicating with each other, passing their linguistic systems on to the next generation, and so on through time. There is no mention of this socio-historical process in most of the accounts we have considered so far. We turn now to consider this process and its role in creating semantic systems.

Artificial life is a form of computational simulation in which populations of agents may interact, learn, and evolve over generations. This allows one to simulate the cultural transmission, or evolution, of particular traits of interest under different conditions – and thus to model the social and historical elements that have been missing in our treatment so far. Simulations of this sort are increasingly used to treat questions of language universals and language evolution (e.g. Barr, 2004; Cangelosi and Parisi, 2002; Hurford, 1989, 2000; Kirby and Hurford, 2001).

Steels and Belpaeme (2005) studied color naming through a series of artificial life simulations. They wished to explore the relative contribution of nonsocial factors (such as accurate *discrimination* of colors) and social factors (such as accurate *communication* of colors) to the development of a color lexicon. They created a population of agents that could perceive and learn to talk about colors. Each agent represented color categories in terms of foci, the positions of which in color space had to be either evolved or learned. They argue on the basis of their simulations that color categories may reflect both real-world structure (Shepard, 1992; Yendrikhovskij, 2001) and social coordination through language. Dowman (2007) applied similar ideas to explaining known color naming universals. He investigated a population of Bayesian learners communicating with each other about color in an idealized color domain, and showed that under some conditions, the distribution of color categories such populations converge on closely matches the pattern of universal tendencies of color naming observed in the world's languages (Kay and Maffi, 1999).

4.5.1 ITERATED LEARNING

Iterated learning (e.g. Kirby and Hurford, 2001; Kirby, Smith, and Brighton, 2004) is a general computational framework for simulations such as these, used to explore the emergence of linguistic universals among a population of learning agents through cultural transmission. In the iterated learning framework, each learner sees utterances produced by other agents, induces a grammar (or other mental representation) on that basis, and then produces utterances from that grammar; these new utterances then become the input for the next generation of agents, who must themselves learn this input, and so on.

A fundamental universal fact about human language is that it is *compositional*: The meaning of a sentence is composed out of the meanings of the words in the sentence. Kirby (2002) reports on iterated learning simulations that probe the origins of compositionality. In these simulations, a population of language learning agents has a set of meanings to convey, and must learn a means of expressing them. One possibility is to express the meanings holistically, that is, noncompositionally. For instance, meanings such as [GIVE BALL] (i.e., "give me the ball" in English), [GIVE LEGO], [TAKE BALL], and [TAKE LEGO] might each be expressed by a single form, all unrelated to each other. Another possible means of expressing these meanings is compositionally, such that each of the constituent meanings GIVE, TAKE, BALL, and LEGO is expressed by a single form, and larger meanings can be expressed by concatenating these forms, as is the case in human language. Kirby finds that in iterated learning simulations, populations of learners settle on compositional rather than holistic expression. He suggests that compositionality emerges in language in part because of constraints introduced by social transmission itself (but see Croft, 2004). Similar simulations (Kirby, 1999) have accounted for other linguistic universals (Dryer, 1992; Greenberg, 1963; Hawkins, 1983). In a population of agents, each of which finds particular sorts of structures easier to parse (Hawkins, 1990), these structures may initially be used by only a minority of "speakers" – but after multiple generations they are eventually adopted by the population as a whole.

4.5.2 WHAT CAN WE CONCLUDE?

What may we conclude from such demonstrations? What exactly is the role of iterated learning, or social transmission more generally, in accounting for linguistic universals? One interpretation is that this process itself provides constraints on language – and thus explanations for universals – beyond those in the mind of the individual learner. However, some recent work suggests a rather different view. Griffiths and Kalish (2007) present a Bayesian analysis of iterated learning and show that under certain assumptions iterated learning converges to a distribution over languages determined solely by the prior bias of the individual learner. In other words, iterated learning has the effect of externalizing, in the form of language, the learning biases in each learner's mind (see also Griffiths, Christian, and Kalish, 2008; Griffiths, Kalish, and Lewandowsky, 2008; Kalish, Griffiths, amd Lewandowsky, 2007) – although possibly in magnified form (Kirby, Dowman, and Griffiths, 2007). These results may help to explain why models grounded in cognitive or perceptual structure, with no iterated learning component at all, nonetheless sometimes fit linguistic data fairly well. Such models are, at least implicitly, models of the learner's prior bias. If iterated learning externalizes the learner's prior bias in the form of language, a good model of the prior bias should also fit linguistic data well.

5 Conclusion

The debate over language and thought has received renewed, and intense, interest recently. The use of computational techniques in addressing these questions is still relatively new, and, with the exception of MDS (a classic) not as widespread as it might be. But that is changing. Models of categorical perception can help in unpacking the Whorf phenomenon; computational statistical methods can help to test for semantic universals; and computational models can help to explain semantic universals in terms of the structure of our minds, the physical world around us, and the nature of communication across historical time. Above all, computational models can help us move beyond the simple universalist versus relativist dichotomy to a detailed understanding of how universal and language-specific forces interact.

Acknowledgments

Thanks to Morten Christiansen, Bill Croft, and Rob Goldstone for help in identifying work relevant to this chapter, and to Michael Spivey and Susanne Gahl for comments on an earlier draft. All errors and oversights are mine. This material is based on work supported by the National Science Foundation under Grant No. 0418283. Address correspondence to Terry Regier, terry.regier@berkeley.edu.

References

Anderson, J. A., Silverstein, J. W., Ritz, S. A., & Jones, R. S. (1977). Distinctive features, categorical perception, and probability learning: Some applications of a neural model. *Psychological Review, 84*, 413–51.

Barr, D. (2004). Establishing conventional communication systems: Is common knowledge necessary? *Cognitive Science, 28*, 937–62.

Berlin, B. & Kay, P. (1969). *Basic Color Terms: Their Universality and Evolution*. Berkeley, CA: University of California Press.

Boroditsky, L., Schmidt, L. A., & Phillips, W. (2003). Sex, Syntax, and Semantics. In Gentner, D. & Goldin-Meadow, S. (Eds.) *Language in Mind: Advances in the Study of Language and Thought* (pp. 61–79). Cambridge, MA: MIT Press.

Bybee, J., Perkins, R., & Pagliuca, W. (1994). The Evolution of Grammar: Tense, Aspect, and Modality in the Languages of the World. Chicago.

Cangelosi, A. & Parisi, D. (2002). *Simulating the Evolution of Language*. London: Springer.

Comrie, B. (1976). Aspect: An introduction to the study of verbal aspect and related problems. Cambridge, UK: Cambridge University Press.

Croft, W. (2003). *Typology and Universals* (2nd Edition). New York: Cambridge University Press.

(2004). Form, meaning, and speakers in the evolution of language: Commentary on Kirby, Smith, and Brighton. *Studies in Language, 28*, 608–11.

Croft, W. & Poole, K. (2008). Inferring universals from grammatical variation: Multidimensional scaling for typological analysis. *Theoretical Linguistics, 34*, 1–37.

Damper, R. & Harnad, S. (2000). Neural network models of categorical perception. *Perception and Psychophysics, 62(4)*, 843–67.

Davidoff, J., Davies, I., & Roberson, D. (1999). Colour categories in a stone-age tribe. *Nature*, 398(6724), 203–4.

Dilkina, K., McClelland, J., & Boroditsky, L. (2007). How language affects thought in a connectionist model. Paper presented at the Proceedings of the 29th Annual Conference of the Cognitive Science Society.

Dowman, M. (2007). Explaining color term typology with an evolutionary model. *Cognitive Science*, 31, 99–132.

Drivonikou, G. V., Kay, P., Regier, T., Ivry, R. B., Gilbert, A. L., Franklin, A., & Davies, IRL (2007). Further evidence that Whorfian effects are stronger in the right visual field than the left. *Proceedings of the National Academy of Sciences*, 104, 1097–102.

Dryer, M. (1992). The Greenbergian word order correlations. *Language*, 68, 81–138.

Feldman, N. H. & Griffiths, T. L. (2007). A rational account of the perceptual magnet effect. Paper presented at the Proceedings of the Twenty-Ninth Annual Conference of the Cognitive Science Society.

Garner, W. R. (1974). *The processing of information and structure*. Potomac, MD: L. Erlbaum Associates.

Gentner, D. & Goldin-Meadow, S. (2003). *Language in Mind: Advances in the Study of Language and Thought*. Cambridge, MA: MIT Press.

Gilbert, A., Regier, T., Kay, P., & Ivry, R. (2006). Whorf hypothesis is supported in the right visual field but not the left. *Proceedings of the National Academy of Sciences*, 103(2), 489–94.

Gilbert, A. L., Regier, T., Kay, P., & Ivry, R. B. (2008). Support for lateralization of the Whorf effect beyond the realm of color discrimination. *Brain and Language*, 105, 91–8.

Goldstone, R. L., Steyvers, M., & Larimer, K. (1996). Categorical perception of novel dimensions, *Proceedings of the 18th Annual Conference of the Cognitive Science Society* (pp. 243–8).

Gordon, P. (2004). Numerical cognition without words: Evidence from Amazonia. *Science*, 306, 496–9.

Greenberg, J. H. (1963). Some universals of grammar with particular reference to the order of meaningful elements. In Greenberg, J. H. (Ed.) *Universals of Language* (pp. 73–113). Cambridge, MA: MIT Press.

Griffin, L. D. (2006). Optimality of the basic colour categories for classification. *Journal of the Royal Society Interface*, 3(6), 71–85.

Griffiths, T. L., Christian, B. R., & Kalish, M. L. (2008). Using Category Structures to Test Iterated Learning as a Method for Identifying Inductive Biases. *Cognitive Science*, 32, 68–107.

Griffiths, T. L. & Kalish, M. L. (2007). Language evolution by iterated learning with Bayesian agents. *Cognitive Science*, 31, 441–80.

Griffiths, T. L., Kalish, M. L., & Lewandowsky, S. (2008). Theoretical and empirical evidence for the impact of inductive biases on cultural evolution. *Philosophical Transactions of the Royal Society B: Biological Sciences*, 363, 3503–14.

Harnad, S. (1987). Categorical Perception: The Groundwork of Cognition. New York: Cambridge University Press.

Harnad, S., Hanson, S. J., & Lubin, J. (1995). Learned Categorical Perception in Neural Nets: Implications for Symbol Grounding. In Honavar, V. & Uhr, L. (Eds.) *Symbol Processors and Connectionist Network Models in Artificial Intelligence and Cognitive Modelling: Steps Toward Principled Integration* (pp. 191–206). New York: Academic Press.

Haspelmath, M. (1997). *Indefinite Pronouns*. Oxford: Oxford University Press.

Hawkins, J. A. (1983). *Word Order Universals*. New York: Academic Press.

(1990). A parsing theory of word order universals. *Linguistic Inquiry*, 21, 223–61.

Heider, E. R. (1972). Universals in color naming and memory. *Journal of Experimental Psychology*, 93, 10–20.

Heider, E. R. & Olivier, D. C. (1972). The structure of the color space in naming and memory for two languages. *Cognitive Psychology*, 3, 337–54.

Hopfield, J. J. (1982). Neural Networks and Physical Systems with Emergent Collective Computational Abilities, *Proceedings of the National Academy of Sciences of the USA* (Vol. 79, pp. 2554–8).

Hopper, P. J. & Traugott, E. C. (1993). *Grammaticalization*. Cambridge, England: Cambridge University Press.

Hurford, J. (1989). Biological evolution of the Saussurean sign as a component of the language acquisition device. *Lingua*, 77(2), 187–222.

(2000). Social transmission favours linguistic generalization. In Knight, D. Studdert-Kennedy, M., & Hurford, J. (Eds.) *The Evolutionary Emergence of Language: Social Function and the Origins of Linguistic Form*. Cambridge, UK: Cambridge University Press.

Huttenlocher, J., Hedges, L., & Duncan, S. (1991). Categories and Particulars: Prototype Effects in Estimating Spatial Location, *Psychological Review* (Vol. 98, pp. 352–76).

Huttenlocher, J., Hedges, L., & Prohaska, V. (1988). Hierarchical organization in ordered domains:

Estimating the dates of events. *Psychological Review*, 95(4), 471–84.

Jameson, K. A. & D'Andrade, R. G. (1997). It's not really red, green, yellow, blue. In Hardin, C. L. & Maffi, L. (Eds.) *Color Categories in Thought and Language* (pp. 295–319). Cambridge: Cambridge University Press.

Kalish, M. L., Griffiths, T. L., & Lewandowsky, S. (2007). Iterated learning: Intergenerational knowledge transmission reveals inductive biases. *Psychonomic Bulletin and Review*, 14, 288–94.

Kay, P. & Kempton, W. (1984). What is the Sapir-Whorf Hypothesis? *American Anthropologist*, 86(1), 65–79.

Kay, P. & Maffi, L. (1999). Color appearance and the emergence and evolution of basic color lexicons. *American Anthropologist*, 101(4), 743–60.

Kay, P. & McDaniel, C. K. (1978). The linguistic significance of the meanings of basic color terms. *Language*, 54(3), 610–46.

Kay, P. & Regier, T. (2003). Resolving the question of color naming universals. *Proceedings of the National Academy of Sciences, USA*, 100(15), 9085–9.

(2007). Color naming universals: The case of Berinmo. *Cognition*, 102, 289–98.

Kirby, S. (1999). Function, Selection, and Innateness: The Emergence of Language Universals. Oxford, UK: Oxford University Press.

(2002). Learning, bottlenecks, and the evolution of recursive syntax. In Briscoe, T. (Ed.) *Linguistic Evolution through Language Acquisition: Formal and Computational Models*. Cambridge: Cambridge University Press.

Kirby, S., Dowman, M., & Griffiths, T. L. (2007). Innateness and culture in the evolution of language. *Proceedings of the National Academy of Sciences*, 104, 5241–5.

Kirby, S. & Hurford, J. (2001). The emergence of linguistic structure: An overview of the iterated learning model. In Cangelosi, A. & Parisi, D. (Eds.) *Simulating the Evolution of Language*. London: Springer.

Kirby, S., Smith, K., & Brighton, H. (2004). From UG to universals: linguistic adaptation through iterated learning. *Studies in Language*, 28, 587–607.

Komarova, N. L., Jameson, K. A., & Narens, L. (2007). Evolutionary models of color categorization based on discrimination. *Journal of Mathematical Psychology*, 51, 359–82.

Kruschke, J. (1992). ALCOVE: An Exemplar-Based Connectionist Model of Category Learning, *Psychological Review* (Vol. 99, pp. 22–44).

Kuhl, P. K., Williams, K. A., Lacerda, F., Stevens, K. N., & Lindblom, B. (1992). Linguistic experience alters phonetic perception in infants by 6 months of age. *Science*, 255, 606–8.

Lakusta, L. & Landau, B. (2005). Starting at the end: The importance of goals in spatial language. *Cognition*, 96(1), 1–33.

Lammens, J. (1994). A computational model of color perception and color naming. Ph.D. dissertation, State University of New York at Buffalo.

Levinson, S. & Meira, S. (2003). "Natural concepts" in the spatial topological domain: Adpositional meanings in crosslinguistic perspective: An exercise in semantic typology. *Language*, 79(3), 485–516.

Liberman, A. M., Harris, K. S., Hoffman, H. S., & Griffith, B. C. (1957). The discrimination of speech sounds within and across phoneme boundaries. *Journal of Experimental Psychology*, 54, 358–68.

Loenneker-Rodman, B. & Narayanan, S. (this volume). Computational approaches to figurative language.

Lucy, J. (1992). Grammatical categories and cognition: A case study of the linguistic relativity hypothesis. Cambridge: Cambridge University Press.

(1997). The Linguistics of "Color." In Hardin, C. L. & Maffi, L. (Eds.) *Color Categories in Thought and Language* (pp. 320–46). Cambridge: Cambridge University Press.

Lupyan, G., Rakison, D. H., & McClelland, J. L. (2007). Language is not just for talking: Redundant labels facilitate learning of novel categories. *Psychological Science*, 18, 1077–83.

Lupyan, G. & Spivey, M. (2008). Perceptual processing is facilitated by ascribing meaning to novel stimuli. *Current Biology*, 18(10), R410–R412.

Malt, B. C., Sloman, S. A., Gennari, S., Shi, M., & Wang, Y. (1999). Knowing versus naming: Similarity and the linguistic categorization of artifacts. *Journal of Memory and Language*, 40(2), 230–62.

Malt, B. C., Sloman, S. A., & Gennari, S. P. (2003). Universality and language specificity in object naming. *Journal of Memory and Language*, 49(1), 20–42.

McClelland, J. & Elman, J. (1986). The TRACE model of speech perception. *Cognitive Psychology*, 18, 1–86.

McClelland, J. & Rumelhart, D. (1981). An Interactive Activation Model of Context Effects in Letter Perception: Part 1. An Account of Basic Findings. *Psychological Review*, 88(5), 375–407.

Merriman, W. (1999). Competition, Attention, and Young Children's Lexical Processing. In MacWhinney, B. (Ed.) *The Emergence of Language* (pp. 331–58). Mahwah, NJ: Erlbaum.

Munnich, E., Landau, B., & Dosher, B. A. (2001). Spatial language and spatial representation: A cross-linguistic comparison. *Cognition, 81(3)*, 171–207.

Narayanan, S. (1997). KARMA: Knowledge-based Action Representations for Metaphor and Aspect. Ph.D. dissertation. University of California at Berkeley.

Nosofsky, R. (1986). Attention, Similarity, and the Identification-Categorization Relationship. *Journal of Experimental Psychology: General, 115(1)*, 39–57.

Papafragou, A., Massey, C., & Gleitman, L. (2002). Shake, rattle, 'n' roll: The representation of motion in language and cognition. *Cognition, 84(2)*, 189–219.

Pastore, R. E. (1987). Categorical perception: Some psychophysical models. In Harnad, S. (Ed.) *Categorical perception: The groundwork of cognition* (pp. 29–52). New York: Cambridge University Press.

Pica, P., Lemer, C., Izard, V., & Dehaene, S. (2004). Exact and Approximate Arithmetic in an Amazonian Indigene Group. *Science, 306*, 499–503.

Pilling, M., Wiggett, A., Özgen, E., & Davies, I. R. (2003). Is color "categorical perception" really perceptual? *Memory & Cognition, 31(4)*, 538–51.

Regier, T. (1996). The human semantic potential: Spatial language and constrained connectionism. Cambridge, MA: The MIT Press.

(2005). The emergence of words: Attentional learning in form and meaning. *Cognitive Science, 29*, 819–65.

Regier, T., Kay, P., & Cook, R. (2005). Focal colors are universal after all. *Proceedings of the National Academy of Sciences, USA, 102(23)*, 8386–91.

Regier, T., Kay, P., Gilbert, A., & Ivry, R. (2010). Language and thought: Which side are you on, anyway? In Malt, B. & Wolff, P. (Eds.), *Words and the World: How words capture human experience*. New York: Oxford University Press.

Regier, T., Kay, P., & Khetarpal, N. (2007). Color naming reflects optimal partitions of color space. *Proceedings of the National Academy of Sciences, 104*, 1436–41.

Regier, T. & Zheng, M. (2007). Attention to end-points: A cross-linguistic constraint on spatial meaning. *Cognitive Science, 31*, 705–19.

Roberson, D. & Davidoff, J. (2000). The categorical perception of colors and facial expressions: The effect of verbal interference. *Memory & Cognition, 28(6)*, 977–86.

Roberson, D., Davidoff, J., Davies, I. R., & Shapiro, L. R. (2005). Color categories: Evidence for the cultural relativity hypothesis. *Cognitive Psychology, 50(4)*, 378–411.

Roberson, D., Davies, I., & Davidoff, J. (2000). Color categories are not universal: Replications and new evidence from a stone-age culture. *Journal of Experimental Psychology: General, 129(3)*, 369–98.

Romney, A. K., Moore, C. C., Batchelder, W. H., & Hsia, T. L. (2000). Statistical methods for characterizing similarities and differences between semantic structures. *Proceedings of the National Academy of Sciences, USA, 97(1)*, 518–23.

Rumelhart, D., Hinton, G., & Williams, R. (1986). Learning Internal Representations by Error Propagation. In Rumelhart, D., McClelland, J., & PDPR. Group (Eds.) *Parallel Distributed Processing: Explorations in the Microstructure of Cognition* (Vol. 1, pp. 318–62). Cambridge, MA.

Shepard, R. (1992). The perceptual organization of colors: An adaptation to regularities of the terrestrial world? In Barkow, J. H., Tooby, J., & Cosmides, L. (Eds.) *The Adapted Mind: Evolutionary Psychology and the Generation of Culture* (pp. 495–532). New York: Oxford University Press.

(2001). Perceptual-cognitive universals as reflections of the world. *Behavioral and Brain Sciences, 24*, 581–601.

Shepard, R., Romney, A. K., & Nerlove, S. B. (1972). *Multidimensional Scaling. Volume 1: Theory*. New York: Seminar Press.

Smith, L. B. (1989). A model of perceptual classification in children and adults, *Psychological Review* (Vol. 96, pp. 125–44).

(2000). Learning how to learn words: An associative crane. In Golinkoff, R., Pasek, K. H., Bloom, L., Smith, L., Woodward, A., Akhtar, N., Tomasello, M., & Hollich, G. (Eds.) *Becoming a Word Learner: A Debate on Lexical Acquisition* (pp. 51–80). New York: Oxford University Press.

Smith, L. B., Jones, S. S., Landau, B., Gershkoff-Stowe, L., & Samuelson, L. (2002). Object name learning provides on-the-job training for attention. *Psychological Science, 13(1)*, 13–19.

Steels, L. & Belpaeme, T. (2005). Coordinating perceptually grounded categories through language: A case study for colour. *Behavioral and Brain Sciences, 28(4)*, 469–529.

Steyvers, M. (2002). Multidimensional scaling: Encyclopedia of Cognitive Science. London: Nature Publishing Group.

Talmy, L. (1996). Fictive motion in language and "ception." Bloom, P., Peterson M. A., et al. (Eds.) *Language and space: Language, speech, and communication* (pp. 211–76). Cambridge, MA: The MIT Press.

Whorf, B. L. (1956). *Language, Thought, and Reality*. Cambridge, MA: MIT Press.

Winawer, J., Witthoft, N., Frank, M. C., Wu, L., Wade, A. R., & Boroditsky, L. (2007). Russian blues reveal effects of language on color discrimination. *Proceedings of the National Academy of Sciences, 104*, 7780–5.

Yendrikhovskij, S. (2001). A computational model of colour categorization. *Color Research & Application, 26(S1)*, S235-S238.

Zheng, M. Y. & Goldin-Meadow, S. (2002). Thought before language: How deaf and hearing children express motion events across cultures. *Cognition, 85(2)*, 145–75.

CHAPTER 33

Language and Cognition in Development

Stella Christie and Dedre Gentner

Introduction

The hypothesis that language can influence thought – generally known as the Whorfian hypothesis – has inspired strong opinions in both directions. Early enthusiasm in the 1950s and 1960s was followed by decades of disregard or worse. Now the wheel has turned again, and the question of whether and how language might influence cognition is openly tested and debated. (See Gentner and Goldin-Meadow, 2003 and Gumperz and Levinson, 1996 for discussions of the forces behind this evolution.) However, work on language and thought remains extremely contentious, and many of the claims reviewed here are under challenge.

In some important ways, the field of cognitive development has been relatively open to the idea that language influences thought. Within adult cognitive psychology, the *language and thought* hypothesis is associated primarily with Benjamin Lee Whorf and his mentor, Edward Sapir (e.g., Whorf, 1956), who proposed that specific properties of a language's grammar and lexicon could influence cognition in speakers of that language:

"We dissect nature along lines laid down by our native language," (Whorf, 1956, p. 213). But in developmental theory, the figure most associated with the view that language influences thought is Russian psychologist Lev Vygotsky (1962). Unlike Piaget, for whom conceptual development proceeded via interactions with experience, with language serving only as a means of communication, Vygotsky saw language and culture as critical to the development of thought. One could say that Piaget viewed the child as a tiny scientist, whereas Vygotsky viewed the child as a cultural apprentice.

Vygotsky's view on the effects of language differed from that of Whorf and Sapir. Rather than focusing on the effects of speaking one language versus another, Vygotsky theorized about the effects of language as such. He proposed that the internalization of language provides children with the means to direct their own thought: to achieve focused attention and will, and a means of introspecting about one's own cognition. Vygotsky offered a view of language as providing scaffolding for new concepts; he suggested that hearing a new term or a new assertion, even when the child has poor initial understanding, might both invite and guide the child to future learning.

Advances in cognitive psychology, linguistics, and linguistic anthropology have led to progress on some classic questions. For example, a perennial question in the development of language and thought is which comes first – the concept or the linguistic term. Scholars like Bowerman (1981; 1989) have long raised challenges to the standing Zeitgeist that concepts come first, with language merely naming them. But until recently there was no way to address this directly. With the recent explosion of techniques for studying infant cognition, it is becoming possible to address the question of whether and how prelinguistic cognition differs from postlinguistic cognition. As another example, comparative studies of apes and young humans are another new source of insight. But this recent progress has also made it clear that the question of whether language influences thought needs to be decomposed into more specific questions.

A set of fine-grained questions has emerged concerning when and how language effects might occur (Gentner and Goldin-Meadow, 2003; Gumperz and Levinson, 1996; Wolff and Holmes, 2011). Taking linguistic determinism – the hypothesis that the language we speak determines how we perceive the world – as the starting point, one way to delimit the hypothesis is to specify *when* we should expect to see effects of language on cognition. This was the move that Slobin (1996; 2003) made in his influential *thinking for speaking* hypothesis, which holds that language influences thought only when language is actively used. The initial statement was couched in terms of "when actually speaking," but later research has broadened the scope to include comprehending language and perhaps even using language internally (though this move makes the thinking-for-speaking view harder to distinguish from linguistic determinism). Another way to delimit the effects of language is to assume that language augments, but does not replace, other ways of construing the world. This is the route taken by the *language as tool kit* view – that acquiring a language provides new representational resources – including new relational schemas as well as new categories – that augment our capacity for encoding and reasoning (Gentner, 2003, 2010; Gentner and Christie, 2010; Loewenstein and Gentner, 2005; see Frank et al., 2008, for a similar view). These linguistically inspired representations may become habitual, so that they are readily accessible even without the internal use of language (Hunt and Agnoli, 1991; Levinson, et al., 2002; Lucy, 1994). In this view, language provides tools that facilitate forming and using particular representations – representations that may be intellectually potent – but does not replace all other encoding formats. Another distinction that needs to be made is that between effects of language on thought, and effects of language on language (Gleitman and Papafragou, 2005). For example, the difference between the naming patterns of English versus Japanese children for substances and objects, as in Imai and Gentner's (1997) work, does not entitle the conclusion that Japanese and English speakers think about objects and substances differently, though it does set the stage for further investigation (e.g., Imai and Mazuka, 2003).

The distinctions among these views make it clear that the language and thought issue is far subtler than the extreme version of the Whorfian hypothesis: that language acts to determine our perception of the world – as a kind of permanent lens on the mind's eye.

From this perspective, the developmental course of language effects is of central interest. In this paper we review evidence that language acts during cognitive development to promote certain kinds of conceptual structures. In terms of the toolkit hypothesis, the question we ask is when and how language facilitates the acquisition of cognitive tools. Our discussion is organized around three domains of active research: space, number, and theory of mind. There are other arenas that could be discussed, including temporal relations (e.g., Boroditsky, 2001), noun learning and object individuation (e.g., Lupyan et al., 2007; Xu, 2002), and object categorization (e.g., Markman, 1989; Waxman, 2002; Waxman and Markow, 1995), but given the limitations of space we prefer to go deeply into a few areas.

1 Space

The domain of space is an obvious place to investigate the question of whether language affects cognition, for several reasons. First, spatial information is universally available to humans regardless of where they live. Indeed, we are all constrained by the same universal laws of physics: An apple placed in a bowl always rests on the bottom of the bowl rather than floating in mid air within the bowl. Second, it is comparatively easy to construct nonlinguistic situations and events to which people can react regardless of their language (Here spatial concepts contrast with, say, counterfactual reasoning or concepts of justice.) Third, spatial knowledge is of fundamental importance in human reasoning, both directly in activities like navigation and manipulation, and through spatial analogies and metaphors, which occur commonly in human language and thought. Finally, a prerequisite for finding language-driven variability in concepts is variability in the language, and here space is an ideal domain. Recent research has revealed an astonishing variety of ways in which languages have categorized spatial configurations (e.g., Bohnemeyer and Brown, 2007; Bowerman, 1989, 1996; Brown, 1994; Levinson and Brown, 1994; Casad and Langacker, 1985; Talmy, 1975, 1985). For all these reasons, space has become an especially active arena of investigation for language and thought. The relational information that constitutes a given spatial configuration can be partitioned differently by different minds and different languages (Gentner, 1982). For example, one can think of an apple in a bowl as being supported by the bottom of the bowl, or as being contained inside the bowl, or as in loose contact with the bowl. All of these possibilities are reflected across human languages.

1.1 *Frames of reference*

Spatial relational terms provide framing structures for the encoding of events and experience. Across a range of languages, Levinson and his colleagues have identified three spatial frames of reference that speakers use to describe the location of an object (Levinson, 1996; Levinson et al., 2002). The *relative* (or *egocentric*) frame describes locations relative to the speaker, as in "the chair is left of the table." The *intrinsic* (or *object-centered*) frame describes locations relative to a landmark object, as in "the chair is in front of the fireplace." Finally the *absolute* (or *geocentric*) frame describes locations relative to a global frame, as in "the chair is in the northwest corner." The term *allocentric* refers to both object-centered and geocentric frames, in contrast to egocentric frames. Languages may use more than one of these frames, but in many cases one frame is dominant. In particular, when discussing close-range locations, the egocentric frame is dominant in English, Dutch, and German, while the geocentric frame predominates in many other languages, including Tzeltal (Mexico), Arrernte (Australia), and Haiɬom (Namibia) (see Majid et al., 2004 for a comprehensive review).

The question here is whether the habitual use of a particular linguistic frame of reference has any more general effect on spatial cognition. Research by Levinson and colleagues (Levinson, 1996, 2003; Levinson and Brown, 1994; Levinson et al., 2002; Pederson, 1995) suggests that the answer is yes; they find that people are influenced by their language's dominant frame of reference even when carrying out a nonlinguistic spatial task, such as copying a scene or tracing a path through a maze (Majid et al., 2004; but see Li and Gleitman, 2002 for a dissenting view).

How do such effects arise in cognitive development? Do we begin life with natural proclivities or instead as "blank slates" on which language, culture, and other experiences impose spatial frames? This question is difficult to answer for a topic like frame of reference, because very young infants are

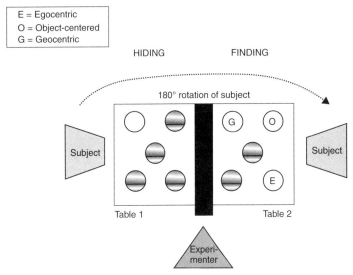

Figure 33.1. Experimental setup for an example trial in Haun et al., 2006. Ten identical cups were placed on two tables (five cups on each table). The participant watched while a target was hidden under the cup depicted as white (HIDING). Then participants moved to the other table and indicated where they thought a second target might be hidden (FINDING).

limited in their response capabilities, while older infants and toddlers may already be influenced by culture and language. The Piagetian tradition holds that there is an initial egocentric bias and a shift from egocentric to allocentric over development (Piaget and Inhelder, 1967; Pick, 1993), although there is also some evidence for flexibility in infants (Acredolo, 1978; Bremner, 1978).

Haun et al., (2006) addressed this in a set of studies that combines cross-linguistic developmental comparisons with cross-species comparisons between humans and our close relatives, the great apes. For the cross-linguistic comparison, Haun et al. compared Dutch speakers, whose language (like English) primarily uses an egocentric frame of reference, with speakers of Haillom (a Khoisan language spoken in Namibia), which primarily uses a geocentric frame. Haun et al. used two-dimensional arrays of five objects, which allowed them to distinguish the three frames of reference (see Figure 33.1).

Participants faced an array of five identical cups on Table 1 and watched as an object was hidden in one of the cups. They then moved around to Table 2, where they saw an identical array of cups, but from the opposite direction. Their task was to retrieve the hidden object. So far this task resembles prior frame of reference tasks. However, a salutary innovation in this research is that, whereas prior research had focused on speakers' preference for using one frame or another, this research utilized a training task, allowing the researchers to compare participants' facility in learning to use one frame over another. Participants received ten consecutive trials in which the correct answer required use of the egocentric frame, then (without any break) ten more using the geocentric frame, then ten using the object-centered frame. This technique thus tests whether people find it easier to learn a spatial task when it is set in the frame of reference dominant in their language. The results paralleled prior findings of language effects in adults: Dutch-speaking adults and eight-to-ten-year-olds were more accurate in the egocentric condition than in the other two, while Haillom-speaking adults and children were most accurate in the geocentric condition. The striking difference between these two groups is just what would be predicted from the dominant frame of reference of the respective languages. (Of course, these differences could have stemmed from other cultural or environmental differences; but see Majid et al. (2004) for arguments against this likelihood.)

Haun et al. then went on to probe the development of frame of reference and to ask how it develops. Their studies built on the prior research of Call and Tomasello (Call, 2001; Tomasello and Call, 1997) comparing human patterns with those of our close cousins among the great apes. They gave both apes (three orangutans, two gorillas, three bonobos, and five chimpanzees) and four-to-five-year-old German-speaking children a simplified search task.[1] Participants saw an object hidden under one of a line of three identical cups on Table 1. As in the prior study, they then moved around to Table 2, where they viewed an identical array from the opposite direction and looked for the hidden target. As before, participants had to discover the rule that determined the correct location on Table 2. There were two conditions: *egocentric*, where the hiding and finding cups maintained the same position relative to the participants' view point (left or right); and *allocentric*, where the hiding and finding cups maintained the same position relative to an external frame. (In this simplified task, we can distinguish between egocentric and allocentric responding, but not between the two kinds of allocentric response, because the geocentric (e.g., the west end) and object-centered (e.g., the end nearest to the experimenter) frames both yield the same response.) The results showed that great apes performed best in the allocentric condition, consistent with research showing that many species use allocentric spatial information to navigate (see Gallistel, 1990). But what is more surprising is that German-speaking children

showed the same allocentric pattern; their performance resembled that of our simian cousins rather than that of older German speakers. As Haun et al. note, this suggests a deep continuity between humans and the great apes in their native cognitive biases with respect to reference frame.

This finding of an allocentric preference in four-year-olds dovetails with evidence that infants can adopt allocentric as well as egocentric frames (Acredolo, 1978; Bremner, 1978). At the same time, this cross-species allocentric bias in young humans and great apes renders the later cross-linguistic divergence all the more striking. By eight years of age, children whose language favors an egocentric frame have diverged from their native pattern and now find the egocentric frame easier to use, while those whose language is geocentric show a correspondingly geocentric bias. Important, this entrainment by language is not absolute. For example, older Dutch children and adults performed above chance in the geocentric condition, and as Li and Gleitman (2002) note, speakers of a given language are also influenced by contextual factors (see also Gleitman and Papafragou, 2005). Nonetheless, the fact that each group performed better on the frame favored by their language is evidence for effects of habitual language on the way we most readily conceptualize space.

1.2 *The semantics of containment and support*

Within cognitive development, Bowerman (1980; 1989) was among the first to challenge the idea that concepts come first in human development and are simply mapped onto language. Noting the variability between languages in how spatial relations are lexicalized (e.g., Bowerman, 1981; 1996; Bowerman and Choi, 2003; Bowerman and Levinson, 2001; Levinson et al., 2002), Bowerman argued against the common assumption that certain words are acquired earlier than others because they correspond to preexisting conceptual categories. Instead, she suggested

---

1 Dutch and German (and also English) use basically the same system of spatial reference, with the egocentric spatial reference frame as dominant.

that concept learning might be guided by language from the start.[2]

One striking example of such semantic diversity is the contrast between Korean and English spatial terms first documented by Choi and Bowerman (1991). In English, spatial attachment is divided into semantic categories of containment and support (*in* and *on*). In contrast, Korean speakers organize spatial attachments according to how the two objects fit with one another, contrasting tight fit with loose fit. In English, putting a videocassette *in* its case or an apple *in* a bowl are both categorized as containment. However, Korean uses two different verbs: a videocassette/case event is described by the verb *kkita* (roughly, to join things tightly), and the apple/bowl event is described by the verb *nehta* (to join things loosely). In the other direction, the English distinction between containment and support is not lexicalized in Korean: for example, the same verb (*kkita*) is used for putting the top *on* a pen and for putting an earplug *into* an ear (Choi and Bowerman, 1991).

If children form particular spatial concepts that are then mapped onto language, then we would expect an advantage for whichever language best matches children's natural concepts. But in fact, Choi and Bowerman found that English and Korean children acquired their very different spatial systems at about the same rate. In both languages, the first relational terms appeared at about fourteen to sixteen months. In English these early relational words were *down, out, on, off,* and *open,* with *come, fall, walk, run, sit,* and *ride* by seventeen to eighteen months. In Korean the early terms were *kkita* (fit), *ppayta* (unfit), *yelta* (open), and *tatta* (close), with *kata* (go), *ancta* (sit), *pwuthita* (juxtapose two surfaces), *kka(k)ta* (peel off), etc., by seventeen to eighteen months. There are some commonalities: Young children like to talk about opening and closing and about

moving around. But although both groups talk about spatial relations, they pick out very different parts of the spatial world to lexicalize, and this selection is guided by their language.

Further work has explored the early effects of language: that is, at what point do infants begin to form different semantic categories corresponding to their linguistic terms? Choi et al. (1999) found that as early as eighteen months, infants are sensitive to language-specific spatial categories. In this study, upon hearing the spatial term *in,* English-speaking children selectively attended to scenes depicting containment (matching scene) as opposed to nonmatching scenes. Similarly, Korean-speaking children attend to scenes depicting tight-fit relations upon hearing *kkita.* During control trials, where the children did not hear the target word (*in* for English or *kkita* for Korean), there was no preference for either the matching or nonmatching scenes, suggesting the absence of nonlinguistic biases. Choi et al. used a variety of different spatial scenes – e.g., for the containment relation (*in*), scenes included putting a peg in a hole, Lego blocks in a box, books in box covers, and rings in a big basket. The fact that eighteen-month-olds could correctly map their respective linguistic spatial terms to this variety of scenes suggests that they have a generalized understanding of the containment relation entailed by the spatial term.

Another line of support for the role of spatial language in shaping spatial semantic categories is a study by Casasola (2005), in which eighteen-month-old English-speaking infants formed an abstract category of support only when they heard the word *on* during habituation trials. Infants in this study were all habituated to four support events, two depicting tight support and two depicting loose support. Infants then viewed four test events in sequence: two depicting support relation (familiar) and two depicting containment (a new relation). Infants who had heard the spatial word *on* during habituation looked longer at the novel relation (containment) with *both* familiar and novel objects, indicating that they had formed an

---

2   Bowerman's recent research has also explored the other direction: that some categories are more natural than others and that these categories will both be more frequent in the world's languages and more readily learned by children (the *typological prevalence* hypothesis) (Gentner and Bowerman, 2009).

abstract representation of the support relation. In contrast, infants who had heard general phrases, novel words, or no words at all during habituation failed to notice the change in relations even for familiar objects; they attended to a change in objects, but not to a change in relations.

These studies suggest that language is instrumental in prompting infants to form stable spatial relational categories. Consistent with this claim, it appears that in the absence of linguistic guidance, young infants are ready to form a variety of spatial categories. McDonough, Choi, and Mandler (2003) familiarized nine-to-fourteen-month-old English- or Korean-learning infants with either pairs of tight containment events or pairs of loose containment events, accompanied only by music. Although the tight–loose distinction is far more central in Korean than in English, both groups of infants were able to extract the category during familiarization: Both groups could distinguish the familiar category from the new category when shown novel test pairs (with new objects) consisting of a tight containment event and a loose containment event.[3]

Hespos and Spelke (2004) studied even younger infants and found that five-month-old English-speaking infants can readily form either the English support/containment distinction or the Korean tight fit/loose fit distinction. The infants were habituated either with a single tight containment event or with a loose containment event: for example, a cylinder entering another container that fit either tightly or loosely. They were then tested with both tight containment and loose containment events (shown sequentially). Infants habituated to tight containment looked longer at the loose containment event and vice versa, indicating that they had abstracted the respective category. More surprisingly, this pattern held up even when infants had to transfer the tight/loose distinction from support to containment. That is, when infants were habituated with either tight or loose *support* events, and

then shown the tight *containment* and loose *containment* test events, they looked longer at the novel test event. This suggests that five-month-old infants can form the Korean tight–loose distinction, even when it cuts across the English *in/on* distinction.

Lining up the developmental studies discussed so far, we have a rather perplexing contrast. Five-month-olds showed sensitivity to the tight–loose distinction unmarked in their native language in Hespos and Spelke's (2004) study. But in Casasola's (2005) study, which also used a habituation paradigm, eighteen-month-olds failed to show sensitivity to the support category which *is* marked in their language, unless they heard the requisite spatial term. We suggest that this difference may rely on the degree of generalization that the infants needed to make (see also Casasola, 2008). In Casasola's study, the habituation events were quite varied and the objects involved were perceptually rich and differed across trials; in the Hespos and Spelke study, the habituation trials utilized highly similar events, both in the motions involved and in the objects (which were varied only slightly). Likewise, the test trials were perceptually quite dissimilar from the habituation trials in Casasola's study (especially in the novel object trials) and perceptually similar to the habituation trials in Hespos and Spelke's study.

One might then ask "So which study is right? When exactly do infants have the category of support?" We suggest that this is the wrong question. Rather, the better question is "When (and under what learning conditions) can infants form a category of support at a given level of abstraction?" If we consider that performance in these studies derives in part from abstractions formed during the study (rather than solely from preexisting categories), then both kinds of study are informative. We can see these studies as spanning a range. At one pole are studies in which the intended relation is perfectly aligned across exemplars with few distracting surface differences (as exemplified in Hespos and Spelke's studies) – an ideal situation in which to form a generalization, albeit one that may not apply far beyond the

---

[3] All ages showed a familiarity preference in both languages.

initial stimuli. At the other pole are studies with complex learning conditions, in which the relation is instantiated over different kinds of objects (as in the Casasola studies). That infants form the abstraction under perfect conditions tells us that this potential is there prior to language; and indeed the Hespos and Spelke results show that infants are multipotential learners at this early stage. But the variable learning experience given to the infants in the Casasola studies more closely matches real-life learning conditions, in which children encounter a given spatial relation instantiated over a wide variety of specific situations.[4] From this perspective, this range of studies from ideal abstraction conditions to perceptually variable conditions can be seen as putting bounds on the conditions under which infants will form the category.

1.3 *Relational language and relational representation*

Gentner and colleagues have theorized that spatial relational language – and relational language in general – can foster the learning and retention of relational patterns (Gentner, 2003, 2010; Loewenstein and Gentner, 2005), thus acting as a "cognitive toolkit." During initial learning, hearing a relational term used for two situations invites children to compare them and derive their common abstraction (*symbolic juxtaposition*). Once learned, a relational term can help to stabilize the abstraction. Gentner (2010) termed this *reification* (see also Lupyan, 2008 for discussions of this idea). The term can then be used to invite a particular construal of a given situation – one that may be advantageous for certain

purposes. One particularly powerful kind of relational construal is a *systematic* representation: one in which the lower-order relations are interconnected by a higher-order constraining relation. For example, the set of terms *top, middle, bottom* form a systematic structure governed by the higher-order relation of monotonicity in the vertical dimension. This kind of connected relational system can be used to support inference and, as discussed later in this chapter, analogical mapping and transfer.

Recent evidence for the benefit of spatial relational language – and especially of systematic relational language – was offered by Loewenstein and Gentner (2005) in a spatial mapping study. Preschool children saw two identical three-tiered boxes; they watched an item being hidden in one box and then searched for a similar item in the corresponding location at the second box (see Figure 33.2). Children's performance was better when they first heard the box described using spatial relational terms such as *on, in, under.* Further, when the task was made more difficult by introducing a competing object match (a *cross-mapping*, Gentner and Toupin, 1986), children performed far better with the terms *top, middle, bottom* (which convey a connected system of relations) than with the terms *on, in, under*, which lack a unifying higher-order structure. We infer that hearing *top, middle, bottom* invited a representation of the monotonic relational structure of the two boxes, and that this higher-order structure helped the children to achieve a relational mapping.

Further evidence of the influence of spatial relational language on spatial cognition comes from a study by Dessalegn and Landau (2008). In this study, four-year-olds were tested with a well-known problem in vision: color and location conjunction (e.g., a split square, with red on the left and green on the right). Children were presented with a target example (e.g., a red (left)-green (right) square); their task was to find the exact match after a one second delay among three choices: the correct match (red-green

---

4   The McDonough et al. study also belongs on the "rich and varied" end of the continuum, with the added important feature that they showed infants pairs of events (for example, two tight containment events) during familiarization. Their finding that even nine-month-old infants given pairs of events can abstract common relations from rich, complex stimuli is consistent with evidence that comparing two exemplars fosters the abstraction of commonalities, particularly common relations (Gentner and Namy, 1999; Oakes and Ribar, 2005).

Neutral

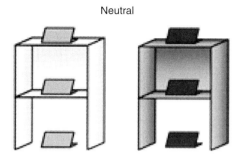

Relational Match Only

Cross-Map

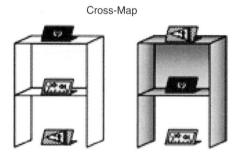

Relational Match with
Competing object Match

Figure 33.2. Experimental setup for the two versions of the Loewenstein and Gentner (2005) spatial mapping task. Children watched the experimenter place the "winner" card in the left box and searched for it in the right box.

square), the reflection (green-red square), or the distractor (red-green diagonal split square). Performance was best when children heard relational language (e.g., "the red is on the left"). Crucial, the advantage of hearing spatial language was not found for potentially salient nonlinguistic attentional cues (flashing, pointing, or changes in size of the red part), suggesting that relational language affected the spatial representation rather than simply increasing attention to the task.[5]

---

[5] However, interestingly, other asymmetric terms such as *prettier* also aided performance – possibly via metaphor mapping to the actual spatial situation.

1.4 *Habitual construals: Beyond thinking for speaking*

The studies reviewed so far suggest that spatial language can influence children's performance on spatial tasks. Some of these effects could be explained by the thinking for speaking account. For example, Dessalegn and Landau's (2008) findings could be accounted for by purely online, temporary effects of language. However, there are also findings that point to longer term effects of language on the development of spatial representations. For example, the effects of language in the Loewenstein and Gentner (2005) spatial mapping task were durable, not fleeting. When children were brought back to the lab two days later to "play the same game," those who had heard systematic language (*top, middle, bottom*) outperformed those who had not, even though the spatial relational terms were never used during the second session. These children were also able to transfer the mapping task to new, rather different-looking boxes. These findings suggest that the relational terms induced a corresponding representation which delineated the internal structure of the boxes. Finally, in a recent study in Istanbul, Gentner et al. (2008) compared five-year-old children who possess normal language with a group of deaf children who had not been taught a sign language, and whose self-developed homesign gestural system (Goldin-Meadow, 2003) was deficient in spatial terms. Neither group was given any spatial language during the task. Nonetheless, the hearing children (who had good command of Turkish spatial terms) performed significantly better on the task than did the deaf children.

There is also evidence from adult studies that language can become internalized and come to influence our default conceptual construals, for instance the frame of reference studies discussed earlier. Studies of support relation provide another example: In contrast to infants, adults show a strong preference for the categories enshrined in their native language. McDonough et al. (2003) gave adults an oddity task in which they had to say which of four events was different from the others. English-speaking adults could do this readily (seventy-eight percent correct) when given three tight containment events and one loose support event; but when given three tight containment events and one loose containment event (so that the choice had to be based on the tight–loose distinction), only thirty-eight percent chose successfully. In contrast, Koreans (for whom the tight–loose distinction is part of habitual language) readily chose the odd item in this latter task (eighty-percent correct). Likewise, Hespos and Spelke (2004) found that in making similarity judgments, English-speaking adults were sensitive only to the English containment–support distinction, and not to the Korean tight–loose distinction.

This development from equipotentiality in infants to linguistically biased similarity in adults suggests that we possess an early ability to form a large number of potential distinctions. Habitual usage of language renders certain spatial categories more dominant. This does not mean that adults cannot learn a new spatial category under favorable learning conditions (e.g., Boroditsky, Schmidt, and Phillips, 2003; Goldstone, 1998); but it does mean that such learning may be difficult in ordinary life. Which relations become easy to notice appears strongly influenced by the language we speak.

2 Number

Mathematical structure seems so compelling that it must be an inevitable aspect of human cognition. Dehaene (1997, p. 242) quotes French mathematician Charles Hermite: "I believe that the numbers and functions of analysis are not the arbitrary product of our spirits; I believe that they exist outside of us with the same character of necessity as the objects of objective reality…" Yet there is evidence that even simple numerical insight is not inevitable and that language plays a role in its development. We begin by describing two possible precursors of number concept, and then discuss how

their interactions with language may give rise to number knowledge.

Two preverbal capacities that have been implicated in accounts of number development are the analog magnitude system and a system for keeping track of small numbers of items. The analog magnitude system is a system shared broadly with other species that allows approximate judgments of quantity. It is what allows us (or a hamster) to choose a larger pile of grain over a smaller pile, or to notice that the amount of liquid in a container has decreased. This skill operates over even very large quantities, but its accuracy is limited by Weber's Law: the discriminability between two amounts is a function of their ratio. Thus, inaccuracies occur for magnitudes that are very close. The analog magnitude system is often modeled with the accumulator model (Meck and Church, 1985).

The other relevant nonverbal capacity is the ability to keep track of a small number of items. This ability can be thought of as a part of our general capacity for representing mental models of the world; some accounts (e.g., Carey, 2004; Spelke, 2000) have also linked it with Pylyshyn's (2001) notion of a preattentive object file system. In contrast to the analog magnitude system, the object file system operates over discrete representations and is capacity limited to roughly three or four objects.

We will consider two main classes of theories that assign a major role to language in number development. One theory centers on language as a link between modules, while a second broad class of theories focuses on the count system and other number terms as a means of promoting numeric insight.

2.1 *Language as link between modules*

Spelke (2000; 2003) and her colleagues theorize that language serves as a combinatorial system that links the two preverbal numeric modules discussed above – the object file and the analog magnitude system. Since neither of these two preverbal modules deals with *exact* large numbers, the combinatorial power of language is needed for the ability to represent exact large numbers. One line of support for this theory comes from a study with adult Russian–English bilinguals (Spelke and Tsivkin, 2001), which showed effects of language in the performance of exact arithmetic calculations. Bilingual participants were trained in one language on two kinds of problems: exact calculation problems and approximation problems. Participants were later tested in similar problems in the other language. Spelke and Tsivkin reasoned that if language is necessary for representing exact large numbers, then performance in exact calculation problems should deteriorate. However, approximate calculation skill should not be affected. This is indeed what they found: Bilinguals were able to transfer the new approximation skills across languages, but not the exact calculation skills.

2.2 Number language as cognitive toolkit

While the view that language acts as a link between modules recruits both the object file and the accumulator system, another view of how language learning supports number development relies primarily on the object file capacity (Carey, 2004; Mix, 2002). These accounts recognize that knowledge of the count routine does not by itself confer an understanding of numbers, but hold that learning the linguistic count sequence is crucial in the development of numbers. The binding of the numbers words to cardinal sets occurs slowly. A child may understand that *one* refers to an individual, but still regard *two*, *three*, and so on as referring to undefined larger sets. Counting seems to begin as a social routine, akin to a chant, and only later to become linked to cardinal numbers (Fuson, 1988; Wynn, 1990). A striking demonstration of this lag is the fact that even when a young child has just correctly counted a set of objects ("one, two, three, four"), she typically cannot respond "four" to the question "So how many are there?"

This suggests an intriguing possibility: that the linguistic count routine serves as an analogy that invites children to organize numerical quantities into an ordinal sequence. This possibility is most clearly articulated by Carey (2004; 2009) in her bootstrapping account (see also Gentner, 2010). According to this account, children first learn the counting routine as a kind of game, with no understanding of how it connects to cardinal numbers. Gradually, the child learns to attach number words to very small set sizes. The learning is at first piecemeal – even after binding *two* to sets of cardinality two, weeks or months may ensue before the child realizes that *three* refers to a set with three items (Carey, 2004; Mix, 2002; Mix, Sandhofer, and Baroody, 2005). But once a child reaches an understanding of roughly *three*, or sometimes *four*, the pattern changes. The child rapidly binds succeeding numbers to their cardinalities, and shows understanding of the successor principle, that every (natural) number has a natural successor. This insight – "If number word X refers to a set with cardinal value n, the next number word in the list refers to a set with cardinal value n + 1" (Carey, 2004) – occurs via an analogy between *counting one further* in the verbal count sequence and *increasing by one* in the set size.

But the analogy between the *counting one further in the count sequence* and *adding one in quantity* is very abstract. As Mix (2002; Mix et al., 2005) documents, children's early insights into how numbers connect to set size are often concrete and context-specific. For example, in Mix's (2002) diary study, at twenty months Spencer spontaneously brought from another room exactly two treats for the family's two dogs, and repeated this feat with perfect accuracy several times over the next few weeks. But he failed when asked to go get "train treats" for his two toy trains, suggesting that his command of "twoness" was highly context-bound.

Mix and colleagues have noted several kinds of early nonverbal experience that contribute to the gradual acquisition of numerical insight, including several kinds of routines that promote one-to-one correspondence (such as distributing candies among several people). They also suggest an important role for language in the development of cardinality: namely, that hearing two sets labeled with the same count word could prompt a comparison process that leads the child to notice their common number (Mix et al., 2005). This line is consistent with the idea that common language invites comparison (Gentner, 2003; Gentner and Namy, 1999; Loewenstein and Gentner, 2005) which in turn can support categorization (Gelman and Markman, 1987; Waxman and Klibanoff, 2000).

In opposition to the above proposals, Gelman and Gallistel argue that language has little if any role in the development of number. In their account, the analog magnitude system is the cognitive foundation of number knowledge (Dehaene, 1997; Gallistel and Gelman, 1992). Gallistel, Gelman, and Cordes (2005) argue further that the analog magnitude system, whose output is continuous rather than discrete, represents the real numbers. As how to language may play a role in number development, Gallistel and Gelman posit that "[A] system for arithmetic reasoning with real numbers evolved before language evolved. When language evolved, it picked out from the real numbers only the integers…" (Gallistel et al., 2005, p. 247). This position reverses the usual supposition of developmentalists and historians that understanding of the natural numbers appears first, followed by the integers, the rationals, and the reals.

2.3 Research on languages that lack full count systems

One line of support for the hypothesis that count terms are causally related to the development of number knowledge comes from studies of the Pirahã (Everett, 2005; Gordon, 2004), an Amazonian tribal group that uses what has been described as a "one-two-many" system of counting (hói, hoí, baagi [or aibai]). (See also Pica et al., 2004 for similar results for the Munduruku). Gordon administered several numerical tasks using objects familiar to the Pirahã, over numbers between one and ten. For example, the experimenter would place, say, five batteries on the table, and ask the participant to "make it the same" with another set of batteries. In another task, some nuts were put in a can, and then nuts were drawn out of the can one by one by the experimenter. After each withdrawal, participants were asked whether the can still contained nuts or was empty. The results were striking. The Pirahã participants performed with good accuracy for up to three items, but performance became merely approximate after three items. Nevertheless, performance beyond three was not random; it was consistent with the Weber fraction found in results of people performing magnitude estimation tasks. The Pirahã have the same ability to estimate numerosity as do English or French speakers; what they lack is a verbal counting system.

Striking as it is, this finding has been replicated by a later study of the Pirahã (Frank et al., 2008). Frank et al. conducted the same tasks as in Gordon's study and again found only approximate performance for numbers beyond three in tasks like the nuts-in-the-can task (though this time the Pirahã performed better on the simpler versions of the one-to-one matching task than they had in Gordon's study). An additional linguistic task administered by Frank et al. suggests that the count system of the Pirahã is even less precise than the previously suggested one-two-many system. In a numeral elicitation task, speakers were shown a series of either increasing (from one to ten) or decreasing (from ten to one) objects, and asked at each stage "how much/many are there?" While in the increasing elicitation condition the word hói was used only for one item, in the decreasing condition the same word was used for quantities as large as six. It appears that the Pirahã terms are not true numbers, but are relative to the size of the set – something more like "a few, more than a few, lots."

2.4 Effects of language on later development of mathematics

If number words are indeed crucial in the development of the number concept, then we might see different developmental patterns in number acquisition depending on the characteristics of number words in a given language. Miller and Stigler (1987) suggest that one important difference is the regularity of the number system. They noted that Chinese is more systematic than English in an important respect: Whereas both languages have unique words for one through ten, Chinese is far more regular in its two-digit numbers than is English. In Chinese, eleven is "ten one," twelve is "ten two," and so on throughout the teens, and the system continues in this regular fashion with "twenty-one," "twenty-two," and so on. Contrast this system with English, in which *eleven* and *twelve* are opaque and although *thirteen* through *nineteen* are partly transparent (if the child recognizes "teen" as "ten"), in addition, the order of tens and units reverses after twenty – we say *twenty-one*, *twenty-two*, and so on. Miller and Stigler hypothesized that a regular system like Chinese would be easier to learn and use (see also Fuson and Kwon, 1992). Consistent with this prediction, they found that Chinese preschoolers (aged four and five) were significantly better than their English-speaking peers in a counting task in which they had to count as high as they could (Miller et al., 1995). Both American children (ninety-four percent) and Chinese children (ninety-two percent) could count to ten, but while seventy-four percent of Chinese children could count to twenty, only forty-eight percent of American children could do so.

What about the effects of linguistic variability *within* a language – does the amount and quality of mathematical language influence children's learning of that domain? To find out, Klibanoff et al. (2006) recorded the kind of mathematical language used by preschool or daycare teachers and related it to measures of the growth of children's conventional mathematical knowledge over the school year. They included language for ordinality (e.g., "Point to the one that has more") and cardinality (e.g., "Point to four," given cards with varying numbers of items), as well as names for geometric shapes, the term "half," and so on. The results showed dramatic differences in how much math-related talk teachers provided, and further,

that the amount of teachers' math-related talk was significantly related to the growth of preschoolers' conventional mathematical knowledge over the school year and unrelated to their math knowledge at the start of the school year.

3 Theory of mind

Theory of mind refers to the ability to reason about mental states – beliefs, desires, intentions, and emotions. In large part, mental states are expressed via language, and hearing conversations about desires and intentions is one way of learning about others' mental states. But some researchers have taken the link between language and theory of mind further and have proposed that language plays a fundamental role in the development of theory of mind. Theories that invoke language differ as to which aspects of language – whether pragmatics and discourse structure, lexical semantics, or syntactic structure – are most fundamental for developing a theory of mind.

A key question in the development of theory of mind is how and when children become aware that other people's minds may not contain the same beliefs as their own mind. Performance on false belief tasks is one standard way of assessing whether children have this understanding. One classic false belief task, first introduced by Wimmer and Perner (1983), is the unseen displacement scenario. For example, three- to nine-year-old children are presented with a story in which Maxi puts his chocolate in the kitchen cupboard. While Maxi is away, his mother moves the chocolate to the drawer. Children are then asked where Maxi will look for his chocolate when he returns – in the cupboard or in the drawer. None of the three-year-olds correctly said that Maxi would look in the cupboard, whereas a majority of four-year-olds gave the correct answer.

Another type of false belief task is the "smarties" study (Gopnik and Astington, 1988; Perner, Leekham, and Wimmer, 1987), which can be used to assess children's insight into their own minds. In this task, the child is shown a smarties box (smarties being a type of candy), and asked what is in the box. The child readily answers "candy" and is then allowed to look inside, whereupon she discovers to her surprise that the box actually contains crayons. When the experimenter asks what the child originally thought was in the box, five-year-olds correctly say "candy," but most three-year-olds insist that they initially expected the candy box to contain crayons; some even claim to have said so out loud.

Many results from theory of mind studies suggest that the ability to represent people's epistemic states does not become firmly established until around four to six years of age.[6] By this age, many cognitive and linguistic skills are already quite advanced. Many theorists emphasize the importance of these skills without assigning language a special role (e.g., Gopnik and Wellman, 1992; Perner 1991). Others have argued that it is theory of mind that precedes language, rather than the reverse. In one version of this position, theory of mind stems from an innately developing module (Baron-Cohen, 1999), which may support children's understanding of mental language but does not require language for its development. A weaker position is that some degree of interpersonal insight – notably a sense of when joint attention is called for – is critical for language development (Baldwin, 1991; Tomasello, 1998).

However, a sizable body of research has argued for a role of language in the development of theory of mind. For example, Milligan, Astington, and Dack (2007) found in a metaanalysis of 104 false belief studies for children under age seven that language ability is a significant predictor of false belief understanding even when age is controlled. Overall, three major views have been proposed for how language may contribute to the development of theory of mind: the discourse pragmatic, the lexical semantic, and

the complementation syntax view. Although these three views are not mutually exclusive, they make different bets as to which aspect of language play a role in the development of theory of mind.

3.1 *Discourse pragmatic*

In the discourse pragmatic account, conversational pragmatics is critical in developing an understanding of other minds (Harris, 1999). Children first become aware of their own mental states, and through simulation or role taking processes, they use this awareness to infer the mental states of others. Back-and-forth discourse allows children to realize that they sometimes know what others do not, and vice versa. One line of support for this view comes from a correlational study that showed that deaf children who had more opportunities to participate in rich discourse interactions with others also performed better in false belief tasks (Peterson and Siegal, 2000). In another study, Dunn et al. (1991) observed naturalistic conversations between two-year-olds and their mothers. Seven months later, the children were queried on the understanding of other minds. They found that children's engagement in family conversation about feeling states was positively correlated with the ability to give correct explanations of false belief behaviors.

3.2 *Lexical semantics*

In the lexical semantics view, the acquisition of mental state terms such as *think, know*, and *believe* plays a crucial role in the development of the understanding of false beliefs (Astington, 1996; Bartsch and Wellman, 1995; Bretherton and Beeghly, 1982). Children begin to use mental state terms at about age two, especially perceptual and emotional terms (*see, hear, happy, sad, angry*). Starting at age three, children also begin to produce cognitive terms such as *think* and *know*, but it is not until the early school years that children show clear discrimination among terms such as *think, know*, and *guess* (Bartsch and Wellman, 1995; Bretherton and Beeghly,

---

[6]   However, some studies have found evidence of an ability to represent at least some mental states of others as early as fifteen months (Onishi and Baillargeon, 2005). How these early sensitivities relate to later patterns remain to be worked out.

1982). The lexical hypothesis is that children acquire these mental state terms in conversation; parents use them to refer to the mental states that the child is experiencing, allowing the child to attach the terms to her own mental states. The child also notices that these terms can apply to other people, inviting the child to attribute the corresponding mental states to others as well as to herself (Astington, 1996).

To test whether mothers' language influences the development of theory of mind, Ruffman, Slade, and Crowe (2002) conducted a longitudinal study in which they asked mothers to describe pictures to eighty-two children at three time points spanning a one-year period. They found that mothers' use of mental state utterances at early time points was correlated with children's later theory of mind understanding. The result held true even when a number of potential intervening factors were accounted for, such as children's age, their language ability, their own use of mental state language, their earlier theory of mind understanding, and also mothers' education and other kinds of mothers' utterances. Ruffman et al. concluded that mothers' mental state utterances play a causal role in the development of theory of mind.

3.3 *Complementation syntax*

Another prominent view is that acquiring the syntax of sentential complements is a critical factor in the development of false belief understanding (de Villiers and de Villiers, 2000). In a sentential complement construction, a sentence takes a full clause as its object complement: for example, "Mary thinks that John is at home." This construction makes it relatively transparent to see that the truth value of the sentence as a whole can differ from that of the embedded proposition: that is, the fact that Mary *thinks* that John is at home does not necessarily mean that John *is* at home. De Villiers and de Villiers note that communication constructions such as "*x says that p*" provide overt evidence for this disassociation when *p* is known to be untrue. In this way, communication verbs can serve

to bootstrap children's understanding of the use of *think*: children learn to deal with false complements via *say*, and by analogy come to understand that *think* too can take a false complement.

One line of evidence for this hypothesis comes from a longitudinal study with preschool children that found that performance on false belief tasks was predicted by performance in interpreting sentences containing mental and communication verbs with complements (de Villiers and Pyers, 2002). To gauge mastery of sentential complements, children were given scenarios like the following: "She said she found a monster under her chair, but it was really the neighbor's dog" and then were asked "What did she say?" Children's responses were counted correct as long as they said "a monster." The children also carried out false belief tasks such as the unseen displacement task and the unexpected content task described earlier. A positive correlation was found between mastery of sentential complements and success in false belief tasks.

Further evidence was found among oral deaf children who are delayed in language learning (de Villiers and de Villiers, 2003). To control for any effects of language required by the false belief tasks themselves, nonverbal false belief tasks were used. In one task, the experimenter hid a sticker in one of the four identical boxes while a screen obscured the hiding from the child. On the test trial, two "helping" adults – one wearing a blindfold and one who could see the hiding event – each pointed to a box after the screen was raised, and the child had to choose whose advice to follow. In the other task, children were shown a sequence of pictures depicting an unexpected content event and had to complete the sequence with either a surprise face (correct) or a neutral face. The performance of these children on false belief tasks was predicted by their performance in the complement comprehension task.

Most recently, Pyers and Senghas (2009) took advantage of a naturally occurring change in the linguistic affordances of an emerging language – Nicaraguan Sign Language (NSL) – to test whether language promotes false belief understanding over and above social experience. NSL first appeared in the 1970s among deaf children entering special education schools (Senghas, Kita, and Özyürek, 2004). When the roughly fifty original children (who typically had developed their own idiosyncratic homesign gesture systems; Goldin-Meadow, 2003) were brought together, they developed an early form of NSL as a common language. This was further enriched by the second cohort of children in the mid-1980s. Senghas and colleagues report that even today, the second cohort exhibits a more developed form of the language than the older first cohort (Senghas and Coppola, 2001; Senghas et al., 2004). In particular, the second cohort's language includes more mental state verbs than the first cohort's version – setting the stage for a test of whether possession of mental state verbs supports reasoning about others' mental states. Important, aside from their language differences, the two cohorts have similar histories of schooling and social interaction.

Pyers and Senghas used a low verbal false belief task to test speakers from the two cohorts of Nicaraguan signers: Participants were given a sequence of pictures depicting unseen displacement events (following a false belief plot), and then had to choose which of two final pictures correctly depicted the final event. The results showed a strong effect of language: The second cohort (average age 17.5 years) by far outperformed the first cohort (average age 26.8 years). Out of four test trials, the second cohort solved on average 3.5 trials, as contrasted with .5 trials for the first cohort. Interesting, when tested two years later, some of the first cohort who had gained mental state verbs also performed better in the false belief task. Overall, these results support the idea that language provides cognitive tools that support theory of mind, even well into adulthood.

4 Summary

While the issues are far from resolved, the evidence reviewed here suggests that language may influence the development of conceptions of space, mind, and number. Language can foster cognitive development through various routes. The language we speak provides us with tools for dissecting space into finer categories, and for connecting those concepts into systems that permit combinatorial inferences. Language can also invite a systematic representation (as in the Chinese numerals, or in the fluent numerical abilities of English speakers as compared to the Pirahã speakers). These representations can support real-world tasks such as navigation and calculation. They also support abstract thinking, such as using spatial relations to reason about time, to plot kinship relations, or to comprehend graphs and other figures that use spatial patterns to depict nonspatial phenomena.

An interesting further question is: What is the time course of this linguistic influence? The available research suggests that language effects are not immediate. It is not enough to simply learn a set of terms (even supposing that their full meanings are understood – a dubious assumption in early development). We suspect that some degree of entrenchment must occur before the new representation is sufficiently robust to have cognitive effects. For example, in the Loewenstein and Gentner (2005) spatial mapping task, hearing spatial terms such as *top*, *middle*, *bottom* improved the performance of younger, but not older, children. Apparently, the younger children knew the terms well enough to benefit from hearing them, but not well enough to access them spontaneously. The performance of the older children is consistent with the possibility that the spatial system conveyed by the terms was sufficiently entrenched to come to mind with or without the terms.

In some cases linguistic patterns may give rise to a habitual mode of construal. But in general, the evidence suggests that the influence of language is far from absolute. Human representation is rich and varied, and no one system of encoding is able to govern all of human representation. There is also reason to believe that there is influence in the reverse direction, from cognition to language. Some systems of categories are more natural – easier to learn and use – than others. For example, Gentner and Bowerman (2009) have suggested that the typological prevalence of a given semantic system across languages may afford an estimate of its cognitive naturalness and concomitant ease of learning.

There are many open questions. For example, in which semantic arenas do we find the largest effects of language – are there larger effects of language in relatively abstract arenas, such as mathematics and time, than in more concrete domains such as color? Does language for emotions and for thought processes influence the way in which we construe our own minds? Does learning a technical language influence adult cognition in ways similar to the developmental patterns discussed here? Addressing these questions will give us a deeper understanding of how language affects the development of thought.

References

Acredolo, L. P. (1978). Development of spatial orientation in infancy. *Developmental Psychology*, 14, 224–34.

Astington, J. W. (1996). What is theoretical about the child's understanding of mind? A Vygotskian view of its development. In Carruthers, P. & Smith, P. K. (Eds.) *Theories of theories of mind* (pp. 184–99). Cambridge University Press.

Baldwin, D. A. (1991). Infants' contribution to the achievement of joint reference. *Child Development*, 62, 875–90.

Bartsch, K. & Wellman, H. (1995). *Children talk about the mind.* New York: Oxford University Press.

Baron-Cohen, S. (1999). The evolution of a theory of mind. In Corballis, M. C. & Lea, SEG (Eds.) *The descent of mind: Psychological perspectives on hominid evolution* (pp. 261–77). New York: Oxford University Press.

Bohnemeyer, J. & Brown, P. (2007). Standing divided: dispositional predicates and locative predications in two Mayan languages. *Linguistics*, 45(5).

Boroditsky, L. (2001). Does language shape thought? Mandarin and English speakers' conceptions of time. *Cognitive Psychology*, 43(1), 1–22.

Boroditsky, L., Schmidt, L., & Phillips, W. (2003). Sex, Syntax, and Semantics. In Gentner, D. & Goldin-Meadow, G. (Eds.) *Language in Mind: Advances in the study of Language and Cognition* (pp. 61–80). Cambridge: MIT Press.

Bowerman, M. (1980). The structure and origin of semantic categories in the language-learning child. In Foster, M. L. & Brande, S. (Eds.) *Symbol as sense* (pp. 277–99). New York: Academic Press.

(1981). The child's expression of meaning: Expanding relationships among lexicon, syntax and morphology. In Winitz, H. (Ed.) *Native language and foreign language acquisition* (Vol. 379, pp. 172–89). New York: New York Academy of Sciences.

(1989). Learning a semantic system: What role do cognitive predispositions play? In Rice, M. L. & Schiefelbusch, R. L. (Eds.) *The teachability of language* (pp. 133–69). Baltimore, MD: Paul H. Brooks.

(1996). Learning how to structure space for language: A crosslinguistic perspective. In Bloom, P., Peterson, M. A., Nadel, L., & Garrett, M. F. (Eds.) *Language and space* (pp. 385–436). Cambridge: MIT Press.

Bowerman, M. & Choi, S. (2003). Space under construction: Language specific spatial categorization in first language acquisition. In Gentner, D. & Goldin-Meadow, S. (Eds.) *Language in Mind: Advances in the study of Language and Cognition* (pp. 387–428). Cambridge: MIT Press.

Bowerman, M. & Levinson, S. (Eds.). (2001). *Language acquisition and conceptual development* (preface, introduction). Cambridge, UK: Cambridge University Press.

Bremner, J. G. (1978). Egocentric versus allocentric spatial coding in nine-month-old infants: Factors influencing the choice of code. *Developmental Psychology*, 14, 346–55.

Bretherton, I. & Beeghly, M. (1982). Talking about internal states: The acquisition of an explicit theory of mind. *Developmental Psychology*, 18, 906–21.

Brown, P. (1994). The ins and ons of Tzeltal locative expressions: The semantics of static descriptions of location. *Linguistics*, 32, 743–90.

Call, J. (2001). Object permanence in orangutans (Pongopygmaeus), chimpanzees (Pantroglodytes), and children (Homosapiens). *Journal of Comparative Psychology*, 115, 159–71.

Carey, S. (2004). Bootstrapping and the origin of concepts. *Daedalus*, 133.

(2009). *The origin of concepts*. Oxford University Press, USA.

Casad, E. H. & Langacker, R. W. (1985). "Inside" and "outside" in Cora Grammar. *International Journal of American Linguistics, 51*, 247–81.

Casasola, M. (2005). Can language do the driving? The effect of linguistic input on infants' categorization of support spatial relations. *Developmental Psychology, 41*, 183–92.

(2008). The development of infants' spatial categories. *Current Directions in Psychological Science, 17*, 21–5.

Choi, S. & Bowerman, M. (1991). Learning to express motion events in English and Korean: The influence of language-specific lexicalization patterns. *Cognition, 41*, 83–121.

Choi, S., McDonough, L., Bowerman, M., & Mandler, J. M. (1999). Early sensitivity to language-specific spatial categories in English and Korean. *Cognitive Development, 14*, 241–68.

Dehaene, S. (1997). *The number sense: How the mind creates mathematics*. New York: Oxford University Press.

Dessalegn, B. & Landau, B. (2008). More than meets the eye: The role of language in binding and maintaining feature conjunctions. *Psychological Science, 19*, 189–95.

de Villiers, J. & de Villiers, P. (2000). Linguistic determinism and the understanding of false beliefs. In Mitchell, P. & Riggs, K. J. (Eds.) *Children's reasoning and the mind* (pp. 191–228). Hove, England: Psychology Press.

(2003) Language for thought: Coming to understand false beliefs. In Gentner, D. & Goldin-Meadow, S. (Eds.) *Language in Mind: Advances in the Study of Language and Thought* (pp. 335–84). Cambridge, MA: MIT Press.

de Villiers, J. G. & Pyers, J. E. (2002). Complements to cognition: A longitudinal study of the relationship between complex syntax and false-belief understanding. *Cognitive Development, 17*, 1037–60.

Dunn, J., Brown, J. R., Slomkowski, C., Tesla, C., & Youngblade, L. (1991). Young children's understanding of other people's feelings and beliefs: Individual differences and their antecedents. *Child Development, 62*, 1352–66.

Everett, D. (2005). Cultural constraints on grammar and cognition in Pirahã: Another look at the design features of human language. *Current Anthropology, 76*, 621–46.

Frank, M. C., Everett, D., Fedorenko, E., & Gibson, E. (2008). Number as a cognitive technology: Evidence from Pirahã language and cognition. *Cognition, 108*, 819–24.

Fuson, K. C. (1988). *Children's counting and concepts of number*. New York: Springer Verlag.

Fuson, K. C. & Kwon, Y. (1992). Learning addition and subtraction: Effects of number words and other cultural tools. In Bideaud, J., Meljac, C., & Fischer, J. P. (Eds.) *Pathways to number: Children's developing numerical abilities* (pp. 283–306). Hillsdale, NJ: Erlbaum.

Gallistel, C. R. (1990). *The organization of learning*. Cambridge, MA: MIT Press.

Gallistel, C. R. & Gelman, R. (1992). Preverbal and verbal counting and computation. *Cognition, 44*, 43–74.

Gallistel, C. R., Gelman, R., & Cordes, S. (2005). The cultural and evolutionary history of the real numbers. In Levinson, S. & Jaisson, P. (Eds.) *Culture and evolution*. Cambridge, MA: MIT Press.

Gelman, S. A. & Markman, E. M. (1987). Young children's inductions from natural kinds: The role of categories and appearances. *Child Development, 58*, 1532–41.

Gentner, D. (1982). Why nouns are learned before verbs: Linguistic relativity versus natural partitioning. In Kuczaj, S. A. (Ed.) *Language development: Vol. 2. Language, thought and culture* (pp. 301–34). Hillsdale, NJ: Lawrence Erlbaum Associates.

(2003). Why we're so smart. In Gentner, D. & Goldin-Meadow, S. (Eds.) *Language in mind: Advances in the study of language and thought* (pp. 195–236). Cambridge, MA: MIT Press.

(2010). Bootstrapping children's learning: Analogical processes and symbol systems. *Cognitive Science, 34(5)*, 752–75.

Gentner, D. & Bowerman, M. (2009). Why some spatial semantic categories are harder to learn than others: The Typological Prevalence hypothesis. In Guo, J., Lieven, E. Ervin-Tripp, S., Budwig, N.,. Özçaliskan, S., & Nakamura, K. (Eds.) *Crosslinguistic approaches to the psychology of language: Research in the tradition of Dan Isaac Slobin* (pp. 465–80). NY: Lawrence Erlbaum Associates.

Gentner, D. & Christie, S. (2010). Mutual bootstrapping between language and analogical processing. *Language and Cognition, 2(2)*, 261–83.

Gentner, D. & Goldin-Meadow, S. (2003). Whither Whorf. In Gentner, D. & Goldin-Meadow, S. (Eds.) *Language in mind: Advances in the study of language and thought* (pp. 3–14). Cambridge, MA: MIT Press.

Gentner, D., & Namy, L. (1999). Comparison in the development of categories. *Cognitive Development, 14*, 487–513.

Gentner, D., Ozyürek, A., Goldin-Meadow, S., & Gurcanli, O. (2008). *Spatial language potentiates spatial cognition: Evidence from deaf home-signers*. Presented at the American Association for the Advancement of Science annual meeting.

Gentner, D. & Toupin, C. (1986). Systematicity and surface similarity in the development of analogy. *Cognitive Science*, 10, 277–300.

Gleitman, L. & Papafragou, A. (2005). Language and thought. In Holyoak, K. & Morrison, B. (Eds.) *Cambridge Handbook of Thinking and Reasoning* (pp. 633–61). Cambridge: Cambridge University Press.

Goldin-Meadow, S. (2003). *The resilience of language: What gesture creation in deaf children can tell us about how all children learn language*. New York: Psychology Press.

Goldstone, R. L. (1998). Perceptual learning. *Annual Review Psychology*, 49, 585–612.

Gopnik, A. & Astington, J. W. (1988). Children's understanding of representational change and its relation to the understanding of false belief and the appearance-reality distinction. *Child Development*, 59, 26–37.

Gopnik, A. & Wellman, H. (1992). Why the child's theory of mind really is a theory. *Mind and Language*, 7, 145–71.

Gordon, P. (2004). Numerical cognition without words: Evidence from Amazonia. *Science*, 306, 406–99.

Gumperz, J. J. & Levinson, S. C. (1996). *Rethinking linguistic relativity*. Cambridge, England: Cambridge University Press.

Harris, P. L. (1999). Individual differences in understanding emotion: the role of attachment status and psychological discourse. *Attachment & Human Development*, 3, 307–24.

Haun, DBM, Rapold, C., Call, J., Janzen, G., Levinson, S. C. (2006). Cognitive cladistics and cultural override in Hominid spatial cognition. *Proceedings of the National Academy of Sciences*, 103, 17568–73.

Hespos, S. & Spelke, E. (2004). Conceptual precursors to language. *Nature*, 430, 453–6.

Hunt, E. & Agnoli, F. (1991). The Whorfian hypothesis: A cognitive psychology perspective. *Psychological Review*, 98, 377–89.

Imai, M. & Gentner, D. (1997). A crosslinguistic study of early word meaning: Universal ontology and linguistic influence. *Cognition*, 62, 169–200.

Imai, M. & Mazuka, R. (2003). Reevaluating linguistic relativity: Language-specific categories and the role of universal ontological knowledge in the construal of individuation. In Gentner, D. & Goldin-Meadow, S. (Eds.) *Language in mind: Advances in the study of language and cognition* (pp. 429–64). Cambridge, MA: MIT Press.

Klibanoff, R. S., Levine, S. C., Huttenlocher, J., Vasilyeva, M., & Hedges, L. V. (2006). Preschool children's mathematical knowledge: The effect of teacher "math talk." *Developmental Psychology*, 42, 50–69.

Levinson, S. C. (1996). Relativity in spatial conception and description. In Gumperz, J. J. & Levinson, S. C. (Eds.) *Rethinking linguistic relativity* (pp. 177–202). Cambridge, MA: Cambridge University Press.

(2003). Language and mind: Let's get the issues straight! In Gentner, D. & Goldin-Meadow, S. (Eds.) *Language in mind: Advances in the study of language and cognition* (pp. 25–46). Cambridge, MA: MIT Press.

Levinson, S., Kita, S., Haun, D., & Rasch, B. (2002). Returning the tables: Language affects spatial reasoning. *Cognition*, 84, 155–88.

Levinson, S. C., & Brown, P. (1994). Immanuel Kant among the Tenejapans: Anthropology as applied philosophy. *Ethos*, 22(1), 3–41.

Loewenstein, J. & Gentner, D. (2005). Relational language and the development of relational mapping. *Cognitive Psychology*, 50, 315–53.

Li, P. & Gleitman, L. (2002). Turning the tables: Language and spatial reasoning. *Cognition*, 83, 265–94.

Lucy, J. A. (1994). *Grammatical categories and cognition*. Cambridge: Cambridge University Press.

Lupyan, G. (2008). From chair to "chair": A representational shift account of object labeling effects on memory. *Journal of Experimental Psychology: General*, 137(2), 348–69.

Lupyan, G., Rakison, D. H., & McClelland, J. L. (2007). Language is not just for talking: labels facilitate learning of novel categories. *Psychological Science*, 18(12), 1077–83.

Majid, A., Bowerman, M., Kita, S., Haun, DBM, & Levinson, S. C. (2004). Can language restructure cognition? The case for space. *TRENDS in Cognitive Sciences*, 8, 108–14.

Markman, E. M. (1989). *Categorization and naming in children: Problems of induction*. Cambridge, MA: MIT Press.

McDonough, L., Choi, S., & Mandler, J. (2003). Understanding spatial relations: Flexible infants, lexical adults. *Cognitive Psychology*, 46, 229–59.

Meck, W. H., Church, R. M., & Gibbon, J. (1985). Temporal integration in duration and number discrimination. *Journal of Experimental Psychology: Animal Behavior Processes*, 11, 591–7.

Miller, K. F. & Stigler, J. W. (1987). Counting in Chinese: Cultural variation in a basic cognitive skill. *Cognitive Development*, 2, 279–305.

Miller, K. F., Smith, C. M., Zhu, J., & Zhang, H. (1995). Preschool origins of cross-national differences in mathematical competence: The role of number-naming systems. *Psychological Science*, 6, 56–60.

Milligan, K., Astington, J. W., & Dack, L. A. (2007). Language and theory of mind: Meta-analysis of the relation between language ability and false-belief understanding. *Child Development*, 77, 622–46.

Mix, K. S. (2002). The construction of number concepts. *Cognitive Development*, 17, 1345–63.

Mix, K. S., Sandhofer, C. M., & Baroody, A. J. (2005) Number words and number concepts: the interplay of verbal and nonverbal quantification in early childhood. In Kail, R. V. (Ed.) *Advances in Child Development and Behavior* (Vol. 33, pp. 305–46). New York: Academic Press.

Oakes, L. M. & Ribar, R. J. (2005). A comparison of infants' categorization in paired and successive presentation familiarization tasks. *Infancy*, 7, 85–98.

Onishi, K. H., & Baillargeon, R. (2005). Do 15-month-old infants understand false beliefs? *Science*, 308, 255–8.

Pederson, E. (1995). Language as context, language as means: Spatial cognition and habitual language use. *Cognitive Linguistics*, 6, 33–62.

Perner, J. (1991). *Understanding the representational mind*. Cambridge, MA: MIT Press.

Perner, J., Leekham, S. R., & Wimmer, H. (1987). Three-year-olds' difficulty with false belief: The case for a conceptual deficit. *British Journal of Developmental Psychology*, 5, 125–37.

Peterson, C. C. & Siegal, M. (2000). Insights into a theory of mind from deafness and autism. *Mind & Language*, 15, 123–45.

Pica, P., Lemer, C., Izard, V., & Dehaene, S. (2004). Exact and approximate arithmetic in an Amazonian indigene group. *Science*, 306, 499–503.

Piaget, J. & Inhelder, B. (1967). *The child's conception of space*. New York: Norton.

Pick, H. L. Jr. (1993). Organization of spatial knowledge in children. In Eilan, N., McCarthy, R., & Brewer, B. (Eds.) *Spatial Representation: Problems in Philosophy and Psychology* (pp. 31–42). Blackwell Publishing.

Pyers, J. & Senghas, A. (2009). Language promotes false-belief understanding: Evidence from Nicaraguan Sign Language. *Psychological Science*, 20, 805–12.

Pylyshyn, Z. (2001). Visual indexes, preconceptual objects, and situated vision. *Cognition*, 80, 127–58.

Ruffman, T., Slade, L., & Crowe, E. (2002). The relation between children's and mothers' mental state language and theory of mind understanding. *Child Development*, 73, 734–51.

Senghas, A. & Coppola, M. (2001). Children creating language: How Nicaraguan Sign Language acquired a spatial grammar. *Psychological Science*, 12, 323–8.

Senghas, A., Kita, S., & Özyürek, A. (2004). Children creating core properties of language: Evidence from an emerging sign language in Nicaragua. *Science*, 305, 1779–82.

Slobin, D. I. (1996). From "thought and language" to "thinking for speaking." In Gumperz, J. J. & Levinson, S. C. (Eds.) *Rethinking linguistic relativity* (pp. 70–96). Cambridge, MA: Cambridge University Press.

(2003). Language and thought online: Cognitive consequences of linguistic relativity. In Gentner, D. & Goldin-Meadow, S. (Eds.) *Language in mind: Advances in the study of language and cognition* (pp. 157–92). Cambridge, MA: MIT Press.

Spelke, E. S. (2000). Core knowledge. *American Psychologist*, 55(11), 1233–43.

(2003). What makes us smart? Core knowledge and natural language. In Gentner, D., & Goldin-Meadow, S. (Eds.) *Language in mind: Advances in the study of language and cognition* (pp. 277–312). Cambridge, MA: MIT Press.

Spelke, E. S. & Tsivkin, S. (2001). Initial knowledge and conceptual change: space and number. In Bowerman, M. & Levinson, S. C. (Eds.) *Language acquisition and conceptual development* (pp. 70–100). Cambridge, UK: Cambridge University Press.

Talmy, L. (1975). Semantics and syntax of motion. In Kimball, J. (Ed.) *Syntax and semantics* (Vol. 4, pp. 181–238). New York: Academic Press.

(1985). Lexicalization patterns: Semantic structure in lexical forms. In Shopen, T. (Ed.) *Language, typology and syntactic description: Vol. 3. Grammatical categories and the lexicon* (pp. 57–149). New York: Cambridge University Press.

Tomasello, M. (1998). Reference: Intending that others jointly attend. *Pragmatics and Cognition*, 6, 229–43.

Tomasello, M. & Call, J. (1997). *Primate Cognition*. New York, NY: Oxford University Press.

Vygotsky, L. S. (1962). *Thought and language*. Cambridge, MA: MIT Press. (Original work published 1934).

Waxman, S. R. (2002). Links between object categorization and naming: Origins and emergence in human infants. In Rakison, D. H. & Oakes, L. M. (Eds.) *Early category and concept development: Making sense of the blooming, buzzing confusion* (pp. 213–41). NY, New York: Oxford University Press.

Waxman, S. R. & Klibanoff, R. S. (2000). The role of comparison in the extension of novel adjectives. *Developmental Psychology*, 36, 571–81.

Waxman, S. R. & Markow, D. B. (1995). Words as invitations to form categories: Evidence from 12- to 13-month-old infants. *Cognitive Psychology*, 29(3), 257–302.

Whorf, B. L. (1956). *Language, thought and reality: Selected writings*. Cambridge, MA: Technology Press of Massachusetts Institute of Technology.

Wimmer, H. & Perner, J. (1983). Beliefs about beliefs: Representation and constraining function of wrong beliefs in young children's understanding of deception. *Cognition*, 13, 41–68.

Wolff, P. & Holmes, K. (2011). Linguistic relativity. *WIREs Cognitive Science*, 2, 253–265.

Wynn, K. (1990). Children's understanding of counting. *Cognition*, 36, 155–193.

Xu, F. (2002). The role of language in acquiring object kind concepts in infancy. *Cognition*, 85, 223–50.

CHAPTER 34

Language, Thought, and … Brain?

Monica Gonzalez-Marquez

Introduction

While addressing a German crowd in Berlin, President Kennedy exclaimed, "*Ich bin ein Berliner.*" Translating directly from English to German, it is completely sensible to imagine he was saying, "I am a person from Berlin," or from a speech act analysis, "I ally myself with the people of Berlin." Actually, when German-speaking people express this sentiment they do not use the indefinite article *ein* but instead say "*Ich bin Berliner.*" What the audience actually heard was, "I am a donut." A Berliner is a German pastry. Imagine what would have happened if he had given the speech in Hamburg!

Humor aside, just what are the implications of the use – or absence – of an indefinite article mapping to concepts as different as *pastry, person from Berlin,* or *ally to people from Berlin?*" Is the use of an article somehow indicative of how thought works? And in contrast with President Kennedy's faux pas, does the article's use point to a difference in thought between English and German speakers? Some language researchers have argued that it does, at least in some

circumstances (Gumperz and Levinson, 1996; Lakoff, 1987; Whorf, 1956. For opposing views see Li and Gleitman, 2002; Munnich and Landau, 2003). But where does the brain fit in? Despite being the seat of language and thought, it is not often included in the equation. Research in linguistics and psychology has focused largely on syntax, pragmatics, polysemy, reading, speech, sentence processing, and the like. And with good reason. Until very recently, the only means for sound investigation was behavior. Whatever questions researchers might have had about the brain were filtered through observations of neural trauma patients. The situation has since changed. New technologies have made it possible to ask pointed questions about how the interaction between language and thought is made manifest in the normal brain. Yet, though research on brain structure and function has increased greatly, there are key questions directly related to language and thought that remain largely unexamined. In this chapter I will explore the possibility of functional and structural neural consequences to speaking a given language. I will then extend this exploration from the case of a single language to the case of multiple languages stored within a single brain. I will conclude by considering recent findings in the cognitive neuroscience of bilingualism.

1 Describing the question

1.1 *Neuroplasticity*

Neuroplasticity is the ability of the brain to restructure itself. Processing centers in the brain can change location in response to learning or trauma. For example, people who become blind and must learn to function without vision report increased sensitivity in the surviving senses. When reading Braille, a tactile activity, blind people show activation of the primary visual cortex (Pons, 1996; Sadato et al., 1996). Something akin occurs with deaf individuals. Area MS-MST (V5) processes visual motion information. Deaf individuals show increased activation in the left hemisphere when processing motion information (Bavelier et al., 2001). The authors attribute the shift to the fact that language tends to be left-hemisphere lateralized, and ASL, as a sign language, uses hand motion configurations instead of sound. They argue that the confluence of language with a motion modality produces increased activity in MS-MST in the left hemisphere. The common finding is that activation in hearing individuals is almost evenly distributed between the hemispheres with a slight bias to the right. Restructuring is also found in people who lose the use of parts of their bodies because of stroke. Though a few years ago patients suffering stroke were told that they would simply have to live with the resulting loss of motor function, now most clinics offer rehabilitation therapy. Patients are guided in teaching their brain to recruit surrounding neural tissue to replace what was damaged with many achieving near normal function.

The expression of plasticity is not limited to sensory adaptation or pathology. FMRI scans of musicians have shown that primary motor cortex, the cerebellum, and the corpus callosum showed structural differences in musicians when compared to nonmusicians (Gaser and Schlaug, 2003). The primary motor cortex and the cerebellum are involved in movement and coordination. The corpus callosum facilitates communication between the brain hemispheres. Presumably, the specialized behavior of musicians imposes a greater processing load on these areas of the brain than in nonmusicians, and the brain responds in much the same way as a muscle would: It gets larger.[1] More recent research has found patterns of relative thickening in the cerebral cortex of people who regularly practice meditation (Lazar, et al., 2005.) Here, neural change appears distributed across the cortex in a consistent configuration, prompting the authors to hypothesize that a different type of meditation might produce a different pattern of thickening.

1.2 *Attention*

At face value the previous examples may seem unrelated. The characteristic they share is their dependence on attention. The blind must redirect attention expectations from vision to the other senses. The deaf using ASL increase attention to hand-based communicative motion. The stroke patient increases attention to parts of the body no longer working properly. The musician increases focus on the elements comprising music.[2] The student of meditation learns to dramatically decrease attention to the mental and physical environment by directing attention to a single element with the goal of mental stillness. Each of these practices results in a measurable neural manifestation. Might the same be possible for speaking a given language or languages?

---

1 For the sake of accuracy, in motor cortex, what increased in size was the intrasulcal length of the posterior bank of the precentral gyrus. No increase in actual neural tissue volume was reported.

2 For those interested, Ross, Olson, and Gore (2003) have conducted research on the interface between being blind and being a musician. The authors claim that the neuroplasticity resulting from increased focus to the other senses, specifically audition, may result in advanced musical skills such as perfect pitch.

Language can also be described as an attention-directing process (Slobin, 1996; Talmy, 2000, 2007a,b). There are well-supported behavioral studies in which the operant component can be described as language as attention. One example comes from phonetics. When infants are first born, they are sensitive to all of the humanly producible language sounds. As a child's exposure to her native language(s) increases, she quickly loses sensitivity to sounds not relevant to those languages. By adulthood, she will not only have difficulty producing them, she will also have difficulty distinguishing them (Werker and Tees, 1984). This phenomenon is responsible for the difficulty most of us experience in learning a new language as adults, that is, we strain our ears to grasp the nuances of the new language's sounds, while contorting our mouths trying to reproduce them, usually to no avail.

Another example comes from Melissa Bowerman's seminal work on spatial language (see Bowerman, 1996 for a review). English uses a system of prepositions to mark spatial relationships between objects. For example *in* is typically used to describe a type of containing relationship, that is, "the marble is in the vase." In Korean, the relationship between objects can also be "tight" or "loose." A key in a keyhole is described as a tight relationship as the keyhole can be thought of as closely wrapped around the key. A small marble in a large vase is a loose relationship because contact between the objects is limited, despite the fact that the vase contains the marble. Studies with infants from both English-speaking and Korean-speaking families have shown that before their native language is cognitively established the infants are sensitive to the differences in relationships. It is only after the infants from English-speaking families have received considerable exposure to English that they lose sensitivity to the tight fit, loose fit relationships. Their attention is concentrated toward spatial relationships deemed relevant to their target language, and thus considerably lessened to those that are not. Because loose/tight relationships are considered important for Korean, the infants

from Korean-speaking families remain sensitive, and learn to mark them linguistically with the appropriate morpheme.

There are obvious differences between language as attention, as described in the examples from phonetics and from spatial cognition, and the examples of neural plasticity described earlier. The most important is that the majority of the neural changes reported have resulted from attentional changes occurring long after the onset of language, with the exception of congenital blindness, where visual cortex is reassigned to other types of sensory processing during development. In normal circumstances, both meditation and music require that development be well advanced before learning can begin. Language is different in that the focusing on different aspects of the environment to the exclusion of others is a normal and necessary component of human development. Ontology aside, there is no single human language that marks every object, process, and relationship in the environment, likely because there is simply too much to mark, and so a language must pick and choose from among the vast possibilities only those elements that it deems important (why "this" and not "that" is the subject of intense speculation). Our question then, is if the attention directing properties of a language might also result in Language-Specific Neural Differences (LSNDs), measurable and significant differences in brain structure and function.[3]

2 Theoretical background

Cognitive science provides two general theoretical frameworks for understanding the relationship between language and thought. The first is modularity, as described by Fodor

---

3 I will reiterate that this chapter is an exploration. Concrete evidence in support or against the question is lacking. I say this now so as to direct the reader away from the suspense of an easy answer and to the nature of the question itself. The question is pursued because it remains largely unconsidered in the literature, a fact that raises other questions about our assumptions about language and its place in cognition.

(1983). The second is linguistic relativity, as put forth by Sapir and Whorf.

2.1 *Modularity*

The brain is arguably structured into different areas responsible for processing different types of information. As such, modularity is a basic tenet of neuroscience. Any introductory course in cognitive neuroscience will spend considerable time discussing how sensory-motor cortex processes sensory-motor information, visual cortex processes visual information, and so forth. Fodor (1983) took this idea one step further, developing a theory in which cognitive processes are genetically specified, functionally independent modules. He argued that a module was a processing center hardwired into the brain, dedicated to taking information from the environment though the senses, and processing it such that it could then be used for domain general processing. Modules were also encapsulated, meaning that though the output of modules could be used by other modules, their internal structure was completely closed off from other brain processes.

In keeping with Fodor's model, language came to be considered a module in light of findings such as the phonetics McGurk effect (McGurk and MacDonald, 1976). Subjects have been shown to integrate visual information of one place of articulation (POA) with auditory information from a second such that the perceived sound appears to occur at a midway point between the two actual POAs. For example, when a subject is presented with a video of someone making the sound *ga* (velar POA) while listening to someone else make the sound *ba* (bilabial POA) what they hear is *da* (alveolar POA). The alveolar ridge is located about halfway between the back palate and the lips. The general idea behind interpreting the effect as evidence for the modularity of language was that the finding was systematic, rather than simply the result of guessing (Frazier, 1999 but see Spivey, Richardson, and Gonzalez-Marquez, 2006 for a different interpretation).

Modularity as applied to language makes predictions on two levels. The first describes the internal structure of language, and the second its relationship to other cognitive processes. In modularity, the variously identified internal components of language are autonomous (Chomsky, 2000; Crain and Lillo-Martin, 1999; Pinker, 1989.) Phonology, syntax, semantics, and the lexicon are considered submodules of the language module. They are completely independent of each other insofar as they do not affect each other's structure or processing, although they do rely on each other for input. Crain and Lillo-Martin(1999) describe their relationship as bottom-up and hierarchical. In this model, the semantics submodule is fed input from syntax strictly unidirectionally. It is never the case that semantics dictates the structure in syntax. In addition, the syntactic submodule holds a privileged position. The structure it produces is believed to be generally the same for all human languages.

According to modularity, the position of language in relation to the rest of cognition is governed largely by three principles (Bates 1994). These are innateness, localization, and domain specificity. Innateness holds that language is genetically predetermined and specific to the human species. To our knowledge, there is no other species on the planet that exhibits the seemingly spontaneous ease with language unremarkable in a four-year-old. Localization posits that language processing occurs only in specific brain areas, with support emerging from legion cases of aphasia resulting from localized neural insult. Domain specificity takes these points as support for language as separate and independent from other cognitive processes, an idea encapsulated as Pinker's (1994, 1997) hypothetical language organ. For thinkers such as Pinker, and the linguist Chomsky, language is not only *sui generis* but independent and nonreliant on other cognitive processes for any aspect of its development. It is couched in an innate language of thought called *mentalese*, which at birth contains all the concepts we are capable of conceiving (Pinker, 1994). Mentalese is thought to be a symbolic propositional system used to order thought. Languages as we know them are simply its external expression. In short, for language modularists, language is a closed symbolic system, innate to the human species, with specific residences in the brain independent of the rest of cognition.

2.2 *Linguistic relativity*

"[T]he 'linguistic relativity principle'… means, in informal terms, that users of markedly different grammars are pointed by their grammars toward different types of observation and different evaluations of externally similar acts of observation, hence not equivalent as observers but must arrive at somewhat different views of the world" (Whorf, 1956, p. 221).

Linguistic relativity is a theory about how language is related to our conceptual system. It posits that culture, through the language we speak, directs the way we think about the world (Whorf, 1956; Gumperz and Levinson, 1996). In other words, that meaning is the product of our cultural interactions. A cursory examination of this statement yields a conception of language and thought neither germane nor antithetical but instead incongruous with that proposed by the modularity hypothesis. Though the two theories are often treated as polar opposites in their interpretation of the relationship between language and thought, they are actually simply different. For modularity, language, although a self-contained module, is an external wrapping for thought. It structures thought in a unidirectional closed relationship flowing from mentalese to actual utterances (Chomsky, 2000). For linguistic relativity, language is one component in a dynamic, densely interconnected network comprising thought, speakers, and the cultures they inhabit. As such, language is seen as an integrated part of cognition, with influences from and to other cognitive processes. This clarification is necessary so as to remove linguistic relativity from its artificially antagonistic position vis-à-vis modularity. For example, generativists/modularists describe the attributes of a given language as

a series of switches that are turned on or off, that is, that a language will have morphological markings for both perfective and imperfective aspects; all the elements that will comprise language are present at birth. The linguistic relativity principle, as described by Whorf takes a somewhat more conservative stance, positing that at least some of the structure exhibited by a language is a reflection and extension of the particular worldview of the population speaking it. In short, there are subparts of the two theoretical positions that could arguably be compatible.

The linguistic relativity principle says that the language someone speaks influences the way they construct reality. It unites two separate claims (Lucy, 1999). The first is that different languages encode the environment differently. This includes both the selection of what is encoded as well as how it is encoded. The second claim is that these differences influence how reality is interpreted. Lucy argues correctly that much of the confusion about evidence for linguistic relativity is due to interpreting differences and similarities between languages as described in claim one as evidence for or against the theory without considering whether the differences or similarities have been shown to actually affect thought. Work by Levinson (1996) illustrates the proper consideration of the two claims. Levinson's work comparing Tzeltal and Dutch showed that the system used to describe spatial relationships in a language had consequences for the way that space was understood in nonlinguistic situations. Languages tend to use either a relative location (left/right, front/back) or absolute location system, akin in meaning to the English cardinal direction system, that is, north, south as their preferred means of description. Dutch uses a relative location system and Tzeltal an absolute one. Levinson developed a task that involved comparing arrows in different orientations set on two different tables under 180-degree rotation. Subjects were asked to point to the arrow in the second table that matched the direction of the arrow in the first. Whereas Dutch speakers tended to choose the arrow that matched the original direction relative to themselves, Tzeltal speakers chose the one that matched the absolute direction of the first, a result which mapped to the spatial system used in the subjects' language.

In its contemporary form, the LRP has taken several different forms. The most common occurs as strong and weak versions of the theory. The strong version, known as linguistic determinism, posits that the language one speaks predetermines the entire contents of thought. The only concepts available to the speaker are those expressed in that language. The weak version concedes that language has limited effects on the contents of thought. Pinker (1989, p. 360) states "Whorf was surely wrong when he said that one's language determines how one conceptualizes reality in general. But he was probably correct in a much weaker sense: one's language does determine how one must conceptualize reality when one has to talk about it."

The reality is that different thinkers make different predictions for the nature of the relationship between language and thought. Pavlenko (2005) aptly states that "what is important...is the shared acknowledgment that speakers' constructions of the world may be influenced by the structural patterns of their language as well as by their discourses." Regardless of the particular incarnation linguistic relativity might take, its position on the relationship between the internal components of language, as well as on the relationship between language and the rest of cognition, is consistent. By definition, the basic premise is that the systems are open. Differences between the interpretations of linguistic relativity emerge as questions about when and how language influences thought, and never if.

The LRP sets the stage for asking how language can influence thought. Lucy (1997) summarizes the possibilities as of three types, semiotic, structural, and functional. The semiotic level focuses on how speaking any natural language can influence thought. The question specifically addresses issues involved with the nature of language, that is, symbolic versus iconic-indexical. Structural

issues comprise possible differences emerging from speaking different natural languages, Turkish versus Italian for example. The last involves differences across social discourse. People tend to not use language the same way when speaking to their children as when speaking to their employees.

3 The theories and LSNDs

3.1 *Modularity*

For our purposes, modularity is interesting because it contains an express account of the role the brain plays in language. There are areas of the brain, typically in the left hemisphere, such as Wernicke's and Broca's, that have been shown to process linguistic information. Wernicke's area is located in the posterior third of the superior temporal gyrus. Damage here results in difficulties understanding language. Broca's area is located in the frontal lobe in the inferior frontal gyrus. Lesions to this area result in problems producing language. Findings such as these have served as the cornerstone for the idea that there are areas of the brain specifically dedicated to given processes (Kandel, Schwartz, and Jessell, 1995). The problem emerges with domain specificity. If we accept the possibility that the areas involved in language processing are hardwired to solve the problem in one particular way, this leaves no room for individual languages to be processed differently, with correlated differences in brain structure and function.

Indeed, since the hypothesis also predicts that the internal components of language are autonomous, with syntax inputting unidirectionally into semantics, the possibility that differences in meaning could repercuss elsewhere within the system itself is also eliminated. An attempt to argue that the theory predicts no differences would actually be inaccurate since this position by definition cannot consider the question in the first place. Posing the question necessitates granting the possibility of the interaction, an argument that cannot exist in the conceptual repertoire of linguistic modularity. This means that the theory in its current form has no basis for pursuing this line of inquiry, and that it unfortunately can offer little to the resolution of the target question.

3.2 *Linguistic relativity*

Since the focus of LRP has been on how external factors, that is, culture, affect thought via language, it finds itself making no specific predictions about the brain. Predicting that a language will affect thought is not the same as predicting that it will affect the brain. It is possible to contemplate a version of linguistic relativity in which brain anatomy and physiology is sufficiently malleable to account for vast differences in language and thought without any overt physical manifestation. That is not to say that linguistic relativity makes this prediction, or any other for that matter. Its focus rests elsewhere. Regardless, one way that it differs from modularity is in the fact that it considers interaction between cognitive processes a reality. Though the theory emphasizes influence from language to thought, it never denies the possibility of a bidirectional relationship. In fact, recent research in LRP leaves open the possibility of measurable neural manifestation. What is missing to move the theory forward is a way to account for the grounding of mental representation in the brain, and specifically, to clarify whether language plays any role in this grounding. I will elaborate on these points later.

4 Asking the question

4.1 *Language and cognition*

There is abundant evidence supporting the hypothesis that language can affect thought. Aside from the Levinson and Bowerman examples on space cited earlier, Boroditsky (2001) studied differences in the way that Mandarin speakers and English speakers conceptualize time. She found that Mandarin speakers, who commonly describe time as vertical, responded more quickly to questions about the succession of months if they were first presented with a vertical array of objects than when presented with a horizontal one. English speakers, for whom time is described horizontally, showed the opposite effect.

Casasanto et al. (2004) followed this study with an investigation of the cross-linguistic differences of low-level discrimination abilities between speakers of languages, such as English and Indonesian, which preferentially describe time uni-dimensionally (e.g., a long time) versus languages, such as Greek and Spanish, that describe time three-dimensionally (e.g., much time). In their experiments participants saw either a line growing outward from the center of the monitor or a container filling with liquid. They were asked to judge how long it took for the line to grow to its maximum displacement or for the container to fill by clicking an hourglass icon, estimating the duration, and then clicking it a second time. As predicted, speakers of languages which described time concepts as uni-dimensional were better at estimating the duration of the growing line than speakers of languages which described time concepts as three-dimensional. In contrast, the second condition demonstrated a reversal in performance between the two groups; Greek and Spanish speakers estimated duration more accurately than English and Spanish speakers in the context of filling a container.

Languages tend to differ in how substances and objects are marked grammatically. Yucatec Maya, for example, treats the referents of nouns as substances. Grammatically, *banana* is treated much the same way as English speakers treat substances such as water. Lucy and Gaskins (2001) investigated whether the grammatical markings would affect the way that objects were categorized. They used a nonverbal categorization task in which they contrasted the shape of the objects with the materials they were made out of. Their findings showed that in contrast to English speakers, the Yucatec Maya consistently classified the objects according to the material they were made of. Languages can also contain conceptual structures that arguably are not explicit cross-linguistically. Sera (1997) found that Spanish-speaking children, when compared to English-speaking ones, were better at distinguishing between real and temporary properties of an object when using the Spanish *to be* verbs *ser* and *estar*, respectively. *Ser* is believed to be used with more permanent attributes and *estar* with more temporary ones, a distinction that does not occur in English. Further evidence comes from work by Choi and Bowerman (1991) and Bowerman (1996). They showed that very young Korean- and English-speaking children used language-specific principles of semantic categorization to understand their environment with no evidence of appeal to universal categorization principles.

In contrast to the previous studies, there is some research on the influence between language and thought that focuses on how concepts, in this case from the English language,[4] affects behavior. Bargh, Chen, and Burrows (1996) showed that having participants engage in a word search task involving terms related to being old caused them to walk down a hallway significantly more slowly than those whose task had involved unrelated words. In a related task involving a general knowledge exam, Dijksterhuis and van Knippenberg (1998) found that participants who had been primed with terms in the professor category performed better on the task than those who had been primed with the soccer hooligan category.

4.2 *Unspoken assumptions*

Despite the abundance of research showing that language affects different types of thought processes, there remains a general unspoken assumption that language is strictly on the receiving end of cognitive processing. That though it can affect

some interpretations of our environment, as shown in the small sample of studies above, the effects are incidental and lie far from suggesting that language participates in an *interdependent* relationship with other cognitive processes. Simply put, it would be difficult to find a researcher willing to argue that spatial cognition, for example, would function abnormally in the absence of language. This is made evident by the organization of any textbook on cognitive psychology or cognitive science. There is typically a chapter, maybe two, dedicated to language. The topics covered are all language encapsulated: speech processing, semantics, syntax, the aphasias. There will be no mention of language contributing in some fashion to the normal function of any cognitive faculty outside of itself, or to development in general.[5] Anywhere else that language might appear, it will be as a predicate calculus, iconic in nature (*eat, marry, apple*). Even in fields in which the subject matter is typically couched in language, such as reasoning, problem solving or analogy, language itself will be considered largely ancillary. This perspective is unsurprising. The accepted view is that cognitive processes are largely independent of each other. Though they may feed input into each other, what they do is self-contained. The possibility that these same processes might also require language in some measure is simply not considered. The dependency is considered unidirectional.

4.3 *Alternative theories*

There are several notable deviations. Carruthers (2002) for example, proposes that the cognitive function of language is to integrate incoming information from the other modules through syntax. His interpretation, though attractive for our purposes, has two general problems. First, accepting modularity as a first principle renders it incapable of addressing our question. The second is functional inconsistency. Specifically, it seems very unlikely that language, as a cognitive

---

4 These studies are classic treatments of language as incidental to the task at hand. Since it is quite possible that the concepts *old, soccer hooligan* and *professor* differ across languages, (and even then, assuming that they all exist in different languages), it is an open question whether the results would hold in a cross-linguistic study. The issue of language as incidental to a task will be taken up later.

5 Vocabulary counts are used primarily to assess language development.

process among other such processes, would have general integrative properties, that is, nonmodular and nondomain specific, absent elsewhere. It is difficult to account for such a dramatic divergence from an evolutionary perspective since it is unclear what would motivate a new process to evolve with such different properties.

Bickerton argues that language is important to thought based on evolutionary arguments (Calvin and Bickerton, 2000). In essence that it is language that has allowed us to have modern complex thought. Unfortunately, his thesis is also not informative to our question as he assumes that language structure is innate and thus not open to language-specific modification.

At this point in the discussion, the potentially interesting question of LSNDs is left unaddressed due to a lack of theoretical motivation and to the weight of the "language as cognitive parasite fallacy" as I will call it, a preconception that relegates language to almost an afterthought in human cognition,[6] merely a means to an end. In order to test whether such a thing as LSNDs were possible, we might begin by testing whether language itself were necessary for normal cognitive development. There may be an experimental setting suited to answering this question. We could deprive one group of children of language, in essence, by constructing a laboratory controlled environment for the rearing of feral children and allow a second group to develop normally, while controlling for social-cultural factors, richness of environment, and so forth. We could then measure neuro-cognitive development and compare the two groups to see if there were any significant differences. Our results would be a pretty strong indicator of the necessity of language for normal neuro-cognitive development, from which we could then go on to discard the question completely or progress to the investigation

of LSNDs. And, of course, it would be monstrous to contemplate this option as anything more than a perverse thought experiment. But is the thought experiment alone even necessary? Seriously considering language-specific neural differences requires first thinking of language as more than an add-on feature. Dale and Spivey (2002) say "[T]he claim that language should be implicated in wider cognition seems almost self-evident.... Indeed, to many researchers in the cognitive sciences, this is an important theoretical primary." We can begin the paradigm shift by asking "why?" Why should it *not* be the case that language should influence thought, that language might produce LSNDs?

Earlier, I wrote that what was necessary to pursue the question of LSNDs was a way to ground mental representation. One possibility is given by embodiment theory.

4.4 *The embodiment option*

Embodiment theory actively takes the view that language is an integral interconnected component of cognition. The theory proposes that cognition emerges as we develop, interacting with our environment through our bodies. It states that our bodies have evolved with sensory systems extremely well attuned to the statistical regularities they will encounter. Further, that these perceptual regularities will become the basis for higher order cognition (Gibbs, 2006; Lakoff and Johnson, 1999; Thelen and Smith, 1994; Varela, Thompson, and Rosch, 1991). The theory, despite having an extensive historical precedent, that is, Heidegger, Merlou-Ponty, Dewey, Gibson, in its current form is actually quite new. This means that there are many different interpretations of what embodiment should be and how it can be used to understand different aspects of cognition (Barsalou, 2008; Gibbs, 2006; Wilson, 2002). Regardless, they tend to share certain assumptions.

4.4.1 GENERAL ASSUMPTIONS
Margaret Wilson (2002) developed an excellent overview of the different general

---

6   Rather ironic considering that language is widely believed to be our species-defining trait, that is, Terrence Deacon's "The symbolic species," Steven Pinker's 'The language instinct," and so on, ad nauseum.

components attributed to embodied cognition, which I have adapted below. They are:

- Cognition is situated.
- Cognition is time-pressured.
- We off-load cognitive work onto the environment.
- The environment is part of the cognitive system.
- Cognition is for action.
- Off-line cognition is body-based.

Situated cognition begins with the observation that cognition occurs in a context. Though sometimes dismissed as a rehashing of the old idea that interpretation of language and action requires a context (Stucky, 1992), more current theory describes it as more than background to a situation, instead proposing that agents need and actively use environmental, contextual information to shape their behavior. (Stucky, 1992; Wilson, 2002). Common examples include interactions at birthday parties or as Wilson says, walking around a room to figure out where the furniture should go. In the first example, the context consists of social components in terms of the other people attending as well as physical ones represented by a birthday cake, streamers, balloons, and so forth. In the second example, the context involves the physical setting of an empty room along with the socially motivated expectation that it should be filled with certain types of furniture to fulfill certain social needs. For example, if the room is to be a living room, then the planning will include a furniture arrangement that will contribute to the ease of activities such as entertaining guests or watching a movie.

Cognition is also thought to be time-pressured. This idea refers specifically to the fact that we live in four dimensions and not three. Conversation, for example, has a given rhythm. Responses are needed and expected at a given pace in order for communication to flow. Lapses lead to corrective behaviors such as repeating one's self and so forth. Too many lapses lead to a breakdown in communication. Other examples include Kirsh and Maglio's (1994) research on spatial arrangement decisions made while playing the game *Tetris*.

The next claim is that we off-load cognitive work onto the environment. There are two common interpretations of this phenomenon. This first is that we use objects such as dictionaries, encyclopedias, and address books to hold information for us for later use. This form is considered uncontroversial and of little theoretical interest (Wilson, 2002). The second is that we use the environment to reduce our cognitive workload by leaving information out there as a guide to be used whenever we need it. Strong proponents of this view, Ballard et al. (1997) worked with what they called *deictic representation*. They described it as "a system of implicit reference, whereby the body's pointing movements bind objects in the world to cognitive programs." An experiment was developed in which participants were instructed to reproduce an arrangement of color blocks in a different location. The authors found that the most commonly used technique involved memorizing as little information as possible, relying instead on frequent eye movements to the target blocks to reproduce the arrangement. This finding indicated that as little information processing as possible was occurring with participants instead using the environmental information on a strictly as needed basis. Further evidence of this type of behavior in an abstract task is given in work by Richardson and Spivey (2000). In their eye-tracking study, participants were presented with a screen containing a "talking head" speaking a piece of information pulled from an encyclopedia, such as "Although the largest city in Australia is Sydney, the capital is Canberra," one of four predetermined locations. Later when participants were asked a question about one of the pieces of information, they made a significant number more saccades to the area on the screen where the "talking head" had been located than to other areas despite the fact that the screen was now blank, indicating that participants were referencing the information at its previous location in a manner akin to that done by participants in the Ballard et al. task.

The claim that the environment is part of the cognitive system is very close to the claim about situated cognition. One of the original proponents of situated cognition was J. J. Gibson (1979). In his theory of ecological psychology, he argued that the environment was crucial to the development of cognitive mechanisms. He followed what we would today call a systems approach in that he believed that in order to understand the behavior of an organism we also needed to understand its environment. In essence, that there was no real separation between the two. A simple example comes from trying to understand how a fish swims. It is not enough to understand the fish's musculature and nervous system responses. We must understand the dynamics of water so as to explain the how and why of the fish's motion. These ideas have been explored quite productively by robotics researchers, who have used them to produce more and more accurate models of biological behavior (Clark, 1997; Nolfi, Migliano, and Parisi, 1994; Thelen and Smith, 1994). Clark and Chalmers (1998) have formalized this claim as active externalism. The general claim is that the environment plays an active role in driving cognition, and that as such, cognition as we actually use it is a system coupled with the environment, and to be understood, should be studied as such.

The claim that cognition is for action is grounded in Thelen and Smith's (1994) developmental research. The authors conducted a series of experiments exploring how children solved various problems associated with functioning in their environments. For example, one study compared the process of learning to grasp an object in two different children. One child, Gabriel, was described as very active. He was so active that it was very difficult for him to grasp a toy because he kept overshooting his goal. In order for him to achieve grasping the toy, he had to learn to better control the motions of his arms and hands. Another child, Hannah, had a different disposition. She was much less active, with her motions much more controlled. Her problem in reaching the toy involved having her body generate enough

force to propel her forward such that she could reach the toy. The authors say that though superficially different, the children had the same problem. They needed to combine the different forces generated by their bodies to reach the toy. Specifically, the different degrees of control they had over these forces meant that they would each have to develop solutions unique to them that could not have been genetically prespecified. Instead the solutions for both children emerged out of their acting on their environment in their own way.

The process of perception and action begun at the earliest exploration of the environment remains at the core of cognition throughout the lifespan. "Biological brains are first and foremost the control systems for biological bodies. Biological bodies move and act in rich real-world surroundings" (Clark, 1997). We do not experience our environment by sitting still but by exploring, moving, and interacting with it (Barsalou, 2008; Gibbs, 2006; Wilson, 2002). The whole of embodiment rests on the idea that higher order cognition emerges from the patterns gathered from perceiving and acting in our environments. This becomes evident in experiments such as that developed by Tucker and Ellis (1998). In their experiment, participants were asked to judge whether an object was inverted or not. These were common household objects such as teapots and pans. The authors used photographs. The target variable was that these typically had a handle of sorts used to grasp it. What the authors found was that participants were significantly faster at judging whether an object was inverted or upright if the location of the object's handle corresponded with the participant's dominant hand, that is, if the handle was on the right side and the participant was right-handed. This experiment suggests that regardless of the task at hand, in this case a simple orientation judgment, we tend to process information about what surrounds us with action in mind. Although there was no way any of these objects could be grasped because they were in fact images, information about their physical accessibility was still processed.

One of the arguments against situated cognition is that there are many cognitive behaviors that do not necessarily occur in an immediate situated setting (Wilson, 2002). Behaviors such as remembering, planning, and daydreaming, for example, obviously fall outside the rubric. A similar argument emerges against the claim that cognition is for action. There are many things that we perceive that we have never had physical interaction with, and with which it is virtually impossible that we ever will, such as sunsets. The idea that offline cognition is body-based addresses this criticism directly. For many researchers, this is the key idea of embodiment theory. Truth be told, it is almost trivial to consider that cognition should be situated, time-bound, involve action, and so forth, as these are all non-controversial characteristics of nonhuman cognition. Since we are also subject to the same evolutionary norms as other species, it makes sense that these characteristics should apply to our cognition. Embodiment theory takes these premises further and posits that bodily experiences ground offline cognition. In essence, arguing that the grounding for the structure in abstracted thought comes from the cognitive characteristics shared in some fashion by other species. There are three complementary and often overlapping general lines of research exploring this extension. These are cognitive simulation theories, cognitive linguistics, and neuroscience as regards mirror neurons.

4.4.1.1 *Cognitive simulation theories* *Cognitive simulation theories* rest on the assumption that we simulate our own past behaviors. Barsalou (2008) describes them as based on the "reenactment of perceptual, motor and introspective states acquired during experience with the world, body, and mind." When having a cup of soup, for example, it is easy to imagine that our experience is limited to the immediate act of eating the soup, that is, how it tasted, whether we were satiated upon finishing. As embodiment theorists emphasize, there is much more experienced in the act of having a cup of soup. Beginning with the primary senses, we experience not only the sensations of the

soup but of the place where we ate. Was the room warm, cold, drafty, bright, dark? Were there other smells in the room? Where were we? Perhaps at home, or in a new restaurant. There are also the experiences involved with moving our bodies to be able to eat the soup. If we were sitting, then we coordinated movements in our shoulder and arm to allow our hand to collect a spoon from the table, grasp it, and hold it so that it could be filled with soup then brought to our mouth. In the process, we likely inclined our head to meet the spoon, then timed opening our mouth with the moment the spoon reached it. There are also the experiences of our minds as we were eating. Did we enjoy the soup? Were we in good spirits? Perhaps we were so distracted by work that we barely noticed the taste and ate strictly for sustenance. The point of this elaboration is to emphasize the richness of experience associated with even the most mundane tasks. The repeated multimodal aggregates of experiences such as those just described are the foundation of multimodal mental representations.

Multimodal representations are not limited to the foci of our behaviors, that is, eating soup. The use of a spoon, for example, will arguably rarely be the focus of our overt attention, yet it is difficult to imagine a more common tool in Western life. Our experience with spoons extends beyond eating soup. It will include eating ice cream, learning to balance one on our nose, or using one to make half-moon indentations in pottery class and so forth. The overlapping experiences will produce the multimodal representation of a spoon.[7] This is believed to be the generalized process for acquiring concepts about the world.

A final important component of multimodal representations is that they are dynamic. Because they are based on experience, as our experience changes, so will the

---

[7] This discussion leads the way into the postulated mental structures known as *image schemas*, a type of schematized mental representation. Though they are relevant, a general understanding of multimodal representation as described here should suffice for the sake of this chapter.

multimodal representations that emerge. For example, a child's conception of cheese may well be limited to American cheese, that is, processed cheese food. As her experience of the world grows, she will be exposed to other types of cheese: Swiss, camembert, or bleu, and may well come to consider American cheese as not real cheese but as a dairy product with only the vaguest relationship to real cheese.

Mental representations, as based on multimodal experiences, are simulated. This capacity is at the heart of remembering, as Marcel Proust's *A la recherche du temps perdus* so aptly demonstrates. The author sits enjoying a *madeline*, a small pastry, and in so doing remembers, or mentally simulates an ocean of experiences all tied together by the very physical experience of eating. Memory is only one mechanism that uses multimodal representations (Glenberg, 1997). What is proposed is that higher order cognitive processes share a system of multimodal representation (Barsalou, 1999) that allows for processes as diverse as imagery (Kosslyn, 1980), social interaction (Goldman, 2006), and language (Bergen and Chang, 2005;, Boroditsky, 2000; Matlock, 2004) all through the ability to mentally recreate our experiences.

4.4.1.2 *Cognitive linguistics* Cognitive Linguistics (CL) emerged as a reaction to the dominant theory of Generative Linguistics (GL) as proposed by Noam Chomsky (1957), mostly independent of the work being done in psychology. Chomsky's theory is nativist to the extent that it proposes that we are born with a universal linguistic system for which natural languages are cosmetic manifestations. This system, as described earlier, is believed to be independent of the rest of cognition and innate. Cognitive linguists such as Lakoff, Johnson, Talmy, and Langacker argued that GL failed to account for meaning as a major motivating force in language as well as for the systematic recurrence of experiential information in linguistic forms. Beyond reacting to GL it also proposed that language was embodied, that linguistic structure was conceptual, and that language meaning was motivated by use.

CL is actually comprised of several theories addressing different aspects of language. Perhaps the most well-known of these is Conceptual Metaphor Theory (CMT) as developed by Lakoff and Johnson (Lakoff and Johnson, 1980; Lakoff, 1987). CMT proposes that we understand abstract ideas via the metaphoric extension of more basic or bodily experiences. For example, we understand someone saying, "If he says that one more time, I'm going to blow" to mean that the speaker will become very angry should the offending party say X one more time. Our understanding comes from English grounding the experience of anger as heat. As heat increases, an explosion is bound to happen. And so, as the speaker becomes angrier, he will also "blow."

Talmy (2000; 2001) has focused on the importance of perceptual experiences such as space and motion in the structuring of meaning in language. He developed the concept of *fictive motion* when he noticed that people use motion terms to describe the connective relationship between two locations such as in 'The road runs from Los Angeles to San Diego." The *road* here is obviously not going anywhere but is instead simply serving to connect the two sites. He observed that this phenomenon occurred across language with great consistency, and that, though some speakers claimed to not experience motion when using motion verbs to refer to stationary situation consistently, all speakers experienced motion some of the time. The experience Talmy refers to is of simulation. In order for speakers to make the judgment as to whether or not they experienced motion, they need to mentally represent the event in their mind, and this requires simulation. Matlock (2004) took Talmy's ideas a bit further by asking whether the presence or absence of such simulation could be made subject to experimental testing. She found that there was a greater latency when subjects processed sentences involving fictive motion than when they did not, indicating that they were in fact simulating static sentences as if they described a motion event.

4.4.1.3 *Mirror neurons Mirror neurons* comprise one of the most intriguing recent discoveries about the nervous system. They are a type of visuomotor neuron that becomes active when producing a behavior as well as when merely observing it. First discovered in area F5 of the premotor cortex of macaque monkeys (DiPellegrino et al., 1992), their presence is also supported in the human brain although to date there is no direct evidence (Rizzollatti and Craighero, 2004). Some indirect evidence comes from research with TMS or *transcranial magnetic stimulation*. TMS is a noninvasive technique used to electrically stimulate the nervous system. When applied to the motor cortex, it produces MEP or *motor-evoked-potentials*, the amplitude of which can be modulated in experimental settings. Rizzollatti and Craighero describe a series of studies involving increases in MEPs in motor cortex in subjects observing actions as well as performing them, among other related studies.

The central idea behind mirror neurons is that they offer an explanation for how we can understand each other's actions. The hypothesis is that we understand a behavior because we reenact or simulate it. This ability is believed to be at the core of behaviors such as imitation (Rizzolatti and Craighero, 2004), theory of mind (Gallese and Goldman, 1998), and language (Arbib, 2005).

4.4.2 EMBODIMENT

Embodiment theory is a promising first step in addressing the question of LSNDs. It provides the much needed grounding for mental or multimodal representation. Its weakness, for our purposes, lies in not giving enough weight to the differences in human experience. Even as researchers acknowledge that the environment is crucial to normal development, and while they investigate differences in the perception of the many facets of the environment, yet another unspoken assumption persists. Namely that though environmental interaction is important, any manifestation of a human environment will do, which is true

enough, although this discounts the possibility that as a particular environment shapes the mind, it may also shape the brain in significant ways. In a sense, it could be argued that marrying the LRP with embodiment theory, given some of the language specific cognitive differences described earlier (Choi and Bowerman, 1991; Levinson, 1996; Lucy and Gaskell 2001), would suffice to motivate the question. And in a limited way, they do, as evidenced by this chapter. More is required, however, than bringing together two complementary theories. We are left, once again, with one of the possibilities proposed earlier for the LRP, that the brain could be sufficiently malleable to accommodate all of these differences without any outward manifestation. Such an explanation would leave findings such as those from music and mediation unaccounted for. What is necessary is a theory that predicts LSNDs and can account for how they would emerge and what their implications and repercussions for cognition might be. However, evidence that language (albeit not specific languages) can and does shape cognition and the brain, at least to some degree, is available from research with bilinguals.

5 Bilingualism

This chapter has until now focused on the possibility that a given language might produce functional and structural differences in the brain. The possibility that the mere presence of multiple languages in the cognitive repertoire of an individual might also result in such differences has barely begun to be considered. The studies described in this section position bilingualism as one determining factor.

The investigation of bilingualism is fascinating on many fronts. It is a case study in the ways that cultural and political agendas shape the science that is done and how it is interpreted. Early work was arguably motivated to substantiate claims about the cognitive deficiencies thought to emerge from growing up with two languages, the vast majority of bilinguals being poor immigrants and their children.[8] As early as 1923, Saer, among others, presented evidence of the "mental confusion" resulting from bilingualism (Bialystok, 2005). It was not until the mid-1980s that the validity of the early research was questioned and the studies dismissed as poorly designed (Hakuta, 1986). Recent, better controlled studies, along with a more sophisticated understanding of human linguistic history, suggest that bilingualism might not only be an asset to cognition but the norm for the human species.

There are numerous studies to date investigating the effects of bilingualism on cognition. The studies, of which I will offer a sample of in the following sections, are roughly divided into behavioral and neural research.[9]

5.1 *Behavioral studies*

In a study on short-term memory, Thorn and Gathercole (1999) showed that when bilingual, monolingual, and ESL students were tested on a word recall task, the number of recalled words was a function of how well the participant knew the language the words belonged to, indicating that short-term memory is not a language-independent process. Emerging evidence shows what appear to be differences in nonlanguage related cognitive abilities in bilinguals. Bialystok (1992; 1999; 2005) has shown that bilinguals exhibit greater control of attention in the execution of cognitive tasks. In other words, that they are better at identifying and concentrating on the relevant elements of a task while effectively ignoring peripheral details. In terms

of spatial abilities, Bialystok and Majumder (1998) showed that bilinguals were favored over monolinguals in spatial control tasks. Further, McLeay (2004) showed that bilinguals were both faster and more accurate in a mental rotation task involving knots. Also in terms of spatial abilities, Gonzalez-Marquez and Spivey (in preparation) and Gonzalez-Marquez and Spivey (in progress) have gathered evidence that the gender differences in spatial abilities present in monolinguals may not occur in bilinguals.

5.2 *Neural studies*

More relevant to the task at hand is research on the neural implications of bilingualism. Evidence for substantial differences in the brains of bilinguals when compared to those of monolinguals keeps emerging. Early bilinguals have been shown to use cortical areas common to monolinguals for language representation, as well as other areas not active in monolinguals. For example, using fMRI, differences in activation in the cerebellum were found during a noun–verb association task and a rhyming task by Pillai et al. (2004). Kim et al. (1997) found differences in the activation of Wernicke's area during a silent sentence generation task, also using fMRI. Marian, Spivey, and Hirsch (2003), in a study that combined fMRI with eyetracking, found that although there were no differences in the general structures active during the early stages of a word recognition task, that there were differences in the activation patterns within the structures. Specifically, there were differences within the left inferior frontal gyrus. Of special interest are recent findings in brain structure differences in bilinguals. Recent voxel-based morphometry has revealed greater grey matter density in left inferior parietal cortex of bilingual brains when compared to monolinguals (Mechelli et al., 2004). In addition, a study by Coggins, Kennedy, and Armstrong (2004) found a structural difference in the anterior midbody of the corpus callosum, which the authors attributed to accommodating the presence of multiple languages.

---

[8]   It has always struck me as comical that historically bilingualism has only been considered cognitively problematic when it involved the poor, huddled masses. I don't think I have ever come across a similar concern for children reared for leadership positions, such as kings and queens, for whom multilingual educations were par for the course.

[9]   I will not be discussing the literature on bilingualism and language lateralization. I tend to agree with Paradis (2000) that the research is at best equivocal.

6 Conclusion

This chapter has explored the possibility of language-specific neural differences. It has examined the theoretical motivations behind the lack of research into the question, and it has described research tentatively supporting the question's viability. The goal here was not to provide answers, but to consider why this question, which may well seem obvious in hindsight, has remained unasked.

We are in the process of moving away from a model of cognition that assumed the brain to be composed of parts, akin to Lego pieces. The pieces fit together snugly, but had little else to do with each other. More current research is producing an image of cognition in which processes, though partly isolatable, remain interconnected and interdependent with the rest of the cognition system. The studies described here are emblematic of the ways that language behaves as ordinarily as any other process; it affects and is affected by attention, memory, behavior for example. Should this question be pursued, indirectly via neural studies of linguistic relativity (Levinson's research on spatial cognition, for example, seems particularly amenable to neural studies), or directly by developing the necessary theory to account productively for much of the evidence presented here, the findings can only serve to better inform our understanding not only of what language really is in our brains, but also of how deeply intertwined our cognitive system truly is.

References

Arbib, M. A. (2005). From monkey-like action recognition to human language: An evolutionary framework for neurolinguistics. *Behavioral and Brain Sciences*, 28, 105–67.

Ballard, D., Hayhoe, M., Pook, P., & Rao, R. (1997). Deictic codes for the embodiment of cognition. *Behavioral and Brain Sciences*, 20, 723–67.

Bargh, J. A., Chen, M., & Burrows, L. (1996). Automaticity of social behavior: Direct effects of trait construct and stereotype activation on action. *Journal of Personality and Social Psychology*, 71, 230–44.

Barsalou, L. W. (1999). Perceptual symbol systems. *Behavioral and Brain Sciences*, 22, 577–609.

Barsalou, L.W. (2008). Grounded cognition. *Annual Review of Psychology*, 59. Retrieved on May 8, 2007 from http://psychology.emory.edu/cognition/barsalou/onlinepapers.html.

Bates, E. (1994). Modularity, domain specificity, and the development of language. *Discussions in Neuroscience*, 10, 136–49.

Bavelier, D., Brozinsky, C., Tomann, A., Mitchell, T., & Liu, G. (2001). Impact of early deafness and early exposure to sign language on the cerebral organization for motion processing. *The Journal of Neuroscience*, 21, 8931–42.

Bergen, B. & Chang, N. (2005). Embodied construction grammar in simulation-based language understanding. In Östman, J. & Fried, M. (Eds.) *Construction grammars: Cognitive grounding and theoretical extensions* (pp. 147–90). Amsterdam: John Benjamins.

Bialystok, E. (1992). Selective attention in cognitive processing: The bilingual edge. In Harris, R. J. (Ed.) *Cognitive processing in bilinguals* (pp. 501–13). Amsterdam: Elsevier Science.

Bialystok, E. (1999). Cognitive complexity and attentional control in the bilingual mind. *Child Development*, 70, 636–44.

(2005). Consequences of bilingualism for cognitive development. In De Groot, A. & Kroll, J. (Eds.) *Handbook of bilingualism: Psycholinguistic approaches* (pp. 417–32). New York: Oxford University Press.

Bialystok, E. & Majumder, S. (1998). The relationship between bilingualism and the development of cognitive processes in problem-solving. *Applied Psycholinguistics*, 19, 69–85.

Boroditsky, L. (2000). Metaphoric structuring: Understanding time through spatial metaphors. *Cognition*, 75, 1–28.

(2001). Does language shape thought? English and Mandarin speakers' conceptions of time. *Cognitive Psychology*, 43, 1–22.

Bowerman, M. (1996). The origins of children's spatial semantic categories: Cognitive versus linguistic determinants. In Gumperz, J. J. & Stevenson, S. L. (Eds.) *Rethinking linguistic relativity* (pp. 145–76). Cambridge, MA: Cambridge University Press.

Calvin, W. H. & Bickerton, D. (2000). Lingua ex machina: Reconciling Darwin and Chomsky with the human brain. Cambridge, MA: MIT Press.

Carruthers, P. (2002). The cognitive functions of language. *Behavioral and Brain Sciences, 25,* 657–726.

Casasanto, D. & Boroditsky, L. (2003). Do we think about time in terms of space? *Proceedings of the 25th Annual Meeting of the Cognitive Science Society.* Boston, MA.

Casasanto, D., Boroditsky, L., Phillips, W., Greene, J., Goswami, S., Bocanegra-Thiel, et al. (2004). How deep are effects of language on thought? Time estimation in speakers of English, Indonesian, Greek, and Spanish. In K. Forbus, D. Gentner, & T. Regier (Eds.), Proceedings of the 26h Annual Conference Cognitive Science Society (pp. 575–580). Hillsdale, NJ: Lawrence Erlbaum Associates.

Choi, S. & Bowerman, M. (1991). Learning to express motion events in English and Korean: The influence of language specific lexicalization patterns. *Cognition, 41,* 83–122.

Chomsky, N. (1957). *Syntactic Structures.* The Hague: Mouton

(2000). *New Horizons in the study of language and mind.* Cambridge, England: Cambridge University Press.

Clark, A. (1997). *Being there.* Cambridge, MA: MIT Press.

Clark, A. & Chalmers, D. (1998). The extended mind. *Analysis, 58,* 10–23.

Coggins III, P. E., Kennedy, T. J., & Armstrong, T. A. (2004). Bilingual corpus callosum variability. *Brain and Language, 89,* 69–75.

Crain, S. & Lillo-Martin, D. (1999). An introduction to linguistic theory and language acquisition. Oxford: Blackwell.

Dale, R. & Spivey, M. J. (2002). A linguistic module to integrate the senses, or a house of cards? *Behavioral and Brain Sciences, 25,* 681–2.

Dehaene, S., Cohen, L., Sigman, M. & Vinckier, F. (2005) *Trends in Cognitive Sciences, 9,* 335–341.

Di Pellegrino, G., Fadiga L., Fogassi L., Gallese, V., & Rizzolatti, G. (1992). Understanding motor events: A neurophysiological study. *Experimental Brain Research, 91,* 176–80.

Dijksterhuis, A., Aarts, H., Bargh, J.A., & Van Knippenberg, A. (2000). On the relation between associative strength and automatic behavior. *Journal of Experimental Social Psychology, 36,* 531–44.

Fodor, J. A. (1983). The modularity of mind: An essay on faculty psychology. Cambridge, MA: The MIT Press.

Frazier, L. (1999). Modularity and language. In Wilson, R. A. & Keil, F. C. (Eds.) *The MIT encyclopedia of the cognitive sciences* (pp. 557–8). Cambridge, MA: MIT Press.

Gallese, V. & Goldman, A. (1998). Mirror neurons and the simulation theory of mind-reading, *Trends in Cognitive Sciences, 2,* 493–501.

Gaser, C. & Schlaug, G. (2003). Brain structures differ between musicians and non-musicians. *Journal of Neuroscience, 23,* 9240–5.

Gibbs, R. (2006). *Embodiment and cognitive science.* New York: Cambridge University Press.

Gibson, J. J. (1979). *The ecological approach to visual perception.* Boston, MA: Houghton Mifflin.

Glenberg, A. M. (1997). What memory is for. *Brain and Behavioral Sciences, 20,* 1–55.

Godfrey-Smith, P. (1998). *Complexity and the function of mind in nature.* New York, NY: Cambridge University Press.

Goldman, A. (2006). Simulating minds: The philosophy, psychology, and neuroscience of mindreading. New York: Oxford University Press.

Gonzalez-Marquez, M. & Spivey, M. (in preparation). Mapping from real to abstract locations: Experimental evidence from the Spanish verb ESTAR.

(in progress). *Spatial cognition in bilingualism.*

Gumperz, J. J. & Levinson, J. C. (1996). *Rethinking linguistic relativity.* Cambridge, MA: Cambridge University Press.

Hakuta, K. (1986). Mirror of language: The debate on bilingualism. New York: Basic Books.

Kandel, E. R., Schwarts, J. H., & Jessell, T. M. (1995). *Essentials of neuroscience and behavior.* McGraw-Hill/Appleton & Lange.

Kim, KHS, Relkin, N. R., Lee, K. M., & Hirsch, J. (1997). Distinct cortical areas associated with native and second languages. *Nature, 388,* 171–174.

Kirsh, D. & Maglio, P. (1994). On distinguishing epistemic from pragmatic action. *Cognitive Science, 18,* 513–49.

Kosslyn, S. M. (1980). *Image and mind.* Cambridge, MA: MIT Press.

Lakoff, G. (1987). *Women, fire, and dangerous things.* Chicago: University of Chicago.

Lakoff, G. & Johnson, M. (1980). *Metaphors we live by.* Chicago: University of Chicago.

(1999). Philosophy In the flesh: The embodied mind and its challenge to Western thought. New York: Basic Books.

Lazar, S., Kerr, C., Wasserman, R., Gray, J., Greve, D., Treadway, M., et al. (2005). Meditation experience is associated with increased cortical thickness. *Neuroreport, 16,* 1893–1897.

Levinson, S. (1996). Relativity in spatial conception and description. In Gumperz, J. J. & Levinson, S. C. (Eds.) *Rethinking linguistic relativity* (pp. 70–96). Cambridge, MA: Cambridge University Press.

Li, P. & Gleitman, L. (2002). Turning the tables: Language and spatial reasoning. *Cognition*, 83,(3) 265–94.

Lucas, M. (2000). Semantic priming without association: A meta-analytic review. Psychonomic *Bulletin & Review*, 7, 618–630.

Lucy, J. (1997). Linguistic relativity. *Annual Review of Anthropology*, 26, 291–312.

(1999). Linguistic relativity. In Wilson, R. A. & Keil, F. C. (Eds.) *The MIT encyclopedia of the cognitive sciences* (pp. 475–476). Cambridge, MA: The MIT Press.

Lucy, J. & Gaskell, S. (2001). Grammatical categories and development of classification preferences: A comparative approach. In Bowerman, M. & Levinson, S. (Eds.) *Language acquisition and conceptual development* (pp. 257–83). Cambridge, MA: Cambridge University Press.

Marian, V., Spivey, M., & Hirsch, J. (2003). Shared and separate systems in bilingual language processing: Con- verging evidence from eyetracking and brain imaging. *Brain and Language*, 86, 70–82.

Matlock, T. (2004). The conceptual motivation of fictive motion. In Radden, G. & Panther, K. U. (Eds.) *Studies in linguistic motivation* (pp. 221–48). Berlin, Germany: Mouton de Gruyter.

McGurk, H. & MacDonald, J. (1976). Hearing lips and seeing voices. *Nature*, 264, 746–8.

McLeay, H. (2004). The relationship between bilingualism and spatial tasks. *Bilingual Education and Bilingualism*, 6, 423–38.

Mechelli A., Crinion, J. T., Noppeney, U., O'Doherty, J. Ashburner, J. Frackowiak, R. S., & Price, C. J. (2004). Neurolinguistics: Structural plasticity in the bilingual brain. *Nature*, 431, 7010.

Munnich, E. & Landau, B. (2003). The effect of spatial language on spatial representations: Setting some boundaries. In Gentner, D. & Goldin-Meadow, S. (Eds.) *Language in mind: Advances in the study of language and though* (pp. 113–36). Cambridge, MA: MIT Press.

Nolfi S., Floreano D., Miglino O., & Mondada F. (1994). How to evolve autonomous robots: Different approaches in evolutionary robotics. In Brooks, R. A. & Maes, P. (Eds.) *Artificial Life IV*. (190–7). Cambridge, MA: MIT Press.

Paradis, M. (2000). Language lateralization in bilinguals: enough already! In L. Wei (Ed.), *The Bilingualism Reader*. (pp.394–401). London: Routledge, London.

Pavlenko, A. (2005). Bilingualism and thought. In De Groot, A. & Kroll, J. (Eds.) *Handbook of Bilingualism: Psycholinguistic Approaches* (pp. 443–53). New York, NY: Oxford University Press.

Pillai, J. J., Allison, J. D., Sethuraman, S., Araque, J. M., Thiruvaiyaru, D., Ison, et al., (2004). Functional magnetic resonance imaging study of language-related differences in bilingual cerebellar activation. *American Journal of Neuroradiology*, 25, 523–32.

Pinker, S. (1989). *The language instinct*. New York, NY: Harper Collins.

(1994). *The language instinct*. New York: Morrow.

(1997). *How the mind works*. New York, NY: Norton.

Pons, T. (1996). Novel sensations in the congenitally blind. *Nature* 380, 479–80.

Richardson, D. C., & Spivey, M. J. (2000). Representation, space and Hollywood Squares: Looking at things that aren't there anymore. *Cognition*, 76, 269–295.

Richardson, D. C., Spivey, M. J., Edelman, S., & Naples, A. (2001). "Language is spatial": Experimental evidence for image schemas of concrete and abstract verbs. *Proceedings of the Twenty-third Annual Meeting of the Cognitive Science Society* (pp.873–8), Mawhah, NJ: Erlbaum.

Rizzolatti, G. & Craighero, L. (2004). The mirror-neuron system. *Annual Review of Neuroscience*, 27, 169–92.

Ross, D. A., Olson, I. R., & Gore, J. C. (2003). Cortical plasticity in an early blind musician: An fMRI study. *Magnetic Resonance Imaging*, 21, 821–8.

Sadato, N., Pascual-Leone, A., Grafmani, J., Ibañez, V., Deiber, M., Dold, G., & Hallet, M. (1996). Activation of the primary visual cortex by Braille reading in blind subjects. *Nature* 380, 526–8.

Sera, M. D., Bales, D., & Castillo, J. (1997). Ser helps speakers of Spanish identify "real" properties. *Child Development*, 68, 820–31.

Sereno, J. (1991). Graphemic, associative, and syntactic priming effects at a brief stimulus onset asynchrony in lexical decision and naming. *Journal of Experimental Psychology: Learning, Memory, and Cognition*, 17, 459–477.

Slobin, D. I. (1996). From "thought and language" to "thinking to speaking." In Gumperz, J. J. & Levinson, S. C. (Eds.) *Rethinking linguistic relativity* (pp. 70–96). Cambridge, MA: Cambridge University Press.

Spivey, M. J., Richardson, D., & Gonzalez-Marquez, M. (2006). On the perceptual-motor and image-schematic infrastructure of language. In Pecher, D & Zwaan, R. (Eds.)

Grounding cognition (pp. 246–81). New York: Cambridge University Press.

Stucky, S. U. (1992). Situated cognition: A strong hypothesis. In Engel, F.L., Bosser, T., & d'Ydewalle, G. (Eds.) *Cognitive modelling and interactive environments in language learning.* (pp. 27–34). Mierlo, Netherlands: Springer-Verlag.

Talmy, L. (2000). *Toward a Cognitive Semantics Vol. 1.* Cambridge, MA: The MIT Press.

(2001). *Toward a Cognitive Semantics Vol. 2.* Cambridge, MA: The MIT Press.

(2007a). Foreword. In Gonzalez-Marquez, M., Mittleberg, I., Coulson, S., & Spivey, M. (Eds.) *Methods in Cognitive Linguistics.* Amsterdam: John Benjamins

(2007b). Attention phenomena. In Geeraerts, D. & Cuyckens, H. (Eds.) *The handbook of cognitive linguistics* (pp. 264–93).New York: Oxford University Press.

Thelen, E. & Smith, L. B. (1994). A dynamic systems approach to the development of cognition and action. Cambridge, MA: MIT Press.

Thorn, ASC & Gathercole, S. E. (1999). Language-specific knowledge and short-term memory in bilingual and non-bilingual children. *Quarterly Journal of Experimental Psychology, 52,* 303–24.

Tucker, M. & Ellis, R. (1998). On the relations between seen objects and components of potential actions. *Journal of Experimental Psychology: Human Perception and Performance, 24,* 830–46.

Varela, F., Thompson, E., & Rosch, E. (1991). *The Embodied Mind.* Cambridge, MA: MIT Press.

Werker, J. F. & Tees, R. C. (1984). Cross-language speech perception: Evidence for perceptual reorganization during the first year of life. *Infant Behavior and Development, 7,* 49–63.

Whorf, B. (1956). *Language, thought, and reality: Selected writings of Benjamin Lee Whorf.* Cambridge, MA: Technology Press of Massachusetts Institute of Technology.

Wilson, M. (2002). Six views of embodied cognition. *Psychonomic Bulletin and Review, 9,* 625–36.

Index

Abramson, M., 168–9
absolute reference frames
  cognitive development and,
    655–7
  cross-language studies and,
    618–23
abstraction
  conceptual systems of
    semantic memory and, 251
  simulation/embodied/
    situated theories of
    semantic memory and,
    251–2
access, in spoken word
  recognition, 79–80
ACE corpus, metonymy studies
  and, 488
Acheson, D. M., 357
Ackerman, B. P., 509–10
acknowledgment, grounding in
  dialogue and, 547–8
acoustic histories, nonhuman
  speech and human
  nonspeech perception, 12
acoustic speech signals
  auditory enhancement
    theory, 7
  functional imaging studies,
    30–2

language learning and, 49–50
phonetic perception, 3, 4–6
spoken word recognition
  and, 66–7, 76–7
acoustic stream, comprehension
  process and, 127–8
acquired dyslexia
  in brain injured patients,
    219–20
  functional neuroanatomy
    and, 221–3
  semantic impairment and,
    270–1
acquisition via exposure
  hypothesis, idiom
  processing in developing
  children and, 510–11
action-based metaphors,
  childhood acquisition of,
  516
actions and activation
  developmental cognition
    research and, 684
  embodiment theory and,
    298–302
  percept adjustment in
    unwarped space and,
    637–8
  semantic impairment and, 271

suppression mechanisms
  and, 359
triangle connectionist reading
  model and, 211–12
visual word recognition,
  160–4
word production and,
  447–6
activation of units
  spoken word recognition, 62
  spoken word recognition
    and, 76–7
Active Externalism theory, 684
ACT semantic network, 261
Adams, M. J., 190
adaptive resonance theory
  (ART)
  phonetic perception, 16–17
  spoken word recognition
    and, 72, 87–8
additivity, neurobiology of
  sentence comprehension
  and, 368–9
adjacency pair, dialogue and,
  543–5
adult word recognition
  research methods for, 104
  in skilled adult readers,
    159–77